T0189175

Lecture Notes in Computer Science 14265

The series Lecture Notes in Computer Science (LNCS), including its subseries Lecture Notes in Artificial Intelligence (LNAI) and Lecture Notes in Bioinformatics (LNBI), has established itself as a medium for the publication of new developments in computer science and information technology research, teaching, and education.

LNCS enjoys close cooperation with the computer science R & D community, the series counts many renowned academics among its volume editors and paper authors, and collaborates with prestigious societies. Its mission is to serve this international community by providing an invaluable service, mainly focused on the publication of conference and workshop proceedings and postproceedings. LNCS commenced publication in 1973.

Terry R. Payne · Valentina Presutti · Guilin Qi ·
María Poveda-Villalón · Giorgos Stoilos ·
Laura Hollink · Zoi Kaoudi · Gong Cheng ·
Juanzi Li
Editors

The Semantic Web – ISWC 2023

22nd International Semantic Web Conference
Athens, Greece, November 6–10, 2023
Proceedings, Part I

Springer

Editors
Terry R. Payne (ID)
University of Liverpool
Liverpool, UK

Valentina Presutti (ID)
University of Bologna
Bologna, Italy

Guilin Qi (ID)
Southeast University
Nanjing, China

María Poveda-Villalón (ID)
Universidad Politécnica de Madrid
Madrid, Spain

Giorgos Stoilos (ID)
Huawei Technologies R&D UK
Edinburgh, UK

Laura Hollink (ID)
Centrum Wiskunde and Informatica
Amsterdam, The Netherlands

Zoi Kaoudi (ID)
IT University of Copenhagen
Copenhagen, Denmark

Gong Cheng (ID)
Nanjing University
Nanjing, China

Juanzi Li (ID)
Tsinghua University
Beijing, China

ISSN 0302-9743   ISSN 1611-3349 (electronic)
Lecture Notes in Computer Science
ISBN 978-3-031-47239-8   ISBN 978-3-031-47240-4 (eBook)
https://doi.org/10.1007/978-3-031-47240-4

Preface

The International Semantic Web Conference (ISWC), started in 2002, aims to provide a platform for Semantic Web researchers and practitioners from around the world to share and exchange advanced techniques, and experiences in Semantic Web and related areas. Now in its 22nd edition, the ISWC has become the flagship conference for the Semantic Web and Knowledge Graph community to discuss and present the latest advances in machine-understandable semantics, large-scale knowledge resource construction, logical reasoning, and semantic interoperability and multi-agent applications.

ISWC continues its tradition of being the premier international forum, having been hosted in 9 countries and 20 cities worldwide since its inception. This year, ISWC 2023 convened in Athens, Greece, bringing together researchers, practitioners, and enthusiasts in the Semantic Web and Knowledge Graph community for valuable face-to-face interactions and discussions. ISWC 2023 received 411 submissions, authored by 1,457 distinct authors from 46 different countries, reflecting the ever-growing interest and participation in the field. Building on the rigorous reviewing processes of previous editions, our review processes this year were equally comprehensive and constructive. Each submitted paper underwent meticulous evaluation, considering criteria such as originality, novelty, empiricism, and reproducibility. We extend our heartfelt gratitude to all the authors, reviewers, and organizers who have contributed to making this conference possible.

The recent upsurge in Artificial Intelligence (AI) driven by Large Language Models (LLMs) brings new challenges and opportunities to the Semantic Web and Knowledge Graph community. LLMs have massive parameterized knowledge, can generate fluent content, engage in natural language interactions with humans, and have the ability to accomplish multi-scenario tasks. At the same time, we notice that LLMs still have some limitations in terms of knowledge hallucination and interpretability, as well as the planning ability of knowledge reasoning and complex problem-solving. Currently, we need to re-examine the relationship between LLMs and Semantic Web and Knowledge Graphs. This conference also hopes to fully communicate and discuss these problems, and together promote the research and application of combining knowledge-driven and data-driven AI.

In-depth exploration of these various aspects was addressed in invited keynotes given by three distinguished professors, and a panel with invited panelists from industry and academia. The keynote of Gerhard Weikum was entitled "Knowledge Graphs in the Age of Large Language Models" and outlined research opportunities that could leverage synergies between LLMs and Knowledge Graphs. Deborah L. McGuinness's keynote was entitled "Semantic Web Research in the Age of Generative Artificial Intelligence" and rethinks how generative AI holds great potential for Semantic Web research and applications in general and ontology-related work. The keynote entitled "ChatGLM: An Alternative to ChatGPT", presented by Jie Tang, introduced and discussed technical details on how to build a ChatGPT-style intelligent system and shared lessons learned during the development of ChatGLM. A panel led by Vassilis Christophides and Heng Ji delved into the topic of neuro-symbolic AI, which aims to enhance statistical AI (machine learning) with the complementary capabilities of symbolic AI (knowledge and reasoning).

The research track was chaired by Terry Payne and Valentina Presutti, and in keeping with previous conferences, solicited novel and significant research contributions addressing theoretical, analytical, and empirical aspects of the Semantic Web. A total of 170 full paper submissions were received across a broad set of topics. As with previous years, the most popular topics included knowledge representation and reasoning, and the construction and use of Knowledge Graphs. Many submissions focused on the use of reasoning and query answering, with a number addressing engineering, maintenance, and alignment tasks for ontologies. Likewise, there was a healthy batch of submissions on search, query, integration, and the analysis of knowledge. Finally, following the growing interest in neuro-symbolic approaches, there was a rise in the number of studies that focus on the use of Large Language Models and Deep Learning techniques such as Graph Neural Networks.

As ever, the Program Committee (PC) was fundamental in reviewing and providing guidance to the papers, both in determining what should be accepted in terms of maturity and quality, and in shaping the final version of each paper through detailed comments and recommendations. For this, we had the help of 264 PC members from 34 countries, and a further 39 Senior Program Committee (SPC) members who helped oversee the reviewing process and were responsible for drafting the meta-reviews for all of the papers. Finally, an additional 56 external reviewers, solicited by PC members, assisted by contributing valuable additional reviews to the process. Continuing the trend of previous editions of ISWC, the Research Track was double-blind, with each paper receiving at least three reviews, and the majority getting four. Reproducibility and novelty continued to be a fundamental component of every submission, with the requirement to provide supplementary material wherever possible. In the end, 33 papers were accepted, resulting in an acceptance rate of 19.4%, which was consistent with that of previous research tracks at ISWC.

The Resources Track, chaired by Guilin Qi and María Poveda-Villalón, focused on the promotion and sharing of resources that support, enable, or utilize Semantic Web research, and in particular datasets, ontologies, software, and benchmarks, among others. This track received 70 papers for review. Each paper was subject to a rigorous single-blind review process involving at least three PC and SPC members, and program chairs considered both the papers and the author responses. The main review criteria focused on impact (novelty of the resource), reusability, design and technical quality, and availability. Eventually, 17 papers were accepted. The Resources Track was aided by 7 SPC and 54 PC members, and 12 additional reviewers.

The In-Use Track this year was chaired by Giorgos Stoilos and Laura Hollink. This track provides a forum to explore the benefits and challenges of applying Semantic Web and Knowledge Graph technologies in concrete, practical use cases, in contexts ranging from industry to government and society. In total, eight full papers were accepted out of 25 full paper submissions (32% acceptance rate). All submissions were thoroughly reviewed in a single-blind process by at least three and in some cases even four PC members. Submissions were assessed in terms of novelty (of the proposed use case or solution), uptake by the target user group, demonstrated or potential impact, as well as overall soundness and quality. An Objection and Response phase was also implemented this year in line with the other tracks of the conference. Overall, 32 PC members and three additional reviewers participated in a rigorous review process.

The Industry Track, this year chaired by Daniel Garijo and Jose Manuel Gomez-Perez, covers all aspects of innovative commercial or industrial-strength Semantic Technologies and Knowledge Graphs to showcase the state of adoption. This track received 19 papers for review, of which 12 were accepted (63% acceptance rate) following a single-blind review process. The 17 members of the PC assessed each submission in terms of qualitative and quantitative business value, as well as the innovative aspects, impact, and lessons learned of applying Knowledge Graph and semantic technologies in the application domain.

The Workshop and Tutorial Track, chaired by Heiko Paulheim and Bo Fu, presented a total of 10 selected workshops covering established and emerging topics as part of the conference program, including knowledge engineering and management (e.g., ontology design and patterns, knowledge base construction, evolution, and preservation), acquisition, integration, and manipulation of knowledge (e.g., ontology matching, as well as the storing, querying, and benchmarking of knowledge graphs), visualization and representation of knowledge for human users (e.g., interactive visual support for ontologies, linked data, and knowledge graphs), applied emerging areas that assist the advancement of Semantic Web research (e.g., deep learning for knowledge graphs), as well as semantic technologies in use (e.g., industrial information modeling, ontology design for cultural heritage, and open knowledge bases such as Wikidata). In addition, two tutorials were offered as part of the conference program to foster discussions and information exchange for researchers and practitioners working to overcome challenges surrounding knowledge discovery in spatial data and neuro-symbolic artificial intelligence for smart manufacturing.

The Semantic Web Challenges Track was jointly chaired by Valentina Ivanova and Wen Zhang. Four challenges were selected for the track, all of them held before in some of the previous editions of either the ISWC or ESWC conference series. Each of the challenges provides a common environment and datasets to evaluate and compare the systems in various settings and tasks. The challenges covered various topics ranging from reasoners evaluation to creating knowledge graphs from tabular data as well as from pretrained language models and query answering. Two of the challenges were collocated with workshops focusing on similar topics, which provided a ground for extended discussion around emerging research and demonstrating it in proof-of-concept solutions. The accepted challenges were: 2nd edition of LM-KBC: Knowledge Base Construction from Pretrained Language Models (collocated with the 1st Workshop on Knowledge Base Construction from Pre-Trained Language Models (KBC-LM)), 2nd edition of The Scholarly QALD Challenge, 5th edition of SemTab: Semantic Web Challenge on Tabular Data to Knowledge Graph Matching (collocated with the 18th International Workshop on Ontology Matching) and the 3rd edition of Semantic Reasoning Evaluation Challenge (SemREC 2023).

The Posters and Demos Track was chaired by Irini Fundulaki and Kouji Kozaki. This track complements the paper tracks of the conference by offering an opportunity to present late-breaking research results, on-going projects, and speculative as well as innovative work in progress. The Posters and Demos Track encourages presenters and participants to submit papers that have the potential to create discussions about their work that provide valuable input for the future work of the presenters. At the same time, it offers participants an effective way to broaden their knowledge on a variety of research topics and to network with other researchers. This track received 101 papers for review, of which 57 were accepted (56% acceptance rate). Among the accepted papers, 29 were poster papers and 28 were demo papers. The 55 members of the PC were involved in a double-blind review process and assessed each submission based on a variety of criteria such as novelty, relevance to the Semantic Web, impact, technical contribution, and readability.

The Doctoral Consortium (DC) was chaired by Claudia d'Amato and Jeff Pan. The DC is another fundamental event of ISWC. It gives PhD students the opportunity to present their research ideas and initial results and to receive constructive feedback from senior members of the community. This year's DC received 24 submissions. Each submission was reviewed by three members of a PC that consisted of 35 members in total. Based on the reviews, which were managed in agreement with a single-blind review process, 17 submissions were accepted to be published in the DC proceedings edited by CEUR, and the students of these submissions were invited to present their ideas and work during the DC sessions of the conference, where they received further feedback from senior conference attendees. The DC also hosted a career-advice session, consisting of senior researchers providing career advice with an open Q&A session.

Our thanks go to our local organization team, led by local chair Manolis Koubarakis, Dimitris Plexousakis, and George Vouros, who worked tirelessly to ensure a seamless conference experience. Their meticulous management of all conference activities was truly commendable.

We would like to thank the diligent work of Zoi Kaoudi and Gong Cheng, who have been instrumental in the preparation of the ISWC 2023 proceedings. Their efforts have not only ensured the quality of the conference materials but have also facilitated the sharing of conference data in a reusable and open format.

The success of ISWC 2023 has been widely disseminated within the Semantic Web and Knowledge Graph community, thanks to the tireless efforts of Ioannis Chrysakis, Ioannis Karatzanis, and Lei Hou. Their unwavering commitment to spreading news and updates has greatly contributed to the conference's visibility and reach.

Sponsorship plays a pivotal role in bringing the conference to fruition. We would like to express our gratitude to sponsorship chairs Haofen Wang, Andrea Nuzzolese, and Evgeny Kharlamov, who worked tirelessly to secure support and promote the conference to our sponsors, making ISWC 2023 possible in its current form. We also extend our sincerest thanks to all our sponsors for their invaluable contributions. Also, we are especially thankful to our Student Grants Chairs, Cogan Shimizu and Eleni Tsalapati, whose hard work enabled students to actively participate in this conference.

Finally, our heartfelt gratitude extends to the entire organizing committee, a dedicated family of chairs who have embarked on this complex yet remarkable journey to deliver ISWC 2023. We would also like to express our appreciation to the Semantic Web Science Association (SWSA) for their invaluable support and constant presence throughout ISWC's 22 year history.

Juanzi Li, ISWC 2023 General Chair, on behalf of all the editors.

September 2023

Terry R. Payne
Valentina Presutti
Guilin Qi
María Poveda-Villalón
Giorgos Stoilos
Laura Hollink
Zoi Kaoudi
Gong Cheng
Juanzi Li

Organization

General Chair

Juanzi Li   Tsinghua University, China

Local Chairs

Manolis Koubarakis   National and Kapodistrian University of Athens, Greece

Dimitris Plexousakis   Foundation for Research and Technology Hellas and University of Crete, Greece

George Vouros   University of Piraeus, Greece

Research Track Chairs

Terry R. Payne   University of Liverpool, UK
Valentina Presutti   University of Bologna, Italy

Resources Track Chairs

Guilin Qi   Southeast University, China
María Poveda-Villalón   Universidad Politécnica de Madrid, Spain

In-Use Track Chairs

Giorgos Stoilos   Huawei Technologies R&D, UK
Laura Hollink   Centrum Wiskunde & Informatica, The Netherlands

Workshops and Tutorials Chairs

Heiko Paulheim   University of Mannheim, Germany
Bo Fu   California State University Long Beach, USA

Industry Track Chairs

Jose Manuel Gomez-Perez   Expert AI, Spain
Daniel Garijo   Universidad Politécnica de Madrid, Spain

Doctoral Consortium Chairs

Claudia d'Amato   University of Bari, Italy
Jeff Z. Pan   University of Edinburgh, UK

Posters, Demos, and Lightning Talks Chairs

Irini Fundulaki   Foundation for Research and Technology Hellas,
                                     Greece
Kozaki Kouji   Osaka Electro-Communication University, Japan

Semantic Web Challenge Chairs

Valentina Ivanova   RISE Research Institutes of Sweden, Sweden
Wen Zhang   Zhejiang University, China

Panel Chairs

Vassilis Christophides   ENSEA, ETIS, France
Heng Ji   University of Illinois at Urbana-Champaign, USA

Sponsor Chairs

Haofen Wang   Tongji University, China
Andrea Nuzzolese   National Research Council, Italy
Evgeny Kharlamov   Bosch Center for AI, Germany and University of
                                     Oslo, Norway

Proceedings and Metadata Chairs

Zoi Kaoudi   IT University of Copenhagen, Denmark
Gong Cheng   Nanjing University, China

Student Grants Chairs

Cogan Shimizu   Wright State University, USA
Eleni Tsalapati   National and Kapodistrian University of Athens,
                                       Greece

Web Presence and Publicity Chairs

Ioannis Chrysakis   Foundation for Research and Technology Hellas,
                                       Greece and Ghent University and KU Leuven,
                                       Belgium
Ioannis Karatzanis   Foundation for Research and Technology Hellas,
                                       Greece
Lei Hou   Tsinghua University, China

Research Track Senior Program Committee

Maribel Acosta   Ruhr University Bochum, Germany
Irene Celino   Cefriel, Italy
Gong Cheng   Nanjing University, China
Michael Cochez   Vrije Universiteit Amsterdam, The Netherlands
Oscar Corcho   Universidad Politécnica de Madrid, Spain
Julien Corman   Free University of Bozen-Bolzano, Italy
Mauro Dragoni   Fondazione Bruno Kessler - FBK-IRST, Italy
Jérôme Euzenat   Inria and Univ. Grenoble Alpes, France
Aldo Gangemi   University of Bologna - CNR-ISTC, Italy
Chiara Ghidini   Fondazione Bruno Kessler, Italy
Peter Haase   metaphacts, Germany
Olaf Hartig   Linköping University, Sweden
Aidan Hogan   Universidad de Chile, Chile
Wei Hu   Nanjing University, China
Ernesto Jimenez-Ruiz   City, University of London, UK
Sabrina Kirrane   Vienna University of Economics and Business,
                                       Austria

Markus Luczak-Roesch	Victoria University of Wellington, New Zealand
Maria Vanina Martinez	Artificial Intelligence Research Institute (IIIA-CSIC), Spain
Gabriela Montoya	Aalborg University, Denmark
Boris Motik	University of Oxford, UK
Magdalena Ortiz	Vienna University of Technology, Austria
Francesco Osborne	Open University, UK
Matteo Palmonari	University of Milano-Bicocca, Italy
Marta Sabou	Vienna University of Economics and Business, Austria
Elena Simperl	King's College London, UK
Hala Skaf-Molli	University of Nantes - LS2N, France
Kavitha Srinivas	IBM, USA
Valentina Tamma	University of Liverpool, UK
Serena Villata	CNRS - Laboratoire d'Informatique, Signaux et Systèmes de Sophia-Antipolis, France
Domagoj Vrgoc	Pontificia Universidad Católica de Chile, Chile
Kewen Wang	Griffith University, Australia
Yizheng Zhao	Nanjing University, China

Research Track Program Committee

Ibrahim Abdelaziz	IBM Research, USA
Shqiponja Ahmetaj	TU Vienna, Austria
Mirza Mohtashim Alam	Institut für Angewandte Informatik, Germany
Harith Alani	Open University, UK
Panos Alexopoulos	Textkernel B.V., Netherlands
Samah Alkhuzaey	University of Liverpool, UK
João Paulo Almeida	Federal University of Espírito Santo, Brazil
Julián Arenas-Guerrero	Universidad Politécnica de Madrid, Spain
Hiba Arnaout	Max Planck Institute for Informatics, Germany
Luigi Asprino	University of Bologna, Italy
Amr Azzam	WU Vienna, Austria
Carlos Badenes-Olmedo	Universidad Politécnica de Madrid, Spain
Ratan Bahadur Thapa	University of Oslo, Norway
Payam Barnaghi	Imperial College London, UK
Pierpaolo Basile	University of Bari, Italy
Russa Biswas	Karlsruhe Institute of Technology & FIZ Karlsruhe, Germany
Christian Bizer	University of Mannheim, Germany
Eva Blomqvist	Linköping University, Sweden

Carlos Bobed   University of Zaragoza, Spain
Alexander Borgida   Rutgers University, USA
Paolo Bouquet   University of Trento, Italy
Zied Bouraoui   CRIL - CNRS & Univ. Artois, France
Janez Brank   Jožef Stefan Institute, Slovenia
Carlos Buil Aranda   Universidad Técnica Federico Santa María, Chile
Davide Buscaldi   LIPN, Université Sorbonne Paris Nord, France
Jean-Paul Calbimonte   University of Applied Sciences and Arts Western
                                    Switzerland HES-SO, Switzerland
Pablo Calleja   Universidad Politécnica de Madrid, Spain
Antonella Carbonaro   University of Bologna, Italy
Valentina Anita Carriero   University of Bologna, Italy
Pierre-Antoine Champin   Inria/W3C, France
Victor Charpenay   Mines Saint-Etienne, Univ Clermont Auvergne,
                                    INP Clermont Auvergne, France
Vinay Chaudhri   JPMorgan Chase & Co., USA
David Chaves-Fraga   Universidad Politécnica de Madrid, Spain
Jiaoyan Chen   University of Manchester, UK
Sijin Cheng   Linköping University, Sweden
Philipp Cimiano   Bielefeld University, Germany
Andrei Ciortea   University of St. Gallen, Switzerland
Pieter Colpaert   Ghent University – imec, Belgium
Philippe Cudre-Mauroux   U. of Fribourg, Switzerland
Victor de Boer   Vrije Universiteit Amsterdam, The Netherlands
Daniele Dell'Aglio   Aalborg University, Denmark
Danilo Dessì   University of Cagliari, Italy
Stefan Dietze   GESIS - Leibniz Institute for the Social Sciences,
                                    Germany
Anastasia Dimou   KU Leuven, Belgium
Shusaku Egami   National Institute of Advanced Industrial Science
                                    and Technology, Japan
Fajar J. Ekaputra   Vienna University of Economics and Business,
                                    Austria
Paola Espinoza-Arias   BASF, Spain
David Eyers   University of Otago, New Zealand
Alessandro Faraotti   IBM, Italy
Michael Färber   Karlsruhe Institute of Technology, Germany
Daniel Faria   INESC-ID, Instituto Superior Técnico,
                                    Universidade de Lisboa, Portugal
Catherine Faron   Université Côte d'Azur, France
Javier D. Fernández   F. Hoffmann-La Roche AG, Switzerland
Sebastián Ferrada   Linköping University, Sweden

Jan-Christoph Kalo	Vrije Universiteit Amsterdam, The Netherlands
Maulik R. Kamdar	Elsevier Inc., The Netherlands
Takahiro Kawamura	National Agriculture and Food Research Organization, Japan
Maria Keet	University of Cape Town, South Africa
Mayank Kejriwal	University of Southern California, USA
Ilkcan Keles	Aalborg University/TomTom, Denmark
Neha Keshan	Rensselaer Polytechnic Institute, USA
Ankesh Khandelwal	Amazon, USA
Evgeny Kharlamov	University of Oslo, Norway
Elmar Kiesling	Vienna University of Economics and Business, Austria
Craig Knoblock	USC Information Sciences Institute, USA
Haridimos Kondylakis	Foundation of Research & Technology-Hellas, Greece
Stasinos Konstantopoulos	NCSR Demokritos, Greece
Roman Kontchakov	Birkbeck, University of London, UK
Manolis Koubarakis	National and Kapodistrian University of Athens, Greece
Adila A. Krisnadhi	Universitas Indonesia, Indonesia
Markus Krötzsch	TU Dresden, Germany
Benno Kruit	Vrije Universiteit Amsterdam, The Netherlands
Jose Emilio Labra Gayo	Universidad de Oviedo, Spain
André Lamurias	Aalborg University, Denmark
Agnieszka Lawrynowicz	Poznan University of Technology, Poland
Danh Le Phuoc	TU Berlin, Germany
Maxime Lefrançois	Mines Saint-Étienne, France
Huanyu Li	Linköping University, Sweden
Tianyi Li	University of Edinburgh, UK
Wenqiang Liu	Tencent Inc., China
Carsten Lutz	Universität Bremen, Germany
Maria Maleshkova	Helmut-Schmidt-Universität, Germany
Thomas Meyer	University of Cape Town and CAIR, South Africa
Pascal Molli	University of Nantes - LS2N, France
Pierre Monnin	Orange, France
Deshendran Moodley	University of Cape Town, South Africa
Varish Mulwad	GE Research, India
Summaya Mumtaz	University of Oslo, Norway
Raghava Mutharaju	IIIT-Delhi, India
Hubert Naacke	Sorbonne Université, LIP6, France
Shinichi Nagano	Toshiba Corporation, Japan
Axel-Cyrille Ngonga Ngomo	Paderborn University, Germany

Marco Luca Sbodio	IBM Research, Ireland
Francois Scharffe	University of Montpellier, France
Konstantin Schekotihin	Alpen-Adria Universität Klagenfurt, Austria
Ralf Schenkel	Trier University, Germany
Juan F. Sequeda	data.world, USA
Cogan Shimizu	Wright State University, USA
Kuldeep Singh	Cerence GmbH and Zerotha Research, Germany
Nadine Steinmetz	TU Ilmenau, Germany
Armando Stellato	University of Rome Tor Vergata, Italy
Gerd Stumme	University of Kassel, Germany
Mari Carmen Suárez-Figueroa	Universidad Politécnica de Madrid, Spain
Zequn Sun	Nanjing University, China
Vojtěch Svátek	University of Economics, Czech Republic
Ruben Taelman	Ghent University – imec, Belgium
Hideaki Takeda	National Institute of Informatics, Japan
Kerry Taylor	Australian National University, Australia
Andreas Thalhammer	F. Hoffmann-La Roche AG, Switzerland
Krishnaprasad Thirunarayan	Wright State University, USA
Steffen Thoma	FZI Research Center for Information Technology, Germany
Ilaria Tiddi	Vrije Universiteit Amsterdam, The Netherlands
David Toman	University of Waterloo, Canada
Riccardo Tommasini	INSA de Lyon - LIRIS Lab, France
Raphael Troncy	Eurecom, France
Takanori Ugai	Fujitsu Ltd., Japan
Guillermo Vega-Gorgojo	Universidad de Valladolid, Spain
Ruben Verborgh	Ghent University – imec, Belgium
Haofen Wang	Tongji University, China
Zhe Wang	Griffith University, Australia
Yisong Wang	Guizhou University, China
Xiaxia Wang	Nanjing University, China
Meng Wang	Southeast University, China
Peng Wang	Southeast University, China
Xin Wang	Tianjin University, China
Ruijie Wang	University of Zurich, Switzerland
Simon Werner	Trier University, Germany
Xander Wilcke	Vrije Universiteit Amsterdam, The Netherlands
Honghan Wu	University College London, UK
Josiane Xavier Parreira	Siemens AG Österreich, Austria
Ikuya Yamada	Studio Ousia Inc., Japan
Qiang Yang	King Abdullah University of Science and Technology, Saudi Arabia

Fouad Zablith	American University of Beirut, Lebanon
Fadi Zaraket	American University of Beirut, Lebanon
Xiaowang Zhang	Tianjin University, China
Lu Zhou	Flatfeecorp, Inc., USA
Antoine Zimmermann	École des Mines de Saint-Étienne, France

Research Track Additional Reviewers

Mehdi Azarafza	Andrea Mauri
Moritz Blum	Sebastian Monka
Alexander Brinkmann	Simon Münker
Luana Bulla	Sergi Nadal
Yanping Chen	Janna Omeliyanenko
Panfeng Chen	Wolfgang Otto
Sulogna Chowdhury	Trupti Padiya
Fiorela Ciroku	Despina-Athanasia Pantazi
Yuanning Cui	George Papadakis
Hang Dong	Ralph Peeters
Daniel Fernández-Álvarez	Zhan Qu
Giacomo Frisoni	Youssra Rebboud
Carlos Golvano	Qasid Saleem
Abul Hasan	Muhammad Salman
Johannes Hirth	Alyssa Sha
Viet-Phi Huynh	Chen Shao
Monika Jain	Basel Shbita
Varvara Kalokyri	Sarah Binta Alam Shoilee
Keti Korini	Lucia Siciliani
Kyriakos Kritikos	Gunjan Singh
Kai Kugler	Eleni Tsalapati
Kabul Kurniawan	Roderick van der Weerdt
Anh Le-Tuan	Binh Vu
Fandel Lin	Xinni Wang
Anna Sofia Lippolis	Jinge Wu
Pasquale Lisena	Ziwei Xu
Yun Liu	Jicheng Yuan
Tiroshan Madhushanka	Albin Zehe

Resources Track Senior Program Committee

Enrico Daga	Open University, UK
Antoine Isaac	Europeana & VU Amsterdam, The Netherlands
Tong Ruan	ECUST, China

Ruben Taelman   Ghent University, Belgium
Maria-Esther Vidal   TIB, Germany
Xiaowang Zhang   Tianjin University, China
Antoine Zimmermann   École des Mines de Saint-Étienne, France

Resources Track Program Committee

Vito Walter Anelli   Politecnico di Bari, Italy
Ghislain Atemezing   ERA - European Union Agency for Railways,
                              France
Debanjali Biswas   GESIS Leibniz Institute for the Social Sciences,
                              Germany
Oleksandra Bruns   FIZ Karlsruhe, Leibniz Institute for Information
                              Infrastructure & KIT Karlsruhe, Germany
Pierre-Antoine Champin   Inria/W3C, France
David Chaves-Fraga   Universidade de Santiago de Compostela, Spain
Andrea Cimmino Arriaga   Universidad Politécnica de Madrid, Spain
Jérôme David   Université Grenoble Alpes, France
Anastasia Dimou   KU Leuven, Belgium
Elvira Amador-Domínguez   Universidad Politécnica de Madrid, Spain
Pablo Fillottrani   Universidad Nacional del Sur, Argentina
Florian Grensing   University of Siegen, Germany
Tudor Groza   Perth Children's Hospital, Australia
Peter Haase   metaphacts, Germany
Fatma-Zohra Hannou   École des Mines de Saint-Étienne, France
Ana Iglesias-Molina   Universidad Politécnica de Madrid, Spain
Clement Jonquet   MISTEA (INRAE) and LIRMM (U. Montpellier),
                              France
Yavuz Selim Kartal   GESIS Leibniz Institute for Social Sciences,
                              Germany
Zubeida Khan   Council for Scientific and Industrial Research,
                              South Africa
Christian Kindermann   Stanford University, UK
Tomas Kliegr   Prague University of Economics and Business,
                              Czechia
Jakub Klímek   Charles University, Czechia
Agnieszka Lawrynowicz   Poznan University of Technology, Poland
Maxime Lefrançois   École des Mines de Saint-Étienne, France
Allyson Lister   University of Oxford, UK
Zola Mahlaza   University of Cape Town, South Africa
Maria Maleshkova   Helmut-Schmidt-Universität Hamburg, Germany

Milan Markovic	University of Aberdeen, UK
Patricia Martín-Chozas	Ontology Engineering Group, Spain
Hande McGinty	Ohio University, USA
Lionel Medini	University of Lyon1 - LIRIS/CNRS, France
Nandana Mihindukulasooriya	IBM Research AI, USA
Pascal Molli	University of Nantes - LS2N, France
Alessandro Mosca	Free University of Bozen-Bolzano, Italy
Ebrahim Norouzi	FIZ Karlsruhe, Leibniz Institute for Information Infrastructure & KIT Karlsruhe, Germany
Rafael Peñaloza	University of Milano-Bicocca, Italy
María del Mar Roldán-García	Universidad de Málaga, Spain
Catherine Roussey	INRAE, France
Harald Sack	FIZ Karlsruhe, Leibniz Institute for Information Infrastructure & KIT Karlsruhe, Germany
Umutcan Serles	University of Innsbruck, Austria
Patricia Serrano Alvarado	University of Nantes - LS2N, France
Cogan Shimizu	Wright State University, USA
Blerina Spahiu	Università degli Studi di Milano-Bicocca, Italy
Valentina Tamma	University of Southampton, UK
Walter Terkaj	CNR-STIIMA, Italy
Tabea Tietz	FIZ Karlsruhe, Leibniz Institute for Information Infrastructure & KIT Karlsruhe, Germany
Jörg Waitelonis	FIZ Karlsruhe – Leibniz Institute for Information Infrastructure, Germany
Meng Wang	Tongji University, China
Zhichun Wang	Beijing Normal University, China
Tianxing Wu	Southeast University, China
Lan Yang	University of Galway, Ireland
Ondřej Zamazal	Prague University of Economics and Business, Czechia
Ningyu Zhang	Zhejiang University, China
Ziqi Zhang	Accessible Intelligence, UK

Resources Track Additional Reviewers

Cristobal Barba-Gonzalez	Aljosha Köcher
Antonio Benítez-Hidalgo	Edna Ruckhaus
Giovanni Maria Biancofiore Biancofiore	Mayra Russo
Jean-Paul Calbimonte	Andre Valdestilhas
Dario Di Palma	Miel Vander Sande
Florian Grensing	Lei Zhang

In-Use Track Program Committee

Nathalie Aussenac-Gilles	IRIT CNRS, France
Martin Bauer	NEC Laboratories Europe, Germany
Maria Bermudez-Edo	University of Granada, Spain
Stefan Bischof	Siemens AG Österreich, Austria
Carlos Buil Aranda	Universidad Técnica Federico Santa María, Chile
Oscar Corcho	Universidad Politécnica de Madrid, Spain
Philippe Cudre-Mauroux	University of Fribourg, Switzerland
Christophe Debruyne	Université de Liège, Belgium
Jose Manuel Gomez-Perez	expert.ai, Spain
Damien Graux	Huawei Technologies, UK
Daniel Gruhl	IBM Almaden Research Center, USA
Peter Haase	Metaphacts, Germany
Nicolas Heist	University of Mannheim, Germany
Aidan Hogan	Universidad de Chile, Chile
Tomi Kauppinen	Aalto University, Finland
Mayank Kejriwal	University of Southern California, USA
Craig Knoblock	University of Southern California, USA
Maxime Lefrançois	École des Mines de Saint-Étienne, France
Vanessa Lopez	IBM Research Europe, Ireland
Michael Luggen	University of Fribourg, Switzerland
Ioanna Lytra	Semantic Web Company, Austria
Beatrice Markhoff	Université de Tours, France
Andriy Nikolov	AstraZeneca, UK
Declan O'Sullivan	Trinity College Dublin, Ireland
Matteo Palmonari	University of Milano-Bicocca, Italy
Artem Revenko	Semantic Web Company, Austria
Mariano Rico	Universidad Politécnica de Madrid, Spain
Dezhao Song	Thomson Reuters, USA
Danai Symeonidou	INRAE, France
Josiane Xavier Parreira	Siemens AG Österreich, Austria
Matthäus Zloch	GESIS - Leibniz Institute for the Social Sciences, Germany

In-Use Track Additional Reviewers

Basel Shbita
Fandel Lin
Binh Vu

Sponsors

Below we report the list of sponsors that joined before the completion of the proceedings, *i.e.*, September 18th, 2023.

For the final list of sponsors in every category, please visit https://iswc2023.semant icweb.org/sponsors/.

Diamond Sponsor

https://www.createlink.com/

Platinum Sponsor

https://www.zhipuai.cn/

Gold Plus Sponsors

https://www.bosch.com/

IBM **Research**

http://www.research.ibm.com/

Gold Sponsors

metaphacts

https://metaphacts.com/

Google

https://www.google.com/

gesis
Leibniz Institute
for the Social Sciences

https://www.gesis.org/

 **ontotext**

https://www.ontotext.com/

ebay

https://www.ebay.com/

HUAWEI

https://www.huawei.com/

Silver Plus Sponsor

https://www.journals.elsevier.com/artificial-intelligence

Silver Sponsor

https://qualco.group/

Sponsor

https://www.bupsolutions.com/

Best Paper Award Sponsor

https://www.springer.com/series/558

Invited Speaker Support

https://www.eurai.org/

Keynote Speeches and Panels

Knowledge Graphs in the Age of Large Language Models

Gerhard Weikum

Max Planck Institute for Informatics, Saarbruecken, Germany
weikum@mpi-inf.mpg.de

Abstract. Large knowledge graphs (KG's) have become a key asset for search engines and other use cases (see, e.g., [1–5]). They are partly based on automatically extracting structured information from web contents and other texts, using a variety of pattern-matching and machine-learning methods. The semantically organized machine knowledge can be harnessed to better interpret text in news, social media and web tables, contributing to question answering, natural language processing (NLP) and data analytics.

A recent trend that has revolutionized NLP is to capture knowledge latently by billions of parameters of language models (LM's), learned at scale from huge text collections in a largely self-supervised manner (see, e.g., [6, 7]). These pre-trained models form the basis of fine-tuning machine-learning solutions for tasks that involve both input texts and broad world knowledge, such as question answering, commonsense reasoning and human-computer conversations (see, e.g., [8–10]).

This talk identifies major gaps in the coverage of today's KG's, and discusses potential roles of large language models towards narrowing thee gaps and constructing the next KG generation. The talk outlines research opportunities that could leverage synergies between LM's and KG's.

References

1. Hogan, A., et al.: Knowledge graphs. ACM Comput. Surv. **54**(4), 71:1–71:37 (2021)
2. Weikum, G., Dong, X.L., Razniewski, S., Suchanek, F.M.: Machine knowledge: creation and curation of comprehensive knowledge bases. Found. Trends Databases **10**(2–4), 108–490 (2021)
3. Weikum, G.: Knowledge graphs 2021: a data odyssey. Proc. VLDB Endow. **14**(12), 3233–3238 (2021)
4. Noy, N.F., et al.: Industry-scale knowledge graphs: lessons and challenges. Commun. ACM **62**(8), 36–43 (2019)
5. Dong, X.L.: Generations of knowledge graphs: the crazy ideas and the business impact. Proc. VLDB Endow. **16** (2023)

6. Liu, P.: et al.: Pre-train, prompt, and predict: a systematic survey of prompting methods in natural language processing. ACM Comput. Surv. **55**(9), 195:1–195:35 (2023)
7. Zhaom, W.X., et al.: A Survey of Large Language Models. CoRR abs/2303.18223 (2023)
8. Hu, L.: A Survey of Knowledge-Enhanced Pre-trained Language Models. CoRR abs/2211.05994 (2022)
9. Pan, S., et al.: Unifying Large Language Models and Knowledge Graphs: A Roadmap. CoRR abs/2306.08302 (2023)
10. Pan, J.Z., et al.: Large Language Models and Knowledge Graphs: Opportunities and Challenges. CoRR abs/2308.06374 (2023)

Semantic Web Research in the Age of Generative Artificial Intelligence

Deborah L. McGuinness

Rensselaer Polytechnic Institute, Troy, NY, USA
dlm@cs.rpi.edu

We are living in an age of rapidly advancing technology. History may view this period as one in which generative artificial intelligence is seen as reshaping the landscape and narrative of many technology-based fields of research and application. Times of disruptions often present both opportunities and challenges. We will briefly discuss some areas that may be ripe for consideration in the field of Semantic Web research and semantically-enabled applications.

Semantic Web research has historically focused on representation and reasoning and enabling interoperability of data and vocabularies. At the core are ontologies along with ontology-enabled (or ontology-compatible) knowledge stores such as knowledge graphs. Ontologies are often manually constructed using a process that (1) identifies existing best practice ontologies (and vocabularies) and (2) generates a plan for how to leverage these ontologies by aligning and augmenting them as needed to address requirements. While semi-automated techniques may help, there is typically a significant manual portion of the work that is often best done by humans with domain and ontology expertise.

This is an opportune time to rethink how the field generates, evolves, maintains, and evaluates ontologies. It is time to consider how hybrid approaches, i.e., those that leverage generative AI components along with more traditional knowledge representation and reasoning approaches to create improved processes.

The effort to build a robust ontology that meets a use case can be large. Ontologies are not static however and they need to evolve along with knowledge evolution and expanded usage. There is potential for hybrid approaches to help identify gaps in ontologies and/or refine content. Further, ontologies need to be documented with term definitions and their provenance. Opportunities exist to consider semi-automated techniques for some types of documentation, provenance, and decision rationale capture for annotating ontologies.

The area of human-AI collaboration for population and verification presents a wide range of areas of research collaboration and impact. Ontologies need to be populated with class and relationship content. Knowledge graphs and other knowledge stores need to be populated with instance data in order to be used for question answering and reasoning. Population of large knowledge graphs can be time consuming. Generative AI holds the promise to create candidate knowledge graphs that are compatible with the ontology schema. The knowledge graph should contain provenance information at least identifying how the content was populated and where the content came from. Efforts also need to be made to verify that the populated content is correct and current. This is an area of opportunity since language models predict likely completions for prompts and most do not have built in capabilities to check their answers.

While generative AI is evolving, at least one theme is emerging. Many are proposing a human-AI collaborative assistant approach (e.g., Microsoft's Copilot [1], Google's Assistant [2], Zoom's AI Companion [3], etc.). This is not new, expert system assistants and semantic technology assistants have been proposed, implemented, and deployed for decades. However, the interactive nature of the current language models along with the constant coverage in the press have drastically expanded awareness and usage of large language model services and tools. Gartner's latest AI hype cycle [4], for example, has helped increase attention to many areas of AI that are subfields of the Semantic Web or Generative AI or a combination of both. Further, the diversity of users has expanded. People who do not have computer science experience are now experimenting with these tools and the use cases seem to be expanding almost daily.

Opportunities and challenges increase with the wider range of users and usage types. When some content is automatically generated potentially from models that have been trained on data that is either inaccurate, out of date, or that contains assumptions and biases, the need for rigorous validation grows. Further, as these hybrid approaches proliferate, transparency and explainability become even more critical. Transparency should not just include content related to what a model was trained on but also how it was evaluated. While the field of validation and verification has existed for decades, it becomes more essential now as hybrid systems become more pervasive. We expect not only that benchmark research will grow, but also services that provide experimentation and testing will grow. We have experimented with a kind of "sandbox" for checking answers [5] from some of the large language models, connecting the entities to known structured data sources, such as Wikidata, and then exploring services that attempt to support or refute answers. While this is just one kind of exploratory harness, we believe many more will and should arise.

The generative AI conversation and explosion has the potential to accelerate research and applications and may initiate a kind of Semantic Web Renaissance as more people call for transparency and understanding of technology. At the same time, as communities are raising issues related to bias, fairness, and potential regulation, ethical considerations and responsible use must be at the forefront of our efforts. Ultimately, the opportunities may be more boundless than they have ever been in the history of Semantic Web research and technology.

References

1. Copilot. https://news.microsoft.com/reinventing-productivity/
2. Google Assistant. https://assistant.google.com/
3. Zoom Blog. https://blog.zoom.us/zoom-ai-companion/
4. Gartner Hype Cycle. https://www.gartner.com/en/articles/what-s-new-in-artificial-intelligence-from-the-2023-gartner-hype-cycle
5. RPI's Tetherless World Constellation Large Language Model/Knowledge Graph Fact Checker Demo. https://inciteprojects.idea.rpi.edu/chatbs/app/chatbs/

ChatGLM: An Alternative to ChatGPT

Jie Tang

KEG, Tsinghua University, China
jietang@tsinghua.edu.cn

Large Language Models (LLMs), such as ChatGPT, GPT-4, Claude, PaLM, ChatGLM, Llama, Gemini, and Falcon, have revolutionized the field of artificial intelligence (AI) and substantially advanced the state of the art in various AI tasks, such as language understanding, text generation, image processing, and multimodal modeling. However, these powerful models also pose significant challenges to their safe and ethical deployment. The problem has become more serious since Open AI stopped sharing its techniques behind the GPT series. We present ChatGLM, an alternative to ChatGPT. We discuss technical details on how to build a ChatGPT-style system and share lessons we learned during the development of ChatGLM. Models and codes introduced in this paper are publicly available[1].

Base Model. To build ChatGLM, a powerful base model was necessary. We have developed GLM-130B [5], a bilingual (English and Chinese) language model with 130 billion parameters pre-trained using 1 trillion text tokens. Different from GPT-3, its model architecture is based on teh General Language Model (GLM) [2], a new pre-training method based on autoregressive blank-filling. In GLM, we randomly blank out continuous spans of tokens from the input text and train the model to reconstruct the spans using autoregressive pre-training. In this way, both bidirectional and unidirectional attention can be learned in a single framework. With only with three-fourths of the parameters of GPT-3, GLM-130B can achieve comparable, or even better performance on a wide range of benchmarks (112 tasks) and also outperforms PaLM 540B in many cases.

CodeGeex. We augmented the GLM base model with more code data—it is believed that the code data can help enhance the reasoning ability of the base model. Similar to Open AI's Codex, we first developed a separate model called CodeGeeX [6] using 850 billion tokens of 23 programming languages. CodeGeeX can achieve the best performance on HumanEval among all open code generation models. Based on CodeGeeX, we developed extensions on Visual Studio Code, JetBrains, and Cloud Studio with over 200,000 users.

WebGLM. The lack of dynamic information is a challenge for LLMs. One can fool the base model with simple questions such as "What is the weather now?" We present WebGLM [4], to augment the base model with web search and retrieval capabilities. In WebGLM, we have developed an LLM-augmented retriever, a bootstrapped generator,

---

[1] https://github.com/THUDM.

and a human preference-aware scorer, which successfully offers an efficient and cost-effective solution to address the limitation of the lack of dynamic information, with comparable quality to WebGPT.

ChatGLM. The base model cannot perfectly understand human intentions, follow complicated instructions, and communicate in multi-turn dialogues. Hence, the alignment training is critical for developing ChatGLM in practice. We take the following three steps to align the base model to human preference. First, *Supervised Fine-tuning (SFT)*: We collect initial queries by our existing web demonstrations (after data desensitization) and annotators' creation, including both single-round and multi-round. Second, *Feedback Bootstrapping (FB)*: We iteratively improve the quality of ChatGLM using feedback from annotators. We guide annotators to score model responses from different dimensions, including safety, factuality, relevance, helpfulness, and human preferences. Only top-scored responses are finally added to the next iteration of training. Third, *Reinforcement Learning From Human Feedback (RLHF)*: RLHF can help address flaws in specific situations, such as rejecting responses, safety issues, generating mixtures of bilingual tokens, multi-turn coherence, and some typical tasks.

VisualGLM. We further develop VisualGLM to enable ChatGLM with the ability to understand images, an important function in GPT-4. It has a visual encoder EVA-CLIP that produces image feature sequences. A Qformer model has been trained to bridge the vision model and ChatGLM. After pre-training on 330M Chinese and English image-text pairs and fine-tuning with extensive visual question answering (VQA) data, VisualGLM can effectively align visual information with the semantic nuances of natural language.

In future work, we are still trying to combine multi-modality and multi-task learning into a unified pre-training framework [1, 3], and investigate super alignment to help computers *understand* and solve real-world complicated problems.

References

1. Ding, M., et al.: CogView: mastering text-to-image generation via transformers. In: NeurIPS 2021, pp. 19822–19835 (2021)
2. Du, Z., et al.: GLM: general language model pretraining with autoregressive blank infilling. In: ACL 2022, pp. 320–335 (2022)
3. Lin, J., et al.: M6: multi-modality-to-multi-modality multitask mega-transformer for unified pretraining. In: KDD 2021, pp. 3251–3261 (2021)
4. Liu, X., et al.: WebGLM: towards an efficient web-enhanced question answering system with human preferences. In: KDD 2023, pp. 4549–4560 (2023)
5. Zeng, A., et al.: GLM-130B: an open bilingual pre-trained model. In: ICLR 2023 (2023)
6. Zheng, Q., et al.: CodeGeeX: a pre-trained model for code generation with multilingual benchmarking on HumanEval-X. In: KDD 2023, pp. 5673–5684 (2023)

Panel on Neuro-Symbolic AI

Efi Tsamoura[1], Vassilis Christophides[2], Antoine Bosselut[3], James Hendler[4], Ian Horrocks[5], and Ioannis Tsamardinos[6]

[1] Samsung AI, Cambridge, UK
efi.tsamoura@samsung.com
[2] ETIS, ENSEA, France
vassilis.christophides@ensea.fr
[3] EPFL, Switzerland
[4] Rensselaer Polytechnic Institute, USA
[5] University of Oxford, UK
[6] University of Crete, Greece

The emerging paradigm of *neuro-symbolic Artificial Intelligence* (AI) stems from the recent efforts to enhance statistical AI (machine learning) with the complementary capabilities of symbolic AI (knowledge and reasoning). In neuro-symbolic AI, symbolic knowledge is used to guide deep models, while offering a path toward grounding symbols and inducing knowledge from low-level sensory data. Neuro-symbolic AI aims to demonstrate the capability to (i) solve hard problems requiring cognitive capabilities (ii) learn with significantly fewer data, ultimately for a large number of tasks rather than one narrow task (iii) provide inherently understandable and controllable decisions and actions.

The success stories and the research challenges of neuro-symbolic AI are the main topics of a panel that will take place in Athens, in November 2023 as part of the 22nd International Semantic Web Conference (ISWC).

A few indicative questions for the panel are:

- What have been the main reasons for developing neuro-symbolic techniques, e.g., explainability, accuracy, or scalability?
- Are there any success stories of blending logic with neural models? Are there any killer application scenarios in the semantic Web, NLP, computer vision, or other areas?
- Is logic the right formalism to address the limitations of the neural models and vice versa?
- What are the main (foundational) problems involved in integrating deep learning with logic? Are uncertain logics the "glue" between these two paradigms?
- How important is understanding the human brain to develop effective neuro-symbolic techniques and vice versa?
- Do neuro-symbolic techniques relate to other AI paradigms like causal AI, hybrid AI and artificial general intelligence (AGI)?
- How logic can help to explain neural models?

Contents – Part I

Research Track

Link Traversal Query Processing Over Decentralized Environments
with Structural Assumptions 3
   Ruben Taelman and Ruben Verborgh

Dense Re-Ranking with Weak Supervision for RDF Dataset Search 23
   Qiaosheng Chen, Zixian Huang, Zhiyang Zhang, Weiqing Luo,
   Tengteng Lin, Qing Shi, and Gong Cheng

Optimizing SPARQL Queries with SHACL 41
   Ratan Bahadur Thapa and Martin Giese

HAEE: Low-Resource Event Detection with Hierarchy-Aware Event
Graph Embeddings 61
   Guoxuan Ding, Xiaobo Guo, Gaode Chen, Lei Wang, and Daren Zha

Textual Entailment for Effective Triple Validation in Object Prediction 80
   Andrés García-Silva, Cristian Berrío, and Jose Manuel Gómez-Pérez

ASKRL: An Aligned-Spatial Knowledge Representation Learning
Framework for Open-World Knowledge Graph 101
   Ziyu Shang, Peng Wang, Yuzhang Liu, Jiajun Liu, and Wenjun Ke

Rethinking Uncertainly Missing and Ambiguous Visual Modality
in Multi-Modal Entity Alignment 121
   Zhuo Chen, Lingbing Guo, Yin Fang, Yichi Zhang, Jiaoyan Chen,
   Jeff Z. Pan, Yangning Li, Huajun Chen, and Wen Zhang

Disentangled Contrastive Learning for Knowledge-Aware Recommender
System 140
   Shuhua Huang, Chenhao Hu, Weiyang Kong, and Yubao Liu

Dependency-Aware Core Column Discovery for Table Understanding 159
   Jingyi Qiu, Aibo Song, Jiahui Jin, Tianbo Zhang, Jingyi Ding,
   Xiaolin Fang, and Jianguo Qian

Spatial Link Prediction with Spatial and Semantic Embeddings 179
   Genivika Mann, Alishiba Dsouza, Ran Yu, and Elena Demidova

How is Your Knowledge Graph Used: Content-Centric Analysis
of SPARQL Query Logs 197
  Luigi Asprino and Miguel Ceriani

Iterative Geographic Entity Alignment with Cross-Attention 216
  Alishiba Dsouza, Ran Yu, Moritz Windoffer, and Elena Demidova

Entity-Relation Distribution-Aware Negative Sampling for Knowledge
Graph Embedding 234
  Naimeng Yao, Qing Liu, Yi Yang, Weihua Li, and Quan Bai

Negative Sampling with Adaptive Denoising Mixup for Knowledge Graph
Embedding 253
  Xiangnan Chen, Wen Zhang, Zhen Yao, Mingyang Chen, and Siliang Tang

Comparison of Knowledge Graph Representations for Consumer Scenarios 271
  Ana Iglesias-Molina, Kian Ahrabian, Filip Ilievski, Jay Pujara,
  and Oscar Corcho

A Comprehensive Study on Knowledge Graph Embedding over Relational
Patterns Based on Rule Learning 290
  Long Jin, Zhen Yao, Mingyang Chen, Huajun Chen, and Wen Zhang

Compact Encoding of Reified Triples Using HDTr 309
  Jose M. Gimenez-Garcia, Thomas Gautrais, Javier D. Fernández,
  and Miguel A. Martínez-Prieto

Causal Inference-Based Debiasing Framework for Knowledge Graph
Completion 328
  Lin Ren, Yongbin Liu, and Chunping Ouyang

Can ChatGPT Replace Traditional KBQA Models? An In-Depth Analysis
of the Question Answering Performance of the GPT LLM Family 348
  Yiming Tan, Dehai Min, Yu Li, Wenbo Li, Nan Hu, Yongrui Chen,
  and Guilin Qi

Mapping and Cleaning Open Commonsense Knowledge Bases
with Generative Translation 368
  Julien Romero and Simon Razniewski

Integrating Knowledge Graph Embeddings and Pre-trained Language
Models in Hypercomplex Spaces 388
  Mojtaba Nayyeri, Zihao Wang, Mst. Mahfuja Akter,
  Mirza Mohtashim Alam, Md Rashad Al Hasan Rony, Jens Lehmann,
  and Steffen Staab

LLMs4OL: Large Language Models for Ontology Learning 408
  Hamed Babaei Giglou, Jennifer D'Souza, and Sören Auer

Biomedical Knowledge Graph Embeddings with Negative Statements 428
  Rita T. Sousa, Sara Silva, Heiko Paulheim, and Catia Pesquita

Knowledge Graph Enhanced Language Models for Sentiment Analysis 447
  Jie Li, Xuan Li, Linmei Hu, Yirui Zhang, and Jinrui Wang

TEMPORALFC: A Temporal Fact Checking Approach over Knowledge
Graphs 465
  Umair Qudus, Michael Röder, Sabrina Kirrane,
  and Axel-Cyrille Ngonga Ngomo

Assessing the Generalization Capabilities of Neural Machine Translation
Models for SPARQL Query Generation 484
  Samuel Reyd and Amal Zouaq

Linking Tabular Columns to Unseen Ontologies 502
  Sarthak Dash, Sugato Bagchi, Nandana Mihindukulasooriya,
  and Alfio Gliozzo

Neural Multi-hop Logical Query Answering with Concept-Level Answers 522
  Zhenwei Tang, Shichao Pei, Xi Peng, Fuzhen Zhuang,
  Xiangliang Zhang, and Robert Hoehndorf

FORECASTTKGQUESTIONS: A Benchmark for Temporal Question
Answering and Forecasting over Temporal Knowledge Graphs 541
  Zifeng Ding, Zongyue Li, Ruoxia Qi, Jingpei Wu, Bailan He, Yunpu Ma,
  Zhao Meng, Shuo Chen, Ruotong Liao, Zhen Han, and Volker Tresp

SORBET: A Siamese Network for Ontology Embeddings Using
a Distance-Based Regression Loss and BERT 561
  Francis Gosselin and Amal Zouaq

Visualizing Mappings Between Pairwise Ontologies - An Empirical Study
of Matrix and Linked Indented List in Their User Support During Class
Mapping Creation and Evaluation 579
  Bo Fu, Allison Austin, and Max Garcia

FeaBI: A Feature Selection-Based Framework for Interpreting KG
Embeddings 599
  Youmna Ismaeil, Daria Stepanova, Trung-Kien Tran,
  and Hendrik Blockeel

CapsKG: Enabling Continual Knowledge Integration in Language Models
for Automatic Knowledge Graph Completion 618
  Janna Omeliyanenko, Albin Zehe, Andreas Hotho, and Daniel Schlör

Author Index 637

Contents – Part II

Resources Track

HOLY: An Ontology Covering the Hydrogen Market 3
Kiara M. Ascencion Arevalo, Christoph Neunsinger,
Roland Zimmermann, Ralph Blum, and Kendra Weakly

MMpedia: A Large-Scale Multi-modal Knowledge Graph 18
Yinan Wu, Xiaowei Wu, Junwen Li, Yue Zhang, Haofen Wang, Wen Du,
Zhidong He, Jingping Liu, and Tong Ruan

Ontology Repositories and Semantic Artefact Catalogues
with the OntoPortal Technology 38
Clement Jonquet, John Graybeal, Syphax Bouazzouni,
Michael Dorf, Nicola Fiore, Xeni Kechagioglou, Timothy Redmond,
Ilaria Rosati, Alex Skrenchuk, Jennifer L. Vendetti, Mark Musen,
and members of the OntoPortal Alliance

AsdKB: A Chinese Knowledge Base for the Early Screening and Diagnosis
of Autism Spectrum Disorder 59
Tianxing Wu, Xudong Cao, Yipeng Zhu, Feiyue Wu, Tianling Gong,
Yuxiang Wang, and Shenqi Jing

TEC: Transparent Emissions Calculation Toolkit 76
Milan Markovic, Daniel Garijo, Stefano Germano, and Iman Naja

SemOpenAlex: The Scientific Landscape in 26 Billion RDF Triples 94
Michael Färber, David Lamprecht, Johan Krause, Linn Aung,
and Peter Haase

Comprehensive Analysis of Freebase and Dataset Creation for Robust
Evaluation of Knowledge Graph Link Prediction Models 113
Nasim Shirvani-Mahdavi, Farahnaz Akrami, Mohammed Samiul Saeef,
Xiao Shi, and Chengkai Li

The SAREF Pipeline and Portal—An Ontology Verification Framework 134
Maxime Lefrançois and David Gnabasik

The RML Ontology: A Community-Driven Modular Redesign After
a Decade of Experience in Mapping Heterogeneous Data to RDF 152
  Ana Iglesias-Molina, Dylan Van Assche, Julián Arenas-Guerrero,
  Ben De Meester, Christophe Debruyne, Samaneh Jozashoori,
  Pano Maria, Franck Michel, David Chaves-Fraga, and Anastasia Dimou

SPARQL_edit: Editing RDF Literals in Knowledge Graphs
via View-Update Translations 176
  Sascha Meckler and Andreas Harth

LDkit: Linked Data Object Graph Mapping Toolkit for Web Applications 194
  Karel Klíma, Ruben Taelman, and Martin Nečaský

VOYAGE: A Large Collection of Vocabulary Usage in Open RDF Datasets 211
  Qing Shi, Junrui Wang, Jeff Z. Pan, and Gong Cheng

Linked Data Objects (LDO): A TypeScript-Enabled RDF Devtool 230
  Jackson Morgan

Text2KGBench: A Benchmark for Ontology-Driven Knowledge Graph
Generation from Text 247
  Nandana Mihindukulasooriya, Sanju Tiwari, Carlos F. Enguix,
  and Kusum Lata

Benchmarking Geospatial Question Answering Engines Using the Dataset
GEOQUESTIONS1089 266
  Sergios-Anestis Kefalidis, Dharmen Punjani, Eleni Tsalapati,
  Konstantinos Plas, Mariangela Pollali, Michail Mitsios,
  Myrto Tsokanaridou, Manolis Koubarakis, and Pierre Maret

FedShop: A Benchmark for Testing the Scalability of SPARQL Federation
Engines 285
  Minh-Hoang Dang, Julien Aimonier-Davat, Pascal Molli, Olaf Hartig,
  Hala Skaf-Molli, and Yotlan Le Crom

The Polifonia Ontology Network: Building a Semantic Backbone
for Musical Heritage 302
  Jacopo de Berardinis, Valentina Anita Carriero, Nitisha Jain,
  Nicolas Lazzari, Albert Meroño-Peñuela, Andrea Poltronieri,
  and Valentina Presutti

In-Use Track

Solving the IoT Cascading Failure Dilemma Using a Semantic Multi-agent
System 325
    Amal Guittoum, François Aïssaoui, Sébastien Bolle, Fabienne Boyer,
    and Noel De Palma

Aviation Certification Powered by the Semantic Web Stack 345
    Paul Cuddihy, Daniel Russell, Eric Mertens, Kit Siu, Dave Archer,
    and Jenny Williams

The Holocaust Archival Material Knowledge Graph 362
    Herminio García-González and Mike Bryant

Scaling Data Science Solutions with Semantics and Machine Learning:
Bosch Case 380
    Baifan Zhou, Nikolay Nikolov, Zhuoxun Zheng, Xianghui Luo,
    Ognjen Savkovic, Dumitru Roman, Ahmet Soylu, and Evgeny Kharlamov

AIDA-Bot 2.0: Enhancing Conversational Agents with Knowledge Graphs
for Analysing the Research Landscape 400
    Antonello Meloni, Simone Angioni, Angelo Salatino,
    Francesco Osborne, Aliaksandr Birukou, Diego Reforgiato Recupero,
    and Enrico Motta

The Wikibase Approach to the Enslaved.Org Hub Knowledge Graph 419
    Cogan Shimizu, Pascal Hitzler, Seila Gonzalez-Estrecha,
    Jeff Goeke-Smith, Dean Rehberger, Catherine Foley, and Alicia Sheill

The World Literature Knowledge Graph 435
    Marco Antonio Stranisci, Eleonora Bernasconi, Viviana Patti,
    Stefano Ferilli, Miguel Ceriani, and Rossana Damiano

Literal-Aware Knowledge Graph Embedding for Welding Quality
Monitoring: A Bosch Case 453
    Zhipeng Tan, Baifan Zhou, Zhuoxun Zheng, Ognjen Savkovic,
    Ziqi Huang, Irlan-Grangel Gonzalez, Ahmet Soylu,
    and Evgeny Kharlamov

Author Index 473

Research Track

Link Traversal Query Processing Over Decentralized Environments with Structural Assumptions

Ruben Taelman[✉] and Ruben Verborgh

IDLab, Department of Electronics and Information Systems, Ghent University – imec, Ghent, Belgium
ruben.taelman@ugent.be

Abstract. To counter societal and economic problems caused by data silos on the Web, efforts such as Solid strive to reclaim private data by storing it in permissioned documents over a large number of personal vaults across the Web. Building applications on top of such a decentralized Knowledge Graph involves significant technical challenges: centralized aggregation prior to query processing is impossible for legal reasons, and current federated querying techniques cannot handle this large scale of distribution at the expected performance. We propose an extension to Link Traversal Query Processing (LTQP) that incorporates structural properties within decentralized environments to tackle their unprecedented scale. In this article, we analyze the structural properties of the Solid decentralization ecosystem that are relevant for query execution, we introduce novel LTQP algorithms leveraging these structural properties, and evaluate their effectiveness. Our experiments indicate that these new algorithms obtain correct results in the order of seconds, which existing algorithms cannot achieve. This work reveals that a traversal-based querying method using structural assumptions can be effective for large-scale decentralization, but that advances are needed in the area of query planning for LTQP to handle more complex queries. These insights open the door to query-driven decentralized applications, in which declarative queries shield developers from the inherent complexity of a decentralized landscape.

Canonical version: https://comunica.github.io/Article-ISWC2023-SolidQuery/

1 Introduction

Despite transforming our world to be more interconnected than ever before, the Web has become increasingly centralized in recent years, contrary to its original vision [1]. The majority of data on the Web today is flowing towards *data silos*, which are in the hands of large companies. This siloization of data leads to various problems, ranging from issues with cross-silo interoperability and vendor lock-in, to privacy breaches and individuals' data being controlled by companies instead of themselves.

Because of increasing awareness and user-empowering legislation such as the GDPR and CCPA, decentralization initiatives [2–5] are gaining popularity. Their common goal is to give people back control over their own data by guarding it in chosen locations

T. R. Payne et al. (Eds.): ISWC 2023, LNCS 14265, pp. 3–22, 2023.
https://doi.org/10.1007/978-3-031-47240-4_1

on the Web instead of aggregated in silos. Initiatives such as Solid [2] and Bluesky [3] achieve this by allowing users to store any kind of data in their own *personal data vault*, which they fully control. In Solid, these data vaults form personal Knowledge Graphs [6, 7], represented as collections of Linked Data documents [8] containing RDF triples [9]. The presence of such data vaults results in a large-scale distribution of data, where applications involving multiple individuals' data will require accessing thousands or even millions of access-controlled data items in data vaults across the Web.

The state of the art in RDF query processing does not support such applications, as it is unprepared to handle large-scale decentralization. The RDF querying research of the past two decades has focused on data that either *is* or *can be* centralized. Some datasets would be in a private or public quadstore [10], specifically designed to enable efficient query processing. Other datasets would be Linked Open Data with a permissive license, making it possible to copy or cache data in a local quadstore. This permanent option to centralize limited the need for decentralized query techniques that allow data to remain at its source. After all, downloading and aggregating datasets would nearly always be more efficient. Yet when we use Linked Data for permissioned or sensitive data, it becomes impossible to download datasets in their entirety. While *federated* query execution approaches do exist [11–14], they currently handle a *small* number (~10) of *large* sources, whereas decentralized environments such as Solid are characterized by a *large* number ($> 10^3$) of *small* sources. Furthermore, federated query execution techniques assume sources to be known prior to query execution, which is not feasible in decentralized environments due to the lack of a central index. Hence, existing techniques are ill-suited for the envisaged scale of decentralization.

Link Traversal Query Processing (LTQP) [15, 16] is an alternative query execution paradigm that is more promising for uncharted decentralized environments. LTQP allows querying over a continuously growing selection of source documents that are discovered *during* query execution, by following hyperlinks between Linked Data documents using the *follow-your-nose* principle [8]. Although LTQP has been theoretically interesting, it has not seen any practical use so far, in particular because of performance concerns.

Fortunately, decentralized ecosystems such as Solid exhibit additional structural properties in addition to the Linked Data principles, allowing us to improve query performance through assumptions about data, documents, and their organization. For example, Solid makes use of Linked Data Platform [17] containers to provide *completeness guarantees* when finding data within vaults, and provides a Type Index [18] to enable *type-based document discovery*.

In this work, we prove that LTQP can be an effective paradigm for the structured retrieval of data from unindexed decentralized Knowledge Graphs. The key is to exploit the aforementioned structural properties for more effective source discovery and query optimization. While we apply our research to the Solid ecosystem, these concepts may be generalizable to other decentralization initiatives [3–5].

This article is structured as follows. In the next section, we discuss related work, after which we provide an analysis of the structural properties of Solid data vaults in Sect. 3. In Sect. 4, we introduce LTQP algorithms that make use of these structural properties, which are evaluated in Sect. 5. Finally, we conclude in Sect. 6.

2 Related Work

The Link Traversal Query Processing (LTQP) paradigm was introduced more than a decade ago [19] as a way to query over the Web of Linked Open Data as if it was a globally distributed dataspace, without having to first index it in a single location. LTQP does this by employing the *follow-your-nose* principle of Linked Data [8] during query execution, in which new RDF are continuously added to a local dataset while discovering new sources by following links between documents. An iterator-based pipeline [19] allows execution to take place without waiting until all links have been followed.

In contrast to *two-phase* approaches [20, 21] that perform data retrieval and indexing *before* query execution, LTQP is thus an *integrated* approach [22] with *parallel* source discovery and query execution. As a one-phase approach, LTQP cannot rely on traditional pre-execution optimization algorithms that require prior dataset statistics. A zero-knowledge query planning technique [23] instead orders triple patterns in a query based on link traversal-specific heuristics. LTQP is related to the idea of *SQL-based query execution over the Web* [24, 25] and to the concept of *focused crawling* [26, 27]. While LTQP considers the Web of Linked Open Data a large database using the RDF data model, SQL-based approaches focus on querying attributes or content within Web pages. Focused crawlers search for Web pages of specific topics to populate a local database or index, using a two-phase approach where a preprocessing step precedes execution. While two-phase approaches in general are able to produce better query plans using traditional cardinality-based planning techniques, waiting for data retrieval to be completed may be impractical or even impossible for certain queries.

The number of potential links to be followed within the Web of Linked Open Data can become prohibitively large. In the worst case, a single query could theoretically require traversing the entire Web. Therefore, the formal LTQP model [16] enables different *reachability criteria*, which embody strategies for deciding what links to follow, each leading to different result completeness semantics. *cNone* follows no URLs, *cAll* follows all URLs in all encountered triple components, and *cMatch* only follows URLs in triple components for those triples that match a triple pattern within the query. *Context-based semantics* [28] is an extension of these reachability semantics to cope with property path expressions in the SPARQL 1.1 language [29]. Next to query-driven reachability, another extension [30] introduces the ability for data publishers to express which links should be followed using *subweb specifications*.

In addition to filtering links via different semantics, a second methodology for lowering query result arrival times is through *link prioritization* [31]. However, existing techniques only sometimes result in faster query results compared to no prioritization. Even though multiple query languages [32–34] have been introduced specifically for LTQP, its SPARQL-based execution model [19] is still the most widely used. Since SPARQL is the only language among these that is a standard, and the fact that it is more widely known and supported by different tools, we make use of it within this work. Nevertheless, the concepts within this work can be applied to other languages.

In general, LTQP has mostly been applied to querying Linked *Open* Data on the Web. In contrast, our work applies LTQP to decentralized environments with *private* personal data, organized in personal data vaults with specific structural properties.

3   The Solid Ecosystem

In this section, we provide an analysis of the structural properties within the Solid ecosystem that are relevant for query processing. We start by explaining the concept of data vaults and their implications on applications. Next, we explain the WebID, which is used for identifying users. Finally, we discuss the Solid type index; a structural property that improves data discovery.

3.1   Data Vault

The Solid Protocol [35] supports the concept of a personal data vault (also known as *data pod*), which is a user-controlled space in which any kind of public and private data can be stored. Users can choose where and how their vault is stored on the Web, by hosting it themselves [36], or obtaining service-provided space by a company [37] or government [38]. Data vaults are intended to be loosely coupled to applications, and applications must request explicit access to the user for interacting with specific data. This loose coupling enables different applications to use the same data in an interoperable way.

Current data vaults are primarily document-oriented, and are exposed on the Web as a REST API using elements of the Linked Data Platform (LDP) specification [17]. Directories are represented using *LDP Basic Containers*, which can contain any number of resources that correspond to RDF or non-RDF resources (via ldp:contains links), or other nested basic containers. For the remainder of this article, we will only consider the processing of RDF resources and containers within vaults. Resources within vaults can be read by sending HTTP GET requests to their URLs, with optional content negotiation to return the documents in different RDF serializations. Vaults may also support creation and modification using HTTP PATCH and POST requests. An example of such a basic container can be found in Listing 1.

```
PREFIX ldp: <http://www.w3.org/ns/ldp#>
<> a ldp:Container, ldp:BasicContainer, ldp:Resource;
   ldp:contains <file.ttl>, <posts/>, <profile/>.
<file.ttl> a ldp:Resource.
<posts/> a ldp:Container, ldp:BasicContainer, ldp:Resource.
<profile/> a ldp:Container, ldp:BasicContainer, ldp:Resource.
```

Listing 1. An LDP container in a Solid data vault containing one file and two directories in the Turtle serialization.

Data vaults can contain public as well as private data. Users can configure who can access or modify files within their vault using mechanisms such as ACL [39] and ACP [40]. This configuration is usually done by referring to the *WebID* of users.

3.2   WebID Profile

Any agent (person or organization) within the Solid ecosystem can establish their identity through a URI, called a *WebID*. These agents can authenticate themselves using the decentralized Solid OIDC protocol [41], which is required for authorizing access during the reading and writing of resources. Each WebID URI should be dereferenceable, and return a WebID profile document. Next to basic information of the agent such as its name, this document contains links to 1) the vault's LDP container (via pim:storage), and 2) public and private type indexes. An example is shown in Listing 2.

```
PREFIX pim: <http://www.w3.org/ns/pim/space#>
PREFIX foaf: <http://xmlns.com/foaf/0.1/>
PREFIX solid: <http://www.w3.org/ns/solid/terms#>
<#me> foaf:name "Zulma";
      pim:storage </>;
      solid:oidcIssuer <https://solidcommunity.net/>;
      solid:publicTypeIndex </publicTypeIndex.ttl>.
```

Listing 2. A simplified WebID profile in Turtle.

3.3 Type Index

Users are free to organize documents in their vault as they see fit. The Type Index [18] is a document that enables type-based resource discovery within a vault. Users may have public or private type indexes, which respectively refer to data that are and are not publicly discoverable. A type index can contain type registration entries for different classes, where each registration has a link to resources containing instances of the corresponding class. Listing 3 shows a type index example with type registrations for posts and comments, where the posts entry refers to a single posts file, and the comments entry refers to a container with multiple comments files. If an application wants to obtain all posts of a user, it can follow the link within the type index entry corresponding to the *post* class.

```
PREFIX ldp: <http://www.w3.org/ns/ldp#>
<> a solid:TypeIndex ;
   a solid:ListedDocument.
<#ab09fd> a solid:TypeRegistration;
   solid:forClass <http://example.org/Post>;
   solid:instance </public/posts.ttl>.
<#bq1r5e> a solid:TypeRegistration;
   solid:forClass <http://example.org/Comment>;
   solid:instanceContainer </public/comments/>.
```

Listing 3. Example of a type index with entries for posts and comments in Turtle.

4 Approach

In this section, we introduce techniques for handling Solid's structural properties discussed in Sect. 3. We do not introduce any additional components or structural properties to the Solid ecosystem; instead, we use what Solid vaults already provide today, and investigate how to query over them as efficiently as possible. We start by discussing the preliminaries of the formalizations we will introduce. Next, we discuss our pipeline-based link queue approach. Then, we discuss two novel discovery approaches for LTQP. Finally, we discuss their implementations.

4.1 Formal Preliminaries

Hereafter, we summarize the semantics of SPARQL querying [42] and LTQP [16, 30]. The infinite set of *RDF triples* is formalized as T = (I ∪ B) × I × (I ∪ B ∪ L), where I, B, and L respectively denote the disjoint, infinite sets of *IRIs, blank nodes,* and *literals.* Furthermore, V is the infinite set of all variables that is disjoint from I, B, and L. A tuple $tp \in$ (V ∪ I) × (V ∪ I) × (V ∪ I ∪ L) is called a *triple pattern.* A finite set of these triple patterns is called a *basic graph pattern* (BGP). For the formalization, we only consider BGPs since they form the foundational building block of a SPARQL query; our implementation incorporates all of SPARQL 1.1. The query results of a SPARQL query P over a set of RDF triples G are called *solution mappings,* which are denoted by $[[P]]G$, consisting of partial mappings μ: V → (I ∪ B ∪ L). An RDF triple t *matches* a triple pattern tp if $\exists\mu$: $t = \mu[tp]$, where $\mu[tp]$ is the triple pattern that is obtained by replacing all variables from μ in tp.

Formally, the reachability approaches that were discussed in Sect. 2 define which links should be followed during link traversal, and are usually captured as *reachability criteria* [16]. Since these reachability semantics lack expressive power to capture the structural properties we require, we formalize new reachability criteria in this work as *source selectors* within the subweb specification formalization [30]. Within this formalization, a source selector σ is defined as σ: W → 2^I, where W is a Web of Linked Data. The Web of Linked Data W is a tuple $\langle D, data, adoc \rangle$, where D is a set of available documents, *data* a function from D to 2^T associating each document with its contained triples, and *adoc* a partial function from I to D to dereference documents. We define the set of all Solid data vaults as Υ, where each vault $v \in \Upsilon$ is defined by its set of triples [7], where $triples(v) \subseteq$ T. For a vault $vLDP$ exposed through the LDP interface, the triples contained in such a vault are captured in different documents $Dv \subseteq D$. Hereby, $triples(vLDP) = \cup d \in {}_Dvdata(d)$.

4.2 Pipeline-Based Link Queue

To execute a query, our approach builds upon the zero-knowledge query planning technique [23] to construct a logical query plan ahead of query execution. This resulting plan produces a tree of logical query operators representing the query execution order. To execute this plan, the logical operators are executed by specific physical operators. Our physical query execution builds upon the iterator-based pipeline approach [19], which is the most popular among LTQP implementations [43–45]. We consider the execution plan as a pipeline [46] of iterator-based physical operators, where intermediary results flow through chained operators with pull-based results. Instead of letting operators trigger the dereferencing of URIs [19], we follow a link queue-based approach [31]. The architecture of this approach is visualized in Fig. 1. Concretely, we consider a continuously growing *triple source* as the basis of the pipeline tree, which is able to produce a (possibly infinite) stream of RDF triples. This triple source is fed triples originating from a loop consisting of the *link queue, dereferencer,* and a set of *link extractors.* The link queue accepts links from a set of link extraction components, which are invoked for every document that has been dereferenced by the dereferencer. The dereferenced documents containing triples are also sent to the continuously growing triple source.

This link queue is initialized with a set of seed URIs, and the dereferencer continuously dereferences the URIs in the queue until it is empty. Since the link extractors are invoked after every dereference operation, this queue may virtually become infinitely long.

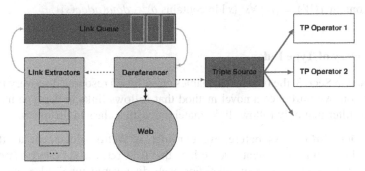

Fig. 1. Link queue, dereferencer, and link extractors feeding triples into a triple source, producing triples to tuple-producing operators in a pipelined query execution.

This link queue and link extractor approach is generic enough to implement other LTQP methods [16, 19, 28, 30, 31] for determining and prioritizing links that need to be followed. For example, one extractor may consider `rdfs:seeAlso` links, while another extractor may consider URIs of a triple that matches with a triple pattern from the query. Optionally, operators in the query pipeline may push links into the link queue, which enables context-based reachability semantics [28]. Link extractors only consider URIs as links, and ignore matching blank nodes and literals.

The triple source is connected to all tuple-producing SPARQL operators [42] in the leaves of the query plan, such as triple patterns and property path operators, into which a stream of triples is sent. The source indexes all triples, to ensure that an operator that is executed later in the execution process does not miss any triples.

4.3 Discovery of Data Vault

Below, we introduce a novel discovery approach for traversing over Solid data vaults.

Intuitive Description. To achieve link traversal within a vault, we assume that the WebID document is available as seed URI, or is discovered through some other reachability approach. As discussed in Sect. 3, the root of a vault can be discovered from a WebID document by dereferencing the object URI referred to by the `pim:storage` predicate. Next, all resources within this vault can be discovered by recursively following `ldp:contains` links from the root container.

We only consider triples for the `pim:storage` and `ldp:contains` predicates that have the current document URI as subject. If subjects contain fragment identifiers, we only consider them if the current document URI had this fragment identifier as well before it was dereferenced. For example, if a WebID with fragment identifier #me was discovered, then we only consider triples with that full WebID as subject.

Formal Description. We can formalize our discovery approach for the roots of datavaults as a following source selector starting from a given WebID with URI i as σ SolidVault$(W) = \{o \mid \langle i$ pim:storage $o\rangle \in data(adoc(i))\}$. Disjunctively coupled with this, we can formalize a source selector that can recursively traverse an LDP container as σ LdpContainer$(W) = \{o \mid \forall s: \langle s$ ldp:contains $o\rangle \in data(adoc(s))\}$.

4.4   Discovery of Type Index

As discussed in Sect. 3, the type index enables class-based resource discovery in a vault. In this section, we introduce a novel method that follows links in the type index, with an optional filter that only follows links matching with a class in the query.

Intuitive Description. As before, we consider a WebID document as the starting point. From this document, we follow the `solid:publicTypeIndex` and `solid:privateTypeIndex` links. For each discovered type index, we consider all `solid:TypeRegistration` resources, and follow their `solid:instance` and `solid:instanceContainer` links.

As an optimization, we can also take into account the type information within the registrations of the type index, to only follow those links for classes that are of interest to the current query. Concretely, this involves considering the objects referred to by `solid:forClass` on each type registration. To know whether or not a class is relevant to the current query, we explicitly check for the occurrence of this class within the query as object within triples using the `rdf:type` predicate. For subjects in the query without `rdf:type` predicate, the matching class is unknown, which is why we consider all type registrations in this case.

Formal Description. To discover and traverse type indexes, we formalize the following source selector from a given WebID with URI s when querying a BGP B:

$$
\begin{aligned}
\sigma_{\text{SolidTypeIndex}}(W) = \{o \mid \; &\forall t, r, c : \phi(B, c) \\
\wedge \quad &(\langle s \text{ solid:publicTypeIndex } t\rangle \in data(adoc(s)) \\
&\vee \langle s \text{ solid:privateTypeIndex } t\rangle \in data(adoc(s))) \\
\wedge \quad &(\langle r \text{ rdf:type solid:TypeRegistration}\rangle \in data(adoc(t)) \\
&\wedge \langle r \text{ solid:forClass } c\rangle \in data(adoc(t))) \\
\wedge \quad &(\langle r \text{ solid:instance } o\rangle \in data(adoc(t)) \\
&\vee \langle r \text{ solid:instanceContainer } o\rangle \in data(adoc(t)))\}
\end{aligned}
$$

Since `solid:instanceContainer` links to LDP containers, σ SolidTypeIndex should be disjunctively combined with σ LdpContainer.

In this formalization, we consider $\phi(B,c)$ a filtering predicate function for determining which classes are considered within the type index. To consider *all* type registrations within the type index, we can implement $\phi(B,c)$ as a predicate always returning `true`. To only consider type registrations that match with a class mentioned in the query, we introduce the following filtering function:

$$\phi_{\text{QueryClass}}(B, c) = \begin{cases} \text{true} & \text{if } \exists tp \in B : \\ & \langle ?v \text{ rdf:type } c \rangle \text{ matches } tp \\ & \text{or if } \exists s : \langle s \ ?p \ ?o \rangle \in B \\ & \wedge \{o \mid \langle s \text{ rdf:type } o \in B\} = \emptyset \\ \text{false} & \text{else.} \end{cases}$$

4.5 Implementation

We have implemented our system as new components for the Comunica SPARQL framework [47]. Concretely, we implemented the pipeline-based link queue as a separate module, and we provide link extractors corresponding to the source selectors introduced in previous sections. We fully support SPARQL 1.1, and have pipelined implementations of all monotonic SPARQL operators. Pipelining is important for iterative tuple processing in a non-blocking manner, as the link queue and the resulting stream of triples may become infinitely long.

Our implementation focuses on the SPARQL query language, instead of alternatives such as LDQL [33] and SPARQL-LD [48] that incorporate link navigation paths into the query. As discussed in Sect. 3, different Solid apps or user preferences may lead to the storage of similar data at different locations within vaults. Hence, link navigation must be *decoupled* from the query to make queries reusable for different Solid users, as link paths to data may differ across different vaults. Our implementation uses LDP container traversal and the type index to replace explicit navigation links.

To provide a stable reference implementation that can be used for the experiments in this work and future research, our implementation focuses on extensibility and reusability. Our implementation builds upon best practices in LTQP and lessons learned from other implementations [43] including, the use of client-side caching [49], the different reachability semantics [16], zero-knowledge query planning [23] applied to arbitrary join operations instead of only triple patterns in BGPs, and more [19]. Furthermore, our implementation allows users to explicitly pass seed URIs, but falls back to query-based seed URIs [43] if no seeds were provided. This fallback considers all URIs within the query as seed URIs.

As Solid performs access control at document-level, we enable users to authenticate to the client-side query engine. This allows the query engine to perform authenticated requests on behalf of the user. Since authenticated requests happen purely on the HTTP layer, other parts of the query engine do not have to be concerned about authentication, and the processing of public and private data can happen together transparently in the client-side query engine.

As a result, our implementation can query over one or more Solid data vaults. To ensure that common HTTP errors that may occur during link traversal don't terminate the query execution process, we enable a default *lenient* mode, which ignores dereference responses with HTTP status code in ranges 400 and 500.

5   Evaluation

In this section, we tackle the research question *"How well does link traversal query processing perform over decentralized environments with structural properties?"*. Within this work, we apply our experiments to the structural properties of the decentralized environment provided by Solid, but findings may be generalizable to other decentralized environments. We provide an answer to this research question by evaluating different approaches based on the implementation discussed in Sect. 4, using a benchmark that simulates Solid data vaults. We first introduce the design of our experiment, followed by presenting our experimental results, and a discussion of our results to answer our research question.

5.1   Experimental Design

Our experimental design is based on the SolidBench benchmark that simulates a realistic decentralized environment based on the Solid ecosystem. Concretely, the benchmark generates a configurable number of data vaults with configurable sizes containing social networking data, where a variety of fragmentation strategies are used to organize files in vaults. By default, it generates 158.233 RDF files over 1.531 data vaults with a total of 3.556.159 triples across all files. Furthermore, it provides SPARQL query templates that simulate a realistic workload for a social networking application. The underlying dataset and query templates are derived from the Social Network Benchmark (SNB) [50]. A full description of all queries can be found on https://github.com/SolidBench/SolidBench.js/blob/master/templates/queries/README.md.

We make use of a factorial experiment containing the following factors and values:

- **Vault Discovery Combinations**: None, LDP, Type Index, Filtered Type Index, LDP + Type Index, LDP + Filtered Type Index
- **Reachability Semantics**: cNone, cMatch, cAll

The LDP strategy corresponds to the disjunction of the source selectors σ SolidVault and σ LdpContainer, the Type Index to σ LdpContainer and σ SolidTypeIndex with $\phi(B,c)$ always returning `true`, and the Filtered Type Index to σ LdpContainer and σ SolidTypeIndex with ϕ QueryClass. Our experiments were performed on a 64-bit Ubuntu 14.04 machine with a 24-core 2.40 GHz CPU and 128 GB of RAM. The Solid vaults and query client were executed in isolated Docker containers on dedicated CPU cores with a simulated network. All queries were configured with a timeout of two minutes, and were executed three times to average metrics over. Each query template in the benchmark was instantiated five times, resulting in 40 discover queries, 35 short queries, and 60 complex queries. These query templates are available in the supplementary material.

We were unable to compare our implementation to existing LTQP engines, because those systems (e.g. Lidaq [21]) would either require significant changes to work over Solid vaults, they depend on a non-standard usage of the SPARQL syntax (e.g. SPARQL-LD [48]), or insufficient documentation was present to make them work (e.g. SQUIN

[43]). Nevertheless, in order to ensure a fair and complete comparison, we have re-implemented the foundational LTQP algorithms (cNone, cMatch, cAll), and compare them against, and in combination with, our algorithms.

5.2 Experimental Results

In this section, we present results that offer insights into our research question. Table 1 and Table 2 show the aggregated results for the different combinations of our setup for the discover and short queries of the benchmark, respectively. We omit results from complex queries, as none of the approaches achieve a level of accuracy significantly higher than 0%. Concretely, each table shows the average $(\bar{t})$ and median $(\tilde{t})$ execution times (ms), the average $(\bar{t}_1)$ and median $(\tilde{t}_1)$ time until first result (ms), average number of HTTP requests per query $(\overline{req})$, total number of results on average per query $(\sum ans)$, average accuracy $(\overline{acc})$, and number of timeouts $(\sum to)$ across all queries. The combinations with the highest accuracy value are marked in bold. The number of HTTP requests is counted across all query executions that did not time out within each combination. The timeout column represents the number of query templates that lead to a timeout for a given combination. The accuracy of each query execution is a percentage indicating the precision and recall of query results to the expected results.

Table 1. Aggregated results for the different combinations across 8 **discover** queries.

	$\bar{t}$	$\tilde{t}$	$\bar{t}_1$	$\tilde{t}_1$	$\overline{req}$	$\sum ans$	$\overline{acc}$	$\sum to$
cnone-base	40	0	N/A	N/A	8	0.00	0.00%	0
cmatch-base	1,791	0	22,946	24,439	1,275	0.00	0.00%	1
call-base	128,320	127,021	28,448	10,554	0	0.63	3.13%	8
cnone-idx	1,448	842	447	351	243	20.50	74.14%	0
cmatch-idx	**12,284**	**2,210**	**2,304**	**1,217**	**2,567**	**39.13**	**99.14%**	**0**
call-idx	124,197	124,811	48,223	9,778	18,022	3.13	17.40%	7
cnone-idx-filt	1,429	755	435	311	230	20.50	74.14%	0
cmatch-idx-filt	**12,114**	**2,312**	**2,397**	**1,075**	**2,554**	**39.13**	**99.14%**	**0**
call-idx-filt	124,003	126,093	43,147	29,937	11,023	4.50	29.78%	8
cnone-ldp	1,606	994	563	386	342	20.50	74.14%	0
cmatch-ldp	13,463	2,288	3,660	1,057	3,625	37.88	86.64%	1
call-ldp	123,712	123,479	37,083	13,733	0	2.00	16.25%	8
cnone-ldp-idx	1,560	1,001	482	349	358	20.50	74.14%	0
cmatch-ldp-idx	**12,417**	**2,529**	**2,333**	**1,189**	**2,709**	**39.13**	**99.14%**	**0**
call-ldp-idx	127,768	125,103	67,577	13,472	12,466	2.38	16.63%	7
cnone-ldp-idx-filt	1,552	1,006	425	331	357	20.50	74.14%	0
cmatch-ldp-idx-filt	**12,483**	**2,372**	**2,309**	**925**	**2,708**	**39.13**	**99.14%**	**0**
call-ldp-idx-filt	123,979	125,235	48,382	10,368	16,623	3.13	17.40%	7

These results show that there are combinations of approaches that achieve a very high level of accuracy for discover queries, and a medium level of accuracy for short queries. We will elaborate on these results in more detail hereafter.

5.3 Discussion

Intra-Vault and Inter-Vault Data Discovery. The results above show that if we desire accurate results, that the combination of cMatch semantics together with at least one of the data vault discovery methods is required. This combination is needed because our

Table 2. Aggregated results for the different combinations across 7 **short** queries.

	$\tilde{t}$	$\bar{t}$	$\tilde{t}_1$	$\bar{t}_1$	$\overline{req}$	$\sum ans$	$\overline{acc}$	$\sum to$
cnone-base	34,364	70	18	2	12	0.14	14.29%	2
cmatch-base	47,700	987	121	92	592	0.43	42.86%	3
call-base	126,794	125,609	1,547	787	0	0.00	0.00%	7
cnone-idx	34,775	540	676	151	71	0.14	14.29%	2
cmatch-idx	70,142	119,114	6,837	530	263	0.43	42.86%	4
call-idx	109,943	123,227	14,290	19,345	0	0.00	0.00%	7
cnone-idx-filt	34,804	534	527	110	71	0.14	14.29%	2
cmatch-idx-filt	69,808	119,032	7,190	434	263	0.43	42.86%	4
call-idx-filt	116,618	123,312	9,764	6,207	0	0.00	0.00%	7
cnone-ldp	34,975	621	816	46	96	0.29	15.71%	2
cmatch-ldp	**70,026**	**119,586**	**6,524**	**636**	**291**	**0.57**	**44.29%**	**4**
call-ldp	127,550	126,587	717	483	0	0.00	0.00%	7
cnone-ldp-idx	34,852	811	521	43	100	0.14	14.29%	2
cmatch-ldp-idx	69,534	119,215	2,936	437	295	0.43	42.86%	4
call-ldp-idx	110,217	122,525	8,841	6,114	0	0.00	0.00%	7
cnone-ldp-idx-filt	34,830	742	402	83	100	0.14	14.29%	2
cmatch-ldp-idx-filt	**70,042**	**119,126**	**6,246**	**663**	**295**	**0.57**	**44.29%**	**4**
call-ldp-idx-filt	114,800	123,058	15,075	17,192	0	0.00	0.00%	7

workload contains queries that either target data within a single vault (e.g. D1), or data spanning multiple data vaults (e.g. D8). While the different data vault discovery methods are able to discover data *within* vaults, the reachability of cMatch is required to discover data *across* multiple vaults.

Due to this, cNone (follow no links) is an ineffective replacement for cMatch (follow links matching query) even when combined with discovery methods, because link traversal across multiple vaults will not take place, which will lead to too few query results. Concretely, for discover queries cNone can only achieve a accuracy of 74.14% for discover queries and 28.57% for short queries, compared to respectively 99.14% and 42.86% for cMatch. However, for those queries that target a single vault, cNone can be used instead of cMatch without a loss of accuracy, leading to a lower number of HTTP requests and lower query execution times.

Since cAll leads to all links being followed, including those followed by cMatch, it is theoretically a sufficient replacement for cMatch. However, our results show that cAll follows too many links, which leads to timeouts for nearly all queries.

Our results show that solely using reachability semantics (cMatch or cAll) without a data discovery method is insufficient for discover queries, where a accuracy of only up to 3.13% can be achieved for discover queries. However, when looking at the short queries category, solely using reachability semantics appears to be sufficient, with the query execution time even being lower. This difference exists because the discover workload contains queries that discover data related to a certain person or resource, while the short queries target only details of specific resources. Discover queries therefore depend on an overview of the vault, while short queries only depend on specific links between resources within a vault. The remainder of this discussion only focuses on discover queries, since these achieve the highest level of accuracy. As such, the short and complex queries highlight opportunities for future improvement.

Type Index and LDP Discovery Perform Similarly. When comparing the number of HTTP requests and query execution times for different data vault discovery approaches under cMatch in Table 1, we can observe that using the type index leads to fewer HTTP requests and faster query execution compared to LDP-based discovery on average. To explain this behaviour in more detail, Subfig. 2.1 shows the average query execution times of each discover query separately, for the different combinations of data vault discovery approaches. To simplify comparability, the execution times within this figure are relative to the maximum query execution time per query [31]. Furthermore, Subfig. 2.2 shows the average number of HTTP requests for each of those discover queries, which are also made relative to the maximum number of requests per query for better comparability.

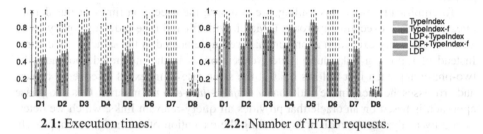

2.1: Execution times.   2.2: Number of HTTP requests.

Fig. 2. Relative measurements for discover queries with different discovery methods under cMatch. Bars indicate average values, whiskers indicate the maxima and minima, and stars indicate average time until first result.

While Subfig. 2.1 shows that for all queries using just the type index is slightly faster or comparable to just LDP-based discovery, this difference has no statistical significance ($p = 0.40$). However, Subfig. 2.2 shows that the number of HTTP requests with the type index is always significantly lower than via LDP ($p = 0.01$).

When the filter-enabled type index approach is used, five queries (D1, D3, D5, D6, D7) are made even faster compared to the non-filtered type index approach. This is because those queries target a possibly empty subset of the type index entries, which means that a significant range of links can be pruned out, which leads to a major reduction in the number of HTTP requests, which is a main bottleneck in link traversal. For the other queries, the filter-enabled approach becomes slightly slower than (D2, D4) or is comparable to (D8) the non-filtered type index approach. For those queries, the processing overhead of type index filtering becomes too high compared to its potential benefit. Statistically, this difference has no significance in terms of execution time ($p = 0.69$) and number of HTTP requests ($p = 0.68$).

These results show that using the type index together with LDP-based discovery is not *significantly* better than the other approaches ($p = 0.71$), which is primarily caused by the statistically significantly higher number of HTTP requests ($p = 0.02$) required for traversing both the type index and nested LDP containers. Query D8 does however show that this combination deserves further investigation, because this query has a result limit that leads to a prioritization of links via the type index, leading to earlier query termination with fewer requests.

In general, results hint that the LDP-based approach combined with filtered type index approach performs better than the other approaches, but this difference is too minor to be significant, hence all approaches can be considered equivalent.

Zero-Knowledge Query Planning is Ineffective. While it may seem obvious to assume that higher query execution times are caused by a higher number of links that need to be dereferenced, we observe only a weak correlation ($\rho = 0.32$) of this within the cMatch-based discovery approaches discussed before. The main bottleneck in this case appears not primarily to be the number of links to traverse. Instead, our analysis suggests that query plan efficiency is the primary influencer of execution times. This is in contrast to earlier research over Linked Open Data [31], where we instead consider structural properties with more selective link traversal.

To empirically prove this finding, we compare the execution times of our default integrated query execution approach (cMatch with filtered type index discovery) with a two-phase query execution approach that we implemented in the same query engine. Instead of following links during query execution as in the integrated approach, the two-phase approach first follows links at the same rate to index all discovered triples, and processes the query in the traditional *optimize-then-execute* manner. This two-phase approach is based on an oracle that provides all query-relevant links, which we determined by analyzing the request logs during the execution of the integrated approach. Therefore, this two-phase approach is merely a theoretical case, which delays time until first results due to prior indexing, and may not always be achievable due to infinitely growing link queues for some queries. The results of this are in Fig. 3.

Query	Integrated	Two-phase	HTTP Requests
D1	1,077.58	403.54	222
D2	1,020.67	567.57	223
D3	1,193.01	821.23	429
D4	3,266.62	505.00	228
D5	522.23	387.24	223
D6	710.16	289.72	122
D7	626.96	340.54	122
D8	2,037.85	1,654.02	420

Fig. 3. Integrated and two-phase execution times (ms) of discover queries, with number of HTTP requests per query.

These results show that the two-phase approach is on average two times faster for all queries compared to the integrated approach, even when taking into account time for dereferencing. The reason for this is that the two-phase approach is able to perform traditional query planning [51, 52], since it has access to an indexed triple store with planning-relevant information such as cardinality estimates. Since the integrated approach finds new triples *during* query execution, it is unable to use them for traditional planning. Instead, our integrated approach makes use of the zero-knowledge query planning technique [23] that uses heuristics to plan the query before execution.

Since the only difference between the integrated and two-phase implementations is in how they plan the query, we can derive that the query plan of the integrated approach is ineffective. Hence, there is a need for better query planning during integrated execution, where performance could ideally become more than two times better.

Zero-knowledge query planning [23] is ineffective in our experiments because it has been designed under the assumptions of Linked Open Data, while it does not match with the structural assumptions of specific decentralized environments such as Solid. For example, one of the heuristics within this planner deprioritizes triple patterns with vocabulary terms, such as `rdf:type`, since they are usually the least selective. However, when a Solid type index is present, such types may instead become *very selective*, which means that those would benefit from prioritization. As such, there is a need for alternative query planners that consider the structural assumptions within specific decentralized environments.

6 Conclusions

User-oriented decentralized applications require results in the order of seconds or less to avoid losing the user's attention [53]. Our work has shown that Link Traversal Query Processing is able to achieve such timings, especially as it is able to produce results in an iterative manner, with first results mostly being produced in less than a second. As such, LTQP with the algorithms introduced in this work is effective for querying over decentralized environments with specific structural properties, but there are open research opportunities for optimizing more complex queries as provided by the benchmark. We have shown this by applying LTQP to simulated Solid environments, for which we have introduced algorithms to capture these structural properties. Before this work, LTQP tended to exclusively focus on Linked Open Data, which centralized quad-stores handle better anyway. After all, in addition to major performance concerns, it was assumed that *"we should never expect complete results"* [19] with LTQP because of the unbounded and distributed nature of the Web. Prior aggregation was therefore always the logical option for efficient queries, limiting the evaluation space to fixed datasets with a compatible license.

However, LTQP becomes relevant again within decentralized environments such as Solid, where aggregation is not an option because of permissioning. Performance concerns can be addressed through the usage of additional assumptions during query execution. For instance, the ability to close the world around Solid vaults, and the data discovery techniques that Solid vaults provide, create opportunities for query execution that allow us to guarantee complete results. While we have investigated the specific case of querying Solid vaults, these concepts may be generalizable to other decentralization efforts [3, 4]. This is possible, because our approach solely relies on the structural properties provided by specifications such as LDP [17] and the Type Index [18], which can be used outside of the Solid ecosystem.

LTQP research over Linked Open Data is exploring the direction of finding query-relevant documents as early as possible [31] due to the possibility of incomplete results. In the context of Solid, we have shown that finding all query-relevant documents is not the main bottleneck during query execution anymore. Instead, the *effectiveness of the query plan* has become the new bottleneck. While finding query-relevant documents is still relevant for specific decentralized environments, we show the need for more research towards better query planning techniques. Since LTQP leads to data being discovered during query execution, adaptive query planning [54] techniques are highly promising.

So far, these techniques have only seen limited adoption within LTQP [31] and SPARQL query processing [55–57].

Our findings indicate that discovery approaches such as the Solid Type Index harbor a great potential for improving query performance, and future work in the direction of *implicit type knowledge* within queries (e.g., through RDFS reasoning) and query decomposition over *different type index entries* could be relevant. Furthermore, alternative structural properties could offer more expressivity, such as *characteristics sets* [58] and other *summarization techniques* [21, 59]. Additionally, more work is needed to investigate the impact of privacy [60] and security [61] during LTQP over decentralized environments. The incorporation of more expressive Linked Data Fragments interfaces [12, 62–66] in certain Solid vaults could introduce interesting trade-offs in terms of server and client query execution effort, especially if they can be combined in a heterogeneous manner [67–69].

In summary, traversal-based querying over decentralized environments can become practically feasible performance-wise. Furthermore, it is useful given the lack of alternatives, because centralization of private data may not be feasible or legal. However, for complex queries, more improvements through future research are needed.

This work provides answers to the increasing need of querying over decentralized environments, and uncovers next steps for resolving current limitations. Hence, it brings us closer to querying a decentralized Web where users are in full control.

Acknowledgements. This work is supported by SolidLab Vlaanderen (Flemish Government, EWI and RRF project VV023/10). Ruben Taelman is a postdoctoral fellow of the Research Foundation – Flanders (FWO) (1274521N).

Supplemental Material Statement

Implementation: https://github.com/comunica/comunica-feature-link-traversal Experiments: https://github.com/comunica/Experiments-Solid-Link-Traversal Benchmark: https://github.com/SolidBench/SolidBench.js.

References

1. Berners-Lee, T.J.: Information management: a proposal (1989)
2. Verborgh, R.: Re-decentralizing the web, for good this time. In: Seneviratne, O., Hendler, J. (eds.) Linking the World's Information: A Collection of Essays on the Work of Sir Tim Berners-Lee. ACM (2022)
3. Bluesky. Bluesky (2023). https://blueskyweb.xyz/
4. Zignani, M., Gaito, S., Rossi, G.P.: Follow the Mastodon: structure and evolution of a decentralized online social network. In: Twelfth International AAAI Conference on Web and Social Media (2018)
5. Kuhn, T., Taelman, R., Emonet, V., Antonatos, H., Soiland-Reyes, S., Dumontier, M.: Semantic micro-contributions with decentralized nanopublication services. PeerJ Comput. Sci. (2021). https://doi.org/10.7717/peerj-cs.387

6. Hogan, A., et al.: Knowledge graphs. In: Synthesis Lectures on Data, Semantics, and Knowledge, vol. 12, pp. 1–257 (2021)
7. Dedecker, R., Slabbinck, W., Wright, J., Hochstenbach, P., Colpaert, P., Verborgh, R.: What's in a Pod? – a knowledge graph interpretation for the Solid ecosystem. In: Saleem, M., Ngonga Ngomo, A.-C. (eds.) Proceedings of the 6th Workshop on Storing, Querying and Benchmarking Knowledge Graphs, pp. 81–96 (2022)
8. Berners-Lee, T.: Linked Data (2009). https://www.w3.org/DesignIssues/LinkedData.html
9. Cyganiak, R., Wood, D., Lanthaler, M.: RDF 1.1: Concepts and Abstract Syntax. W3C (2014). https://www.w3.org/TR/2014/REC-rdf11-concepts-20140225/
10. Feigenbaum, L., Todd Williams, G., Grant Clark, K., Torres, E.: SPARQL 1.1 Protocol. W3C (2013). https://www.w3.org/TR/2013/REC-sparql11-protocol-20130321/
11. Schwarte, A., Haase, P., Hose, K., Schenkel, R., Schmidt, M.: Fedx: optimization techniques for federated query processing on linked data. In: Aroyo, L., et al. (eds.) ISWC 2011. LNCS, vol. 7031, pp. 601–616. Springer, Heidelberg (2011). https://doi.org/10.1007/978-3-642-25073-6_38
12. Verborgh, R., et al.: Triple pattern fragments: a low-cost knowledge graph interface for the web. J. Web Semant. **37**, 184–206 (2016)
13. Saleem, M., Ngonga Ngomo, A.-C.: Hibiscus: hypergraph-based source selection for SPARQL endpoint federation. In: Presutti, V., d'Amato, C., Gandon, F., d'Aquin, M., Staab, S., Tordai, A. (eds.) ESWC 2014. LNCS, vol. 8465, pp. 176–191. Springer, Cham (2014). https://doi.org/10.1007/978-3-319-07443-6_13
14. Görlitz, O., Staab, S.: Splendid: SPARQL endpoint federation exploiting void descriptions. In: Proceedings of the Second International Conference on Consuming Linked Data, vol. 782, pp. 13–24. CEUR-WS.org (2011)
15. Hartig, O.: An overview on execution strategies for linked data queries. Datenbank-Spektrum **13**, 89–99 (2013)
16. Hartig, O., Freytag, J.-C.: Foundations of traversal based query execution over linked data. In: Proceedings of the 23rd ACM Conference on Hypertext and Social Media, pp. 43–52. ACM (2012)
17. Speicher, S., Arwe, J., Malhotra, A.: Linked Data Platform 1.0. W3C (2015). https://www.w3.org/TR/ldp/
18. Turdean, T.: Type Indexes. Solid (2022). https://solid.github.io/type-indexes/
19. Hartig, O.: SPARQL for a web of linked data: semantics and computability. In: Simperl, E., Cimiano, P., Polleres, A., Corcho, O., Presutti, V. (eds.) ESWC 2012. LNCS, vol. 7295, pp. 8–23. Springer, Heidelberg (2012). https://doi.org/10.1007/978-3-642-30284-8_8
20. Harth, A., Hose, K., Karnstedt, M., Polleres, A., Sattler, K.-U., Umbrich, J.: Data summaries for on-demand queries over linked data. In: Proceedings of the 19th International Conference on World Wide Web, pp. 411–420 (2010)
21. Umbrich, J., Hose, K., Karnstedt, M., Harth, A., Polleres, A.: Comparing data summaries for processing live queries over linked data. World Wide Web **14**, 495–544 (2011)
22. Hartig, O., Hose, K., Sequeda, J.: Linked data management. In: Sakr, S., Zomaya, A. (eds.) Encyclopedia of Big Data Technologies, pp. 1–7. Springer, Cham (2018). https://doi.org/10.1007/978-3-319-63962-8_76-1
23. Hartig, O.: Zero-knowledge query planning for an iterator implementation of link traversal based query execution. In: Antoniou, G., et al. (eds.) ESWC 2011. LNCS, vol. 6643, pp. 154–169. Springer, Heidelberg (2011). https://doi.org/10.1007/978-3-642-21034-1_11
24. Mendelzon, A.O., Mihaila, G.A., Milo, T.: Querying the world wide web. In: Fourth International Conference on Parallel and Distributed Information Systems, pp. 80–91. IEEE (1996)
25. Konopnicki, D., Shmueli, O.: Information gathering in the world-wide web: the W3QL query language and the W3QS system. ACM Trans. Datab. Syst. **23**, 369–410 (1998)

26. Chakrabarti, S., Van den Berg, M., Dom, B.: Focused crawling: a new approach to topic-specific Web resource discovery. Comput. Netw. **31**, 1623–1640 (1999)
27. Batsakis, S., Petrakis, E.G.M., Milios, E.: Improving the performance of focused web crawlers. Data Knowl. Eng. **68**, 1001–1013 (2009)
28. Hartig, O., Pirrò, G.: SPARQL with property paths on the web. Semantic Web **8**, 773–795 (2017)
29. Harris, S., Seaborne, A., Prud'hommeaux, E.: SPARQL 1.1 Query Language. W3C (2013). https://www.w3.org/TR/2013/REC-sparql11-query-20130321/
30. Bogaerts, B., Ketsman, B., Zeboudj, Y., Aamer, H., Taelman, R., Verborgh, R.: Link traversal with distributed subweb specifications. In: Proceedings of the Rules and Reasoning: 5th International Joint Conference, RuleML+RR 2021, Leuven, 8–15 September 2021 (2021)
31. Hartig, O., Özsu, M.T.: Walking without a map: optimizing response times of traversal-based linked data queries (extended version). arXiv preprint arXiv:1607.01046 (2016)
32. Schaffert, S., Bauer, C., Kurz, T., Dorschel, F., Glachs, D., Fernandez, M.: The linked media framework: Integrating and interlinking enterprise media content and data. In: Proceedings of the 8th International Conference on Semantic Systems, pp. 25–32 (2012)
33. Hartig, O., Pérez, J.: LDQL: a query language for the web of linked data. J. Web Semant. **41**, 9–29 (2016)
34. Fionda, V., Pirrò, G., Gutierrez, C.: NautiLOD: a formal language for the web of data graph. ACM Trans. Web (TWEB) **9**, 1–43 (2015)
35. Capadisli, S., Berners-Lee, T., Verborgh, R., Kjernsmo, K.: Solid Protocol. Solid (2020). https://solidproject.org/TR/protocol
36. Van Herwegen, J., Verborgh, R., Taelman, R., Bosquet, M.: Community Solid Server (2022). https://github.com/CommunitySolidServer/CommunitySolidServer
37. Inrupt. PodSpaces (2022). https://docs.inrupt.com/pod-spaces/
38. Flanders, D.: The Flemish Data Utility Company (2022). https://www.vlaanderen.be/digitaal-vlaanderen/het-vlaams-datanutsbedrijf/the-flemish-data-utility-company
39. Capadisli, S.: Web Access Control. Solid (2022). https://solid.github.io/web-access-control-spec/
40. Bosquet, M.: Access Control Policy (ACP). Solid (2022). https://solid.github.io/authorization-panel/acp-specification/
41. Coburn, A., Pavlik, E., Zagidulin, D.: Solid-OIDC. Solid (2022). https://solid.github.io/solid-oidc/
42. Pérez, J., Arenas, M., Gutierrez, C.: Semantics and complexity of SPARQL. ACM Trans. Datab. Syst. **34**, 1–45 (2009)
43. Hartig, O.: SQUIN: a traversal based query execution system for the web of linked data. In: Proceedings of the 2013 ACM SIGMOD International Conference on Management of Data, pp. 1081–1084 (2013)
44. Ladwig, G., Tran, T.: SIHJoin: querying remote and local linked data. In: Antoniou, G., et al. (eds.) ESWC 2011. LNCS, vol. 6643, pp. 139–153. Springer, Heidelberg (2011). https://doi.org/10.1007/978-3-642-21034-1_10
45. Miranker, D.P., Depena, R.K., Jung, H., Sequeda, J.F., Reyna, C.: Diamond: a SPARQL query engine, for linked data based on the Rete match. In: Proceedings of the Workshop on Artificial Intelligence Meets the Web of Data (AImWD) (2012)
46. Wilschut, A.N., Apers, P.M.G.: Pipelining in query execution. In: Proceedings. PARBASE-90: International Conference on Databases, Parallel Architectures, and Their Applications, p. 562. IEEE (1990)
47. Taelman, R., Van Herwegen, J., Vander Sande, M., Verborgh, R.: Comunica: a Modular SPARQL query engine for the web. In: Proceedings of the 17th International Semantic Web Conference (2018)

48. Fafalios, P., Yannakis, T., Tzitzikas, Y.: Querying the web of data with SPARQL-LD. In: Fuhr, N., Kovács, L., Risse, T., Nejdl, W. (eds.) TPDL 2016. LNCS, vol. 9819, pp. 175–187. Springer, Cham (2016). https://doi.org/10.1007/978-3-319-43997-6_14

49. Hartig, O.: How caching improves efficiency and result completeness for querying linked data. In: LDOW (2011)

50. Erling, O., et al.: The LDBC social network benchmark: interactive workload. In: Proceedings of the 2015 ACM SIGMOD International Conference on Management of Data, pp. 619–630 (2015)

51. Schmidt, M., Meier, M., Lausen, G.: Foundations of SPARQL query optimization. In: Proceedings of the 13th International Conference on Database Theory, pp. 4–33. ACM (2010)

52. Stocker, M., Seaborne, A., Bernstein, A., Kiefer, C., Reynolds, D.: SPARQL basic graph pattern optimization using selectivity estimation. In: Proceedings of the 7th International Conference on World Wide Web, pp. 595–604. ACM (2008)

53. Nielsen, J.: Response times: the three important limits. Usabil. Eng. (1993)

54. Deshpande, A., Ives, Z., Raman, V.: Adaptive query processing. Found. Trends® Databases **1**, 1–140 (2007)

55. Acosta, M., Vidal, M.-E., Lampo, T., Castillo, J., Ruckhaus, E.: ANAPSID: an adaptive query processing engine for SPARQL endpoints. In: Aroyo, L., et al. (eds.) ISWC 2011. LNCS, vol. 7031, pp. 18–34. Springer, Heidelberg (2011). https://doi.org/10.1007/978-3-642-25073-6_2

56. Acosta, M., Vidal, M.-E.: Networks of linked data eddies: an adaptive web query processing engine for RDF data. In: Arenas, M., et al. (eds.) ISWC 2015. LNCS, vol. 9366, pp. 111–127. Springer, Cham (2015). https://doi.org/10.1007/978-3-319-25007-6_7

57. Heling, L., Acosta, M.: Robust query processing for linked data fragments. Semantic Web 1–35 (2022)

58. Neumann, T., Moerkotte, G.: Characteristic sets: accurate cardinality estimation for RDF queries with multiple joins. In: 2011 IEEE 27th International Conference on Data Engineering, pp. 984–994. IEEE (2011)

59. Prud'hommeaux, E., Bingham, J.: Shape Trees Specification. W3C (2021). https://shape-trees.org/TR/specification/

60. Taelman, R., Steyskal, S., Kirrane, S.: Towards querying in decentralized environments with privacy-preserving aggregation. In: Proceedings of the 4th Workshop on Storing, Querying, and Benchmarking the Web of Data (2020)

61. Taelman, R., Verborgh, R.: A prospective analysis of security vulnerabilities within link traversal-based query processing. In: Proceedings of the 6th International Workshop on Storing, Querying and Benchmarking Knowledge Graphs (2022)

62. Azzam, A., Fernández, J.D., Acosta, M., Beno, M., Polleres, A.: SMART-KG: hybrid shipping for SPARQL querying on the web. In: Proceedings of the Web Conference 2020, pp. 984–994 (2020)

63. Minier, T., Skaf-Molli, H., Molli, P.: SaGe: web preemption for public SPARQL query services. In: The World Wide Web Conference, pp. 1268–1278 (2019)

64. Azzam, A., Aebeloe, C., Montoya, G., Keles, I., Polleres, A., Hose, K.: WiseKG: balanced access to web knowledge graphs. In: Proceedings of the Web Conference 2021, pp. 1422–1434 (2021)

65. Aebeloe, C., Keles, I., Montoya, G., Hose, K.: Star pattern fragments: accessing knowledge graphs through star patterns. arXiv preprint arXiv:2002.09172 (2020)

66. Hartig, O., Buil-Aranda, C.: Bindings-restricted triple pattern fragments. In: Debruyne, C., et al. (eds.) OTM 2016. LNCS, vol. 10033, pp. 762–779. Springer, Cham (2016). https://doi.org/10.1007/978-3-319-48472-3_48

67. Heling, L., Acosta, M.: Federated SPARQL query processing over heterogeneous linked data fragments. In: Proceedings of the ACM Web Conference 2022, pp. 1047–1057 (2022)

68. Cheng, S., Hartig, O.: FedQPL: A language for logical query plans over heterogeneous federations of RDF data sources. In: Proceedings of the 22nd International Conference on Information Integration and Web-based Applications and Services, pp. 436–445 (2020)
69. Montoya, G., Aebeloe, C., Hose, K.: Towards efficient query processing over heterogeneous RDF interfaces. In: 2nd Workshop on Decentralizing the Semantic Web, DeSemWeb 2018. CEUR Workshop Proceedings (2018)

Dense Re-Ranking with Weak Supervision for RDF Dataset Search

Qiaosheng Chen, Zixian Huang, Zhiyang Zhang, Weiqing Luo, Tengteng Lin, Qing Shi, and Gong Cheng(✉) ⓘ

State Key Laboratory for Novel Software Technology, Nanjing University, Nanjing, China
{qschen,zixianhuang,zhiyangzhang,wqluo,tengtenglin, qingshi}@smail.nju.edu.cn, gcheng@nju.edu.cn

Abstract. Dataset search aims to find datasets that are relevant to a keyword query. Existing dataset search engines rely on conventional sparse retrieval models (e.g., BM25). Dense models (e.g., BERT-based) remain under-investigated for two reasons: the limited availability of labeled data for fine-tuning such a deep neural model, and its limited input capacity relative to the large size of a dataset. To fill the gap, in this paper, we study dense re-ranking for RDF dataset search. Our re-ranking model encodes the metadata of RDF datasets and also their actual RDF data—by extracting a small yet representative subset of data to accommodate large datasets. To address the insufficiency of training data, we adopt a coarse-to-fine tuning strategy where we warm up the model with weak supervision from a large set of automatically generated queries and relevance labels. Experiments on the ACORDAR test collection demonstrate the effectiveness of our approach, which considerably improves the retrieval accuracy of existing sparse models.

Keywords: Dataset search · Dense re-ranking · Data augmentation

1 Introduction

As data plays an increasingly crucial role in many domains, the capability to search for relevant datasets has become critical [5]. To satisfy this need, dataset search engines such as Google Dataset Search [2,3] have emerged. The Semantic Web community is particularly interested in RDF dataset search, and has also developed a few such solutions [6,24,30] and made benchmarking efforts [18].

Motivation. Existing RDF dataset search solutions employ conventional sparse models (e.g., BM25 [26]) to retrieve lexically relevant datasets, which cannot capture the semantic relationships between query and dataset. By contrast, building on the semantic matching capability of pre-trained language models (e.g., BERT [10]) to understand text, dense ranking models (e.g., DPR [12]) have achieved remarkable performance in document retrieval [33]. It inspires us to study *dense models for RDF dataset search* and investigate their effectiveness.

© The Author(s), under exclusive license to Springer Nature Switzerland AG 2023
T. R. Payne et al. (Eds.): ISWC 2023, LNCS 14265, pp. 23–40, 2023.
https://doi.org/10.1007/978-3-031-47240-4_2

Challenges. Applying dense models to RDF dataset search is a nontrivial task. Indeed, we identify the following two challenges. Note that these difficulties also face dataset search in general, not limited to RDF dataset search.

- Unlike documents, (RDF) datasets are structured and commonly *very large*, e.g., containing thousands or millions of RDF triples. It remains unclear how to effectively feed such a huge amount of data into a dense ranking model which typically allows a maximum input length of only 512 tokens, and we should not simply drop the data but rely solely on the metadata of a dataset since this has been proven to hurt accuracy [6,18].
- Unlike document retrieval which is an established research task with many large test collections, (RDF) dataset search is relatively new and is now accompanied by only a few relatively small test collections [13,18]. The *limited labeled data* in these test collections is insufficient for tuning a dense ranking model having at least hundreds of millions of trainable parameters.

Our Work. We propose to study dense ranking models for RDF dataset search and address the above two challenges. Our approach adopts a popular retrieval-then-reranking architecture, and we use dense models in the re-ranking step. To feed the metadata and content of an RDF dataset into the model, we concatenate metadata fields as well as a small subset of RDF triples extracted from the data as a representative data sample. To tune the model, besides the limited labeled data provided by existing test collections, we adopt a coarse-to-fine tuning strategy and we propose two methods for automatically generating a large amount of possibly noisy labeled data to weakly supervise the model in the preliminary coarse-tuning phase. We refer to our approach as DR^2, short for Dense Rdf Dataset Re-ranking. To summarize, our contributions include

- the first research attempt to adapt dense ranking models to RDF dataset search, by encoding representative RDF triples extracted from large datasets,
- two methods for automatically generating labeled data to coarse-tune the model, one based on distant supervision and the other based on self-training,
- experiments on a public test collection, empirically comparing a variety of triple extraction methods, dense ranking models, and tuning strategies.

Outline. The remainder of the paper is organized as follows. Section 2 introduces our retrieval-then-reranking approach for RDF dataset search. Section 3 details our coarse-to-fine tuning strategy. Section 4 presents evaluation results. Section 5 discusses related work. Section 6 concludes the paper with future work.

2   Dense Re-Ranking for RDF Dataset Search

In this section, we describe our retrieval-then-reranking approach for RDF dataset search. We begin with an overview of the approach. Then we detail its two major steps: compact document representation and dense re-ranking.

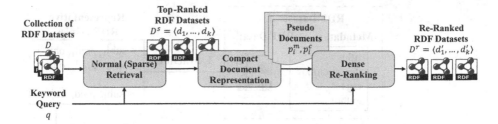

Fig. 1. Our retrieval-then-reranking approach for RDF dataset search.

2.1 Overview

Figure 1 presents an overview of our approach for RDF dataset search. We follow best practice [17] to adopt a *retrieval-then-reranking* design. Specifically, given a keyword query q and a collection D of RDF datasets, the first step is to perform a *normal retrieval* by using a conventional off-the-shelf method for RDF dataset search to retrieve k top-ranked RDF datasets from D that are the most relevant to q, denoted by $D^s = \langle d_1, \ldots, d_k \rangle$. For each retrieved RDF dataset $d_i \in D^s$, the second step is to construct its *compact document representation* to be fed into the downstream dense re-ranking model. We construct two pseudo documents in this step: p_i^m representing the metadata of d_i, and p_i^c representing the content of d_i, i.e., the actual RDF data in d_i. The last step is to employ a dense ranking model to *re-rank* each RDF dataset $d_i \in D^s$ based on the relevance of p_i^m and p_i^c to q, and output the re-ranked results denoted by $D^r = \langle d_1', \ldots, d_k' \rangle$.

The retrieval model in the first step is out of our research focus. In the experiments we will use existing implementations provided in the literature [18]. In the following we will focus on the second and the third steps.

2.2 Compact Document Representation

An RDF dataset contains RDF data and typically has metadata description. Both metadata and RDF data are structured. They need to be linearized into pseudo documents so that they can be processed by the downstream dense re-ranking model. We call them *compact documents* because, relatively to the possibly large size of an RDF dataset (e.g., millions of RDF triples), the length of such a document has to be bounded to fit the maximum input length of the downstream dense model which is usually a small number (e.g., 512 tokens).

Metadata Document. For a retrieved RDF dataset $d_i \in D^s$, we construct its metadata document p_i^m, i.e., a pseudo document representing its metadata.

Specifically, recall that metadata commonly consists of a set of fields. Following [18], we choose four fields that should contain human-readable information and hence are used in the computation of query relevance: `title`, `description`, `tags`, and `author`. The values of these fields are concatenated into p_i^m as illustrated in Fig. 2, where `[CLS]` and `[SEP]` are standard separating tokens used

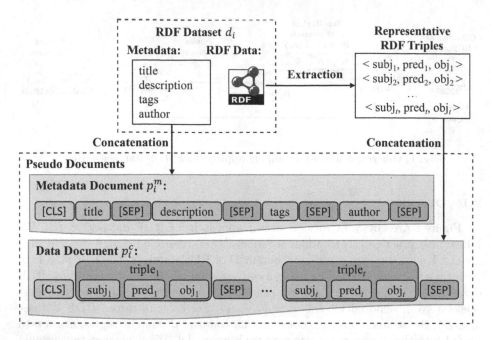

Fig. 2. Compact document representation for an RDF dataset.

in BERT-based models [10]. They can be replaced by their counterparts when other families of language models are used as a substitute for BERT.

Metadata is usually short enough to fit the maximum input length of a dense model. If exceeded, the metadata document will be truncated to the maximum input length in a normal way, i.e., its end will be cut off.

Data Document. For a retrieved RDF dataset $d_i \in D^s$, we construct its data document p_i^c, i.e., a pseudo document representing its RDF data content.

Specifically, recall that RDF data consists of a set of RDF triples. An RDF dataset may easily contain too many triples to fit the maximum input length of a dense model. Indeed, a median of 2k RDF triples was observed in the literature [18]. Instead of performing arbitrary truncation, we want to identify and keep the most important information in RDF data by extracting a representative subset of RDF triples. This resembles the research objective of *RDF dataset snippet generation* [29]. Therefore, we choose and implement two state-of-the-art solutions to this research problem: IlluSnip [8,19] and PCSG [28]. In a nutshell, IlluSnip computes a ranking of the RDF triples in an RDF dataset such that the top-ranked triples cover the most frequent classes, properties, and entities in the data. PCSG relies on entity description pattern (EDP) which is a set of classes and properties used to describe an entity in an RDF dataset. It selects a smallest number of subsets of RDF triples—each subset covering an EDP—such that the selected subsets of triples cover all the EDPs in the data. We further rank these subsets by the frequency of covered EDP.

From a possibly large RDF dataset d_i, subject to the maximum input length of a dense model, we extract the largest possible number of top-ranked RDF triples returned by IlluSnip, or the largest possible number of top-ranked subsets of triples returned by PCSG, depending on which algorithm is used. We will compare IlluSnip and PCSG in the experiments. We concatenate the human-readable forms of the subject, predicate, and object in each extracted RDF triple into p_i^c as illustrated in Fig. 2, separated by [CLS] and [SEP]. The human-readable form of an IRI or blank node refers to its `rdfs:label` (if available) or local name, and the human-readable form of a literal refers to its lexical form.

Moreover, a single RDF triple may occasionally be very long, e.g., containing a long literal. We need to find a trade-off between the number of extracted RDF triples and the maximum allowed length of a triple. Our implementation empirically truncates each RDF triple to at most 45 tokens because, by sampling RDF datasets used the literature [18], we find that more than 99% of the sampled RDF triples contain at most 45 tokens, i.e., truncation would be very rare in our setting so that the completeness of most triples could be guaranteed.

2.3 Dense Re-Ranking

Given a keyword query q and a set of retrieved k top-ranked RDF datasets D^s, we employ a dense ranking model to re-rank each dataset $d_i \in D^s$ based on the relevance of its metadata document p_i^m and data document p_i^c to q.

Specifically, we consider using dense models for re-ranking because, compared with normal sparse models which rely on *lexical features* for measuring query relevance, dense models are expected to extract *semantic features* from queries and documents to more accurately compute their relevance. We choose and adapt two dense ranking models, DPR [12] and ColBERT [14], because they have been widely used in information retrieval research. In a nutshell, DPR and ColBERT both based on BERT [10] perform sentence-level and token-level semantic matching, respectively. We will compare them in the experiments. They can also be substituted by other dense ranking models [33].

Let `DenseRel`($\cdot, \cdot$) be a dense ranking model, i.e., DPR or ColBERT, which computes the relevance of a document to a keyword query. We calculate the re-ranking score of an RDF dataset d_i by computing the relevance of its metadata document p_i^m to q and the relevance of its data document p_i^c to q, and then take their maximum value:

$$\text{Score}(d_i) = \max\{\text{DenseRel}(q, p_i^m), \text{DenseRel}(q, p_i^c)\}. \tag{1}$$

3   Coarse Tuning with Weak Supervision

Dense ranking models are supervised. Although they are based on pre-trained language models such as BERT, it is still expected to fine-tune them with task-specific training data to achieve better performance. However, RDF dataset

search is a relatively new research problem. The labeled data provided by existing test collections such as [18] may be sufficient for testing but not sufficient for
fine-tuning a deep neural model. Therefore, we propose to warm up our dense
re-ranking model with *weak supervision*, i.e., with a large set of automatically
generated labeled data which, however, possibly contains some noise.

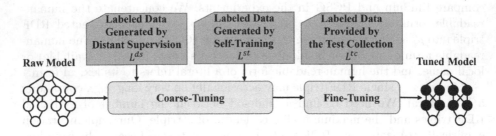

Fig. 3. Our coarse-to-fine strategy for tuning our dense re-ranking model.

In this section, we begin with an overview of our coarse-to-fine tuning strategy. Then we detail two methods for generating labeled data for coarse-tuning:
one based on distant supervision, and the other based on self-training.

3.1   Overview

Figure 3 presents an overview of our strategy for tuning our dense re-ranking
model. We adopt a *coarse-to-fine* design which has been popularly used in other
tasks but not yet in RDF dataset search. Specifically, given a raw (i.e., untuned)
model, in the first step, we employ a large set of automatically generated labeled
data to tune the model. Such labeled data is generated by two methods: L^{ds} generated by distant supervision, and L^{st} generated by self-training. They are automatically generated and hence may contain noise, i.e., incorrect labels. Therefore,
we refer to this step as *coarse-tuning*. In the second step, we employ the labeled
data L^{tc} provided by the training and validation sets of a test collection for RDF
dataset search to *fine-tune* the model in a normal way.

Each $L \in \{L^{ds}, L^{st}, L^{tc}\}$ is a set of *query-document-label triples* $\{\langle q, p_i, l \rangle\}$
where q is a keyword query, p_i is a pseudo document, i.e., the metadata docu-
ment p_i^m or the data document p_i^c constructed for an RDF dataset d_i according
to Sect. 2.2, and l is a Boolean label indicating whether d_i is relevant to q. Note
that for L^{ds} and L^{st}, we will only focus on the generation of positive labels,
i.e., $\langle q, p_i, \text{true} \rangle$. It is then common practice to automatically generate negative labels by randomly pairing keyword queries with pseudo documents. For
example, DPR [12] is associated with such a built-in generator called in-batch
negatives.

3.2 Coarse-Tuning Based on Distant Supervision

Our first method for generating labeled data is inspired by the concept of *distant supervision*, which was originally applied to the task of relation extraction [22]. The idea is that by treating the title of a dataset d_i as a query q, the metadata document p_i^c for d_i should be relevant to q. Therefore, although the availability of labeled data for training RDF dataset search is limited, it is relatively easy to collect metadata for a large number of datasets from the Web, and they are not even restricted to RDF datasets since only their metadata will be used. In this way, a large number of labeled data can be automatically generated.

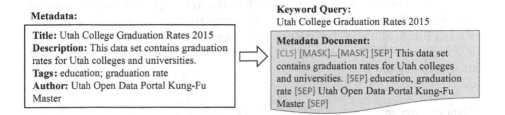

Fig. 4. An example of generating labeled data by distant supervision.

Specifically, with the metadata of each collected dataset d_i, as illustrated in Fig. 4, we take d_i's title as a query q, and construct d_i's metadata document p_i^m according to Sect. 2.2. In particular, we *mask* the title field in p_i^m because otherwise the relevance of p_i^m to q would be too explicit to be useful when being used in tuning. We mask the title field by replacing each token in this field with [MASK] which is a standard masking token used in BERT-based models [10]. Finally, we add the triple $\langle q, p_i^m, \texttt{true} \rangle$ to L^{ds}.

To use L^{ds} to coarse-tune our dense re-ranking model, we randomly split L^{ds} into 90% for training and 10% for validation.

3.3 Coarse-Tuning Based on Self-training

Our second method for generating labeled data adopts a *self-training* design. The idea is to exploit both the labeled and unlabeled data in a test collection for RDF dataset search, by training a *document-to-query generator* on the labeled data and then applying it to generate a query q from the metadata document p_i^m or the data document p_i^c for each unlabeled RDF dataset d_i; these two documents should be relevant to q. Since unlabeled data is often in large amounts in a test collection, e.g., 80% of the RDF datasets in [18] are unlabeled (i.e., not involved in any query-document-label triple in L^{tc}), a large number of labeled data can be automatically generated in this way.

Specifically, recall that L^{tc} denotes the set of labeled data in the training and validation sets of a test collection for RDF dataset search. Let $L^{tc/t/m}, L^{tc/v/m} \subseteq$

L^{tc} be the subsets of labeled data in the training and validation sets, respectively, where query-document-label triples are about metadata documents. Let $L^{tc/t/c}, L^{tc/v/c} \subseteq L^{tc}$ be the subsets of labeled data in the training and validation sets, respectively, where query-document-label triples are about data documents. We separately train two document-to-query generators: $\mathcal{G}^m$ for metadata documents and $\mathcal{G}^c$ for data documents. We reduce document-to-query generation to a *text-to-text generation* task. We train $\mathcal{G}^m$ by employing $L^{tc/t/m}$ as the training set and $L^{tc/v/m}$ as the validation set to fine-tune a T5 model [25], which is a pre-trained text-to-text model. Model selection based on the validation set relies on the ROUGE score, i.e., the mean of ROUGE-1, ROUGE-2, and ROUGE-L, which are standard metrics for evaluating text generation. Then we apply the fine-tuned T5 model as $\mathcal{G}^m$ to the metadata document p_i^m constructed for each unlabeled RDF dataset d_i in the test collection to generate a query q, as illustrated in Fig. 5, and add the triple $\langle q, p_i^m, \texttt{true} \rangle$ to L^{st}. Analogously, we train $\mathcal{G}^c$ on $L^{tc/t/c}$ and $L^{tc/v/c}$, and apply it to the data documents of unlabeled RDF datasets to expand L^{st}.

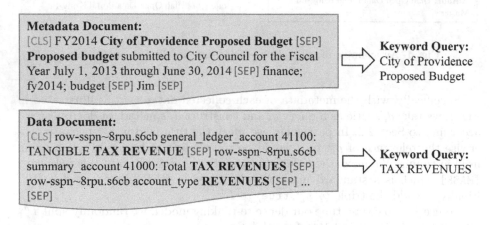

Fig. 5. An example of generating labeled data by a document-to-query generator.

To use L^{st} to coarse-tune our dense re-ranking model, we use L^{st} as the training set and use the original validation set $L^{tc/v/m} \cup L^{tc/v/c}$ in the test collection as the validation set.

4   Evaluation

4.1   Test Collection

We conducted experiments on ACORDAR [18], the currently largest test collection for RDF dataset search, providing 493 queries and 10,671 labeled relevance judgments over 31,589 RDF datasets. Following [18], we conducted five-fold cross-validation using the official train-valid-test splits provided by ACORDAR.[1]

---
[1] https://github.com/nju-websoft/ACORDAR.

4.2 Labeled Data for Coarse-Tuning

We implemented the method for generating labeled data L^{ds} based on distant supervision described in Sect. 3.2 by collecting metadata of datasets from open data portals (ODPs). Specifically, to collect metadata for as many datasets as possible, inspired by [18], we found ODPs by looking up five large catalogues: CKAN,[2] DKAN,[3] DataPortals.org,[4] Open Data Portal Watch,[5] and Socrata.[6] We collected all the ODPs listed in these catalogues, and additionally took the Linked Open Data Cloud[7] into account as an ODP. We identified a total of 570 ODPs that were accessible at the time of experimentation. For each ODP, we used its API to download the metadata for all the datasets registered in the ODP. We successfully collected metadata for 704,370 datasets, but had to remove 354 due to their empty titles. We constructed metadata documents for the remaining 704,016 datasets to generate query-document-label triples as L^{ds}.

   We implemented the method for generating labeled data L^{st} based on self-training described in Sect. 3.3 by exploiting the labeled and unlabeled data in ACORDAR. Specifically, we trained document-to-query generators on the training and validation sets in ACORDAR, and applied them to the metadata and data documents constructed for the 25,380 unlabeled RDF datasets in ACORDAR to generate queries and form query-document-label triples in L^{st}.

4.3 Implementation Details

Our document-to-query generators were implemented based on the T5-Base model.[8] We searched batch size in $\{8, 16\}$, learning rate in $\{1e-6, 5e-6, 1e-5\}$, and trained 10 epochs. We used the Adam optimizer [15]. We ran T5 on an NVIDIA GeForce RTX 3090 GPU with 24 GB memory.

   For DPR and ColBERT in our dense re-ranking model, we used their open-source code.[9][10] For DPR, we trained 1 epoch in the coarse-tuning phase and 10 epochs in the fine-tuning phase, considering the different sizes of training data for different phases. We searched batch size in $\{2, 4\}$ and learning rate in $\{1e-5, 2e-5\}$. For ColBERT, we followed [14] to train 1 epoch in each phase. We searched batch size in $\{8, 16\}$ and learning rate in $\{1e-6, 3e-6, 7e-6\}$. We used the Adam optimizer. We ran DPR and ColBERT on eight NVIDIA Tesla V100 GPUs with 32 GB memory. Based on Faiss indexes,[11] the mean re-ranking time used by DPR and ColBERT for a query was 62 ms and 139 ms, respectively.

---

[2] https://ckan.org/.
[3] https://getdkan.org/.
[4] http://dataportals.org/.
[5] https://data.wu.ac.at/portalwatch/.
[6] https://dev.socrata.com/.
[7] http://cas.lod-cloud.net/.
[8] https://huggingface.co/t5-base.
[9] https://github.com/facebookresearch/DPR.
[10] https://github.com/stanford-futuredata/ColBERT.
[11] https://github.com/facebookresearch/faiss.

4.4   Experimental Settings

We evaluated with the following settings of our approach.

For normal retrieval, we directly reused the 10 top-ranked RDF datasets outputted by each of the four sparse retrieval models provided by ACORDAR: TF-IDF, BM25, LMD, and FSDM. TF-IDF (Term Frequency—Inverse Document Frequency) is a weighting scheme giving large weights to locally frequent (i.e., within the current dataset) but globally infrequent (across all datasets) words; based on TF-IDF vector representations, datasets are ranked by their cosine similarity with the query. BM25 is a ranking function that combines term frequency, inverse document frequency, and document length normalization. LMD (Language Model with Dirichlet Smoothing) is a retrieval model that estimates the probability of generating a query given a document, incorporating smoothing techniques to handle unseen terms. FSDM (Fielded Sequential Dependence Model) is a retrieval model for structured document retrieval which considers term dependencies and optimizes document field weights.

For RDF triple extraction in compact document representation, we compared Illusnip and PCSG.

For the dense ranking model in re-ranking, we compared DPR and ColBERT.

For tuning the dense re-ranking model, we compared coarse-tuning based on distant supervision (denoted by ds), coarse-tuning based on self-training (denoted by st), and normal fine-tuning (denoted by ft).

4.5   Evaluation Metrics

Following [18], we used Normalized Discounted Cumulative Gain (NDCG) and Mean Average Precision (MAP). We calculated and reported the mean NDCG@5, NDCG@10, MAP@5, and MAP@10 scores over all the queries.

4.6   Evaluation Results

In the presented results tables, we highlight the best result in each setting **in bold**, and underline the second best result.

Effectiveness of Re-Ranking. As shown in Table 1, re-ranking brings improvements in all the settings, and the improvements in most settings are statistically significant. The best results are achieved with PCSG and ColBERT. Compared with the original sparse retrieval model, this dense re-ranking model raises NDCG@5 by 0.0218–0.0610 (4%–11%), NDCG@10 by 0.0088–0.0326 (1%–6%), MAP@5 by 0.0175–0.0476 (5%–17%), and MAP@10 by 0.0132–0.0363 (3%–9%). In particular, by re-ranking the outputs of FSDM with this model, we obtain the current state-of-the-art results on ACORDAR. The second best results are mostly achieved with IlluSnip and ColBERT. *These results demonstrate the effectiveness of our dense re-ranking for RDF dataset search.*

Table 1. Effectiveness of Re-Ranking (* indicating a significant improvement after re-ranking according to paired t-test under $p < 0.05$)

Retrieval	Re-Ranking	Tuning	NDCG@5	NDCG@10	MAP@5	MAP@10
TF-IDF	before re-ranking	-	0.5088	0.5452	0.2871	0.3976
	Illusnip+DPR	ds+st+ft	0.5579*	0.5720*	0.3295*	0.4319*
	Illusnip+ColBERT	ds+st+ft	0.5610*	0.5749*	0.3329*	**0.4339***
	PCSG+DPR	ds+st+ft	0.5521*	0.5704*	0.3234*	0.4280*
	PCSG+ColBERT	ds+st+ft	**0.5659***	**0.5753***	**0.3347***	**0.4339***
BM25	before re-ranking	-	0.5538	0.5877	0.3198	0.4358
	Illusnip+DPR	ds+st+ft	0.5888*	0.6082*	0.3481*	0.4592*
	Illusnip+ColBERT	ds+st+ft	0.6028*	0.6136*	0.3553*	0.4623*
	PCSG+DPR	ds+st+ft	0.5880*	0.6065*	0.3462*	0.4567*
	PCSG+ColBERT	ds+st+ft	**0.6079***	**0.6173***	**0.3625***	**0.4680***
LMD	before re-ranking	-	0.5465	0.5805	0.3266	0.4324
	Illusnip+DPR	ds+st+ft	0.5959*	0.6055*	0.3563*	0.4571*
	Illusnip+ColBERT	ds+st+ft	0.5963*	0.6083*	0.3564*	0.4585*
	PCSG+DPR	ds+st+ft	0.5908*	0.6003*	0.3498*	0.4509*
	PCSG+ColBERT	ds+st+ft	**0.6075***	**0.6131***	**0.3671***	**0.4654***
FSDM	before re-ranking	-	0.5932	0.6151	0.3592	0.4602
	Illusnip+DPR	ds+st+ft	0.6088	0.6204	0.3709	0.4713
	Illusnip+ColBERT	ds+st+ft	0.6121	0.6184	0.3677	0.4645
	PCSG+DPR	ds+st+ft	0.6061	0.6149	0.3655	0.4637
	PCSG+ColBERT	ds+st+ft	**0.6150**	**0.6239**	**0.3767**	**0.4734**

Effectiveness of Coarse-Tuning. For space reasons, Table 2 and Table 3 only show the results obtained with ColBERT. The results with DPR are similar.

As shown in Table 2, compared with fine-tuning (ft), adding coarse-tuning brings improvements in almost all the settings. In particular, such improvements are not an effect of longer training since naively increasing the number of epochs in the fine-tuning phase from 1 to 3 (ft^3) only brings marginal differences. In some settings, adding coarse-tuning based on distant supervision (ds+ft) or self-training (st+ft) brings larger improvements than adding both of them (ds+st+ft). However, the latter is more robust as it achieves the first or second best result in most settings. Interestingly, for IlluSnip-based re-ranking models, self-training (st+ft) generally brings larger improvements than distant supervision (ds+ft), whereas for PCSG-based re-ranking models, opposite results are observed. *These results demonstrate the effectiveness of our two coarse-tuning methods which complement fine-tuning and also complement each other.*

As shown in Table 3, coarse-tuning alone based on self-training without fine-tuning (st) is generally comparable with fine-tuning (ft), *which demonstrates the quality of our augmented labeled data via self-training.* However, there are noticeable gaps between fine-tuning (ft) and coarse-tuning alone based on distant supervision without fine-tuning (ds), *which shows difficulty in dense re-ranking for RDF dataset search solved as a zero-shot learning task.*

Table 2. Effectiveness of Coarse-Tuning in Complementing Fine-Tuning

Retrieval	Re-Ranking	Tuning	NDCG@5	NDCG@10	MAP@5	MAP@10
TF-IDF	Illusnip+ColBERT	ft	0.5530	0.5696	0.3287	0.4307
		ft^3	0.5558	0.5703	0.3320	0.4320
		ds+ft	**0.5632**	**0.5754**	<u>0.3343</u>	<u>0.4343</u>
		st+ft	<u>0.5625</u>	0.5746	**0.3368**	**0.4355**
		ds+st+ft	0.5610	<u>0.5749</u>	0.3329	0.4339
	PCSG+ColBERT	ft	0.5621	0.5738	<u>0.3372</u>	<u>0.4356</u>
		ft^3	0.5578	0.5716	0.3345	0.4336
		ds+ft	**0.5688**	**0.5784**	**0.3379**	**0.4368**
		st+ft	0.5566	0.5687	0.3294	0.4297
		ds+st+ft	<u>0.5659</u>	<u>0.5753</u>	0.3347	0.4339
BM25	Illusnip+ColBERT	ft	0.5976	0.6113	0.3522	0.4603
		ft^3	0.6027	<u>0.6137</u>	<u>0.3581</u>	<u>0.4640</u>
		ds+ft	0.6022	0.6124	0.3544	0.4605
		st+ft	**0.6081**	**0.6163**	**0.3602**	**0.4658**
		ds+st+ft	<u>0.6028</u>	0.6136	0.3553	0.4623
	PCSG+ColBERT	ft	0.6045	0.6163	0.3602	0.4671
		ft^3	0.5961	0.6099	0.3534	0.4608
		ds+ft	**0.6103**	**0.6195**	**0.3636**	**0.4694**
		st+ft	0.6047	0.6154	0.3608	0.4672
		ds+st+ft	<u>0.6079</u>	<u>0.6173</u>	<u>0.3625</u>	<u>0.4680</u>
LMD	Illusnip+ColBERT	ft	0.5918	0.6037	0.3514	0.4544
		ft^3	0.5978	0.6068	0.3574	0.4574
		ds+ft	<u>0.5989</u>	0.6064	<u>0.3582</u>	0.4569
		st+ft	**0.6096**	**0.6121**	**0.3666**	**0.4637**
		ds+st+ft	0.5963	<u>0.6083</u>	0.3565	<u>0.4585</u>
	PCSG+ColBERT	ft	0.6029	0.6077	0.3596	0.4578
		ft^3	0.5933	0.6051	0.3562	0.4572
		ds+ft	<u>0.6067</u>	<u>0.6122</u>	<u>0.3656</u>	<u>0.4636</u>
		st+ft	0.6035	0.6104	0.3642	0.4625
		ds+st+ft	**0.6075**	**0.6131**	**0.3671**	**0.4654**
FSDM	Illusnip+ColBERT	ft	0.5981	0.6119	0.3615	0.4608
		ft^3	0.6058	**0.6187**	<u>0.3695</u>	**0.4673**
		ds+ft	0.6030	0.6134	0.3610	0.4592
		st+ft	<u>0.6090</u>	0.6182	**0.3704**	**0.4673**
		ds+st+ft	**0.6121**	<u>0.6184</u>	0.3677	0.4645
	PCSG+ColBERT	ft	**0.6152**	0.6195	<u>0.3766</u>	0.4695
		ft^3	0.6064	0.6181	0.3690	0.4662
		ds+ft	0.6133	0.6223	0.3732	0.4703
		st+ft	0.6128	<u>0.6224</u>	0.3755	<u>0.4725</u>
		ds+st+ft	<u>0.6150</u>	**0.6239**	**0.3767**	**0.4734**

Table 3. Effectiveness of Coarse-Tuning in Replacing Fine-Tuning

Retrieval	Re-Ranking	Tuning	NDCG@5	NDCG@10	MAP@5	MAP@10
TF-IDF	Illusnip+ColBERT	ft	0.5530	0.5696	**0.3287**	**0.4307**
		ds	0.4928	0.5344	0.2757	0.3878
		st	**0.5589**	**0.5708**	0.3276	0.4284
	PCSG+ColBERT	ft	**0.5621**	**0.5738**	**0.3372**	**0.4356**
		ds	0.5095	0.5416	0.2844	0.3937
		st	0.5538	0.5680	0.3209	0.4236
BM25	Illusnip+ColBERT	ft	0.5976	**0.6113**	**0.3522**	**0.4603**
		ds	0.5376	0.5752	0.3031	0.4211
		st	**0.5998**	0.6108	0.3517	0.4597
	PCSG+ColBERT	ft	**0.6045**	**0.6163**	**0.3602**	**0.4671**
		ds	0.5495	0.5849	0.3087	0.4275
		st	0.5948	0.6115	0.3484	0.4594
LMD	Illusnip+ColBERT	ft	0.5918	0.6037	0.3514	0.4544
		ds	0.5332	0.5692	0.2993	0.4115
		st	**0.6001**	**0.6072**	**0.3551**	**0.4552**
	PCSG+ColBERT	ft	**0.6029**	0.6077	**0.3596**	**0.4578**
		ds	0.5477	0.5805	0.3128	0.4243
		st	0.5980	**0.6087**	0.3541	0.4560
FSDM	Illusnip+ColBERT	ft	0.5981	0.6119	0.3615	0.4608
		ds	0.5380	0.5807	0.3103	0.4221
		st	**0.6033**	**0.6168**	**0.3667**	**0.4645**
	PCSG+ColBERT	ft	**0.6152**	0.6195	**0.3766**	**0.4695**
		ds	0.5505	0.5878	0.3158	0.4269
		st	0.6079	**0.6212**	0.3666	0.4670

Table 4. Comparison between Triple Extraction Methods

Retrieval	Re-Ranking	NDCG@5	NDCG@10	MAP@5	MAP@10
TF-IDF	Illusnip+*	**0.5594**	**0.5734**	**0.3312**	**0.4329**
	PCSG+*	0.5590	0.5729	0.3290	0.4309
BM25	Illusnip+*	0.5958	0.6109	0.3517	0.4608
	PCSG+*	**0.5979**	**0.6119**	**0.3543**	**0.4624**
LMD	Illusnip+*	0.5961	**0.6069**	0.3564	0.4578
	PCSG+*	**0.5992**	0.6067	**0.3585**	**0.4582**
FSDM	Illusnip+*	0.6105	0.6194	0.3693	0.4679
	PCSG+*	**0.6106**	**0.6194**	**0.3711**	**0.4686**

Comparison Between Triple Extraction Methods. Table 4 aggregates the results in Table 1 by IlluSnip and PCSG. There is no clear winner between them. In fact, according to Table 1, IlluSnip outperforms PCSG when accompanying DPR, whereas opposite results are observed when accompanying ColBERT, suggesting that extracting representative RDF triples in the context of dataset search deserves to be further studied in the future.

Table 5. Comparison between Dense Ranking Models

Retrieval	Re-Ranking	NDCG@5	NDCG@10	MAP@5	MAP@10
TF-IDF	*+DPR	0.5550	0.5712	0.3264	0.4299
	*+ColBERT	**0.5659**	**0.5753**	**0.3347**	**0.4339**
BM25	*+DPR	0.5884	0.6074	0.3471	0.4580
	*+ColBERT	**0.6053**	**0.6154**	**0.3589**	**0.4652**
LMD	*+DPR	0.5934	0.6029	0.3531	0.4540
	*+ColBERT	**0.6019**	**0.6107**	**0.3618**	**0.4620**
FSDM	*+DPR	0.6074	0.6177	0.3682	0.4675
	*+ColBERT	**0.6136**	**0.6211**	**0.3722**	**0.4690**

Table 6. An Example of Top-Ranked RDF Datasets Before and After Re-Ranking (**bold**: highly relevant; <u>underlined</u>: partially relevant)

Keyword Query: nitrogen reduction plan in MaryLand

	Top-Ranked RDF Datasets by TF-IDF	Re-Ranked by PCSG+ColBERT
1	[ID-46561] Plan Review	[ID-42421] **Percent of required nitrogen reduction achieved: Line Chart**
2	[ID-11683] Plan Review	<u>[ID-41757] Chesapeake Bay Pollution Loads - Nitrogen</u>
3	[ID-86273] January Water Reduction Chart	<u>[ID-03531] Chesapeake Bay Pollution Loads - Nitrogen</u>
4	[ID-08199] Class Size Reduction Projects	[ID-86273] January Water Reduction Chart
5	<u>[ID-03531] Chesapeake Bay Pollution Loads - Nitrogen</u>	[ID-40742] Watershed Contaminant Reduction Index
6	<u>[ID-41757] Chesapeake Bay Pollution Loads - Nitrogen</u>	[ID-08199] Class Size Reduction Projects
7	[ID-07248] 2019 NYC Open Data Plan: Removed Datasets	[ID-79232] Open Publishing Plan Dataset
8	[ID-79232] Open Publishing Plan Dataset	[ID-46561] Plan Review
9	[ID-40742] Watershed Contaminant Reduction Index	[ID-11683] Plan Review
10	[ID-42421] **Percent of required nitrogen reduction achieved: Line Chart**	[ID-07248] 2019 NYC Open Data Plan: Removed Datasets

Comparison Between Dense Ranking Models. Table 5 aggregates the results in Table 1 by DPR and ColBERT. ColBERT consistently outperforms DPR in all the settings, showing its relative suitability for RDF dataset search.

4.7   Case Study

Table 6 illustrates and compares the top-ranked RDF datasets before and after re-ranking for the keyword query "nitrogen reduction plan in MaryLand" which is sampled from our experiments. Before re-ranking, the four top-ranked datasets retrieved by a sparse model (i.e., TF-IDF) are actually irrelevant to the query, although in their metadata, the query keyword "plan" or "reduction" has a misleadingly very high lexical frequency. After re-ranking by our dense model (i.e., PCSG+ColBERT), these datasets fall noticeably, while the three relevant datasets rise to the top. It is expected since they exhibit better semantic matching with the query, which is satisfyingly captured by the dense model.

5   Related Work

5.1   Dataset Search

Researchers have explored various principles and methods for dataset search [5]. For example, Koesten et al. [16] studied the user behavior of seeking structured data on the Web, based on interviews with participants and analyses of search logs. Google Dataset Search [3] is a dataset search engine providing keyword search over reconciled metadata of datasets discovered on the Web.

The Semantic Web community is interested in RDF dataset search, and has developed several prototype systems. LODAtlas [24] allows users to search for RDF datasets and browse a retrieved dataset through a summary visualization. CKGSE [30] supports full-text search over RDF datasets and presents extracted data snippets and summaries. All these systems employ a sparse retrieval model such as BM25. Moreover, Lin et al. [18] constructed the ACORDAR test collection for RDF dataset search and evaluated a set of retrieval methods—all based on sparse models. By contrast, our work is distinguished by *studying dense ranking models* for RDF dataset search and addressing the encountered challenges.

5.2   Dense Ranking

Benefiting from the progress of pre-trained language models like BERT [10], dense ranking models have exhibited higher accuracy than sparse models in document retrieval [12,14]. However, one factor that restricts the application of dense models to boarder tasks is their limited input length of 512 tokens. ANCE [31] addressed it by splitting a document into segments and then pooling segment-level scores, where the semantic dependency among segments was ignored. SeDR [7] used segment interaction to capture document-level representations, but only extended the maximum input length to 2,048 tokens. This capacity still cannot fit the possibly large size of an RDF dataset. Differently, we addressed this challenge by *extracting a subset of representative RDF triples*.

Another factor affecting the performance of dense models is the availability of labeled data for training. Indeed, as reported in [12], accuracy dropped largely after reducing training samples from 59k to 1k. To alleviate this challenge, [11] fine-tuned on a large set of out-of-domain labeled data such as MS MARCO [23], and then transferred the model to the target domain. However, existing labeled data is mainly for document retrieval which differs greatly from RDF dataset search, and our preliminary experiments have confirmed this concern. Therefore, we chose a different direction partially inspired by self-training [21], i.e., we adopted a coarse-to-fine tuning strategy and devised two methods for *generating in-domain (i.e., task-specific) labeled data* for coarse tuning.

6 Conclusion and Future Work

Our exploration of applying dense ranking models to RDF dataset search has brought an improvement of up to 11% in NDCG@5 and 17% in MAP@5 compared with conventional sparse retrieval, considerably pushing the state of the art on the ACORDAR test collection. It represents an encouraging start to connect the task of RDF dataset search with recent advances in pre-trained language models and dense text retrieval. Our empirical findings are expected to expand the understanding of dense dataset search as a promising research pathway, and our code and generated labeled data are shared to facilitate future studies.

As for future work, we identify the following three research directions. First, for compact document representation, it remains unknown whether our selected IlluSnip or PCSG is most suitable for sampling RDF data in the context of dataset search. There are other snippet extraction and data summarization methods [4,9,20,27,29] which deserve to be investigated, and a new specialized method may be more helpful. Besides, beyond simple concatenation, a better way of verbalizing RDF data into a document may also be helpful. Second, contrastive learning is known to be useful for enhancing dense ranking models [31]. However, to boost training, it relies on high-quality (i.e., hard) negative samples [32]. Their generation in the scenario of dataset search is still an open problem. Third, we plan to extend our approach to a more general setting of dataset search going beyond RDF datasets. One major challenge to be overcome is how to encode different formats of data in a universal way. A possible solution is to convert all types of data into graphs [1].

Supplemental Material Statement: Source code for all the dense re-ranking models, their outputs, and all the generated labeled data are available from GitHub at https://github.com/nju-websoft/DR2.

Acknowledgments. This work was supported by the NSFC (62072224).

References

1. Anadiotis, A.G., et al.: Graph integration of structured, semistructured and unstructured data for data journalism. Inf. Syst. **104**, 101846 (2022). https://doi.org/10.1016/j.is.2021.101846
2. Benjelloun, O., Chen, S., Noy, N.F.: Google dataset search by the numbers. In: ISWC 2020, vol. 12507, pp. 667–682 (2020). https://doi.org/10.1007/978-3-030-62466-8_41

3. Brickley, D., Burgess, M., Noy, N.F.: Google dataset search: building a search engine for datasets in an open Web ecosystem. In: WWW 2019, pp. 1365–1375 (2019). https://doi.org/10.1145/3308558.3313685
4. Cebiric, S., Goasdoué, F., Kondylakis, H., Kotzinos, D., Manolescu, I., Troullinou, G., Zneika, M.: Summarizing semantic graphs: a survey. VLDB J. **28**(3), 295–327 (2019). https://doi.org/10.1007/s00778-018-0528-3
5. Chapman, A., Simperl, E., Koesten, L., Konstantinidis, G., Ibáñez, L., Kacprzak, E., Groth, P.: Dataset search: a survey. VLDB J. **29**(1), 251–272 (2020). https://doi.org/10.1007/s00778-019-00564-x
6. Chen, J., Wang, X., Cheng, G., Kharlamov, E., Qu, Y.: Towards more usable dataset search: From query characterization to snippet generation. In: CIKM 2019, pp. 2445–2448 (2019). https://doi.org/10.1145/3357384.3358096
7. Chen, J., Chen, Q., Li, D., Huang, Y.: Sedr: segment representation learning for long documents dense retrieval. CoRR abs/2211.10841 (2022). https://doi.org/10.48550/arXiv.2211.10841
8. Cheng, G., Jin, C., Ding, W., Xu, D., Qu, Y.: Generating illustrative snippets for open data on the Web. In: WSDM 2017, pp. 151–159 (2017). https://doi.org/10.1145/3018661.3018670
9. Cheng, G., Jin, C., Qu, Y.: HIEDS: a generic and efficient approach to hierarchical dataset summarization. In: IJCAI 2016, pp. 3705–3711 (2016)
10. Devlin, J., Chang, M., Lee, K., Toutanova, K.: BERT: pre-training of deep bidirectional transformers for language understanding. In: NAACL-HLT 2019, vol. 1, pp. 4171–4186 (2019). https://doi.org/10.18653/v1/n19-1423
11. Izacard, G., et al.: Unsupervised dense information retrieval with contrastive learning. CoRR abs/2112.09118 (2021). 10.48550/arXiv.2112.09118
12. Karpukhin, V., et al.: Dense passage retrieval for open-domain question answering. In: EMNLP 2020, pp. 6769–6781 (2020). https://doi.org/10.18653/v1/2020.emnlp-main.550
13. Kato, M.P., Ohshima, H., Liu, Y., Chen, H.: A test collection for ad-hoc dataset retrieval. In: SIGIR 2021, pp. 2450–2456 (2021). https://doi.org/10.1145/3404835.3463261
14. Khattab, O., Zaharia, M.: ColBERT: efficient and effective passage search via contextualized late interaction over BERT. In: SIGIR 2020, pp. 39–48 (2020). https://doi.org/10.1145/3397271.3401075
15. Kingma, D.P., Ba, J.: Adam: a method for stochastic optimization. In: ICLR 2015 (2015)
16. Koesten, L.M., Kacprzak, E., Tennison, J.F.A., Simperl, E.: The trials and tribulations of working with structured data - a study on information seeking behaviour. In: CHI 2017, pp. 1277–1289 (2017). https://doi.org/10.1145/3025453.3025838
17. Lin, J., Nogueira, R.F., Yates, A.: Pretrained Transformers for Text Ranking: BERT and Beyond. Synthesis Lectures on Human Language Technologies, Morgan & Claypool Publishers, San Rafael (2021). https://doi.org/10.2200/S01123ED1V01Y202108HLT053
18. Lin, T., et al.: ACORDAR: a test collection for ad hoc content-based (RDF) dataset retrieval. In: SIGIR 2022, pp. 2981–2991 (2022). https://doi.org/10.1145/3477495.3531729
19. Liu, D., Cheng, G., Liu, Q., Qu, Y.: Fast and practical snippet generation for RDF datasets. ACM Trans. Web **13**(4), 19:1–19:38 (2019). https://doi.org/10.1145/3365575

20. Liu, Q., Cheng, G., Gunaratna, K., Qu, Y.: Entity summarization: state of the art and future challenges. J. Web Semant. **69**, 100647 (2021). https://doi.org/10.1016/j.websem.2021.100647

21. Luo, H., Li, S., Gao, M., Yu, S., Glass, J.R.: Cooperative self-training of machine reading comprehension. In: NAACL 2022, pp. 244–257 (2022). https://doi.org/10.18653/v1/2022.naacl-main.18

22. Mintz, M., Bills, S., Snow, R., Jurafsky, D.: Distant supervision for relation extraction without labeled data. In: ACL 2009, pp. 1003–1011 (2009)

23. Nguyen, T., et al.: MS MARCO: a human generated machine reading comprehension dataset. In: CoCo 2016, vol. 1773 (2016)

24. Pietriga, E., et al.: Browsing linked data catalogs with LODAtlas. In: ISWC 2018, pp. 137–153 (2018). https://doi.org/10.1007/978-3-030-00668-6_9

25. Raffel, C., Shazeer, N., Roberts, A., Lee, K., Narang, S., Matena, M., Zhou, Y., Li, W., Liu, P.J.: Exploring the limits of transfer learning with a unified text-to-text transformer. J. Mach. Learn. Res. **21**, 140:1-140:67 (2020)

26. Robertson, S., Zaragoza, H.: The probabilistic relevance framework: Bm25 and beyond. Found. Trends Inf. Retr. **3**(4), 333–389 (2009). https://doi.org/10.1561/1500000019

27. Wang, X., Cheng, G., Kharlamov, E.: Towards multi-facet snippets for dataset search. In: PROFILES & SEMEX 2019, pp. 1–6 (2019)

28. Wang, X., et al.: PCSG: pattern-coverage snippet generation for RDF datasets. In: ISWC 2021, pp. 3–20 (2021). https://doi.org/10.1007/978-3-030-88361-4_1

29. Wang, X., Cheng, G., Pan, J.Z., Kharlamov, E., Qu, Y.: BANDAR: benchmarking snippet generation algorithms for (RDF) dataset search. IEEE Trans. Knowl. Data Eng. **35**(2), 1227–1241 (2023). https://doi.org/10.1109/TKDE.2021.3095309

30. Wang, X., Lin, T., Luo, W., Cheng, G., Qu, Y.: CKGSE: a prototype search engine for chinese knowledge graphs. Data Intell. **4**(1), 41–65 (2022). https://doi.org/10.1162/dint_a_00118

31. Xiong, L., et al.: Approximate nearest neighbor negative contrastive learning for dense text retrieval. In: ICLR 2021 (2021). https://openreview.net/forum?id=zeFrfgyZln

32. Zhan, J., Mao, J., Liu, Y., Guo, J., Zhang, M., Ma, S.: Optimizing dense retrieval model training with hard negatives. In: SIGIR 2021, pp. 1503–1512 (2021). https://doi.org/10.1145/3404835.3462880

33. Zhao, W.X., Liu, J., Ren, R., Wen, J.: Dense text retrieval based on pretrained language models: a survey. CoRR abs/2211.14876 (2022). https://doi.org/10.48550/arXiv.2211.14876

Optimizing SPARQL Queries with SHACL

Ratan Bahadur Thapa$^{(\boxtimes)}$ and Martin Giese

Department of Informatics, University of Oslo, Oslo, Norway
{ratanbt,martingi}@ifi.uio.no

Abstract. We propose a set of optimizations that can be applied to a given SPARQL query, and that guarantee that the optimized query has the same answers under bag semantics as the original query, provided that the queried RDF graph validates certain SHACL constraints. Our optimizations exploit the relationship between graph patterns in the SPARQL queries and the SHACL constraints that describe those patterns in the RDF graph. We prove the correctness of these optimizations and show how they can be propagated to larger queries while preserving answers. Further, we prove the confluence of rewritings that employ these optimizations, guaranteeing convergence to the same optimized query regardless of the rewriting order.

1 Introduction

The Resource Description Framework (RDF) [37] has seen increasing adoption in recent years, prompting the W3C standardization of the SPARQL [24,45] query language for RDF. Since the W3C standardization in 2008, SPARQL has been recognised as a key technology for the Semantic Web and the current version SPARQL 1.1 [24] is well-adopted in both academia and industries, e.g., query engines for AllegroGraph [22], Apache Jena [16], Sesame [11] and OpenLink Virtuoso [21].

The RDF model, as an abstract knowledge representation, doesn't explicitly distinguish between data and metadata, such as schema and constraints. To address this, the W3C has recommended the SHACL [32] constraint language for RDF. SHACL validation relies on "shapes," which define a set of constraints and indicate which nodes in an RDF graph should be validated against these constraints. Since its recommendation in 2017, SHACL has been widely used to verify compliance of RDF datasets w.r.t. certain policies, such as GDPR requirements [39], and to generate guarantees for data transformation [53,54], facilitating data repairs [4] and others [40]. Additionally, a set of SHACL constraints can function as a "schema" for RDF datasets that satisfy these constraints, enhancing the understandability and usability of the data represented in RDF.

However, the potential of utilizing SHACL to optimize SPARQL queries, similar to how relational constraints optimize queries in relational databases [3], remains largely unexplored. While hand-written SPARQL queries are often tailored to the structure of the RDF graph being queried, queries generated by user interfaces [31,38] or query translators [28,57] and rewriting engines [26,36,52] may contain redundant parts that are not necessary for a specific graph. SHACL can capture information about the structure of an RDF graph, similar to relational database constraints. As a result, triple stores

T. R. Payne et al. (Eds.): ISWC 2023, LNCS 14265, pp. 41–60, 2023.
https://doi.org/10.1007/978-3-031-47240-4_3

that have built-in support for SHACL can then use this information to enforce SHACL constraints as well as incorporate them into query processing to optimize queries. To address this issue, we propose a set of optimizations that maintain the correctness of query results and can be applied to a SPARQL query prior to processing, provided that the RDF graph conforms to a specified set of SHACL shapes.

SPARQL queries consist of three main components: (a) pattern matching, which includes optional parts, unions, joins, nesting, and filtering values to find possible matches, (b) solution modifiers, which allow for modifying matched values using operators such as projection and distinct, and (c) output mode, which can be a boolean answer or selections of values from variables that match the patterns, constructing new values, or describing existing data through constraints. To optimize SPARQL queries, we focus on those containing semantically redundant graph patterns that can be minimized or restructured in the query definition based on SHACL descriptions of these patterns in RDF.

The optional operator is a crucial feature in SPARQL queries, commonly used to handle missing or unavailable information [6]. By using optional, query answers can include available information instead of failing to give an answer when parts of the pattern do not match. This feature is particularly important in semantic web applications, where partial knowledge about data is often assumed. However, optional is also a source of complexity in query answering, as it is PSPACE-hard for optional alone [43,50]. As a result, it has been actively studied [29,34] and optimized [15,56] in various query circumstances. In this work, we focus on the Left-Join intuition applied by Xiao et al. [56] for the treatment of optional. However, instead of relying on SQL not null constraint information in their SPARQL-to-SQL translation, we use SHACL constraints to reduce optional patterns to joins. We illustrate this approach using an example below.

Example 1. *Consider an RDF graph on the left that validates a SHACL shape s on the right, written in Turtle syntax:*

```
:Ida a :Student;
    :hasID "001"^^xsd:int;
    :hasAddress "Oslo".
:Ingrid a :Student;
    :hasID "002"^^xsd:int;
    :hasAddress "Bergen".
```

```
:StudentNode a sh:NodeShape;
    sh:targetClass :Student;
    sh:property [ sh:path :hasAddress;
        sh:nodeKind sh:Literal;
        sh:maxCount 1; sh:minCount 1 ; ];
    sh:property [ sh:path :hasID;
        dash:uniqueValueForClass
            :Student ; ].
```

The node shape, ':StudentNode' declares (a) a class-based target, indicating that all the members of Student class are target nodes, (b) cardinality path constraint requiring all students to have exactly one address, and (c) dash:uniqueValueForClass[1] path constraint stating that no two students can share the same id. Instances of Student validate against the shape if they satisfy both stated constraints.

Consider an information need to retrieve the ids of students including their addresses if available, which could be expressed as the following SPARQL query Q,

SELECT ?y ?z WHERE {?x a Student. ?x :hasID ?y. Optional {?x :hasAddress ?z}}.

---

[1] https://datashapes.org/constraints.html.

Q retrieves ids *of students including their* addresses *if possible from the graph, i.e., in the absence of* address, ids *are still retrieved with variable* ?z *left undefined in the answer. Observe a scenario, where Q is to be evaluated over a graph that satisfies the shape s. Since the shape s guarantees that for each student* ?x, *irrespective of their* ids ?y, *variable* ?z *will always bind to an address (i.e., will never be left unbound), the query Q can be rewritten as follows without the* Optional,

SELECT ?y ?z *WHERE* {?x a Student . ?x :hasID ?y . ?x :hasAddress ?z .}

Similarly, consider finding the ids *of those students who have addresses, such as,*

SELECT ?y *WHERE* {?x a Student . ?x :hasID ?y . ?x :hasAddress ?z .}

Since shape s guarantees an address ?z *for every student* ?x, *the original query can be rewritten as follows without changing the solutions,*

SELECT ?y *WHERE* {?x a Student . ?x :hasID ?y .}

Consider the query SELECT DISTINCT ?y *WHERE* {?x a Student . ?x :hasID ?y .}. *Then, the distinct operator can be removed from the query definition since the shape s guarantees a unique id* ?y *for every student* ?x.

Our approach to optimizing joins in SPARQL is similar to that of query containment concerning inclusion dependencies [27] in relational databases. In particular, when dealing with two query patterns $\mathcal{P}_1$ and $\mathcal{P}_2$ under set (resp., bag) semantics, we can simplify their join by reducing it to $\mathcal{P}_2$ if the answers to $\mathcal{P}_1$ are included in the answers to $\mathcal{P}_2$ for any graph. To achieve this, we draw on intuitions from previous literature [9, 13, 33, 49, 51] on join optimization. Specifically, we focus on the task of pruning join patterns that do not affect the output of a query, resulting in reduced query execution costs. Finally, eliminating distinct patterns can also improve query performance significantly as it can be a bottleneck in SPARQL processing, requiring substantial resources to eliminate duplicate rows, particularly with large datasets [7]. We remove distinct if the original query's result is guaranteed to be free of duplicate rows by SHACL. For instance, when joining two triple patterns with a unique one-to-one (resp., one to at most one) relation, applying distinct over the join may not have any effect. An example of this optimization is illustrated in Example 1.

The rest of the paper is organized as follows: In Sect. 2, we review fundamental concepts of SPARQL algebra and SHACL constraints. Query optimizations are presented in Sect. 3. Section 4 contains a discussion of our results, and Sect. 5 concludes the paper. Due to space constraints, the paper includes only partial proofs of the results. For details proofs, we refer the reader to [55].

2   Preliminaries

We next recapitulate the SPARQL algebra and SHACL constraints that we deal with in this paper.

RDF Graph. Assume that $\mathbf{I}$, $\mathbf{B}$ and $\mathbf{L}$ are countably infinite disjoint sets of *Internationalized Resource Identifiers* (IRIs), *Blank nodes* and *Literals*, respectively. The set of RDF terms $\mathbf{T}$ is $\mathbf{I} \cup \mathbf{B} \cup \mathbf{L}$. An *RDF triple* is an element $\langle s, p, o \rangle$ of $(\mathbf{I} \cup \mathbf{B}) \times \mathbf{I} \times \mathbf{T}$, where s is called the subject, p the predicate and o the object. An RDF graph $G \subseteq (\mathbf{I} \cup \mathbf{B}) \times \mathbf{I} \times \mathbf{T}$ is a finite set of RDF triples. We assume that all RDF graphs are non-empty, which we do not see as a limitation in practice since querying empty graphs has no use in most applications. For simplicity, we represent RDF triples as binary relations in first-order logic, except the triple of the form $\langle s, \mathrm{rdf{:}type}, C \rangle$. We write $P(s, o)$ (resp., $C(s)$) for the RDF triple $\langle s, P, o \rangle$ (resp., $\langle s, \mathrm{rdf{:}type}, C \rangle$) and $P^-(s, o)$ for the inverse of triple $P(o, s)$.

Definition 1. *The set N_G of nodes of an RDF graph G is the union of sets of subjects and objects of triples of the form $\langle s, P, o \rangle$ and subjects of triples of the form $\langle s, \mathrm{rdf{:}type}, C \rangle$ in the graph, i.e., $\{s, o \mid P(s, o) \in G \text{ or } C(s) \in G\}$.*

SPARQL Algebra. We formally adopt the bag-based (rather than the set-based [43]) semantics for SPARQL as in the W3C specification [24,45] and studied in the literature [5,30].

Assume a countably infinite set $\mathbf{V}$ of variables disjoint from $\mathbf{T}$. A triple pattern is defined as a triple in $(\mathbf{I} \cup \mathbf{L} \cup \mathbf{V}) \times (\mathbf{I} \cup \mathbf{V}) \times (\mathbf{I} \cup \mathbf{L} \cup \mathbf{V})$. We use the same notations $P(x, y)$, $P^-(x, y)$, $C(x)$ for triple patterns as we do for RDF triples. A *basic graph pattern (BGP)* is a finite set of triple patterns. For simplicity, we only consider project and distinct solution modifiers and treat SPARQL query as a graph pattern $\mathcal{P}$, defined by the grammar

$$\mathcal{P} ::= \mathcal{B} \mid \mathrm{Filter}_{\mathcal{F}}(\mathcal{P}) \mid \mathrm{Union}(\mathcal{P}_1, \mathcal{P}_2) \mid \mathrm{Join}(\mathcal{P}_1, \mathcal{P}_2) \mid \mathrm{Minus}(\mathcal{P}_1, \mathcal{P}_2) \mid$$
$$\mathrm{Diff}_{\mathcal{F}}(\mathcal{P}_1, \mathcal{P}_2) \mid \mathrm{Opt}_{\mathcal{F}}(\mathcal{P}_1, \mathcal{P}_2) \mid \mathrm{Proj}_L(\mathcal{P}) \mid \mathrm{Dist}(\mathcal{P}),$$

where $\mathcal{B}$ is a BGP, $L \subseteq \mathbf{V}$ and $\mathcal{F}$, called *filter*, is a formula constructed using the logical connectives $\wedge$ and $\neg$ from atoms of the form $\mathrm{bound}(v)$, $(v = c)$, $(v = v')$ for $v, v' \in \mathbf{V}$ and $c \in \mathbf{T}$. Let $\mathit{var}(\mathcal{P})$ (resp., $\mathit{var}(\mathcal{F})$) be the set of variables occurring in a graph pattern $\mathcal{P}$ (resp. filter $\mathcal{F}$). In the rest of the article, we assume that all filter constraints are safe, i.e., $\mathit{var}(\mathcal{F}) \subseteq \mathit{var}(\mathcal{P})$ for every pattern $\mathrm{Filter}_{\mathcal{F}}(\mathcal{P})$.

Given a SPARQL query Q and graph pattern $\mathcal{P}$, we write $\mathcal{P} \trianglelefteq Q$ if either $\mathcal{P}$ is Q or $\mathcal{P}$ appears in Q. Similarly, we denote by $Q^{\mathcal{P} \mapsto \mathcal{P}'}$ the rewriting of $\mathcal{P} \trianglelefteq Q$ to graph pattern $\mathcal{P}'$ in Q, $Q^{X \mapsto Y}$ the renaming of $X \subseteq \mathit{var}(Q)$ to a set Y of variables in Q (i.e., renaming $\rho : X \to Y$ s.t. $\forall y \in Y, \exists x \in X$ and $\rho(x) = y$), $\mathit{var}(Q \setminus \mathcal{P})$ the set of variables that occur in Q excluding the pattern $\mathcal{P} \trianglelefteq Q$ and $\mathit{var}(Q \cup \mathcal{P}) := \mathit{var}(Q) \cup \mathit{var}(\mathcal{P})$. For readability, we also write nested Join expressions as *concatenation* whenever required, e.g., the graph pattern $\mathcal{P} = \mathrm{Join}(\ldots \mathrm{Join}(\mathcal{P}_1, \mathcal{P}_2), \ldots \mathcal{P}_n)$ may be written as $\mathcal{P}_1 \mathcal{P}_2 \ldots \mathcal{P}_n$, and the $\mathcal{P}_i$ are called inner graph patterns of $\mathcal{P}$.

The semantics of graph patterns is defined in terms of (solution) mappings, partial functions, $\mu : \mathbf{V} \to \mathbf{T}$ with (possibly empty) domain dom_μ. Let $\mu_{|L}$ (resp., $\mu_{|\bar{L}}$) be the restriction of mapping μ to $L \subseteq \mathbf{V}$ (resp. $\mathbf{V} \setminus L$) . Two mappings μ_1 and μ_2 are called compatible, denoted by $\mu_1 \sim \mu_2$, if $\mu_1(v) = \mu_2(v)$, for all $v \in \mathrm{dom}_{\mu_1} \cap \mathrm{dom}_{\mu_2}$, in which case $\mu_1 \oplus \mu_2$ denotes a solution mapping with domain $\mathrm{dom}_{\mu_1} \cup \mathrm{dom}_{\mu_2}$ s.t. $\mu_1 \oplus \mu_2 : v \to \mu_1(v)$ for $v \in \mathrm{dom}_{\mu_1}$, and $\mu_1 \oplus \mu_2 : v \to \mu_2(v)$ for $v \in \mathrm{dom}_{\mu_2}$. The truth-value $\mathcal{F}^\mu \in \{\top, \bot, \varepsilon\}$ (i.e., ε stands for "error") of a filter $\mathcal{F}$ under a mapping μ is defined inductively,

$$\square \ (\text{bound}(v))^\mu = \begin{cases} \top, & \text{if } v \in \text{dom}_\mu, \\ \bot, & \text{otherwise.} \end{cases}$$

$$\square \ (v = c)^\mu = \begin{cases} \top, & \text{if } \mu(v) = c, \\ \bot, & \text{if } \mu(v) \neq c, \quad \text{and } (v = v')^\mu = \begin{cases} \top, & \text{if } \mu(v) = \mu(v'), \\ \bot, & \text{if } \mu(v) \neq \mu(v'), \\ \varepsilon, & \text{if } \{v, v'\} \nsubseteq \text{dom}_\mu. \end{cases} \\ \varepsilon \ (\text{error}), & \text{if } v \notin \text{dom}_\mu, \end{cases}$$

$$\square \ (\neg \mathcal{F})^\mu = \begin{cases} \top, & \text{if } \mathcal{F}^\mu = \bot, \\ \bot, & \text{if } \mathcal{F}^\mu = \top, \quad \text{and } \ (\mathcal{F}_1 \wedge \mathcal{F}_2)^\mu = \begin{cases} \top, & \text{if } \mathcal{F}_1^\mu = \mathcal{F}_2^\mu = \top, \\ \bot, & \text{if } \mathcal{F}_1^\mu = \bot \text{ or } \mathcal{F}_2^\mu = \bot, \\ \varepsilon, & \text{if } \mathcal{F}_1^\mu = \varepsilon \text{ or } \mathcal{F}_2^\mu = \varepsilon. \end{cases} \\ \varepsilon, & \text{if } \mathcal{F}^\mu = \varepsilon, \end{cases}$$

The evaluation of a SPARQL graph pattern $\mathcal{P}$ over an RDF graph G, denoted by $\mathcal{P}^G$, returns a multiset (i.e., bag) of mappings. Let $|\mu, \mathcal{P}^G|$ be the multiplicity of a mapping μ in the multiset $\mathcal{P}^G$. In this sense, we also write $\mu \in \mathcal{P}^G$ when $|\mu, \mathcal{P}^G| > 0$ and $\mu \notin \mathcal{P}^G$ when $|\mu, \mathcal{P}^G| = 0$. Then, the $|\mu, \mathcal{P}^G|$ is defined recursively as follows:

1. Let $\mathcal{P}$ be a BGP. Then, $|\mu, \mathcal{P}^G| = 1$ for every μ if $\text{dom}_\mu = var(\mathcal{P})$ and $\mu(\mathcal{P}) \subseteq G$, and 0 otherwise;

2. $|\mu, \text{Proj}_L(\mathcal{P})^G| = \sum_{\mu = \mu'_{|L}} |\mu', \mathcal{P}^G|$;

3. $|\mu, \text{Dist}(\mathcal{P})^G| = \begin{cases} 1, & \text{if } |\mu, \mathcal{P}^G| > 0, \\ 0, & \text{otherwise;} \end{cases}$

4. $|\mu, \text{Filter}_{\mathcal{F}}(\mathcal{P})^G| = \begin{cases} |\mu, \mathcal{P}^G|, & \text{if } \mathcal{F}^\mu = \top, \\ 0, & \text{otherwise;} \end{cases}$

5. $|\mu, \text{Union}(\mathcal{P}_1, \mathcal{P}_2)^G| = |\mu, \mathcal{P}_1^G| + |\mu, \mathcal{P}_2^G|$;

6. $|\mu_1 \oplus \mu_2, \text{Join}(\mathcal{P}_1, \mathcal{P}_2)^G| = \sum_{\mu_1 \in \mathcal{P}_1^G, \mu_2 \in \mathcal{P}_2^G \text{ with } \mu_1 \sim \mu_2} |\mu_1, \mathcal{P}_1^G| \times |\mu_2, \mathcal{P}_2^G|$;

7. $|\mu, \text{Minus}(\mathcal{P}_1, \mathcal{P}_2)^G| = \begin{cases} |\mu, \mathcal{P}_1^G|, & \text{if } \forall \mu_2 \in \mathcal{P}_2^G.(\mu \nsim \mu_2 \text{ or } \text{dom}_\mu \cap \text{dom}_{\mu_2} = \emptyset), \\ 0, & \text{otherwise;} \end{cases}$

8. $|\mu, \text{Diff}_{\mathcal{F}}(\mathcal{P}_1, \mathcal{P}_2)^G| = \begin{cases} |\mu, \mathcal{P}_1^G|, & \text{if } \forall \mu_2 \in \mathcal{P}_2^G.(\mu \nsim \mu_2 \text{ or } \mathcal{F}^{\mu \oplus \mu_2} \neq \top), \\ 0, & \text{otherwise;} \end{cases}$

9. $|\mu, \text{Opt}_{\mathcal{F}}(\mathcal{P}_1, \mathcal{P}_2)^G| = |\mu, \text{Filter}_{\mathcal{F}}(\text{Join}(\mathcal{P}_1, \mathcal{P}_2))^G| + |\mu, \text{Diff}_{\mathcal{F}}(\mathcal{P}_1, \mathcal{P}_2)^G|$.

The support of a multiset M is the underlying set $\sup(M) = \{\mu \mid |\mu, M| > 0\}$. The domain of a multiset M of mappings is defined as $\text{dom}_M = \bigcup_{\mu \in M} \text{dom}_\mu$. We denote by $M_{|\bar{X}}$ the multiset of mappings $\mu \in M$ restricted to $\mathbf{V} \setminus X$, i.e., $|\mu, M_{|\bar{X}}| = \sum_{\mu = \mu'_{|\bar{X}}} |\mu', M|$.

Finally, Proj and Dist operators capture the query nesting functionality, called *subqueries* [30, Sect. 3], in SPARQL, which can be arbitrarily deep and may lead to a complex layered structure. We thus adopt the *simple normal form* (SNF) of SPARQL queries from [30, Defn. 3.8] that is suitable for optimizations presented in Sect. 3.

Definition 2. *A SPARQL query is in SNF if it has the form* $\text{Dist}(\text{Proj}_X(\mathcal{P}))$ *with subquery-free pattern* $\mathcal{P}$ *or the form* $\text{Proj}_X(\mathcal{P})$*, where all subquery patterns in* $\mathcal{P}$ *are of the form* $\text{Dist}(\text{Proj}_{X'}(\mathcal{P}'))$ *with* $\mathcal{P}'$ *subquery-free.*

Any SPARQL query Q can be brought into *SNF* by following two steps of normalisation as illustrated below, where $n \geq i \geq 1$:

1. If Q is a query of the form $\text{Dist}(\text{Proj}_X(\mathcal{P}))$ s.t. $\mathcal{P}$ is subquery $\text{Dist}(\mathcal{P}')$, then Q can be simplified to $\text{Dist}(\text{Proj}_X(\mathcal{P}'))$.
2. If Q is a query of the form $\text{Proj}_X(\mathcal{P})$ s.t. $\mathcal{P} = \{\mathcal{P}_1 \ldots \text{Proj}_Y(\mathcal{P}_i) \ldots \mathcal{P}_n\}$, then Q can be simplified to $\text{Proj}_X(\mathcal{P}')$, where $\mathcal{P}' = \{\mathcal{P}_1 \ldots \mathcal{P}_i^{W \mapsto W'} \ldots \mathcal{P}_n\}$ s.t. $W = (var(P_i) \setminus Y) \cap var(Q \setminus P_i)$ and $w' \notin var(Q)$ for all $w' \in W'$.

Step 1 removes redundant `Dist` from inner graph pattern $\mathcal{P}'$ since the outermost `Dist` already guarantees a duplicate-free result. To avoid conflicts with variables outside of $\mathcal{P}_i$ in Q, step 2 renames variables in inner graph pattern $\mathcal{P}_i$ before removing the inner `Proj`.

Henceforth, we assume that all SPARQL queries are in their *SNF*.

Example 2. *Consider a SPARQL query that retrieves the name of employees and their office addresses, such as,*

$$\text{Proj}_{yz}(\text{Join}(hasName(x, y), \text{Proj}_{xz}(\text{Join}(hasOffice(x, y), hasAddress(y, z))))),$$

which can be brought into SNF by renaming the variable y of subquery to n, thus removing clashes with any variables outside of the subquery, as follows,

$$\text{Proj}_{yz}(hasName(x, y) \, hasOffice(x, n) \, hasAddress(n, z)).$$

SHACL Constraint. We adopt the abstract syntax for the *core constraints* of SHACL [32] introduced by Corman et al. [19]. In addition, we incorporate a non-standard SPARQL-based constraint component called `dash:uniqueValuesForClass`. Let **S**, **C** and **P** be countably infinite and mutually disjoint sets of SHACL *shape*, *class* and *property* names, respectively. Each SHACL constraint is a set of conditions, usually referred to as shape, defined as a triple $\langle s, \tau_s, \phi_s \rangle$ consisting of:

☐ *name s,*
☐ *target definition* τ_s is a SPARQL query with a single output variable, which retrieves the target entities of s from the RDF graph G that is being validated. There are two types of τ_s that we consider:
- The first type corresponds to the 'sh:targetClass' of the SHACL specification. In this case, τ_s is a SPARQL query of the form:

    "SELECT ?x WHERE ?x rdf:type/subClassOf* C".

- The second type corresponds to the 'sh:targetSubjectOf' or 'sh:targetObjectOf' of the SHACL specification, as shown in Example 3. In this case, τ_s is a SPARQL query of the form:

    "SELECT ?x WHERE ?x P ?y" or "SELECT ?x WHERE ?y P ?x".

In abstract syntax, we express τ_s using the following grammar:

$$\tau_s ::= C \mid \exists P \mid \exists P^-$$

where τ_s being C, $\exists P$ and $\exists P^-$ represent 'sh:targetClass C', 'sh:targetSubjectOf P', and 'sh:targetObjectOf P' in the SHACL specification, respectively. Given a target expression τ_s, we say that $n \in \mathcal{N}_G$ is a target of the shape s, written $G \models \tau_s(n)$, iff $\exists \mu \in \tau_s{}^G$ s.t. $n \in \mu(var(\tau_s))$.

□ *constraint definition* ϕ_s, which can be represented as a boolean SPARQL query as described in [10, 17, 18], indicating whether the target node under validation violates the graph pattern defined by the ϕ_s or not. The constraint ϕ_s is an expression defined according to the following grammar:

$$\phi_s ::= \geq_n \alpha.\beta \mid \leq_n \alpha.\beta \mid \triangleright_{\tau_s} \alpha \mid \alpha_1 = \alpha_2 \mid \phi_s \wedge \phi_s$$

$$\beta ::= \top \mid C \mid s' \mid \neg\beta$$

where $\top$ stands for the *Boolean* true value, $\alpha, \alpha_1, \alpha_2 \in (\mathbf{P} \cup \{P^- \mid P \in \mathbf{P}\})$, $C \in \mathbf{C}$, $s' \in \mathbf{S}$, $\neg$ stands for *negation*, $n \in \mathbb{N}$, $(\geq_n \alpha.\beta)$ requires that there must be at least n α-successors verifying β, $(\triangleright_{\tau_s} \alpha)$ that the value node of α-successor must be unique among target nodes defined by the τ_s, e.g., dash:uniqueValueForClass constraint for the class-based target, and $(\alpha_1 = \alpha_2)$ means equality of the sets of nodes reachable via the respective properties α_1 and α_2. As syntactic sugar, we write $\phi_1 \vee \phi_2$ for $\neg(\neg\phi_1 \wedge \neg\phi_2)$ and $=_n \alpha.\phi$ for $(\geq_n \alpha.\phi) \wedge (\leq_n \alpha.\phi)$. For a constraint expression ϕ_s and a node $n \in \mathcal{N}_G$, we say that n validates against ϕ_s, written $G \models \phi_s(n)$, iff n does not violate the graph pattern, aka constraints, defined by ϕ_s. For any constraints ϕ and ϕ', we say that ϕ implies ϕ', rewritten $\phi \longrightarrow \phi'$, iff for all graphs G and nodes $n \in \mathcal{N}_G$, if $G \models \phi(n)$ then $G \models \phi'(n)$.

A SHACL document is a set of SHACL shapes. An RDF graph G validates against a shape $\langle s, \tau_s, \phi_s \rangle$, if $G \models \phi_s(n)$ for all $n \in \mathcal{N}_G$ with $G \models \tau_s(n)$. An RDF graph G validates against a SHACL document $\mathcal{S}$, written $G \models \mathcal{S}$, iff G validates against all shapes in $\mathcal{S}$.

Example 3. *Assume an RDF graph on the left that validates a shape with a 'property-based target,' i.e.,* sh:targetSubjectOf :hasID, *on the right written in Turtle syntax:*

```
:Ida a :Student;                  :TargetSubjectShape a sh:NodeShape;
   :hasID "001"^^xsd:int;         sh:targetSubjectOf :hasID;
   :hasAddress "Oslo".            sh:property [ sh:path :hasAddress;
:Nora a :Student;                              sh:nodeKind sh:Literal;
   :hasAddress "Oslo".                          sh:minCount 1;    ];
:Ingrid a :Student;               sh:property [ sh:path :hasID;
   :hasID "002"^^xsd:int;                       dash:uniqueValueForClass
   :hasAddress "Bergen".                          :Student ; ].
```

Observe that '**Nora**' is not subject of a '**hasID**' triple, and therefore, is not a target node of the shape '**TargetSubjectShape**'. Since the target nodes, i.e., '**Ida**' and '**Ingrid**', of the shape have an address and unique ids, they validate against the shape.

3 Optimizations

The goal is to optimize a SPARQL query with respect to a SHACL document, by identifying smaller or more efficient queries that have the same answers for all RDF graphs that satisfy the SHACL document.

Next we will present SPARQL query optimizations that resemble SQL query rewriting using relational constraints. They only differ in how SPARQL graph patterns interact with SHACL constraints describing these graph patterns in the RDF graph. For instance, when property path cardinality constraints imply that the first argument of an Opt-pattern will always find at least one solution on the second, we can substitute Opt with a more straightforward join operator, as shown in Lemmas 1.1, 3.1 and 6.1. In the case of a distinct projection, with an 'at least one' property path cardinality constraint, we can infer that every solution mapping from the first argument of the join expression is guaranteed to find at least one solution on the second argument. This guarantee on the graph patterns allows us to reduce the entire joint expression to the first argument, as shown in Lemmas 1.2 and 3.2. In the case of an 'exactly one' property path cardinality constraint, the described optimization of join patterns occurs even in the absence of distinct projection, as shown in Lemmas 2 and 4. If all possible mappings for the first argument of the optional pattern can find a compatible solution with the second argument, and if the variables used in filter are limited to the first argument, then it is possible to replace the entire optional pattern with the filter expression applied to the first argument, as shown in Lemma 5.2, Corollaries 2.2, 4.2 and 5.2.

Let $\mathcal{U}$ and $\mathcal{V}$ be two graph patterns and S a SHACL document.

Definition 3. $\mathcal{U} \equiv_S \mathcal{V}$ iff $\mathcal{U}^G = \mathcal{V}^G$ for all graphs G with $G \models S$.

Definition 4. $\mathcal{U} \equiv_{S,y} \mathcal{V}$ iff, for all graphs G with $G \models S$,

1. $\mathcal{U}^G_{|\bar{y}} = \mathcal{V}^G_{|\bar{y}}$ and
2. $(\mu_{|\bar{y}} = \mu'_{|\bar{y}}) \longrightarrow (\mu = \mu')$ for all $\mu, \mu' \in \mathcal{U}^G$ and $\mu, \mu' \in \mathcal{V}^G$.

Definition 5. $\mathcal{U} \cong_{S,y} \mathcal{V}$ iff $sup(\mathcal{U}^G_{|\bar{y}}) = sup(\mathcal{V}^G_{|\bar{y}})$ for all graphs G with $G \models S$.

In Theorem 1, we will prove that an $\equiv_S$ equivalence is applicable to all queries, while $\equiv_{S,y}$ is restricted to the placement of variable y within the query, and $\cong_{S,y}$ is exclusive to the distinct graph patterns with restrictions on the placement of variable y. In the subsequent Lemmas 1 to 7, we will establish these equivalences under various constraints, and illustrate their application along with counterexamples when restrictions on the placement of variables are violated in the query.

Let $\mathcal{B}$ and $\mathcal{B}'$ be two BGPs and $\mathcal{P}$ a graph pattern. Then, we write $\mathcal{B} \blacktriangleleft \mathcal{P}$ (resp., $\mathcal{B}, \mathcal{B}' \blacktriangleleft \mathcal{P}$) if $\mathcal{P} = \mathcal{B}$ or $\mathcal{P} = \mathcal{B}\mathcal{P}_1 \dots \mathcal{P}_n$ (resp., $\mathcal{P} = \mathcal{B}\mathcal{B}'$ or $\mathcal{P} = \mathcal{B}\mathcal{B}'\mathcal{P}_1 \dots \mathcal{P}_n$), where $\mathcal{P}_i$ s.t. $n \geq i \geq 1$ are inner graph patterns. Let $C, C' \in \mathbf{C}$ and $P, R \in (\gamma \cup \{\gamma^- \mid \gamma \in \mathbf{P}\})$. Then, in the lemmas that follow, given an arbitrary shape $\langle s, \tau_s, \phi_s \rangle$ with target τ_s definition, let T be a triple pattern s.t.,

$$T = \begin{cases} C(x), & \text{if } \tau_s = C, \\ R(x, z), & \text{if } \tau_s = \exists R, \\ R^-(x, z), & \text{if } \tau_s = \exists R^-. \end{cases}$$

Lemma 1. *Let $\langle s, \tau_s, \phi_s \rangle \in S$ with $(\geq_n P.\top) \in \phi_s$ s.t. $n \geq 1$, and $\mathcal{P}$ a graph pattern s.t. $T \blacktriangleleft \mathcal{P}$. If $y \notin var(\mathcal{P})$, then*

1. $\text{OPT}_{\mathcal{F}}(\mathcal{P}, P(x, y)) \equiv_S \text{FILTER}_{\mathcal{F}}(\text{JOIN}(\mathcal{P}, P(x, y)))$
2. $\text{JOIN}(\mathcal{P}, P(x, y)) \cong_{S,y} \mathcal{P}$

Proof. Assuming $T \blacktriangleleft \mathcal{P}$ w.r.t. the target τ_s of the shape $\langle s, \tau_s, \phi_s \rangle \in S$, we know that x is the only variable shared between $\mathcal{P}$ and $P(x, y)$, and y is not in $var(\mathcal{P})$. Let G be a graph s.t. $G \models S$.

Clause 1: Using the definition of OPT, we can split the solutions of $\text{OPT}_{\mathcal{F}}(\mathcal{P}, P(x, y))$ into two parts: finding solutions that satisfy both $\mathcal{P}$ and $P(x, y)$, and finding solutions that satisfy only $\mathcal{P}$. For any mapping in the first part $\mathcal{P}^G$, we can find at least n mappings in the second part $P(x, y)^G$, where $n \geq 1$ is guaranteed by the constraint $(\geq_n P.\top) \in \phi_s$. Therefore, any solution that satisfies $\mathcal{P}$ and $P(x, y)$ will also be part of the solutions that satisfy only $\mathcal{P}$ w.r.t. G and vice-versa, which means that $|\mu, \text{OPT}_{\mathcal{F}}(\mathcal{P}, P(x, y))^G| = |\mu, \text{FILTER}_{\mathcal{F}}(\text{JOIN}(\mathcal{P}, P(x, y)))^G|$. Thus, $\text{OPT}_{\mathcal{F}}(\mathcal{P}, P(x, y)) \equiv_S \text{FILTER}_{\mathcal{F}}(\text{JOIN}(\mathcal{P}, P(x, y)))$ by Definition 3 if $y \notin var(\mathcal{P})$.

Clause 2: Starting from the left-hand side $\text{JOIN}(\mathcal{P}, P(x, y))$, we have $y \notin var(\mathcal{P})$. Using the definition of JOIN, the problem is to find all possible combinations of solutions that satisfy $\mathcal{P}$ and $P(x, y)$. Since constraint $(\geq_n P.\top) \in \phi_s$ together with conditions $T \blacktriangleleft \mathcal{P}$ and $y \notin var(\mathcal{P})$ guarantees that there exist least n mappings $\mu_2 \in P(x, y)^G$ for $\forall \mu_1 \in \mathcal{P}^G$ s.t. $\mu_1 \sim \mu_2$, we can deduce that any solution that satisfies $\mathcal{P}$ will also satisfy $\text{JOIN}(\mathcal{P}, P(x, y))$ w.r.t. G. Thus, we can claim that $\sup(\text{JOIN}(\mathcal{P}, P(x, y))^G_{|\bar{y}})$ is equal to $\sup(\mathcal{P}^G_{|\bar{y}})$, i.e., $\text{JOIN}(\mathcal{P}, P(x, y)) \cong_{S,y} \mathcal{P}$ by Definition 4.

Corollary 1 follows from Lemma 1.

Corollary 1. *Let $\langle s, \tau_s, \phi_s \rangle \in S$ with $(\geq_n P.\top) \in \phi_s$ s.t. $n \geq 1$, and $\mathcal{P}$ a graph pattern s.t. $T \blacktriangleleft \mathcal{P}$. If $y \notin var(\mathcal{P} \cup \mathcal{F})$, then*

1. $\text{FILTER}_{\mathcal{F}}(\text{JOIN}(\mathcal{P}, P(x, y))) \cong_{S,y} \text{FILTER}_{\mathcal{F}}(\mathcal{P})$
2. $\text{OPT}_{\mathcal{F}}(\mathcal{P}, P(x, y)) \cong_{S,y} \text{FILTER}_{\mathcal{F}}(\mathcal{P})$

Example 4. *Let G be a graph such that $G \models \langle \text{Student}, \tau_{\text{Student}}, \phi_{\text{Student}} \rangle$ with $(\geq_n :hasAddress.\top) \in \phi_{\text{Student}}$ s.t. $n \geq 1$. Then, let Q be a query that asks for all students who do not have a postal address, where $\top$ denotes the tautological filter (true),*

$$\text{PROJ}_x(\text{FILTER}_{\neg bound(y)}(\text{OPT}_\top(\text{Student}(x), \text{hasAddress}(x, y))))$$

over G. As per the constraint ϕ_{Student}, all students in G have a postal address. Hence, the optimal solution would be to replace the entire query with an empty query. However, in our setting, the OPT-pattern of Q can be reduced to an equivalent JOIN-pattern by following the clause 1 of Lemma 1 since y does not appear in the first part of the OPT-pattern,

$$\text{PROJ}_x(\text{FILTER}_{\neg bound(y)}(\text{JOIN}(\text{Student}(x), \text{hasAddress}(x, y)))).$$

In a scenario where y also appears in the first part of the OPT-pattern, such as

$$\text{PROJ}_x(\text{FILTER}_{\neg bound(y)}(\text{OPT}_\top(\text{Student}(x) \text{ enrolledIn}(x, y), \text{hasAddress}(x, y)))).$$

A counter-example $G = \{$Student$(a),$ enrolledIn$(a, b),$ hasAddress$(a, d)\}$ s.t. $G \models$ $\langle$Student$, \tau_{Student}, \phi_{Student}\rangle$ can be constructed, where a solution can be found that yields "Student(a)" for the OPT *pattern but none when* OPT *is reduced to* JOIN-*pattern. Similarly, assume a query that asks for students who have postal addresses, such as*

$$\text{DIST}(\text{PROJ}_{xy}(\text{JOIN}(Student(x)\ hasName(x, y), hasAddress(x, z))))$$

over the graph G. Then, clause 2 of Lemma 1 allows us to safely remove the pattern hasAddress(x, z) *from the '*DIST*' query, given that variable z only appears in this pattern and all students in the graph G satisfying $\langle$Student$, \tau_{Student}, \phi_{Student}\rangle$ have at least n postal addresses., i.e.,*

$$\text{DIST}(\text{PROJ}_{xy}(Student(x)\ hasName(x, y)))\,.$$

However, a counter-example can be found for the $\cong_{S,y}$ equivalence when variable z appears outside of the pattern hasAddress(x, z) *in the* DIST *query above, such as*

$$\text{DIST}(\text{PROJ}_{xy}(\text{FILTER}_{\neg bound(z)}(\text{JOIN}(Student(x)\ hasName(x, y), hasAddress(x, z)))))\,.$$

Finally, assume a query scenario over the G as per required by the 'if-condition' in Corollary 1,

$$\text{DIST}(\text{PROJ}_{xz}(\text{OPT}_{z='A'}(Student(x)\ hasGrade(x, z), hasAddress(x, y))))\,.$$

Then, the equivalent "$\text{DIST}(\text{PROJ}_{xz}(\text{FILTER}_{z='A'}(Student(x)\ hasGrade(x, z))))$*" query can be deduced by using Corollary 1.2, which reduces the entire '*OPT*'-pattern to the first part of the pattern with the filter applied (i.e., $\cong_{S,y}$ equivalence).*

Lemma 2 follows from the same reasoning as Lemma 1.

Lemma 2. *Let $\langle s, \tau_s, \phi_s \rangle \in S$ with $(=_1 P.\top) \in \phi_s$ and $\mathcal{P}$ a graph pattern s.t. $T \blacktriangleleft \mathcal{P}$. If $y \notin var(\mathcal{P})$, then* JOIN$(\mathcal{P}, P(x, y)) \equiv_{S,y} \mathcal{P}$.

Corollary 2 follows from Lemma 1 and Lemma 2.

Corollary 2. *Let $\langle s, \tau_s, \phi_s \rangle \in S$ with $(=_1 P.\top) \in \phi_s$ s.t. $n \geq 1$, and $\mathcal{P}$ a graph pattern s.t. $T \blacktriangleleft \mathcal{P}$. If $y \notin var(\mathcal{P} \cup \mathcal{F})$, then*

1. FILTER$_{\mathcal{F}}(\text{JOIN}(\mathcal{P}, P(x, y))) \equiv_{S,y}$ FILTER$_{\mathcal{F}}(\mathcal{P})$
2. OPT$_{\mathcal{F}}(\mathcal{P}, P(x, y)) \equiv_{S,y}$ FILTER$_{\mathcal{F}}(\mathcal{P})$

Example 5. *consider a SPARQL query that asks for the names of those who have postal addresses, such as*

$$\text{PROJ}_y(\text{JOIN}(hasName(x, y), hasAddress(x, z)))\,,$$

over a graph G s.t. $G \models \langle\exists$hasName$, \tau_{\exists hasName}, \phi_{\exists hasName}\rangle$ and $(=_1 $:hasAddress$.\top) \in \phi_{\exists hasName}$. Since the constraint $\phi_{\exists hasName}$ ensures that individuals with names have exactly one postal address, we can deduce the following equivalent query based on Lemma 2:

$$\text{PROJ}_y(hasName(x, y))\,.$$

In Lemmas 3 to 5,

- let β be either C' or s' s.t. $s' \in S$, and
- let $\mathcal{P}'$ be a graph pattern s.t. $\mathcal{P}'$ is either $P(x, y)$ or $P(x, y)C'(y)$ if $\beta = s'$, and $P(x, y)C'(y)$ if $\beta = C'$.

Lemma 3. *Let $\langle s, \tau_s, \phi_s \rangle \in S$ with $(\geq_n P.\beta) \in \phi_s$ s.t. $n \geq 1$, and $\mathcal{P}$ a graph pattern s.t. $T \blacktriangleleft \mathcal{P}$. If $y \notin var(\mathcal{P})$, then*

1. $\text{OPT}_{\mathcal{F}}(\mathcal{P}, \mathcal{P}') \equiv_S \text{FILTER}_{\mathcal{F}}(\text{JOIN}(\mathcal{P}, \mathcal{P}'))$
2. $\text{JOIN}(\mathcal{P}, \mathcal{P}') \cong_{S,y} \mathcal{P}$

In contrast to Lemma 1, Lemma 3 also handles type constraints on the value node of a property predicate P. Corollary 3 follows from Lemma 3.

Corollary 3. *Let $\langle s, \tau_s, \phi_s \rangle \in S$ with $(\geq_n P.\beta) \in \phi_s$ s.t. $n \geq 1$, and $\mathcal{P}$ a graph pattern s.t. $T \blacktriangleleft \mathcal{P}$. If $y \notin var(\mathcal{P} \cup \mathcal{F})$, then*

1. $\text{FILTER}_{\mathcal{F}}(\text{JOIN}(\mathcal{P}, \mathcal{P}')) \cong_{S,y} \text{FILTER}_{\mathcal{F}}(\mathcal{P})$
2. $\text{OPT}_{\mathcal{F}}(\mathcal{P}, \mathcal{P}') \cong_{S,y} \text{FILTER}_{\mathcal{F}}(\mathcal{P})$

Example 6. *Suppose we have a SPARQL query that asks the names of individuals who have valid addresses, such as*

$$\text{DIST}(\text{PROJ}_y(\text{JOIN}(hasName(x, y), hasAddress(x, z) \, Address(z)))),$$

over a graph G s.t. $G \models \langle \exists hasName, \tau_{\exists hasName}, \phi_{\exists hasName} \rangle$ and $(\geq_1 \; :hasAddress.\, Address) \in \phi_{People}$. Then, we can use Lemma 3, specifically clause 2, to simplify the query to:

$$\text{DIST}(\text{PROJ}_y(hasName(x, y))).$$

Lemma 4. *Let $\langle s, \tau_s, \phi_s \rangle \in S$ with $(=_1 P.\beta) \in \phi_s$, and $\mathcal{P}$ a graph pattern s.t. $T \blacktriangleleft \mathcal{P}$. If $y \notin var(\mathcal{P})$, then $\text{JOIN}(\mathcal{P}, \mathcal{P}') \equiv_{S,y} \mathcal{P}$.*

Lemma 4 follows from the same reasoning as Lemma 3, and Corollary 4 follows from Lemma 3 and Lemma 4.

Corollary 4. *Let $\langle s, \tau_s, \phi_s \rangle \in S$ with $(=_1 P.\beta) \in \phi_s$ s.t. $n \geq 1$, and $\mathcal{P}$ a graph pattern s.t. $T \blacktriangleleft \mathcal{P}$. If $y \notin var(\mathcal{P} \cup \mathcal{F})$, then*

1. $\text{FILTER}_{\mathcal{F}}(\text{JOIN}(\mathcal{P}, \mathcal{P}')) \equiv_{S,y} \text{FILTER}_{\mathcal{F}}(\mathcal{P})$
2. $\text{OPT}_{\mathcal{F}}(\mathcal{P}, \mathcal{P}') \equiv_{S,y} \text{FILTER}_{\mathcal{F}}(\mathcal{P})$

Lemma 5. *Let $\langle s, \tau_s, \phi_s \rangle \in S$ with $(\geq_n P.\beta) \in \phi_s$ s.t. $n \geq 1$ or $(\leq_0 P. \neg\beta) \in \phi_s$, and $\mathcal{P}$ a graph pattern s.t. $T, P(x, y) \blacktriangleleft \mathcal{P}$. Then,*

1. $\text{JOIN}(\mathcal{P}, C'(y)) \equiv_S \mathcal{P}$
2. $\text{OPT}_{\mathcal{F}}(\mathcal{P}, C'(y)) \equiv_S \text{FILTER}_{\mathcal{F}}(\mathcal{P})$

Proof. Assuming $T, P(x, y) \blacktriangleleft \mathcal{P}$ w.r.t. the target τ_s of the shape $\langle s, \tau_s, \phi_s \rangle \in \mathcal{S}$, we have $var(\mathcal{P}) \cap var(C'(y)) = \{y\}$. Let G be a graph s.t. $G \models \mathcal{S}$. Then,

Clause 1: Starting from the left-hand side pattern $\text{JOIN}(\mathcal{P}, C'(y))$, the constraint $(\geq_n P.\beta) \in \phi_s$ (resp., $(\leq_0 P.\neg\beta) \in \phi_s$) s.t. $n \geq 1$ together with the condition $P(x, y) \blacktriangleleft \mathcal{P}$ guarantees that there exists exactly one mapping $\mu_2 \in C'(y)^G$ for $\forall \mu_1 \in \mathcal{P}^G$ s.t. $\mu_1 \sim \mu_2$. Thus, we can deduce $|\mu, \text{JOIN}(\mathcal{P}, P(x, y))^G| = |\mu, \mathcal{P}^G|$, which implies $\text{JOIN}(\mathcal{P}, P(x, y)) \equiv_S \mathcal{P}$ by Definition 3.

Clause 2: For the pattern $\text{OPT}_{\mathcal{F}}(\mathcal{P}, C'(y))$, constraint $(\geq_n P.\beta) \in \phi_s$ (resp., $(\leq_0 P.\neg\beta) \in \phi_s$) together with the condition $P(x, y) \blacktriangleleft \mathcal{P}$ guarantees that for any mapping in the first part $\mathcal{P}^G$, we can find exactly one mapping in the second part $C'(y)^G$. Thus, any solution that satisfies $\mathcal{P}$ and $C'(y)$ will also be part of the solutions that satisfy only $\mathcal{P}$ w.r.t. G and vice-versa, which means that $|\mu, \text{OPT}_{\mathcal{F}}(\mathcal{P}, C'(y))^G| = |\mu, \text{FILTER}_{\mathcal{F}}(\text{JOIN}(\mathcal{P}, C'(y)))^G|$, i.e., $\text{OPT}_{\mathcal{F}}(\mathcal{P}, C'(y)) \equiv_S \text{FILTER}_{\mathcal{F}}(\text{JOIN}(\mathcal{P}, C'(y)))$ by Definition 3.

Further, the restriction of solutions to $\mathcal{F}^\mu = \top$ is identical for both $\text{JOIN}(\mathcal{P}, C'(y))^G$ and $\mathcal{P}^G$ since $var(\mathcal{F}) \subseteq var(\mathcal{P})$ can be deduced from the fact $var(C'(y)) \subseteq var(\mathcal{P})$. Then, using clause 1, i.e., $\text{JOIN}(\mathcal{P}, C'(y)) \equiv_S \mathcal{P}$, we can infer that $\text{FILTER}_{\mathcal{F}}(\text{JOIN}(\mathcal{P}, C'(y))) \equiv_S \text{FILTER}_{\mathcal{F}}(\mathcal{P})$. Thus,

$$\text{OPT}_{\mathcal{F}}(\mathcal{P}, C'(y)) \equiv_S \text{FILTER}_{\mathcal{F}}(\text{JOIN}(\mathcal{P}, C'(y))) \equiv_S \text{FILTER}_{\mathcal{F}}(\mathcal{P}).$$

Example 7. *Let G be a graph that satisfies the shapes $\langle \exists hasName, \tau_{\exists hasName}, \phi_{\exists hasName} \rangle$ and $\langle Program, \tau_{Program}, \phi_{Program} \rangle$, where $(\leq_0 : enrolledIn.\neg, Program) \in \phi_{\exists hasName}$. Consider the query,*

$$\text{PROJ}_{xz}(\text{OPT}_{\top}(hasName(x, y) \; enrolledIn(x, z), \; Program(z)))$$

over the G. According to the constraint $\phi_{\exists hasName}$, all enrollments are only in the 'Program'. Hence, using clause 1 and 2 of Lemma 5, we can obtain the following equivalent query:

$$\text{PROJ}_{xz}(hasName(x, y) \; enrolledIn(x, z)).$$

Given a shape $\langle s, \tau_s, \phi_s \rangle \in \mathcal{S}$, let $\mathcal{K}$ be a graph pattern s.t.,

$$\mathcal{K} = \begin{cases} C(x)R(x, z), & \text{if } \tau_s = C, \\ R(x, z), & \text{if } \tau_s = \exists R, \\ R^-(x, z), & \text{if } \tau_s = \exists R^-. \end{cases}$$

Lemma 6. *Let $\langle s, \tau_s, \phi_s \rangle \in S$ with $(R = P) \in \phi_s$, and $\mathcal{P}$ a graph pattern s.t. $\mathcal{K} \blacktriangleleft \mathcal{P}$. If $y \notin var(\mathcal{P})$, then*

1. $\text{OPT}_{\mathcal{F}}(\mathcal{P}, P(x, y)) \equiv_S \text{FILTER}_{\mathcal{F}}(\text{JOIN}(\mathcal{P}, P(x, y)))$
2. $\text{JOIN}(\mathcal{P}, P(x, y)) \cong_{S,y} \mathcal{P}$

Proof. Assuming $\mathcal{K} \blacktriangleleft \mathcal{P}$ w.r.t. the target τ_s of the shape $\langle s, \tau_s, \phi_s \rangle \in \mathcal{S}$, we have $var(\mathcal{P}) \cap var(P(x, y)) = \{x\}$ since $R(x, z) \blacktriangleleft \mathcal{K}$. Let G be a graph s.t. $G \models \mathcal{S}$.

Clause 1: For $\text{OPT}_{\mathcal{F}}(\mathcal{P}, P(x, y))$ s.t. $y \notin var(\mathcal{P})$, the constraint $(R = P) \in \phi_s$ together with the condition $R(x, z) \blacktriangleleft \mathcal{P}$ guarantees that for any mapping in the first part $\mathcal{P}^G$, we can find exactly one mapping in the second part $P(x,y)^G$. Thus, any solution that satisfies $\mathcal{P}$ and $P(x,y)$ will also be part of the solutions that satisfy only $\mathcal{P}$ w.r.t. G and vice-versa, which means that $|\mu, \text{OPT}_{\mathcal{F}}(\mathcal{P}, P(x,y))^G| = |\mu, \text{FILTER}_{\mathcal{F}}(\text{JOIN}(\mathcal{P}, P(x,y)))^G|$ if $y \notin var(\mathcal{P})$, i.e.,

$$\text{OPT}_{\mathcal{F}}(\mathcal{P}, P(x,y)) \equiv_S \text{FILTER}_{\mathcal{F}}(\text{JOIN}(\mathcal{P}, P(x,y))) \text{ by Definition 3.}$$

Clause 2: Consider the left-hand side $\text{JOIN}(\mathcal{P}, P(x,y))$ s.t. $y \notin var(\mathcal{P})$. Then, the constraint $(R = P) \in \phi_s$ together with the condition $R(x,z) \blacktriangleleft \mathcal{P}$ guarantees that there exists exactly one mapping $\mu_2 \in P(x,y)^G$ for $\forall \mu_1 \in \mathcal{P}^G$ s.t. $\mu_1 \sim \mu_2$. From this, we can deduce that $\sup(\text{JOIN}(\mathcal{P}, P(x,y))^G) = \sup(\mathcal{P}^G)$, which in turn implies $\text{JOIN}(\mathcal{P}, P(x,y)) \cong_{S,y} \mathcal{P}$ by Definition 5, if $y \notin var(\mathcal{P})$.

Corollary 5 follows from Lemma 6.

Corollary 5. *Let $\langle s, \tau_s, \phi_s \rangle \in S$ with $(R = P) \in \phi_s$, and $\mathcal{P}$ a graph pattern s.t. $\mathcal{K} \blacktriangleleft \mathcal{P}$. If $y \notin var(\mathcal{P} \cup \mathcal{F})$, then*

1. $\text{FILTER}_{\mathcal{F}}(\text{JOIN}(\mathcal{P}, P(x,y))) \cong_{S,y} \text{FILTER}_{\mathcal{F}}(\mathcal{P})$
2. $\text{OPT}_{\mathcal{F}}(\mathcal{P}, P(x,y)) \cong_{S,y} \text{FILTER}_{\mathcal{F}}(\mathcal{P})$

Example 8. *Consider a SPARQL query,*

$$\text{DIST}(\text{PROJ}_{xy}(\text{JOIN}(Employee(x) \; insuredBy(x,y), employedBy(x,z))))$$

over G s.t. $G \models \langle Employee, \tau_{Employee}, \phi_{Employee} \rangle$ with $(insuredBy = employedBy) \in \phi_{Employee}$. Then, using clause 2 of Lemma 6, we can obtain the following equivalent query:

$$\text{DIST}(\text{PROJ}_{xy}(Employee(x) \; insuredBy(x,y))).$$

Similarly, assume an optional query scenario where variable z only occurs within the pattern '$employedBy(x,z)$,' such as

$$\text{DIST}(\text{PROJ}_{xy}(\text{OPT}_{\top}(Employee(x) \; insuredBy(x,y), employedBy(x,z)))).$$

Using Corollary 5.2, which applies $\cong_{S,y}$ equivalence to reduce the entire 'OPT'-pattern to the first part of the Opt-pattern with the filter applied, we can deduce the following equivalent query:

$$\text{DIST}(\text{PROJ}_{xy}(\text{FILTER}_{\top}(Employee(x) \; insuredBy(x,y)))).$$

In Lemma 7, let $\phi' = \begin{cases} \top, & \text{if } \mathcal{P} = T, \\ \bigwedge_{i=1}^{n}(\leq_1 P_i. \top), & \text{if } \mathcal{P} = (T \; P_1(x,z_1) \ldots P_i(x,z_i) \ldots P_n(x,z_n)). \end{cases}$

Lemma 7. *Let $\langle s, \tau_s, \phi_s \rangle \in S$ with $\{(\rhd_{\tau_s} P), \phi'\} \subseteq \phi_s$ and $\mathcal{P}$ a graph pattern s.t. $\mathcal{P} = T$ or $\mathcal{P} = (T \; P_1(x,z_1) \ldots P_i(x,z_i) \ldots P_n(x,z_n))$ for $n \geq i \geq 1$. Then,*

$$\text{DIST}(\text{PROJ}_X(\text{JOIN}(\mathcal{P}, P(x,y)))) \equiv_S \text{PROJ}_X(\text{JOIN}(\mathcal{P}, P(x,y))).$$

Proof. For the pattern $\text{Proj}_X(\text{Join}(\mathcal{P}, P(x, y)))$, we can observe that $var(\mathcal{P}) \cap var(P(x, y)) = \{x\}$ because: (a) $\mathcal{P} = T$ or $T \blacktriangleleft \mathcal{P}$, and (b) T is either $C(x)$ or $R(x, z)$ or $R^-(x, z)$ based on the target τ_s of a shape $\langle s, \tau_s, \phi_s \rangle \in S$. Using the definition of Join and Proj, the solution of $\text{Proj}_X(\text{Join}(\mathcal{P}, P(x, y)))$ is all possible combinations of solutions that satisfy $\mathcal{P}$ and $P(x, y)$, and restricted to variable set X. Let G be a graph s.t. $G \models S$. Then, constraint $(\rhd_{\tau_s} P) \in \phi_s$ ensures that all P-successors binding to y are unique (i.e., distinct) among the target nodes τ_s over G. Therefore, for each mapping in $\mathcal{P}^G$, we can only find at most one corresponding mapping in $P(x, y)^G$ when $\mathcal{P} = T$. This implies $|\mu, \text{Proj}_X(\text{Join}(\mathcal{P}, P(x, y)))^G| = 1$ for $\forall \mu \in \sup(\text{Proj}_X(\text{Join}(\mathcal{P}, P(x, y)))^G)$. Hence, $\text{Dist}(\text{Proj}_X(\text{Join}(\mathcal{P}, P(x, y)))) \equiv_S \text{Proj}_X(\text{Join}(\mathcal{P}, P(x, y)))$.

In the case of $\mathcal{P} = \{T P_1(x, z_1) \ldots P_i(x, z_i) \ldots P_n(x, z_n)\}$ s.t. $n \geq 1$, the constraint component $\bigwedge_{i=1}^{n}(\leq_1 P_i. T) \in \phi_s$ guarantees the absence of duplicate mappings $\mu \in \text{Proj}_X(\text{Join}(\mathcal{P}, P(x, y)))^G$ that could have originated from the join operations with the (inner) patterns $P_1(x, z_1) \ldots P_i(x, z_i) \ldots P_n(x, z_n)$. Thus, equivalence $\equiv_S$ holds.

Example 9. *Consider the SPARQL query,*

$$\text{Dist}(\text{Proj}_{yz}(\textit{Employee}(x) \textit{ hasName}(x, y) \textit{ hasID}(x, z)))$$

over a graph $\mathcal{G} \models \langle \textit{Employee}, \tau_{Employee}, \phi_{Employee} \rangle$ *such that* $\{(\rhd_{Employee} \textit{ hasID}), (\leq_1 \textit{hasName.}\top)\} \subseteq \phi_{Employee}$ *(resp.,* $\mathcal{G} \models \langle \exists \textit{hasName}, \tau_{\exists hasName}, \phi_{\exists hasName} \rangle$ *s.t.* $\{(\rhd_{Employee} \textit{ hasID}), (\leq_1 \textit{ hasName.}\top)\} \subseteq \phi_{\exists hasName}$*). Then, 'Dist' modifier of the query can be removed by using Lemma 7,*

$$\text{Proj}_{yz}(\textit{Employee}(x) \textit{ hasName}(x, y) \textit{ hasID}(x, z)).$$

Definition 6. *Let Q be a SPARQL query, and let $\mathcal{P}$ and $\mathcal{U}$ be two graph patterns. Then, we write $U \trianglelefteq Q$ if $\text{Dist}(\text{Proj}_X(\mathcal{P})) \trianglelefteq Q$ and $\mathcal{U} \trianglelefteq \mathcal{P}$.*

Theorem 1 specifies query rewriting, outlining the necessary conditions for applying and propagating the established equivalences from Lemmas 1 to 7 to a larger query.

Theorem 1. *Let Q be a SPARQL query and S a SHACL document. Let $\mathcal{U}$ and $\mathcal{V}$ be two graph patterns. Then,*

1. $Q \equiv_S Q^{\mathcal{U} \mapsto \mathcal{V}}$ *if* $\mathcal{U} \equiv_S \mathcal{V}$
2. $\text{Proj}_X(Q) \equiv_S \text{Proj}_X(Q)^{\mathcal{U} \mapsto \mathcal{V}}$ *if* $\mathcal{U} \trianglelefteq Q$, $\mathcal{U} \equiv_{S,y} \mathcal{V}$ *and* $y \notin var(\text{Proj}_X(Q) \setminus \mathcal{U})$
3. $Q \equiv_S Q^{\mathcal{U} \mapsto \mathcal{V}}$ *if* $\mathcal{U} \trianglelefteq Q$, $\mathcal{U} \cong_{S,y} \mathcal{V}$ *and* $y \notin var(Q \setminus \mathcal{U})$

Example 10. *Consider a query that asks for all distinct combinations of student ids and their corresponding advisors (if available), for those who are currently enrolled in a university program, such as*

$$\text{Dist}(\text{Proj}_{zk}(\text{Opt}_\top(\textit{Student}(x) \textit{ enrolledIn}(x, y) \textit{ Program}(y) \textit{ hasID}(x, z),$$
$$\textit{hasAdvisor}(x, k))))$$

over a graph $G \models \langle \textit{Student}, \tau_{Student}, \phi_{Student} \rangle$ *with* $\{(\geq_1 \textit{ enrolledIn.}$ $\textit{Program}), (\rhd_{Student} \textit{ hasID}), (=_1 \textit{ hasAdvisor.}\top)\} \subseteq \phi_{Student}$*. Then, using clause 1* *of Lemma 1 (i.e., $\equiv_S$), we can reduce 'Opt' to 'Join' pattern as follows,*

$$\text{Dist}(\text{Proj}_{zk}(\text{Join}(\texttt{Student}(x)\ \texttt{enrolledIn}(x,y)\ \texttt{Program}(y)\ \texttt{hasID}(x,z),$$
$$\texttt{hasAdvisor}(x,k)))).$$

Similarly, using clause 2 of Lemma 3 (i.e., $\cong_{S,y}$), we can remove the join clause '$\texttt{enrolledIn}(x,y)\ \texttt{Program}(y)$' *from the query,*

$$\text{Dist}(\text{Proj}_{zk}(\text{Join}(\texttt{Student}(x)\ \texttt{hasID}(x,z),\texttt{hasAdvisor}(x,k)))).$$

Finally, 'Dist' modifier can be removed by using Lemma 7 (i.e., $\equiv_S$),

$$\text{Proj}_{zk}(\text{Join}(\texttt{Student}(x)\ \texttt{hasID}(x,z),\texttt{hasAdvisor}(x,k))).$$

Theorems 2 and 3 state the *confluence* [8, Chapter 6] property, which guarantees that the query rewriting, defined by employing equivalences from Lemmas 1–7, is deterministic and results in the same optimized query, regardless of the order in which the rewriting rules (i.e., replacing left-hand-side of equivalences with the right-hand-side) are applied. In this context, the query rewriting defined by Lemmas 1–6 (resp., 1–7) freely employs equivalence $\equiv_S$ for rewriting graph patterns anywhere within a query, permits the use of equivalence $\equiv_{S,y}$ when y is confined within the joint (or optional) triples pattern to be removed (or transformed into a join), and exclusively employs equivalence $\cong_{S,y}$ for rewriting distinct patterns, as described in Theorem 1.

Theorem 2. *Query rewriting defined by Lemmas 1 to 6 is a confluent reduction.*

Proof. The main point of the proof is to establish that all overlapping rewriting rules (i.e., application of equivalences) defined by Lemmas 1 to 6 always yield the same uniquely simplified pattern when applied to a graph pattern. Taking $\mathcal{P}' = P(x,y)$ into account, observe that satisfying the constraint $\phi = (\geq_n P.\beta)$ with $\beta = s'$ in Lemma 3.1 also satisfies $(\geq_n P.\top)$ in Lemma 1.1, and applying either lemma to an optional pattern of the form $\text{Opt}_{\mathcal{F}}(\mathcal{P}, P(x,y))$ where $y \notin var(\mathcal{P})$ results in the same pattern, namely $\text{Filter}_{\mathcal{F}}(\text{Join}(\mathcal{P}, P(x,y)))$. Similarly, fulfilling $(=_1 P.\beta)$ s.t. $\beta = s'$ in Lemma 4 satisfies $(=_1 P.\top)$ in Lemma 2, and applying either lemma leads to the same optimized join pattern. This property also applies to the implied constraint case, e.g., $(=_1 P.\top) \longrightarrow (\geq_1 P.\top)$. Likewise, satisfying ϕ in Lemma 3.2 satisfies the condition $(\geq_n P.\top)$ in Lemma 1.2, and applying either lemma produces the same optimized joint pattern.

Due to the implication $(=_1 P.\top) \longrightarrow (\geq_1 P.\top)$, when the condition of Lemma 2 is fulfilled, the rewriting of Lemma 1.2 also applies. As Lemma 2 can be applied to all patterns (Clause 1 of Theorem 2), applying both rewritings to a distinct query pattern leads to the same optimized pattern. A similar situation arises for Lemmas 2.2 and 4 due to the implication $(=_1 P.\beta) \longrightarrow (\geq_1 P.\beta)$, and they also lead to the same optimized pattern.

Theorem 3. *Query rewriting defined by Lemmas 1 to 7 is a confluent reduction iff*
$$\phi' = \begin{cases} \top, & \text{if } \mathcal{P} = T, \\ \bigwedge_{i=1}^{n}(=_1 P_i.\top), & \text{if } \mathcal{P} = (T\,P_1(x,z_1)\ldots P_i(x,z_i)\ldots P_n(x,z_n)) \end{cases} \text{ in Lemma 7.}$$

The rewriting employing equivalence supported by Lemma 7 transforms a distinct pattern into a distinct-free pattern. However, certain rewritings, such as Lemmas 1.2, 3.2 and 6.2, are exclusive to distinct patterns. Hence, the introduction of constraint $\bigwedge_{i=1}^{n}(=_1 P_i. \top)$ in Theorem 3 becomes necessary to ensure the application of complementary rewritings, particularly based on equivalences supported by Lemmas 2 and 4, when the aforementioned rewritings cannot be directly applied after Lemma 7.

Example 11. *Consider a SPARQL query,*

$$\text{Dist}(\text{Proj}_{xy}(\texttt{employeeID}(x, y)\,\texttt{hiredBy}(x, k)\,\texttt{insuredBy}(x, z)))$$

over a graph G s.t. $G \models \langle \exists \texttt{employeeID}, \tau_{\exists \texttt{employeeID}}, \phi_{\exists \texttt{employeeID}} \rangle$ with $\{(\triangleright_{\exists \texttt{employeeID}}$ $\texttt{employeeID}), (=_1 \texttt{insuredBy}. \top), (\texttt{hiredBy} = \texttt{insuredBy})\} \subseteq \phi_{\exists \texttt{employedID}}$. Subsequently, the constraint $(=_1 \texttt{hiredBy}. \top)$ can be inferred from the $(=_1 \texttt{insuredBy}. \top)$ and $(\texttt{hiredBy} = \texttt{insuredBy})$. Based on Theorem 1, the query is subject to optimization using the Lemmas 1.2 (i.e., $\cong_{S,y}$), 2 (i.e., $\equiv_{S,y}$), 6.2 (i.e., $\cong_{S,y}$) and 7 (i.e., $\equiv_S$). Then, there are seven possible rewriting combinations that can be applied using the lemmas mentioned above: (Lemmas (1.2, 1.2, 7), Lemmas (1.2, 2, 7), Lemmas (2, 1.2, 7), Lemmas (2, 2, 7), Lemmas (6.2, 1.2, 7), Lemmas (6.2, 2, 7), and Lemmas (7, 2, 2)). All these combinations result in a uniquely optimized query, which is

$$\text{Proj}_{xy}(\texttt{employeeID}(x, y)).$$

Note that Lemmas 1.2 and 6.2 cannot be applied after Lemma 7. This information is further useful in determining the cheapest order in complex query optimization, which is a topic related to our future goals.

4 Discussion

We have presented a set of query rewriting rules that exploit the relation between the SPARQL queries containing graph patterns and SHACL constraints describing these graph patterns in the RDF. By treating each lemma as a set of rules under distinct constraints, we emphasized the significance of each constraint-enabled rule and made it easier to track and analyze their order and individual contributions to the overall robust query rewriting process, see Example 10. They also offer a clearer understanding of the different orders and strategies that can be employed while rewriting complex queries, see Example 11.

Constraints, known for restricting data to useful relations [23], can be used to rewrite queries into more efficient equivalents [50]. Leveraging constraints for optimizing queries has become a well-established practice in knowledge graphs [13,20,56], deductive databases [14], relational databases [3,25] and other fields [48]. Regarding SHACL, Rabbani et al. [47] were the first to propose shapes as global statistics for estimating cardinality and optimizing SPARQL query plans for the RDF graph under query. Further, Abbas et al. [1] studied the containment of restricted classes of SPARQL queries under set semantics, while considering ShEx constraints [46]. They also leveraged information obtained from ShEx schemas to optimize the execution of SPARQL queries [2]. In their work [2] (resp., [1]), a notion of well-formed ShEx schemas (resp., query patterns), especially suitable for query optimization (resp., containment), was first introduced, then subsequently used to reorganise execution orders (resp., to determine subsumption) of triple patterns in a SPARQL query. In contrast to previous studies [1,2,47], we have prioritized optimizing a much larger class of queries, and subsequently, introduced an explicit set of core rewriting rules for optimizing SPARQL queries under bag semantics when SHACL constraints are satisfied, and proved their correctness. We have further shown that our proposed query rewriting rules are confluent and always lead to a unique simplified form. We plan to investigate the potential benefits of integrating these rewriting rules into a query processing engine to enhance query execution in the near future. Additionally, we intend to extend our results to cover the broader expressivity and more general cases of SPARQL queries.

5 Conclusion

In this paper, we have proposed a set of optimizations for SPARQL query constructed from core operators of SPARQL 1.1 under the SHACL constraints. We believe that the proposed optimizations could play a crucial role in simplifying and answering SPARQL queries over large-scale RDF triples when SHACL descriptions of the underlying RDF dataset are available. In future, we aim to investigate an optimal normal form of SPARQL 1.1 [24] queries studied in [12,30] (which includes nesting, assignment, construct [35,44] and aggregation as in online analytical processing cube and window-based queries) with respect to (full) SHACL constraints [32] formalized in [19,41,42] that should allow us to introduce a confluent set of query rewriting [50, Sect. 5] rules.

Acknowledgements. This work is supported by the Norwegian Research Council via the SIRIUS SFI (237898). We thank Egor Kostylev for many fruitful discussions.

References

1. Abbas, A., Genevès, P., Roisin, C., Layaïda, N.: SPARQL query containment with ShEx constraints. In: Kirikova, M., Nørvåg, K., Papadopoulos, G.A. (eds.) ADBIS 2017. LNCS, vol. 10509, pp. 343–356. Springer, Cham (2017). https://doi.org/10.1007/978-3-319-66917-5_23
2. Abbas, A., Genevès, P., Roisin, C., Layaïda, N.: Selectivity estimation for SPARQL triple patterns with shape expressions. In: Mikkonen, T., Klamma, R., Hernández, J. (eds.) ICWE 2018. LNCS, vol. 10845, pp. 195–209. Springer, Cham (2018). https://doi.org/10.1007/978-3-319-91662-0_15
3. Abiteboul, S., Hull, R., Vianu, V.: Foundations of Databases, vol. 8. Addison-Wesley, Reading (1995)
4. Ahmetaj, S., David, R., Polleres, A., Šimkus, M.: Repairing SHACL constraint violations using answer set programming. In: Sattler, U., et al. (eds.) ISWC 2022. LNCS, vol. 13489, pp. 375–391. Springer, Cham (2022). https://doi.org/10.1007/978-3-031-19433-7_22
5. Angles, R., Gutierrez, C.: The multiset semantics of SPARQL patterns. In: Groth, P., et al. (eds.) ISWC 2016. LNCS, vol. 9981, pp. 20–36. Springer, Cham (2016). https://doi.org/10.1007/978-3-319-46523-4_2

6. Arias, M., Fernández, J.D., Martínez-Prieto, M.A., de la Fuente, P.: An empirical study of real-world SPARQL queries. *arXiv preprint* https://arxiv.org/pdf/1103.5043.pdf (2011)
7. Atre, M.: For the DISTINCT clause of SPARQL queries. In: Proceedings of the 25th International Conference Companion on World Wide Web, pp. 7–8 (2016)
8. Baader, F., Nipkow, T.: Term Rewriting and All That. Cambridge University Press, Cambridge (1998)
9. Bilidas, D., Koubarakis, M.: Efficient duplicate elimination in SPARQL to SQL translation. In: Description Logics (2018)
10. Bogaerts, B., Jakubowski, M., Van den Bussche, J.: Expressiveness of SHACL features and extensions for full equality and disjointness tests. *arXiv preprint* https://arxiv.org/pdf/2212.03553.pdf (2022)
11. Broekstra, J., Kampman, A., Van Harmelen, F.: Sesame: an architecture for storing and querying RDF data and schema information. In: Spinning the Semantic Web, pp. 197–222 (2001)
12. Buil-Aranda, C., Arenas, M., Corcho, O., Polleres, A.: Federating queries in SPARQL 1.1: syntax, semantics and evaluation. J. Web Semant. **18**(1), 1–17 (2013)
13. Calvanese, D., et al.: Ontop: answering SPARQL queries over relational databases. Semantic Web **8**(3), 471–487 (2017)
14. Chakravarthy, U.S., Grant, J., Minker, J.: Foundations of semantic query optimization for deductive databases. In: Foundations of Deductive Databases and Logic Programming, pp. 243–273. Elsevier (1988)
15. Cheng, S., Hartig, O.: OPT+: a monotonic alternative to OPTIONAL in SPARQL. J. Web Eng. (2019)
16. W3C Consortium. Apache Jena (2016). https://jena.apache.org
17. Corman, J., Florenzano, F., Reutter, J.L., Savkovic, O.: SHACL2SPARQL: validating a SPARQL endpoint against recursive SHACL constraints. In: ISWC (Satellites), pp. 165–168 (2019)
18. Corman, J., Florenzano, F., Reutter, J.L., Savković, O.: Validating Sʜᴀᴄʟ constraints over a Sᴘᴀʀǫʟ endpoint. In: Ghidini, C., et al. (eds.) ISWC 2019. LNCS, vol. 11778, pp. 145–163. Springer, Cham (2019). https://doi.org/10.1007/978-3-030-30793-6_9
19. Corman, J., Reutter, J.L., Savković, O.: Semantics and validation of recursive SHACL. In: Vrandečić, D., et al. (eds.) ISWC 2018. LNCS, vol. 11136, pp. 318–336. Springer, Cham (2018). https://doi.org/10.1007/978-3-030-00671-6_19
20. Di Pinto, F., et al.: Optimizing query rewriting in ontology-based data access. In: Proceedings of the 16th International Conference on Extending Database Technology, pp. 561–572 (2013)
21. Erling, O.: Implementing a SPARQL compliant RDF triple store using a SQLORDBMS. OpenLink Software Virtuoso (2001)
22. Inc Franz. AllegroGraph (2017). *Compatible Semantic Technologies*, https://allegrograph.com
23. Grefen, P.W.P.J., Apers, P.M.G.: Integrity control in relational database systems-an overview. Data Knowl. Eng. **10**(2), 187–223 (1993)
24. Harris, S., Seaborne, A., Prud'hommeaux, E.: SPARQL 1.1 query language. W3C Recommendation **21**(10), 778 (2013)
25. Jarke, M., Koch, J.: Query optimization in database systems. ACM Comput. Surv. (CsUR) **16**(2), 111–152 (1984)
26. Jian, X., Wang, Y., Lei, X., Zheng, L., Chen, L.: SPARQL rewriting: towards desired results. In: Proceedings of the 2020 ACM SIGMOD International Conference on Management of Data, pp. 1979–1993 (2020)
27. Johnson, D.S., Klug, A.: Testing containment of conjunctive queries under functional and inclusion dependencies. In: Proceedings of the 1st ACM SIGACT-SIGMOD Symposium on Principles of Database Systems, pp. 164–169 (1982)

28. Jung, H., Kim, W.: Automated conversion from natural language query to SPARQL query. J. Intell. Inf. Syst. **55**(3), 501–520 (2020). https://doi.org/10.1007/s10844-019-00589-2
29. Kaminski, M., Kostylev, E.V.: Beyond well-designed SPARQL. In: 19th International Conference on Database Theory (ICDT 2016). Schloss Dagstuhl-Leibniz-Zentrum fuer Informatik (2016)
30. Kaminski, M., Kostylev, E.V., Grau, B.C.: Query nesting, assignment, and aggregation in SPARQL 1.1. ACM Trans. Database Syst. (TODS) **42**(3), 1–46 (2017)
31. Kaufmann, E., Bernstein, A., Zumstein, R.: Querix: a natural language interface to query ontologies based on clarification dialogs. In: 5th International Semantic Web Conference (ISWC 2006), pp. 980–981. Citeseer (2006)
32. Knublauch, H., Kontokostas, D.: Shapes constraint language (SHACL). W3C Candidate Recommend. **11**(8) (2017)
33. Kontchakov, R., Rezk, M., Rodríguez-Muro, M., Xiao, G., Zakharyaschev, M.: Answering SPARQL queries over databases under OWL 2 QL entailment regime. In: Mika, P., et al. (eds.) ISWC 2014. LNCS, vol. 8796, pp. 552–567. Springer, Cham (2014). https://doi.org/10.1007/978-3-319-11964-9_35
34. Kostylev, E.V., Reutter, J.L., Romero, M., Vrgoč, D.: SPARQL with property paths. In: Arenas, M., et al. (eds.) ISWC 2015. LNCS, vol. 9366, pp. 3–18. Springer, Cham (2015). https://doi.org/10.1007/978-3-319-25007-6_1
35. Kostylev, E.V., Reutter, J.L., Ugarte, M.: CONSTRUCT queries in SPARQL. In: 18th International Conference on Database Theory (ICDT 2015). Schloss Dagstuhl-Leibniz-Zentrum fuer Informatik (2015)
36. Le, W., Duan, S., Kementsietsidis, A., Li, F., Wang, M.: Rewriting queries on SPARQL views. In: Proceedings of the 20th International Conference on World Wide Web, pp. 655–664 (2011)
37. Manola, F., Miller, E., McBride, B., et al.: RDF primer. W3C Recommend. **10**(1–107), 6 (2004)
38. Mohamed, A., Abuoda, G., Ghanem, A., Kaoudi, Z., Aboulnaga, A.: RDFFrames: knowledge graph access for machine learning tools. VLDB J. **31**(2), 321–346 (2022)
39. Pandit, H.J., O'Sullivan, D., Lewis, D.: Test-driven approach towards GDPR compliance. In: Acosta, M., Cudré-Mauroux, P., Maleshkova, M., Pellegrini, T., Sack, H., Sure-Vetter, Y. (eds.) SEMANTiCS 2019. LNCS, vol. 11702, pp. 19–33. Springer, Cham (2019). https://doi.org/10.1007/978-3-030-33220-4_2
40. Pareti, P., Konstantinidis, G.: A review of SHACL: from data validation to schema reasoning for RDF graphs. Reasoning Web International Summer School, pp. 115–144 (2021)
41. Pareti, P., Konstantinidis, G., Mogavero, F.: Satisfiability and containment of recursive SHACL. J. Web Semantics **74**, 100721 (2022)
42. Pareti, P., Konstantinidis, G., Mogavero, F., Norman, T.J.: SHACL satisfiability and containment. In: Pan, J.Z., et al. (eds.) ISWC 2020. LNCS, vol. 12506, pp. 474–493. Springer, Cham (2020). https://doi.org/10.1007/978-3-030-62419-4_27
43. Pérez, J., Arenas, M., Gutierrez, C.: Semantics and complexity of SPARQL. ACM Trans. Database Syst. (TODS) **34**(3), 1–45 (2009)
44. Polleres, A., Reutter, J., Kostylev, E.: Nested constructs vs. sub-selects in SPARQL. In: CEUR Workshop Proceedings (2016)
45. Prud'Hommeaux, E., Seaborne, A.: SPARQL query language for RDF. W3C Recommendation, January 15, 2008 (2011)
46. Prud'hommeaux, E., Gayo, J.E.L., Solbrig, H.: Shape expressions: an RDF validation and transformation language. In: Proceedings of the 10th International Conference on Semantic Systems, pp. 32–40 (2014)
47. Rabbani, K., Lissandrini, M., Hose, K.: Optimizing SPARQL qeries using shape statistics (2021)

48. Reiter, R.: Nonmonotonic reasoning. In: Exploring Artificial Intelligence, pp. 439–481. Elsevier (1988)
49. Rodriguez-Muro, M., Rezk, M.: Efficient SPARQL-to-SQL with R2RML mappings. J. Web Semantics **33**, 141–169 (2015)
50. Schmidt, M., Meier, M., Lausen, G.: Foundations of SPARQL query optimization. In: Proceedings of the 13th International Conference on Database Theory, pp. 4–33 (2010)
51. Sequeda, J.F., Miranker, D.P.: Ultrawrap: SPARQL execution on relational data. J. Web Semantics **22**, 19–39 (2013)
52. Taelman, R., Van Herwegen, J., Vander Sande, M., Verborgh, R.: Comunica: a modular SPARQL query engine for the web. In: Vrandečić, D., et al. (eds.) ISWC 2018. LNCS, vol. 11137, pp. 239–255. Springer, Cham (2018). https://doi.org/10.1007/978-3-030-00668-6_15
53. Thapa, R.B., Giese, M.: A source-to-target constraint rewriting for direct mapping. In: Hotho, A., et al. (eds.) ISWC 2021. LNCS, vol. 12922, pp. 21–38. Springer, Cham (2021). https://doi.org/10.1007/978-3-030-88361-4_2
54. Thapa, R.B., Giese, M.: Mapping relational database constraints to SHACL. In: The Semantic Web-ISWC 2022: 21st International Semantic Web Conference, Virtual Event, October 23–27, 2022, Proceedings, pp. 214–230 (2022)
55. Thapa, R.B., Giese, M.: Optimizing SPARQL queries with SHACL (extended version). Research Report 504, Dept. of Informatics, University of Oslo, July 2023
56. Xiao, G., Kontchakov, R., Cogrel, B., Calvanese, D., Botoeva, E.: Efficient handling of SPARQL OPTIONAL for OBDA. In: Vrandečić, D., et al. (eds.) ISWC 2018. LNCS, vol. 11136, pp. 354–373. Springer, Cham (2018). https://doi.org/10.1007/978-3-030-00671-6_21
57. Yin, X., Gromann, D., Rudolph, S.: Neural machine translating from natural language to SPARQL. Futur. Gener. Comput. Syst. **117**, 510–519 (2021)

HAEE: Low-Resource Event Detection with Hierarchy-Aware Event Graph Embeddings

Guoxuan Ding[1,2], Xiaobo Guo[1(✉)], Gaode Chen[1,2], Lei Wang[1], and Daren Zha[1]

[1] Institute of Information Engineering, Chinese Academy of Sciences, Beijing, China
{dingguoxuan,guoxiaobo,chengaode,wanglei,zhadaren}@iie.ac.cn
[2] School of Cyber Security, University of Chinese Academy of Sciences, Beijing, China

Abstract. The event detection (ED) task aims to extract structured event information from unstructured text. Recent works in ED rely heavily on annotated training data and often lack the ability to construct semantic knowledge, leading to a significant dependence on resource. In this paper, we propose a hierarchy-aware model called HAEE by constructing event graph embeddings. We utilize two relations (*cause* and *subevent*) to help model events on two dimensions of polar coordinates, so as to distinguish events and establish event-event relations. Specifically, events under the *cause* relation are constructed at the same level of the hierarchy through rotation, while events under the *subevent* relation are constructed at different levels of the hierarchy through modulus. In this way, coexistence and interactions between relations in time and space can be fully utilized to enhance event representation and allow the knowledge to flow into the low-resource samples. The experiments show that HAEE has high performance in low-resource ED task, and the analysis of different dimensions of embeddings proves that HAEE can effectively model the semantic hierarchies in the event graph.

Keywords: Event detection · Low resource · Hierarchy-aware · Event graph

1 Introduction

Event detection [14] (ED) is an important task in natural language processing, as it aims to extract structured event information from unstructured text to support downstream tasks such as question answering systems [2,12], information retrieval [11,33], knowledge graph construction [1,28] and so on. For example, in the sentence "Stewart's first marriage to Alana Hamilton lasted about five years.", the event detection task requires identifying the event type "marry" where the word "marriage" triggers the event.

© The Author(s), under exclusive license to Springer Nature Switzerland AG 2023
T. R. Payne et al. (Eds.): ISWC 2023, LNCS 14265, pp. 61–79, 2023.
https://doi.org/10.1007/978-3-031-47240-4_4

There are two major challenges in practical applications of ED. One such challenge is the problem of data scarcity [4]. ED requires a large amount of labeled data to train models. However, in real-world scenarios, some event types have limited samples, which can hinder models from effectively extracting event information. Therefore, there is a need to explore techniques that can facilitate learning knowledge from limited or even absent data.

On the other hand, learning existing knowledge is no longer a difficult problem due to the development of large-scale language models. Instead, constructing knowledge with semantic features is a more challenging problem [34]. Training models to capture profound semantic associations and extract potential information can enhance ED model performance. Therefore, it is necessary to investigate hierarchy-aware approaches for ED task.

Using more abstract event relations as an extra knowledge is a promising direction in low-resource ED scenarios. By learning event-event relations, it can provide a higher-level understanding of events that can be used to build better event representations and guide ED models. OntoED [5] is a classic and important model that formulates ED as an event ontology population task. By introducing three types of relations (*temporal*, *cause*, and *subevent*), it establishes associations between events to let the information flow into the low-resource events. To some extent, it addresses the problem of data scarcity. However, OntoED still has some limitations. Event relations can coexist and interact simultaneously in time and space, but 1) OntoED only considers and calculates each relation separately without discussing whether there are interactions between them. Additionally, 2) OntoED only involves one level of *subevent* without considering whether it has multi-level feature, which may result in the loss of relation knowledge.

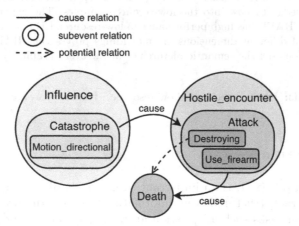

Fig. 1. Event graph with *cause* and *subevent*, potential relations are invisible in the knowledge set, but are real and can be mined. Color zones indicate events that are in the same time and space and are related through *subevent* (Color figure online)

To tackle these problems, we build a knowledge set with the *cause* and *subevent* relations and consider their characteristics of correlation. We do not consider *temporal* because it is relatively weak in terms of logical correlation. As illustrated in Fig. 1, *Cause* (e.g., *Attack* $\xrightarrow{cause}$ *Death*) means head events lead to the occurrence of tail events, and *subevent* (e.g., *Attack* $\xrightarrow{subevent}$ *Destroying*) indicates that child events are components of parent events, note that it can be a multi-level relation due to the transitivity of *subevent*. By modeling both *cause* and *subevent* together, we can observe the coexistence and interaction between relations: Events occurring in the same time and space may have an effect on events that occur in another time and space. Building *cause-subevent* relations not only makes the correlation closer but also helps to explore potential connections between events.

In this paper, we propose a novel hierarchy-aware model called HAEE (**H**ierarchy-**A**ware with **E**vent graph **E**mbedding) by combining *cause-subevent* relations and event graph embeddings. HAEE is expected to distinguish events and establish event-event relations by rotation and modulus, which operate at the same level and different levels of the hierarchy, respectively. For *cause*, we adopt a rotation-based approach [23] in which the event pairs are set at opposite positions on the circle. For *subevent*, we adopt a contrastive learning approach [20] where the distance between child events is as close as possible compare to the distance from child events to their parents. We perform convolution operations on embeddings to enhance the representation of events. In this way, further and hierarchical relation knowledge between events can be learned. We calculate multiple loss functions using Uncertainty to Weigh Losses [9] to obtain the final loss, which helps us balance the importance of each loss in the final ED task.

Applying these ideas, HAEE can start from a tiny amount of labeled samples and gradually discover more and more potential knowledge contained in event graph (e.g., *Destroying* $\xrightarrow{relation}$ *Death*), thereby improving the performance of low-resource ED task. The experiments demonstrate that HAEE outperforms existing models in data-scarce scenarios. To further analyze the effectiveness of our model, we conduct a module-wise analysis that examines each component of the model and its contribution to the overall performance. We find that our model has good modeling and semantic hierarchies on event embeddings, which is a key factor in accurately extracting events from text.

In summary, our contributions are as follows:

- We propose a novel hiearchy-aware model called HAEE. By constructing the knowledge set with *cause* and *subevent*, it can discover more potential information and allow the knowledge to flow into the low-resource events to solve the problem of ED in low-resource scenarios.
- To fully utilize coexistence and interactions between relations in time and space, we leverage *cause-subevent* relations by learning event embedding in the polar coordinates, which lead to a hierarchical event graph on dimensions of rotation and modulus.
- The experiments demonstrate that HAEE can achieve better performance in low-resource ED task. We conduct a module-wise analysis that examines

each component of the model and its contribution to the overall performance, showing that our model has good modeling and semantic hierarchies on event graph.

2   Related Work

In low-resource scenarios, exploiting stronger models and data augmentation are two main directions to improve the ED task [4]. Exploiting stronger models is to design a model that can improve its learning ability, thereby making full use of a small amount of samples and reducing its dependence on data. Data augmentation is expected to enhance the quality of samples as well as contribute more semantic representations.

Compare to traditional machine learning methods that have difficulty handling complex event structures and semantic relations, most recent ED works are based on neural networks [16,18], which can automatically learning useful features from data. DMCNN [3] is designed with a vocabulary expression model for capturing sentence-level clues by extracting lexical and sentence-level features using CNNs. Nguyen et al. [19] propose an improved non-continuous CNN that uses a joint-based paradigm to learn potential feature representations. JRNN [21] is presented with a bidirectional RNNs to link grammar-related vocabulary without using vocabulary itself. Feng et al. [8] use LSTM's long-term memory to capture text sequence information at the document level. However, both RNN-based and CNN-based models only consider the semantic information of individual samples without considering their relations with other samples. The powerful text learning ability enables the pre-training models [31,36] to win a widely attention and achieve a rapid development. ED tasks have shifted from constructing lexical representations for identifying triggers to representing samples as a whole. For example, CLEVE [27] is designed with a contrastive learning method based on pre-training frameworks that makes full use of event knowledge in large amounts of unsupervised data to construct semantic structures. While these techniques have shown promise, they encounter obstacles such as the requirement for significant quantities of annotated data and the inability to explore more suitable strategies for learning with limited data.

Another research direction to improve model performance is through data augmentation [17]. PathLM [13] provides an event pattern representation semantic framework that connects events together through multiple paths. OntoED [5] uses an ontology-based event construction method to enhance data by introducing multiple event relations. K-HPN [6] embeds *cause* into a knowledge-aware hypersphere prototype network. Ye et al. [32] use external knowledge graphs to transform structured knowledge into text to address the problem of knowledge scarcity. However, these techniques have primarily focused on enhancing samples at a local level, without improving sample quality from a higher-level perspective. Recent works [30,35] on entity graphs provide the possibility of constructing event knowledge in a higher-dimensional space. By doing so, it may facilitate the investigation of events from a more abstract and holistic perspective.

3   Methodology

In this section, we formally present the proposed model HAEE. We first introduce a) *Event Detection* as the main task of our model. Afterwards, we introduce b) *Graph Embedding* including rotation and modulus part for hierarchy-aware event graph modeling. Finally, we introduce c) *Embedding Convolution* and d) *Loss Function* to complete the rest of our model.

3.1   Problem Formulation

For an ED task, the given input includes a sample set $T = \{X_i | i = 1, \ldots, N\}$ and an event type set $\mathcal{E} = \{e_i | i = 1, \ldots, M\}$. Each sample X_i in T is a token sequence $\{x_i^1, \ldots, x_i^L\}$ with trigger x_i^k, where L is the maximum length of the sequence, and k is the position of the trigger in the sequence. The event type set $\mathcal{E}$ consists of different event types e, and each X_i belongs to an event type label e_i. The goal of the event detection task is to predict the event type label corresponding to each sample.

Event relation refer to the higher-level knowledge and more abstract connections between events. The relation set $\mathcal{R}$ includes the *cause* set $\mathcal{R}_c$ and the *subevent* set $\mathcal{R}_s$. The *cause* set $\mathcal{R}_c$ includes *cause* r_{cause} and *caused by* $r_{causedby}$, while the *subevent* set $\mathcal{R}_s$ includes *subevent* $r_{subevent}$ and *superevent* $r_{superevent}$.

Based on the event type set $\mathcal{E}$ and the relation set $\mathcal{R}$, the knowledge set $\mathcal{K}$ about events and relations is constructed, consisting of triples $(e_h, r, e_t) \in \mathcal{E} \times \mathcal{R} \times \mathcal{E}$, where e_h and e_t respectively refer to the head event and tail event under the relation r.

3.2   Model Overview

In this paper, we propose a general model called HAEE with three modules: event detection, graph embedding and embedding convolution. The key information for each module is shown in Fig. 2. Graph embedding contains rotation part and modulus part, and each part including event detection can be divided into three steps: graph modeling, score mapping, and loss calculation.

For event detection, we obtain the contextual representation of the sample from BERT and calculate the probability between sample and its event to form the event detection loss.

For graph embedding, we model event embeddings in the polar coordinates, find events that are in the *cause* or *subevent* relation with the query event from the knowledge set and calculate corresponding distance scores to form the loss function.

For embedding convolution, we convolve distant events in a certain weight to learn further and hierarchical relation knowledge.

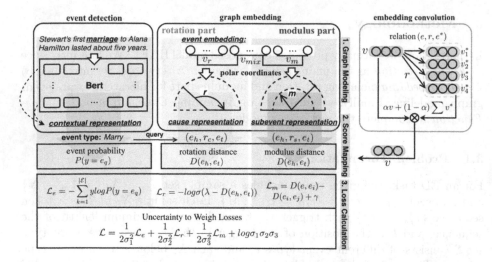

Fig. 2. Detailed example for the process of HAEE. Green zone represent the event detection. Yellow zone represent the rotation part in graph embedding. Blue zone represent the modulus part in graph embedding. Each space contains three steps: **Step 1 (Graph Modeling)** form sample representation and model event embedding to graph. **Step 2 (Score Mapping)** calculate event probability, rotation distance and modulus distance. **Step 3 (Loss Calculation)** form three loss functions and combine them to obtain the final loss (Color figure online)

3.3 Event Detection

To obtain the representation of each X_i, We use a pre-trained BERT model [7]. Specifically, we take the average of the word embeddings from the first and last layers of BERT's transformer to form the sentence representation. This approach maximally preserves semantic information for words and sentences in original samples, ultimately enhancing event representation [22,29].

We share the same formula to that of OntoED [5] for the calculation of event probability. For a given token sequence X_i, the probability of it belonging to event type e_k is

$$P(y = e_k) = \frac{exp(-||X_i - v_k||)}{\sum_{j=1}^{|\mathcal{E}|} exp(-||X_i - v_j||)}, \tag{1}$$

and the event detection loss is

$$\mathcal{L}_e = -\sum_{k=1}^{|\mathcal{E}|} y log P(y = e_q). \tag{2}$$

where e_q is the ground-truth label for X_i.

3.4 Graph Embedding

Based on the characteristics of *cause* and *subevent*, we choose two dimensions of polar coordinates to model them. Polar coordinates [35] is a position system in a two-dimensional space, consisting of rotation and modulus. By determining the rotation and modulus of a point, we can determine its position in the two-dimensional space.

To map event type to polar coordinates, we divide the embedding v of an event type e into rotation embedding v_r, modulus embedding v_m, and confuse embedding v_{mix} of equal size. The addition of the confuse embedding is to synthesize the characteristics of both dimensions and enhance the generalization ability of event representation. Specifically, we map $[v_r, v_{mix}]$ to the rotation as the *cause* representation and $[v_m, v_{mix}]$ to the modulus as the *subevent* representation. This modeling approach enhances interactions between two relations, helps discover potential relations between events, and ultimately enhances the model's semantic understanding ability.

Rotation Part. *Cause* refer to the occurrence of head events leading to the occurrence of tail events, indicating a obvious *cause* between them. Through the *cause* set R_c, we model events on the rotation of polar coordinates. Specifically, to represent *cause* between two events, we learn their opposite positions on the circle.

Given a query event e and *cause* r_c, we find all events e_c in the knowledge set $\mathcal{K}$ that satisfy (e, r_c, e_c) to form an event type set $\mathcal{E}_c$. For embeddings v and v_c of event types e and e_c, respectively, we have

$$(v - v_c) \, mod \, 2\pi = \pi, \tag{3}$$

where $v, v_c \in [0, 2\pi)$. We define the distance between events as

$$D(e_h, e_t) = \|sin((v_h - v_t + \pi)/2)\|_1. \tag{4}$$

The rotation loss [23] is then defined as

$$\mathcal{L}_r = \sum_{e_c \in \mathcal{E}_c} -log\sigma(\lambda - D(e, e_c)), \tag{5}$$

where $\sigma(\cdot)$ represents the sigmoid function and λ is a fixed threshold under rotation.

Modulus Part. *Subevent* means head events contain tail events in time and space, where tail events are components of head events. For the *subevent* set R_s, we assume that *subevent* have multi-level feature, meaning that events at the same level should have similar properties, while there is a certain distance between events and their parents. The *subevent* has transitivity, i.e., $(a, r, b), (b, r, c), then(a, r, c)$. We model this on the modulus of polar coordinates to represent events level. To achieve this goal, we use contrastive learning [20] to make events at the same level closer and events at different levels farther apart.

Given a query event e and *subevent* r_s, we find all events e_s in the knowledge set $\mathcal{K}$ that satisfy (e, r_s, e_s) to form an event type set $\mathcal{E}_s$. We define the different-level event pairs set $\mathcal{P}_d = \{(e, e_i)|e_i \in \mathcal{E}_s\}$ and the same-level event pairs set

$\mathcal{P}_s = \{(e_i, e_j)|e_i, e_j \in \mathcal{E}_s, i \neq j\}$. The distance between events as

$$D(e_h, e_t) = \|v_h - v_t\|_2. \tag{6}$$

Then the modulus loss is defined as

$$\mathcal{L}_m = \sum_{(e,e_i)\in\mathcal{P}_d} \sum_{(e_i,e_j)\in\mathcal{P}_s} max(D(e, e_i) - D(e_i, e_j) + \gamma, 0). \tag{7}$$

where γ represents an interval threshold under modulus.

3.5   Embedding Convolution

For an event relation chain $(a, r, b), (b, r, c) \in \mathcal{K}$, and $(a, r, c) \notin \mathcal{K}$, the event c may play a role in learning the relation (a, r, b) for the event a. To enhance the representation of events, obtain further and hierarchical knowledge in relation learning, given a query event e, a relation r, and the event relation knowledge (e, r, e_r), we find all events e^* in the knowledge set $\mathcal{K}$ that satisfy (e_r, r, e^*) to form an event set $\mathcal{E}^*$. We then calculate embedding of e_r as

$$v = \alpha v + (1 - \alpha)\frac{1}{|\mathcal{E}^*|} \sum_{e^* \in \mathcal{E}^*} v^*, \tag{8}$$

where v^* is a embedding of e^* and $\alpha \in [0, 1]$ is the weight for distant events. Through this approach, when calculating relations between events e and e_r, more knowledge can be learned.

3.6   Loss Function

For each event that undergoes relation calculation, its relation distribution may not be uniform, resulting in some events having many relations while others have few. To balance three losses, we introduce the Uncertainty to Weigh Losses multi-task optimization strategy [9]. By introducing weight coefficients into losses and adjusting their weights based on the prediction uncertainty of different module, we can express the final loss function as

$$\mathcal{L} = \frac{1}{2\sigma_1^2}\mathcal{L}_e + \frac{1}{2\sigma_2^2}\mathcal{L}_r + \frac{1}{2\sigma_3^2}\mathcal{L}_m + log\sigma_1\sigma_2\sigma_3, \tag{9}$$

where $\sigma_1, \sigma_2, \sigma_3$ are learnable parameters.

4   Experiments

In this section, we first introduce two datasets (OntoEvent and MAVEN-Few) and the baseline methods. Then we report the experimental results on ED task in different scenarios including a) *Overall Evaluation* and b) *Low-resource Evaluation*.

4.1 Datasets

Two datasets are used for the model evaluation: the OntoEvent dataset and the selected MAVEN-ERE dataset, called MAVEN-Few. Both of these datasets are composed of English samples. OntoEvent [5] is an event dataset with event relations, used to demonstrate that introducing ontology helps with event detection. MAVEN-ERE [24] is a unified large-scale dataset for event relation detection based on the original MAVEN [26] dataset, containing a large number of event types and their relations. To facilitate comparison with OntoED, we select event types from MAVEN-ERE that exist in OntoEvent, which has 71 event types, and their corresponding samples to conduct MAVEN-Few dataset for the evaluation. For the construction of knowledge set, we selected all involved events relations from MAVEN-ERE, which has 277 *cause* and 83 *subevent* for experiment. Compared to OntoEvent's 9 *cause* and no multi-level *subevent* involved, relations in MAVEN-Few are richer and it may be much more easier to mine more potential associations between events. In this paper, we will use these two datasets and the knowledge set to evaluate the performance of HAEE (Table 1).

Table 1. Statistics of OntoEvent and MAVEN-Few datasets. (Doc: document, Train: training set, Valid: validation set, Test: test set, Class: event types, Caus-Rel: *cause* relations, Sub-Rel: muti-level *subevent* relations.)

Dataset	#Doc	#Train	#Valid	#Test	#Class	#Caus-Rel	#Sub-Rel
OntoEvent [5]	4115	48436	6055	6055	100	9	–
MAVEN-Few	–	4416	552	551	71	277	83

4.2 Experiments Settings

We test the results of the validation set under different dimensions in {50,100,200, 500}, and finally choose 100 as the dimension of event embedding. The maximum token sequence length of the training sample is set to 128, and a dropout ratio of 0.2 is set to prevent overfitting. The learning rate is 1×10^3, and the initial values of uncertainty values $\sigma_1, \sigma_2, \sigma_3$ are set to -0.5. In terms of hyperparameter selection, we use a grid search on the validation set. Specifically, convolution weight $\alpha \in [0.2, 0.8]$ with a step size of 0.2, rotation threshold $\lambda \in [0.06, 0.12]$ with a step size of 0.02, and modulus threshold $\gamma \in [0.06, 0.12]$ with a step size of 0.02 are searched on the validation set to find optimal values for α, λ, γ, which are ultimately set to 0.4, 0.08, and 0.08 respectively for testing purposes. We randomly divide dataset into training set (80%), validation set (10%), and test set (10%), using the SGD optimizer [10] with the batch size of 42 samples per training iteration for a total of 5000 iterations to obtain the final result. We evaluate the performance of model with Precision, Recall and F1 Score for sample classification to the correct event label [5].

4.3 Baselines

For overall evaluation, we compare the proposed model with the following baseline methods in ED task.

- AD-DMBERT [25] is an adversarial training model that enhances distantly supervised event detection models and automatically constructs more diverse and accurate training data for semi-supervised event detection models.
- OneIE [15] is a joint neural model for information extraction. It explicitly models cross-subtask and cross-instance inter-dependencies and predicts the result as a unified graph instead of isolated knowledge elements.
- PathLM [13] is an auto-regressive language model and is designed to induce graph schemas that connect two event types through multiple paths involving entities.
- OntoED [5] formulates ED as an event ontology population task, and inferred more enriched samples and event-event relations with ontology learning.

For low-resource evaluation, we simply select OntoED [5] model for comparison due to its superior performance compared to other models and its utilization of event relations as extra knowledge, similar to HAEE.

4.4 Results

Overall Evaluation. From Table 2, it can be seen that on the OntoEvent dataset, HAEE obtains a better result than other models on all three indicators, such as BERT-based AD-DMBERT. This indicates the effectiveness of the HAEE framework built on BERT, which can better establish the connection between events. It also has a better performance than graph-based OneIE and PathLM, which only convert sentences into instance graphs and ignore potential relations between events. For ontology-based OntoED, it only explains event relations at the semantic level without considering whether there are interactions between relations and has weak modeling of *cause* and *subevent*. It is due to the comprehensive consideration of both *cause* and *subevent* between events and the implicit associations in the whole event graph in HAEE.

Table 2. Evaluation of event detection with overall OntoEvent dataset. †: results are produced with codes referred to Deng et al. [5]; ‡: results are produced with official implementation.

Model	Precision	Recall	F1 Score
AD-DMBERT† [25]	0.6735	0.7346	0.7189
OneIE† [15]	0.7194	0.6852	0.7177
PathLM† [13]	0.7351	0.6874	0.7283
OntoED‡ [5]	0.7756	0.7844	0.78
HAEE	**0.8882**	**0.8868**	**0.8875**

Low-Resource Evaluation. In low-resource scenarios, HAEE still maintains better performance. From Table 3, it can be seen that when the training samples of the OntoEvent dataset are reduced to 50%, OntoED's F1 score drops by 6.5% while HAEE only drops by 1.3%. When the training set is reduced to 25%, OntoED's F1 score drops by 16% while HAEE only drops by 2.4%. Even when the training set is reduced to 10%, HAEE only drops by 7.6%, with an F1 score of 0.831, which is much higher than OntoED's F1 score of 0.78 on the full training set.

Table 3. F1 Score of event detection on different ratios of OntoEvent and MAVEN-Few training data.

Model	OntoEvent				MAVEN-Few			
	Full	50%	25%	10%	Full	50%	25%	10%
OntoED [5]	0.78	0.7154	0.6198	0.4989	0.7725	0.6034	0.5195	0.2534
HAEE	**0.8875**	**0.8747**	**0.8634**	**0.831**	**0.8722**	**0.8577**	**0.8165**	**0.5993**

In the low-resource MAVEN-Few dataset, HAEE still performs well. The F1 values in each scenario are higher than those of OntoED. In terms of model stability, OntoED has already shown a significant decline when the training set is reduced to 50%, while for HAEE, when the training set is reduced to 50% and 25%, F1 only decreases by 2.5% and 5.6%, respectively. Only when it is reduced to 10%, does F1 show a significant decrease of 27%. However, compared with OntoED, HAEE still has a significant advantage at this point as its F1 value at a data ratio of 25% is higher than that of OntoED on the full dataset by 4.4%.

It can be seen that HAEE can maintain great and stable performance in low-resource scenarios while OntoED relies solely on semantic relations, which means that explicit event relations are not enough to support event representation in low-resource scenarios due to not considering implicit interactions between relations. Owing to modeling events in graph, HAEE can fully utilize event relations to enhance event representation in low-resource scenarios, thereby helping the model perform better in event detection task and enhancing its robustness.

5   Analysis

In this section, we analysis the semantic hierarchies and performance of HAEE from different perspectives including a) *Cause Representation*, b) *Subevent Representation* and c) *Ablation Studies*. We also provide possible explanations for our findings.

5.1   Cause Representation

Due to complex one-to-many and many-to-one *cause*, event pairs in relation may not fully reflect opposite position in polar coordinates modeling. To study

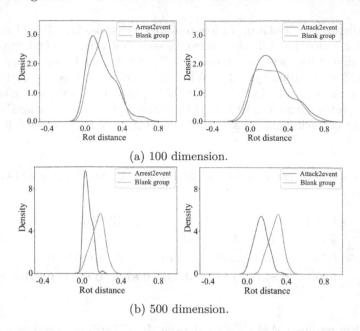

(a) 100 dimension.

(b) 500 dimension.

Fig. 3. Rotation distance density of two events (*Arrest* and *Attack*) in different embedding dimensions. Blue lines represent distance to other events. Red lines represent distance to blank control group. (Color figure online)

the effect of *cause* representation on rotation, we select two events, *Attack* and *Arrest*, to calculate their *cause* distance density to other events and set up 30 blank events as a control group. The blank events are only established during model initialization and do not participate in relation calculations. By comparing the distance to other events and the distance to the blank group, it can not only reflect the effect of *cause* calculation on events but also reflect the *cause* information of events themselves based on the blank control group.

Figure 3 shows the *cause* distance density of *Attack* and *Arrest* at 100 and 500 dimensions. It can be seen that as the dimension increases, the variance of blank control group tends to be more similar, indicating that *cause* representation becomes more stable, while event *cause* features become more prominent, means the distinction between events becomes obvious. This proves that the model does have an effect on modeling *cause*.

To further analyze the semantic hierarchy of *cause* representation, we select 20 positive events and 20 negative events from 100 events, as well as the aforementioned 30 blank control events, to form their respective event groups. We calculate the average distance from each event to the positive group, negative group, and blank control group and test the model's clustering effect on positive and negative events in *cause* modeling.

From the Table 4, it can be seen that positive events have a more unified clustering tendency, with 16 positive events tending to be far from negative

Table 4. The average rotation distance from each event to different groups. (p.g: positive group, b.g: blank control group, n.g:negative group. The bold numbers represent groups with a greater distance.)

Positive Events	Distance			Negative Events	Distance		
	p.g	b.g	n.g		p.g	b.g	n.g
come_together	0.45	0.55	**0.59**	destroying	**0.34**	0.23	0.24
elect	0.34	0.42	**0.47**	kidnapping	**0.30**	0.22	0.23
committing_crime	0.19	0.21	**0.28**	violence	**0.28**	0.21	0.22
employment	0.19	0.19	**0.23**	theft	**0.45**	0.32	0.33
award	**0.27**	0.20	0.21	robbery	0.18	0.19	**0.24**
arriving	0.31	0.38	**0.44**	hostile_encounter	0.18	0.20	**0.26**
contact	**0.51**	0.36	0.35	killing	0.23	0.29	**0.37**
recovering	0.21	0.19	**0.22**	terrorism	0.28	0.37	**0.45**
commerce_sell	0.28	0.34	**0.40**	conquering	**0.26**	0.20	0.22
exchange	0.19	0.20	**0.26**	arrest	0.19	0.19	**0.23**
marry	0.37	0.46	**0.51**	divorce	0.18	0.19	**0.25**
cure	0.25	0.30	**0.37**	bodily_harm	**0.38**	0.23	0.25
breathing	0.18	0.20	**0.25**	military_operation	**0.26**	0.20	0.22
communication	0.20	0.19	**0.22**	catastrophe	0.19	0.19	**0.23**
education_teaching	0.18	0.19	**0.24**	prison	**0.58**	0.47	0.46
traveling	0.19	0.21	**0.28**	use_firearm	**0.72**	0.60	0.59
resolve_problem	0.20	0.19	**0.22**	confronting_problem	**0.35**	0.23	0.25
be_born	**0.24**	0.20	0.21	death	0.41	0.53	**0.60**
placing	0.19	0.20	**0.24**	damaging	0.27	0.36	**0.44**
sending	**0.57**	0.42	0.40	revenge	**0.36**	0.24	0.26

events, and only 4 positive events showing the opposite result. This means that if an event shows obvious positivity, the model's accuracy in predicting the polarity of the event can reach up to 80%. For negative events, the clustering tendency is not particularly obvious, but it can be observed from the data in the table that compared with the blank control group, the clustering effect of events is significant. This means that the farther away an event's *cause* distance is from negative events, the more obvious its unified positivity or negativity is.

Compared with distant event groups, close event groups do not have particularly distinction from blank control group, but for some specific events, they can also effectively distinguish close groups. For example, *Death* has a distance difference of 0.12 between close group and blank group while that of only 0.07 between distant group and blank group.

Cause representation calculated through rotation can cluster event polarity. One possible explanation for this phenomenon is that *cause* representation carry *subevent* information through confuse embedding, and *subevent* have obvious clustering effects on events of the same type through learning distant relation of events. On the other hand, learning through a large number of samples also affects event representation. This ultimately leads to *cause* having polarity clustering effects as well. This means that the model can fully combine the characteristics of *cause-subevent* relations and event samples to enhance event representation, ultimately enhance semantic understanding of events by the model.

5.2 Subevent Representation

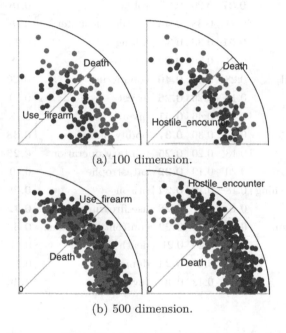

(a) 100 dimension.

(b) 500 dimension.

Fig. 4. Modulus distance of two event pairs (*Death, Use_firearm*) and (*Death, Hostile_encounter*) in different embedding dimensions. Note that the modulus in 100 dimension does not start from 0.

To demonstrate the hierarchy of *subevent* representation, we model other events based on the modulus of *Attack*. Specifically, we calculate the *subevent* distance between *Attack* and other events as the modulus of each event, while compressing the rotation to better demonstrate the effect of representation modeling. We select three events for graph embedding mapping: *Death, Use_firearm* and *Hostile_encounter*. It should be noted that *Death* and the other two events do not have a direct *subevent* in the knowledge set and can only indirectly reflect their *subevent* through *Attack*.

As shown in Fig. 4, in different dimensions, it can be seen that *Death* has a clear hierarchical distinction from the other two events. This proves that through *cause* information in confuse embedding, model can utilize *cause* to learn more event knowledge in *subevent* and ultimately enhance event representation.

5.3 Ablation Studies

To study the effect of each module on the model, we remove modulus part, rotation part, and use only the basic architecture of the model for testing in different resource scenarios on the OntoEvent [5] dataset. As shown in the Table 5, when there is sufficient data, the improvement of modules on accuracy is not significant. This may be because the sample set itself already contains enough information, which makes it difficult to demonstrate the effects of rotation and modulus. However, when resources are limited, combining rotation and modulus can effectively improve F1 score. It can be observed that under extremely low-resource conditions (10%), using only rotation can increase F1 score by 2.2% compared to not using graph embedding at all. But if we combine rotation and modulus, it can increase F1 score by 7.3%. Also, it can be observed that modulus provides more gain when there is sufficient data, while rotation provides more gain under low-resource conditions. By combining rotation and modulus, HAEE can fully utilize the relations between events to enhance representation.

Table 5. Effect of different modules of HAEE in low-resource scenarios. (rot: rotation part, mod: modulus part).

Model	Full	50%	25%	10%
HAEE	0.8875	0.8747	0.8634	0.831
HAEE w/o mod	0.8696	0.8593	0.8477	0.7808
HAEE w/o rot	0.8801	0.8641	0.8495	0.7578
HAEE w/o mod & rot	0.8741	0.8637	0.8474	0.7579

6   Conclusions and Future Work

This paper proposes a new hierarchy-aware model HAEE, which establishes *cause-subevent* relations by rotation and modulus, and maps event embeddings to polar coordinates to enhance event representation. To learn further and hierarchical relation knowledge, we convolve distant events together. We combine three loss functions by balance the importance of each loss in the final ED task. Through experiments, we demonstrate that HAEE has high performance under low-resource conditions, and analyze the modeling effects of each module, proving that the model has good modeling and semantic effects on event graph. In the future, we intend to enhance our work by more event relations and more complicated structures, and extend it to other information extraction tasks.

Supplemental Material Statement: Source code for HAEE and the MAVEN-Few dataset is available from Github at https://github.com/cdmelon/HAEE. Source code for OntoED and the OntoEvent dataset is available from Github at https://github.com/231sm/Reasoning_In_EE.

References

1. Bosselut, A., Le Bras, R., Choi, Y.: Dynamic neuro-symbolic knowledge graph construction for zero-shot commonsense question answering. In: Proceedings of the AAAI Conference on Artificial Intelligence, vol. 35, pp. 4923–4931 (2021)
2. Boyd-Graber, J., Börschinger, B.: What question answering can learn from trivia nerds. In: Proceedings of the 58th Annual Meeting of the Association for Computational Linguistics, pp. 7422–7435. Association for Computational Linguistics, Online (2020). https://doi.org/10.18653/v1/2020.acl-main.662. https://aclanthology.org/2020.acl-main.662
3. Chen, Y., Xu, L., Liu, K., Zeng, D., Zhao, J.: Event extraction via dynamic multi-pooling convolutional neural networks. In: Proceedings of the 53rd Annual Meeting of the Association for Computational Linguistics and the 7th International Joint Conference on Natural Language Processing (Volume 1: Long Papers), Beijing, China, pp. 167–176. Association for Computational Linguistics (2015). https://doi.org/10.3115/v1/P15-1017. https://aclanthology.org/P15-1017
4. Deng, S., et al.: Low-resource extraction with knowledge-aware pairwise prototype learning. Knowl.-Based Syst. **235**, 107584 (2022)
5. Deng, S., et al.: OntoED: low-resource event detection with ontology embedding. In: Proceedings of the 59th Annual Meeting of the Association for Computational Linguistics and the 11th International Joint Conference on Natural Language Processing (Volume 1: Long Papers), pp. 2828–2839. Association for Computational Linguistics, Online (2021). https://doi.org/10.18653/v1/2021.acl-long.220. https://aclanthology.org/2021.acl-long.220
6. Deng, S., Zhang, N., Xiong, F., Pan, J.Z., Chen, H.: Knowledge extraction in low-resource scenarios: survey and perspective. arXiv preprint abs/2202.08063 (2022). https://arxiv.org/abs/2202.08063
7. Devlin, J., Chang, M.W., Lee, K., Toutanova, K.: BERT: pre-training of deep bidirectional transformers for language understanding. In: Proceedings of the 2019 Conference of the North American Chapter of the Association for Computational Linguistics: Human Language Technologies, Volume 1 (Long and Short Papers), Minneapolis, Minnesota, pp. 4171–4186. Association for Computational Linguistics (2019). https://doi.org/10.18653/v1/N19-1423. https://aclanthology.org/N19-1423
8. Feng, X., Huang, L., Tang, D., Ji, H., Qin, B., Liu, T.: A language-independent neural network for event detection. In: Proceedings of the 54th Annual Meeting of the Association for Computational Linguistics (Volume 2: Short Papers), Berlin, Germany, pp. 66–71. Association for Computational Linguistics (2016). https://doi.org/10.18653/v1/P16-2011. https://aclanthology.org/P16-2011
9. Kendall, A., Gal, Y., Cipolla, R.: Multi-task learning using uncertainty to weigh losses for scene geometry and semantics. In: 2018 IEEE Conference on Computer Vision and Pattern Recognition, CVPR 2018, Salt Lake City, UT, USA, 18–22 June 2018, pp. 7482–7491. IEEE Computer Society (2018). https://doi.org/10.1109/CVPR.2018.00781. https://openaccess.thecvf.com/content_cvpr_2018/html/Kendall_Multi-Task_Learning_Using_CVPR_2018_paper.html

10. Ketkar, N., Ketkar, N.: Stochastic gradient descent. Deep learning with Python: a hands-on introduction, pp. 113–132 (2017)
11. Kuhnle, A., Aroca-Ouellette, M., Basu, A., Sensoy, M., Reid, J., Zhang, D.: Reinforcement learning for information retrieval. In: Proceedings of the 44th International ACM SIGIR Conference on Research and Development in Information Retrieval, pp. 2669–2672 (2021)
12. Li, F., et al.: Event extraction as multi-turn question answering. In: Findings of the Association for Computational Linguistics: EMNLP 2020, pp. 829–838. Association for Computational Linguistics, Online (2020). https://doi.org/10.18653/v1/2020. findings-emnlp.73. https://aclanthology.org/2020.findings-emnlp.73
13. Li, M., et al.: Connecting the dots: event graph schema induction with path language modeling. In: Proceedings of the 2020 Conference on Empirical Methods in Natural Language Processing (EMNLP), pp. 684–695. Association for Computational Linguistics, Online (2020). https://doi.org/10.18653/v1/2020.emnlp-main. 50. https://aclanthology.org/2020.emnlp-main.50
14. Li, Q., et al.: A survey on deep learning event extraction: approaches and applications. IEEE Trans. Neural Netw. Learn. Syst. (2022)
15. Lin, Y., Ji, H., Huang, F., Wu, L.: A joint neural model for information extraction with global features. In: Proceedings of the 58th Annual Meeting of the Association for Computational Linguistics, pp. 7999–8009. Association for Computational Linguistics, Online (2020). https://doi.org/10.18653/v1/2020.acl-main.713. https:// aclanthology.org/2020.acl-main.713
16. Liu, X., Luo, Z., Huang, H.: Jointly multiple events extraction via attention-based graph information aggregation. In: Proceedings of the 2018 Conference on Empirical Methods in Natural Language Processing, Brussels, Belgium, pp. 1247–1256. Association for Computational Linguistics (2018). https://doi.org/10.18653/v1/ D18-1156. https://aclanthology.org/D18-1156
17. Lu, Y., et al.: Text2Event: controllable sequence-to-structure generation for end-to-end event extraction. In: Proceedings of the 59th Annual Meeting of the Association for Computational Linguistics and the 11th International Joint Conference on Natural Language Processing (Volume 1: Long Papers), pp. 2795–2806. Association for Computational Linguistics, Online (2021). https://doi.org/10.18653/v1/ 2021.acl-long.217. https://aclanthology.org/2021.acl-long.217
18. Nguyen, T.H., Cho, K., Grishman, R.: Joint event extraction via recurrent neural networks. In: Proceedings of the 2016 Conference of the North American Chapter of the Association for Computational Linguistics: Human Language Technologies, San Diego, California, pp. 300–309. Association for Computational Linguistics (2016). https://doi.org/10.18653/v1/N16-1034. https://aclanthology.org/N16-1034
19. Nguyen, T.H., Grishman, R.: Modeling skip-grams for event detection with convolutional neural networks. In: Proceedings of the 2016 Conference on Empirical Methods in Natural Language Processing, Austin, Texas, pp. 886–891. Association for Computational Linguistics (2016). https://doi.org/10.18653/v1/D16-1085. https://aclanthology.org/D16-1085
20. Schroff, F., Kalenichenko, D., Philbin, J.: FaceNet: a unified embedding for face recognition and clustering. In: IEEE Conference on Computer Vision and Pattern Recognition, CVPR 2015, Boston, MA, USA, 7–12 June 2015, pp. 815–823. IEEE Computer Society (2015). https://doi.org/10.1109/CVPR.2015.7298682
21. Sha, L., Qian, F., Chang, B., Sui, Z.: Jointly extracting event triggers and arguments by dependency-bridge RNN and tensor-based argument interaction. In: McIlraith, S.A., Weinberger, K.Q. (eds.) Proceedings of the Thirty-Second AAAI

Conference on Artificial Intelligence, (AAAI 2018), The 30th Innovative Applications of Artificial Intelligence (IAAI 2018), and The 8th AAAI Symposium on Educational Advances in Artificial Intelligence (EAAI 2018), New Orleans, Louisiana, USA, 2–7 February 2018, pp. 5916–5923. AAAI Press (2018). www.aaai.org/ocs/index.php/AAAI/AAAI18/paper/view/16222

22. Su, J., Cao, J., Liu, W., Ou, Y.: Whitening sentence representations for better semantics and faster retrieval. arXiv preprint abs/2103.15316 (2021). arxiv:2103.15316

23. Sun, Z., Deng, Z., Nie, J., Tang, J.: Rotate: knowledge graph embedding by relational rotation in complex space. In: 7th International Conference on Learning Representations, ICLR 2019, New Orleans, LA, USA, 6–9 May 2019. OpenReview.net (2019). https://openreview.net/forum?id=HkgEQnRqYQ

24. Wang, X., et al.: MAVEN-ERE: a unified large-scale dataset for event coreference, temporal, causal, and subevent relation extraction. arXiv preprint abs/2211.07342 (2022). arxiv:2211.07342

25. Wang, X., Han, X., Liu, Z., Sun, M., Li, P.: Adversarial training for weakly supervised event detection. In: Proceedings of the 2019 Conference of the North American Chapter of the Association for Computational Linguistics: Human Language Technologies, Volume 1 (Long and Short Papers), Minneapolis, Minnesota, pp. 998–1008. Association for Computational Linguistics (2019). https://doi.org/10.18653/v1/N19-1105. https://aclanthology.org/N19-1105

26. Wang, X., et al.: MAVEN: a massive general domain event detection dataset. In: Proceedings of the 2020 Conference on Empirical Methods in Natural Language Processing (EMNLP), pp. 1652–1671. Association for Computational Linguistics, Online (2020). https://doi.org/10.18653/v1/2020.emnlp-main.129. https://aclanthology.org/2020.emnlp-main.129

27. Wang, Z., et al.: CLEVE: contrastive pre-training for event extraction. In: Proceedings of the 59th Annual Meeting of the Association for Computational Linguistics and the 11th International Joint Conference on Natural Language Processing (Volume 1: Long Papers), pp. 6283–6297. Association for Computational Linguistics, Online (2021). https://doi.org/10.18653/v1/2021.acl-long.491. https://aclanthology.org/2021.acl-long.491

28. Wu, X., Wu, J., Fu, X., Li, J., Zhou, P., Jiang, X.: Automatic knowledge graph construction: a report on the 2019 ICDM/ICBK contest. In: 2019 IEEE International Conference on Data Mining (ICDM), pp. 1540–1545. IEEE (2019)

29. Wu, X., Gao, C., Zang, L., Han, J., Wang, Z., Hu, S.: ESimCSE: enhanced sample building method for contrastive learning of unsupervised sentence embedding. arXiv preprint abs/2109.04380 (2021). arXiv:2109.04380

30. Yang, J., et al.: Learning hierarchy-aware quaternion knowledge graph embeddings with representing relations as 3D rotations. In: Proceedings of the 29th International Conference on Computational Linguistics, pp. 2011–2023 (2022)

31. Yang, S., Feng, D., Qiao, L., Kan, Z., Li, D.: Exploring pre-trained language models for event extraction and generation. In: Proceedings of the 57th Annual Meeting of the Association for Computational Linguistics, Florence, Italy, pp. 5284–5294. Association for Computational Linguistics (2019). https://doi.org/10.18653/v1/P19-1522. https://aclanthology.org/P19-1522

32. Ye, H., et al.: Ontology-enhanced prompt-tuning for few-shot learning. In: Proceedings of the ACM Web Conference 2022, pp. 778–787 (2022)

33. Zhang, W., Zhao, X., Zhao, L., Yin, D., Yang, G.H.: DRL4IR: 2nd workshop on deep reinforcement learning for information retrieval. In: Proceedings of the 44th

International ACM SIGIR Conference on Research and Development in Information Retrieval, pp. 2681–2684 (2021)

34. Zhang, W., et al.: Iteratively learning embeddings and rules for knowledge graph reasoning. In: Liu, L., et al. (eds.) The World Wide Web Conference, WWW 2019, San Francisco, CA, USA, 13–17 May 2019, pp. 2366–2377. ACM (2019). https:// doi.org/10.1145/3308558.3313612

35. Zhang, Z., Cai, J., Zhang, Y., Wang, J.: Learning hierarchy-aware knowledge graph embeddings for link prediction. In: Proceedings of the AAAI Conference on Artificial Intelligence, vol. 34, pp. 3065–3072 (2020)

36. Zheng, S., Cao, W., Xu, W., Bian, J.: Doc2EDAG: an end-to-end document-level framework for Chinese financial event extraction. In: Proceedings of the 2019 Conference on Empirical Methods in Natural Language Processing and the 9th International Joint Conference on Natural Language Processing (EMNLP-IJCNLP), Hong Kong, China, pp. 337–346. Association for Computational Linguistics (2019). https://doi.org/10.18653/v1/D19-1032. https://aclanthology.org/D19-1032

Textual Entailment for Effective Triple Validation in Object Prediction

Andrés García-Silva(✉), Cristian Berrío, and Jose Manuel Gómez-Pérez

Expert.ai, Language Technology Research Lab, Poeta Joan Maragall 3, 28020
Madrid, Spain
{agarcia,cberrio,jmgomez}@expert.ai
https://www.expert.ai

Abstract. Knowledge base population seeks to expand knowledge graphs with facts that are typically extracted from a text corpus. Recently, language models pretrained on large corpora have been shown to contain factual knowledge that can be retrieved using cloze-style strategies. Such approach enables zero-shot recall of facts, showing competitive results in object prediction compared to supervised baselines. However, prompt-based fact retrieval can be brittle and heavily depend on the prompts and context used, which may produce results that are unintended or hallucinatory. We propose to use textual entailment to validate facts extracted from language models through cloze statements. Our results show that triple validation based on textual entailment improves language model predictions in different training regimes. Furthermore, we show that entailment-based triple validation is also effective to validate candidate facts extracted from other sources including existing knowledge graphs and text passages where named entities are recognized.

Keywords: Object Prediction · Knowledge Base Population · Recognizing Textual Entailment

1 Introduction

Knowledge Graphs arrange entities and relationships in a graph structure to represent knowledge [29,43]. The edges of the graph describe relations between subject and object entities that are encoded as *<subject relation object>* triples. Knowledge graphs have applications in many areas, including search[1], recommendation, and natural language processing [22]. Nowadays the collaboration between editors and bots to curate and extend knowledge graphs has become common [50]. However, this is a complex and never-ending task and as a consequence, knowledge graphs are often incomplete [12,52].

Knowledge Base Completion KBC [3] aims at predicting relations between existing entities. Similarly, the goal of the Knowledge Base Population KBP task

---

[1] https://blog.google/products/search/introducing-knowledge-graph-things-not/.

T. R. Payne et al. (Eds.): ISWC 2023, LNCS 14265, pp. 80–100, 2023.
https://doi.org/10.1007/978-3-031-47240-4_5

[21] is to expand knowledge graphs with new facts discovered from text corpora. While in recent years a plethora of embeddings-based approaches have emerged for KBC [22], KBP research has not progressed at the same speed due to the complexity of the pipelines [14,21] and the lack of established benchmarks.[2]

Recently, language models have been revealed as promising resources for KBP. Language models trained on large text corpora encode different types of knowledge including syntactic [26], semantic [47], commonsense [57], and factual knowledge [31]. To elicit facts from the internal memory of a language model, researchers typically use cloze statements to make the language model fill in the masked tokens, e.g., John Lennon plays <MASK>. Cloze statements, also known as prompts in this context, enable zero-shot fact retrieval without any fine-tuning [31]. Nevertheless, the knowledge encoded in the language model is limited to the data it has seen during pretraining. Additionally, prompt-based fact retrieval can be brittle [32] and heavily depend on the prompts and context used [9], which may produce results that are unintended or hallucinatory. For example, as a response to the previous prompt, BERT would return guitar, piano, drums, himself, harmonica. Lennon played percussion overdubs on some tracks, but he never actually played the drums. Further, while all of the remaining statements are true, "John Lennon plays himself" relates to his acting side, while we are interested in musical instruments. An apparently more specific prompt like John Lennon plays instrument <MASK> returns here, there, too, himself, onstage, adding even more noise.

To address such limitations we propose to validate candidate triples using textual entailment [34] against evidence retrieved from the Web. Within KBP, we focus on the object prediction task [42]. Given a subject entity and a relation, the goal is to predict every object that renders a valid triple, where such objects may not have been contained in the knowledge graph yet. In this paper we present our system SATORI (Seek And enTail for Object pRedIction). As shown in Fig. 1, SATORI obtains candidate objects from language models using cloze statements and generates candidate triples. To improve recall SATORI also considers other sources of candidate objects including external knowledge bases and named entities recognized in relevant text passages. A language model fine-tuned on the entailment task is used to validate whether the generated triples can be entailed from passages retrieved from the web. The objects of the triples validated by the model as entailment are the output of the system.

SATORI relies on templates to convert the input subject and relation pair into search engine queries to retrieve text passages, language model prompts to get candidate objects, and hypotheses describing candidate triples. Templates need to be defined only once per relation, and in its most basic form a template can be re-used across all the system components. For example, given the input pair *(John Lennon, PersonIntrument)* and a relation template {X} *plays*, we can submit the query *John Lennon plays* to the search engine, prompt the language model with *John Lennon plays <MASK>* for a candidate object, e.g., *Guitar,*

---

[2] The KBP evaluation track of the TAC [14] is a long running initiative. However, manual system evaluation makes it hard to reproduce evaluation for new systems.

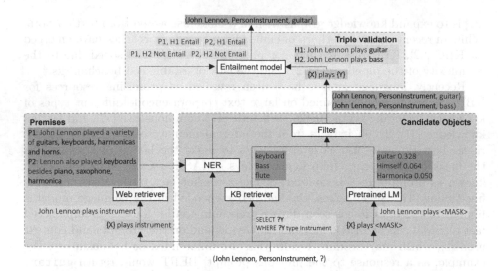

Fig. 1. SATORI architecture exemplified using as input pair *John Lennon* in the subject and *PersonInstrument* in the relation.

and validate the entailment of the hypothesis *John Lennon plays Guitar* against the premises retrieved through our web search. Using language models as a source of factual knowledge, SATORI could also leverage breakthroughs in prompting and knowledge-based enhancement of language models [32].

Validating candidate triples generated from objects predicted using language models raises the following main research questions:

- Q1: Does candidate triple validation through textual entailment improve object prediction results over prompting a pretrained language model?
- Q2: How do further pretraining the language model and fine-tuning for entailment-based triple validation under different data regimes impact object prediction?
- Q3: How do language models compare to other potential sources of structured knowledge, as well as to methods based on extracting information from text, for the generation of candidate triples?

In this paper, we investigate such research questions and present the following contributions. First, an approach for object prediction including the validation of triples using textual entailment. Second, an experimental study where different configurations of SATORI and baseline systems are evaluated using a gold dataset for object prediction [42]. In such experiments we show that triple validation through textual entailment improves the performance of facts extracted from pretrained language models and also when additional training data is available. Finally, we compare language models with other sources including structured knowledge and unstructured text, which we process using extractive techniques repurposed for object prediction.

2 Related Work

Knowledge Base Population. A prototypical KBP architecture [4,21] applies *entity linking* [54] on a corpus to recognize the entities mentioned in the text. Then a *slot filling* process [44] predicts an object, either an entity or a value for each subject entity and named relation, given the text where the entity appears. A key component of slot filling is a *relation extraction* model [1,18] that identifies the relation between the entity and the candidate object. Thus, in KPB object prediction could complement the slot filling task since both share the goal of getting entities or values for a given subject and predicate. However, while slot filling leverages a large corpus to get the objects, in object prediction we rely on a language model to get objects and neither entity linking, relation extraction nor a text corpus are required.

Similar to our work West et al. [52] extract values from web search snippets although using question-answering (QA). Nevertheless, they experiment only with relations of subject type PERSON, and their approach only predict entities already in the knowledge graph. Unlike West et al., our work is framed in open world KBP [39], where predicted entities are not restricted to existing entities.

Knowledge Base Completion. KBC [22] mostly refers to *relation prediction* [3,56] where the goal is to recognize a relation between two existing entities. However, KBC de facto evaluation turns relation prediction into a ranking task where triples with right objects (or subjects) are expected at the top [6,55]. Such evaluation could lead to confusing KBC goal with object prediction. However in KBC the predicted objects are already part of the knowledge graph, while in object prediction they are not necessarily known.

Prompts and Entity-Enhanced Languages Models. To elicit relational knowledge from language models Petroni et al. [31] use prompting. They show that prompting BERT achieves competitive results againts non-neural and supervised alternatives. Prompts can be hand-crafted [31], mined from a large corpus [7] or learned [33,40]. Li et al. [25] decompose prompts to split the task into multiple steps, and use task-specific pretraining for object prediction. Similar to our work Alivanistos et al. [2] add a fact probing step. However rather than using entailment for the validation, they ask a generative language model whether the generated fact is correct. Other works such as KnowBERT [30], and E-BERT [32] enhance BERT with pretrained entity embeddings, showing that such enhanced versions improve BERT results on LAMA [31].

Textual Entailment. It aims at recognizing, given two text fragments, whether the meaning of one text can be inferred (entailed) from the other [11]. The state of the art for textual entailment [51] is to fine-tune language models on datasets such as SNLI [8] or MNLI [53]. Researchers have reformulated several task as entailment. Wang et al. [51] convert single-sentence and sentence-pair classification tasks into entailment style. Entailment has been also used for zero-shot and few-shot relation extraction [37], answer validation [35], event argument extraction [36], and claim verification in fact checking [16]. Preliminary experiments suggest that a slot filling validation filter using textual entailment could be useful for KBP systems [5]. To the best of our knowledge we are the first to use textual entailment to validate object prediction results.

Fact Checking. Fact checking [16], originally proposed for assessing whether claims made in written or spoken language are true, have been applied also to check the trustworthiness of facts in knowledge graphs. Approaches for truth scoring of facts can be broadly classified into two types [23]: approaches that use unstructured textual data to find supporting evidential sentences for a given statement [13, 46, 48], and approaches that use a knowledge graph to find supporting evidential paths for a given statement [41, 45]. Fact checking, is a step beyond our triple validation approach, where trustworthiness of the triples and the sources is evaluated. Trustworthiness analysis is out of the scope of out work that is defined in the research questions that we pose.

3   Object Prediction

3.1   Task Definition

Let $F \subset E \times R \times E$ be the set of facts in a knowledge graph, where E is the set of entities and R the set of relations. Given $s \in E$ and $r \in R$, the goal of the object prediction task is to find every $o \in E \cup E'$ where E' is the complement of E such that the triple (s, r, o) is a valid fact. Valid triples are added to F, and E is expanded when o is not an existing entity in the graph. In object prediction, as in other KBP tasks, the knowledge graph schema is available. The schema defines the relations in the knowledge graph including their range[3]. The range indicates that the objects of a particular relation are instances of a designated class. For example, the range of the *PersonInstrument* relation is the class *MusicalInstrument*.

3.2   SATORI: Seek and Entail for Object Prediction

Recognizing textual entailment (RTE) is central in SATORI to validate triples. RTE is the task to determine whether a hypothesis H is true given a premise P. Typically for an input pair P and H, an RTE model assigns the labels Entailment (true), Contradiction (false) or Neutral [27]. We consider as hypothesis a natural language description of the candidate triple that we are validating, and as premises relevant text retrieved from the web. Thus SATORI has three major steps (see Fig. 1): i) retrieving premises, ii) getting candidate objects to generate new triples, and iii) validating triples using RTE. Along this section we use the input pair $s = JohnLennon$, $r = PersonInstrument$ as an example for the object prediction task.

Retrieving Premises. The goal is to query a search engine using the input pair s and r to retrieve relevant text passages (featured snippets). For a relation

---

[3] See RDF schema in https://www.w3.org/TR/rdf-primer/#properties.

r we define a search template $t_{search,r}$ as a keyword-based query including a placeholder for the subject. The subject s is replaced in the template $t_{search,r}$ and the output query is sent to the search engine API. We retrieve the top k featured snippets to use them as premises. For the example input pair and template $t_{search,r} = X$ *plays instrument*, our query is *John Lennon plays instrument*.

Getting Candidate Objects. Our first source of candidate objects is a pre-trained language model. For each relation we define a template $t_{lm,r}$ of a prompt for the language model. The prompt is obtained by replacing the subject s in the template $t_{lm,r}$. For example the template $t_{lm,r} = X$ *plays <MASK>* becomes the prompt *John Lennon plays <MASK>*. In a bidirectional transformer like BERT the output vectors corresponding to the mask tokens are fed into an output softmax layer over the vocabulary. Hence the language model output for a mask token is the words in the vocabulary and the score indicating the probability of being the mask token in the input sequence. We use a per-relation threshold $T_{lm,r}$ on the word score. Predicted words with a score above the threshold are added to the set of candidate objects $objs = \{o_i\}$. Given an input pair (s, r) and each candidate object o_i we create a candidate triple (s, r, o_i)

In addition, we consider existing knowledge graphs as source of candidate objects. We use instances of the classes defined in the relation range as candidate objects. To retrieve such instances we use SPARQL queries. First, we get the classes C_j in the relation range from the schema of the knowledge graph that we are populating. Next, for each class in the relation range we send the following SPARQL query to the knowledge graph from where we want to obtain candidates: *SELECT ?y WHERE ?y rdf:type C_j.*[4] The retrieved entities are added to the set of candidate objects $objs = \{o_i\}$. For example, the relation *person-Instrument* expects entities of class *MusicalInstrument* in the range. Thus, the SPARQL query generated for the example input pair is *SELECT ?y WHERE ?y rdf:type MusicalInstrument*.

Both language models and knowledge graphs can generate a high number of non-relevant candidate objects. We use heuristics to filter out unrelated objects. The most basic filter is a stop word list including punctuation marks. Language models are known for assigning high probability to punctuation marks and articles. In addition, we filter out objects which are not explicitly mentioned in the text passages gathered in the premise retrieval stage.

Named Entity Recognition NER can also be used to identify candidate objects for some relations depending on the classes in the relation range. Standard NER recognizes People, Locations, and Organizations[5]. We apply NER on the texts passages retrieved from the web for the input pair. If there is a match between the classes in the relation range and the classes of the recognized entities then we add such entities to the set of candidate objects $objs = \{o_i\}$.

---

[4] While rdf:type is the standard property used to state that a resource is an instance of a class, some knowledge graphs could use other ad-hoc property.

[5] Due to the diverse nature of the MISC category we do not consider it.

Validating Triples. We generate a short text description of a candidate triple (s, r, o_i) to be used as hypothesis to validate against the premises through RTE. We define per-relation templates $t_{h,r}$ to generate hypotheses containing place-holders for the subject (X) and object (Y). Then we replace the subject (X) and object (Y) placeholders with s and o_i to generate a hypothesis H_l. Given the candidate triple *(John Lennon, PersonInstrument, Guitar)*, and template $t_{h,r} = X$ *plays* Y, the generated hypothesis is $H_l =$ *John Lennon plays guitar*. Next, we use a language model fine-tuned for the RTE task to evaluate whether H_l is entailed on average by the k premises. The objects o_i corresponding to an entailed hypothesis are the final objects for the input tuple (s, r).

Language models fine-tuned for RTE address the task as a multi-class classi-fication of premise and hypothesis pairs into Entailment, Contradiction and Neu-tral classes. For transformers like BERT the input is a sequence *[CLS] premise [SEP] hypothesis [SEP]*. The [CLS] output vector $C \in R^H$, where H is the hid-den size in the transformer, acts as the aggregated representation of the input sequence, and is connected to an output layer for classification $W \in^{K \times H}$, where K is the number of classes. Softmax is the activation function of the output layer and cross-entropy the loss function. In SATORI we focus on the Entailment and Contradiction classes, and softmax is applied only to the corresponding outputs. For each pair of premise and hypothesis the classifier generates scores for each of the classes. We use a per-relation threshold $T_{e,r}$ on the Entailment class score to accept the prediction as valid.

4   Evaluation Setup

4.1   Dataset

The datasets used in the TAC KBP [14] evaluation series are tightly coupled with the text corpus used to mine facts: only information extracted from the corpus is considered valid to populate the knowledge graph. We discard such datasets since SATORI's web-based approach does not rely on a particular corpus. In addition, the evaluation of the slot-filling task, which is the most closely related to object prediction, is carried out manually.

Other triple-based datasets like LAMA [31], FB15K-237 [49] and WN18 [6], and their derived versions, were also discarded since they do not guarantee the completeness of objects for subject and relation pairs. Completeness of objects is important to evaluate precision and recall in object prediction. For instance, when predicting objects for relation *PersonInstrument* we want to predict all the instruments and not only some instruments for a given individual. In LAMA triples are randomly sampled, while in FB15K-237 and WN18 only frequent entities and relations are selected.

Moreover, optional relations that do not apply to every subject in the domain play an important role in object prediction evaluation. For example, the optional *PlaceOfDeath* relation only applies to people that have passed away, not to all the instances of people. Thus, to evaluate whether an object prediction system must produce or not an object for a subject and relation pair, the dataset needs to include pairs for which an object is not expected.

Therefore, we resort to the recently introduced LM_KBC22 [42] dataset[6] that includes all expected objects for a given subject and relation pair, is not tied to a particular corpus, and comprises subject-relation pairs for which objects are not expected. The dataset includes 12 relations exemplified by a set of subjects and a complete list of ground-truth objects per subject and relation pair. Five relations also contain subjects without any correct ground truth objects. In this dataset relation domains are diverse, including *Person, Organization*, or *Chemical compound*. Similarly the range of relations includes *Country, Language, Chemical element, Profession, Musical Instruments*, or *Companies* to name a few classes. The training set includes 100 subjects per relation, and development and test sets each contain 50 subjects per relation.

4.2   Metrics

KBP systems are required to make accurate decisions with good coverage of the predicted entities. Rank-aware metrics customary used in KBC such as Mean Rank, and Mean Recriprocal Rank are of little use in a real KBP setting. They indicate how high in the ranking of predicted objects are the right ones. However in KBP we are interested in making actual predictions. Therefore, we use standard classification metrics that are good indicators of system accuracy and coverage: precision, recall, and F1.

4.3   SATORI Configuration

We use the duckduckgo.com search engine to gather premises from the Web for each subject-relation pair. We leverage its python library[7] to send queries to the text search service. This service returns the web page title, url, and featured snippet that we keep as a premise. The duckduckgo library is very convenient since it can be used straightaway in Python programs and does not require registration in a cloud-based platform, unlike with leading search engines. We set k = 3 to gather at least three different premises that we can use to evaluate the hypotheses that we generate.

We evaluate three sources of candidate objects: pretrained language model (LM), knowledge graph (KG) and NER. We use BERT large cased as pretrained LM since it allows us to compare SATORI with the baseline model in the LM-KBC22 dataset. KG and NER are used together since NER recognizes a limited number of entity types and some entity types might not be covered in a KG. To perform NER we use a transformer model fine-tuned on the task[8]. We use NER to get candidate locations for relations *StateSharesBorderState* and *PersonPlace-OfDeath*, and candidate organizations for relations *CompanyParentOrganization*

---

[6] https://lm-kbc.github.io/2022/.

[7] https://pypi.org/project/duckduckgo-search/.

[8] https://spacy.io/models/en#en_core_web_trf.

and *PersonEmployer*. We use Wikidata [50] as KG for the rest of the relations in the dataset. Wikidata includes instances of all classes in the ranges of the remaining relations: *Language, Country, ChemicalElement, MusicalInstrument, Profession*, and *CauseOfDeath*.

To validate candidate triples we test three language models fine-tuned for the entailment task. We choose the models according to their performance on the entailment task and the number of parameters in the model. We use a DeBERTa Extra Large (XL) model[9] with 900M parameters that reports 91.7 accuracy on the MNLI dataset [53]. We also use DeBERTa Extra Small (XS)[10] model with 22M parameters that reports 88.1 accuracy on the same dataset. The final model that we test is a BERT large model[11] with 336M parameters that reports 86.7 accuracy on MNLI.

Templates $t_{lm,r}$, $t_{search,r}$, and $t_{h,r}$ used in the experiments are listed in the paper repository.[12] Particularly, templates $t_{lm,r}$ are reused from the language model baseline that we describe below.

4.4   Baselines

The first baseline that we use is prompting a language model. Such baseline allows to test our hypothesis that triple validation through textual entailment can benefit object prediction from language models. In addition, we are interested in comparing the knowledge in language models with other sources of knowledge including knowledge graphs and text passages related to the input subject and relation pair. Thus, we use as baselines a state of the art extractive question answering model and a relation extraction model repurposed for object prediction.

LM-Baseline. We reuse the baseline system from the LM_KBC challenge [42], which prompts a BERT-large-cased model. We use the templates to transform triples into prompts made available in the challenge repository.[13] The baseline uses a threshold $T_{lm,r}$ on the likelihood of words to fill in the mask token. Stop words are also filtered out. In addition, following Li et al. [25] we further-pretrain the language model on the masked language modeling objective using training data from the LM_KBC22 dataset. We transform triples in the training dataset into prompts where the objects are masked, and train the model to predict the right objects (see Sect. 4.5 for further pretraining details).

The BERT-based system that scored highest in the LM_KBC22 challenge trains several BERT models (one model per relation) and further pretrains the models with data from Wikidata [25]. While we could have used such approach as a baseline and integrated it in SATORI as source of candidate objects, we

---

[9] https://huggingface.co/microsoft/deberta-v2-xlarge-mnli.
[10] https://huggingface.co/microsoft/deberta-v3-xsmall.
[11] https://huggingface.co/boychaboy/MNLI_bert-large-cased.
[12] https://github.com/satori2023/Textual-Entailment-for-Effective-Triple-Validation-in-Object-Prediction.
[13] https://github.com/lm-kbc/dataset.

decided against it since we think such approach does not scale due to the number of models being trained.

QA-Baseline. We use an extractive Question Answering (QA) system as baseline. To this end, we transform each subject-relation pair using per-relation templates into a question, where the answer is the expected object. The QA system then attempts to extract the answer from the text passages that we gather from the Web as premises in SATORI for the same input pair (see Sect. 3 for the premise retrieval procedure). QA per-relation templates $t_{qa,r}$ have a placeholder (X) for the subject entity and follow a similar basic pattern with minor variations: *What relation* X?*, where relation* is a text fragment derived from the relation label. For example, the template for the *PlaysInstrument* relation is: *What instruments plays X?*. The complete set of QA templates is available in the paper repository.

As QA model we use DeBERTa large[14] fine-tuned on SQUAD 2.0. DeBERTa is the highest scoring single model in the SQuAD 2.0 leaderboard[15] (F1 = 90.3) that is available on hugginface.co. We slightly post-process DeBERTa's answers containing lists of items to extract each item. For example, for the question *What instruments plays John Lennon?*, DeBERTa extracts the answer *guitar, keyboard, harmonica and horn*. From such list we extract each single instrument as a possible answer. Along with the answer span DeBERTa generates a score that indicates the probability of the answer. We use a per-relation threshold $T_{qa,r}$ on that score to accept or reject an answer. In addition we further fine-tune the QA model using questions and answers derived from the training set and the premise retrieved in SATORI as text passages from where the answers can be extracted (see Sect. 4.5 for further details on QA fine-tuning).

RE-Baseline. We also test the state of the art relation extraction system REBEL [19] in the object prediction task. REBEL is a sequence to sequence model based on BART [24] that performs end-to-end relation extraction for more than 200 different relation types. REBEL autoregressively generates each triple present in the input text. To use REBEL we need to map the relations it supports with relations in the LM_KBC22 dataset. From the 12 relations in LM_KBC22 we find 10 relations with the same or very similar semantics in REBEL.[16] For the *ChemicalCompoundElement*, one of the remaining relations, we establish a mapping with the broader *has part* relation. The *PersonCauseOfDeath* relation could not be mapped. We use REBEL to generate triples from the text passages previously retrieved as premises for input subject-relation pairs. Finally, we extract the objects from those triples as the predicted objects.

4.5 Pretrained Models and Training Regimes

We evaluate pretrained models off the shelf and once they are further trained using the LM_KBC22 dataset. Since the test set is withheld by the dataset

---

[14] https://huggingface.co/deepset/deberta-v3-large-squad2.

[15] https://rajpurkar.github.io/SQuAD-explorer/.

[16] The relation mapping can be found in the paper repository.

authors, we test on the development set and use a held-out 20% of the training set as a new development set, leaving the remaining 80% as training data.

First we evaluate SATORI and the baselines using available pretrained models (see Sects. 4.3 and 4.4). To adjust the parameters that control the predictions of the different models for each relation, i.e. $T_{lm,r}$, $T_{e,r}$ in SATORI, $T_{lm,r}$ in the LM_baseline and $T_{qa,r}$ in the QA_baseline, we search for the best thresholds F1-wise in the range 0.01 to 0.99 with 0.01 increments over the union of training and development sets.

In addition, we train the models that we use in SATORI and the baselines on random samples of 5%, 10% and 20% of the training set corresponding on average to 4, 8, and 16 examples per relation. We also use 100% of the training data. The same percentages are used to sample the development set in each training scenario. Each training scenario is repeated 10 times, and evaluation metrics are averaged. We follow the same strategy to adjust the parameter that we use for pretrained models using the training and development sets. In the following we describe how we train the models.

Language Model. The language model used in SATORI and the LM-baseline (BERT large) is further trained on the masked language model objective using the data from the training set in each scenario. We transform triples in the training and development set into prompts using the per-relation templates $t_{lm,r}$ and train the model to fill in the mask tokens with the corresponding objects. For the masked language modeling training objective, we set the hyper-parameters following [25]. That is, we train the model for 10 epochs, use a learning rate of 5e-6, an a batch size of 32. We save checkpoints at the end of every epoch, considering as the best checkpoint the one with the lowest development set loss.

Entailment Model. An entailment training instance comprises a premise, hypothesis, and a label indicating Entailment or Contradiction. We create entailment training instances as follows. For each triple in the training set we use the text passages retrieved as premises for the subject and relation in the triple. If the subject and object are mentioned in the text passage we generate a positive entailment example using the passage as premise and the hypothesis that we generate using the corresponding template $t_{h,r}$. To generate negative examples, i.e., contradictions, we replace the object in the positive example with an incorrect object, and use a premise retrieved for the input pair where such object is mentioned. To obtain the incorrect object we prompt the language model using the per-relation template $t_{lm,r}$ where we replace the input subject. We keep objects appearing in any of the premises for the input pair, that are not related to the input subject-relation pair in the training set. If we do not find any object from the language model that satisfies the previous condition, we look for incorrect objects in the training set for the same relation.

To train the entailment model, we reuse the classification scripts available in HuggingFace.[17] We use the default hyper-parameters: 3 epochs, learning rate

---

[17] https://github.com/huggingface/transformers/tree/v4.24.0/examples/pytorch/text-classification.

of 2e-5, and maximum sequence length of 128. Due to hardware limitations we use a batch size of 8, and gradient accumulation steps of 4. Particularly, to fine-tune the DeBERTa xlarge model, we reduce further the batch size to 1 and increase gradient accumulation steps to 32, applying gradient checkpointing, and use "Adafactor" optimizer instead of the default "AdamW".

QA-Baseline. A training instance for an extractive QA model includes a question, an answer and a text from where the answer is extracted. To generate training instances we first pre-process the training set and obtain for each subject and relation the complete lists of objects. Next, we get the text passages retrieved as premises for each subject and relation pair. For entries with empty object lists, we use the first retrieved passage and also use the empty gold answer.

If there is only one object for the input subject and relation pair, and there is a text passage where the object appears, we generate a training example with the passage, the question that we generate using the template $t_{qa,r}$ and the object as answer. If there is more than one object for the subject and relation the only way to extract them from a passage using a QA model is if they are arranged as a list of terms in a contiguous text span. Therefore we look for text passages containing every object with the condition that they must be located at most three tokens away from each other. We select the passage with the span containing the highest number of objects, and generate the training example with such passage, the question that we generate using the template $t_{qa,r}$, and the text span where objects appear as answer.

To train the question answering model we leverage HuggingFace scripts[18], and use the default hyper-parameters: batch size of 12, learning rate of 3e-5, 2 training epochs, and a maximum sequence length of 384.

RE-Baseline. Training instances for REBEL consist of a short text, followed by the triples that can be extracted from that text. Triples are described in a REBEL-specific format using special tokens. Relations in triples are indicated using their text descriptions. To transform instances from the LB_KBC22 dataset into REBEL training instances we first obtain for each subject and relation the complete lists of objects. Next, we get the text passages retrieved as premises for each subject and relation pair. If we find a text passage containing some of the objects related to subject and relation pair we create a REBEL training instance with such text, and the triples for the subject, relation and objects found in the text. To train the model we use the script[19] provided by the REBEL authors. We use the default training parameters in the script.

5   Evaluation Results

Table 1 shows evaluation results in the object prediction task for SATORI and baselines using pretrained models and models further trained on the different

---

[18] https://github.com/huggingface/transformers/tree/v4.24.0/examples/pytorch/question-answering.

[19] https://github.com/Babelscape/rebel/blob/main/src/train.py.

training regimes. Note that SATORI is evaluated using different RTE models for triple validation and also using different sources of candidate objects.

5.1 Language Model Prompting and Triple Validation

Let us start with Q1 (does candidate triple validation through textual entailment improve object prediction results over pretrained language model prompting?). We compare SATORI using RTE for triple validation and a pretrained language model as source of candidate objects (Table 1: first three rows in the Pretrained column) against the LM_baseline using only a pretrained language model.

Results show that in such scenario triple validation using any RTE model improves the LM_baseline in all evaluation metrics. The largest gain is in precision, with an improvement that ranges from 14 to 15.5 points depending on the RTE model. Recall is also improved, although to a lesser extent, in the range of 1.9 to 3.2. Improvement in precision shows that triple validation using RTE is effective to filter out non-relevant objects predicted by the language model. Since the system is more precise, the threshold limiting the number of objects predicted per relation $T_{lm,r}$ is actually lower in SATORI than in the LM_baseline. A lower $T_{lm,r}$ allows obtaining more candidates from the language model, thus the improvement on recall. Overall, triple validation using RTE improves over the LM_baseline with a margin ranging between 4.7 and 5.4 F1 points and research question Q1 is therefore satisfactorily addressed.

Table 1. Object prediction using pretrained models vs. such models additionally trained in different scenarios. The models include the LM from where we get objects and the entailment model that we use for triple validation. The SATORI versions evaluated include three sources of candidate objects (Language Model LM, Knowledge Graph KG, Named Entities NER) and three entailment models (DeBERTa xs, BERT large, DeBERTa xl).

SATORI		Pretrained			Training Data											
					5%			10%			20%			100%		
RTE Model	Obj. Source	P	R	F	P	R	F	P	R	F	P	R	F	P	R	F
DeBERTa xs	LM	83.6	48.6	47.9	80.5	51.7	47.9	81.9	51.5	48.4	84.1	51.3	50.3	**91.3**	44.7	46.8
BERT large	LM	82.1	49.9	48.6	79.9	52.2	48.1	81.7	51.8	48.7	84.8	51.2	50.6	89.3	46.0	47.1
DeBERTa xl	LM	83.0	49.5	48.5	82.4	51.9	48.5	**84.3**	52.1	50.1	**87.0**	52.0	51.4	91.1	47.8	48.4
DeBERTa xs	KG+NER	67.7	61.8	55.2	67.0	60.9	52.1	69.5	60.1	52.6	71.0	60.8	53.8	73.5	60.4	54.7
BERT large	KG+NER	67.0	62.9	55.2	68.2	61.8	52.2	70.0	61.1	52.9	69.9	63.0	54.9	66.9	64.8	55.1
DeBERTa xl	KG+NER	70.0	62.5	**55.9**	71.4	62.2	**54.9**	72.6	62.3	**55.1**	70.7	63.6	**56.5**	68.3	64.0	54.8
DeBERTa xs	LM+KG+NER	66.6	62.0	54.4	65.4	61.2	51.5	67.1	60.8	51.8	69.1	61.5	53.4	73.3	60.5	54.6
BERT large	LM+KG+NER	64.5	63.2	54.7	65.7	**62.6**	51.5	68.2	61.6	52.7	68.6	63.5	54.8	67.2	**65.1**	55.7
DeBERTa xl	LM+KG+NER	63.5	**64.3**	53.9	69.4	62.6	54.2	70.6	**63.1**	54.8	69.5	**64.2**	56.5	70.0	64.3	**56.6**
LM-baseline		68.1	46.7	43.2	59.9	50.8	43.3	63.6	49.0	44.3	67.2	49.6	46.9	52.2	48.1	41.4
QA-baseline		67.1	42.3	40.9	54.1	45.2	38.5	57.9	45.4	40.6	57.6	46.5	41.7	57.4	52.7	47.3
RE-baseline		**85.5**	33.3	31.8	**83.8**	41.8	40.6	81.3	43.0	42.0	78.6	44.7	43.2	70.0	54.9	48.2

5.2 Additional Pretraining and Fine-Tuning Scenarios

To address research question Q2 (how do further pretraining the language model and fine-tuning for entailment-based triple validation under different data regimes impact object prediction?) we analyse evaluation results when models are further trained. In Fig. 2c we can see that triple validation using any RTE model improves F1 across all training scenarios compared to LM_baseline. Interestingly the LM_baseline F1 is lower in full training than the pretrained version and the other low data training regimes. Pending further experimentation, this can indicate a case of catastrophic forgetting [15, 28, 38], where, upon further pretraining, language models might lose some of the (in this case, factual) knowledge previously acquired during pretraining.

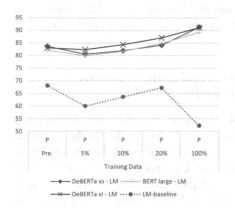

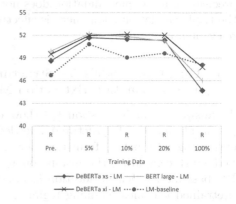

(a) Precision: LM baseline and SATORI using different RTE models and objects from LM.

(b) Recall: LM baseline and SATORI using different RTE models and objects from LM.

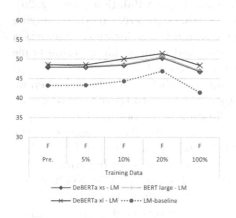

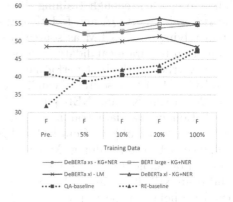

(c) F1: LM baseline and SATORI using different RTE models and objects from LM

(d) F1: best SATORI getting objects from LM, vs. using other knowledge sources and the QA and RE baselines.

Fig. 2. Object prediction evaluation on the LM_KBC22 dataset

The more training data available, the more precise the predicted objects using triple validation are (see Fig. 2a). Triple validation also improves recall, although in a narrower margin, across most training scenarios except in full training (see Fig. 2b). Nevertheless, the use of more training data does not imply an improvement in recall for SATORI. Such recall pattern reflects the higher precision the system achieves when more training data is used. That is, the triple validation filter becomes more and more strict, thus accepting less predicted objects. In low data regimes (5% of the training data) the LM_baseline precision decreases compared to results achieved with pretrained models. However, the precision using triple validation does not fall at the same rate. This shows that the triple validation component is effective in low data regimes to filter out non relevant predicted objects.

5.3   Language Models Vs Structured Knowledge Sources and Information Extraction Methods

To answer research question Q3 (how do language models compare to other potential sources of structured knowledge, as well as to methods based on extracting information from text, for the generation of candidate triples?) we first start comparing the evaluation results of LM_baseline and the QA and RE baselines, which in addition leverage text passages. Table 1 shows that in pretrained and most training regimes, except in full training, the QA and RE baselines achieve worse F1 than retrieving objects from the language models. Nevertheless, in a full training scenario the QA and RE baselines achieve an F1 score that is higher than the one obtained with LM_baseline and similar to the one that we obtained with SATORI, using triple validation (see Fig. 2d). Therefore, when enough training data is available extractive methods relying on state-of-the art QA and Relation Extraction are better for object prediction than relying only on LM as source of objects, and comparable to using triple validation to curate candidate objects retrieved from a LM.

Nevertheless, the best performance in object prediction is achieved when we use KG and NER as source of candidate objects along with triple validation (see Fig. 2d). Using KG and NER plus triple validation is the best option for object prediction in low data training regimes (5%, 10% and 20%). Enhancing the list of candidate objects from KG and NER including objects from LM slightly enhances F1 in full training. Manual inspection shows that in full training, the number of candidate objects obtained from the LM is 794, from the KG it is 2338 and from NER it is 3506. While the number of objects from LM is lower due to the thresholds on the LM score and filters, such objects contribute to slightly increase the overall performance when combined with objects from KG and NER. The large number of objects obtained from KG+NER and the evaluation results shows that triple validation is effective to filter out non-relevant objects. In fact, if we remove the triple validation component and use objects from LM, NER and KG in the full training scenario we get 0.276 precision, 0.761 recall, and 0.327 F1. Such training scenario without triple validation is even worse than the LM_baseline in terms of F1.

6   Conclusions

In this paper we posit that object prediction relying on prompting language models can be enhanced through triple validation using textual entailment. Our experiments show that triple validation provides a boost in object prediction performance using pretrained models and when such models are further fine-tuned under different training regimes. In addition, we compare language models with other sources of knowledge including existing knowledge graphs and relevant text passages where techniques such as named entity recognition NER, question answering QA and relation extraction RE can be applied for object prediction.

We find that in low data regimes, getting objects using language model prompting with or without triple validation is better than using extractive QA and RE models. However in full training the performance of the QA and RE models surpass language model prompting and reach the performance achieved when we validate the triples proposed by the language model. Moreover, using existing knowledge graphs and NER on text passages as source of candidate objects along with triple validation shows the overall best performance when pretrained models and models fine-tuned in low data regimes are evaluated. Adding candidate objects from language models to the ones found on KG and using NER is the best option in full training.

The results presented in this paper are limited to the language model that we use, particularly BERT large, as primary source of candidate objects. Further research is needed to understand whether triple validation will continue having a positive effect in the object prediction task using a language model with a larger number of parameters and if this could balance the current gap between LMs and KGs when it comes to proposing candidate objects that we identified here. As future work, we think Entailment Graphs [10,17] could be useful to get better per-relation templates or to improve the entailment model used in triple validation. In addition, we plan to assess how triple classification [20] compares to textual entailment for triple validation, and whether fact checking techniques [13] applied to triple validation brings new improvements. Finally, another research avenue is to use triple validation along with the QA and RE models given the good results that we obtained in full training when we use them for object prediction.

Supplemental Material Statement: All necessary resources to reproduce the experiments presented in Sect. 5 are available in Github.[20] The repository includes code, templates and text passages that we use as premises in triple validation, and as input in the QA and RE baselines.

Acknowledgement. We are grateful to the European Commission (EU Horizon 2020 EXCELLENT SCIENCE - Research Infrastructure under grant agreement No. 101017501 RELIANCE) and ESA (Contract No. 4000135254/21/NL/GLC/kk FEPOSI) for the support received to carry out this research.

---

[20] https://github.com/expertailab/Textual-Entailment-for-Effective-Triple-Validation-in-Object-Prediction.

References

1. Adel, H., Schütze, H.: Type-aware convolutional neural networks for slot filling. J. Artif. Intell. Res. **66**, 297–339 (2019)
2. Alivanistos, D., Santamaría, S., Cochez, M., Kalo, J., van Krieken, E., Thanapalasingam, T.: Prompting as probing: using language models for knowledge base construction. In: Singhania, S., Nguyen, T.P., Razniewski, S. (eds.) LM-KBC 2022 Knowledge Base Construction from Pre-trained Language Models 2022, pp. 11–34. CEUR Workshop Proceedings, CEUR-WS.org (2022)
3. Balazevic, I., Allen, C., Hospedales, T.: TuckER: tensor factorization for knowledge graph completion. In: Proceedings of the 2019 Conference on Empirical Methods in Natural Language Processing and the 9th International Joint Conference on Natural Language Processing (EMNLP-IJCNLP), Hong Kong, China, pp. 5185–5194. Association for Computational Linguistics (2019). https://doi.org/10.18653/v1/D19-1522. https://aclanthology.org/D19-1522
4. Balog, K.: Populating knowledge bases. In: Balog, K. (ed.) Entity-Oriented Search. TIRS, vol. 39, pp. 189–222. Springer, Cham (2018). https://doi.org/10.1007/978-3-319-93935-3_6
5. Bentivogli, L., Clark, P., Dagan, I., Giampiccolo, D.: The seventh pascal recognizing textual entailment challenge. In: Theory and Applications of Categories (2011)
6. Bordes, A., Usunier, N., Garcia-Duran, A., Weston, J., Yakhnenko, O.: Translating embeddings for modeling multi-relational data. In: Advances in Neural Information Processing Systems, vol. 26. Curran Associates, Inc. (2013). https://papers.nips.cc/paper/2013/hash/1cecc7a77928ca8133fa24680a88d2f9-Abstract.html
7. Bouraoui, Z., Camacho-Collados, J., Schockaert, S.: Inducing relational knowledge from BERT. In: Proceedings of the AAAI Conference on Artificial Intelligence, vol. 34, pp. 7456–7463 (2020)
8. Bowman, S.R., Angeli, G., Potts, C., Manning, C.D.: A large annotated corpus for learning natural language inference. In: Proceedings of the 2015 Conference on Empirical Methods in Natural Language Processing, Lisbon, Portugal, pp. 632–642. Association for Computational Linguistics (2015). https://doi.org/10.18653/v1/D15-1075. https://aclanthology.org/D15-1075
9. Cao, B., et al.: Knowledgeable or educated guess? Revisiting language models as knowledge bases. In: Proceedings of the 59th Annual Meeting of the Association for Computational Linguistics and the 11th International Joint Conference on Natural Language Processing (Volume 1: Long Papers), Online, pp. 1860–1874. Association for Computational Linguistics (2021). https://doi.org/10.18653/v1/2021.acl-long.146. https://aclanthology.org/2021.acl-long.146
10. Chen, Z., Feng, Y., Zhao, D.: Entailment graph learning with textual entailment and soft transitivity. In: Proceedings of the 60th Annual Meeting of the Association for Computational Linguistics (Volume 1: Long Papers), Dublin, Ireland, pp. 5899–5910. Association for Computational Linguistics (2022). https://doi.org/10.18653/v1/2022.acl-long.406. https://aclanthology.org/2022.acl-long.406
11. Dagan, I., Glickman, O., Magnini, B.: The PASCAL recognising textual entailment challenge. In: Quiñonero-Candela, J., Dagan, I., Magnini, B., d'Alché-Buc, F. (eds.) MLCW 2005. LNCS (LNAI), vol. 3944, pp. 177–190. Springer, Heidelberg (2006). https://doi.org/10.1007/11736790_9
12. Galárraga, L., Razniewski, S., Amarilli, A., Suchanek, F.M.: Predicting completeness in knowledge bases. In: Proceedings of the Tenth ACM International Conference on Web Search and Data Mining, WSDM 2017, New York, NY, USA, pp.

375–383. Association for Computing Machinery (2017). https://doi.org/10.1145/3018661.3018739

13. Gerber, D., et al.: Defacto-temporal and multilingual deep fact validation. Web Semant. **35**(P2), 85–101 (2015). https://doi.org/10.1016/j.websem.2015.08.001

14. Getman, J., Ellis, J., Strassel, S., Song, Z., Tracey, J.: Laying the groundwork for knowledge base population: nine years of linguistic resources for TAC KBP. In: Proceedings of the Eleventh International Conference on Language Resources and Evaluation (LREC 2018), Miyazaki, Japan. European Language Resources Association (ELRA) (2018). https://aclanthology.org/L18-1245

15. Goodfellow, I.J., Mirza, M., Da, X., Courville, A.C., Bengio, Y.: An empirical investigation of catastrophic forgetting in gradient-based neural networks. CoRR abs/1312.6211 (2013)

16. Guo, Z., Schlichtkrull, M., Vlachos, A.: A survey on automated fact-checking. Trans. Assoc. Comput. Linguist. **10**, 178–206 (2022). https://doi.org/10.1162/tacl_a_00454

17. Hosseini, M.J., Cohen, S.B., Johnson, M., Steedman, M.: Open-domain contextual link prediction and its complementarity with entailment graphs. In: Findings of the Association for Computational Linguistics: EMNLP 2021, Punta Cana, Dominican Republic, pp. 2790–2802. Association for Computational Linguistics (2021). https://doi.org/10.18653/v1/2021.findings-emnlp.238. https://aclanthology.org/2021.findings-emnlp.238/

18. Huang, L., Sil, A., Ji, H., Florian, R.: Improving slot filling performance with attentive neural networks on dependency structures. In: EMNLP (2017)

19. Huguet Cabot, P.L., Navigli, R.: REBEL: relation extraction by end-to-end language generation. In: Findings of the Association for Computational Linguistics: EMNLP 2021, Punta Cana, Dominican Republic, pp. 2370–2381. Association for Computational Linguistics (2021). https://doi.org/10.18653/v1/2021.findings-emnlp.204. https://aclanthology.org/2021.findings-emnlp.204

20. Jaradeh, M.Y., Singh, K., Stocker, M., Auer, S.: Triple classification for scholarly knowledge graph completion. In: Proceedings of the 11th on Knowledge Capture Conference, pp. 225–232 (2021)

21. Ji, H., Grishman, R.: Knowledge base population: successful approaches and challenges. In: Proceedings of the 49th Annual Meeting of the Association for Computational Linguistics: Human Language Technologies, Portland, Oregon, USA, pp. 1148–1158. Association for Computational Linguistics (2011). https://aclanthology.org/P11-1115

22. Ji, S., Pan, S., Cambria, E., Marttinen, P., Yu, P.S.: A survey on knowledge graphs: representation, acquisition, and applications. IEEE Trans. Neural Netw. Learn. Syst. **33**(2), 494–514 (2022). https://doi.org/10.1109/TNNLS.2021.3070843

23. Kim, J., Choi, K.s.: Unsupervised fact checking by counter-weighted positive and negative evidential paths in a knowledge graph. In: Proceedings of the 28th International Conference on Computational Linguistics, Barcelona, Spain, pp. 1677–1686. International Committee on Computational Linguistics (2020). https://doi.org/10.18653/v1/2020.coling-main.147. https://aclanthology.org/2020.coling-main.147

24. Lewis, M., et al.: BART: denoising sequence-to-sequence pre-training for natural language generation, translation, and comprehension. In: Proceedings of the 58th Annual Meeting of the Association for Computational Linguistics, Online, pp. 7871–7880. Association for Computational Linguistics (2020). https://doi.org/10.18653/v1/2020.acl-main.703. https://aclanthology.org/2020.acl-main.703

25. Li, T., Huang, W., Papasarantopoulos, N., Vougiouklis, P., Pan, J.Z.: Task-specific pre-training and prompt decomposition for knowledge graph population with language models. arXiv abs/2208.12539 (2022)
26. Liu, N.F., Gardner, M., Belinkov, Y., Peters, M.E., Smith, N.A.: Linguistic knowledge and transferability of contextual representations. In: Proceedings of the 2019 Conference of the North American Chapter of the Association for Computational Linguistics: Human Language Technologies, Volume 1 (Long and Short Papers), Minneapolis, Minnesota, pp. 1073–1094. Association for Computational Linguistics (2019). https://doi.org/10.18653/v1/N19-1112. https://aclanthology.org/N19-1112
27. MacCartney, B., Manning, C.D.: Modeling semantic containment and exclusion in natural language inference. In: Proceedings of the 22nd International Conference on Computational Linguistics (Coling 2008), Manchester, UK, pp. 521–528. Coling 2008 Organizing Committee (2008). https://aclanthology.org/C08-1066
28. McCloskey, M., Cohen, N.J.: Catastrophic interference in connectionist networks: the sequential learning problem. In: Psychology of Learning and Motivation, vol. 24, pp. 109–165. Elsevier (1989)
29. Miller, G.A.: Wordnet: a lexical database for english. Commun. ACM **38**(11), 39–41 (1995)
30. Peters, M.E., et al.: Knowledge enhanced contextual word representations. In: Proceedings of the 2019 Conference on Empirical Methods in Natural Language Processing and the 9th International Joint Conference on Natural Language Processing (EMNLP-IJCNLP), pp. 43–54 (2019)
31. Petroni, F., et al.: Language models as knowledge bases? In: Proceedings of the 2019 Conference on Empirical Methods in Natural Language Processing and the 9th International Joint Conference on Natural Language Processing (EMNLP-IJCNLP), Hong Kong, China, pp. 2463–2473. Association for Computational Linguistics (2019). https://doi.org/10.18653/v1/D19-1250. https://aclanthology.org/D19-1250
32. Poerner, N., Waltinger, U., Schütze, H.: E-BERT: efficient-yet-effective entity embeddings for BERT. In: Findings of the Association for Computational Linguistics: EMNLP 2020, pp. 803–818 (2020)
33. Qin, G., Eisner, J.: Learning how to ask: querying LMs with mixtures of soft prompts. In: Proceedings of the 2021 Conference of the North American Chapter of the Association for Computational Linguistics: Human Language Technologies, Online, pp. 5203–5212. Association for Computational Linguistics (2021). https://doi.org/10.18653/v1/2021.naacl-main.410. https://aclanthology.org/2021.naacl-main.410
34. Richardson, K., Hu, H., Moss, L., Sabharwal, A.: Probing natural language inference models through semantic fragments. In: Proceedings of the AAAI Conference on Artificial Intelligence, vol. 34, no. 05, pp. 8713–8721 (2020). https://doi.org/10.1609/aaai.v34i05.6397. https://ojs.aaai.org/index.php/AAAI/article/view/6397
35. Rodrigo, Á., Peñas, A., Verdejo, F.: Overview of the answer validation exercise 2008. In: Peters, C., et al. (eds.) CLEF 2008. LNCS, vol. 5706, pp. 296–313. Springer, Heidelberg (2009). https://doi.org/10.1007/978-3-642-04447-2_35
36. Sainz, O., Gonzalez-Dios, I., Lopez de Lacalle, O., Min, B., Agirre, E.: Textual entailment for event argument extraction: zero- and few-shot with multi-source learning. In: Findings of the Association for Computational Linguistics: NAACL 2022, Seattle, United States, pp. 2439–2455. Association for Computational Linguistics (2022). https://doi.org/10.18653/v1/2022.findings-naacl.187. https://aclanthology.org/2022.findings-naacl.187/

37. Sainz, O., de Lacalle, O.L., Labaka, G., Barrena, A., Agirre, E.: Label verbalization and entailment for effective zero and few-shot relation extraction. arXiv abs/2109.03659 (2021)
38. Serra, J., Suris, D., Miron, M., Karatzoglou, A.: Overcoming catastrophic forgetting with hard attention to the task. In: International Conference on Machine Learning, pp. 4548–4557. PMLR (2018)
39. Shi, B., Weninger, T.: Open-world knowledge graph completion. In: Proceedings of the AAAI Conference on Artificial Intelligence, vol. 32, no. 1 (2018). https://doi.org/10.1609/aaai.v32i1.11535. https://ojs.aaai.org/index.php/AAAI/article/view/11535
40. Shin, T., Razeghi, Y., Logan IV, R.L., Wallace, E., Singh, S.: AutoPrompt: eliciting knowledge from language models with automatically generated prompts. In: Proceedings of the 2020 Conference on Empirical Methods in Natural Language Processing (EMNLP), Online, pp. 4222–4235. Association for Computational Linguistics (2020). https://doi.org/10.18653/v1/2020.emnlp-main.346. https://aclanthology.org/2020.emnlp-main.346
41. Shiralkar, P., Flammini, A., Menczer, F., Ciampaglia, G.L.: Finding streams in knowledge graphs to support fact checking. In: 2017 IEEE International Conference on Data Mining (ICDM), pp. 859–864 (2017). https://doi.org/10.1109/ICDM.2017.105
42. Singhania, S., Nguyen, T.P., Razniewski, S.: LM-KBC: knowledge base construction from pre-trained language models. In: the Semantic Web Challenge on Knowledge Base Construction from Pre-trained Language Models 2022 co-located with the 21st International Semantic Web Conference (ISWC 2022), Hanghzou, China, vol. 3274 (2022). https://ceur-ws.org/Vol-3274/paper1.pdf
43. Speer, R., Chin, J., Havasi, C.: Conceptnet 5.5: an open multilingual graph of general knowledge. In: Thirty-First AAAI Conference on Artificial Intelligence (2017)
44. Surdeanu, M., Ji, H.: Overview of the english slot filling track at the TAC2014 knowledge base population evaluation. In: Proceedings of Text Analysis Conference (TAC 2014) (2014)
45. Syed, Z.H., Röder, M., Ngomo, A.-C.N.: Unsupervised discovery of corroborative paths for fact validation. In: Ghidini, C., et al. (eds.) ISWC 2019. LNCS, vol. 11778, pp. 630–646. Springer, Cham (2019). https://doi.org/10.1007/978-3-030-30793-6_36
46. Syed, Z.H., Röder, M., Ngonga Ngomo, A.C.: Factcheck: validating RDF triples using textual evidence. In: Proceedings of the 27th ACM International Conference on Information and Knowledge Management, CIKM 2018, pp. 1599–1602. Association for Computing Machinery, New York (2018). https://doi.org/10.1145/3269206.3269308
47. Tenney, I., et al.: What do you learn from context? Probing for sentence structure in contextualized word representations. In: International Conference on Learning Representations (2019). https://openreview.net/forum?id=SJzSgnRcKX
48. Thorne, J., Vlachos, A.: Automated fact checking: task formulations, methods and future directions. In: Proceedings of the 27th International Conference on Computational Linguistics, Santa Fe, New Mexico, USA, pp. 3346–3359. Association for Computational Linguistics (2018). https://aclanthology.org/C18-1283
49. Toutanova, K., Chen, D., Pantel, P., Poon, H., Choudhury, P., Gamon, M.: Representing text for joint embedding of text and knowledge bases. In: Proceedings of the 2015 Conference on Empirical Methods in Natural Language Processing, Lisbon, Portugal, pp. 1499–1509. Association for Computational Linguistics (2015). https://doi.org/10.18653/v1/D15-1174. https://aclanthology.org/D15-1174

50. Vrandečić, D., Krötzsch, M.: Wikidata: a free collaborative knowledgebase. Commun. ACM **57**(10), 78–85 (2014)
51. Wang, S., Fang, H., Khabsa, M., Mao, H., Ma, H.: Entailment as Few-Shot Learner (2021). arXiv:2104.14690
52. West, R., Gabrilovich, E., Murphy, K., Sun, S., Gupta, R., Lin, D.: Knowledge base completion via search-based question answering. In: Proceedings of the 23rd International Conference on World Wide Web, WWW 2014, pp. 515–526. Association for Computing Machinery, New York (2014). https://doi.org/10.1145/2566486. 2568032
53. Williams, A., Nangia, N., Bowman, S.: A broad-coverage challenge corpus for sentence understanding through inference. In: Proceedings of the 2018 Conference of the North American Chapter of the Association for Computational Linguistics: Human Language Technologies, Volume 1 (Long Papers), New Orleans, Louisiana, pp. 1112–1122. Association for Computational Linguistics (2018). https://doi.org/ 10.18653/v1/N18-1101. https://aclanthology.org/N18-1101
54. Wu, L., Petroni, F., Josifoski, M., Riedel, S., Zettlemoyer, L.: Scalable zero-shot entity linking with dense entity retrieval. In: Proceedings of the 2020 Conference on Empirical Methods in Natural Language Processing (EMNLP), pp. 6397–6407 (2020)
55. Yao, L., Mao, C., Luo, Y.: KG-BERT: BERT for knowledge graph completion. arXiv preprint arXiv:1909.03193 (2019)
56. Zha, H., Chen, Z., Yan, X.: Inductive Relation Prediction by BERT. In: Proceedings of the First MiniCon Conference (2022). https://aaai-022.virtualchair.net/ poster_aaai7162
57. Zhou, X., Zhang, Y., Cui, L., Huang, D.: Evaluating commonsense in pre-trained language models. In: AAAI (2020)

ASKRL: An Aligned-Spatial Knowledge Representation Learning Framework for Open-World Knowledge Graph

Ziyu Shang[1], Peng Wang[1,2]($\boxtimes$), Yuzhang Liu[1], Jiajun Liu[1], and Wenjun Ke[1,2]

[1] School of Computer Science and Engineering, Southeast University, Nanjing, China
{ziyus1999,yuzhangliu,jiajliu,kewenjun}@seu.edu.cn
[2] Key Laboratory of New Generation Artificial Intelligence Technology and Its Interdisciplinary Applications (Southeast University), Ministry of Education, Nanjing, China
pwang@seu.edu.cn

Abstract. Knowledge representation learning (KRL) aims to project entities and relations in knowledge graphs (KGs) to densely distributed embedding space. As the knowledge base expands, we are often presented with zero-shot entities, often with textual descriptions. Although many closed-world KRL methods have been proposed, most of them focus on connections between entities in the existing KGs. Therefore, they cannot handle zero-shot entities well, resulting in the inability of bringing zero-shot entities to existing KGs. To address this issue, this paper proposes ASKRL, a straightforward yet efficient open-world knowledge representation learning framework. ASKRL learns representations of entities and relations in both structured and semantic spaces, and subsequently aligns the semantic space with the structured space. To begin with, ASKRL employs the off-the-shelf KRL models to derive entity and relation embeddings in the structured embedding space. Afterward, a Transformer-based encoder is applied to obtain contextualized representations of existing entities and relations in semantic space. To introduce structure knowledge of KG into the contextualized representations, ASKRL aligns semantic embedding space to structured embedding space from the perspective of common properties (i.e., angle and length). Additionally, it aligns the output distribution of the score function between the two spaces. To further learn representations of zero-shot entities effectively, a sophisticated three-stage optimization strategy is devised in the training phase. In the inference phase, representations of zero-shot entities can be directly derived from the Transformer-based encoder. ASKRL is plug-and-play, enabling off-the-shelf closed-world KRL models to handle the open-world KGs. Extensive experiments demonstrate that ASKRL significantly outperforms strong baselines in open-world datasets, and the results illuminate that ASKRL is simple and efficient in modeling zero-shot entities.

Keywords: Knowledge Graph · Knowledge Representation Learning · Knowledge Graph Completion

T. R. Payne et al. (Eds.): ISWC 2023, LNCS 14265, pp. 101–120, 2023.
https://doi.org/10.1007/978-3-031-47240-4_6

1   Introduction

In knowledge graphs (KGs) [6,9], entities and relations are organized in a graph structured form. KGs consist of a large number of factual triples (h, r, t), where h and t represent head and tail entities, respectively, and r represents the relationship between h and t. Some large-scale KGs such as DBpedia [1], Freebase [2], and YAGO [20] have been widely used in many applications including natural language understanding [26], question answering [14], and recommender systems [27]. Meanwhile, many knowledge representation learning (KRL) methods [3,11,13,21,24] have been proposed to embed entities and relations into densely low-dimensional spaces.

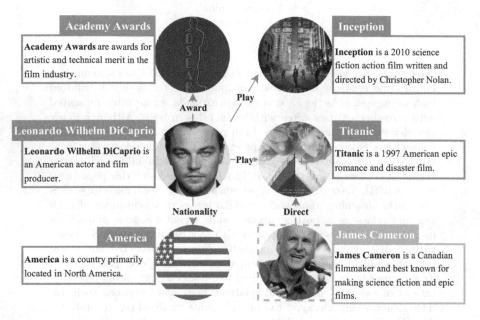

Fig. 1. Open-world knowledge graph examples with entity descriptions. The blue boxes represent in-KG entities and their descriptions, and the pink box represents the zero-shot entity and corresponding description to be added to the existing knowledge base. (Color figure online)

With the development of information extraction [10,30,36], many zero-shot (new) entities, which are out of the pre-defined entity set, have been mined. These zero-shot entities can empower the current KGs to provide more value for downstream applications. However, most of the existing KRL models follow closed-world assumption [16], which means that they can only handle the entities in the pre-defined entity set, and fail to process zero-shot entities. To handle zero-shot entities, the closed-world models must be retrained when zero-shot entities are added to existing KGs. In real-world scenarios, this paradigm is prone to inefficiency. Moreover, it is intractable to model the zero-shot entities with only the entity-self information such as entity name. To effectively process zero-shot entities, it usually needs more extra entity-related information. Fortunately, besides entities and relations, there are many textual descriptions of entities in most KGs. For a zero-shot entity, there is usually descriptive text as well [31]. As the example shown in Fig. 1, entity descriptions are informative, and the previously unseen entity *James Cameron* contains a textual description *James Cameron is a Canadian filmmaker and best known for making science fiction and epic films*. Valuable information is contained in this entity description such as *Canadian filmmaker*, *science fiction* and *epic films* to help to link with the correct entities in KGs, namely (*James Cameron, director, Titanic*). However, such helpful entity descriptions providing further contextual information have not been exploited effectively in existing closed-world KRL models.

To model zero-shot entities, some open-world models exploiting entity descriptions have been proposed. DKRL [31] proposes using CNN to learn knowledge representations with both triples and descriptions. By this design, even though no embeddings have been learned for zero-shot entities, representations of zero-shot entities can be derived from their entity descriptions. Although DKRL can handle the zero-shot entities using entity descriptions, it neglects the noise of descriptions. To alleviate the impact of noisy entity descriptions, Con-Mask [19] proposes a relation-dependent content masking model to extract relevant content segments and then trains a CNN to model the extracted segments with entities in KGs. Despite the success of previous methods, they can only work for specific KRL models (e.g., TransE [3]) and cannot be migrated to other backbone models. To mitigate this problem, OWE [18] proposes an open-world extension for closed-world KRL models. OWE combines a regular closed-world KRL model learned from KGs with a simple word embedding model learned from the descriptions of entities. In OWE, the goal is to learn a mapping function from the textual description representations of entities to the structural representations learned by the closed-world KRL model. Therefore, closed-world KRL models are able to handle the open-world problem with this plug-and-play extension. However, in terms of the choice of the closed-world KRL model, it is not modular but is trained separately and independently from the contextualized representation model, so there may be a problem of error-propagating in OWE. Moreover, OWE attempts to map the word vector embedding space directly to the structural embedding space learned by the close-world KRL model via a linear layer. By mapping the semantic space directly to the structured space, we argue that a significant amount of semantic information is lost. In addition, the simple word embedding model might not be effective to model text descriptions. To deal with this deficiency, Caps-OWKG [29] applies capsule networks to encode entity descriptions better. It can be seen that these open-world models handle zero-shot entities by encoding entity descriptions. However, these models employ static word embedding trained on the domain?specific data, e.g., Wikipedia2Vec [33] is trained on Wikipedia. Therefore, if the zero-shot entities and their corresponding descriptions are derived from other domains, the existing models suffer from the generalization problem.

To address the above issues, we propose a novel Aligned-Spatial Knowledge Representation Learning framework ASKRL. This framework aligns the semantic space with the structural space from two distinct perspectives. The first perspective takes into consideration the common properties of different embedding spaces, i.e., the angle and length, while the second perspective focuses on the output distribution of distinct spaces on KRL. Specifically, ASKRL consists of three layers: a structured embedding layer, a description encoding layer, and an embedding space alignment layer. Firstly, it employs widely-used closed-world KRL models to learn the embeddings of entities and relations in the structured knowledge embedding layer. Then, it applies a Transformer-based model such as BERT [5] to encode the description of entities and relations, and then fine-tunes representations in the description encoding layer. Finally, in the embedding space alignment layer, we align common properties in different embedding spaces in a structure-to-structure manner, while aligning the output distribution of the KRL model on different embedding spaces in a distribution-to-distribution manner. Besides, to effectively learn representations of zero-shot entities, a three-stage optimization strategy is proposed. In the first stage, ASKRL focuses on optimizing the backbone KRL model in the structured embedding layer. In the second stage, ASKRL further optimizes the Transformer-based encoder in the description encoding layer and aligns semantic embedding space to structured embedding space in both structure-to-structure and distribution-to-distribution ways. In the third stage, in order to exploit the potential of the Transformer-based encoder, ASKRL only optimizes the description representation model to learn richer representations from textual descriptions. Because the Transformer-based encoder is usually trained on massive corpora by self-supervised tasks such as masked language model and next sentence prediction [5], they can learn rich prior knowledge within corpora. Thus the proposed ASKRL is more powerful than the previous several open-world models encoding the entity descriptions. Extensive experiments illuminate that ASKRL consistently achieves better performance than strong baseline models in widely-adopted open-world knowledge graph completion datasets. This evidence demonstrates that ASKRL is competent in modeling zero-shot entities.

In summary, our main contributions are twofold: (1) We propose a straightforward yet efficient open-world embedding framework, ASKRL, which proposes a novel approach to align two different embedding spaces to solve the zero-shot entity problem. (2) ASKRL is plug-and-play and can enable most KRL models under the closed-world assumption to be modular and efficient to produce embeddings of the zero-shot entities.

2 Related Work

2.1 Closed-World KRL Models

TransE [3] treats relations as translation operations from head entities to tail entities. It can model inverse and compositional relationship patterns, but it is too simple to handle complex relations such as 1-to-N, N-to-1, and N-to-N. To alleviate this problem, Yang et al. [34] proposed a bilinear diagonal model DistMult to capture the interaction between head entities, relations, and tail entities using the product of corresponding elements. DistMult can model symmetric relational patterns but fails to process the antisymmetric patterns. To solve antisymmetric patterns, Trouillon et al. [24] proposed ComplEx and introduced the concept of complex space to learn the representations of entities and relations in complex space. Liu et al. [13] proposed a triple-level self-attention model to handle the symmetric and antisymmetric patterns. Besides symmetric and antisymmetric patterns, Sun et al. [21] proposed RotatE to model more complex patterns including inversion, and composition. RotatE regards relations as rotations from source to target entities in complex space.

2.2 Open-World KRL Models

In real-world scenarios, entities and relations are constantly added, removed, or changed over time. The unseen added entities cannot be handled by closed-world models. Some open-world models have been proposed to model zero-shot entities. Xie et al. [31] first notice that there are descriptions for most zero-shot entities. To exploit entity descriptions, Xie et al. [31] proposed a model DKRL which employs CNN to encode entity descriptions and learns entity embedding from both entities and their descriptions. In this way, DKRL can model zero-shot entities using entity descriptions. To mitigate the effect of noise in descriptions, Shi et al. [19] proposed ConMask using a relation-dependent content masking mechanism to extract relevant segments and fuse them with entities in KGs by CNN. Recently, OWE [18] trains graph embeddings and text embeddings separately, and then learns the transformation function between the two embedding spaces. Because OWE ignores the unequal nature of different words in entity descriptions, WOWE [37] improves OWE by replacing the average aggregator with an attention mechanism to capture the weights of different words in entity descriptions. Furthermore, Caps-OWKG [29] combines text descriptions and KGs by using capsule networks to capture known and unknown triple features in open-world KGs.

2.3 Inductive KRL Models

The open-world setting emphasizes that the KRL model can deal with entities that are not seen during training, whereas the KRL model in the inductive setting focuses on the ability to leverage knowledge learned from the source KG to the target KG. Specifically, the sets of entities of the target and source KGs are disjoint, while the sets of relations are completely overlapping [22]. Therefore, inductive setting can be considered as a subset of open-world setting. Inductive KRL models can be divided into three main families: external resources-based models, logical rule-based models, and graph neural network-based models. The external resource-based models [4,28] mainly utilize accessible corpus about the target KG to assist in KRL. Logical rule-based methods [7,8] model logical rules with explicit frequent patterns, which are inherently inductive since logical rules are entity-independent. Neural LP [35] and DRUM [17] extract logical rules and confidence that are scored by differentiable rule learners in an end-to-end paradigm. Nevertheless, the neighbor structures surrounding the missing factual triples are ignored by these methods. Representative among the graph neural network-based models are GraIL [22] and SNIR [32], which extract the enclosing subgraphs around the target links to learn entity-independent features to deal with unseen entities.

3   Methodology

3.1   Preliminary

Definition 1. *(Knowledge Graph). A knowledge graph (KG) $\mathcal{G} = \{\mathcal{E}, \mathcal{R}, \mathcal{T}\}$ is defined by the set of entities $\mathcal{E}$, relations $\mathcal{R}$, and triples $\mathcal{T}$. A triple is usually denoted as (h, r, t) $\in \mathcal{T}$, where $h \in \mathcal{E}$, $t \in \mathcal{E}$ and $r \in \mathcal{R}$ denote the head entity, and the tail entity, and the relation between them, respectively.*

Definition 2. *(Closed-World Assumption and Open-World Assumption). For a world $W(\mathcal{E}_W, \mathcal{R}_W)$, closed-world assumption believes that a KG $\mathcal{G}_C$ under the closed world is the closure of the world, which can be formulated as follows:*

$$\mathcal{G}_C = \bigcup_{\mathcal{G}' \in W} \mathcal{G}' \tag{1}$$

where the union is defined on the triple set. And for a KG $\mathcal{G}''$, if $\mathcal{G}'' \neq \mathcal{G}_C$, then $\mathcal{G}''$ is open-world KG under open-world assumption.

Keeping in line with the previous open-world KG setup [18], only new entities are required to appear and the type of relations does not change, i.e., for an open-world KG $\mathcal{G}''$, $\mathcal{E}_{\mathcal{G}''} \nsubseteq \mathcal{E}_{\mathcal{G}_C}$ and $\mathcal{R}_{\mathcal{G}''} \subseteq \mathcal{R}_{\mathcal{G}_C}$.

Definition 3. *(Open-Wrold Knowledge Graph Completion). Given an incomplete open-world Knowledge Graph $\mathcal{G}_O = \{\mathcal{E}_O, \mathcal{R}_O, \mathcal{T}_O\}$, where $\mathcal{E}_O \subset \mathcal{E}_W$ and $\mathcal{R}_O = \mathcal{R}_W$, open-world knowledge graph completion completes $\mathcal{G}_O$ by predicting a set of missing triple $\mathcal{T}' = \{(h, r, t) | (h, r, t) \notin \mathcal{T}_O, h \in \mathcal{E}_W, r \in \mathcal{R}_O, t \in \mathcal{E}_W\}$.*

In this paper, given a triple (h, r, t), h, r, and t represent the head entity, relation, and tail entity, respectively, and $\mathbf{h}_{stru}, \mathbf{r}_{stru}, \mathbf{t}_{stru} \in \mathbb{R}^{d_s}$ denote their corresponding structured embedding vectors. For textual description, we denote the head entity description as $X_h = [x_1^h, x_2^h, ..., x_{|h|}^h]$, where $|h|$ is the description length of all words in the head entity, the tail entity description as $X_t =$

$[x_1^t, x_2^t, ..., x_{|t|}^t]$, where the $|t|$ stands for the length of all words in the tail description, and the relation description as $X_r = [x_1^r, x_2^r, ..., x_{|r|}^r]$, where the $|r|$ stands for the length of all words in the relation description. The $\mathbf{h}_{desc}, \mathbf{r}_{desc}, \mathbf{t}_{desc} \in \mathbb{R}^{d_t}$ denote the description representations of the head entity, relation, and tail entity, respectively.

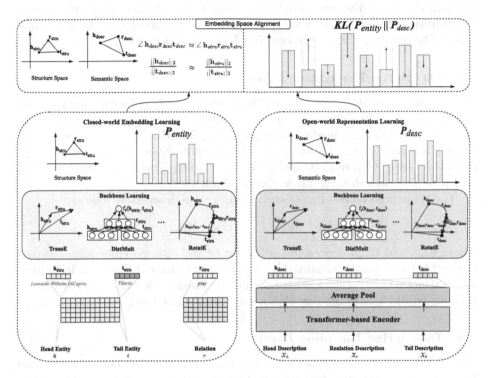

Fig. 2. The generic framework of ASKRL. The lower-left block is the component of closed-world embedding learning. The structured embedding is learned in this phase. The lower-right block is the component of open-world representation learning. The description representation is learned in this phase. The upper block is the component of embedding space alignment.

3.2   Framework Overview

This paper proposes a framework following the open-world assumption, namely ASKRL. There are three layers in ASKRL: the structured embedding layer, the description encoding layer, and the embedding space alignment layer. Firstly, the structured embedding layer is applied to learn embeddings of entities and relations in structured space. Then, the description encoding layer is used to produce embeddings of entities and relations in semantic space by encoding corresponding textual descriptions. Finally, in the embedding space alignment layer, we align the semantic space to the structured space in two steps. Firstly, we align the common properties of the semantic space and the structured space, such as angle and length. Concretely, ASKRL aligns the angle formed between the head, tail embeddings, and the relation embedding in the semantic space with the structured space, as well as aligning the ratio of the lengths of the head and tail embeddings with the structured space. Secondly, based on the score function defined in the structured embedding layer, ASKRL aligns the output distribution of the semantic space with the output distribution of the structured space. The overview framework of ASKRL is depicted in Fig. 2.

3.3   Structured Embedding Layer

The purpose of the structured embedding layer is to project entities and relations in KGs into densely embedding space. The procedure of this layer is similar to most closed-world KRL models. In other words, ASKRL can apply most closed-world KRL models to enable them for the open-world KGs. Specifically, we adopt the widely-used KRL models in this layer, including TransE [3], DistMult [34], ComplEx [21], and RotatE [21] as the backbone model.

The structured embedding of each entity can be learned as follows:

$$\mathbf{E}_{stru}, \mathbf{R}_{stru} = \phi(\mathbf{E}_{init}, \mathbf{R}_{init}) \tag{2}$$

where $\mathbf{E}_{init}$ and $\mathbf{R}_{init}$ denote the initial entity and relation embedding, respectively. They are usually initialized by a uniform initializer or Gaussian initializer, and ϕ denotes the transformation function of closed-world KRL models. In this way, for triple (h, r, t), we can obtain structured embedding $\mathbf{h}_{stru}, \mathbf{r}_{stru}, \mathbf{t}_{stru}$.

3.4   Description Encoding Layer

The description encoding layer aims to learn rich textual semantic information from entity and relation descriptions. In this paper, we apply a Transformer-based encoder [5] to encode the description. More specifically, we first use the Transformer-based encoder to encode the textual description, and then we input each word vector in the description representation obtained by the encoder to the average pooling layer, which can be formulated as follows:

$$\mathbf{E}_{desc} = \text{AvgPool}(\text{Transformer-Enc}([x^{[\text{CLS}]}, X_{h/t}, x^{[\text{SEP}]}]))$$
$$\mathbf{R}_{desc} = \text{AvgPool}(\text{Transformer-Enc}([x^{[\text{CLS}]}, X_r, x^{[\text{SEP}]}])) \tag{3}$$

In this way, for triple (h, r, t), we can get the head entity description representation $\mathbf{h}_{desc}$, the relation description representation $\mathbf{r}_{desc}$, the tail entity description representation $\mathbf{t}_{desc}$.

3.5   Embedding Space Alignment Layer

For KRL, the Transformer-based models usually need to be trained longer than conventional KRL models (e.g., TransE) due to the larger number of model parameters [25]. Moreover, there is a lack of KGs structural information in the contextualized representations of entities and relations obtained by encoding the corresponding descriptions using a textual encoder. Intuitively, the embedding space learned by the conventional KRL model and learned by the text-based encoder is different, the former being the structure space and the latter the semantic space. To introduce graph structure knowledge into the contextualized representations of entities, previous methods attempt to learn the mapping function from the textual description representation space to the structure space by minimizing the L2 norm of the corresponding embedding of the same entity in the transformation space. Nevertheless, it is worth noting that the dimensions of the semantic space and the structure space are often different, and therefore, mapping the semantic space onto the structure space could lead to the loss of significant semantic information. To this end, we propose a new approach to aligning structure embedding space and semantic embedding space in a soft alignment manner, while can accelerate the training of text-based learning. Specifically, we argue that the common properties in different embedding spaces are angle and length [15]. Given triple (h, r, t) in different embedding spaces, we have two objectives: firstly, to minimize the difference in the angles between the head entity, tail entity, and relation in different embedding spaces, and secondly, to minimize the differences in the ratio of the length between the head and tail entity in different embedding spaces. Therefore, in heterogeneous spaces, both the angle and length ratio can measure structural similarity, rather than the absolute replicability. Therefore, the objective of embedding space common property alignment can be expressed as follows:

$$\mathcal{L}_{property} = l_{\mathcal{H}}(f_A(\mathbf{h}_{stru}, \mathbf{r}_{stru}, \mathbf{t}_{stru}), f_A(\mathbf{h}_{desc}, \mathbf{r}_{desc}, \mathbf{t}_{desc})) \\ + l_{\mathcal{H}}(f_{DR}(\mathbf{h}_{stru}, \mathbf{t}_{stru}), f_{DR}(\mathbf{h}_{desc}, \mathbf{t}_{desc})) \tag{4}$$

where $f_A(\mathbf{h}., \mathbf{r}., \mathbf{t}.) = < \frac{\mathbf{h}.-\mathbf{r}.}{||\mathbf{h}.-\mathbf{r}.||_2}, \frac{\mathbf{r}.-\mathbf{t}.}{||\mathbf{r}.-\mathbf{t}.||_2} >$ and $f_{DR}(\mathbf{h}., \mathbf{t}.) = \frac{||\mathbf{h}.||_2}{||\mathbf{t}.||_2}$, $l_{\mathcal{H}}$ is Huber loss which is defined in Eq. 5.

$$l_{\mathcal{H}}(a, b) = \begin{cases} \frac{1}{2}(a-b)^2, & |a-b| \leq 1 \\ |a-b| - \frac{1}{2}, & |a-b| > 1 \end{cases} \tag{5}$$

In addition to the alignment of embedding space common properties, the output distribution of the score function in the semantic space and the output distribution of the score function in the structure space also need to be aligned. Taking the prediction of missing triples $(h, r, ?)$ as an example, we input the Transformer-based contextualized representation and structured embedding corresponding to the candidate entities into the score function $f_{\mathbf{r}}(\cdot, \cdot)$ defined in the structured embedding layer to obtain logits of the candidate entities $\mathbf{P}_{entity}$ and $\mathbf{P}_{desc}$, and then align $\mathbf{P}_{desc}$ to $\mathbf{P}_{entity}$ as follows:

$$\mathcal{L}_{output} = \mathcal{L}_{KL}(\mathbf{P}_{stru} \| \mathbf{P}_{desc}) = \sum_{i=1}^{m} \mathbf{P}_{stru}^i log \frac{\mathbf{P}_{stru}^i}{\mathbf{P}_{desc}^i} \tag{6}$$

where m is the candidate entity size, and $\mathbf{P}^i_{stru}$ and $\mathbf{P}^i_{desc}$ can be defined as follows:

$$\mathbf{P}^i_{stru} = \frac{\exp f_{\mathbf{r}}(\mathbf{h}_{stru}, \mathbf{E}^i_{stru})}{\sum_{j=1}^m \exp f_{\mathbf{r}}(\mathbf{h}_{stru}, \mathbf{E}^j_{stru})}$$

$$\mathbf{P}^i_{desc} = \frac{\exp f_{\mathbf{r}}(\mathbf{h}_{desc}, \mathbf{E}^i_{desc})}{\sum_{j=1}^m \exp f_{\mathbf{r}}(\mathbf{h}_{desc}, \mathbf{E}^j_{desc})} \tag{7}$$

3.6 Training Optimization

Structured Embedding Optimization. We follow the settings of previous closed-world KRL models [21] to optimize the structured embedding layer. We first gather positive triples and build their corresponding negative samples to compute the rank-based hinge loss function. Considering each positive triple (h, r, t), the impact of their negative triples is different. We apply the self-adversarial negative sampling method [21] to measure the impact as follows:

$$p((h'_j, r, t'_j)|(h_i, r_i, t_i)) = \frac{exp(\alpha f_r(\mathbf{h}'_{stru_j}, \mathbf{t}'_{stru_j}))}{\sum_i exp(\alpha f_r(\mathbf{h}'_{stru_i}, \mathbf{t}'_{stru_i}))} \tag{8}$$

where α denotes the temperature coefficient of sampling, $f_r(\mathbf{h}'_{stru_i}, \mathbf{t}'_{stru_i})$ denotes the score of the i-th negative triple in the negative sample candidate set, and $f_r(\mathbf{h}'_{stru_j}, \mathbf{t}'_{stru_j})$ denotes the score of the j-th negative sample. The hinge loss is calculated as follows:

$$\begin{aligned}
\mathcal{L}_{stru} = &-log\ \sigma(\gamma - f_r(\mathbf{h}_{stru}, \mathbf{t}_{stru})) \\
&- \sum_{i=1}^n p(h'_i, r, t'_i) log\ \sigma(f_r(\mathbf{h}'_{stru_i}, \mathbf{t}'_{stru_i}) - \gamma)
\end{aligned} \tag{9}$$

where γ denotes the margin of the hinge loss.

Transformer-Based Encoder Optimization. Similar to the structured embedding optimization, we also adopt the self-adversarial negative sampling to optimize the Transformer-based encoder, as follows:

$$p((h'_j, r, t'_j)|(h_i, r_i, t_i)) = \frac{exp(\alpha f_r(\mathbf{h}'_{desc_j}, \mathbf{t}'_{desc_j}))}{\sum_i exp(\alpha f_r(\mathbf{h}'_{desc_i}, \mathbf{t}'_{desc_i}))} \tag{10}$$

The loss function is calculated as follows:

$$\begin{aligned}
\mathcal{L}_{desc} = &-log\ \sigma(\gamma - f_r(\mathbf{h}_{desc}, \mathbf{t}_{desc})) \\
&- \sum_{i=1}^n p(h'_i, r, t'_i) log\ \sigma(f_r(\mathbf{h}'_{desc_i}, \mathbf{t}'_{desc_i}) - \gamma)
\end{aligned} \tag{11}$$

where γ is the margin of the hinge loss.

3.7   Three-Stage Optimization Strategy

To model the zero-shot entities effectively, this paper proposes a three-stage optimization strategy. In the first stage, ASKRL is trained following the closed-world setting, i.e., only the structured embedding layer is trained in this stage. Specifically, it is optimized only using the structured embedding optimization and the loss is calculated by $\mathcal{L}_{stru}$. The first stage ends when the validation set's MRR score calculated by structured embedding essentially remains unchanged. In the second stage, the Transformer-based encoder is participated in encoding the descriptions of entities and relations via the Transformer-based encoder optimization $\mathcal{L}_{desc}$. It is usually more time-consuming for Transformer-based to fine-tune descriptions than structured embedding layer learning. To alleviate this problem and introduce graph structure knowledge into contextualized representations, we apply the embedding space alignment layer to align the semantic embedding space to the structure embedding space, and the loss in the second stage is calculated by $\mathcal{L}_{property} + \mathcal{L}_{output} + \mathcal{L}_{desc}$. The second stage ends when the validation set's MRR calculation using the text semantic embedding is substantially unaffected. In the third stage, to continuously activate the power of the Transformer-based encoder to encode the description, ASKRL is optimized only by $\mathcal{L}_{desc}$. The third stage finishes until the validation set's MRR calculated with the semantic embedding stays essentially unchanged. In a nutshell, the three-stage training objectives of the ASKRL can be formulated as follows:

$$\mathcal{L} = \begin{cases} \mathcal{L}_{stru} & , \text{FirstStage} \\ \mathcal{L}_{property} + \mathcal{L}_{output} + \mathcal{L}_{desc} & , \text{SecondStage} \\ \mathcal{L}_{desc} & , \text{ThirdStage} \end{cases} \tag{12}$$

4   Experiment

4.1   Datasets and Evaluation Metrics

To evaluate the performance of ASKRL, we conduct experiments on widely-used open-world knowledge graph completion datasets, including FB20k [31], DBPedia50k [19], and FB15k-237-OWE [18]. Particularly, FB20k is built on top of the FB15k [3] dataset by adding triples with new entities, which are selected to have long textual descriptions. DBPedia50k contains approximately 50k entities and is constructed from DBPedia [1]. FB15k-237-OWE is built upon the FB15k-237 [23] dataset, where redundant inverse relations have been removed and new entities with short descriptions are added. The statistics of these datasets are summarized in Table 1. The code of ASKRL and the datasets can be accessed via https://github.com/seukgcode/ASKRL.

We evaluate baselines and our proposed ASKRL in the open-world link prediction task. For a fair comparison, we evaluate the performance of all models on tail prediction following to [18]. We report the MRR (Mean Reciprocal Rank), and Hits@N (the proportion of correct entities ranked in the top N) metrics as most baselines do. Notice that metrics in the main experiment are reported in

Table 1. The statistics of datasets. $|E|$ stands for the entity size, $|R|$ denotes the relation size, $|L_{desc}|$ is the average length of all words in entity descriptions, and $|E^{open}|$ is the set of new entities which are not in KGs. Head Pred. is Head Prediction, and Tail Pred. denotes Tail Prediction.

Dataset	$|R|$	$|E|$	$|E^{open}|$	$|L_{desc}|$	Number of triples				
					Train	Head Pred.		Tail Pred.	
						Valid	Test	Valid	Test
FB20k	1,341	149,04	5,019	147	472,860	1,800	18,753	1,000	11,586
DBPedia50k	351	24,624	3,636	454	32,388	55	2,139	164	4,320
FB15k-237-OWE	235	12,324	2,081	5	242,489	1,539	13,857	9,424	22,393

the target filter setting [19] for a fair comparison with baselines. In the target filter setting, when evaluating a test triple (h, r, t), a candidate tail t' is only included in the ranked result list if the triple $(?, r, t')$ exists in the training data, otherwise, it is removed.

4.2 Baselines

We compare the proposed model ASKRL with the following widely-adopted open-world state-of-the-art models: DKRL [31] uses a two-layer CNN to encode entity descriptions. ConMask [19] employs the relation-dependent content masking mechanism to extract relevant content description segments and applies CNNs to encode the entity descriptions. OWE [18] maps the text-based entity description representation to the pre-trained graph embedding space. WOWE [37] applies the attention mechanism instead of the average aggregator to model entity descriptions. Caps-OWKG [29] uses the capsule network to capture known and unknown triples features in open-world KGs.

4.3 Implementation Details

All experiments are obtained on the single NVIDIA RTX 3090Ti GPU. The hyper-parameters are tuned by grid search and the range of hyper-parameters is set as follows: embedding size $d \in \{300, 400, 500, 600, 1000\}$, the initial learning rate of backbone models: $lr_1 \in \{1e-3, 2e-3, 3e-3, 4e-3, 5e-3\}$, the initial learning rate of Transformer-based encoder: $lr_2 \in \{1e-4, 5e-4, 1e-5, 5e-5\}$, batch size $b \in \{16, 32, 256, 512, 1024\}$, temperature coefficient $\alpha \in \{0.1, 0.5, 1.0\}$, and margin $\gamma \in \{3, 6, 9, 12, 18, 24\}$. There are two types of negative samples in the training process: (1) Other entities within the same batch as negative samples. (2) The current entity as a difficult negative sample, e.g., taking the predicted tail entity (h, r, t) as an example, we consider (h, r, h) as a difficult negative sample. We use the popular library HuggingFace Transformers[1] to load the Transformer-based encoder and fine-tune it. For the default setting, we apply the RotatE as

---

[1] https://github.com/huggingface/transformers.

the KRL model and BERT-base-uncased [5]² as the default Transformer-based encoder. In our experiments, we utilize the textual descriptions of entities that are available in the dataset, while the relation name is considered as the textual description of the corresponding relation. For those entities in the datasets that do not have textual descriptions, we directly use text mentions of their name as the corresponding descriptions.

Table 2. Tail prediction results of baselines models on FB20k, DBPedia50k, and FB15k-237-OWE datasets (with target filter). † stands for results obtained from [18] , and ‡ denotes results retrieved from original papers. The numbers in bold indicate the best performances, whereas the second-best performances are underlined

Model	FB20k				DBPedia50k				FB15k-237-OWE			
	MRR	H@1	H@3	H@10	MRR	H@1	H@3	H@10	MRR	H@1	H@3	H@10
Target Filt. Base. †	27.2	17.5	32.1	41.2	11.0	4.5	9.7	23.0	12.7	6.4	14.2	23.3
DKRL †	–	–	–	67.4	23.0	–	–	40.0	–	–	–	–
ConMask †	53.3	42.3	57.3	71.7	58.4	47.1	64.5	<u>81.0</u>	29.9	21.5	39.9	45.8
OWE ‡	53.1	44.8	57.1	69.1	60.3	51.9	65.2	76.0	40.1	31.6	43.9	56.0
Caps-OWKG ‡	–	–	–	–	59.6	48.8	64.8	75.8	35.2	25.5	39.0	50.8
WOWE ‡	54.1	45.2	58.3	70.0	61.2	<u>52.7</u>	<u>66.5</u>	76.9	40.4	31.9	44.1	56.4
ASKRL-LSTM	<u>56.2</u>	<u>47.3</u>	<u>61.4</u>	<u>75.2</u>	<u>61.3</u>	52.3	<u>66.5</u>	77.9	<u>42.4</u>	<u>33.5</u>	<u>45.9</u>	<u>58.2</u>
ASKRL-BERT$_{base}$	**61.5**	**52.9**	**69.8**	**81.4**	**68.7**	**60.3**	**73.6**	**82.9**	**44.3**	**34.5**	**47.6**	**61.8**

4.4   Main Results

We evaluate models with different settings to provide a multi-perspective analysis. In Table 2, we compute metrics in the target filter setting. We can see that our proposed ASKRL-BERT$_{base}$ achieves new state-of-the-art performance in Table 2. ASKRL-BERT$_{base}$ outperforms all baselines on the FB20k dataset. More specifically, ASKRL-BERT$_{base}$ achieves approximately 7.4% gain to 61.5 on MRR against WOWE. For the DBPedia50k dataset, ASKRL-BERT$_{base}$ achieves approximately 7.5% gain to 68.7 on MRR against WOWE. Besides, we can also find that ASKRL-BERT$_{base}$ achieves a 3.9% gain to 44.3 on MRR than WOWE on the FB15k-237-OWE dataset. Furthermore, to verify whether the performance of ASKRL is brought by the pre-trained language model, we replace BERT$_{base}$ with an LSTM encoder and use 300-dimensional Wiki-pedia2Vec word embedding. The results are reported in Table 2. We can see that ASKRL-LSTM beats most of the baselines except Hits@3 and Hits@10 on the DBPedia50k dataset, which shows the effectiveness of the proposed approach of aligning two different representation spaces by aligning both common properties and the output distribution of the score function. However, compared to on the FB20k and DBPedia50k datasets, using BERT$_{base}$ on the FB15k-237-OWE is not a significant improvement compared to using LSTM. The reason for this can be seen in

---

² https://github.com/google-research/bert.

Table 1, where the average length of all words in entity descriptions for FB15k-237-OWE is 5. Most of the descriptions are even just entity names, which do not contain more additional information that can be used.

Apart from the target filter setting, we also report the metrics in the normal setting (without target filter) on the FB15k-237-OWE dataset in Table 3. We can find that ASKRL-BERT$_{base}$ still consistently achieves better results than the baseline model OWE in the normal setting. Notably, ASKRL-BERT$_{base}$ achieves 4.6% gain than OWE on the MRR, which suggests that ASKRL-BERT$_{base}$ can process zero-shot entities effectively. Besides, the MRR of ASKRL-LSTM is improved by 2.9% compared to OWE, which indicates that the performance of ASKRL is not entirely attributable to the pre-trained Transformer-based encoder.

Table 3. Tail prediction results on the FB15k-237-OWE dataset without target filter. † marks results retrieved from the original paper.

Model	MRR	H@1	H@3	H@10
OWE †	35.2	27.8	38.6	49.1
ASKRL-LSTM	**38.1**	**30.5**	**41.2**	**52.8**
ASKRL-BERT$_{base}$	**39.8**	**31.0**	**43.9**	**57.6**

Table 4. Comparison of ASKRL based on different KRL models on the FB15k-237-OWE (with target filter).

Model	MRR	H@1	H@3	H@10
ASKRL-TransE	38.3	30.6	42.3	53.9
ASKRL-DistMult	39.8	31.2	43.3	55.6
ASKRL-ComplEx	40.3	32.2	43.9	55.6
ASKRL-RotatE	**44.3**	**34.5**	**47.6**	**61.8**

4.5   Results of Ablation Study

Effect of KRL Models. One of our critical insights is to design a plug-and-play strategy that can be seamlessly adapted to diverse KRL methods, such as TransE and RotatE. Specifically, ASKRL encodes the raw entity semantics with a Transformer-based encoder and augments their comparability in the perspective of spatial aspects (angles and length ratios). Such a design can be easily integrated as an auxiliary loss to fine-tune the BERT efficiently. Despite the different geometric suppositions made by different structured-based KRL models, their corresponding output distribution remains generally applicable across the semantic-spatial transformation. Thus, the alignment space mechanism is also applicable. To verify the effectiveness of ASKRL for different KRL models, we conduct experiments on different backbone KRL models. The results are shown in Table 4. It can be seen that ASKRL can be applied to off-the-shelf KRL models with different geometrical assumptions and that the results are slightly different in terms of different backbone KRL models. In general, the performance ranking of KRL models is as follows: RotatE > ComplEx > DisMult > TransE. Our results follow the above rank. In our results, RotatE-based ASKRL achieves the best results.

Table 5. Comparison results of different Transformer-based encoders on FB15k-237-OWE dataset (with target filter).

Encoder	MRR	H@1	H@3	H@10
ASKRL-BERT$_{tiny}$	34.0	27.1	37.6	48.9
ASKRL-BERT$_{small}$	42.5	32.1	45.7	59.5
ASKRL-BERT$_{base}$	44.3	34.5	47.6	61.8
ASKRL-BERT$_{large}$	**44.9**	**35.0**	**47.9**	**62.3**
ASKRL-RoBERTa$_{base}$	**45.3**	**36.2**	**48.5**	**63.8**
ASKRL-RoBERTa$_{large}$	44.7	35.8	47.6	62.7

Effect of Transformer-Base Encoder Models. Furthermore, we conduct experiments on the effect of different Transformer-base encoders on ASKRL. We use two families of Transformer-base encoders, i.e., BERT [5] and RoBERTa [12], with ASKRL. In general, RoBERTa is superior to BERT in terms of the performance of pre-trained language models on downstream tasks [5,12]. The results, shown in Table 5, fit with our common sense. Specifically, ASKRL-RoBERTa$_{base}$ achieves the best MRR in all encoder settings, with a 0.4% improvement compared to the second-best result. However, we find that ASKRL-RoBERTa$_{large}$ does not perform better than ASKRL-RoBERTa$_{base}$. The main reason could be that there are too many parameters in RoBERTa$_{base}$, making it difficult to train to converge to a globally optimal parameter.

Effect of Embedding Space Alignment Layer. To explore the effect of aligning the semantic space to the structure space by aligning the common properties and the output distribution of score function proposed in this paper, we removed the corresponding parts from the default settings of ASKRL. The experimental results are shown in Table 6. After removing the alignment of spatial properties (refer to -$\mathcal{L}_{property}$), the performance of ASKRL drops significantly on all datasets. Concretely, the MRR of ASKRL decreases by 3.1%, 3.2%, and 1.4%

Table 6. Experimental results on the ablation of embedding space alignment layer, where Time refers to the time (hours) required to train the model until the MRR of validation set is essentially unchanged.

Model	FB20k			DBPedia50k			FB15k-237-OWE		
	MRR	H@10	Time	MRR	H@10	Time	MRR	H@10	Time
ASKRL-BERT$_{base}$	61.5	81.4	20.58 h	68.7	82.9	8.97 h	44.3	61.8	15.30 h
-$\mathcal{L}_{property}$	58.4	79.6	20.36 h	65.5	80.9	8.33 h	42.9	59.3	14.62 h
-$\mathcal{L}_{output}$	59.1	80.2	20.49 h	66.8	81.5	8.67 h	43.8	60.6	15.21 h
BERT$_{base}$	50.0	63.8	28.33 h	58.6	70.3	12.90 h	35.8	50.0	19.63 h
BERT$_{large}$	51.3	64.2	35.95 h	59.9	71.6	16.47 h	36.3	51.2	25.71 h

on FB20K, DBPedia50K, and FB15k-237-OWE datasets, respectively, compared to the default setting. Meanwhile, after removing the alignment of output distribution (refer to -$\mathcal{L}_{output}$), the performance degradation of ASKRL is not too significant, which indicates that it is necessary to introduce the common structural information of the triples into the semantic space.

Furthermore, we remove the entire embedding space alignment layer, and then only optimize $\mathcal{L}_{desc}$ (refer to BERT$_{base}$ and BERT$_{large}$). The following conclusions can be drawn: (1) Optimizing solely $\mathcal{L}_{desc}$ results in a significant decline in performance for ASKRL, suggesting that relying solely on features from the semantic space is inadequate for modeling zero-shot entities. (2) There is a substantial difference in training time between BERT$_{base}$ and ASKRL-BERT$_{base}$ in FB20K, DBPedia50k, and FB15k-237-OWE datasets, with the former taking as much as 37.7%, 43.8%, and 28.3% longer than the latter, respectively. This suggests that our proposed embedding space alignment layer can provide a more explicit optimization direction and accelerate the convergence of the Transformer-based encoder.

Effect of the Three-Stage Optimization Strategy. This paper introduces a three-stage optimization strategy to train the model effectively. Each stage includes unique and luminous optimization targets, i,e., structured, semantic, and continual fine-tuning relative to the 1st, 2nd, and 3rd stages, respectively. Meanwhile, such a pipeline training strategy makes ASKRL converge successfully and efficiently. Moreover, the effectiveness of the three-stage optimization strategy has also been validated in the experiments. In the first optimization stage, the structured KRL model is trained to learn representations of entities and relations. After training, the backbone model will learn an experienced prior distribution. In the second optimization stage, the experienced prior distribution is applied to the embedding space alignment, in which the distribution of the Transformer-based encoder is aligned to the experienced prior distribution of the trained structured KRL model. Moreover, the average MRR experiences a decrease of 10.0% without the first and second Stages. This design not only accelerates the convergence of the Transformer-based encoder, but also introduces the knowledge of the KGs structure into the textual encoder. In our experiment, it usually needs to be trained five or more epochs to converge for the Transformer-based encoder without the embedding space alignment layer. In the third optimization stage, the Transformer-based encoder is continuously trained to achieve better performance. In our experiment, there is approximately 0.2% to 0.7% improvement in MRR with the third stage optimization than without it.

Table 7. Case Study: The actual tail prediction results on the FB15k-237-OWE dataset of ASKRL

Test Triples	Head Description	Top-k Predicted Tails
(The Mask of Zorro, /film/film/language, English)	1998 American swashbuckler film	1.English 2.Russian 3.French 4.Spanish 5.United States of America
(Bury My Heart at Wounded Knee, /film/film/language, English)	2007 US TV film	1.English 2.Library of Congress Classification 3.Birdie Kim 4.United States of America 5.French
(Daytona Beach, /base/biblioness /bibs_location/country, United States of America)	city in Florida, United States	1.Library of Congress Classification 2.United States of America 3.actor 4.CE Campos 5.EA Vancouver
(Thomas Jefferson, /influence/influence_node /peers./influence /peer_relationship/peers , John Adams)	3rd President of the United States of America	1.Europe 2.marriage 3.New York University 4.New York City 132.John Adams
(Christopher McDonald, /people/person /spouse_s./people /marriage/type_of_union, marriage)	American actor	1.actor 2.film producer 3.United States of America 4.Warner Bros. 249.marriage

4.6   Case Study

To intuitively explain how ASKRL solves the zero-shot entities, we provide some prediction cases of ASKRL on the FB15k-237-OWE dataset, as shown in Table 7.

Supposed that *The Mask of Zorro* is a zero-shot entity with description *1998 American swashbuckler film*. Because the *The Mask of Zorro* does not belong to the predefined entity set, the entity-based structured backbone model cannot encode it. At this time, ASKRL can encode its description *1998 American swashbuckler film* by the Transformer-based encoder to obtain its embedding. Table 7 shows that the top-1 tail prediction of ASKRL is *English* when the input relation is */film/film/language*, which is equal to the ground-truth tail entity. We can also see that the first three examples show good performance: the ground truth is in the top five predicted results. These actual prediction cases intuitively prove that the proposed model ASKRL is capable of modeling zero-shot entities effectively.

However, we notice that some complicated relations consist of multiple sub-relations in the FB15k-237-OWE dataset. For instance, there are two sub-relations: */people/person/spouse_s* and */people/marriage/type_of_union* in the relation */people/person/spouse_s./people/marriage/type_of_union*. It is still challenging for ASKRL to handle relations with multiple sub-relations, e.g., the fourth and fifth examples.

5   Conclusion

In this paper, we propose a novel model ASKRL to handle the knowledge representation learning of zero-shot entities. For given zero-shot entities, ASKRL uses the Transformer-based encoder to encode their descriptions as input. ASKRL can be a plug-and-play extension for off-the-shelf closed-world KRL models to enable them to handle zero-shot entities. We conduct extensive experiments on widely-used open-world KGC datasets to demonstrate the effectiveness of ASKRL.

References

1. Auer, S., Bizer, C., Kobilarov, G., et al.: Dbpedia: a nucleus for a web of open data. In: Proceedings of the 6th International Semantic Web Conference (2007)
2. Bollacker, K., Evans, C., Paritosh, P., et al.: Freebase: a collaboratively created graph database for structuring human knowledge. In: Proceedings of the 27th ACM SIGMOD International Conference (2008)
3. Bordes, A., Usunier, N., García-Durán, A., et al.: Translating embeddings for modeling multi-relational data. In: Proceedings of the 27th Neural Information Processing Systems (2013)
4. Daza, D., Cochez, M., Groth, P.: Inductive entity representations from text via link prediction. In: Proceedings of the Web Conference 2021 (2021)
5. Devlin, J., Chang, M., Lee, K., et al.: Bert: pre-training of deep bidirectional transformers for language understanding. In: Proceedings of the 2019 Conference of the North American Chapter of the Association for Computational Linguistics (2019)
6. Dong, X.L., Gabrilovich, E., Heitz, G., et al.: Knowledge vault: a web-scale approach to probabilistic knowledge fusion. In: Proceedings of the 20th ACM SIGKDD International Conference (2014)

7. Galárraga, L., Teflioudi, C., Hose, K., Suchanek, F.M.: Fast rule mining in onto-logical knowledge bases with AMIE+. VLDB J. **24**(6), 707–730 (2015)
8. Galárraga, L.A., Teflioudi, C., Hose, K., Suchanek, F.: Amie: association rule min-ing under incomplete evidence in ontological knowledge bases. In: Proceedings of the Web Conference 2013 (2013)
9. Hogan, A., Blomqvist, E., Cochez, M., et al.: Knowledge graphs. ACM Comput. Surv. **54**(4), 1–37 (2021)
10. Li, X., Luo, X., Dong, C., et al.: TDEER: an efficient translating decoding schema for joint extraction of entities and relations. In: Proceedings of the 2021 Conference on Empirical Methods in Natural Language Processing (2021)
11. Li, Z., Liu, H., Zhang, Z., Liu, T., Xiong, N.N.: Learning knowledge graph embed-ding with heterogeneous relation attention networks. IEEE Trans. Neural Netw. Learn. Syst. **33**(8), 3961–3973 (2022)
12. Liu, Y., et al.: Roberta: a robustly optimized BERT pretraining approach. arXiv preprint arXiv:1907.11692 (2019)
13. Liu, Y., Wang, P., Li, Y., et al.: Aprile: attention with pseudo residual connec-tion for knowledge graph embedding. In: Proceedings of the 28th International Conference on Computational Linguistics (2020)
14. Mohammed, S., Shi, P., Lin, J.: Strong baselines for simple question answering over knowledge graphs with and without neural networks. In: Proceedings of the 16th North American Chapter of the Association for Computational Linguistics (2018)
15. Park, W., Kim, D., Lu, Y., Cho, M.: Relational knowledge distillation. In: Proceed-ings of the IEEE/CVF Conference on Computer Vision and Pattern Recognition (2019)
16. Reiter, R.: On closed world data bases. In: Webber, B.L., Nilsson, N.J. (eds.) Readings in Artificial Intelligence, pp. 119–140. Morgan Kaufmann (1981)
17. Sadeghian, A., Armandpour, M., Ding, P., Wang, D.Z.: Drum: end-to-end dif-ferentiable rule mining on knowledge graphs. In: Proceedings of the 33th Neural Information Processing Systems (2019)
18. Shah, H., Villmow, J., Ulges, A., et al.: An open-world extension to knowledge graph completion models. In: Proceedings of the 33rd AAAI Conference on Arti-ficial Intelligence (2019)
19. Shi, B., Weninger, T.: Open-world knowledge graph completion. In: Proceedings of the 32nd AAAI Conference on Artificial Intelligence (2018)
20. Suchanek, F.M., Kasneci, G., Weikum, G.: Yago: a core of semantic knowledge. In: Proceedings of the 16th International Conference on World Wide Web (2007)
21. Sun, Z., Deng, Z., Nie, J., et al.: Rotate: knowledge graph embedding by relational rotation in complex space. In: Proceedings of the 7th International Conference on Learning Representations (2019)
22. Teru, K.K., Denis, E.G., Hamilton, W.L.: Inductive relation prediction by sub-graph reasoning. In: Proceedings of the 37th International Conference on Machine Learning (2020)
23. Toutanova, K., Chen, D., Pantel, P., et al.: Representing text for joint embedding of text and knowledge bases. In: Proceedings of the 2015 Conference on Empirical Methods in Natural Language Processing (2015)
24. Trouillon, T., Welbl, J., Riedel, S., et al.: Complex embeddings for simple link pre-diction. In: Proceedings of the 33nd International Conference on Machine Learning (2016)
25. Wang, B., Shen, T., Long, G., Zhou, T., Wang, Y., Chang, Y.: Structure-augmented text representation learning for efficient knowledge graph completion. In: Proceed-ings of the Web Conference 2021 (2021)

26. Wang, J., Wang, Z., Zhang, D., et al.: Combining knowledge with deep convolutional neural networks for short text classification. In: Proceedings of the 26th International Joint Conference on Artificial Intelligence (2017)
27. Wang, X., He, X., Cao, Y., et al.: KGAT: knowledge graph attention network for recommendation. In: Proceedings of the 25th ACM SIGKDD International Conference (2019)
28. Wang, X., et al.: Kepler: a unified model for knowledge embedding and pre-trained language representation. Trans. Assoc. Comput. Linguist. 9, 176–194 (2021)
29. Wang, Y., Xiao, W.D., Tan, Z., Zhao, X.: Caps-OWKG: a capsule network model for open-world knowledge graph. Int. J. Mach. Learn. Cybern. 12, 1627–1637 (2021)
30. Wei, Z., Su, J., Wang, Y., Tian, Y., et al.: A novel cascade binary tagging framework for relational triple extraction. In: Proceedings of the 58th Annual Meeting of the Association for Computational Linguistics (2020)
31. Xie, R., Liu, Z., Jia, J., et al.: Representation learning of knowledge graphs with entity descriptions. In: Proceedings of the 30th AAAI Conference on Artificial Intelligence (2016)
32. Xu, X., Zhang, P., He, Y., Chao, C., Yan, C.: Subgraph neighboring relations infomax for inductive link prediction on knowledge graphs. In: Proceedings of the Thirty-First International Joint Conference on Artificial Intelligence (2022)
33. Yamada, I., Shindo, H., Takeda, H., Takefuji, Y.: Joint learning of the embedding of words and entities for named entity disambiguation. In: Proceedings of the 20th SIGNLL Conference on Computational Natural Language Learning (2016)
34. Yang, B., Yih, W., He, X., et al.: Embedding entities and relations for learning and inference in knowledge bases. In: Proceedings of the 3rd International Conference on Learning Representations (2015)
35. Yang, F., Yang, Z., Cohen, W.W.: Differentiable learning of logical rules for knowledge base reasoning. In: Proceedings of the 31th Neural Information Processing Systems (2017)
36. Zhong, Z., Chen, D.: A frustratingly easy approach for entity and relation extraction. In: Proceedings of the 2021 Conference of the North American Chapter of the Association for Computational Linguistics (2021)
37. Zhou, Y., Shi, S., Huang, H.: Weighted aggregator for the open-world knowledge graph completion. In: Proceedings of the 6th International Conference of Pioneering Computer Scientists (2020)

Rethinking Uncertainly Missing and Ambiguous Visual Modality in Multi-Modal Entity Alignment

Zhuo Chen[1], Lingbing Guo[1], Yin Fang[1], Yichi Zhang[1], Jiaoyan Chen[4,5], Jeff Z. Pan[6], Yangning Li[7], Huajun Chen[1,2], and Wen Zhang[3(✉)]

[1] College of Computer Science, Zhejiang University, Hangzhou, China
{zhuo.chen,lbguo,fangyin,zhangyichi2022,huajunsir}@zju.edu.cn
[2] Donghai laboratory, Zhoushan, China
[3] School of Software Technology, Zhejiang University, Hangzhou, China
zhang.wen@zju.edu.cn
[4] The University of Manchester, Manchester, UK
jiaoyan.chen@manchester.ac.uk
[5] University of Oxford, Oxford, UK
[6] School of Informatics, The University of Edinburgh, Edinburgh, UK
[7] Shenzhen International Graduate School, Tsinghua University, Shenzhen, China
liyn20@mails.tsinghua.edu.cn
https://knowledge-representation.org/j.z.pan/

Abstract. As a crucial extension of entity alignment (EA), multi-modal entity alignment (MMEA) aims to identify identical entities across disparate knowledge graphs (KGs) by exploiting associated visual information. However, existing MMEA approaches primarily concentrate on the fusion paradigm of multi-modal entity features, while neglecting the challenges presented by the pervasive phenomenon of missing and intrinsic ambiguity of visual images. In this paper, we present a further analysis of visual modality incompleteness, benchmarking latest MMEA models on our proposed dataset MMEA-UMVM, where the types of alignment KGs covering bilingual and monolingual, with standard (non-iterative) and iterative training paradigms to evaluate the model performance. Our research indicates that, in the face of modality incompleteness, models succumb to overfitting the modality noise, and exhibit performance oscillations or declines at high rates of missing modality. This proves that the inclusion of additional multi-modal data can sometimes adversely affect EA. To address these challenges, we introduce UMAEA, a robust multi-modal entity alignment approach designed to tackle uncertainly missing and ambiguous visual modalities. It consistently achieves SOTA performance across all 97 benchmark splits, significantly surpassing existing baselines with limited parameters and time consumption, while effectively alleviating the identified limitations of other models. Our code and benchmark data are available at https://github.com/zjukg/UMAEA.

Keywords: Entity Alignment · Knowledge Graph · Multi-modal Learning · Uncertainly Missing Modality

© The Author(s), under exclusive license to Springer Nature Switzerland AG 2023
T. R. Payne et al. (Eds.): ISWC 2023, LNCS 14265, pp. 121–139, 2023.
https://doi.org/10.1007/978-3-031-47240-4_7

1   Introduction

Recently entity alignment (EA) has attracted wide attention as a crucial task for aggregating knowledge graphs (KGs) from diverse data sources. Multi-modal information, particularly visual images, serves as a vital supplement for entities. However, achieving visual modality completeness always proves challenging for automatically constructed KGs both on the Internet and domain-specific KGs. For instance, in the DBP15K datasets [28] for EA, only a portion of the entities have attached images (e.g., 67.58% in DBP15K$_{JA-EN}$ [21]). This incompleteness is inherent to the DBpedia KG [17], as not every entity possesses an associated image. Furthermore, the intrinsic ambiguity of visual images also impacts the alignment quality. As illustrated in Fig. 1, the movie *THOR* can be represented by a snapshot of the movie (star) poster or an image of the movie title itself. While individuals familiar with the Marvel universe can effortlessly associate these patterns, machines struggle to discern significant visual feature association without the aid of external technologies like OCR and linking knowledge bases [7], posing challenges for alignment tasks. This phenomenon primarily arises from the abstraction of single-modal content, e.g., country-related images could be either national flags, landmarks or maps.

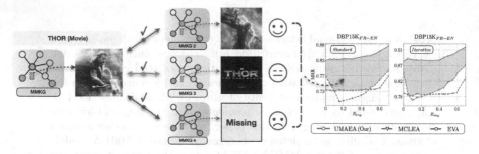

Fig. 1. Phenomenon for missing and ambiguous visual modality in MMEA, where our UMAEA attains superior performance compared to MCLEA [20] and EVA [21].

In this paper, we deliver an in-depth analysis of potential missing visual modality for MMEA. To achieve this, we propose the MMEA-UMVM dataset, which contains seven separate datasets with a total of 97 splits, each with distinct degrees of visual modality incompleteness, and benchmark several latest MMEA models. To ensure a comprehensive comparison, our dataset encompasses bilingual, monolingual, as well as normal and high-degree KG variations, with standard (non-iterative) and iterative training paradigms to evaluate the model performance. The robustness of the models against ambiguous images is discussed by comparing their performance under complete visual modality.

In our analysis, we identify two critical phenomena: (i) Models may succumb to overfitting noise during training, thereby affecting overall performance. (ii)

Models exhibit performance oscillations or even declines at high missing modality rates, indicating that sometimes the additional multi-modal data negatively impacts EA and leads to even worse results than when no visual modality information is used. These findings provide new insights for further exploration in this field. Building upon these observations, we propose our model UMAEA, which alleviates those shortcomings of other models via introducing multi-scale modality hybrid and circularly missing modality imagination. Experiments prove that our model can consistently achieve SOTA results across all benchmark splits with limited parameters and runtime, which supports our perspectives.

2   Related Work

Entity Alignment (EA) [10, 29] is the task of identifying equivalent entities across multiple knowledge graphs (KGs), which can facilitate knowledge integration.

Typical Entity Alignment methods mainly rely on the relational, attribute, and surface (or literal) features of KG entity for alignment. Specifically, symbol logic-based technologies are used [13,24,27] to constrain the EA process via manually defined prior rules (e.g., logical reasoning and lexical matching). Embedding-based methods [29] eschew the ad-hoc heuristics of logic-based approaches, employing learned embedding space similarity measures for rapid alignment decisions. Among these, GNN-based EA models [9,18,23,32,37,38] emphasize local and global structural KG characteristics, primarily utilizing graph neural networks (GNNs) for neighborhood entity feature aggregation. While translation-based EA methods [2,12,31,39,43] use techniques like TransE [1] to capture the pairwise information from relational triples, positing that relations can be modeled as straightforward translations in the vector space.

Multi-Modal Entity Alignment (MMEA) normally leverages visual modality as supplementary information to enhance EA, with each entity accompanied by a related image. Specifically, Chen et al. [4] propose to combine knowledge representations from different modalities, minimizing the distance between holistic embeddings of aligned entities. Liu et al. [21] use a learnable attention weighting scheme to assign varying importance to each modality. Chen et al. [5] incorporate visual features to guide relational feature learning while weighting valuable attributes for alignment. Lin et al. [20] further improve intra-modal learning with contrastive learning. Shi et al. [36] filter out mismatched images with pre-defined ontologies and an image type classifier. Chen et al. [8] dynamically predict the mutual modality weights for entity-level modality fusion and alignment.

These approaches substantiate that visual information indeed contributes positively to EA. However, we notice that all of them are based on two ideal assumptions: (i) Entities and images have a one-to-one correspondence, meaning that a single image sufficiently encapsulates and conveys all the information about an entity. (ii) Images are always available, implying that an entity consistently possesses a corresponding image.

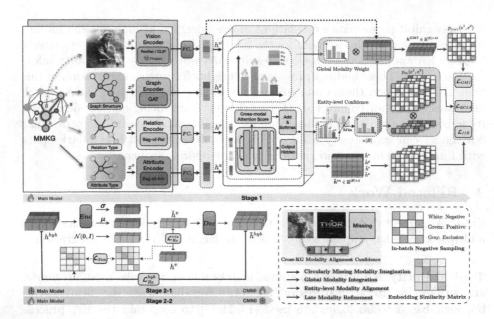

Fig. 2. The overall framework of UMAEA.

In real-world KGs, the noise is an inherent issue. Even for the standard MMEA datasets [4,21,22,28], they are hard to satisfy those two ideal conditions mentioned above. Consequently, we focus on two more pragmatic and demanding issues: (i) In MMKGs, entity images might be missing uncertainly, implying a varying degree of image absence. (ii) In MMKGs, images of the entities could be uncertainly ambiguous, suggesting that a single entity might have heterogeneous visual representations. To tackle these challenges, we present a benchmark consisting of seven datasets on which extensive experiments are conducted, and introduce our model UMAEA against these problems.

Incomplete Multi-modal Learning aims to tackle classification or reconstruction tasks, like multi-modal emotion recognition [44] and cross-modal retrieval [14], by leveraging information from available modalities when one modality is missing (e.g., a tweet may only have images or text content). In multi-modal alignment tasks, missing modality significantly impacts the performance as the symmetry of paired multi-modal data leads to noise accumulation when it is uncertain which side has modality incompleteness, further hindering model training. Prior MMEA studies [5,8,20,21] calculate mean and variance from available visual features, enabling random generation of those incomplete features using a normal distribution. In this paper, we develop an adaptive method for optimal training under the conditions with uncertainly missing or noisy visual modality, meanwhile providing a comprehensive benchmark.

3   Method

3.1   Preliminaries

We define a MMKG as a five-tuple $\mathcal{G}=\{\mathcal{E}, \mathcal{R}, \mathcal{A}, \mathcal{V}, \mathcal{T}\}$, where $\mathcal{E}, \mathcal{R}, \mathcal{A}$ and $\mathcal{V}$ denote the sets of entities, relations, attributes, and images, respectively. $\mathcal{T} \subseteq \mathcal{E} \times \mathcal{R} \times \mathcal{E}$ is the set of relation triples. Given two MMKGs $\mathcal{G}_1 = \{\mathcal{E}_1, \mathcal{R}_1, \mathcal{A}_1, \mathcal{V}_1, \mathcal{T}_1\}$ and $\mathcal{G}_2 = \{\mathcal{E}_2, \mathcal{R}_2, \mathcal{A}_2, \mathcal{V}_2, \mathcal{T}_2\}$, MMEA aims to discern each entity pair (e_i^1, e_i^2), $e_i^1 \in \mathcal{E}_1$, $e_i^2 \in \mathcal{E}_2$ where e_i^1 and e_i^2 correspond to an identical real-world entity e_i. For clarity, we omit the superscript symbol denoting the source KG of an entity in our context, except when explicitly required in statements or formulas. A set of pre-aligned entity pairs is provided, which is proportionally divided into a training set (i.e., seed alignments $\mathcal{S}$) and a testing set $\mathcal{S}_{te}$ based on a given seed alignment ratio (R_{sa}). We denote $\mathcal{M} = \{g, r, a, v\}$ as the set of available modalities. Commonly, in typical KG datasets for MMEA, each entity is associated with multiple attributes and 0 or 1 image, and the proportion (R_{img}) of entities containing images is uncertain (e.g., 67.58% in DBP15K$_{JA\text{-}EN}$ [21]). In this study, in order to facilitate a comprehensive evaluation, dataset MMEA-UMAM is proposed where we define R_{img} as a controlled variable for benchmarking.

3.2   Multi-modal Knowledge Embedding

Graph Structure Embedding. Let $x_i^g \in \mathbb{R}^d$ represent the randomly initialized graph embedding of entity e_i where d is the predetermined hidden dimension. We employ the Graph Attention Network (GAT) [35] with two attention heads and two layers to capture the structural information of $\mathcal{G}$, equipped with a diagonal weight matrix [40] $W_g \in \mathbb{R}^{d \times d}$ for linear transformation. We define $h_i^g = GAT(W_g, M_g; x_i^g)$, where M_g denotes to the graph adjacency matrix.

Relation, Attribute, and Visual Embedding. To mitigate the information contamination arising from blending relation/attribute representations in GNN-like networks [21], we employ separate fully connected layers, parameterized by $W_m \in \mathbb{R}^{d_m \times d}$, for embedding space harmonization via $h_i^m = FC_m(W_m, x_i^m)$, where $m \in \{r, a, v\}$ and r, a, v, represent relation, attribute, visual modalities, respectively. Furthermore, $x_i^m \in \mathbb{R}^{d_m}$ denotes the input feature of entity e_i for the corresponding modality m. We follow Yang et al. [41] to use the bag-of-words features for relation (x^r) and attribute (x^a) representations (see Sect. 4.1 for details). While for the visual modality, we employ a pre-trained (frozen) visual model as the encoder (Enc_v) to obtain the visual embeddings x_i^v for each available image of the entity e_i. For entities without image data, we generate random image features using a normal distribution parameterised by the mean and standard deviation of other available images [5,8,20,21].

3.3 Multi-scale Modality Hybrid

This section describes the detailed architecture of the multi-scale modality hybrid for aligning multi-modal entities between MMKGs. The model comprises three modality alignment modules operating at different scales, each associated with a training objective as depicted in Fig. 2.

Global Modality Integration (GMI) emphasizes global alignment for each multi-modal entity pair, where the multi-modal embeddings for an entity are first concatenated and then aligned using a learnable global weight, allowing the model to adaptively learn the relative quality of each modality across two MMKGs. Let w_m be the global weight for modality m. We formulate the GMI joint embedding h_i^{GMI} for entity e_i as:

$$h_i^{GMI} = \bigoplus_{m \in \mathcal{M}} [w_m h_i^m], \tag{1}$$

where $\bigoplus$ refers to the vector concatenation operation. To enhance model's sensitivity to feature differences between unaligned entities, we introduce a unified entity alignment contrastive learning framework, inspired by Lin et al. [20], to consolidate the training objectives of the modules. For each entity pair (e_i^1, e_i^2) in $\mathcal{S}$, we define $\mathcal{N}_i^{ng} = \{e_j^1 | \forall e_j^1 \in \mathcal{E}_1, j \neq i\} \cup \{e_j^2 | \forall e_j^2 \in \mathcal{E}_2, j \neq i\}$ as its negative entity set. To improve efficiency, we adopt the in-batch negative sampling strategy [6], restricting the sampling scope of $\mathcal{N}_i^{ng}$ to the mini-batch $\mathcal{B}$. Concretely, we define the alignment probability distribution as follows:

$$p_m(e_i^1, e_i^2) = \frac{\gamma_m(e_i^1, e_i^2)}{\gamma_m(e_i^1, e_i^2) + \sum_{e_j \in \mathcal{N}_i^{ng}} \gamma_m(e_i^1, e_j)}, \tag{2}$$

where $\gamma_m(e_i, e_j) = \exp(h_i^{m\top} h_j^m / \tau)$ and τ represents the temperature hyperparameter. To account for the alignment direction of entity pairs in (2), we establish a bi-directional alignment objective as:

$$\mathcal{L}_m = -\mathbb{E}_{i \in \mathcal{B}} \log[p_m(e_i^1, e_i^2) + p_m(e_i^2, e_i^1)]/2, \tag{3}$$

where m denotes a modality or an embedding type. We denote the training objective as $\mathcal{L}_{GMI}$ when the GMI join embedding is used, i.e., $\gamma_{GMI}(e_i, e_j)$ is set to $\exp(h_i^{GMI\top} h_j^{GMI} / \tau)$.

We note that the global adaptive weighting allows the model to capitalize on high-quality modalities while minimizing the impact of low-quality modalities, such as the redundant information within attributes / relations, and noise within images. Concurrently, it ensures the preservation of valuable information to a certain extent, ultimately contributing to the stability of the alignment process.

Entity-Level Modality Alignment aims to perform instance-level modality weighting and alignment, utilizing minimum cross-KG confidence measures from seed alignments to constrain the modality alignment objectives. It allows the model to dynamically assign lower training weights to missing or ambiguous modality information, thereby reducing the risk of encoder misdirection arising from uncertainties. To achieve this, we follow Chen et al. [8] to adapt the vanilla Transformer [34] for two types of sub-layers: the multi-head cross-modal attention (MHCA) block and the fully connected feed-forward networks (FFN).

Specifically, MHCA operates its attention function across N_h parallel heads. The i-th head is parameterized by modally shared matrices $\boldsymbol{W}_q^{(i)}$, $\boldsymbol{W}_k^{(i)}$, $\boldsymbol{W}_v^{(i)}$ $\in \mathbb{R}^{d \times d_h}$, transforming the multi-modal input h^m into modal-aware query $Q_m^{(i)}$, key $K_m^{(i)}$, and value $V_m^{(i)}$ in $\mathbb{R}^{d_h}$ $(d_h = d/N_h)$:

$$Q_m^{(i)}, K_m^{(i)}, V_m^{(i)} = h^m \boldsymbol{W}_q^{(i)}, h^m \boldsymbol{W}_k^{(i)}, h^m \boldsymbol{W}_v^{(i)}. \tag{4}$$

MHCA generates the following output for a given feature of modality m:

$$\text{MHCA}(h^m) = \bigoplus_{i=1}^{N_h} \text{head}_i^m \cdot \boldsymbol{W}o, \tag{5}$$

$$\text{head}_i^m = \sum_{j \in \mathcal{M}} \beta_{mj}^{(i)} V_j^{(i)}, \tag{6}$$

where $\boldsymbol{W}_o \in \mathbb{R}^{d \times d}$. The attention weight (β_{mj}) between an entity's modality m and j in each head is calculated as:

$$\beta_{mj} = \frac{\exp(Q_m^\top K_j / \sqrt{d_h})}{\sum_{i \in \mathcal{M}} \exp(Q_m^\top K_i / \sqrt{d_h})}. \tag{7}$$

Besides, layer normalization (LN) and residual connection (RC) are incorporated to stabilize training:

$$\hat{h}^m = LayerNorm(\text{MHCA}(h^m) + h^m). \tag{8}$$

The FFN consists of two linear transformation layers and a ReLU activation function with LN and RC applied afterwards:

$$\text{FFN}(\hat{h}^m) = ReLU(\hat{h}^m \boldsymbol{W}_1 + b_1)\boldsymbol{W}_2 + b_2, \tag{9}$$

$$\hat{h}^m \leftarrow LayerNorm(\text{FFN}(\hat{h}^m) + \hat{h}^m), \tag{10}$$

where $\boldsymbol{W}_1 \in \mathbb{R}^{d \times d_{in}}$ and $\boldsymbol{W}_2 \in \mathbb{R}^{d_{in} \times d}$. Notably, we define the entity-level confidence $\tilde{w}^m$ for each modality m as:

$$\tilde{w}^m = \frac{\exp(\sum_{j \in \mathcal{M}} \sum_{i=0}^{N_h} \beta_{mj}^{(i)} / \sqrt{|\mathcal{M}| \times N_h})}{\sum_{k \in \mathcal{M}} \exp(\sum_{j \in \mathcal{M}} \sum_{i=0}^{N_h} \beta_{kj}^{(i)} \sqrt{|\mathcal{M}| \times N_h})}, \tag{11}$$

which captures crucial inter-modal interface information and adaptively adjusts model's cross-KG alignment confidence for different modalities from each entity. To facilitate learning these dynamic confidences and incorporating them into the training process, we devise two distinct training objectives: $\mathcal{L}_{ECIA}$ and $\mathcal{L}_{IIR}$. The first objective is *explicit confidence-augmented intra-modal alignment*

(ECIA), while the second is *implicit inter-modal refinement* (IIR), which will be discussed in the following subsection. For the ECIA, we design the following training target which is the variation of Eq. (3):

$$\mathcal{L}_{ECIA} = \sum_{m \in \mathcal{M}} \widetilde{\mathcal{L}}_m \,, \tag{12}$$

$$\widetilde{\mathcal{L}}_m = -\mathbb{E}_{i \in \mathcal{B}} \log[\,\phi_m(e_i^1, e_i^2) * (p_m(e_i^1, e_i^2) + p_m(e_i^2, e_i^1))\,]/2 \,. \tag{13}$$

Considering the symmetric nature of EA and the varying quality of aligned entities and their modality features within each KG, we employ the minimum confidence value to minimize errors. For example, e_i^1 may possess high-quality image data while e_i^2 lacks image information, as illustrated in Fig. 1. In such cases, using the original objective for feature alignment will inadvertently align meaningful features with random noise, thereby disrupting the encoder training process. To mitigate this issue, we define $\phi_m(e_i^1, e_i^2)$ as the minimum confidence value for entities e_i^1 and e_i^2 in modality m, calculated by $\phi_m(e_i, e_j) = Min(\tilde{w}_i^m, \tilde{w}_j^m)$.

Late Modality Refinement leverages the transformer layer outputs to further enhance the entity-level adaptive modality alignment through an *implicit inter-modal refinement* (IIR) objective, enabling the refinement of attention scores by directly aligning the output hidden states. Concretely, we define the hidden state embedding of modality m for entity e_i as $\hat{h}^m$, following Eq. (10). We define:

$$\mathcal{L}_{IIR} = \sum_{m \in \mathcal{M}} \widehat{\mathcal{L}}_m \,, \tag{14}$$

where $\widehat{\mathcal{L}}_m$ is also a variant of $\mathcal{L}_m$, as illustrated in Eq. (3), with only the following modification: $\hat{\gamma}_m(e_i, e_j) = \exp(\hat{h}_i^{m\top} \hat{h}_j^m / \tau)$.

As depicted in Fig. 2, we designate the entire process so far as the first stage of our (main) model, with the training objective formulated as:

$$\mathcal{L}_1 = \mathcal{L}_{GMI} + \mathcal{L}_{ECIA} + \mathcal{L}_{IIR} \,. \tag{15}$$

3.4   Circularly Missing Modality Imagination

Note that our primary target of the first stage is to alleviate the impact of modality noise and incompleteness on the alignment process throughout training. Conversely, the second stage draws inspiration from VAE [15,26] and CycleGAN [45], which accentuates generative modeling and unsupervised domain translation. Expanding upon these ideas, we develop our circularly missing modality imagination (CMMI) module, aiming to enable the model to proactively complete missing modality information.

To reach our goal, we develop a variational multi-modal autoencoder framework, allowing the hidden layer output between the encoder MLP_{Enc} and decoder MLP_{Dec} (parameterized by $\boldsymbol{W}_{Enc} \in \mathbb{R}^{3d \times 2d}$ and $\boldsymbol{W}_{Dec} \in \mathbb{R}^{d \times 3d}$, respectively) to act as an imagined pseudo-visual feature $\bar{h}_i^v$, using reparameterization strategy [15] with tri-modal hybrid feature $h_i^{hyb} = [h_i^r \oplus h_i^a \oplus h_i^g]$ as the input:

$$[\mu_i \oplus \log(\sigma_i)^2] = MLP_{Enc}(h_i^{hyb}), \tag{16}$$

$$\bar{h}_i^v = z \odot \sigma_i + \mu_i, \quad z \sim \mathcal{N}(\mathbf{0}, \mathbf{I}), \tag{17}$$

$$\bar{h}_i^{hyb} = MLP_{Dec}(\bar{h}_i^v). \tag{18}$$

Concretely, two reconstruction objectives $\mathcal{L}_{Re}^{vis}$ and $\mathcal{L}_{Re}^{hyb}$ are utilized to minimize $|h_i^{hyb} - \bar{h}_i^{hyb}|$ and $|h_i^v - \bar{h}_i^v|$, where h_i^v represents the real image feature. Besides, we adhere to the standard VAE algorithm [15] to regularize the latent space by encouraging it to be similar to a Gaussian distribution through minimizing the Kullback-Leibler (KL) divergence:

$$\mathcal{L}_{KL} = \mathbb{E}_{i \in \bar{\mathcal{B}}}((\mu_i)^2 + (\sigma_i)^2 - \log(\sigma_i)^2 - 1)/2, \tag{19}$$

where $\bar{\mathcal{B}}$ refers to those entities with complete images within a mini-batch.

Furthermore, we exploit the internal embedding similarity matrix obtained from the hybrid embeddings h^{hyb}, and distill this information into the virtual image feature similarity matrix based on $\bar{h}^v$:

$$\mathcal{L}_{Sim} = \mathbb{E}_{i \in \bar{\mathcal{B}}} D_{KL}(p_{hyb}(e_i^1, e_i^2) || \bar{p}_v(e_i^1, e_i^2)), \tag{20}$$

where p_{hyb} and $\bar{p}_v$ all follow Eq. (2) with $\gamma_{hyb}(e_i, e_j) = \exp(h_i^{hyb\top} h_j^{hyb}/\tau)$ and $\bar{\gamma}_v(e_i, e_j) = \exp(\bar{h}_i^{v\top} \bar{h}_j^v/\tau)$. This strategy not only curbs the overfitting of visible visual modalities in the autoencoding process, but also emphasizes the differences between distinct characteristics. Crucially, the knowledge mapping of original tri-modal hybrid features to the visual space is maximally preserved, thereby mitigating modal collapse when most of the visual content is missing and the noise is involved. The final loss in stage two is formulated as:

$$\mathcal{L}_2 = \mathcal{L}_{KL} + \mathcal{L}_{Re}^{vis} + \mathcal{L}_{Re}^{hyb} + \mathcal{L}_{Sim}. \tag{21}$$

3.5   Training Details

Pipeline. As previously mentioned, the training process consists of two stages. In the first stage, the primary model components are trained independently, while in the second stage, the CMMI module is additionally incorporated. The training objective $\mathcal{L}$ is defined as follows:

$$Stage\ 1 : \mathcal{L} \leftarrow \mathcal{L}_1, \tag{22}$$

$$Stage\ 2\text{-}1/2\text{-}2 : \mathcal{L} \leftarrow \mathcal{L}_1 + \mathcal{L}_2, \tag{23}$$

where the second stage is further divided into two sub-stages. Concretely, in order to stabilize model training and avoid knowledge forgetting caused by the cold-start of module insertion [42], as shown in Fig. 2, the models from stage 1 (i.e., main model) are frozen to facilitate CMMI training when entering stage 2-1. While in stage 2-2, the CMMI is frozen and the main model undergoes further refinement to establish the entire pipeline. This process is easy to implement, just by switching the range of learnable parameters during model training.

Entity Representation. During evaluation, we replace the original random vectors with the generated μ_i for those entities without images. While in the second training stage, we employ the pseudo-visual embedding $\bar{h}_i^v$ (rather than μ_i) as a substitute as we observe that actively introducing noise during training could introduce randomness and uncertainty into the reconstruction process, which has been demonstrated to be beneficial in learning sophisticated distributions and enhances the model's robustness [16]. Furthermore, we select h_i^{GMI}, as formulated in Eq. (1), for the final multi-modal entity representation.

4   Experiment

4.1   Experiment Setup

To guarantee a fair assessment, we use a total of seven MMEA datasets derived from three major categories (bilingual, monolingual, and high-degree), with two representative pre-trained visual encoders (ResNet-152 [11] and CLIP [25]), and evaluated the performance of four models under two distinct settings (standard (non-iterative) and iterative). In this research, we intentionally set aside the surface modality (literal information) to focus on understanding the effects of absent visual modality on model performance.

Datasets. DBP15K [28] contains three datasets ($R_{sa} = 0.3$) built from the multilingual versions of DBpedia, including DBP15K$_{ZH\text{-}EN}$, DBP15K$_{JA\text{-}EN}$ and DBP15K$_{FR\text{-}EN}$. We adopt their multi-model variants [21] with entity-matched images attached. Besides, four Multi-OpenEA datasets ($R_{sa} = 0.2$) [19] are used, which are the multi-modal variants of the OpenEA benchmarks [33] with entity images achieved by searching the entity names through the Google search engine. We include two bilingual datasets { EN-FR-15K, EN-DE-15K } and two monolingual datasets { D-W-15K-V1, D-W-15K-V2 }, where V1 and V2 denote two versions with distinct average relation degrees. To create our **MMEA-UMVM** (uncertainly missing visual modality) datasets, we perform random image dropping on MMEA datasets. Specifically, we randomly discard entity images to achieve varying degrees of visual modality missing, ranging from 0.05 to the maximum R_{img} of the raw datasets with a step of 0.05 or 0.1. Finally, we get a total number of 97 data split. See appendix[1] for more details.

Iterative Training. Following Lin et al. [20], we adopt a probation technique for iterative training. The probation can be viewed as a buffering mechanism, which maintains a temporary cache to store cross-graph mutual nearest entity pairs from the testing set. Concretely, every K_e (where $K_e = 5$) epochs, we propose cross-KG entity pairs that are mutual nearest neighbors in the vector space and add them to a candidate list $\mathcal{N}^{cd}$. Furthermore, an entity pair in $\mathcal{N}^{cd}$ will be added into the training set if it remains a mutual nearest neighbour for K_s ($= 10$) consecutive rounds.

---

[1] The appendix is attached with the arXiv version of this paper.

Baselines. Six prominent EA algorithms proposed in recent years are selected as our baseline comparisons, excluding the surface information for a parallel evaluation. We further collect 3 latest MMEA methods as the strong baselines, including EVA [21], MSNEA [5], and MCLEA [20]. Particularly, we reproduce them with their original pipelines unchanged in our benchmark.

Table 1. Non-iterative results of four models with "w/o CMMI" setting indicating the absence of the stage-2. The best results within the baselines are marked with underline, and we highlight our results with **bold** when we achieve SOTA

Models	$R_{img} = 0.05$			$R_{img} = 0.2$			$R_{img} = 0.4$			$R_{img} = 0.6$		
	H@1	H@10	MRR	H@1	H@10	MRR	H@1	H@10	MRR	H@1	H@10	MRR
DBP15K$_{ZH-EN}$												
MSNEA [5]	.413	.722	.517	.411	.725	.518	.446	.743	.546	.520	.786	.611
EVA [21]	.623	.878	.715	.624	.878	.716	.623	.875	.714	.625	.876	.717
MCLEA [20]	.638	.905	.732	.588	.865	.686	.611	.874	.704	.661	.896	.744
w/o CMMI	.703	.934	.787	.710	.937	.793	.721	.939	.801	.753	.949	.825
UMAEA	.720	.938	.800	.727	.941	.806	.727	.941	.806	.758	.951	.829
Improve ↑	8.2%	3.3%	.068	10.3%	6.3%	.090	10.4%	6.6%	.092	9.7%	5.5%	.085
DBP15K$_{JA-EN}$												
MSNEA [5]	.313	.643	.425	.311	.644	.422	.369	.678	.472	.480	.744	.569
EVA [21]	.615	.877	.708	.616	.877	.710	.616	.878	.711	.624	.881	.716
MCLEA [20]	.599	.897	.706	.579	.846	.675	.613	.867	.703	.686	.898	.761
w/o CMMI	.708	.943	.794	.712	.947	.798	.730	.950	.810	.772	.962	.843
UMAEA	.725	.949	.807	.726	.949	.808	.732	.952	.813	.775	.963	.845
Improve ↑	11.0%	5.2%	.099	11.0%	7.2%	.098	11.6%	7.4%	.102	8.9%	6.5%	.084
DBP15K$_{FR-EN}$												
MSNEA [5]	.297	.690	.427	.304	.690	.428	.360	.710	.474	.478	.772	.574
EVA [21]	.624	.895	.720	.624	.895	.720	.626	.898	.721	.634	.900	.728
MCLEA [20]	.634	.930	.741	.582	.863	.682	.601	.879	.702	.675	.901	.757
w/o CMMI	.727	.956	.813	.733	.960	.817	.746	.961	.828	.790	.968	.857
UMAEA	.752	.970	.830	.755	.960	.832	.763	.962	.838	.792	.970	.859
Improve ↑	11.8%	4.0%	.089	13.1%	6.7%	.112	13.7%	6.4%	.117	11.7%	6.9%	.102
OpenEA$_{EN-FR}$												
MSNEA [5]	.200	.431	.278	.213	.439	.290	.260	.477	.334	.360	.560	.427
EVA [21]	.528	.833	.634	.533	.835	.638	.539	.835	.642	.547	.830	.647
MCLEA [20]	.545	.852	.653	.547	.852	.655	.531	.839	.637	.597	.852	.688
w/o CMMI	.587	.893	.695	.590	.893	.697	.614	.900	.715	.664	.912	.753
UMAEA	.605	.898	.708	.604	.896	.708	.618	.899	.718	.665	.914	.753
Improve ↑	6.0%	4.6%	.055	5.7%	4.4%	.053	7.9%	6.1%	.076	6.8%	6.2%	.065
OpenEA$_{EN-DE}$												
MSNEA [5]	.242	.486	.323	.253	.495	.333	.309	.542	.387	.412	.622	.484
EVA [21]	.717	.917	.787	.718	.918	.788	.721	.920	.791	.734	.921	.800
MCLEA [20]	.723	.918	.791	.721	.915	.789	.697	.907	.771	.745	.906	.803
w/o CMMI	.752	.938	.818	.757	.941	.822	.771	.946	.833	.804	.954	.858
UMAEA	.757	.942	.823	.759	.943	.824	.774	.947	.835	.804	.957	.860
Improve ↑	3.4%	2.4%	.032	3.8%	2.5%	.035	5.3%	2.7%	.044	5.9%	3.6%	.057
OpenEA$_{D-W-V1}$												
MSNEA [5]	.238	.452	.31	.254	.465	.326	.318	.514	.385	.432	.601	.490
EVA [21]	.570	.801	.653	.575	.806	.658	.567	.797	.650	.595	.811	.673
MCLEA [20]	.585	.834	.675	.574	.824	.663	.581	.813	.665	.655	.848	.726
w/o CMMI	.640	.879	.727	.644	.882	.730	.667	.891	.749	.722	.908	.790
UMAEA	.647	.881	.733	.649	.882	.735	.669	.892	.750	.724	.908	.791
Improve ↑	6.2%	4.7%	.058	7.4%	5.8%	.072	8.8%	7.9%	.085	6.9%	6.0%	.065
OpenEA$_{D-W-V2}$												
MSNEA [5]	.397	.690	.497	.405	.695	.503	.454	.727	.546	.545	.781	.626
EVA [21]	.775	.952	.839	.767	.947	.832	.773	.950	.837	.788	.954	.848
MCLEA [20]	.771	.965	.842	.753	.957	.827	.757	.935	.822	.800	.948	.855
w/o CMMI	.828	.983	.883	.829	.982	.885	.844	.984	.896	.857	.986	.905
UMAEA	.840	.984	.890	.832	.982	.887	.844	.984	.896	.859	.987	.905
Improve ↑	6.5%	1.9%	.048	6.5%	2.5%	.055	7.1%	3.4%	.059	5.9%	3.3%	.050

Implementation Details. To ensure fairness, we consistently reproduce or implement all methods with the following settings: (i) The hidden layer dimensions d for all networks are unified into 300. The total epochs for baselines are set to 500 with an optional iterative training strategy applied for another 500 epochs, following [20]. Training strategies including cosine warm-up schedule (15% steps for LR warm-up), early stopping, and gradient accumulation are adopted. The AdamW optimizer ($\beta_1 = 0.9$, $\beta_2 = 0.999$) is used, with a fixed batch size of 3500. (ii) To demonstrate model stability, following [4,20], the vision encoders Enc_v are set to ResNet-152 [11] on DBP15K where the vision feature dimension d_v is 2048, and set to CLIP [25] on Multi-OpenEA with $d_v = 512$. (iii) An alignment editing method is employed to reduce the error accumulation [30]. (iv) Following Yang et al. [41], Bag-of-Words (BoW) is selected for encoding relations (x^r) and attributes (x^a) as fixed-length (i.e., $d_r = d_a = 1000$) vectors. Specially, we firstly sort relations/attributes across KGs by frequencies in descending order. At rank d_r/d_a, we truncated or padded the list to discard the long-tail relations/attributes and obtain fixed-length all-zero vectors x^r and x^a. For entity e_i: if it includes any of the top-k attributes, the corresponding position in x_i^a is set to 1; if a relation of e_i is among the top-k, the corresponding position in x_i^r is incremented by 1.

In our UMAEA model, τ is set to 0.1 which determines how much attention the contrast loss pays to difficult negative samples. Besides, the head number N_h in MHCA is set to 1, and the training epochs are set to {250, 50, 100} for stage 1, 2-1, 2-2, respectively. Despite potential performance variations resulting from parameter searching, our focus remained on achieving broad applicability rather than fine-tuning for specific datasets. During iterative training, the pipeline is repeated; but the expansion of the training set occurs exclusively in stage 1. For MSNEA, we eliminate the attribute values for input consistency, and extend MSNEA with iterative training capability. All experiments are conducted on RTX 3090Ti GPUs.

4.2 Overall Results

Uncertainly Missing Modality. Our primary experiment focuses on the model performances with varying missing modality proportions R_{img}. In Table 1, we select four representative proportions: $R_{img} \in \{0.05, 0.2, 0.4, 0.6\} \times 100\%$ to simulate the degree of uncertainly missing modality that may exist in real-world scenarios, and evaluate the robustness of different models. Our UMAEA demonstrates stable improvement on the DBP15K datasets across different R_{img} values in comparison to the top-performing benchmark model: 10.3% ($R_{img} = 0.05$), 11.6% ($R_{img} = 0.2$), 11.9% ($R_{img} = 0.4$), and 10.3% ($R_{img} = 0.6$). We note that it exhibits the most significant improvement when the R_{img} lies between 20% and 40%. For the Multi-OpenEA datasets, our average improvement is: 5.5% ($R_{img} = 0.05$), 5.9% ($R_{img} = 0.2$), 7.3% ($R_{img} = 0.4$), and 6.4% ($R_{img} = 0.6$). Although the improvement is slightly lower than in DBP15K, the overall advantage range remains consistent, aligning with our motivation. Besides, Fig. 3 visualizes performance variation curves for three models. The overall performance trend fits the conclusions drawn in Table 1, showing that our method outperforms the baseline in terms of significant performance gap, regardless of whether iterative or non-iterative learning is employed.

Additionally, we notice a phenomenon that existing models exhibit performance oscillations (EVA) or even declines (MCLEA) at higher modality missing rates. This kind of adverse effect peaks within a particular R_{img}^1 range and gradually recovers and gains benefits as R_{img} rises to a certain level R_{img}^2. In other words, when $0 \leq R_{img} \leq R_{img}^2$, the additional multi-modal data negatively impacts EA. This observation seems counterintuitive since providing more information leads to side effects, but it is also logical. Introducing images for half of the entities means that the remaining half may become noise, which calls for a necessary trade-off. Under the standard (non-iterative) setting, MCLEA's R_{img}^2 averages 63.6%, which is 57.14% for MSNEA and 46.43% for EVA across seven datasets. Our method, augmented with the CMMI module, reaches 20.71% for R_{img}^2. Even without CMMI, the R_{img}^2 of UMAEA remains at 34.29%. This implies that our method can gain benefits with fewer visual modality data in entity. Meanwhile, UMAEA exhibits less oscillation and greater robustness than other methods, as further evidenced by the entity distribution analysis in Sect. 4.3.

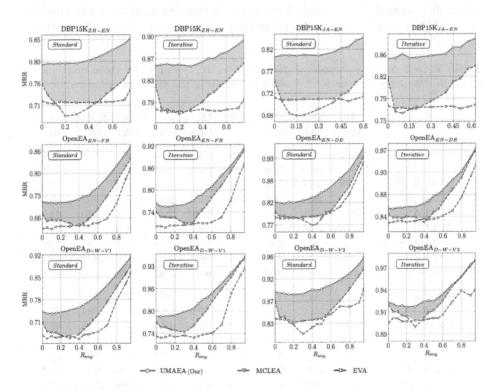

Fig. 3. The overall standard (non-iterative) and iterative model performance under the setting of uncertainly missing modality with $R_{img} \in \{0.2, 0.4, 0.6\}$. The performance of DBP15K$_{FR\text{-}EN}$ are shown in Fig. 1.

We observe that our performance improvement on Multi-OpenEA is less pronounced compared to the DBP15K dataset. This may be due to the higher image feature quality of CLIP compared to ResNet-152, which in turn diminishes the relative benefit of our model in addressing feature ambiguity. Additionally, as the appendix shows, these datasets have fewer relation and attribute types, allowing for better feature training with comparable data sizes (with a fixed 1000-word bag size, long tail effects are minimized) which partially compensates for missing image modalities. This finding can also explain why, as seen in Fig. 3, our model's performance improvement decreases as R_{img} increases, and our enhancement in the dense graph (D-W-V2) is slightly less pronounced than in the sparse graph (D-W-V1) which has richer graph structure information.

Complete Modality. We also evaluate our model on the standard multi-modal DBP15K [21] dataset, achieving satisfactory results with or without the visual modality (w/o IMG), as shown in Table 2. It is noteworthy that the DBP15K dataset only has part of the entities with images attached (e.g., 78.29% in DBP15K$_{ZH-EN}$, 70.32% in DBP15K$_{FR-EN}$, and 67.58% in DBP15K$_{JA-EN}$), which is inherent to the DBPedia database. To further showcase our method's adaptability, in Table 3, we evaluate it on the standard Multi-OpenEA dataset with 100% image data attached, demonstrating that our method can be superior in the (MM)EA task against the potentially ambiguous modality information.

Table 2. Non-iterative (Non-iter.) and iterative (Iter.) results on three multi-modal DPB15K [28] datasets, where " * " refers to involving the visual information for EA.

	Models	DBP15K$_{ZH-EN}$			DBP15K$_{JA-EN}$			DBP15K$_{FR-EN}$		
		H@1	H@10	MRR	H@1	H@10	MRR	H@1	H@10	MRR
Non-iter.	AlignEA [30]	.472	.792	.581	.448	.789	.563	.481	.824	.599
	KECG [18]	.478	.835	.598	.490	.844	.610	.486	.851	.610
	MUGNN [3]	.494	.844	.611	.501	.857	.621	.495	.870	.621
	AliNet [32]	.539	.826	.628	.549	.831	.645	.552	.852	.657
	MSNEA* [5]	.609	.831	.685	.541	.776	.620	.557	.820	.643
	EVA* [21]	.683	.906	.762	.669	.904	.752	.686	.928	.771
	MCLEA* [20]	.726	.922	.796	.719	.915	.789	.719	.918	.792
	UMAEA*	**.800**	**.962**	**.860**	**.801**	**.967**	**.862**	**.818**	**.973**	**.877**
	w/o IMG	**.718**	**.930**	**.797**	**.723**	**.941**	**.803**	**.748**	**.956**	**.826**
Iter.	BootEA [30]	.629	.847	.703	.622	.854	.701	.653	.874	.731
	NAEA [46]	.650	.867	.720	.641	.873	.718	.673	.894	.752
	MSNEA* [5]	.648	.881	.728	.557	.804	.643	.583	.848	.672
	EVA* [21]	.750	.912	.810	.741	.921	.807	.765	.944	.831
	MCLEA* [20]	.811	.957	.865	.805	.958	.863	.808	.963	.867
	UMAEA*	**.856**	**.974**	**.900**	**.857**	**.980**	**.904**	**.873**	**.988**	**.917**
	w/o IMG	**.793**	**.952**	**.852**	**.794**	**.960**	**.857**	**.820**	**.976**	**.880**

Table 3. Non-iterative (Non-iter.) and iterative (Iter.) results on four standard Multi-OpenEA [19] datasets with $R_{img} = 1.0$

	Models	OpenEA$_{EN-FR}$			OpenEA$_{EN-DE}$			OpenEA$_{D-W-V1}$			OpenEA$_{D-W-V2}$		
		H@1	H@10	MRR	H@1	H@10	MRR	H@1	H@10	MRR	H@1	H@10	MRR
Non-iter.	MSNEA* [5]	.692	.813	.734	.753	.895	.804	.800	.874	.826	.838	.940	.873
	EVA* [21]	.785	.932	.836	.922	.983	.945	.858	.946	.891	.890	.981	.922
	MCLEA* [20]	.819	.943	.864	.939	.988	.957	.881	.955	.908	.928	.983	.949
	UMAEA*	**.848**	**.966**	**.891**	**.956**	**.994**	**.971**	**.904**	**.971**	**.930**	**.948**	**.996**	**.967**
Iter.	MSNEA* [5]	.699	.823	.742	.788	.917	.835	.809	.885	.836	.862	.954	.894
	EVA* [21]	.849	.974	.896	.956	.985	.968	.915	.986	.942	.925	.996	.951
	MCLEA* [20]	.888	.979	.924	.969	.993	.979	.944	.989	.963	.969	.997	.982
	UMAEA*	**.895**	**.987**	**.931**	**.974**	**998**	**.984**	**.945**	**.994**	**.965**	**.973**	**.999**	**.984**

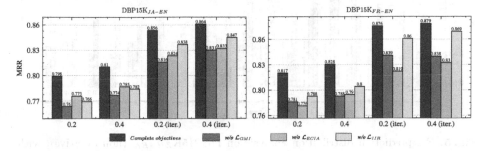

Fig. 4. The component analysis of UMAEA (w/o CMMI), where the scales on the horizontal axis represent $R_{img} \in \{0.2, 0.4\}$ and "iter." represents the model performance on iterative setting

4.3   Details Analysis

Component Analysis. We further analyze the impact of each training objective on our model's performance in Fig. 4, where the absence of any objective results in varying performance degradation. As mentioned in Sect. 3.3, IIR serves as an enhancement for ECIA, and its influence is comparatively less significant than that of $\mathcal{L}_{GMI}$ and $\mathcal{L}_{ECIA}$. The CMMI module's influence is detailed in Table 1, where it becomes more significant when R_{img} is low. CMMI's primary function is to mitigate noise in the missing modalities, facilitating efficient learning at high noise levels and minimizing the noise to existing information.

Efficiency Analysis. Concurrently, we briefly compare the relationship between model parameter size, training time, and performance. Our model improves the performance with only a minor increase in parameters and time consumption. This indicates that in many cases, our method can directly substitute these models with minimal additional overhead. While there is potential for enhancing UMAEA's efficiency, we view this as a direction for future research (Table 4).

Table 4. Efficiency Analysis. Non-iterative model performance on three datasets with $R_{img} = 0.4$, where "Para." refers to the number of learnable parameters and "Time" refers to the total time required for model to reach the optimal performance

Models	DBP15K$_{JA-EN}$			DBP15K$_{FR-EN}$			OpenEA$_{EN-FR}$		
	Para. (M)	Time (Min)	MRR	Para. (M)	Time (Min)	MRR	Para. (M)	Time (Min)	MRR
EVA* [21]	13.27	30.9	.711	13.29	30.8	.721	9.81	17.8	.642
MCLEA* [20]	13.22	15.3	.703	13.24	15.7	.702	9.75	19.5	.637
w/o CMMI	13.82	30.2	.810	13.83	28.8	.828	10.35	17.9	.715
UMAEA	14.72	33.4	.813	14.74	32.7	.838	11.26	23.1	.718

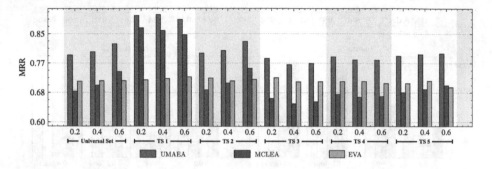

Fig. 5. EA prediction distribution analysis on DBP15K$_{ZH-EN}$ (non-iterative), with $R_{img} \in \{0.2, 0.4, 0.6\}$. "TS" denotes the testing set, where: TS 1 (both entities in an alignment pair have images); TS 2 (at least one entity in an alignment pair has images); TS 3 (only one entity in an alignment pair has images); TS 4 (at least one entity in an alignment pair loss images); TS 5 (neither entity in an alignment pair has images)

Entity Distribution Analysis. To further evaluate the robustness of our method, we analyze the model's prediction performance under different distributions of entity's visual modality. Concretely, we compare five testing sets under $R_{img} \in \{0.2, 0.4, 0.6\}$ with details presented in Fig. 5, where we exclude the CMMI module during the comparison. We observe that EVA's performance is generally stable but underperforms when visual modality is complete (TS 1), suggesting its overfitting to modality noise in the training stage. In contrast, MCLEA exhibits more extreme performance fluctuations, performing worse than EVA does when there's incomplete visual information within the entity pairs (TS 2, 3, 4, 5). Our superior performance reflects the intuition that the optimal performance occurs in TS 1, with tolerable fluctuations in other scenarios.

5   Conclusion

In this work, we discussed the challenges and limitations of existing MMEA methods in dealing with modality incompleteness and visual ambiguity. Our analysis revealed that certain models overfit to modality noise and suffer from oscillating or declining performance at high modality missing rates, emphasizing the need for a more robust approach. Thus, we introduced UMAEA which introduces multi-scale modality hybrid and circularly missing modality imagination to tackle this problem, performing well across all benchmarks. There remain opportunities for future research, such as evaluating our techniques for the incompleteness of other modalities (e.g., attribute), and investigating effective techniques to utilize more detailed visual contents for MMEA.

Acknowledgments. This work was supported by the National Natural Science Foundation of China (NSFCU19B2027/NSFC91846204), joint project DH-2022ZY0012 from Donghai Lab, and the EPSRC project ConCur (EP/V050869/1).

References

1. Bordes, A., Usunier, N., García-Durán, A., Weston, J., Yakhnenko, O.: Translating embeddings for modeling multi-relational data. In: NIPS, pp. 2787–2795 (2013)
2. Cai, W., Ma, W., Zhan, J., Jiang, Y.: Entity alignment with reliable path reasoning and relation-aware heterogeneous graph transformer. In: IJCAI, pp. 1930–1937. ijcai.org (2022)
3. Cao, Y., Liu, Z., Li, C., Li, J., Chua, T.: Multi-channel graph neural network for entity alignment. In: ACL (1), pp. 1452–1461. Association for Computational Linguistics (2019)
4. Chen, L., Li, Z., Wang, Y., Xu, T., Wang, Z., Chen, E.: MMEA: entity alignment for multi-modal knowledge graph. In: Li, G., Shen, H.T., Yuan, Y., Wang, X., Liu, H., Zhao, X. (eds.) KSEM 2020. LNCS (LNAI), vol. 12274, pp. 134–147. Springer, Cham (2020). https://doi.org/10.1007/978-3-030-55130-8_12
5. Chen, L., et al.: Multi-modal siamese network for entity alignment. In: KDD, pp. 118–126. ACM (2022)
6. Chen, T., Kornblith, S., Norouzi, M., Hinton, G.E.: A simple framework for contrastive learning of visual representations. In: ICML. Proceedings of Machine Learning Research, vol. 119, pp. 1597–1607. PMLR (2020)
7. Chen, Z., Chen, J., Geng, Y., Pan, J.Z., Yuan, Z., Chen, H.: Zero-shot visual question answering using knowledge graph. In: Hotho, A., et al. (eds.) ISWC 2021. LNCS, vol. 12922, pp. 146–162. Springer, Cham (2021). https://doi.org/10.1007/978-3-030-88361-4_9
8. Chen, Z., et al.: Meaformer: multi-modal entity alignment transformer for meta modality hybrid. In: ACM Multimedia. ACM (2023)
9. Gao, Y., Liu, X., Wu, J., Li, T., Wang, P., Chen, L.: Clusterea: scalable entity alignment with stochastic training and normalized mini-batch similarities. In: KDD, pp. 421–431. ACM (2022)
10. Guo, L., Chen, Z., Chen, J., Chen, H.: Revisit and outstrip entity alignment: a perspective of generative models. CoRR abs/2305.14651 (2023)
11. He, K., Zhang, X., Ren, S., Sun, J.: Deep residual learning for image recognition. In: CVPR, pp. 770–778. IEEE Computer Society (2016)
12. Huang, J., Sun, Z., Chen, Q., Xu, X., Ren, W., Hu, W.: Deep active alignment of knowledge graph entities and schemata. CoRR abs/2304.04389 (2023)
13. Jiménez-Ruiz, E., Cuenca Grau, B.: LogMap: logic-based and scalable ontology matching. In: Aroyo, L., et al. (eds.) ISWC 2011. LNCS, vol. 7031, pp. 273–288. Springer, Heidelberg (2011). https://doi.org/10.1007/978-3-642-25073-6_18
14. Jing, M., Li, J., Zhu, L., Lu, K., Yang, Y., Huang, Z.: Incomplete cross-modal retrieval with dual-aligned variational autoencoders. In: ACM Multimedia, pp. 3283–3291. ACM (2020)

15. Kingma, D.P., Welling, M.: Auto-encoding variational bayes. In: ICLR (2014)
16. Lee, H., Nam, T., Yang, E., Hwang, S.J.: Meta dropout: learning to perturb latent features for generalization. In: ICLR. OpenReview.net (2020)
17. Lehmann, J., et al.: DBpedia - a large-scale, multilingual knowledge base extracted from Wikipedia. Semant. Web 6(2), 167–195 (2015)
18. Li, C., Cao, Y., Hou, L., Shi, J., Li, J., Chua, T.: Semi-supervised entity alignment via joint knowledge embedding model and cross-graph model. In: EMNLP/IJCNLP (1), pp. 2723–2732. Association for Computational Linguistics (2019)
19. Li, Y., Chen, J., Li, Y., Xiang, Y., Chen, X., Zheng, H.: Vision, deduction and alignment: an empirical study on multi-modal knowledge graph alignment. CoRR abs/2302.08774 (2023)
20. Lin, Z., Zhang, Z., Wang, M., Shi, Y., Wu, X., Zheng, Y.: Multi-modal contrastive representation learning for entity alignment. In: COLING, pp. 2572–2584. International Committee on Computational Linguistics (2022)
21. Liu, F., Chen, M., Roth, D., Collier, N.: Visual pivoting for (unsupervised) entity alignment. In: AAAI, pp. 4257–4266. AAAI Press (2021)
22. Liu, Y., Li, H., Garcia-Duran, A., Niepert, M., Onoro-Rubio, D., Rosenblum, D.S.: MMKG: multi-modal knowledge graphs. In: Hitzler, P., et al. (eds.) ESWC 2019. LNCS, vol. 11503, pp. 459–474. Springer, Cham (2019). https://doi.org/10.1007/978-3-030-21348-0_30
23. Liu, Z., Cao, Y., Pan, L., Li, J., Chua, T.: Exploring and evaluating attributes, values, and structures for entity alignment. In: EMNLP (1), pp. 6355–6364. Association for Computational Linguistics (2020)
24. Qi, Z., et al.: Unsupervised knowledge graph alignment by probabilistic reasoning and semantic embedding. In: IJCAI, pp. 2019–2025 (2021)
25. Radford, A., et al.: Learning transferable visual models from natural language supervision. In: ICML. Proceedings of Machine Learning Research, vol. 139, pp. 8748–8763. PMLR (2021)
26. Sohn, K., Lee, H., Yan, X.: Learning structured output representation using deep conditional generative models. In: NIPS, pp. 3483–3491 (2015)
27. Suchanek, F.M., Abiteboul, S., Senellart, P.: PARIS: probabilistic alignment of relations, instances, and schema. Proc. VLDB Endow. 5(3), 157–168 (2011)
28. Sun, Z., Hu, W., Li, C.: Cross-lingual entity alignment via joint attribute-preserving embedding. In: d'Amato, C., et al. (eds.) ISWC 2017. LNCS, vol. 10587, pp. 628–644. Springer, Cham (2017). https://doi.org/10.1007/978-3-319-68288-4_37
29. Sun, Z., Hu, W., Wang, C., Wang, Y., Qu, Y.: Revisiting embedding-based entity alignment: a robust and adaptive method. IEEE Trans. Knowl. Data Eng. 1–14 (2022). https://doi.org/10.1109/TKDE.2022.3200981
30. Sun, Z., Hu, W., Zhang, Q., Qu, Y.: Bootstrapping entity alignment with knowledge graph embedding. In: IJCAI, pp. 4396–4402. ijcai.org (2018)
31. Sun, Z., Huang, J., Hu, W., Chen, M., Guo, L., Qu, Y.: TransEdge: translating relation-contextualized embeddings for knowledge graphs. In: Ghidini, C., et al. (eds.) ISWC 2019. LNCS, vol. 11778, pp. 612–629. Springer, Cham (2019). https://doi.org/10.1007/978-3-030-30793-6_35
32. Sun, Z., et al.: Knowledge graph alignment network with gated multi-hop neighborhood aggregation. In: AAAI, pp. 222–229. AAAI Press (2020)
33. Sun, Z., et al.: A benchmarking study of embedding-based entity alignment for knowledge graphs. Proc. VLDB Endow. 13(11), 2326–2340 (2020)
34. Vaswani, A., et al.: Attention is all you need. In: NIPS, pp. 5998–6008 (2017)
35. Velickovic, P., Cucurull, G., Casanova, A., Romero, A., Liò, P., Bengio, Y.: Graph attention networks. In: ICLR (Poster). OpenReview.net (2018)

36. Wang, M., Shi, Y., Yang, H., Zhang, Z., Lin, Z., Zheng, Y.: Probing the impacts of visual context in multimodal entity alignment. Data Sci. Eng. **8**(2), 124–134 (2023)

37. Wang, Y., et al.: Facing changes: continual entity alignment for growing knowledge graphs. In: Sattler, U., et al. (eds.) ISWC. LNCS, vol. 13489, pp. 196–213. Springer, Cham (2022). https://doi.org/10.1007/978-3-031-19433-7_12

38. Wu, Y., Liu, X., Feng, Y., Wang, Z., Zhao, D.: Neighborhood matching network for entity alignment. In: ACL, pp. 6477–6487. Association for Computational Linguistics (2020)

39. Xin, K., Sun, Z., Hua, W., Hu, W., Zhou, X.: Informed multi-context entity alignment. In: WSDM, pp. 1197–1205. ACM (2022)

40. Yang, B., Yih, W., He, X., Gao, J., Deng, L.: Embedding entities and relations for learning and inference in knowledge bases. In: ICLR (Poster) (2015)

41. Yang, H., Zou, Y., Shi, P., Lu, W., Lin, J., Sun, X.: Aligning cross-lingual entities with multi-aspect information. In: EMNLP/IJCNLP (1), pp. 4430–4440. Association for Computational Linguistics (2019)

42. Ye, Q., et al.: mPLUG-Owl: modularization empowers large language models with multimodality. CoRR abs/2304.14178 (2023)

43. Zhang, Q., Sun, Z., Hu, W., Chen, M., Guo, L., Qu, Y.: Multi-view knowledge graph embedding for entity alignment. In: IJCAI, pp. 5429–5435. ijcai.org (2019)

44. Zhao, J., Li, R., Jin, Q.: Missing modality imagination network for emotion recognition with uncertain missing modalities. In: ACL/IJCNLP (1), pp. 2608–2618. Association for Computational Linguistics (2021)

45. Zhu, J., Park, T., Isola, P., Efros, A.A.: Unpaired image-to-image translation using cycle-consistent adversarial networks. In: ICCV, pp. 2242–2251. IEEE Computer Society (2017)

46. Zhu, Q., Zhou, X., Wu, J., Tan, J., Guo, L.: Neighborhood-aware attentional representation for multilingual knowledge graphs. In: IJCAI, pp. 1943–1949. ijcai.org (2019)

Disentangled Contrastive Learning for Knowledge-Aware Recommender System

Shuhua Huang[1], Chenhao Hu[1], Weiyang Kong[1], and Yubao Liu[1,2]([✉])

[1] Sun Yat-Sen University, Guangzhou, China
{huangshh33,huchh8,kongwy3}@mail2.sysu.edu.cn, liuyubao@mail.sysu.edu.cn
[2] Guangdong Key Laboratory of Big Data Analysis and Processing, Guangzhou, China

Abstract. Knowledge Graphs (KGs) play an increasingly important role as useful side information in recommender systems. Recently, developing end-to-end models based on graph neural networks (GNNs) becomes the technical trend of knowledge-aware recommendation. However, we argue that prior methods are insufficient to discover multi-faceted user preferences based on diverse aspects of item attributes, since they only learn a single representation for each user and item. To alleviate this limitation, we focus on exploring user preferences from multiple aspects of item attributes, and propose a novel disentangled contrastive learning framework for knowledge-aware recommendation (DCLKR). Technically, we first disentangle item knowledge graph into multiple aspects for the knowledge view, and user-item interaction graph for the collaborative view, equipped with attentive neighbor assignment and embedding propagation mechanisms. Then we perform intra-view contrastive learning to encourage differences among disentangled representations in each view, and inter-view contrastive learning to transfer knowledge between the two views. Extensive experiments conducted on three benchmark datasets demonstrate the superior performance of our proposed method over the state-of-the-arts. The implementations are available at: https://github.com/Jill5/DCLKR..

Keywords: Recommender System · Knowledge Graphs · Disentangled Representation Learning · Contrastive Learning · Graph Neural Networks

1 Introduction

Recommender systems are crucial for many online services to discover interested items for users. For developing effective recommendation approaches, learning high-quality user and item representations is of great significance. In recent years, a great deal of research effort is devoted to utilizing knowledge graphs (KGs) to improve the representation learning of recommendation [28,33,45]. A KG is a

T. R. Payne et al. (Eds.): ISWC 2023, LNCS 14265, pp. 140–158, 2023.
https://doi.org/10.1007/978-3-031-47240-4_8

semantic network of real-world entities, and illustrates the relationship between them. The rich entity and relation information can not only reveal various relatedness among items (e.g., co-directed by a director) but also be used to interpret user preference (e.g., attributing a user's choice of a movie to its director).

Early studies on knowledge-aware recommendation focus on bridging different knowledge graph embedding (KGE) models [2,16,39] with recommendation models, by pre-processing KGs with KGE models and feeding the learned entity embeddings into recommendation frameworks. Some follow-on studies [10,36,42] propose to construct multi-hop paths along with multiple relations in KGs from users to items, exploiting the high-order KG connectivity to model user-item relations better. More recently, due to the powerful capabilities of graph neural networks (GNNs) [7,15,25], the information aggregation schemes of GNNs become the mainstream in knowledge-aware recommendation [23,32–34]. Such methods unify user-item interactions and KGs as user-item-entity graphs, then recursively integrate multi-hop neighbors into node representations.

However, we argue that prior methods are insufficient to discover multi-faceted user preferences. The key reason is that each item contains diverse relation and entity information, but prior methods only learn a single representation for each item, which is further used to characterize user preferences. An underlying fact has been ignored that user preferences are multi-faceted based on diverse aspects of item attributes, and a user likes an item doesn't mean he/she likes all the attributes of the item. Taking Fig. 1 as an example, the movie *Batman Begins* has multiple aspects of relation and entity information, user u_1 saw the movie *Batman Begins* because he liked its *genre*, while user u_2 saw this movie for its *director* and *star*. Ignoring the diverse facets behind user preferences limits the performance of recommendation. To solve this limitation, we propose to explore user preferences at a more granular level, by disentangling item knowledge graph and user-item interaction graph under multiple aspects of item attributes, which form the knowledge view and the collaborative view, respectively. The main challenge is how to learn such disentangled representations of users and items in two views, while transferring knowledge between these two views for knowledge-aware recommendation.

Recently, contrastive learning, one of the classical self-supervised learning (SSL) methods, shows excellent performance on learning discriminative representations from unlabeled data, via maximizing the distance between negative samples while minimizing the distance between positive samples [17]. Besides, contrastive learning enables knowledge transferring between views by maximizing the mutual information between those augmented views of the same instance (*i.e.*, user or item) [47].

Motivated by the advantage of contrastive learning in representation learning, we develop a novel **D**isentangled **C**ontrastive **L**earning framework for **K**nowledge-aware **R**ecommendation (DCLKR). More specifically, we first initialize multi-aspect embeddings via multiple gate units, coupling each gate unit with an aspect. We then apply graph disentangling modules in the knowledge view and collaborative view separately, equipped with attentive neighbor assign-

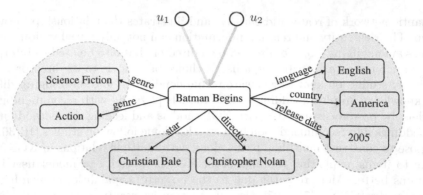

Fig. 1. A toy example of different facets of user preferences. Best viewed in color.

ment and embedding propagation mechanisms. In particular, attentive neighbor assignment exploits node-neighbor affinity to refine the graph in each aspect, highlighting the importance of influential connections, *i.e.*, user-item interactions and KG triplets. In turn, embedding propagation on such graphs updates a node embedding relevant to a certain aspect. By iteratively performing such disentangling operations, we establish a set of disentangled representations under multiple aspects. Simultaneously, a contrastive learning module is introduced, consisting of intra-view contrastive learning and inter-view contrastive learning. The intra-view contrastive learning is performed to encourage differences among disentangled representations in each view. Besides, the inter-view contrastive learning is conducted to align item representations between two views, for transferring item knowledge to the collaborative view as well as collaborative signals to the knowledge view.

Our contributions are summarized as follows:

- This work emphasizes the significance of exploring multi-faceted user preferences based on different aspects of item attributes, and presents the idea of modeling multi-faceted user preferences by disentangled representation learning.
- We propose a novel model DCLKR, which builds a disentangled contrastive learning framework for knowledge-aware recommendation. DCLKR learns disentangled representations of users and items from the knowledge view and the collaborative view. Besides, it performs intra-view and inter-view contrastive learning to enhance representation learning.
- We conduct extensive experiments on three benchmark datasets to demonstrate the advantages of our DCLKR in recommendation, and investigate the effectiveness of each component with ablation studies.

2   Preliminaries

In this section, we introduce main notations used throughout the paper and formulate the knowledge-aware recommendation task.

In a typical recommendation scenario, let $\mathcal{U}$ be a set of users and $\mathcal{I}$ be a set of items, respectively. Let $\mathcal{O}^+ = \{(u,i)|u \in \mathcal{U}, i \in \mathcal{I}\}$ be a set of observed feedback, where each (u,i) pair indicates that user u has engaged item i before.

KGs store plentiful real-world facts associated with items, *e.g.*, item attributes, or external commonsense knowledge, in the form of heterogeneous graphs. Let a KG be a collection of triplets $\mathcal{G} = \{(h,r,t)|h,t \in \mathcal{V}, r \in \mathcal{R}\}$, where each triplet (h,r,t) indicates that a relation r exists from head entity h to tail entity t; $\mathcal{V}$ and $\mathcal{R}$ refer to the sets of entities and relations in $\mathcal{G}$, respectively. Here, $\mathcal{V}$ is comprised of items $\mathcal{I}$ and non-item entities $\mathcal{V}/\mathcal{I}$. For example, the triplet (*Batman Begins, star, Christian Bale*) describes that *Christian Bale* is the *star* of movie *Batman Begins*.

Given the user-item interaction data $\mathcal{O}^+$ and the knowledge graph $\mathcal{G}$, our task of knowledge-aware recommendation is to learn a function that can predict the probability that a user $u \in \mathcal{U}$ would interact with an item $i \in \mathcal{I}$.

3 Methodology

In this section, we present the proposed DCLKR. It aims to incorporate contrastive learning into knowledge-aware recommendation to model disentangled multi-faceted user preferences. The framework of DCLKR is illustrated in Fig. 2, which consists of three key components: (1) **Knowledge Graph Disentangling Module**. It incorporates an attentive neighbor assignment mechanism into a path-aware GNN to encode disentangled knowledge-aware representations of items. (2) **Interaction Graph Disentangling Module**. It applies an attentive light aggregation scheme to encode the interaction graphs, under the guidance of the multi-faceted representations from the knowledge view. (3) **Contrastive Learning Module**. First, it separately performs intra-view contrastive learning in the two views, then conducts inter-view contrastive learning to aligned item representations between the two views. We next present the three components in details.

3.1 Multi-aspect Embeddings Initialization

Before the graph disentangling, we need to initialize embeddings for multiple aspects. Formally, we assume that there are total K aspects. Instead of slicing ID embeddings into K chunks [35], we utilize element-wise self-gating units to control the information flow from ID embeddings to each aspect, as follow:

$$\mathbf{e}_{i,k} = f_{gate}^k(\mathbf{e}_i) = \mathbf{e}_i \odot \sigma(\mathbf{W}_k\mathbf{e}_i + \mathbf{b}_k), \tag{1}$$

where $\mathbf{e}_i$ is ID embedding of item i, $\mathbf{e}_{i,k}$ is the initial embedding of item i under the k-th aspect, $\mathbf{W}_k \in \mathbb{R}^{d \times d}$ and $\mathbf{b}_k \in \mathbb{R}^d$ are parameters to be learned, $\odot$ denotes the element-wise product and σ is the sigmoid function. Analogously, $\mathbf{e}_{u,k}$, $\mathbf{e}_{v,k}$, $\mathbf{e}_{r,k}$, are established for user u, entity v and relation r, respectively. The self-gating mechanism effectively learns non-linear gates to modulate ID

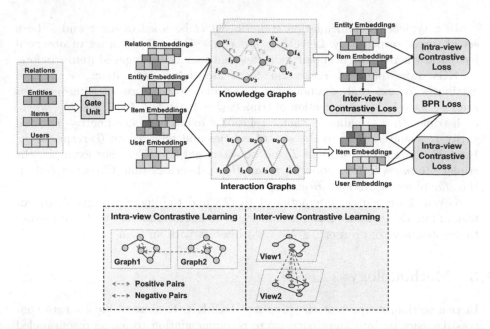

Fig. 2. Illustration of the proposed DCLKR model. The upper part is the model framework of DCLKR, and the lower part is the details of intra-view and inter-view contrastive learning mechanism. Best viewed in color.

embeddings under different aspects at element-wise granularity through dimension re-weighting, which is more adaptive than simply dividing embeddings into multiple chunks.

3.2 Knowledge Graph Disentangling Module

In this component, we aim to learn disentangled knowledge-aware representations to distinguish different aspects of relations and entities. Inspired by [34], we propose a path-aware GNN to encode the relation information in item knowledge graphs. The path-aware GNN aggregates neighboring information for L times, $i.e.$, aggregation depth, meanwhile preserving the path information, $i.e.$, long-range connectivity such as item-relation-entity-relation-item.

However, in the knowledge graph disentanglement task, we should not aggregate all the neighbors when re-constructing node representations in one aspect, as only a subset of neighbors are highly correlated with this aspect. Taking Fig. 1 as an example, movie *Batman Begins*'s neighbors, (*genre, Science Fiction*) and (*genre, Action*) are strongly relevant to the aspect of *genre*, while (*language, English*) and (*release date, 2005*) are weakly correlated. Thus, in order to better capture the affinity between item i and its neighbors in each aspect, we leverage an attentive neighbor assignment mechanism to infer the importance of each neighbor in aggregation. Here we simply adopt the similarity-based attention based on the hypothesis that the more similar the item i and the neighbor (r, v)

are in the k-th aspect, the better neighbor (r, v) characterizes the feature of item i in terms of the k-th aspect. The attention score of item i's neighbor (r, v) in the k-th aspect is formulated as:

$$\alpha_{(i,r,v)}^{k} = \frac{\exp(\mathbf{e}_{i,k}^{\top}(\mathbf{e}_{r,k} \odot \mathbf{e}_{v,k}))}{\sum_{k' \in K} \exp(\mathbf{e}_{i,k'}^{\top}(\mathbf{e}_{r,k'} \odot \mathbf{e}_{v,k'}))}. \tag{2}$$

With the attention score, the l-th layer aggregation in the k-th aspect can be formulated as:

$$\mathbf{e}_{i,k}^{(l+1)} = \frac{1}{|\mathcal{N}_i^s|} \sum_{(r,v) \in \mathcal{N}_i^s} \alpha_{(i,r,v)}^{k} \mathbf{e}_{r,k} \odot \mathbf{e}_{v,k}^{(l)}, \tag{3}$$

where $\mathcal{N}_i^s$ represents a set of item i's neighbors in the knowledge graph, $\mathbf{e}_{i,k}^{(l+1)}$ denotes the k-th representation of item i after $l + 1$ layers aggregation, and representation $\mathbf{e}_{v,k}^{(l)}$ of entity v is obtained by l layers aggregation in a similar way.

Then we sum all layers' representations up to obtain the final representations specific to the k-th aspect:

$$\mathbf{x}_{i,k}^{s} = \mathbf{e}_{i,k}^{(0)} + \cdots + \mathbf{e}_{i,k}^{(L)}, \tag{4}$$

where $\mathbf{e}_{i,k}^{(0)}$ is equal to the initial embedding of item i under the k-th aspect.

3.3   Interaction Graph Disentangling Module

The collaborative view lays stress on collaborative signals in user-item interactions, *i.e.*, user-item-user and item-user-item co-occurrences. As a result, collaborative information could be captured by modeling long-range connectivity in the user-item interaction graphs, where an edge between a user and an item indicates that the user has interacted with the item. Thus, we adopt a light aggregation scheme referred to LightGCN [9], which adopts a simple message passing and aggregation mechanism without feature transformation and non-linear activation, effective and computationally efficient.

However, like knowledge graph disentangling, it is unwise to aggregate all the interacted neighbors under one aspect when disentangling interaction graphs, as only a subset of neighbors are strongly correlated with this aspect. Taking Fig. 1 as an example, the relations and entities of the *genre* aspect are the main factors leading to the interaction between user u_1 and movie *Batman Begins*, while those of other aspects are not. Thus, we also leverage an attentive neighbor assignment mechanism to refine the interaction graph by inferring the importance of each interaction under different aspects, which is based on disentangled knowledge-aware representations. In particular, the attention score of an interaction (u, i) under the k-th aspect is formulated as:

$$\alpha_{(u,i)}^{k} = \frac{\exp(\mathbf{e}_{u,k}^{\top} \mathbf{x}_{i,k}^{s})}{\sum_{k' \in K} \exp(\mathbf{e}_{u,k'}^{\top} \mathbf{x}_{i,k'}^{s})}. \tag{5}$$

At the l-th layer under the k-th aspect, the aggregation can be formulated as:

$$\mathbf{e}_{u,k}^{(l+1)} = \frac{1}{|\mathcal{N}_u^c|} \sum_{i \in \mathcal{N}_u^c} \alpha_{(u,i)}^k \mathbf{e}_{i,k}^{(l)}, \quad \mathbf{e}_{i,k}^{(l+1)} = \frac{1}{|\mathcal{N}_i^c|} \sum_{u \in \mathcal{N}_i^c} \alpha_{(u,i)}^k \mathbf{e}_{u,k}^{(l)}, \quad (6)$$

where $\mathcal{N}_u^c$ and $\mathcal{N}_i^c$ represent sets of user u's neighbors and item i's neighbors in the interaction graph.

Then representations at different layers are summed up as the collaborative representations of the k-th aspect, as follows:

$$\mathbf{x}_{u,k}^c = \mathbf{e}_{u,k}^{(0)} + \cdots + \mathbf{e}_{u,k}^{(L)}, \quad \mathbf{x}_{i,k}^c = \mathbf{e}_{i,k}^{(0)} + \cdots + \mathbf{e}_{i,k}^{(L)}, \quad (7)$$

where $\mathbf{e}_{u,k}^{(0)}$ and $\mathbf{e}_{i,k}^{(0)}$ are equal to the initial embeddings of user u and item i in the k-th aspect.

3.4 Contrastive Learning Module

Intra-view Contrastive Learning. We expect that there should be a weak dependence among disentangled representations from different aspects. In general, disentangled representations with unique information will be able to supply diverse and complementary angles to characterize node features. Otherwise, they might be less informative and not capable of achieving comprehensive disentanglement.

Here we utilize contrastive learning among disentangled knowledge graphs, as well as among disentangled interaction graphs, to guide the independent representation learning. First, we define the positive and negative samples. In particular, for any node in one view, its representations under the same aspect form the positive pairs, and its representations under different aspects form the negative pairs. With the positive and negative samples, we have the following contrastive loss in the knowledge view:

$$\mathcal{L}_{intra}^s = \sum_{v \in \mathcal{V}} \sum_{k \in K} -\log \frac{e^{s(\mathbf{x}_{v,k}^s, \mathbf{x}_{v,k}^s)/\tau}}{\sum_{k' \in K} e^{s(\mathbf{x}_{v,k}^s, \mathbf{x}_{v,k'}^s)/\tau}}, \quad (8)$$

where $s(\cdot)$ denotes the cosine similarity calculating, and τ denotes a temperature parameter. In a similar way, we can obtain the contrastive loss of the collaborative view as follow:

$$\mathcal{L}_{intra}^c = \sum_{n \in \mathcal{U} \cup \mathcal{I}} \sum_{k \in K} -\log \frac{e^{s(\mathbf{x}_{n,k}^c, \mathbf{x}_{n,k}^c)/\tau}}{\sum_{k' \in K} e^{s(\mathbf{x}_{n,k}^c, \mathbf{x}_{n,k'}^c)/\tau}}. \quad (9)$$

The complete intra-view contrastive loss is the sum of the above two losses:

$$\mathcal{L}_{intra} = \mathcal{L}_{intra}^s + \mathcal{L}_{intra}^c. \quad (10)$$

In this way, we successfully learn discriminative disentangled node representations from various perspectives with the guidance of contrastive learning.

Inter-view Contrastive Learning. In order to transfer item knowledge to the collaborative view, as well as collaborative signals to the knowledge view, we conduct inter-view contrastive learning to align item representations between these two views. For any item in one view, the same item embedding learned by the other view forms the positive sample, and the item embeddings except itself in the other view are naturally regarded as negative samples. With the positive and negative samples, we have the following inter-view contrastive loss:

$$\mathcal{L}_{inter} = \sum_{i \in \mathcal{I}} \sum_{k \in K} - \log \frac{e^{s(\mathbf{x}_{i,k}^s, \mathbf{x}_{i,k}^c)/\tau}}{\sum_{i' \in \mathcal{I}} e^{s(\mathbf{x}_{i',k}^s, \mathbf{x}_{i,k}^c)/\tau} + \sum_{i' \in \mathcal{I}} e^{s(\mathbf{x}_{i,k}^s, \mathbf{x}_{i',k}^c)/\tau}} . \tag{11}$$

3.5 Model Prediction

In this module, we first conduct aspect-level prediction and then leverage an attentive scoring mechanism to guide the fusion of results from different aspects. For the aspect-level prediction, we combine embeddings from two views, and predict their matching scores through inner product as follows:

$$\mathbf{z}_{u,k} = \mathbf{x}_{u,k}^c , \quad \mathbf{z}_{i,k} = \mathbf{x}_{i,k}^s + \mathbf{x}_{i,k}^c , \quad \hat{y}_{(u,i)}^k = \mathbf{z}_{u,k}^\top \mathbf{z}_{i,k} . \tag{12}$$

As discussed in Sect. 3.3, each interaction has different correlation with different aspects. Thus, we adopt an attentive fusion of prediction scores from different aspects to get the final results, as follows:

$$\beta_{(u,i)}^k = \frac{\exp((\mathbf{e}_u \odot \mathbf{e}_i)^\top (\mathbf{e}_{u,k} \odot \mathbf{e}_{i,k}))}{\sum_{k' \in K} \exp((\mathbf{e}_u \odot \mathbf{e}_i)^\top (\mathbf{e}_{u,k'} \odot \mathbf{e}_{i,k'}))} ,$$

$$\hat{y}_{(u,i)} = \sum_{k \in K} \beta_{(u,i)}^k \hat{y}_{(u,i)}^k . \tag{13}$$

3.6 Multi-task Training

We apply a multi-task learning strategy to jointly train the recommendation loss and the contrastive losses. For the knowledge-aware recommendation task, we employ a pairwise BPR loss [22] as follow:

$$\mathcal{L}_{BPR} = \sum_{(u,i,j) \in \mathcal{O}} - \ln \sigma(\hat{y}_{(u,i)} - \hat{y}_{(u,j)}) , \tag{14}$$

where $\hat{y}_{(u,i)}$ and $\hat{y}_{(u,j)}$ are predicted scores, $\mathcal{O} = \{(u,i,j) | (u,i) \in \mathcal{O}^+, (u,j) \in \mathcal{O}^-\}$ is the training dataset consisting of the observed interactions $\mathcal{O}^+$ and unobserved counterparts $\mathcal{O}^-$; σ is the sigmoid function. By combining the intra-view and inter-view contrastive losses with BPR loss, we minimize the following objective function to learn the model parameters:

$$\mathcal{L}_{DCLKR} = \mathcal{L}_{BPR} + \lambda_1 \mathcal{L}_{intra} + \lambda_2 \mathcal{L}_{inter} + \lambda_3 \|\Theta\|_2^2 , \tag{15}$$

where Θ is the model parameter set, λ_1 and λ_2 are the hyper-parameters to control the weights of the intra-view and inter-view contrastive losses, λ_3 is the hyper-parameter to control L_2 regularization term, respectively.

Table 1. Statistics and hyper-parameter settings for the three datasets.

		Book-Crossing	MovieLens-1M	Last.FM
User-item Interaction	# users	17,860	6,036	1,872
	# items	14,967	2,445	3,846
	# interactions	139,746	753,772	42,346
Knowledge Graph	# entities	77,903	182,011	9,366
	# relations	25	12	60
	# triplets	151,500	1,241,996	15,518
Hyper-parameter Settings	# K	3	3	3
	# L	2	3	2
	# λ_1	0.1	0.01	0.01
	# λ_2	0.1	0.01	0.01

4 Experiment

Extensive experiments are performed on three public datasets, which are widely used in knowledge-aware recommender systems, to evaluate the effectiveness of our proposed DCLKR by answering the following research questions:

- **RQ1:** How does DCLKR perform, compared with the state-of-the-art knowledge-aware recommender models?
- **RQ2:** Are the key components in our DCLKR framework really improving the overall performance?
- **RQ3:** How do different hyper-parameter settings affect DCLKR?

4.1 Experiment Settings

Dataset Description. Three benchmark datasets are Book-Crossing[1], MovieLens-1M[2], and Last.FM[3], which vary in size, interaction sparsity and knowledge graph characteristics, making our experiments more convincing. Table 1 presents the statistical information of our experimented datasets.

We follow RippleNet [28] to transform the explicit ratings into the implicit marks where 1 indicates that the user has rated the item (the threshold of the rating to be viewed as positive is 4 for MovieLens-1M, but no threshold is set for Book-Crossing and Last.FM due to their sparsity). Closely following RippleNet, we use Microsoft Satori[4] to construct the KGs for three datasets. We gather

---

[1] http://www2.informatik.uni-freiburg.de/~cziegler/BX/.

[2] https://grouplens.org/datasets/movielens/1m/.

[3] https://grouplens.org/datasets/hetrec-2011/.

[4] https://searchengineland.com/library/bing/bing-satori.

Satori IDs of all valid items through their names, and match the IDs with the heads and tails of all KG triplets to extract all well-matched triplets.

Evaluation Metrics. We conduct the evaluation in two experimental scenarios: (1) In click-through rate (CTR) prediction, we adopt two widely used metrics AUC and $F1$. (2) In top-N recommendation, we choose $Recall@N$ to evaluate the recommended lists, where N is set to 5, 10, 20, 50, and 100 for consistency.

Baselines. To comprehensively demonstrate the effectiveness of our proposed DCLKR, we compare it with different types of recommender system methods:

- BPRMF [22]: It is a conventional collaborative filtering method that uses pairwise matrix factorization for implicit feedback optimized by the pairwise ranking loss.
- CKE [45]: This method first encodes items' semantic knowledge, then unifies knowledge embeddings, text embeddings, and image embeddings into recommendation framework.
- RippleNet [28]: This method propagates users' preferences along with paths in KGs to encode user embeddings.
- KGAT [33]: This GNN-based method designs an attentive message passing scheme over the user-item-entity graph for embedding fusion.
- CKAN [38]: This GNN-based method utilizes different neighbor aggregation schemes over the user-item interaction graphs and KGs, respectively.
- KGIN [34]: It is a state-of-the-art GNN-based knowledge-aware method, which performs relational path-based aggregation on the user-intent-item-entity graph to identify latent intention of users.
- KDR [20]: This method utilizes KGs to guide the implicit disentangled representation learning on the user-item interaction graph.
- KGIC [48]: This method constructs local and non-local graphs for users and items in KGs, and conducts layer-wise contrastive learning on these graphs.
- MCCLK [47]: It is a state-of-the-art knowledge-aware method with contrastive learning, which generates three different graph views and performs contrastive learning across three views on both local and global levels.

Parameter Settings. Our proposed DCLKR is implemented with PyTorch. For a fair comparison, we fix the embedding dimensionality as 64 for all models, and the embedding parameters are initialized with the Xavier method [6]. We optimize our method with Adam [14] with the learning rate of $1e^{-3}$ and the batch size of 2048. And λ_3 of L_2 regularization term is set to $1e^{-5}$. Other hyper-parameter settings are provided in Table 1, including the number of disentangled aspects K, aggregation depth L, intra-view contrastive loss weight λ_1, and inter-view contrastive loss weight λ_2. The best settings for hyper-parameters in all comparison methods are researched by either empirical study or following the original papers.

Table 2. The results of AUC and $F1$ in CTR prediction.

Model	Book-Crossing		MovieLens-1M		Last.FM	
	AUC	$F1$	AUC	$F1$	AUC	$F1$
BPRMF	0.6583	0.6117	0.8920	0.7921	0.7563	0.7010
CKE	0.6759	0.6235	0.9065	0.8024	0.7471	0.6740
RippleNet	0.7211	0.6472	0.9190	0.8422	0.7762	0.7025
KGAT	0.7314	0.6544	0.9140	0.8440	0.8293	0.7424
CKAN	0.7439	0.6676	0.9091	0.8466	0.8421	0.7607
KGIN	0.7225	0.6730	0.9321	0.8601	0.8602	0.7803
KDR	0.7246	0.6528	0.9265	0.8463	0.8550	0.7790
KGIC	<u>0.7573</u>	0.6723	0.9252	0.8560	0.8590	0.7802
MCCLK	0.7508	<u>0.6774</u>	<u>0.9325</u>	<u>0.8603</u>	<u>0.8742</u>	<u>0.7908</u>
DCLKR	**0.7910***	**0.6983***	**0.9445***	**0.8703***	**0.8936***	**0.8105***
%Imp	4.45%	3.09%	1.29%	1.16%	2.22%	2.49%

4.2 Performance Comparison (RQ1)

We report the overall performance evaluation of all methods in Table 2 and Fig. 3, where %Imp. denotes the relative improvements of the best performing method (starred) over the strongest baselines (underlined). By analyzing the results, we summarize the following observations:

- **Our proposed DCLKR achieves the best results.** DCLKR consistently performs better than other baselines in all cases of measures. More specifically, it achieves considerable improvements over the strongest baselines *w.r.t.* AUC by 4.45%, 1.29%, and 2.22% in Book-Crossing, MovieLens-1M and Last.FM datasets, respectively. In top-N recommendation scenario, DCLKR also achieves best performance *w.r.t. Recall@N* ($N = 5, 10, 20, 50, 100$). We attribute such improvements to the following aspects: (1) By disentangling the user-item interaction graphs and KGs, DCLKR is able to capture users' multi-faceted preferences based on diverse aspects of item attributes. (2) The contrastive mechanism preserves features from both knowledge view and collaborative view, hence prompting the representations to be more informative for DCLKR.
- **Incorporating KGs benefits recommender systems.** We can observe that all the models that incorporate KGs perform better than conventional CF methods. Compared with BPRMF, CKE simply incorporating KG embeddings into matrix factorization elevates the model performance, which clarifies the significance of bringing in KGs as side information.
- **Extracting more informative KG facts boosts the model performance.** KGIN disentangles user-item interactions at the fine granularity of user intents which related to semantic relations in KGs, so that KGIN is the state-of-the-art in GNN-based knowledge-aware methods. The truth inspires

us to explore user preferences on different aspects of item attributes implicit in KGs. KDR also learns disentangled representations from the knowledge and collaborative view, but ignores different importance of the connections in graphs, which degrades its performance.

– **Contrastive learning benefits graph learning.** We can observe that the methods based on contrastive learning paradigm achieve better performance than the GNN-based methods in most cases, which indicates that contrastive learning brings benefits to the graph learning of recommendation.

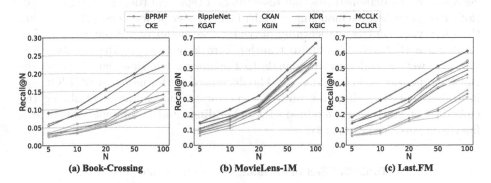

Fig. 3. The results of *Recall@N* in top-*N* recommendation.

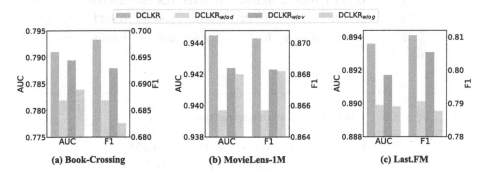

Fig. 4. Effect of ablation study.

4.3   Ablation Studies (RQ2)

We investigate the effect of main components in our model to the final performance by comparing DCLKR with the following three variants:

- DCLKR$_{w/od}$: the variant of DCLKR without disentangled representation learning. Naturally, the intra-view contrastive learning is also removed.
- DCLKR$_{w/ov}$: the variant of DCLKR without the inter-view contrastive learning.
- DCLKR$_{w/og}$: the variant of DCLKR which removes the self-gating units and initializes multi-aspect embeddings by simply slicing ID embeddings into multiple chunks.

As shown in Fig. 4, we have the following observations: (1) Without disentangled representation learning, DCLKR$_{w/od}$ leads to a significant performance decrease, which demonstrates that disentangled representation learning is propitious to comprehensive modeling of multi-faceted user preferences. (2) Removing the inter-view contrastive learning degrades the model performance. It makes sense since DCLKR$_{w/ov}$ fails to transfer item knowledge to the collaborative view, as well as collaborative signals to the knowledge view, which is beneficial for representation learning. (3) The decreased performance of DCLKR$_{w/og}$ indicates that the self-gating units is superior to the operation of slicing the embeddings, since it can modulate ID embeddings under different aspects at a finer element-wise granularity.

Table 3. Effect of disentangled aspects number K.

	Book-Crossing		MovieLens-1M		Last.FM	
	AUC	*F1*	*AUC*	*F1*	*AUC*	*F1*
$K = 2$	0.7862	0.6893	0.9436	0.8690	0.8925	0.8064
$K = 3$	**0.7910**	**0.6983**	**0.9445**	**0.8703**	**0.8936**	**0.8105**
$K = 4$	0.7906	0.6916	0.9430	0.8696	0.8928	0.8071
$K = 5$	0.7844	0.6903	0.9435	0.8660	0.8919	0.8058

Table 4. Effect of aggregation depth L.

	Book-Crossing		MovieLens-1M		Last.FM	
	AUC	*F1*	*AUC*	*F1*	*AUC*	*F1*
$L = 1$	0.7828	0.6939	0.9332	0.8634	0.8777	0.7937
$L = 2$	**0.7910**	**0.6983**	0.9420	0.8696	**0.8936**	**0.8105**
$L = 3$	0.7908	0.6668	**0.9445**	**0.8703**	0.8892	0.7803
$L = 4$	0.7840	0.6691	0.9424	0.8685	0.8889	0.7782

4.4 Sensitivity Analysis (RQ3)

Effect of Disentangled Aspects Number. To analyze the effect of disentangled aspects number, we vary K in range of $\{2, 3, 4, 5\}$ and illustrate the performance comparison on Book-Crossing, MovieLens-1M and Last.FM in Table 3. We observe that increasing the number of disentangled aspects enhances the predictive results, as it enables model to capture user preferences from more diverse perspectives. However, excessive number of disentangled aspects impairs model performance, as it is detrimental to the independence among disentangled aspects. DCLKR performs best on all three datasets when $K = 3$.

Effect of Aggregation Depth. To study the influence of graph aggregation depth, we vary L in range of $\{1, 2, 3, 4\}$ and demonstrate the performance comparison on Book-Crossing, MovieLens-1M and Last.FM in Table 4. We can observe that DCLKR substantially achieves improvements on Book-Crossing, MovieLens-1M and Last.FM when $L = 2, 3, 2$, respectively. But further stacking more layers leads to performance degradation, cause neighbors in too long distance may introduce noise to node representations.

Effect of Contrastive Loss Weights. The trade-off parameters λ_1 and λ_2 control the influence of intra-view and inter-view contrastive losses in final loss, respectively. To study the effect of contrastive loss weights, we vary both λ_1 and λ_2 in $\{0.001, 0.01, 0.1, 1\}$. According to the results shown in Fig. 5 and Fig. 6, we can observe that DCLKR performs best when $\lambda_1 = 0.1, 0.01, 0.01$ and $\lambda_2 = 0.1, 0.01, 0.01$ on Book-Crossing, MovieLens-1M and Last.FM, respectively. The intra-view contrastive learning is deployed to encourage the independence among disentangled representations from different aspects, and the inter-view contrastive learning is adopted to transfer knowledge between the knowledge and collaborative views. Tuning the contributions of these two contrastive losses to a proper degree could boost the model performance.

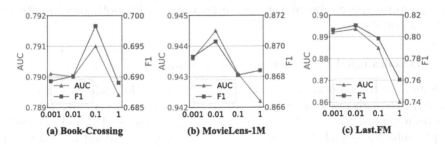

(a) Book-Crossing   (b) MovieLens-1M   (c) Last.FM

Fig. 5. Effect of intra-view contrastive loss weight λ_1.

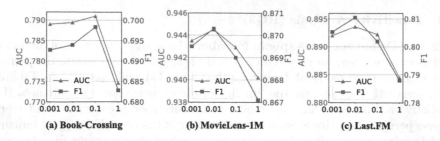

Fig. 6. Effect of inter-view contrastive loss weight λ_2.

5   Related Work

5.1   Knowledge-Aware Recommendation

In recent years, there is a surge of interest in the knowledge-aware recommendation. A typical approach is to pre-train the entity embeddings with knowledge graph embedding (KGE) algorithms [2,16,39], then incorporate them into recommendation frameworks [3,11,27,29,31,45]. CKE [45] adopts TransR [16] to encode items' semantic knowledge, and then combines knowledge embeddings, text embeddings, and image embeddings together for collaborative filtering. Besides, some methods [4,10,19,24,28,36,44] focus on exploring various patterns of connections among items to afford supplementary assistance for recommendation. RippleNet [28] propagates users' historical interacted items along with paths in KGs to explore users' potential long-range preferences via a memory-like neural model. More recently, the information aggregation mechanisms of GNNs [7,15,25] become the technical trend of knowledge-aware recommendation [12,30,32–34,38]. KGAT [33] unifies user-item interactions and KGs as user-item-entity graphs, then utilizes GCN with an attention mechanism to perform aggregation on it. But, CKAN [38] separately applies different neighbor aggregation schemes over the user-item interaction graphs and KGs. KGIN [34] disentangles user-item interactions at the granularity of user intents, and further performs the relational path-aware aggregation for both user-intent-item and KG triplets.

5.2   Disentangled Representation Learning

Disentangled representation learning aims to separate the underlying factors in the data through embedding objects from multiple perspectives [1,18], which has been applied to many fields, such as texts [13], images [5], and knowledge graph embeddings [41]. There are also some effort [20,35,40,46] has been done towards disentangled representation learning on recommendation. DGCF [35] disentangles the intents hidden in the user-item interaction graphs and learns the intent-aware disentangled representations. KDR [20] leverages KGs to guide the disentangled representation learning in recommendation, making the disentangled representations interpretable. MDKE [46] is proposed to disentangle the knowledge-aware recommendation into semantic-level and structural-level subspaces, and then utilize two levels disentangled representations to enhance recommendation. Our work considers the fact that relations and entities in KGs have different correlation with different aspects which is ignored by KDR and MDKE, and emphasizes influential relations and entities by attention mechanisms.

5.3   Contrastive Learning

Contrastive learning methods [8,21,26,37] learn discriminative node representations from unlabeled data by maximizing the distance between negative pairs while minimizing the distance between positive pairs. Recently, there are several efforts [43,47,48] that apply contrastive learning on knowledge-aware recommendation. KGCL [43] proposes a KG augmentation schema to suppress KG noise in information aggregation to derive more robust knowledge-aware representations for items, and exploits the KG augmentation to guide cross-view contrastive learning. MCCLK [47] generates three different graph views from collaborative interactions and KGs, then performs contrastive learning across three views on both local and global levels. KGIC [48] constructs local and non-local graphs for users and items in KGs, and conducts layer-wise contrastive learning on these graphs. All the above methods conduct contrastive learning to align node representations among different views, but do not perform contrastive learning among the disentangled graphs, which helps to distinguish user preferences under different semantic aspects.

6   Conclusion

In this work, we focus on exploring user preferences from multiple aspects of item attributes, and propose a novel disentangled contrastive learning framework for knowledge-aware recommendation, DCLKR, which achieves better recommendation performance from two dimensions: (1) It disentangles the knowledge graph and the user-item interaction graph into multiple aspects, and uses attentive neighbor assignment mechanisms to highlight the importance of influential connections. (2) It performs intra-view and inter-view contrastive learning to enhance the disentangled representation learning. The experimental results on three public datasets demonstrate the superior performance of our proposed method over the state-of the-arts.

Acknowledgments. The authors would like to thank the anonymous reviewers for their helpful comments. This work was supported by the National Nature Science Foundation of China (NSFC 61572537), and the CCF-Huawei Populus Grove Challenge Fund (CCF-HuaweiDBC202305).

References

1. Bengio, Y., Courville, A.C., Vincent, P.: Representation learning: a review and new perspectives. IEEE Trans. Pattern Anal. Mach. Intell. **35**(8), 1798–1828 (2013)

2. Bordes, A., Usunier, N., Garcia-Duran, A., Weston, J., Yakhnenko, O.: Translating embeddings for modeling multi-relational data. In: Advances in Neural Information Processing Systems, vol. 26 (2013)
3. Cao, Y., Wang, X., He, X., Hu, Z., Chua, T.S.: Unifying knowledge graph learning and recommendation: towards a better understanding of user preferences. In: The World Wide Web Conference, pp. 151–161 (2019)
4. Catherine, R., Cohen, W.: Personalized recommendations using knowledge graphs: a probabilistic logic programming approach. In: Proceedings of the 10th ACM Conference on Recommender Systems, pp. 325–332 (2016)
5. Chen, X., Duan, Y., Houthooft, R., Schulman, J., Sutskever, I., Abbeel, P.: Infogan: interpretable representation learning by information maximizing generative adversarial nets. In: Advances in Neural Information Processing Systems 29: Annual Conference on Neural Information Processing Systems 2016, December 5–10, 2016, Barcelona, Spain, pp. 2172–2180 (2016)
6. Glorot, X., Bengio, Y.: Understanding the difficulty of training deep feedforward neural networks. In: Proceedings of the Thirteenth International Conference on Artificial Intelligence and Statistics, pp. 249–256 (2010)
7. Hamilton, W., Ying, Z., Leskovec, J.: Inductive representation learning on large graphs. In: Advances in Neural Information Processing Systems, vol. 30 (2017)
8. Hassani, K., Khasahmadi, A.H.: Contrastive multi-view representation learning on graphs. In: International Conference on Machine Learning, pp. 4116–4126 (2020)
9. He, X., Deng, K., Wang, X., Li, Y., Zhang, Y., Wang, M.: LightGCN: simplifying and powering graph convolution network for recommendation. In: Proceedings of the 43rd International ACM SIGIR Conference on Research and Development in Information Retrieval, pp. 639–648 (2020)
10. Hu, B., Shi, C., Zhao, W.X., Yu, P.S.: Leveraging meta-path based context for top-n recommendation with a neural co-attention model. In: Proceedings of the 24th ACM SIGKDD International Conference on Knowledge Discovery & Data Mining, pp. 1531–1540 (2018)
11. Huang, J., Zhao, W.X., Dou, H., Wen, J.R., Chang, E.Y.: Improving sequential recommendation with knowledge-enhanced memory networks. In: The 41st International ACM SIGIR Conference on Research & Development in Information Retrieval, pp. 505–514 (2018)
12. Jin, J., et al.: An efficient neighborhood-based interaction model for recommendation on heterogeneous graph. In: Proceedings of the 26th ACM SIGKDD International Conference on Knowledge Discovery & Data Mining, pp. 75–84 (2020)
13. John, V., Mou, L., Bahuleyan, H., Vechtomova, O.: Disentangled representation learning for non-parallel text style transfer. In: Proceedings of the 57th Conference of the Association for Computational Linguistics, ACL 2019, Florence, Italy, July 28- August 2, 2019, Volume 1: Long Papers, pp. 424–434 (2019)
14. Kingma, D.P., Ba, J.: Adam: a method for stochastic optimization. In: 3rd International Conference on Learning Representations, ICLR 2015, San Diego, CA, USA, May 7–9, 2015, Conference Track Proceedings (2015)
15. Kipf, T.N., Welling, M.: Semi-supervised classification with graph convolutional networks. In: 5th International Conference on Learning Representations, ICLR 2017, Toulon, France, April 24–26, 2017, Conference Track Proceedings (2017)
16. Lin, Y., Liu, Z., Sun, M., Liu, Y., Zhu, X.: Learning entity and relation embeddings for knowledge graph completion. In: Proceedings of the AAAI Conference on Artificial Intelligence, vol. 29 (2015)
17. Liu, X., et al.: Self-supervised learning: generative or contrastive. IEEE Trans. Knowl. Data Eng. **35**(1), 857–876 (2023)

18. Locatello, F., et al.: Challenging common assumptions in the unsupervised learning of disentangled representations. In: Proceedings of the 36th International Conference on Machine Learning, ICML 2019, 9–15 June 2019, Long Beach, California, USA, pp. 4114–4124 (2019)
19. Ma, W., et al.: Jointly learning explainable rules for recommendation with knowledge graph. In: The World Wide Web Conference, pp. 1210–1221 (2019)
20. Mu, S., Li, Y., Zhao, W.X., Li, S., Wen, J.: Knowledge-guided disentangled representation learning for recommender systems. ACM Trans. Inf. Syst. $40(1)$, 6:1–6:26 (2022)
21. Peng, Z., Huang, W., Luo, M., Zheng, Q., Rong, Y., Xu, T., Huang, J.: Graph representation learning via graphical mutual information maximization. In: Proceedings of The Web Conference, vol. 2020, pp. 259–270 (2020)
22. Rendle, S., Freudenthaler, C., Gantner, Z., Schmidt-Thieme, L.: BPR: bayesian personalized ranking from implicit feedback. In: UAI 2009, Proceedings of the Twenty-Fifth Conference on Uncertainty in Artificial Intelligence, Montreal, QC, Canada, June 18–21, vol. 2009, pp. 452–461 (2009)
23. Sha, X., Sun, Z., Zhang, J.: Hierarchical attentive knowledge graph embedding for personalized recommendation. Electron. Commer. Res. Appl. 48, 101071 (2021)
24. Sun, Z., Yang, J., Zhang, J., Bozzon, A., Huang, L.K., Xu, C.: Recurrent knowledge graph embedding for effective recommendation. In: Proceedings of the 12th ACM Conference on Recommender Systems, pp. 297–305 (2018)
25. Veličković, P., Cucurull, G., Casanova, A., Romero, A., Lio, P., Bengio, Y., et al.: Graph attention networks. Stat $1050(20)$, 10–48550 (2017)
26. Velickovic, P., Fedus, W., Hamilton, W.L., Liò, P., Bengio, Y., Hjelm, R.D.: Deep graph infomax. ICLR (Poster) $2(3)$, 4 (2019)
27. Wang, H., Zhang, F., Hou, M., Xie, X., Guo, M., Liu, Q.: Shine: signed heterogeneous information network embedding for sentiment link prediction. In: Proceedings of the eleventh ACM International Conference on Web Search and Data Mining, pp. 592–600 (2018)
28. Wang, H., et al.: RippleNet: propagating user preferences on the knowledge graph for recommender systems. In: Proceedings of the 27th ACM International Conference on Information and Knowledge Management, pp. 417–426 (2018)
29. Wang, H., Zhang, F., Xie, X., Guo, M.: Dkn: deep knowledge-aware network for news recommendation. In: Proceedings of the 2018 World Wide Web Conference, pp. 1835–1844 (2018)
30. Wang, H., et al.: Knowledge-aware graph neural networks with label smoothness regularization for recommender systems. In: Proceedings of the 25th ACM SIGKDD International Conference on Knowledge Discovery & Data Mining, pp. 968–977 (2019)
31. Wang, H., Zhang, F., Zhao, M., Li, W., Xie, X., Guo, M.: Multi-task feature learning for knowledge graph enhanced recommendation. In: The World Wide Web Conference, pp. 2000–2010 (2019)
32. Wang, H., Zhao, M., Xie, X., Li, W., Guo, M.: Knowledge graph convolutional networks for recommender systems. In: The world Wide Web Conference, pp. 3307–3313 (2019)
33. Wang, X., He, X., Cao, Y., Liu, M., Chua, T.S.: Kgat: Knowledge graph attention network for recommendation. In: Proceedings of the 25th ACM SIGKDD International Conference on Knowledge Discovery & Data Mining, pp. 950–958 (2019)
34. Wang, X., ct al.: Learning intents behind interactions with knowledge graph for recommendation. In: Proceedings of the Web Conference 2021, pp. 878–887 (2021)

35. Wang, X., et al.: Disentangled graph collaborative filtering. In: Proceedings of the 43rd International ACM SIGIR Conference on Research and Development in Information Retrieval, pp. 1001–1010 (2020)
36. Wang, X., Wang, D., Xu, C., He, X., Cao, Y., Chua, T.S.: Explainable reasoning over knowledge graphs for recommendation. In: Proceedings of the AAAI Conference on Artificial Intelligence, vol. 33, pp. 5329–5336 (2019)
37. Wang, X., Liu, N., Han, H., Shi, C.: Self-supervised heterogeneous graph neural network with co-contrastive learning. In: Proceedings of the 27th ACM SIGKDD Conference on Knowledge Discovery & Data Mining, pp. 1726–1736 (2021)
38. Wang, Z., Lin, G., Tan, H., Chen, Q., Liu, X.: CKAN: collaborative knowledge-aware attentive network for recommender systems. In: Proceedings of the 43rd International ACM SIGIR Conference on Research and Development in Information Retrieval, pp. 219–228 (2020)
39. Wang, Z., Zhang, J., Feng, J., Chen, Z.: Knowledge graph embedding by translating on hyperplanes. In: Proceedings of the AAAI Conference on Artificial Intelligence, vol. 28 (2014)
40. Wu, J., Fan, W., Chen, J., Liu, S., Li, Q., Tang, K.: Disentangled contrastive learning for social recommendation. In: Proceedings of the 31st ACM International Conference on Information & Knowledge Management, Atlanta, GA, USA, October 17–21, 2022, pp. 4570–4574 (2022)
41. Wu, J., et al.: DisenKGAT: knowledge graph embedding with disentangled graph attention network. In: CIKM '21: The 30th ACM International Conference on Information and Knowledge Management, Virtual Event, Queensland, Australia, November 1–5, vol. 2021, pp. 2140–2149 (2021)
42. Xian, Y., Fu, Z., Muthukrishnan, S., De Melo, G., Zhang, Y.: Reinforcement knowledge graph reasoning for explainable recommendation. In: Proceedings of the 42nd international ACM SIGIR Conference on Research and Development in Information Retrieval, pp. 285–294 (2019)
43. Yang, Y., Huang, C., Xia, L., Li, C.: Knowledge graph contrastive learning for recommendation. In: SIGIR '22: The 45th International ACM SIGIR Conference on Research and Development in Information Retrieval, Madrid, Spain, July 11–15, vol. 2022, pp. 1434–1443 (2022)
44. Yu, X., et al.: Personalized entity recommendation: a heterogeneous information network approach. In: Proceedings of the 7th ACM International Conference on Web Search and Data Mining, pp. 283–292 (2014)
45. Zhang, F., Yuan, N.J., Lian, D., Xie, X., Ma, W.Y.: Collaborative knowledge base embedding for recommender systems. In: Proceedings of the 22nd ACM SIGKDD International Conference on Knowledge Discovery and Data Mining, pp. 353–362 (2016)
46. Zhou, H., Liu, Q., Gao, X., Chen, G.: MDKE: multi-level disentangled knowledge-based embedding for recommender systems. In: Database Systems for Advanced Applications - 27th International Conference, DASFAA 2022, Virtual Event, April 11–14, 2022, Proceedings, Part II, pp. 3–18 (2022)
47. Zou, D., et al.: Multi-level cross-view contrastive learning for knowledge-aware recommender system. In: SIGIR '22: The 45th International ACM SIGIR Conference on Research and Development in Information Retrieval, Madrid, Spain, July 11–15, 2022, pp. 1358–1368 (2022)
48. Zou, D., et al.: Improving knowledge-aware recommendation with multi-level interactive contrastive learning. In: Proceedings of the 31st ACM International Conference on Information & Knowledge Management, pp. 2817–2826 (2022)

Dependency-Aware Core Column Discovery for Table Understanding

Jingyi Qiu[1], Aibo Song[1], Jiahui Jin[1(✉)], Tianbo Zhang[1], Jingyi Ding[1], Xiaolin Fang[1], and Jianguo Qian[2]

[1] School of Computer Science and Engineering, Southeast University, Nanjing, China
{jingyi_qiu,absong,jjin,tianbozhang,jingyi_ding,
xiaolin}@seu.edu.cn
[2] State Grid Zhejiang Electric Power Company, LTD, Hangzhou, China
qian_jianguo@zj.sgcc.com.cn

Abstract. In a relational table, core columns represent the primary subject entities that other columns in the table depend on. While discovering core columns is crucial for understanding a table's semantic column types, column relations, and entities, it is often overlooked. Previous methods typically rely on heuristic rules or contextual information, which can fail to accurately capture the dependencies between columns and make it difficult to preserve their relationships. To address these challenges, we introduce Dependency-aware Core Column Discovery (DaCo), an iterative method that uses a novel *rough matching* strategy to identify both inter-column dependencies and core columns. Unlike other methods, DaCo does not require labeled data or contextual information, making it suitable for practical scenarios. Additionally, it can identify multiple core columns within a table, which is common in real-world tables. Our experimental results demonstrate that DaCo outperforms existing core column discovery methods, substantially improving the efficiency of table understanding tasks.

Keywords: table understanding · core column · semantic dependency

1 Introduction

Tabular data, which includes web tables, CSV files, and data lake tables, is a valuable resource for developing knowledge graphs [11,27] and question answering systems [41]. However, as tabular data often lacks well-defined schemas, the process of table understanding (also known as table interpretation or table annotation) is critical in assigning semantic tags from knowledge graphs to mentions within the table [21,32]. To do this effectively, it is necessary to identify the core columns [53], also known as subject columns, which represent the primary subject entities on which other columns in the table depend [50,51,54]. Once these core columns have been identified, understanding the remaining non-core columns becomes significantly simplified [13,38]. Existing methods for discovering core columns mainly rely on heuristic rules, such as the leftmost rule [52], or contextual information [6,12]. However, these methods may not be practical or applicable in scenarios like data lakes or enterprise tables [19,20], where

T. R. Payne et al. (Eds.): ISWC 2023, LNCS 14265, pp. 159–178, 2023.
https://doi.org/10.1007/978-3-031-47240-4_9

structures are often incomplete, data is noisy, and there may be multiple core columns. Therefore, identifying inter-column dependencies and discovering core columns can be challenging.

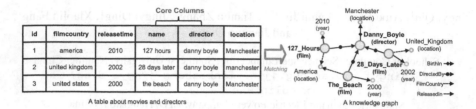

Fig. 1. A table about movies and directors. Prior works usually choose the leftmost column *i.e.,* "id" as the core column, but the values within the "id" column are general and do not refer to entities in the knowledge graph [18]. In contrast, our method selects the "name" and "movie director" columns as core columns because they correspond to the entities on which the entities listed in the "filmcountry", "releasetime", and "location" columns depend, according to the knowledge graph.

This paper aims to tackle the problem of core column discovery for table understanding by identifying the minimum set of columns that other columns depend on[1]. While discovering core columns is crucial for table understanding, it is often overlooked [6]. Existing methods rely on heuristic rules [16,52,54] or machine learning techniques [45], but these may not capture true dependencies [24,47] or require large amounts of labeled data. Pre-trained models show promise [10,12,44,48], but their effectiveness depends on the corpus they were trained on and may not adapt well to specific domains. Unlike keys discovered based on uniqueness in data profiling, core column discovery focuses more on semantic inter-column dependency, *i.e.,* whether there are entity-attribute relationships [24,53,54]. Furthermore, research on discovering multiple core columns often suffers from poor performance due to their reliance on exact matching [18,46].

Identifying core columns while preserving their dependencies is a challenging task. Using a knowledge graph (KG) as a reference may appear to be a solution, but it is intricate due to *(1) Data incompleteness and inconsistency.* Real-life KGs are inherently incomplete, which means that a significant portion of mentions in a table may not have corresponding entries in the KG, named unlinkable mention [36]. Additionally, inconsistencies in representation between tables and KGs can make it challenging to map these mentions accurately. *(2) Noisy table metadata.* Noisy column names, captions, or lack of metadata [17] in tables make it difficult to annotate column types accurately, which is crucial for determining dependent relationships among columns. *(3) Multiple core columns.* Detecting multiple core columns [18,46] in tabular data is challenging due to their unpredictable number and locations. Although prior

---

[1] By dependency, we are implying that column y is an attribute of column x if y depends on x [28].

research [8, 26, 27, 36, 49, 55] has attempted to tackle these issues, they are computationally expensive and rely on the success of core column discovery, leading to a dilemma.

We propose a solution called Dependency-Aware Core Column Discovery (DaCo) to address the above challenges. DaCo is a two-level iterative process that identifies inter-column dependencies and core columns. Outer iteration performs sampling and discovery iteratively until the termination test is satisfied, which considerably reduces computational complexity when matching tables to knowledge graphs. Inner iteration identifies the core columns based on the sampled rows. It establishes a rough matching between each mention (column type) and a set of candidate KG entities (KG types), providing a coarse understanding of the table, which is necessary for DaCo to handle situations where the table has only small portions of overlaps with the KG[2]. Based on this rough matching, DaCo calculates the dependency score for each pair of columns. If the score exceeds a certain threshold, we consider the existence of an dependent relationship between the columns and identify the core column set according to the inter-column dependencies. Once a core column is found, we update the threshold and repeat the inner iteration until the core column set size converges. *To the best of our knowledge,* DaCo *is the first approach to discover the core column for table understanding while preserving inter-column dependencies without requiring table metadata, contextual information and exact table-to-KG matching.*

Overall, our contributions are as follows. *(1) Rough matching and dependency scoring.* We propose a novel approach that combines rough matching and dependency scoring to explore the semantic dependencies between columns, which enables the extraction of a core column based on inter-column dependencies. *(2) Two-level iterative algorithm.* To improve the effectiveness and efficiency of the dependency and core column discovery, we introduce a two-level iterative algorithm, named DaCo, that performs sampling in outer iteration and discovery in inner iteration until convergence. *(3) Extensive evaluations.* Extensive experiments were conducted on core column discovery and table understanding, revealing that DaCo outperforms other approaches in terms of effectiveness with precision of 85%-90% on core column set discovery and nearly 40% improvement on fine grained column type prediction and relation extraction tasks. Source code is provided on github[3].

The rest of our paper is organized as follows. Sect. 2 provides a definition of the core column discovery problem. Rough matching strategy and the dependency score are presented in Sect. 3. The two-level iterative algorithm is presented in Sect. 4. Our experimental results and related works are showcased in Sect. 5 and 6, respectively. Finally, we conclude our paper in Sect. 7.

2   Preliminary

A review of basic notations is listed in Table 1. Assume three infinite alphabets, Υ, Θ, and Φ for table mentions, graph node labels, and graph edge labels.

---

[2] Our solution can be applied to table understanding tasks since research on table understanding assumes an overlap between the table and the KG.

[3] https://github.com/barrel-0314/daco.

Definition 1 (Table and Column Set). *A table T is a collection of data organized into m rows and n columns, each cell contains a mention, which refers to the textual content for representing an entity in KG and often shares relationships with other mentions in the same row. The mention in i^{th} row and the xth column of table T is denoted by $t_{i,x}$, where $t_{i,x} \in \Upsilon$. $S \subseteq X$ is a column set of T, where set X is defined as the set of all possible column indices in the table, ranging from 1 to n. The projection of T on column x is represented as $T[x]$.*

Table 1. Notations and their descriptions.

Notations	Descriptions
$T, T[x], t_{i,x}$	a table, the xth column of table T, the mention located in the ith row and the xth column in T
C, G, v, τ	core column set, KG, matching function for mention and type
$\text{dep}(x, y), \zeta$	semantic dependency score between column x and y, threshold of semantic dependency
$\hat{v}_{i,x}^{k}, \theta_x$	the kth entity in rough matching of $t_{i,x}$, a type in $\tau(x)$
q, η, γ	parameter for calculating $\text{dep}_\tau(\cdot, \cdot)$, the threshold and decay parameter of iterations
$a, \hat{a}, \varepsilon$	the ground truth, the sample and a threshold of d
T_s, m_s	sampled table and the number of sampling rows

To avoid the influence of noisy metadata, we exclude headers and captions from our definition, which distinguishes our approach from previous works [12,54]. Without contextual information, annotating mentions, column types, and inter-column relationships by matching tables to a KG is crucial for accurately identifying inter-column dependencies.

Remark: We assume that each cell in the table refers to a specific entity. However, it's common for tables to include cells that do not correspond to any particular entity. For example, in Fig. 1, the values in the "id" column may not have corresponding entities in a KG. Even if numerical strings can be treated as text for candidate selection, they often matches literals in the KG rather than entities, which means it lacks type attributes or does not share consistent type in the same column. Besides, the "id" column lacks connecting edges with mentions in the KG within the same row. In this case, the content of the "id" column cannot be considered as mentions and does not provide entity information. Therefore, when computing the semantic dependency relationships and identifying the core columns, we exclude columns where every cell cannot be matched to the KG.

Definition 2 (Knowledge Graph). *A knowledge graph, denoted by $G = (V, E, L)$, is a directed graph that contains nodes representing entities and edges connecting the nodes. The set of nodes and edges are denoted by V and E respectively. A labeling function represented by L is also present in the graph. Each node $v \in V$ and edge $e \in E$ has a label denoted by $L(v) \in \Theta$ and $L(e) \in \Phi$ respectively. We can represent the type of a node v as the value of its "type" attribute. We use θ to denote a type. Because an entity may be related to multiple types, we use set $\tau(v)$ to denote the type set of v.*

Assuming that the KG is complete and that the table can completely overlap the KG, we can match the table and KG exactly by using table annotation. To achieve this, we use the entity annotation function $v(\cdot)$ to map a table mention to a corresponding entity in the KG. In other words, for any given table mention $t_{i,x}$, we have $v(t_{i,x}) \in V$. Additionally, we use the type annotation function $\tau(\cdot)$ to assign a set of semantic types to each column in the table. Specifically, for any given column x, we have $\tau(x) \subseteq \cup_{v \in V}(\tau(v))$. Furthermore, we use the relationship annotation function $\rho(\cdot, \cdot)$ to assign a property from the KG to the relationship between two columns. In other words, for any two columns x and y, we have $\rho(x, y) \in \cup_{e \in E}(\{L(e)\})$. If this is no relationship between x and y, we let $\rho(x, y) = null$. With the exact table annotation, we define the semantic dependency between two columns as follows:

Definition 3 (Semantic Dependency). *Given two columns x and y in the same table, we can determine if column y is semantically dependent on column x by examining each pair of mentions $t_{i,x}$ and $t_{i,y}$. If there exists a KG edge e_i starting from the entity represented by $t_{i,x}$ and pointing to the entity represented by $t_{i,y}$ for every row i, we establish that column y is semantically dependent on column x. Formally, if each edge $e_i = (v(t_{i,x}), v(t_{i,y})) \in E$ satisfies the relation label $L(e_i) = \rho(x, y)$, then we denote this semantic dependency as $x \rightarrow y$.*

We expand the idea of column-wise semantic dependency to include column-set-wise semantic dependency. We denote the semantic dependency between two sets of columns, S_1 and S_2, as $S_1 \rightarrow S_2$. Here, S_1 and S_2 are subsets of X, and for each y in S_2, there exists an x in S_1 that satisfies $x \rightarrow y$. Also we let column x depend on itself, *i.e.*, $x \rightarrow x$. In the subsequent sections, we will refer to semantic dependency as "dependency" if there is no confusion.

Example 1. Consider the table in Fig. 1. There is a semantic dependency between the 5th and 6th columns, specifically, *i.e.*,$5 \rightarrow 6$. This relationship stems from the presence of an edge labeled as "BirthIn" between $v("dannyboyle")$ and $v("manchester")$, meaning that $\rho(5, 6) = "BirthIn"$. Additionally, we can also observe a semantic dependency between the "name" column and several other columns (*i.e.*,"filmcountry", and "releasetime"), resulting in a column-set-wise dependency of $\{4, 5\} \rightarrow \{2, 3, 6\}$.

Because KG is far from complete and overlapping for real-life table to be matched, accurately identifying inter-column dependencies becomes infeasible. To account for real-world situations, we propose a dependency score $\text{dep}(x, y)$ that gauges the possibility of column y being dependent on column x. If the value of $\text{dep}(x, y)$ surpasses a predetermined threshold ζ, then we establish a relation between x and y, such that $(\text{dep}(x, y) > \zeta) \Rightarrow (x \rightarrow y)$. Sect. 3 explains how to calculate $\text{dep}(x, y)$. By utilizing these dependency scores, we can define the core column discovery problem as follows.

Definition 4 (Core Column Discovery Problem). *Given a table with the set of columns (denoted by X), the problem is to discover a set of core columns C that is the smallest subset of X on which all other columns in the table depend, i.e.,$C \rightarrow X$ and for all C' that satisfies $C' \rightarrow X$, $|C| \leq |C'|$.*

Determining the core column remains an NP-hard problem even when the dependency scores $\text{dep}(\cdot, \cdot)$ and the threshold ζ are provided. This can be demonstrated through a reduction from the directed dominating set problem [39]. In the next sections, we show how to measure $\text{dep}(\cdot, \cdot)$ (Sect. 3) and how to iteratively compute $\text{dep}(\cdot, \cdot)$ to discover the core column (Sect. 4).

3   Rough Matching and Dependency Scores

This section aims at measuring the dependency score $\text{dep}(\cdot, \cdot)$. The semantic dependency definition implies that if column y depends on column x, each pair of corresponding entities $v(t_{i,x})$ and $v(t_{i,y})$ should share the same relationship as the columns themselves. In other words, $\rho(x, y) = L((v(t_{i,x}), v(t_{i,y})))$, where $t_{i,x}$ and $t_{i,y}$ are mentions in the ith row of columns x and y, respectively. However, this entity-centric matching approach may be too strict for real-life tables and KGs, since the mentions in the table may not always be linkable to entities in the KG. Additionally, there might not exist a shared relationship capable of connecting all pairs of matched entities due to the incompleteness of KG.

To overcome these limitations, we propose a column-centric strategy called *rough matching* to replace the fine-grained entity-centric matching. By taking the column-centric approach, we can relax the constraints on linkability and account for the incompleteness of KGs which provides a more flexible and robust method for measuring the dependency score of real-world tables.

3.1   Rough Matching

The rough matching approach generate candidate entities for each mention and assigns potential types $\tau(x)$ to each column x, rather than providing precise annotations. Let $t_{i,x}$ be the ith mention in column x. In this approach, we produce the top-K candidate entities for $t_{i,x}$, denoted as $\hat{\mathbf{v}}(t_{i,x}) = \{\hat{v}^k(t_{i,x})\}_{k=1}^{K}$, where $\hat{v}^k(t_{i,x})$ represents the kth candidate entity. Note that any label similarity function can be employed to select candidates by comparing the mention and the entity name, and we use edit distance as the label similarity measure here. For simplicity, we represent $\hat{v}^k(t_{i,x})$ as $\hat{v}_{i,x}^k$. To determine a potential type set for column x, we extract the types of mentions' candidate entities from the knowledge graph by using the edges labeled "type" and then merge the type sets. We accomplish this by combining the sets $\tau(\hat{v}_{i,x}^k)$ for all $i \in [1, m]$ and $k \in [1, K]$, where m is the number of rows and $\tau(\cdot)$ is a function that assigns type sets to entities and columns. The resulting union is the type set of column x, *i.e.*,$\tau(x)$.

In our approach, the type sets $\tau(x)$ and $\tau(y)$ are essential for calculating $\text{dep}(x, y)$. Nevertheless, $\tau(\cdot)$ may include many irrelevant types as the top-k candidates chosen for each mention might not pertain to the table's topic. To filter those irrelevant types, we define a score function $s_\tau(\theta, x)$ to determine the relevance of a particular type θ to column x as follows:

$$s_\tau(\theta, x) = \frac{1}{mK} \sum_{i=1}^{m} \sum_{k=1}^{K} w_{i,x}^k s_\tau^v(\theta, \hat{v}_{i,x}^k), \tag{1}$$

where $s_\tau^v(\theta, \hat{v}_{i,x}^k) = \mathbb{I}[\theta \in \tau(\hat{v}_{i,x}^k)]$ and $\mathbb{I}[\cdot]$ is the indicator function that takes the value 1 if its argument is true and 0 otherwise determines whether $\theta \in \tau(\hat{v}_{i,x}^k)$ and takes the value 1 if it does, otherwise it is 0. $s_\tau(\theta, x)$ can be seen as the weighted sum of the $s_\tau^v(\theta, \hat{v}_{i,x}^k)$ for each candidate.

We employ the weight $w_{i,x}^k$ to distinguish whether $\hat{v}_{i,x}^k$ is a correct match for $t_{i,x}$. Ideally, all correct entities corresponding to the same column should have the same set of types. Therefore, we use the Jaccard function to measure the similarity between the type set of $\hat{v}_{i,x}^k$ and those of other candidates. If the types of $\hat{v}_{i,x}^k$ are more consistent with those of other candidates, it is more likely to be a correct match. To compute $w_{i,x}^k$, we use the following equation:

$$w_{i,x}^k = \frac{\sigma_{i,x}^k}{mK} \sum_{j=1}^{m} \sum_{l=1}^{K} Jaccard(\tau(\hat{v}_{i,x}^k), \tau(\hat{v}_{j,x}^l)), \tag{2}$$

where the weight $\sigma_{i,x}^k$ evaluates whether $\hat{v}_{i,x}^k$ correctly matches $t_{i,x}$ based on the inter-column relationship. Since the inter-column relationship is not predetermined, our algorithm adjusts $\sigma_{i,x}^k$'s value dynamically with Eq.(7).

After computing $s_\tau(\theta, x)$ for each type θ, we cluster the types into two groups using k-means ($k = 2$) and select the types with the highest scores as $\tau(x)$. We also select candidate entities whose types belong to the updated $\tau(x)$. Here, k-means is used rather than selecting top-k types or setting a threshold because k-means eliminates the need to set parameter values.

3.2 Dependency Score

After performing a rough matching, we proceed to calculate the dependency score $dep(x, y)$ for columns x and y. To consider that the semantic dependencies between corresponding entities have similar relationships as the columns themselves, we divide the score into two parts. The first part, denoted as $dep_{\hat{v}}(x, y)$, considers the dependencies between candidate entities in $\hat{\mathbf{v}}_{i,x}$ and $\hat{\mathbf{v}}_{i,y}$. The second part, denoted as $dep_\tau(x, y)$, evaluates the dependency between two columns based on $\tau(x)$ and $\tau(y)$. Then $dep(x, y)$ is a linear combination of the two part of scores, which is as follows.

$$dep(x, y) = \alpha dep_{\hat{v}}(x, y) + (1 - \alpha)dep_\tau(x, y) \tag{3}$$

where $\alpha \in [0, 1]$ is a parameter for balancing $dep_{\hat{v}}(\cdot, \cdot)$ and $dep_\tau(\cdot, \cdot)$ and defaults to 0.5.

We show how to compute $dep_{\hat{v}}(x, y)$. Our main idea is to count the number of edges in the KG that link the candidate entities of column x with those of column y. When there are more edges present, it suggests a stronger likelihood of interdependence between these columns. Formally, if there exists a relationship $\rho(x, y) \in \Phi$ connecting x and y, the corresponding entities should be connected by edges in E between two columns, i.e., $(v(t_{i,x}), v(t_{i,y})) \in E$. However, it is difficult to calculate an exact value for $\rho(x, y)$ using $\hat{v}_{i,x}$ and $\hat{v}_{i,y}$. Nonetheless, since the number of edges $|E|$ is considerably smaller $|V|^2$ in a KG, there are barely any edges existed between two randomly selected entities. Hence, if y does not depend on x, it is difficult for there to exist edges from $\hat{\mathbf{v}}_{i,x}$ to $\hat{\mathbf{v}}_{i,y}$. Conversely, x has a higher dependency with y when there are several edges from $\hat{\mathbf{v}}_{i,x}$ to $\hat{\mathbf{v}}_{i,y}$, which can be used as an indicator for the existence of $\rho(x, y)$. Based on this observation, we compute $\text{dep}_{\hat{v}}(x, y)$ as follows:

$$\text{dep}_{\hat{v}}(x, y) = \frac{n_e(x, y) - \min\{n_e\}}{\max\{n_e\} - \min\{n_e\}} \tag{4}$$

where $n_e(x, y) = \sum_{i=1}^{m} \sum_{\hat{v}_{i,x}^k \in \hat{\mathbf{v}}_{i,x}} \sum_{\hat{v}_{i,y}^l \in \hat{\mathbf{v}}_{i,y}} \mathbb{I}[(\hat{v}_{i,x}^k, \hat{v}_{i,y}^l) \in E]$. $n_e(x, y)$ represents the total number of edges between candidates $\hat{\mathbf{v}}_{i,x}$ and $\hat{\mathbf{v}}_{i,y}$ in each row of columns x and y. To normalize $\text{dep}_{\hat{v}}(x, y)$ to the range of $[0, 1]$, we apply min-max normalization to $n_e(x, y)$. Here, $\max\{n_e\}$ and $\min\{n_e\}$ represent the max and min values of n_e over all pairs of columns, respectively.

Next, we demonstrate the computation of $\text{dep}_{\tau}(x, y)$, which tackles scenarios where a relationship exists between two columns, but there are no direct connections among the candidate entities. Our main idea is to assess the inter-column dependency by examining the correlation between the candidate types of column x, $i.e., \tau(x)$, and the candidate types of column y, $i.e., \tau(y)$ based on the KG ontology. This involves computing the correlation of θ_x and θ_y for each type pair (θ_x, θ_y) where $\theta_x \in \tau(x)$ and $\theta_y \in \tau(y)$. The correlation, denoted as $Corr(\theta_x, \theta_y)$, takes into account the ontology and can be computed using the method described in [58], which considers the specificity of types and the distance between types in the ontology graph. However, the method presented in [58] can only determine the existence of a relationship between columns x and y, without indicating its direction, $i.e.,$ whether it is $x \rightarrow y$ or $y \rightarrow x$. To address this issue, we calculate the proportion of head nodes with type θ_x and θ_y, denoted as $h(\theta_x)$ and $h(\theta_y)$, respectively. The ratio of $h(\theta_x)/(h(\theta_x) + h(\theta_y))$ serves as a useful reference for determining the direction of dependency between x and y. If this value is greater, it signifies that θ_x has more head entities and θ_y has fewer head entities, implying that the direction of dependency is more likely to be $x \rightarrow y$ rather than $y \rightarrow x$. Overall, we have

$$\text{dep}_{\tau}(x, y) = \frac{\mathcal{T}(x, y) - \min_{x', y' \in X, x' \neq y'} \mathcal{T}(x', y')}{\max_{x', y' \in X, x' \neq y'} \mathcal{T}(x', y') - \min_{x', y' \in X, x' \neq y'} \mathcal{T}(x', y')} \tag{5}$$

where $\mathcal{T}(x, y) = \sum_{\theta_x \in \tau(x)} \sum_{\theta_y \in \tau(y)} \frac{h(\theta_x)}{h(\theta_x) + h(\theta_y)} \sqrt[q]{Corr(\theta_x, \theta_y)}$. To balance the scores, we introduce the parameter q due to the exponential nature of $Corr(\theta_x, \theta_y)$ as calculated by [58], where $q > 0$. This equation considers potential type matches, computes scores for each pair, and normalizes them to 0 to 1. The score is determined by a combination of the relationship between the two column types in the ontology graph and the proportion in which the two column types appear as head entities in the knowledge graph. Moreover, since the values of $\text{dep}_{\tau}(\cdot, \cdot)$ for different (θ_x, θ_y) pairs are always greater than zero, it is possible to identify the core column using $\text{dep}(x, y)$ even if $\text{dep}_{\hat{v}}(x, y) = 0$.

4 DaCo: A Two-Level Iterative Algorithm

This section presents DaCo, a two-level iterative algorithm for identifying core columns based on dependency scores. The algorithm includes an outer iteration and an inner iteration (Alg. 1). The outer iteration handles large tables using a sampling method with a termination check to avoid biased samples. The inner iteration refines rough matching results to discover core columns. An example of applying DaCo is shown in Fig. 2, which demonstrates the process of discovering core columns from the table of Fig. 1.

4.1 Outer Iteration

In the process, the outer iteration randomly selects rows from a table and proceeds with the inner iteration until the termination check is met. To be specific, every cycle of the outer iteration involves the following steps.

- **Initialization** (lines 2–5). We randomly select m_s rows for T to form a sub-table T_s and generate the candidate entities for each mention in T_s.

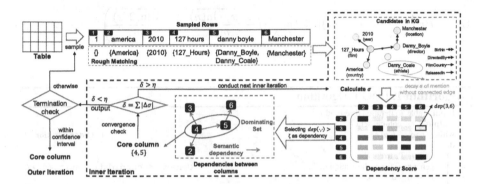

Fig. 2. An example of DaCo algorithm : (i) In the outer iteration, it keeps sampling rows and discovering the core columns from the table until the results are unbiased. Before inner iteration, it conducts rough matching for each mention of the sampled rows. If one column (*e.g.*, column 1) cannot generate entity candidates in KG or its candidates do not connect with candidates in other columns, this column will be excluded for the following operations. (ii) In the inner iteration, the weights of candidate entities are adjusted based on their connecting edges in the KG, and the dependency scores are computed. Based on the calculated dependency scores, core column discovery can be transformed into a problem of finding the dominating set in a directed graph: Set a threshold and consider each column as a vertex, connecting two columns if their dependency score exceeds the threshold. The inner iteration terminates and outputs the set of core columns when erroneous candidates such as *Danny_Coale* are filtered out, and the candidates' weights are stabilize, ensuring the convergence of the process.

- **Perform Inter Iteration** (lines 6–13). We iteratively determine the core column set C based on the sampled rows with detailed information in Sect. 4.2.
- **Termination Check** (line 14). To confidently terminate the algorithm, it is necessary to verify that the core column set C discovered from T_s is equivalent to that obtained from T. We represent a core column set as an n-bit feature vector $\mathcal{C}$, where if x is a core column, then $\mathcal{C}[x] = 1$, otherwise $\mathcal{C}[x] = 0$. The feature vectors of the core column sets discovered from T_s, T, and row i, are denoted by $\mathcal{C}$, $\mathcal{C}_T$, and $\mathcal{C}_i$, respectively. Since $\mathcal{C}_T$ is not known in advance, it must be discovered from each row. For each column x, we have defined a function $a(x)$ to measure the degree of consistency between $\mathcal{C}_T[x]$ and $\mathcal{C}_i[x]$ for all rows i, such that $a(x) = \frac{1}{m} \sum_{1 \leq i \leq m} [\mathcal{C}_T[x] \equiv \mathcal{C}_i[x]]$.

By introducing $a(x)$ and Rademacher random variables [33], we can estimate the confidence interval of the samples, *i.e.*, whether the core column of the sample is consistent with the one of the entire table. If a sample falls within the confidence interval, it indicates that the sample is unbiased and the result can be returned. Otherwise, it suggests that the biased sample causes its core column inconsistent with the one of the entire table, requiring a new round of sampling. Additionally, we compute $\hat{a}(x) = \frac{1}{m} \sum_{1 \leq i \leq m_s} [\mathcal{C}[x] \equiv \mathcal{C}_i[x]]$ for T_s. We have the following theorem regarding the confidential interval of $\hat{a}(x)$.

Theorem 1. *Given a confidence level $1-\varepsilon > 0$, the confidence interval of $\hat{a}(x)$ satisfies the following bound:*

$$Pr\left(\sup_{x \in X} |\hat{a}(x) - a(x)| \leq 2 \max_{x \in X} \sqrt{\frac{2\hat{a}(x) \cdot \ln(n)}{m_s}} + \sqrt{\frac{2\ln(2/\varepsilon)}{m_s}} \right) \geq 1 - \varepsilon. \qquad (6)$$

Algorithm 1: DaCo Algorithm

Input: Table T, iteration threshold η
Output: Core column set C
1 **while** $flag = False$;   /* **Outer iteration** */
2 **do**
3   sample T_s from T;
4   generate $\hat{v}$ for each mention in T_s;   /* Generate candidate entities */
5      $r \leftarrow 0, \quad \delta \leftarrow \infty$;
6   **while** $\delta > \eta$;   /* **Inner iteration** */
7   **do**
8   calculate σ with Eq. (7);   /* Compute weights of candidates */
9   calculate dep$(\cdot, \cdot)$ with Eq. (3);   /* Compute dependency scores */
10         $\zeta \leftarrow$ k-means(dep$(\cdot, \cdot)$);   /* Update ζ */
11         $C \leftarrow$ CoreColumnSet$(\zeta, \text{dep}(\cdot, \cdot))$;   /* Discover core column set */
12         $r \leftarrow r + 1$;
13         $\delta \leftarrow$ ConvergenceCheck(ζ);
14     $flag \leftarrow$ TerminationCheck(C, T_s, ε);
15 **return** C

Sketch of Proof. Theorem 1 can be proved by introducing Rademacher random variable and Massart's lemma [33].

The termination check of the algorithm involves computing a bound based on Theorem 1. This bound is evidently determined by ε, C, and T_s. If the resulting bound is less than a predetermined threshold, the algorithm terminates.

4.2 Inner Iteration

During the inner iteration, we use sampled sub-table to generate core column sets. The following steps are repeated in each iteration.

- **Update Dependency Scores** (lines 8–9). In each iteration, we update the dependency scores dep$(\cdot, \cdot)$ of all pairs of columns by adjusting the weights of candidate entities through Eq. (2). This involves changing the value of $\sigma_{i,x}^k$ which evaluates candidate entities based on the relationship between the two columns. To achieve this, we initialize $\sigma_{i,x}^{k,0}$ as 1 and compute $\sigma_{i,x}^{k,r}$ in the rth iteration by Eq. (7) using the core column set discovered in the previous iteration.

The main idea of Eq. (7) is to determine whether a candidate is a correct match entity by examining the existence of connecting edges between candidates, and to lower the weight of candidates that are more likely to be incorrect matches. Assuming $t_{i,x}$ is a mention in a core column, we determine the correctness of $\hat{v}_{i,x}^k$ by examining whether there exists an edge between it and a candidate of any non-core column. If such an edge exists, we set $\sigma_{i,x}^{k,r}$ to $\sigma_{i,x}^{k,r-1}$. Otherwise, we reduce the importance of $\hat{v}_{i,y}^k$ by multiplying it with factor γ, where $0 < \gamma < 1$. Consequently, we compute $\sigma_{i,x}^{k,r}$ as either $\sigma_{i,x}^{k,r-1}$ or $\gamma\sigma_{i,x}^{k,r-1}$:

$$\sigma_{i,x}^{k,r} = \begin{cases} 1, & \text{if } r = 0 \\ \sigma_{i,x}^{k,r-1}, & \text{if } r > 0 \wedge \exists \hat{v}_{i,y'}^l \text{ such that } (\hat{v}_{i,x}^k, \hat{v}_{i,y'}^l) \in E \\ \gamma\sigma_{i,x}^{k,r-1}, & \text{otherwise,} \end{cases} \quad (7)$$

where y' is any non-core columns. In a similar way, we compute the weight $\sigma_{i,y}^{k,r}$ for candidate entities in the non-core columns. Once all the weights have been computed, we update the dependency scores with Eq. (3).

- **Discover Core Column Set** (lines 10–11). After dep$(\cdot, \cdot)$ is updated, we utilize a k-means ($k = 2$) cluster algorithm to divide dep$(\cdot, \cdot)$ into two groups, one with higher dep$(\cdot, \cdot)$ and the other with lower dep$(\cdot, \cdot)$. ζ is set as the smallest value in the higher-score group. Then, C can discovered by finding the minimize size of core column set that satisfies dep$(x, y) > \zeta$ for $\forall x \in C, y \in X\backslash C$. Since the problem is NP-hard, we apply a heuristic method where we repeatedly identify and mark a column as the core column if it results in the determination of the maximum number of non-core columns.

- **Convergence Check** (line 13). The inner iteration stops when the core column set remains unchanged. To track the progress of convergence, we use the change of $\sigma_{i,x}^{k,r}$ as a metric. When $\sigma_{i,x}^{k,r}$ doesn't change, the output of $s_\tau(\theta, x)$, $\tau(x)$, dep(x, y) also remain unchanged, which leads to a converged core column C. Therefore, to check for convergence, we need to identify any differences in σ, specifically $|\sigma_{i,x}^{k,r} - \sigma_{i,x}^{k,r-1}|$. We define the check variable δ as $\sum_{x\in X}\sum_{i=1}^m\sum_{k=1}^K(|\sigma_{i,x}^{k,r} - \sigma_{i,x}^{k,r-1}|)/(mnK)$. Convergence of $\sigma_{i,x}^{k,r}$ can be proved by applying Cauchy's convergence criterion [30]. It follows that both $\tau(x)$ for every column x, dep(x, y) and C are also convergent, indicating the guaranteed convergence of the inner iteration. To terminate the inner iteration, we set the threshold η to stop at $\delta < \eta$. In Sect. 5.6, we discuss the impact of η.

5   Experiment

We conduct experiments to evaluate the performance of DaCo. There are four research questions to seek in this section:

- **RQ1:** How does DaCo perform compared with other baselines of core column set discovery task?

– **RQ2:** To what extent do multiple core columns, unlinkable mention portion, and the number of sampled rows impact the effectiveness of DaCo?
– **RQ3:** What is the impact of parameter settings on the performance of DaCo?
– **RQ4:** How does DaCo improve the performance of table understanding?

5.1 Experimental Settings

Dataset: We use two main data sources:

– **Table Corpus:** We conducted experiments for core column set discovery on SEM[4] [3], T2D [1], GIT [2], WIKI [4] and TUS [34]. In all datasets, except T2D, we manually identified the single core column in each table. We excluded blank tables and tables without core columns in GIT. For TUS, we labeled it by sampling 300 tables. Additionally, we introduce a new dataset called MULTICC, consisting of 94 tables, which is collected from SEM and WIKI for multiple core column discovery, by adding new columns generated with reference to the KG. The statistics of these datasets are summarized in Table 2. We use the portion of unlinkable mentions (UMP) in each table corpus to indicate the overlap between tables and KGs.
– **Knowledge Graphs:** We use subsets of DBpedia [25], *i.e.,mappingbased_objects_en, mappingbased_literals_en, instance_types_en, DBpedia Ontology*.

Table 2. Statistics of table datasets.

Dataset	$|T|$	$\bar{m}$	$\bar{n}$	$\max_m$	$\max_n$	$\sum m$	$\sum n$	$UMP[\%]$
SEM	180	1080.21	4.46	15,478	8	194,438	803	6.74
T2D	233	121.60	4.950	586	14	28,333	1,153	30.53
GIT	460	47.27	18.00	1,015	75	38,478	14,652	53.92
WIKI	428	35.55	3.79	465	6	15,215	1,622	61.10
TUS	5049	1932.12	10.98	4,987	44	9,755,274	55,438	>72.12
MULTICC	94	1132.23	3.47	15,477	7	106,430	326	28.99

Baselines: We compared DaCo with ten baseline methods, including five heuristic-based methods (LEFT, UNI, SUP, CONN, MIX [14]), two database-based methods (HPIValid (HPI) [5], GORDIAN (GOR) [40]), and three machine learning-based methods (SVM [45], NK [6], TURL [12]). SUP, CONN, and MIX are based on disambiguation results and linked edges between columns. HPI and GOR are key discovery approaches in data profiling, where we implement modules such as preprocessing, sampling, tree search and validation of HPI, prefix tree creation and merging, finding non-keys, pruning, and computing keys from non-keys of GOR. SVM and NK are supervised learning methods. TURL is a pretrained table representation model, which

---

[4] It includes tough tables generated from SemTab for dealing with the tabular data to KG matching problem.

Table 3. Precision, accuracy and recall of core column discovery. Pre, Acc and Rec represent precision, accuracy and recall, respectively. The bolds denote the best results.

	Method	SEM			T2D			GIT			WIKI			TUS		
		Pre	Acc	Rec	Pre	Acc	Rec	Pre	Acc	Rec	Pre	Acc	Rec	Pre	Acc	Rec
Heuristic	LEFT	.811	.898	.811	.906	.941	.906	.594	.865	.594	.624	.778	.624	.380	.862	.380
	UNI	.617	.816	.617	.644	.790	.644	.757	.911	.757	.675	.794	.675	.280	.859	.280
	SUP	.378	.590	.378	.498	.663	.498	.622	.868	.622	.304	.601	.304	.200	.825	.200
	CONN	.439	.628	.439	.451	.642	.451	.639	.878	.639	.344	.631	.344	.180	.816	.180
	MIX	.361	.571	.361	.506	.671	.506	.598	.857	.598	.278	.584	.278	.160	.814	.160
DB	HPI	.633	.810	.633	.691	.812	.691	.735	.904	.735	.703	.811	.703	.400	.882	.400
	GOR	.628	.817	.628	.640	.778	.640	.737	.903	.737	.668	.789	.668	.337	.862	.337
ML	SVM	.400	.498	.400	.652	.474	.652	.587	.854	.587	.175	.482	.175	.060	.661	.060
	NK	.806	.810	.806	.871	.902	.871	.535	.761	.535	.643	.726	.643	.360	.858	.360
	TURL	.683	.689	.683	.652	.776	.652	.613	.834	.613	.591	.695	.591	.080	.760	.080
DaCo		**.850**	**.901**	**.850**	**.949**	**.970**	**.949**	**.798**	**.930**	**.798**	**.918**	**.959**	**.918**	**.800**	**.959**	**.800**

we fine-tuned it by using the cross-entropy loss function and 70 tables in T2D with their core column labels.

Parameter Default Configurations: Parameter q for calculating $d(x, y)$ is 1, convergence threshold $\eta=0.01$, decay parameter $\gamma=0.85$ [4], sample number $m_s=10$.

5.2 Overall Performance (RQ1)

In this study, precision, accuracy, and recall results of different approaches are reported on five table corpora (Table 3). Notice that all tables in the corpus have a single core column, resulting in identical precision and recall values.

The evaluation of various methods indicates DaCo's superiority over state-of-the-art baselines in all five benchmark datasets. DaCo attains precision improvements ranging from 3.9%-40% and accuracy improvements from 0.3%-14.8%. Precision ranges between 80% to 95% and accuracy varies from 90%-97% across different table corpora. DaCo performs better than baselines even with incomplete data (e.g., WIKI and TUS), making it effective for various types of tables, particularly those with more unlinkable mentions. These results demonstrate DaCo's robustness for core column detection in table understanding.

5.3 Effects of Unlinkable Mentions (RQ2-1)

We conducted an experiment to study the impact of Unlinkable Mention Portion (UMP) in tables by randomly setting cells to blank with varying rates to simulate UMP. The results of this experiment are presented in Fig. 3.

Our experimental findings demonstrate that DaCo outperforms existing approaches, particularly when dealing with tables containing numerous unlinkable mentions. Despite a decrease in precision with an increase in UMP, DaCo achieves a precision of over 70% and yields improvements of approximately 10% and 20% on GIT and WIKI, respectively, when UMP is 90%. The superior performance of DaCo can be

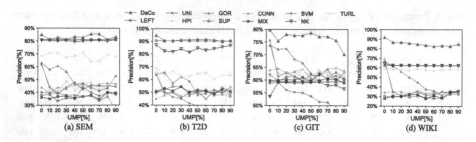

Fig. 3. Effects of unlinkable mention. Precision of four table corpus are depicted with UMP ranging from 10% to 90%.

attributed to its ability to extract valid dependencies using rough matching, even in the presence of a scarcity of linkable mentions. Additionally, our results highlight that DaCo has a distinct advantage in processing real-life tables with incomplete data.

5.4   Effects of Row Sampling (RQ2-2)

In order to further investigate the effectiveness of DaCo, we conduct experiments within the range of sampled row numbers ($m_s = [2, 20]$) in each outer iteration. For comparison, baselines sample m_s rows in this experiment. As shown in Fig. 4, we compare the results with DaCo$^-$, which represents our model without termination check module, *i.e.,*running once in outer iteration.

Based on the results shown in Fig. 4, DaCo outperforms other methods in most cases, with its precision gradually increasing and leveling off as the number of sampled rows increases. Even only with two rows, DaCo reports precision about 75%-90%. On GIT and WIKI, DaCo outperforms other methods on any of m_s with an improvement of at least 3% and 18% respectively. This further demonstrates that DaCo can achieve good results even with a small number of sampled rows on tables with many unlinkable mentions, making it suitable for real-life tables with various size.

Comparing DaCo with DaCo$^-$, DaCo achieves higher precision, especially with a lower number of sampled rows, *e.g.,*it brings an improvement on precision to DaCo$^-$ about 10%, 12%, 11% and 8% on different table corpus. This is because a smaller

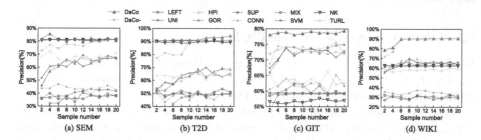

Fig. 4. Sample number effect on core column discovery. Sample number m_s is ranged from 2 to 20. The whole table will be input when it has less number of rows than m_s.

number of sampled rows is more likely to result in biased samples. Termination check can prevent this. Therefore, the existence of the termination check module improves the precision of results, particularly when working with small tables.

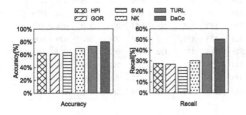 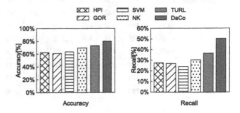

Fig. 5. Results on MULTICC   **Fig. 6.** Effects of varying q and η

5.5 Effects of Multiple Core Columns (RQ2-3)

In order to evaluate the performance of DaCo in identifying multiple core column from tables, we conducted experiments on MULTICC. We extend the DB and ML approaches to support multi core columns discovery for comparison of accuracy and recall, as shown in Fig. 5. DB is designed to implement the identification of unique column combinations, which inherently allows for the discovery of multiple core columns. ML involves classifying each column, and in cases where multiple columns in a table are classified as core columns, it provides results for multiple core column discovery.

The evaluation results show that DaCo outperforms state-of-the-art methods in identifying tables with multiple core columns, achieving an accuracy improvement of 8% and a recall improvement of 13%. Specifically, DaCo achieves an accuracy of 80% and a recall of 50% for multiple core column discovery, which indicates its effectiveness in discovering multiple core columns even without metadata and complete data.

5.6 Effects of Varying Parameter Settings (RQ3)

We investigated the impact of parameter settings, specifically the values of q in $\mathrm{dep}_\tau(\cdot, \cdot)$ and η in the inner iteration. Figure 6 reveals an initial increase, followed by fluctuation within a certain range, and eventually a decrease in precision on both of q and η. We found that the highest precision for core column discovery in both datasets was achieved when $q=1.00$ and $\eta=0.01$.

Table 4. Effects on table understanding tasks' precision.

Method		Column Type Prediction						Entity Linking						Relation Extraction		
		T2K			Hybrid I			T2K			Hybrid I			T2K		
		SEM	T2D	WIKI	SEM	T2D	WIKI	SEM	T2D	WIKI	SEM	T2D	WIKI	SEM	T2D	WIKI
Heuristic	LEFT	.320	.220	.620	.381	.354	.380	.438	.312	.217	.582	.100	.178	.326	.096	.153
	UNI	.330	.142	.553	.381	.241	.391	.334	.178	.234	.410	.073	.206	.278	.104	.170
	SUP	.300	.152	.448	.356	.288	.201	.330	.183	.165	.218	.047	.070	.120	.054	.082
	CONN	.305	.114	.306	.332	.202	.191	.324	.123	.131	.231	.053	.076	.166	.079	.079
	MIX	.282	.156	.435	.349	.302	.198	.319	.188	.175	.192	.048	.067	.104	.073	.075
DB	HPI	.339	.188	.553	.380	.259	.423	.334	.226	.224	.385	.075	.207	.260	.131	.190
	GOR	.314	.149	.541	.385	.239	.392	.345	.169	.219	.413	.077	.199	.255	.118	.181
DaCo		**.795**	**.646**	**.630**	**.795**	**.646**	**.630**	**.457**	**.347**	**.290**	**.590**	**.114**	**.287**	**.733**	**.533**	**.442**

5.7 Performance on Table Understanding Tasks (RQ4)

We present various experiments to demonstrate the effectiveness of DaCo in three primary tasks in table understanding [53]: Column Type Prediction (CTP), Entity Linking (EL), and Relation Extraction (RE). We integrate DaCo with two core column-based table understanding methods, T2K [38] and Hybrid I [13], and evaluate the results. We do not compare Hybrid I's RE task as it does not include a RE implementation. Both methods are core column based table understanding approaches. The CTP and RE tasks are subsequently completed based on these linked entities or entity candidate sets. Table 4 summarizes the precision of the two table understanding models using core column discovery.

The table shows that DaCo significantly outperforms state-of-the-art baselines in CTP, achieving precision values of 60%-80% compared to the precision values of T2K and Hybrid I. This is because DaCo returns a more accurate or fine-grained column type than baselines. For example, in Fig. 1, DaCo returns "Director" while T2K returns "Person" for the 5th column , where we identify "Director" as the correct result. DaCo's advantage in CTP is due to the use of dependency analysis and two-level iteration to refine the type of each column during core column discovery, which yields more precise column types. T2K and Hybrid I often predict a general type by majority voting of top-1 results. In EL, DaCo also achieves a slight improvement in precision by 0.8%, 3.5%, and 5.6% over state-of-the-art baselines when inputting the core columns identified by DaCo. For RE, DaCo again outperforms the state-of-the-art baselines, achieving precision values of 44%-73% and improving RE by 30%-50%.

6 Related Work

Table Understanding. The comprehension of table semantics for downstream applications is essential, and this task often involves referencing a knowledge graph [53]. Table understanding research can be divided into core column-based and core column-free. Core column-free techniques generate representations from supervised learning or context in table surroundings [9,35,37,42]. In contrast, core column-based methods integrate semantics more efficiently from core column entities to non-core column attributes [16,27,31,56,57]. We consider discovering core columns is a crucial task for successful table understanding. However, there is currently a lack of deep investigation into this area [6].

Core Column Discovery. Core column discovery is a crucial task in web table understanding [53] that can provide input to multiple downstream applications [18,26, 27,36,51]. There are three main categories approaches for core column discovery: (1) heuristic-based. Heuristic approaches often select the leftmost column [7,52,54] or the most unique column [16,23,55]. However, these approaches only focus on a single core column and lack explanation; (2) machine learning-based. They treat core column discovery as a binary classification problem for each column [6,45], which suffer from the unavailability of training data due to the limited labeled tables and the lack of metadata; (3) databased-based. These methods aim to identify core columns based on unique column detection and functional dependency [22,29], which often demand numerous tables to explore inter-table information for reducing noise. Our approach is based on the perspective of mining inter-column dependencies semantically, which is ignored by most previous work.

Dependencies in Database. Functional dependencies are fundamental to discover keys, rules, and schema in relational data. They allow for the determination of whether one column set can uniquely determine the value of another column set [24]. In response to the growing demands of real-world datasets, extensions to functional dependencies have been proposed [15,24,43,47]. However, semantic dependencies are defined on tables using KG and discovered by relations in KG but not value uniqueness in functional dependency studies.

7   Conclusion

DaCo is a novel method for discovering core column that can handle challenges such as incomplete and inconsistent data, lack of metadata, and multiple core columns. This is achieved by defining a new semantic dependency that measures the inter-column relationship and a two-level iterative algorithm to obtain the core columns. Extensive experiments demonstrate the effectiveness of our model on various aspects and improvements in table understanding tasks.

Supplemental Material Statement: Code for our DaCo and dataset are available from GitHub at https://github.com/barrel-0314/daco.git.

Acknowledgements. We would like to thank Jiaoyan Chen for his useful comment on this paper. This work is supported by the State Grid Technology Project "research and application of key technologies for automatic graphic construction of power grid control system driven by model and data", the National Natural Science Foundation of China under the grant numbers [62061146001, 62072099, 62232004], the "Zhishan" Scholars Programs of Southeast University, and the Fundamental Research Funds for the Central Universities.

References

1. T2d gold standard for matching web tables to dbpedia (2015). http://webdatacommons.org/webtables/goldstandard.html
2. Gittables benchmark-column type detection (2021). https://zenodo.org/record/5706316#.YxAVU9NBw2x
3. Semtab 2021: Semantic web challenge on tabular data to knowledge graph matching (2021), http://www.cs.ox.ac.uk/isg/challenges/sem-tab/2021/
4. Bhagavatula, C.S., Noraset, T., Downey, D.: TabEL: entity linking in web tables. In: Arenas, M., et al. (eds.) ISWC 2015. LNCS, vol. 9366, pp. 425–441. Springer, Cham (2015). https://doi.org/10.1007/978-3-319-25007-6_25
5. Birnick, J., Blasius, T., Friedrich, T., Naumann, F., Papenbrock, T., Schirneck, M.: Hitting set enumeration with partial information for unique column combination discovery. In: Proceedings of the VLDB Endowment, vol. 13, pp. 2070–2083 (2020)
6. Bornemann, L., Bleifuß, T., Kalashnikov, D.V., Naumann, F., Srivastava, D.: Natural key discovery in wikipedia tables. In: Proceedings of The Web Conference 2020, pp. 2789–2795 (2020)
7. Cafarella, M.J., Halevy, A., Wang, D.: WebTables: exploring the power of tables on the web. In: Proceedings of the VLDB Endowment, pp. 538–549 (2008)
8. Cafarella, M.J., Halevy, A., Wang, D., Wu, E., Zhang, Y.: Uncovering the relational web. In: Proceedings of the 11th International Workshop on Web and Databases (2008)
9. Chen, J., Jiménez-Ruiz, E., Horrocks, I., Sutton, C.: ColNet: embedding the semantics of web tables for column type prediction. In: Proceedings of the AAAI Conference on Artificial Intelligence, vol. 33, pp. 29–36 (2019)
10. Chen, Z., Trabelsi, M., Heflin, J., Xu, Y., Davison, B.D.: Table search using a deep contextualized language model. In: Proceedings of the 43rd International ACM SIGIR Conference on Research and Development in Information Retrieval. pp. 589–598 (2020)
11. Chirigati, F., Liu, J., Korn, F., Wu, Y., Yu, C., Zhang, H.: Knowledge exploration using tables on the web. In: Proceedings of the VLDB Endowment, vol. 10, pp. 193–204 (2016)
12. Deng, X., Sun, H., Lees, A., Wu, Y., Yu, C.: TURL: table understanding through representation learning. In: Proceedings of the 2022 ACM SIGMOD International Conference on Management of Data, vol. 14, pp. 33–40 (2022)
13. Efthymiou, V., Hassanzadeh, O., Rodriguez-Muro, M., Christophides, V.: Matching web tables with knowledge base entities: from entity lookups to entity embeddings. In: Proceedings of the International Semantic Web Conference, pp. 260–277 (2017)
14. Ermilov, I., Ngomo, A.-C.N.: TAIPAN: automatic property mapping for tabular data. In: Blomqvist, E., Ciancarini, P., Poggi, F., Vitali, F. (eds.) EKAW 2016. LNCS (LNAI), vol. 10024, pp. 163–179. Springer, Cham (2016). https://doi.org/10.1007/978-3-319-49004-5_11
15. Fan, W., Wu, Y., Xu, J.: Functional dependencies for graphs. In: Proceedings of the 2016 ACM SIGMOD International Conference on Management of Data, pp. 1843–1857 (2016)
16. Gentile, A.L., Ristoski, P., Eckel, S., Ritze, D., Paulheim, H.: Entity matching on web tables: a table embeddings approach for blocking. In: Proceedings of the 20th International Conference on Extending Database Technology, pp. 510–513 (2017)
17. Harmouch, H., Papenbrock, T., Naumann, F.: Relational header discovery using similarity search in a table corpus. In: 2021 IEEE 37th International Conference on Data Engineering, pp. 444–455. IEEE (2021)
18. Ho, V.T., Pal, K., Razniewski, S., Berberich, K., Weikum, G.: Extracting contextualized quantity facts from web tables. In: Proceedings of the Web Conference 2021, pp. 4033–4042 (2021)

19. Ibrahim, Y., Riedewald, M., Weikum, G., Zeinalipour-Yazti, D.: Bridging quantities in tables and text. In: Proceedings of IEEE 35th International Conference on Data Engineering, pp. 1010–1021 (2019)
20. Khatiwada, A., et al.: Santos: relationship-based semantic table union search. CoRR abs/2209.13589 (2022)
21. Korini1, K., Peeters, R., Bizer, C.: SOTAB: the WDC schema.org table annotation benchmark. In: Proceedings of the Semantic Web Challenge on Tabular Data to Knowledge Graph Matching co-located with the 21st International Semantic Web Conference, vol. 3320, pp. 14–19 (2022)
22. Kruit, B., Boncz, P., Urbani, J.: Extracting N-ary facts from wikipedia table clusters. In: Proceedings of the 29th ACM International Conference on Information & Knowledge Management, pp. 655–664 (2020)
23. Kruit, B., Boncz, P., Urbani, J.: TAKCO: a platform for extracting novel facts from tables. In: Companion Proceedings of the Web Conference, pp. 705–707 (2021)
24. Kruse, S., Naumann, F.: Efficient discovery of approximate dependencies. In: Proceedings of the VLDB Endowment, vol. 11, pp. 759–772 (2018)
25. Lehmann, J., et al.: Dbpedia - a large-scale, multilingual knowledge base extracted from wikipedia. Semantic Web 6(2), 167–195 (2014)
26. Lehmberg, O., Bizer, C.: Web table column categorisation and profiling. In: Proceedings of the 19th International Workshop on Web and Databases, pp. 1–7 (2016)
27. Lehmberg, O., Bizer, C.: Stitching web tables for improving matching quality. In: Proceedings of the VLDB Endowment, vol. 10, pp. 1502–1513 (2017)
28. Lehmberg, O., Bizer, C.: Profiling the semantics of N-ary web table data. In: Proceedings of the International Workshop on Semantic Big Data, vol. 5, pp. 1–6 (2019)
29. Lehmberg, O., Bizer, C.: Synthesizing N-ary relations from web tables. In: Proceedings of the 9th International Conference on Web Intelligence, Mining and Semantics, vol. 17, pp. 1–12 (2019)
30. Li, Z.: Cauchy convergence topologies on the space of continuous functions. Topol. Appl. 161, 321–329 (2014)
31. Luzuriaga, J., Munoz, E., Rosales-Mendez, H., Hogan, A.: Merging web tables for relation extraction with knowledge graphs. IEEE Trans. Knowl. Data Eng. 35(2), 1803–1816 (2023)
32. Marzocchi, M., Cremaschi, M., Pozzi, R., Avogadro, R., Palmonari, M.: MammoTab: a giant and comprehensive dataset for semantic table interpretation. In: Proceedings of the Semantic Web Challenge on Tabular Data to Knowledge Graph Matching co-located with the 21st International Semantic Web Conference, vol. 3320, pp. 28–33 (2022)
33. Mohri, M., Rostamizadeh, A., Talwalkar, A.: Foundations of Machine Learning. The MIT Press (2018)
34. Nargesian, F., Zhu, E., Pu, K.Q., Miller, R.J.: Table union search on open data. In: Proceedings of the VLDB Endowment, vol. 11, pp. 813–825 (2018)
35. Neumaier, S., Umbrich, J., Parreira, J.X., Polleres, A.: Multi-level semantic labelling of numerical values. In: Groth, P., et al. (eds.) Proceedings of the 15th International Semantic Web Conference, pp. 428–445 (2016)
36. Nguyen, P., Kertkeidkachorn, N., Ichise, R., Takeda, H.: TabEAno: table to knowledge graph entity annotation. CoRR abs/2010.01829 (2020)
37. Pham, M., Alse, S., Knoblock, C.A., Szekely, P.: Semantic labeling: a domain-independent approach. In: Groth, P., et al., (eds.) Proceedings of the 15th International Semantic Web Conference, pp. 446–462 (2016)
38. Ritze, D., Lehmberg, O., Bizer, C.: Matching html tables to DBpedia. In: Proceedings of the 5th International Conference on Web Intelligence, Mining and Semantics, pp. 1–6 (2015)
39. Shyu, S.j., Yin, P., Lin, B.M.T.: An ant colony optimization algorithm for the minimum weight vertex cover problem. Ann. Oper. Res. 131, 283–304 (2004)

40. Sismanis, Y., Brown, P., Haas, P.J., Reinwald, B.: GORDIAN: efficient and scalable discovery of composite keys. In: Proceedings of the VLDB Endowment, pp. 691–702 (2006)
41. Sun, H., Ma, H., Yih, W.t., Yan, X.: Table cell search for question answering. In: Proceedings of the 25th International Conference on World Wide Web, pp. 771–782 (2016)
42. Takeoka, K., Oyamada, M., Nakadai, S., Okadome, T.: Meimei: an efficient probabilistic approach for semantically annotating tables. In: Proceedings of the AAAI Conference on Artificial Intelligence, vol. 33, pp. 281–288 (2019)
43. Tan, Z., Ran, A., Ma, S., Qin, S.: Fast incremental discovery of pointwise order dependencies. In: Proceedings of the VLDB Endwment, vol. 13, pp. 1669–1681 (2020)
44. Trabelsi, M., Chen, Z., Zhang, S., Davison, B.D., Heflin, J.: StruBERT: structure-aware BERT for table search and matching. In: Proceedings of the Web Conference 2022, pp. 442–451 (2021)
45. Venetis, P., et al.: Recovering semantics of tables on the web. In: Proceedings of the VLDB Endowment, vol. 4, pp. 528–538 (2011)
46. Wang, N., Ren, X.: Identifying multiple entity columns in web tables. Int. J. Softw. Eng. Knowl. Eng. 28(3), 287–309 (2018)
47. Wei, Z., Hartmann, S., Link, S.: Discovery algorithms for embedded functional dependencies. In: Proceedings of the 2020 ACM SIGMOD International Conference on Management of Data, pp. 833–843 (2020)
48. Yin, P., Neubig, G., Yih, W.T., Riedel, S.: TaBERT: pretraining for joint understanding of textual and tabular data. In: Proceedings of the 58th Annual Meeting of the Association for Computational Linguistics, ACL 2020, pp. 8413–8426 (2020)
49. Zhang, M., Chakrabarti, K.: InfoGather+ semantic matching and annotation of numeric and time-varying attributes in web tables. In: Proceedings of the 2013 ACM SIGMOD International Conference on Management of Data, pp. 145–156 (2013)
50. Zhang, S., Balog, K.: Ad hoc table retrieval using semantic similarity. In: Proceedings of the World Wide Web Conference, pp. 1553–1562 (2018)
51. Zhang, S., Balog, K.: On-the-fly table generation. In: Proceedings of the 41st International ACM SIGIR Conference on Research & Development in Information Retrieval, pp. 595–604 (2018)
52. Zhang, S., Balog, K.: Auto-completion for data cells in relational tables. In: Proceedings of the 28th ACM International Conference on Information and Knowledge Management, pp. 761–770 (2019)
53. Zhang, S., Balog, K.: Web table extraction, retrieval, and augmentation: a survey. ACM Trans. Intell. Syst. Technol. 11, 13:1-13:35 (2020)
54. Zhang, S., Meij, E., Balog, K., Rernanda, R.: Novel entity discovery from web tables. In: Proceedings of International World Wide Web Conference, pp. 1298–1308 (2020)
55. Zhang, X., Chen, Y., Chen, J., Du, X., Zou, L.: Mapping entity-attribute web tables to web-scale knowledge bases. In: Meng, W., Feng, L., Bressan, S., Winiwarter, W., Song, W. (eds.) DASFAA 2013. LNCS, vol. 7826, pp. 108–122. Springer, Heidelberg (2013). https://doi.org/10.1007/978-3-642-37450-0_8
56. Zhang, Z.: Towards efficient and effective semantic table interpretation. In: Mika, P., et al. (eds.) ISWC 2014. LNCS, vol. 8796, pp. 487–502. Springer, Cham (2014). https://doi.org/10.1007/978-3-319-11964-9_31
57. Zhang, Z.: Effective and efficient semantic table interpretation using TableMiner+. Semantic Web 8(6), 921–957 (2017)
58. Zhu, G., Iglesias, C.A.: Computing semantic similarity of concepts in knowledge graphs. IEEE Trans. Knowl. Data Eng. 29(1), 72–89 (2017)

Spatial Link Prediction with Spatial and Semantic Embeddings

Genivika Mann[1], Alishiba Dsouza[1](✉), Ran Yu[1,2],
and Elena Demidova[1,2]

[1] Data Science & Intelligent Systems (DSIS), University of Bonn, Bonn, Germany
{genivika.mann,dsouza,elena.demidova}@cs.uni-bonn.de, ran.yu@uni-bonn.de
[2] Lamarr Institute for Machine Learning and Artificial Intelligence, Bonn, Germany
https://lamarr-institute.org/

Abstract. Semantic geospatial applications, such as geographic question answering, have benefited from knowledge graphs incorporating information regarding geographic entities and their relations. However, one of the most critical limitations of geographic knowledge graphs is the lack of semantic relations between geographic entities. The most extensive knowledge graphs specifically tailored to geographic entities are extracted from unstructured sources, with these graphs often relying on datatype properties to describe the entities, resulting in a flat representation that lacks entity relationships. Therefore, predicting links between geographic entities is essential for advancing semantic geospatial applications. Existing neural link prediction methods for knowledge graphs typically rely on pre-existing entity relations, making them unsuitable for scenarios where such information is absent. In this paper, we tackle the challenge of predicting spatial links in sparsely interlinked knowledge graphs by introducing two novel approaches: supervised spatial link prediction (SSLP) and unsupervised inductive spatial link prediction (USLP). These approaches leverage the wealth of literal values in geographic knowledge graphs through spatial and semantic embeddings. To assess the effectiveness of our proposed methods, we conduct evaluations on the WorldKG geographic knowledge graph, which incorporates geospatial data extracted from OpenStreetMap. Our results demonstrate that the SSLP and USLP approaches substantially outperform state-of-the-art link prediction methods.

Keywords: Knowledge Graph Completion · Spatial Link Prediction · Literals

1 Introduction

Knowledge graphs (KGs) serve as standardized semantic knowledge representations that facilitate the integration, inference, and relationship establishment among heterogeneous data sources. Domain-specific geographic knowledge graphs are specialized knowledge graphs that focus on representing locations on Earth. Although knowledge graphs are widely adopted in various semantic applications, their incompleteness remains a challenging problem. Link prediction in

© The Author(s) 2023
T. R. Payne et al. (Eds.): ISWC 2023, LNCS 14265, pp. 179–196, 2023.
https://doi.org/10.1007/978-3-031-47240-4_10

knowledge graphs has attracted a lot of research attention recently [7,21,28,30]. However, existing link prediction methods primarily focus on well-connected graphs with well-defined and structured object properties. Such methods often neglect rich semantic information in datatype properties that capture essential attributes of geographic entities such as names, descriptions, and spatial coordinates.

An example of a recently proposed geographic knowledge graph is WorldKG [8], which includes various entities representing geographic locations extracted from OpenStreetMap (OSM)[1]. As illustrated in Fig. 1, WorldKG contains the entity *wkg:10021976* representing the city of Leicester, located in the county of Leicestershire in the United Kingdom. Although WorldKG also contains the entities *wkg:838090640* representing the United Kingdom and *wkg:302324104* representing the county of Leicestershire, there are no links between these entities in the knowledge graph. The entity representing Leicester includes the spatial relations *wkgs:isInCountry* and *wkgs:isInCounty* associating this entity with the literals *"United Kingdom"* and *"Leicestershire"*, while lacking the links to the corresponding entities. Spatial link prediction can help interlink these geographic entities to further exploit the information in the knowledge graph.

In the context of link prediction to identify spatial relations between geographic entities, for instance, *wkgs:capitalCity*, *wkgs:isInCountry*, *wkgs:isInCounty*, spatial and literal values are critical. These values play a vital role in indicating entity proximity and the types of spatial relationships. Spatial link prediction can enhance the expressiveness of knowledge graphs, making it possible to solve complex spatial queries, reveal transitive relations, and eliminate geographic disambiguation issues. Downstream tasks in geospatial question answering, data retrieval, and cross-domain semantic data-driven applications in mobility, tourism, logistics, and city planning can also benefit significantly from accurate representations of spatial semantics in knowledge graphs.

Only few link prediction methods utilize textual entity descriptions [4,12] or numeric literals [23,27,28] to supplement the information provided through the graph structure. However, these approaches do not perform well without structural information from entity relations or in the presence of heterogeneous textual and numerical datatype properties of varied lengths [10]. Name disambiguation is another challenge when linking geographic entities, primarily due to the presence of homonymous names, synonyms, and variations. For instance, *Toronto* is a city's name in Canada and the USA. Similarly, *Germany*, *DE*, and *Deutschland* refer to the same country. Explicit spatial and contextual information is crucial for accurate spatial linking. Furthermore, existing approaches typically operate in transductive settings, aiming to predict the links between entities known at training time, whereas predicting links in the inductive settings, where the entities unseen during training appear, is a more difficult task [2].

---

[1] OpenStreetMap, OSM and the OpenStreetMap magnifying glass logo are trademarks of the OpenStreetMap Foundation, and are used with their permission. We are not endorsed by or affiliated with the OpenStreetMap Foundation.

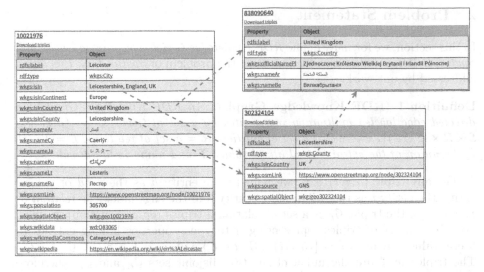

Fig. 1. An excerpt from the WorldKG knowledge graph [8], illustrating three entities *wkg:10021976, wkg:838090640, wkg:302324104* representing Leicester, United Kingdom and Leicestershire, respectively. Arrows in orange indicate potential spatial links currently missing in the WorldKG knowledge graph.

In this paper, we tackle the problem of spatial link prediction and introduce two novel approaches: Supervised Spatial Link Prediction (SSLP) and Unsupervised Spatial Link Prediction (USLP). These approaches are designed to operate in different modes, namely transductive and inductive link prediction. The SSLP architecture leverages location embedding and word embeddings to capture literal and spatial semantics, followed by enhancement of the tail embeddings using multi-head attention and a hierarchy-based scoring function to learn the containment hierarchy of geographic entities. In USLP, we score the tail entities for a given triple by computing the similarity between head, relation, and tail in different latent spaces based on geographic proximity and literal properties.

In summary, the main contributions of this paper are as follows:

– We propose two novel approaches, SSLP and USLP, for supervised and unsupervised spatial link prediction. These approaches leverage literal and geospatial semantics by incorporating spatial and semantic embeddings.
– We assess the performance of existing knowledge graph completion methods on the task of spatial link prediction in real-world scenarios where the knowledge graph lacks entity relationships.
– Through extensive experiments, we demonstrate that our proposed approaches outperform the baseline methods by a significant margin in terms of the Hits@k metric. These results highlight the effectiveness of our proposed approaches in spatial link prediction tasks.

2   Problem Statement

In this section, we formally define *RDF Knowledge Graph*, *Geographic Entity* and *Spatial Relation*, following which we state the problem of *Spatial Link Prediction* addressed by our work.

Definition 1 (RDF Knowledge Graph). *An RDF Knowledge Graph is a directed edge labeled multigraph represented by a set of triples* $\mathcal{G} = \{(h, r, t) \in \mathcal{E} \times \mathcal{R} \times (\mathcal{E} \cup \mathcal{L})\}$, *where* $\mathcal{E} = $ *a set of entities,* $\mathcal{R} = $ *a set of relations,* $\mathcal{L} = \mathcal{T} \cup \mathcal{N}$ *is the union of the set of textual literal values* $\mathcal{T}$ *and numeric literal values* $\mathcal{N}$.

For any triple $(h, r, t) \in \mathcal{G}$, we refer to the entity h as the *head* or *subject* entity, the entity t as the *tail* or *object* entity and the edge label r as *relation* or *predicate* of the triple. $\mathcal{G}_E$ is a set of relational triples representing object links, and $\mathcal{G}_L$ is a set of triples representing datatype properties linking entities to literal values. Hence, $\mathcal{G}_E = \{(h, r, t) \in \mathcal{G} \mid t \in \mathcal{E}\}$ and $\mathcal{G}_L = \{(h, r, t) \in \mathcal{G} \mid t \in \mathcal{L}\}$. The triples in $\mathcal{G}$ are the union of the two disjoint sets $\mathcal{G}_E$ and $\mathcal{G}_L$, therefore $\mathcal{G} = \mathcal{G}_E \cup \mathcal{G}_L$ and $\mathcal{G}_E \cap \mathcal{G}_L = \emptyset$.

Let $\mathcal{E}_{geo} \subseteq \mathcal{E}$ be the set of all geographic entities in the knowledge graph.

Definition 2 (Geographic Entity). *An entity* $e \in \mathcal{E}_{geo}$ *is a geographic entity* $\Leftrightarrow \exists r \in \mathcal{R}$ *such that r associates e to geographic coordinates (latitude and longitude).*

Spatial relations are connections between two geographic entities. These connections can imply physical entity relations such as containment, intersection, and adjacency, or conceptual relations such as capital, country, and suburb.

Definition 3 (Spatial Relation). *Let* $\mathcal{R}_{spatial} \subset \mathcal{R}$ *be a set of all spatial relations. A relation* $r_{sp} \in \mathcal{R}_{spatial}$ *is a spatial relation if* $\forall (h, r_{sp}, t) \in \mathcal{G}$ *it holds* $h, t \in \mathcal{E}_{geo}$, *i.e., h and t are geographic entities.*

Spatial link prediction is the task of predicting spatial relations between geographic entities in a knowledge graph.

Definition 4 (Spatial Link Prediction). *Given a knowledge graph* $\mathcal{G}$, *a geographic entity* $h \in \mathcal{E}_{geo}$ *and spatial relation* $r_{sp} \in \mathcal{R}_{spatial}$, *find the geographic entity* $t \in \mathcal{E}_{geo}$ *such that* $(h, r_{sp}, t) \in \mathcal{G}$ *holds.*

3   Approach

We tackle the spatial link prediction problem with spatial and semantic embeddings and propose novel supervised and unsupervised approaches. In this section, we describe the embedding generation process and the proposed approaches. The supervised SSLP approach operates in the *transductive* link prediction setup. In transductive link prediction, the model predicts links between entities known during training; hence, training and prediction are conducted on the same set of

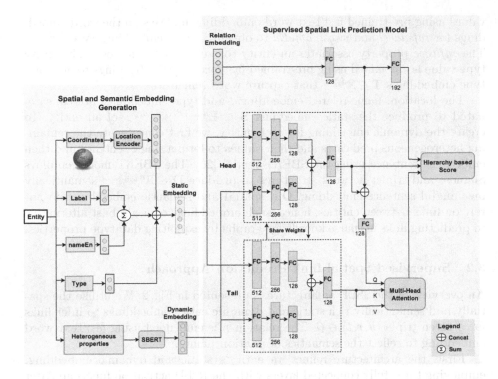

Fig. 2. Overview of spatial and semantic embedding generation of an entity and the architecture of SSLP model.

entities [2]. However, novel entities can emerge in knowledge graphs over time. The *inductive* link prediction setup reflects this scenario by facilitating spatial link prediction for unseen entities that do not appear during model training. Hence, in contrast to the transductive mode, links are predicted between seen and unseen entities of the knowledge graph. Our unsupervised USLP approach operates in this setting.

3.1   Spatial and Semantic Embedding of Entities

We utilize the datatype properties of a geographic entity to compute entity embeddings that capture its spatial and semantic information. The embedding generation process overview is illustrated in Fig. 2.

A geographic entity in a knowledge graph has geographic coordinates (latitude and longitude) associated with it. We embed these coordinates using the location encoding scheme proposed by Mai et al. [16] as a d_{loc} dimensional vector. Using sine and cosine functions of different frequencies, the location coordinates $x \in \mathbb{R}^2$ in 2D space are embedded as $\mathbf{X} \in \mathbb{R}^{d_{loc}}$-dimensional distributed representation. We consider the *rdfs:label* and *wkgs:nameEn* properties, which contain the entity label and name in the English language, and embed each of these values using pre-trained fastText word embedding [6]. We sum the word embeddings for *rdfs:label* and *wkgs:nameEn* to obtain a single embedding $\mathbf{W} \in \mathbb{R}^{d_{label}}$. The *rdf:type* property associates an entity to a class in an ontology. The entity type value is embedded using pre-trained fastText word embeddings to generate type embeddings $\mathbf{T} \in \mathbb{R}^{d_{type}}$ that capture word semantics.

The location, name-related embeddings, and type embeddings are concatenated to produce the static embedding $\mathbf{S} \in \mathbb{R}^{d_{loc}+d_{label}+d_{type}}$ of an entity. To create the dynamic embedding for each entity, we first concatenate the remaining heterogeneous predicates and their values to form a single sentence and then embed the sentence using the SBERT model [20]. The SBERT model employs Siamese and triplet network structures to produce $\mathbf{D} \in \mathbb{R}^{d_{dynamic}}$ semantically meaningful sentence embedding. Our spatial and semantic embeddings do not rely on links between entities; hence, such embeddings offer a robust alternative to predicting links in sparse knowledge graphs by exploiting datatype properties.

3.2   Supervised Spatial Link Prediction Approach

An overview of the SSLP architecture is presented in Fig. 2. We utilize the spatially and semantically rich static and dynamic entity embeddings to infer links for a given triple $(h, r, t) \in \mathcal{G}$. The relation r is embedded using fastText word embedding to reflect the semantics of relation names.

First, the architecture refines an entity's static and dynamic embedding, employing three fully connected layers with the ReLU activation function. After refinement, the static and dynamic embeddings are concatenated and passed through a fully connected layer to facilitate their fusion. This refinement and fusion operation is applied on both the head and tail entity embeddings, and weights are shared as done in a Siamese network to transform both head and tail embeddings to the same vector space. This ensures the feature learning from the head and tail entity occurs similarly, regardless of whether the entity appears in the head or tail position.

The head embedding obtained at this stage is used for scoring and does not pass through further layers, while multi-head attention is applied to the tail embedding to incorporate head and relation information in the tail embedding and to focus on relevant sections of the embedding. The head and relation embeddings are concatenated and passed through a linear layer to serve as the query, while the tail embedding serves as the key and value input for attention computation. The output of the attention block is treated as the final tail embedding. The head, relation, and tail embeddings are then projected into polar coordinates using a hierarchy-based score function.

The HAKE (Zhang et al. 2020 [30]) score function learns a hierarchy in an embedding space by only using triples to project entities to polar coordinates. We divide entities into hierarchical levels using *rdf:type* and modify the score function f_r to explicitly perform type-based hierarchical penalization using a hierarchy term f_{hterm}. This enables the modeling of semantic hierarchies of geographic entities in the embedding space. For instance, continents should be placed at the highest level, followed by countries, states, and districts, and finally, containing suburbs and burroughs at the lower hierarchy levels. The score function is formulated as follows:

$$f_r(h,t) = -\|\mathbf{h}_m \circ \mathbf{r}_m - \mathbf{t}_m\|_2 - \lambda \|\sin((\mathbf{h}_p + \mathbf{r}_p - \mathbf{t}_p)/2)\|_1 + \eta f_{hterm}. \tag{1}$$

Here, $\mathbf{h}_m, \mathbf{t}_m \in \mathbb{R}^k$, $\mathbf{r}_m \in \mathbb{R}_+^k$ are the radial coordinates, $\mathbf{h}_p, \mathbf{t}_p, \mathbf{r}_p \in [0, 2\pi)^k$ are the angular coordinates of head, tail, and relation embeddings respectively and $\lambda \in \mathbb{R}$ is a learnable weight of phase term. f_{hterm} is the hierarchical penalization term weighed by the learnable parameter $\eta \in \mathbb{R}$. The hierarchical penalization is computed as:

$$f_{hterm}(h, r, t) = \mathbf{r}_{dir} (\mathbf{h}_{level} - \mathbf{t}_{level}), \tag{2}$$

where $\mathbf{h}_{level}, \mathbf{t}_{level} \in \mathbf{Z}_+$ are hierarchy levels using *rdf:type* of head and tail entity respectively and $\mathbf{r}_{dir} \in [-1, +1]$ controls whether the head or tail entity should have a higher hierarchy level for the given relation.

Sampling negative triples is crucial for training models. In our approach, we sample our space to include a diversity of classes by sampling tails that have a different *rdf:type* than the true tail entity and also address hard cases by sampling tails of the same *rdf:type* as the true tail. Sampling tails from different classes allows us to incorporate class distribution during learning. The loss is computed using self-adversarial negative sampling loss (Sun et al. 2019 [22]):

$$L = -\log \sigma(\gamma - f_r(\mathbf{h}, \mathbf{t})) - \sum_{i=1}^{n} p(h'_i, r, t'_i) \log \sigma(f_r(\mathbf{h}'_i, \mathbf{t}'_i) - \gamma). \tag{3}$$

The parameter γ is a fixed margin, σ is the sigmoid function and (h'_i, r, t'_i) is the ith negative triple. The probability distribution of sampling negative triples with α temperature of sampling is given by (Sun et al. 2019 [22]):

$$p(h'_j, r, t'_j | \{(h_i, r, t_i)\}) = \frac{\exp \alpha f_r(\mathbf{h}'_j, \mathbf{t}'_j)}{\sum_i \exp \alpha f_r(\mathbf{h}'_i, \mathbf{t}'_i)}. \tag{4}$$

3.3 Unsupervised Spatial Link Prediction Approach

An overview of the USLP architecture is presented in Fig. 3.

In contrast to the supervised SSLP approach, the unsupervised USLP approach does not require training data for link prediction and operates in the inductive mode. The triple scores are computed by comparing the similarity of head entity, relation, and tail entity features in three spaces, namely *geographic space*, *name space*, and *class space*. In the *geographic space*, the coordinates of head and tail entities are represented using geohash. A geohash is an alphanumeric string that serves as a unique identifier and compact representation of regions using bounding boxes on the Earth surface [9]. This method splits the Earth surface into grid cells of various sizes depending on the length of the geohash.

The precision of the geohash is selected based on the relation in the triple, such that relations that may have a larger spatial distance between the entities are assigned a shorter geohash length to represent a larger area. Similarly, relations where the entities are assumed to be spatially closer, for example, *addrSuburb*, *addrHamlet*, are represented using longer geohash values. The centroid of the rectangular geohash grid is computed for both head and tail entities, and the Haversine distance between the geohash centroids serves as the similarity score in the *geographic space*.

Knowledge graphs often contain spatial relations where the object is a literal string representing the tail entity instead of the link to the entity. This literal value can match candidate tail entities based on their *rdfs:label* and *wkgs:nameEn* properties. In the *name space*, the pre-trained fastText word embeddings of the tail entity generated using *rdfs:label* and *wkgs:nameEn* property are compared with the embeddings of the literal string present in the object position of the spatial relation. The cosine similarity between the two embeddings is used to score the triples in this space. The *class space* also computes the cosine similarity between the embeddings of relation name and tail *rdf:type* class to assign a higher score to entities whose *rdf:type* is semantically similar to relation names in the shared semantic latent space. For example, the relation *wkgs:isInCountry* has a high similarity score with all entities of *rdf:type* country.

The final triple score is computed as the sum of the similarity scores of the embeddings in all three spaces. Tail entities closer to the triple head and relation in the spatial and semantic vector spaces have a higher likelihood of being linked and will therefore achieve a higher score using this scoring scheme.

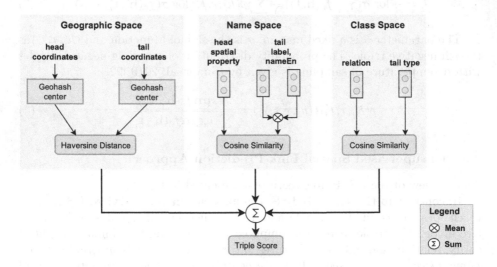

Fig. 3. Architecture of the USLP model.

4   Evaluation Setup

This section describes datasets, ground truth creation, baselines, and evaluation metrics. All experiments were conducted on AMD Ryzen 9 3900X 12-Core processor @ 2.2 GHz and 128 GB of memory using NVIDIA RTX A6000 GPU, CUDA 12.1, Python 3.10.9, and PyTorch 2.0.0. The SSLP model was trained for 3000 epochs with a batch size of 64, a learning rate of 0.001 optimized using Adam optimizer.

4.1   Datasets

For our spatial link prediction experiments, we use the WorldKG knowledge graph constructed by Dsouza et al. [8] using data from OpenStreetMap (OSM), one of the richest sources of openly available semantic volunteered geographic information. Each entity in WorldKG has geographic coordinates and heterogeneous spatial and non-spatial properties with textual and numeric literal values indicating entity names in different languages, areas, populations, geographic divisions such as a county, state, district, hamlet, and links to Wikipedia, Wikidata, and OSM.

4.2   Ground Truth Creation

In the current dataset version, the WorldKG knowledge graph (version 1.0) contains information extracted from OSM tags and does not contain any object property triples, lacking links between entities. All spatial relations are represented as datatype properties, with a string as the object representing a geographic entity. We extracted all triples with predicates that indicate spatial relations in the knowledge graph and prepared a set of candidate entities that were subclasses of *wkgs:Place*. Rule-based matching, using Haversine distance from subject entities, string matching of literal strings in the object position with entity names, and the type and relation-based filtering of subject/object entities, was performed on a subset of triples containing instances covering all spatial relations. We also used the identity link *wkgs:wikidata*, which links entities present in Wikidata and WorldKG, for matching a subset of spatial relations using equivalent relations present in the former knowledge graph.

The ground truth was used to create two transductive datasets, namely **TD1** and **TD2**, for evaluating the supervised approaches. The dataset **TD1** contains ground truth triples generated using WorldKG only, while **TD2** additionally contains triples created using WorldKG and Wikidata identity links. Furthermore, we created the inductive dataset **ID1** containing novel entities in the test triples for evaluating the unsupervised approaches. The test triples of **ID1** are generated by a stratified sampling of 133 triples from the ground truth. Table 1 contains statistics regarding the number of entities, relations, and triples in the three datasets.

Table 1. Dataset statistics. Rows indicate the count of each statistic.

Statistic	Dataset		
	TD1	TD2	ID1
#Entities	223297	284305	313385
#Spatial relations	14	14	14
#Literal relations	354	431	128
#Literal triples	1571175	1077982	1853
#Train triples	247419	323066	323066
#Validation triples	6145	10493	39943
#Test triples	26087	15931	133

4.3   Baselines

We consider state-of-the-art and well-established link prediction methods that can be classified into the following categories as our baselines:

- Translation distance model **TransE** [7] treats relations as a translation from head entity to tail entity. Roto-translational models **RotatE** [22] and **HAKE** [30] consider relations as rotations in a complex vector space.
- Tensor Decomposition models **RESCAL** [18], **DistMult** [29] and **ComplEx** [24].
- Deep learning models such as **ConvKB** [17] which uses convolutional neural networks and **CompGCN** [25] employing graph neural networks.
- **LiteralE** [12] and **Literal2Entity-DistMult** variant proposed by [5] where the former uses literal values to enrich KG embeddings and the latter performs graph transformations using literals.
- For the unsupervised approach, a naive baseline **Levenshtein similarity** (LS) computes string similarity between *rdfs:label* and *wkgs:nameEn* properties of the entities to score tail triples.

All baselines were trained using the default hyperparameters and the evaluation settings reported in the respective publications.

4.4   Evaluation Metrics

We evaluate our models on the spatial link prediction task by following the standard link prediction setup. For each triple $(h, r_{sp}, t) \in \mathcal{G}_{test}$, the set of corrupted triples $\mathcal{T}^-$ is generated by replacing the true tail entity t with all other geographic entities in the knowledge graph, hence $\mathcal{T}^- = \{(h, r_{sp}, t') \mid t' \in (\mathcal{E}_{geo} - \{t\})\}$. The model scores the true triple (h, r_{sp}, t) and corrupted triples in $\mathcal{T}^-$. The triples' scores are then sorted to obtain the rank of the true triple. We use the *filtered* evaluation setting [7] and filter the corrupted triples $\mathcal{T}^-$ to exclude the triples present in the training and validation set. We summarize the overall performance of the models using *Mean rank* (MR), *Mean reciprocal rank* (MRR), and *Hits@k* for $k \in \{1, 3, 5, 10\}$. *Mean rank* is the average rank of the test triples. *Mean reciprocal rank* is the mean over the reciprocal of individual ranks of test triples. *Hits@k* is the ratio of test triples present among the top k ranked triples.

5 Evaluation

This section aims to assess the performance of our proposed SSLP and USLP approaches against prominent baselines.

5.1 Performance in Transductive Setting

The link prediction results in the transductive setting for datasets TD1 and TD2 are summarized in Table 2. Our proposed USLP approach outperforms all baselines on both datasets regarding MRR and Hits@k and achieves the second-best mean rank on TD1. Its performance is closely followed by the proposed SSLP approach, with Hits@3,5,10 lying around three percentage points below the unsupervised model for TD1 and TD2. This result can be attributed to the additional spatial and literal information exploited by our approaches, along with triples for link prediction. The Literal2Entity variant with DistMult score function [5] also utilizes KG literals to transform the knowledge graph and performs well compared to other baselines, which only consider relational triples. It achieves a competitive MRR and Hits@1 compared to USLP on TD1; however, all other metrics are relatively lower than SSLP and USLP on both datasets. A possible reason for its performance lag is the absence of spatial semantics and hierarchical information in the literal transformations and scoring function used in this model, which can be beneficial when predicting spatial links. The LiteralE baseline fails on all metrics, despite utilizing literal triples. A possible reason for its negligible performance can be the inability of the model to scale to a large number of literal relations present in our datasets.

The remaining baselines use knowledge graph triples for predicting links, with their performance lying below a margin of around 20% points in terms of Hits@k compared to USLP and SSLP on both datasets. The sparsity of graph neighborhood and lack of sufficient structural information affects the link prediction ability of the baselines CompGCN and ConvKB employing graph neural networks and convolutions. Simple models such as TransE, RotatE, and HAKE, which treat relations as geometric operations, perform poorly regarding all metrics on TD1 and TD2. These approaches randomly initialize entity and relation embeddings and transform them based on observed triples in the graph, causing performance drop when predicting links in sparse knowledge graphs. DistMult achieves better Hits@k and MRR than other baselines on TD1 and TD2; overall, its results are lower than our approaches by a considerable margin on the TD2 dataset, especially in the case of Hits@1 and Hits@3 metrics.

The ablation study results of SSLP on dynamic embedding, multi-head attention, scoring function, and hierarchy penalization are shown in Table 3. Removing

Table 2. Spatial link prediction performance in transductive setting. The best results are highlighted in bold, and runner-up results are underlined.

Model	TD1 Dataset						TD2 Dataset					
	MR	MRR	H@1	H@3	H@5	H@10	MR	MRR	H@1	H@3	H@5	H@10
TransE	1104	0.147	0.065	0.174	0.229	0.306	12594	0.199	0.114	0.237	0.286	0.357
DistMult	1328	0.861	0.780	0.934	0.968	0.977	22005	0.660	0.568	0.747	0.799	0.808
HAKE	1592	0.327	0.214	0.426	0.475	0.499	13194	0.305	0.235	0.366	0.402	0.409
RotatE	1730	0.791	0.743	0.831	0.849	0.865	31671	0.010	0.002	0.004	0.006	0.021
ComplEx	34410	0.005	0.002	0.005	0.007	0.012	41360	0.025	0.016	0.026	0.032	0.041
CompGCN	750	0.095	0.000	0.004	0.078	0.396	17508	0.229	0.020	0.396	0.485	0.580
ConvKB	2555	0.099	0.019	0.132	0.179	0.249	11348	0.247	0.022	0.405	0.531	0.655
RESCAL	446	0.006	0.000	0.001	0.001	0.000	12337	0.002	0.000	0.000	0.000	0.000
LiteralE	70129	0.000	0.000	0.000	0.000	0.000	43276	0.022	0.016	0.018	0.022	0.039
L2E-DistMult	986	_0.936_	_0.919_	0.951	0.958	0.963	7113	0.797	0.776	0.811	0.820	0.830
SSLP	**144**	0.894	0.823	_0.962_	_0.972_	_0.978_	_6505_	_0.819_	_0.805_	_0.831_	_0.836_	_0.844_
USLP	_188_	**0.964**	**0.941**	**0.990**	**0.995**	**0.996**	**68**	**0.856**	**0.845**	**0.862**	**0.866**	**0.872**

Table 3. Ablation study of SSLP. The best results are highlighted in bold, and runner-up results are underlined.

Component	TD1 Dataset						TD2 Dataset					
	MR	MRR	H@1	H@3	H@5	H@10	MR	MRR	H@1	H@3	H@5	H@10
w/o Dynamic Embedding	212	0.669	0.527	0.781	0.851	0.903	6304	0.508	0.383	0.599	0.658	0.684
w/o Attention	_170_	0.839	0.798	0.859	0.894	0.923	9787	0.682	0.639	0.702	0.725	0.758
w/ DistMult score	327	0.336	0.104	0.434	0.616	0.802	13969	0.226	0.034	0.333	0.604	0.633
w/o Hierarchy term ($\eta = 0$)	280	0.876	0.816	0.922	0.934	0.964	_5444_	0.582	0.423	0.713	0.743	0.786
w/ Hierarchy term ($\eta = 0.25$)	224	_0.886_	**0.831**	0.929	_0.959_	0.974	6732	0.649	0.458	**0.832**	**0.853**	**0.867**
w/ Hierarchy term ($\eta = 0.5$)	213	0.802	0.658	_0.937_	0.951	_0.976_	**4635**	_0.754_	_0.688_	0.813	0.825	0.836
SSLP	**144**	**0.894**	_0.823_	**0.962**	**0.972**	**0.978**	6505	**0.819**	**0.805**	_0.831_	_0.836_	_0.844_

dynamic embedding in SSLP results in a decline in performance across all metrics in both datasets. This result highlights the expressiveness of these embeddings in serving as a latent representation for the heterogeneous predicates present in entities and capturing valuable supplementary information such as provenance, description, population, currency, etc., which boosts link prediction performance. The removal of the Multi-head attention component resulted in a sharp decline in performance for TD1 and TD2, with Hits@k for all k falling by a margin of at least ten percentage points compared to SSLP on the latter dataset. Replacing our hierarchy-based scoring function with the DistMult score also causes a performance drop across all metrics, especially in the case of Hits@1, showcasing the benefit of our hierarchy-based scoring function. To examine the effect of incorporating hierarchy penalization in the scoring function, we experimented with different values for the weight parameter η. The hierarchy penalization in our scoring caused a significant improvement in the performance of SSLP, which uses $\eta = 0.8$ on both datasets, with a rise of Hits@1 by around 38% points for TD2 compared to scoring with $\eta = 0$. The weight initialization of $\eta = 0.25$ also produced the highest Hits@k for k = 3, 5, 10 in TD2.

Table 4. Spatial link prediction performance in the inductive setting. The best results are highlighted in bold, and runner-up results are underlined.

Model	ID1 Dataset					
	MR	MRR	H@1	H@3	H@5	H@10
LS w/ rdfs:label	89	0.051	0.000	0.053	0.083	0.135
LS w/ wkgs:nameEn	121	0.035	0.000	0.023	0.045	0.105
USLP	**3**	**0.832**	**0.774**	**0.857**	**0.902**	**0.939**

5.2   Performance in Inductive Setting

Table 4 shows the results of unsupervised approaches on the ID1 dataset. The naive baseline computes string similarity using Levenshtein distance between *rdfs:label* and *wkgs:nameEn*, showing poor results across all metrics. String matching using literal values for predicting entity links introduces ambiguity with no mechanism to disambiguate candidate entities. Our proposed approach, USLP, fuses spatial proximity with entity naming semantics and type information aiding in precise disambiguation and substantially improved results on the ID1 dataset.

Table 5 reports the results of feature analysis on the USLP model. We compute the evaluation metrics for different combinations of spaces and the inclusion of dynamic embeddings along with the spaces of USLP. We observe that for all spaces except *name space*, each space considered individually is unsuitable for the spatial link prediction task, with the Hits@1 metric lying close to zero. On the other hand, the *name space* attains Hits@k values for all k in the range of around 65 to 75% points. The *geographic space* captures vital information for predicting spatial links, with its Hits@k values significantly higher than *class space* and latent space of dynamic embeddings considered individually or together. Combining *geographic* and *name* spaces further improves the performance. The combination of *geographic*, *name*, and *class* space used in USLP is the most effective for spatial link prediction, as indicated by their consistently higher performance in terms of all metrics. Our approach aligns entities along multiple semantic spaces by considering their similarity and is robust against disambiguation challenges. By incorporating dynamic embeddings with USLP, Hits@k metrics for $k = 1, 3, 5$ are lower; however, Hits@10 increases. This result can be due to noise present in the heterogeneous properties of entities, which reduces the recall of the model but increases Hits@10 with more true entities scoring in the top 10 ranks.

6   Related Work

In this section, we discuss related work in knowledge graph link prediction.

Link Prediction. Traditional knowledge graph link prediction methods are based on rule mining or generating random walks in knowledge graphs. Rule mining approaches [1] mine generic and conditional declarative rules using KG triples, while random walk-based approaches [13] perform combinations of constrained, weighed, random walks and use path ranking algorithms to tune the weights of these walks. These methods directly exploit observable features of the graph but do not consider latent features of entities. Embedding-based approaches transform the high-dimensional knowledge graph to low-dimensional vector spaces, while preserving semantic information and considering latent features of entities. Rossi et al. [21] classify these approaches as Tensor Decomposition, Geometric, and Deep learning models. Tensor Decomposition models view the knowledge graph as a 3D adjacency matrix and decompose this tensor to low dimensional vectors to generate entity and relation representations, with the scoring function a formulation of a bilinear product [24] or non-bilinear [3]. Geometric models interpret relations as a geometric operation in a latent space, where the operation can be a form of translation in the case of Translational models [7] or rotation-like transformations either separately or along with translations for Roto-translational models [22,30]. Deep Learning models use convolutional neural networks, reinforcement learning, or graph neural networks to predict links [17,25]. However, all these approaches do not consider the literal values in a knowledge graph and rely on the connectivity between entities.

Link Prediction Using Literals. Few approaches use the literal values present in knowledge graphs for link prediction. Kristiadi et al. in [12] propose an extension module over existing link prediction methods, named LiteralE, to directly enrich entity embeddings with literal information using a learnable parameterized function. Li et al. [14] perform numeric link prediction by considering the attribute semantics of literals in KG embeddings with a more comprehensive representation of attribute semantics. These approaches face scalability issues due to constructing a literal vector or an attribute matrix. The papers [23,27,28] also predict numeric literals in knowledge graphs using ensemble learning, attribute value regression, or by simultaneously adding numerical attribute prediction loss to triple loss. Blum et al. [5] propose three knowledge graph transformations and add additional entities and relations in the knowledge graph to enable existing approaches to leverage literals. Biswas et al. [4] use attentive bidirectional Gated Recurrent Unit (GRU)-based encoder-decoder for link prediction and consider textual entity descriptions and graph walks of KG. Literal-based approaches consider either numeric literals or require long textual entity descriptions and only utilize this information to supplement the structural information provided by the existing links in the graph.

Table 5. Feature analysis of USLP. The best results are highlighted in bold, and runner-up results are underlined.

Feature	ID1 Dataset					
	MR	MRR	H@1	H@3	H@5	H@10
Geographic Space	14	0.340	0.150	0.414	0.541	0.692
Name Space	22	0.695	0.669	0.692	0.699	0.752
Class Space	48	0.043	0	0.015	0.030	0.045
Dynamic Embedding	69	0.091	0	0.090	0.150	0.316
Geographic & Name	<u>4</u>	<u>0.769</u>	<u>0.714</u>	0.767	0.842	0.887
Geographic & Class	9	0.355	0.143	0.489	0.654	0.842
Geographic & Dynamic Embedding	18	0.151	0	0.173	0.278	0.489
Name & Class	13	0.695	0.662	0.669	0.729	0.797
Name & Dynamic Embedding	10	0.627	0.511	0.707	0.774	0.835
Class & Dynamic Embedding	51	0.128	0.023	0.143	0.195	0.383
USLP w/ Dynamic Embedding	**3**	0.701	0.571	<u>0.797</u>	<u>0.887</u>	**0.962**
USLP	**3**	**0.832**	**0.774**	**0.857**	**0.902**	<u>0.939</u>

Link Prediction Using Spatial Information. Huang et al. [11] propose a method containing an enhancer, encoder, and decoder where the enhancer converts relations to relation expressions using lexical, spatial, structural, and attribute similarity networks, followed by the encoder to obtain vector representations and a decoder to perform relation prediction. SE-KGE by Mai et al. [15] is a location-aware embedding model designed for geographic question answering. The method encodes spatial footprints (coordinates and bounding boxes) using a location-encoder based on Space2Vec and positional encoding of the transformer model. Qiu et al. [19] perform geographic link prediction by encoding geospatial distance restriction as a weighing term based on Euclidean distance in the objective function of translational embedding models. In contrast, Wang et al. [26] add geographic constraints such as inclusion, adjacency, and intersection for optimizing existing models such as TransE and RESCAL. The link prediction approaches using spatial information involve the construction of multiple similarity networks [11] or geographic constraints such as intersection [26], making them infeasible on our datasets containing a large number of entities and datatype properties.

7 Conclusion

In this paper, we proposed two novel approaches, SSLP and USLP, for transductive and inductive spatial link prediction, respectively. Our approaches address a crucial gap in the state-of-the-art by considering literal values and spatial semantics of geographic entities. SSLP and USLP outperform all baselines in terms of Hits@k. Our results demonstrate that effective fusion of spatial and literal semantics in knowledge graphs can facilitate the completion of sparse KGs that lack connectivity, including knowledge graphs from the geographic domain.

In future research, we would like to explore the adoption of our proposed spatial and semantic embeddings for answering complex semantic spatial queries.

Supplemental Material Statement: Our source code, experimental data, and instructions for repeating all experiments are available at GitHub[2].

Acknowledgements. This work was partially funded by the DFG, German Research Foundation ("WorldKG", 424985896), the Federal Ministry for Economic Affairs and Climate Action (BMWK), Germany ("ATTENTION!", 01MJ22012C), and DAAD/BMBF, Germany ("KOALA", 57600865).

References

1. Ahmadi, N., Huynh, V., Meduri, V.V., Ortona, S., Papotti, P.: Mining expressive rules in knowledge graphs. ACM J. Data Inf. Qual. **12**(2), 8:1–8:27 (2020)
2. Ali, M., et al.: Improving inductive link prediction using hyper-relational facts. In: Hotho, A., et al. (eds.) ISWC 2021. LNCS, vol. 12922, pp. 74–92. Springer, Cham (2021). https://doi.org/10.1007/978-3-030-88361-4_5
3. Balažević, I., Allen, C., Hospedales, T.: TuckER: tensor factorization for knowledge graph completion. In: Proceedings of the 2019 Conference on Empirical Methods in Natural Language Processing and the 9th International Joint Conference on Natural Language Processing, pp. 5185–5194 (2019)
4. Biswas, R., Sack, H., Alam, M.: MADLINK: attentive multihop and entity descriptions for link prediction in knowledge graphs. Semantic Web J. 2960–4174 (2022)
5. Blum, M., Ell, B., Cimiano, P.: Exploring the impact of literal transformations within knowledge graphs for link prediction. In: Proceedings of the 11th International Joint Conference on Knowledge Graphs, pp. 48–54. ACM (2022)
6. Bojanowski, P., Grave, E., Joulin, A., Mikolov, T.: Enriching word vectors with subword information. Trans. Assoc. Comput. Linguist. **5**, 135–146 (2017)
7. Bordes, A., Usunier, N., García-Durán, A., Weston, J., Yakhnenko, O.: Translating embeddings for modeling multi-relational data. In: Proceedings of the 27th Annual Conference on Neural Information Processing Systems, pp. 2787–2795 (2013)
8. Dsouza, A., Tempelmeier, N., Yu, R., Gottschalk, S., Demidova, E.: WorldKG: a world-scale geographic knowledge graph. In: Proceeding of the 30th ACM International Conference on Information and Knowledge Management, pp. 4475–4484. ACM (2021)
9. Ganti, R.K., Srivatsa, M., Agrawal, D., Zerfos, P., Ortiz, J.: MP-trie: fast spatial queries on moving objects. In: Proceedings of the Industrial Track of the 17th International Middleware Conference, p. 1. ACM (2016)
10. Gesese, G.A., Biswas, R., Alam, M., Sack, H.: A survey on knowledge graph embeddings with literals: which model links better literal-ly? Semantic Web **12**(4), 617–647 (2021)
11. Huang, Z., Qiu, P., Yu, L., Lu, F.: MSEN-GRP: a geographic relations prediction model based on multi-layer similarity enhanced networks for geographic relations completion. ISPRS Int. J. Geo Inf. **11**(9), 493 (2022)

---

12. Kristiadi, A., Khan, M.A., Lukovnikov, D., Lehmann, J., Fischer, A.: Incorporating literals into knowledge graph embeddings. In: Ghidini, C., et al. (eds.) ISWC 2019. LNCS, vol. 11778, pp. 347–363. Springer, Cham (2019). https://doi.org/10.1007/978-3-030-30793-6_20
13. Lao, N., Mitchell, T.M., Cohen, W.W.: Random walk inference and learning in A large scale knowledge base. In: Proceedings of the 2011 Conference on Empirical Methods in Natural Language Processing, pp. 529–539. ACL (2011)
14. Li, M., Gao, N., Tu, C., Peng, J., Li, M.: Incorporating attributes semantics into knowledge graph embeddings. In: Proceedings of the 24th International Conference on Computer Supported Cooperative Work in Design, pp. 620–625. IEEE (2021)
15. Mai, G., et al.: SE-KGE: a location-aware knowledge graph embedding model for geographic question answering and spatial semantic lifting. Trans. GIS **24**(3), 623–655 (2020)
16. Mai, G., Janowicz, K., Yan, B., Zhu, R., Cai, L., Lao, N.: Multi-scale representation learning for spatial feature distributions using grid cells. In: Proceedings of the 8th International Conference on Learning Representations. OpenReview.net (2020)
17. Nguyen, D.Q., Nguyen, D.Q., Nguyen, T.D., Phung, D.: A convolutional neural network-based model for knowledge base completion and its application to search personalization. Semantic Web **10**(5), 947–960 (2019)
18. Nickel, M., Tresp, V., Kriegel, H.: A three-way model for collective learning on multi-relational data. In: Proceedings of the 28th International Conference on Machine Learning, pp. 809–816. Omnipress (2011)
19. Qiu, P., Gao, J., Yu, L., Lu, F.: Knowledge embedding with geospatial distance restriction for geographic knowledge graph completion. ISPRS Int. J. Geo Inf. **8**(6), 254 (2019)
20. Reimers, N., Gurevych, I.: Sentence-BERT: Sentence embeddings using Siamese BERT-networks. In: Proceedings of the 2019 Conference on Empirical Methods in Natural Language Processing and the 9th International Joint Conference on Natural Language Processing, pp. 3980–3990. ACM (2019)
21. Rossi, A., Barbosa, D., Firmani, D., Matinata, A., Merialdo, P.: Knowledge graph embedding for link prediction: a comparative analysis. ACM Trans. Knowl. Discov. Data **15**(2), 14:1–14:49 (2021)
22. Sun, Z., Deng, Z., Nie, J., Tang, J.: Rotate: knowledge graph embedding by relational rotation in complex space. In: Proceedings of the 7th International Conference on Learning Representations, OpenReview.net (2019)
23. Tay, Y., Tuan, L.A., Phan, M.C., Hui, S.C.: Multi-task neural network for non-discrete attribute prediction in knowledge graphs. In: Proceedings of the Conference on Information and Knowledge Management, pp. 1029–1038. ACM (2017)
24. Trouillon, T., Welbl, J., Riedel, S., Gaussier, É., Bouchard, G.: Complex embeddings for simple link prediction. In: Proceedings of the 33rd International Conference on Machine Learning, pp. 2071–2080. JMLR.org (2016)
25. Vashishth, S., Sanyal, S., Nitin, V., Talukdar, P.P.: Composition-based multi-relational graph convolutional networks. In: Proceedings of the 8th International Conference on Learning Representations, OpenReview.net (2020)
26. Wang, Y., Zhang, H., Xie, H.: Geography-enhanced link prediction framework for knowledge graph completion. In: Zhu, X., Qin, B., Zhu, X., Liu, M., Qian, L. (eds.) CCKS 2019. CCIS, vol. 1134, pp. 198–210. Springer, Singapore (2019). https://doi.org/10.1007/978-981-15-1956-7_18
27. Wu, Y., Wang, Z.: Knowledge graph embedding with numeric attributes of entities. In: Proceedings of The Third Workshop on Representation Learning for NLP, pp. 132–136. ACM (2018)

28. Xue, B., Li, Y., Zou, L.: Introducing semantic information for numerical attribute prediction over knowledge graphs. In: Proceedings of the 21st International Semantic Web Conference, pp. 3–21. Springer, Cham (2022). https://doi.org/10.1007/978-3-031-19433-7_1
29. Yang, B., Yih, W., He, X., Gao, J., Deng, L.: Embedding entities and relations for learning and inference in knowledge bases. In: Proceedings of the 3rd International Conference on Learning Representations (2015)
30. Zhang, Z., Cai, J., Zhang, Y., Wang, J.: Learning hierarchy-aware knowledge graph embeddings for link prediction. In: Proceedings of the Thirty-Fourth Conference on Artificial Intelligence, pp. 3065–3072. AAAI Press (2020)

How is Your Knowledge Graph Used: Content-Centric Analysis of SPARQL Query Logs

Luigi Asprino[1] and Miguel Ceriani[2,3]

[1] University of Bologna, Via Zamboni 33, Bologna, Italy
luigi.asprino@unibo.it
[2] University of Bari Aldo Moro, Via Orabona 4, Bari, Italy
[3] ISTC-CNR, Via S. Martino della Battaglia 44, Roma, Italy
miguel.ceriani@cnr.it

Abstract. Knowledge graphs (KGs) are used to integrate and persist information useful to organisations, communities, or the general public. It is essential to understand how KGs are used so as to evaluate the strengths and shortcomings of semantic web standards, data modelling choices formalised in ontologies, deployment settings of triple stores etc. One source of information on the usage of the KGs is the query logs, but making sense of hundreds of thousands of log entries is not trivial. Previous works that studied available logs from public SPARQL endpoints mainly focused on the general syntactic properties of the queries disregarding the semantics and their intent. We introduce a novel, content-centric, approach that we call *query log summarisation*, in which we group the queries that can be derived from some common pattern. The type of patterns considered in this work is *query templates*, i.e. common blueprints from which multiple queries can be generated by the replacement of parameters with constants. Moreover, we present an algorithm able to summarise a query log as a list of templates whose time and space complexity is linear with respect to the size of the input (number and dimension of queries). We experimented with the algorithm on the query logs of the Linked SPARQL Queries dataset showing promising results.

Keywords: SPARQL · Query log summarisation · Linked SPARQL queries

1 Introduction

Knowledge Graphs (KGs) are pervasive assets used by organisations and communities to share information with other stakeholders. For knowledge engineers, it is essential to understand how KGs are used so as to assess their strengths and shortcomings, but, neither established methodologies nor tools are available. We

An extended version of this paper (pre-print) is available at https://doi.org/10.6084/m9.figshare.23751243.

observe that it is customary to make KGs accessible via SPARQL endpoints, therefore their query logs, i.e. the list of queries evaluated by the endpoint, are a valuable source from which the use of the KGs can be pictured. Compared to logs of "traditional" (centralised) databases (both relational and NoSQL), logs of public SPARQL endpoints bear much more information because they show usage of a dataset by multiple agents (human or robotic), for multiple applications, in different ways, and even in the context of multiple domains (especially if the dataset is generic).

Several works had already analysed the available SPARQL logs [2,9–11,16,29,32,37,38]. Most of them centred the analysis on the general structure of the queries (usage of specific SPARQL clauses, the shape of the basic graph patterns). The output of the analyses is mostly quantitative, possibly coupled by some examples. Relatively less focus has been so far given to aspects that go beyond the general query syntactic structure and relate to the actual content, such as aspects ranging from the usage of specific RDF terms (both classes, properties, and individuals), to specific (sub)query patterns, to inference of template usage and query evolution. Analysis of the actual content of queries can lead to further quantitative results, but most importantly can be used as a tool for qualitative analysis of one or multiple query logs: different levels of abstractions on the queries enable a meaningful exploration of the given data set.

The potential usage contexts for such analysis are manifold. For example, maintainers of SPARQL endpoints could optimise the execution of common queries by caching results or indexing predicates; designers of ontologies could assess what predicates are actually used thus allowing reshaping the model with shortcuts or removing unused predicates; designers of semantic web standards could introduce new constructs and operators in order to address common query patterns; and, researchers of the field could design benchmark to assess the performance of SPARQL endpoints.

The present work introduces a novel general approach to analyse query logs with a focus on query content and qualitative information. Specifically, we frame the *query log summarisation* as the problem of finding a list of templates modelling a query log. We introduce an algorithm able to solve the problem whose time and space complexity is linear in the size of the input. Finally, we experiment with the algorithm on the logs available in the LSQ dataset [37] to evaluate its usefulness. The analysis of the results shows that the method is able to provide more concise representations of the logs and novel insights on the usage of 28 public SPARQL endpoints.

The rest of the paper is organised as follows. Section 2 gives an overview of the existing work on query logs analysis. Section 3 lays the theoretical foundation of the work and introduces the problem of query log summarisation. The proposed algorithm to address the problem is presented in Sect. 4. Section 5 describes the experimental evaluation and its results, discussing strengths and opportunities enabled by the proposed approach. Section 6 concludes and outlines the ongoing and future work.

2   Related Work

Query logs are insightful sources for profiling the access to datasets. Although there are no approaches that aim to summarise SPARQL query logs as a list of query templates, an overview of the main approaches to analysing query logs is worthwhile. We classify the approaches according to the target query language.

Approaches Targeting SQL Query Logs. Even if not directly applicable to assess the usage of knowledge graphs, techniques analysing query logs of relational databases may be adapted as SQL and SPARQL have syntactic similarities. These techniques have been used for detecting anomalous access patterns [21], preventing insider attacks [26] and optimising the workload of database management systems [14] thus becoming standard features for automatic indexing in commercial relational databases [28,31]. All the approaches can be generalised as feature extraction methods needed for clustering queries and profiling user behaviour. In most cases, the features extracted are basic, such as the SQL command used (e.g. SELECT, INSERT), the list of relations queried, and the operators used. Nevertheless, similarly to our approach, query templates and structural features are also used for computing query similarity [22,44], albeit still in a clustering approach. Some issues of such feature-based clustering approaches are that finding a useful way to convey the meaning of the clusters is not trivial, that scalability can be a problem as the worst-case cost is quadratic, and that some aspects of the query are scraped since the beginning for performance reasons, while they may be a relevant facet of a common pattern. Specifically, some methods [22,43,44] replace all the constants in the query with placeholders as a pre-processing step, which for SPARQL would hide the intent of most of the queries. Our method also replaces the constants with placeholders in an initial phase but, crucially, keeps the mapping with the original constants and puts them back if they have always the same value in a group of queries.

Approaches Targeting SPARQL Query Logs. Analyses of SPARQL query logs have been performed since the early years of the Semantic Web. These studies fall into a more general line of research adopting empirical methods for observing typical characteristics of data [4,6], identifying common patterns in data [5], assessing the usage and identifying shortcomings of data [3,24] and using the obtained insights for developing better tools [20]. This kind of analysis has been also promoted by international workshops, such as USEWOD[1] which from 2011 to 2016 fostered research on mining the usage of the Web of Data [25]. Most of the existing work focus on quantitative and syntactic characteristics, such as the types of clients requesting semantic data [29] (including analyses of the characteristics of queries issues by humans, called organic, and those sent by artificial agents, robotic queries [9,36]), the user profile [19], the number of triple patterns per query [2,16,29,32,41], the use of predicates [2,29,32], the use of SPARQL operators [2,16,32,41] or a specific function (e.g. REGEX [1]), the

---

[1] http://usewod.org/workshops.html.

structure of the Basic Graph Patterns (e.g. the out-degree of nodes, the number of join vertices) [2,41], the monotonicity of the queries [16], the probabilistic safeness [38], and the presence of non-conjunctive queries [32]. However, the analysis is limited at the triple-pattern level by paying less attention to the structural and semantic characteristics of the queries, thus making it difficult to figure out what the prototypical queries submitted to the endpoints look like. A noteworthy exception is [35], in which the author, while analysing queries at the triple pattern level, attempts to extract generic query patterns.

Bonifati et al. [11] investigate the structural characteristics related to the graph and hypergraph representation of queries by outlining the most common shapes. Moreover, they analyse the evolution of queries over time, by introducing the notion of the streak, i.e., a sequence of queries that appear as subsequent modifications of a seed query. By grouping queries based on similarity, this aspect of their work is akin to the approach presented in this work.

The existing studies are valuable for assessing the usage of SPARQL as a standard query language or for benchmarking and optimising the query engines. However, none of the existing approaches provides any insight into how KG is actually queried in terms of KG patterns queried by the users, and, therefore are of little help in designing the KGs. This paper investigates an alternative approach aiming at extracting query templates from SPARQL logs that may help designers to characterise the prototypical queries submitted by the users.

3   Preliminaries

This Section lays the theoretical foundation of this work.

RDF and SPARQL. For the sake of completeness, we introduce the basic notions of RDF [13] and SPARQL [17] needed to understand the methods and analysis described in this work. We defer the reader to the corresponding documentation for a complete description of these standards. Formally, let I, B, and L be infinite sets of IRIs, blank nodes, and literals. The sets are assumed to be pairwise disjoint and we will collectively refer to them as *RDF terms*. A tuple $(s, p, o) \in (I \cup B) \times (I) \times (I \cup B \cup L)$ is called *(RDF) triple* and we say s is the *subject* of the triple, p the *predicate*, and o the *object*. An *RDF graph* is a set of RDF triples, whereas an *RDF dataset* is a collection of named RDF graphs, each one identified by IRI, and a default RDF graph.

SPARQL is based on the idea of defining patterns to be matched against an input RDF dataset. Formally, considering the set of variables V, disjoint from the previously defined I, B, and L, a *triple pattern* is a tuple of the form $(s, p, o) \in (I \cup B \times V) \times (I \times V) \times (I \cup B \cup L \times V)$. A *basic graph pattern (BGP)* is a set of triple patterns. A SPARQL query Q is composed of the following components: *(i)* the query type (i.e. SELECT, ASK, DESCRIBE, CONSTRUCT); *(ii)* the dataset clause; *(iii)* the graph pattern (recursively defined as being a BGP or the result of the composition of one or more graph patterns through one of several SPARQL operators that modify and combine the obtained results); *(iv)* the solution modifiers (i.e. LIMIT, GROUP BY, OFFSET).

3.1 Query Templates

Intuitively, a query template is a SPARQL query containing a set of placeholders which are meant to be substituted with RDF terms. The placeholders are called *parameters* of the query template and will be represented in queries using variable names starting with "$_"[2]. For example, consider the following queries 1.1 and 1.2[3]. The intent of both queries is to retrieve the types of a given entity. Such intent can be expressed via the Template 1.1.

Query 1.1.	Query 1.2.

`SELECT ?type WHERE {`
`  dbr:Barack_Obama rdf:type ?type`
`}`
	`SELECT ?type WHERE {`
	`  dbr:Interstellar_(film) rdf:type ?type`
	`}`

Template 1.1.	Query 1.3.	Template 1.2.

`SELECT ?type WHERE {`
`  $_1 rdf:type ?type`
`}`
	`SELECT ?p WHERE {`
	`  ?p rdf:type foaf:Person`
	`}`
		`SELECT ?type WHERE {`
		`  $_1 $_2 ?type`
		`}`

We say that a query template q^t *models* a query q, indicated as $q^t \prec q$, if there exists a partial bijective function m^t, called *mapping*, that maps parameters P^t in q^t onto RDF terms of q such that applying m^t onto q^t gives q, i.e. $m^t : P^t \rightarrow (I \cup L)$ and $m(q^t) = q$. For example, the following mappings m_1 and m_2 transform the Template 1.1 into the queries 1.1 and 1.2 respectively: $m_1(\$_1)$:= dbr:Barack_Obama and $m_2(\$_1)$:= dbr:Interstellar_(film).

It is worth noticing that, to preserve the intent of the query, templates do not substitute variables and blank nodes (as they are considered non-distinguished variables) with parameters, reduce the number of triple patterns, or replace SPARQL operators. As a result, a template for modelling a set of queries does not always exist (e.g. a single template modelling queries 1.1, 1.2, and 1.3 can not exist). Moreover, multiple templates may model the same set of queries. For example, the Template 1.2 models the queries 1.1 and 1.2 (in this case m_1 and m_2 must also map $\$_2$ onto rdf:type, i.e. $m_1(\$_2)$:= rdf:type and $m_2(\$_2)$:= rdf:type). In fact, the number of parameters of a template allows us to formalise the intuition of more specific/generic template. We say that the Template 1.2 is more generic (or, less specific) of Template 1.1 as it maps a

---

[2] Using the initial underscore in the variable name to identify parameters matches with existing practice [27], while using "$" visually helps distinguish the parameters from query variables that often start with "?".

[3] For brevity, the queries omit prefix declarations:

  - dbr: <http://dbpedia.org/resource/>
  - rdf: <http://www.w3.org/1999/02/22-rdf-syntax-ns#>
  - foaf: <http://xmlns.com/foaf/0.1/>
  - dbo: <https://dbpedia.org/ontology/>

higher number of parameters. As a result, given a query q, the *most generic template* modelling q is the template in which all the IRIs and literals of q are substituted by parameters. Therefore, it is easy to see that given a set of queries (that can be modelled by a single template) it is always possible to derive the most generic template by substituting all literals and IRIs by parameters.

We characterised templates as queries having placeholders that are to be replaced by IRIs or literals. However, there are two extensions to this rule which are needed to capture very common patterns for paginating the results and injecting values into a query. One is the usage of placeholders in LIMIT and OFFSET clauses, which are the solution modifiers used to get a specific slice of all the results. Both clauses are always followed by an integer, specifying respectively the number and initial position of the query solutions. By allowing this, integers to be replaced by parameters, multiple versions of the same query in which only one or both are changed (e.g., changing the OFFSET to perform pagination) can be represented by the same template.

The second extension to the rule has been defined for another specific clause: VALUES. This clause is used to bind one or more variables with a multiset of RDF terms. It is thus a way to give constraints to a query with multi-valued data that could come from previous computations, possibly also other queries[4]. In the case of a VALUES clause, rather than replacing single RDF terms, a placeholder either replace the whole corresponding multiset of terms or none.

Even if they are not explicitly mentioned, all the SPARQL clauses and operators (FILTERs, OPTIONALs, UNIONs etc.) can be part of a query template. We only mentioned the VALUE, LIMIT, and OFFSET operators as they deserve special treatment.

One of the main intuitions behind the usage of query templates to study a log is that it can help to "reverse engineer" the methods and processes used to generate the queries. In order to discuss this aspect, we define a *query-source* as a specific and unique piece of code (which could nevertheless span multiple software components in complex cases) that is responsible for the generation (possibly based on parameters) and execution of a query. A template that models many queries in a log may capture a common usage pattern that spans multiple query sources or a broadly used single query source. Both cases can be of interest in the analysis of a query log.

3.2   Query Log Summarisation Problem

We formally describe a query log and frame its summarisation as a theoretical problem. A SPARQL Query Log $l = [e_1, e_2, .., e_n]$ is a list of entries $e_i = (q, t, s, m)$ each representing the execution at a certain time t of a query q by a SPARQL endpoint s with associated metadata m. For the purpose of the algorithm presented below, the information of the SPARQL endpoint executing the query is only used to group together queries evaluated over the same KG, and we do not consider time and metadata. Therefore, for brevity, SPARQL

---

[4] It is for example a recommended way to perform query federation [34].

query logs reduce to a sequence of queries $l = [q_1, q_2, .., q_n]$. Note that queries can be repeated in a log, so for convenience, we define an operator Q to get them as a set (hence without repetitions): $Q(l) = \{q_i | q_i \in l\}$.

Given a query log $l = [q_1, q_2.., q_n]$, the *SPARQL log summarisation* is the problem of finding a set of query templates $Q_t = \{q_1^t, q_2^t, .., q_m^t\}$ (with $m \leq n$), called *log model*, such that for each query $q_i \in l$, there exists a query template q_j^t such that $q_j^t \prec q_i$. It is worth noticing that, since each query is the template of itself (in this case the mapping from placeholders to RDF terms is empty), a trivial solution to the problem is $Q_t = Q(l)$. Therefore, we have that the size of log model Q_t may range from 1, in the case that all the queries in the log are modelled by a single template, to $|Q(l)|$, when a common template for any pair of queries does not exist.

It is worth noticing that summarising a query log differs from evaluating the containment/equivalence of a pair of queries [12,33]. In fact, given a query q and its template q^t (i.e. $q^t \prec q$), q and q^t are (except for constants and parameters) the exact same query. Whereas evaluating the query containment/equivalence requires deciding if the result set of one query is always (i.e. for any dataset) contained into/equivalent to the result set of a *different* query. Of course, the two approaches, log summarisation and query containment/equivalence can be potentially combined to derive more succinct log models, but this is outside the scope of this paper.

Metrics. The aim of summarising a query log is to assist KG engineers in understanding how their KGs are queried. To do so, a KG engineer has ideally to go through the list of all the queries. Obviously, the shorter the list of queries to examine, the less effort from the KG engineer is required for the analysis. Intuitively, the benefit of using a log model instead of a full query log is to reduce the list of queries to examine. This benefit is proportional to the difference between the size of the log model and the size of the query log. However, one must consider that not all the query templates have the same informational value. In fact, we can consider that the more log entries a template models, the more informative it is (in other words, it allows the KG engineer to have an indication of a larger portion of the query log). Therefore, if the templates are ordered according to their informational value, the KG engineer would be able to analyse a large portion of the log by going only through the most informative templates.

To measure the impact of this on the informational value of a model we employ the concept of *entropy*. The entropy over a discrete random variable X, taking values in the alphabet $\mathcal{X}$ and distributed according to $p : \mathcal{X} \to [0, 1]$, is defined as follows [39]:

$$\mathrm{H}(X) := - \sum_{x \in \mathcal{X}} p(x) \log p(x)$$

Given a query log l and a model Q_t over it, we consider a random variable T taking values over the "alphabet" Q_t and distributed as the templates of Q_t

are distributed over the log l. That is, with probability distribution p_{Q_t} defined as follows:

$$p_{Q_t}(q_i^t) = \frac{|\{q_j | q_j \in l, q_i^t \prec q_j\}|}{|l|}$$

We can thus measure the entropy of this distribution, which depends both on the log l and the model Q_t. The entropy corresponds to the average number of bits (considering base 2 for log) used to encode an item, which in our case is a template, in an optimal encoding. For a uniform distribution over n values, the entropy is $log(n)$, which is the number of bits required for a simple encoding of n values. If the values are not uniformly distributed a more efficient representation (as in a lossless compression) can be used, where more frequent values are represented with shorter encodings.

Recalling that the set of queries $Q(l)$ is already a model of l, the one created by simply taking all the queries as they are, we can compute the entropy for this model. The aim of another computed model Q_t of l is to achieve a more concise representation of the log and thus lower entropy. In the experiments with a dataset of logs (cf. Sect. 5), we measure the entropy of $Q(l)$ (indicated as $H(Q)$) as opposed to that of a derived log model Q_t (indicated as $H(T)$). The difference between $H(Q)$ and $H(T)$ indicates how much less information needs to be screened by the KG engineer to examine the log.

4 Approach

We describe the procedure for query log summarisation. Appendix A of the extended version of the paper contains the complete pseudo-code for the algorithm, the sketch of the proof of soundness, the detailed complexity analysis, and other formal considerations on the output of the algorithm. To convey the intuition, we use the following log as a running example $l =$ [Query 1.1, Query 1.2, Query 1.1, Query 1.4, Query 1.2, Query 1.5] where Queries 1.1 and 1.2 are defined above and Queries 1.4 and 1.5 follow.

Query 1.4.

```
SELECT ?director ?starring WHERE {
    dbr:Pulp_Fiction dbo:director ?
        director .
    dbr:Pulp_Fiction dbo:starring ?
        starring .
}
```

Query 1.5.

```
SELECT ?director ?starring WHERE {
    dbr:Django_Unchained dbo:director
        ?director .
    dbr:Django_Unchained dbo:starring
        ?starring .
}
```

Template 1.3.

```
SELECT ?director ?starring WHERE {
    $_1 $_2 ?director .
    $_3 $_4 ?starring .
}
```

Template 1.4.

```
SELECT ?director ?starring WHERE {
    $_1 dbo:director  ?director .
    $_1 dbo:starring ?starring .
}
```

Intuitively, the algorithm performs two steps, called GENERALISE() and SPE-CIALISE(). The function GENERALISE() creates a generic template for a query, replacing each occurrence of IRIs and literals with a different new parameter. Therefore, the generated template is the most generic that models the query. At the same time a mapping is created, associating each parameter with the RDF term that was replaced. For example, GENERALISE(Query 1.1) returns the Template 1.2 and the mapping m_1 defined as follows: $m_1(\$\_1) :=$ dbr:Barack_Obama, $m_1(\$\_2) :=$ rdf:type; GENERALISE(Query 1.2) returns the Template 1.2 and the mapping m_2 defined as follows: $m_2(\$\_1) :=$ dbr:Interstellar_(film), $m_2(\$\_2) :=$ rdf:type; GENERALISE(Query 1.4) returns the Template 1.3 and the mapping m_4 defined as follows: $m_4(\$\_1) :=$ dbr:Pulp_Fiction, $m_4(\$\_2) :=$ dbo:director, $m_4(\$\_3) :=$ dbr:Pulp_Fiction, $m_4(\$\_4) :=$ dbo:starring; GEN-ERALISE(Query 1.5) returns the Template 1.3 and the mapping m_5 defined as follows: $m_5(\$\_1) :=$ dbr:Django_Unchained, $m_5(\$\_2) :=$ dbo:director, $m_5(\$\_3) :=$ dbr:Django_Unchained, $m_5(\$\_4) :=$ dbo:starring.

The function SPECIALISE() takes as input a template and an associated set of mappings and, by just analysing the set of mappings, it establishes if the number of parameters can be reduced. There are two interesting cases for this purpose: *(i)* for a parameter, all the mappings in the set map it to the same RDF term (it is thus a constant); *(ii)* for a pair of parameters of a template, each mappings in the set maps them to a common RDF term (one parameter is actually a duplicate of the other). For each instance of these cases, the template and the mappings are updated accordingly: *(i)* in the first case (the parameter is constant), the parameter in the template is replaced by the constant and removed from the mappings; *(ii)* in the second case (two parameters mapped to the same RDF terms), one parameter in the template is replaced by the other and removed from the mappings. For example, both m_1 and m_2 map $\$\_2$ to rdf:type which can be considered as a constant (i.e. $m_1(\$\_2) = m_2(\$\_2) =$ rdf:type), therefore the Template 1.2 can be specialised as Template 1.1 and the parameter $\$\_2$ replaced with rdf:type. Concerning the Template 1.3 and the mappings m_4 and m_5, the SPECIALISE function replaces $\$\_2$ and $\$\_4$ with two constants (dbo:director and dbo:starring) and unifies $\$\_1$ and $\$\_3$ in both mappings as they map to the same RDF term (dbr:Pulp_Fiction and dbr:Django_Unchained respectively for m_4 and m_5). The function returns the Template 1.4 and m_4 and m_5 updated.

The main function DISCOVERTEMPLATES(): *(i)* takes a set of queries; *(ii)* extracts a pair (template, mapping) for each query by invoking GENERALISE; *(iii)* accumulates the mappings associated with the same template into a dictionary (the dictionary uses the templates as keys and mapping sets as values); *(iv)* then, for each pair (template, mapping set), calls SPECIALISE() and, possibly, replaces the pair with a specialised one.

Furthermore, along with the mappings, the algorithm maintains the original query ids, which in turn allows to find the data of each corresponding execution in the log. Keeping track of this relationship is crucial so that is later possible to derive statistics based on their usage or explore the detail of specific executions.

Properties of the Extracted Log Model. It is worth noticing that, given a query log, the algorithm first maximizes the number of queries a single template can represent, by grouping each query under its most generic template. Then, the algorithm minimizes the number of parameters of each template, by returning the most specific template modelling that group of queries (in other words, it keeps a minimal set of parameters needed to represent the set of queries). This ensures that for any pair queries of the log, if a single template can model the queries, then, the template is in the log model and the template is the most specific one.

Moreover, since the algorithm does not perform any normalisation of the input queries, syntactic differences affect the templates, e.g. two queries having the same triple patterns in a different order result in two different templates. This implies that the extracted templates generalise over fewer input queries (hence the algorithm tends to extract more templates) in respect to what could be if some normalisation was adopted, but the extracted templates are closer to the queries sent by the clients (which is desirable for identifying queries sent from the same process). Some form query normalisation can then be included as a preliminary step for different perspectives, but this is left to future work.

Implementation of the Algorithm. The algorithm has been implemented in Javascript, relying on the SPARQL.js library[5] for SPARQL parsing. Both the LSQ dataset in input and the discovered templates are represented as RDF in a local triple store, namely Apache Jena Fuseki[6]. The code is freely available on GitHub[7]

5   Experimentation

The LSQ dataset, already briefly introduced in Sect. 2, is the de-facto state-of-the-art collection of SPARQL query logs. We tested our method by using it to analyse all the logs available in the latest version of the LSQ dataset. In this section, we describe and discuss the dataset, its analysis, and the findings, focusing on the high level view and the details that can be useful to discuss the algorithm. For the detailed description of the results obtained for each endpoint and the full code of all the templates we refer the reader respectively to Appendix B and C of the extended version of the paper.

5.1   The Dataset

The LSQ 2.0 dataset[8] contains information about approximately 46M query executions and is composed of logs extracted from 28 public SPARQL endpoints. 24 of the endpoints are part of **Bio2RDF**, a project aimed at converting to

---

[5] https://github.com/RubenVerborgh/SPARQL.js.
[6] https://jena.apache.org/documentation/fuseki2.
[7] https://github.com/miguel76/sparql-clustering.
[8] http://lsq.aksw.org/.

RDF different collections of heterogeneously formatted structured biomedical data [8]. The other four endpoints are the following ones: **DBpedia**, a well-known knowledge base automatically extracted from Wikipedia [7]; **Wikidata**, an encyclopedic knowledge graph built collaboratively [42]; **Semantic Web Dog Food (SWDF)**, a dataset describing research in the area of the semantic web [30]; **LinkedGeoData** [40], an RDF mapping of OpenStreetMap, which is, in turn, a user-curated geographical knowledge base [15].

The LSQ project provides the collection of these SPARQL logs and their conversion to a common (RDF-based) format. In the process of conversion, the LSQ software performs also some filtering (e.g., only successful queries are considered) and anonymisation (e.g., client host information is hidden). The main information items offered by LSQ from each entry of a query log are the following ones: the endpoint against which the query was executed; the actual *SPARQL query*, the *timestamp* of execution, and an anonymised identifier of the client *host* which sent the query.

Table 1. Statistics on the LSQ 2.0 dataset before/after summarisation.

Dataset	Execs	Hosts	Queries	H(Q)	Templ.s	H(T)	ΔH
Bio2RDF	33 829 184	2 306	1 899 027	15.22	12 296	3.73	11.49
DBpedia	6 999 815	37 056	4 257 903	21.16	17 715	5.58	15.59
DBpedia-2010	518 717	1 649	358 955	17.99	2 223	5.66	12.33
DBpedia-2015/6	6 481 098	35 407	3 903 734	21.01	15 808	5.21	15.80
Wikidata	3 298 254	–	844 260	12.26	167 578	7.47	4.80
LinkedGeoData	501 197	25 431	173 043	14.24	2 748	4.78	9.46
SWDF	1 415 568	921	101 422	14.54	1 826	1.03	13.51

Table 1 shows some statistics about the data in the LSQ dataset, organised by endpoints[9]. The column *Execs* indicates the number of query executions contained in the log. Column *Hosts* is the total number of client hosts and *Queries* is the number of unique queries. The column H(Q) is the entropy of the unique queries distribution across the executions.

5.2   Methodology of Analysis

The aforementioned templates-mining algorithm was applied separately on each query log in the LSQ 2.0 dataset, with the corresponding set of queries as input.

---

[9] In the table, for conciseness, the statistics of the Bio2RDF endpoints are shown only aggregated for the whole project. In Appendix B the extended version of the paper there is a more detailed version of the table showing the statistics endpoint by endpoint..

Furthermore, the queries of Bio2RDF were also considered as a whole, on top of analysing each specific endpoint[10]

The templates obtained with our method can be analysed in a variety of ways. Different statistics can be computed on top of this summarised representation of the original data. Furthermore, the templates can be explored in several ways to have a content-based insight of how an endpoint has been used. In this study we will focus on two main aspects:

- a quantitative analysis of the effectiveness of the summarisation by measuring for each log 1) the number of templates in comparison with the number of queries and 2) the entropy of the templates distribution in comparison with the entropy of the query distribution;
- a qualitative analysis of the templates obtained, choosing for each log the ten most executed ones and discussing the possible intent of the queries, what they say about the usage of the endpoint, which ones probably come from a single code source, which ones instead probably correspond to common usage patterns, if and how some of them are related between each other.

It should be noted many other perspectives are possible (some of them will be sketched among the future work in Sect. 6).

5.3   Results

The execution of the algorithm overall took approximately nine hours on consumer hardware. Statistics about the results for each log or set of logs are shown in Table 1, alongside the previously described information. The column *Templ.s* corresponds to the number of templates generated, while the column $H(T)$ is the entropy of the templates distribution across the log and ΔH is the difference between the entropy according to the unique queries and the one according to the templates ($\Delta H = H(Q) - H(T)$).

For all the logs the number of templates is significantly smaller than the number of unique queries, with a reduction amounting to around two orders of magnitude (the ratio going from ∼56 to ∼240) for all cases but Wikidata (for which the reduction is smaller, namely five-fold). The reduction in entropy considering the distribution using templates shows even more strongly the effectiveness of the summarisation, as the value is in all the cases greater than $log_2 \frac{|Q|}{|T|}$, which would be the reduction in entropy in case of uniform distributions, showing that the algorithm is able to merge the most relevant (in terms of executions) queries.

Furthermore, it is worth noticing that, regarding the DBpedia log, while there is a significant difference in the query entropy from the data of 2010 (17.99) to the ones of 2015/6 (21.01), in line with a ten-fold increase in both executions and unique queries, the respective entropies measured on templates distribution

---

[10] This choice is motivated by the fact that the Bio2RDF endpoints are part of the same project, the collected logs refer roughly to the same period, and there is considerable overlap in the clients querying the endpoints.

are much closer, actually sightly decreasing from 2010 (5.66) to 2015/6 (5.21). This is interesting because it shows that the template diversity remains stable, while the number and diversity of specific queries increase roughly as the volume of the executions. In our opinion this case also manifests the importance of using the entropy as an index of diversity, rather than just counting the total number templates (which is instead quite different between the two datasets, ~2.2K against ~16K).

Then, for each endpoint[11], we performed the qualitative analysis of the ten most frequently executed templates. As part of the interpretation of these templates, we labelled them using a functional syntax composed of the a name given to the function (template) and a name given to each parameter. Interestingly, the most executed templates are quite vary across different endpoints and fulfil different kinds of purposes. Some templates correspond to generic, content-independent, patterns, like the template from SWDF log labelled PROPERTIESANDVALUES(*resource*) that list all properties and values associated to a resource and has been executed ~17K times. Others are specific of some triple store software as they use specific extensions, as it is the case for as in the template COMMONSUPERCLASSANDDISTANCE(*class1,class2*) from Wikidata, executed ~107K times, which employs a feature specific of Blazegraph, the software used for this dataset. Others are specific of some domain that the dataset encompasses, like CLOSEPOIS(*latitude,longitude*) from LinkedGeoData, executed ~81K times, that looks for points of interest close to a geographic location. Some of them, finally, are specific of a certain application, like AIRPORTSFORCITY(*cityLabel,lang*) in DBpedia, executed ~1.4M times.

As previously mentioned, it can be of interest to understand if a template correspond to a single query-source or instead arises from a pattern which is common in the usage of an endpoint. While we do not propose a specific metric for this purpose, nor we have a general way to check the ground truth, the qualitative analysis of the most executed templates offers a chance to reason on this topic. The generality of the template, as accessed above, offers a hint: the more general the more likely that it correspond to commonly adopted pattern rather than a single query-source. But the analysis of the general-purpose templates found show that they are not necessarily simple and may not correspond to the most straightforward solution to design a certain query. The structural complexity is perhaps then a better predictor of the usage of a template. For example, the template TRIPLES(*subject*) in Bio2RDF is a CONSTRUCT that return all the triples for which *subject* is the subject. The query is hence functionally generic but it is peculiar for being in a form slightly more complex than necessary: it is composed of a triple pattern and a filter instead of using directly a triple pattern with fixed subject. This template has been executed across most of the endpoints of Bio2RDF, for a total of ~9.3M times.

Another interesting aspect that emerges from the qualitative analysis is the evidence of relationships between different templates. For each endpoint, even considering just the most executed templates, it is possible to find one or more

---

[11] With the exception of the Bio2RDF endpoints, which are considered as a whole.

groups of templates that for structure, function, number of executions, hosts, period of use show many commonalities and can reasonably be conjectured to be part of a common process. For example among the most executed templates on SWDF four of them have been executed the same number of times and have the same kind of parameter (a researcher) albeit they extract different kind of data (respectively general information, affiliations, participation to events, publications). Still on SWDF, there are other two groups of templates having the same aspects in common (with a group having as common parameter an article and another having as common parameter an organisation). While in this case the grouped templates are probably part of a single process that executes multiple queries, in other cases the related templates could testify the evolution of a process. The template COMMONSUBCLASSES($class1$, $class2$) from the LinkedGeoData log is executed ~17K times across a span of ~7 h, then it is "replaced" by the template COMMONSUBCLASSES($class1$, $class2$, $class3$) that fulfills the same purpose but having one class more as parameter. The second version is then executed ~17K times across a span of other ~7 h.

Such hypothesises about the relationship between among a group of queries are reinforced in all the cases we found by the fact that the templates are executed by a common set of hosts. In most of the cases it is a single host that execute all the templates in a group, but not necessarily: on DBpedia the templates COUNTLINKSBETWEEN($res1$, $res2$) and COUNTCOMMONLINKS($res1$, $res2$) have different but related functions[12] on the same kind of parameters, they are both executed ~181K times by the same set of ~1130 hosts.

The complete results are available online for download[13] The templates found for each endpoint are represented both as CSVs and RDF. The RDF representation of the templates is meant to be used alongside the RDF representation of LSQ and is based on the Provenance Vocabulary [18], a specialisation of the standard W3C provenance ontology (PROV-O) [23] dealing with web data and in particular SPARQL queries and query templates.

5.4 Discussion

The aim of the analysis of the LSQ dataset was to prove that our method is able to effectively summarise the given logs, that the inferred templates often correspond to broadly used patterns or single query-sources, and that their analysis can give new insights on the usage of the considered endpoints. We quantitatively measured the efficacy of the summarisation through the ratio of original queries per template and the reduction in entropy when considering each log entry as an instance of a template, rather than as an instance of a query. Both measures show that the summarisation had a noteworthy impact on all the considered logs. Moreover, the qualitative analysis of a selected sample of templates (specifically the most executed) shows how their function may be appropriately analysed and discussed, without the need to check the thousands of corresponding queries.

---

[12] One counts the triples in which one resource is subject and the other object, the other counts the triples in which they replace each other or have symmetric role.

[13] https://doi.org/110.6084/m9.figshare.23751138.

Regarding the accuracy of the predicted templates in identifying a single source for a set of queries, there is no gold standard or previous attempt to compare with. Thus the qualitative analysis resorts to educated guesses, where we decide if an inferred template corresponds plausibly to a single source based on the syntactic distinctness and relationship with other templates and data from the log. For many of the described templates, it is possible to reasonably infer a single origin. In terms of the usefulness of the inferred templates to gain insights, the qualitative analysis has shown multiple ways in which the analysis of the templates gives direct access to information that was previously not straightforward and stimulates further study.

Finally, another finding has been that this template-based analysis paves the way to the analysis of another level of relationships between queries, namely when different queries are applied to the same (or related) data items as part of a (possibly automatic) process. Evidence of such relationships has been found in the qualitative analysis of all the considered logs.

6   Conclusions

In this work, we address the *query log summarisation* problem, i.e. identifying a set of *query templates* (i.e. queries with placeholder meant to be replaced with RDF terms) describing the queries of a log. We designed and implemented a method to perform the summarisation of a query log in linear time, based on the use of a hash table to group sets of queries that can be derived from a common query template. The approach has been experimented with the available logs of the LSQ dataset. The representation of the logs using templates has been shown to be significantly more concise. A qualitative analysis performed on the most executed templates enabled the characterisation of the log in ways that would not have been directly possible by analysing just the single queries.

Besides further exploring possible extensions of the template-mining algorithm for normalising the input log (e.g. reordering triple patterns), the analysis of the discovered templates brought forward some interesting issues that we consider deserving of further research.

One aspect worth investigating is the relationships between the execution patterns of each template. In the qualitative analysis, we found groups of templates being executed by the same set of hosts, often at similar times, and many times with the same parameters. Such analysis may, for example, allow to mine the prototypical interactions (namely, processes) with data, beyond the single query or template.

Moreover, many more interesting levels of abstraction are possible beyond the query templates: e.g., a common part of the query, the usage of certain BGP, a property, and so on. The general idea of the approach and the structure of the algorithm can be still applied. Apart from computing these multiple levels, which can be done by extending the presented algorithm, it is interesting to understand if some measure may be used to select the more relevant abstractions, rather than leaving the choice entirely to the user.

Another direction worth exploring is to assess the possible benefits of combining log summarisation with strategies for bot detection (e.g. templates can help characterise the features of queries and thus favouring the classification of robotic queries) or for optimising the execution of a sequence of queries (once prototypical interaction with data is delineated, one could imagine triple stores being able to predict workload and optimise query execution).

In this work, we mainly focussed on the most frequent queries, but, future analyses may also investigate what insights can be extracted from the rare ones (for example, a long tail of rare queries may indicate a high variety of clients and data exposed by the endpoint).

Finally, the proposed method and algorithm are applicable without much change to other query languages, thus offering an approach for the analysis of logs of, e.g. relational databases.

Supplemental Material Statement. The extended version of this paper (pre-print) is publicly available (see title note), as well as the dataset with the experimentation results (see note 13). The query logs used in the experimentation can be downloaded from the LSQ website[14]. The code is available from a public git repository (see note 7).

Acknowledgements. This work was partially supported by the PNRR project "Fostering Open Science in Social Science Research (FOSSR)" (CUP B83C22003950001) and by the PNRR MUR project PE0000013-FAIR.

References

1. Aljaloud, S., Luczak-Rösch, M., Chown, T., Gibbins, N.: Get all, filter details-on the use of regular expressions in SPARQL queries. In: Proceedings of the Workshop on Usage Analysis and the Web of Data (USEWOD 2014) (2014)
2. Arias, M., Fernandez, J.D., Martinez-Prieto, M.A., de la Fuente, P.: An empirical study of real-world SPARQL queries. In: Proceedings of Usage Analysis and the Web of Data (USEWOD 2011) (2011)
3. Asprino, L., Basile, V., Ciancarini, P., Presutti, V.: Empirical analysis of foundational distinctions in linked open data. In: Proceedings of the 27th International Joint Conference on Artificial Intelligence and the 23rd European Conference on Artificial Intelligence (IJCAI-ECAI 2018), pp. 3962–3969 (2018). https://doi.org/10.24963/ijcai.2018/551
4. Asprino, L., Beek, W., Ciancarini, P., van Harmelen, F., Presutti, V.: Observing LOD using equivalent set graphs: it is mostly flat and sparsely linked. In: Ghidini, C., et al. (eds.) ISWC 2019, Part I. LNCS, vol. 11778, pp. 57–74. Springer, Cham (2019). https://doi.org/10.1007/978-3-030-30793-6_4
5. Asprino, L., Carriero, V.A., Presutti, V.: Extraction of common conceptual components from multiple ontologies. In: Proceedings of the International Conference on Knowledge Capture (K-CAP 2021), pp. 185–192 (2021). https://doi.org/10.1145/3460210.3493542

---

[14] http://lsq.aksw.org/.

6. Asprino, L., Presutti, V.: Observing LOD: its knowledge domains and the varying behavior of ontologies across them. IEEE Access **11**, 21127–21143 (2023). https://doi.org/10.1109/ACCESS.2023.3250105

7. Auer, S., Bizer, C., Kobilarov, G., Lehmann, J., Cyganiak, R., Ives, Z.: DBpedia: a nucleus for a web of open data. In: Aberer, K., et al. (eds.) ASWC/ISWC -2007. LNCS, vol. 4825, pp. 722–735. Springer, Heidelberg (2007). https://doi.org/10.1007/978-3-540-76298-0_52

8. Belleau, F., Nolin, M.A., Tourigny, N., Rigault, P., Morissette, J.: Bio2RDF: towards a mashup to build bioinformatics knowledge systems. J. Biomed. Inform. **41**(5), 706–716 (2008)

9. Bielefeldt, A., Gonsior, J., Krötzsch, M.: Practical linked data access via SPARQL: the case of wikidata. In: Proceedings of the Workshop on Linked Data on the Web co-located with the Web Conference (LDOW@WWW 2018) (2018)

10. Bonifati, A., Martens, W., Timm, T.: Navigating the maze of wikidata query logs. In: Proceedings of The Web Conference (WWW 2019), pp. 127–138 (2019). https://doi.org/10.1145/3308558.3313472

11. Bonifati, A., Martens, W., Timm, T.: An analytical study of large SPARQL query logs. VLDB J. **29**(2–3), 655–679 (2020). https://doi.org/10.1007/s00778-019-00558-9

12. Chekol, M.W., Euzenat, J., Genevès, P., Layaïda, N.: SPARQL query containment under SHI axioms. In: Proceedings of the Twenty-Sixth AAAI Conference on Artificial Intelligence (AAAI 2012) (2012)

13. Cyganiak, R., Wood, D., Lanthaler, M.: RDF 1.1 Concepts and Abstract Syntax. http://www.w3.org/TR/2014/REC-rdf11-concepts-20140225/

14. Deep, S., Gruenheid, A., Koutris, P., Viglas, S., Naughton, J.F.: Comprehensive and efficient workload summarization. Datenbank-Spektrum **22**(3), 249–256 (2022). https://doi.org/10.1007/s13222-022-00427-w

15. Haklay, M., Weber, P.: Openstreetmap: user-generated street maps. IEEE Pervasive Comput. **7**(4), 12–18 (2008). https://doi.org/10.1109/MPRV.2008.80

16. Han, X., Feng, Z., Zhang, X., Wang, X., Rao, G., Jiang, S.: On the statistical analysis of practical SPARQL queries. In: Proceedings of the 19th International Workshop on Web and Databases (2016). https://doi.org/10.1145/2932194.2932196

17. Harris, S., et al.: SPARQL 1.1 Query Language. http://www.w3.org/TR/2013/REC-sparql11-query-20130321/

18. Hartig, O.: Provenance information in the web of data. In: Proceedings of the Workshop on Linked Data on the Web (LDOW 2009) (2009). http://ceur-ws.org/Vol-538/ldow2009_paper18.pdf

19. Hoxha, J., Junghans, M., Agarwal, S.: Enabling semantic analysis of user browsing patterns in the web of data. In: Proceedings of Usage Analysis and the Web of Data (USEWOD 2012) (2012)

20. Huelss, J., Paulheim, H.: What SPARQL query logs tell and do not tell about semantic relatedness in LOD - or: the unsuccessful attempt to improve the browsing experience of DBPedia by exploiting query logs. In: Proceedings of ESWC 2015, Revised Selected Papers, pp. 297–308 (2015). https://doi.org/10.1007/978-3-319-25639-9_44

21. Kamra, A., Terzi, E., Bertino, E.: Detecting anomalous access patterns in relational databases. VLDB J. **17**(5), 1063–1077 (2008). https://doi.org/10.1007/s00778-007-0051-4

22. Kul, G., et al.: Summarizing large query logs in Ettu. CoRR (2016). http://arxiv.org/abs/1608.01013

23. Lebo, T., Sahoo, S., McGuinness, D.: PROV-O: The PROV Ontology. https://www.w3.org/TR/2013/REC-prov-o-20130430/
24. Luczak-Rösch, M., Bischoff, M.: Statistical analysis of web of data usage. In: Joint Workshop on Knowledge Evolution and Ontology Dynamics (EvoDyn 2011) (2011)
25. Luczak-Rösch, M., Hollink, L., Berendt, B.: Current directions for usage analysis and the web of data: the diverse ecosystem of web of data access mechanisms. In: Proceedings of the 25th International Conference on World Wide Web (WWW 2016), pp. 885–887 (2016). https://doi.org/10.1145/2872518.2891068
26. Mathew, S., Petropoulos, M., Ngo, H.Q., Upadhyaya, S.J.: A data-centric approach to insider attack detection in database systems. In: Proceedings of the 13th International Symposium on Recent Advances in Intrusion (RAID 2010), pp. 382–401 (2010). https://doi.org/10.1007/978-3-642-15512-3_20
27. Meroño-Peñuela, A., Hoekstra, R.: grlc makes GitHub taste like linked data APIs. In: Proceedings of ESWC 2016, pp. 342–353 (2016)
28. Microsoft: Automatic Tuning - Microsoft SQL Server. https://learn.microsoft.com/en-us/sql/relational-databases/automatic-tuning/automatic-tuning?view=sql-server-ver16
29. Möller, K., Hausenblas, M., Cyganiak, R., Handschuh, S.: Learning from linked open data usage: patterns & metrics. In: Proceedings of the Web Science Conference (2010)
30. Möller, K., Heath, T., Handschuh, S., Domingue, J.: Recipes for semantic web dog food - the ESWC and ISWC metadata projects. In: Proceedings of the 6th International Semantic Web Conference and the 2nd Asian Semantic Web Conference, ISWC-ASWC 2007, pp. 802–815 (2007). https://doi.org/10.1007/978-3-540-76298-0_58
31. Oracle: Automatic Indexing - Oracle SQL Developer Web. https://docs.oracle.com/en/database/oracle/sql-developer-web/19.2.1/sdweb/automatic-indexing-page.html#GUID-8198E146-1D87-4541-8EC0-56ABBF52B438
32. Picalausa, F., Vansummeren, S.: What are real SPARQL queries like? In: Proceedings of the International Workshop on Semantic Web Information Management (SWIM 2011) (2011). https://doi.org/10.1145/1999299.1999306
33. Pichler, R., Skritek, S.: Containment and equivalence of well-designed SPARQL. In: Proceedings of the 33rd ACM SIGMOD-SIGACT-SIGART Symposium on Principles of Database Systems (PODS 2014), pp. 39–50 (2014). https://doi.org/10.1145/2594538.2594542
34. Prud'hommeaux, E., Buil-Aranda, C.: SPARQL 1.1 Federated Query. http://www.w3.org/TR/2013/REC-sparql11-federated-query-20130321/
35. Raghuveer, A.: Characterizing machine agent behavior through SPARQL query mining. In: Proceedings of the Workshop on Usage Analysis and the Web of Data (USEWOD 2012) (2012)
36. Rietveld, L., Hoekstra, R., et al.: Man vs. machine: differences in SPARQL queries. In: Proceedings of the Workshop on Usage Analysis and the Web of Data (USEWOD 2014) (2014)
37. Saleem, M., Ali, M.I., Hogan, A., Mehmood, Q., Ngomo, A.-C.N.: LSQ: the linked SPARQL queries dataset. In: Arenas, M., et al. (eds.) ISWC 2015, Part II. LNCS, vol. 9367, pp. 261–269. Springer, Cham (2015). https://doi.org/10.1007/978-3-319-25010-6_15
38. Schoenfisch, J., Stuckenschmidt, H.: Analyzing real-world SPARQL queries and ontology-based data access in the context of probabilistic data. Int. J. Approx. Reason. **90**, 374–388 (2017). https://doi.org/10.1016/j.ijar.2017.08.005

39. Shannon, C.E.: A mathematical theory of communication. Bell Syst. Tech. J. **27**(3), 379–423 (1948). https://doi.org/10.1002/j.1538-7305.1948.tb01338.x

40. Stadler, C., Lehmann, J., Höffner, K., Auer, S.: LinkedGeoData: a core for a web of spatial open data. Semant. Web **3**(4), 333–354 (2012). https://doi.org/10.3233/SW-2011-0052

41. Stadler, C., et al.: LSQ 2.0: a linked dataset of SPARQL query logs (Preprint) (2022). https://aidanhogan.com/docs/lsq-sparql-logs.pdf

42. Vrandečić, D.: WikiData: a new platform for collaborative data collection. In: Proceedings of the 21st International Conference on World Wide Web (WWW 2012), pp. 1063–1064 (2012). https://doi.org/10.1145/2187980.2188242

43. Wang, J., et al.: Real-time workload pattern analysis for large-scale cloud databases. arXiv e-prints arXiv:2307.02626, July 2023. https://doi.org/10.48550/arXiv.2307.02626

44. Xie, T., Chandola, V., Kennedy, O.: Query log compression for workload analytics. VLDB Endow. **12**(3), 183–196 (2018). https://doi.org/10.14778/3291264.3291265

Iterative Geographic Entity Alignment
with Cross-Attention

Alishiba Dsouza[1]($\boxtimes$) , Ran Yu[1,2] , Moritz Windoffer[1],
and Elena Demidova[1,2]

[1] Data Science & Intelligent Systems (DSIS), University of Bonn, Bonn, Germany
{dsouza,elena.demidova}@cs.uni-bonn.de, {ran.yu,s5mowind}@uni-bonn.de
[2] Lamarr Institute for Machine Learning and Artificial Intelligence, Bonn, Germany
https://lamarr-institute.org/

Abstract. Aligning schemas and entities of community-created geographic data sources with ontologies and knowledge graphs is a promising research direction for making this data widely accessible and reusable for semantic applications. However, such alignment is challenging due to the substantial differences in entity representations and sparse interlinking across sources, as well as high heterogeneity of schema elements and sparse entity annotations in community-created geographic data. To address these challenges, we propose a novel cross-attention-based iterative alignment approach called IGEA in this paper. IGEA adopts cross-attention to align heterogeneous context representations across geographic data sources and knowledge graphs. Moreover, IGEA employs an iterative approach for schema and entity alignment to overcome annotation and interlinking sparsity. Experiments on real-world datasets from several countries demonstrate that our proposed approach increases entity alignment performance compared to baseline methods by up to 18% points in F1-score. IGEA increases the performance of the entity and tag-to-class alignment by 7 and 8% points in terms of F1-score, respectively, by employing the iterative method.

Keywords: Geographic Knowledge Graph · Iterative Neural Entity Alignment

1 Introduction

Knowledge graphs provide a backbone for emerging semantic applications in the geographic domain, including geographic question answering and point of interest recommendations. However, general-purpose knowledge graphs such as Wikidata [23], DBpedia [14], and YAGO [19] contain only a limited number of popular geographic entities, restricting their usefulness in this context. In contrast, OpenStreetMap (OSM)[1][2] is a community-created world-scale geographic

---

[1] https://www.openstreetmap.org/.
[2] OpenStreetMap, OSM and the OpenStreetMap magnifying glass logo are trademarks of the OpenStreetMap Foundation, and are used with their permission. We are not endorsed by or affiliated with the OpenStreetMap Foundation.

© The Author(s) 2023
T. R. Payne et al. (Eds.): ISWC 2023, LNCS 14265, pp. 216–233, 2023.
https://doi.org/10.1007/978-3-031-47240-4_12

data source containing millions of geographic entities. However, the community-driven nature of OSM leads to highly heterogeneous and sparse annotations at both the schema and instance levels, which lack machine-interpretable semantics and limit the accessibility and reusability of OSM data. Knowledge graphs extracted from OSM and dedicated to geographic entities such as LinkedGeoData [1] and WorldKG [7] focus on a selection of well-annotated geographic classes and entities and do not take full advantage of OSM data. Tighter interlinking of geographic data sources with knowledge graphs can open up the rich community-created geographic data sources to various semantic applications.

Interlinking geographic data sources with knowledge graphs is challenging due to the heterogeneity of their schema and entity representations, along with the sparsity of entity annotations and links between sources. Knowledge graphs such as Wikidata adopt ontologies to specify the semantics of entities through classes and properties. Taking the entity Berlin as an example, Table 1a and 1b illustrate its representation in OSM and Wikidata. The property wdt:P31 (instance of) in Wikidata specifies the entity type. In contrast, OSM annotates geographic entities using key-value pairs called tags, often without clear semantics. The distinction of whether a key-value pair represents an entity type or an attribute is not provided. For instance, in Table 1, the key *capital* in OSM corresponds to a binary value specifying whether the location is the capital of a country. In contrast, the Wikidata property wdt:P1376 (*capital of*) is an object property linked to an entity of type country. Moreover, user-defined key-value pairs in OSM lead to highly heterogeneous and sparse annotations, where many entities do not have comprehensive annotations and many key-value pairs are rarely reused. Finally, sparse and often inaccurate interlinking makes training supervised alignment algorithms difficult. As illustrated in the example, the values, such as the geo-coordinates of the same real-world entity Berlin, differ between sources. Such differences in representation, coupled with the heterogeneity and sparsity of OSM annotations and the lack of links, make schema and entity alignment across sources extremely challenging.

Recently, several approaches have been proposed to interlink knowledge graphs to OSM at the entity and schema level, to lift the OSM data into a semantic representation, and to create geographic knowledge graphs [1, 6, 13, 21]. For example, LinkedGeoData [1] relies on manual schema mappings and provides high-precision entity alignment using labels and geographic distance for a limited number of well-annotated classes. OSM2KG [21] – a linking method for geographic entities, embeds the tags of geographic entities for entity representation and interlinking. The NCA tag-to-class alignment [6] enables accurate matching of frequent tags to classes, but does not support the alignment of rare tags. The recently proposed WorldKG knowledge graph [7] incorporates the information extracted by NCA and OSM2KG, but is currently limited to the well-annotated geographic classes and entities. Overall, whereas several approaches for linking geographic entities and schema elements exist, they are limited to well-annotated classes and entities, they rely on a few properties and do not sufficiently address the representation heterogeneity and annotation sparsity.

Table 1. An excerpt of the Berlin representation in OSM and Wikidata.

(a) OSM tags.

Key	Value
name	Berlin
place	city
population	3769962
way	POINT(52.5183 13.4179)
capital	yes

(b) Wikidata triples. `wd:Q64` identifies Berlin.

Subject	Predicate	Object
wd:Q64	rdfs:label (*label*)	Berlin
wd:Q64	wdt:P31 (*instance of*)	wd:Q515 (*city*)
wd:Q64	wdt:P1082 (*population*)	3677472
wd:Q64	wdt:P625 (*coordinate location*)	52°31'N, 13°23'E
wd:Q64	wdt:P1376 (*capital of*)	wd:Q183 (*Germany*)

In this paper, we propose IGEA – a novel iterative geographic entity alignment approach. IGEA relies on a cross-attention mechanism to align heterogeneous context representations across community-created geographic data and knowledge graphs. This model learns the representations of the entities through the tags and properties and reduces the dependency on specific tags and labels. Furthermore, to overcome the annotation and interlinking sparsity problem, IGEA employs an iterative approach for tag-to-class and entity alignment that starts from existing links and enriches the links with alignment results from previous iterations. We evaluate our approach on real-world OSM, Wikidata, and DBpedia datasets. The results demonstrate that, compared to state-of-the-art baselines, the proposed approach can improve the performance of entity alignment by up to 18% points, in terms of F1-score. By employing the iterative method, IGEA increases the performance of the entity and tag-to-class alignment by 7 and 8% points in terms of F1-score, respectively.

In summary, our contributions are as follows:

- We propose IGEA – a novel iterative cross-attention-based approach to interlink geographic entities, bridging the representation differences in community-created geographic data and knowledge graphs.
- To overcome the sparsity of annotations and links, IGEA employs an iterative method for tag-to-class and entity alignment, with integrated candidate blocking mechanisms for efficiency and noise reduction.
- We demonstrate that IGEA substantially outperforms the baselines in F1-score through experiments on several real-world datasets.

2   Problem Statement

In this section, we introduce the relevant concepts and formalize the problem addressed in this paper.

Definition 1 (Knowledge Graph). *A knowledge graph $KG = (E, C, P, L, F)$ consists of a set of entities E, a set of classes $C \subset E$, a set of properties P, a set of literals L and a set of relations $F \subseteq E \times P \times (E \cup L)$.*

Entities of knowledge graph KG with geo-coordinates L_{geo} are referred to as geographic entities E_{geo}.

Definition 2 (Geographic Entity Alignment). *Given an entity n from a geographic data source G (n ∈ G), and a set of geographic entities E_{geo} from a knowledge graph KG, $E_{geo} \subseteq KG$, determine the entity e ∈ E_{geo} such that sameAs(n, e) holds.*

In the example in Table 1, as a result of the geographic entity alignment, Berlin from OSM will be linked to Berlin from Wikidata with a *sameAs* link.

Definition 3 (Geographic Class Alignment). *Given a geographic data source G and a knowledge graph KG, find a set of pairs of class elements of both sources, such that elements in each pair (s_i, s_j), $s_i \in G$ and $s_j \in KG$, describe the same real-world concept.*

In the example illustrated in Table 1, the tag place=city from OSM will be linked to the *city* (wd:Q515) class of Wikidata.

In this paper, we address the task of geographic entity alignment through iterative learning of class and entity alignment.

3   The *IGEA* Approach

In this section, we introduce the proposed IGEA approach. Figure 1 provides an approach overview. In the first step, IGEA conducts geographic class alignment based on known linked entities between OSM and KG with the NCA approach [6]. The resulting tag-to-class alignment is further adopted for blocking in the candidate generation step. Then IGEA applies the cross-attention-based entity alignment module to the candidate set to obtain new links. IGEA repeats this process iteratively with the resulting high-confidence links for several iterations. In the following, we present the proposed IGEA approach in more detail.

3.1   Geographic Class Alignment

We adopt the NCA alignment approach introduced in [6] to conduct tag-to-class alignment. The NCA approach aligns OSM tags with the KG classes. NCA relies on the linked entities from both sources, OSM and a KG, and trains a neural model to learn the representations of the tags and classes. The NCA model creates the shared latent space while classifying the OSM entities into the knowledge graph classes. NCA then probes the resulting classification model to obtain the tag-to-class alignments. NCA selects all matches above a certain threshold value. After applying NCA, we obtain a set of tag-to-class alignments, i.e., (s_i, s_j), $s_i \in G$, and $s_j \in KG$.

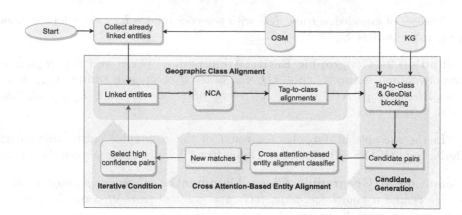

Fig. 1. Overview of the proposed IGEA approach.

3.2   Candidate Generation

OSM contains numerous geographic entities for which we often do not have a match in the KGs. IGEA applies candidate blocking to reduce the search space to make the algorithm more time and complexity efficient. In our task, the objective of the blocking module is to generate a set of candidate entity pairs that potentially match. We built the candidate blocking module based on two strategies, namely entity-type-based and distance-based candidate selection. Entities with a *sameAs* link should belong to the same class. Therefore, we use the tag-to-class alignments produced by the NCA module to select the entities of the same class from both sources to form candidate pairs. Secondly, since we consider only geographic entities, we use spatial distance to reduce the candidate set further and only consider the entities within a threshold distance. Past works observed that a threshold value of around 2000 to 2500 m can work well for most classes [1,13,21]. We choose the threshold of 2500 m as mentioned in [21]. The candidate pairs generated after the candidate blocking step are passed to the cross-attention-based entity alignment module.

3.3   Cross-Attention-Based Entity Alignment

We build a cross-attention-based classification model for entity alignment by classifying a pair of entities into a match or a non-match. Figure 2 illustrates the overall architecture of the entity alignment model. The components of the model are described in detail below.

Entity Representation Module: In this module, we prepare entity representations to serve as the model input. For a given OSM node, we select all tags and create a sentence by concatenating the tags. For a given KG entity, we select all predicates and objects of the entity and concatenate all pairs of predicates and objects to form a sentence. We set the maximum length of a sentence to be input to the model to N_w, where N_w is calculated as the average number of

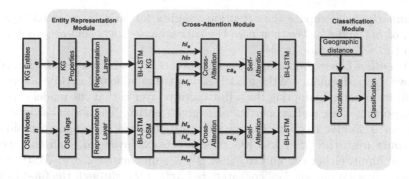

Fig. 2. Cross-attention-based entity alignment model.

words of all entities in the current candidate set. We pass these sentences to the representation layer for each pair of OSM node n and KG entity e.

In the representation layer, the model creates embeddings for the given sentence. We adopt pre-trained fastText word embeddings [3] for the embedding layer. For any word not present in the pre-trained embeddings, we assign a zero vector of size d, where d is the embeddings dimension. In this step, we obtain an array of size $N_w * d$ for each entity.

Cross-Attention Module: We initiate our cross-attention module with a Bidirectional LSTM (BI-LSTM) layer. BI-LSTM models have been demonstrated to perform well on sequential data tasks such as named entity recognition and speech recognition [4,10]. We adopt BI-LSTM since we want the model to learn to answer what comes after a particular key or a property to help the cross-attention layer. We incorporate BI-LSTM layers after the embedding layers for each of the inputs. As an output, the BI-LSTM layer can return the final hidden state or the full sequence of hidden states for all input words. We select the full sequence of hidden states hl_n, hl_e since we are interested in the sequence and not a single output. These sequences of hidden states hl_n, hl_e are then passed to the cross-attention layer.

Cross-Attention Layer: This layer implements the cross-attention mechanism [22] that helps understand the important properties and tags for aligning the entities. As explained in [22], attention scores are built using keys, values, and queries along with their dimensions. For OSM, we adopt the output of the BI-LSTM layer hl_e as key k and query q and hl_n becomes the value v. For KGs, we adopt the output of the BI-LSTM layer hl_n as key k and query q and hl_e becomes the value v. We initialize the weight vectors w_q, w_k, w_v using the Xavier uniform initializer [9]. We then compute the cross-attention weights for OSM as:

$$Q = hl_e * w_q, K = hl_e * w_k, V = hl_n * w_v,$$

$$att = Q \cdot K, att_w = softmax(att), att_c = att_w \cdot V,$$

where att_w is the attention weights and att_c is the context.

Similarly, we compute the attention weights for KGs by interchanging the values of hl_n and hl_e. We then pass the concatenated att_w and att_c as ca_n and ca_e to the self-attention model.

Self-Attention Layer: Adopting both cross-attention and self-attention layers can improve the performance of the models in multi-modal learning [15]. In our case, the intuition behind adopting the self-attention layer is that the model can learn the important tags and properties of a given entity. The formulation of self-attention is similar to that of cross-attention. Instead of using a combination of outputs from the OSM and KG cross-attention layers ca_n and ca_e, we use only one input, either ca_n and ca_e that is the same across k, q, v. We then pass the self-attention output, i.e., concatenated att_w, att_c, through the final layer of Bi-directional LSTM.

Once we have both inputs parsed through all layers, we concatenate the outputs of the Bi-directional LSTM layers along with the distance input that defines the haversine distance between the input entities.

Classification Module: We utilize the linked entities as the supervision for the classification. Each true pair is labeled one, and the remaining pairs generated by the candidate blocking step are labeled zero. The classification layer predicts whether the given pair is a match or not. We pass the concatenated output through a fully connected layer, which is then passed through another fully connected layer with one neuron to predict the final score. We use a sigmoid activation function with binary cross-entropy loss to generate the score for the final match.

3.4   Iterative Geographic Entity Alignment Approach

We create an end-to-end iterative pipeline for aligning KG and OSM entities and schema elements to alleviate the annotation and interlinking sparsity. We apply the IGEA approach at the country level. For a selected country, we collect all entities having geo-coordinates from the KG. In the first iteration, the already linked entities are used as supervision to link unseen entities that are not yet linked. After selecting candidate pairs and classifying them into match and non-match classes, we use a threshold th_a to only select high confidence pairs from the matched class. In the subsequent iterations, we add these high-confidence matched pairs to the linked entities and then run the pipeline starting from NCA-based class alignment again. By doing so, we aim to enhance the performance of entity alignment with tag-to-class alignment-based candidate blocking and tag-to-class alignment with additional newly linked entities. Algorithm 1 provides details of the IGEA approach.

Algorithm 1 The IGEA Algorithm

Input: n, e OSM and KG linked Entities
              th_a Alignment threshold
              itr number of iterations
              con Country
              kg KG
Output: $align$ Final entity alignment

1: $align \Leftarrow \emptyset$
2: load(n, e, con)
3: $KG_e \Leftarrow$ getCountryEntities(con, kg)
4: $GT \Leftarrow$ getSeedAlignment(con,kg)
5: **while** $i < itr$ **do**
6:     $tag\text{-}to\text{-}class \Leftarrow$ NCA(con,kg,GT)
7:     $view \Leftarrow$ createView($tag\text{-}to\text{-}class$)
8:     **for all** $ent \in KG_e$ **do**
9:         $candidates \Leftarrow$ generateCandidates(ent, $view$, 2500)
10:        **if** $candidates \cap GT \neq \emptyset$ **then**
11:            $SeenEnt \Leftarrow candidates$
12:        **else**
13:            $UnseenEnt \Leftarrow candidates$
14:        **end if**
15:    **end for**
16:    $model \Leftarrow$ classificationModel($seenEnt$)
17:    $prediction \Leftarrow model(UnseenEnt)$
18:    **for all** $pair \in prediction$ **do**
19:        **if** $pair_{confidence} > th_a$ **then**
20:            $align \Leftarrow align \cup \{pair\}$
21:            $GT \Leftarrow GT \cup \{pair\}$
22:        **end if**
23:    **end for**
24:    $i = i + 1$
25: **end while**
26: **return** $align$

---

4   Evaluation Setup

This section describes the experimental setup, including datasets, ground truth generation, baselines, and evaluation metrics. All experiments were conducted on an AMD EPYC 7402 24-Core Processor with 1 TB of memory. We implement the framework in Python 3.8. For data storage, we use the PostgreSQL database (version 15.2). We use TensorFlow 2.12.0 and Keras 2.12.0 for neural model building.

4.1   Datasets

For our experiments, we consider OSM, Wikidata, and DBpedia datasets across various countries, including Germany, France, Italy, USA, India, Netherlands,

Table 2. Ground truth size for Wikidata and DBpedia.

	France	Germany	India	Italy	Netherlands	Spain	USA
WIKIDATA	19082	21165	7001	16584	4427	14145	73115
DBPEDIA	10921	165	1870	2621	110	4319	14017

and Spain. All datasets were collected in April 2023. For OSM data, we use OSM2pgsql[3] to load the nodes of OSM into the PostgreSQL database. The OSM datasets are collected from GeoFabrik download server[4]. For Wikidata[5] and DBpedia[6], we rely on the SPARQL endpoints. Given a country, we select all entities that are part of the country with property *P17* for Wikidata and *dbo:country* for DBpedia along with geo-coordinates (*P625* for Wikidata and *geo:geometry* for DBpedia).

4.2   Ground Truth

We select the existing links between geographic entities in OSM and KGs as ground truth. Since we consider geographic entities from the already linked entities identified through "wikidata" and "wikipedia" tags, we select entities with geo-coordinates. Table 2 displays the number of ground truth entities for Wikidata and DBpedia knowledge graphs. We consider only those datasets where the number of links in the ground truth data exceeds 1500 to have sufficient data to train the model. For tag-to-class alignment, we use the same ground truth as in the NCA [6] approach.

4.3   Baselines

This section introduces the baselines to which we compare our work, including similarity-based and deep learning-based approaches.

GeoDistance: In this baseline, we select the OSM node for each KG geographic entity so that the distance between the KG entity and the OSM node is the least compared to all other OSM nodes. We consider the distance calculated using the *st_distance* function of PostgreSQL that calculates the minimum geodesic distance as the distance metric.

LGD [1]: LinkedGeoData approach utilizes geographic and linguistic distance to match the entities in OSM and KG. Given a pair of geographic entities $e1$ and $e2$, LinkedGeoData considers $\frac{2}{3}ss(e1, e2) + \frac{1}{3}gd(e1, e2) > 0.95$ as a match, where ss is the Jaro-Winkler distance and gd is the logistic geographical distance.

---

[3] https://osm2pgsql.org/.

[4] https://download.geofabrik.de/.

[5] https://query.wikidata.org/.

[6] https://dbpedia.org/sparql.

Yago2Geo: Yago2Geo [13] considers both string and geographic distance while matching entities by having two filters, one based on Jaro-Winkler similarity (s) between the labels and the second filter based on the Euclidean distance (ed) between the geo-coordinates of the two entities. Given entities $e1$ and $e2$, if $s(e1, e2) > 0.82$ and $ed(e1, e2) < 2000$ $meters$, the two entities are matched.

DeepMatcher: DeepMatcher [17] links two entities from different data sources having similar schema. The model learns the similarity between two entities by summarizing and comparing their attribute embeddings. Since our data sources do not follow the same schema, we select the values of keys name, addressCountry, address, and population for OSM. For KGs, we select the values of the equivalent properties label, country, location, and population.

HierMatcher: This baseline [8] aligns entities by jointly matching at token, attribute, and entity levels. At the token level, the model performs the cross-attribute token alignment. At the attribute level, the attention mechanism is applied to select contextually important information for each attribute. Finally, the results from the attribute level are aggregated and passed through fully connected layers that predict the probability of two entities being a match.

OSM2KG: OSM2KG [21] implements a machine learning-based model for the entity alignment between OSM and KGs. The model generated key-value embeddings using the occurrences of the tags and created a feature vector including entity type and popularity of KG entities. We use the default th_{dist} 2500 m and the random forest classification model adopted in the original paper.

OSM2KG-FT: This baseline is a variation of the OSM2KG model where we replace the key-value embeddings of OSM entities with fastText embeddings.

4.4   Evaluation Metrics

The standard evaluation metrics for entity and tag-to-class alignment are precision, recall, and F1-score computed against a reference alignment (i.e., ground truth). We calculate **precision** as the ratio of all correctly identified pairs to all identified pairs. We calculate **recall** as the fraction of all correctly identified pairs to all pairs in the ground truth alignment. **F1-score** is the harmonic mean of recall and precision. The F1-score is most relevant for our analysis since it considers both precision and recall. We use macro averages for the metrics because we have imbalanced datasets in terms of classes.

5   Evaluation

In this section, we discuss the performance of the IGEA model. First, we evaluate the performance of the approach for entity alignment against baselines.

Furthermore, we assess the impact of the number of iterations and thresholds. Finally, we demonstrate the approach effectiveness on unseen entities through a manual assessment. To facilitate the evaluation, we split our data into 70:10:20 for training, validation, and test data with a random seed of 42.

Table 3. Entity alignment performance on the OSM to Wikidata linking.

Name	France			Germany			India			Italy			Netherlands			Spain			USA		
	P	R	F1	P	R	F1	P	R	F1	P	R	F1	P	R	F1	P	R	F1	P	R	F1
GEODIST	0.65	0.65	0.65	0.56	0.56	0.56	0.75	0.75	0.75	0.68	0.68	0.68	0.67	0.67	0.67	0.71	0.71	0.71	0.88	0.88	0.88
LGD	0.63	0.61	0.62	0.83	0.81	0.82	0.87	0.68	0.72	0.90	0.68	0.77	0.81	0.79	0.80	0.82	0.40	0.82	0.87	0.84	0.85
YAGO2GEO	0.5	0.51	0.50	0.53	0.51	0.50	0.61	0.60	0.60	0.52	0.51	0.50	0.50	0.88	0.64	0.63	0.70	0.65	0.88	0.69	0.73
DEEPMATCHER	0.62	0.58	0.60	0.74	0.67	0.71	0.77	0.79	0.78	0.89	0.55	0.68	0.83	0.78	0.80	0.87	0.75	0.80	0.93	0.91	0.91
HIERARMATCH	0.51	0.71	0.59	0.64	0.79	0.70	0.71	0.88	0.79	0.62	0.83	0.71	0.8	0.83	0.81	0.80	0.77	0.78	0.92	0.93	0.92
OSM2KG	0.81	0.79	0.80	0.83	0.82	0.82	0.87	0.81	0.84	0.87	0.79	0.83	0.82	0.69	0.75	0.83	0.82	0.82	0.92	0.81	0.86
OSM2KG-FT	0.83	0.81	0.81	0.89	0.82	0.85	0.91	0.75	0.82	0.89	0.85	0.87	0.89	0.71	0.77	0.88	0.82	0.85	0.95	0.87	0.91
IGEA-1	0.95	0.91	<u>0.94</u>	0.93	0.95	<u>0.94</u>	0.88	0.87	<u>0.87</u>	0.93	0.97	<u>0.94</u>	0.94	0.86	<u>0.90</u>	0.89	0.91	<u>0.90</u>	0.93	0.95	<u>0.94</u>
IGEA-3	0.98	0.99	**0.99**	0.93	0.96	**0.95**	0.96	0.90	**0.93**	0.99	0.97	**0.98**	0.94	0.94	**0.94**	0.98	0.93	**0.95**	0.97	0.97	**0.97**

5.1 Entity Alignment Performance

Tables 3 and 4 present the performance of the IGEA approach and the baselines in terms of precision, recall, and F1-score on the various country datasets for Wikidata and DBpedia knowledge graphs, respectively. IGEA-1 and IGEA-3 indicate the results obtained with the 1st and 3rd iterations of the IGEA approach, respectively. The results demonstrate that the proposed IGEA approach outperforms all the baselines in terms of the F1-score. We achieve up to 18% points F1-score improvement on Wikidata and up to 14% points improvement over DBpedia KGs. IGEA also achieves the best recall and precision on several datasets. Regarding the baselines, as expected, GeoDist performs poorly since the geo-coordinates of the same entity are presented with different precision in OSM and in KGs and are not always in closer proximity to each other. OSM2KG-FT performs the best among the baselines for both KGs. We notice that using the tags with fastText embeddings slightly improves the performance of the OSM2KG over using the occurrence-based key-value embeddings. The deep-learning-based baselines perform on par with the other baselines. The absence of the features such as name and country limits the performance of these deep-learning-based baselines that rely on specific properties. The performance of the name-based baselines such as Yago2Geo and LGD is inconsistent across datasets; a potential reason is the absence of labels in the same language.

Regarding the datasets, the IGEA approach achieved the highest performance improvement on the France and Spain datasets for Wikidata and DBpedia KGs, respectively. The smallest performance improvement over the best-performing baselines is produced on the USA dataset. Data in the USA dataset is mostly in English; furthermore, the USA dataset has the highest percentage of name tags among given countries, which makes string similarity-based baseline approaches more effective. We notice that India achieves the lowest performance across datasets and KGs. The number of overall properties and tags for entities in India are lower than in other datasets, making IGEA less beneficial. DBpedia results demonstrate better model performance compared to Wikidata. Since DBpedia contains more descriptive properties, it benefits more from employing the cross-attention-based mechanism.

Table 4. Entity alignment performance on the OSM to DBpedia linking.

Name	France			India			Italy			Spain			USA		
	P	R	F1	P	R	F1	P	R	F1	P	R	F1	P	R	F1
GEODIST	0.39	0.39	0.39	0.35	0.35	0.35	0.58	0.58	0.58	0.40	0.40	0.40	0.64	0.64	0.64
LGD	0.84	0.76	0.79	0.83	0.63	0.72	0.87	0.69	0.76	0.91	0.72	0.78	0.70	0.61	0.64
YAGO2GEO	0.70	0.63	0.66	0.67	0.65	0.65	0.73	0.69	0.71	0.73	0.76	0.74	0.54	0.54	0.54
DEEPMATCHER	0.79	0.85	0.82	0.78	0.85	0.81	0.83	0.73	0.77	0.81	0.73	0.77	0.85	0.86	0.85
HIERARMATCH	0.69	0.84	0.76	0.73	0.85	0.79	0.66	0.90	0.76	0.55	0.87	0.67	0.81	0.90	0.85
OSM2KG	0.80	0.82	0.80	0.84	0.79	0.81	0.80	0.84	0.81	0.82	0.77	0.79	0.87	0.82	0.84
OSM2KG-FT	0.82	0.87	0.84	0.84	0.82	0.83	0.81	0.89	0.85	0.82	0.82	0.82	0.90	0.91	0.90
IGEA-1	0.92	0.91	0.91	0.89	0.91	0.90	0.95	0.89	0.92	0.96	0.97	0.96	0.97	0.95	0.96
IGEA-3	0.95	0.99	**0.97**	0.96	0.97	**0.97**	0.95	0.98	**0.96**	0.96	0.95	**0.95**	0.99	0.97	**0.98**

Table 5. Ablation study results for the DBpedia datasets.

Name	France			India			Italy			Spain			USA		
	P	R	F1	P	R	F1	P	R	F1	P	R	F1	P	R	F1
W/O CROSS-ATTENTION	0.86	0.81	0.83	0.83	0.82	0.82	0.86	0.77	0.81	0.82	0.81	0.81	0.83	0.84	0.83
W/O DISTANCE	0.85	0.89	0.86	0.81	0.87	0.82	0.81	0.83	0.82	0.79	0.86	0.82	0.82	0.87	0.84
W/O CLASS-BLOCKING	0.81	0.93	0.87	0.73	0.94	0.82	0.78	0.93	0.85	0.75	0.92	0.83	0.79	0.96	0.86
IGEA-3	0.95	0.99	**0.97**	0.96	0.97	**0.97**	0.95	0.98	**0.96**	0.96	0.95	**0.95**	0.99	0.97	**0.98**

5.2 Ablation Study

Table 5 displays the results of an ablation study to better understand the impact of individual components. We observe that removing the cross-attention layer significantly reduces the performance of the model. The class-based blocking improves the recall but has a sharp decrease in precision, as it creates many noisy matches. Removing geographic distance also results in worse performance compared to the IGEA. The results of the ablation study confirm that the components introduced in the IGEA approach help to achieve the best performance.

5.3 Impact of the Number of Iterations

In this section, we evaluate the impact of the number of iterations on the IGEA performance. Figure 3 displays the F1-scores for the entity alignment after each iteration. We observe that the scores increase in all configurations with the increased number of iterations; after the 3rd iteration, the trend is not continuing. We notice the performance drops for a few countries. After manually checking such drops, we found that the model removes the wrong matches that are part of the ground truth data, which leads to a drop in the evaluation metrics. By adopting an iterative approach, we obtain a maximum improvement of 6 and 7% points in F1-score over Wikidata and DBpedia, respectively. Figure 4 displays the F1-scores for tag-to-class alignment after each iteration. We obtain a maximum increase of 4 and 8% points in the F1-score over Wikidata and DBpedia, respectively. We observe a similar trend as the entity alignment, such that the model performance increases up to the 3rd or 4th iteration. The increased number of aligned tag-class pairs provides more evidence for entity alignment.

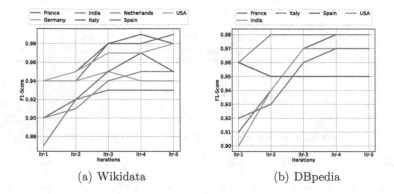

(a) Wikidata   (b) DBpedia

Fig. 3. Entity alignment performance: F1-scores for 1–5 iterations.

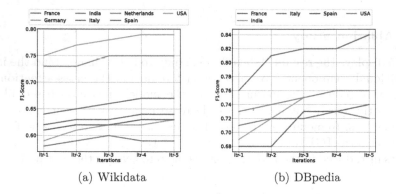

(a) Wikidata   (b) DBpedia

Fig. 4. Tag-to-class alignment performance: F1-scores for 1–5 iterations.

5.4 Alignment Threshold Tuning

We assess the importance of the alignment threshold th_a regarding the F1-score to select the appropriate value of th_a. Figure 5 depicts the F1-scores obtained after the third iteration for threshold values ranging between 0.50 and 0.90 with a gap of 0.1. Overall, the model performs well for all threshold values. Comparing the performance of different th_a values, the highest F1-score is achieved with a $th_a = 0.60$ for both KGs across all datasets. Therefore, in the experiments in other parts of this paper, we set th_a to 0.6.

5.5 Manual Assessment of New Links

We manually assess the quality of the links obtained on unseen data. We create the unseen dataset by considering the entities of Wikidata that are tagged with the country Germany and have a geo-coordinate, but are not present in the ground truth links. We randomly select 100 entities from all iterations and manually verify the correctness of the links. Out of 100 matches, we obtained 89 correct matches. We observe that 6 of the wrong matches are mostly located closer to each other or contained in one another. These entities contain similar property and tag values, making it difficult for the model to understand the difference. For example, Wikidata entity *Q1774543 (Klingermühle)* is contained in OSM node *114219911 (Bessenbach)*. The lack of an English label also hinders the performance. Meanwhile, we observed that IGEA discovers new links between entities and corrects the previously wrong-linked entities. OSM node *1579461216 (Beuel-Ost)* has a Wikidata tag as *Q850834 (Beuel-Mitte)* but using IGEA, the correct Wikidata entity *Q850829 (Beuel-Ost)* has been linked to the OSM node. The performance of the unseen entities demonstrates the effectiveness of the proposed IGEA approach.

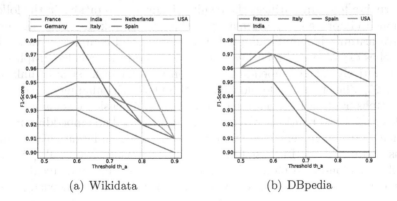

(a) Wikidata   (b) DBpedia

Fig. 5. Entity alignment performance in terms of F1-Score with different threshold values.

6   Related Work

This section discusses related work in geographic entity alignment, ontology alignment, and iterative learning.

Geographic entity alignment aims to align geographic entities across different geographic sources that refer to the same real-world object. In the past, approaches often relied on geographic distance and linguistic similarity between the labels of the entities [1,13]. LIMES [20] relies on rules to rate the similarity between entities and uses these rules in a supervised model to predict the links. Tempelmeier et al. [21] proposed the OSM2KG algorithm – a machine-learning model to learn a latent representation of OSM nodes and align them with knowledge graphs. OSM2KG also uses KG features such as name, popularity, and entity type to produce more precise links. Recently, deep learning-based models have gained popularity for the task of entity alignment on tabular data. DeepMatcher [8] and HierMatcher [17] use an embedding-based deep learning approach for predicting the matches for tabular datasets. Peeters et al. [18] use contrastive learning with supervision to match entities in small tabular product datasets. In contrast, IGEA adopts the entire entity description, including KG properties and OSM tags, to enhance the linking performance.

Ontology and schema alignment refer to aligning elements such as classes, properties, and relations between ontologies and schemas. Such alignment can be performed at the element and structural levels. Many approaches have been proposed for tabular and relational data schema alignment and rely on the structural and linguistic similarity between elements [5,12,16,26]. Lately, deep learning methods have also gained popularity for the task of schema alignment [2]. Due to the OSM schema heterogeneity and flatness, applying these methods to OSM data is difficult. Recently, Dsouza et al. [6] proposed the NCA model for OSM schema alignment with knowledge graphs using adversarial learning. We adopt NCA as part of the proposed IGEA approach.

Iterative learning utilizes the results of previous iterations in the following iterations to improve the performance of the overall task. In knowledge graphs, iterative learning is mainly adopted in reasoning and completion tasks. Many approaches exploit rule-based knowledge to generate knowledge graph embeddings iteratively. These embeddings are then used for tasks such as link prediction [11,27]. Zhu et al. [28] developed a method for entity alignment across knowledge graphs by iteratively learning the joint low-dimensional semantic space to encode entities and relations. Wang et al. [24] proposed an embedding model for continual entity alignment in knowledge graphs based on latent entity representations and neighbors. In cross-lingual entity alignment, Xie et al. [25] created a graph attention-based model. The model iteratively and dynamically updates the attention score to obtain cross-KG knowledge. Unlike knowledge graphs, OSM does not have connectivity between entities. Therefore, the aforementioned methods are not applicable to OSM. In IGEA, we employ class and entity alignment iteratively to alleviate the data heterogeneity as well as annotation and interlinking sparsity to improve the results of the geographic entity and schema alignment.

7 Conclusion

In this paper, we presented IGEA – a novel iterative approach for geographic entity alignment based on cross-attention. IGEA overcomes the differences in entity representations between community-created geographic data sources and knowledge graphs by using a cross-attention-based model to align heterogeneous context information and predict identity links between geographic entities. By iterating schema and entity alignment, the IGEA approach alleviates the annotation and interlinking sparsity of geographic entities. Our evaluation results on real-world datasets demonstrate that IGEA is highly effective and outperforms the baselines by up to 18% points F1-score in terms of entity alignment. Moreover, we observe improvement in the results of tag-to-class alignment. We make our code publicly available to facilitate further research[7].

Supplemental Material Statement: Sect. 4 provides details for baselines and datasets. Source code, instructions on data collection, and for repeating all experiments are available from GitHub (see footnote 7).

Acknowledgements. This work was partially funded by the DFG, German Research Foundation ("WorldKG", 424985896), the Federal Ministry for Economic Affairs and Climate Action (BMWK), Germany ("ATTENTION!", 01MJ22012C), and DAAD/BMBF, Germany ("KOALA", 57600865).

References

1. Auer, S., Lehmann, J., Hellmann, S.: LinkedGeoData: adding a spatial dimension to the web of data. In: Bernstein, A., et al. (eds.) ISWC 2009. LNCS, vol. 5823, pp. 731–746. Springer, Heidelberg (2009). https://doi.org/10.1007/978-3-642-04930-9_46
2. Bento, A., Zouaq, A., Gagnon, M.: Ontology matching using convolutional neural networks. In: Proceedings of the 12th Language Resources and Evaluation Conference, pp. 5648–5653. ELRA (2020)
3. Bojanowski, P., Grave, E., Joulin, A., Mikolov, T.: Enriching word vectors with subword information. Trans. Assoc. Comput. Linguistics 5, 135–146 (2017)
4. Chiu, J.P.C., Nichols, E.: Named entity recognition with bidirectional LSTM-CNNs. Trans. Assoc. Comput. Linguistics 4, 357–370 (2016)
5. Demidova, E., Oelze, I., Nejdl, W.: Aligning freebase with the YAGO ontology. In: 22nd ACM International Conference on Information and Knowledge Management, pp. 579–588 (2013)
6. Dsouza, A., Tempelmeier, N., Demidova, E.: Towards neural schema alignment for OpenStreetMap and knowledge graphs. In: Hotho, A., et al. (eds.) ISWC 2021. LNCS, vol. 12922, pp. 56–73. Springer, Cham (2021). https://doi.org/10.1007/978-3-030-88361-4_4
7. Dsouza, A., Tempelmeier, N., Yu, R., Gottschalk, S., Demidova, E.: Worldkg: a world-scale geographic knowledge graph. In: CIKM '21: The 30th ACM International Conference on Information and Knowledge Management, pp. 4475–4484. ACM (2021)

---

[7] https://github.com/alishiba14/IGEA.

8. Fu, C., Han, X., He, J., Sun, L.: Hierarchical matching network for heterogeneous entity resolution. In: Proceedings of the Twenty-Ninth International Joint Conference on Artificial Intelligence,. pp. 3665–3671 (2020)
9. Glorot, X., Bengio, Y.: Understanding the difficulty of training deep feedforward neural networks. In: Proceedings of the Thirteenth International Conference on Artificial Intelligence and Statistics, pp. 249–256 (2010)
10. Graves, A., Jaitly, N., Mohamed, A.: Hybrid speech recognition with deep bidirectional LSTM. In: Proceedings of the IEEE Workshop on Automatic Speech Recognition and Understanding, pp. 273–278 (2013)
11. Guo, S., Wang, Q., Wang, L., Wang, B., Guo, L.: Knowledge graph embedding with iterative guidance from soft rules. In: Proceedings of the 22nd AAAI Conference on Artificial Intelligence, pp. 4816–4823 (2018)
12. Jiménez-Ruiz, E., Agibetov, A., Chen, J., Samwald, M., Cross, V.: Dividing the ontology alignment task with semantic embeddings and logic-based modules. In: Proceedings of the 24th European Conference on Artificial Intelligence, pp. 784–791. FAIA, IOS Press (2020)
13. Karalis, N., Mandilaras, G., Koubarakis, M.: Extending the YAGO2 knowledge graph with precise geospatial knowledge. In: Ghidini, C., et al. (eds.) ISWC 2019. LNCS, vol. 11779, pp. 181–197. Springer, Cham (2019). https://doi.org/10.1007/978-3-030-30796-7_12
14. Lehmann, J., et al.: Dbpedia - a large-scale, multilingual knowledge base extracted from wikipedia. Semantic Web 6(2), 167–195 (2015)
15. Li, P., et al.: Selfdoc: self-supervised document representation learning. In: Proceedings of the IEEE Conference on Computer Vision and Pattern Recognition, pp. 5652–5660 (2021)
16. Madhavan, J., Bernstein, P.A., Rahm, E.: Generic schema matching with cupid. In: Proceedings of the 27th International Conference on Very Large Data Bases, pp. 49–58. Morgan Kaufmann (2001)
17. Mudgal, S., et al.: Deep learning for entity matching: a design space exploration. In: Proceedings of the 2018 International Conference on Management of Data, pp. 19–34. ACM (2018)
18. Peeters, R., Bizer, C.: Supervised contrastive learning for product matching. In: Companion of the Web Conference 2022, pp. 248–251. ACM (2022)
19. Rebele, T., et al.: YAGO: a multilingual knowledge base from wikipedia, wordnet, and geonames. In: Proceedings of the 15th International Semantic Web Conference, pp. 177–185 (2016)
20. Sherif, M.A., Ngomo, A.N., Lehmann, J.: Wombat - a generalization approach for automatic link discovery. In: Proceedings of the 14th Extended Semantic Web Conference, pp. 103–119 (2017)
21. Tempelmeier, N., Demidova, E.: Linking OpenStreetMap with knowledge graphs - link discovery for schema-agnostic volunteered geographic information. Future Gener. Comput. Syst. 116, 349–364 (2021)
22. Vaswani, A., et al.: Attention is all you need. In: Proceedings of the Annual Conference on Neural Information Processing Systems, pp. 5998–6008 (2017)
23. Vrandecic, D., Krötzsch, M.: Wikidata: a free collaborative knowledgebase. Commun. ACM 57(10), 78–85 (2014)
24. Wang, Y., et al.: Facing changes: continual entity alignment for growing knowledge graphs. In: Sattler, U., et al. The Semantic Web - ISWC 2022. ISWC 2022. LNCS, vol. 13489, pp. 196–213. Springer, Cham (2022). https://doi.org/10.1007/978-3-031-19433-7_12

25. Xie, Z., Zhu, R., Zhao, K., Liu, J., Zhou, G., Huang, J.X.: Dual gated graph attention networks with dynamic iterative training for cross-lingual entity alignment. ACM Trans. Inf. Syst. **40**(3), 44:1–44:30 (2022)
26. Zhang, S., Balog, K.: Web table extraction, retrieval, and augmentation: a survey. ACM Trans. Intell. Syst. Technol. **11**(2), 13:1–13:35 (2020)
27. Zhang, W., et al.: Iteratively learning embeddings and rules for knowledge graph reasoning. In: Proceedings of the World Wide Web Conference, pp. 2366–2377. ACM (2019)
28. Zhu, H., Xie, R., Liu, Z., Sun, M.: Iterative entity alignment via joint knowledge embeddings. In: Proceedings of the 26th International Joint Conference on Artificial Intelligence, pp. 4258–4264 (2017)

Entity-Relation Distribution-Aware Negative Sampling for Knowledge Graph Embedding

Naimeng Yao[1]([✉])[iD], Qing Liu[2][iD], Yi Yang[3][iD], Weihua Li[4][iD], and Quan Bai[1][iD]

[1] University of Tasmania, Hobart, Australia
{naimeng.yao,quan.bai}@utas.edu.au
[2] Data61, CSIRO, Hobart, Australia
q.liu@data61.csiro.au
[3] Hefei University of Technology, Hefei, China
yyang@hfut.edu.cn
[4] Auckland University of Technology, Auckland, New Zealand
weihua.li@aut.ac.nz

Abstract. Knowledge Graph Embedding (KGE) is a powerful technique for mining knowledge from knowledge graphs. Negative sampling plays a critical role in KGE training and significantly impacts the performance of KGE models. Negative sampling methods typically preserve a pair of **Entity-Relation (ER)** in each positive triple and replace the other entity with negative entities selected randomly from the entity set to create a consistent number of negative samples. However, the distribution of ER pairs is often long-tailed, making it problematic to assign the same number of negative samples to each ER pair, which is overlooked in most related works. This paper investigates the impact of assigning the same number of negative samples to ER pairs during training and demonstrates that this approach impedes the training from reaching the optimal solution in the negative sampling loss function and undermines the objective of the trained model. To address this issue, we propose a novel ER distribution-aware negative sampling method that can adaptively assign a varying number of negative samples to each ER pair based on its distribution characteristics. Furthermore, our proposed method also mitigates the issue of introducing false negative samples commonly found in many negative sampling methods. Our approach is founded on theoretical analysis and practical considerations and can be applied to most KGE models. We validate the effectiveness of our proposed method by testing it on conventional KGE and Neural Network-based KGE models. Our experimental results outperform most state-of-the-art negative sampling methods.

Keywords: Knowledge Graph Embedding · Negative Sampling · Knowledge Graph

Supplementary Information The online version contains supplementary material available at https://doi.org/10.1007/978-3-031-47240-4_13.

1   Introduction

A Knowledge Graph (KG) is a graph composed of entities as nodes and relations as edges that connect entities [25, 27]. It is typically represented in the form of triples, denoted as $(h, r, t) \in \mathcal{F}$, where $\mathcal{F}$ is a set of facts, h and t are head and tail entities from an entity set $\mathcal{E}$, and r is drawn from a relation set $\mathcal{R}$. Knowledge Graph Embedding (KGE) represents entities and relations as vectors or matrices, which can be used to perform downstream tasks such as KG completion, relation extraction, and question answering [27, 32, 33]. KGE has shown promising results in various KG-related applications.

In KGE training, the scoring function, loss function, and negative sampling are crucial components. The scoring function models entity relation interactions and evaluate the likelihood of a triple's truth. The loss function processes positive and negative triple embeddings during training, assigning higher scores (from the scoring function) to positive triples and lower scores to negative ones. Simple negative sampling methods like uniform sampling [2] generate negative samples by randomly substituting t or h in each positive triple (h, r, t). The preserved Entity-Relation pair, denoted as (e, r), can represent both **Head-Relation (HR)** and **Tail-Relation (TR)** pairs, which are denoted as (h, r) and (t, r). The replaced entity is denoted as q, and the generated negative entities in negative samples are denoted as $\bar{q}$.

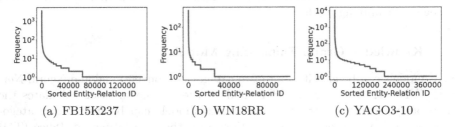

(a) FB15K237   (b) WN18RR   (c) YAGO3-10

Fig. 1. The long-tailed distribution of ER pairs in FB15K237, WN18RR, and YAGO3-10 datasets. The y-axis represents the frequency $\#(e, r)$ of each (e, r) pair, and the x-axis shows the sorted ER ID.

Current negative sampling approaches, such as works [3, 26, 34], create quality negative samples that KGE models can hardly differentiate from positive triples, while others, like those mentioned in [1, 10, 21], demand a substantial number of negative samples for training. However, these methods typically generate the same number of negative samples for all triples, ignoring that the distribution of ER pairs is long-tailed in most datasets (Fig. 1), with a large proportion of ER pairs appearing less frequently in triples, while a few ER pairs have a higher frequency of occurrence. Recent studies have shown that imbalanced data distribution, also known as long-tailed distribution, poses a challenge to accurate model learning [4, 32]. The imbalanced distribution also challenges the generation of negative samples in KGE models. Intuitively, it is unreasonable to generate the same number of negative entities $\bar{q}$ for the triple (*messi, profession, q*) with infrequent HR pair (*messi, profession*) and the triple (*q, profession, footballer*) with frequent and common TR pair (*footballer, profession*). A small number may not be sufficient for the former due to its rarity, while a large number may introduce false negative samples (i.e., true but non-observed triples) for the latter. We discover that this hinders KGE models from reaching their optimal solution, subsequently affecting their performances on downstream tasks. The main contributions of this work are as follows:

- We investigated the problem of assigning the same number of negative samples N to ER pairs for KGE training given a long-tailed distribution in KGs from a theoretical standpoint.
- We proposed an ER distribution-aware negative sampling method that is effective for a broad range of KGE models, including both conventional and Neural Network-based models.
- We conducted comprehensive experiments on six different KGE models and three benchmark KGs to validate our proposed method. The results show that our method outperforms state-of-the-art negative sampling methods.

2 Related Work

This section begins with an overview of KGE models, followed by a discussion of negative sampling methods.

2.1 Knowledge Graph Embedding Models

KGE models can be classified into two categories: conventional and Neural Network (NN)-based models. In KGE models, the scoring function calculates the plausibility score for a triple. Conventional models can be further subcategorized according to their scoring functions into the translational distance (TD) and semantic matching (SM) models. Examples of TD models include TransE [2], TransD [8], TransR [15], and RotatE [21], while popular SM models include DistMult [30], ComplEx [23], and SimplE [11]. NN-based KGE models can be broadly categorized into Convolutional NN-based (CNN) and Graph NN-based (GNN) models. Examples of CNN-based models are ConvKB [18], ConvE [5], and InteractE [24], while CompGCN [5] is a generalized version of several existing GNN methods [19,20]. GNN models usually use scoring functions from conventional KGE models as decoders for the link prediction task.

2.2 Negative Sampling Methods

The uniform sampling method selects negative entities $\bar{q}$ for (e, r) with equal probability. To avoid zero gradients in the effective training process, several negative sampling methods prioritize selecting a smaller set of quality negative samples with higher scores [3,26,34], or assigning greater weights to high score samples within multiple negative samples [1,21], which share a similar idea to train word embeddings by choosing negative words based on ranking scores in natural language processing (NLP) [7]. KBGAN [3], IGAN [26], and NSCaching [34] create a negative candidate set $C_{(e,r)}$ for (e,r) in each positive triple and employ their specific distribution functions $p_\phi(\bar{q}_i|(e,r))$ to choose negative samples. Despite minor differences in their distribution functions, their negative sampling distribution $p_n\big(\bar{q}_i|(e,r)\big)$ could be collectively represented as:

$$p_n\big(\bar{q}_i|(e,r)\big) = p_\phi\big(\bar{q}_i|(e,r)\big) = \frac{exp\Big(\alpha f\big(\bar{q}_i,(e,r)\big)\Big)}{\sum_{\big(\bar{q}_i,(e,r)\big)\in C_{(e,r)}} exp\Big(\alpha f\big(\bar{q}_i,(e,r)\big)\Big)}, (\bar{q}_i,(e,r)) \notin \mathcal{F},$$

$$(1)$$

where $f(\cdot)$ is the scoring function of KGE models and α is the sampling temperature. Likewise, the distribution function serves as weights assigned to negative samples in the loss function in Self-Adv [21] and SANS [1]. However, these approaches primarily stem from experimental observations and frequently face false negative samples. Distinguishing between quality and false negative samples is difficult, as both exhibit high scores. Also, multiple negative samples can inadvertently introduce false negative samples.

Other works have analyzed the impact of the number of negative samples on the performance of KGEs. For instance, Bernoulli sampling [29] assigns different probabilities to replace the head or tail entity in a triple to construct negative samples, reducing the number of false negative samples. Trouillon et al. [23] find that increasing the number of negative samples within a certain range can improve the KGE performance. More recently, a Subsampling work [10] explores the hyperparameter tuning for the negative sampling (NS) loss function, and a Non-Sampling work [14] adds all of the negative instances in the KG for model learning.

Previous studies have not investigated the effect of assigning the same number N of negative samples to ER pairs with an imbalanced distribution, nor have they tackled the challenge of producing quality negative samples while minimizing false negative samples. To our knowledge, this study is the first to analyze the effect and attempt to resolve this issue while simultaneously mitigating false negative samples.

3   Theoretical Analysis

This section introduces the NS loss function and its optimal solution, discusses the problem of allocating an equal number of negative samples to all ER pairs, and presents our proposed solution.

3.1   Optimal Solution for the Negative Sampling Loss Function

The NS loss function was initially introduced for word-representation learning [17] and has been widely adopted in training SM models [23] for its effectiveness. Recently, the work [21] adapted it for TD models by introducing a margin term κ. The variant of the NS loss function is defined as follows:

$$L = -\frac{1}{|\mathcal{F}|} \sum_{(q,(e,r)) \in \mathcal{F}} \left[\log \sigma \big(g(q, (e,r)) \big) + w \sum_{\bar{q}_i \sim p_n \big(\bar{q}_i | (e,r) \big)}^{N} \log \sigma \big(-g(\bar{q}_i, (e,r)) \big) \right], \quad (2)$$

where N represents the number of negative samples for each positive triple, $\sigma(\cdot)$ denotes the sigmoid activation function, and $g\big(q, (e,r)\big) = f\big(q, (e,r)\big) + \kappa$. In TD models, the value of κ is greater than 0, whereas it is set to 0 for SM models. When $w = p_\phi(\bar{q}|(e,r))$ (Eq. (1)), it aligns with the loss function employed in the Self-Adv method [21]. The original NS loss function corresponds to the case with $w = 1$. Recent studies [9,10,13,31] suggest that within the NS loss function ($w = 1$), the optimal embedding, denoted by $(q, (e,r))^*$ for each triple, satisfies the following condition:

$$f\big(q, (e,r)\big)^* = \log \frac{p_d\big(q|(e,r)\big)}{N \exp(\kappa) p_n\big(q|(e,r)\big)}, \quad (3)$$

where $p_d(q, (e,r))$ is the true distribution of all observed triples $(q, (e,r))$ in $\mathcal{F}$. Moreover, while $(q, (e,r))^*$ denotes the optimal embedding for a given triple, $f(q, (e,r))^*$ stands for its corresponding optimal solution in KGE models. The optimal solution guarantees the **monotonicity** property (objective) of the trained model. In the context of uniform sampling, where $p_n(q|(e,r)) = \frac{1}{|\mathcal{E}|}$,[1] and $|\mathcal{E}|$ is the size of the entity set, given any ER pair (e,r) and two distinct triples $(q_m, (e,r))$ and $(q_n, (e,r))$, if it is established that $p_d(q_m|(e,r)) > p_d(q_n|(e,r))$, then $f(q_m, (e,r))^* > f(q_n, (e,r))^*$ can be inferred.

3.2   Inaccessible Optimal Solution

During the KGE training, negative sampling methods typically generate negative samples for each triple by randomly retaining either the TR or the HR pair with an even chance. This process can be carried out simultaneously or alternately. Consequently, the optimal solution for each triple should align with Eq. (3) from both the TR and HR perspectives. Yet, for a given triple (h, r, t) and referencing Eq. (3), the optimal solution would yield two distinct values if $p_d(h|(t, r))$ is not the same as $p_d(t|(h, r))$. Nonetheless, it is impractical for a single triple to possess dual scores simultaneously, making attaining the optimal solution infeasible. Moreover, a model optimized in this manner loses its **monotonicity** trait, leading to a decline in the performance of KGE in downstream tasks.

Indeed, the distributions of $p_d(h|(t, r))$ and $p_d(t|(h, r))$ could differ significantly in most triples. Even though obtaining the explicit values of $p_d(h|(t, r))$

---

[1]   In the implementation, observed positive entities are filtered out. However, since the total number of entities $|\mathcal{E}|$ is significantly larger than the frequency $\#(e, r)$ of ER pairs, for the sake of simplification in theoretical analysis, we set $p_n(q|(e,r)) = \frac{1}{|\mathcal{E}|}$.

and $p_d(t|(h,r))$ is not feasible due to incomplete knowledge graphs, their distributions can be implicitly inferred from the dataset. For a simplified explanation, we use the frequency of ER pairs $\#(e,r)$ as a proxy for the distribution, assuming that for $(q,(e,r)) \in \mathcal{F}$, $p_d(q|(e,r)) = \frac{1}{\#(e,r)}$, and for $(q,(e,r)) \notin \mathcal{F}$, $p_d(q|(e,r)) = 0$. As shown in Fig. 1, ER pairs follow an imbalanced distribution, so $p_d(h|(t,r))$ and $p_d(t|(h,r))$ can differ significantly in most triples. This problem has been ignored in most research.

3.3   Assigning Varying $N_{(e,r)}$ to Entity-Relation Pair (e,r)

In pursuit of ensuring $f(h,(t,r))^* = f(t,(h,r))^*$ as per Eq. (3), a straightforward adjustment is modifying N to $N_{(e,r)}$ and assigning $N_{(e,r)}$ to each input (e,r) in proportion to $p_d(q|(e,r))$, when $\exp(\kappa)$ and p_n are constant. Nevertheless, one prerequisite to consider is the persistence of Eq. (3) when $N_{(e,r)}$ is no longer a uniform, constant number N in Eq. (2). We find modifying N to $N_{(e,r)}$ will not disrupt Yang's proof process [31] for Eq. (3), so the subsequent proposition remains valid.

Proposition 1. *Within the NS loss where $N_{(e,r)}$ represents the number of negative samples for each ER pair (e,r), the optimal solution can still be formulated as follows:*

$$f\big(q,(e,r)\big)^* = \log \frac{p_d\big(q|(e,r)\big)}{N_{(e,r)} exp(\kappa) p_n\big(q|(e,r)\big)}. \tag{4}$$

The complete proof is available in the supplementary material. This optimal solution still guarantees the **monotonicity** property of the trained model. Moreover, practical realization is attainable by adhering to the proposition below, which outlines the suitable number of negative samples for the TR and HR pairs:

Proposition 2. *To guarantee $f(h,(t,r))^* = f(t,(h,r))^*$, the number of negative samples $N_{(h,r)}$ and $N_{(t,r)}$ should conform to the following equation when utilizing the frequency of ER pairs $\#(e,r)$ as a proxy for the distribution.*

$$\frac{N_{(t,r)}}{N_{(h,r)}} = \frac{p_d(h|(t,r))}{p_d(t|(h,r))} \approx \frac{\#(h,r)}{\#(t,r)} \Rightarrow N_{(t,r)}\#(t,r) = N_{(h,r)}\#(h,r). \tag{5}$$

For instance, considering the triple (*messi, profession, footballer*), the number of corresponding negative samples should adhere to $N_{(messi,profession)}\#(messi, profession) = N_{(footballer,profession)}\#(footballer, profession)$. Here, we refer to the collection of all observed HR pairs sharing the same TR pair as the Share Tail-Relation (STR) for (t,r), represented by $S_{(t,r)}$. Similarly, the Share Head-Relation (SHR) for (h,r) is denoted as $S_{(h,r)}$. By using the transitive property of equality, we present the following proposition:

Proposition 3. *For any HR pairs* $(h_m, r), (h_n, r) \in S_{(t,r)}$, *the numbers of negative samples* $N_{(h_m,r)}$ *and* $N_{(h_n,r)}$ *should satisfy:*

$$N_{(h_m,r)} \#(h_m, r) = N_{(t,r)} \#(t, r) = N_{(h_n,r)} \#(h_n, r). \tag{6}$$

Similar conclusions can be reached for TR pairs in $S_{(h,r)}$.

Considering HR pairs (*messi, profession*) and (*maradona, profession*) that share TR (*footballer, profession*), the numbers of their negative samples also conform to $N_{(messi,profession)} \#(messi$, profession$) = N_{(maradona,profession)} \#(maradona,$ *profession*). Equation (5) and (6) provide guidelines for assigning numbers of negative sampling within a triple as well as within $S_{(t,r)}$ (or $S_{(h,r)}$). However, designing batches within each Share Entity-Relation (SER) during training can be challenging and may introduce bias, so we propose a global ER distribution-aware negative sampling method that considers ER pairs' distribution across the entire dataset rather than just within a single triple or SER.

4   Entity-Relation Distribution-Aware Negative Sampling Method (ERDNS)

In this section, we apply the theoretical result to practical implementation, discuss the challenges faced during method development, and present the proposed method's details.

4.1   From Theory to Practice: Two-Step Expansion

Among ER pairs Share the Same Relation r. Through the mechanism of the transitive property of equality, the association between $N_{(e,r)}$ and the frequency $\#(e, r)$ can be generalized across all HR and TR pairs that have the same r. For example, while the HR pairs (*messi, profession*) and (*parreira, profession*) do not have a shared TR pair, they are each in STR sets $S_{(footballer,profession)}$ and $S_{(coach,profession)}$, both of which intersect at the HR pair (*maradona, profession*). Through the transitive property of equality, $N_{(messi,profession)} \#(messi,$ *profession*$) = N_{(parreira,profession)} \#(parreira, profession)$ holds. On a broader scale, this inference is plausible for most relationships in the dataset.

Among All ER pairs. Assigning negative samples to ER pairs with the same r is still inefficient, so we propose extending Eq. (5) and (6) to apply among all ER pairs, as shown below:

$$N_{(e_m,r_m)} \#(e_m, r_m) = N_{(e_n,r_n)} \#(e_n, r_n), \tag{7}$$

where (e_m, r_m) and (e_n, r_n) represent any ER pairs in the dataset. Expanding the scope of Eq. (5) and (6) only extends the relationship without affecting its maintenance within a triple and within $S_{(t,r)}$ (or $S_{(h,r)}$). It is worth noting that the practical expansion does not affect the attainment of the optimal solution for the NS loss, nor does it compromise the **monotonicity** property of the trained model.

The concept introduced in Eq. (7) reflects that ER pairs that occur more frequently in the dataset should be given fewer negative samples during training, and those that occur less frequently should be given more negative samples. As noted earlier, in the case of research [1,3,21,26,34], a potential issue is the introduction of false negative samples. This drawback can negatively impact the convergence rate of the model, increase computational expenses, and ultimately reduce the overall performance. Our method also effectively reduces the likelihood of generating false negative samples. While Bernoulli sampling can also reduce false negative samples, our method has a broader scope and stronger theoretical support. Instead of emphasizing the average frequency of heads per tail hpt or tails per head tph for each r in Bernoulli sampling, we focus on the frequency of ER pairs. The average frequency hpt or tph can be distinctively different from $\#(e,r)$ in the dataset. Moreover, we assign different $N_{(e,r)}$ values to each (e,r) in the dataset, unlike Bernoulli sampling, which only considers ER pairs within a single triple. In the following subsection, we provide details about our proposed method ERDNS.

4.2   The Proposed Method

Previous negative sampling methods commonly assign N negative samples to each positive triple in a training mini-batch $\mathcal{F}_{batch}$, resulting in a total of $N_a = N \times |\mathcal{F}_{batch}|$ negative samples for triples in a mini-batch. Equation (7) demonstrates that the number of negative samples $N_{(e_i,r_i)}$ for each triple $(q_i, (e_i, r_i)) \in \mathcal{F}_{batch}$, $i \in [1, |\mathcal{F}_{batch}|]$, is inversely proportional to $\#(e_i, r_i)$. We propose a new allocation strategy to address this issue. Instead of dividing the N_a samples according to the ratio of $\frac{1}{\#(e_i,r_i)}$, we treat the N_a negative samples as N_a independent statistical experiments, denoted as x_j, where $j \in [1, N_a]$. For each of these experiments, there are $|\mathcal{F}_{batch}|$ possible outcomes labeled as i. We then assign $N_{(e_i,r_i)}$ based on how frequently outcome i appears in the N_a experiments. The resulting allocation can be modeled using a multinomial distribution shown below.

$$p(x_j = i) = p(e_i, r_i) = \frac{\frac{1}{\#(e_i,r_i)}}{\sum_{i=1}^{|\mathcal{F}_{batch}|} \frac{1}{\#(e_i,r_i)}}, \sum_{i=1}^{|\mathcal{F}_{batch}|} p(e_i, r_i) = 1,$$

$$N_{(e_i,r_i)} = \sum_{j=1}^{|\mathcal{F}_{batch}|} I(x_j = i),$$

(8)

where $I(\cdot)$ is the indicator function.

0 **Negative Sample Problem.** During the pre-processing of the dataset, we compute the frequency $\#(e,r)$ for both (h,r) and (t,r) pairs by traversing the dataset and indexing them by the respective (c,r). However, the frequency distribution of these pairs is often highly skewed, with the maximum value being

significantly larger than the minimum value. This can cause some ER pairs to struggle to receive even a single negative sample, which in turn can severely impact the performance of KGE models. Thus, it is crucial to devise a reliable and effective ER distribution-aware negative sampling method that satisfies two key **requirements**: 1) generating a varying $N_{(e,r)}$ for each (e,r) by using Eq. (8); 2) ensuring fewer ER pairs (e,r) obtain zero negative samples. To meet the two requirements, we introduce a hyperparameter $\alpha \in (0, 1]$:

$$p(e_i, r_i) = \frac{\frac{1}{\#(e_i, r_i)^{\alpha}}}{\sum_{i=1}^{|\mathcal{F}_{batch}|} \frac{1}{\#(e_i, r_i)^{\alpha}}}. \tag{9}$$

A smaller value of α can help meet the second requirement, ensuring that fewer pairs get zero negative samples. Our proposed strategy enhances the adaptability and robustness of the model, especially in handling the long-tailed distribution of ER pairs. We use Algorithm 1 to train KGE models based on the distribution-aware negative sampling method. Our proposed method centers around the generation of varying numbers of negative samples $N_{(e_i, r_i)}$ according to the probability of $p(e_i, r_i)$ (Step 5). The probability is dynamically calculated based on the inclusion of (e_i, r_i) in $\mathcal{F}_{batch}$ using Eq. (9). Once $N(e_i, r_i)$ are determined for each (e_i, r_i) in the triple, negative entities $\bar{q}_i$ are randomly chosen from the entity set. The remaining training processes adhere to standard KGE training steps. Our method follows unbiased uniform sampling and allocates fewer negative samples to high-frequency ER pairs to reduce the likelihood of generating false negative samples. Instead of assessing the scores of negative samples for each individual triple, our method evaluates the quality of all negative samples from a data augmentation perspective. While our method does not guarantee that every generated negative sample has a high score, the proposed allocation strategy can effectively address the issue caused by the long-tail nature, which

---

Algorithm 1. Entity-Relation Distribution-aware Negative Sampling Method (ERDNS).

Input: Training set $\mathcal{F} = \{(q, (e, r))\}$, embeddings of entities and relations, scoring function $f(q, (e, r))$, and frequency $\#(e, r)$. Hyperparameters: α, average number of negative samples N, dimension d, mini-batch size b, and training step Q.
Output: Trained embeddings.
1: Initialize the embeddings.
2: **for** $step = 1, \ldots, Q$ **do**
3:     Sample a mini-batch $\mathcal{F}_{batch} \in \mathcal{F}$.
4:     Calculate the probability $p(e_i, r_i)$ for each triple $(q_i, (e_i, r_i,))$ in $\mathcal{F}_{batch}$.
5:     Calculate the negative samples $N_{(e_i, r_i)}$ based on $p(e_i, r_i)$ in Eq. (9).
6:     Randomly sample $N_{(e_i, r_i)}$ negative entities $\bar{q}_i$ for each triple.
7:     Feed positive triples $(q_i, (e_i, r_i,))$ into the NS loss function ($w = 1$).
8:     Feed negative samples $(\bar{q}_i, (e_i, r_i))$ with size $N_{(e_i, r_i)}$ into the NS loss function.
9:     Update embeddings.
10: **end for**

is prevalent for many datasets, and improves the overall quality of negative samples.

Computational Cost. We examine computational space to store intermediate computation results and computational time of ERDNS using the DistMult model as a reference. The scoring function of this model is $f(q, (e, r)) = \langle e, r, q \rangle$, where $\langle \cdot \rangle$ is the inner product. The computational space and time of ERDNS and other state-of-the-art methods in each mini-batch are detailed in Table 1. The notation "1" indicates the space required to store the embedding of $\langle e, r \rangle$, and "N" represents the space for the embeddings of negative samples $\bar{q}$s. In the computational process, ERDNS needs to expand the embedding of $\langle e, r \rangle$ to align with the size of embeddings of $\bar{q}$s. This results in a manageable doubling of the standard cache space. The computation time of ERDNS is the same as others with the same average "N" negative samples. The computation cost of ERDNS is comparable to the existing negative sampling methods. Additionally, by applying ERDNS, there is an opportunity to reduce the number of negative samples, potentially lowering its computational cost compared to other methods. Therefore, ERDNS proves to be scalable for large-scale knowledge graphs.

Table 1. Comparison of the proposed method with the state-of-the-art regarding computational space and time in each mini-batch. N_1 and N_2 are the cache size and randomly sampled negative triples in NSCaching.

Method	NSCaching	KBGAN	unif	Bernoulli	Self-Adv	Subsampling	ERDNS
Space	$\mathcal{O}(b(N_1 + N_2 + 1)d)$	$\mathcal{O}(b(N + 1)d)$					$\mathcal{O}(b(2N)d)$
Time	$\mathcal{O}(b(N_1 + N_2)d)$	$\mathcal{O}(bNd)$					

5 Experiments

In this section, we detail our experimental setup, present our method's outcomes, analyze the findings, and assess our approach's impact through ablation and extension studies.

5.1 Experimental Setting

Datasets. We evaluate our proposed method on three commonly used knowledge graphs: FB15K237 [22], WN18RR [28], and YAGO3-10 [16]. The statistics for these KGs are presented in Table 2, and their ER distributions are illustrated in Fig. 1.

Table 2. Statistics of the datasets.

Dataset	Entity	Relation	Train	Valid	Test
FB15K237	14,541	237	272,115	17,535	20,466
WN18RR	40,943	11	86,835	3,034	3,134
YAGO3-10	123,182	37	1,079,040	5,000	5,000

Models. To evaluate the efficacy of our proposed method ERDNS, we integrate it into six different models: four conventional KGE models and two NN-based models. These models are as follows: TD models (TransE and RotatE), SM models (DistMult and ComplEx), a CNN model (ConvE), and a GNN model (CompGCN). CompGCN has used TransE, DistMult, and ConvE as decoders.

Compared Methods. We compare our proposed method ERDNS with two categories of negative sampling methods.
With Single Negative Sample: These methods only generate one negative sample per positive triple.

- KBGAN [3] computes a probability distribution over candidate negative triples for each positive triple and selects a single negative sample by sampling from the distribution.
- NSCaching [34] uses caches to store and update quality negative samples for each ER during training and selects a negative sample from the cache.
  With Multiple Negative Samples: These methods generate more than one negative sample per positive triple.
- Uniform Sampling [2] randomly selects a set of entities to serve as negative samples with an equal probability assigned to all entities in the KG.
- Bernoulli Sampling [29] generates negative samples for a positive triple (h, r, t) by replacing the head and tail according to the probabilities $\frac{tph}{tph+hpt}$ and $\frac{hpt}{tph+hpt}$.
- Self-Adv [21] generates multiple negative samples per positive triple and assigns higher weights to high score negative samples during training.
- Subsampling [10] is specialized for the NS loss and studied theoretically. It incorporates Self-Adv in its implementation.

Hyperparameter Settings. We utilized the Adam optimizer [12] to optimize the KGE models. To establish baseline hyperparameters for conventional models, we adopt settings from prior research [10,21]. These settings consist of the embedding dimension d, batch size b, learning rate lr, number of negative samples N, margin λ (for TD models), and regularization factor μ (for SM models). The results for uniform Sampling, Bernoulli Sampling, Self-Adv and Subsampling are obtained using the inherited hyperparameters. For KBGAN and NSCaching, we directly take the results from their works because the best settings were not provided. The hyperparameters for NSCaching (RotatE) were optimized based on the settings provided in its original paper. ConvE and CompGCN initially used a complete entity set for training, so we only used negative sampling methods with multiple samples in comparison. We also inherited the hyperparameters from their prior works. We identified two critical hyperparameters in our method: the average number of negative samples N per positive triple and α. We performed a grid search to evaluate the range of values, with N having options of $\{50, 128, 256, 512, 1024\}$ (Conventional models) and $\{1024, 2048, 4096, 8192\}$ (NN-based models), and α having options of $\{0.25, 0.5, 0.75, 1\}$.

Evaluation Setting. We evaluate the proposed negative sampling method using the link prediction task designed to predict the missing entity in a positive triple (h, r, t). To assess the performance of the method, we employ standard evaluation metrics, including Mean Reciprocal Rank (MRR), and Hits@N (N=1, 3, 10). The evaluation is performed with the filtered setting.

5.2   Main Results

Conventional Models. Table 3 displays the results of compared methods with conventional KGE models. ERDNS consistently outperforms other models on all three KGs, achieving the average highest MRR and Hits@N across different ranks. Negative sampling methods employing multiple samples generally perform better than those using single samples. Even though the latter often utilize quality negative samples, their performance may still be inferior to uniform sampling with multiple samples. Regarding negative sampling methods with multiple samples, Bernoulli sampling demonstrates superior performance over uniform sampling in reducing the number of false negative samples, particularly in the case of SM models rather than TD models. This indicates that false negative samples have a more substantial impact on SM models. The Subsampling model integrates Self-Adv in implementation, its enhancement through the subsampling technique is less effective than our method when compared to Self-Adv, even though our approach does not use Self-Adv.

The effectiveness of ERDNS is more pronounced on the FB15K237 and YAGO3-10 datasets compared to WN18RR, primarily due to the broader range of frequency values in the former datasets and the relatively lower percentage of (e, r) pairs with a frequency of 1. Both of these factors contribute to increased diversity in all $\#(e, r)$, making the optimal solution more challenging to obtain. Consequently, ERDNS demonstrates greater improvement on these datasets. Despite relying solely on dynamic allocation, our method surpasses more complex sampling methods, such as candidate selection in KBGAN, caching in NSCaching, Subsampling, and Self-Adv.

Neural Network-based Models. Table 4 presents the performance of negative sampling methods with NN-based KGE models. For CompGCN, Bernoulli sampling is not applicable due to incompatibility with the framework. Interestingly, unlike conventional KGE models, Self-Adv does not consistently outperform the uniform sampling method, which might be attributed to incorporating false negative samples, adversely affecting the learning of global features in NN-based

Table 3. Performance comparison on DistMult, ComplEx, TransE and RotatE.

Dataset	KGE model	DistMult				ComplEx			
	Method	MRR	Hits@1	Hits@3	Hits@10	MRR	Hits@1	Hits@3	Hits@10
FB15K237	KBGAN	26.7	-	-	45.3	28.2	-	-	45.4
	NSCaching	28.3	-	-	45.6	30.2	-	-	48.1
	unif	21.9	13.1	23.4	41.1	22.7	13.7	24.5	42.1
	Bernoulli	25.9	17.4	28.3	43.3	31.0	21.2	34.3	51.3
	Self-Adv	30.9	22.1	33.6	48.4	32.2	23.0	35.1	51.0
	Subsampling	29.9	21.2	32.7	47.5	32.8	23.6	36.1	51.2
	ERDNS	**35.0**	**25.7**	**38.3**	**53.7**	**35.7**	**26.2**	**39.3**	**54.7**
WN18RR	KBGAN	38.5	-	-	44.3	42.9	-	-	47.0
	NSCaching	41.3	-	-	45.5	44.6	-	-	50.9
	unif	42.7	39.0	43.7	50.7	44.8	41.5	46.4	51.7
	Bernoulli	40.0	37.3	40.7	45.2	46.0	42.4	47.8	53.0
	Self-Adv	43.9	39.4	45.2	53.8	47.1	42.8	48.9	55.7
	Subsampling	44.6	40.0	45.9	54.4	47.6	43.3	49.3	56.3
	ERDNS	**45.5**	**41.1**	**46.7**	**54.6**	**48.4**	**44.3**	**50.0**	**56.4**
YAGO3-10	NSCaching	40.3	-	-	56.6	40.5	-	-	57.8
	unif	45.4	35.7	51.0	64.5	46.4	36.6	51.9	64.8
	Bernoulli	49.0	39.4	54.2	67.2	50.3	40.9	55.5	68.0
	Self-Adv	44.8	34.7	50.4	64.3	47.3	37.4	53.2	66.1
	Subsampling	45.9	34.6	52.7	66.2	49.1	38.1	56.0	68.5
	ERDNS	**52.6**	**43.7**	**57.8**	**69.4**	**54.6**	**45.9**	**59.8**	**70.3**
Dataset	KGE model	TransE				RotatE			
	Method	MRR	Hits@1	Hits@3	Hits@10	MRR	Hits@1	Hits@3	Hits@10
FB15K237	KBGAN	29.4	-	-	46.7	-	-	-	-
	NSCaching	30.0	-	-	47.4	30.9	22.1	34.1	48.6
	unif	31.4	21.5	35.2	51.5	31.9	22.3	35.3	51.7
	Bernoulli	33.4	23.9	37.0	52.6	33.6	24.1	37.1	52.7
	Self-Adv	32.9	23.0	36.8	52.7	33.6	23.9	37.4	53.0
	Subsampling	33.6	24.0	37.3	52.9	34.0	24.5	37.6	53.2
	ERDNS	**34.2**	**24.8**	**37.9**	**53.0**	**34.5**	**25.2**	**37.9**	**53.7**
WN18RR	KBGAN	18.6	-	-	45.4	-	-	-	-
	NSCaching	20.0	-	-	47.8	47.1	42.9	48.9	55.3
	unif	22.4	1.5	40.1	51.9	47.1	42.8	48.6	55.5
	Bernoulli	23.2	2.2	41.4	52.2	47.5	43.1	49.1	56.0
	Self-Adv	22.3	1.3	40.1	52.8	47.6	43.1	49.5	57.3
	Subsampling	23.0	1.9	40.7	**53.7**	47.8	42.9	**49.8**	**57.4**
	ERDNS	**23.8**	**3.0**	**41.8**	52.8	**47.9**	**43.5**	49.4	56.5
YAGO3-10	NSCaching	30.7	-	-	50.7	42.3	33.8	47.1	59.7
	unif	48.2	37.4	55.1	67.3	49.8	40.2	55.2	67.7
	Bernoulli	50.3	40.6	56.3	67.9	50.2	40.8	55.8	67.9
	Self-Adv	51.2	41.5	57.6	68.3	50.8	41.8	56.5	67.6
	Subsampling	51.3	41.9	57.2	68.1	51.0	41.9	56.5	67.8
	ERDNS	**51.7**	**42.2**	**57.6**	**68.7**	**51.8**	**42.7**	**57.0**	**68.8**

models. Nevertheless, ERDNS continues to outperform the uniform sampling method in most conditions, highlighting its effectiveness and universality. Incorporating global trainable feature matrices might diminish the impact of negative samples during training, resulting in a modest performance enhancement of ERDNS on NN-based models.

Table 4. Performance comparison on ConvE and CompGCN.

KGE model	Dataset	FB15K237				WN18RR			
	Method	MRR	Hits@1	Hits@3	Hits@10	MRR	Hits@1	Hits@3	Hits@10
ConvE	unif	31.5	22.6	34.4	49.8	41.0	36.9	42.4	**49.0**
	Bernoulli	29.8	21.4	32.5	46.9	39.7	35.9	41.0	47.9
	Self-Adv	31.9	22.7	34.8	**50.4**	40.3	37.0	41.4	47.0
	ERDNS	**32.3**	**23.4**	**35.4**	50.2	**41.3**	**38.0**	**42.6**	48.4
CompGCN (TransE)	unif	32.9	24.1	36.1	50.1	18.9	**5.6**	25.6	47.5
	Self-Adv	28.5	20.0	31.2	45.7	20.4	5.3	29.6	49.3
	ERDNS	**33.6**	**24.2**	**36.2**	**50.9**	**24.5**	4.9	**39.0**	**53.1**
CompGCN (DistMult)	unif	33.3	24.4	36.4	51.2	42.0	37.3	43.3	52.1
	Self-Adv	29.2	21.0	31.8	45.9	43.0	**39.2**	43.1	51.8
	ERDNS	**34.2**	**25.2**	**37.4**	**52.3**	**43.4**	**39.2**	**44.3**	**52.5**
CompGCN (ConvE)	unif	35.2	26.2	38.5	53.1	46.6	43.4	47.7	**53.0**
	Self-Adv	30.3	22.6	32.9	46.2	43.7	40.7	44.7	49.4
	ERDNS	**35.3**	**26.3**	**38.9**	**53.6**	**46.8**	**43.8**	**47.8**	53.1

5.3   Ablation Study

Investigating the Impact of α and N. As mentioned in Sect. 4, the parameter α is crucial in meeting the two requirements of the proposed method. A large value of α prioritizes sampling according to the distribution of ER pairs, while a small value prevents the allocation of 0 negative samples to ER pairs with high frequency. We find that N impacts the optimal value of α. When N is relatively low, setting $\alpha = 1$ may not yield the best MRR, despite being consistent with the principle, as higher values of α can lead to the "0 negative sample problem". The MRR results on RotatE (R) and ComplEx (C) for all values of α exhibit a similar trend as N increases in Fig. 2. Initially, the MRR gradually improves until it reaches its peak when N attains a sufficiently large value, denoted as N_α^*, because the "0 negative sample problem" gradually diminishes as N increases. The sufficiently large value of N_α^* for different values of α follows the trend $N_{0.25}^* < N_{0.5}^* < N_{0.75}^* < N_1^*$. The exact value of N_α^* varies depending on the model and dataset.

Entity-Relation Pairs with Different Frequencies. We conduct experiments to examine the impact of our method on the number of negative samples $N_{(e,r)}$ for ER pairs with different frequencies during training and its effect on the performance of ER pairs with different frequencies during testing. We categorize ER pairs in the training set into three groups based on their frequencies: G_t^1

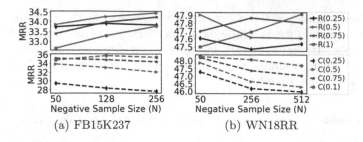

Fig. 2. MRR of ERDNS on RotatE (R) and ComplEx (C) with different α.

contains ER pairs with the highest frequency, where $\#(e, r) > 50$; G_t^3 contains ER pairs with the lowest frequency, where $\#(e, r) = 1$; and G_t^2 contains ER pairs with moderate frequency, where $\#(e, r) \in (1, 50]$. Additionally, we group ER pairs in the testing set into three categories, G_{te}^1, G_{te}^2, and G_{te}^3, to observe the performance of ER pairs with different frequencies. G_{te}^1 and G_{te}^2 are subsets of G_t^1 and G_t^2 respectively, while G_{te}^3 consists of ER pairs that do not appear in the training set.

Figure 3(a) presents the average number of negative samples $N_{(e,r)}$ for G_t with and without ERDNS (w/ and w/o N), and the average link prediction results of G_{te} with and without ERDNS (w/ or w/o MRR), and Self-Adv (S MRR). With ComplEx, dynamic allocation significantly reduces the average $N_{(e,r)}$ for G_t^1 from 256 to 17, and for G_t^3, it increases from 256 to 600. The change of $N_{(e,r)}$ is slightly different for RotatE because its best result is achieved when $\alpha = 0.5$, and ComplEx performs best when $\alpha = 1$. This demonstrates that the allocation strategy significantly impacts the average $N_{(e,r)}$ in different groups. We observe that MRR of G_{te}^1, G_{te}^2, and G_{te}^3 improve with dynamic allocation, which is also better than Self-Adv, indicating that obtaining the optimal solution resulted in the overall performance improvements across ER pairs with all frequency ranges since with our method the optimal solution of all triples in the NS loss is attainable. Surprisingly, MRR of G_{te}^1 improves despite the substantial drop in average $N_{(e,r)}$ for $(e, r) \in G_{te}^1 \subset G_t^1$, suggesting that excessive negative samples may introduce false negative samples, negatively impacting the performance.

False Negative Sample. We discussed the average MRR of G_{te}^1 increases with ERDNS even though only a few negative samples are given because of introducing false negative samples. To demonstrate this, we present the average number of false negative samples in G_t^1 during training using various negative sampling methods such as NSCaching, uniform sampling, Bernoulli sampling, Self-Adv, and ERDNS in Fig. 3(b). It is worth noting that for NSCaching, the average number increases during training because false negative samples with high-value scores can become trapped in the caches. In the case of uniform sampling and Self-Adv (U&S), negative samples are randomly chosen from the entity set, resulting in the same average number, which is higher than that of Bernoulli

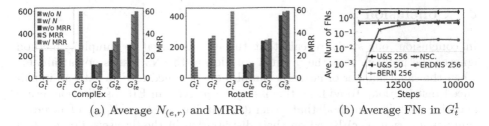

(a) Average $N_{(e,r)}$ and MRR   (b) Average FNs in G_t^1

Fig. 3. Average $N_{(e,r)}$ and MRR of three groups on different models and average numbers of false negative samples.

sampling when N equals 256. Additionally, ERDNS shows significantly fewer false negative samples on average, almost one-hundredth of the number of uniform sampling and Self-Adv, and even much lower than them with $N = 50$.

Statistical Analysis. We conduct a paired t-test on the results obtained from 10-fold cross-validation [6] of KGE models, namely ComplEx, RotatE, and ConvE, using the FB15K237 and WN18RR datasets. Table 5 displays the average evaluation metrics from this 10-fold cross-validation and the associated paired t-test p-values. We observe that varying the train-test split percentage affects KGE model performance. Specifically, performance on the FB15K237 dataset improves, while it declines for WN18RR. However, consistent comparative results are achieved. ERDNS still exhibits the best results for SM models on FB15K237, as explained in Sect. 5.2. It is worth noting that the p-values consistently remain under the 0.05 threshold, which is the conventional threshold for denoting statistical significance, and frequently drop to values less than 0.0001. This suggests that even minor performance improvements exhibit statistical differences. Apart from two exceptions, our method's average results surpass those of other methods, indicating the overall ERDNS performances are better than others.

Table 5. Mean results of 10-fold cross-validation and its paired t-test p-values.

KGE model	Dataset	FB15K237				WN18RR			
	Method	MRR	Hits@1	Hits@3	Hits@10	MRR	Hits@1	Hits@3	Hits@10
ComplEx	Subsampling(Mean)	37.6	26.0	43.4	60.4	41.0	37.2	42.5	**48.6**
	ERDNS(Mean)	**41.8**	**30.4**	**47.8**	**64.0**	**41.3**	**37.9**	**42.7**	47.8
	p-value	0.00	0.00	0.00	0.00	0.00	0.00	0.00	0.00
RotatE	Subsampling(Mean)	40.1	28.3	46.8	63.0	41.7	37.5	43.1	50.2
	ERDNS(Mean)	**40.3**	**28.4**	**47.2**	**63.3**	**41.9**	**37.6**	**43.3**	**50.4**
	p-value	0.00	0.03	0.00	0.00	0.00	0.03	0.01	0.00
ConvE	Self-Adv(Mean)	38.3	26.9	43.7	**61.1**	33.9	31.5	34.8	38.8
	ERDNS(Mean)	**38.7**	**27.9**	**43.9**	59.8	**34.7**	**31.7**	**35.9**	**40.6**
	p-value	0.00	0.00	0.00	0.00	0.00	0.02	0.00	0.00

6 Conclusion

In conclusion, our study reveals that the current negative sampling method ignores the problem that the optimal solution in the NS loss is not attainable when the same number of negative samples are assigned to ERs with an imbalanced distribution. To address this issue, we present an ER distribution-aware negative sampling method that generates varying numbers $N_{(e,r)}$ of negative samples for each (e, r) based on their distribution in the dataset. The method also can effectively alleviate the problem of introducing false negative samples in many negative sampling methods. The proposed method takes into account both theoretical and practical aspects and is applicable to a wide range of KGE models. Experimental results on the link prediction task demonstrate the effectiveness of the proposed method on both conventional and NN-based KGE models.

The results of NN-based models indicate that incorporating global trainable features may impact the effectiveness of negative samples in the KGE training process. In future research, we aim to investigate this issue and explore methods further to enhance the effectiveness of our approach to NN-based models.

Supplemental Material Statement: Detailed proofs, source code, scoring functions of KGE models, best hyperparameter settings, and full 10-fold cross-validation results are all available at https://github.com/for4ever44/ERDNS.

References

1. Ahrabian, K., Feizi, A., Salehi, Y., Hamilton, W.L., Bose, A.J.: Structure aware negative sampling in knowledge graphs. In: Proceedings of the 2020 Conference on Empirical Methods in Natural Language Processing (EMNLP), pp. 6093–6101 (2020)
2. Bordes, A., Usunier, N., Garcia-Duran, A., Weston, J., Yakhnenko, O.: Translating embeddings for modeling multi-relational data. In: Advances in Neural Information Processing Systems, vol. 26 (2013)
3. Cai, L., Wang, W.Y.: KBGAN: adversarial learning for knowledge graph embeddings. CoRR (2017)
4. Chen, X., et al.: Imagine by reasoning: A reasoning-based implicit semantic data augmentation for long-tailed classification. In: Proceedings of the AAAI Conference on Artificial Intelligence, vol. 36, pp. 356–364 (2022)
5. Dettmers, T., Minervini, P., Stenetorp, P., Riedel, S.: Convolutional 2d knowledge graph embeddings. In: Proceedings of the AAAI Conference on Artificial Intelligence, vol. 32 (2018)
6. Dietterich, T.G.: Approximate statistical tests for comparing supervised classification learning algorithms. Neural Comput. **10**(7), 1895–1923 (1998)
7. Guo, G., Ouyang, S., Yuan, F., Wang, X.: Approximating word ranking and negative sampling for word embedding. In: Proceedings of the 27th International Joint Conference on Artificial Intelligence, pp. 4092–4098 (2018)

8. Ji, G., He, S., Xu, L., Liu, K., Zhao, J.: Knowledge graph embedding via dynamic mapping matrix. In: Proceedings of the 53rd Annual Meeting of the Association for Computational Linguistics and the 7th International Joint Conference on Natural Language Processing (Volume 1: Long Papers), pp. 687–696 (2015)

9. Kamigaito, H., Hayashi, K.: Unified interpretation of softmax cross-entropy and negative sampling: with case study for knowledge graph embedding. In: Proceedings of the 59th Annual Meeting of the Association for Computational Linguistics and the 11th International Joint Conference on Natural Language Processing (Volume 1: Long Papers), pp. 5517–5531 (2021)

10. Kamigaito, H., Hayashi, K.: Comprehensive analysis of negative sampling in knowledge graph representation learning. In: International Conference on Machine Learning, pp. 10661–10675. PMLR (2022)

11. Kazemi, S.M., Poole, D.: Simple embedding for link prediction in knowledge graphs. In: Advances in Neural Information Processing Systems, vol. 31 (2018)

12. Kingma, D.P., Ba, J.: Adam: a method for stochastic optimization. Technical report (2014)

13. Levy, O., Goldberg, Y.: Neural word embedding as implicit matrix factorization. In: Advances in Neural Information Processing Systems, vol. 27 (2014)

14. Li, Z., et al.: Efficient non-sampling knowledge graph embedding. In: Proceedings of the Web Conference 2021, pp. 1727–1736 (2021)

15. Lin, Y., Liu, Z., Sun, M., Liu, Y., Zhu, X.: Learning entity and relation embeddings for knowledge graph completion. In: Proceedings of the Twenty-Ninth AAAI Conference on Artificial Intelligence, January 25–30, 2015, Austin, Texas, USA, pp. 2181–2187 (2015)

16. Mahdisoltani, F., Biega, J., Suchanek, F.: Yago3: A knowledge base from multilingual Wikipedia's. In: 7th Biennial Conference on Innovative Data Systems Research. CIDR Conference (2014)

17. Mikolov, T., Sutskever, I., Chen, K., Corrado, G., Dean, J.: Distributed representations of words and phrases and their compositionality. In: Advances in Neural Information Processing Systems, vol. 26 (2013)

18. Nguyen, D.Q., Nguyen, T.D., Nguyen, D.Q., Phung, D.: A novel embedding model for knowledge base completion based on convolutional neural network. In: Proceedings of the 2018 Conference of the North American Chapter of the Association for Computational Linguistics: Human Language Technologies, Volume 2 (Short Papers), pp. 327–333 (2018)

19. Schlichtkrull, M., Kipf, T.N., Bloem, P., Berg, R., Titov, I., Welling, M.: Modeling relational data with graph convolutional networks. In: European Semantic Web Conference, pp. 593–607 (2018)

20. Shang, C., Tang, Y., Huang, J., Bi, J., He, X., Zhou, B.: End-to-end structure-aware convolutional networks for knowledge base completion. In: Proceedings of the AAAI Conference on Artificial Intelligence, vol. 33, pp. 3060–3067 (2019)

21. Sun, Z., Deng, Z.H., Nie, J.Y., Tang, J.: Rotate: Knowledge graph embedding by relational rotation in complex space. In: International Conference on Learning Representations (2019)

22. Toutanova, K., Chen, D.: Observed versus latent features for knowledge base and text inference. In: Proceedings of the 3rd Workshop on Continuous Vector Space Models and Their Compositionality, pp. 57–66 (2015)

23. Trouillon, T., Welbl, J., Riedel, S., Gaussier, É., Bouchard, G.: Complex embeddings for simple link prediction. In: International Conference on Machine Learning, pp. 2071–2080. PMLR (2016)

24. Vashishth, S., Sanyal, S., Nitin, V., Agrawal, N., Talukdar, P.: Interacte: improving convolution-based knowledge graph embeddings by increasing feature interactions. In: Proceedings of the AAAI Conference on Artificial Intelligence, vol. 34, pp. 3009–3016 (2020)
25. Wang, M., Qiu, L., Wang, X.: A survey on knowledge graph embeddings for link prediction. Symmetry **13**(3), 485 (2021)
26. Wang, P., Li, S., et al.: Incorporating GAN for negative sampling in knowledge representation learning. CoRR (2018)
27. Wang, Q., Mao, Z., Wang, B., Guo, L.: Knowledge graph embedding: a survey of approaches and applications. IEEE Trans. Knowl. Data Eng. **29**(12), 2724–2743 (2017)
28. Wang, Y., Ruffinelli, D., Gemulla, R., Broscheit, S., Meilicke, C.: On evaluating embedding models for knowledge base completion. In: Proceedings of the 4th Workshop on Representation Learning for NLP (RepL4NLP-2019) (2019)
29. Wang, Z., Zhang, J., Feng, J., Chen, Z.: Knowledge graph embedding by translating on hyperplanes. In: Proceedings of the AAAI Conference on Artificial Intelligence, vol. 28 (2014)
30. Yang, B., Yih, W., He, X., Gao, J., Deng, L.: Embedding entities and relations for learning and inference in knowledge bases. In: 3rd International Conference on Learning Representations (ICLR) (2015)
31. Yang, Z., Ding, M., Zhou, C., Yang, H., Zhou, J., Tang, J.: Understanding negative sampling in graph representation learning. In: Proceedings of the 26th ACM SIGKDD International Conference on Knowledge Discovery & Data Mining, pp. 1666–1676 (2020)
32. Zhang, N., et al.: Long-tail relation extraction via knowledge graph embeddings and graph convolution networks. In: Proceedings of the 2019 Conference of the North American Chapter of the Association for Computational Linguistics: Human Language Technologies, Volume 1 (Long and Short Papers), pp. 3016–3025 (2019)
33. Zhang, W., et al.: Iteratively learning embeddings and rules for knowledge graph reasoning. In: The World Wide Web Conference, pp. 2366–2377 (2019)
34. Zhang, Y., Yao, Q., Shao, Y., Chen, L.: NSCaching: simple and efficient negative sampling for knowledge graph embedding. In: 2019 IEEE 35th International Conference on Data Engineering (ICDE), pp. 614–625 (2019)

Negative Sampling with Adaptive Denoising Mixup for Knowledge Graph Embedding

Xiangnan Chen, Wen Zhang, Zhen Yao, Mingyang Chen, and Siliang Tang[✉]

Zhejiang University, Hangzhou, China
{xnchen2020,zhang.wen,22151303,mingyangchen,siliang}@zju.edu.cn

Abstract. Knowledge graph embedding (KGE) aims to map entities and relations of a knowledge graph (KG) into a low-dimensional and dense vector space via contrasting the positive and negative triples. In the training process of KGEs, negative sampling is essential to find high-quality negative triples since KGs only contain positive triples. Most existing negative sampling methods assume that non-existent triples with high scores are high-quality negative triples. However, negative triples sampled by these methods are likely to contain noise. Specifically, they ignore that non-existent triples with high scores might also be true facts due to the incompleteness of KGs, which are usually called false-negative triples. To alleviate the above issue, we propose an easily pluggable denoising mixup method called **DeMix**, which generates high-quality triples by refining sampled negative triples in a self-supervised manner. Given a sampled unlabeled triple, DeMix firstly classifies it into a marginal pseudo-negative triple or a negative triple based on the judgment of the KGE model itself. Secondly, it selects an appropriate mixup partner for the current triple to synthesize a partially positive or a harder negative triple. Experimental results on the knowledge graph completion task show that the proposed DeMix is superior to other negative sampling techniques, ensuring corresponding KGEs a faster convergence and better link prediction results.

Keywords: Knowledge graph embeddings · Negative sampling · Mixup

1 Introduction

Recently, knowledge graphs (KGs) have been successfully profitable in many practical applications, including question answering [12], information retrieval [27] and dialogue systems [29]. However, the KGs constructed manually or automatically still suffer from incompleteness. Thus, completing KGs through efficient representation learning has been a hot topic. For flexible and efficient KG representation learning, knowledge graph embedding (KGE) [4,31] aims to represent entities and relations in KGs with real-valued vectors, also called embeddings. KGEs have shown promising performance in KG related tasks, such as

T. R. Payne et al. (Eds.): ISWC 2023, LNCS 14265, pp. 253–270, 2023.
https://doi.org/10.1007/978-3-031-47240-4_14

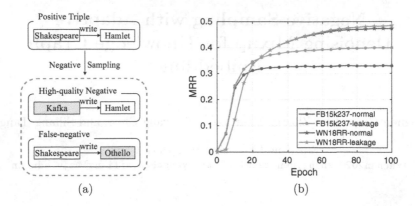

(a)   (b)

Fig. 1. (a) The example of sampling false-negative triples. (b) Testing MRR performance v.s. Epoch based on RotatE. Normal means self-adversarial negative sampling. Leakage means ensuring sampled negative triples are not contained in the validation or test set. We regard triples in the validation and test sets as false-negative triples during training.

triple classification [15] and link prediction [19]. They generally follow the same training paradigm. Specifically, they define a score function to measure the plausibility of triples through calculation with entity and relation embeddings, then learn the embeddings with the training objective of enlarging the gap between the scores of the positive and negative triples.

Since KGs only contain positive triples, negative sampling methods for KGEs usually regard non-existent triples as negative triples. Formally, given a fact (h, r, t) of a KG $\mathcal{G}$, negative sampling methods sample an entity e among all candidate entities and replace the head entity h or tail entity t with e to form a corrupted triple $(e, r, t) \notin \mathcal{G}$ or $(h, r, e) \notin \mathcal{G}$ as a negative triple. Previous works [24,32] have proved the quality of negative triples significantly affects the performance of KGEs, such as low-quality negative triples can cause gradient vanishing problems [24]. Therefore, searching for high-quality negative triples is not only necessary but also vital for learning KGEs.

Many negative sampling methods [6,32] assume that non-existent triples with high scores are high-quality negative triples. These methods optimize the mechanism of negative sampling from different perspectives to search for non-existent triples with high scores. For example, KBGAN [6] and IGAN [24] introduce a generative adversarial network (GAN) [11] to generate negative triples with high scores, and NSCaching [32] introduces a caching mechanism to store corrupted triples with large scores, etc. However, these negative sampling methods for KGEs neglect the issue of sampling noisy triples, especially when they regard non-existing triples with high scores as high-quality negative triples. Because those corrupted triples with high scores might also be true facts with high probability due to the complementary capability of KGEs, which are usually called false-negative triples. As shown in Fig. 1(a), given a positive triple (*Shakespeare, write, Hamlet*), the false-negative triple such as (*Shakespeare, write, Othello*) may be sampled, which will give imprecise supervision signals to KGE models' training. Furthermore, we set up a toy experiment[1] to quantify the effect of false-negative triples on KGEs' training. As shown in Fig. 1(b), compared with normal negative sampling, negative sampling with data leakage can improve MRR by 21.3% and 1.2% on FB15K237 and WN18RR respectively. This phenomenon indicates that although the probability of sampling false-negative triples is very low, the false-negative triples do mislead the learning of KGE and degrade the inference ability of KGE models.

Therefore, it is important to consider the challenging denoising problem when sampling high-quality negative triples. In this paper, to address the above issue, we propose a novel and easily pluggable framework **DeMix** which could generate high-quality triples that are beneficial for models' training by refining negative triples. Specifically, DeMix contains two modules, namely Marginal Pseudo-Negative triple Estimator (MPNE) and Adaptive Mixup (AdaMix). Given sampled corrupted triples (h, r, e) or (e, r, t), the MPNE module firstly leverages the current predictive results of the KGE model to estimate whether these corrupted triples contain noisy triples, then divides them into marginal pseudo-negative triples which more likely contain noisy triples and true-negative ones which are more likely negative triples. Then, in order to refine corrupted triples, the AdaMix module selects an appropriate mixup partner e' for e, then mixes them in the entity embedding space. Overall, DeMix generates partially positive triples for marginal pseudo-negative triples and harder negative triples for true negative ones as high-quality triples to help the training of KGEs.

In summary, the contributions of our work are as follows:

- We propose a simple and efficient denoising framework, named **DeMix**. It generates high-quality triples by refining sampled negative triples without additional information.
- We design two pluggable modules MPNE and AdaMix, which are general to be combined with other negative sampling methods and are efficient for not wasting training time on additional parameters.
- We conduct extensive experiments on two benchmark datasets to illustrate the effectiveness and the superiority of our whole framework and each module.

2   Preliminaries

Notations. We use lower-case letters h, r, and t to represent the head entity, relation, and tail entity in triples respectively, and the corresponding boldface lower-case letters $\mathbf{h}$, $\mathbf{r}$ and $\mathbf{t}$ indicate their embeddings. Let $\mathcal{E}$ and $\mathcal{R}$ represent the set of entities and relations respectively, we denote a knowledge graph as $\mathcal{G} = \{\mathcal{E}, \mathcal{R}, \mathcal{T}\}$ where $\mathcal{T} = \{(h, r, t)\} \subseteq \mathcal{E} \times \mathcal{R} \times \mathcal{E}$ is the set of facts in KG. For training of KGEs, a dataset $\mathcal{D}$ of triples with labels is used $\mathcal{D} = \{((h_i, r_i, t_i), y_i)\}_{i=1}^{n_p+n_u}$,

---

[1] We use the official open source code of RotatE model with the best config parameters: https://github.com/DeepGraphLearning/KnowledgeGraphEmbedding.

which includes n_p positive triples with label $y = 1$ and n_u negative triples with label $y = 0$. n_p usually is equivalent to the size of fact set that $n_p = |\mathcal{T}|$. Since negative triples are not included in $\mathcal{G}$, thus they are usually created by negative sampling methods.

Negative Sampling for KGE. Unlike the negative sampling at the instance level in the computer vision domain [9], the negative sampling for KGE is sampling and replacing entities in facts. More specifically, based on the fact set $\mathcal{T}$, the negative sampling for KGE sample entities $e \in \mathcal{E}$ and replace either h or t in facts with e to construct a set of corrupted triples $\mathcal{T}_u$ which is computed as follows:

$$\mathcal{T}_u = \bigcup_{(h,r,t)\in\mathcal{T}} \{(e,r,t) \notin \mathcal{T}\} \cup \{(h,r,e) \notin \mathcal{T}\}. \tag{1}$$

Following the closed-world assumption [15], the majority of negative sampling methods for KGE treat all non-existent triples as negative triples. Thus,

$$\begin{aligned}
\mathcal{D} =&\{((h,r,t),y = 1)|(h,r,t) \in \mathcal{T}\} \\
&\cup \{((h',r,t'),y = 0)|(h',r,t') \in \mathcal{T}_u\}.
\end{aligned} \tag{2}$$

Therefore, the optimization objective for KGE models learning based on closed-world assumption(CWA) can be formulated as follows [19]:

$$\mathcal{L} = -\log \sigma(f(h,r,t)) - \sum_{(h',r,t')\in\mathcal{T}_u} \log \sigma(-f(h',r,t')), \tag{3}$$

where $f(h,r,t)$ denotes the score function of KGEs to assess the credibility of (h,r,t).

KGE Score Function. The two most typical score functions for a triple (h,r,t) are:

(1) The **distance**-based score function which evaluates the score of triples based on the Euclidean distance between vectors, such as the score function of RotatE [19]:

$$f(h,r,t) = \gamma - \|\mathbf{h} \circ \mathbf{r} - \mathbf{t}\|, \tag{4}$$

where γ is the margin, $\circ$ indicates the hardmard product.

(2) The **similarity**-based score function which evaluates the score of triples based on dot product similarity between vectors, such as the score function of DistMult [28]:

$$f(h,r,t) = \mathbf{h}^\top diag(\mathbf{M}_r)\mathbf{t}, \tag{5}$$

where $diag(\mathbf{M}_r)$ represents the diagonal matrix of the relation r.

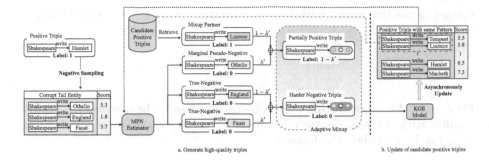

Fig. 2. An overview of the DeMix framework based on corupting tail entity.

3 Methodology

In this section, we introduce the proposed method **DeMix**, which is a novel and easily pluggable framework for generating high-quality triples. Recalling the denoising challenge in sampling high-quality negative triples, we design two modules to address the above challenge, namely Marginal Pseudo-Negative Triple Estimator (MPNE) and Adaptive Mixup(AdaMix) modules. The MPNE module leverages the current predictive results of the KGE models to divide unlabeled corrupted triples into pseudo-negative triples and true-negative triples. Then, the AdaMix module selects a suitable mixup partner for each corrupted triple and mixes them in the entity embedding space to generate partially correct triples or harder negative triples to help train the KGE model. The overview of DeMix is shown in Fig. 2.

3.1 Marginal Pseudo-Negative Triple Estimator (MPNE)

Motivated by sampled corrupted triples with high scores more likely to contain noise due to the incompleteness of KGs, we aim to leverage the predictive results of the KGE model itself to recognize noisy triples. In this work, we divide sampled corrupted triples into two subsets, such as marginal pseudo-negative triples which are likely to contain noise according to the current predictive results of the KGE model, and true-negative triples which are more likely negative triples. Because the KGE model has different learning levels for each relation pattern due to the long-tail distribution in KGs [26] and the phenomenon that the discriminative ability of the KGE model is continuously improving during the training process. We need to design a module to dynamically estimate noisy triples. Considering negative sampling for KGE is to replace the head entity or tail entity in a positive triple, the unreplaced binary terms in a positive triple are invariant. We call the invariant binary terms a pattern. So $\mathcal{T}_u$ can be reformulated as follows:

$$\mathcal{T}_u = \{(e, pattern)|e \in \mathcal{E}, pattern = (r, t)\}$$
$$\cup \{(pattern, e)|e \in \mathcal{E}, pattern = (h, r)\}. \tag{6}$$

The set of positive triples with the same pattern $((h, r)$ or $(r, t))$ as follows:

$$\mathcal{T} = \mathcal{T}_{pattern}^{rt} \cup \mathcal{T}_{pattern}^{hr},$$
$$\mathcal{T}_{pattern}^{rt} = \{(e_i, r, t) \in \mathcal{T} | e_i \in \mathcal{E}\}, \tag{7}$$
$$\mathcal{T}_{pattern}^{hr} = \{(h, r, e_j) \in \mathcal{T} | e_j \in \mathcal{E}\}.$$

Then we treat corrupted triples whose scores are close to the scores of the positive samples with the same pattern as marginal pseudo-negative triples $\mathcal{T}_{mpn}$. So $\mathcal{T}_{mpn}$ can be formulated as follows:

$$\mathcal{T}_{mpn} = \{((h', r, t'), y = 0) | (h', r, t') \in \mathcal{T}_u,$$
$$- \delta_T + [f^{\mathcal{T}_{pattern}}]_{min} \leqslant f(h', r, t') \leqslant [f^{\mathcal{T}_{pattern}}]_{mean}\}, \tag{8}$$

where $f^{\mathcal{T}_{pattern}}$ is the collection of scores of positive triples with the same pattern, i.e., $f^{\mathcal{T}_{pattern}} = \{f(h, r, t) | (h, r, t) \in \mathcal{T}_{pattern}\}$, and $[X]_{min}$ and $[X]_{mean}$ is the minimum and mean value of X. δ_T is a hyper-parameter controlling the estimation range at the T-th training epoch. Specifically, $\delta_T = \delta \cdot min(\beta, T/T_0)$, where T_0 denotes the threshold of stopping increase, δ and β are hyper-parameters. Notably, inspired by the characteristics of complex relations in KG, namely 1-N, N-1, 1-1, and N-N defined in TransH [25], we record the num of positive triples with the same pattern. When $|\mathcal{T}_{pattern}|$ is lower, the probability that the corrupted triples based on this pattern are noisy triples is lower. So after sampling negative triples $\mathcal{T}_u$, we set a threshold μ to decide whether to estimate the set $\mathcal{T}_{mpn}$ from $\mathcal{T}_u$ as follows:

$$\mathcal{T}_u = \begin{cases} \mathcal{T}_{mpn} \cup \mathcal{T}_{\widetilde{u}} & if |\mathcal{T}_{pattern}| >= \mu, \\ \mathcal{T}_{\widetilde{u}} & if |\mathcal{T}_{pattern}| < \mu, \end{cases} \tag{9}$$

where $\mathcal{T}_{\widetilde{u}}$ contains triples which are regarding as true-negative triples.

3.2   Adaptive Mixup(AdaMix)

To address the denoising challenge in sampling high-quality negative triples, an intuitive approach is to directly label the triples in $\mathcal{T}_{mpn}$ as 1. However, when the KGE model does not have the strong distinguishable ability, especially in the early training stage. This approach can give the wrong supervisory signal to the KGE model. Inspired by the recent progress of mixup [13], we aim to adapt the mixup technique to alleviate the wrong supervisory signal issue. Since the triples in $\mathcal{T}_{mpn}$ are more likely to be positive triples than $\mathcal{T}_{\widetilde{u}}$, we develop an adaptive mixup mechanism to guide the selection of a suitable mixup partner for each corrupted triple, to generate high-quality triples containing rich information. In specific, we first build a pool of candidate positive triples $\mathcal{T}_{cap}$ for each pattern from $\mathcal{T}_{pattern}$. $\mathcal{T}_{cap}$ contains the positive triples around the current learned boundary of the KGE model. $\mathcal{T}_{cap}$ can be formulated as follows:

$$\mathcal{T}_{cap} = \{((h, r, t), y = 1) | (h, r, t) \in \mathcal{T}_{pattern},$$
$$f(h, r, t) \leqslant [f^{\mathcal{T}_{pattern}}]_{mean}\}. \tag{10}$$

Since the embeddings of the KGE model are continually updated, we thus propose to update $\mathcal{T}_{cap}$ every epoch. Then, we select a mixup partner with the same pattern for each corrupted triple in $\mathcal{T}_u$. For marginal pseudo-negative triples in $\mathcal{T}_{mpn}$, which are more likely to be positive but annotated by negative, we uniformly choose a mixup partner from $\mathcal{T}_{cap}$ to generate a partially positive triple to take more precise supervision to the KGE model. Besides, for true-negative triples in $\mathcal{T}_{\widetilde{u}}$, we select another true-negative triple as a mixup partner to construct harder negative triples using a non-existent mixing entity in KG. It is worth noting that since the pattern of the mixup partner is the same as the pattern of the corrupted triple, the actual mixing object is mixing between corrupted candidate entity and the entity in the corresponding position of the mixup partner. Let $\mathbf{e}_i$, $\mathbf{e}_j$ denote the entity to be mixed in the corrupted triple and the corresponding mixup partner respectively, the overall mixup partner selection is formulated as follows:

$$(\mathbf{e}_j, y_j) \sim \begin{cases} \text{Uniform } (\mathcal{T}_{cap}) & \text{if } (\mathbf{e}_i, y_i) \in \mathcal{T}_{mpn}, \\ \text{Uniform } (\mathcal{T}_{\widetilde{u}}) & \text{if } (\mathbf{e}_i, y_i) \in \mathcal{T}_{\widetilde{u}}. \end{cases} \tag{11}$$

Finally we mix each corrupted triple $(h_i', r_i, t_i') \in \mathcal{T}_{mpn} \cup \mathcal{T}_{\widetilde{u}}$ with its corresponding mixup partner (h_j, r_j, t_j) in the entity embedding space of the KGE model to generate an augmented triple set $\widehat{\mathcal{T}}_u$. Motivated by the modified mixup operator [2], the mixup operation is as follows:

$$\widehat{\mathbf{e}}_i = \lambda' \mathbf{e}_i + (1 - \lambda') \mathbf{e}_j, \quad \widehat{y}_i = \lambda' y_i + (1 - \lambda') y_j,$$
$$\lambda' = \max(\lambda, 1 - \lambda), \lambda \sim \text{Beta}(\alpha, \alpha), \alpha \in (0, \infty), \tag{12}$$

where λ' is a balance parameter. λ' can guarantee that the feature of each augmented entity $\widehat{\mathbf{e}}_i$ is closer to $\mathbf{e}_i$ than the mixup partner $\mathbf{e}_j$.

3.3 Traning the KGE Model

Because our framework is pluggable, we can combine other negative sampling methods to train the KGE model. Here we show the training objectives based on the uniform negative sampling [4] and self-adversarial sampling [19]. The loss function based on uniform sampling is as follows:

$$\mathcal{L} = \ell(f(h, r, t), 1) + \sum_{(\widehat{h}_i, r, \widehat{t}_i) \in \widehat{\mathcal{T}}_u} \ell(f(\widehat{h}_i, r, \widehat{t}_i), \widehat{y}_i). \tag{13}$$

The loss function based on self-adversarial sampling is as follows:

$$\mathcal{L} = \ell(f(h, r, t), 1)$$
$$+ \sum_{(\widehat{h}_i, r, \widehat{t}_i) \in \widehat{\mathcal{T}}_u} p(\widehat{h}_i, r, \widehat{t}_i) \ell(f(\widehat{h}_i, r, \widehat{t}_i), \widehat{y}_i), \tag{14}$$

Algorithm 1. Training procedure of DeMix

Input: training set $\mathcal{P} = \{(h, r, t)\}$, entity set $\mathcal{E}$, relation set $\mathcal{R}$, embedding dimension d, scoring function f, the size of epoches E, the size of warm-up epoches W.
Output: embeddings for each $e \in \mathcal{E}$ and $r \in \mathcal{R}$

1: **Initialize** embeddings for each $e \in \mathcal{E}$ and $r \in \mathcal{R}$;
2: Get $\mathcal{T}_{pattern}$ from $\mathcal{T}$;
3: **while** epoch < W **do**
4:    Warm up model using uniform sampling with K negative samples;
5: **end while**
6: **while** epoch < E **do**
7:    Sample a mini-batch $\mathcal{T}_{\text{batch}} \in \mathcal{T}$;
8:    **while** $(h, r, t) \in \mathcal{T}_{\text{batch}}$ **do**
9:       Uniformly sample M entities from $\mathcal{E}$ to form unlabeled corrupted triplets $\mathcal{T}_u = \{(h_m, r, t'_m), m = 1, 2...M\}$;
10:      Estimate marginal pseudo-negative triples $\mathcal{T}_{mpn}$ using Eq.(9)(8);
11:      Select the mixup partners for each corrupted triples using Eq.(11);
12:      Construct $\widehat{\mathcal{T}}_u$ applying Eq.(12) to corrupted triples and their mixup partners;

13:      calculate loss functions using Eq.(13), then update the embeddings of entites and relations via gradient descent;
14:    **end while**
15:    Update $\mathcal{T}_{cap}$ using Eq.(10);
16: **end while**

---

where $\widehat{\mathcal{T}}_u = \text{AdaptiveMixup}\,(\mathcal{T}_u, \mathcal{T}_{pattern}, \alpha)$ and $\ell(.,.)$ is the cross-entropy loss. Movever, the probability distribution of sampling high-quality triples is as follows:

$$p(\widehat{h}_j, r, \widehat{t}_j | \{(\widehat{h}_i, r, \widehat{t}_i)\}) = \frac{\exp \alpha_t f(\widehat{h}_j, r, \widehat{t}_j))}{\sum_i \exp \alpha_t f(\widehat{h}_i, r, \widehat{t}_i)}, \tag{15}$$

where α_t is the temperature of sampling. The full training procedure is shown in Algorithm 1

4   Experiment

In this section, we perform detailed experiments to demonstrate the effectiveness of our proposed framework DeMix by answering the following questions. **Q1**: Does DeMix can mitigate the noisy triples issue? **Q2**: Whether DeMix can be effectively plugged into other negative sampling methods? **Q3**: How does each of designed modules influence the performance of DeMix?

4.1   Experiment Settings

Datasets. Two public datasets are utilized for experiments, including WN18RR [10] and FB15K237 [21]. WN18RR is a subset of WN18 [4], where inverse relations are deleted. Similarly, FB15k237 is a subset of FB15K [4], which comes

Table 1. Statistics of two benchmarks. #Rel, #Ent, represent the number of relations, and entities of each dataset, respectively.

Dataset	#Rel	#Ent	#Train	#Valid	#Test
WN18RR	11	40,943	86,835	3,034	3,134
FB15K237	237	14,541	272,115	17,535	20,466

from FreeBase [3]. FB15K237 is denser than WN18RR, so it is more affected by false-negative triples. The statistics of the two datasets are given in Table 1.

Baseline Methods. We compare DeMix to seven negative sampling baselines. The details of baseline methods are presented as follows:

- *Uniform Sampling* [4]. The basic negative sampling method, which samples negative triples from a uniform distribution.
- *Bernoulli Sampling* [25]. Which sample negative triples from a Bernoulli distribution considering false-negative triples.
- *NSCaching* [32]. The NSCaching introduces the cache strategy as a general negative sampling scheme.
- *Self-adversarial Sampling* [19]. It utilizes a self-scoring function and samples negative triples according to the current embedding model.
- *RW-SANS* [1]. It samples negative triples from the k-hop of the node neighborhood by utilizing the graph structure.
- *CANS* [17]. The CANS is a component of CAKE [17] responsible for solving the invalid negative sampling challenge. Considering our method focuses on negative sampling for KGEs, we mainly compare CANS instead of CAKE.
- *ESNS* [30]. It takes semantic similarities among entities into consideration to tackle the issue of false-negative samples.

Evaluation Protocol. Following the previous work [17], we calculate the score of triples in the test dataset by employing the learned KG embeddings and the score function. Then we can get the rank of the correct entity for each test triple based on the filtered setting, where all corrupted triples in the dataset are removed. The performance is evaluated by four metrics: mean reciprocal rank (MRR) and Hits at 1,3,10 (Hits@N). Higher MRR and Hits@N mean better performance.

Implementation Details. We firstly use the negative sampling method to warm-up[2] 8 epochs to give the KGE model discriminative ability, and then use our method to generate high-quality triples for further training. We use PyTorch [18] framework to implement our method and Adam [16] optimizer for model training. The mixup balance hyperparameter α is fixed to 1. In addition, we

---

[2] We will discuss warm-up in the ablation study.

Table 2. Link prediction results for TransE on two datasets. **DeMix-Adv** denotes DeMix based on self-adversarial sampling, **Bold** numbers are the best results for each type of model. Underlined numbers mean the best performances of baselines.

Translational Distance-based Models	WN18RR		FB15K237	
	MRR	Hits@10	MRR	Hits@10
Neglecting False-negative Triples				
TransE+Uniform	0.175*	0.445*	0.171$^\square$	0.323$^\square$
TransE+NSCaching	0.200*	0.478*	0.205$^\square$	0.353$^\square$
TransE+Self-Adv	0.215$^\triangle$	0.516$^\triangle$	0.268$^\square$	0.454 $^\square$
TransE+RW-SANS$^\triangle$	0.218	0.510	0.295	0.483
Considering False-negative Triples				
TransE+Bernoulli*	0.178	0.451	0.256	0.419
TransE+CANS$^\square$	-	-	0.298	0.490
Ours				
TransE+**DeMix-Adv**	**0.220**	**0.521**	**0.318**	**0.510**

Table 3. Link prediction results on RotatE and HAKE. **DeMix-Adv** denotes DeMix based on self-adversarial sampling, **Bold** numbers are the best results for each type of model. Underlined numbers mean the best performances of baselines.

Translational Distance-based	WN18RR				FB15K237			
	MRR	Hits@10	Hits@3	Hits@1	MRR	Hits@10	Hits@3	Hits@1
RotatE+Uniform$^\triangle$	0.471	0.560	0.488	0.424	0.282	0.462	0.314	0.191
RotatE+Self-Adv	0.476$^\triangle$	0.570$^\triangle$	0.490$^\triangle$	0.428$^\triangle$	0.269$^\square$	0.452$^\square$	0.298$^\square$	0.179$^\square$
RotatE+RW-SANS$^\triangle$	0.478	0.572	**0.494**	**0.430**	0.295	0.481	0.327	0.202
RotatE+CANS$^\square$	-	-	-	-	0.296	0.486	0.329	0.202
RotatE+**DeMix-Adv**	**0.479**	**0.576**	0.492	0.428	**0.329**	**0.518**	**0.366**	**0.235**
HAKE+Uniform$^\triangle$	0.493	0.580	0.510	0.450	0.304	0.482	0.333	0.216
HAKE+Self-Adv	0.495$^\triangle$	0.580$^\triangle$	0.513$^\triangle$	0.450$^\triangle$	0.306$^\square$	0.486$^\square$	0.337$^\square$	0.216$^\square$
HAKE+RW-SANS$^\triangle$	0.492	0.579	0.507	0.446	0.305	0.488	0.336	0.214
HAKE+CANS$^\square$	-	-	-	-	0.315	0.501	0.344	0.221
HAKE+**DeMix-Adv**	**0.498**	**0.584**	**0.514**	**0.451**	**0.337**	**0.533**	**0.374**	**0.239**

use grid search to tune hyper-parameters on the validation dataset. Specifically, we choose β from $\{1, 3\}$, δ from $\{0, 0.1, 1\}$, μ from $\{1, 3, 5\}$. The learning rate is tuned from 0.00001 to 0.01. The margin is chosen from $\{3, 6, 9, 12\}$. To make a fair comparison, the negative sampling size of each baseline is the same as generated negative triples size in our method. Specifically, for translational distance-based models, we follow the experimental setup in CANS [17]. The negative sampling size is 16. For semantic matching-based approaches, we set the negative sampling size as 50 following ESNS [30].

4.2 Experimental Results (Q1)

We compare the overall performance of DeMix applied to different KGE models in the link prediction task to answer Q1. X^*, $X^\square$, and $X^\triangle$ indicate the results are

Table 4. Link prediction results for semantic matching KGE models on two datasets. **DeMix-Adv** denotes DeMix based on self-adversarial sampling, **Bold** numbers are the best results for each type of model. Underlined numbers mean the best performances of baselines. All baseline results are from ESNS [30].

Semantic Matching Models	WN18RR		FB15K237	
	MRR	Hits@10	MRR	Hits@10
DistMult+Uniform	0.412	0.463	0.213	0.383
DistMult+Bernoulli	0.396	0.437	0.262	0.430
DistMult+NSCaching	0.413	0.455	0.288	0.458
DistMult+Self-Adv	0.416	0.463	0.215	0.395
DistMult+ESNS	<u>0.424</u>	<u>0.488</u>	<u>0.296</u>	<u>0.465</u>
DistMult+**DeMix-Adv**	**0.439**	**0.535**	**0.301**	**0.470**
ComplEx+Uniform	0.429	0.478	0.214	0.387
ComplEx+Bernoulli	0.405	0.441	0.268	0.442
ComplEx+NSCaching	0.446	0.509	0.302	**0.481**
ComplEx+Self-Adv	0.435	0.493	0.211	0.395
ComplEx+ESNS	<u>0.450</u>	<u>0.512</u>	<u>0.303</u>	0.471
ComplEx+**DeMix-Adv**	**0.468**	**0.552**	**0.307**	0.479

taken from [32], [17] and official code reproduction based on same setting respectively. First, we conduct experiments with translational distance-based KGE models. The link prediction results of TransE with different negative sampling methods on the two datasets are shown in Table 2. We can observe that DeMix can effectively improve the performance of the TransE model on each dataset. Compared with the best method without considering false-negative triples, our DeMix method improves MRR by 0.9%, 7.8% on WN18RR, and FB15K237. Even compared to CANS which reduces false-negative triples with commonsense, our method improves MRR by 6.7% on FB15K237. Besides, the improvement of our method on WN18RR is not as pronounced as on FB15K237, which is consistent with the observation that false-negative triples have a lower effect on WN18RR than the degrading effect on FB15K237 in Fig. 1(b). Furthermore, we conduct experiments with recently proposed KGE models such as RotatE and HAKE on two datasets. From the results shown in Table 3, our DeMix outperforms all the other negative sampling methods on FB15K237 dataset and achieves competitive results on WN18RR. Second, we conduct experiments with semantic matching KGE models. As shown in Table 4, we can observe that our method DeMix outperforms ESNS, which specifically aim to tackle the issue of false-negative triples, on both datasets incorporating DistMult and ComplEx as backbones. These results demonstrate the superiority and effectiveness of our method. The results combined with different KGE models also illustrate the generalizability of our approach.

Table 5. DeMix upon different negative sampling methods on FB15K237 with HAKE as KGE.

	MRR	Hits@10	Hits@3	Hits@1
HAKE+Uniform	0.304	0.482	0.333	0.216
HAKE+DeMix-Uni	**0.332**	**0.524**	**0.368**	**0.236**
HAKE+RW-SANS	0.305	0.488	0.336	0.214
HAKE+DeMix-RW-SANS	**0.322**	**0.515**	**0.353**	**0.228**

Table 6. Ablation study of DeMix on FB15K237 with HAKE as KGE.

Models	MRR	Hits@10	Hits@3	Hits@1
DeMix	**0.337**	0.533	**0.374**	**0.239**
-WARM	0.336	**0.534**	**0.374**	0.237
-MPNE	0.306	0.509	0.341	0.207
-AdaMix	0.288	0.471	0.318	0.198

4.3 Combine with Other NS (Q2)

To verify whether our approach is plug-and-play, we implement DeMix upon other negative sampling methods to answer Q2. From the results shown in Table 5, our proposed method can be effectively combined with different negative sampling methods, and all of them can obtain significant improvements. Such results demonstrate that DeMix can be a plug-and-play component for existing negative sampling methods.

4.4 Ablation Study (Q3)

We conduct ablation studies to show the contribution of different modules in DeMix to answer Q3. We choose HAKE [33] model as the backbone since it has high performance. Specifically, we integrate our framework into HAKE based on the following three ablation settings: 1) removing warm up the KGE model (-WARM); 2) neglecting marginal pseudo-negative triples (-MPNE); 3) directly using the label information of noisy triples (-AdaMix). The results of ablation studies using HAKE on FB15K237 are shown in Table 6. The results show that all ablation settings lead to degraded performance. In specific, we observe that the warm-up has a slight effect on the training of the KGE model. AdaMix module is essential for model performance, indicating the adaptive mixup mechanism can take more precise supervision to the KGE model. Moreover, we also find that the performance drops significantly after removing the MPNE module, which indicates the validity of estimating marginal pseudo-negative triples.

4.5   Further Analysis

Convergence Speed. First, we demonstrate the generating manner of DeMix can help the KGE model converge quickly. To ensure a clear observation, we compare the convergence speed of our method with other negative sampling methods using the same batch size and learning rate on WN18RR. Figure 3 shows the convergence of evaluating Hits@10 of HAKE based on WN18RR. We can observe our method help the KGE model converge more quickly compared with other searching-based methods. This means that even on WN18RR where the effect of false-negative triples is small, our method can help the model converge faster by generating high-quality triples, while not wasting training time on additional parameters.

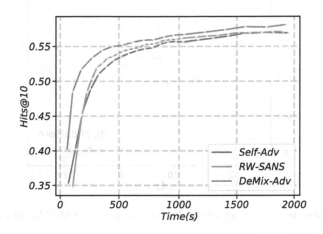

Fig. 3. Evaluating Hits@10 performance v.s. clock time (in seconds) of HAKE based on WN18RR.

Estimation Accuracy. In order to investigate whether the MPNE module in DeMix can indeed identify false-negative triples, we inject triples from the validation set and test dataset into the MPNE module, then observe the estimation accuracy of the MPNE module for these false-negative triples as the training time increases. In specific, we calculate the estimation accuracy separately according to two patterns, i.e. (h, r) and (r, t). Especially if a pattern does not exist in $\mathcal{T}_{pattern}$, we do not estimate this triple based on this pattern. Finally, the number of false-negative triples are 28926 and 34410 based on (h, r) pattern and (r, t) pattern respectively. As shown in Fig. 4, After warming up HAKE 8 epochs, the estimation accuracy increases along the training, which implies our method can leverage the judgment power of the model itself to efficiently estimate false-negative triples.

Visualization of Entity Embeddings. We visualize entities embeddings to verify the validity of our adaptive denoising mixup mechanism. In specific, we random sample an input (h, r) pattern from FB15K237, namely (*marriage, location*), then retrieve 20 positive triples, in the training set, near the decision boundary, 10 false-negative triples, in the validation set and test set, with the lowest scores, and 10 true-negative triples with the highest scores. We visualize tail entities embeddings of these triples. From Fig. 5, we can notice that our method can push the false-negative triples closer to the positive triples and away from the true-negative triples, which indicates our adaptive denoising mixup mechanism can alleviate the noisy triples issue.

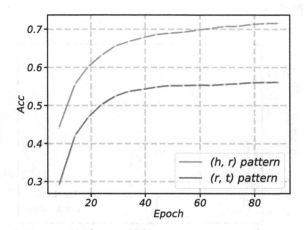

Fig. 4. The estimating accuracy of the MPNE module of HAKE based on FB15K237 with warming up 8 epochs.

5   Related Work

KGE Models. The general learning approach of KGEs is to define a score function to measure the plausibility of triples. Traditional KGE Methods consist of translational distance-based models and semantic matching models. Translational distance-based models such as TransE [4] and SE [5] calculate the Euclidean distance between the relational projection of entities. Semantic matching models such as DistMult [28] and ComplEx [22] use similarity-based scoring function to measure the correctness of triples. The recent KGE approach attempt to model some of the properties present in KGs, such as RotatE [19] aims to model and infer various relation patterns by projecting entities into complex space, HAKE [33] aims to model semantic hierarchies in KGs by mapping entities into the polar coordinate system, and COMPGCN [23] uses deep neural networks to embed KGs. KGE approaches can be effectively applied to the task of knowledge graph complementation, also known as the link prediction task.

However, the ability of KGE models to discriminate whether a triple is correct is often affected by the quality of the negative triples used in the training phase.

Negative Sampling for KGE. The existing negative sampling techniques for KGE can be classified into two categories: 1) Negative sampling methods that ignore false-negative triples. This kind of approach is based on the closed-world assumption, where all unlabeled corrupted triples are considered as negative triples, and search for high-quality negative triples. Uniform sampling [4] method samples negative triples from a uniform distribution. KBGAN [6] and IGAN [24] use the generative adversarial framework to feed the model with high-quality negative triples. Self-adversarial sampling [19] performs similarly to KBGAN, but it gives different training weights to negative triples. To achieve effectiveness and efficiency, NSCaching [32] maintains a cache containing candidates of negative triples. 2) Negative sampling considering false-negative triples. This type of method aims to minimize the chance of sampling false-negative triples, such as Bernoulli sampling [25], ESNS [30] and CANS [17]. For example, CANS leverages external commonsense information and the characteristics of complex relations to model false-negative triples' distribution, then give lower training weights to false-negative triples following the self-adversarial negative sampling loss [19]. However, all previous negative sampling methods are searching-based methods, which inefficiently search for high-quality negative triples from a large set of unlabeled corrupted triples. Besides, CANS requires costly manual effort to gather valuable external information, and Bernoulli sampling does not use external information, but this method is a fixed sampling scheme. Our approach

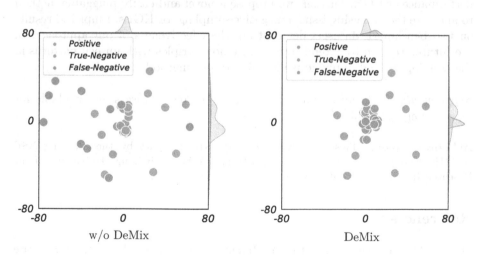

Fig. 5. 2D t-SNE visualisation of tail entities with their embeddings of positive triples near the decision boundary, false-negative triples, and true-negative triples with the same pattern (*marriage, location*).

differs from these methods in that we do not avoid sampling false-negative triples, but rather refine negative triples to high-quality triples as much as possible.

Mixup Method. Mixup [13] is a data augmentation method that generates a new instance by convex combinations of pairs of training instances. Despite its simplicity, it has shown that it can improve the generalization and Robustness of the model in many applications [7,20]. Further, a number of modified mixup versions have been proposed for supervised and unsupervised learning. For supervised learning, Mixup [13] for the first time linearly interpolates two samples and their corresponding labels to generate virtual samples, and experimental results show that mixup is generally applicable to image, speech, and table datasets. In unsupervised scenarios, mixup method is mainly used to construct high-quality virtual negative samples to effectively improve the generalization and robustness of models. MixGCF [14] integrates multiple negative samples to synthesize a difficult negative sample by positive mixing and hop mixing to improve the performance of GNN-based recommendation models. More similar to us are methods that leverage off-the-shelf mixup methods to generate harder negative triples for KGE such as MixKG [8]. Different from existing methods, DeMix design an adaptive mixup mechanism to dynamically refine noisy negative triples.

6   Conclusion and Future Work

In this paper, we explore the denoising issue in sampling high-quality negative triples for KGEs and find these noisy triples have a significant impact on the performance of KGE. Further, we propose a novel and easily pluggable method to alleviate the denoising issue in negative sampling for KGEs. Empirical results on two benchmark datasets demonstrate the effectiveness of our approach. In the future, we plan to extend to recognize noisy triples with unseen patterns in the training set and apply active learning to our method.

Supplemental Material Statement: Source code and datasets are available for reproducing the results.[3]

Acknowledgment. This work has been supported in part by the Zhejiang NSF (LR21F020004), the NSFC (No. 62272411), Alibaba-Zhejiang University Joint Research Institute of Frontier Technologies, and Ant Group.

References

1. Ahrabian, K., Feizi, A., Salehi, Y., Hamilton, W.L., Bose, A.J.: Structure aware negative sampling in knowledge graphs. In: Proceedings of the Conference on Empirical Methods in Natural Language Processing, pp. 6093–6101 (2020)

---

[3] https://github.com/DeMix2023/Demix.

2. Berthelot, D., Carlini, N., Goodfellow, I., Papernot, N., Oliver, A., Raffel, C.A.: MixMatch: a holistic approach to semi-supervised learning. In: Advances in Neural Information Processing Systems, vol. 32 (2019)
3. Bollacker, K., Evans, C., Paritosh, P., Sturge, T., Taylor, J.: Freebase: a collaboratively created graph database for structuring human knowledge. In: Proceedings of the ACM Conference on Management of Data, pp. 1247–1250 (2008)
4. Bordes, A., Usunier, N., Garcia-Duran, A., Weston, J., Yakhnenko, O.: Translating embeddings for modeling multi-relational data. In: Proceedings of the Annual Conference on Neural Information Processing Systems, pp. 2787–2795 (2013)
5. Bordes, A., Weston, J., Collobert, R., Bengio, Y.: Learning structured embeddings of knowledge bases. In: Proceedings of the AAAI Conference on Artificial Intelligence, pp. 301–306 (2011)
6. Cai, L., Wang, W.Y.: KBGAN: adversarial learning for knowledge graph embeddings. In: NAACL-HLT, pp. 1470–1480 (2018)
7. Carratino, L., Cissé, M., Jenatton, R., Vert, J.P.: On mixup regularization. arXiv preprint arXiv:2006.06049 (2020)
8. Che, F., Yang, G., Shao, P., Zhang, D., Tao, J.: MixKG: mixing for harder negative samples in knowledge graph. arXiv preprint arXiv:2202.09606
9. Chen, T.S., Hung, W.C., Tseng, H.Y., Chien, S.Y., Yang, M.H.: Incremental false negative detection for contrastive learning (2021)
10. Dettmers, T., Pasquale, M., Pontus, S., Riedel, S.: Convolutional 2D knowledge graph embeddings. In: Proceedings of the AAAI Conference on Artificial Intelligence, pp. 1811–1818 (2018)
11. Goodfellow, I., et al.: Generative adversarial nets. In: Advances in Neural Information Processing Systems, pp. 2672–2680 (2014)
12. Hao, Y., et al.: An end-to-end model for question answering over knowledge base with cross-attention combining global knowledge. In: Proceedings of Annual Meeting of the Association for Computational Linguistics, pp. 221–231 (2017)
13. Zhang, H., Cisse, M., Dauphin, Y.N., Lopez-Paz, D.: Mixup: beyond empirical risk minimization. In: Proceedings of the International Conference on Learning Representations (2018)
14. Huang, T., et al.: MixGCF: an improved training method for graph neural network-based recommender systems. In: Proceedings of the ACM Knowledge Discovery and Data Mining (2021)
15. Ji, S., Pan, S., Cambria, E., Marttinen, P., Yu, P.S.: A survey on knowledge graphs: representation, acquisition, and applications. IEEE Trans. Neural Netw. Learn. Syst. 33(2), 494–514 (2022)
16. Kingma, D.P., Ba, J.: Adam: a method for stochastic optimization. In: Proceedings of the International Conference on Learning Representations (2015)
17. Niu, G., Li, B., Zhang, Y., Pu, S.: Cake: A scalable commonsense-aware framework for multi-view knowledge graph completion. In: Proceedings of the Annual Meeting of the Association for Computational Linguistics (2022)
18. Paszke, A., et al.: Pytorch: an imperative style, high-performance deep learning library. In: Proceedings of the Annual Conference on Neural Information Processing Systems, pp. 8024–8035 (2019)
19. Sun, Z., Deng, Z., Nie, J., Tang, J.: Rotate: knowledge graph embedding by relational rotation in complex space. In: Proceedings of the International Conference on Learning Representations (2019)

20. Thulasidasan, S., Chennupati, G., Bilmes, J.A., Bhattacharya, T., Michalak, S.: On mixup training: Improved calibration and predictive uncertainty for deep neural networks. In: Proceedings of the Annual Conference on Neural Information Processing Systems, pp. 13888–13899 (2019)
21. Toutanova, K., Chen, D., Pantel, P., Poon, H., Choudhury, P., Gamon, M.: Representing text for joint embedding of text and knowledge bases. In: Proceedings of the Conference on Empirical Methods in Natural Language Processing, pp. 1499–1509 (2015)
22. Trouillon, T., Welbl, J., Riedel, S., Gaussier, É., Bouchard, G.: Complex embeddings for simple link prediction. In: Proceedings of the International Conference on Machine Learning, pp. 2071–2080 (2016)
23. Vashishth, S., Sanyal, S., Nitin, V., Talukdar, P.: Composition-based multi-relational graph convolutional networks. In: International Conference on Learning Representations (2020)
24. Wang, P., Li, S., Pan, R.: Incorporating GAN for negative sampling in knowledge representation learning. In: Proceedings of the Thirty-Second AAAI Conference on Artificial Intelligence, pp. 2005–2012 (2018)
25. Wang, Z., Zhang, J., Feng, J., Chen, Z.: Knowledge graph embedding by translating on hyperplanes. In: Proceedings of the Twenty-Eighth AAAI Conference, pp. 1112–1119 (2014)
26. Wang, Z., Lai, K., Li, P., Bing, L., Lam, W.: Tackling long-tailed relations and uncommon entities in knowledge graph completion. In: Proceedings of the 2019 Conference on Empirical Methods in Natural Language Processing and the 9th International Joint Conference on Natural Language Processing (EMNLP-IJCNLP), pp. 250–260 (2019)
27. Xiong, C., Power, R., Callan, J.: Explicit semantic ranking for academic search via knowledge graph embedding. In: Proceedings of the International World Wide Web Conferences, pp. 1271–1279 (2017)
28. Yang, B., Yih, W., He, X., Gao, J., Deng, L.: Embedding entities and relations for learning and inference in knowledge bases. In: Proceedings of the International Conference on Learning Representations (2015)
29. Yang, S., Zhang, R., Erfani, S.: GraphDialog: integrating graph knowledge into end-to-end task-oriented dialogue systems. In: Proceedings of the 2020 Conference on Empirical Methods in Natural Language Processing (EMNLP), pp. 1878–1888 (2020)
30. Yao, N., Liu, Q., Li, X., Yang, Y., Bai, Q.: Entity similarity-based negative sampling for knowledge graph embedding. In: Proceedings of the 19th Pacific Rim International Conference on Artificial Intelligence, PRICAI, pp. 73–87 (2022)
31. Zhang, W., Deng, S., Wang, H., Chen, Q., Zhang, W., Chen, H.: Xtranse: explainable knowledge graph embedding for link prediction with lifestyles in e-commerce. In: Proceedings of the Joint International Semantic Technology Conference, vol. 1157, pp. 78–87 (2019)
32. Zhang, Y., Yao, Q., Shao, Y., Chen, L.: Nscaching: simple and efficient negative sampling for knowledge graph embedding. In: Proceedings of the IEEE International Conference on Data Engineering, pp. 614–625 (2019)
33. Zhang, Z., Cai, J., Zhang, Y., Wang, J.: Learning hierarchy-aware knowledge graph embeddings for link prediction. In: Thirty-Fourth AAAI Conference on Artificial Intelligence, pp. 3065–3072 (2020)

Comparison of Knowledge Graph Representations for Consumer Scenarios

Ana Iglesias-Molina[1]([✉])[iD], Kian Ahrabian[2][iD], Filip Ilievski[2][iD], Jay Pujara[2][iD], and Oscar Corcho[1][iD]

[1] Ontology Engineering Group, Universidad Politécnica de Madrid, Madrid, Spain
{ana.iglesiasm,oscar.corcho}@upm.es
[2] Information Sciences Institute, University of Southern California, Marina del Rey, CA, USA
{ahrabian,ilievski,jpujara}@isi.edu

Abstract. Knowledge graphs have been widely adopted across organizations and research domains, fueling applications that span interactive browsing to large-scale analysis and data science. One design decision in knowledge graph deployment is choosing a representation that optimally supports the application's consumers. Currently, however, there is no consensus on which representations best support each consumer scenario. In this work, we analyze the fitness of popular knowledge graph representations for three consumer scenarios: knowledge exploration, systematic querying, and graph completion. We compare the accessibility for knowledge exploration through a user study with dedicated browsing interfaces and query endpoints. We assess systematic querying with SPARQL in terms of time and query complexity on both synthetic and real-world datasets. We measure the impact of various representations on the popular graph completion task by training graph embedding models per representation. We experiment with four representations: Standard Reification, N-Ary Relationships, Wikidata qualifiers, and RDF-star. We find that Qualifiers and RDF-star are better suited to support use cases of knowledge exploration and systematic querying, while Standard Reification models perform most consistently for embedding model inference tasks but may become cumbersome for users. With this study, we aim to provide novel insights into the relevance of the representation choice and its impact on common knowledge graph consumption scenarios.

Keywords: Knowledge Graphs · Knowledge Representation · User Study · Graph Completion

1 Introduction

The growth of the knowledge graph (KG) user base has triggered the emergence of new representational requirements. While RDF is the traditional and standard model for KG representation, alternative models such as property graphs [25], the Wikidata model [34], and RDF-star [12] have also become recently popular. The

© The Author(s) 2023
T. R. Payne et al. (Eds.): ISWC 2023, LNCS 14265, pp. 271–289, 2023.
https://doi.org/10.1007/978-3-031-47240-4_15

promise of these alternative and complementary representation models is that they can provide more flexibility to address certain use cases, such as statement annotation, for which RDF-based representations are not straightforward [17]. While the plurality of knowledge representation (KR) models provides the means to address a wider range of possibilities in consumer scenarios, there is currently no consensus nor sufficient empirical evidence on which representations are most suitable for different KG consumer tasks [16].

Previous studies comparing knowledge representations have focused primarily on query performance [2,6,14,26,28] and graph interoperability [3,4]. For this scenario, the representations need to ensure efficiency to minimize performance time. However, applications relating to exploration by end users and machine learning over KGs have not been taken into account [16,22]. Knowledge exploration scenarios, e.g., browsing, are impacted by representational choices, and therefore the selected representations should reduce the cognitive load and user expertise needed to explore, access, and acquire knowledge. Similarly, many embedding models-based tasks such as knowledge graph completion [1,29,37] require adequate representations to maximize the performance of the models on downstream predictive tasks.

In this paper, we address the research question: **How do different knowledge representation models impact common KG consumer scenarios?** Based on three complementary KG consumer tasks (knowledge exploration, systematic querying, and knowledge graph completion), we define four concrete questions: **(RQ1)** Which representations facilitate faster knowledge exploration and acquisition? **(RQ2)** Are certain representations more intuitive for building accurate queries efficiently? **(RQ3)** How do representational query patterns impact query evaluation time? **(RQ4)** How do different representations affect the performance of KG embedding models for a KG completion task?

We investigate these research questions by assessing the fitness of four popular KR approaches: Standard Reification, N-Ary Relationships, Wikidata qualifiers, and RDF-Star, for the needs of the abovementioned scenarios. First, to understand user preferences in knowledge exploration tasks, we run a user study where participants interact with a web browser interface and a query endpoint to determine the representation that improves knowledge acquisition for real-world questions. Then, to assess the differential performance of the representations, we test several queries using synthetic and real-world data. Lastly, to estimate the impact on KG embedding model performance, we train and evaluate a selection of these models for the KG completion task with different representations.

The rest of the paper is structured as follows: Sect. 2 introduces the four representation models. Section 3 describes the datasets used in the evaluation. The experimental setup and evaluation are organized by scenario, for knowledge exploration in Sect. 4, systematic querying in Sect. 5, and knowledge graph embedding models in Sect. 6. Section 7 reviews related work. The conclusions and limitations are discussed in Sect. 8.

2   Knowledge Representation Models

In this section, we describe different representation models that can be used for statement annotation, i.e., making statements about statements, a challenge that has motivated the development of several different KG representation approaches [7,12,24,26,27]. Figure 1 illustrates instances of these models for the main statement *Jodie Foster received the Academy Award for Best Actress* annotated with the additional statement *for the work The "Silence of the Lambs."*

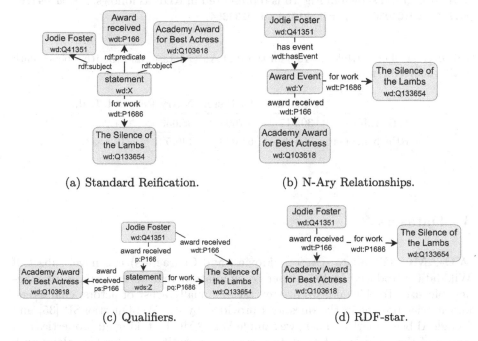

(a) Standard Reification.   (b) N-Ary Relationships.

(c) Qualifiers.   (d) RDF-star.

Fig. 1. Representation models shown as RDF graphs: (a) Standard Reification, (b) N-Ary Relationships, (c) Qualifiers (Wikidata model) and (d) RDF-star.

Standard Reification. [24] (Fig. 1a) explicitly declares a resource to denote an `rdf:Statement`. This statement has `rdf:subject`, `rdf:predicate`, and `rdf:object` attached to it and can be further annotated with additional statements. The resource is typically a blank node; we simplify the encoding using a Wikidata Item identifier (shown as `wd:X` in the figure for brevity).

N-Ary Relationships. [27] (Fig. 1b) converts a relationship into an instance that describes the relation, which can have attached both the main object and additional statements. This representation is widely used in ontology engineering as an ontology design pattern [10].

The Wikidata Model. [7] (Fig. 1c) is organized around the notion of Items. An Item is the equivalent of either a Class or an Instance in RDF and is described with labels, descriptions, aliases, statements, and site links. Statements represent triples (comprised of `item-property-value`) and can be further enriched with qualifiers and references. Qualifiers are `property-value` pairs that attach additional information to the triple. From this point onward, we refer to this representation as "Qualifiers".

RDF-Star. [12] (Fig. 1d) extends RDF to introduce triple reification in a compact manner. It introduces the notion of triple recursiveness with `Quoted Triples`, which can be used as subjects and/or objects of other triples. The RDF-star graph shown in Fig. 1d is represented in RDF as follows: <<`wd:Q41351 wd:P166 wd:Q103618`>> `wdt:P1686 wd:Q133654`.

Table 1. Number of triples ($\times 10^6$) for the WD-AMC dataset and the REF benchmark in the analysed representations.

	Qualifiers	RDF-star	N-Ary Rel.	Std. Reif.
WD-AMC	30.917	5.700	35.653	51.266
REF benchmark	268.965	61.033	140.521	175.592

3   Datasets

WD-AMC. (Wikidata - Actors, Movies, and Characters) is a novel subset of Wikidata introduced in this paper to simulate a real-world scenario of manageable size. To this end, we first extract manually a list of actors, characters, and movies present in the questions provided by the WebQuestionSP [35] and GoogleAI benchmarks.[1] Then, we sample WD-AMC by taking all properties and values of the main Wikidata statements for the entities in this list, along with their qualifier properties and values. The WD-AMC subset and all its variants are created using the Knowledge Graph Toolkit (KGTK) [21].

For the query evaluation performance scenario, we use the **REF benchmark** [28], which is proposed to compare different reifications providing the Biomedical Knowledge Repository (BKR) dataset [30] in three representations: Standard Reification, Singleton Property, and RDF-star. We extend the available representations in REF to include Qualifiers and N-Ary Relationships approaches. Table 1 presents the number of triples of both datasets in each representation. We make all datasets and their corresponding queries available online [19, 20].

---

[1] https://ai.google.com/research/NaturalQuestions/dataset.

4   Knowledge Exploration Scenario

We define *knowledge exploration* as the process of interactively discovering and obtaining information available in knowledge graphs. We distinguish and study two knowledge exploration scenarios by asking users to (i) interact with a user-friendly interface, and (ii) build queries to systematically access the KG. We measure the time and accuracy of the participant responses for both scenarios.

4.1   Experimental Setup

User Study Setup. We conduct a user study composed of two tasks. The *browser interaction task* consists of answering 5 natural language questions by looking for the information in Wikidata via a KGTK browser interface. The answer should be provided as a Wikidata identifier (QXXXX). The *endpoint interaction task* consists of building SPARQL queries for the same natural language questions answered in the previous task, providing a machine-executable query as a response. In this task, participants can build and test the query in a triplestore provided for them. For both tasks, answers are submitted in free-text boxes, with no predefined options to choose from. Participants are provided with representative example responses in order to ensure that they submit the queries in a useful format for the posterior evaluation. We measure the time spent solving each query and the accuracy of the responses.

Table 2. Set 1 of questions used in the user study with their corresponding identifier (ID) and from which QA benchmark they were extracted (Source).

ID	Questions	Source
Q1	Cast of the 2005 version of Pride and Prejudice	GoogleAI
Q2	What character did Natalie Portman play in The Phantom Menace?	WebQSP
Q3	Who won the academy award for best actor in 2020?	GoogleAI
Q4	Who is the Australian actress in Orange Is The New Black?	GoogleAI
Q5	How many movies have Woody Harrelson and Bill Murray been in together?	GoogleAI

Data. For both tasks, we use the WD-AMC dataset described in Sect. 3. For the *browser interaction task*, we adapt the dataset to create three instances (one per representation) of the KGTK Browser,[2] an adaptive user interface similar to Wikidata. For the *endpoint interaction task*, we generate the corresponding RDF graphs and upload them to a triplestore. We do not include RDF-star explicitly since its visualization in the first task is equivalent to the Qualifier model representation. All resources are accessible online for the participants.[3,4]

---

[2] https://github.com/usc-isi-i2/kgtk-browser/.
[3] https://kgtk.isi.edu/krhc1/, https://kgtk.isi.edu/krhc2/, https://kgtk.isi.edu/krhc3/.
[4] https://setting1.krhc.linkeddata.es/sparql.

Queries. We prepare 4 sets of 5 queries, extracting them from the QA benchmarks WebQuestionsSP [35] and GoogleAI(see footnote 1), which contain real questions from users. One set of queries is presented in Table 2 in natural language. Each of the 4 sets contains variants of the same 5 queries to minimize participants' risk of copying, by altering specific elements in the questions, e.g., years, movies; while maintaining the structure.[5] These 4 versions are applied to the three representations, resulting in 12 different sets of queries. We map these query sets to 12 groups of participants. Participants are provided with the same set of natural language questions for completing both tasks.

Participants. The user study is carried out with 45 students of a Master's level course on Knowledge Graphs. All students have similar backgrounds, are enrolled in a University Computer Science or Data Science program, and have learned about the KG representations in the course. The students first sign up for a voluntary assignment and are randomly divided into 12 groups, 4 groups per representation and each of them with a different query set. Then, they are sent a Google questionnaire with representation description, instructions, questions for both tasks, and text boxes for the answers. These groups contain: 16 participants for Qualifiers, 16 for N-Ary Relationships, and 13 for Standard Reification.

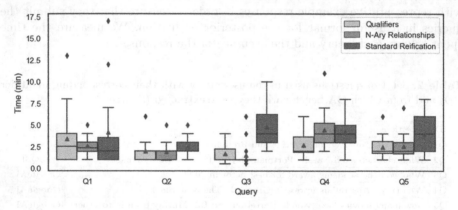

Fig. 2. Measured time that participants spent for retrieving the answers to the questions proposed in the *browser interaction task*.

Metrics. We analyze the results using ANOVA and t-test for the response time measurements to look for significant differences among representation approaches per query. Both ANOVA and t-test are used under the assumptions of (i) normality, (ii) sameness of variance, (iii) data independence, and (iv) variable continuity. ANOVA is first used for the three variables (Qualifiers, N-Ary Relationships and Standard Reification). Then, the t-test is used to test pairs of representations per query. To test the significance of accuracy, we use

---

[5] https://github.com/oeg-upm/kg-scenarios-eval/blob/main/WD-AMC/README.md

the chi-squared test of independence and look into whether the accuracy and representation variables are independent. It is used under the following assumptions: (i) the variables are categorical, (ii) all observations are independent, (iii) cells in the contingency table are mutually exclusive, and (iv) the expected value of cells in the contingency table should be 5 or greater in at least 80% of the cells.

4.2 Results

Browser Interaction Results. Figure 2 shows participants' time spent finding the answer in the browser interface for each query. We observe that the results for the three representations are overall similar, with significant differences in individual queries. The ANOVA test shows significant differences between the representation models (p-value< 0.05) for queries Q3-5 (Table 3). Our t-tests for pairs of representation models confirm the results of ANOVA for Q1-2, showing no significant differences. For Q3 and Q5, the measured time is significantly higher for Standard Reification, while for Q4, Qualifiers take significantly less time compared to the other representations. Thus, we observe that the time spent answering questions with the Standard Reification is significantly higher for Q3-5; and the average time in Q1 and Q2 is slightly (but not significantly) higher, which makes this representation less fit than the other two for this task. To obtain the accuracy of the responses, we measure the proportion of correct responses retrieved. Nearly all of the received answers are correct. Only in one query with N-Ary Relationships and Standard Reification, a wrong answer is submitted. We run a chi-squared test per query, and the results show no significant differences among the approaches in terms of accuracy.

Table 3. P-values of ANOVA and t-test for the time that participants spent for retrieving the answers to the questions proposed in *browser interaction task*. The significant values (p-value < 0.05) are highlighted in **bold**.

		Q1	Q2	Q3	Q4	Q5
ANOVA		0.437	0.429	**7.87E-06**	**0.034**	**0.047**
t-test	Qualifiers - N-Ary Rel.	0.323	0.964	0.715	**0.013**	0.817
	Qualifiers - Std. Reif.	0.621	0.289	**1.42E-04**	**0.034**	**0.034**
	N-Ary Rel. - Std. Reif.	0.216	0.220	**1.80E-04**	0.735	**0.064**

Answering **RQ1**, we conclude that, while participants can find the correct answers with any of the three representations, answering questions via knowledge exploration takes longer with the Standard Reification representational model. This finding is intuitive, as Standard Reification divides a triple into three triples, where only the object is the relevant element. The information is thus scattered and does not follow the "natural" direction of relationships between the elements. For instance, for answering Q3 "Who won the academy award for best actor in 2020?", in Qualifiers and N-Ary Relationships the information stems from the *Academy Award for Best Actor* (Q103916) node using the *winner* property (P1346); while for Standard Reification, the statement holds this information in separate relations: `<wd:Statement rdf:subject wd:Q103916; rdf:predicate wdt:P1346>`. Thus, the answer can be only accessed by referencing from the statement node, rather than directly as for the other representations.

Endpoint Interaction Results. Figure 3 shows the distribution of time spent on building the SPARQL queries and Table 4 shows the accuracy of the results obtained when running the SPARQL queries submitted by the participants. In terms of time, we note small variations among the three representations, which are not significant according to the ANOVA test. In terms of accuracy, the results for this task show a higher portion of errors compared to the *browser interaction task*, and they vary highly among approaches and queries. The largest differences are observed for the queries Q1 and Q5, where the Qualifiers model performs the best (accuracy of 1 and 0.71) and the Standard Reification model has an accuracy of 0.36. In such queries, Standard Reification requires a `UNION` clause

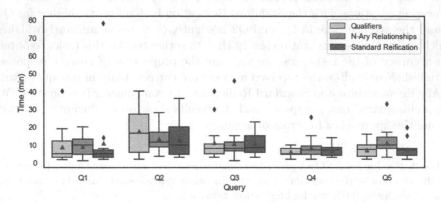

Fig. 3. Measured time that participants spent for building the SPARQL queries corresponding to *endpoint interaction task*.

Table 4. Proportion of correct responses returned by the SPARQL queries built in the *endpoint interaction task*. The highest accuracy per query is highlighted in **bold**, and the lowest is underlined. The p-values of the chi-squared test are also shown. Significant values (p-value <0.05) are marked with *.

	Q1	Q2	Q3	Q4	Q5	Average
Qualifiers	**1.000**	0.786	0.786	0.786	**0.714**	0.814
N-Ary Rel.	0.938	**0.875**	0.813	**0.938**	0.563	**0.825**
Std. Reif.	0.364	0.818	**0.909**	0.818	0.364	0.655
Chi-squared test	4.340E-05*	0.874	0.756	0.532	0.133	0.022*

to retrieve the complete set of results, which is not needed for the other representations, and thus, increases the relative complexity of the correct query. The
results of the other three queries are relatively close between the three representation models, with Qualifiers performing the worst on all of them. However, on
average Standard Reification produces the lowest accuracy, while N-Ary Relationships the highest. To test the significance of the accuracy results, we apply
chi-squared tests Table 4), showing significant values for Q1 and on average.
Thus, the accuracy of results is in general dependent on the representation.

Addressing **RQ2**, we observe that all three representations perform similarly
in terms of the time it takes to interact with a SPARQL endpoint. However, for
queries with a higher complexity, Standard Reification is more error-prone, as it
requires additional clauses (e.g., UNION) to retrieve the complete set of results.
Curiously, these results are similar to those for the *browser interaction task* in
RQ1, in the sense that Standard Reification fares the worst among the three
models, while Qualifiers and N-Ary Relationships perform alternatively best
depending on the query. Yet, the granular performance on individual queries
and metrics overlaps only partially: in the *browser interaction task*, the gap
is observed in terms of time and affects queries Q3–Q5; while in the *endpoint
interaction task*, it is manifested in terms of accuracy for the queries Q1 and Q5.
These findings provide initial insights into the suitability of different representation models for knowledge exploration. We leave a more systematic comparison
between queries in terms of their properties for future work.

Table 5. Characteristics of the WD-AMC queries in terms of the number of triple
patterns and SPARQL clauses used per query. The RDF-star queries with quoted
triples are marked with "*", while "^{SR}" only applies to Std. Reif. The number of
checkmarcks (✓) indicates the number of times the clause appears.

		Q1	Q2	Q3	Q4	Q5	Q6	Q7	Q8	Q9	Q10
#TP	**Qualifiers**	1	3	3	3	2	3	3	3	2	6
	RDF-Star	1	1*	1*	3	2	1*	3	3	2	2*
	N-Ary Rel.	2	3	3	6	4	3	3	4	4	6
	Std. Reif.	3	3	4	5	8	4	4	2	2	8
Clauses	**FILTER**	–	–	✓	–	–	–	–	✓✓	–	–
	FUNCTION	–	–	✓	–	–	–	–	✓✓	–	–
	UNION	–	–	–	–	✓^{SR}	–	–	–	–	–
	OPTIONAL	–	–	–	–	–	–	✓	–	–	–

Table 6. Characteristics of queries of the REF benchmark regarding the number of triple patterns and SPARQL clauses used per query. The number of checkmarcks ($\checkmark$) indicates the number of times the clause appears. GT stands for the *greater than* operator.

		A-Q1	A-Q2	A-Q3	A-Q4	B-Q1	B-Q2	B-Q3	F-Q1	F-Q2	F-Q3	F-Q4	F-Q5
#TP	Qualifiers	3	2	4	4	3	6	9	3	4	6	9	6
	RDF-Star	1	1	2	2	1	2	3	1	2	2	3	2
	N-Ary Rel.	4	4	5	5	4	8	12	4	5	7	12	8
	Std. Reif.	4	5	5	6	4	10	15	5	6	10	15	10
Clauses	COUNT	–	–	$\checkmark$	$\checkmark$	–	–	–	–	–	–	–	–
	GROUP BY	–	–	$\checkmark$	–	–	–	–	–	–	–	–	–
	FILTER	–	–	–	$\checkmark$	–	–	–	$\checkmark$	$\checkmark$	$\checkmark$	$\checkmark$	$\checkmark\checkmark$
	FUNCTION	–	–	–	$\checkmark$	–	–	–	$\checkmark$	$\checkmark$	–	–	–
	Operator (GT)	–	–	–	–	–	–	–	–	–	$\checkmark$	$\checkmark$	$\checkmark\checkmark$

5 Systematic Querying Scenario

The *systematic querying* scenario refers to the assessment of information retrieval efficiency with diverse query loads and structures. We analyze the differential behaviour of diverse series of queries over realistic and synthetic data for each representation, measuring its performance time.

5.1 Experimental Setup

Data. We use both datasets presented in Sect. 3. The WD-AMC dataset is used for analysing the behaviour with real-world queries in real-world data. We reuse the REF benchmark to validate our results with their previously reported analysis [28], and extend the resources to test and analyse two additional representations, Qualifiers and N-Ary Relationships.

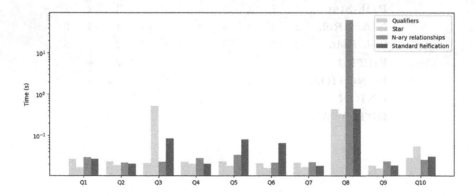

Fig. 4. Measured query evaluation time for the SPARQL WD-AMC dataset.

Queries. For WD-AMC, we use 10 series of queries. Each series is comprised of 20 variants of one query extracted from the QA benchmarks WebQuestion-sSP [35] and GoogleAI[3], which contain real questions from users made over Google. We use the first queries shown in Table 2, and we introduce five additional queries, extracted from the same QA benchmarks, to study a wider variety of query structures. The query variants are created by altering specific elements in the query (e.g., years, actors, movies, characters) while maintaining the triple patterns intact. Their characteristics are shown in Table 5. They are selected to apply to the patterns that differentiate the representations variants of WD-AMC. We note that, being extracted from real questions and not designed by us, not all queries require the use of the reification solution in all representations. This is especially remarkable for RDF-star, which is highlighted in the table, and directly affects the results described below. Still, all queries are different across the four representations.

The REF benchmark contains 12 queries divided into three series per approach (A, B, and F). These series contain queries with variable length, complexity, and computationally expensive clauses such as COUNT or FILTER, or operators such as *greater than* (Table 6). For more details on the queries, we refer to [30] for series A, [26] for series B, and [28] for series F.

Implementation. Previous studies [14] show no significant differences between the proposed representations across different triplestores. For that reason, we only use Jena Fuseki, which is an open-source implementation that can process all four representations. Both datasets were uploaded to a Jena Fuseki v4.6.1 triplestore running on a single-node VM with a 4-cores CPU and 16GB of main memory. To measure the efficiency of each representation, we measure the evaluation time while assessing the query complexity. Each set of queries for both datasets is run in warm mode three times, and the average is shown as a result.

5.2   Results

Results on WD-AMC. Figure 4 shows the average query evaluation time on the WD-AMC benchmark. As all queries are naturally asked by users, they are typically not computationally expensive, returning results in less than 100 ms. Q8 is the only exception, requiring more time as it contains additional clauses (2 functions and 2 FILTER; cf. Table 5). In this case, N-Ary Relationships take longer (around 1 min) as it contains more triple patterns than the other representations. Most of the remaining queries show similar times, with Qualifiers providing the quickest response on average[7]. In some queries, Standard Reification needs a higher number of triple patterns compared to the other representations, resulting in higher response times. For Q5, in addition, this representation requires the UNION clause to provide the complete set of results, a clause that is not needed in the other representations. RDF-star performs the best for nearly all queries, which may be due to having the smallest size and lowest number of triple patterns per query. The queries for which this representation shows a significantly increased response time involve expensive clauses or joins.

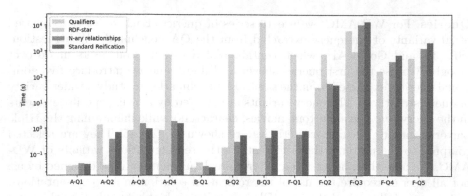

Fig. 5. Measured query evaluation time for the REF benchmark.

Results on the REF Benchmark. Figure 5 depicts the results obtained for the evaluation using the REF benchmark. RDF-star and Standard Reification show similar results to those reported by Orlandi et al. [28]. We observe that for Qualifiers, N-Ary Relationships, and Standard Reification, the measured times follow a similar pattern in query evaluation time for all queries in contrast to RDF-star. Qualifiers obtain the best results for almost all queries, presenting a total execution time reduced by half compared to the other representations.[6] The measured response times for RDF-star show a completely different behavior. Most of the queries for which this representation presents an increased time response involve joins. Meanwhile, RDF-star is not affected as much as the other representations by the use of operators such as *greater than* (Table 6).

Addressing **RQ3**, query performance on both datasets is sensitive to the choice of representation. The Qualifiers representation shows the quickest results for demanding queries on average. Together with N-Ary Relationships and Standard Reification, these representations are usually less differentially affected by a particular clause or pattern compared to RDF-star, as these three show similar behaviour per query. RDF-star stands out for good performance for simple queries (i.e., with one quoted triple) and logical operators such as *greater than*, but it becomes highly inefficient when joins and clauses like FILTER or COUNT are involved. RDF-star introduces quoted triples, a new element in the syntax that implies different processing by triplestores compared to the other representations, and makes it the most susceptible to change between queries.

6   Knowledge Graph Embedding Scenario

Machine learning applications over graphs have relied on the idea of *knowledge graph embedding* (KGE). KGE provides a mechanism to map the nodes and edges in a KG into a high-dimensional vector space. The resulting vector representations are then used for a variety of tasks, including link prediction, node

---

[6] https://github.com/oeg-upm/kg-scenarios-eval/blob/main/REF-Benchmark/README.md

classification, graph classification, and entity resolution. In this section, we evaluate popular KGE methods on the task of *knowledge graph completion* (KGC), which addresses the sparsity of a KG by predicting an object node given a subject node and a relation. We study the impact of the different KG representations on KGC performance in terms of mean reciprocal rank (MRR) and hits@K.

6.1 Experimental Setup

Data. We use the WD-AMC dataset described in Sect. 3. RDF-star is not used in this evaluation because the models that use this representation as their input are not fir for large-scale data. To create the evaluation data, we first extract all the triples containing a statement node and an object node from each representation. In the example shown in Fig. 1, this would yield the triples <wd:X, rdf:object, wd:Q103618>, <wd:Y, wdt:P166, wd:Q103618>, and <wds:Z, ps:P166, wd:Q10361>. Next, for each representation, we randomly sample 10% of the respective triples into a test and validation set, and combine the rest with the remaining triples of each representation to create the training sets. After this procedure, we end up with the following number of triples for our experiments: 1) validation set: 189,839, 2) test set: 189,839, 3) qualifiers train set: 5,128,864, 4) n-ary train set: 3,610,155, and 5) standard reification train set: 5,440,482.

Methodology. KGE models learn a mathematical relationship between entities and relationships that allow them to produce a likelihood score for an arbitrary triple. The most common architecture for these models is the encoder-decoder framework [11]. Traditionally, the encoder consists of learnable shallow embeddings $(\mathcal{E}, \mathcal{R})$ that map each entity or relation to a high-dimensional vector, and the decoder is a function that takes in the high-dimensional representations and produces the likelihood score. Formally, these models could be defined as $\mathcal{L}(s, r, o) = \psi(\mathcal{E}(s), \mathcal{R}(r), \mathcal{E}(o))$, where (s, r, o) is the given arbitrary triple, $\mathcal{E}$ is the shallow embedding for entities, $\mathcal{R}$ is the shallow embedding for relations, ψ is the decoder function, and $\mathcal{L}$ is the produced likelihood score. For our experiments, we use three of the most common KGE models with publicly accessible large-scale implementations [23, 36], namely RotatE [31], ComplEx [32], and TransE [5]. We exclude graph neural network models from this study as none had any publicly accessible implementation that could operate on the scale of our dataset in a reasonable time [18].

Implementation. In the evaluation phase, we compare each positive sample with 4,096 negative samples and report the object prediction results on the test set. Moreover, to mitigate the effect of random negative sampling in the evaluation phase, we run each experiment five times and report the best result. To make a fair comparison, we fix the following hyperparameters: *training steps* = 300 k and *batch size* = 1024. As for the rest of the hyperparameters, they were tuned on the following ranges: *embedding dimension* $\in \{50, 100, 200\}$ *learning rate* $\in \{0.003, 0.01, 0.03, 0.1\}$, *regularization coefficient*

Table 7. KGC results for three KGE models. We bold the best result for a model.

	RotatE				ComplEx				TransE			
	MRR	H@1	H@3	H@10	MRR	H@1	H@3	H@10	MRR	H@1	H@3	H@10
Qualifiers	**0.716**	0.678	**0.744**	**0.778**	0.426	0.364	0.453	0.546	0.599	0.518	0.658	0.739
N-Ary Rel.	0.714	**0.683**	0.736	0.765	0.261	0.232	0.277	0.310	**0.721**	**0.678**	**0.752**	**0.793**
Std. Reif.	0.697	0.653	0.726	0.773	**0.518**	**0.468**	**0.542**	**0.613**	0.622	0.567	0.655	0.725

$\in \{1e{-}4, 1e{-}5, 1e{-}6, 1e{-}7, 1e{-}8, 1e{-}9\}$, *negative samples size* $\in \{512, 1024\}$, *adversarial temperature* $\in \{0.5, 1.0\}$, and *gamma* $\in \{18, 12, 9, 6, 3, 2, 1\}$.

6.2 Results

Table 7 presents the experimental results of the models above on the KGC task. We observe that each model has a specific best-performing representation with significant performance differences compared to the other representations. However, the performance gap decreases as the expressive power of the model increases, indicating that the sheer expressive power of the models could potentially overcome representational disadvantages. From the perspective of representations, we observe that although two of the top three best-performing models use N-Ary Relationships, Standard Reification is the best representation on average. This phenomenon showcases the potential downfall of randomly mix-and-matching models with representations.

Regarding **RQ4**, our experimental results showcase the importance of associating models with a suitable representation. Failing to do so may lead to degraded performance, as evident from the results obtained on N-Ary Relationships with ComplEx. Throughout our experiments, no single representation consistently achieves the highest performance; however, we observe that a model with superior expressive power, i.e., RotatE, can overcome potential representational shortcomings and perform consistently well over all representations.

7 Related Work

Multiple studies have assessed the efficiency of different representations in terms of data management efficiency with computationally expensive queries, measuring metrics such as execution time, storage size, or number of triples. The Singleton Properties [26] model is compared in its inception with Standard Reification [24] using two series of queries of increasing complexity. Hernández et al. [14] test Wikidata represented in N-Ary Relationships, Standard Reification, Singleton Properties and Named Graphs over multiple triplestores. They remark the processing difficulties for Singleton Properties due to the high number of created properties. In a follow-up work, Hernández et al. [15] investigate how Wikidata in the same representations as their previous study performed on two SPARQL triplestores (Virtuoso and Blazegraph), a relational database (PostgreSQL), and a graph database (Neo4J), reporting that Virtuoso performed best among the data stores. Frey et al. [9] extends this work's evaluation to the DBpedia dataset and its representations to include their proposal Companion Property and Blaze-graph's Reification Done Right,[7] which is currently known as RDF-star) This work employs several data stores, highlighting which representation performs best in each store. More recently, the REF-benchmark [28] is proposed to evaluate different reification approaches with the inclusion of RDF-star, providing a version of the Biomedical Knowledge Repository (BKR) dataset [30] and three series of queries for each representation that can be applied to different triple-stores. Additionally, there are studies that compare Property Graphs and RDF with regards to query performance [2,6] and model interoperability [3,4], highlighting the advances of Property Graphs.

Hence, studies so far focus on the behavior of multiple representations over triplestores, and occasionally relational databases or other graph databases. To the best of our knowledge, there is no comprehensive evaluation of KG representations across consumer scenarios beyond triplestores and studies of query efficiency, a gap filled in by the extensive evaluation of different representations and scenarios in this paper. Yet, we include the systematic querying scenario in our work to (i) validate our experimental setup with the REF benchmark, obtaining similar results to ones previously reported, (ii) enrich it with two new representations (N-Ary Relationships and Wikidata qualifiers), and (iii) mimic a real-world scenario with real data and queries.

8   Discussion and Conclusions

8.1   Summary of Results

In this paper, we assessed the fitness of different knowledge graph representations in three consumer scenarios: knowledge exploration, systematic querying, and KG embedding. While no single representation model was optimal for all scenarios, we found significant differences for particular consumer scenarios, summarized in Table 8. We can extract the following conclusions from our study: (i) Standard Reification is the least suitable for users. Its anti-intuitive structure results time-consuming to navigate with, and it introduces additional complexity to retrieve correct and complete information. (ii) RDF-star still needs improved support in all studies scenarios, as it is underway of becoming part of the RDF 1.2 specification [13]. At the moment, it is risky to use it in high-demanding scenarios. (iii) Qualifiers obtain steadily better results for retrieving results in high-demanding querying scenarios. Despite being restricted to Wiki-data at the moment, its representation could be considered to be adopted in more knowledge graphs. (iv) Analysing and understanding how each embedding model works is key to select a representation for graph completion (and hence, additional embedding-based tasks). While for the other scenarios all representations showed acceptable behaviour, here the decision is critical. (v) Promoting the use of interfaces such as browsers highly improves the user experience in knowledge

---

[7] https://github.com/blazegraph/database/wiki/Reification_Done_Right.

Table 8. Summary of the fitness for each representation evaluated in the studied scenarios, where ✓ means suitable, ⌣ is acceptable, X is avoidable and * indicates that the value is not tested but equivalent to Qualifiers.

	User interaction	Simple graphs and queries	Large graphs and demanding queries	Graph completion
Qualifiers	✓	✓	✓	✓ (RotatE)
RDF-star	✓*	✓	⌣	–
N-Ary Rel.	✓	✓	⌣	✓ (TransE)
Std. Reif.	X	✓	⌣	✓ (ComplEx)

exploration. These interfaces help mask the representation complexity and differences, which directly influences the adoption and usability of semantic resources, an aspect usually overlooked. (vi) Despite the lack of a good-for-all solution, promoting interoperability among representations when knowledge graphs are consumed for very different purposes is potentially useful.

8.2 Limitations

Knowledge graphs are built for reuse across different applications, and their fitness for these applications depends on representational choices. Our paper provided insights into the fitness of four representations for three diverse consumption scenarios. We reflect on three key design decisions and point to future extensions of this study that can increase the significance of its findings.

1. Representational choices - Our study considered a subset of representations, prioritized for their popularity in prior work. Namely, we selected two RDF-based representations (the Standard Reification proposed in the first RDF Recommendation and the widely used N-Ary Relationships); the Wikidata model, and RDF-star. Other RDF-based representations (e.g. Singleton Properties) and property graphs were out of scope of this paper, but their inclusion in follow-up work is valuable. The choice of representations directly influences the selection of particular techniques and tools, as a representation may be limited to a single technology and cannot be processed by others. This prevents evaluating all existing representations under the exact same conditions. To ensure fair evaluation conditions, property graphs were not included in this work. Hence, further work is needed to include additional relevant representations while ensuring that differences in performance are due to the representation and not the underlying implementation.

2. Task choices - The tasks studied in this paper were derived by surveying popular KG tasks from recent research and associating them with three consumer scenarios. For knowledge exploration, we selected two representative tasks, yet, it remains to be seen whether our findings will generalize to other exploratory tasks, e.g., graph navigation visualization. For systematic querying, we extend previous studies to address a real-world scenario. The generality of this scenario can be increased with a complete real-world dataset instead of a subset with increasingly complex queries and with additional query languages (e.g., Cypher [8] or

Linked Data Fragments [33]). For KG embedding, a vibrant research community has explored a vast space of learning methods, applications, and benchmarks. We limit the task to KG completion and investigate simpler, widely used models to focus on a common real-world scenario. We believe these choices balance the likely trade-offs in many deployed settings, where institutional knowledge and dataset size preclude the adoption of more advanced techniques. Alternatives in the task space (e.g., node classification or entity resolution) and the model space, where graph neural network-based architectures can more directly represent complex graph structures, are promising extensions we hope to investigate in future work.

3. Participant sample - The remaining limitation refers to the sample of participants in the knowledge exploration user study. For this first study, we chose Master students because of their short and comparable experience with knowledge graph representations and tasks. We considered them a better sample than colleague practitioners, who may be already biased toward the representations and technologies they use. As a next step of this work, we plan to include a more varied sample of participants, i.e., to include industry experts, junior students, academics, and software developers.

Supplemental Material Statement: Datasets are available from Zenodo [19], queries and supplementary resources from GitHub [20].

Acknowledgement. We would like to thank Pedro Szekely for the inception and preliminar conceptualization of this work; Daniel Garijo and Edna Ruckhaus for the feedback provided for improving this work. This work was partially funded by the project *Knowledge Spaces* (Grant PID2020-118274RB-I00 funded by MCIN/AEI/10.130 39/501100011033).

References

1. Alivanistos, D., Berrendorf, M., Cochez, M., Galkin, M.: Query embedding on hyper-relational knowledge graphs. arXiv preprint: arXiv:2106.08166 (2021)
2. Alocci, D., Mariethoz, J., Horlacher, O., Bolleman, J.T., Campbell, M.P., Lisacek, F.: Property graph vs RDF triple store: a comparison on glycan substructure search. PLoS ONE **10**(12), e0144578 (2015)
3. Angles, R., Thakkar, H., Tomaszuk, D.: RDF and property graphs interoperability: status and issues. AMW **2369**, 1–11 (2019)
4. Angles, R., Thakkar, H., Tomaszuk, D.: Mapping RDF databases to property graph databases. IEEE Access **8**, 86091–86110 (2020)
5. Bordes, A., Usunier, N., Garcia-Duran, A., Weston, J., Yakhnenko, O.: Translating embeddings for modeling multi-relational data. In: Advances in Neural Information Processing Systems, vol. 26 (2013)
6. Das, S., Srinivasan, J., Perry, M., Chong, E.I., Banerjee, J.: A tale of two graphs: property graphs as RDF in oracle. In: EDBT, pp. 762–773 (2014)
7. Erxleben, F., Günther, M., Krötzsch, M., Mendez, J., Vrandečić, D.: Introducing Wikidata to the linked data web. In: Mika, P., et al. (eds.) ISWC 2014. LNCS, vol. 8796, pp. 50–65. Springer, Cham (2014). https://doi.org/10.1007/978-3-319-11964-9_4

8. Francis, N., et al.: Cypher: an evolving query language for property graphs. In: Proceedings of the 2018 International Conference on Management of Data, pp. 1433–1445 (2018)
9. Frey, J., Müller, K., Hellmann, S., Rahm, E., Vidal, M.E.: Evaluation of metadata representations in RDF stores. Semantic Web **10**(2), 205–229 (2019)
10. Gangemi, A., Presutti, V.: A multi-dimensional comparison of ontology design patterns for representing n-ary relations. In: van Emde Boas, P., Groen, F.C.A., Italiano, G.F., Nawrocki, J., Sack, H. (eds.) SOFSEM 2013. LNCS, vol. 7741, pp. 86–105. Springer, Heidelberg (2013). https://doi.org/10.1007/978-3-642-35843-2_8
11. Hamilton, W.L.: Graph Representation Learning. Synthesis Lectures on Artifical Intelligence and Machine Learning, vol. 14, no. 3, pp. 1–159 (2020)
12. Hartig, O.: Foundations of RDF* and SPARQL* (An Alternative Approach to Statement-Level Metadata in RDF). In: Proceedings of the 11th Alberto Mendelzon International Workshop on Foundations of Data Management and the Web. CEUR Workshop Proceedings, vol. 1912 (2017)
13. Hartig, O., Champin, P.A., Kellog, G.: RDF 1.2 concepts and abstract syntax. W3C Working Draft, World Wide Web Consortium (2023). https://www.w3.org/TR/rdf12-concepts/
14. Hernández, D., Hogan, A., Krötzsch, M.: Reifying RDF: what works well with Wikidata? vol. 1457, pp. 32–47 (2015)
15. Hernández, D., Hogan, A., Riveros, C., Rojas, C., Zerega, E.: Querying Wikidata: comparing SPARQL, relational and graph databases. In: Groth, P., et al. (eds.) ISWC 2016. LNCS, vol. 9982, pp. 88–103. Springer, Cham (2016). https://doi.org/10.1007/978-3-319-46547-0_10
16. Hogan, A.: The semantic web: two decades on. Semantic Web **11**(1), 169–185 (2020)
17. Hogan, A., et al.: Knowledge graphs. ACM Comput. Surv. (CSUR) **54**(4), 1–37 (2021)
18. Hu, W., Fey, M., Ren, H., Nakata, M., Dong, Y., Leskovec, J.: OGB-LSC: a large-scale challenge for machine learning on graphs. arXiv preprint: arXiv:2103.09430 (2021)
19. Iglesias-Molina, A.: Comparison of knowledge graph representations for consumer scenarios - datasets. https://doi.org/10.5281/zenodo.7443836 (2023)
20. Iglesias-Molina, A.: oeg-upm/kg-scenarios-eval: v1.0.0. https://github.com/oeg-upm/kg-scenarios-eval, https://doi.org/10.5281/zenodo.8179156 (2023)
21. Ilievski, F., et al.: KGTK: a toolkit for large knowledge graph manipulation and analysis. In: Pan, J.Z., et al. (eds.) ISWC 2020. LNCS, vol. 12507, pp. 278–293. Springer, Cham (2020). https://doi.org/10.1007/978-3-030-62466-8_18
22. Karger, D.R.: The semantic web and end users: what's wrong and how to fix it. IEEE Internet Comput. **18**(6), 64–70 (2014)
23. Lerer, A.: PyTorch-BigGraph: a large scale graph embedding system. Proc. Mach. Learn. Syst. **1**, 120–131 (2019)
24. Manola, F., Miller, E.: RDF primer. W3C Recommendation, World Wide Web Consortium (W3C) (2004). https://www.w3.org/TR/rdf-primer/
25. Miller, J.J.: Graph database applications and concepts with Neo4j. In: Proceedings of the Southern Association for Information Systems Conference, Atlanta, GA, USA, vol. 2324 (2013)
26. Nguyen, V., Bodenreider, O., Sheth, A.: Don't like RDF reification? Making statements about statements using singleton property. In: Proceedings of the 23rd International Conference on World Wide Web, pp. 759–770 (2014)

27. Noy, N., Rector, A.: Defining N-ary relations on the semantic web: use with individuals. Technical report, W3C (2006). https://www.w3.org/TR/swbp-n-aryRelations/
28. Orlandi, F., Graux, D., O'Sullivan, D.: Benchmarking RDF metadata representations: reification, singleton property and RDF. In: 2021 IEEE 15th International Conference on Semantic Computing (ICSC), pp. 233–240. IEEE (2021)
29. Ren, H., et al.: SMORE: knowledge graph completion and multi-hop reasoning in massive knowledge graphs. In: Proceedings of the 28th ACM SIGKDD Conference on Knowledge Discovery and Data Mining, pp. 1472–1482 (2022)
30. Sahoo, S.S., Bodenreider, O., Hitzler, P., Sheth, A., Thirunarayan, K.: Provenance context entity (PaCE): scalable provenance tracking for scientific RDF data. In: Gertz, M., Ludäscher, B. (eds.) SSDBM 2010. LNCS, vol. 6187, pp. 461–470. Springer, Heidelberg (2010). https://doi.org/10.1007/978-3-642-13818-8_32
31. Sun, Z., Deng, Z.H., Nie, J.Y., Tang, J.: RotatE: knowledge graph embedding by relational rotation in complex space. In: International Conference on Learning Representations (2019). https://openreview.net/forum?id=HkgEQnRqYQ
32. Trouillon, T., Welbl, J., Riedel, S., Gaussier, É., Bouchard, G.: Complex embeddings for simple link prediction. In: International Conference on Machine Learning, pp. 2071–2080. PMLR (2016)
33. Verborgh, R., Vander Sande, M., Colpaert, P., Coppens, S., Mannens, E., Van de Walle, R.: Web-scale querying through linked data fragments. In: LDOW (2014)
34. Vrandečić, D., Krötzsch, M.: Wikidata: a free collaborative knowledgebase. Commun. ACM 57(10), 78–85 (2014)
35. Yih, W.T., Richardson, M., Meek, C., Chang, M.W., Suh, J.: The value of semantic parse labeling for knowledge base question answering. In: Proceedings of the 54th Annual Meeting of the Association for Computational Linguistics (Volume 2: Short Papers), pp. 201–206 (2016)
36. Zheng, D., et al.: DGL-KE: training knowledge graph embeddings at scale. In: Proceedings of the 43rd International ACM SIGIR Conference on Research and Development in Information Retrieval, pp. 739–748 (2020)
37. Zhu, Z., Galkin, M., Zhang, Z., Tang, J.: Neural-symbolic models for logical queries on knowledge graphs. In: International Conference on Machine Learning, pp. 27454–27478. PMLR (2022)

A Comprehensive Study on Knowledge Graph Embedding over Relational Patterns Based on Rule Learning

Long Jin[1], Zhen Yao[1], Mingyang Chen[2], Huajun Chen[2,3], and Wen Zhang[1(✉)]

[1] School of Software Technology, Zhejiang University, Hangzhou, China
[2] College of Computer Science and Technology, Zhejiang University, Hangzhou, China
[3] Donghai laboratory, Hangzhou, China
{longjin,yz0204,mingyangchen,huajunsir,zhang.wen}@zju.edu.cn

Abstract. Knowledge Graph Embedding (KGE) has proven to be an effective approach to solving the Knowledge Graph Completion (KGC) task. Relational patterns which refer to relations with specific semantics exhibiting graph patterns are an important factor in the performance of KGE models. Though KGE models' capabilities are analyzed over different relational patterns in theory and a rough connection between better relational patterns modeling and better performance of KGC has been built, a comprehensive quantitative analysis on KGE models over relational patterns remains absent so it is uncertain how the theoretical support of KGE to a relational pattern contributes to the performance of triples associated to such a relational pattern. To address this challenge, we evaluate the performance of 7 KGE models over 4 common relational patterns on 2 benchmarks, then conduct an analysis in theory, entity frequency, and part-to-whole three aspects and get some counter-intuitive conclusions. Finally, we introduce a training-free method Score-based Patterns Adaptation (SPA) to enhance KGE models' performance over various relational patterns. This approach is simple yet effective and can be applied to KGE models without additional training. Our experimental results demonstrate that our method generally enhances performance over specific relational patterns. Our source code is available from GitHub at https://github.com/zjukg/Comprehensive-Study-over-Relational-Patterns.

Keywords: Relational patterns · Knowledge graph embedding · Rule mining · Knowledge graph completion

1 Introduction

Knowledge Graphs (KGs) are used to organize triples and represent various types of information about the real world. A typical triple consists of a head entity, a relation, and a tail entity, expressed in the format (h, r, t). Several

© The Author(s), under exclusive license to Springer Nature Switzerland AG 2023
T. R. Payne et al. (Eds.): ISWC 2023, LNCS 14265, pp. 290–308, 2023.
https://doi.org/10.1007/978-3-031-47240-4_16

well-known KG projects, including FreeBase [1], WordNet [21], YAGO [30], and DBpedia [18], have gained attention for their successful use in natural language processing [40], question answering [3], recommendation systems [35], and other downstream tasks.

Despite the vast number of triples in large-scale KGs, they suffer from the problem of incompleteness. To address this problem, the Knowledge Graph Completion (KGC) task, such as link prediction, aims to predict missing triples based on known triples. Knowledge Graph Embedding (KGE) [34] has proven to be an effective approach to solving the KGC task by capturing semantic representations of entities and relations in a low-dimensional vector space.

Most KGE methods utilizing triples as learning resources derive the semantics of entities and relations from graph structures. Relations with specific semantics typically exhibit corresponding graph patterns, which we call relational patterns in this paper, such as symmetry/antisymmetry, inversion, and composition [31]. The performance of KGE models is widely regarded as being closely tied to their capacity for capturing relational patterns within the KG [4,19,27,31,44]. Previous studies have endeavored to explore whether KGE models truly learned the relational patterns among triples. Some works [41,44] use the learned relation embeddings to mine rules corresponding to different relational patterns and prove that the mined rules are of high quality, showing KGE models successfully learned the relational patterns among triples. Some works [31,45] utilize distribution histograms to reveal that embeddings of relations associated with relational patterns tend to converge towards specific positions within the vector space. Although previous studies have theoretically analyzed KGE models' capabilities in addressing various relational patterns and established a rough connection between better relational patterns modeling and better performance of KGC, a comprehensive quantitative analysis of KGE models to relational patterns remains absent. In the absence of such research, it is uncertain how the theoretical support of KGE for a specific relational pattern contributes to the prediction results of triples associated with that pattern. Consequently, quantifying KGE models' performance over particular relational patterns poses a significant challenge.

In this paper, we propose a methodology to classify triples into relational patterns based on rules mined from training data, then the capacity of KGE models in reasoning over different patterns can be quantified with the performance of triples belonging to specific patterns. We conduct numerous experiments, in theory, entity frequency, and part-to-whole aspects, to assess KGE models' performance over relational patterns, leading to the following conclusions: **1)** Theoretical support for a relational pattern in a KGE model does not guarantee superior performance compared to another KGE model lacking such support. **2)** The influence of entity frequency on the performance of different relational patterns varies. Performance for symmetric patterns diminishes as entity frequency increases, while for other patterns, performance improves with increasing frequency. **3)** If one KGE model significantly outperforms another, the superior model will exhibit better performance overall relational patterns. Conversely, when two KGE models exhibit similar overall performance, their performance over relational patterns may diverge considerably. Lastly, we introduce a training-free method, Score-based Patterns Adaptation (SPA), to enhance KGE models' performance over various relational patterns. Our experimental results demonstrate that SPA generally improves performance over specific relational patterns.

The contributions of this paper are summarized as follows:

1. To our best knowledge, we are the first to conduct a comprehensive quantitative analysis over relational patterns;
2. We evaluate the performance of 7 KGE models over 4 common relational patterns on 2 benchmarks, then provide an analysis in theory, entity frequency, and part-to-whole three aspects, and get some counterintuitive conclusions;
3. We introduce a training-free method, Score-based Patterns Adaptation (SPA), designed to enhance KGE models' performance over various relational patterns. This approach is simple yet effective and can be applied to KGE models without additional training.

This article is structured as follows: Sect. 2 introduces the related work and Sect. 3 introduces preliminaries and background. Sections 4 and 5 are the main part of the paper, presenting our methodology, the comprehensive quantitative analysis of patterns, and SPA results. Section 6 presents conclusions and an outlook for future work.

2   Related Work

In this section, we concentrate on the related work of this paper, which encompasses the process of KGE, the definition of various relational patterns, and rule mining for relational patterns.

Knowledge Graph Embedding. Knowledge Graph Embedding (KGE) models strive to capture the semantic meanings of entities and relations by mapping them to continuous vectors, allowing for effective information retrieval and knowledge discovery. The process of KGE generally initializes the entity and relation embeddings and subsequently updates them with the score function and loss function. **Score function** measures the plausibility of a triple (h, r, t) with embeddings. These functions can be classified into two categories: translational distance based and semantic matching based models [15,34]. The translational distance based model primarily includes TransE and its extensions (such as TransH [36], TransR [20], TransD [14]), RotatE [31], and others. Semantic matching based models mainly comprise RESCAL [24], DistMult [41], ComplEx [33] and more. Table 3 presents some common score functions of KGE models. **Negative sampling** is the process of generating negative samples as most KGs predominantly contain positive triples. Negative triples are produced by corrupting a positive triple (h, r, t) through the replacement of either h or t.

Established methods encompass uniform negative sampling [2], Bernoulli negative sampling [36], and so on. **Loss functions** strive to minimize the scores of negative triples while maximizing those of positive triples. Principal loss function methods mainly include pointwise logistic loss [33], pairwise hinge loss [2], softplus loss [23], self-adversarial negative sampling loss [31] and others.

Relational Patterns. Relational patterns serve as a crucial metric for evaluating the performance of KGE models. Our comprehension of relational patterns becomes deepening over time. Wang et al. [36] highlight several mapping properties of relations that ought to be considered when embedding a knowledge graph, including **reflexive, one-to-many, many-to-one,** and **many-to-many**. Xie et al. [37] introduce a method called Type-embodied Knowledge Representation Learning (TKRL) that leverages **hierarchical entity types** to enhance the representation learning of knowledge graphs. Minervini et al. [22] incorporate **equivalence and inversion axioms** to improve the training of neural embeddings for knowledge graphs. The purpose of these axioms is to improve the accuracy and generalization abilities of neural embeddings by utilizing external background knowledge. Sun et al. [31] discuss **relational patterns** such as **symmetry/antisymmetry, inversion,** and **composition**. Then RotatE is proposed and demonstrates higher performance on various benchmarks. Qu et al. [27] examine the **subrelational pattern** in the context of exploring the impact of different rule patterns on knowledge graph reasoning. Cao et al. [4] suggest that **multiple relations** and propose DualE to model multiple relations using a combination of translation and rotation with greater performance. Some common relational patterns with their conditions are listed in Table 1.

Rule Mining. Rule mining can be employed to uncover non-obvious structures in data with logical rules [42]. The logical rules serve as a flexible declarative language for conveying high-level cognition [13,39], which can enhance the accuracy of reasoning or contribute to the generation of new triples [6,43]. Various rule mining methods have been developed to efficiently extract rules from large-scale knowledge graphs. The WARMR [8] and ALEPH [29] discover association rules over a limited set of queries. AMIE [10] and Ontological Path-finding [5] mine rule based on an exhaustive top-down search with pruning strategies. AMIE+ [9] improves the precision of the forecasts by using joint reasoning and type information. RARL [26] uses relatedness between predicates to improve search efficiency. These mined logical rules can correspond to the majority of relational patterns we proposed (the relationships between them will be detailed in Sect. 3). In this paper, we employ the latest version of AMIE called AMIE3 [17] to achieve length control and a trade-off between efficiency and quality.

3 Preliminaries and Background

Knowledge Graph. With a set of entities $\mathcal{E}$ and a set of relations $\mathcal{R}$, Knowledge Graph $\mathcal{G}$ can be represented as a set of triplets $\mathcal{G} = \{(h, r, t)\}$ in which $h \in \mathcal{E}$

and $t \in \mathcal{E}$ represent the head and tail entity respectively, $r \in \mathcal{R}$ represents the relationship between h and t. A triple (h, r, t) can also be represented as $r(h, t)$. Most KGs are far from complete. KGC comes into play as a powerful application to infer missing links. For example, predicting the missing head or tail entities given (h, r) or (r, t) pairs.

Relational Patterns. We gave definitions of six key patterns [27,31] that could be written in regular rule form concerned in Table 1, including symmetric, antisymmetric, inverse, equivalent, subrelation, and compositional patterns.

Table 1. Conditions for relational patterns and its rule formulation. $EN(r)$ refers to the set of entity pairs with $(head\ entity, tail\ entity)$ that satisfy $r(head\ entity, tail\ entity)$. $\emptyset$ refers to the empty set. The r in each row is represented as the relation belonging to the corresponding pattern. Note that the n in parentheses after the compositional indicates the number of relations in the hypothesis.

Relational Patterns	Condition	Rule Form
symmetric	$EN(r) = \{(t,h)\|(h,t) \in EN(r)\}$	$r(H,T) \leftrightarrow r(T,H)$
antisymmetric	$EN(r) \cap \{(t,h)\|(h,t) \in EN(r)\} = \emptyset$	$r(H,T) \not\leftrightarrow r(T,H)$
inverse	$EN(r') \subseteq \{(t,h)\|(h,t) \in EN(r)\}$	$r(H,T) \leftarrow r'(T,H)$
equivalent	$EN(r') = EN(r)$	$r(H,T) \leftrightarrow r'(H,T)$
subrelation	$EN(r') \subseteq EN(r)$	$r(H,T) \leftarrow r'(H,T)$
compositional(n)	$\{(h,t)\|(h,a_1) \in EN(r_1)\dots$	$r(H,T)$
	$(a_n,t) \in EN(r_n)\} \subseteq EN(r)$	$\leftarrow r_1(H,X_1), \dots r_n(X_n, T)$

Closed-Path Rules The rule has the property of a closed path [41] if and only if the sequence in the hypotheses creates a path from the subject argument to the object argument of the conclusion predicate without any cycles or repeated nodes. Closed-path rules are a type of rule that is used to capture complex relationships between entities in KGs. A closed-path rule τ is of the form:

$$r(H,T) \leftarrow r_1(H,X_1) \wedge r_2(X_1,X_2) \wedge \dots \wedge r_n(X_{n-1},T) \tag{1}$$

where H, T, X_i are variables. We usually represent hypotheses $r_1(H,X_1) \wedge r_2(X_1,X_2) \wedge \dots \wedge r_n(X_{n-1},T)$ as the body and denote the conclusion $r(H,T)$ as the head of the rule. Rule quality could be evaluated through statistical metrics such as standard confidence, partial-close-world assumption (PCA) Confidence, and Head Coverage [10].

4   Methodology

The overall architecture of our methodology is shown in Fig. 1. Our work pipeline can be divided into the following three steps. **1)** In the training stage, train the KGE model on the training set to get entities' and relations' embeddings.

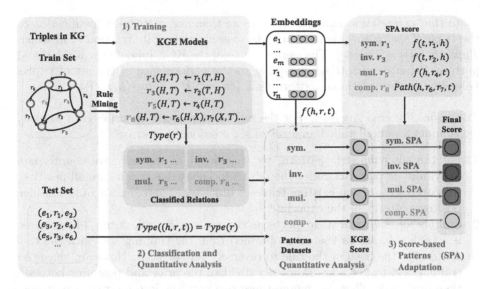

Fig. 1. The overall architecture of our methodology. Sym, inv, mul, comp2, and comp3 are abbreviations for symmetric, inverse, multiple, compositional2, and compositional3 respectively.

2) In the classification and analysis stage, classify triple (h, r, t) into patterns datasets based on the classification of r. Then the performance of different KGE models over different patterns is analyzed comprehensively and quantitatively through experiments on specific pattern datasets. **3)** Compute the final score by combining the SPA score and KGE score without requiring additional training.

The training of KGE models in step 1 follows the standard process, thus we omit the training details of KGE models and refer readers to the original papers of these methods. Next, we will describe Steps 2, and 3 of the architecture of our methodology in detail.

4.1 Classification of Triples

In this subsection, we focus on classifying triples into different relational pattern datasets to realize the comprehensive quantitative capabilities analysis of KGE models over various relational patterns. We first give a more detailed explanation of the classification method. Then we make an analysis of the relational pattern from the perspective of rule form and KG's property.

Classification Method. The rule form of relational patterns often takes the form of Horn rules with closed paths (as seen in Table 1), which are similar to the rules mined by rule mining in KGs. Therefore, we decide to utilize rule mining to classify relations $Type(r)$ based on the rule form of distinct patterns. For example, if we get a rule $\tau : r(H, T) \leftarrow r(T, H)$ which is similar to the rule form of symmetric pattern $r(H, T) \leftrightarrow r(T, H)$, we will get $Type(r) = \{symmetric\}$

(note that one relation may belong to more than one pattern). Classification of the triple $Type((h, r, t))$ is based on the classification of its relation r, in which $Type((h, r, t)) = Type(r)$. The performance of the KGE model over a relational pattern P can be quantified according to the performance of the set of triples belonging to this relational pattern that $\{(h, r, t) | P \in Type((h, r, t))\}$.

Relational Patterns Analysis. For the relational patterns mentioned in Table 1, we conduct a more detailed analysis of six relational patterns:

1. For the antisymmetric pattern, we consider it as the negative counterpart of symmetric patterns. Since the triples in knowledge graphs are all positive, the correctness of non-existing triples is unknown. Therefore, we only consider positive patterns in the experiments.
2. Subrelation and equivalent patterns share a similar rule form. The test set is classified based on the rules obtained from the training set, with the test set used as the head of the rule to reversely get the body. However, since the training and test sets are randomly divided, the prior and posterior between them are weak. Thus, we merge these two patterns into `multiple` patterns, following the expression by Cao et al. [4].
3. In the compositional pattern, if the length of the rule is 1, it can become the previous pattern form. Some works [6,32] incorporated language biases, such as restricting the length of rules up to 3 to deal with the vast search space and self-loops. We also set the length of rules to 2 and 3 in subsequent experiments.

4.2 Score-Based Patterns Adaptation (SPA)

To explicitly enhance the capability of KGE models over relational patterns, we aim to propose a simple approach to specifically promote KGE models on different patterns. Therefore, we introduce a training-free method, **Score-based Patterns Adaptation (SPA)**, which combines information from specific relational patterns and KGE score to modify the score function of models. The fundamental premise of SPA is that if the head triple is true, the triples within the body are also likely to be true with a high probability as the rule's head can be inferred from the body using established rules. Consequently, we propose to utilize the result derived from the rule's body as SPA score to enhance the inference over specific patterns. We also consider the rule confidence of rule mining as the confidence of relational patterns to measure the credibility of the modified score. The details are as follows:

Table 2 shows the SPA score with rule τ on different relational patterns. Compared to Table 1, Table 2 is refined based on the relational patterns analysis in Table 1. For the `symmetric` pattern, if we have the rule $\tau : r(H, T) \leftarrow r(T, H)$, we consider this relation r in the rule to be symmetric and can contribute to reasoning by calculating `symmetric` SPA score $f(t, r, h)$. And for the `inverse` pattern, we consider the relation r to be inverse with relation r' on rule $\tau : r(H, T) \leftarrow r'(T, H)$, and the semantic information in the body is $f(t, r', h)$

Table 2. Correspondence between SPA score and rules in relational patterns. `Multiple` is the combination of subrelation and equivalent patterns mentioned in Table 1.

Relational Patterns	Rule τ	SPA score $S_p(h, r, t)$
`Symmetric`	$r(H, T) \leftarrow r(T, H)$	$f(t, r, h)$
`Inverse`	$r(H, T) \leftarrow r'(T, H)$	$f(t, r', h)$
`Multiple`	$r(H, T) \leftarrow r'(H, T)$	$f(h, r', t)$
`Compositional`	$r(H, T) \leftarrow r_1(H, X_1), ... r_n(X_n, T)$	$Path(h, r_1...r_n, t)$

when computing the credibility of (h, r, t). Similarly to `symmetric` and `inverse` patterns, we can get SPA score $f(h, r', t)$ for the `multiple` and $Path(h, r_1...r_n, t)$ for the `compositional`.

Nevertheless, the compositional rules mined by the majority of existing open-source techniques are not readily applicable, largely due to their not chain-like structure [25]. Take the rule $\tau : r(H, T) \leftarrow r_1(X, H), r_2(X, T)$ as an example, we need first convert the body part $r_1(X, H)$ into $r_1^{-1}(H, X)$, where r_1^{-1} denotes the inverse relation of r_1, then we can obtain a compositional chain rule $r(H, T) \leftarrow r_1^{-1}(H, X), r_2(X, T)$, and see Appendix A for more details on the implementation of `Compositional` SPA.

Table 3. The details of KGE models, where $\| \cdot \|_1$ and $\| \cdot \|_2$ denote the absolute-value norm and Euclidean norm respectively. The expression of **h,r,t** in bold is denoted as their embedding vectors.

Model	$f_{kge}(h, r, t)$	$Path(h, r_1...r_n, t)$
TransE	$-\|\mathbf{h} + \mathbf{r} - \mathbf{t}\|_1$	$-\|\mathbf{h} + \mathbf{r_1}... + \mathbf{r_n} - \mathbf{t}\|_1$
RotatE	$-\|\mathbf{h} \circ \mathbf{r} - \mathbf{t}\|_2$	$-\|\mathbf{h} \circ \mathbf{r_1}... \circ \mathbf{r_n} - \mathbf{t}\|_2$
HAKE	$-\|\mathbf{h}_m \circ \mathbf{r}_m - \mathbf{t}_m\|_2 -$	$-\|\mathbf{h}_m \circ \mathbf{r_1}_m... \circ \mathbf{r_n}_m - \mathbf{t}_m\|_2 -$
	$\lambda \|\sin((\mathbf{h}_p + \mathbf{r}_p - \mathbf{t}_p)/2)\|_1$	$\lambda \|\sin((\mathbf{h}_p + \mathbf{r_1}_p... + \mathbf{r_n}_p - \mathbf{t}_p)/2)\|_1$
ComplEx	$\text{Re}\left(h^\top \text{diag}(r)\bar{t}\right)$	$\text{Re}\left(h^\top \text{diag}(r_1)...\text{diag}(r_n)\bar{t}\right)$
DualE	$< Q_h \otimes W_r^0, Q_t >$	$< Q_h \otimes W_{r_1}^0...\otimes W_{r_n}^0, Q_t >$
PairRE	$-\left\|\mathbf{h} \circ \mathbf{r}^H - \mathbf{t} \circ \mathbf{r}^T\right\|_1$	$-\left\|\mathbf{h} \circ \mathbf{r_1}^H... \circ \mathbf{r_n}^H - \mathbf{t} \circ \mathbf{r_1}^T... \circ \mathbf{r_n}^T\right\|_1$
DistMult	$\mathbf{h}^\top \text{diag}(\mathbf{r})\mathbf{t}$	$\mathbf{h}^\top \text{diag}(\mathbf{r_1})...\text{diag}(\mathbf{r_n})\mathbf{t}$

We predict any missing fact jointly with the KGE score (Table 3) and SPA score (Table 2). For a query $(h, r, ?)$, we substitute the tail entity with all candidate entities (h, r, t') and compute their KGE scores $f(h, r, t)$ and compute the SPA score $s_p(h, r, t)$ if relation r belongs to specific p patterns. There may be many relations with the relation r showing specific patterns, so we need to consider all of them. The final scores can be presented as:

$$s(h, r, t) = s_{kge}(h, r, t) +$$

$$\lambda_p \frac{1}{\sum_{\tau \in Set_p(r)} MC_\tau} \sum_{\tau \in Set_p(r)} MC_\tau (s_p(h, r, t) - s_{kge}(h, r, t)) \quad (2)$$

where the function s_{kge} represents the score function of KGE models and $s_p(h, r, t)$ represents the SPA score of the p pattern. $Set_p(r)$ represents the p pattern rule set of relation r. λ_p represents the hyper-parameters of the p pattern, and MC_τ represents the mean confidence of the rule τ to measure the credibility of the modified score.

5   Experiments

In this section, we introduce the experiment results with analysis. Specifically, in Subsect. 5.1, we introduce the datasets, metrics, and implementation first. Next in Subsect. 5.2, we analyze the performance of the KGE models over relational patterns with three questions. Last, in Subsect. 5.3 and 5.4, we compare the performance of using SPA to optimize the score function on specific patterns and analyze SPA with the case study.

5.1   Evaluation Setup

Datasets. We have chosen two benchmark datasets, FB15k-237 and WN18RR, which are commonly used for evaluating Knowledge Graph Embedding (KGE) models. A summary of these datasets is presented in Appendix B.

Evaluation Protocol. Following the same protocol as in TransE [2], we evaluate link prediction performance by assessing the ranking quality of each test triple. For a given triple (h, r, t) in the test set, we replace either the head (h', r, t) or the tail entity (h, r, t') with all entities and rank the candidate triples in descending order according to their scores. We select Mean Reciprocal Rank (MRR) as the evaluation metric. Furthermore, we use the "filtered" setting [2] to eliminate the reconstructed triples that are already present in the KG.

Implementation Details. In our experiments, we employ the combination of PCA confidence and HC thresholds to mine rules with AMIE3 [17] and classify relations and triples then conduct quantitative analysis. The best models are chosen by early stopping on the validation set using MRR over different patterns. As our SPA method optimizes the score function based on the embedding information from the trained KGE model without retraining or parameter adjustment, we do not modify the learning rate, margin, or other hyper-parameters. Instead, we only adjust the hyper-parameter λ for the four patterns (symmetric, inverse, multiple, and compositional). Our settings for hyper-parameter selection are as follows: the hyper-parameters of symmetric pattern λ_{sym}, inverse pattern λ_{inv}, and multiple pattern λ_{sub} are adjusted within the set $\{\pm 1, \pm 2, \pm 3, \pm 4, \pm 5, \pm 10, \pm 50, \pm 100\}$, while the hyper-parameter for the compositional pattern λ_{comp2} is adjusted within the set $\{\pm 1e{-}5, \pm 1e{-}4, \pm 1e{-}3, \pm 0.01, \pm 0.02, \pm 0.05, \pm 0.1, \pm 0.2, \pm 0.5, \pm 1, \pm 2, \pm 5\}$. It should be noted that to ensure a fair comparison, experiments with the SPA strategy have the same hyper-parameters and implementation as the original models, except for pattern hyper-parameters. For more details about hyper-parameters in different KGE models, please refer to Appendix C.

Table 4. Statistics of the number of rules and relations for different relational patterns. #Rule, #r(P) denote the number of the mined rules and relations in pattern P $\#\{r|P \in Type(r)\}$ respectively. Sym, inv, mul, comp2, and comp3 are abbreviations for **symmetric**, **inverse**, **multiple**, and **compositional** patterns respectively. The mining results of relational patterns on FB15k-237 and WN18RR with five prescribed thresholds, where the symbol means the symbolization of different thresholds. i.e., the symbol of "PCA=0.9 and HC=0.6 thresholds" can be written as θ_1.

Confidence Thresholds			FB15k-237 / WN18RR					
Symbol	PCA	HC	# Rule	#r(sym)	#r(inv)	#r(sub)	#r(comp2)	#r(comp3)
θ_1	0.9	0.5	6k/5	6/3	4/0	14/0	49/0	111/1
θ_2	0.8	0.5	6k/10	26/3	11/0	22/0	62/0	147/3
θ_3	0.6	0.3	13k/41	28/3	26/0	32/0	96/0	203/7
θ_4	0.4	0.1	39k/84	31/3	48/0	55/0	162/1	233/10
θ_5	0.2	0.1	54k/115	31/3	67/0	73/0	185/1	233/10

5.2 Quantitative Analysis over Relational Patterns

Table 4 displays the number of rules mined in the two benchmarks at different confidence thresholds. We can obviously observe that the number of rules in FB15k-237 is much more than that in WN18RR, and there are all five relational patterns. While there are only two relational patterns in WN18RR, indicating that the data in FB15k-237 is more miscellaneous than that in WN18RR.

Following the suggestions of RUGE [11] and taking HC in the middle position, the evaluation of performance over patterns will be based on θ_2 (PCA=0.8 and HC=0.5).

Figure 2 illustrates the heat map of relation distribution to show the overlapping between patterns. More details about the heat map can be found in Appendix D. In FB15k-237, the overlap between **compositional3** and others are close to 1, while the overlap between other relations is small, which means that relations in **compositional3** are massive. The relationships in WN18RR

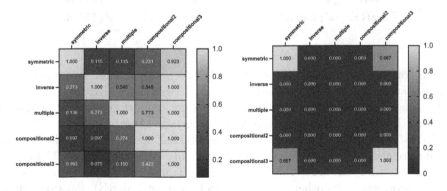

Fig. 2. The heat map of the relations' distribution in five relational patterns. From left to right are the statistical results under FB15k-237 and WN18RR datasets.

are simpler without `inverse` or `multiple`. Furthermore, we closely examine the rules of `compositional3` in WN18RR and find that the body of rules consists of the head relation with two symmetric relations [7], which causes the `compositional3` pattern to lose its compositional meaning.

Considering the significant overlap of `compositional3` with other patterns in FB15k-237 and its meaninglessness in WN18RR, we discard the `compositional3` pattern and conduct further experiments with the remaining four patterns.

Our analysis is driven by the form of three questions.

Q1: Does a KGE model supporting a specific relational pattern in theory achieve better link prediction results on triples related to the relational pattern compared to another KGE model that does not support such a relational pattern?

Table 5. Comparison of seven KGE models over various relational patterns with θ_2. ✓ indicates that the model supports the pattern while ✗ indicates unsupported. The numbers with Star(∗) indicate the baseline in each pattern. The percentages in parentheses represent the MRR ratios compared to the baseline while the radio of baseline in each pattern is always 100%. If the model gets better performance than the baseline, it indicates in **bold**, otherwise in gray.

Model	Relation Patterns			
	Symmetric	Inverse	Multiple	Composition2
TransE	✗(100%)∗	✓(98%)	✗(105%)	✓(119%)
RotatE	✓(98%)	✓(98%)	✗(102%)	✓(120%)
HAKE	✓(98%)	✓(96%)	✗(104%)	✓(124%)
DistMult	✓(94%)	✗(100%)∗	✗(106%)	✗(100%)∗
ComplEx	✓ (61%)	✓(49%)	✗(52%)	✗(100%)
DualE	✓(90%)	✓(93%)	✓(100%)∗	✓(117%)
PairRE	✓(105%)	✓(99%)	✓(104%)	✓(125%)

We consider the answer to be **NO**. Intuition suggests that if a model itself does not support one relational pattern, it may have a lower MRR in the link prediction task compared to other KGE models that support the related relational pattern. However, the experimental results contradict our intuition.

Table 5 shows the comparison between seven KGE models. Due to the absence of some relational patterns in WN18RR, we only consider FB15k-237 for this experiment. In `symmetric`, the benchmark is TransE which does not support this pattern, while the other six KGE models (except PairRE) that do support it perform worse than TransE. The same result also appears in `inverse` and multiple. Only in `compositional2`, KGE models show significantly better performance for the supported than unsupported ones. Moreover, it is difficult to judge the capability of KGE models over patterns when comparing those that support the same pattern. For instance, in `symmetric`, all supporting models perform around 90% except for ComplEx, which also achieves 90% in `inverse`, 105% in `multiple`, and 120% in `compositional2`.

We consider that one of the reasons for this phenomenon is the complexity of the relations. The complex relatedness between relations makes relational patterns less discernible. As shown in Fig. 2, expect `compositional3`, the overlap between patterns is still not small and part overlaps values up to 50–70%. This suggests that a single pattern is insufficient to construct the semantics of relations in complex KGs. Also, the issue of sparsity presents a significant challenge for KGE models in reasoning processes [28,38]. Generally, the infrequency of an entity correlates with diminished reasoning accuracy [44]. This prompts an investigation into the extent to which entity frequency impacts relational patterns, thus leading to our second research question.

Q2: What is the impact of entity frequency for different KGE models over patterns?

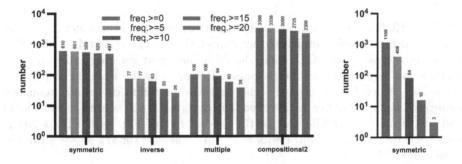

Fig. 3. Statistics of triples in four patterns with entity frequency under θ_2. From left to right are the results on FB15k-237 and WN18RR. (Note that the vertical axis is exponential)

The statistics for the number of triples over patterns are shown in Fig. 3. For a triple (h, r, t), the threshold limit is the total number of occurrences of h and t in the KG. The `symmetric` pattern is significantly reduced from 0 to 5 frequency and the number of triples in the `compositional2` pattern is large with little change in entity frequency. In WN18RR, it only contains the `symmetric` pattern without `inverse` and `multiple` patterns. The number of `symmetric` triples is large and decreases sharply with increasing frequency. The subsequent experiments in this question will be based on the data mentioned above.

Figure 4 illustrates the performance of seven KGE models over different patterns with varying entity frequencies on two datasets. In FB15k-237, we observe that the performance of ComplEx is significantly worse than the other models.

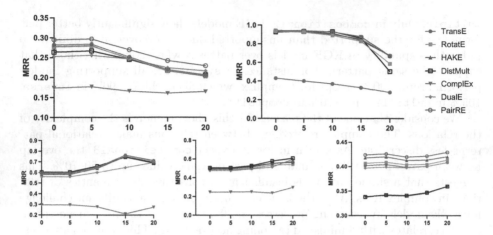

Fig. 4. MRR of seven KGE models(TransE, RotatE, HAKE, DistMult, ComplEx, DualE, and PairRE) with varying entity frequency over patterns. The two figures in the first row, from left to right, are the experimental results of the symmetric pattern in FB15k-237 and WN18RR respectively. The second line from left to right is the results over inverse, multiple, and compositional2 patterns in FB15k-237 respectively.

In WN18RR, TransE, which does not support symmetric, is considerably worse than the other models. Intuitively, we expect that as the constraints on entity frequency increase, the KGE model should be better at learning embeddings of entities and result in better performance. However, in the symmetric pattern, there is a noticeable downward trend as the constraints on entity frequency increase. The performance on inverse (the first plot in the second row of Fig. 4) and multiple (the middle plot in the second row of Fig. 4) in FB15k-237 is consistent with our intuition. Performance on compositional2 shows an initial drop followed by a rise.

We find that the impact of entity frequency on different models (except ComplEx) is similar. Additionally, different patterns (except symmetric) generally improve as the constraint on entity frequency increases. We consider the reason for the downward trend as the increasing entity frequency is that the symmetric pattern relation solution is usually unitary. For example, in RotatE [31] and HAKE [45], the symmetric relation tends to be π to realize the rotation in complex space. With the increase in the entity frequency, the relations involved in the entities may also increase, resulting in the entity is not in the center symmetric position, which makes the model less effective.

Subsequently, we aim to examine the correlation between pattern-specific performance and overall performance in KGE inference, thereby formulating our final research question.

Q3: If one KGE model performs better than another one on link prediction, is it because it improves uniformly across different relational patterns?

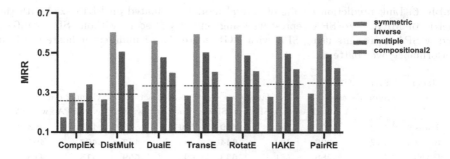

Fig. 5. Comparison of seven KGE models under relational patterns with the overall performance in FB15k-237. The dotted lines in each model represent the performance under the complete test set of FB15k-237.

We compare seven KGE models over relational patterns with the full set of MRR in FB15k-237, as shown in Fig. 5. We find there are two scenarios. First, if one model demonstrates overall improvement compared to another, there will be significant enhancements in all relational patterns. For instance, when comparing ComplEx to DistMult, MRR has increased from 0.26 to 0.29, and it is evident that DistMult has improved in all patterns relative to ComplEx. Second, the relational pattern capability may be poor even when the overall performance is similar. Taking TransE, RotatE, and HAKE as examples, the overall performance of the three models is similar (0.33 for TransE, 0.333 for RotatE, and 0.329 for HAKE), but the capability of HAKE is slightly weaker than the other two models overall patterns.

5.3   Score-Based Patterns Adaptation Results

We compare the effectiveness of using SPA to optimize the score function on specific pattern datasets. We observe that different KGE models with SPA achieve greater performance in various pattern datasets on FB15K237 and WN18RR. Table 6 displays the experimental result on FB15k-237.

On FB15k-237, our SPA strategy attains the best performance, demonstrating that it can effectively learn all patterns in specific pattern datasets. In the performance comparison of the **symmetric** pattern, KGE models with SPA, such as TransE, RotatE, and PairRE, achieve a 2% improvement in MRR. For the **inverse** pattern, KGE models with SPA, such as TransE, RotatE, HAKE, and PairRE, show MRR improvements of 5–8%. For the **multiple** pattern, KGE models with SPA, such as TransE, RotatE, HAKE, and PairRE, exhibit MRR improvements of around 6%. For the **compositional2** pattern, we find that SPA gets only slight improvements in DualE and PairRE. A possible explanation for this phenomenon is that during the experiment, we calculate the contribution of the **compositional2** pattern in the form of 2-hops, which may further amplify errors and make the effect less pronounced. The experimental result of WN18RR is presented in Appendix E and is consistent with our conclusions in FB15k-237.

Table 6. Link prediction results of several models evaluated on FB15k-237 with the metric of MRR. w/o SPA represents using only KGE score without SPA strategy and w SPA represents using SPA with KGE score. **Bold** numbers indicate the best performance over patterns.

Model	FB15k-237							
	Sym. dataset		Inv. dataset		Sub. dataset		Comp.2 dataset	
	w/o. SPA	w. SPA	w/o. SPA	w. SPA	w/o. SPA	w. SPA	w/o. SPA	w. SPA
TransE	.282	**.301**	.592	**.649**	.500	**.546**	.402	**.403**
RotatE	.277	**.293**	.590	**.644**	.485	**.543**	.407	**.407**
HAKE	.278	**.288**	.581	**.633**	.495	**.559**	.418	**.418**
DistMult	**.264**	**.264**	.603	**.622**	.505	**.529**	.338	**.338**
ComplEx	.174	**.179**	.296	**.296**	.247	**.273**	.339	**.339**
DualE	.253	**.254**	.559	**.564**	.475	**.483**	.397	**.399**
PairRE	.295	**.316**	.597	**.676**	.494	**.555**	.424	**.425**

5.4 Case Study

Score-based Patterns Adaptation (SPA) utilizes the information from relational patterns, which is simple but effective to be applied to KGE models without further training. As Table 7 shows, we provide an intuitive demonstration for SPA. We select an example case (1980 Summer Olympics, /olympics/olympic_games/ sports, ?) from the FB15k-237 and list the tail prediction rank on $s_{kge}(h, r, t)$, $s_p(h, r, t)$, and $s(h, r, t)$ based on RotatE.

Firstly, we get the rule τ: /user/jg/default_domain/olympic_games/sports(H, T) $\rightarrow$ /olympics/olympic_games/sports(H, T) with PCA = 0.83 and HC = 0.72 from test set which means relations in the head and body of rule τ with high similarity. The rank of the correct answer (Rowing) is 5,6, and 2 with different

Table 7. The rank of part entities in different score functions. The reasoning task is (1980 Summer Olympics, /olympics/olympic_games/sports, ?) from the FB15k-237, and we list the tail prediction rank in KGE score $s_{kge}(h, r, t)$, SPA score $s_p(h, r, t)$, and KGE with SPA score $s(h, r, t)$ based on RotatE. The rankings are sorted from highest to lowest with "filter" and the "**Rowing**" entity is the grounding.

Q: (1980 Summer Olympics, /olympics/olympic_games/sports, ?) A: **Rowing**		
Rank	KGE score $s_{kge}(h, r, t)$ SPA score $s_p(h, r, t)$	KGE and SPA $s(h, r, t)$
1	Artistic gymnastics Artistic gymnastics	Canoe Slalom
2	Swimming Swimming	**Rowing**
3	Volleyball Freestyle wrestling	Swimming
4	Freestyle wrestling Volleyball	Artistic gymnastics
5	**Rowing** Archery	Cycling
6	Archery **Rowing**	Volleyball

scores respectively, while confusing answers such as Artistic gymnastics, Swimming, and Volleyball are decreased in the rank of the $s(h, r, t)$, which means that SPA calculates the SPA score from the body of rules with the KGE score can achieve more accurate in reasoning.

6   Conclusion and Future Work

We study KGC tasks in KGE models based on relational patterns and analyze the result in theory, entity frequency, and part-to-whole three aspects with some counterintuitive and interesting conclusions. Firstly, theoretical backing for a KGE model's relational pattern doesn't ensure its superiority over models without such support. Secondly, entity frequency differently affects relational patterns' performance; it decreases for symmetric patterns yet increases for others with rising frequency. Finally, a significantly outperforming KGE model consistently excels across all relational patterns otherwise doesn't.

In the future, we believe that the research of KGE should not be confined to relational patterns. Greater attention should be given to analyzing the correlations between overall relations from a macro perspective, negative sampling [12, 16], and loss function.

Supplemental Material Statement: Our source code, datasets and results of study with SPA are all available from GitHub at https://github.com/zjukg/Comprehensive-Study-over-Relational-Patterns.

Acknowledgements. This work is funded by Zhejiang Provincial Natural Science Foundation of China (No. LQ23F020017), Yongjiang Talent Introduction Programme (2022A-238-G), the National Natural Science Foundation of China (NSFCU19B2027, NSFC91846204), joint project DH-2022ZY0012 from Donghai Lab.

References

1. Bollacker, K., Evans, C., Paritosh, P., Sturge, T., Taylor, J.: Freebase: a collaboratively created graph database for structuring human knowledge. In: Proceedings of the 2008 ACM SIGMOD International Conference on Management of Data, pp. 1247–1250 (2008)
2. Bordes, A., Usunier, N., Garcia-Duran, A., Weston, J., Yakhnenko, O.: Translating embeddings for modeling multi-relational data. In: Advances in Neural Information Processing Systems, vol. 26 (2013)
3. Bordes, A., Weston, J., Usunier, N.: Open question answering with weakly supervised embedding models. In: Calders, T., Esposito, F., Hüllermeier, E., Meo, R. (eds.) ECML PKDD 2014. LNCS (LNAI), vol. 8724, pp. 165–180. Springer, Heidelberg (2014). https://doi.org/10.1007/978-3-662-44848-9_11
4. Cao, Z., Xu, Q., Yang, Z., Cao, X., Huang, Q.: Dual quaternion knowledge graph embeddings. In: Proceedings of the AAAI Conference on Artificial Intelligence, vol. 35, pp. 6894–6902 (2021)

5. Chen, Y., Goldberg, S., Wang, D.Z., Johri, S.S.: Ontological pathfinding. In: Proceedings of the 2016 International Conference on Management of Data, pp. 835–846 (2016)
6. Cheng, K., Yang, Z., Zhang, M., Sun, Y.: Uniker: a unified framework for combining embedding and definite horn rule reasoning for knowledge graph inference. In: Proceedings of the 2021 Conference on Empirical Methods in Natural Language Processing, pp. 9753–9771 (2021)
7. Cui, W., Chen, X.: Instance-based learning for knowledge base completion. arXiv preprint arXiv:2211.06807 (2022)
8. Dehaspe, L., Toivonen, H.: Discovery of frequent datalog patterns. Data Min. Knowl. Disc. **3**, 7–36 (1999)
9. Galárraga, L., Teflioudi, C., Hose, K., Suchanek, F.M.: Fast rule mining in ontological knowledge bases with AMIE+. VLDB J. **24**(6), 707–730 (2015)
10. Galárraga, L.A., Teflioudi, C., Hose, K., Suchanek, F.: AMIE: association rule mining under incomplete evidence in ontological knowledge bases. In: Proceedings of the 22nd International Conference on World Wide Web, pp. 413–422 (2013)
11. Guo, S., Wang, Q., Wang, L., Wang, B., Guo, L.: Knowledge graph embedding with iterative guidance from soft rules. In: Proceedings of the AAAI Conference on Artificial Intelligence, vol. 32 (2018)
12. Hajimoradlou, A., Kazemi, M.: Stay positive: knowledge graph embedding without negative sampling. arXiv preprint arXiv:2201.02661 (2022)
13. Hu, Z., Ma, X., Liu, Z., Hovy, E., Xing, E.: Harnessing deep neural networks with logic rules. arXiv preprint arXiv:1603.06318 (2016)
14. Ji, G., He, S., Xu, L., Liu, K., Zhao, J.: Knowledge graph embedding via dynamic mapping matrix. In: Proceedings of the 53rd Annual Meeting of the Association for Computational Linguistics and the 7th International Joint Conference on Natural Language Processing (Volume 1: Long Papers), pp. 687–696 (2015)
15. Ji, S., Pan, S., Cambria, E., Marttinen, P., Philip, S.Y.: A survey on knowledge graphs: representation, acquisition, and applications. IEEE Trans. Neural Netw. Learn. Syst. **33**(2), 494–514 (2021)
16. Kamigaito, H., Hayashi, K.: Comprehensive analysis of negative sampling in knowledge graph representation learning. In: International Conference on Machine Learning, pp. 10661–10675. PMLR (2022)
17. Lajus, J., Galárraga, L., Suchanek, F.: Fast and exact rule mining with AMIE 3. In: Harth, A., Kirrane, S., Ngonga Ngomo, A.-C., Paulheim, H., Rula, A., Gentile, A.L., Haase, P., Cochez, M. (eds.) ESWC 2020. LNCS, vol. 12123, pp. 36–52. Springer, Cham (2020). https://doi.org/10.1007/978-3-030-49461-2_3
18. Lehmann, J., et al.: DBPedia-a large-scale, multilingual knowledge base extracted from Wikipedia. Semantic web **6**(2), 167–195 (2015)
19. Li, R., Cao, Y., Zhu, Q., Li, X., Fang, F.: Is there more pattern in knowledge graph? exploring proximity pattern for knowledge graph embedding. arXiv preprint arXiv:2110.00720 (2021)
20. Lin, Y., Liu, Z., Sun, M., Liu, Y., Zhu, X.: Learning entity and relation embeddings for knowledge graph completion. In: Proceedings of the AAAI Conference on Artificial Intelligence, vol. 29 (2015)
21. Miller, G.A.: Wordnet: a lexical database for English. Commun. ACM **38**(11), 39–41 (1995)
22. Minervini, P., Costabello, L., Muñoz, E., Nováček, V., Vandenbussche, P.-Y.: Regularizing knowledge graph embeddings via equivalence and inversion axioms. In: Ceci, M., Hollmén, J., Todorovski, L., Vens, C., Džeroski, S. (eds.) ECML PKDD

2017. LNCS (LNAI), vol. 10534, pp. 668–683. Springer, Cham (2017). https://doi.org/10.1007/978-3-319-71249-9_40

23. Mohamed, S.K., Nováček, V., Vandenbussche, P.Y., Muñoz, E.: Loss functions in knowledge graph embedding models. DL4KG@ ESWC. **2377**, 1–10 (2019)

24. Nickel, M., Tresp, V., Kriegel, H.P., et al.: A three-way model for collective learning on multi-relational data. In: ICML, vol. 11, pp. 3104482–3104584 (2011)

25. Niu, G., et al.: Rule-guided compositional representation learning on knowledge graphs. In: Proceedings of the AAAI Conference on Artificial Intelligence, vol. 34, pp. 2950–2958 (2020)

26. Pirrò, G.: Relatedness and TBOX-driven rule learning in large knowledge bases. In: Proceedings of the AAAI Conference on Artificial Intelligence, vol. 34, pp. 2975–2982 (2020)

27. Qu, M., Tang, J.: Probabilistic logic neural networks for reasoning. In: Advances in Neural Information Processing Systems, vol. 32 (2019)

28. Sharma, A., Talukdar, P., et al.: Towards understanding the geometry of knowledge graph embeddings. In: Proceedings of the 56th Annual Meeting of the Association for Computational Linguistics (Volume 1: Long Papers), pp. 122–131 (2018)

29. Srinivasan, A.: The aleph manual (2001)

30. Suchanek, F.M., Kasneci, G., Weikum, G.: YAGO: a core of semantic knowledge. In: Proceedings of the 16th International Conference on World Wide Web, pp. 697–706 (2007)

31. Sun, Z., Deng, Z.H., Nie, J.Y., Tang, J.: Rotate: Knowledge graph embedding by relational rotation in complex space. arXiv preprint arXiv:1902.10197 (2019)

32. Suresh, S., Neville, J.: A hybrid model for learning embeddings and logical rules simultaneously from knowledge graphs. In: 2020 IEEE International Conference on Data Mining (ICDM), pp. 1280–1285. IEEE (2020)

33. Trouillon, T., Welbl, J., Riedel, S., Gaussier, É., Bouchard, G.: Complex embeddings for simple link prediction. In: International Conference on Machine Learning, pp. 2071–2080. PMLR (2016)

34. Wang, Q., Mao, Z., Wang, B., Guo, L.: Knowledge graph embedding: a survey of approaches and applications. IEEE Trans. Knowl. Data Eng. **29**(12), 2724–2743 (2017)

35. Wang, X., Wang, D., Xu, C., He, X., Cao, Y., Chua, T.S.: Explainable reasoning over knowledge graphs for recommendation. In: Proceedings of the AAAI Conference on Artificial Intelligence, vol. 33, pp. 5329–5336 (2019)

36. Wang, Z., Zhang, J., Feng, J., Chen, Z.: Knowledge graph embedding by translating on hyperplanes. In: Proceedings of the AAAI Conference on Artificial Intelligence, vol. 28 (2014)

37. Xie, R., Liu, Z., Sun, M., et al.: Representation learning of knowledge graphs with hierarchical types. In: IJCAI, vol. 2016, pp. 2965–2971 (2016)

38. Xiong, C., Power, R., Callan, J.: Explicit semantic ranking for academic search via knowledge graph embedding. In: Proceedings of the 26th International Conference on World Wide Web, pp. 1271–1279 (2017)

39. Xu, Z., Ye, P., Chen, H., Zhao, M., Chen, H., Zhang, W.: Ruleformer: context-aware rule mining over knowledge graph. In: Proceedings of the 29th International Conference on Computational Linguistics, pp. 2551–2560 (2022)

40. Yang, B., Mitchell, T.: Leveraging knowledge bases in LSTMS for improving machine reading. arXiv preprint arXiv:1902.09091 (2019)

41. Yang, B., Yih, W.t., He, X., Gao, J., Deng, L.: Embedding entities and relations for learning and inference in knowledge bases. arXiv preprint arXiv:1412.6575 (2014)

42. Zhang, W., Chen, J., Li, J., Xu, Z., Pan, J.Z., Chen, H.: Knowledge graph reasoning with logics and embeddings: survey and perspective. arXiv preprint arXiv:2202.07412 (2022)
43. Zhang, W., Chen, M., Xu, Z., Zhu, Y., Chen, H.: Explaining knowledge graph embedding via latent rule learning (2021)
44. Zhang, W., et al.: Iteratively learning embeddings and rules for knowledge graph reasoning. In: The World Wide Web Conference, pp. 2366–2377 (2019)
45. Zhang, Z., Cai, J., Zhang, Y., Wang, J.: Learning hierarchy-aware knowledge graph embeddings for link prediction. In: Proceedings of the AAAI Conference on Artificial Intelligence, vol. 34, pp. 3065–3072 (2020)

Compact Encoding of Reified Triples Using HDTr

Jose M. Gimenez-Garcia[1,2]([envelope])[iD], Thomas Gautrais[2][iD], Javier D. Fernández[3][iD], and Miguel A. Martínez-Prieto[4][iD]

[1] Group of Intelligent and Cooperative Systems, Univ. of Valladolid, Valladolid, Spain
jm.gimenez.garcia@gsic.uva.es
[2] Univ. de Lyon, CNRS, UMR 5516, Lab. Hubert-Curien, Saint-Étienne, France
thomas.gautrais@univ-st-etienne.fr
[3] Data Science Acceleration (DSX), F. Hoffman-La Roche, Basel, Switzerland
javier_d.fernandez@roche.com
[4] Department of Computer Science, Univ. of Valladolid, Valladolid, Spain
miguelamp@uva.es

Abstract. Contextual information about a statement is usually represented in RDF knowledge graphs via *reification:* creating a fresh 'anchor' term that represents the statement and using it in the triples that describe it. Current approaches make the connection between the reified statement and its anchor by either extending the RDF syntax, resulting in non-compliant RDF, or via additional triples to connect the anchor with the terms of the statement, at the cost of size and complexity.

This work tackles this challenge and presents HDTr, a binary serialization format for reified triples that is model-agnostic, compact, and queryable. HDTr is based on, and compatible with, the counterpart HDT format, leveraging its underlying structure to connect the reified statements with the terms that represent them. Our evaluation shows that HDTr improves compression and retrieval time of reified statements *w.r.t.* several triplestores and HDT serialization of different reification approaches.

Keywords: Knowledge Graphs · RDF · Reification · Contextual Data · HDT · Compression · Compact Data Structures

1 Introduction

Knowledge Graphs (KG) are increasingly being used to build innovative data-driven applications (semantic search, question answering, product recommendation, etc.) thanks to their ability to store and communicate the semantics of real-world knowledge. KGs represent information as a graph of entities and relationships, typically modeled as a directed labelled graph due to its relative succinctness [22]. The *Resource Data Framework* (RDF) [7] has been used extensively to model such KGs in terms of `<subject>`, `<predicate>`, `<object>` *statements*, also called *triples*. Thus, each statement establishes the relationship

T. R. Payne et al. (Eds.): ISWC 2023, LNCS 14265, pp. 309–327, 2023.
https://doi.org/10.1007/978-3-031-47240-4_17

(labeled in the predicate) between the two resources declared in the subject and object values. However, it does not natively allow information (such as validity time, provenance, certainty...) about the triple itself to be expressed [28].

The most common solution to express this information is to *reify* the statement; *i.e.*, to introduce a new element that represents the statement, which we call the *anchor*. Then, this anchor is used as subject and/or object in a set of triples that describe the statement, which we refer to as the *contextual annotation*. Existing approaches to represent reified statements fall in two categories. The first approach can be seen as applying a *reification function* to the triple and its contextual annotation, to obtain a new RDF graph where the original statement is replaced by a set of triples connecting the anchor to both the terms of the statement and the contextual annotation (*e.g.*, RDF reification [4]). However, the introduction of different sets of triples per reified statement can degrade performance by increasing the size and complexity of the graph, and introduce interoperability problems between the results of two or more contextualization functions. A second alternative is to extend the syntax (and possibly the semantics) of RDF to cover the reification needs, at the cost of obtaining non-compliant RDF graphs (*e.g.*, RDF-Star [17]).

The management of reified statements is therefore an emerging challenge with increasingly large KGs, which account billions of triples that are subject to reification; e.g. Wikidata contains more than 100 million different subjects and more than 1.2 billion statements, from which at least 900 million are reified.[1] A simple but effective approach to deal with this complexity in regular KGs (without reification) is *knowledge graph compression*, *i.e.*, "*encoding a KG using less bits than its original representation*" [25]. Managing compressed KGs leads to more efficient storage and lower transmission costs due to space savings. In addition, some compressors, such as HDT *(Header-Dictionary-Triples)* [11], allow efficient access to triples without prior decompression due to their self-indexed internal structures. Unfortunately, none of these solutions natively support reification. A practical approach is to compress the graph produced by a reification function at the cost of encoding potentially much larger datasets, with the consequent impact that this has on space requirements and, in particular, the retrieval time of a reified statement and its anchor.

This paper presents HDTr, an extension of HDT for compressing and querying reified triples. This approach enhances HDT components to link statements to their anchors, without adding new triples nor adapting to a new syntax. The resulting HDTr compressed files comply with the HDT *standard*, allowing HDTr to be used in applications that consume HDT (see Sect. 4 for some examples). Our evaluation comparing HDTr with an HDT-based deployment, and with triplestores using named graphs to encode contextual annotations, shows that HDTr outperforms both approaches in terms of space and performance.

The rest of the paper is organized as follows. Sections 2 and 3 provide a basic background on reification and review practical solutions to manage reified KGs. Section 4 explains the foundations of HDT, which is extended into HDTr

---

[1] https://wikidata-todo.toolforge.org/stats.php.

in Sect. 5. A comprehensive evaluation is provided in Sect. 6, and we conclude
and provide future work in Sect. 7.

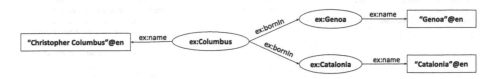

Fig. 1. Example of RDF graph

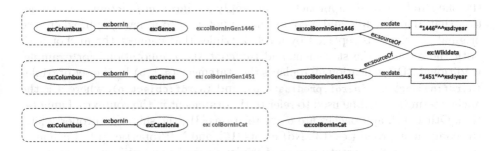

Fig. 2. Example of abstract reification

2 Reifying RDF Statements

RDF can only represent binary relations between two entities, but does not
natively allow to express information about the relations themselves [28].
Figure 1 shows an RDF graph composed of five statements that describe *Christopher Columbus*. It gives his *name* and two birthplaces (using the predicate
`ex:bornIn`), which correspond to those given by two information sources. So,
what is his real birthplace? We cannot answer this question with the information we have.

In order to state something about the context of a statement itself, it is
necessary to resort to reification. *Reification* stands for the mechanism by which
a new term (that we call the *anchor*) is used to represent the statement [18].
The anchor is used as subject and/or object in other triples to provide the
contextual annotation (*e.g.*, the source of the information, a temporal or spatial
dimension, etc.). Figure 2 shows an abstract representation of the reification of
two of the triples in Fig. 1, one of them associated with an anchor and the other
with two (left), and their contextual annotations (right). As can be seen, the
triple that says *Columbus* was born in *Genoa* is now qualified with two different
contextual annotations, each indicating a different date, and both using *Wikidata*
as their source. On the contrary, for the statement that *Columbus* was born in

Table 1. Triples introduced by each reification function

RDF Reification	N-Ary Relations	Singleton Properties	NdFluents
(a,rdf:subject,s)	(s,p_1,a)	(s,a,o)	(s_a,nd:contextualPartOf,s)
(a,rdf:predicate,p)	(a,p_2,o)	(a,rdf:singletonPropertyOf,p)	(o_a,nd:contextualPartOf,o)
(a,rdf:object,o)	(p,subjectProperty,p_s)	(a,rdf:type,rdf:SingletonProperty)	(s_a,nd:contextualExtent,a)
(a,rdf:type,rdf:Statement)	(p,objectProperty,p_o)		(o_a,nd:contextualExtent,a)
			(s_a,rdf:type,nd:ContextualPart)
			(o_a,rdf:type,nd:ContextualPart)
			(a,rdf:type,nd:ContextualExtent)

Catalonia, there is actually no information in the contextual annotation (the anchor ex:ccBornInCat is not connected to anything).

Current reification approaches can be categorized into two main families. On the one hand, there are approaches that apply a *reification function, i.e.*, a function that maps a triple and a contextual annotation to a new graph, where the original statement is replaced by a set of triples that connect the anchor with both the terms of the statement and the contextual annotation. For example, traditional RDF reification [4] replaces the statement (s,p,o) by the set of triples (a,rdf:subject,s), (a,rdf:predicate,p), and (a,rdf:object,o), where a is the anchor term that will be used to refer to the statement in the contextual annotation. Other such approaches are n-ary relations [31], the singleton property [30], the companion properties [13], NdFluents [16], and NdProperties [14]. Each approach generates a different number of triples to implement reification, as shown in Table 1, which lists the triples added by RDF reification, n-ary relations, singleton property, and NdFluents (evaluated in Sect. 6).[2] On the other hand, other approaches extend the RDF syntax and/or semantics to link the statements and their corresponding anchors. For example, RDF-Star [17] extends the definition of term to allow for a triple itself to be used as subject or object in other statements. Other such approaches are Notation 3 [2] or using Named Graphs [6], with each named graph containing only a reified statement.

Finally, note that RDF-Star and N3 follow a *"quoted triples"* model, where the triple (or a unique identifier thereof) can be used as a term in the subject or object position of another statement. This means that a statement can have at most one contextual annotation. On the other hand, reification functions and Named Graphs follow a model of *"contextualized statements"*, allowing a triple to be represented by different anchors, and therefore to have an indefinite number of different contextual annotations for it, each one in a different context. Some approaches, such as NdFluents, go even further, creating contextual versions of individuals to allow inference for sets of statements within the same context.

3   Related Work on Efficient Reification Representation

Efficiently representing KGs containing reified statements remains an open challenge. Hernández et al. [19,20] compare the management of several reification

---

[2] Note that the triples that indicate the types of some individuals can be considered as optional, since they can be inferred by the semantics of the vocabularies.

approaches by different triplestores, concluding that using *named graphs* is the most efficient solution. Moreover, triplestores commonly support named graphs natively, hence this is a relatively simple and practical approach, at the cost of losing named graphs for other purposes (*e.g.*, versioning). On the other hand, there are some triplestores (such as AnzoGraph[3], Blazegraph[4], GraphDB[5], or Stardog[6]) which are able to manage the RDF-Star [17] extension, so they can be used to store and query reified statements modeled in this way.

HDTQ [12] allows multiple named graphs to be managed and queried in compressed form. Like our approach, HDTQ extends HDT, but in this case, it proposes a *Quad Information* component that indexes whether a particular triple appears in a particular graph, allowing quad pattern queries (triple patterns augmented with graph information) to be performed efficiently in-memory.

TrieDF [32] also proposes an in-memory architecture to handle RDF data augmented with any type of metadata. For this purpose, it regards tuples of arbitrary length: `<subject>`, `<predicate>`, `<object>`, `<a`$_1$`>` ... `<a`$_n$`>`, where `<a`$_i$`>` are annotations, and models them using tries [3]. The resulting representation is able to compress shared prefixes (of any length) between tuples, and supports fast prefix-based retrieval. TrieDF shows competitive performance for managing statements with 1 and 2 annotations, consolidating a first step toward managing arbitrary levels of metadata in an application-agnostic manner.

Finally note that all of the approaches mentioned in this section follow the *"contextualized statements"* model, except for triplestores that support RDF-Star, which implements the *"quoted triples"* model.

4   HDT

HDT (Header-Dictionary-Triples) is a framework originally designed to optimize the storage and transmission of RDF data [11], and then enhanced to support efficient querying of triple patterns [23]. This versatility has allowed HDT to be adopted as backend for many tools in the Semantic Web community, such as Triple Pattern Fragments for client-based triple pattern querying over the Web [34], in natural language query answering systems such as WDAqua-core1 [9], or in SPARQL endpoints in commodity hardware [36]. It has also been used for data archiving [1,35], encoding one of the largest datasets from the LOD cloud (with more than 28 billion triples) [10], and for efficiently computing the PageRank summarization of datasets [8], among other applications.

HDT transforms the RDF graph into two main elements, illustrated in Fig. 3, which are then independently encoded to remove their respective redundancies: (i) the *dictionary*, which maps each RDF term used in the dataset (*i.e.*, its vocabulary) to a unique integer ID, and (ii) the *ID-graph*, which replaces the original terms in the RDF graph by their corresponding IDs in the dictionary.

---

[3] https://cambridgesemantics.com/anzograph/.
[4] https://www.blazegraph.com/.
[5] http://graphdb.ontotext.com/.
[6] https://www.stardog.com/.

That is, each triple is transformed into a tuple of 3-integer IDs (*ID-triples*): $< id_s, id_p, id_o >$; where id_s, id_p, and id_o are the IDs of the subject, predicate, and object in the dictionary, respectively.

HDT Dictionary. HDT proposes a practical dictionary implementation, called *Four Section Dictionary*, where each section *SO*, *S*, *O*, and *P* is independently sorted and compressed using Front Coding [24]. In this way, each section has its own mapping to exclusively identify its terms:

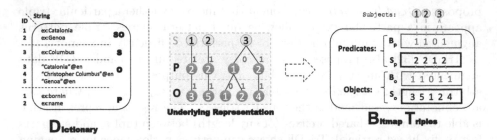

Fig. 3. HDT Dictionary and Triples components

- The section *SO* maps shared *subjects-objects* (*i.e.*, terms that play both subject and object roles) to $[1, |SO|]$, where $|SO|$ is the number of RDF terms that appear as subject and object in the set of triples.
- The section *S* maps single *subjects* (not appearing as objects) to $[|SO| + 1, |SO| + |S|]$, where $|S|$ is the number of RDF terms that act only as subjects.
- The section *O* maps single *objects* (not appearing as subjects) to $[|SO| + 1, |SO| + |O|]$, where $|O|$ is the number of RDF terms that act only as objects.
- The section *P* maps *predicate* to $[1, |P|]$, where $|P|$ is the number of RDF terms that appear as predicate in the triples.

The number of RDF terms in each section and how they are serialized are stored in the HDT *Header*, together with other HDT metadata. Figure 3 (left) shows the resulting Dictionary for the example given in Fig. 1. Note that the mapping ID-term is implicitly encoded by the position of the term in its section.

The Dictionary is encoded using compact data structures [29], which self-index each section and efficiently resolve two main operations:

- *locate*(*term*, *role*) returns the unique ID for the given term and role (*subject*, *predicate*, or *object*), if their combination exists in the dictionary.
- *extract*(*id*, *role*) returns the term for the given ID and role, if their combination exists in the dictionary.

HDT Triples. They provide an interface for accessing the ID-graph using SPARQL triple patterns [33]. A practical implementation, called *Bitmap Triples*, transforms the ID-graph into a forest of three-level trees, where each tree is rooted by a subject ID with its adjacency list of predicates in the second level and, for each of them, the adjacency list of related objects in the third (leaf) level. Figure 3 (middle) illustrates this organization.

In practice, the entire SPO forest is then encoded using compact data structures [29] to ensure efficient data retrieval in minimal space. On the one hand, two *integer sequences* are used to encode each level of the forest: S_p for predicate IDs and S_o for object IDs. On the other hand, two *bitsequences* are used to encode the shape of each tree: B_p encodes the number of branches hanging from each subject, and B_o encodes the number of leaves in each branch. This is easily done by simply marking the last children of the parent node (in the previous level) with 1 bits and the rest with 0 bits. This is illustrated in Fig. 3 (right). Note that this representation allows each triple to be identified by the position of its object in S_o, a fundamental feature for building HDTr, as described in the next section.

All structures used in Bitmap Triples support positional access to their values, and bitsequences provide two additional operations, which are essential for traversing the SPO forest:

- $rank_a(B, i)$ counts the number of occurrences of $a \in \{0, 1\}$ in $B[1, i]$, for any $1 \leq i \leq n$; $rank_a(B, 0) = 0$.
- $select_a(B, j)$ returns the position of the jth occurrence of $a \in \{0, 1\}$ in B, for any $1 \leq j \leq n$; $select_a(B, 0) = 0$ and $select_a(B, j) = n+1$, if $j > rank_a(B, n)$.

Bitmap Triples is able to resolve the four SPARQL triple patterns binding the subject[7]: (s,p,o), (s,p,?o), (s,?p,o), and (s,?p,?o). First, it translates the bound terms in the triple pattern to their corresponding IDs: $< id_s, id_p, id_o >$, using the Dictionary locate(term,role) method, and then traverses the $id_s{}^{th}$ tree, as follows:

1. Predicates related to the subject id_s are located at $S_p[p_x, p_y]$, $p_x = select_1(B_p, id_s - 1) + 1$ and $p_y = select_1(B_p, id_s)$. If the predicate is bound, id_p is binary searched in $S_p[p_s, p_y]$, returning pos_p if there is any triple connecting id_s and id_p ($p_x \leq pos_p \leq p_y$).
2. Objects related to a pair $< id_s, id_p >$ are located at $S_o[o_x, o_y]$, $o_x = select_1(B_o, pos_p - 1) + 1$ and $o_y = select_1(B_o, pos_p)$. If the object is also bound, id_o is binary searched in $S_o[o_x, o_y]$, returning pos_o if the triple $< id_s, id_p, id_o >$ exists in the graph ($o_x \leq pos_o \leq o_y$).

Finally, the original terms in the returned triples are retrieved using the existing *extract*(*id, role*) method in the Dictionary.

Note that the pattern (?s,?p,?o), which returns all existing triples, can also be resolved by traversing all trees sequentially and retrieving the original terms from the Dictionary. To resolve the remaining triple patterns with unbound subject (*i.e.*, (?s,p,o), (?s,p,?o), and (?s,?p,o)), *HDT-FoQ* (HDT Focused on Querying) [23] extends Bitmap Triples with additional structures, which ensure efficient predicate- and object-based retrieval while keeping the Triples component in compressed form.

---

[7] ? is used to indicate variables in the triple pattern.

5   Extending HDT for Reified Triples: HDTr

In this section we present HDTr, a binary serialization for reified statements. HDTr takes advantage of the structure of the Triples component in HDT, where an RDF statement is implicitly identified by the position of its object in S_o, to connect reified statements with their anchors in the Dictionary. HDTr files are backward compatible with HDT, so HDTr can be easily adopted by existing HDT-based applications that need to manage reified triples.

Table 2. Five Section Dictionary configuration

Section	IDs	
SO $= SO_T \cup SO_A$	$[1, |SO|]$,	where $SO = |SO_T| + |SO_A|$
S $= S_T \cup S_A$	$[|SO + 1|, |SO + S|]$,	where $|S| = |S_T| + |S_A|$
O $= O_T \cup O_A$	$[|SO + 1|, |SO + O|]$,	where $|O| = |O_T| + |O_A|$
P $= P_T$,	$[1, |P|]$,	where $|P| = |P_T|$
A $= SO_A \cup S_A \cup O_A \cup U_A$	$[1, |A|]$,	where $|A| = |SO_A| + |S_A| + |O_A| + |U_A|]$

5.1   The HDTr Dictionary

Reified statements include terms used as anchors, which can then be used in the subject and/or object position in contextual annotation triples. The HDTr Dictionary extends the logical model of the Four Section Dictionary into a *Five Section Dictionary*, adding a new section for the anchors, referred to as A, while preserving SO, S, O and P, which now encode the terms used in regular and contextual triples, according to their respective roles.

The Five Section Dictionary is implemented in practice as two subdictionaries. On the one hand, the *Triples Dictionary* rearranges all terms that do not play as anchors in a Four Section Dictionary: SO_T, S_T, O_T, and P_T.[8]. This component is essential to ensure HDT and HDTr compatibility. On the other hand, the *Anchors Dictionary* manages only anchor terms, so they are organized in sections for shared subject-objects, subjects and objects: SO_A, S_A, and O_A, as well as U_A for "unused" anchors (*i.e.*, not used as terms in any triple).[9]. At the physical level, each section of both subdictionaries is also compressed using Front Coding [24], as in HDT, so it is lexicographically sorted before encoding it. This decision also ensures that $locate(element, role)$ and $extract(id, role)$ operations are performed efficiently in all dictionary sections.

Figure 4 (left) shows the resulting Five Section Dictionary and its corresponding implementation as two subdictionaries for our example. Note that all anchor terms (shown in Fig. 2) are organized in the section corresponding to their role in the contextual annotation triples, while the Triples subdictionary contains the same terms as the HDT Dictionary had for the non-reified statements (Fig. 3) plus the additional terms appearing in the contextual annotation (Table 2).

---

[8] The subscript T is added to the names of the sections to indicate that they belong to the Triples Dictionary.

[9] The subscript A refers to the Anchors Dictionary.

5.2   The HDTr Triples

The Triples component must handle the need of compactly connecting reified statements to their anchors. This can be done by identifying each triple by the position of its object in S_o; *i.e.*, the object of the ith triple is encoded at $S_o[i]$. This HDT feature allows reification to be efficiently implemented in the Triples component by adding two compact data structures: (i) a bitsequence B_a, that marks with 1 bits the positions corresponding to reified triples ($B_a[i] = 1$, *iff* the ith triple is reified); and (ii) a sequence P_a that encodes anchor IDs (in the Dictionary) for all reified triples. At the physical level, B_a is implemented as B_p and B_o in BitmapTriples, while P_a is implemented as a compact permutation [27] that provides two basic methods:

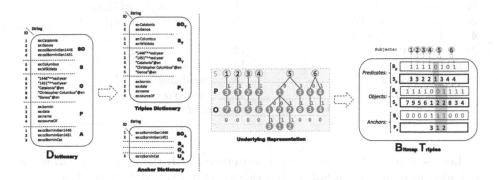

Fig. 4. HDTr Dictionary and Triples components

- $\pi(P_a, j)$: returns the value at $P_a[j]$; it allows to efficiently retrieve the anchor ID for the reified statement j^{th}.
- $\pi^{-1}(P_a, k)$: returns the position at where value k is stored in P_a; it allows to efficiently find the (reified) statement connected to the anchor with ID k.

It is worth noting the particular case where a triple $< id_s, id_p, id_o >$ is annotated with two or more different anchors. In this situation, each pair (triple, anchor) is considered as a different statement, and id_o is encoded in S_o as many times as anchors are related to the triple.

Figure 4 (right) illustrates the HDTr Triples configuration that encodes the statements from the running example. The "Underlying Representation" shows how (the 3rd, the 4th, and the 6th) statements are logically connected to their anchors, while the Anchors level (at the "Bitmap Triples" representation) illustrates its physical encoding; note that $B_a[3] = B_a[4] = B_a[6] = 1$ and $Pa[1] = 3$ because the first reified triple is connected to anchor 3, $Pa[2] = 2$ because the second reified triple is connected to anchor 2, and so on. For example, the highlighted statement states that *Christopher Columbus* (subject 5) *was born in* (predicate 1) *Genoa* (object 2), and it is identified with ex:ccBornInGen1446 (anchor 1) and ccBornInGen1451 (anchor 2).

5.3   Querying HDTr

HDT files can be loaded as HDTr files, so that all SPARQL triple patterns can be resolved efficiently. However, the HDT retrieval methods needs to be extended to query reified statements, *i.e.*, a query containing a triple pattern (tp) and an anchor (a), where any component of tp and a can be a variable. Algorithm 1 describes the proposed method for querying reified statements[10], with two main flows depending on whether the anchor is provided (Line 1–5) or not (Lines 6–18).

Algorithm 1. query(tp, a)

1: **if** *bound*(a) **then**	10: $pos_a \leftarrow rank_1(B_a, pos_t)$
2: $pos_a \leftarrow \pi^{-1}(P_a, a)$	11: $id_a \leftarrow \pi(P_a, pos_a)$
3: $pos_t \leftarrow select_1(B_a, pos_a)$	12: $r.add(t, id_a)$
4: $t \leftarrow check(pos_t, tp)$	13: **else**
5: **return**(t, a)	14: $r.add(t)$
6: **else**	15: **end if**
7: $T \leftarrow search(tp)$	16: **end for**
8: **for** $t \in T$ **do**	17: **return** r
9: **if** $(B_a[pos_t] = 1)$ **then**	18: **end if**

Let us suppose that we search a statement with the subject ex:Columbus and identified by the anchor ex:ccBornInGen1451 $(tp =< 5, ?p, ?o >, a = 2)$. Intuitively, we need to navigate the tree in Fig. 4 (right) from bottom (once we locate the anchor) to top (the subject). In line 2, the anchor ID is used to find its single occurrence in P_a: $pos_a \leftarrow \pi^{-1}(P_a, 2) = 3$ and then, in line 3, its reified statement is obtained from B_a: $pos_t \leftarrow select_1(B_a, 3) = 7$. The pos_t is then used to traverse up the tree encoding the triple (as in HDT [23]), checking that the variables are satisfied (line 4); all variables in tp are bound to their corresponding IDs $(?p = 1, ?o = 2)$ and the result is returned (line 5), as $(< 5, 1, 2 >; 2)$.

In the second case, let us suppose that we search the *birth place* of *Christopher Columbus* and all related annotations $(tp =< 5, 1, ?o >, a = ?a)$. In this situation, we proceed top to bottom in Fig. 4 (right), so tp is first searched (line 7) using the original HDT methods [23]. Note that, in HDT, for each matching triple t (line 8), its position, pos_t, is immediately known, *e.g.*, <5,1,1> has position 5. Thus, the algorithm iterates over each matching triple and checks if it is reified (line 9); otherwise the triple is returned with no anchor value (line 14). In our example, three statements are annotated: $B_a[5] = B_a[6] = B_a[7] = 1$. In line 10, the anchor of the triple is identified in B_a (for the first triple, $pos_a \leftarrow rank_1(B_a, 5) = 1$) and its ID is retrieved from P_a in line 11 $(id_a \leftarrow \pi(P_a, 1) = 3)$. Finally, the matching triple and anchor are added to the resultset, in our example $(< 3, 1, 1 >; 3), (< 3, 1, 2 >; 1), (< 3, 1, 2 >; 2)$.

---

[10] For the sake of simplicity, we assume that tp and a have previously mapped to IDs and, conversely, the returned resultset is then mapped to their corresponding terms.

6 Evaluation

HDTr extends the theoretical specification of HDT to incorporate reified triples, including a dictionary interface separate from the implementation, and retrieval algorithms. The implementation itself makes several design choices: using two subdictionaries, leveraging the structure of Bitmap Triples by using the object positions to reference triples, using a permutation as a bidirectional link between anchors and triples, and adapted serialization and query algorithms. In this section, we analyze the performance of HDTr[11] and we evaluate the impact of these decisions against a selected state-of-the-art baseline. For that, we use data from *NELL* [5,26], a system that learns categories and relations from the Web, keeping track of their provenance. Specifically, we use *NELL2RDF* [15], which extracts the beliefs of NELL and their provenance contextual information into RDF. In order to test the impact of the proportion of reified triples, we create two evaluation scenarios: (i) we keep in the dataset all triples extracted from NELL, including their contextual annotations, to ensure a low proportion of refied statements *w.r.t.* the total number or triples ($reif_{CA}$ scenario); and (ii) we remove the contextual annotations, leaving only the reified triples, to achieve a high proportion of reified statements ($reif_\emptyset$ scenario). All KGs are generated using the reification functions provided by NELL2RDF: RDF reification (*Reif*), n-ary relations (*N-Ary*), singleton properties (*SP*), and NdFluents (*NdF*), as well as *n-quads*. Finally, we use three randomized slices of NELL's beliefs: the *full* dataset, *half* of the statements, and a *quarter* of the statements, with the goal of testing the scalability of our design choices. The resulting KGs are described in Table 3, showing the number of statements per dataset, its size, and either

Table 3. Summary of NELL2RDF datasets (in # millions of statements, GB, and percentage)

File		Full Data			Half Data			Quarter Data		
		#	Size	Prop.	#	Size	Prop.	#	Size	Prop.
Reif	$reif_{CA}$	1,069.6	239.2	8.00%	551.7	123.1	8.16%	284.2	63.3	8.23%
	$reif_\emptyset$	113.7	21.5	75.26%	59.7	11.3	75.37%	31.0	5.8	75.42%
N-Ary	$reif_{CA}$	1,012.7	229.1	2.84%	521.8	117.8	2.91%	268.7	60.5	2.93
	$reif_\emptyset$	56.8	11.4	50.52%	29.9	6.0	50.75%	15.5	3.1	50.85
SP	$reif_{CA}$	1,041.1	234.4	5.49%	536.7	120.6	5.61%	276.4	62.0	5.65%
	$reif_\emptyset$	85.3	16.7	67.01%	44.8	8.7	67.16%	23.2	4.5	67.23%
NdF	$reif_{CA}$	1173.3	254.0	16.14%	600.7	130.0	15.65%	308.3	66.6	15.40%
	$reif_\emptyset$	217.5	36.3	87.07%	108.7	18.1	86.47%	55.1	9.2	86.17%
Quads	$reif_{CA}$	984.0	224.6	2.18%	506.6	115.4	2.90%	260.8	59.3	2.92%
	$reif_\emptyset$	28.1	6.9	100%	14.7	3.6	2.90%	7.6	1.8	2.92%

---

[11] We use a HDTr prototype implemented in C++. See the supplemental material statement at the end of the document.

the proportion of triples that are generated by the reification function or the proportion of quads in the dataset.

We first assess the performance of HDTr with respect to encoding with HDT[12] the KG resulting from the application of any reification function. This is an important comparison because HDTr files can directly replace HDT files in applications that use reified KGs.

We then measure space-time tradeoffs of HDTr against some well-known triplestores. Arguably, HDT and HDTr are not directly comparable with triplestores, since they are production systems that include additional overheads to fully conform to SPARQL (including datatype filter expressions). However, this evaluation allows us to show in a quantitative way how an index such as HDTr compares with those used in such triplestores, as well as to position HDTr in the context of similar HDT comparisons. The triplestore experiments were made loading and querying quads, using named graphs to store the anchor, since this is reportedly the most efficient approach for triplestores to manage reified triples [19,20].

HDTQ and TrieDF were also included in the planned evaluation, but HDTQ failed in all the experiments performed due to memory limitations,[13] while the published code of TrieDF does not allow to serialize files different to those provided for their experiments.

All experiments were performed in a cluster in which the same resources are always reserved: 2 cores and 320 GB of RAM. The same installation and configuration is used for HDT, HDTr, and all triplestores, which received basic optimizations to use the reserved resources according to the instructions by their publishers. To avoid as much skew as possible, we report the average of 10 independent executions.

6.1 HDTr vs. HDT

We first compare HDTr with its counterpart HDT in terms of space requirements and retrieval performance.

Space Requirements. Figure 5 compares the space requirements of HDTr with those of HDT for all reification functions in the two $reif_{CA}$ and $reif_\emptyset$ scenarios: Figs. 5 a-b compare the size of the serialized KG, whereas Figs. 5 c-d report the size of the indexes required for efficient triple pattern resolution [23].

HDTr clearly outperforms HDT in the $reif_\emptyset$ scenario, because it represents the same information with fewer triples and encodes them more compactly. We can observe that the size of the HDTr files is smaller than the HDT files with any

---

[12] We use the HDT C++ library. Please find the concrete forked version and additional details in the supplemental material statement specified at the end of this document.

[13] Our hypothesis is that HDTQ was designed to encode named graphs, making assumptions (*e.g.*, the proportion of named graphs to triples or the use of named graphs as terms in statements) that have a negative impact in its ability to encode reified statements.

contextualization approach, ranging 6% for n-ary relations to 237% for NdFluents. The difference for the indexes is even more pronounced, going from 263% to 1461% for the same approaches. However, if we look at $reif_{CA}$ scenario, we see that the HDTr and the HDT files for RDF reification and n-ary relations have similar size, and the space savings for the singleton property and NdFluents have been reduced. Index sizes are also lower for HDTr, although to a lesser extent than in the $reif_\emptyset$ case. This shows that the HDTr savings, due to its additional structures to identify reified statements by its position and connect them with their anchor in the dictionary, are proportional to the number of statements that are reified and the number of triples introduced by each reification function.

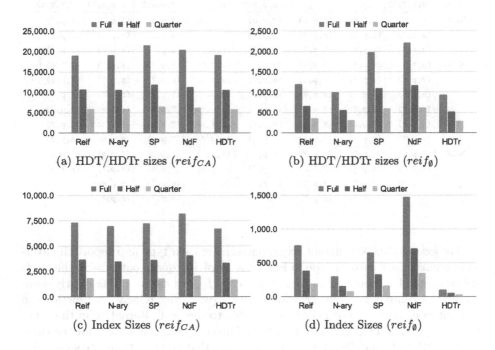

Fig. 5. Size of HDT and HDTr files and their indexes (in MB)

Retrieval Performance. HDTr is able to identify reified triples and connect them with their anchor in the dictionary thanks to the additional bitsequence and permutation. This allows to efficiently obtain a triple and its anchor with a single quad pattern. However, HDT needs to translate them into a set of triple patterns, depending on the reification approach that they encode. Table 4 lists the set of triple patterns that must be resolved to answer the equivalent quad pattern for each reification function; for example, to resolve the pattern (s,?,?,?), which asks for all statements related to subject s and their anchors, *HDT+Reif* resolves (?,rdf:subject,s) to get the anchors of the statement (corresponding to the pattern type (?,p,o) in the table) and then (a,rdf:predicate, ?) and (a,rdf:object,?) for each anchor (corresponding to the pattern type (s,p,?) twice). To estimate a lower bound for HDT, we compute, for each triple, the average retrieval time for each triple pattern, and sum together the times for all of them, ignoring the cost of the joint operations. Note that this is an optimistic estimate in favor of HDT. We then average this time and compare it to the average retrieval time of a quad pattern type for the same set of statements in HDTr.

Table 4. Types of patterns needed to obtain a triple and its anchor

Quad	(s,?,?,?)	(?,p,?,?)	(?,?,o,?)	(s,p,?,?)	(s,?,o,?)	(?,p,o,?)	(s,p,o,?)	(?,?,?,a)
Reif	(?,p,o)	(?,p,o)	(?,p,o)	(?,p,o)	(?,p,o)	(?,p,o)	(?,p,o)	(s,p,?)
	(s,p,?)	(s,p,?)	(s,p,?)	(s,p,o)	(s,p,?)	(s,p,o)	(s,p,o)	(s,p,?)
	(s,p,?)	(s,p,?)	(s,p,?)	(s,p,?)	(s,p,?)	(s,p,?)	(s,p,o)	(s,p,?)
N-Ary	(s,?,?)	(s,p,?)	(?,?,o)	(s,p,?)	(s,?,?)	(s,p,?)	(s,p,?)	(?,?,o)
	(?,p,o)	(s,p,?)	(?,p,o)	(s,p,?)	(s,?,?)	(s,p,?)	(s,p,?)	(?,p,o)
	(s,p,?)	(?,p,?)	(s,p,?)	(s,p,?)	(s,p,?)	(?,p,o)	(s,p,?)	(s,p,?)
	(s,p,?)	(s,p,?)	(?,p,o)	(s,p,?)	(s,p,?)	(?,p,o)	(s,p,o)	(s,p,?)
SP	(s,?,?)	(?,p,o)	(?,?,o)	(s,p,?)	(s,?,o)	(?,p,o)	(?,p,o)	(?,p,?)
	(s,p,?)	(?,p,?)	(?,p,o)	(?,p,o)	(s,p,?)	(?,p,o)	(s,p,o)	(s,p,?)
NdF	(?,p,o)	(?,p,?)	(s,p,?)	(?,p,o)	(?,p,o)	(s,p,o)	(?,p,o)	(?,p,o)
	(s,?,?)	(s,p,?)	(?,?,o)	(s,p,?)	(?,p,o)	(?,p,o)	(s,p,?)	(s,?,o)
	(s,p,?)	(s,p,?)	(s,p,?)	(s,p,?)	(s,?,o)	(s,p,?)	(s,p,o)	
		(s,p,?)	(s,p,?)	(s,p,?)	(s,p,?)	(s,p,?)	(s,p,?)	

We extract 10,000 different triple patterns of each type and report the average execution per pattern type in Fig. 7 for resolving query patterns in the $reif_\emptyset$ scenario (similar results are obtained in the $reif_{CA}$ scenario). HDTr clearly dominates the comparison, outperforming HDT (with any reification function) in five out of eight cases and being comparable to the best alternative in the other three: (s,?,o,?), (s,p,o), and (?,?,?,a). The comparison is similar for the three slices (*Full*, *Half*, and *Quarter*), demonstrating that HDTr retains the scalability features of HDT.

6.2   HDTr vs. Triplestores

We now compare HDTr against a representative baseline of four well-known triplestores: Virtuoso 7.2.6, Blazegraph 11.0.19, GraphDB 8.8.1, and Fuseki 3.10, using the quads datasets for all of them. Comparison is also performed in terms of space requirements and retrieval performance.

Space Requirements. Fig. 6 compares the space requirements of HDTr (including data and indexes) with respect to the evaluated triplestores. HDTr dominates the comparison in both scenarios. *HDTr* exploits its compressibility and uses more than 3 times less space than *Virtuoso* (for the *Full* slice) but up to 13 times less space than *Blazegraph* or *Fuseki*. These numbers demonstrate HDTr's ability to save disk space, which in turn enable scalable and efficient in-memory data management.

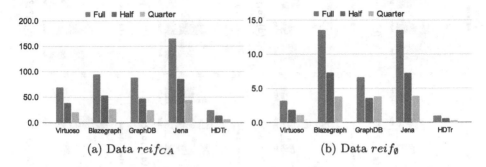

(a) Data $reif_{CA}$ (b) Data $reif_{\emptyset}$

Fig. 6. Size of HDTr files and triplestores data (in GB)

Retrieval performance. Figure 8 reports query times for HDTr and the triplestores in the $reif_{\emptyset}$ scenario, using a testbed containing 10,000 randomly generated quad patterns, as explained earlier. HDTr's performance is clearly superior for seven out of eight patterns, with reported query times between 2 and 4 orders of magnitude faster, depending on the pattern and the triplestore. HDTr shows slower performance only with the pattern (?,p,?,?), which is a known weakness of HDT [21]. The same conclusions can be drawn for the $reif_{CA}$ scenario, and are consistent with the previous results comparing HDT and triplestores [23], confirming that HDTr is able to compete with the most prominent state-of-the-art solutions with guarantees.

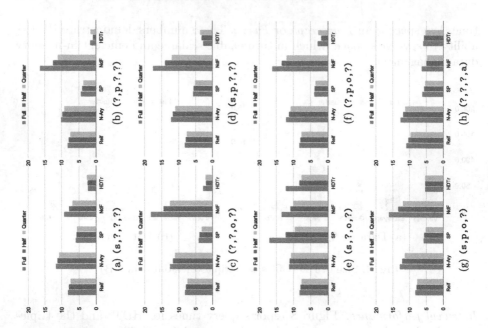

Fig. 7. HDTr vs HDT estimated retrieval time (in μs.)

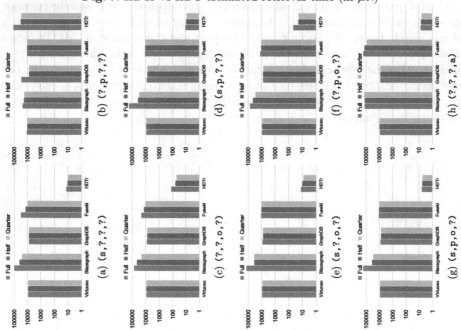

Fig. 8. HDTr vs triplestores quad retrieval time (in μs.)

7   Conclusions and Future Work

This work presents HDTr, an extension of HDT to serialize reified statements in a model-agnostic binary representation that is compact and queryable. Our proposal is HDT compatible and leverages its current compact structures to make a connection between the reified statements and the anchors to their contextual annotations. Our evaluation against four triplestores, Virtuoso, Blazegraph, GraphDB, and Jena Fuseki, shows that HDTr is between two and four orders of magnitude faster than all triplestores when querying for reified triples for all patterns patterns but one, keeping the compelling compression (at least 350% gains) and loading results of HDT.

As future work, we plan to leverage, even more, the existing redundancies in the data. First, we aim at exploring the possibility of splitting the reified and non-reified statements in the HDT components. Then, we plan to extend HDTr with the option of not storing anchors terms that are merely a placeholder. This would be specially useful for reification approaches where this is given (such as RDF-star). Extensions for full SPARQL resolution and using HDTr as a support to convert between different reification approaches are also considered.

Supplemental Material Statement: Source code is available at https://github. com/jm-gimenez-garcia/hdtr-cpp. The HDT source code at fork time is available at https://github.com/jm-gimenez-garcia/hdtr-cpp/tree/base. Data and instructions to replicate the evaluation, as well as additional experimental results on loading times, are available at https://doi.org/10.6084/m9.figshare.22787495.

Acknowledgments. This work has been partially funded by the Spanish Ministry of Science and Innovation through LOD.For.Trees (TED2021-130667B-I00), EXTRA-Compact (PID2020-114635RB-I00), and PLAGEMIS-UDC (TED2021-129245B-C21) projects, and from the EU H2020 research and innovation program under the Marie Skłodowska-Curie grant No 642795.

References

1. Beek, W., Rietveld, L., Bazoobandi, H.R., Wielemaker, J., Schlobach, S.: LOD laundromat: a uniform way of publishing other people's dirty data. In: ISWC (2014)
2. Berners-Lee, T., Connolly, D.: Notation3 (N3): A readable RDF syntax. W3C (2011)
3. Briandais, R.D.L.: File searching using variable length keys. In: IRE-AIEE-ACM (1959)
4. Brickley, D., Guha, R.V.: RDF vocabulary description language 1.0: RDF schema. In: W3C (2004)
5. Carlson, A., Betteridge, J., Hruschka, E.R., Mitchell, T.M.: Coupling Semi-supervised Learning of Categories and Relations. In: SSLNLP (2009)
6. Carroll, J.J., Bizer, C., Hayes, P.J., Stickler, P.: Named graphs. JWS **3**(4), 247–267 (2005)
7. Cyganiak, R., Wood, D., Lanthaler, M.: RDF 1.1 concepts and abstract syntax. In: W3C (2014)

8. Diefenbach, D., Both, A., Singh, K., Maret, P.: Towards a question answering system over the Semantic Web. Semantic Web **11**(3), 421–439 (2020)
9. Diefenbach, D., Thalhammer, A.: PageRank and Generic Entity Summarization for RDF Knowledge Bases. In: ESWC (2018)
10. Fernández, J.D., Beek, W., Martínez-Prieto, M.A., Arias, M.: LOD-a-lot: a queryable dump of the LOD cloud. In: ISWC (2017)
11. Fernández, J.D., Martínez-Prieto, M.A., Gutiérrez, C., Polleres, A., Arias, M.: Binary RDF representation for publication and exchange (HDT). JWS **19**, 22–41 (2013)
12. Fernández, J.D., Martínez-Prieto, M.A., Polleres, A., Reindorf, J.: HDTQ: Managing RDF Datasets in Compressed Space. In: ESWC (2018)
13. Frey, J., Müller, K., Hellmann, S., Rahm, E., Vidal, M.-E.: Evaluation of metadata representations in RDF stores. SWJ **10**(2), 205–229 (2017)
14. Giménez-García, J.M., Duarte, M., Zimmermann, A., Gravier, C., Hruschka Jr., E.R., Maret, P.: NELL2RDF: Reading the web, tracking the provenance, and publishing it as linked data. In: CKG (2018)
15. Giménez-García, J.M., Zimmermann, A.: NdProperties: encoding contexts in RDF predicates with inference preservation. In: CKG (2018)
16. Giménez-García, J.M., Zimmermann, A., Maret, P.: NdFluents: an ontology for Annotated Statements with Inference Preservation. In: ESWC (2017)
17. Hartig, O., et al.: RDF-star and SPARQL-star. In: W3C (2021)
18. Hayes, P.J., Patel-Schneider, P.F.: RDF 1.1 semantics. In: W3C (2014)
19. Hernández, D., Hogan, A., Krötzsch, M.: Reifying RDF: What Works Well With Wikidata? SSWS (2015)
20. Hernández, D., Hogan, A., Riveros, C., Rojas, C., Zerega, E.: Querying Wikidata: Comparing SPARQL. Relational and Graph Databases, ISWC (2016)
21. Hernández-Illera, A., Martínez-Prieto, M.A., Fernández, J.D., Fariña, A.: iHDT++: improving HDT for SPARQL triple pattern resolution. JIFS **39**(2), 2249–2261 (2020)
22. Hogan, A., et al.: Knowledge Graphs. Springer, Cham (2021). https://doi.org/10.1007/978-3-031-01918-0
23. Martínez-Prieto, M., Arias, M., Fernández, J.: Exchange and consumption of huge RDF Data. In: ESWC (2012)
24. Martínez-Prieto, M.A., Brisaboa, N.R., Cánovas, R., Claude, F., Navarro, G.: Practical compressed string dictionaries. IS **56**, 73–108 (2016)
25. Martínez-Prieto, M.A., Fernández, J.D., Hernández-Illera, A., Gutierrez, C.: Knowledge graph compression for big semantic data. In: Encyclopedia of Big Data Technologies (2022)
26. Mitchell, T.M., et al.: Never-ending learning. In: AAAI (2015)
27. Munro, J.I., Raman, R., Raman, V., Rao, S.S.: Succinct representations of permutations and functions. TCS **438**, 74–88 (2012)
28. Nardi, D., Brachman, R.J.: An Introduction to Description Logics. Theory, Implementation, and Applications, The Description Logic Handbook (2003)
29. Navarro, G.: Compact Data Structures - A Practical Approach. Cambridge University Press, Cambridge (2016)
30. Nguyen, V., Bodenreider, O., Sheth, A.: Don't like RDF reification?: Making statements about statements using singleton property. In: WWW (2014)
31. Noy, N., Rector, A., Hayes, P., Welty, C.: Defining N-ary relations on the semantic web. In: W3C (2006)
32. Pelgrin, O.P., Hose, K., Galárraga, L.: TrieDF: Efficient in-memory indexing for metadata-augmented RDF. In: MEPDaW (2021)

33. Prud'hommeaux, E., Seaborne, A.: SPARQL Query Language for RDF (2008)
34. Verborgh, R., et al.: Triple pattern fragments: a low-cost knowledge graph interface for the web. JWS **37–38**, 184–206 (2016)
35. Verborgh, R., Vander Sande, M., Shankar, H., Balakireva, L., Van de Sompel, H.: Devising affordable and functional linked data archives. TCDL. **13**(1), 1–8 (2017)
36. Willerval, A., Diefenbach, D., Bonifati, A.: qEndpoint: A Wikidata SPARQL endpoint on commodity hardware. WWW_Demo (2023)

Causal Inference-Based Debiasing Framework for Knowledge Graph Completion

Lin Ren, Yongbin Liu$^{(\boxtimes)}$, and Chunping Ouyang

University of South China, Hengyang, China
yongbinliu03@gmail.com

Abstract. The task of Knowledge Graph Completion (KGC) entails inferring missing relations and facts in a partially specified graph to discover new knowledge. However, the discrepancy in the targets between the training and inference phases might lead to in-depth bias and in-breadth bias during inference, potentially resulting in incorrect outcomes. In this work, we conduct a comprehensive analysis of these biases to determine their extent of impact. To mitigate these biases, we propose a novel debiasing framework called Causal Inference-based Debiasing Framework for KGC (CIDF) by formulating a causal graph and utilizing it for causal analysis of KGC tasks. The framework incorporates In-Depth Bias Mitigation to diminish the bias on feature representations by measuring the bias during inference, and In-Breadth Bias Mitigation to increase the distinguishability between feature representations by introducing a novel loss function. We evaluate the effectiveness of our proposed method on four benchmark datasets - WN18RR, FB15k-237, Wikidata5M-Trans, and Wikidata5M-Ind, achieving improvements of 2.5%, 0.9%, 3.2%, and 1.5% on Hit@1 respectively. Our results demonstrate that CIDF leads to significant improvements on these datasets, with more substantial gains observed in the biased settings on WN18RR achieving a 3.4% improvement in Hit@1.

Keywords: Knowledge Graph Completion · Causal Inference · Link Prediction

1 Introduction

Knowledge Graphs (KGs) are structured representations of factual knowledge, currently often represented by triples consisting of head entities, relations, and tail entities, as well as their descriptions. They are widely applied in various fields, such as question answering [9,48], dialogue systems [13,24], recommender systems [38,42], and so on. Some examples of available KGs include WordNet [23], Freebase [1], and DBpedia [18]. Building high-quality KGs often relies on human-curated structured or semi-structured data. Although many resources have been expended to refine the KGs, they remain incomplete.

© The Author(s), under exclusive license to Springer Nature Switzerland AG 2023
T. R. Payne et al. (Eds.): ISWC 2023, LNCS 14265, pp. 328–347, 2023.
https://doi.org/10.1007/978-3-031-47240-4_18

Knowledge Graph Completion (KGC) is a vital task for constructing and enhancing KGs, as it involves inferring missing factual triples. Existing KGC methods generally consist of three steps: firstly, formulating a score function to measure the plausibility of triples; secondly, learning representations of entities and relations from established knowledge graphs by optimizing the scores of all factual triples; finally, using the score function to measure the plausibility of the missing triples (either a relation or entity is unknown) given the rest of the information [45], such as TransE [2], RotatE [34], HAKE [49], and ConvE [7]. In addition, due to the powerful semantic acquisition capability of Pre-training Language Models (PLMs) [8,11,31], some KGC approaches use PLMs as Knowledge Bases to leverage the semantic information from the descriptions of entities and relations such as KEPLER [39] and SimKGC [37].

However, since the training strategy for KGC tasks aims to obtain feature representations of entities and relations that fit the original knowledge graph, the process's positive and negative selection depends solely on the original knowledge graph's structure, which can often increase the correlation among factual triples' entities and relations while decreasing the correlation between those that are not within factual triples. In other words, within the knowledge graph (KG), the homophily and structural equivalence of labeled nodes and edges cause feature representations to be more sensitive to connection patterns among structurally equivalent or homophilic nodes and edges during the training process [12]. This often leads to spurious correlations in the features, creating a preference for certain connection patterns during the inference process. Additionally, the entities associated with a large number of other entities may be more likely to receive preferences in KG inference. In this study, we term the preference as **Structure Preference**, which results in the dissemination of correlation through two distinct mechanisms: in-depth diffusion and in-breadth aggregation.

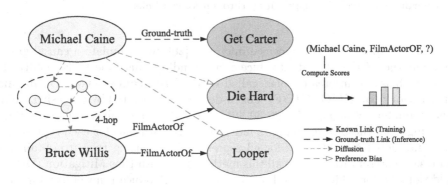

Fig. 1. A simple example from dataset FB15k-237 [35] for **in-depth bias**. *Diffusion* means the correlation diffusion along known links.

In the context of in-depth diffusion, the phenomenon may introduce a bias, which arises from the diffusion of correlation along relations between distantly connected entities. As shown in Fig. 1, there will be a relatively high correlation between *Michael Caine* and *Bruce Willis* after training. As a result, the prediction for the triple *(Michael Caine, FilmActorOf, ?)* is inaccurately classified as *Lopper* or *Die Hard* instead of the ground-truth prediction of *Get Carter*. We refer to this phenomenon as **in-depth bias**.

In the context of in-breadth aggregation, the entities tend to aggregate information from the neighboring entities and their corresponding relations. As a consequence of the training objective, the feature representations of entities will display a higher degree of similarity if there are similar bipartite graph structures between two head entities in a certain relation and a large overlap of tail entities for this relation in the knowledge graph. This phenomenon, termed **in-breadth bias**, results in prediction biases during inference. As shown in Fig. 2, *Michael Caine* and *Joseph Gordon-Levitt* have similar topological structures, and if we want to extend the *FilmActorOf* relation for these two entities, their outcomes will exhibit a high degree of similarity, which could potentially lead to errors.

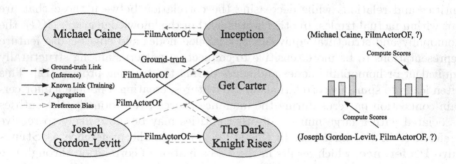

Fig. 2. A simple example from dataset FB15k-237 [35] for **in-breadth bias**. *Aggregation* means the correlation aggregation through known links.

In this paper, inspired by causal inference [28], we formulate a causal graph to model the KGC task and introduce corresponding causal methods to mitigate in-depth bias and in-breadth bias, called **Causal Inference-based Debiasing Framework for KGC (CIDF)**. For in-depth bias, inspired by debiasing methods of counterfactual analysis [26,30,40], we leverage the trained representations suffering from the bias to compute individual in-depth bias for each representation and global in-depth bias for all representations, using them to obtain the debiased representations. We call this method In-Depth Bias Mitigation (DBM). Additionally, for addressing in-breadth bias, we introduce a novel loss function in the training phase to reduce the similarity among feature representations, enhancing the distinguishability of different entities and relations. We call this method In-Breadth Bias Mitigation (BBM).

We evaluate the effectiveness of our proposed CIDF on four commonly used datasets, namely WN18RR, FB15k-237, Wikidata5M-Trans, and Wikidata5M-Ind, through a series of experiments. By applying CIDF to SimKGC [37], we observe improved performance across all evaluation metrics, including MRR, Hit@1, Hit@3, and Hit@10, with improvements of 2.5%, 0.9%, 3.2%, and 1.5%, respectively, over the Hit@1 baseline on the aforementioned datasets. Notably, our framework shows greater improvement in a biased setting.

2   Related Work

2.1   Knowledge Graph Completion

Knowledge graph completion (KGC) involves automatically inferring missing or uncertain facts in a given knowledge graph. Different models have been proposed to tackle this problem, such as translational models like TransE [2], TransH [41], and RotatE [34], which interpret relations as translation or rotation operations, and tensor decompositional models like RESCAL [27], DistMult [43], and ComplEx [14,17,36], which treat KGC as a tensor factorization problem. More recent approaches, such as LP-BERT [19], KEPLER [39], and SimKGC [37], attempt to exploit textual information. However, the majority of the above models focus on acquiring feature representations to fit original KGs and fail to consider in-depth bias and in-breadth bias.

2.2   Bias in Knowledge Graph

Entity and relation representations in a knowledge graph are obtained by statistically fitting existing facts and summarizing their distributional characteristics [16]. Consequently, the representation may be influenced by biases introduced through the use of statistical methods. Several works have emerged with a focus on mitigating biases in knowledge graphs. Some of these works include [20,33,50], which concentrate on mitigating the degree bias; [3,10], which address gender bias reduction; [21,32], which consider sensitive information in KGs; and [15], which aims to detect biases automatically. In this work, we concentrate on in-depth bias and in-breadth bias, and propose a method to mitigate them.

2.3   Causal Inference

Causal inference is a statistical technique that enables the identification of causal relationships between variables in complex systems. This method has found extensive applications in various fields, including semantic segmentation [46], video grounding [25], stable learning [47], text classification [30], medical Q&A [44], and information extraction [26,40]. Recently, causal inference has also been employed in KGC, such as KGCF [4] which utilizes causal inference for data augmentation on NBFNet [52] to achieve improvement. Additionally, GEAR [21] and CFLP [51] have introduced counterfactual inference in KGC, demonstrating substantial enhancements in performance. In this work, we employ causal inference to mitigate in-depth and in-breadth biases present in KGC tasks.

3 Preliminaries

This section intends to offer a comprehensive overview of the notation employed, the inference process of knowledge graph completion methods, and the specific setting selected for this study.

3.1 Notation

We denote a Knowledge Graph as $G = (E, R, T)$, where E represents the set of entities, R refers to the set of relations, and T is the set of triples that constitute the knowledge graph. A triple consists of a head entity, a relation, and a tail entity, $(head\ entity, relation, tail\ entity)$, where the head entity is the initiator of the relation and the tail entity is the recipient of the relation, in which the order of the two entities cannot be reversed. To simplify the description, h, r, and t are used to represent $head\ entity$, $relation$, and $tail\ entity$, respectively, with (h, r, t) denoting a triple.

The evaluation protocol for entity ranking has gained widespread adoption in the field of KGC, which aims to rank all entities based on their relevance to a given entity and relation pair. Specifically, KGC tasks include tail entity prediction, represented as $(h, r, ?)$, and head entity prediction, represented as $(?, r, t)$. To reformulate $(?, r, t)$ as $(t, r^{-1}, ?)$, where r^{-1} is the inverse relation of r, we can focus solely on tail entity prediction task [22].

3.2 Inference Process of KGC Methods

KGC methods propose various scoring functions to optimize entity and relation representations. These methods strive to learn representations that capture the underlying semantic information in the knowledge graph, facilitating more accurate predictions of missing factual triples. To offer a thorough understanding of these methods, we present an overview of several KGC approaches below.

TransE [2] is a traditional translational method for representation learning in knowledge representation, which considers relation as translational operations. To achieve this, the optimization target in the training phase is the minimization of the distance between the expected tail entity and the translated head entity after applying the relation representation, expecting $h + r = t$ established finally if (h, r, t) is a missing factual triple. In RotatE [34], relations between entities are modeled as rotation operations within complex space, with the primary goal of satisfying the equation $h \odot r = t$ where $\odot$ denotes the Hadamard product. SimKGC [37] employs the BERT [8] model to extract the fusion feature of the head entity and relation, denoted as f_{hr}, and the representation of the tail entity, denoted as f_t. The objective of SimKGC is to maximize the similarity between f_{hr} and f_t. Table. 1 presents a comprehensive overview of the score functions utilized by the KGC methods outlined above.

To guarantee a clear causal analysis and modeling process, we opt for the SimKGC framework as the fundamental setting due to its simplicity and effectiveness. Employing this framework as a foundation allows us to build upon it for comprehensive analysis and modeling.

Table 1. Score functions for KGC methods. Where $cossim(\cdot)$ means cosine similarity function, and ↑ indicates that higher values are better.

Methods	Score Function ↑
TransE [2]	$-\|h + r - t\|_{l_1/l_2}$
RotatE [34]	$-\|h \odot r - t\|$
SimKGC [37]	$cossim(f_{hr}, f_t)$

4 Methodology

4.1 Bias Analysis

The majority of KGC techniques rely on crafted scoring functions to act as optimization targets for learning entity and relation representations. Typically, these methods partition the data into two distinct groups: positive samples, which correspond to triples that present in the knowledge graph, and negative samples, which correspond to non-existent triples, and then they seek to maximize the aggregate score of all positive samples while minimizing the aggregate score of all negative samples, as shown in Eq. 1. This training process yields a learned representation of entities and relations that can then be used to determine the missing factual triples in the KG. By optimizing the scoring functions and learning robust entity and relation representations through machine learning, KGC methods have achieved significant success in accurately and efficiently inferring missing information to complement KGs.

$$\underset{Rep_E, Rep_R}{argmax} \sum_{(h,r,t) \in T} f(e_h, e_r, e_t) - \sum_{(h,r,t) \notin T} f(e_h, e_r, e_t) \tag{1}$$

Where $f(\cdot)$ denotes the score function, Rep_E and Rep_R represent representation sets of E and R respectively; T denotes factual triples of the training set; $e_h, e_t \in Rep_E$ are the representations of entities h and t; $e_r \in Rep_R$ is the representation of relation r.

However, optimizing the aforementioned objective may cause issues in KGC tasks. Specifically, the absent triples in the original knowledge graph are treated as negative samples, leading to their scores being diminished in the training process. This not only affects non-factual triples but also impacts missing factual triples. Additionally, the entities will be correlated during training if there are paths connecting them in the KG. Consequently, during the inference phase, given a task $(h, r, ?)$, the entities connected with h in the original KG will more likely receive high scores, while ineligible entities will receive relatively lower scores, resulting in an unfair issue as shown in Fig. 1. Although addressing this bias may be hard for the KGC methods which solely rely on the structure of KGs, such as TransE [2], it can be measured and mitigated in methods that leverage descriptions of entities and relations as additional information.

Furthermore, it's noteworthy that the aforementioned phenomenon may also present an additional issue when dealing with entities that exhibit similar topological structures within a KG. Consequently, given two tasks with the form $(h_1, r, ?)$ and $(h_2, r, ?)$, where h_1 is topologically similar to h_2, it is reasonable to expect that the outcomes of these tasks will exhibit significant similarity. Figure 2 shows a simple example of this issue, we call it **in-breadth bias** in this paper.

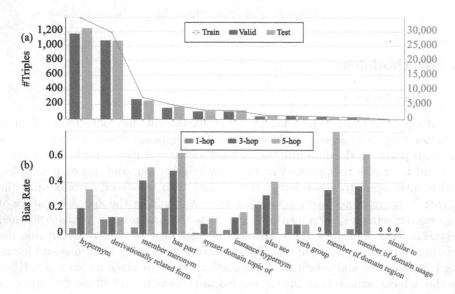

Fig. 3. The statistic of WN18RR where the x-axis represents relation names, noting that the x-axis for (a) and (b) is the same. (a) Quantity statistics for each relation in the dataset where the y-axis means the number of triples in train, validation, and test sets respectively. The red y-axis corresponds to the value of *Train*. (b) Bias statistic for each relation in the dataset where the y-axis means *bias rate* in different settings. (Color figure online)

In order to assess the degree of bias presented in KGs, we conduct a statistical analysis on datasets commonly used in KGC tasks. Specifically, we focus on the WN18RR dataset, which has been widely employed in KGC research with relatively few relations, as shown in Fig. 3. Firstly, we conduct an analysis of the quantity statistics and discovered a significant long-tail distribution among the relations in the dataset. In particular, as shown in Fig. 3(a), we observe that while the *hypernym* relation appears in tens of thousands of triples in the training set, the *similar to* relation appears only in tens of triples, and the proportions of relation numbers are similar in the validation and test sets. Moreover, to measure the degree of in-depth bias in KG datasets, we employ a function to quantify the *bias rate* of each relation as follows:

$$BiasCount_{r_i}^{hop} = \sum_{(h,r,t) \in Res_t} \mathbb{I}((h,r,t) \notin FT \wedge C(h,t,hop) \wedge r = r_i) \quad (2)$$

$$SampleCount_{r_i} = \sum_{(h,r,t)\in Res_t} \mathbb{I}((h,r,t) \notin FT \wedge r = r_i) \qquad (3)$$

$$BiasRate_{r_i}^{hop} = BiasCount_{r_i}^{hop}/SampleCount_{r_i} \qquad (4)$$

where $hop \in \{1,3,5\}$ denotes whether two entities are $\{1,3,5\}$-hop neighbors; $C(h,r,k)$ denotes an indicator function that the value is 1 if h and t are k-hop neighbors, 0 if not; $\mathbb{I}(\cdot)$ represents indicator function that the value is 1 if the condition holds, 0 if not; $r_i \in R$ denotes a specific relation; FT denotes the factual triples of the testing set; Res_t means the prediction results of the testing set from SimKGC framework; r^{-1} is viewed as the same relation type as r. In a nutshell, *bias rate* refers to the ratio of prediction tasks that may be impacted by in-depth bias during inference.

As depicted in Fig. 3, a significant proportion of relations in the WN18RR datasets may be affected by the issue of in-depth bias. This issue is especially pronounced for specific relations, such as *member meronym* and *has part* in the 3-hop setting. In the 5-hop context, these bias rates exhibit a greater increase.

4.2 Causal Analysis

As a foundation of causal analysis, we select SimKGC's framework [37], which has a relatively simple structure in inference, referring to $\underline{hr}$ as a fuse representation for h and r which is utilized to measure the rank of all entities. As shown in Fig. 4, we formulate a **causal graph** [28,29] for KGC tasks. The causal graph is denoted as a directed acyclic graph which consists of a variable set and a directed edge set, which can provide a comprehensive visualization of causal relationships.

In the causal graph, we consider the dependencies of feature representations of hr and t on both the training set (KG), which comprises the factual triples (topological structures) of the original KG, and the textual descriptions (S_{hr} and S_t), which define as the semantic information of hr and t. Furthermore, the score calculation (SC) of a given pair of hr and t is accomplished by utilizing their feature representations (F_{hr} and F_t).

The causal graph demonstrates that feature representation learning is affected not only by the structure of the knowledge but also by the semantic information of entities and relations. The biases that arise from in-depth and in-breadth both relate to the path $F_{hr} \leftarrow KG \rightarrow F_t$. Consequently, the mitigation of the above biases can be achieved by exerting influence over the aforementioned path.

4.3 In-Depth Bias Mitigation

The cause of in-depth bias in KGC tasks lies in the structural equivalence preference during training, where the correlation between entities and relations will gradually diffuse along links of KGs. Consequently, entities that are distant from each other may result in incorrect outcomes due to high correlations. This bias can be reduced by modifying the feature representations of hr according to the structure preference during inference.

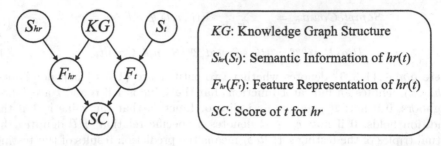

Fig. 4. The causal graph of knowledge graph completion. KG can be seen as the training set; S_{hr} and S_t are the text description of corresponding entities and relations. It should be noted that unobserved biases which can not be observed and interfered with are ignored in this figure.

Inspired by **Counterfactual Analysis** [26, 28, 30, 40], it incorporates a counterfactual scenario into the debiasing process for a given task. The construction of the scenario serves as a guiding factor in mitigating bias in the inference. To this end, we construct a counterfactual inference scenario for the KGC task and present a factual inference scenario, the original inference scenario of KGC tasks, for comparison:

- **Factual Inference:** *Given $(h, r, ?)$, what will the missing entity be if seeing the original KG?*
- **Counterfactual Inference:** *Given $(h, r, ?)$, what will the missing entity be if seeing the original KG and knowing that in-depth bias may cause incorrect outcomes?*

In order to enable the hr to effectively "recognize" the correlated tail entities (t) caused by the structure preference, we leverage the phenomenon that the triples consisting of correlated entities and relations tend to exhibit relatively high scores while other triples demonstrate relatively low scores. Through leveraging the aforementioned phenomenon, it becomes possible to measure and quantify the extent of in-depth bias that exists for hr and t during the inference process. Following this way, we introduce two measurable in-depth biases, namely, **individual in-depth bias** and **global in-depth bias**, and their description are as follows:

- **Individual In-Depth Bias (IDB):** The bias caused by the path $KG \rightarrow F_{hr}$ indicates the overall feature of the set of t that can be correlated with hr during training. It is different for each hr.
- **Global In-Depth Bias (GDB):** The bias caused by path $KG \rightarrow F_t$ indicates the overall bias of the KG that the entities correlated with more other entities are predisposed to attain higher scores. This bias has uniqueness for each dataset.

To assess the **individual in-depth bias**, we employ hr to assign weights to all entities, and then calculate the weighted average of these weights to serve as the bias feature:

$$F_{IDB}^{hr} = norm(\sigma(\sum_{E}^{t} w_t^{hr} * F_t))$$

$$w_t^{hr} = \exp(\hat{w}_t^{hr})/\sum_{E}^{i} \exp(\hat{w}_i^{hr}) \tag{5}$$

$$\hat{w}_t^{hr} = cossim(F_{hr}, F_t)$$

where F_{IDB}^{hr} means the individual in-depth bias of hr; $cossim(\cdot)$ means cosine similarity function; i and t means a entity in E; $\sigma(\cdot)$ means nonlinear activation function $tanh$; $norm(\cdot)$ denotes the L_2 normalization function.

In order to access the **global in-depth bias**, the bias feature is represented by the average feature of all entities which represents the overall preference of the dataset:

$$F_{GDB} = \frac{1}{N} \sum_{E}^{t} F_t \tag{6}$$

where F_{GDB} means the global in-depth bias of the KG and N means the number of entities.

Finally, F_{IDB}^{hr} and F_{GDB} are used to compute the debiasing result of F_{hr}:

$$F_{hr}^{db} = F_{hr} - \lambda_{IDB}F_{IDB}^{hr} - \lambda_{GDB}F_{GDB} \tag{7}$$

where F_{hr}^{db} is the debiasing feature of hr after in-depth bias mitigation; λ_{IDB} and λ_{GDB} are hyperparameters. F_{hr}^{db}, replacing F_{hr}, is used to predict the missing entity.

4.4   In-Breadth Bias Mitigation

The in-breadth bias obtained during inference can be attributed to the training strategy adopted. In a certain relation, there are similar bipartite graph structures and a large overlap of tail entities. Specifically, those hr or t with similar topological structures are likely to acquire similar feature representations.

The bias results in the path $F_{hr} \leftarrow KG \rightarrow F_t$, as illustrated by the causal graph Fig. 4. The main cause of this bias lies in the fact that the training strategy employed does not sufficiently account for the potential overlap in features between hr or t that are structurally similar.

To reduce this bias, **causal intervention** [28] is used to block paths $KG \rightarrow F_{hr}$ and $KG \rightarrow F_t$ by keeping F_{hr} and F_t as constants during training. But it is impossible in KGC tasks due to the necessity of learning feature representations through the structure of KGs. Therefore, we reduce the restriction of the aforementioned method and mitigate the impact from $F_{hr} \leftarrow KG \rightarrow F_t$ by respectively lowering the similarities between representations of hr and between those of t during training. In practice, we introduce a novel loss function that quantifies the level of similarity among feature representations within a batch, and minimize it to reduce **in-breadth bias (BB)** during the training phase as follows:

$$L_{BB} = \frac{1}{2N} \sum_{N}^{i} \sum_{N}^{j} (cossim(F_{hr}^i, F_{hr}^j) + cossim(F_t^i, F_t^j)) \tag{8}$$

where N means the sample number of one batch during training; F_{hr}^i and F_t^i mean the $i - th$ F_{hr} and F_t respectively in the batch; $cossim(\cdot)$ means cosine similarity function. L_{BB} is used as an extra loss in the original training phase.

5 Experiment

5.1 Datasets

We conduct experiments to evaluate the performance of our method **CIDF** including **In-Depth Bias Mitigation (DBM)** and **In-Breadth Bias Mitigation (BBM)** on three widely used KGC datasets: WN18RR [7], FB15k-237 [35], and Wikidata5M[1] [39]. The data statistics of each dataset are shown in Table. 2. WN18RR and FB15k-237 are revised by WN18 and FB15k datasets [2], respectively, which suffer from test set leakage. For the Wikidata5M dataset, there exist two distinct settings available, namely transductive and inductive. In the transductive setting, the set of entities is identical between the training and inference phases, whereas, in the inductive setting, entities encountered during training will not appear during inference.

Table 2. Statistics of datasets we use in experiments. Wikidata5M-Trans and Wikidata5M-Ind denote the transductive and inductive settings of Wikidata dataset respectively.

Dataset	#Entity	#Relation	#Taining	#Valid	#Test
WN18RR	40,943	11	86,835	3,304	3,314
FB15k-237	14,541	237	272,115	17,535	20,466
Wikidata5M-Trans	4,594,485	822	20,614,279	5,163	5,163
Wikidata5M-Ind	4,579,609	822	20,496,514	6,699	6,894

5.2 Evaluation Metrics

Following previous KGC works, we evaluate the performance of our proposed method with the entity ranking task. In practice, for each task $(h, r, ?)$ during test phase, it is required to predict the ranks of all entities as the result of t given h and r, which is similar for task $(t, r^{-1}, ?)$. For evaluating the overall performance of datasets, we use four evaluation metrics as follows: Mean Reciprocal Rank (MMR), and Hit@k ($k \in \{1, 3, 10\}$), where MRR is determined by the average reciprocal rank of all test triples and Hit@k is calculated from the proportion of correct entities ranked among the top-k. Additionally, in main comparative experiments, MRR and Hit@k are computed following the *filtered setting* [2] which excludes the factual triples when ranking.

---

[1] https://deepgraphlearning.github.io/project/wikidata5m.

5.3   Baselines

For comparison, we select a series of strong baselines as follows:

- KGC methods that integrate head entity and relation as a whole in score computing, including SimKGC [37], Hitter [5], and LP-BERT [19].
- KGC methods that treat relations as operations in score computing, including TransE [2], RotatE [34], DistMult [43], and KEPLER [39].

5.4   Hyperparameters

Given that our proposed method, CIDF, is primarily applied within the SimKGC framework, we maintain the existing hyperparameters setting within SimKGC, which aims to ensure that the comparison is consistent and fair. The two encoders for hr and t are both the pre-training language model called *bert-base-uncased* [8]. The descriptions in both hr and t are restricted to a maximum token number of 50. Any portion of the descriptions that exceeds this limit will be truncated. Within the hyperparameters of CIDF, we conduct grid searches on λ_{IDB} and λ_{GDB} with ranges $[0.1, 1]$ at 0.1 intervals. The training epochs for datasets WN18RR, FB15k-237, and Wikidata5M are 50, 10, and 1 respectively. In the training phase, the models are run on 4 V100 GPU (32G) with batch size 1024.

Table 3. Main results for datasets WN18RR and FB15k-237. "CIDF" refers to our proposed method Causal Inference based KGC Debiasing Framework;"-BB", "-GDB" and "-IDB" refer to the result after mitigating In-Breadth Bias, Global In-Depth Bias, and Individual In-Depth Bias respectively. SimKGC is the setting SimKGC$_{IB+PB+SN}$ [37].

Method	WN18RR				FB15k-237			
	MRR	Hit@1	Hit@3	Hit@10	MRR	Hit@1	Hit@3	Hit@10
TransE(2013) [2]	22.2	1.2	40.1	52.9	32.9	23.0	36.8	52.7
DisMult(2015) [43]	44.0	39.6	45.2	53.6	30.1	22.1	33.8	48.3
RotatE(2019) [34]	47.7	42.9	49.4	57.2	33.5	23.7	37.3	53.1
LP-BERT(2022) [19]	48.2	34.3	**56.3**	**75.2**	31.0	22.3	33.6	49.0
Hitter(2021) [5]	**49.9**	**45.7**	51.3	58.7	**37.2**	**27.8**	**40.8**	**55.8**
CIDF								
SimKGC(2022) [37]	66.5	58.6	71.5	80.2	33.6	24.9	36.2	51.1
-BB	67.8	60.6	72.0	80.3	33.8	25.3	36.6	51.4
-BB-GDB	67.9	60.9	72.1	80.4	34.4	25.6	37.1	52.3
-BB-GDB-IDB	**68.1**	**61.2**	**72.2**	**80.4**	**34.6**	**25.8**	**37.4**	**52.7**

5.5   Main Results

The results of the KGC tasks conducted on WN18RR and FB15k-237 datasets are presented in Table. 3. It indicates that the CIDF applied to the SimKGC framework enhances all evaluation metrics across both two datasets. In comparison to $\text{SimKGC}_{\text{IB+PB+SN}}$, applying CIDF for WN18RR shows improvements of 1.6%, 2.6%, 0.7%, and 0.2% in MRR, Hit@1, Hit@3, and Hit@10, correspondingly. Similarly, for FB15k-237, applying CIDF offers enhancements of 1.0%, 0.9%, 1.2%, and 1.6% in MRR, Hit@1, Hit@3, and Hit@10, respectively.

Table 4. Main results for dataset Wikidata5M.

Method	Wikidata5M-Trans				Wikidata5M-Ind			
	MRR	Hit@1	Hit@3	Hit@10	MRR	Hit@1	Hit@3	Hit@10
TransE(2013) [2]	25.3	17.0	31.1	39.2	-	-	-	-
RotatE(2019) [34]	**29.0**	**23.4**	**32.2**	**39.0**	-	-	-	-
KEPLER(2021) [39]	21.0	17.3	22.4	27.7	40.2	22.2	51.4	73.0
BLP-ComplEx(2021) [6]	-	-	-	-	48.9	26.2	**66.4**	**87.7**
BLP-SimplE(2021) [6]	-	-	-	-	**49.3**	**28.9**	63.9	86.6
CIDF								
SimKGC(2022) [37]	35.8	31.3	37.6	44.1	71.4	60.9	78.5	91.7
-BB	36.8	32.2	38.2	44.7	**72.6**	**62.4**	**79.8**	**91.7**
-BB-GDB	37.4	32.9	39.0	45.5	-	-	-	-
-BB-GDB-IDB	**38.7**	**34.5**	**40.2**	**46.7**	-	-	-	-

Furthermore, we present the performance results of our proposed method on the Wikidata5M dataset, presented in both the transductive and inductive settings, as depicted in Table. 4. In the Wikidata5M-Trans setting, our method displays a notable increase of 2.9%, 3.2%, 2.6%, and 2.6% improvements in MRR, Hit@1, Hit@3, and Hit@10, respectively. On the other hand, in the Wikidata5M-Ind setting, since the entities utilized during the training and inference phases are mutually exclusive, we only conduct in-breadth bias mitigation (-BB) in this setting and achieve enhancements in MRR, Hit@1, and Hit@3 by 1.2%, 1.5%, and 1.3%, respectively.

In summary, the experimental results presented above indicate that our proposed method, Causal Inference based KGC Debiasing Framework (CIDF), effectively enhances the performance of KGC tasks.

6   Analysis

In this section, we aim to further illuminate the effectiveness of our proposed method by carrying out a series of analytical experiments from various perspectives.

6.1   Fine-Grained Analysis

We conduct a series of fine-grained analytical experiments on WN18RR, a knowledge graph with a relatively smaller number of relations with well-defined label descriptions. We calculate the performance metrics for each relation specifically, using the mean reciprocal rank (MRR), as our primary evaluation metric.

Table 5. The fine-grained results of WN18RR basing SimKGC framework. "**Bias Rate**" is computed by Eq. 4; "**Prop.**" denotes the proportion for each relation in the training set; "**overall**" denotes measuring the results for all samples while "**k-hop**" ($k \in \{3,5\}$) denotes measuring the results only for the samples with k-hop in-depth bias; "**w/o.**" and "**w.**" denote the results without and with CIDF respectively; "**avg. Hit@1**" denotes the average Hit@1 for all relations; ↑ (↓) means the result is better when the value is higher (lower). Relation abbreviation: "derivational .. form" = "derivationally related form", "synset .. of" = "synset domain topic of", "member .. region" = "member of domain region", and "member .. usage" = "member of domain usage". ◇♡♣♠ are the markers for facilitating locating the specific part of this table in the paper.

| Relation | Prop.(%) | MRR ↑ | | | | Bias Rate ↓ | | | |
| | | overall◇ | | biased♡ | | 3-hop♣ | | 5-hop ♠ | |
		w/o.	w	w/o.	w	w/o.	w	w/o.	w
hypernym	39.9	48.9	**50.0**	37.2	**38.1**	20.2	18.8	34.8	32.6
derivationally .. form	34.3	90.3	**93.2**	89.4	**92.3**	13.2	10.8	13.6	11.3
member meronym	8.1	58.9	**62.8**	52.0	**56.2**	41.9	38.7	52.2	48.6
has part	5.5	45.9	**49.0**	41.0	**48.2**	49.4	47.1	63.4	61.6
synset .. of	3.9	61.7	**63.2**	36.1	**40.6**	7.9	6.1	12.3	9.6
instance hypernym	3.6	66.8	**71.4**	55.9	**63.2**	13.1	9.0	17.2	12.3
also see	1.8	**67.7**	64.5	**69.9**	65.9	30.4	26.8	41.1	37.5
verb group	1.2	92.8	**96.5**	84.2	**88.0**	7.7	5.1	7.7	5.1
member .. region	0.8	46.6	**48.7**	17.6	**22.4**	34.6	30.8	80.8	76.9
member .. usage	0.8	53.2	**60.7**	32.4	**35.6**	37.5	33.3	62.5	62.5
similar to	0.1	100.0	100.0	100.0	100.0	0.0	0.0	0.0	0.0
avg	-	66.6	**69.1**	56.0	**59.1**	23.3	20.6	35.0	32.6
avg. Hit@1	-	60.0	**63.4**	47.7	**52.1**	-	-	-	-

Conventional Results. In the filtered setting, our analysis, as presented in Table. 5 ◇, demonstrates that after applying our proposed method CIDF, nearly all of the relations exhibit performance improvements. More specifically, on average, we observe an enhancement of 2.5% and 3.4% for MRR and Hit@1 respectively, which underscores the effectiveness of CIDF. Furthermore, when considering the symmetric relation *also see*, whereby $(A, also\ see, B)$ and $(B, also\ see, A)$ are both factual triples when one of them holds, there is a notable decrease of 3.1% in MRR that may be attributed to the effects of DBM. To further investigate this performance drop, we conduct a supplementary experiment consisting of solely using BBM of CIDF without DBM. As a result, we observe a significant increase in the MRR of *alse see* relation, which improves from 64.5% to 67.8% (+3.2%).

Biased Results. In order to assess the efficacy of our proposed method in tacking in-depth bias, we conduct performance measurements exclusively on the samples which are potentially susceptible to this bias. Table. 5 ♡ shows the results in the biased setting on the performance of relations. In the biased setting, we only evaluate the hr that exists in both the training and inference phases. By applying CIDF, there are improvements of 3.2% and 4.4% on average MRR and Hit@1 respectively, which means CIDF is more effective in the biased setting.

Bias Rate Results. To assess the efficacy of CIDF in bias mitigation, bias rates for individual relations in 3-hop and 5-hop settings are measured. The results, presented in Table. 5 ♣ and ♠, demonstrate a reduction in bias rates for most relations by applying CIDF. Specifically, the average bias rates decrease by 2.7% and 2.4% in the respective hop settings.

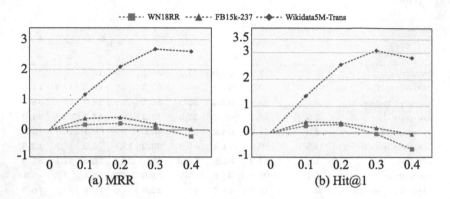

Fig. 5. Detail results of MRR and Hit@1. The x-axis means the value of λ_{IDB}; the y-axis represents the difference in performance compared with $\lambda_{IDB} = 0$.

6.2   Effect of In-Depth Bias Mitigation

For the better adaptation of DBM to different datasets, we use two hyperparameters to control the degree of bias mitigation (Eq. 5). Specifically, we conduct beam searches for λ_{IDB} and λ_{GDB} to gain the optimal setting for different datasets as depicted in Eq. 5. To effectively determine the optimal settings for various datasets, we employ beam searches for λ_{IDB} and λ_{GDB} with ranges $[0.1, 1]$ at 0.1 intervals. As shown in Fig. 5, the optimal λ_{IDB} is 0.1 for WN18RR and FB15k-237 datasets and is 0.3 for Wikidata5M-Trans. For λ_{GDB}, the optimal values of all datasets used in this paper are 1.0.

7   Conclusion and Future Work

In this paper, we present a bias analysis of Knowledge Graph Completion tasks and identify two biases, in-depth and in-breadth, during the training phase that may lead to erroneous outcomes during inference. To mitigate these biases, we conduct a causal analysis and formulate a causal graph for KGC tasks. Building on this, we propose a novel debiasing framework, the Causal Inference-biased

KGC Debiasing Framework, which incorporates In-Depth Bias Mitigation and In-Breadth Bias Mitigation. Applying CIDF results in significant improvements on three benchmark datasets, namely WN18RR, FB15k-237, and Wikidata5M, particularly in the biased setting. In the future, we intend to conduct a more comprehensive analysis of KGC task biases and develop a general causal debiasing framework applicable to various KGC methods directly.

Supplemental Material Statement: Source code, datasets and results are available at https://github.com/HomuraT/CIDF.

Acknowledgements. National Natural Science Foundation of China, Grant/Award Number: 61402220; The Philosophy and Social Science Foundation of Hunan Province, Grant/Award Number: 16YBA323; Natural Science Foundation of Hunan Province, Grant/Award Number: 2020JJ4525,2022JJ30495; Scientific Research Fund of Hunan Provincial Education Department, Grant/Award Number: 18B279,19A439,22A0316.

References

1. Bollacker, K., Evans, C., Paritosh, P., Sturge, T., Taylor, J.: Freebase: a collaboratively created graph database for structuring human knowledge. In: Proceedings of the 2008 ACM SIGMOD International Conference on Management of Data, pp. 1247–1250. SIGMOD 2008, Association for Computing Machinery, New York, NY, USA (2008). https://doi.org/10.1145/1376616.1376746

2. Bordes, A., Usunier, N., Garcia-Duran, A., Weston, J., Yakhnenko, O.: Translating embeddings for modeling multi-relational data. In: Burges, C., Bottou, L., Welling, M., Ghahramani, Z., Weinberger, K. (eds.) Advances in Neural Information Processing Systems. vol. 26. Curran Associates, Inc. (2013). https://proceedings.neurips.cc/paper_files/paper/2013/file/1cecc7a77928ca8133fa24680a88d2f9-Paper.pdf

3. Bourli, S., Pitoura, E.: Bias in knowledge graph embeddings. In: 2020 IEEE/ACM International Conference on Advances in Social Networks Analysis and Mining (ASONAM), pp. 6–10 (2020). https://doi.org/10.1109/ASONAM49781.2020.9381459

4. Chang, H., Cai, J., Li, J.: Knowledge graph completion with counterfactual augmentation. In: Proceedings of the ACM Web Conference 2023, pp. 2611–2620. WWW 2023, Association for Computing Machinery, New York, NY, USA (2023). https://doi.org/10.1145/3543507.3583401

5. Chen, S., Liu, X., Gao, J., Jiao, J., Zhang, R., Ji, Y.: HittER: hierarchical transformers for knowledge graph embeddings. In: Proceedings of the 2021 Conference on Empirical Methods in Natural Language Processing, pp. 10395–10407. Association for Computational Linguistics, Online and Punta Cana, Dominican Republic, November 2021. https://doi.org/10.18653/v1/2021.emnlp-main.812

6. Daza, D., Cochez, M., Groth, P.: Inductive entity representations from text via link prediction. In: Proceedings of the Web Conference 2021, pp. 798–808. WWW 2021, Association for Computing Machinery, New York, NY, USA (2021). https://doi.org/10.1145/3442381.3450141

7. Dettmers, T., Minervini, P., Stenetorp, P., Riedel, S.: Convolutional 2d knowledge graph embeddings. In: McIlraith, S.A., Weinberger, K.Q. (eds.) Proceedings of the Thirty-Second AAAI Conference on Artificial Intelligence, (AAAI-2018), the 30th innovative Applications of Artificial Intelligence (IAAI-2018), and the 8th AAAI Symposium on Educational Advances in Artificial Intelligence (EAAI-2018), New Orleans, Louisiana, USA, February 2–7, 2018, pp. 1811–1818. AAAI Press (2018). https://www.aaai.org/ocs/index.php/AAAI/AAAI18/paper/view/17366

8. Devlin, J., Chang, M.W., Lee, K., Toutanova, K.: BERT: pre-training of deep bidirectional transformers for language understanding. In: Proceedings of the 2019 Conference of the North American Chapter of the Association for Computational Linguistics: Human Language Technologies, Volume 1 (Long and Short Papers). pp. 4171–4186. Association for Computational Linguistics, Minneapolis, Minnesota, June 2019. https://doi.org/10.18653/v1/N19-1423

9. Ding, M., Zhou, C., Chen, Q., Yang, H., Tang, J.: Cognitive graph for multi-hop reading comprehension at scale. In: Proceedings of the 57th Annual Meeting of the Association for Computational Linguistics, pp. 2694–2703. Association for Computational Linguistics, Florence, Italy, July 2019. https://doi.org/10.18653/v1/P19-1259

10. Du, Y., Zheng, Q., Wu, Y., Lan, M., Yang, Y., Ma, M.: Understanding gender bias in knowledge base embeddings. In: Proceedings of the 60th Annual Meeting of the Association for Computational Linguistics (Volume 1: Long Papers), pp. 1381–1395. Association for Computational Linguistics, Dublin, Ireland, May 2022. https://doi.org/10.18653/v1/2022.acl-long.98

11. Du, Z., Qian, Y., Liu, X., Ding, M., Qiu, J., Yang, Z., Tang, J.: GLM: general language model pretraining with autoregressive blank infilling. In: Proceedings of the 60th Annual Meeting of the Association for Computational Linguistics (Volume 1: Long Papers), pp. 320–335. Association for Computational Linguistics, Dublin, Ireland, May 2022. https://doi.org/10.18653/v1/2022.acl-long.26

12. Grover, A., Leskovec, J.: node2vec: Scalable feature learning for networks. In: Proceedings of the 22nd ACM SIGKDD International Conference on Knowledge Discovery and Data Mining, pp. 855–864 (2016)

13. Guo, D., Tang, D., Duan, N., Zhou, M., Yin, J.: Dialog-to-action: conversational question answering over a large-scale knowledge base. In: Bengio, S., Wallach, H., Larochelle, H., Grauman, K., Cesa-Bianchi, N., Garnett, R. (eds.) Advances in Neural Information Processing Systems, vol. 31. Curran Associates, Inc. (2018). https://proceedings.neurips.cc/paper_files/paper/2018/file/d63fbf8c3173730f82b150c5ef38b8ff-Paper.pdf

14. Jia, T., Yang, Y., Lu, X., Zhu, Q., Yang, K., Zhou, X.: Link prediction based on tensor decomposition for the knowledge graph of COVID-19 antiviral drug. Data Intell. 4(1), 134–148 (2022). https://doi.org/10.1162/dint_a_00117

15. Keidar, D., Zhong, M., Zhang, C., Shrestha, Y.R., Paudel, B.: Towards automatic bias detection in knowledge graphs. In: Findings of the Association for Computational Linguistics: EMNLP 2021. pp. 3804–3811. Association for Computational Linguistics, Punta Cana, Dominican Republic, November 2021. https://doi.org/10.18653/v1/2021.findings-emnlp.321

16. Kraft, A., Usbeck, R.: The lifecycle of "facts": a survey of social bias in knowledge graphs. In: Proceedings of the 2nd Conference of the Asia-Pacific Chapter of the Association for Computational Linguistics and the 12th International Joint Conference on Natural Language Processing (Volume 1: Long Papers), pp. 639–652. Association for Computational Linguistics, Online only, November 2022. https://aclanthology.org/2022.aacl-main.49

17. Lacroix, T., Usunier, N., Obozinski, G.: Canonical tensor decomposition for knowledge base completion. In: Dy, J.G., Krause, A. (eds.) Proceedings of the 35th International Conference on Machine Learning, ICML 2018, Stockholmsmässan, Stockholm, Sweden, July 10–15, 2018. Proceedings of Machine Learning Research, vol. 80, pp. 2869–2878. PMLR (2018). http://proceedings.mlr.press/v80/lacroix18a.html

18. Lehmann, J., et al.: DBPedia - a large-scale, multilingual knowledge base extracted from Wikipedia. Semant. Web 6(2), 167–195 (2015). https://doi.org/10.3233/SW-140134

19. Li, D., Yang, S., Xu, K., Yi, M., He, Y., Wang, H.: Multi-task pre-training language model for semantic network completion. arXiv preprint arXiv:2201.04843 (2022). https://arxiv.org/abs/2201.04843

20. Liu, Z., Nguyen, T.K., Fang, Y.: Tail-GNN: tail-node graph neural networks. In: Proceedings of the 27th ACM SIGKDD Conference on Knowledge Discovery & Data Mining, pp. 1109–1119. KDD 2021, Association for Computing Machinery, New York, NY, USA (2021). https://doi.org/10.1145/3447548.3467276

21. Ma, J., Guo, R., Wan, M., Yang, L., Zhang, A., Li, J.: Learning fair node representations with graph counterfactual fairness. In: Proceedings of the Fifteenth ACM International Conference on Web Search and Data Mining, pp. 695–703. WSDM 2022, Association for Computing Machinery, New York, NY, USA (2022). https://doi.org/10.1145/3488560.3498391

22. Malaviya, C., Bhagavatula, C., Bosselut, A., Choi, Y.: Commonsense knowledge base completion with structural and semantic context. Proc. AAAI Conf. Artif. Intell. 34(03), 2925–2933 (2020). https://doi.org/10.1609/aaai.v34i03.5684

23. Miller, G.A.: WordNet: a lexical database for English. In: Speech and Natural Language: Proceedings of a Workshop Held at Harriman, New York, 23–26 February 1992 (1992). https://aclanthology.org/H92-1116

24. Moon, S., Shah, P., Kumar, A., Subba, R.: OpenDialKG: explainable conversational reasoning with attention-based walks over knowledge graphs. In: Proceedings of the 57th Annual Meeting of the Association for Computational Linguistics, pp. 845–854. Association for Computational Linguistics, Florence, Italy, July 2019. https://doi.org/10.18653/v1/P19-1081

25. Nan, G., Qiao, R., Xiao, Y., Liu, J., Leng, S., Zhang, H., Lu, W.: Interventional video grounding with dual contrastive learning. In: Proceedings of the IEEE/CVF Conference on Computer Vision and Pattern Recognition (CVPR), pp. 2765–2775, June 2021

26. Nan, G., Zeng, J., Qiao, R., Guo, Z., Lu, W.: Uncovering main causalities for long-tailed information extraction. In: Proceedings of the 2021 Conference on Empirical Methods in Natural Language Processing, pp. 9683–9695. Association for Computational Linguistics, Online and Punta Cana, Dominican Republic, November 2021. https://doi.org/10.18653/v1/2021.emnlp-main.763

27. Nickel, M., Tresp, V., Kriegel, H.: A three-way model for collective learning on multi-relational data. In: Getoor, L., Scheffer, T. (eds.) Proceedings of the 28th International Conference on Machine Learning, ICML 2011, Bellevue, Washington, USA, June 28–July 2, 2011, pp. 809–816. Omnipress (2011). https://icml.cc/2011/papers/438_icmlpaper.pdf

28. Pearl, J., Glymour, M., Jewell, N.P.: Causal Inference in Statistics: A Primer. John Wiley & Sons, New York (2016)

29. Pearl, J., Mackenzie, D.: The Book of Why: The New Science of Cause and Effect. Basic Books (2018)

30. Qian, C., Feng, F., Wen, L., Ma, C., Xie, P.: Counterfactual inference for text classification debiasing. In: Proceedings of the 59th Annual Meeting of the Association for Computational Linguistics and the 11th International Joint Conference on Natural Language Processing (Volume 1: Long Papers), pp. 5434–5445. Association for Computational Linguistics, Online, August 2021. https://doi.org/10.18653/v1/2021.acl-long.422

31. Radford, A., Wu, J., Child, R., Luan, D., Amodei, D., Sutskever, I.: Language models are unsupervised multitask learners. OpenAI blog (2019). https://d4mucfp ksywv.cloudfront.net/better-language-models/language-models.pdf

32. Radstok, W., Chekol, M.W., Schäfer, M.T.: Are knowledge graph embedding models biased, or is it the data that they are trained on? In: Kaffee, L., Razniewski, S., Hogan, A. (eds.) Proceedings of the 2nd Wikidata Workshop (Wikidata 2021) co-located with the 20th International Semantic Web Conference (ISWC 2021), Virtual Conference, October 24, 2021. CEUR Workshop Proceedings, vol. 2982. CEUR-WS.org (2021). https://ceur-ws.org/Vol-2982/paper-5.pdf

33. Shomer, H., Jin, W., Wang, W., Tang, J.: Toward degree bias in embedding-based knowledge graph completion. In: Proceedings of the ACM Web Conference 2023, pp. 705–715. WWW 2023, Association for Computing Machinery, New York, NY, USA (2023). https://doi.org/10.1145/3543507.3583544

34. Sun, Z., Deng, Z.H., Nie, J.Y., Tang, J.: Rotate: Knowledge graph embedding by relational rotation in complex space. In: International Conference on Learning Representations (2019). https://openreview.net/forum?id=HkgEQnRqYQ

35. Toutanova, K., Chen, D.: Observed versus latent features for knowledge base and text inference. In: Proceedings of the 3rd Workshop on Continuous Vector Space Models and their Compositionality, pp. 57–66. Association for Computational Linguistics, Beijing, China, July 2015. https://doi.org/10.18653/v1/W15-4007

36. Trouillon, T., Welbl, J., Riedel, S., Gaussier, E., Bouchard, G.: Complex embeddings for simple link prediction. In: Balcan, M.F., Weinberger, K.Q. (eds.) Proceedings of The 33rd International Conference on Machine Learning. In: Proceedings of Machine Learning Research, vol. 48, pp. 2071–2080. PMLR, New York, New York, USA, 20–22 June 2016. https://proceedings.mlr.press/v48/trouillon16.html

37. Wang, L., Zhao, W., Wei, Z., Liu, J.: SimKGC: simple contrastive knowledge graph completion with pre-trained language models. In: Proceedings of the 60th Annual Meeting of the Association for Computational Linguistics (Volume 1: Long Papers), pp. 4281–4294. Association for Computational Linguistics, Dublin, Ireland, May 2022. https://doi.org/10.18653/v1/2022.acl-long.295

38. Wang, X., Wang, D., Xu, C., He, X., Cao, Y., Chua, T.S.: Explainable reasoning over knowledge graphs for recommendation. Proc. AAAI Conf. Artif. Intell. **33**(01), 5329–5336 (2019). https://doi.org/10.1609/aaai.v33i01.33015329

39. Wang, X., et al.: KEPLER: a unified Model for Knowledge Embedding and Pre-trained Language Representation. Trans. Assoc. Comput. Linguist. 9, 176–194 (2021). https://doi.org/10.1162/tacl_a_00360

40. Wang, Y., et al.: Should we rely on entity mentions for relation extraction? Debiasing relation extraction with counterfactual analysis. In: Proceedings of the 2022 Conference of the North American Chapter of the Association for Computational Linguistics: Human Language Technologies, pp. 3071–3081. Association for Computational Linguistics, Seattle, United States, July 2022. https://doi.org/10.18653/v1/2022.naacl-main.224

41. Wang, Z., Zhang, J., Feng, J., Chen, Z.: Knowledge graph embedding by translating on hyperplanes. In: Brodley, C.E., Stone, P. (eds.) Proceedings of the Twenty-Eighth AAAI Conference on Artificial Intelligence, 27–31 July 2014, Québec City, Québec, Canada, pp. 1112–1119. AAAI Press (2014). http://www.aaai.org/ocs/index.php/AAAI/AAAI14/paper/view/8531

42. Xian, Y., Fu, Z., Muthukrishnan, S., de Melo, G., Zhang, Y.: Reinforcement knowledge graph reasoning for explainable recommendation. In: Proceedings of the 42nd International ACM SIGIR Conference on Research and Development in Information Retrieval, pp. 285–294. SIGIR 2019, Association for Computing Machinery, New York, NY, USA (2019). https://doi.org/10.1145/3331184.3331203

43. Yang, B., Yih, W., He, X., Gao, J., Deng, L.: Embedding entities and relations for learning and inference in knowledge bases. In: Bengio, Y., LeCun, Y. (eds.) 3rd International Conference on Learning Representations, ICLR 2015, San Diego, CA, USA, 7–9 May 2015, Conference Track Proceedings (2015). http://arxiv.org/abs/1412.6575

44. Yang, Z., Liu, Y., Ouyang, C., Ren, L., Wen, W.: Counterfactual can be strong in medical question and answering. Inf. Process. Manage. **60**(4), 103408 (2023). https://doi.org/10.1016/j.ipm.2023.103408

45. Zamini, M., Reza, H., Rabiei, M.: A review of knowledge graph completion. Information. **13**(8), 396 (2022). https://doi.org/10.3390/info13080396

46. Zhang, D., Zhang, H., Tang, J., Hua, X.S., Sun, Q.: Causal intervention for weakly-supervised semantic segmentation. In: Larochelle, H., Ranzato, M., Hadsell, R., Balcan, M., Lin, H. (eds.) Advances in Neural Information Processing Systems, vol. 33, pp. 655–666. Curran Associates, Inc. (2020). https://proceedings.neurips.cc/paper_files/paper/2020/file/07211688a0869d995947a8fb11b215d6-Paper.pdf

47. Zhang, X., Cui, P., Xu, R., Zhou, L., He, Y., Shen, Z.: Deep stable learning for out-of-distribution generalization. In: Proceedings of the IEEE/CVF Conference on Computer Vision and Pattern Recognition (CVPR), pp. 5372–5382, June 2021

48. Zhang, Y., Dai, H., Kozareva, Z., Smola, A., Song, L.: Variational reasoning for question answering with knowledge graph. Proc. AAAI Conf. Artif. Intell. **32**(1), 1–8 (2018). https://doi.org/10.1609/aaai.v32i1.12057

49. Zhang, Z., Cai, J., Zhang, Y., Wang, J.: Learning hierarchy-aware knowledge graph embeddings for link prediction. Proc. AAAI Conf. Artif. Intell. **34**(03), 3065–3072 (2020). https://doi.org/10.1609/aaai.v34i03.5701

50. Zhao, T., Zhang, X., Wang, S.: GraphSmote: Imbalanced node classification on graphs with graph neural networks. In: Proceedings of the 14th ACM International Conference on Web Search and Data Mining. p. 833–841. WSDM 2021, Association for Computing Machinery, New York, NY, USA (2021). https://doi.org/10.1145/3437963.3441720

51. Zhao, T., Liu, G., Wang, D., Yu, W., Jiang, M.: Learning from counterfactual links for link prediction. In: Chaudhuri, K., Jegelka, S., Song, L., Szepesvari, C., Niu, G., Sabato, S. (eds.) Proceedings of the 39th International Conference on Machine Learning. Proceedings of Machine Learning Research, vol. 162, pp. 26911–26926. PMLR, 17–23 July 2022. https://proceedings.mlr.press/v162/zhao22e.html

52. Zhu, Z., Zhang, Z., Xhonneux, L.P., Tang, J.: Neural bellman-ford networks: a general graph neural network framework for link prediction. In: Ranzato, M., Beygelzimer, A., Dauphin, Y., Liang, P., Vaughan, J.W. (eds.) Advances in Neural Information Processing Systems, vol. 34, pp. 29476–29490. Curran Associates, Inc. (2021). https://proceedings.neurips.cc/paper_files/paper/2021/file/f6a673f09493afcd8b129a0bcf1cd5bc-Paper.pdf

Can ChatGPT Replace Traditional KBQA Models? An In-Depth Analysis of the Question Answering Performance of the GPT LLM Family

Yiming Tan[1,4], Dehai Min[2,4], Yu Li[2,4], Wenbo Li[3], Nan Hu[2,4],
Yongrui Chen[2,4], and Guilin Qi[2,4(✉)]

[1] School of Cyber Science and Engineering, Southeast University, Nanjing, China
tt_yymm@seu.edu.cn
[2] School of Computer Science and Engineering, Southeast University, Nanjing, China
{zhishanq,yuli_11,nanhu,yrchen,gqi}@seu.edu.cn
[3] School of Computer Science and Technology, Anhui Unviersity, Hefei, China
wenboli@stu.ahu.edu.cn
[4] Key Laboratory of New Generation Artificial Intelligence Technology and Its
Interdisciplinary Applications, Southeast University, Ministry of Education, Nanjing,
China

Abstract. ChatGPT is a powerful large language model (LLM) that
covers knowledge resources such as Wikipedia and supports natural language question answering using its own knowledge. Therefore, there is
growing interest in exploring whether ChatGPT can replace traditional
knowledge-based question answering (KBQA) models. Although there
have been some works analyzing the question answering performance of
ChatGPT, there is still a lack of large-scale, comprehensive testing of various types of complex questions to analyze the limitations of the model.
In this paper, we present a framework that follows the black-box testing specifications of CheckList proposed by [38]. We evaluate ChatGPT
and its family of LLMs on eight real-world KB-based complex question
answering datasets, which include six English datasets and two multilingual datasets. The total number of test cases is approximately 190,000.
In addition to the GPT family of LLMs, we also evaluate the well-
known FLAN-T5 to identify commonalities between the GPT family and
other LLMs. The dataset and code are available at https://github.com/
tan92hl/Complex-Question-Answering-Evaluation-of-GPT-family.git.

Keywords: Large language model · Complex question answering ·
Knowledge base · ChatGPT · Evaluation · Black-box testing

Y. Tan and D. Min—Contribute equally to this work.

T. R. Payne et al. (Eds.): ISWC 2023, LNCS 14265, pp. 348–367, 2023.
https://doi.org/10.1007/978-3-031-47240-4_19

1   Introduction

Given its extensive coverage of knowledge from Wikipedia as training data and its impressive natural language understanding ability, ChatGPT has demonstrated powerful question-answering abilities by leveraging its own knowledge. Additionally, a study conducted by [30] suggests that language models can be considered as knowledge bases (KBs) to support downstream natural language processing (NLP) tasks. This has led to growing interest in exploring whether ChatGPT and related large language models (LLMs) can replace traditional Knowledge-Based Question Answering (KBQA) models.

There have been many evaluations of ChatGPT [2, 7, 16, 19, 26, 33, 46, 47, 52, 54], some of which include the testing of question answering tasks and have yielded interesting conclusions: for example, [26] showed that ChatGPT has lower stability than traditional KBQA models on a test set of 200 questions, and [2] found that ChatGPT is a "lazy reasoner" that suffers more with induction after analyzing 30 samples. However, due to the limited number of test cases, it is difficult to perform a comprehensive evaluation of ChatGPT's performance on the KBQA task based on these findings. Moreover, the reliability of these findings still requires further testing for validation. We find that the difficulty in answer evaluation is the main reason why existing works have not conducted large-scale KBQA tests on ChatGPT, which outputs sentences or paragraphs that contain answers rather than an exact answer. Furthermore, due to the influence of the generated textual context, the answer sequence of ChatGPT may not necessarily correspond strictly to entity names in the knowledge base. Therefore, the traditional Exact Match (EM) metric cannot directly evaluate the output of ChatGPT for question-answering. Consequently, most of the works mentioned above rely on manual evaluation.

In this paper, we select the KB-based Complex Question Answering (KB-based CQA) task to comprehensively evaluate the ability of LLMs to answer complex questions based on their own knowledge. This task requires the model to use compositional reasoning to obtain the answer to the question, which includes multi-hop reasoning, attribute comparison, set operations, and other complex reasoning. We believe that evaluating ChatGPT's performance in complex knowledge question answering using its own knowledge can help us understand whether existing LLMs have the potential to surpass traditional KBQA models or whether ChatGPT is already capable of replacing the current best KBQA models. Therefore, we collect test data from existing KB-based CQA datasets and establish an evaluation framework.

Our evaluation framework consists of two parts: 1) the feature-driven unified labeling method is established for the KBQA datasets involved in the testing; and 2) the evaluation of answers generated by LLMs. Inspired by the approach of using multiple scenario tags to evaluate language models in the HELM framework [21], we label each test question with unified answer-type, inference-type, and language-type tags. In the answer evaluation part, we first improve the Exact Match (EM) method so that it can be used to evaluate the accuracy of LLMs' output. The main process of improved EM is to extract potential answer phrases from the LLM output through constituent trees as the candidate answer pool, and then match them with the reference answer pool formed by annotated answers and aliases provided by wikidata. Next, we follow the CheckList testing specification [38] and set up three tests: the minimal functionality test (MFT), invariance test (INV) [40], and directional expectation test (DIR). Along with an overall evaluation, these tests assess the LLMs' capability, stability, and control when answering questions and performing specific reasoning operations.

Finally, we collect six English real-world KB-based CQA datasets and two multilingual real-world KB-based CQA datasets for our evaluation experiment, with a scale of approximately 190,000 questions, including approximately 12,000 multilingual questions covering 13 languages. In the experiment, we mainly compare the QA performance differences between the traditional the current state-of-the-art (SOTA) models and the GPT family models [4,27,28]. In addition, we also introduce the open-source LLM FLAN-T5 [9] model as a representative of the non-GPT family for comparison. Like ChatGPT, all the LLMs involved in the comparison in this paper use their own knowledge to answer questions and are considered unsupervised models.

Our key findings and insights are summarized as follows:

ChatGPT and the LLMs of GPT family outperform the best traditional models on some old datasets like WQSP and LC-quad2.0, but they still lag behind the current state-of-the-art on the latest released KBQA datase such as KQApro and GrailQA.

GPT family LLMs and the FLAN-T5 model tend to have similar tendencies in terms of strengths and weaknesses when answering different types of questions.

Using chain-of-thought prompts in CheckList testing enhances GPT LLMs' ability to answer specific questions but may negatively impact other question types, suggesting their potential and sensitivities for future task-specific applications.

2 Related Work

2.1 Large Language Models and Prompting

In recent years, LLMs and prompt learning have attracted considerable attention. Groundbreaking studies such as [4,17,30] revealed that LLMs, when given appropriate textual prompts, can perform a wide range of NLP tasks with zero-shot or few-shot learning without gradient updates. On the one hand, improved prompting can enable the information contained in the LLM to be more accurately applied to the target task, and early representative works include [34,37] The chain-of-thought (CoT) [48] method is a distinguished approach in effective prompt research. CoT enables LLMs to have a better understanding and think more when answering questions. On the other hand, much work has been done to improve the natural language understanding ability of LLMs, including Gopher [35] and PaLM [8], which aim to extend LLMs. Undoubtedly, ChatGPT has garnered significant attention as a prominent LLM due to its remarkable natural language understanding abilities. It is trained on the GPT-3.5 series of models [11] using RLHF.

2.2 Evaluation of the Large Language Model

While LLMs have demonstrated outstanding natural language understanding and generation capabilities, it is still necessary to further research their strengths, limitations, and potential risks to fully understand their advantages. Recently, many works aimed at evaluating LLMs have been proposed [6], including general benchmarks like HELM [21], Bigbench [41], Promptbench [53], and MME [10]. These aim to categorize and summarize multiple existing tasks, providing a macro-level assessment of LLM performance and potential biases. Other studies focus on specific NLP tasks, such as summarization [2], question-answering [1, 2,26], and machine translation [23]. In these existing works, the advantages of the general benchmark approaches lie in their fine-grained sample classification and high testing efficiency. However, these benchmarks are limited by the use of automated metrics, which restrict the diversity of testing objectives. On the other hand, evaluating task-specialized LLMs introduces more manually defined testing objectives, such as interpretability, determinism, robustness, and question understanding. Nevertheless, due to manual testing costs, these evaluations often rely on small samples (less than 10k) and coarsely categorized datasets.

In this paper, we combine the strengths of both benchmark studies and task-specific manual evaluations to test the GPT family LLMs. To achieve this, we adopt a strategy inspired by HELM [21], which uses multiple feature labels to describe and categorize task types, especially complex problem types. Additionally, we incorporate the manually predefined testing objectives from [26] and combine them with the CheckList natural language model's black-box testing strategy. This comprehensive and diverse testing approach allows us to draw more comprehensive and valuable conclusions.

2.3 Black-Box Testing of the NLP Model

The prohibitive expense associated with training LLMs renders white-box testing an impractical approach. Consequently, the majority of assessment efforts presently concentrate on black-box evaluation approaches for LLMs. For example, the methods used by [3,39] for evaluating robustness, the methods used by [49] for adversarial changes, and attention and interpretability within LLMs research conducted by [45]. The most comprehensive approach currently available is the CheckList approach proposed by [38], which categorizes evaluation targets into three parts: the minimum functionality test (MFT), invariance test (INV), and directional expectation test (DIR). The MFT examines a model's basic functionality, INV examines whether the model can maintain functional correctness when non-answer-affecting information is added to the input, and DIR examines whether the model can output the expected result when the input is modified. In this work, we follow the idea of CheckList and use CoT prompting to generate test cases for DIR.

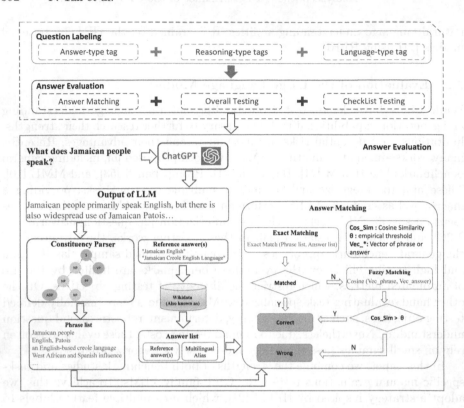

Fig. 1. Overview of proposed Evaluation Framework.

3 Evaluation Framework

As mentioned in Sect. 1, our KBQA evaluation framework consists of two parts. The first part aims to assign uniform feature labels to the questions in the datasets. The second part includes an improved Exact Match answer evaluation strategy and an extended CheckList test. Figure 1 illustrates the overall process of the framework. The detailed process is described in the following section.

3.1 Feature-Driven Unified Question Labeling

We collect multiple existing KB-based CQA datasets for the evaluation. However, due to the different annotation rules used for features such as answer and reasoning type in each dataset, we need to establish a standardized and unified set of question feature tags for evaluating and analyzing question types.

Referring to the question tags provided by existing KBQA datasets [5, 22, 24, 51], we categorize the tags that describe the features of complex questions into three types, including answer type, reasoning type and language type. Table 1 lists the eight answer type tags and seven reasoning type tags we defined. Generally, a question contains one answer type tag, one language type tag and several

Table 1. The feature-driven question tags defined in this paper.

Answer type	Description
MISC	The answer to the question is the miscellaneous fact defined by the named entity recognition task
PER	The answer to the question is the name of a person
LOC	The answer to the question is a location
WHY	The answer explains the reasons for the facts mentioned in the question
DATE	The answer to the question is a date or time
NUM	The answer to the question is a number
Boolean	The answer to the question is yes or no
ORG	The answer to the question is the name of a organization
UNA	The input question is unable to answer.

Reasoning type	Description
SetOperation	The process of obtaining answers involves set operations
Filter	The answer is obtained through condition filtering
Counting	The process of obtaining an answer involves counting operations
Comparative	The answer needs to be obtained by comparing or sorting numerical values
Single-hop	Answering questions requires a single-hop Reasoning
Multi-hop	Answering questions requires multi-hop Reasoning
Star-shape	The reasoning graph corresponding to inputting question is star-shape

reasoning type tags. Figure 2 presents the label distribution of the data collected in this paper. For an input question, our labeling process is as follows: when the dataset provides question type tags, we simply match them to our feature tag list. When no tag is provided, we use an existing bert-base-NER model [18,44] to identify the type of answer, and use keywords in SPARQL to identify the type of inference.

3.2 Answer Evaluation

The output of traditional KBQA models typically takes two forms: either a SPARQL query or a precise answer. The evaluation strategy for traditional KBQA models is based on exact match (EM), which involves comparing the model's output with a reference answer or to assess its accuracy. However, without adding additional prompts, LLMs generate text paragraphs containing answers, rather than precise answers. Furthermore, this answer may be a restatement of the reference answer.

Extended Answer Matching. To obtain evaluation results on KBQA outputs of LLMs resembling exact match, we propose an extended answer matching

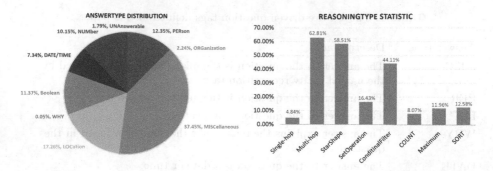

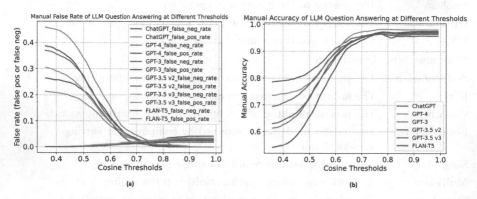

Fig. 2. The distribution of feature labels in the collect KB-based CQA datasets

Fig. 3. (a) The GPT family and T5 models show changing error rates on sampled questions as the threshold varies. (b) LLMs' QA accuracy (evaluated manually) on sampled questions varies with the threshold.

approach. This approach consists of three main parts: 1) Parsing LLMs' output using constituent trees [14] to extract NP or VP root node phrases as the candidate answer pool. 2) Expanding each reference answer using multilingual alias lists from Wikidata, including various names and aliases. 3) Using m-bert [18] to calculate the maximum Cosine similarity between reference and candidate answers for precise match evaluation, with a fuzzy matching strategy applied only to non-"NUM, DATE, Boolean" answer types.

Threshold Selection and Sensitivity Analysis. As shown in Fig. 3 (a), the analysis of various models reveals that using only EM evaluation for answers (threshold = 1) may result in 2.38%–4.17% (average 3.89%) false negative cases. To address this issue, we opt for establishing a fuzzy matching process based on cosine similarity to alleviate the problem. However, selecting an inadequate threshold may introduce additional false positive issues. Therefore, we followed the steps below to find an empirical threshold that minimizes the overall false rate (false pos + false neg) across all models: (1) We randomly sampled 3000 question samples from the test data of answer types involved in fuzzy matching

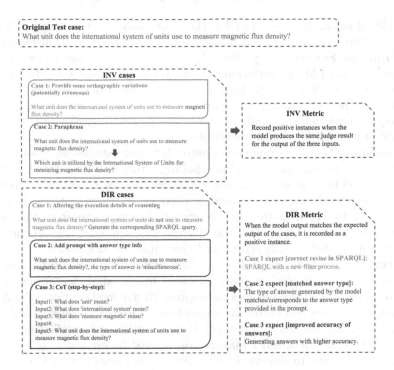

Fig. 4. Test cases design for INV and DIR.

and manually verified the correctness of the six LLM output answers shown in Fig. 3(a) (binary labels, correct/incorrect). (2) We calculate the minimum cosine similarity (the value is 0.38) between the gold answer and its aliases, and used it as the lower bound for finding the threshold. (3) We observed the changes in false rates for each model as the threshold increased from 0.38 to 1 and selected the threshold of 0.78 that minimized the average false rate across models. From the Fig. 3(a), it can be observed that the false rates of each model stabilize around this value. To evaluate the sensitivity of model performance to the threshold, as shown in Fig. 3(b), we compared the accuracy of each model on the test data as the threshold varied. The accuracy of each model tended to stabilize when the threshold was >0.7. Finally, we use 0.78 as the empirical threshold for further experiments. Sampling tests show that this threshold decreases the average false rate from 3.89% to 2.71%.

3.3 CheckList Testing

Following the idea of CheckList, we also evaluate ChatGPT and other LLMs with three distinct objectives: (1) to evaluate the ability of LLMs to handle each feature in KB-based CQA through the MFT; (2) to evaluate the robustness of LLMs' ability to handle various features in KB-based CQA scenarios through the INV; and (3) to evaluate whether the outputs of LLMs meet human expectations for modified inputs through the DIR, the controllability. The specific INV and DIR procedures are presented as follows, and Fig. 4 presents the instances:

Minimum Functionality Test. In this work, we choose to examine the performance of LLMs in performing basic reasoning tasks by only including questions that involve a single type of reasoning operation. We then compare and analyze the performance differences of the models in answering questions that require performing a single reasoning operation versus those that require performing multiple reasoning operations.

Invariance Test. We designe two methods to generate test cases for INV: the first method is to randomly introduce spelling errors into the original sentence, and the second method is to generate a question that is semantically equivalent (paraphrased) to the original sentence. Subsequently, we evaluate the invariance of the LLMs by checking the consistency of their correctness in the outputs generated from three inputs, i.e. the original test sentence, the version of the question with added spelling errors, and the paraphrased question.

Directional Expectation Test. In this study, we designed three modes for DIR test cases: (1) Replacing phrases related to reasoning operations in questions, to observe if LLMs' outputs correspond to our modifications. (2) Adding prompts with answer types after the original question text to check LLMs' ability to control the output answer type. (3) Using multi-round questioning inspired by CoT, where LLMs consider information related to key nouns before asking the original question, to observe the effectiveness and sensitivity of CoT prompts for different question types.

4   Experiments

4.1   Datasets

To highlight the complexity of the testing questions and the breadth of the testing dataset, after careful consideration, we selected six representative English monolingual KBQA datasets and two multilingual KBQA datasets for evaluation. These datasets include classic datasets such as WebQuestionSP [51], ComplexWebQuestions [43], GraphQ [42] and QALD-9 [24], as well as newly proposed datasets such as KQApro [5], GrailQA [12] and MKQA [22]. Due to the limitations of the OpenAI API, we sampled some datasets, such as MKQA (sampled by answer type) and GrailQA (only using the test set). The collection size for each dataset and the scale we collected are summarized in Table 2.

4.2   Comparative Models

State-of-the-Art Models for Each Dataset. We introduce current SOTA models' report scores from the KBQA leaderboard [29] for each dataset as traditional KBQA models in this paper for comparison. This primarily reflects the comparison between LLMs and traditional KBQA models in terms of the overall results.

Table 2. The Statistical of collected KB-based CQA datasets, "Col. Size" represents the size of the dataset we collected in our experiments. "Size" denotes the original size of the dataset.

Datasets	Size	Col. Size	Lang
KQApro	117,970	106,173	EN
LC-quad2.0	26,975	26,975	EN
WQSP	4737	4,700	EN
CWQ	31,158	31,158	EN
GrailQA	64,331	6,763	EN
GraphQ	4,776	4,776	EN
QALD-9	6,045	6,045	Mul
MKQA	260,000	6,144	Mul
Total Collected		194,782	

Large-Language Models of the GPT Family. ChatGPT is a landmark model in the GPT family, and we believe that comparing it to its predecessors and subsequent versions is very valuable. By doing so, we can observe and analyze the technical increments of the GPT family at each stage and the benefits they bring. In this paper, we compare the GPT family models, which include GPT-3, GPT-3.5 v2, GPT-3.5 v3, ChatGPT (Their names on OpenAI's Model Index document are: text-davinci-001, text-davinci-002, text-davinci-003, gpt-3.5-turbo-0301) and the newest addition, GPT-4 [27].

Large-Language Model Not Belongs to GPT Family. The LLM we have chosen is the famous FLAN-T5 (Text-to-Text Transfer Transformer 11B, [7]), which does not belong to the GPT family. Considering its multilingual question-answering ability and open-source nature, we have chosen it to participate in the comparison in this paper. FLAN-T5 is an encoder-decoder transformer language model that is trained on a filtered variant of CommonCrawl (C4) [36]. The release date and model size for this model are also based on [36].

4.3   Overall Results

The overall results are presented in Table 3. First, ChatGPT outperforms the current SOTA traditional models on three of the eight test sets, and the subsequently released GPT-4 surpasses on four test sets. By comparing the performance of GPT-4 and SOTA models, we can see that as LLMs represented by the GPT family, their zero-shot ability is constantly approaching and even surpassing traditional deep learning and knowledge representation models.

Second, comparing models in the GPT family, the newer models perform better than the previous ones, as expected. Interestingly, the performance improvement of the new GPT models is relatively consistent across all datasets, as shown in Fig. 5(a), where the line shapes of all GPT models are almost identical. This means that each generation of GPT models retains some commonalities. Based

Table 3. Overall results of the evaluation. We compare the exact match of ChatGPT with current SOTA traditional KBQA models (fine-tuned (FT) and zero-shot (ZS)), GPT family LLMs, and Non-GPT LLM. In GraphQ, QALD-9 and LC-quad2, the evaluation metric used is F1, while other datasets use Accuracy (Exact match).

Datasets	KQApro	LC-quad2	WQSP	CWQ	GrailQA	GraphQ	QALD-9	MKQA
	Acc	F1	Acc	Acc	Acc	F1	F1	Acc
SOTA(FT)	**93.85** [29]	33.10 [31]	73.10 [15]	**72.20** [15]	76.31‡	31.8 [13]	**67.82** [32]	46.00 [22]
SOTA(ZS)	94.20 [25]	-	62.98 [50]	-	-	-	-	-
FLAN-T5	37.27	30.14	59.87	46.69	29.02	32.27	30.17	20.17
GPT-3	38.28	33.04	67.68	51.77	27.58	38.32	38.54	26.97
GPT-3.5v2	38.01	33.77	72.34	53.96	30.50	40.85	44.96	30.14
GPT-3.5v3	40.35	39.04	79.60	57.54	35.43	47.95	46.19	39.05
ChatGPT	47.93	42.76	83.70	64.02	46.77	53.10	45.71	44.30
GPT-4	57.20	**54.95**	**90.45**	71.00	51.40	**63.20**	57.20	**59.20**

‡ https://dki-lab.github.io/GrailQA/.

Table 4. Comparison of LLMs on multilingual test sets.

Languages	FLAN-T5	GPT-3	GPT-3.5v2	GPT-3.5v3	ChatGPT	GPT-4
en	30.29	57.53	56.99	64.16	**66.49**	66.09
nl	20.75	50.47	54.58	60.56	65.05	**69.72**
de	22.40	50.54	54.48	57.17	62.54	**73.91**
es	21.68	48.22	55.70	58.50	**61.87**	57.69
fr	26.16	49.46	55.02	57.89	**62.19**	62.00
it	24.19	47.67	52.33	58.06	58.96	**73.91**
ro	22.28	44.38	50.94	54.12	59.55	**63.41**
pt_br	15.38	38.46	38.46	42.31	50.00	**66.67**
pt	20.58	37.70	44.26	50.27	**52.64**	52.25
ru	7.29	20.58	29.69	21.68	32.24	**49.58**
hi_in	3.61	9.93	19.13	13.54	21.48	**25.00**
fa	2.45	6.59	21.09	11.49	22.03	**31.71**
zh_cn	3.65	17.45	22.40	24.87	33.46	**44.62**

on the known cases, these commonalities may come from the transformer-based encoding. We will discuss in detail the impact they have in Sect. 4.5. In addition, we can observe that the newer versions of the GPT model show increasingly significant improvements compared to the previous generations.

Third, as shown in Fig. 5(a), although FLAN-T5's overall performance is weaker than that of the GPT family, its line shape is quite similar to that of the GPT family. This further supports our inference that the transformer-based architecture leads to commonalities in the abilities of current LLMs.

4.4   Multilingual KBQA Results

Based on the results from MKQA and QALD-9, we further present the performance of LLMs on multilingual QA in Table 4. Despite the overall trend showing

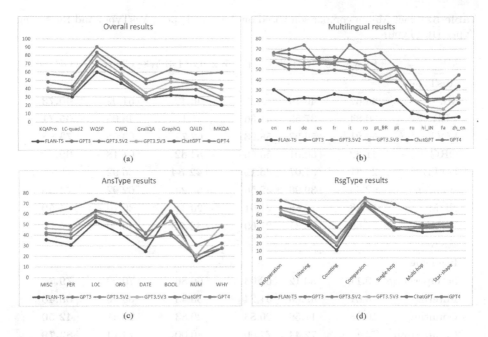

Fig. 5. (a) is the line chart based on Table 3, showing the EM scores of each model on different datasets. (b) corresponds to Table 5, with lines representing the EM scores of each model in different languages. (c) and (d) correspond to Table 4, reflecting the trend of EM scores of each model on different types of questions.

improvement in the model's ability to answer questions in different languages as the GPT family continues to iterate, we observe that GPT-4 has not surpassed ChatGPT in the four languages. This suggests that the evolution of GPT's multilingual capabilities may be starting to slow down. Figure 5(b) shows the line chart of the EM scores of the models in each language. We can find that the shapes of the lines for GPT-3 and ChatGPT are very similar, while there is a significant change in the shape of the line for GPT-4. We believe that the main reason for this change is due to the introduction of multimodal data in GPT-4, which plays a positive role in mapping between some languages.

4.5   Feature Tags Based Results

The results in Table 5 show the performance of ChatGPT and other LLMs when answering different types of questions. As such, traditional models are not compared in this section. Overall, models from the GPT family are better at answering questions with boolean (yes/no) answers, questions about organizations and locations, as well as those involving set operations and numerical comparisons. However, they do not perform well when answering questions that require precise dates or involve numerical calculations. From the performance of models in the GPT family and Flan-T5, it can be found that Flan-T5 performs worse

Table 5. Exact Match comparison based on Answer Types (AnsType) and Reasoning Types (RsgType)

MF	FLAN-T5	GPT-3	GPT-3.5v2	GPT-3.5v3	ChatGPT	GPT-4
AnsType						
MISC	35.67	40.79	42.35	46.42	51.02	**60.73**
PER	30.84	37.53	41.36	45.10	48.65	**65.71**
LOC	52.91	56.92	58.93	62.71	63.55	**73.98**
ORG	41.62	50.01	50.58	54.62	61.18	**69.20**
DATE	24.81	37.07	36.15	**42.54**	36.92	41.57
Boolean	62.43	39.96	42.56	53.23	62.92	**72.28**
NUM	16.08	19.66	21.01	20.31	30.70	**44.59**
WHY	27.69	32.31	27.69	**49.23**	40.00	47.83
UNA	-	-	-	-	-	-
RsgType						
SetOperation	60.11	60.12	62.03	66.86	70.00	**79.70**
Filtering	45.01	49.06	51.24	55.43	63.40	**68.40**
Counting	10.68	17.56	20.83	20.83	28.41	**42.50**
Comparison	72.13	72.44	74.00	80.00	74.74	**82.79**
Single-hop	41.00	38.72	42.54	49.22	54.00	**74.14**
Multi-hop	35.68	41.09	42.98	47.06	44.88	**57.20**
Star-shape	37.23	42.28	43.96	48.17	47.43	**60.91**

in all cases except for questions with boolean answer types. This is consistent with the conclusion of [21]: The performance of knowledge-intensive tasks is closely related to the size of the model. For comparisons within the GPT family of models, following the iteration process of the GPT model summarized in [11], we also observe some positive effects of certain technical introductions on the model, including: (1) [11] point out that GPT-3.5 v3 has better in-context learning abilities, while ChatGPT sacrifices these abilities in order to model dialogue history. This may explain why GPT-3.5 v3 performs better in answering multi-hop and star-shaped questions that require distinguishing entity mentions through context. (2) ChatGPT's dialogue learning helps it better answer short questions (Single-hop). (3) The GPT-3.5 v2, obtained through language model and code training followed by supervised instruction tuning, but its overall capabilities do not appear to have significantly improved compared to GPT-3. The possible reason could be that alignment harms performance, and the alignment tax offsets the increase in zero-shot ability obtained through training [21,28]. (4) One possible reason why the successor models outperform GPT3.5 V2 in most aspects is that the complex reasoning ability acquired through training on code, which did not manifest prominently in GPT3.5 V2, but were unlocked after the introduction of instruction tuning with RLHF [9,28].

Figures 5(c) and (d) respectively show line chart of the EM scores formed by each model in answering questions of different answer and reasoning types. The two Figures are consistent with what we observed in the Overall results, that is, various models of the GPT family and FLAN-T5 have similar line shapes. In addition, we also find that the performance of the new GPT models has improved significantly in some specific types of questions, such as Boolean-type (ChatGPT, GPT-4) and WHY-type (GPT-3.5 v3). However, in some other types of questions, there is no significant improvement for the multi-generation models of GPT, such as Num-type and Counting-type. This indicates that there is still a significant room for improvement for LLMs, and the iteration is far from over. Another interesting finding is that FLAN-T5 performs similarly to ChatGPT in answering boolean questions, but performs worse than the GPT family in other types of answers. Due to the difference in their training data, we cannot accurately determine in the current evaluation whether the reason for this situation is the difference in training data or whether certain training strategies used by the GPT family have a negative impact on specific types of questions.

Table 6. MFT results of ChatGPT

	SetOperation	Filtering	Counting	Comparison	Single-hop	Multi-hop	Star-shape
Single Reasoning	60.22	51.39	24.16	31.48	44.07	**48.27**	**50.75**
Multiple Reasoning	**70.00**	**63.40**	**28.41**	**74.74**	**54.00**	44.88	47.43

4.6   CheckList Results

MFT Results. In the MFT tests, we only evaluate questions that contain a single type of reasoning or multiple reasoning labels of the same type (such as SetOperation+Comparison and SetOperation+Filtering). Based on the results of MFT, we compared the performance of ChatGPT in answering single and multiple reasoning questions. Table 6 shows the following findings. (1) Except for multi-hop and star type questions, ChatGPT performs better in executing multiple reasoning than in performing single reasoning in answering questions involving other types of reasoning operations. (2) ChatGPT is not good at answering counting questions despite the improvements generated by multiple reasoning.

INV Results. Table 7 presents the stability of LLMs from the GPT family across three runs on three different test cases. As a reference, [26] noted that the stability of traditional KBQA models is 100. The results in Table 7 are reported using the following symbols: 'CCC' indicates that all answers to the three inquiries are correct, while 'WWW' indicates that none of the three

Table 7. INV results of GPT family

LLM	CCC	CCW	CWC	CWW	WCC	WCW	WWC	WWW	Stability Rate
GPT-3	434	64	59	52	42	43	73	666	76.76
GPT-3.5 v2	495	44	65	42	43	30	58	656	80.30
GPT-3.5 v3	604	46	43	49	34	35	49	583	82.83
ChatGPT	588	49	72	68	52	27	32	545	79.06
GPT-4	798	0	0	65	54	0	0	516	**91.70**

Table 8. DIR results for RsgType, the score represents the percentage of expected output produced by the LLMs.

	SetOperation	Filtering	Counting	Comparison	Overall
GPT-3.5 v3	45%	75%	65%	**65%**	62.5%
ChatGPT	**75%**	85%	**70%**	**65%**	**73.75%**
GPT-4	65%	**90%**	**70%**	60%	71.25%

inquiries received correct answers or the model did not return any useful answers. Only when the correctness of the three queries is consistent, the model's performance on the problem is considered stable. As shown in Tables 7, the overall stability of the GPT models has improved from GPT-3 to GPT-4, and GPT-4 has reached a stability rate of 91.70, which is very close to that of traditional KBQA models. The stability rate of ChatGPT is slightly lower than that of GPT-3.5, and we infer that this is due to the fact that the ChatGPT model focuses more on conversation training, resulting in higher instability (randomness) in the output.

DIR Results. As mentioned in Fig. 4, we designed three DIR modes to examine the controllability of LLMs from the GPT family. In the first mode, we manually observe whether the SPARQL statements output by the model contain the expected keywords, and calculate the failure rate of the model's expected reasoning operations. Since GPT-3.5 v2 and its earlier versions did not undergo code learning, it is difficult for them to generate correct SPARQL queries. Therefore, in this test, we compare the GPT-3.5 v3, ChatGPT, and GPT-4. As shown in Table 8, the scores of around 73% indicate that even the latest GPT model still has a high degree of randomness in performing reasoning operations, which will affect its applicable scenarios.

In the second mode, we provide prompts to the model's input indicating the answer type and observe the change in the EM score. In Table 9, red values indicate that adding prompts increases the EM score, while blue values indicate negative effects. For most models, prompts have a relatively stable positive effect on Boolean and NUM type questions, while the answers to MISC type questions are mostly negatively affected. In addition, in new models such as ChatGPT and GPT-4, the effect of answer type prompts is much worse than in GPT-3.5 and earlier models. This suggests that different models have different internal

Table 9. DIR results for AnsType prompting

	MISC	PER	LOC	ORG	DATE	Boolean	NUM	WHY
GPT-3	+1.43	0	+5.71	+4.29	+4.29	+15.71	+17.14	0
GPT-3.5 v2	-4.28	+2.85	+7.14	+14.28	+2.86	-8.57	+14.28	+12.13
GPT-3.5 v3	-12.86	+10.00	+18.57	-7.14	+4.71	+17.14	+22.85	+9.09
ChatGPT	+6.78	-3.64	-1.72	-5.35	-8.58	+4.28	+7.15	-3.03
GPT-4	-4.29	-2.86	+11.43	+5.71	0	+7.14	+4.29	-6.06

Table 10. DIR results for CoT prompting

	MISC	PER	LOC	ORG	DATE	Boolean	NUM	WHY
GPT-3	-1.40	-2.00	-2.67	+2.73	-3.77	+3.36	+35.66	+6.06
GPT-3.5 v2	-0.35	-5.33	+1.78	-3.64	+0.76	-5.04	+32.95	0
GPT-3.5 v3	0	-2.00	-1.33	-1.82	-1.51	-2.10	+34.12	0
ChatGPT	-1.75	-4.66	+0.89	-3.63	-1.50	+3.36	+30.62	+6.06
GPT-4	-3.00	+11.11	+2.22	+3.3	-2.71	0	+20.00	+2.62

	SetOperation	Filtering	Counting	Comparison	Multi-hop	Star-shape		
GPT-3	+10.79	+10.43	+35.66	+1.35	-1.60	-1.69		
GPT-3.5 v2	+4.86	+5.46	+38.54	-2.26	-1.18	-0.85		
GPT-3.5 v3	+6.34	+8.18	+38.99	-1.13	-1.61	-1.26		
ChatGPT	+7.82	+9.47	+35.78	+0.45	-1.47	-1.41		
GPT-4	+2.05	+0.93	+11.11	-1.88	+2.82	+2.68		

knowledge and understanding of the same input text, and the effectiveness and helpfulness of the same prompt vary among different models. More powerful models are more sensitive to the content of prompts because of their powerful natural language understanding ability. It may be difficult to design simple and universally effective prompts that work well across all models.

In the third mode, we guide the model step by step through a naive CoT-guided process to first provide the crucial information required to answer the question, and then answer the original question. Table 10 shows the difference in EM scores of the GPT model's answers before and after using CoT-guided process for each type of questions. We can observe that positive impact brought by CoT to GPT-4 is greater than that of other models, and the improvement of CoT on the model's ability to answer NUM-type questions is significant and stable. In terms of reasoning types, CoT improves the ability of all models in set operations, conditional filtering, and counting, but it doesn't help much with multi-hop and star-shape questions. Specifically, the most significant improvement introduced by CoT for the GPT family of models is a score increase of over 30.00 for answer types that are numerical (NUM). This result strongly supports the importance of CoT for using LLMs to solve numerical-related questions [20].

5   Conclusion

In this paper, we extensively tested the ability of ChatGPT and other LLMs to answer questions on KB-based CQA datasets using their own knowledge. The experimental results showed that the question-answering performance and reliability of the GPT model have been continuously improving with version iterations, approaching that of traditional models. CheckList testing showed that current LLMs still have a lot of room for improvement in some reasoning abilities, and CoT-inspired prompts can improve the performance of the original model on certain types of questions. Consequently, this evaluation serves as a valuable reference for future research in the relevant community. In future work, we need to further expand on the following two points: Firstly, conduct tests in various domains to validate which conclusions obtained from open-domain KBQA are universal and which are domain-specific. Secondly, perform tests on various types of models. With ongoing LLM research, besides the GPT family, many new large-scale open-source models have been proposed. It requires further exploration and summarization to determine if they possess better mechanisms for self-knowledge organization or stronger capabilities to accept human prompts and find answers.

Acknowledgments. This work is supported by the Natural Science Foundation of China (Grant No. U21A20488). We thank the Big Data Computing Center of Southeast University for providing the facility support on the numerical calculations in this paper.

References

1. Bai, Y., et al.: Benchmarking foundation models with language-model-as-an-examiner. arXiv preprint arXiv:2306.04181 (2023)
2. Bang, Y., et al.: A multitask, multilingual, multimodal evaluation of ChatGPT on reasoning, hallucination, and interactivity. arXiv e-prints, arXiv-2302 (2023)
3. Belinkov, Y., Glass, J.: Analysis methods in neural language processing: a survey. Trans. Assoc. Comput. Linguist. **7**, 49–72 (2019)
4. Brown, T., et al.: Language models are few-shot learners. Adv. Neural. Inf. Process. Syst. **33**, 1877–1901 (2020)
5. Cao, S., et al.: KQA Pro: a dataset with explicit compositional programs for complex question answering over knowledge base. In: Proceedings ACL Conference, pp. 6101–6119 (2022)
6. Chang, Y., et al.: A survey on evaluation of large language models. arXiv preprint arXiv:2307.03109 (2023)
7. Chen, X., et al.: How robust is GPT-3.5 to predecessors? A comprehensive study on language understanding tasks. arXiv e-prints, arXiv-2303 (2023)
8. Chowdhery, A., et al.: PaLM: scaling language modeling with pathways. arXiv e-prints, arXiv-2204 (2022)
9. Chung, H.W., et al.: Scaling instruction-finetuned language models. arXiv preprint arXiv:2210.11416 (2022)
10. Fu, C., et al.: MME: a comprehensive evaluation benchmark for multimodal large language models. arXiv preprint arXiv:2306.13394 (2023)
11. Fu, Y., Peng, H., Khot, T.: How does GPT obtain its ability? Tracing emergent abilities of language models to their sources. Yao Fu's Notion (2022)

12. Gu, Y., et al.: Beyond IID: three levels of generalization for question answering on knowledge bases. In: Proceedings WWW Conference, pp. 3477–3488 (2021)
13. Gu, Y., Su, Y.: ArcaneQA: dynamic program induction and contextualized encoding for knowledge base question answering. In: Proceedings COLING Conference, pp. 1718–1731 (2022)
14. He, H., Choi, J.D.: The stem cell hypothesis: dilemma behind multi-task learning with transformer encoders. In: Proceedings EMNLP Conference, pp. 5555–5577 (2021)
15. Hu, X., Wu, X., Shu, Y., Qu, Y.: Logical form generation via multi-task learning for complex question answering over knowledge bases. In: Proceedings ICCL Conference, pp. 1687–1696 (2022)
16. Huang, F., Kwak, H., An, J.: Is ChatGPT better than human annotators? Potential and limitations of ChatGPT in explaining implicit hate speech. arXiv e-prints, arXiv-2302 (2023)
17. Jiang, Z., Xu, F.F., Araki, J., Neubig, G.: How can we know what language models know? Trans. Assoc. Comput. Linguist. 8, 423–438 (2020)
18. Kenton, J.D.M.W.C., Toutanova, L.K.: BERT: pre-training of deep bidirectional transformers for language understanding. In: Proceedings NAACL-HLT Conference, pp. 4171–4186 (2019)
19. Kocoń, J., et al.: ChatGPT: jack of all trades, master of none. arXiv e-prints, arXiv-2302 (2023)
20. Kojima, T., Gu, S.S., Reid, M., Matsuo, Y., Iwasawa, Y.: Large language models are zero-shot reasoners. arXiv preprint arXiv:2205.11916 (2022)
21. Liang, P., et al.: Holistic evaluation of language models. arXiv e-prints, arXiv-2211 (2022)
22. Longpre, S., Lu, Y., Daiber, J.: MKQA: a linguistically diverse benchmark for multilingual open domain question answering. Trans. Assoc. Comput. Linguist. 9, 1389–1406 (2021)
23. Lyu, C., Xu, J., Wang, L.: New trends in machine translation using large language models: case examples with ChatGPT. arXiv preprint arXiv:2305.01181 (2023)
24. Ngomo, N.: 9th challenge on question answering over linked data (QALD-9). Language 7(1), 58–64 (2018)
25. Nie, L., et al.: GraphQ IR: unifying the semantic parsing of graph query languages with one intermediate representation. In: Proceedings EMNLP Conference, pp. 5848–5865 (2022)
26. Omar, R., Mangukiya, O., Kalnis, P., Mansour, E.: ChatGPT versus traditional question answering for knowledge graphs: current status and future directions towards knowledge graph chatbots. arXiv e-prints, arXiv-2302 (2023)
27. OpenAI: GPT-4 technical report (2023)
28. Ouyang, L., et al.: Training language models to follow instructions with human feedback. arXiv e-prints, arXiv-2203 (2022)
29. Perevalov, A., Yan, X., Kovriguina, L., Jiang, L., Both, A., Usbeck, R.: Knowledge graph question answering leaderboard: a community resource to prevent a replication crisis. In: Proceedings LREC Conference, pp. 2998–3007 (2022)
30. Petroni, F., et al.: Language models as knowledge bases? In: Proceedings IJCAI Conference, pp. 2463–2473 (2019)
31. Pramanik, S., Alabi, J., Saha Roy, R., Weikum, G.: UNIQORN: unified question answering over RDF knowledge graphs and natural language text. arXiv e-prints, arXiv-2108 (2021)

32. Purkayastha, S., Dana, S., Garg, D., Khandelwal, D., Bhargav, G.S.: A deep neural approach to KGQA via SPARQL silhouette generation. In: Proceedings IJCNN Conference, pp. 1–8. IEEE (2022)
33. Qin, C., Zhang, A., Zhang, Z., Chen, J., Yasunaga, M., Yang, D.: Is ChatGPT a general-purpose natural language processing task solver? arXiv e-prints, arXiv-2302 (2023)
34. Qin, G., Eisner, J.: Learning how to ask: querying LMS with mixtures of soft prompts. In: Proceedings NAACL-HLT Conference (2021)
35. Rae, J.W., et al.: Scaling language models: methods, analysis & insights from training gopher. arXiv e-prints, arXiv-2112 (2021)
36. Raffel, C., et al.: Exploring the limits of transfer learning with a unified text-to-text transformer. J. Mach. Learn. Res. **21**(1), 5485–5551 (2020)
37. Reynolds, L., McDonell, K.: Prompt programming for large language models: beyond the few-shot paradigm. In: Proceedings CHI EA Conference, pp. 1–7 (2021)
38. Ribeiro, M.T., Wu, T., Guestrin, C., Singh, S.: Beyond accuracy: behavioral testing of NLP models with checklist. In: Proceedings ACL Conference, pp. 4902–4912 (2020)
39. Rychalska, B., Basaj, D., Gosiewska, A., Biecek, P.: Models in the wild: on corruption robustness of neural NLP systems. In: Proceedings ICONIP Conference, pp. 235–247 (2019)
40. Segura, S., Fraser, G., Sanchez, A.B., Ruiz-Cortés, A.: A survey on metamorphic testing. IEEE Trans. Software Eng. **42**(9), 805–824 (2016)
41. Srivastava, A., et al.: Beyond the imitation game: quantifying and extrapolating the capabilities of language models. arXiv preprint arXiv:2206.04615 (2022)
42. Su, Y., et al.: On generating characteristic-rich question sets for QA evaluation. In: Proceedings EMNLP Conference, pp. 562–572 (2016)
43. Talmor, A., Berant, J.: The web as a knowledge-base for answering complex questions. In: Proceedings ACL Conference, pp. 641–651 (2018)
44. Tjong Kim Sang, E.F., De Meulder, F.: Introduction to the CoNLL-2003 shared task: language-independent named entity recognition. In: Proceedings NAACL-HLT Conference, pp. 142–147 (2003)
45. Wang, A., et al.: SuperGLUE: a stickier benchmark for general-purpose language understanding systems. In: Proceedings NeurIPS Conference, pp. 3266–3280 (2019)
46. Wang, J., Liang, Y., Meng, F., Li, Z., Qu, J., Zhou, J.: Cross-lingual summarization via chatgpt. arXiv e-prints, arXiv-2302 (2023)
47. Wang, S., Scells, H., Koopman, B., Zuccon, G.: Can ChatGPT write a good Boolean query for systematic review literature search? arXiv e-prints, arXiv-2302 (2023)
48. Wei, J., et al.: Chain of thought prompting elicits reasoning in large language models. arXiv preprint arXiv:2201.11903 (2022)
49. Wu, T., Ribeiro, M.T., Heer, J., Weld, D.S.: Errudite: scalable, reproducible, and testable error analysis. In: Proceedings ACL Conference, pp. 747–763 (2019)
50. Ye, X., Yavuz, S., Hashimoto, K., Zhou, Y., Xiong, C.: RNG-KBQA: generation augmented iterative ranking for knowledge base question answering. In: Proceedings ACL Conference, pp. 6032–6043 (2022)
51. Yih, W.T., Richardson, M., Meek, C., Chang, M.W., Suh, J.: The value of semantic parse labeling for knowledge base question answering. In: Proceedings ACL Conference, pp. 201–206 (2016)
52. Zhong, Q., Ding, L., Liu, J., Du, B., Tao, D.: Can ChatGPT understand too? A comparative study on ChatGPT and fine-tuned BERT. arXiv e-prints, arXiv-2302 (2023)

53. Zhu, K., et al.: PromptBench: towards evaluating the robustness of large language models on adversarial prompts. arXiv preprint arXiv:2306.04528 (2023)
54. Zhuo, T.Y., Huang, Y., Chen, C., Xing, Z.: Exploring AI ethics of ChatGPT: a diagnostic analysis. arXiv e-prints, arXiv-2301 (2023)

Mapping and Cleaning Open Commonsense Knowledge Bases with Generative Translation

Julien Romero[1]([✉])[iD] and Simon Razniewski[2][iD]

[1] Téléom SudParis, IPParis, Palaiseau, France
julien.romero@telecom-sudparis.eu
[2] Bosch Center for AI, Renningen, Germany
simon.razniewski@de.bosch.com

Abstract. Structured knowledge bases (KBs) are the backbone of many knowledge-intensive applications, and their automated construction has received considerable attention. In particular, open information extraction (OpenIE) is often used to induce structure from a text. However, although it allows high recall, the extracted knowledge tends to inherit noise from the sources and the OpenIE algorithm. Besides, OpenIE tuples contain an open-ended, non-canonicalized set of relations, making the extracted knowledge's downstream exploitation harder. In this paper, we study the problem of mapping an open KB into the fixed schema of an existing KB, specifically for the case of commonsense knowledge. We propose approaching the problem by *generative translation*, i.e., by training a language model to generate fixed-schema assertions from open ones. Experiments show that this approach occupies a sweet spot between traditional manual, rule-based, or classification-based canonicalization and purely generative KB construction like COMET. Moreover, it produces higher mapping accuracy than the former while avoiding the association-based noise of the latter. Code and data are available. (https://github.com/Aunsiels/GenT, julienromero.fr/data/GenT)

Keywords: Open Knowledge Bases · Generative Language Models · Schema Matching

1 Introduction

Motivation and Problem Open Information Extraction (OpenIE) automatically extracts knowledge from a text. The idea is to find explicit relationships, together with the subject and the object they link. For example, from the sentence "In nature, fish swim freely in the ocean.", OpenIE could extract the triple *(fish, swim in, the ocean)*. Here, the text explicitly mentions the subject, the predicate, and the object. Therefore, if one uses OpenIE to construct a knowledge base (we call it an Open Knowledge Base, open KB) from a longer text, one obtains many predicates, redundant statements, and ambiguity.

OpenIE is often used for commonsense knowledge base (CSKB) construction. Previous works such as TupleKB [18], Quasimodo [27,28] or Ascent [19–21] use OpenIE to extract knowledge from different textual sources (textbooks,

T. R. Payne et al. (Eds.): ISWC 2023, LNCS 14265, pp. 368–387, 2023.
https://doi.org/10.1007/978-3-031-47240-4_20

query logs, question-answering forums, search engines, or the Web), and then add additional steps to clean and normalize the obtained data. Another example is ReVerb [10], which was used to get OpenIE triples from a Web crawl. The output of OpenIE typically inherits noise from sources and extraction, and the resulting KBs contain an open-ended set of predicates. This generally is not the case for knowledge bases with a predefined schema. Famous instances of this type are manually constructed, like ConceptNet [31] and ATOMIC [15]. They tend to have higher precision. Besides, they are frequently used in downstream applications such as question-answering [11,42], knowledge-enhanced text generation [43], image classification [40], conversation recommender systems [47], or emotion detection [46]. These applications assume there are a few known predicates so that we can learn specialized parameters for each relation (a matrix or embeddings with a graph neural network). This is not the case for open KBs.

Still, many properties of open KBs, such as high recall and ease of construction, are desirable. In this paper, we study *how to transform an open KB into a KB with a predefined schema*. More specifically, we study the case of commonsense knowledge, where ConceptNet is by far the most popular resource. From an open KB, we want to generate a KB with the same relation names as ConceptNet. This way, we aim to increase precision and rank the statements better while keeping high recall. Notably, as we reduce the number of relations, we obtain the chance to make the statements corroborate. For example, *(fish, live in, water, freq:1)*, *(fish, swim in, water, freq:1)* and *(fish, breath in, water, freq:1)* can be transformed into *(fish, LocatedIn, water, freq:3)*, and therefore they all help to consolidate that statement.

Transforming open triples to a predefined schema raises several challenges. In the simplest case, the subject and object are conserved, and we only need to predict the correct predefined predicate. This would be a classification task. For example, *(fish, live in, water)* can be mapped to *(fish, LocatedAt, water)* in ConceptNet. We could proceed similarly in cases where subject and object are inverted, like mapping *(ocean, contain, fish)* to *(fish, LocatedAt, ocean)*, with just an order detection step. However, in many cases, the object is not expressed in the same way or only partially: *(fish, live in, the ocean)* can be mapped to *(fish, LocatedAt, ocean)*. In other cases, part or all of the predicate is in the object, like *(fish, swim in, the ocean)* that can be mapped to *(fish, CapableOf, swim in the ocean)*. Here, the initial triple could also be mapped to *(fish, LocatedAt, ocean)*, showing that the mapping is not always unique. Other problems also arise, like with (near) synonyms. For example, we might want to map *(fish, live in, sea)* to *(fish, LocatedAt, ocean)*.

Approach and Contribution. We propose to approach the mapping of an open KB to a predefined set of relations as a translation task. We start by automatically aligning triples from the source and target KB. Then, we use these alignments to finetune a generative language model (LM) on the translation task: Given a triple from an open KB, the model produces one or several triples in the target schema. The generative nature of the LM allows it to adapt to the abovementioned problems while keeping a high faithfulness w.r.t. the source KB. Besides, we show that this improves the precision of the original KB and provides a better ranking for the statements while keeping a high recall. Our contributions are:

1. We define the problem of open KB mapping, delineating it from the more generic KB canonicalization and the more specific predicate classification.
2. We propose a generative translation model based on pre-trained language models trained on automatically constructed training data.
3. We experimentally verify the advantages of this method compared to traditional manual and rule-based mapping, classification, and purely generative methods like COMET.

2   Previous Work

2.1   Commonsense Knowledge Bases

ConceptNet. ConceptNet [31], built since the late 1990s via crowdsourcing, is arguably today's most used commonsense knowledge base. Due to user-based construction, it has high precision. ConceptNet comprises a limited set of predefined relations and contains non-disambiguated entities and concepts. For example, we find *(mouse, PartOf, computer)* and *(mouse, PartOf, rodent family)*. Thus, when mapping an open KB to ConceptNet, one needs to focus mainly on the predicates and, to some extent, the modification of the subject and object.

Open Knowledge Base. An open knowledge base (open KB) is a collection of SPO triples *(subject, predicate, object)* with no further constraints on the components. This means that they are not canonicalized. For example, the triples *(The Statue of Liberty, is in, New York)* and *(Statue of Liberty, located in, NYC)*, although equivalent, could be present in the same knowledge base. The subject and the object are noun phrases (NP), whereas the predicate is a relational phrase (RP). As a comparison, knowledge bases with a predefined schema like Wikidata [36], YAGO [33] or ConceptNet [31] come with a set of predefined predicates and/or entities for the subjects and the objects. This paper will call such a knowledge base a *Closed Knowledge Base* (closed KB).

This paper will use two open KBs: Quasimodo and Ascent++. Quasimodo [28] is an open commonsense knowledge base constructed automatically from query logs and question-answering forums. Ascent++ [19] is also an open commonsense knowledge base created from Web content. The extraction follows a classical pipeline and outputs an open KB in both cases.

2.2   From Open KBs to Closed KBs

Open Knowledge Base Canonicalization. The task of open KB canonicalization [12] consists of turning an open triple (s, p, o), where s and o are an NP and p is an RP, into an equivalent (semantically) new triple (s_e, p_e, o_e), where s_e and o_e represent entities (generally through a non-ambiguous NP), and p_e is a non-ambiguous and unique representation of a predicate. It means there is no other p'_e such that (s_e, p_e, o_e) is semantically equivalent to (s_e, p'_e, o_e). For example, we would like to map *(Statue of Liberty, located in, NYC)* to *(The Statue of Liberty, AtLocation, New York City)*, where "The Statue of Liberty" represents only the famous monument in New York City, "New York City" represents the American city unambiguously, and "AtLocation" is a predicate used to give the location of the subject.

NP canonicalization is more studied than RP canonicalization, but the task is generally treated as a clusterization problem [12]. It is essential to notice that an NP or an RP does not necessarily belong to a single cluster, as this cluster may depend on the context. For example, in *(Obama, be, president of the US)*, "Obama" refers to the entity "Barack Obama", whereas in *(Obama, wrote, Becoming)*, "Obama" refers to "Michele Obama". Also, we must notice that canonicalization does not have a target: *The transformation does not try to imitate the schema of an existing knowledge base.* The main goal is to reduce redundancy, but the number of predicates (and entities) might remain high.

Entity Linking. Entity Linking is the task of mapping an entity name to an entity in a knowledge base. For example, we would like to map *Paris* in *(Paris, be, city of love)* to Q90 in Wikidata, the entity that represents the capital of France. In the triple *(Paris, be, a hero)*, *Paris* should be mapped to Q167646 in Wikidata, the entity that represents the son of Priam. When mapping an open KB to a closed KB, most systems first perform entity linking before processing the predicate [6,44]. This supposes that the subject and the object remain unchanged during the mapping. This is a problem when we want to map to ConceptNet as this KB is not canonicalized, and the subject and object might be modified.

Knowledge Base Construction. Knowledge base construction can be done manually by asking humans to fill in the KB [15,31] or automatically using pattern matching [1,33] or OpenIE [18,19,28]. In general, manual approaches have higher accuracy but struggle to scale. Translating an open KB to a closed KB can be seen as an additional stage in an OpenIE extraction pipeline like Quasimodo or Ascent++. By doing so, we make the KB match a predefined schema. The same result would be possible directly from the corpus using traditional IE techniques. However, this approach is more human-labor intensive, depends on the domain, and does the scale [48].

Ontology Matching. Ontology matching is the task of mapping one structured schema into another [9]. This task has a long history in databases and semantic web research. However, due to the input being of little variance in predicates, it is typically approached as a structured graph alignment problem [5,8]. We cannot simply map one predicate to another in the present problem, as textual predicates are generally ambiguous. The mapping may differ for different s-o-pairs with the same p.

2.3 Existing Systems

In this paper, we are interested in a task that was barely tackled by previous works: We want to map an *entire* open KB to the schema of an existing closed KB. In the Ascent++ paper [19], the authors noticed that using an open KB in practice was difficult due to the lack of existing frameworks. Therefore, they proposed to map Ascent++ to ConceptNet's schema. However, they did a straightforward manual mapping that involved translating as many relations as possible manually. This approach is simplistic and does not yield good results, as we will see later. KBPearl [17] did a variation of the manual mapping in which they used the existing labels of entities and predicates, which greatly limits the system.

When we look at similar tasks, we find two main ideas to transition between an open KB and a closed KB. First, some authors approached this problem via rule mining, a generalization of the manual mapping of predicates. Previous systems [6,29,30] often use a rule mining system (automatic or manual) that relies on the type of subject and object and keywords in the triple. They often return a confidence score. The main issues with these frameworks are that they generalize poorly (particularly to unseen predicates) and require significant human work.

The second way to see our problem is as a classification task: Given an open triple (s, p, o), we want to predict a semantically equivalent/related triple (s, p', o) that would be in the considered closed KB. OpenKI [44] used neighbor relations as input of their classifier. Later [41], word embeddings were included to represent the predicate and help with the generalization. However, their training and testing dataset is constructed using an open KB and a closed KB with entities already aligned by humans (ReVerb [10] and Freebase in the original paper). This is not generally the case in practice. Besides, this approach considers that the subject and object remain the same, thus ignoring modification of the subject and object, inverse relations, or closely related entities.

In [24], the authors propose a method to compute the similarity between a triple in an open KB and a triple in a closed KB. This differs from our approach because we do not know potential candidates in the closed KB in advance. Indeed, the closed KB is often incomplete, and we want to generate new triples thanks to the open KB. Therefore, we focus more on the generation rather than the comparison. However, it is essential to notice that this approach integrates word embeddings for comparison. Besides, the authors use the distant supervision approach to create a dataset automatically: Given a close triple, they find sentences (in a different corpus) containing both entities from the triple. Then, they apply an OpenIE algorithm to obtain an open triple. This triple is used as a ground truth. In our case, we do not have this additional textual source: The inputs are the open KB and the closed KB.

T-REx [7] aligns Wikipedia abstracts with the Wikidata triples using a rule-based system. However, it comes with several limitations. First, it takes as input text and not open triples. Even if we were to take the documents used for constructing Ascent++ (a web crawl), the computation time would be much longer because of the difference in scale. Second, T-REx needs to perform named-entity recognition which does not apply to commonsense. Third, there is a strong dependency between Wikipedia and Wikidata. Some pages are even created automatically from Wikidata. Despite these limitations, we can consider the rule-based alignment presented in Sect. 4.1 as a generalization of their AllEnt aligner. T-REx was used for evaluating language models in a zero-shot fashion [23,38], or for OpenIE [37].

In [13], the authors introduce a methodology to manually evaluate the alignment of triples from an open KB with a closed KB. Besides, they studied how much an open KB (OPIEC [14] in their case) can be expressed by a closed KB (DBpedia [1]). They found that the open triples can often be aligned to DBpedia facts, but they are generally more specific. Also, one can usually express an OpenIE fact in the DBpedia schema. Still, this expressivity is limited if we consider only a single relation rather than a conjunction (or even a more expressive logical formula).

3   Problem Formulation

An open triple t consists of a subject s, a predicate p, and an object o. An open knowledge base $\mathcal{K}_O$ is a set of open triples. A closed schema $\mathcal{R}_C$ is a set of relations $\{R_1, \ldots, R_n\}$. A triple mapping m is a function that takes an open triple t and a closed schema $\mathcal{R}_C$ and produces a set of triples with predicates from $\mathcal{R}_C$.

Note that m is not defined as producing a single output triple per input triple - depending on the closed schema's structure, some open triples may give rise to several closed triples. Besides, the subject and object are not guaranteed to remain the same.

Problem. Given an open KB $\mathcal{K}_O$ and a closed set of relations $\mathcal{R}_C$, the task is to find a mapping m that enables to build a closed KB $\mathcal{K}_C = m(\mathcal{K}_O, \mathcal{R}_C)$, with the following properties:

1. **Preserves source recall.** In other words, ensure that as many triples as possible are mapped to a nonempty set, maximizing $| \{t_O \in \mathcal{K}_O \mid m(t_O, \mathcal{R}_C) \neq \emptyset) | $.
2. **Remains source-faithful.** In other words, ensure that each triple in the output stems from one or several semantically similar statements in the input, that is, that for each $t_c \in \mathcal{K}_C$, $m^{-1}(t_C, \mathcal{R}_C)$ is semantically similar to t_C.
3. **Corrects errors.** In other words, the goal is to minimize the set of triples in $\mathcal{K}_C$ that are factually wrong.

The definition above hinges on the concept of semantic similarity. In line with previous work [13], we specifically refer to semantic equivalence or entailment. In summary, the truth of t_O should be a sufficient condition for the truth of t_C. However, our method does not desire the opposite direction, i.e. producing t_C statements that are sufficient conditions for t_O.

4   Methodology

As we saw in Sect. 2 and will describe in more detail in Sect. 5.2, previous works propose to tackle the open KB mapping task in three different ways: manual mapping, rule mining mapping, or classifier mapping. However, these methods all come with challenges: They require much human work, cannot modify the subject and the object, cannot cover all cases, and, as we will see, have low performance. Therefore, we introduce here a new methodology to tackle these issues. We present in Fig. 1 our approach. It is composed of four steps:

1. *Alignment*: We automatically create a dataset of alignments using the open KB and the closed KB.
2. *Finetuning*: We use this dataset to finetune a generative language model (GPT-2 here) to generate alignments.
3. *Generation*: We generate one or several mappings for each triple in the open KB.
4. *Ranking*: Using the score in the original KB, the generation score, and the rank of the generated alignment, we create a final score for each closed triple.

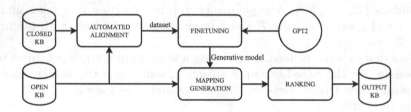

Fig. 1. The Steps of Our Methodology.

4.1   Creating Weakly-Labelled Training Data

The generative translation mapping and existing classification and rule mining approaches require a training dataset of alignments, that is, pairs of open triples and semantically equivalent or entailed closed triples. Creating this at scale manually is hardly feasible. Therefore, we decided to adopt two automatic approaches to generate a broader dataset, even if they contain some noise.

Rule-Based Alignment. The first approach we consider is based on rules. To align an open KB with ConceptNet, we used the following algorithm:

1. Lemmatization and stopwords removal.
2. For each triple (s, p, o) in our open KB, we create one or several alignments (we used _ as a general placeholder):

- s, _, o is in Conceptnet (standard alignment)
- o, _, s is in Conceptnet (reverse alignement)
- s, _, p + o is in Conceptnet (predicate in the object)
- p + o, _, s is in Conceptnet (reverse predicate in the object)

This approach has the advantage of not creating divergence in the alignment: We have hard constraints (words) that do not allow us to align statements that are too different. However, this is not true with the following technique.

LM-Based Alignment. Here, we propose an entirely unsupervised method. First, we compute the embeddings of each triple in both KBs and then align each open triple with the nearest close triple. For computing the triple embeddings, we used a sentence embeddings neural network fed with the subject, the predicate, and the object, separated by a comma. The Python library SBert provides a MiniLM [39] model finetuned on a paraphrasing task. Then, we used Scikit-learn [22] K-nearest neighbor algorithm to find the nearest neighbor in a closed KB for each triple in an open KB (or the opposite, marked as INV later) and the distance between the two triples. Finally, as considering all the alignments might introduce noise, we assess several scenarios in which we only take the top 1k, 10k, and 100k alignments according to the distance score. As generating the mapping is expensive, we will not finetune this parameter more.

With this technique, we might have alignments that are not related. However, compared to the previous method, we will be able to have a larger dataset, and we might get semantic relatedness coming from using different wording (e.g., with synonyms) that was not captured before.

4.2 Generative Translation Mapping

The second step consists in finetuning a generative language model to generate the mappings. This can be seen as a translation problem, similar to machine translation. We formatted our input by separating the OpenIE triple and its aligned ConceptNet triple with a *[SEP]* token. In our experiments, we used the GPT-2 model [25] and the script provided by HuggingFace to finetune GPT-2. Unfortunately, GPT-3 [3] is not publicly available. We also tried T5 [26], but we did not obtain better results (see T5-GenT in Table 1). We also accessed a very large language model, LLaMa [35], following Alpaca [34,45]. However, this model failed to adapt to the structure of the closed KB, even when given various explicit prompts. We hypothesize that such a model lost flexibility as it better understood natural language. Succeeding in reintroducing structured information in very large LM can lead to exciting future works. Another disadvantage of very large LMs is their computation cost at training and during inference.

The third step is the actual generation. We used a beam search for the generation part to obtain the top K results for each statement in our knowledge base. We filter the results to keep only well-formed triples and triples so that the subject and object differ. Considering more than one alignment per triple can help in many ways. First, a triple can have several translations. Second, the system learned to generate related statements that might help rank the final statements.

Finally, once we have all the translations to ConceptNet triples, we compute a score for each triple based on the frequency at which it appeared (several OpenIE triples generally generate the same closed triple) and the inverse rank among the predictions. More formally, we obtain the score of a triple t using:

$$\text{FinalScore}(t) = \sum_{t' \text{ generates } t} \frac{\text{score}(t')}{\text{rank}(t',t)+1}$$

We will also consider two other scores in Sect. 6. The first only considers the open KB score part of the previous formula (a sum of scores), while the second only considers the ranks (a sum of reciprocal ranks). Here, it is essential to notice that the score of an open triple is provided by the open KB. Therefore, if the open KB is not good at scoring triples, we will inherit negative signals that we hope to compensate with the ranks.

In the end, we can generate a ranking for all our statements. Moreover, using a generative LM allows for having friendly properties missing in previous works. For example, it can adapt the subject and the object to match the new predicate. Besides, it can also correct the original statement if it contains a mistake (spelling or truth). Furthermore, it can inverse the subject and the object without additional help. Finally, it can generate multiple outputs from one input, bringing value to the end KB. We will demonstrate these properties in Sect. 6.

5   Experiment Setup

5.1   Evaluation

Automatic Global Metrics. To get a general understanding of the generated KB after the mapping, we compute the size of the KB. However, as the size is insufficient to evaluate the recall [28], we consider that ConceptNet is our gold standard as humans filled it. Then, we measure the number of triples from ConceptNet we can generate. We call it the *automatic recall*. Likewise, we create the *automatic precision*:

$$R_a(KB_{trans}) = \frac{|KB_{trans} \cap KB_{target}|}{|KB_{target}|} \qquad P_a(KB_{trans}) = \frac{|KB_{trans} \cap KB_{target}|}{|KB_{trans}|}$$

As a part of the target KB can be used in the training dataset, we also define $\bar{R}_a$ as:

$$\overline{R}_a(KB_{trans}) = \frac{|KB_{trans} \cap KB_{target} - D_{train}|}{|KB_{target} - D_{train}|}$$

We also define $\overline{P_a}$ following the same rationale as $\overline{R}_a$. However, this metric does not capture the ranking of our statements. The ranking is crucial in open KBs as these KBs are often noisy. Ideally, we want to have correct and important statements with a high score. We introduce metrics to measure that property. First, we will also use an *automatic precision at K* where, instead of considering the entire KB_{trans}, we will only consider its top K statements. However, these metrics do not consider the entire KB. Therefore, we introduce a generalized mean reciprocal rank of the final ranked KB as follows:

$$MRR(KB_{trans}) = \frac{\sum_{KB_{trans}[i]\in KB_{target}} \frac{1}{i}}{|KB_{target}|} \qquad \overline{MRR}(KB_{trans}) = \frac{\sum_{KB_{trans}[i]\in KB_{target}-D_{train}} \frac{1}{i}}{|KB_{target}-D_{train}|}$$

These metrics allow us to measure the recall, but it gives more weight to correct high-ranked statements.

All the metrics presented depend on the quality and coverage of the original open knowledge base. Therefore, when considering a translated KB, we prefer relative metrics where the metric is divided by the metric computed for the open knowledge base, ignoring the relations.

Automatic Triple Alignment Metrics. In Sect. 4.1, we suggested methods to align an open KB with a closed KB. These techniques generate a dataset of alignments that can be split into a training and a testing set used to evaluate the MRR, the precision (@K), and the recall (@K).

Manual Metrics. The automatic metrics we presented above are cheap to run but give a coarse approximation of the quality of the resulting knowledge. Therefore, we introduce manual metrics here. They are more expensive to run as they require human work but will provide a more precise evaluation.

Manual Triple Metrics. Inspired by [13], we would like to evaluate the quality of the triple mapping according to three parameters:

- *Correct mapping*: Is the generated triple a correct mapping of the open triple, i.e., is it semantically equivalent/related to the original triple?
- *Correct prediction*: Is the resulting triple true? Independently of whether the mapping is correct, we would like to know if the resulting triple is accurate. This can be useful for several reasons. First, even if the mapping is incorrect, we would prefer that it does not hurt the quality of the knowledge base we construct next. Second, as the input triple may be noisy and incorrect, we would prefer that the system generates a correct statement rather than a correct mapping. Finally, if such a property holds, it will prove that the system has some cleaning properties that will help improve the quality of the open KB.
- *Correct open triple*: Is the original open triple correct? This information will help evaluate what the system predicts depending on the quality of the input triple (see the point above).

Knowledge Base Level Metrics. Precision and recall are crude automated heuristics w.r.t. another data source. To evaluate the quality of novel CSK resources meaningfully, we rely on the *typicality* notion of previous works [20,28]: We ask humans how often a statement holds for a given subject. Possible answers are: Invalid (the statement makes no sense) or Never / Rarely / Sometimes / Often / Always. Each answer has a score between 0 and 4 to compute a mean.

5.2   Baselines

Manual Mapping. For this baseline, we manually map the relations in an open KB to relations in ConceptNet. It is inspired by an idea from [19]. Given a predicate p in an open knowledge base, we ask humans to turn it into a predicate p' in ConceptNet (including inverse relations). There are many relations in an open KB, so we only mapped the top relations. We also notice that, in many cases, a triples *(s, p, o)* can directly be mapped to the triple *(s, CapableOf, p + o)*. For example, *(elephant, live in, Africa)* could be mapped to *(elephant, CapableOf, live in Africa)*. If we cannot find a better translation, we default to this translation. This approach is a simple rule system. In our case, we annotated 100 predicates for Quasimodo and Ascent++. By doing so, we cover 82% of triples in Quasimodo and 57% of triples in Ascent++.

Rule Mining. Given that no previous work made their implementation public, we propose a rule mining approach inspired by previous works [6,29,30]. Our method requires a training dataset of mappings. In our case, this dataset was constructed automatically (see Sect. 4.1) using the rule-based alignment method. The LM-based alignment is inappropriate as the subject and object must remain unchanged with the rule mining approach. Like in previous works, we also used WordNet to get the type of the concepts.

We use AMIE [16] to mine Horn rules of the form $B \Rightarrow r(x,y)$. The PCA confidence proposed in AMIE yields poor results. Therefore, we used the standard confidence. Ultimately, we only keep rules with a confidence score greater than 0.5. An advantage of this method is that it provides high interpretability: For each final generation, we can see which open triples were used to generate it and which rules were applied.

Classification Task. For this baseline inspired by OpenKI [44], we want to use a classifier to predict the ConceptNet relation of an open triple. Given a triple *(s, p, o)* in an open KB, we want to predict a relation p' (including inverse relations) in ConceptNet such that (s, p', o) would be in ConceptNet. To do so, we used a classifier based on BERT [4] and trained it with a dataset created automatically (see Sect. 4.1). Building this dataset by hand would be possible, but it would take much time, and we would get problems getting enough examples for each predicate. Besides, we will use the same training dataset with the translation models.

5.3   Implementation

We implemented the baselines using Python3 (except for AMIE, written in Java). For the generative LM, we used GPT-2-large given by Huggingface. We ran our code on machines with NVIDIA Quadro RTX 8000 GPUs. Finetuning a language model required a single machine for a maximum of two days. We used three training epochs in our experiments. However, mapping an open KB to ConceptNet was much longer and took up to 30 days on a single GPU. Nevertheless, the computations can easily be parallelized on several GPUs by splitting the input data, which allows us to speed up the process. In our experiments, we used Quasimodo and ASCENT++ as open KBs and mapped them to ConceptNet commonsense relations. The code (github.com/Aunsiels/GenT) and data (julienromero.fr/data/GenT) are available. .

6   Results and Discussion

6.1   Comparison with Baselines

Table 1 shows the results of the automated metrics for all baselines. The first thing to notice is that the metrics seem "low". We recall that they are in fact relative to the open KB with the relations ignored, as mentioned in Sect. 5.1. Therefore, they only have a relative interpretation. Even with the generous evaluation of the open KB, many metrics have a value of more than one, showing a significant improvement, particularly for the recall. For precision, a value less than one mainly comes with the growth of the KB size.

Our proposed approach clearly outperforms the various baselines. The basic models are not flexible and do not tackle the challenges we mentioned earlier. For manual mapping, the annotation process depends on humans and is not trivial, as translating a predicate often depends on the context. The classifier model performs better than the two other baselines when we look at the recall. Still, we observe problems to generalize as $\overline{R_a}$ is low.

Table 1. Automatic (Relative) Recall And Precision (* ignores the predicates).

KB	Method	Training data	R_a	$\overline{R_a}$	P_a	$\overline{P_a}$	P_a@10	P_a@100	P_a@1000	P_a@10k	$\overline{P_a}$@10k	MRR	$\overline{MRR}$	Size
ConceptNet	KB itself	-	-	-	-	-	-	-	-	-	-	-	-	232,532
Quasimodo	KB itself	-	2.54%*	-	0.271%*	-	10%*	17%*	11%*	4.79%*	-	4.63e^{-6} *	-	5,930,628
Ascent++	KB itself	-	1.63%*	-	0.430%*	-	10%*	10%*	6.6%*	3.13%*	-	3.56e^{-6} *	-	1,967,126
KB	**Method**	**Training data**	$R_{a,rel}$	$\overline{R}_{a,rel}$	$P_{a,rel}$	$\overline{P}_{a,rel}$	$P_{a,rel}$@10	$P_{a,rel}$@100	$P_{a,rel}$@1000	$P_{a,rel}$@10k	$\overline{P}_{a,rel}$@10k	MRR$_{rel}$	$\overline{MRR}_{rel}$	**Size**
Quasimodo	Manual Mapping [19]	-	0.231	-	0.103	-	1.000	0.471	0.455	0.315	-	0.592	-	4,925,792
	Rule Mining [6,29,30]	Rule-based	0.161	0.006	0.509	0.020	3.000	1.235	0.645	0.365	0.004	1.259	0.002	689,146
	Classifier [44]	Rule-based	0.752	0.042	0.299	0.016	2.000	1.000	0.855	0.672	0.002	1.419	0.001	5,478,028
	GenT@1	Rule-based	1.465	0.425	**0.771**	0.217	8.000	4.471	4.127	3.361	0.201	4.816	0.098	4,135,349
	GenT@10	Rule-based	2.563	1.319	0.176	0.085	9.000	4.588	4.227	**3.612**	0.234	**4.968**	0.097	33,425,732
	GenT@10	LM-based@10k	2.370	1.677	0.347	**0.235**	2.000	2.294	3.227	2.777	0.357	2.505	0.069	15,647,853
	GenT@10	LM-based@10k-INV	**2.787**	**1.933**	0.241	0.162	1.000	1.059	1.391	1.939	**0.660**	1.333	0.216	25,798,594
	T5-GenT@10	LM-based@10k-INV	1.843	1.020	0.123	0.065	-	-	-	1.094	0.236	0.670	0.070	33,874,204
Ascent++	Manual Mapping [19]	-	0.287	-	0.205	-	0.000	0.500	0.485	0.415	-	0.351	-	1,228,001
	Rule Mining [6,29,30]	Rule-based	0.223	0.060	0.705	0.190	2.000	0.600	0.394	0.511	0.045	1.306	0.034	277,835
	Classifier [44]	Rule-based	0.663	0.180	0.340	0.105	2.000	1.200	0.652	0.649	0.026	0.784	0.016	1,722,441
	GenT@1	Rule-based	1.706	0.785	**1.147**	**0.523**	4.000	4.800	3.091	2.722	0.396	2.949	0.278	1,277,065
	GenT@10	Rule-based	3.055	1.933	0.260	0.160	5.000	4.800	3.803	3.073	0.454	3.989	0.500	10,193,040
	GenT@10	LM-based@10k	3.497	2.546	0.444	0.319	6.000	4.700	3.803	**3.450**	1.096	**4.494**	0.216	7,000,135
	GenT@10	LM-based@10k-INV	**4.000**	**2.613**	0.428	0.272	4.000	2.000	2.727	**3.450**	**1.326**	2.736	**0.556**	8,305,861

Table 2. Manual Alignment Evaluation On Quasimodo (left) and Typicality (right).

Dataset	Sem. Rel.	Open Correct	Close Correct	Both Correct
Rule-based	53.0%	85.3%	69.3%	64.8%
GenT@10k	45.7%	85.3%	75.7%	68.0%
GenT@10k-INV	**55.3%**	85.3%	**77.3%**	**69.7%**

KB	Alignment	Typicality
ConceptNet	-	**3.18**
Quasimodo	-	2.70
Quasimodo	Rule-based	2.91
Quasimodo	GenT@10k-INV	2.88
Ascent++	-	2.31
Ascent++	Rule-based	2.68
Ascent++	GenT@10k-INV	2.88

Table 3. Automatic Triple Alignment MRR, Recall And Precision (as usually defined).

KB	Method	Dataset	MRR	R@1	R@5	R@10	P@1	P@5	P@10
Quasimodo	Manual	Manual	$1.56e^{-2}$	1.51%	–	–	1.56%	–	–
	Rule Mining	Rule-based	$5.96e^{-2}$	5.55%	17.8%	24.8%	5.68%	3.63%	2.52%
	Classifier	Rule-based	0.194	19.0%	–	–	19.4%	–	–
	GenT@10	Rule-based	**0.381**	**31.6%**	**46.7%**	**49.5%**	**31.1%**	**9.67%**	**5.12%**
	GenT@10	LM-based@10k	0.279	23.1%	34.5%	36.9%	23.1%	6.91%	3.69%
	GenT@10	LM-based@100k	0.319	27.5%	38.0%	39.8%	27.5%	7.60%	3.98%
	GenT@10	LM-based@1k-INV	0.211	15.4%	26.9%	34.6%	15.4%	5.38%	3.46%
	GenT@10	LM-based@10k-INV	0.123	8.48%	17.1%	20.4%	8.77%	3.51%	2.09%
	T5-GenT@10	LM-based@10k-INV	0.129	10.0%	16.6%	19.9%	10.1%	3.40%	2.05%

Table 4. SO Conservation For Quasimodo.

	First gen.			At least one gen.			All gens.		
Alignment	S	O	SO	S	O	SO	S	O	SO
Rule-based	36.8%	48.5%	**26.6%**	57.9%	76.2%	**48.3%**	25.0%	**35.3%**	**12.4%**
LM-based@1k	27.5%	21.0%	7.37%	45.3%	41.7%	17.9%	22.3%	12.3%	2.37%
LM-based@1k-INV	**38.7%**	**53.6%**	22.4%	55.2%	**77.5%**	42.0%	**27.0%**	31.9%	5.84%

6.2   What Is the Best Alignment Method?

In Sect. 4.1, we presented two automatic alignment methods. The first is based on a rule system, whereas the second aligns with the closest triples in a latent space using embeddings. We refer to the first as Rule-based and the second as LM-based@K(-INV) when we used top K statements of the complete dataset obtained by aligning each open triple with a close triple (INV means we align each close triple with an open triple).

Do They Allow the Model to Generate Accurate Alignments? Table 3 gives the performance of the model on a test dataset derived from the complete dataset. Therefore, it is not the same for all models and depends on the alignment method. Still, it gives us some valuable insights. We can see that the Rule-based alignment is the easiest to learn. This is due to the strong correlation created by the rules between the open and the closed triples. According to the metrics, the INV methods perform worse than non-INV ones. A reason might be that the INV alignment has more diversity: A triple from ConceptNet can appear only once in the dataset (we align each close triple with a single open triple). Therefore, it might be harder to learn.

Table 4 shows the conservation of the subject S and object O during the generation phase. We want to observe if they remain the same for the first generation, for at least one generation, or for all generations. The rule-based system encodes these constraints and should therefore outperform the other baselines. However, interestingly, we observe that the INV methods have excellent conservation, competing with the rule-based system (except for SO conservation), and largely beating non-INV alignments. This is surprising as it contains no prior constraint. It is a property that we expect from a good alignment method as we do not want the generated close triples to diverge from the original triples.

All these evaluations are automatic and only approximate the model's capabilities. We additionally performed manual annotations of the generations to check if the generated close triples are correct alignments (according to semantic relatedness, as discussed in Sect. 5.1). We sampled 300 triples from the top 10k triples in Quasimodo and looked at the first generation for three models. The results are presented in Table 2. We observed that the rule-based and INV alignments have similar performances for generating related close triples. Only the non-INV model underperforms, which matches what we noticed for SO conservation. Here, semantic relatedness is relatively low because it is quite constraining. However, we observe that the generated triples share most of the time part of the subject or object with the original triple.

What Is the Impact of the Training Dataset Size? We sampled the top-K samples with $K \in \{1k, 10k, 100k\}$ in the training dataset and picked the best size. We observed that the model performs best for 10k samples. Note that finding the optimal size would take too much time as, with these metrics, we need to generate the entire mapping. The testing dataset used in Table 3 gives a faster heuristic for finding a good K.

6.3   What Are the Properties of Our Model?

In Sect. 1 and Sect. 3, we described properties we want our new system to have, such as high recall and precision, flexibility thanks to the LM, and good generalization. We will investigate these advantages here in more detail.

What Are the Advantages of Using a Generative Translation Model? When we use traditional models like manual mapping, rule mining, or classifiers, we encounter problems coming from their lack of flexibility: The subject and object often remain unchanged, the mapping is often unique, mistakes are not corrected, etc. With a generative translation model, we can tackle some of these challenges. In Table 5, we present examples of nice and unique properties we observed in the final results. This shows that using LMs with open KBs lets us get the best of both worlds. LMs are more flexible and contain knowledge that is not easily extractable [23]. The open KB helps guide the LM.

Can We Improve the Quality of an Open KB with a Generative Translation Model? To evaluate the evolution of the quality of an open KB, we asked humans to annotate the typicality of statements. We sampled 300 statements out of the top 10k statements for each KB and then computed the mean typicality. The results are reported in Table 2. As we can see, the generative translation methods significantly improve the quality of the statements. The best-performing alignment method seems to depend on the open KB. As expected, ConceptNet still outperforms our approach as it was manually generated. However, it does not have the same scaling capabilities.

Table 5. Examples of Mappings from GenT.

Property	Open triple	Generated closed triple
The mapping depends on the context	(elephant, has_property, decorated)	(elephant, ReceivesAction, decorated)
Adapt the subject/object	(elephant, be in, africa killed) (doctor, write, prescription) (doctor, be in, training) (doctor, keep, from getting sick)	(elephant, AtLocation, africa) (doctor, CapableOf, prescribe) (doctor, AtLocation, medical school) (doctor, CapableOf, keep patient healthy)
Inversion subject/object	(elephant, have, tusks)	(tusk, PartOf, elephant)
Correct the subject/object	(elephant, have, ivory tusks answers)	(elephant, HasA, ivory tusk)
Put the predicate in the object	(doctor, wear, coat)	(doctor, CapableOf, wear coat)
Good triples from nonsense	(doctor, has_property, as a career)	(doctor, HasProperty, well respected)
Generate related triples	(doctor, wear, mask)	(doctor, CapableOf, wear lab coat)
Turn s/o into standard form	(apartment, be in, nyc)	(apartment, AtLocation, new york city)

Can GenT Generalize Across Open KBs? Table 6 shows the results of models trained on one open KB, Quasimodo or Ascent++, and used to generate a closed KB from triples in another open KB. We chose the LM-based@10k-INV alignment. In most cases, the original model trained with the same open KB outperforms the foreign model. This is understandable as the data sources and processing steps used to generate the open KBs differ, and therefore the style of the open triples is different. So, the model might have difficulties adapting. Still, the new results are close to the original ones, showing that we can have the reusability of our models with entirely new data. Finally, some metrics seem less impacted by the change of the original open KBs. From what we can see, the ranking capabilities, expressed through P_a and MRR, vary but not necessary for the worst. It shows that the generation and the scoring stage allow selecting good close triples, whatever the new data is.

Table 6. Performances when evaluating with a model trained for another KB.

KB	Method	$R_{a,rel}$	$\overline{R}_{a,rel}$	$P_{a,rel}$	$\overline{P}_{a,rel}$	$P_{a,rel}$@10	$P_{a,rel}$@100	$P_{a,rel}$@1000	$P_{a,rel}$@10k	$\overline{P}_{a,rel}$@10k	MRR_{rel}	$\overline{MRR}_{rel}$
Quasimodo	GenT@1	1.35	0.81	0.77	0.46	70%	67%	37.3%	0.73	0.76	4.28	0.98
Quasimodo	GenT@10	2.44	1.77	0.18	0.13	70%	71%	38.6%	2.92	0.84	4.41	0.96
Ascent++	GenT@1	1.95	0.77	1.28	0.50	80%	56%	25.2%	3.17	0.38	4.69	0.08
Ascent++	GenT@10	3.62	1.96	0.30	0.16	80%	65%	32.4%	3.87	0.44	5.37	0.10

Generalization to Sentences. In Table 7, we took sentences or paragraphs from several sources (Wikipedia, New York Times, GenericsKB [2]) and used our model trained on Quasimodo with the LM-based@10k-INV alignment method. Surprisingly, the model can correctly extract knowledge from sentences. This could lead to several interesting future works: Information extraction directly from sentences, aligning sentences rather than open triples, or commonsense inference.

Table 7. Examples of Generations From Sentences.

Source	First Generation
Elephants are the largest existing land animals	(elephants, DefinedAs, largest land animal)
A lawyer or attorney is a person who practices law	(lawyer, CapableOf, represent client)
Elon Musk Races to Secure Financing for Twitter Bid	(elon musk, CapableOf, bid for twitter)
South Africa's Government Shifts to Rebuilding After Disastrous Flooding. Nearly 4,000 homes have been destroyed and more than twice as many damaged in the Durban area after a week of punishing rains and mudslides. The death toll is now 448, with about four dozen people unaccounted for	(people, CapableOf, die from flooding)
Some air pollutants fall to earth in the form of acid rain	(air pollution, CapableOf, cause acid rain)

6.4 How Does GenT Compare with Direct LM Generation Methods?

As previous works like LAMA [23] suggested, a powerful language model could serve as a knowledge base. Then, aligning this "knowledge base" with a target knowledge base requires finetuning the language model. COMET [15] finetunes GPT-2 [25] to generate triples in ConceptNet. Here, we consider two kinds of input: A subject alone (denoted as COMET S) or a subject/predicate pair (designated as COMET SP). COMET initially accepted only subject/predicates pairs. However, it makes the generation of relevant triples harder as it is not always possible to associate all subjects to all predicates (for example, "elephant" and "HasSubEvent"). Then, we generate ten candidate statements for each subject or subject/predicate pair in ConceptNet. They all come with a generation score that we use for an overall ranking. In addition to the raw COMET, we used the translation models described above to generate a KB (GenT COMET). The inputs are the same as COMET. We additionally parse the output to keep the triple on the right of the *[SEP]* token.

It turns out that our translation model is a clever scheme in between traditional IE-based KB construction and a general COMET-style generation. It overcomes the limitation of IE that requires a text as input (it can generate more triples without requiring that each is seen in input text). It also tackles some COMET challenges by providing more robust guidance on what to generate based on the input triples.

In Table 8, we observe that GenT consistently outperforms COMET in all metrics but R_a. This is easily understandable: As we do not require alignments, we can get 5 to 10 times more training data than the translation models. These data points are guaranteed to represent different ConceptNet triples (not necessarily the case for the translation models). However, if we look at $\bar{R}_a$, the translation models generalize better. Besides, we have a ranking capability lacking in the original COMET. This could be explained by the fact that the translation models first try to generate an open triple closer to natural language and then map this triple to ConceptNet. Therefore, it can better leverage its prior knowledge to focus on what is essential.

Table 8. Direct Generation Comparison, non-relative metrics

KB	Method	Dataset	R_a	$\bar{R}_a$	P_a	$\bar{P}_a$	$P_a@10$	$P_a@100$	$P_a@1k$	$P_a@10k$	$\overline{P_a@10k}$	MRR	$\overline{MRR}$
Quasimodo	GenT COMET S	Rule-based	1.09%	0.222%	**3.72%**	0.137%	**100%**	**83%**	42.2%	**13.3%**	1.66%	**$2.59e^{-5}$**	$2.96e^{-7}$
Quasimodo	GenT COMET SP	Rule-based	2.33%	0.803%	0.403%	0.782%	30%	24%	18.6%	11.3%	1.24%	$8.15e^{-6}$	$2.66e^{-7}$
Quasimodo	GenT COMET S	LM-based@10-INV	0.657%	0.285%	2.20%	0.975%	20%	17%	15.8%	7.14%	2.86%	$9.59e^{-6}$	$5.20e^{-6}$
Quasimodo	GenT COMET SP	LM-based@10-INV	1.71%	1.07%	0.261%	0.163%	20%	21%	15.5%	6.46%	3.12%	$7.16e^{-6}$	$3.61e^{-7}$
Ascent++	GenT COMET S	Rule-based	0.977%	0.358%	3.10%	**1.15%**	**100%**	81%	**43%**	12.5%	3.90%	$2.63e^{-5}$	$2.68e^{-6}$
Ascent++	GenT COMET SP	Rule-based	2.15%	**1.11%**	0.345%	0.177%	100%	74%	38.7%	12.6%	4.14%	$1.11e^{-5}$	**$6.77e^{-6}$**
Ascent++	GenT COMET S	LM-based@10-INV	0.825%	0.326%	2.74%	0.326%	20%	26%	28.8%	8.94%	3.50%	$6.44e^{-6}$	$1.26e^{-6}$
Ascent++	GenT COMET SP	LM-based@10-INV	2.09%	1.10%	0.340%	0.178%	40%	24%	19.6%	10.7%	**4.69%**	$8.74e^{-6}$	$3.52e^{-6}$
–	Comet S	ConceptNet	1.11%	0.144%	2.96%	0.401%	20%	25%	20.1%	7.65%	0.891%	$6.30e^{-6}$	$3.04e^{-7}$
–	Comet SP	ConceptNet	**2.87%**	0.504%	0.179%	0.504%	10%	2%	3.2%	3.36%	0.510	$1.43e^{-6}$	$1.28e^{-7}$

7   Conclusion

We studied the problem of mapping an open commonsense knowledge base to a fixed schema. We proposed a generative translation approach that carries novel properties such as flexibility and cleaning ability. In the process, we compared different ways to create training data and analyzed their advantages and disadvantages. Finally, we experimentally verified the strengths of the proposed approach both in automated and manual evaluation.

We provided the first solution for the mapping task, and there is still room for improvement. For example, we could study how to adapt state-of-the-art translation models. We could also check how the output of the generative model can be constrained to provide closed triples that are not too far from the original triples. Also, as we observed that LM-based models have cleaning capabilities, we could include a negative sample in the training dataset to predict cases where a triple has no translation (e.g. because it is incorrect).

Supplemental Material Statement: We provide mappings to ConceptNet of Quasimodo and Ascent++ as additional resources (julienromero.fr/data/GenT), in addition to the code (github.com/Aunsiels/GenT) and input data. We hope they will help improve tasks such as commonsense question answering that currently use ConceptNet, which can sometimes be problematic as some of these datasets are constructed from ConceptNet (e.g., CommonsenseQA [32]).

Limitations. Our work is based on the GPT-2 model, which is not considered state-of-the-art when this paper is released. Using newer and bigger language models raises additional challenges: Computation time (currently approx. one month on a single GPU with a beam search), training complexity (bigger models have more weights, do not fit on a single GPU, and take more space during training), or hyperparameters hard to finetune. In this paper, we laid the foundations of a new task, and we believe more complex architectures can improve upon our baselines.

In this article, we studied the case of commonsense knowledge bases that generally contain uncanonicalized entities. Our study could be extended to other kinds of knowledge base.

Acknowledgements. This work was partially funded by the Hi!Paris center, and the experiments were performed using HPC resources from GENCI-IDRIS (Grant 2022-AD010613537).

References

1. Auer, S., Bizer, C., Kobilarov, G., Lehmann, J., Cyganiak, R., Ives, Z.: Dbpedia: a nucleus for a web of open data. In: ISWC (2007)
2. Bhakthavatsalam, S., Anastasiades, C., Clark, P.: Genericskb: a knowledge base of generic statements. arXiv preprint (2020)
3. Brown, T., et al.: Language models are few-shot learners. In: NeurIPS (2020)
4. Devlin, J., Chang, M.W., Lee, K., Toutanova, K.: BERT: pre-training of deep bidirectional transformers for language understanding. In: NAACL (2019)
5. Doan, A., Madhavan, J., Domingos, P., Halevy, A.: Ontology matching: a machine learning approach. In: Staab, S., Studer, R. (eds.) Handbook on ontologies. Springer, Heidelberg (2004). https://doi.org/10.1007/978-3-540-24750-0_19
6. Dutta, A., Meilicke, C., Stuckenschmidt, H.: Semantifying triples from open information extraction systems. In: STAIRS (2014)
7. Elsahar, H., et al.: T-rex: a large scale alignment of natural language with knowledge base triples. In: Proceedings of the Eleventh International Conference on Language Resources and Evaluation (LREC 2018) (2018)
8. Euzenat, J., Meilicke, C., Stuckenschmidt, H., Shvaiko, P., Trojahn, C.: Ontology alignment evaluation initiative: six years of experience. In: Spaccapietra, S. (ed.) Journal on Data Semantics XV. LNCS, vol. 6720, pp. 158–192. Springer, Heidelberg (2011). https://doi.org/10.1007/978-3-642-22630-4_6
9. Euzenat, J., Shvaiko, P., et al.: Ontology Matching. Springer, Heidelberg (2007). https://doi.org/10.1007/978-3-642-38721-0

10. Fader, A., Soderland, S., Etzioni, O.: Identifying relations for open information extraction. In: EMNLP (2011)
11. Feng, Y., Chen, X., Lin, B.Y., Wang, P., Yan, J., Ren, X.: Scalable multi-hop relational reasoning for knowledge-aware question answering. EMNLP (2020)
12. Galárraga, L., Heitz, G., Murphy, K., Suchanek, F.M.: Canonicalizing open knowledge bases. In: CIKM (2014)
13. Gashteovski, K., Gemulla, R., Kotnis, B., Hertling, S., Meilicke, C.: On aligning openie extractions with knowledge bases: a case study. In: Eval4NLP (2020)
14. Gashteovski, K., Wanner, S., Hertling, S., Broscheit, S., Gemulla, R.: Opiec: an open information extraction corpus. AKBC (2019)
15. Hwang, J.D., et al.: (Comet-)Atomic 2020: On symbolic and neural commonsense knowledge graphs. In: AAAI (2021)
16. Lajus, J., Galárraga, L., Suchanek, F.: Fast and exact rule mining with amie 3. In: ESWC (2020)
17. Lin, X., Li, H., Xin, H., Li, Z., Chen, L.: Kbpearl: a knowledge base population system supported by joint entity and relation linking. VLDB (2020)
18. Mishra, B.D., Tandon, N., Clark, P.: Domain-targeted, high precision knowledge extraction. TACL (2017)
19. Nguyen, T.P., Razniewski, S., Romero, J., Weikum, G.: Refined commonsense knowledge from large-scale web contents. arXiv (2021)
20. Nguyen, T.P., Razniewski, S., Weikum, G.: Advanced semantics for commonsense knowledge extraction. In: WWW (2021)
21. Nguyen, T.P., Razniewski, S., Weikum, G.: Inside ascent: exploring a deep commonsense knowledge base and its usage in question answering. ACL (2021)
22. Pedregosa, F., et al.: Scikit-learn: machine learning in python. JMLR (2011)
23. Petroni, F., et al.: Language models as knowledge bases? In: EMNLP (2019)
24. Putri, R.A., Hong, G., Myaeng, S.H.: Aligning OpenIE relations and KB relations using a SIAMESE network based on word embedding. In: IWCS (2019)
25. Radford, A., et al.: Language models are unsupervised multitask learners. OpenAI blog (2019)
26. Raffel, C., Shazeer, N., Roberts, A., Lee, K., Narang, S., Matena, M., Zhou, Y., Li, W., Liu, P.J., et al.: Exploring the limits of transfer learning with a unified text-to-text transformer. J. Mach. Learn. Res. **21**(140), 1–67 (2020)
27. Romero, J., Razniewski, S.: Inside quasimodo: exploring construction and usage of commonsense knowledge. In: Proceedings of the 29th ACM International Conference on Information & Knowledge Management. CIKM 2020, New York, NY, USA, pp. 3445–3448. Association for Computing Machinery (2020). https://doi.org/10.1145/3340531.3417416
28. Romero, J., Razniewski, S., Pal, K., Z. Pan, J., Sakhadeo, A., Weikum, G.: Commonsense properties from query logs and question answering forums. In: CIKM (2019)
29. Soderland, S., Gilmer, J., Bart, R., Etzioni, O., Weld, D.S.: Open information extraction to KBP relations in 3 hours. In: TAC (2013)
30. Soderland, S., Roof, B., Qin, B., Xu, S., Etzioni, O., et al.: Adapting open information extraction to domain-specific relations. AI magazine (2010)
31. Speer, R., Chin, J., Havasi, C.: Conceptnet 5.5: An open multilingual graph of general knowledge. In: AAAI (2017)
32. Talmor, A., Herzig, J., Lourie, N., Berant, J.: Commonsenseqa: A question answering challenge targeting commonsense knowledge. NAACL (2019)
33. Tanon, T.P., Weikum, G., Suchanek, F.: Yago 4: a reason-able knowledge base. In: ESWC (2020)

34. Taori, R., et al.: Stanford alpaca: an instruction-following llama model (2023). https://github.com/tatsu-lab/stanford_alpaca
35. Touvron, H., et al.: Llama: Open and efficient foundation language models. arXiv preprint arXiv:2302.13971 (2023)
36. Vrandečić, D., Krötzsch, M.: Wikidata: a free collaborative knowledgebase. Commun. ACM (2014)
37. Wang, C., Liu, X., Chen, Z., Hong, H., Tang, J., Song, D.: Zero-shot information extraction as a unified text-to-triple translation. arXiv preprint arXiv:2109.11171 (2021)
38. Wang, C., Liu, X., Chen, Z., Hong, H., Tang, J., Song, D.: Deepstruct: pretraining of language models for structure prediction. arXiv preprint arXiv:2205.10475 (2022)
39. Wang, W., Wei, F., Dong, L., Bao, H., Yang, N., Zhou, M.: Minilm: deep self-attention distillation for task-agnostic compression of pre-trained transformers. In: NeurIPS (2020)
40. Wang, Y., et al.: Multi-label classification with label graph superimposing. In: AAAI (2020)
41. Wood, I., Johnson, M., Wan, S.: Integrating lexical information into entity neighbourhood representations for relation prediction. In: NAACL (2021)
42. Yasunaga, M., Ren, H., Bosselut, A., Liang, P., Leskovec, J.: QA-GNN: reasoning with language models and knowledge graphs for question answering. In: NAACL (2021)
43. Yu, W., et al.: A survey of knowledge-enhanced text generation. ACM Comput. Surv. (2022)
44. Zhang, D., Mukherjee, S., Lockard, C., Dong, X.L., McCallum, A.: Openki: Integrating open information extraction and knowledge bases with relation inference. NAACL (2019)
45. Zhang, R., et al.: Llama-adapter: efficient fine-tuning of language models with zero-init attention. arXiv preprint arXiv:2303.16199 (2023)
46. Zhong, P., Wang, D., Miao, C.: Knowledge-enriched transformer for emotion detection in textual conversations. In: EMNLP. Hong Kong, China (2019)
47. Zhou, K., Zhao, W.X., Bian, S., Zhou, Y., Wen, J., Yu, J.: Improving conversational recommender systems via knowledge graph based semantic fusion. In: KDD (2020)
48. Zhou, S., Yu, B., Sun, A., Long, C., Li, J., Sun, J.: A survey on neural open information extraction: Current status and future directions. arXiv preprint arXiv:2205.11725 (2022)

Integrating Knowledge Graph Embeddings and Pre-trained Language Models in Hypercomplex Spaces

Mojtaba Nayyeri[1], Zihao Wang[1(✉)], Mst. Mahfuja Akter[2],
Mirza Mohtashim Alam[3], Md Rashad Al Hasan Rony[2], Jens Lehmann[4],
and Steffen Staab[1,5]

[1] University of Stuttgart, Stuttgart, Germany
{mojtaba.nayyer,zihao.wang,steffen.staab}@ki.uni-stuttgart.de
[2] University of Bonn, Bonn, Germany
s39mrony@uni-bonn.de
[3] Karlsruhe Institute of Technology, Karlsruhe, Germany
[4] Amazon (work done outside of Amazon), TU Dresden, Germany
jlehmnn@amazon.com
[5] University of Southampton, Southampton, UK

Abstract. Knowledge graphs comprise structural and textual information to represent knowledge. To predict new structural knowledge, current approaches learn representations using both types of information through knowledge graph embeddings and language models. These approaches commit to a single pre-trained language model. We hypothesize that heterogeneous language models may provide complementary information not exploited by current approaches. To investigate this hypothesis, we propose a unified framework that integrates multiple representations of structural knowledge and textual information. Our approach leverages hypercomplex algebra to model the interactions between (i) graph structural information and (ii) multiple text representations. Specifically, we utilize Dihedron models with 4*D dimensional hypercomplex numbers to integrate four different representations: structural knowledge graph embeddings, word-level representations (e.g., Word2vec and FastText), sentence-level representations (using a sentence transformer), and document-level representations (using FastText or Doc2vec). Our unified framework score the plausibility of labeled edges via Dihedron products, thus modeling pairwise interactions between the four representations. Extensive experimental evaluations on standard benchmark datasets confirm our hypothesis showing the superiority of our two new frameworks for link prediction tasks.

Keywords: Knowledge Graph Embedding · Pre-trained Language Model · Textual Information

---

M. Nayyeri, Z. Wang and Mst. M. Akter—These authors contributed equally to this work.

T. R. Payne et al. (Eds.): ISWC 2023, LNCS 14265, pp. 388–407, 2023.
https://doi.org/10.1007/978-3-031-47240-4_21

1   Introduction

Knowledge Graphs (KGs) have become an integral part of many AI systems, ranging from question answering and named entity recognition to recommendation systems [8,12,22]. KGs represent knowledge in the form of multi-relational directed labeled graphs, where nodes with labels can represent entities (e.g., "Q5220733"), and labeled edges represent relations between entities (e.g., P19). Therefore, a fact can be represented as a triple, (node, edge label, node), such as (Q5220733, P19, Q621549) in Wikidata.

In order to enable machine learning to act on KGs with symbolic information [34], Knowledge Graph embeddings (KGE) map nodes and edge labels to a low-dimensional vector space. These embeddings are assumed to capture semantic and structural knowledge and can support machine learning tasks such as link prediction, entity linking, and question answering. However, despite the large number of facts contained in KGs, they are still incomplete compared to the facts that exist in the world, which can have a negative impact on downstream tasks. Consider Fig. 1 and assume that the purple dashed edge (Q5220733, P19, Q621549) is unknown because the entity "Q5220733" is only connected to one other entity, "Q193592". Although structural graph information alone cannot help bridge the gap between "Q5220733" and "Q621549", a second textual representation, such as additional information from a source like Wikipedia[1], could be used to provide a solution.

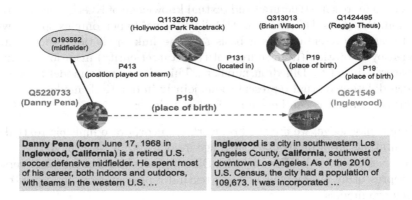

Fig. 1. Knowledge Graph with textual descriptions of entities. The entity "Q5220733" lacks proper structural information, but it comes with a rich textual description, which may help to predict the place of birth.

Early approaches such as DKRL [37] and ConMask [27], have gone beyond structural graph knowledge and incorporated textual information for link prediction using deep learning methods, such as convolutional neural networks (CNNs)

---

[1] https://en.wikipedia.org/wiki/Danny_Pena.

and attention mechanisms to transform textual information into joint latent representations with structure-based KGEs. More recent approaches [18,35,39,41] have incorporated pre-trained language models into KGE models by unifying their two loss functions. However, these approaches only represent texts with a single pre-trained language model, which may lead to inferior performance when encoding textual information in certain KGs. For example, while BERT is employed in [35,39,41], evaluations [11,33] demonstrate that fastText [2], Glove [23] or their combination outperform BERT on some datasets.

In this paper, we contend that relying on a single pre-trained language model is inadequate for KGE models for two main reasons. Firstly, the textual information available in different knowledge graphs can vary significantly, which can lead to varying performance of pre-trained language models. For example, entity descriptions in Freebase may consist of multiple sentences, whereas in Wikidata, they may be just a short sentence. Secondly, different pre-trained language models excel in different levels of information. For example, while BERT excels in extracting word and sentence-level information, Doc2Vec [17] captures the document-level information. As a result, the use of multiple pre-trained language models is crucial in improving the performance of KGE models. Therefore, we extend previous KGE models that integrate textual information by incorporating multiple textual representations. These representations capture different levels of semantics through the use of different pre-trained language models for word, sentence, and document embeddings. In order to integrate these various representations efficiently, we employ a 4*D dimensional space of hypercomplex numbers to represent structured and textual knowledge of KGs in a unified representation. We utilize Dihedrons as 4*D dimensional hypercomplex spaces, where each textual representation is a basis and the link prediction process can be modeled by a rotation (from source entity to target entity) in various geometric subspaces induced by Dihedron numbers. This allows us to model interactions between different textual representations jointly in our KGE model.

Our contributions can be summarized as follows:

1. To our knowledge, we are the first work to incorporate multiple textual representations from pre-trained language models into a KGE model.
2. We develop a novel KGE model with Dihedron algebra, which is more versatile in representing interactions between textual representations from pre-trained language models.
3. We conduct informative experiments, ablation studies, and analyses on various datasets to investigate the impact of incorporating different pre-trained language models into KGE models.

2   Related Work

2.1   Structural Knowledge Graph Embedding Models

We will begin by introducing KGE models that consider only structural information from knowledge graphs. TransE [3] and TransH [36] are early KGE models that score triples using different distance-based scoring functions. These models minimize the distance between the tail entity and the query, which is formulated by adding the head entity and the relation (edge) label. TransH [36] further improves on TransE by projecting entities onto relation-specific hyperplanes, resulting in different representations of an entity with respect to different relation labels. ComplEx [31] uses the Hermitian dot product in complex space to model the scoring function, which characterizes the asymmetric relations in knowledge graphs. RotatE [28] is more expressive than previous approaches, as it can represent a relation composed of the natural join between two other relations. To achieve this, it models relations using rotations in the complex space. AttE and AttH [7] incorporate an attention mechanism on rotation and reflection in hyperbolic space. QuatE [40] and Dihedral [20,38] model KGEs using Quaternions and Dihedrons, respectively. While these models rely on structural knowledge in knowledge graphs, they do not exploit the advantages of complementary knowledge such as text. On the contrary, our method jointly utilizes both structural and textual information of KGs. As a result, we are better equipped to tackle the incompleteness of KGs.

2.2 Text-Enhanced Knowledge Graph Embedding Models

Several KGE approaches have been proposed that integrate textual information, such as textual descriptions and names of entities, along with the structural information of KGs. As an early work, DKRL [37] extends TransE by considering entity descriptions. Entity descriptions are encoded by a Convolutional Neural Network (CNN) and jointly optimized together with the TransE scoring function. ConMask [27] claims that an entity may involve multiple relations. It extracts relation-specific information from the entity description by training a network that computes attention over entity descriptions. However, these approaches were proposed before the emergence of large-scale pre-trained language models like BERT, and as a result, their performance is limited.

Recent approaches have exploited large-scale pre-trained language models to enhance the performance of KGE models. KG-BERT [39] and LAnguage Model Analysis (LAMA) [24] demonstrate that structural knowledge in KGs can be stored in pre-trained language models. They treat triples in the KG as a sequence of text and obtain the representation of triplets with BERT. PretrainKGE [41] extracts knowledge from BERT by representing entity descriptions and relation names with BERT embeddings, which can be utilized to enhance different KGE algorithms. MLMLM [9] claims that KG-BERT cannot generalize well on unseen entities. This work proposes a novel masked language model that yields strong results with unseen entities of arbitrary length in the link prediction task. StAR [32] argues that previous work such as KG-BERT may not be effective in learning the structural knowledge in KGs well, and the evidence is that KG-BERT can achieve good results on Top-K recall when K is relatively large (Top-10) but performs poorly when K is small (Top-1). To address this issue, StAR proposes a hybrid framework that combines pre-trained language models with KGE methods such as RotatE, which aims to obtain the benefits of both approaches. More recent approaches [5,18,26] also explore different methods to combine pre-trained language models and KGE to improve the performance of link prediction tasks in KGs. However, all the KGE approaches mentioned above only incorporate one pre-trained language model, which may not be optimal for all KGs. Evaluations [11,33] have shown that pre-trained language models perform differently on different datasets, indicating that there is no single optimal pre-trained language model for all KGs. In contrast, our approach incorporates multiple pre-trained language models. This allows us to not only capture different levels of information (word/sentence/document) in a single text but also better fit the different textual information present in various KGs.

3 Preliminaries

In this section, we introduce the preliminaries necessary to understand our proposed models.

Knowledge Graph: A knowledge graph is a collection of triples $\mathcal{K} = \{(h,r,t)|h,t \in \mathcal{E}, r \in \mathcal{R}\} \subset \mathcal{E} \times \mathcal{R} \times \mathcal{E}$, where $\mathcal{E}$ and $\mathcal{R}$ are the sets of all entities and relation labels in the KG, respectively.

Textual Knowledge Graph: For a given KG $\mathcal{K}$, we can collect words, sentences, or documents associated with each node or relation label to construct a textual KG $\mathcal{TK}$ defined as $\mathcal{TK} = \{(h^T, r^T, t^T)|h^T, t^T \in \mathcal{E}^T, r^T \in \mathcal{R}^T\} \subset \mathcal{E}^T \times \mathcal{R}^T \times \mathcal{E}^T$, where h^T, r^T, t^T denote the word ($T = W$), sentence ($T = S$), or document ($T = D$) representations of entities and relation labels. For instance, consider an entity $h = $ *"Berlin"* in the KG that has the word representation $h^W = $ *"Berlin"*, sentence representation $h^S = $ *"Berlin is the capital and largest city of Germany by both area and population"*, and document representation $h^D = $ *"Berlin is the capital and largest city of Germany by both area and population. Its 3.7 million inhabitants make it the most populous city in the European Union..."*.

Knowledge Graph Embedding: A knowledge graph $\mathcal{K}$ can be represented by a low-dimensional vector embedding, denoted as $\mathcal{KGE} = \{(\mathbf{h},\mathbf{r},\mathbf{t})|\mathbf{h},\mathbf{t} \in \mathbf{E}, \mathbf{r} \in \mathbf{R}\} \subset \mathbf{E} \times \mathbf{R} \times \mathbf{E}$, where $\mathbf{E}, \mathbf{R}$ are the sets of entity and relation label embeddings in the KG, respectively. These embeddings are $n_e \times D$ and $n_r \times D$ dimensional, respectively, where n_e and n_r are the number of entities and relation labels, and D is the embedding dimension.

Pre-trained Language Model KG Embedding: The word, sentence, and document representations of triples can be vectorized using pre-trained language models. Thus, we represent the embedding of $\mathcal{TK}$ as a set $\mathcal{TKE} = \{(\mathbf{h}^T, \mathbf{r}, \mathbf{t}^T)|\mathbf{h}^T, \mathbf{t}^T \in \mathbf{E}^T, \mathbf{r} \in \mathbf{R}\} \subset \mathbf{E}^T \times \mathbf{R} \times \mathbf{E}^T$, where $\mathbf{E}^T$ represents the embeddings of all word/sentence/document representations of entities in the KG. These embeddings are generated by feeding the word/sentence/document representation of an entity into the corresponding pre-trained language model.

Quaternion and Dihedron Algebra: To integrate the structural, word, sentence, and document representations of an entity or a relation label into a unified representation, we utilize a 4*D dimensional algebra, which has been extensively studied in the field of hypercomplex numbers. Specifically, we employ Quaternion $\mathcal{Q}$ [40] and Dihedron $\mathcal{D}$ [20,29,38] algebra as 4*D dimensional hypercomplex numbers, which are defined as $u = s + xi + yj + zk$, where i, j, and k are the three imaginary parts. In Quaternion and Dihedron representations, we have, respectively, $i^2 = j^2 = k^2 = ijk = \bar{1}$, $ij = k$, $jk = i$, $ki = j$, $ji = \bar{k}$, $kj = \bar{i}$, $ik = \bar{j}$, and $i^2 = \bar{1}$, $j^2 = k^2 = 1$, $ij = k$, $jk = \bar{i}$, $ki = j$, $ji = \bar{k}$, $kj = i$, $ik = \bar{j}$, where $\bar{a} = -a$, $a \in i, j, k$. The prime operators of Quaternion and Dihedron are defined in the following paragraphs.

Quaternion Product: This product is also known as the Hamilton product. Let $u = s_u + x_u i + y_u j + z_u k, v = s_v + x_v i + y_v j + z_v k$ be two Quaternion numbers. The Hamilton product between u, v is defined as follows:

$$
\begin{aligned}
u \otimes_{\mathcal{Q}} v := &(s_u s_v - x_u x_v - y_u y_v - z_u z_v) + (s_u x_v + x_u s_v + y_u z_v - z_u y_v)\,\mathbf{i} \\
&+ (s_u y_v - x_u z_v + y_u s_v + z_u x_v)\,\mathbf{j} + (s_u z_v + x_u y_v - y_u x_v + z_u s_v)\,\mathbf{k}.
\end{aligned}
\tag{1}
$$

Dihedron Product: Let u, v be two Dihedron numbers. The Dihedron product is defined as

$$
\begin{aligned}
u \otimes_{\mathcal{D}} v := &(s_u s_v - x_u x_v + y_u y_v + z_u z_v) + (s_u x_v + x_u s_v - y_u z_v + z_u y_v)\,\mathbf{i} \\
&+ (s_u y_v - x_u z_v + y_u s_v + z_u x_v)\,\mathbf{j} + (s_u z_v + x_u y_v - y_u x_v + z_u s_v)\,\mathbf{k}.
\end{aligned}
\tag{2}
$$

Inner Product: In both the Dihedron and the Quaternion spaces, the inner product is defined as $\langle u, v \rangle = u \cdot v := s_u s_v + x_u x_v + y_u y_v + z_u z_v$.

Conjugate: The conjugate in both representations is $\bar{u} = s - xi - yj - zk$.

Norm: The norm in the representations of the Quaternions and Dihedrons is defined as $\|u\| = \langle u, \bar{u} \rangle$ which are $\sqrt{s_u^2 + x_u^2 + y_u^2 + z_u^2}$ and $\sqrt{s_u^2 + x_u^2 - y_u^2 - z_u^2}$, respectively.

Previous approaches [6,40] employed Quaternion as another algebra in the hypercomplex space. Both the Quaternion and Dihedron spaces offer various geometric representations. Quaternion numbers of equal length represent hyperspheres, while Dihedron numbers of equal length can represent various shapes, including spheres, one-sheets, two-sheets, and conical surfaces. Therefore, the Dihedron space is more expressive than the Quaternion space in terms of geometric representation.

4   Our Method

In this section, we introduce a family of embedding models based on the Quaternion or Dihedron algebra that operate in 4*D dimensional spaces. These spaces capture the four types of entity representations, namely graph, word, sentence,

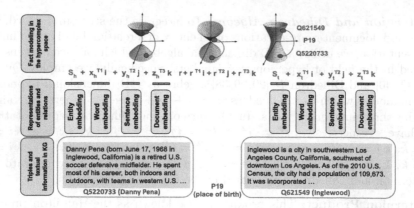

Fig. 2. The proposed model's overall architecture considers various entity representations, such as word, sentence, and document levels, and maps them into a joint geometric space using the Quaternion or Dihedron algebra. This joint space can be either spherical or hyperbolic.

and document embeddings, and allow for modeling the interactions between different elements, resulting in a comprehensive feature representation that can be used to assess the plausibility score of links. As shown in Fig. 2, our framework involves splitting a triple, such as (Q5220733, P19, Q621549), into a triple pattern, e.g., (Q5220733, P19, ?), and a tail, e.g., Q621549, which corresponds to a query such as "Where was Danny Pena born?". We then compute embeddings for the query and the tail using both textual and structural information, and calculate the plausibility score by measuring the distance between them in the embedding space.

In the rest of this section, we will present our embedding model and provide technical details on the dimension adjustment that aligns the different representations of entities in the same geometric space. This process is accomplished through the following order: a) Entity, Relation, and Query Representation, b) Dimension Adjustment and c) Triple Plausibility Score and Training. The purpose of b) is to match the dimensions of the KGE model with the pre-trained vectors from language models in cases where the dimensions do not match.

4.1 Entity, Relation, and Query Representation

We represent each entity e as a Quaternion or Dihedron vector with dimensions $4 * D$, which captures its structural and textual information at different levels of granularity, as follows:

$$\mathbf{e} = \mathbf{s}_e + \mathbf{x}_e^{\mathcal{T}_1} \boldsymbol{i} + \mathbf{y}_e^{\mathcal{T}_2} \boldsymbol{j} + \mathbf{z}_e^{\mathcal{T}_3} \boldsymbol{k}, \tag{3}$$

where $\mathbf{s}_e$ is the node representation in the graph embedding of the KG and $\mathcal{T}_i, i = 1, 2, 3$ are pre-trained language models. For one entity description, we feed the text into a set of pre-trained language models $\mathcal{T}_i$ and initialize corresponding embeddings $\mathbf{x}_e^{\mathcal{T}_1}, \mathbf{y}_e^{\mathcal{T}_2}, \mathbf{z}_e^{\mathcal{T}_3}$.

In Fig. 1, the entities "Q5220733" and "Q621549" both possess textual descriptions. To extract word, sentence, and document representations from these descriptions, we use a variety of pre-trained language models. By doing so, we obtain a comprehensive representation of the entities.

Each relation is represented as a rotation in the hypercomplex space, which is

$$\mathbf{r} = \frac{\mathbf{s}_r + \mathbf{x}_r^{\mathcal{T}_1}i + \mathbf{y}_r^{\mathcal{T}_2}j + \mathbf{z}_r^{\mathcal{T}_3}k}{\sqrt{\mathbf{s}_r^2 + (\mathbf{x}_r^{\mathcal{T}_1})^2 + (\mathbf{y}_r^{\mathcal{T}_2})^2 + (\mathbf{z}_r^{\mathcal{T}_3})^2}}. \tag{4}$$

To calculate the plausibility score of a triple (h, r, t), we divide it into a triple pattern $(h, r, ?)$ and a tail entity t. Both the triple pattern and the tail entity are represented in a 4*D dimensional space. Table 1 presents three different approaches for representing the triple pattern $(h, r, ?)$ in our model. The following methods are proposed for the representation of the query:

Table 1. Query representations derived by our models.

Name	query $(h, r, ?)$	embedding $\mathbf{h}, \mathbf{r} \in \mathcal{D}^d$
Tetra	$q = \mathbf{h} \otimes \mathbf{r}^\triangleleft$	$\mathbf{h} = \mathbf{s}_h + \mathbf{x}_h^{\mathcal{T}_1}i + \mathbf{y}_h^{\mathcal{T}_2}j + \mathbf{z}_h^{\mathcal{T}_3}k, \mathbf{r}^\triangleleft = \frac{\mathbf{r}}{|\mathbf{r}|}$
Robin	$q = \mathbf{h} \otimes h_{lt}^{\triangleleft \mathcal{T}_1} + h_l^{\mathcal{T}_0} + h_t^{\mathcal{T}_1} + r^\triangleleft$	$h_{lt}^{\mathcal{T}_1} = s_h^{\mathcal{T}_0} + x_h^{l\mathcal{T}_0}i + y_h^{t\mathcal{T}_1}j + z_h^{t\mathcal{T}_1}k, h_{lt}^{\triangleleft \mathcal{T}_1} = \frac{h_{lt}^{\mathcal{T}_1}}{|h_{lt}^{\mathcal{T}_1}|}$
Lion	$q = \mathbf{h} \otimes h_t^{\triangleleft \mathcal{T}_1 \mathcal{T}_2} + h_t^{\mathcal{T}_1} + h_t^{\mathcal{T}_2} + r^\triangleleft$	$h_t^{\mathcal{T}_1 \mathcal{T}_2} = s_h^{t\mathcal{T}_1} + x_h^{t\mathcal{T}_1}i + y_h^{t\mathcal{T}_2}j + z_h^{t\mathcal{T}_2}k, h_t^{\triangleleft \mathcal{T}_1 \mathcal{T}_2} = \frac{h_t^{\mathcal{T}_1 \mathcal{T}_2}}{|h_t^{\mathcal{T}_1 \mathcal{T}_2}|}$

Text-enhanced relaTional RotAtion (Tetra): This model comprises four parts for representing each entity. For each head entity, node representation $\mathbf{s}_h$ is learned from a graph embedding of the KG structure, and the components $(\mathbf{x}_h^{\mathcal{T}_1}, \mathbf{y}_h^{\mathcal{T}_2}, \mathbf{z}_h^{\mathcal{T}_3})$ are learned from textual embeddings (word, sentence, and document) of the entities using three pre-trained language models. Likewise, for each tail entity, $\mathbf{s}_t$ and $(\mathbf{x}_t^{\mathcal{T}_1}, \mathbf{y}_t^{\mathcal{T}_2}, \mathbf{z}_t^{\mathcal{T}_3})$ are also learned. The Tetra model represents the query by learning relation-specific rotations of the head in Quaternion or Dihedron space, and $\otimes$ refers to the Quaternion or Dihedron products (see Eq. 1, 2) in Quaternion or Dihedron space. The resulting query inherently contains pairwise correlations between each of $\mathbf{s}_h, \mathbf{x}_h^{\mathcal{T}_1}, \mathbf{y}_h^{\mathcal{T}_2}, \mathbf{z}_h^{\mathcal{T}_3}$, thus providing a rich feature representation for the corresponding query.

Multi-texts RelatiOn-Based rotatIon and translatioN (Robin): In this model, we incorporate both the vector of the entity name (e.g., "Berlin") indexed by l (i.e., $h_l^{\mathcal{T}_0}$) and the vector of the textual description indexed by t (i.e., $h_t^{\mathcal{T}_1}$). We perform a rotation of the form $h \otimes h_{lt}^{\triangleleft \mathcal{T}_1}$ and a translation of the form $h_l^{\mathcal{T}_0} + h_t^{\mathcal{T}_1} + r^\triangleleft$ derived from these two sources of information. Specifically, $h_{lt}^{\triangleleft \mathcal{T}_1}$ is obtained by normalizing $h_{lt}^{\mathcal{T}_1}$. We always use Word2Vec ($\mathcal{T}_0$) to embed entity names, but we use a different pre-trained language model for embedding entity descriptions, which is selected based on performance in experiments (details provided in the experimental section). We utilize two distinct neural networks (details in Sect. 4.2) to generate distinct representations $\mathbf{s}_h^{l^{T_0}}$ and $\mathbf{x}_h^{l^{T_0}}$ given the same embedding from Word2Vec T_0. Similarly, $\mathbf{y}_h^{t^{T_1}}$ and $\mathbf{z}_h^{t^{T_1}}$ are distinct representations given the same embedding from another pre-trained language model T_1. Consequently, the query is computed by combining the head entity embedding from the KG, relation label embedding, entity name, and entity description through translation and rotation in Quaternion or Dihedron space: $\mathbf{q} = h \otimes h_{lt}^{\triangleleft^{T_1}} + h_l^{T_0} + h_t^{T_1} + \mathbf{r}^{\triangleleft}$, where h is the graph embedding of the head entity. Incorporating both translation and rotation improves the model's expressiveness compared to utilize only a single rotation [7,21].

Multi-language Models relatIon rOtation and translatioN (Lion): In this model, we utilize two pre-trained language models (T_1, T_2) to embed the same entity description and adjust their dimensions using NNs (detailed in Sect. 4.2). We then construct a vector for rotation as follows: $h^{T_1 T_2} = \mathbf{s}_h^{t^{T_1}} + \mathbf{x}_h^{t^{T_1}} i + \mathbf{y}_h^{t^{T_2}} j + \mathbf{z}_h^{t^{T_2}} k, h^{T_1 T_2 \triangleleft} = \frac{h^{T_1 T_2}}{|h^{T_1 T_2}|}$. Together with the rotation $h \otimes h_t^{\triangleleft^{T_1 T_2}}$, we use the embedding of the entity description $h_t^{T_1}, h_t^{T_2}$ to represent a translation for query representation in Quaternion or Dihedron spaces: $\mathbf{q} = h \otimes h_t^{\triangleleft^{T_1 T_2}} + h_t^{T_1} + h_t^{T_2} + \mathbf{r}^{\triangleleft}$.

The query representations mentioned above are related to the triple pattern $(h, r, ?)$. For the triple pattern $(?, r, t)$, we adopt the approach of using $(t, r^{-1}, ?)$ for query representation, where r^{-1} is a reverse relation label corresponding to the relation label r. To create a set of $|R|$ embeddings of reverse relation labels R^{-1}, we add an additional triple (t, r^{-1}, h) to the training set for each embedding of the reverse relation label $r^{-1} \in R^{-1}$, following the approach used in previous works [13,15]. When representing queries for these triples, we use the equations presented in Table 1, but with h replaced by t and r replaced by r^{-1}. It is worth noting that the choice of the appropriate model from Table 1 may depend on various characteristics of the KG, such as sparsity and density, quality of textual description, etc. For instance, if the KG has a complex structure, a more expressive model like the Robin and Lion may be required, because they mix both the translation and the rotation, which could be preferred over the Tetra relying solely on the rotation.

4.2   Dimension Adjustment

The underlying assumption of Eq. 3 is that the vectors $\mathbf{s}_e, \mathbf{x}_e^{T_1}, \mathbf{y}_e^{T_2}$, and $\mathbf{z}_e^{T_3}$ have the same dimension D. However, since pre-trained language models may produce vectors of different dimensions, we use a neural network to adjust their dimensions. Thus, we can rewrite Eq. 3 as follows:

$$\mathbf{e} = \mathbf{s}_e + NN(\mathbf{x}_e^{T_1})i + NN(\mathbf{y}_e^{T_2})j + NN(\mathbf{z}_e^{T_3})k, \tag{5}$$

where NN is a multilayer perceptron whose input and output dimensions are D_{T_i} and D, respectively.

In our dimension-adjustment module, we use an individual multi-layer network NN for each embedding from pre-trained language models. The input and output dimension of each NN are D_{T_i} and D, respectively. Among all embeddings, the largest embedding from BERT has size of 512, so we always adapt all embedding dimension D to 512. Our NN has two layers, each layer consists of a linear transformation and then a non-linear transformation. For the activation function in the non-linear transformation, we simply use hyperbolic tangent function.

4.3   Triple Plausibility Score and Training

To measure the plausibility score of a triple (h, r, t), we calculate the distance between the query $\mathbf{q}$ and the corresponding tail t as follows:

$$f(h, r, t) = -d(\mathbf{q}, \mathbf{t}) + b_h + b_t, \tag{6}$$

where b_h, b_t are entity-specific biases proposed in [1].

In Fig. 1, a series of geometric representations are presented (located on top of the figure) in which the query and corresponding tail are matched (from the blue dot to the red dot). The textual description of "Q5220733" mentions the entity "Q621549" and the term "born", which is closely related to the "P19" relation label. Similarly, the textual description of "Q621549" includes the entities "Inglewood". These descriptions are strongly correlated and effectively cover the mention of the triple elements (head, relation label, tail). Consequently, based on the textual descriptions of these entities, it can be inferred that "Q5220733" was born in "Inglewood".

During the training phase, we minimize the cross-entropy loss function with uniform negative sampling as described in [7]. In particular, for a positive triple (h, r, t), we obtain negative triples by uniformly sampling negative tail entities $t' \in E$ such that $(h, r, t') \notin \mathcal{K}$. Besides, for any positive triple, we always train another triple involving inverse relation (t, r^{-1}, h'), where we similarly perform negative sampling to obtain negative head entities h'. This is based on previous work [16] that suggests the inclusion of triples with inverse relations can improve model performance.

Given positive and negative triples, the loss function can be defined as follows:

$$\mathcal{L} = -\sum_{h,r,t;t'} y^{t;t'} \log f(h, r, t; t') - \sum_{t,r^{-1},h;h'} y^{h;h'} \log f(t, r^{-1}, h; h') \tag{7}$$

where $y^{t;t'} = \pm 1$ is the label for positive or negative triples when sampling tail entities, and $y^{h;h'}$ is similarly for head entities. During the training process, we employ the Adagrad optimizer [10] to optimize the model parameters. Furthermore, we utilize early stopping on the validation dataset to prevent overfitting.

5   Experiments

5.1   Experimental Setup

Datasets, Environments and Hyperparameters: We evaluate our proposed models on two domain-specific KG datasets: **NATIONS** [14], **Diabetes** [42], and two commonsense KG datasets: **FB15k-237** [30], and **YAGO-10**. Table 2 provides a summary of types and other statistic details of each dataset. Other details of datasets can be found in Appendix A. Besides, the details of our environments and hyperparameters can be found in Appendix B.

Table 2. The statistics of our datasets.

Dataset	Type	#ent	#rel	#train	#val	#test
NATIONS	domain specific	14	55	1,592	199	201
Diabetes	domain specific	7,886	67	56,830	1,344	1,936
FB15k-237	commonsense	14,904	237	271,431	17,503	20,427
YAGO-10	commonsense	103,222	30	490,214	2,295	2,292

Evaluation Metrics: We evaluated our models using the link prediction task and the following standard evaluation metrics: Mean Reciprocal Rank (MRR) and Hits@K, where K is set to 1, 3, and 10. MRR calculates the mean reciprocal rank of the correct tail entity across all queries, while Hits@K measures the proportion of correct tail entities that rank in the top K positions. In accordance with prior work, we also employed the filtering setup [4] during evaluation to remove existing triples in the dataset from the ranking process.

Baselines and Our Ablation Models: We compare our proposed models against four baselines that do not consider textual information: TransE [3], ComplEx [31], AttE, and AttH [7]. We also compare against baselines that incorporate textual information: DKRL [37], ConMask [27], PretrainKGE [41], KG-BERT [39], and StAR [32]. We reimplemented ConMask and PretrainKGE and obtained the codes for DKRL, KG-BERT and StAR online.

We conducted an ablation study to evaluate different variants of our model with different combinations of pre-trained language models. To simplify, we use the abbreviations $\{W, F, D, S\}$ to represent the pre-trained language models Word2Vec, FastText, Doc2Vec, SentenceTransformer, respectively. We compared four variants of Robin that utilize one of $\{W, F, S, D\}$ individually for modeling the entity descriptions and always use W for modeling the entity names, namely, *Robin_W*, *Robin_F*, *Robin_S* and *Robin_D*. We further compared two variants of Lion that use $\{S, D\}$ or $\{F, S\}$, namely, *Lion_SD* and *Lion_SF*. We also compare three variants of Tetra that use only $\{S, F\}$ for *Tetra_SF* and use $\{W, S, F\}$ for *Tetra_WSF*. Besides, we do not incorporate any pre-trained language model into *Tetra_zero*. All our variants employ the Dihedron representation for better performance. By comparing the performance of our ablation models, we evaluated different aspects of our model, as shown in Table 3:

Table 3. The design of our ablation models.

Ablation models to compare	Purpose of evaluation
different variants of Robin	difference from each individual pre-trained language model
different variants of Lion	different combinations of two pre-trained language models
different variants of Tetra	difference from numbers of incorporated pre-trained language models
Robins and Lions	different numbers of texts (name, description) utilized in our model

5.2 Link Prediction Results and Analysis

Table 4 presents the results of the link prediction task for the embedding dimensions $D = 32$ and $D = 500$, respectively. Our proposed models consistently outperform all baselines on all datasets.

However, the performance of our ablation variants varies across different datasets. In the small NATIONS dataset, Tetra outperforms Robin and Lion by a significant margin. This is due to the fact that on smaller datasets, the amount of structural information from the KG is limited, and the incorporation of additional textual information becomes more crucial. Tetra performs better in this scenario because it incorporates three different pre-trained language models, allowing for a more comprehensive exploitation of textual information. The results on the three KGs suggest that Lion generally outperforms Robin, with the most significant improvement of a 3% higher MRR observed on YAGO-10 in the low-dimensional setting. These results demonstrate that incorporating more pre-trained language models to extract information from the same text is more effective than incorporating more types of text, such as entity names and descriptions. Additionally, Tetra's performance is comparable to Lion in the high-dimensional setting on FB15k-237, with Tetra_SF even achieving the best performance among all ablation variants on YAGO-10 in the high-dimensional setting. Since the primary difference between the Tetra and Lion variants is the mixture of translation and rotation, these results suggest that this mixture is more suitable in the low-dimensional setting.

We also compared all the different variants of Robin and Lion models together since they all use two pre-trained language models. We observed that their performances on smaller datasets such as NATIONS and Diabetes were quite similar, but on larger datasets, there were more noticeable differences. For instance, on the YAGO-10 dataset, Lion_SD outperformed Robin_S by 3.4% in terms of MRR in the low dimensional setting, and Lion_SF had 9% higher MRR than Robin_D in the high dimensional setting. These results suggest that the selection of the incorporated pre-trained language models is more critical on larger datasets.

For various Tetra variants, our findings indicate that Tetra_zero consistently underperforms, which highlights the significance of incorporating pre-trained language models. Comparing Tetra_SF and Tetra_WSF, we observe that the former generally exhibits superior performance on smaller datasets, while the latter performs better on larger datasets. This evidence suggests that incorporating more pre-trained language models is more appropriate when the structural information is insufficient, such as on smaller datasets.

Table 4. Link prediction results for both low (D = 32) and high (D = 500) dimensional settings. In each dimensional setting, numbers are the best results for each dataset.

Elements	Model	Nations				Diabetes				FB15k-237				YAGO-10			
		MRR	H@1	H@3	H@10	MRR	H@1	H@3	H@10	MRR	H@1	H@3	H@10	MRR	H@1	H@3	H@10
Baselines D=32	TransE	0.684	0.542	0.779	0.990	0.166	0.089	0.182	0.322	0.274	0.197	0.298	0.428	0.368	0.284	0.403	0.534
	ComplEx	0.610	0.460	0.697	0.978	0.136	0.069	0.144	0.273	0.250	0.178	0.275	0.395	0.344	0.277	0.365	0.480
	AttE	0.648	0.488	0.741	0.980	0.125	0.060	0.135	0.259	0.283	0.205	0.307	0.436	0.364	0.289	0.394	0.518
	AttH	0.728	0.610	0.804	0.990	0.120	0.058	0.124	0.247	0.280	0.200	0.307	0.443	0.380	0.300	0.415	0.538
	DKRL	0.660	0.505	0.774	0.998	0.158	0.085	0.171	0.310	0.230	0.159	0.250	0.368	0.339	0.255	0.373	0.509
	ConMask	0.662	0.505	0.761	0.988	0.155	0.083	0.169	0.305	0.245	0.171	0.268	0.390	0.362	0.294	0.389	0.504
	PretrainKGE	0.674	0.540	0.756	0.985	0.151	0.078	0.164	0.300	0.251	0.175	0.276	0.397	0.349	0.274	0.380	0.502
Ours D=32	Robin_W	0.730	0.610	0.801	0.990	0.173	0.096	0.188	0.333	0.290	0.208	0.317	0.449	0.363	0.281	0.396	0.528
	Robin_F	0.732	0.609	0.811	0.993	0.173	0.095	0.186	0.338	0.300	0.213	0.329	0.471	0.365	0.285	0.397	0.524
	Robin_S	0.732	0.612	0.799	0.980	0.173	0.095	0.188	0.333	0.304	0.222	0.331	0.465	0.363	0.282	0.398	0.528
	Robin_D	0.728	0.610	0.789	0.993	0.173	0.097	0.187	0.333	0.294	0.213	0.321	0.452	0.366	0.286	0.401	0.528
	Lion_SD	0.736	0.624	0.801	0.988	0.167	0.090	0.180	0.330	0.304	0.217	0.333	0.478	0.397	0.314	0.441	0.554
	Lion_SF	0.727	0.605	0.801	0.993	0.175	0.097	0.190	0.340	0.301	0.214	0.330	0.475	0.395	0.314	0.439	0.548
	Tetra_zero	0.547	0.356	0.647	0.978	0.134	0.069	0.141	0.266	0.264	0.187	0.288	0.414	0.330	0.274	0.349	0.451
	Tetra_SF	0.773	0.652	0.856	0.990	0.157	0.086	0.166	0.299	0.278	0.196	0.304	0.439	0.255	0.178	0.274	0.421
	Tetra_WSF	0.780	0.669	0.858	0.995	0.155	0.084	0.169	0.302	0.266	0.188	0.289	0.421	0.169	0.113	0.180	0.288
Baselines D=500	TransE	0.712	0.590	0.789	0.990	0.178	0.100	0.194	0.341	0.318	0.231	0.350	0.492	0.421	0.351	0.461	0.556
	ComplEx	0.626	0.483	0.699	0.978	0.144	0.077	0.155	0.283	0.308	0.223	0.337	0.482	0.410	0.341	0.443	0.550
	AttE	0.795	0.699	0.858	0.993	0.187	0.105	0.205	0.355	0.272	0.195	0.295	0.429	0.356	0.294	0.389	0.471
	AttH	0.789	0.684	0.861	0.995	0.185	0.102	0.202	0.354	0.265	0.188	0.287	0.420	0.313	0.256	0.336	0.431
	DKRL	0.706	0.582	0.786	0.990	0.162	0.083	0.176	0.328	0.239	0.169	0.260	0.375	0.333	0.239	0.371	0.520
	ConMask	0.713	0.587	0.808	0.993	0.165	0.086	0.180	0.335	0.258	0.183	0.284	0.405	0.381	0.306	0.421	0.519
	PretrainKGE	0.718	0.592	0.803	0.993	0.159	0.082	0.172	0.323	0.262	0.187	0.287	0.407	0.320	0.231	0.353	0.495
Ours D=500	Robin_W	0.731	0.614	0.796	0.993	0.192	0.111	0.207	0.363	0.328	0.235	0.362	0.514	0.402	0.327	0.442	0.541
	Robin_F	0.721	0.597	0.791	0.995	0.192	0.110	0.208	0.366	0.331	0.236	0.366	0.520	0.402	0.327	0.442	0.541
	Robin_S	0.730	0.614	0.786	0.993	0.192	0.109	0.208	0.368	0.325	0.231	0.360	0.512	0.436	0.365	0.471	0.571
	Robin_D	0.729	0.612	0.801	0.995	0.191	0.107	0.208	0.368	0.332	0.237	0.370	0.522	0.35	0.272	0.395	0.500
	Lion_SD	0.726	0.605	0.801	0.993	0.193	0.110	0.209	0.369	0.330	0.235	0.366	0.519	0.433	0.363	0.471	0.562
	Lion_SF	0.725	0.602	0.801	0.993	0.194	0.111	0.209	0.369	0.332	0.237	0.367	0.521	0.440	0.366	0.478	0.577
	Tetra_zero	0.787	0.689	0.851	0.995	0.179	0.099	0.196	0.343	0.324	0.234	0.356	0.503	0.356	0.279	0.384	0.516
	Tetra_SF	0.816	0.709	0.884	0.995	0.181	0.102	0.195	0.345	0.336	0.245	0.368	0.518	0.445	0.367	0.489	0.593
	Tetra_WSF	0.822	0.731	0.893	0.993	0.186	0.102	0.204	0.360	0.323	0.233	0.353	0.501	0.443	0.365	0.482	0.588

Table 5. Comparison of LM-based baselines and our best results. In each dimensional setting, numbers are the best results for each dataset.

Model	Nations				Diabetes				FB15k-237				YAGO-10			
	MRR	H@1	H@3	H@10	MRR	H@1	H@3	H@10	MRR	H@1	H@3	H@10	MRR	H@1	H@3	H@10
KG-BERT	0.592	0.420	0.716	0.982	0.063	0.022	0.057	0.143	-	-	-	0.420	-	-	-	0.292
StAR	0.545	0.348	0.677	0.950	0.102	0.033	0.103	0.229	0.296	0.205	0.322	0.482	0.254	0.169	0.271	0.426
Our best	0.822	0.731	0.893	0.995	0.194	0.111	0.209	0.369	0.336	0.245	0.370	0.522	0.445	0.367	0.489	0.593

Results of Models Purely Based on Pre-trained Language Models: We also conduct a comparison of the results obtained by KG-BERT [39] and StAR [32] in Tables 5. Please note that these approaches do not explicitly provide embeddings for entities and relation labels, and thus the embedding dimension D is not applicable. We obtained these results by replicating their experiments on the other three datasets, while their results on FB15k-237 were obtained from the original papers. The KG-BERT takes too much time running on the YAGO-10, so we can only report its intermediate testing result of Hits@10. These results from both baselines are lower than our best results. The reason for this is that approaches such as KG-BERT and StAR model triples as sequences of text using pre-trained language models, disregarding the structural information in KGs. As a result, they encounter entity ambiguity problems on larger datasets. Unlike these approaches, KGE models that explicitly model entity embeddings naturally possess a unique representation for each entity. In contrast, models like KG-BERT and StAR only have a unique representation for each word, and entities are represented as a sequence of words. This become noisy with long entity descriptions, leading to noisy entity representations.

The Importance of Integration in the Hypercomplex Space: To demonstrate the significance of integrating different features from texts in the hypercomplex space, we construct an ablation model, *TransE_Concat*, by concatenating four representations $\{W, F, D, S\}$ and treating it as the input for TransE. The purpose of *TransE_Concat* is to assess whether the performance gain truly arises from the integration of the hypercomplex space or not. We reused the low-dimensional results of TransE and the Dihedron version of our models from Tables 4. Simultaneously, we re-run the *TransE_Concat* model, and the results are presented in Table 6. We observe that *TransE_Concat* outperforms TransE on the smallest dataset, Nations, but it falls short in comparison to our best model, Tetra_WSF. For the other larger datasets, *TransE_Concat* yield inferior results compared to Lion and even TransE. These findings suggest that the simple concatenation strategy fails to efficiently capture the interaction between different features. In contrast, our approach inherently accounts for such interactions due to the essence of the Dihedron product in Eq. 2, along with various geometric perspectives illustrated in Fig. 2.

Table 6. Ablation study results of concatenating representations for the low ($D = 32$) dimensional setting, where numbers are the best results for each dataset.

Model	Nations				Diabetes				FB15k-237				YAGO-10			
	MRR	H@1	H@3	H@10	MRR	H@1	H@3	H@10	MRR	H@1	H@3	H@10	MRR	H@1	H@3	H@10
TransE	0.684	0.542	0.779	0.990	0.166	0.089	0.182	0.322	0.274	0.197	0.298	0.428	0.368	0.284	0.403	0.534
TransE_Concat	0.726	0.612	0.786	0.983	0.161	0.088	0.174	0.312	0.257	0.182	0.278	0.406	0.149	0.087	0.160	0.272
Lion_SD	0.736	0.624	0.801	0.988	0.167	0.090	0.180	0.330	**0.304**	**0.217**	**0.333**	**0.478**	**0.397**	**0.314**	**0.441**	**0.554**
Lion_SF	0.727	0.605	0.801	0.993	**0.175**	**0.097**	**0.190**	**0.340**	0.301	0.214	0.330	0.475	0.395	**0.314**	0.439	0.548
Tetra_WSF	**0.780**	**0.669**	**0.858**	**0.995**	0.155	0.084	0.169	0.302	0.266	0.188	0.289	0.421	0.169	0.113	0.180	0.288

Comparison of Quaternion and Dihedron: We conducted a comparison of the query representation using Quaternion and Dihedron on three variants of our model (Robin_S, Lion_SF, and Tetra_WSF) by performing link prediction experiments on FB15k-237. We reused the results of the Dihedron version of each model from Tables 4, while rerunning the Quaternion version. The results, as shown in Table 7, indicate that Dihedron generally outperforms Quaternion, which is in line with our earlier claim in the Preliminary that Dihedron is a more expressive representation than Quaternion.

5.3 Effect of Textual Information in Entity Representation

In this visualization, we demonstrate the impact of pre-trained language models on the Tetra_WSF model's performance. We selected two datasets, FB15k-237 and YAGO-10, and computed the average cosine similarities on all testing triples of each dataset. The heat maps in Fig. 3 and 4 show the cosine similarities

Table 7. Link prediction results on FB15k-237 with both dimensions. Each model use Quaternion product in Eq. 1 or Dihedron product in Eq. 2.

Model	FB15k-237 (D=32)				FB15k-237 (D=500)			
	MRR	H@1	H@3	H@10	MRR	H@1	H@3	H@10
Robin_S (Quaternion)	0.290	0.205	0.317	0.459	0.322	0.229	0.355	0.505
Robin_S (Dihedron)	**0.304**	**0.222**	**0.331**	**0.465**	**0.325**	**0.231**	**0.360**	**0.512**
Lion_SF (Quaternion)	0.295	0.208	0.322	0.465	0.320	0.228	0.353	0.505
Lion_SF (Dihedron)	**0.301**	**0.214**	**0.330**	**0.475**	**0.332**	**0.237**	**0.367**	**0.521**
Tetra_WSF (Quaternion)	**0.270**	0.192	**0.294**	**0.420**	0.318	0.227	0.351	0.499
Tetra_WSF (Dihedron)	0.269	**0.192**	**0.295**	0.419	**0.328**	**0.237**	**0.361**	**0.509**

between the four parts of our 4*D dimensional representation: *entity embedding*, *word embedding*, *sentence embedding*, and *document embedding*. By examining the similarities on the diagonal of the heat maps, we can assess the contribution of each part when matching the query and the tail in the link prediction task.

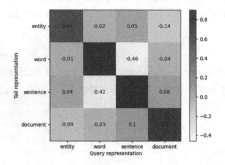

Fig. 3. Cosine similarities of the query and tail of triples on FB15k-237.

Fig. 4. Cosine similarities of the query and tail of triples on YAGO-10.

Among the four types of embeddings, the similarities between word-word, sentence-sentence, and document-document embeddings are higher than the similarity between entity-entity embeddings, indicating that semantic information at the word, sentence, and document levels are helpful in matching queries and tails. We conclude that all three levels of textual information from entity descriptions capture important semantic information during the matching between queries and tails.

5.4   Contribution of Individual Sentences

In this analysis, we aim to investigate how our Robin_S model leverages sentence-level representations by selecting important sentences. Specifically, we evaluate the model's performance on the YAGO-10 dataset for link prediction and collect sentences from the descriptions of the head and tail entities for each triple. We then compute the importance of each sentence using the Shapley value method

[25] and rank them in descending order of importance. Finally, we manually inspect the semantics of each highly ranked sentence, and conclude that our model effectively exploits sentence-level information for the corresponding triple if a semantically important sentence receives a high rank.

Table 8 presents the top-3 important sentences from the entity descriptions, as identified by the Shapley value, in the YAGO-10 dataset. For the first triple (MarsCallahan, created, Zigs(film)), the top-ranked sentence comes from the tail description and contains the keywords "directed by Mars Callahan," which is about the head entity. For the second triple (MargaretOfGeneva, isMarriedTo, ThomasCountOfSavoy), the top-1 and top-2 sentences refer to the definition of both entities. Notably, the keywords "escorting" and "carried her off" in the top-3 sentence provide information about the relation label "isMarriedTo." These examples demonstrate how our model effectively exploits sentence-level information from the entity descriptions for link prediction.

Table 8. Examples about sentence contribution of our model, where a sentence with higher rank (smaller number) is more important. The source of the sentence indicates whether a sentence comes from the description of a head or tail entity.

Triple	Sentence rank	Sentence source	Sentence
MarsCallahan, created, Zigs(film)	1	tail	**Zigs** is a 2001 English language drama starring Jason Priestley Peter Dobson and Richard Portnow and **directed by Mars Callahan**.
	2	tail	The film received an r rating by the MPAA
	3	head	At the age of eleven Callahan toured with a children's musical group through thirty-seven states.
MargaretOfGeneva, isMarriedTo, ThomasCountOfSavoy	1	tail	**Thomas Tommaso I was count of savoy** from 1189 to 1233 he is sometimes numbered Thomas I to distinguish him from his son of the same name who governed savoy but was not count.
	2	head	**Margaret of Geneva** 1180–1252 countess of savoy was the daughter of William I count of Geneva
	3	head	When her father was **escorting** her to France in May 1195 Thomas I of savoy **carried her off**

6   Conclusion

In this study, we investigated the effectiveness of incorporating multi-level textual information by using multiple pre-trained language models in a KGE model. Our novel KGE model based on the Dihedron algebra captures the interactions between embeddings from pre-trained language models, resulting in better representations for incomplete KGs. Our experiments demonstrate that the incorporation of more pre-trained language models is beneficial for extracting information from text in KGs, particularly on small or sparse KGs. While other recent work [19] focuses on unifying information from multiple sources, our work is the first to explore the use of multiple pre-trained language models in the representation learning of KGs. In future work, we plan to investigate the incorporation of multi-source information in multi-hop KG completion scenarios. Beside the KG completion task, we also plan to apply our model to various other tasks. For instance, we can adapt it to predict entity types given a schema or to facilitate complex logical query answering.

Supplemental Material Statement: The datasets and our implementation are available at https://github.com/ZihaoWang/text_enhanced_KGE. The Appendix can be found in our full Arxiv version https://arxiv.org/abs/2208.02743.

Acknowledgement. The authors thank the International Max Planck Research School for Intelligent Systems (IMPRS-IS) for supporting Zihao Wang. Zihao Wang and Mojtaba Nayyeri have been funded by the German Federal Ministry for Economic Affairs and Climate Action under Grant Agreement Number 01MK20008F (Service-Meister) and ATLAS project funded by Bundesministerium für Bildung und Forschung (BMBF).

References

1. Balazevic, I., Allen, C., Hospedales, T.: Multi-relational poincaré graph embeddings. In: Advances in Neural Information Processing Systems, vol. 32 (2019)
2. Bojanowski, P., Grave, E., Joulin, A., Mikolov, T.: Enriching word vectors with subword information. Trans. Assoc. Comput. Linguistics **5**, 135–146 (2017)
3. Bordes, A., Usunier, N., Garcia-Duran, A., Weston, J., Yakhnenko, O.: Translating embeddings for modeling multi-relational data. In: Advances in Neural Information Processing Systems, vol. 26 (2013)
4. Bordes, A., Usunier, N., Garcia-Duran, A., Weston, J., Yakhnenko, O.: Translating embeddings for modeling multi-relational data. In: Burges, C.J.C., Bottou, L., Welling, M., Ghahramani, Z., Weinberger, K.Q. (eds.) Advances in Neural Information Processing Systems, vol. 26. Curran Associates, Inc. (2013). https://proceedings.neurips.cc/paper/2013/file/1cecc7a77928ca8133fa24680a88d2f9-Paper.pdf
5. Brayne, A., Wiatrak, M., Corneil, D.: On masked language models for contextual link prediction. In: Agirre, E., Apidianaki, M., Vulic, I. (eds.) Proceedings of Deep Learning Inside Out: The 3rd Workshop on Knowledge Extraction and Integration for Deep Learning Architectures, DeeLIO@ACL 2022, Dublin, Ireland and Online, May 27, 2022, pp. 87–99. Association for Computational Linguistics (2022)
6. Cao, Z., Xu, Q., Yang, Z., Cao, X., Huang, Q.: Dual quaternion knowledge graph embeddings. In: AAAI, pp. 6894–6902. AAAI Press (2021)
7. Chami, I., Wolf, A., Juan, D., Sala, F., Ravi, S., Ré, C.: Low-dimensional hyperbolic knowledge graph embeddings. In: Jurafsky, D., Chai, J., Schluter, N., Tetreault, J.R. (eds.) Proceedings of the 58th Annual Meeting of the Association for Computational Linguistics, ACL 2020, Online, July 5–10, 2020, pp. 6901–6914. Association for Computational Linguistics (2020)

8. Choudhary, S., Luthra, T., Mittal, A., Singh, R.: A survey of knowledge graph embedding and their applications. arXiv preprint arXiv:2107.07842 (2021)
9. Clouâtre, L., Trempe, P., Zouaq, A., Chandar, S.: MLMLM: link prediction with mean likelihood masked language model. In: Zong, C., Xia, F., Li, W., Navigli, R. (eds.) Findings of the Association for Computational Linguistics: ACL/IJCNLP 2021, Online Event, August 1–6, 2021. Findings of ACL, vol. ACL/IJCNLP 2021, pp. 4321–4331. Association for Computational Linguistics (2021)
10. Duchi, J.C., Hazan, E., Singer, Y.: Adaptive subgradient methods for online learning and stochastic optimization. J. Mach. Learn. Res. **12**, 2121–2159 (2011)
11. Ethayarajh, K.: How contextual are contextualized word representations? comparing the geometry of Bert, Elmo, and GPT-2 embeddings. In: EMNLP/IJCNLP (1), pp. 55–65. Association for Computational Linguistics (2019)
12. Ji, S., Pan, S., Cambria, E., Marttinen, P., Philip, S.Y.: A survey on knowledge graphs: representation, acquisition, and applications. IEEE Trans. Neural Networks Learn. Syst. **33**, 494–514 (2021)
13. Kazemi, S.M., Poole, D.: Simple embedding for link prediction in knowledge graphs. In: Advances in Neural Information Processing Systems, vol. 31 (2018)
14. Kok, S., Domingos, P.: Statistical predicate invention. In: Proceedings of the 24th International Conference on Machine Learning, pp. 433–440 (2007)
15. Lacroix, T., Usunier, N., Obozinski, G.: Canonical tensor decomposition for knowledge base completion. In: International Conference on Machine Learning, pp. 2863–2872. PMLR (2018)
16. Lacroix, T., Usunier, N., Obozinski, G.: Canonical tensor decomposition for knowledge base completion. In: Dy, J.G., Krause, A. (eds.) Proceedings of the 35th International Conference on Machine Learning, ICML 2018, Stockholmsmässan, Stockholm, Sweden, July 10–15, 2018. Proceedings of Machine Learning Research, vol. 80, pp. 2869–2878. PMLR (2018). https://proceedings.mlr.press/v80/lacroix18a.html
17. Le, Q., Mikolov, T.: Distributed representations of sentences and documents. In: International Conference on Machine Learning, pp. 1188–1196. PMLR (2014)
18. Li, M., Wang, B., Jiang, J.: Siamese pre-trained transformer encoder for knowledge base completion. Neural Process. Lett. **53**(6), 4143–4158 (2021)
19. Li, X., Zhao, X., Xu, J., Zhang, Y., Xing, C.: IMF: interactive multimodal fusion model for link prediction. In: WWW, pp. 2572–2580. ACM (2023)
20. Nayyeri, M., et al.: Dihedron algebraic embeddings for spatio-temporal knowledge graph completion. In: Groth, P., et al. (eds.) ESWC 2022. LNCS, vol. 13261, pp. 253–269. Springer, Cham (2022). https://doi.org/10.1007/978-3-031-06981-9_15
21. Nayyeri, M., et al.: Fantastic knowledge graph embeddings and how to find the right space for them. In: Pan, J.Z., et al. (eds.) ISWC 2020. LNCS, vol. 12506, pp. 438–455. Springer, Cham (2020). https://doi.org/10.1007/978-3-030-62419-4_25
22. Nickel, M., Murphy, K., Tresp, V., Gabrilovich, E.: A review of relational machine learning for knowledge graphs. Proc. IEEE **104**(1), 11–33 (2015)
23. Pennington, J., Socher, R., Manning, C.D.: Glove: global vectors for word representation. In: EMNLP, pp. 1532–1543. ACL (2014)
24. Petroni, F., et al.: Language models as knowledge bases? In: Proceedings of the 2019 Conference on Empirical Methods in Natural Language Processing and the 9th International Joint Conference on Natural Language Processing (EMNLP-IJCNLP), Hong Kong, China, pp. 2463–2473. Association for Computational Linguistics (2019)
25. Shapley, L.S.: 17. A value for n-person games. Princeton University Press, Princeton (2016)

26. Shen, J., Wang, C., Gong, L., Song, D.: Joint language semantic and structure embedding for knowledge graph completion. In: Calzolari, N., et al. (eds.) Proceedings of the 29th International Conference on Computational Linguistics, COLING 2022, Gyeongju, Republic of Korea, October 12–17, 2022, pp. 1965–1978. International Committee on Computational Linguistics (2022)

27. Shi, B., Weninger, T.: Open-world knowledge graph completion. In Proceedings of the AAAI Conference on Artificial Intelligence, vol. 32, no. 1. AAAI (2018)

28. Sun, Z., Deng, Z., Nie, J., Tang, J.: Rotate: knowledge graph embedding by relational rotation in complex space. In: 7th International Conference on Learning Representations, ICLR 2019, New Orleans, LA, USA, May 6–9, 2019. OpenReview.net (2019)

29. Toth, G., Tâoth, G.: Glimpses of Algebra and Geometry, vol. 1810. Springer, New York (2002). https://doi.org/10.1007/b98964

30. Toutanova, K., Chen, D.: Observed versus latent features for knowledge base and text inference. In: CVSC, pp. 57–66. Association for Computational Linguistics (2015)

31. Trouillon, T., Welbl, J., Riedel, S., Gaussier, É., Bouchard, G.: Complex embeddings for simple link prediction. In: International Conference on Machine Learning, pp. 2071–2080 (2016)

32. Wang, B., Shen, T., Long, G., Zhou, T., Wang, Y., Chang, Y.: Structure-augmented text representation learning for efficient knowledge graph completion. In: Leskovec, J., Grobelnik, M., Najork, M., Tang, J., Zia, L. (eds.) WWW 2021: The Web Conference 2021, Virtual Event/Ljubljana, Slovenia, April 19–23, 2021, pp. 1737–1748. ACM/IW3C2 (2021)

33. Wang, C., Nulty, P., Lillis, D.: A comparative study on word embeddings in deep learning for text classification. In: NLPIR, pp. 37–46. ACM (2020)

34. Wang, Q., Mao, Z., Wang, B., Guo, L.: Knowledge graph embedding: a survey of approaches and applications. IEEE Trans. Knowl. Data Eng. **29**(12), 2724–2743 (2017)

35. Wang, X., et al.: Kepler: a unified model for knowledge embedding and pre-trained language representation. Trans. Assoc. Comput. Linguist. **9**, 176–194 (2021)

36. Wang, Z., Zhang, J., Feng, J., Chen, Z.: Knowledge graph embedding by translating on hyperplanes. In: AAAI, pp. 1112–1119. Citeseer (2014)

37. Xie, R., Liu, Z., Jia, J., Luan, H., Sun, M.: Representation learning of knowledge graphs with entity descriptions. In: Proceedings of the AAAI Conference on Artificial Intelligence, vol. 30 (2016)

38. Xu, C., Li, R.: Relation embedding with dihedral group in knowledge graph. In: Korhonen, A., Traum, D.R., Màrquez, L. (eds.) Proceedings of the 57th Conference of the Association for Computational Linguistics, ACL 2019, Florence, Italy, July 28- August 2, 2019, Volume 1: Long Papers, pp. 263–272. Association for Computational Linguistics (2019)

39. Yao, L., Mao, C., Luo, Y.: Kg-Bert: Bert for knowledge graph completion. arXiv preprint arXiv:1909.03193 (2019)

40. Zhang, S., Tay, Y., Yao, L., Liu, Q.: Quaternion knowledge graph embeddings. In: NeurIPS (2019)

41. Zhang, Z., Liu, X., Zhang, Y., Su, Q., Sun, X., He, B.: Pretrain-KGE: learning knowledge representation from pretrained language models. In: Findings of the Association for Computational Linguistics: EMNLP 2020, pp. 259–266. Association for Computational Linguistics (2020)

42. Zhu, C., Yang, Z., Xia, X., Li, N., Zhong, F., Liu, L.: Multimodal reasoning based on knowledge graph embedding for specific diseases. Bioinformatics **38**(8), 2235–2245 (2022). https://doi.org/10.1093/bioinformatics/btac085

LLMs4OL: Large Language Models for Ontology Learning

Hamed Babaei Giglou[✉] , Jennifer D'Souza , and Sören Auer

TIB Leibniz Information Centre for Science and Technology, Hannover, Germany
{hamed.babaei,jennifer.dsouza,auer}@tib.eu

Abstract. We propose the LLMs4OL approach, which utilizes Large Language Models (LLMs) for Ontology Learning (OL). LLMs have shown significant advancements in natural language processing, demonstrating their ability to capture complex language patterns in different knowledge domains. Our LLMs4OL paradigm investigates the following hypothesis: *Can LLMs effectively apply their language pattern capturing capability to OL, which involves automatically extracting and structuring knowledge from natural language text?* To test this hypothesis, we conduct a comprehensive evaluation using the zero-shot prompting method. We evaluate nine different LLM model families for three main OL tasks: term typing, taxonomy discovery, and extraction of non-taxonomic relations. Additionally, the evaluations encompass diverse genres of ontological knowledge, including lexicosemantic knowledge in WordNet, geographical knowledge in GeoNames, and medical knowledge in UMLS.

The obtained empirical results show that foundational LLMs are not sufficiently suitable for ontology construction that entails a high degree of reasoning skills and domain expertise. Nevertheless, when effectively fine-tuned they just might work as suitable assistants, alleviating the knowledge acquisition bottleneck, for ontology construction.

Keywords: Large Language Models · LLMs · Ontologies · Ontology Learning · Prompting · Prompt-based Learning

1 Introduction

Ontology Learning (OL) is an important field of research in artificial intelligence (AI) and knowledge engineering, as it addresses the challenge of knowledge acquisition and representation in a variety of domains. OL involves automatically identifying terms, types, relations, and potentially axioms from textual information to construct an ontology [30]. Numerous examples of human-expert created ontologies exist, ranging from general-purpose ontologies to domain-specific ones, e.g., Unified Medical Language System (UMLS) [9], WordNet [41], GeoNames [53], Dublin Core Metadata Initiative (DCMI) [66], schema.org [20], etc. Traditional ontology creation relies on manual specification by domain experts, which can be time-consuming, costly, error-prone, and impractical when knowledge constantly evolves or domain experts are unavailable. Consequently, OL techniques have emerged to automatically acquire knowledge from unstructured or semi-structured sources, such as text documents and the web, and transform it into a structured ontology. A quick review of the field shows that traditional approaches to OL are based on lexico-syntactic pattern mining and clustering [2, 4, 21, 23, 24, 26, 28, 37, 42, 54, 61, 67]. In contrast, recent advances in natural language processing (NLP) through Large Language Models (LLMs) [46] offer a promising alternative to traditional OL methods. The ultimate goal of OL is to provide a cost-effective and scalable solution for knowledge acquisition and representation, enabling more efficient and effective decision-making in a range of domains. To this end, we introduce the LLMs4OL paradigm and empirically ground it as a foundational first step.

Currently, there is no research explicitly training LLMs for OL. Thus to test LLMs for OL for the first time, we made some experimental considerations. The first being: *Do the characteristics of LLMs justify ontology learning?* First, LLMs are trained on extensive and diverse text, similar to domain-specific knowledge bases [51]. This aligns with the need for ontology developers to have extensive domain knowledge. Second, LLMs are built on the core technology of transformers that have enabled their higher language modeling complexity by facilitating the rapid scaling of their parameters. These parameters represent connections between words, enabling LLMs to comprehend the meaning of unstructured text like sentences or paragraphs. Further, by extrapolating complex linguistic patterns from word connections, LLMs exhibit human-like response capabilities across various tasks, as observed in the field of "emergent" AI. This behavior entails performing tasks beyond their explicit training, such as generating executable code, diverse genre text, and accurate text summaries [59, 64]. Such ability of LLMs to extrapolate patterns from simple word connections, encoding language semantics, is crucial for OL. Ontologies often rely on analyzing and extrapolating structured information connections, such as term-type taxonomies and relations, from unstructured text [18]. Thus LLMs4OL hypothesis of LLMs' fruitful application for OL appeared conceptually justified.

LLMs are being developed at a rapid pace. At the time of writing of this work, at least 60 different LLMs are reported [5]. This led to our second main experimental consideration. *Which LLMs to test for the LLMs4OL task hypothesis?* Empirical validation of various LLMs is crucial for NLP advancements and selecting suitable models for research tasks. Despite impressive performances in diverse NLP tasks, LLM effectiveness varies. For the foundational groundwork of LLMs4OL, we comprehensively selected eight diverse model families based on architecture and reported state-of-the-art performances at the time of this writing. The three main LLM architectures are encoder, decoder, and encoder-decoder. The selected LLMs for validation are: BERT [16] (encoder-only); BLOOM [56], MetaAI's LLaMA [60], OpenAI's GPT-3 [10], GPT-3.5 [46], GPT-4 [47] (all decoder-only); and BART [33] and Google's Flan-T5 [11] (encoder-decoder). Recent studies show that BERT excels in text classification and named entity recognition [16], BART is effective in text generation and summarization [33], and LLaMA demonstrates high accuracy in various NLP tasks, including reasoning, question answering, and code generation [60]. Flan-T5 emphasizes instruction tuning and exhibits strong multi-task performance [11]. BLOOM's unique multilingual approach achieves robust performance in tasks like text classification and sequence tagging [56]. Lastly, the GPT series stands out for its human-like text generation abilities [10,46,47]. In this work, we aim to comprehensively unify these LLMs for their effectiveness under the LLMs4OL paradigm for the first time.

With the two experimental considerations in place, we now introduce the LLMs4OL paradigm and highlight our contributions. LLMs4OL is centered around the development of ontologies that comprise the following primitives [39]: **1.** a set of strings that describe terminological lexical entries L for conceptual types; **2.** a set of conceptual types T; **3.** a taxonomy of types in a hierarchy H_T; **4.** a set of non-taxonomic relations R described by their domain and range restrictions arranged in a heterarchy of relations H_R; and **5.** a set of axioms A that describe additional constraints on the ontology and make implicit facts explicit. The LLMs4OL paradigm, introduced in this work, addresses three core aspects of OL as tasks, outlined as the following research questions (RQs).

- **RQ1:** *Term Typing Task* – How effective are LLMs for automated type discovery to construct an ontology?
- **RQ2:** *Type Taxonomy Discovery Task* – How effective are LLMs to recognize a type taxonomy i.e. the "is-a" hierarchy between types?
- **RQ3:** *Type Non-Taxonomic Relation Extraction Task* – How effective are LLMs to discover non-taxonomic relations between types?

The diversity of the empirical tests of this work are not only w.r.t. LLMs considered, but also the ontological knowledge domains tested for. Specifically, we test LLMs for lexico-semantic knowledge in WordNet [41], geographical knowledge in GeoNames [1], biomedical knowledge in UMLS [8], and web content type representations in schema.org [48]. For our empirical validation of LLMs4OL, we seize the opportunity to include PubMedBERT [19], a domain-specific LLM designed solely for the biomedical domain and thus applicable only to UMLS. This addition complements the eight domain-independent model families introduced earlier as a ninth model type. Summarily, our main contributions are:

- The LLMs4OL task paradigm as a conceptual framework for leveraging LLMs for OL.
- An implementation of the LLMs4OL concept leveraging tailored prompt templates for zero-shot OL in the context of three specific tasks, viz. term typing, type taxonomic relation discovery, and type non-taxonomic relation discovery. These tasks are evaluated across unique ontological sources well-known in the community. Our code source with templates and datasets per task are released here https://github.com/HamedBabaei/LLMs4OL.
- A thorough out-of-the-box empirical evaluation of eight state-of-the-art domain-independent LLM types (10 models) and a ninth biomedical domain-specific LLM type (11th model) for their suitability to the various OL tasks

considered in this work. Furthermore, the most effective overall LLM is fine-tuned and subsequently finetuned LLM results are reported for our three OL tasks.

2 Related Work

There are three avenues of related research: ontology learning from text, prompting LLMs for knowledge, and LLM prompting methods or prompt engineering.

Ontology Learning from Text. One of the earliest approaches [23] used lexicosyntactic patterns to extract new lexicosemantic concepts and relations from large collections of unstructured text, enhancing WordNet [41]. WordNet is a lexical database comprising a lexical ontology of concepts (nouns, verbs, etc.) and lexico-semantic relations (synonymy, hyponymy, etc.). Hwang [24] proposed an alternative approach for constructing a dynamic ontology specific to an application domain. The method involved iteratively discovering types and taxonomy from unstructured text using a seed set of terms representing high-level domain types. In each iteration, newly discovered specialized types were incorporated, and the algorithm detected relations between linguistic features. The approach utilized a simple ontology algebra based on inheritance hierarchy and set operations. Agirre et al. [2] enhanced WordNet by extracting topically related words from web documents. This unique approach added topical signatures to enrich WordNet. Kietz et al. [28] introduced the On-To-Knowledge system, which utilized a generic core ontology like GermaNet [22] or WordNet as the foundational structure. It aimed to discover a domain-specific ontology from corporate intranet text resources. For concept extraction and pruning, it employed statistical term frequency count heuristics, while association rules were applied for relation identification in corporate texts. Roux et al. [54] proposed a method to expand a genetics ontology by reusing existing domain ontologies and enhancing concepts through verb patterns extracted from unstructured text. Their system utilized linguistic tools like part-of-speech taggers and syntactic parsers. Wagner [61] employed statistical analysis of corpora to enrich WordNet in non-English languages by discovering relations, adding new terms to concepts, and acquiring concepts through the automatic acquisition of verb preferences. Moldovan and Girju [43] introduced the Knowledge Acquisition from Text (KAT) system to enrich WordNet's finance domain coverage. Their method involved four stages: (1) discovering new concepts from a seed set of terms, expanding the concept list using dictionaries; (2) identifying lexical patterns from new concepts; (3) discovering relations from lexical patterns; and (4) integrating extracted information into WordNet using a knowledge classification algorithm. In [4], an unsupervised method is presented to enhance ontologies with domain-specific information using NLP techniques such as NER and WSD. The method utilizes a general NER system to uncover a taxonomic hierarchy and employs WSD to enrich existing synsets by querying the internet for new terms and disambiguating them through cooccurrence frequency. Khan and Luo [26] employed clustering techniques to find new terms, utilizing WordNet for typing. They used the self-organizing tree algorithm [17], inspired by molecular evolution, to establish an ontology hierarchy. Additionally, Xu et al. [67] focused on automatically acquiring domain-specific terms and relations through a TFIDF-based single-word term classifier, a lexico-syntactic pattern finder based on known relations and collocations, and a relation extractor utilizing discovered lexico-syntactic patterns.

Predominantly, the approaches for OL [62] that stand out so far are based on lexico-syntactic patterns for term and relation extraction as well as clustering for type discovery. Otherwise, they build on seed-term-based bootstrapping methods. The reader is referred to further detailed reviews [6,38] on this theme for a comprehensive overall methodological picture for OL. Traditional NLP was defined by modular pipelines by which machines were equipped step-wise with annotations at the linguistic, syntactic, and semantic levels to process text. LLMs have ushered in a new era of possibilities for AI systems that obviate the need for modular NLP systems to understand natural language which we tap into for the first time for the OL task in this work.

Prompting LLMs for Knowledge. LLMs can process and retrieve facts based on their knowledge which makes them good zero-shot learners for various NLP tasks. Prompting LLMs means feeding an input x using a *template function* $f_{prompt}(x)$, a textual string prompt input that has some unfilled slots, and then the LLMs are used to probabilistically fill the unfilled information to obtain a final string x', from which the final output y can be derived [35]. The LAMA: LAnguage Model Analysis [52] benchmark has been introduced as a probing technique for analyzing the factual and commonsense knowledge contained in unidirectional LMs (i.e. Transformer-XL [13]) and bidirectional LMs (i.e. BERT and ELMo [49]) with cloze prompt templates from knowledge triples. They demonstrated the potential of pre-trained language models (PLMs) in probing facts – where facts are taken into account as subject-relation-object triples or question-answer pairs – with querying LLMs by converting facts into a cloze template which is used as an input for the LM to fill the missing token. Further studies extended LAMA by the automated discovery of prompts [25], finetuning LLMs for better probing [3,32,68], or a purely unsupervised way of probing knowledge from LMs [50]. These studies analyzed LLMs for their ability to encode various linguistic and non-linguistic facts. This analysis was limited to predefined facts that reinforce the traditional linguistic knowledge of the LLMs, and as a result do not reflect how concepts are learned by the LLMs. In response to this limitation, Dalvi et al. [14] put forward a proposal to explore and examine the latent concepts learned by LLMs, offering a fresh perspective on BERT. They defined concepts as "a group of words that are meaningful," i.e. that can be clustered based on relations such as lexical, morphological, etc. In another study [55], they propose the framework *ConceptX* by extending their studies on seven LLMs in latent space analysis with the alignment of the grouped concepts to human-defined concepts. These works show that using LLMs and accessing the concept's latent spaces, allows us to group concepts and align them to predefined types and type relations discovery.

Prompt Engineering. As a novel discipline, prompt engineering focuses on designing optimal instructions for LLMs to enable successful task performance. Standard prompting [63] represents a fundamental approach for instructing LLMs. It allows users to craft their own customized "self-designed prompts" to effectively interact with LLMs [10] and prompt them to respond to the given prompt instruction straightaway with an answer. Consider the manually crafted FLAN collection [36] addressing diverse NLP tasks other than OL as an exemplar. Notably, the nature of some problems naturally encompass a step-by-step thought process for arriving at the answer. In other words, the problem to be solved can be decomposed as a series of preceding intermediate steps before arriving at the final solution. E.g., arithmetic or reasoning problems. Toward explainability and providing language models in a sense "time to think" helping it respond more accurately, there are advanced prompt engineering methods as well. As a first, as per the Chain-of-Thought (CoT) [65] prompting method, the prompt instruction is so crafted that the LLM is instructed to break down complex tasks as a series of incremental steps leading to the solution. This helps the LLM to reason step-by-step and arrive at a more accurate and logical conclusion. On the other hand Tree-of-Thoughts (ToT) [69] has been introduced for tasks that require exploration or strategic lookahead. ToT generalizes over CoT prompting by exploring thoughts that serve as intermediate steps for general problem-solving with LLMs. Both CoT and ToT unlock complex reasoning capabilities through intermediate reasoning steps in combination with few-shot or zero-shot [29] prompting. Another approach for solving more complex tasks is using decomposed prompting [27], where we can further decompose tasks that are hard for LLMs into simpler solvable sub-tasks and delegate these to subtask-specific LLMs.

Given the LLMs4OL task paradigm introduced in this work, complex prompting is not a primary concern, as our current focus is on the initial exploration of the task to identify the areas where we need further improvement. We want to understand how much we have accomplished so far before delving into more complex techniques like CoT, ToT, and decomposed prompting. Once we have a clearer picture of the model's capabilities and limitations in a standard prompting setting, we can then consider other than standard prompt engineering approaches by formulating OL as a stepwise reasoning task.

3 The LLMs4OL Task Paradigm

The Large Language Models for Ontology Learning (LLMs4OL) task paradigm offers a conceptual framework to accelerate the time-consuming and expensive construction of ontologies exclusively by domain experts to a level playing field involving powerful AI methods such as LLMs for high-quality OL results; consequently and ideally involving domains experts only in validation cycles. In theory, with the right formulations, all tasks pertinent to OL fit within the LLMs4OL task paradigm. OL tasks are based on ontology primitives [39], including lexical entries L, conceptual types T, a hierarchical taxonomy of types H_T, non-taxonomic relations R in a heterarchy H_R, and a set of axioms A to describe

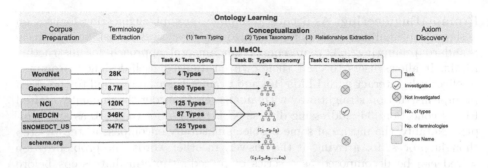

Fig. 1. The LLMs4OL task paradigm is an end-to-end framework for ontology learning in various knowledge domains, i.e. lexicosemantics (WordNet), geography (GeoNames), biomedicine (NCI, MEDICIN, SNOMEDCT), and web content types (schema.org). The three OL tasks empirically validated in this work are depicted within the blue arrow, aligned with the greater LLMs4OL paradigm.(Color figure online)

the ontology's constraints and inference rules. To address these primitives, OL tasks [45] include: 1) Corpus preparation - selecting and collecting source texts for ontology building. 2) Terminology extraction - identifying and extracting relevant terms. 3) Term typing - grouping similar terms into conceptual types. 4) Taxonomy construction - establishing "is-a" hierarchies between types. 5) Relationship extraction - identifying semantic relationships beyond "is-a." 6) Axiom discovery - finding constraints and inference rules for the ontology. This set of six tasks forms the LLMs4OL task paradigm. See Fig. 1 for the proposed LLMs4OL conceptual framework.

In this work, we empirically ground three core OL tasks using LLMs as a foundational basis for future research. However, traditional AI paradigms rely on testing models only on explicitly trained tasks, which is not the case for LLMs. Instead, we test LLMs for OL as an "emergent" behavior [59,64], where they demonstrate the capacity to generate responses on a wide range of tasks despite lacking explicit training. The key to unraveling the emergent abilities of LLMs is to prompt them for their knowledge, as popularized by GPT-3 [10], via carefully designed prompts. As discussed earlier (see Sect. 2), prompt engineering for LLMs is a new AI sub-discipline. In this process, a pre-trained language model receives a prompt, such as a natural language statement, to generate responses without further training or gradient updates to its parameters [35]. Prompts can be designed in two main types based on the underlying LLM pre-training objective: cloze prompts [12,51], which involve filling in blanks in an incomplete sentence or passage per masked language modeling pre-training; and prefix prompts [31,34], which generate text following a given starting phrase and offer more design adaptability to the underlying model. The earlier introduced LLMs4OL paradigm is empirically validated for three select OL tasks using respective prompt functions $f_{prompt}(.)$ suited to each task and model.

Task A - *Term Typing.* A generalized type is discovered for a lexical term.

The generic cloze prompt template is $f^A_{c-prompt}(L) := [S?].\ [L]\ [P_{domain}]$ *is a* $[MASK]$. where S is an optional context sentence, L is the lexical term prompted for, P_{domain} is a domain specification, and the special $MASK$ token is the type output expected from the model. Since prompt design is an important factor that determines how the LLM responds, eight different prompt template instantiations of the generic template were leveraged with final results reported for the best template. E.g., if WordNet is the base ontology, the part-of-speech type for the lexical term is prompted. In this case, template 1 is "[S]. [L] POS is a [MASK]." Note here "$[P_{domain}]$" is POS. Template 2 is "[S]. [L] part of speech is a [MASK]." Note here "$[P_{domain}]$" is "part of speech." In a similar manner, eight different prompt variants from the generic template were created. However, the specification of "$[P_{domain}]$" depended on the ontology's knowledge domain.

The prefix prompt template reuses the cloze prompt template but appends an additional "instruction" sentence and replaces the special [MASK] token with a blank or a "?" symbol. Generically, it is $f^A_{p-prompt}(T) = [instruction] + f^A_{c-prompt}(T)$, where the instruction is "Perform a sentence completion on the following sentence:" Based on the eight variations created from the generic cloze template prompt, subsequently eight template variations were created for the prefix prompting of the LLMs as well with best template results reported.

Task B - *Taxonomy Discovery.* Here a taxonomic hierarchy between pairs of types is discovered.

The generic cloze prompt template is $f^B_{c-prompt}(a,b) := [a|b]$ *is* $[P_{hierarchy}]$ *of* $[b|a]$. *This statement is* $[MASK]$. Where (a,b) or (b,a) are type pairs, $P_{hierarchy}$ indicates superclass relations if the template is initialized for top-down taxonomy discovery, otherwise indicates subclass relations if the template is initialized for bottom-up taxonomy discovery. In Task B, the expected model output for the special [MASK] token for a given type pair was true or false.

Similar to term typing, eight template variations of the generic template were created. Four of which were predicated on the top-down taxonomy discovery. E.g., "[a] is the superclass of [b]. This statement is [MASK]." Note here, $[P_{hierarchy}]$ is "superclass". Other three templates were based on $[P_{hierarchy}] \in$ parent class, supertype, ancestor class. And four more template instantiations predicated on the bottom-up taxonomy discovery were based on $[P_{hierarchy}] \in$ subclass, child class, subtype, descendant class. Thus eight experiments per template instantiation for the applicable LLM were run and the results from the best template were reported.

The prefix prompt template, similarly, reuses the cloze prompt template with the [MASK] token replaced with a blank or "?" symbol. It is $f^B_{p-prompt}(a,b) = [instruction] + f^B_{c-prompt}(a,b)$, with instruction "Identify whether the following statement is true or false:"

Task C - *Non-Taxonomic Relation Extraction.* This task discovers non-taxonomic semantic heterarchical relations between types.

The cloze prompt template is $f^C_{c-prompt}(h,r,t) := [h]\ is\ [r]\ [t].\ This$ *statement is* $[MASK]$. Where h is a head type, t is a tail type, and r is a non-taxonomic relationship between h and r. To support the discovery of a het-erarchy that can consist of a 1-M relational cardinality, for a given relation, all possible type pairs of the ontology were created. The expected output for the [MASK] token was again true or false. Note, unlike in Task A and B, the given template was used as is and no variations of it were created.

Again, the prefix prompt template reuses the cloze prompt template as the other tasks, with instructions similar to task B. It is $f^C_{p-prompt}(h, r, t) = [instruction] + f^C_{c-prompt}(h, r, t)$

4   LLMs4OL - Three Ontology Learning Tasks Evaluations

4.1   Evaluation Datasets - Ontological Knowledge Sources

To comprehensively assess LLMs for the three OL tasks presented in the previous section, we cover a variety of ontological knowledge domain sources. Generally, across the tasks, four knowledge domains are represented, i.e. lexicosemantic – WordNet [41], geographical – GeoNames [1], biomedicine – Unified Medical Language System (UMLS) [8] teased out as the National Cancer Institute (NCI) [44], MEDCIN [40], and Systematized Nomenclature of Medicine – Clinical Terms United States (SNOMEDCT_US) [57] subontologies, and content representa-tions in the web – schema.org [48]. Tasks A, B, and C applied only to UMLS. In other words, the ontology has a supporting knowledge base with terms that can be leveraged in the test prompts for term typing as Task A, taxonomic hierar-chical relational prompts as Task B, and non-taxonomic heterarchical relational prompts as Task C. The GeoNames source came with a knowledge base of terms instantiated for types and taxonomic relations, therefore, was leveraged in the Task A and B as OL tests with LLMs of this work. The WordNet source could be leveraged only in Task A since it came with an instantiated collection of lexical terms for syntactic types. It was not applicable in the Tasks B and C for OL defined in this work since the semantic relations in WordNet are lexicosemantic, in other words, between terms directly and not their types. Finally, since the schema.org source offered only typed taxonomies as standardized downloads, it was leveraged only in the OL Task B of this work. In this case, we refrained from scraping the web for instantiations of the schema.org taxonomy. For all other ontological knowledge sources considered in this work that were relevant to Task A, the term instantiations were obtained directly from the source. This facilitates replicating our Task A dataset easily. Detailed information on the ontological knowledge sources per task with relevant dataset statistics are pre-sented next.

Task A Datasets. Table 1 shows statistical insights for the Task A dataset where we used terms from WordNet, GeoNames, and UMLS. For WordNet we used the WN18RR data dump [15] that is derived from the original WordNet but released as a benchmark dataset with precreated train and test splits. Overall, it consists of 40,943 terms with 18 different relation types between the terms and four term types (noun, verb, adverb, adjective). We combined the original validation and test sets as a single test dataset. GeoNames comprises 680 categories of geographical locations, which are classified into 9 higher-level categories, e.g. H for stream, lake, and sea, and R for road and railroad. UMLS contains almost three million concepts from various sources which are linked together by semantic relationships. UMLS is unique in that it is a greater semantic ontological network that subsumes other biomedical problem-domain restricted subontologies. We grounded the term typing task to the semantic spaces of three select subontological sources,i.e. NCI, MEDCIN, and SNOMEDCT_US.

Table 1. Task A term typing dataset counts across three core ontological knowledge sources, i.e. WordNet, GeoNames, and UMLS, where for Task A UMLS is represented only by the NCI, MEDCIN, and SNOMEDCT_US subontological sources. The unique term types per source that defined Task A Ontology Learning is also provided.

Parameter	WordNet	GeoNames	NCI	MEDCIN	SNOMEDCT_US
Train Set Size	40,559	8,078,865	96,177	277,028	278,374
Test Set Size	9,470	702,510	24,045	69,258	69,594
Types	4	680	125	87	125

The train datasets were reserved for LLM fine-tuning. Among the 11 models, we selected the most promising one based on its zero-shot performance. The test datasets were used for evaluations in both zero-shot and fine-tuned settings.

Task B Datasets. From GeoNames, UMLS, and schema.org we obtained 689, 127, and 797 term types forming type taxonomies. Our test dataset was constructed as type pairs, where half represented the taxonomic hierarchy while the other half were not in a taxonomy. This is based on the following formulations.

$$\forall (a \in T_n, b \in T_{n+1}) \longmapsto (aRb \wedge b\neg Ra)$$

$$\forall (a \in T_n, b \in T_{n+1}, c \in T_{n+2}); (aRb \wedge bRc) \longmapsto aRc$$

$$\forall (a \in T_n, b \in T_{n+1}, c \in T_{n+2}); (c\neg Rb \wedge b\neg Ra) \longmapsto c\neg Ra$$

Where a, b, and c are types at different levels in the hierarchy. T is a collection of types at a particular level in the taxonomy, where $n + 2 > n + 1 > n$ and n is the root. The symbol R represents "a is a super class of type b" as a true taxonomic relation. Conversely, the $\neg R$ represents "b is a super class of type a" as a false taxonomic relation. Furthermore, transitive taxonomic relations, $(aRb \wedge bRc) \longmapsto aRc$, were also extracted as true relations, while their converse, i.e. $(c\neg Rb \wedge b\neg Ra) \longmapsto c\neg Ra$ were false relations.

Task C Datasets. As alluded to earlier, Task C evaluations, i.e. non-taxonomic relations discovery, were relegated to the only available ontological knowledge source among those we considered i.e. UMLS. It reports 53 non-taxonomic relations across its 127 term types. The testing dataset comprised all pairs of types for each relation, where for any given relation some pairs are true while the rest are false candidates. Task B and Task C datasets' statistics are in Table 2.

Table 2. Dataset statistics as counts per reported parameter for Task B type taxonomic hierarchy discovery and Task C type non-taxonomic heterarchy discovery across the pertinent ontological knowledge sources respectively per task.

Task	Parameter	GeoNames	UMLS	schema.org
Task B	Types	689	127	797
	Levels	2	3	6
	Positive/Negative Samples	680/680	254/254	2,670/2,670
	Train/Test split	272/1,088	101/407	1,086/4,727
Task C	Non-Taxonomic Relations	–	53	–
	Positive/Negative Samples	–	5,641/1,896	–
	Train/Test Split	–	1,507/6,030	–

4.2   Evaluation Models-Large Language Models (LLMs)

As already introduced earlier, in this work, we comprehensively evaluate eight main types of domain-independent LLMs reported as state-of-the-art for different tasks in the community. They are: BERT [16] as an encoder-only architecture, BLOOM [56], LLaMA [60], GPT-3 [10], GPT-3.5 [46], and GPT-4 [47] as decoder-only models, and finally BART [33] and Flan-T5 [11] as encoder-decoder models. Note these LLMs are released at varying parameter sizes. Thus qualified by the size in terms of parameters written in parenthesis, in all, we evaluate seven LLMs: 1. BERT-Large (340M), 2. BART-Large (400M), 3. Flan-T5-Large (780M), 4. Flan-T5-XL (3B), 5. BLOOM-1b7 (1.7B), 6. BLOOM-3b (3B), 7. GPT-3 (175B), 8. GPT-3.5 (174B), 9. LLaMA (7B), and GPT-4 (>1T). Additionally, we also test an eleventh biomedical domain-specific model Pub-MedBERT [19].

In this work, since we propose the LLMs4OL paradigm for the first time, in a sense postulating OL as an emergent ability of LLMs, it is important for us to test different LLMs on the new task. Evaluating different LLMs supports: 1) Performance comparison - this allows us to identify which models are effective for OL, 2) Model improvement - toward OL one can identify areas where the models need improvement, and 3) Research advancement - with our results from testing and comparing different models, researchers interested in OL could potentially identify new areas of research and develop new techniques for improving LLMs.

4.3   Evaluations

Metrics. Evaluations for Task A are reported as the mean average precision at k (MAP@K), where k = 1, since this metric was noted as being best suited to the task. Specifically, in our case, for term typing, MAP@1 measures the average precision of the top-1 ranked term types returned by an LLM for prompts initialized with terms from the evaluation set. And evaluations for Tasks B and C are reported in terms of the standard F1-score based on precision and recall.

Results-Three Ontology Learning Tasks Zero-Shot Evaluations. The per task overall evaluations are reported in Table 3. The three main rows of the table marked by alphabets A, B, and C correspond to term typing, type taxonomy discovery, and type non-taxonomic relational hetrarchy discovery results, respectively. The five subrows against Task A shows term typing results for WordNet, GeoNames, and the three UMLS subontologies, viz. NCI, SNOMEDCT_US, and MEDCIN. The three subrows against Task B shows type taxonomy discovery results for GeoNames, UMLS, and schema.org, respectively. Task C evaluation results are provided only for UMLS. We first examine the results in the zero-shot setting, i.e. for LLMs evaluated out-of-the-box, w.r.t. three RQs.

Table 3. Zero-shot results across 11 LLMs and finetuned Flan-T5-Large and Flan-T5-XL LLMs results reported for ontology learning Task A i.e. term typing in MAP@1, and as F1-score for Task B i.e. type taxonomy discovery, and Task C i.e. type non-taxonomic relation extraction. The results are in percentages.

Task	Dataset					Zero-Shot Testing							Finetuned	
		BERT-Large	PubMedBERT	BART-Large	Flan-T5-Large	Flan-T5-XL	BLOOM-1b7	BLOOM-3b	GPT-3	GPT-3.5	LLaMA-7B	GPT-4	Flan-T5-Large*	Flan-T5-XL*
A	WordNet	27.9	–	2.2	31.3	52.2	79.2	79.1	37.9	**91.7**	81.4	90.1	76.9	**86.3**
	GeoNames	38.3	-	23.2	13.2	33.8	28.5	28.8	22.4	35.0	29.5	**43.3**	16.9	18.4
	NCI	11.1	5.9	9.9	9.0	9.8	12.4	15.6	12.7	14.7	7.7	**16.1**	31.9	**32.8**
	SNOMEDCT_US	21.1	28.5	19.8	24.3	31.6	37.0	**37.7**	24.4	25.0	13.8	27.8	33.4	**43.4**
	MEDCIN	8.7	15.6	12.7	13.0	18.5	28.8	**29.8**	25.7	23.9	4.9	23.7	38.4	**51.8**
B	GeoNames	54.5	-	55.4	59.6	52.4	36.7	48.3	53.2	**67.8**	33.5	55.4	62.5	59.1
	UMLS	48.2	33.7	49.9	55.3	64.3	38.3	37.5	51.6	70.4	32.3	**78.1**	53.4	**79.3**
	schema.org	44.1	–	52.9	54.8	42.7	48.6	51.3	51.0	**74.4**	33.8	74.3	91.7	**91.7**
C	UMLS	40.1	42.7	42.4	46.0	**49.5**	43.1	42.7	38.8	37.5	20.3	41.3	49.1	**53.1**

RQ1: How Effective are LLMs for Task A, i.e. Automated Type Discovery?. We examine this question given the results in 5 subrows against the row A, i.e. corresponding to the various ontological datasets evaluated for Task A. Of the five ontological sources, the highest term typing results were achieved on the 4-typed WordNet at 91.7% MAP@1 by GPT-3.5. This high performance can be attributed in part to the simple type space of WordNet with only 4 types.

However, looking across the other LLMs evaluated on WordNet, in particular even GPT-3, scores in the range of 30% MAP@1 seem to be the norm with a low of 2.2% by BART-Large. Thus LLMs that report high scores on WordNet should be seen as more amenable to syntactic typing regardless of the WordNet simple type space. Considering all the ontological sources, Geonames presents the most fine-grained types taxonomy of 680 types. Despite this, the best result obtained on this source is 43.3% from GPT-4 with BERT-Large second at 38.3%. This is better than the typing evaluations on the three biomedical datasets. Even the domain-specific PubMedBERT underperforms. In this regard, domain-independent models with large-scale parameters such a BLOOM (3B) are more amenable to this complex task. Since biomedicine entails deeper domain-specific semantics, we hypothesize better performance not just from domain-specific fine-tuning but also strategically for task-specific reasoning.

The results overview is: 91.7% WordNet by GPT-3.5 > 43.3% GeoNames by GPT-4 > 37.7% SNOMEDCT_US by BLOOM-3b > 29.8% MEDCIN by BLOOM-3b > 16.1% NCI by GPT-4.

Notably this work addresses Task A as a text generation task for the term types. We wish to highlight that Task A can alternatively be tackled as a classification task. For instance, given the set of types for Task A: WordNet - 4, GeoNames - 680, NCI - 125, MEDICIN - 87, and SNOMED_CT - 125, the task can be respectively formulated as a multiclass classification task. We anticipate the classification task complexity to grow with the number of classes. Generally, our only reservation here is that the set of types needs to be known in advance. By following the LLM generation approach instead, we allow the LLM to generate the closest class it thinks applicable and in this work then evaluate how close its generated class is to the one the human-annotated or typed for the term.

RQ2: How Effective are LLMs to Recognize a Type Taxonomy i.e. the "is-a" Hierarchy Between Types?. We examine this question given the results in the 3 subrows against the main row B, i.e. corresponding to the three ontological sources evaluated for Task B. The highest result was achieved for UMLS by GPT-4 at 78.1%. Of the open-source models, Flan-T5-XL achieved the best result at 64.3%. Thus for term taxonomy discovery, LLMs on average have proven most effective in the zero-shot setting on the biomedical domain.

The results overview is: 78.1% UMLS by GPT-4 > 74.4% schema.org by GPT-3.5 > 67.8% GeoNames by GPT-3.5. Note the three GPT models were not open-sourced and thus we tested them with a paid subscription. For the open-source models, the results overview is: 64.3% UMLS by Flan-T5-XL > 59.6% GeoNames by Flan-T5-XL > 54.8% schema.org by Flan-T5-Large.

RQ3: How Effective are LLMs to Discover Non-Taxonomic Relations Between Types?. We examine this question given the results in Table 3 row for Task C, i.e. for UMLS. The best result achieved is 49.5% by Flan-T5-XL. We consider this a fairly good result over a sizeable set of 7,537 type pairs that are in true non-taxonomic relations or are false pairs.

Finally, over all the three tasks considered under the LLMs4OL paradigm, term typing proved the hardest obtaining the lowest overall results for most of its ontological sources tested including the biomedical domain in particular. Additionally in our analysis, GPT, Flan-T5, and BLOOM variants showed improved scores with increase in parameters, respectively. This held true for the closed-sourced GPT models, i.e. GPT-3 (175B) and GPT-3.5 (175B) to GPT-4 (>1T) and the open-sourced models, i.e. Flan-T5-Large (780M) to Flan-T5-XL (3B) and BLOOM from 1.7B to 3B. Thus it seems apparent that with an increased number of LLM parameters, we can expect an improvement in ontology learning.

Note, UMLS offers a robust empirical foundation for Task C. In future work, we propose ConceptNet [58] encompassing commonsense knowledge facts and DBpedia [7] encompassing general knowledge on wide range of topics, including but not limited to geography, history, science, literature, arts, and sports.

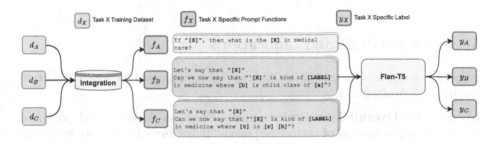

Fig. 2. An illustration of the LLM finetuning workflow on tasks for ontology learning.

Results-Three Ontology Learning Tasks Finetuned LLM Evaluations. Our zero-shot test results indicate that while LLMs seem promising for OL they would need task-specific finetuning to be a practically viable solution. To this end, we adopt the method of "instruction tuning" proposed as the FLAN collection which is the only known systematically deconstructed, effective way to finetune LLMs [36]. For finetuning, we choose the Flan-T5 LMM for two reasons: 1) it is open-source: we intend to foster future research directions for models unhidden behind paywalls to aid in democratizing LLM research, and 2) it showed consistently good performance across all tasks. The finetuning instructions were instantiated from a small selection of eight samples of each knowledge source' reserved training set and fed in a finetuning workflow shown in Fig. 2. The finetuned Flan models' results (see last two columns in Table 3) are significantly boosted across almost all tasks. For task A, we observed an average improvement of 25% from zero-shot to the finetuned model for both Flan-T5 variants. Notably, SNOMEDCT_US showed least improvement of 9%, while the WordNet showed the most improvement of 45%. For task B we marked an average improvement of 18%, and for task C 3%. Given an illustration of the results in Fig. 3 shows that on average finetuned models, even with fewer parameters outperforms models with 1000x or more parameters across the three OL tasks. These insights appear crucial to expedite developmental research progress for practical tools for OL using LLMs which we plan to leverage in our future work.

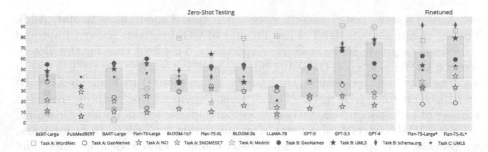

Fig. 3. Comparative visual of the zero-shot and finetuned results. Unfilled shapes, filled shapes, and small filled stars represent performances in tasks A, B, and C, respectively.

5   Error Analysis and Limitations

For error analysis, our evaluation results are summarized in Fig. 3 depicting comparable model ranks.

LLaMA-7B Overall Low Performance. For Task A, the model produced code or prompts instead of correct responses. It performed relatively better on GeoNames due to term types present in location names (e.g., "Huggins Church" includes the type "church"). For Tasks B and C, it exhibited a bias towards the false category. A limitation in our experiments is the absence of few-shot testing. We hypothesize that models like LLaMA can achieve better performance if shown task examples within the prompt.

Dataset Specific Error Analysis (WN18RR) – Task A. WordNet consists of ≈7k nouns, ≈2K verbs, and ≈0.4K rest of POS tags (adjective and adverbs). Note LLMs tested for Task A are tested for a generation task, which means they can generate text for types that do not map one-to-one to the gold standard. E.g., the best model i.e. GPT-3.5 for 9k test samples generated 43 distinct texts as types with the most frequent being: noun, verb, noun phrase, and adjective. This points out a second limitation of our work, i.e. the possibility for heuristics-based generated answer set mapping to the gold standard.

BERT, showing among the lowest performance on the task (63% lower than the best), generated 177 different answer texts with "verb" being the most frequent (7k times), followed by: noun, joke, and pun. Thus the BERT-based models, including BART, seem to not grasp the syntactic typing task directly from a zero-shot prompt, thus pointing toward the earlier identified limitation of our work for few-shot tests as the alternative method for better results.

Dataset Specific Error Analysis (NCI) – Task A. Overall, the LLMs are least effective on Task A for the NCI biomedical knowledge source. The best-performing open-source BLOOM-3B LLM generated 4k distinct answer texts for a test set of 24k instances, with the most frequently generated texts being: "protein that is involved in," "drug that is used to," "rare disease," and "common problem." On the other hand, the best-performing closed-sourced GPT-4 model generated 17k different answer texts from the identical test set, with the most frequently generated texts being: "term that does not exist," "term that does not exist or is not recognized in," and "term that does not exist or is not commonly used." Both models show varying proficiency and limitations in the NCI biomedical ontology. The NCI Thesaurus covers cancer-related topics, including diseases, agents, and substances. The low LLM performance could be attributed to high domain specialization. Even domain-specific LLMs like PubMedBERT did not yield promising results, suggesting a need for task-specific training or finetuning. While our finetuning experiments obtained boosted scores offering credence to our hypothesis, a limitation is the low number of training samples used which can be addressed by using a large training set.

6   Conclusions and Future Directions

Various initiatives benchmark LLM performance, revealing new task abilities [59,64]. These benchmarks advance computer science's understanding of LLMs. We explore LLMs' potential for Ontology Learning (OL) [18,39] through our introduced conceptual framework, LLMs4OL. Extensive experiments on 11 LLMs across three OL tasks demonstrate the paradigm's proof of concept. Our codebase facilitates replication and extension of methods for testing new LLMs. Our empirical results are promising to pave future work for OL.

Future research directions in the field of OL with LLMs can focus on several key areas. First, there is a need to enhance LLMs specifically for OL tasks, exploring novel architectures and fine-tuning to capture ontological structures better. Second, expanding the evaluation to cover other diverse knowledge domains would provide a broader understanding of LLMs' generalizability. Third, hybrid approaches that combine LLMs with traditional OL techniques, such as lexico-syntactic pattern mining and clustering, could lead to more accurate and comprehensive ontologies. Fourth, further research can delve into the extraction of specific semantic relations, like part-whole relationships or causality, to enhance the expressiveness of learned ontologies. Standardizing evaluation metrics, creating benchmark datasets, exploring dynamic ontology evolution, and domain-specific learning are important directions. Additionally, integrating human-in-the-loop approaches with expert involvement would enhance ontology relevance and accuracy. Exploring these research directions will advance LLM-based OL, enhancing knowledge acquisition and representation across domains.

Supplemental Material Statement: Our LLM templates, detailed results, and codebase are publicly released as supplemental material on Github https:// github.com/HamedBabaei/LLMs4OL.

Acknowledgements. We thank the anonymous reviewers for their detailed and insightful comments on an earlier draft of the paper. This work was jointly supported by the German BMBF project SCINEXT (ID 01lS22070), DFG NFDI4DataScience (ID 460234259), and ERC ScienceGraph (ID 819536).

Author contributions. Hamed Babaei Giglou: Conceptualization, Methodology, Software, Validation, Investigation, Resources, Data Curation, Writing - Original Draft, Visualization. Jennifer D'Souza: Conceptualization, Methodology, Investigation, Resources, Writing - Original Draft, Writing - Review & Editing, Supervision, Project administration, Funding acquisition. Sören Auer: Conceptualization, Methodology, Investigation, Resources, Review & Editing, Supervision, Project administration, Funding acquisition.

References

1. Geonames geographical database (2023). http://www.geonames.org/
2. Agirre, E., Ansa, O., Hovy, E., Martínez, D.: Enriching very large ontologies using the www. In: Proceedings of the First International Conference on Ontology Learning, vol. 31. pp. 25–30 (2000)
3. Akkalyoncu Yilmaz, Z., Wang, S., Yang, W., Zhang, H., Lin, J.: Applying BERT to document retrieval with birch. In: Proceedings of the 2019 Conference on Empirical Methods in Natural Language Processing and the 9th International Joint Conference on Natural Language Processing (EMNLP-IJCNLP): System Demonstrations, pp. 19–24. Association for Computational Linguistics, Hong Kong, China (Nov 2019). https://doi.org/10.18653/v1/D19-3004, https://aclanthology.org/D19-3004
4. Alfonseca, E., Manandhar, S.: An unsupervised method for general named entity recognition and automated concept discovery. In: Proceedings of the 1st International Conference on General WordNet, Mysore, India, pp. 34–43 (2002)
5. Amatriain, X.: Transformer models: an introduction and catalog. arXiv preprint arXiv:2302.07730 (2023)
6. Asim, M.N., Wasim, M., Khan, M.U.G., Mahmood, W., Abbasi, H.M.: A survey of ontology learning techniques and applications. Database 2018, bay101 (2018)
7. Auer, S., Bizer, C., Kobilarov, G., Lehmann, J., Cyganiak, R., Ives, Z.: DBpedia: a nucleus for a web of open data. In: Aberer, K., et al. (eds.) ASWC/ISWC -2007. LNCS, vol. 4825, pp. 722–735. Springer, Heidelberg (2007). https://doi.org/10.1007/978-3-540-76298-0_52
8. Bodenreider, O.: The unified medical language system (UMLS): integrating biomedical terminology. Nucleic Acids Res. **32**(suppl_1), D267–D270 2004). https://doi.org/10.1093/nar/gkh061
9. Bodenreider, O.: The unified medical language system (umls): integrating biomedical terminology. Nucleic Acids Res. **32**(suppl_1), D267–D270 (2004)
10. Brown, T.B., et al.: Language models are few-shot learners (2020)
11. Chung, H.W., et al.: Scaling instruction-finetuned language models (2022)
12. Cui, L., Wu, Y., Liu, J., Yang, S., Zhang, Y.: Template-based named entity recognition using bart. arXiv preprint arXiv:2106.01760 (2021)
13. Dai, Z., Yang, Z., Yang, Y., Carbonell, J., Le, Q.V., Salakhutdinov, R.: Transformer-xl: attentive language models beyond a fixed-length context (2019)
14. Dalvi, F., Khan, A.R., Alam, F., Durrani, N., Xu, J., Sajjad, H.: Discovering latent concepts learned in BERT. In: International Conference on Learning Representations (2022). https://openreview.net/forum?id=POTMtpYI1xH
15. Dettmers, T., Pasquale, M., Pontus, S., Riedel, S.: Convolutional 2d knowledge graph embeddings. In: Proceedings of the 32th AAAI Conference on Artificial Intelligence, pp. 1811–1818 (February 2018), https://arxiv.org/abs/1707.01476
16. Devlin, J., Chang, M.W., Lee, K., Toutanova, K.: Bert: Pre-training of deep bidirectional transformers for language understanding (2019)

17. Dopazo, J., Carazo, J.M.: Phylogenetic reconstruction using an unsupervised growing neural network that adopts the topology of a phylogenetic tree. J. Mol. Evol. **44**(2), 226–233 (1997)
18. Gruber, T.R.: Toward principles for the design of ontologies used for knowledge sharing? Int. J. Hum Comput Stud. **43**(5–6), 907–928 (1995)
19. Gu, Y., et al.: Domain-specific language model pretraining for biomedical natural language processing. ACM Trans. Comput. Healthcare (Health) **3**(1), 1–23 (2021)
20. Guha, R.V., Brickley, D., Macbeth, S.: Schema. org: evolution of structured data on the web. Commun. ACM **59**(2), 44–51 (2016)
21. Hahn, U., Markó, K.G.: Joint knowledge capture for grammars and ontologies. In: Proceedings of the 1st International Conference on Knowledge Capture, pp. 68–75 (2001)
22. Hamp, B., Feldweg, H.: Germanet-a lexical-semantic net for german. In: Automatic Information Extraction and Building Of Lexical Semantic Resources for NLP Applications (1997)
23. Hearst, M.A.: Automated discovery of wordnet relations. WordNet: an electronic lexical database, vol. 2 (1998)
24. Hwang, C.H.: Incompletely and imprecisely speaking: using dynamic ontologies for representing and retrieving information. In: KRDB, vol. 21, pp. 14–20. Citeseer (1999)
25. Jiang, Z., Xu, F.F., Araki, J., Neubig, G.: How can we know what language models know? Trans. Asso. Comput. Ling. **8**, 423–438 (2020). https://doi.org/10.1162/tacl_a_00324, https://aclanthology.org/2020.tacl-1.28
26. Khan, L., Luo, F.: Ontology construction for information selection. In: 14th IEEE International Conference on Tools with Artificial Intelligence, 2002. (ICTAI 2002). Proceedings, pp. 122–127. IEEE (2002)
27. Khot, T., et al.: Decomposed prompting: A modular approach for solving complex tasks (2023)
28. Kietz, J.U., Maedche, A., Volz, R.: A method for semi-automatic ontology acquisition from a corporate intranet. In: EKAW-2000 Workshop "Ontologies and Text", Juan-Les-Pins, France (October 2000)
29. Kojima, T., Gu, S.S., Reid, M., Matsuo, Y., Iwasawa, Y.: Large language models are zero-shot reasoners (2023)
30. Konys, A.: Knowledge repository of ontology learning tools from text. Proc. Comput. Sci. **159**, 1614–1628 (2019)
31. Lester, B., Al-Rfou, R., Constant, N.: The power of scale for parameter-efficient prompt tuning. arXiv preprint arXiv:2104.08691 (2021)
32. Levy, O., Seo, M., Choi, E., Zettlemoyer, L.: Zero-shot relation extraction via reading comprehension. In: Proceedings of the 21st Conference on Computational Natural Language Learning (CoNLL 2017), pp. 333–342. Association for Computational Linguistics, Vancouver, Canada (Aug 2017). https://doi.org/10.18653/v1/K17-1034, https://aclanthology.org/K17-1034
33. Lewis, M., et al.: Bart: denoising sequence-to-sequence pre-training for natural language generation, translation, and comprehension (2019)
34. Li, X.L., Liang, P.: Prefix-tuning: optimizing continuous prompts for generation. arXiv preprint arXiv:2101.00190 (2021)
35. Liu, P., Yuan, W., Fu, J., Jiang, Z., Hayashi, H., Neubig, G.: Pre-train, prompt, and predict: a systematic survey of prompting methods in natural language processing. ACM Comput. Surv. **55**(9) (2023). https://doi.org/10.1145/3560815
36. Longpre, S., et al.: The flan collection: designing data and methods for effective instruction tuning. arXiv preprint arXiv:2301.13688 (2023)

37. Lonsdale, D., Ding, Y., Embley, D.W., Melby, A.: Peppering knowledge sources with salt: Boosting conceptual content for ontology generation. In: Proceedings of the AAAI Workshop on Semantic Web Meets Language Resources, Edmonton, Alberta, Canada (2002)

38. Lourdusamy, R., Abraham, S.: A survey on methods of ontology learning from text. In: Jain, L.C., Peng, S.-L., Alhadidi, B., Pal, S. (eds.) ICICCT 2019. LAIS, vol. 9, pp. 113–123. Springer, Cham (2020). https://doi.org/10.1007/978-3-030-38501-9_11

39. Maedche, A., Staab, S.: Ontology learning for the semantic web. IEEE Intell. Syst. **16**(2), 72–79 (2001)

40. Medicomp Systems: MEDCIN (January 2023). https://medicomp.com

41. Miller, G.A.: Wordnet: a lexical database for English. Commun. ACM **38**(11), 39–41 (1995)

42. Missikoff, M., Navigli, R., Velardi, P.: The usable ontology: an environment for building and assessing a domain ontology. In: Horrocks, I., Hendler, J. (eds.) ISWC 2002. LNCS, vol. 2342, pp. 39–53. Springer, Heidelberg (2002). https://doi.org/10.1007/3-540-48005-6_6

43. Moldovan, D.I., GiRJU, R.C.: An interactive tool for the rapid development of knowledge bases. Inter. J. Artifi. Intell. Tools **10**(01n02), 65–86 (2001)

44. National Cancer Institute, National Institutes of Health: NCI Thesaurus (September 2022). http://ncit.nci.nih.gov

45. Noy, N.F., McGuinness, D.L., et al.: Ontology development 101: A guide to creating your first ontology (2001)

46. OpenAI: Chatgpt (2023). https://openai.com/chat-gpt/ (Accessed 5 May 2023)

47. OpenAI: Gpt-4 technical report (2023)

48. Patel-Schneider, P.F.: Analyzing Schema.org. In: Mika, P., et al. (eds.) ISWC 2014. LNCS, vol. 8796, pp. 261–276. Springer, Cham (2014). https://doi.org/10.1007/978-3-319-11964-9_17

49. Peters, M.E., et al.: Deep contextualized word representations. In: Proceedings of the 2018 Conference of the North American Chapter of the Association for Computational Linguistics: Human Language Technologies, Volume 1 (Long Papers), pp. 2227–2237. Association for Computational Linguistics, New Orleans, Louisiana (Jun 2018). https://doi.org/10.18653/v1/N18-1202, https://aclanthology.org/N18-1202

50. Petroni, F., et al.: How context affects language models' factual predictions. In: Automated Knowledge Base Construction (2020). https://openreview.net/forum?id=025X0zPfn

51. Petroni, F., et al.: Language models as knowledge bases? arXiv preprint arXiv:1909.01066 (2019)

52. Petroni, F., et al.: Language models as knowledge bases? In: Proceedings of the 2019 Conference on Empirical Methods in Natural Language Processing and the 9th International Joint Conference on Natural Language Processing (EMNLP-IJCNLP). Association for Computational Linguistics (2019)

53. Rebele, T., Suchanek, F., Hoffart, J., Biega, J., Kuzey, E., Weikum, G.: YAGO: a multilingual knowledge base from wikipedia, wordnet, and geonames. In: Groth, P., et al. (eds.) ISWC 2016. LNCS, vol. 9982, pp. 177–185. Springer, Cham (2016). https://doi.org/10.1007/978-3-319-46547-0_19

54. Roux, C., Proux, D., Rechenmann, F., Julliard, L.: An ontology enrichment method for a pragmatic information extraction system gathering data on genetic interactions. In: ECAI Workshop on Ontology Learning (2000)

55. Sajjad, H., Durrani, N., Dalvi, F., Alam, F., Khan, A.R., Xu, J.: Analyzing encoded concepts in transformer language models (2022)
56. Scao, T.L., et al.: Bloom: A 176b-parameter open-access multilingual language model. arXiv preprint arXiv:2211.05100 (2022)
57. SNOMED International: US Edition of SNOMED CT (March 2023). https://www.nlm.nih.gov/healthit/snomedct/us_edition.html
58. Speer, R., Chin, J., Havasi, C.: Conceptnet 5.5: an open multilingual graph of general knowledge. In: Proceedings of the AAAI conference on Artificial Intelligence. vol. 31 (2017)
59. Srivastava, A., et al.: Beyond the imitation game: quantifying and extrapolating the capabilities of language models. arXiv preprint arXiv:2206.04615 (2022)
60. Touvron, H., et al.: Llama: open and efficient foundation language models. arXiv preprint arXiv:2302.13971 (2023)
61. Wagner, A.: Enriching a lexical semantic net with selectional preferences by means of statistical corpus analysis. In: ECAI Workshop on Ontology Learning, vol. 61. Citeseer (2000)
62. Wątróbski, J.: Ontology learning methods from text-an extensive knowledge-based approach. Proc. Comput. Sci. **176**, 3356–3368 (2020)
63. Wei, J., et al.: Finetuned language models are zero-shot learners. In: International Conference on Learning Representations (2022). https://openreview.net/forum?id=gEZrGCozdqR
64. Wei, J., et al.: Emergent abilities of large language models. arXiv preprint arXiv:2206.07682 (2022)
65. Wei, J., et al.: Chain-of-thought prompting elicits reasoning in large language models. In: Koyejo, S., Mohamed, S., Agarwal, A., Belgrave, D., Cho, K., Oh, A. (eds.) Advances in Neural Information Processing Systems, vol. 35, pp. 24824–24837. Curran Associates, Inc. (2022). https://proceedings.neurips.cc/paper_files/paper/2022/file/9d5609613524ecf4f15af0f7b31abca4-Paper-Conference.pdf
66. Weibel, S.L., Koch, T.: The dublin core metadata initiative. D-lib magazine **6**(12), 1082–9873 (2000)
67. Xu, F., Kurz, D., Piskorski, J., Schmeier, S.: A domain adaptive approach to automatic acquisition of domain relevant terms and their relations with bootstrapping. In: LREC (2002)
68. Yang, W., Zhang, H., Lin, J.: Simple applications of bert for ad hoc document retrieval (2019)
69. Yao, S., Yu, D., Zhao, J., Shafran, I., Griffiths, T.L., Cao, Y., Narasimhan, K.: Tree of thoughts: deliberate problem solving with large language models (2023)

Biomedical Knowledge Graph Embeddings with Negative Statements

Rita T. Sousa[1](✉)⬤, Sara Silva[1]⬤, Heiko Paulheim[2]⬤, and Catia Pesquita[1]⬤

[1] LASIGE, Faculdade de Ciências da Universidade de Lisboa, Lisbon, Portugal
{risousa,sgsilva,clpesquita}@ciencias.ulisboa.pt
[2] Data and Web Science Group, Universität Mannheim, Mannheim, Germany
heiko.paulheim@uni-mannheim.de

Abstract. A knowledge graph is a powerful representation of real-world entities and their relations. The vast majority of these relations are defined as positive statements, but the importance of negative statements is increasingly recognized, especially under an Open World Assumption. Explicitly considering negative statements has been shown to improve performance on tasks such as entity summarization and question answering or domain-specific tasks such as protein function prediction. However, no attention has been given to the exploration of negative statements by knowledge graph embedding approaches despite the potential of negative statements to produce more accurate representations of entities in a knowledge graph.

We propose a novel approach, TrueWalks, to incorporate negative statements into the knowledge graph representation learning process. In particular, we present a novel walk-generation method that is able to not only differentiate between positive and negative statements but also take into account the semantic implications of negation in ontology-rich knowledge graphs. This is of particular importance for applications in the biomedical domain, where the inadequacy of embedding approaches regarding negative statements at the ontology level has been identified as a crucial limitation.

We evaluate TrueWalks in ontology-rich biomedical knowledge graphs in two different predictive tasks based on KG embeddings: protein-protein interaction prediction and gene-disease association prediction. We conduct an extensive analysis over established benchmarks and demonstrate that our method is able to improve the performance of knowledge graph embeddings on all tasks.

Keywords: Knowledge Graph · Knowledge Graph Embedding · Negative Statements · Biomedical Applications

1 Introduction

Knowledge Graphs (KGs) represent facts about real-world entities and their relations and have been extensively used to support a range of applications from question-answering and recommendation systems to machine learning and analytics [17]. KGs have taken to the forefront of biomedical data through their ability to describe and interlink information about biomedical entities such as genes, proteins, diseases and

T. R. Payne et al. (Eds.): ISWC 2023, LNCS 14265, pp. 428–446, 2023.
https://doi.org/10.1007/978-3-031-47240-4_23

patients, structured according to biomedical ontologies. This supports the analysis and interpretation of biological data, for instance, through the use of semantic similarity measures [32]. More recently, a spate of KG embedding methods [42] have emerged in this space and have been successfully employed in a number of biomedical applications [28]. The impact of KG embeddings in biomedical analytics is expected to increase in tandem with the growing volume and complexity of biomedical data. However, this success relies on the expectation that KG embeddings are semantically meaningful representations of the underlying biomedical entities.

Regardless of their domain, the vast majority of KG facts are represented as positive statements, e.g. (hemoglobin, hasFunction, oxygen transport). Under a Closed World Assumption, negative statements are not required, since any missing fact can be assumed as a negative. However, real-world KGs reside under the Open World Assumption where non-stated negative facts are formally indistinguishable from missing or unknown facts, which can have important implications across a variety of tasks.

The importance of negative statements is increasingly recognized [2, 10]. For example, in the biomedical domain, the knowledge that a patient does not exhibit a given symptom or a protein does not perform a specific function is crucial for both clinical decision-making and biomedical insight. While ontologies are able to express negation and the enrichment of KGs with interesting negative statements is gaining traction, existing KG embedding methods are not able to adequately utilize them [21], which ultimately results in less accurate representations of entities.

We propose True Walks, to the best of our knowledge, the first-ever approach that is able to incorporate negative statements into the KG embedding learning process. This is fundamentally different from other KG embedding methods, which produce negative statements by negative random sampling strategies to train representations that bring the representations of nodes that are linked closer, while distancing them from the negative examples. TrueWalks uses explicit negative statements to produce entity representations that take into account both existing attributes and lacking attributes. For example, for the negative statement (Bruce Willis, NOT birthPlace, U.S.), our representation would be able to capture the similarity between Bruce Willis and Ryan Gosling, since neither was born in the U.S (see Fig. 1). The explicit declaration of negative statements such as these is an important aspect of more accurate representations, especially when they capture unexpected negative statements (i.e., most people would expect that both actors are U.S. born). Using TrueWalks, Bruce Willis and Ryan Gosling would be similar not just because they are both actors but also because neither was born in the U.S.

True Walks generates walks that can distinguish between positive and negative statements and consider the semantic implications of negation in KGs that are rich in ontological information, particularly in regard to inheritance. This is of particular importance for applications in the biomedical domain, where the inadequacy of embedding approaches regarding negative statements has been identified as a crucial limitation [21]. We demonstrate that the resulting embeddings can be employed to determine semantic similarity or as features for relation prediction. We evaluate the effectiveness of our approach in two different tasks, protein-protein interaction prediction and gene-disease association prediction, and show that our method improves performance over state-of-the-art embedding methods and popular semantic similarity measures.

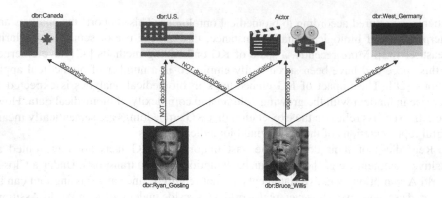

Fig. 1. A DBPedia example motivating the negative statements problem. The author of Bruce Willis' picture is Gage Skidmore.

Our contributions are as follows:

- We propose TrueWalks, a novel method to generate random walks on KGs that are aware of negative statements and results in the first KG embedding approach that considers negative statements.
- We develop extensions of popular path-based KG embedding methods implementing the TrueWalks approach.
- We enrich existing KGs with negative statements and propose benchmark datasets for two popular biomedical KG applications: protein-protein interaction (PPI) prediction and gene-disease association (GDA) prediction.
- We report experimental results that demonstrate the superior performance of True-Walks when compared to state-of-the-art KG embedding methods.

2   Related Work

2.1   Exploring Negative Statements

Approaches to enrich existing KGs with interesting negative statements have been proposed both for general-purpose KGs such as Wikidata [3] and for domain-specific ones such as the Gene Ontology (GO) [11,44]. Exploring negative statements has been demonstrated to improve the performance of various applications. [2] developed a method to enrich Wikidata with interesting negative statements and its usage improved the performance on entity summarization and decision-making tasks. [44] have designed a method to enrich the GO [14] with relevant negative statements indicating that a protein does not perform a given function and demonstrated that a balance between positive and negative annotations supports a more reasonable evaluation of protein function prediction methods. Similarly, [11] enriched the GO with negative statements and demonstrated an associated increase in protein function prediction performance. The relevance of negative annotations has also been recognized in the prediction of gene-phenotype associations in the context of the Human-Phenotype Ontology

(HP) [22], but the topic remains unexplored [25]. It should be highlighted that KG embedding methods have not been employed in any of these approaches to explore negative statements.

2.2 Knowledge Graph Embeddings

KG embedding methods map entities and their relations expressed in a KG into a lower-dimensional space while preserving the underlying structure of the KG and other semantic information [42]. These entity and relation embedding vectors can then be applied to various KG applications such as link prediction, entity typing, or triple classification. In the biomedical domain, KG embeddings have been used in machine learning-based applications in which they are used as input in classification tasks or to predict relations between biomedical entities. [21] provides an overview of KG embedding-based approaches for biomedical applications.

Translational models, which rely on distance-based scoring functions, are some of the most widely employed KG embedding methods. A popular method, TransE [6], assumes that if a relation holds between two entities, the vector of the head entity plus the relation vector should be close to the vector of the tail entity in the vector space. TransE has the disadvantage of not handling one-to-many and many-to-many relationships well. To address this issue, TransH [43] introduces a relation-specific hyperplane for each relation and projects the head and tail entities into the hyperplane. TransR [23] builds entity and relation embeddings in separate entity space and relation spaces.

Semantic matching approaches are also well-known and use similarity-based scoring functions to capture the latent semantics of entities and relations in their vector space representations. For instance, DistMult [48] employs tensor factorization to embed entities as vectors and relations as diagonal matrices.

2.3 Walk-Based Embeddings

More recently, random walk-based KG embedding approaches have emerged. These approaches are built upon two main steps: (i) producing entity sequences from walks in the graph to produce a corpus of sequences that is akin to a corpus of word sequences or sentences; (2) using those sequences as input to a neural language model [27] that learns a latent low-dimensional representation of each entity within the corpus of sequences.

DeepWalk [31] first samples a set of paths from the input graph using uniform random walks. Then it uses those paths to train a skip-gram model, originally proposed by the word2vec approach for word embeddings [27]. Node2vec [16] introduces a different biased strategy for generating random walks and exploring diverse neighborhoods. The biased random walk strategy is controlled by two parameters: the likelihood of visiting immediate neighbors (breadth-first search behavior), and the likelihood of visiting entities that are at increasing distances (depth-first search behavior). Neither DeepWalk nor node2vec take into account the direction or type of the edges. Metapath2vec [8] proposes random walks driven by metapaths that define the node type order by which the random walker explores the graph. RDF2Vec [35] is inspired by the node2vec strategy but it considers both edge direction and type making it particularly suited to KGs.

OWL2Vec* [7] was designed to learn ontology embeddings and it also employs direct walks on the graph to learn graph structure.

2.4   Tailoring Knowledge Graph Embeddings

Recent KG embedding approaches aim to tailor representations by considering different semantic, structural or lexical aspects of a KG and its underlying ontology. Approaches such as EL [20] and BoxEL [45] embeddings are geometric approaches that account for the logical structure of the ontology (e.g., intersection, conjunction, existential quantifiers). OWL2Vec* [7] and OPA2Vec [37] take into consideration the lexical portion of the KG (i.e., labels of entities) when generating graph walks or triples. OPA2Vec also offers the option of using a pre-trained language model to bootstrap the KG embedding. Closer to our approach, OLW2Vec* contemplates the declaration of inverse axioms to enable reverse path traversal, however, this option was found lacking for the biomedical ontology GO. Finally, different approaches have been proposed to train embeddings that are aware of the order of entities in a path, such as [51] and [34], which extend TransE and RDF2Vec, respectively.

3   Methods

3.1   Problem Formulation

In this work, we address the task of learning a relation between two KG entities (which can belong to the same or different KGs) when the relation itself is not encoded in the KG. We employ two distinct approaches: (1) using the KG embeddings of each entity as features for a machine learning algorithm and (2) comparing the KG embeddings directly through a similarity metric.

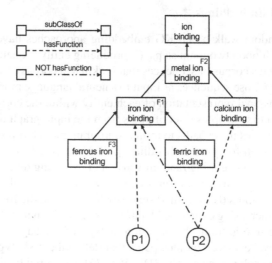

Fig. 2. A GO KG subgraph motivating the *reverse inheritance* problem.

We target ontology-rich KGs that use an ontology to provide rich descriptions of real-world entities instead of focusing on describing relations between entities themselves. These KGs are common in the biomedical domain. As a result, the KG's richness lies in the TBox, with a comparatively less complex ABox, since entities have no links between them. We focus on Web Ontology Language (OWL) [15] ontologies since biomedical ontologies are typically developed in OWL or have an OWL version.

Biomedical entities in a KG are typically described through positive statements that link them to an ontology. For instance, to state that a protein P performs a function F described under the GO, a KG can declare the axiom $P \sqsubseteq \exists hasFunction.F$. However, the knowledge that a given protein does not perform a function can also be relevant, especially to declare that a given protein does not have an activity typical of its homologs [12]. Likewise, the knowledge that a given disease does not exhibit a particular phenotype is also decisive in understanding the relations between diseases and genes [25]. We consider the definition of grounded negative statements proposed by [2] as $\neg(s, p, o)$ which is satisfied if $(s, p, o) \notin KG$ and expressed as a *NegativeObjectPropertyAssertion*[1]. Similar to what was done in [2], we do not have a negative object property assertion for every missing triple. Negative statements are only included if there is clear evidence that a triple does not exist in the domain being captured. Taking the protein example, negative object property assertions only exist when it has been demonstrated that a protein does not perform a particular function.

An essential difference between a positive and a negative statement of this kind is related to the implied inheritance of properties exhibited by the superclasses or subclasses of the assigned class. Let us consider that $(P_1, \text{hasFunction}, F_1)$ and $(F_1, \text{subClassOf}, F_2)$. This implies that $(P_1, \text{hasFunction}, F_2)$, since an individual with a class assignment also belongs to all superclasses of the given class, e.g., a protein that performs iron ion binding also performs *metal ion binding* (see Fig. 2). This implication is easily captured by directed walk generation methods that explore the declared subclass axioms in an OWL ontology. However, when we have a negative statement, such as $\neg(P_2, \text{hasFunction}, F_1)$, it does not imply that $\neg(P_2, \text{hasFunction}, F_2)$. There are no guarantees that a protein that does not perform *iron ion binding* also does not perform *metal ion binding*, since it can very well, for instance, perform *calcium ion binding*. However, for $(F_3, \text{subClassOf}, F_1)$ the negative statement $\neg(P_2, \text{hasFunction}, F_1)$ implies that $\neg(P_2, \text{hasFunction}, F_3)$, as a protein that does not perform *iron ion binding* also does not perform *ferric iron binding* nor *ferrous iron binding*. Therefore, we need to be able to declare that protein P_1 performs both functions F_1 and F_3, but that P_2 performs F_1 but not F_3. Since OWL ontologies typically declare subclass axioms, there is no opportunity for typical KG embedding methods to explore the reverse paths that would more accurately represent a negative statement.

The problem we tackle is then two-fold: how can the *reverse inheritance* implied by negative statements be adequately explored by walk-based KG embedding methods, and how can these methods distinguish between negative and positive statements.

---

[1] https://www.w3.org/TR/owl2-syntax/#Negative_Object_Property_Assertions.

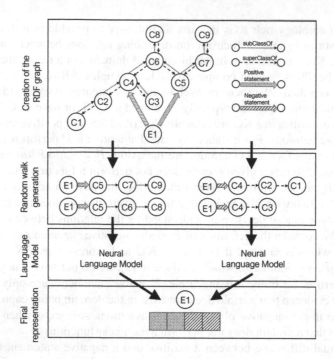

Fig. 3. Overview of the TrueWalks method with the four main steps: (i) creation of the RDF graph, (ii) random walk generation with negative statements; (iii) neural language models, and (iv) final representation.

3.2   Overview

An overview of TrueWalks, the method we propose, is shown in Fig. 3. The first step is the transformation of the KG into an RDF Graph. Next, our novel random walk generation strategy that is aware of positive and negative statements is applied to the graph to produce a set of entity sequences. The positive and negative entity walks are fed to neural language models to learn a dual latent representation of the entities. TrueWalks has two variants: one that employs the classical skip-gram model to learn the embeddings (TrueWalks), and one that employs a variation of skip-gram that is aware of the order of entities in the walk (TrueWalksOA, i.e. order-aware).

3.3   Creation of the RDF Graph

The first step is the conversion of an ontology-rich KG into an RDF graph. This is a directed, labeled graph, where the edges represent the named relations between two resources or entities, represented by the graph nodes[2]. We perform the transformation according to the *OWL to RDF Graph Mapping* guidelines defined by the W3C[3]. Simple axioms can be directly transformed into RDF triples, such as subsumption axioms

---

[2] https://www.w3.org/RDF/.
[3] https://www.w3.org/TR/owl2-mapping-to-rdf/.

for atomic entities or data and annotation properties associated with an entity. Axioms involving complex class expressions are transformed into multiple triples which typically require blank nodes.

Let us consider the following existential restriction of the class *obo:GO_0034708 (methyltransferase complex)* that encodes the fact that a methyltransferase complex is part of at least one intracellular anatomical structure:

ObjectSomeValuesFrom(obo:BFO_0000050 (part of),
obo:GO_0005622 (intracellular anatomical structure))

Its conversion to RDF results in three triples:

(obo:GO_0034708, rdfs:subClassOf, _:x)
(_:x, owl:someValuesFrom,obo:GO_0005622)
(_:x, owl:onProperty,obo:BFO_0000050)

where _:x denotes a blank node.

3.4 Random Walk Generation with Negative Statements

The next step is to generate the graph walks that will make up the corpus (see Algorithm 1). For a given graph $G = (V, E)$ where E is the set of edges and V is the set of vertices, for each vertex $v_r \in V_r$, where V_r is the subset of individuals for which we want to learn representations, we generate up to w graph walks of maximum depth d rooted in vertex v_r. We employ a depth-first search algorithm, extending on the basic approach in [35]. At the first iteration, we can find either a positive or negative statement. From then on, walks are biased: a positive statement implies that whenever a subclass edge is found it is traversed from subclass to superclass, whereas a negative statement results in a traversal of subclass edges in the opposite direction (see also Fig. 3). This generates paths that follow the pattern $v_r \rightarrow e_{1i} \rightarrow v_{1i} \rightarrow e_{2i}$. The set of walks is split in two, negative statement walks and positive statement walks. This will allow the learning of separate latent representations, one that captures the positive aspect and one that captures the negative aspect.

An important aspect of our approach is that, since OWL is converted into an RDF graph for walk-based KG embedding methods, a negative statement declared using a simple object property assertion (e.g. *notHasFunction*) could result in the less accurate path: *Protein P → notHasFunction → iron ion binding → subClassOf → ion binding*. Moreover, random walks directly over the *NegativeObjectPropertyAssertion*, since it is decomposed into multiple triples using blank nodes, would also result in inaccurate paths. However, our algorithm produces more accurate paths, e.g.: *Protein P → notHasFunction → iron ion binding → superClassOf → ferric iron binding* by adequately processing the *NegativeObjectPropertyAssertion*.

3.5 Neural Language Models

We employ two alternative approaches to learn a latent representation of the individuals in the KG. For the first approach, we use the skip-gram model [27], which predicts the context (neighbor entities) based on a target word, or in our case a target entity.

Algorithm 1. Walk generation for one entity using TrueWalks. The function GET NON VISITED NEIGHBOURS(status) is used to generate the random walks using a depth-first search. It gets the neighbors of a given node that have not yet been visited in previous iterations. If the status is negative (which means that the first step in the walk was made with a negative statement), the neighbors will include all the non-visited neighbors except those connected through subclass statements, and if the status is positive, it will include all the neighbors except those connected through superclass statements.

1: $d \leftarrow max\_depth\_walks$
2: $w \leftarrow max\_number\_of\_walks$
3: $ent \leftarrow root\_entity$
4: **function** GET TRUEWALKS(ent)
5:     $pos\_walks \leftarrow$ GET RANDOM WALKS($ent, positive$)
6:     $neg\_walks \leftarrow$ GET RANDOM WALKS($ent, negative$)
7:     **return** pos_walks, neg_walks

8: **function** GET RANDOM WALKS($ent, status$)
9:     **while** $len(walks) < w$ **do**
10:        $walk \leftarrow ent$
11:        $depth \leftarrow 1$
12:        **while** $depth < d$ **do**
13:            $last \leftarrow len(walk) == d$
14:            $e, v \leftarrow$ GET NEIGHBOR($walk, status, last$)
15:            **if** $e, v == None$ **then**
16:                break
17:            $walk$.append(e, v)
18:            $depth + +$
19:        $walks$.append($walk$)
20:     **return** $walks$
21: **function** GET NEIGHBOR($walk, status, last$)
22:     $n \leftarrow$ GET NON VISITED NEIGHBORS($status$)
23:     **if** $len(n) == 0$ & $len(walk) > 2$ **then**
24:        $e, v \leftarrow walk[-2], walk[-1]$
25:        ADD VISITED NEIGHBORS($e, v, len(walk) - 2, status$)
26:        **return** $None$
27:     $e, v \leftarrow n[rand()]$
28:     **if** $last$ **then**
29:        ADD VISITED NEIGHBORS($e, v, len(walk), status$)
30:     **return** e, v

Let $f : E \rightarrow \mathbb{R}^d$ be the mapping function from entities to the latent representations we will be learning, where d is the number of dimensions of the representation (f is then a matrix $|E| \times d$). Given a context window c, and a sequence of entities $e_1, e_2, e_3, ..., e_L$, the objective of the skip-gram model is to maximize the average log probability p:

$$\frac{1}{L} \sum_{l=1}^{L} \log p(e_{l+c}|e_l) \tag{1}$$

where $p(e_{l+c}|e_l)$ is calculated using the softmax function:

$$p(e_{l+c}|e_l) = \frac{\exp(f(e_{l+c}) \cdot f(e_l))}{\sum_{e=1}^{E} \exp(f(e) \cdot f(e_l))} \tag{2}$$

where $f(e)$ is the vector of the entity e.

To improve computation time, we employ a negative sampling approach based in [27] that minimizes the number of comparisons required to distinguish the target entity, by taking samples from a noise distribution using logistic regression, where there are k negative samples for each entity.

The second approach is the structured skip-gram model [24], a variation of skip-gram that is sensitive to the order of words, or in our case, entities in the graph walks. The critical distinction of this approach is that, instead of using a single matrix f, it creates $c \times 2$ matrices, $f_{-c}, ..., f_{-2}, f_{-1}, f_1, ..., f_c$, each dedicated to predicting a specific relative position to the entity. To make a prediction $p(e_{l+c}|e_l)$, the method selects the appropriate matrix f_l.

The neural language models are applied separately to the positive and negative walks, producing two representations for each entity.

3.6 Final Representations

The two representations of each entity need to be combined to produce a final representation. Different vector operations can, in principle, be employed, such as the Hadamard product or the L1-norm. However, especially since we will employ these vectors as inputs for machine learning methods, we would like to create a feature space that allows the distinction between the negative and positive representations, motivating us to use a simple concatenation of vectors.

4 Experiments

We evaluate our novel approach on two biomedical tasks: protein-protein interaction (PPI) prediction and gene-disease association (GDA) prediction [39]. These two challenges have significant implications for understanding the underlying mechanisms of biological processes and disease states.

Both tasks are modeled as relation prediction tasks. For PPI prediction, we employ TrueWalks embeddings both as features for a supervised learning algorithm and directly for similarity-based prediction. For GDA prediction, since embeddings for genes and diseases are learned over two different KGs, we focus only on supervised learning. We employ a Random Forest algorithm across all classification experiments with the same parameters (see the supplementary file for details).

4.1 Data

Our method takes as input an ontology file, instance annotation file and a list of instance pairs. We construct the knowledge graph (KG) using the RDFlib package [5], which parses the ontology file in OWL format and processes the annotation file to add edges to the RDFlib graph. The annotation file contains both positive and negative statements which are used to create the edges in the graph.

Table 1. Statistics for each KG regarding classes, instances, nodes, edges, positive and negative statements.

	GO_{PPI}	GO_{GDA}	HP_{GDA}
Classes	50918	50918	17060
Literals and blank nodes	532373	532373	442246
Edges	1425102	1425102	1082859
Instances	440	755	162
Positive statements	7364	10631	4197
Negative statements	8579	8966	225

Protein-Protein Interaction Prediction. Predicting protein-protein interactions is a fundamental task in molecular biology that can explore both sequence and functional information [18]. Given the high cost of experimentally determining PPI, computational methods have been proposed as a solution to the problem of finding protein pairs that are likely to interact and thus provide a selection of good candidates for experimental analysis. In recent years, a number of approaches for PPI prediction based on functional information as described by the GO have been proposed [20,21,37,38,50]. The GO contains over 50000 classes that describe proteins or genes according to the molecular functions they perform, the biological processes they are involved in, and the cellular components where they act.

The GO KG is built by integrating three sources: the GO itself [14], the Gene Ontology Annotation (GOA) data [13], and negative GO annotations [44] (details on the KG building method and data sources are available in the supplementary file). A GO annotation associates a Uniprot protein identifier with a GO class that describes it. We downloaded the GO annotations corresponding to positive statements from the GOA database for human species. For each protein P in the PPI dataset and each of its association statements to a function F in GOA, we add the assertion $(P, hasFunction, F)$. We employ the negative GO associations produced in [44], which were derived from expert-curated annotations of protein families on phylogenetic trees. For each protein P in the PPI dataset and each of its association statements to a function F in the negative GO associations dataset, we add a negative object property assertion. To do so, we use metamodeling (more specifically, punning[4]) and represent each ontology class as both a class and an individual. This situation translates into using the same IRI. Then, we use a negative object property assertion to state that the individual representing a biomedical entity is not connected by the object property expression to the individual representing an ontology class. Table 1 presents the GO KG statistics.

The target relations to predict are extracted from the STRING database [40]. We considered the following criteria to select protein pairs: (i) protein interactions must be extracted from curated databases or experimentally determined (as opposed to computationally determined); (ii) interactions must have a confidence score above 0.950 to retain only high confidence interaction; (iii) each protein must have at least one pos-

---

[4] https://www.w3.org/TR/owl2-new-features/#F12:_Punning.

itive GO association and one negative GO association. The PPI dataset contains 440 proteins, 1024 interacting protein pairs, and another 1024 pairs generated by random negative sampling over the same set of proteins.

Gene-Disease Association Prediction. Predicting the relation between genes and diseases is essential to understand disease mechanisms and identify potential biomarkers or therapeutic targets [9]. However, validating these associations in the wet lab is expensive and time-consuming, which fostered the development of computational approaches to identify the most promising associations to be further validated. Many of these explore biomedical ontologies and KGs [4,26,36,41,49] and some recent approaches even apply KG embedding methods such as DeepWalk [1] or OPA2Vec [30,37].

For GDA prediction, we have used the GO KG, the Human Phenotype Ontology (HP) KG (created from the HP file and HP annotations files), and a GDA dataset. Two different ontologies are used to describe each type of entity. Diseases are described under the HP and genes under the GO. We built GO KG in the same fashion as in the PPI experiment, but instead of having proteins linked to GO classes, we have genes associated with GO classes. Regarding HP KG, HP [22] describes phenotypic abnormalities found in human hereditary diseases. The HP annotations link a disease to a specific class in the HP through both positive and negative statements.

The target relations to predict are extracted from DisGeNET [33], adapting the approach described in [30] to consider the following criterion: each gene (or disease) must have at least one positive GO (or HP) association and one negative GO (or HP) association. This resulted in 755 genes, 162 diseases, and 107 gene-disease relations. To create a balanced dataset, we sampled random negative examples over the same genes and diseases. Table 1 describes the created KGs.

4.2   Results and Discussion

We compare TrueWalks against ten state-of-the-art KG embedding methods: TransE, TransH, TransR, ComplEx, distMult, DeepWalk, node2vec, metapath2vec, OWL2Vec* and RDF2Vec. TransE, TransH and TransR are representative methods of translational models. ComplEx and distMult are semantic matching methods. They represent a bottom-line baseline with well-known KG embedding methods. DeepWalk and node2vec are undirected random walk-based methods, and OWL2Vec* and RDF2Vec are directed walk-based methods. These methods represent a closer approach to ours, providing a potentially stronger baseline. Each method is run with two different KGs, one with only positive statements and one with both positive and negative statements. In this second KG, we declare the negative statements as an object property, so positive and negative statements appear as two distinct relation types. The size of all the embeddings is 200 dimensions across all experiments (details on parameters can be found in the supplementary file), with TrueWalks generating two 100-dimensional vectors, one for the positive statement-based representation and one for the negative, which are concatenated to produce the final 200-dimensional representation.

Relation Prediction Using Machine Learning To predict the relation between a pair of entities e_1 and e_2 using machine learning, we take their vector representations and combine them using the binary Hadamard operator to represent the pair: $r(e_1, e_2) = v_{e_1} \times v_{e_2}$. The pair representations are then fed into a Random Forest algorithm for training using Monte Carlo cross-validation (MCCV) [46]. MCCV is a variation of traditional k-fold cross-validation in which the process of dividing the data into training and testing sets (with β being the proportion of the dataset to include in the test split) is repeated M times. Our experiments use MCCV with $M = 30$ and $\beta = 0.3$. For each run, the predictive performance is evaluated based on recall, precision and weighted average F-measure. Statistically significant differences between TrueWalks and the other methods are determined using the non-parametric Wilcoxon test at $p < 0.05$.

Table 2. Median precision, recall, and F-measure (weighted average F-measure) for PPI and GDA prediction. TrueWalks performance values are italicized/underlined when improvements are statistically significant with p-value < 0.05 for the Wilcoxon test against the positive (Pos)/positive and negative (Pos+Neg) variants of other methods. The best results are in bold.

	Method	PPI Prediction			GDA Prediction		
		Precision	Recall	F-measure	Precision	Recall	F-measure
Pos	TransE	0.553	0.546	0.554	0.533	0.538	0.531
	TransH	0.566	0.562	0.566	0.556	0.563	0.548
	TransR	0.620	0.607	0.616	0.594	0.600	0.592
	ComplEx	0.680	0.659	0.679	0.597	0.625	0.598
	distMult	0.765	0.737	0.754	0.585	0.600	0.575
	DeepWalk	0.813	0.836	0.822	0.618	0.646	0.629
	node2vec	0.826	0.741	0.794	0.643	0.616	0.644
	metapath2vec	0.562	0.563	0.561	0.554	0.531	0.549
	OWL2Vec*	0.833	0.806	0.823	0.652	0.656	0.646
	RDF2Vec	0.831	0.826	0.828	0.623	0.625	0.615
Pos+Neg	TransE	0.584	0.582	0.585	0.597	0.585	0.586
	TransH	0.573	0.572	0.570	0.563	0.554	0.554
	TransR	0.722	0.678	0.704	0.633	0.625	0.630
	ComplEx	0.750	0.720	0.740	0.549	0.545	0.545
	distMult	0.813	0.740	0.784	0.530	0.523	0.534
	DeepWalk	0.843	0.834	0.841	0.615	0.646	0.630
	node2vec	0.847	0.734	0.798	0.614	0.594	0.621
	metapath2vec	0.557	0.569	0.558	0.527	0.531	0.522
	OWL2Vec*	0.860	0.812	0.840	0.654	0.600	0.645
	RDF2Vec	0.847	**0.844**	0.845	0.625	**0.661**	0.630
	TrueWalks	*0.870*	0.817	*0.846*	*0.667*	0.625	*0.661*
	TrueWalksOA	*0.868*	0.836	*0.858*	*0.661*	0.616	*0.654*

Table 2 reports the median scores for both PPI and GDA prediction. The top half contains the results of the first experiment where we compare state-of-the-art methods using only the positive statements to TrueWalks (at the bottom) which uses both types. The results reveal that the performance of TrueWalks is significantly better than the other methods, improving both precision and F-measure. An improvement in precision, which is not always accompanied by an increase in recall, confirms the hypothesis that embeddings that consider negative statements produce more accurate representations of entities, which allows a better distinction of true positives from false positives.

A second experiment employs a KG with both negative and positive statements for all methods. Our method can accurately distinguish between positive statements and negative statements, as discussed in Subsect. 3.4. For the remaining embedding methods, we declare the negative statements as an object property so that these methods distinguish positive and negative statements as two distinct types of relation. This experiment allows us to test whether TrueWalks, which takes into account the positive or negative status of a statement, can improve the performance of methods that handle all statements equally regardless of status.

The bottom half of Table 2 shows that both variants of TrueWalks improve on precision and F-measure for both tasks when compared with the state-of-the-art methods using both positive and negative statements. This experiment further shows that the added information given by negative statements generally improves the performance of most KG embedding methods. However, no method surpasses TrueWalks, likely due to its ability to consider the semantic implications of inheritance and walk direction, especially when combined with the order-aware model.

Comparing the two variants of TrueWalks demonstrates that order awareness does not improve performance in most cases. However, TrueWalksOA improves on precision and F-measure for all other state-of-the-art methods. These results are not unexpected since the same effect was observed in other order-aware embedding methods [34].

Regarding the statistical tests, TrueWalks performance values are italicized/underlined in Table 2 when improvements over all other methods are statistically significant, except when comparing TrueWalks with OWL2Vec* for GDA, since in this particular case the improvement is not statistically significant.

Relation Prediction Using Semantic Similarity. We also evaluate all methods in PPI prediction using KG embedding-based semantic similarity, computed as the cosine similarity between the vectors of each protein in a pair. Adopting the methodology employed by [20] and [45], for each positive pair e_1 and e_2 in the dataset, we compute the similarity between e_1 and all other entities and identify the rank of e_2. The performance was measured using recall at rank 10^5, recall at rank 100, mean rank, and the area under the ROC curve (Table 3). Results show that TrueWalksOA achieves the top performance across all metrics, but TrueWalks is bested by RDF2Vec on all metrics except Hits@10, by OWL2Vec* on Hits@100 and by node2vec on Hits@10.

---

[5] Since we compute the similarity score for all possible pairs to simulate a more realistic scenario where a user is presented with a ranked list of candidate interactions, the task is several degrees more difficult to performant and all KG embedding methods have a recall score of 0 at rank 1. As a result, we have excluded the results for this metric from our analysis.

Table 3. Hits@10, Hits@100, mean rank, and ROC-AUC for PPI prediction using cosine similarity obtained with different methods. In bold, the best value for each metric.

	Method	Hits@10	Hits@100	MeanRank	AUC
Pos	TransE	0.013	0.125	103.934	0.538
	TransH	0.013	0.134	102.703	0.543
	TransR	0.037	0.196	81.916	0.636
	ComplEx	0.080	0.261	64.558	0.689
	distMult	0.112	0.340	46.512	0.803
	DeepWalk	0.125	0.380	35.406	0.847
	node2vec	0.163	0.375	37.275	0.827
	metapath2vec	0.017	0.151	98.445	0.558
	OWL2Vec*	0.152	0.386	33.192	0.860
	RDF2Vec	0.133	0.391	32.419	0.870
Pos + Neg	TransE	0.022	0.161	94.809	0.576
	TransR	0.100	0.274	60.120	0.732
	TransH	0.025	0.174	91.553	0.594
	ComplEx	0.132	0.334	45.268	0.805
	distMult	0.149	0.378	35.351	0.853
	DeepWalk	0.148	0.383	35.365	0.849
	node2vec	**0.166**	0.389	34.305	0.840
	metapath2vec	0.020	0.165	93.374	0.578
	OWL2Vec*	0.160	0.397	32.234	0.869
	RDF2Vec	0.155	0.401	30.281	0.879
TrueWalks		0.161	0.392	32.089	0.869
TrueWalksOA		**0.166**	**0.407**	**28.128**	**0.889**

To better understand these results, we plotted the distribution of similarity values for positive and negative pairs in Fig. 4. There is a smaller overlap between negative and positive pairs similarities for TrueWalksOA, which indicates that considering both the status of the function assignments and the order of entities in the random walks results in embeddings that are more meaningful semantic representations of proteins. Furthermore, the cosine similarity for negative pairs is consistently lower when using both variants of TrueWalks, which supports that the contribution of negative statement-based embeddings is working towards filtering out false positives.

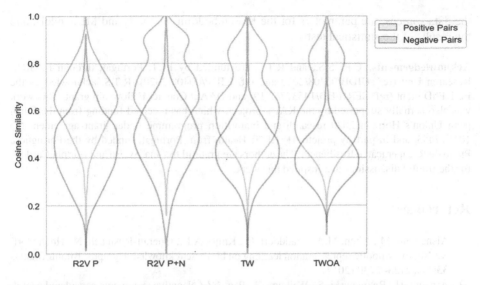

Fig. 4. Violin plot with embedding similarity obtained with RDF2Vec with positive statements (R2V P), RDF2Vec with both positive and negative statements (R2V P+N), TrueWalks (TW), and TrueWalksOA (TWOA).

5   Conclusion

Knowledge graph embeddings are increasingly used in biomedical applications such as the prediction of protein-protein interactions, gene-disease associations, drug-target relations and drug-drug interactions [28]. Our novel approach, TrueWalks, was motivated by the fact that existing knowledge graph embedding methods are ill-equipped to handle negative statements, despite their recognized importance in biomedical machine learning tasks [21]. TrueWalks incorporates a novel walk-generation method that distinguishes between positive and negative statements and considers the semantic implications of negation in ontology-rich knowledge graphs. It generates two separate embeddings, one for each type of statement, enabling a dual representation of entities that can be explored by downstream ML, focusing both on features entities have and those they lack. TrueWalks outperforms representative and state-of-the-art knowledge graph embedding approaches in the prediction of protein-protein interactions and gene-disease associations.

We expect TrueWalks to be generalizable to other biomedical applications where negative statements play a decisive role, such as predicting disease-related phenotypes [47] or performing differential diagnosis [19]. In future work, we would also like to explore counter-fitting approaches, such as those proposed for language embeddings [29], to consider how opposite statements can impact the dissimilarity of entities.

Supplemental Material Statement: The source code for True Walks is available on GitHub (https://github.com/liseda-lab/TrueWalks). All datasets are available on Zenodo (https://doi.org/10.5281/zenodo.7709195). A supplementary file contains the links to the data sources, the parameters for the KG embedding methods and ML models, and the results of the statistical tests.

Acknowledgements. C.P., S.S., and R.T.S. are funded by FCT, Portugal, through LASIGE Research Unit (ref. UIDB/00408/2020 and ref. UIDP/00408/2020). R.T.S. acknowledges the FCT PhD grant (ref. SFRH/BD/145377/2019) and DAAD Contact Fellowship grant. This work was also partially supported by the KATY project, which has received funding from the European Union's Horizon 2020 research and innovation programme under grant agreement No 101017453, and in part by projeto 41, HfPT: Health from Portugal, funded by the Portuguese Plano de Recuperação e Resiliência. The authors are grateful to Lina Aveiro and Carlota Cardoso for the fruitful discussions that inspired this work.

References

1. Alshahrani, M., Khan, M.A., Maddouri, O., Kinjo, A.R., Queralt-Rosinach, N., Hoehndorf, R.: Neuro-symbolic representation learning on biological knowledge graphs. Bioinformatics **33**(17), 2723–2730 (2017)
2. Arnaout, H., Razniewski, S., Weikum, G., Pan, J.Z.: Negative statements considered useful. J. Web Semant. **71**, 100661 (2021)
3. Arnaout, H., Razniewski, S., Weikum, G., Pan, J.Z.: Wikinegata: a knowledge base with interesting negative statements. Proc. VLDB Endow. **14**(12), 2807–2810 (2021)
4. Asif, M., Martiniano, H., Couto, F.: Identifying disease genes using machine learning and gene functional similarities, assessed through Gene Ontology. PLoS ONE **13**, e0208626 (2018)
5. Boettiger, C.: rdflib: a high level wrapper around the redland package for common rdf applications (2018)
6. Bordes, A., Usunier, N., Garcia-Durán, A., Weston, J., Yakhnenko, O.: Translating embeddings for modeling multi-relational data. In: Proceedings of NIPS 2013, pp.. 2787–2795. Curran Associates Inc., Red Hook, NY, USA (2013)
7. Chen, J., Hu, P., Jimenez-Ruiz, E., Holter, O.M., Antonyrajah, D., Horrocks, I.: OWL2Vec*: Embedding of OWL ontologies. Machine Learning, pp. 1–33 (2021)
8. Dong, Y., Chawla, N.V., Swami, A.: metapath2vec: scalable representation learning for heterogeneous networks. In: Proceedings of the 23rd ACM SIGKDD International Conference on Knowledge Discovery and Data Mining, pp. 135–144 (2017)
9. Eilbeck, K., Quinlan, A., Yandell, M.: Settling the score: variant prioritization and mendelian disease. Nat. Rev. Genet. **18**(10), 599–612 (2017)
10. Flouris, G., Huang, Z., Pan, J.Z., Plexousakis, D., Wache, H.: Inconsistencies, negations and changes in ontologies. In: Proceedings of the 21st National Conference on Artificial Intelligence, vol. 2, pp. 1295–1300 (2006)
11. Fu, G., Wang, J., Yang, B., Yu, G.: NegGOA: negative GO annotations selection using ontology structure. Bioinformatics **32**(19), 2996–3004 (2016)
12. Gaudet, P., Dessimoz, C.: Gene ontology: pitfalls, biases, and remedies. In: The Gene Ontology Handbook, pp. 189–205. Humana Press, New York (2017)
13. GO Consortium: The gene ontology resource: enriching a gold mine. Nucleic Acids Res. **49**(D1), D325–D334 (2021)
14. GO Consortium: The gene ontology resource: 20 years and still going strong. Nucleic Acids Res. **47**(D1), D330–D338 (2018)
15. Grau, B.C., Horrocks, I., Motik, B., Parsia, B., Patel-Schneider, P., Sattler, U.: OWL 2: the next step for OWL. J. Web Seman. **6**(4), 309–322 (2008)

16. Grover, A., Leskovec, J.: node2vec: scalable feature learning for networks. In: Proceedings of the 22nd ACM SIGKDD International Conference on Knowledge Discovery and Data Mining, pp. 855–864 (2016)
17. Hogan, A., et al.: Knowledge graphs. ACM Comput. Surv. (CSUR) **54**(4), 1–37 (2021)
18. Hu, L., Wang, X., Huang, Y.A., Hu, P., You, Z.H.: A survey on computational models for predicting protein-protein interactions. Briefings Bioinform. **22**(5), bbab036 (2021)
19. Köhler, S.: Encoding clinical data with the Human Phenotype Ontology for computational differential diagnostics. Curr. Protoc. Hum. Genet. **103**(1), e92 (2019)
20. Kulmanov, M., Liu-Wei, W., Yan, Y., Hoehndorf, R.: EL embeddings: geometric construction of models for the description logic EL++. In: Proceedings of the Twenty-Eighth International Joint Conference on Artificial Intelligence (2019)
21. Kulmanov, M., Smaili, F.Z., Gao, X., Hoehndorf, R.: Semantic similarity and machine learning with ontologies. Brief. Bioinform. **22**(4), bbaa199 (2021)
22. Köhler, S., Gargano, M., Matentzoglu, N., Carmody, L.C., Lewis-Smith, D., Vasilevsky, N.A., Danis, D.e.a.: The Human Phenotype Ontology in 2021. Nucleic Acids Research **49**(D1), D1207–D1217 (12 2020)
23. Lin, Y., Liu, Z., Sun, M., Liu, Y., Zhu, X.: Learning entity and relation embeddings for knowledge graph completion. Proceedings of the AAAI Conference on Artificial Intelligence, vol. 29(1) (2015)
24. Ling, W., Dyer, C., Black, A.W., Trancoso, I.: Two/too simple adaptations of word2vec for syntax problems. In: Proceedings of the 2015 Conference of the North American Chapter of the Association for Computational Linguistics: Human Language Technologies, pp. 1299–1304 (2015)
25. Liu, L., Zhu, S.: Computational methods for prediction of human protein-phenotype associations: a review. Phenomics **1**(4), 171–185 (2021)
26. Luo, P., Xiao, Q., Wei, P.J., Liao, B., Wu, F.X.: Identifying disease-gene associations with graph-regularized manifold learning. Front. Genetics **10** (2019)
27. Mikolov, T., Chen, K., Corrado, G., Dean, J.: Efficient estimation of word representations in vector space. arXiv preprint arXiv:1301.3781 (2013)
28. Mohamed, S.K., Nounu, A., Nováček, V.: Biological applications of knowledge graph embedding models. Brief. Bioinform. **22**(2), 1679–1693 (2021)
29. Mrksic, N., et al.: Counter-fitting word vectors to linguistic constraints. In: HLT-NAACL (2016)
30. Nunes, S., Sousa, R.T., Pesquita, C.: Predicting gene-disease associations with knowledge graph embeddings over multiple ontologies. In: ISMB Annual Meeting - Bio-Ontologies (2021)
31. Perozzi, B., Al-Rfou, R., Skiena, S.: Deepwalk: online learning of social representations. In: Proceedings of the 20th ACM SIGKDD International Conference on Knowledge Discovery and Data Mining, pp. 701–710 (2014)
32. Pesquita, C., Faria, D., Falcao, A.O., Lord, P., Couto, F.M.: Semantic similarity in biomedical ontologies. PLoS Comput. Biol. **5**(7), e1000443 (2009)
33. Piñero, J., et al.: The DisGeNET knowledge platform for disease genomics: 2019 update. Nucleic Acids Res. **48**(D1), D845–D855 (2019)
34. Portisch, J., Paulheim, H.: Putting RDF2Vec in order. In: CEUR Workshop Proceedings, vol. 2980, pp. 1–5. RWTH (2021)
35. Ristoski, P., Paulheim, H.: RDF2Vec: RDF graph embeddings for data mining. In: Groth, P., et al. (eds.) ISWC 2016. LNCS, vol. 9981, pp. 498–514. Springer, Cham (2016). https://doi.org/10.1007/978-3-319-46523-4_30
36. Robinson, P., et al.: Improved exome prioritization of disease genes through cross-species phenotype comparison. PCR Methods Appl. **24**(2), 340–348 (2014)

37. Smaili, F.Z., Gao, X., Hoehndorf, R.: OPA2Vec: combining formal and informal content of biomedical ontologies to improve similarity-based prediction. Bioinformatics **35**(12), 2133–2140 (2019)
38. Sousa, R.T., Silva, S., Pesquita, C.: Evolving knowledge graph similarity for supervised learning in complex biomedical domains. BMC Bioinform. **21**(1), 1–19 (2020)
39. Sousa, R.T., Silva, S., Pesquita, C.: Benchmark datasets for biomedical knowledge graphs with negative statements (2023)
40. Szklarczyk, D., et al.: The STRING database in 2021: customizable protein-protein networks, and functional characterization of user-uploaded gene/measurement sets. Nucleic Acids Res. **49**(D1), D605–D612 (2020)
41. Vanunu, O., Magger, O., Ruppin, E., Shlomi, T., Sharan, R.: Associating genes and protein complexes with disease via network propagation. PLoS Comput. Biol/ **6** (2010)
42. Wang, Q., Mao, Z., Wang, B., Guo, L.: Knowledge graph embedding: a survey of approaches and applications. IEEE Trans. Knowl. Data Eng. **29**(12), 2724–2743 (2017)
43. Wang, Z., Zhang, J., Feng, J., Chen, Z.: Knowledge graph embedding by translating on hyperplanes. In: Proceedings of the 28th AAAI Conference on Artificial Intelligence, pp. 1112–1119. AAAI Press (2014)
44. Warwick Vesztrocy, A., Dessimoz, C.: Benchmarking gene ontology function predictions using negative annotations. Bioinformatics **36**(Supplement_1), i210–i218 (2020)
45. Xiong, B., Potyka, N., Tran, T.K., Nayyeri, M., Staab, S.: Faithful embeddings for EL++ knowledge bases. In: International Semantic Web Conference. pp. 22–38. Springer (2022). https://doi.org/10.1007/978-3-031-19433-7_2
46. Xu, Q.S., Liang, Y.Z.: Monte Carlo cross validation. Chemom. Intell. Lab. Syst. **56**(1), 1–11 (2001)
47. Xue, H., Peng, J., Shang, X.: Predicting disease-related phenotypes using an integrated phenotype similarity measurement based on HPO. BMC Syst. Biol. **13**(2), 1–12 (2019)
48. Yang, B., tau Yih, W., He, X., Gao, J., Deng, L.: Embedding entities and relations for learning and inference in knowledge bases (2015)
49. Zakeri, P., Simm, J., Arany, A., ElShal, S., Moreau, Y.: Gene prioritization using bayesian matrix factorization with genomic and phenotypic side information. Bioinformatics **34**, i447–i456 (2018)
50. Zhang, S.B., Tang, Q.R.: Protein-protein interaction inference based on semantic similarity of Gene Ontology terms. J. Theor. Biol. **401**, 30–37 (2016)
51. Zhu, Y., Liu, H., Wu, Z., Song, Y., Zhang, T.: Representation learning with ordered relation paths for knowledge graph completion. In: Proceedings of the 2019 Conference on Empirical Methods in Natural Language Processing and the 9th International Joint Conference on Natural Language Processing (EMNLP-IJCNLP), pp. 2662–2671 (2019)

Knowledge Graph Enhanced Language Models for Sentiment Analysis

Jie Li[1], Xuan Li[1], Linmei Hu[2(✉)], Yirui Zhang[1], and Jinrui Wang[1]

[1] Beijing University of Posts and Telecommunications, Beijing, China
{Jli,lixuan20000530,zhangyirui,wangjr}@bupt.edu.cn
[2] Beijing Institute of Technology, Beijing, China
hulinmei@bit.edu.cn

Abstract. Pre-trained language models (LMs) have been widely used in sentiment analysis, and some recent works have focused on injecting sentiment knowledge from sentiment lexicons or structured commonsense knowledge from knowledge graphs (KGs) into pre-trained LMs, which have achieved remarkable success. However, these works often only obtain knowledge from a single source in either the sentiment lexicon or the KG, and only perform very shallow fusion of LM representations and external knowledge representations. Therefore, how to effectively extract multiple sources of external knowledge and fully integrate them with the LM representations is still an unresolved issue. In this paper, we propose a novel knowledge enhanced model for sentiment analysis (KSA), which simultaneously incorporates commonsense and sentiment knowledge as external knowledge, by constructing a heterogeneous Commonsense-Senti Knowledge Graph. Additionally, a separate global token and global node are added to the text sequence and constructed knowledge graph respectively, and a fusion unit is used to enable global information interaction between the different modalities, allowing them to perceive each other's information and thereby improving the ability to perform sentiment analysis. Experiments on standard datasets show that our proposed KSA significantly outperforms the strong pre-trained baselines, and achieves new state-of-the-art results on most of the test datasets.

Keywords: Knowledge Graph · Knowledge Fusion · Sentiment Analysis

1 Introduction

Sentence-level sentiment analysis strives to extract the overall sentiment, which has garnered considerable attention in natural language processing (NLP) [1,2]. Recently, pre-trained language models (LMs) [3–6] have shown their power in learning general semantic representations, leading to significant advancements in most NLP tasks, including sentiment analysis. These models learn encoders on large-scale corpora via well-designed pre-training tasks [7]. However, the application of general purposed pre-trained LMs in sentiment analysis is limited, because they neglect to consider the importance of external knowledge [8].

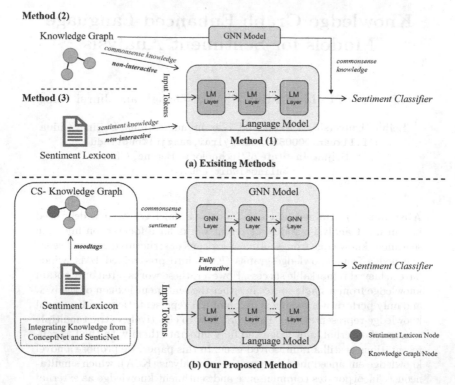

Fig. 1. Illustration of comparison of existing methods and our proposed method. Method (1) directly performs sentiment analysis using pretrained LMs. Method (2) injects commonsense knowledge from the knowledge graph into LMs in a non-interactive manner. It can either encode LM representations and graph representations separately, where graph representations directly participate in the final sentiment analysis, or enhance text encoding representations using commonsense knowledge during the LM encoding stage. Method (3) enhances text encoding representations using sentiment knowledge from the sentiment lexicon. Our proposed method utilizes knowledge from both sources to construct a CS-knowledge graph and effectively integrates graph representations and LM representations for sentiment analysis.

Some recent works attempt to integrate various knowledge into pre-trained LMs (see Fig. 1). On the one hand, some researches [9, 10] have infused commonsense knowledge using massive knowledge graphs (KG), such as ConceptNet [11], Freebase [12]. On the other hand, sentiment lexicons, such as SenticNet [13], SentiWordNet [14], have been injected into pre-trained LMs [15–18]. These researches have demonstrated the significant role of KGs or sentiment lexicons in sentiment polarity prediction. However, these methods still have two problems: 1) Using only one kind of knowledge. Prior methods typically inject one kind of knowledge into LMs, but whether the KG that provides a rich source of background concepts or the sentiment lexicon that provides specific moodtags is helpful to enhance the sentiment polarity prediction. For example, in the case of a movie review, KG can provide commonsense information such as director, cast, plot, and themes, while sentiment lexicon can offer corresponding positive or negative moodtags to the words in the review. Therefore, there are still challenges in how to acquire knowledge from both sources. 2) How to effectively fuse the external knowledge. The existing methods can only fuse the external knowledge representations and LM representations in a shallow and non-interactive manner, which constrain the performance of the model. Exploring how to effectively integrate two representations in a truly unified manner is still an underexplored area.

In this work, we present KSA, a novel knowledge enhanced model for sentiment analysis that addresses the two problems mentioned above. Our KSA has two key insights: (i) Constructing a heterogeneous Commonsense-Senti knowledge graph(CS-knowledge graph). We construct a CS-knowledge graph by integrating knowledge from the commonsense KG ConceptNet and the sentiment lexicon SenticNet to represent external knowledge that may contribute to sentiment polarity prediction. Based on the input, we first retrieve the corresponding entities from ConceptNet. Then, we iterate through these entities and search for their moodtags in SenticNet. The retrieved entities and moodtags are then used as nodes in the CS-knowledge graph. Corresponding edges are retrieved from ConceptNet to connect these nodes, resulting in the CS-knowledge graph that encompasses both commonsense and sentiment knowledge. (ii) Deep fusion of LM representations and graph representations. Our proposed KSA includes multiple stacked fusion layers, each of which is composed of a LM layer, a GNN layer, and a fusion unit. We encode the input text and the CS knowledge graph separately using LM and GNN. Additionally, the text sequence and CS knowledge graph are equipped with a global token and a global node, respectively, to capture global information. After each layer of LM and GNN encoding, the global token and global node are input into a special fusion unit, where a deep fusion of the two modalities is performed. The fused global token and global node then enter the next round of representation update, integrating global information from each other into their own modality representations, bridging the gap between the two sources of information.

Our contributions are outlined below.

- To the best of our knowledge, we propose for the first time to enhance sentiment classification using both commonsense and sentiment knowledge. Specifically, we construct a Commonsense-Senti knowledge graph for each input and employ GNN layers to learn the rich external knowledge in the graph. By integrating external knowledge representations with text representations, we effectively improve the performance of sentiment classification.
- In our KSA model, we designed a specialized fusion mechanism. The representations of the global token and global node are extracted, concatenated, and fed into the fusion unit to mix their representations. In subsequent layers, the mixed information from the global elements is combined with their respective modality representations. Through this mechanism, our model fully and effectively integrates knowledge.

- We conduct extensive experiments and achieve new state-of-the-art results on most of the test datasets, which proves the effectiveness of the KSA fusion approach and the significance of simultaneously injecting commonsense and sentiment knowledge.

2   Related Work

2.1   Incorporating External Knowledge for NLP

Various works have incorporated knowledge to augment NLP systems [19–23]. For example, ERNIE 3.0 [19] augments the original input sentence with triples, such as (Andersen, Write, Nightingale), which are then used as the basis for designing tasks that aim to predict the relationship between the entities in the triple, in this case the relation "Write". K-BERT [20] attaches triples to entities in the input sentence to create a sentence tree, and uses soft-position and visible matrix to reduce knowledge noise. SenseBERT [21] integrates word-supersense knowledge by predicting the supersense of masked words in the input, where candidates are nouns and verbs, and ground truth is derived from WordNet. KnowBERT [22] integrates knowledge bases into BERT by employing Knowledge Attention and Recontextualization mechanisms. The knowledge sources used are derived from synset-synset and lemma-lemma relationships in WordNet, as well as entity linking information extracted from Wikipedia. K-Adapter [23] develops adapters and treats them as add-ons with knowledge representations. These adapters are separated from the backbone pre-trained LMs and are trained from scratch through self-designed task. The above-mentioned methods for knowledge fusion are often unidirectional. To be more specific, while their fusion units empower the LMs with external knowledge, they miss out on the potential benefits of integrating contextual information from the LMs into the KG. A more comprehensive and bidirectional knowledge fusion process could be highly advantageous.

2.2   Incorporating External Knowledge for Sentiment Analysis

Analogously, external knowledge can be typically used as a source for enhancing the sentiment feature representations in the task of sentiment analysis (i.e., structured commonsense knowledge and sentiment knowledge). On the one hand, a line of works utilize commonsense knowledge from KGs to enhance sentiment analysis. Some of them [10,24] encode structured knowledge representations and language representations respectively, where graph representations directly participate in the final sentiment analysis. For example, KinGDOM [10] concatenates the graph feature representations learned through graph convolutional autoencoder and the language representations learned through DANN autoencoder to perform sentiment classification task. KGAN [24] integrates the knowledge graph into the embedding space, which is then fed into a hierarchical fusion module to fuse the learned multiview representations. Others [9,25,26] seek to use encoded representations of a linked KG to augment the textual representations. SEKT [9] uses the external knowledge to construct a knowledge graph, which is then fed into a graph convolutional network to learn graph representations, and it is fully integrated into the bidirectional long short-term memory (BiLSTM) stance classifier to enhance the text representations. SAKG-BERT [25] model constructs an SAKG in which triples are injected into sentences as domain knowledge to improve the interpretability of the deep learning algorithm. KG-MPOA [26] proposes a matching and filtering method to distill useful knowledge in the ConceptNet, and a bi-directional long-short term memory model with multipolarity orthogonal attention is adopted to fuse the distilled knowledge with the semantic embedding, effectively enriching the representations of sentences. On the other hand, sentiment lexicons are usually injected into LMs by designing sentiment-aware tasks [8,27–30]. For example, SKEP [27] integrates sentiment information at the word, polarity, and aspect levels into pre-trained sentiment representations. SentiLARE [28] incorporates linguistic knowledge at the word-level, such as part-of-speech tags and sentiment polarity (derived from SentiWordNet) into pre-trained LMs.

However, the existing methods still fall short in exploring the knowledge to augment the sentiment analysis. One main reason for this is that the interaction between external knowledge and LMs is limited as information between them only flows in one direction, often relying on external knowledge to enhance text representation. In addition, existing methods often choose one of sentiment lexicon or KG as external knowledge, but we think it is possible to combine the two to enrich the feature representations of external knowledge.

In contrast to prior works, we synergistically combine the LMs with both KG and sentiment knowledge by constructing CS-knowledge graph to obtain richer feature representations and effectively boost the performance of sentiment analysis. Additionally, both the text representations sent to LM and the CS-knowledge graph representations sent to GNN are attached with a global information extraction section, which can fuse the two modalities after each layer of LM and GNN, so that both modalities can reflect specific aspects of the other.

3 Methodology

3.1 Task Definition and Model Overview

We aim to determine the sentiment polarity of sentences by leveraging knowledge from a pre-trained LM and a structured KG. In the task of sentence-level sentiment classification (SSC), the dataset is typically composed of examples of a text sentence s and a digital label l. In particular, in this work, we will convert the numerical labels in the examples into textual labels, denoted by a. For example, in binary classification problems, label "1" corresponds to "It is positive" and label "0" corresponds to "It is negative", thus connecting textual label a with the sentence s to form a pure text input (s, a). Note that we link all text-based label a options in the dataset with s in turn as input to judge the polarity of the sentence by scores. Furthermore, the external knowledge graph that we access is referred to as $\mathcal{G}$, which offers background knowledge relevant to the sentences being analyzed.

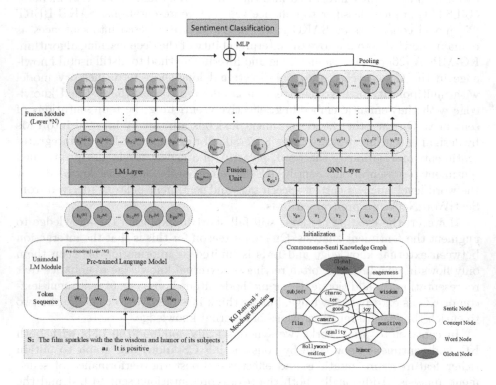

Fig. 2. Overview of our approach. The input tokens are attached with a special global token to extract the global information of the LM representations, and pre-encoding is performed through LM layers. At the same time, the corresponding CS-Knowledge Graph is extracted based on the input, and word nodes are connected to the global node to capture the global information of the graph. Then, both modalities enter the Fusion Module, with the language representations continuing to be updated through the LM layers, and the KG being processed using GNN Layers for information propagation between nodes. In each layer, after the representations of both modalities are updated, global token and node are extracted to exchange global information through the Fusion Unit. In subsequent layers, the mixed global token allows knowledge from the KG to influence the representations of other tokens, while the mixed global node allows language context to influence the node representations in the GNN.

As illustrated in Fig. 2, our model consists of three primary components: (1) a Commonsense-Senti knowledge graph (CS-knowledge graph) building module, (2) a unimodal LM module that learns an initial representation of the input tokens, and (3) a fusion module which learns to update representations of the input sequence and retrieved CS-knowledge graph, enabling the mixing of the textual representations derived from the underlying LM module with the graph representations. The unimodal module is composed of M stacked LM layers, while the fusion module is composed of N stacked layers, each includes a LM layer, a GNN layer and a fusion unit.

Given a textual input (s, a), first, we build a CS-knowledge graph (denoted $\mathcal{G}^{cs}$) from the KG ConceptNet and the sentiment lexicon SenticNet (Sect. 3.2). Meanwhile, we tokenize the combined sequence into $\{w_1, ..., w_T\}$, where T is the total number of tokens, which are then fed into the LM to obtain a pre-encoding representations (Sect. 3.4). Then the pre-encoding token representations denoted as $\{h_1^M, ..., h_T^M\}$, where M is the total number of layers in the LM unimodal module, and the set of nodes denoted as $\{v_1, ..., v_K\}$, where K is the total number of nodes, are fed into the fusion module. Within this module, LM is utilized to update textual representations, and GNN is employed to learn graph representations that capture semantic connections between nodes. Additionally, we introduce a special global token w_{glo} and a special global node v_{glo} to propagate global information from both modalities. The global token is added to the token sequence, and the global node is connected to all the KG entities mentioned in the given input sequence (Sect. 3.5). Finally, we utilize the w_{glo} token representation, v_{glo} node representation, and a pooled $\mathcal{G}^{cs}$ representation to make the final prediction (Sect. 3.6).

3.2 Commonsense-Senti Knowledge Graph Construction

In addition to the general knowledge provided by the LM, sentiment analysis often requires external knowledge such as world knowledge and specific sentiment knowledge. While language models excel at understanding human-like text, they may lack the contextual understanding necessary to accurately determine sentiment. By incorporating external knowledge sources, such as knowledge graphs, sentiment lexicons, we can enhance the LM's sentiment analysis capabilities. World knowledge helps the LM interpret language nuances and understand the connotations associated with certain words or phrases. For example, understanding that certain events or cultural references may have a positive or negative sentiment can greatly improve the accuracy of sentiment analysis. Meanwhile, by incorporating specific sentiment knowledge into the LM, it can better understand the sentiment orientation of words and phrases, enabling more precise sentiment analysis. Therefore, we construct a Commonsense-Senti knowledge graph (CS-knowledge graph) to represent the external knowledge that may contribute to sentiment polarity prediction.

Algorithm 1 describes the details of constructing the CS-Knowledge Graph. Given each input sequence (s, a), we retrieve the knowledge graph $\mathcal{G}^{cs}$ from $\mathcal{G}$. First, we perform entity linking to $\mathcal{G}$ based on (s, a) in order to identify the word nodes. We iterate through each word in the input, and if it appears in ConceptNet, we select it as an entity in our CS-knowledge graph. Next, we consider all entities that appear in any two-hop paths between the mentioned entity pairs as nodes in the CS knowledge graph. Then we attempt to assign moodtags to the entities retrieved above by looking for the sentiment lexicon

SenticNet. These moodtags are referred to as sentic nodes. For example, for a word "wisdom" in word entity, its corresponding moodtag from Senticnet is "#eagerness". Then we prune the set of nodes retrieved above. We calculate the relevance score by combining the node name with the context of the input example and feeding it through a pre-trained LM. We consider the output score of the node name as the relevance score and only keep the top 200 nodes with the highest scores while discarding the rest. Afterwards, we retrieve the edges in $\mathcal{G}$ based on the prunned nodes to form the retrieved knowledge graph. In this way, we construct a CS-knowledge graph that contains both commonsense knowledge and specific sentiment knowledge at the same time. Additionally, a global node v_{glo} (the dark yellow node in Fig. 2) is added to connect to all the word nodes to capture the global information in $\mathcal{G}^{cs}$ and fully integrate it with the contextual knowledge from LM (Sect. 3.5).

Algorithm 1. Construct CS-knowledge graph

    Input: Sentence sequence (s, a)
    Output: knowledge graph $\mathcal{G}_{cs}$
1: $\mathcal{G}_{cs} \leftarrow$ create empty graph
2: Initialize a set of nodes N_{pruned} to store pruned nodes based on relevance scores
3: $entities \leftarrow$ entity_linking$(s, a, \text{ConceptNet})$
4: $\mathcal{G}_{cs}$.add_nodes($entities$)
5: **for** each entity in $\mathcal{G}_{cs}$ **do**
6:     $moodtag \leftarrow$ senticnet_lookup($entity$)
7:     **if** $moodtag$ is not None **then**
8:         $\mathcal{G}_{cs}$.add_nodes($moodtag$)
9: **for** each entity in $\mathcal{G}_{cs}$ **do**
10:     $context \leftarrow$ get_context($entity, (s, a)$)
11:     $score \leftarrow$ pre_trained_LM($context$)
12:     N_{pruned}.add(entity, score)
13: N_{pruned}.sort_by_score()
14: $top\_200\_nodes \leftarrow N_{pruned}[: 200]$
15: $\mathcal{G}_{cs} \leftarrow$ empty existing entities
16: $\mathcal{G}_{cs}$.add_nodes(top_200_nodes)
17: **for** each head-entity in $\mathcal{G}_{cs}$ **do**
18:     **for** each tail-entity in $\mathcal{G}_{cs}$ **do**
19:         **if** check_relation(entity1, entity2) **then**
20:             $\mathcal{G}_{cs}$.add_edge(entity1, entity2)
21: $global\_node \leftarrow$ create_global_node($\mathcal{G}_{cs}$)
22: $\mathcal{G}_{cs}$.add_node($global\_node$)
23: **for** each entity in $\mathcal{G}_{cs}$ **do**
24:     **if** $entity$ is in (s, a) **then**
25:         $\mathcal{G}_{cs}$.add_edge($global\_node$, $entity$)
26: **return** $\mathcal{G}_{cs}$

3.3   CS-Knowledge Graph Initialization

Generating initial node embeddings for entities in the CS-knowledge graph is a crucial step in our model. To begin with, we convert knowledge triples in $\mathcal{G}^{cs}$ into sentences using pre-defined templates for each relation. These templates ensure that the resulting sentences preserve the semantics of the original triples. Then, we feed these sentences into a BERT-large LM, which computes embeddings for each sentence. These sentence embeddings capture the semantic meaning of the knowledge triples in $\mathcal{G}^{cs}$. Subsequently, we extract all token representations of the entity's mention spans in sentences containing that entity, mean pool over these representations, and project the resulting mean-pooled representation. Finally, we initialize the embedding of the global node $v_{glo}^{(0)}$ randomly.

3.4   Textual Pre-embedding

In the M-Layer unimodal LM module, we provide the input sequence of tokens as $\{w_{glo}, w_1, ..., w_T\}$. The representation of a token w_t in the ℓ-th layer of the model is donated as $h_t^{(\ell)}$. The input representation for layer $\ell=0$ is computed by summing the token, segment, and positional embeddings for each token, resulting in $\{h_{glo}^{(0)}, h_1^{(0)}, ..., h_T^{(0)}\}$. For each subsequent layer $\ell+1$, the input representation is updated using the following process:

$$\left\{h_{glo}^{(\ell+1)}, h_1^{(\ell+1)}, ..., h_T^{(\ell+1)}\right\} = \text{LM-Layer}\left(\left\{h_{glo}^{(\ell)}, h_1^{(\ell)}, ..., h_T^{(\ell)}\right\}\right) \tag{1}$$
$$\text{for } \ell = 1, ..., M-1$$

where LM-Layer $(\cdot)$ represents a single encoder layer of the LM, and its parameters are initialized with a pre-trained model.

3.5   Fusion Module

After initializing and pre-encoding respectively, the structured CS-knowledge graph and the input text are fed into the fusion module. The fusion module draws inspiration from previous work which focused on enhancing text representations using external knowledge. However, these approaches only implemented one-way information propagation. In order to enrich the representations further, our work introduces a bidirectional fusion mechanism in the fusion module. The fusion module facilitates the interaction of global information between textual representations and KG representations, enabling the two modalities to integrate information from each other. Specifically, pre-encoded tokens are further encoded through the LM layers in the fusion module, while the initialized $\mathcal{G}^{cs}$ is fed into the GNN network for node information propagation. It is worth noting that after each LM and GNN layer, an additional fusion operation is performed on the h_{glo} and the v_{glo} to exchange global information between the two modalities. Therefore, our fusion module mainly consists of the LM layers, GNN layers, and fusion units, and we will introduce the specific operations of each.

The fusion module is specifically designed to separately encode information for both modalities. Specifically, in a N-Layer fusion module, the input textual embeddings from the M-th unimodal LM layer are further processed by additional transformer LM encoder blocks. The textual embedding of the $(M+\ell+1)$-th layer is updated using the following process:

$$\left\{\tilde{h}_{glo}^{(M+\ell+1)}, h_1^{(M+\ell+1)}, \ldots, h_T^{(M+\ell+1)}\right\} = \text{LM-Layer}\left(\left\{h_{glo}^{(M+\ell)}, h_1^{(M+\ell)}, \ldots, h_T^{(M+\ell)}\right\}\right)$$
$$\text{for } \ell = 1, \ldots, N-1$$
(2)

where $\tilde{h}_{glo}$ refers to the global token that have not undergone interaction in the current layer. As $\tilde{h}_{glo}$ interacts with the nodes $\tilde{v}_{glo}$ in the knowledge graph representation and encodes the received global graph information, this allows for token representations to mix with $\mathcal{G}^{cs}$ representations in the later LM layers, which will be explained in detail later.

Meanwhile, in the fusion module, the graph representations that are initialized above are fed into GNN layers to perform information propagation over the CS-knowledge graph, aiming to fully exploit the commonsense knowledge and emotional connections between the nodes. Our GNN network utilizes the graph attention network (GAT) framework [31] to learn the graph representations. This framework uses iterative message passing to induce the learning of node representations among graph neighbors. Specifically, in the fusion module, for each layer, we update the representation of each node $v_k^{(\ell)}$ by

$$\left\{\tilde{v}_{glo}^{(\ell+1)}, v_1^{(\ell+1)}, \ldots, v_K^{(\ell+1)}\right\} = \text{GNN}\left(\left\{v_{glo}^{(\ell)}, v_1^{(\ell)}, \ldots, v_K^{(\ell)}\right\}\right)$$
$$\text{for } \ell = 1, \ldots, N-1$$
(3)

where $\tilde{v}_{glo}$ refers to the global node that have not undergone interaction in the current layer. Importantly, since our GNN layer performs message passing on the graph, it will simultaneously utilize the representations of both the textual context and CS-knowledge graph through global node $v_{glo}^{(\ell)}$. Further elaboration on this will be provided later.

After updating token embeddings and node embeddings using a LM layer and a GNN layer respectively, we use a fusion unit (FU) to enable the two modalities to exchange information through h_{glo} that captures text global information and v_{glo} that captures knowledge graph global information. We concatenate the unmixed embeddings of $\tilde{h}_{glo}^{(\ell)}$ and $\tilde{v}_{glo}^{(\ell)}$, apply a mixing operation (FU) to the joint representation, and then separate the fused embeddings into $h_{glo}^{(\ell)}$ and $e_{glo}^{(\ell)}$.

$$\left[h_{glo}^{(\ell)}; v_{glo}^{(\ell)}\right] = \text{FU}\left(\left[\tilde{h}_{glo}^{(\ell)}; \tilde{v}_{glo}^{(\ell)}\right]\right)$$
(4)

where FU adopts a two-layer MLP operation. Of course, besides the global token h_{glo} and the global nodes v_{glo}, other tokens and nodes do not directly participate in fusion. Instead, in the next layer when they are separately encoded, they obtain information from each other through their respective h_{glo} and v_{glo}. For the textual representations, the fused h_{glo} and the rest of them are sent to the next layer of the LM, where they undergo the next round of modal propagation (i.e., Eqs. 2), which allows for the fusion with commonsense knowledge and specific sentiment knowledge from the knowledge graph. For the graph representations, the fused v_{glo} and the rest of the nodes are fed into the next GNN layer, where its propagation mechanism enables each node to integrate contextual information from the LM (i.e., Eqs. 3). As a result, LM and KG form a bidirectional information propagation mechanism that reinforces each other.

3.6   Inference and Learning

Given a sentence s and a textualized label a, we leverage the information from both the context and the external knowledge to calculate the probability of it being the correct polarity $p(a \mid q) \propto \exp(\mathrm{MLP}(h_{glo}^{(M+N)}, v_{glo}^{(N)}, g))$, where g denotes the pooling of $\{v_k^{(N)} \mid v_k \in \mathcal{G}^{cs}\}$. The cross entropy loss is utilized to optimize the entire model in an end-to-end manner.

4   Experiment

4.1   Datasets and External Knowledge

To verify the effectiveness of KSA, we examine the model on four popular sentence-level sentiment analysis datasets. Table 1 summarizes the statistics of the datasets used in the experiments, which contain the amount of training/validation/test sets and the number of classes. The datasets include Stanford Sentiment Treebank (SST2 and SST5) [32], IMDB [33] and Movie Review (MR) [34]. For MR and IMDB, there is no validation set in the original dataset, so we randomly select a subset from the training set for validation. The accuracy of the model is used as the metric to assess its performance.

Table 1. Statistics of datasets used in our experiments.

Dataset	Amount(Train/Dev/Test)	classes
SST-2	67,349/872/1,821	2
IMDB	22,500/2,500/25,000	2
MR	8,534/1,078/1,050	2
SST-5	8,544/1,101/2,210	5

Given that our approach is adaptable to all pre-trained models of BERT-style, we opt to utilize RoBERTa [35] as the foundational framework to construct Transformer blocks in this paper. And we utilize two external sources of knowledge in our study: ConceptNet [11], a general-domain knowledge graph with 799,273 nodes and 2,487,810 edges, and moodtags from the sentiment lexicon SenticNet [13] which provides us with specific sentiment knowledge. After receiving each textual input (sentence s and textual label a), we follow the pre-processing step outlined in §3.2 to construct the CS-knowledge graph from $\mathcal{G}$, with a hop size of k = 2. We subsequently prune the CS-knowledge graph, retaining only the top 200 nodes based on their node relevance scores.

4.2   Comparison Methods

In order to demonstrate the effectiveness of the proposed method for sentence-level sentiment analysis, we compare our model with both general pre-trained models and knowledge-aware pre-trained models. For general pre-trained models, we use vanilla BERT [36], XLNet [6] and RoBERTa [35] as our baselines, which are knowledge-agnostic. For knowledge-aware pre-trained models, we adopt some methods focusing on leveraging external knowledge as baselines, i.e., SentiX [8], SentiLARE [28], SentiBERT [37], KESA [38] and SentiWSP [39]. The key difference between our model and these baseline methods is that they only incorporate one type of knowledge, while our model integrates both structured knowledge and sentiment knowledge. Additionally, they do not integrate the representations of both modalities across multiple fusion layers, thus not enabling the representations of the two modalities to affect each other (Sect. 3.5).

4.3   Implementation Details

We implement our model utilize RoBERTa as the foundational framework to construct Transformer blocks and graph attention network(GAT) as the foundational framework to construct GNN blocks. According to the experiments, the GNN module for the IMDB dataset and other datasets was set to 5 layers and 7 layers, respectively, with a dimensionality of 200. And we applied a dropout rate of 0.3 to each layer of GNN module. We train the model with the RAdam optimizer using two GPUs (NVIDIA A30). The batch size is set to 64 and 128 for IMDB and other datasets. The learning rate for the LM module is set to 1e-5 for SST2 and MR, and 5e-5 for SST5 and IMDb. And the learning rate for the GNN module is set to 1e-3. To ensure coverage of over 90% of the samples, we set the input sequence length to 512 for the IMDb dataset and 128 for other datasets. The experimental results were reported as the mean values averaged over 5 runs.

In addition, capturing multi-hop semantic relationships is one of the crucial aspects of our model's overall performance. Therefore, we conducted experimental research to investigate the impact of the number of hops. We evaluated the model's performance by varying the number of hops from 1 to 4. We found that the optimal results were obtained when using 2 or 3 hops. This could be attributed to the fact that graph neural networks with intermediate hops can effectively capture the semantic relationships between words while preventing the introduction of unnecessary noise.

4.4   Overall Results

Table 2 shows that our results improved across four datasets. We find that our base model's test performance improves by (1.11%, 0.81%, 2.64%, 2.32%) on (SST2, IMDB, MR, SST5) over LMs which are knowledge-agnostic. Furthermore, on most of the datasets, KSA has also shown improvements over the best previous model equipped with external knowledge. These results demonstrate the effectiveness of incorporating two external knowledge sources, i.e., structured KGs and sentiment lexicons. Meanwhile, it also verifies the effectiveness of the proposed global information fusion approach between LM representations and graph representations. Additionally, our proposed KSA model is highly sensitive to parameter size. Compared to the basic version, significant improvements can be achieved by increasing the model layers. Moreover, KSA-large can achieve competitive results on dataset leaderboards compared to systems with similar or even larger parameter sizes, particularly demonstrating state-of-the-art performance on SST5.

Table 2. Overall accuracy on sentence-level sentiment classification benchmarks(%). The note * means our model significantly outperforms the reproduced baselines based on t-test (p < 0.01).

Model	SST-2	IMDB	MR	SST-5
BERT	91.38	93.45	86.62	53.52
XLNet	92.75	94.99	88.83	54.95
RoBERTa	94.00	95.13	89.84	57.09
SentiX	92.23	94.62	86.81	55.59
SentiLARE	94.58	95.73	90.50	58.54
SentiBERT	94.72	94.04	88.59	56.87
KESA	94.96	95.83	91.26	59.26
SentiWSP	–	96.26	92.41	59.32
KSA (ours)	95.11	95.94	92.48	59.41
KSA-large (ours)	**96.67***	**96.42***	**93.52***	**62.17***

4.5   Ablation Results

To investigate the impact of each component on our KSA model, we perform the ablation test by separately removing the sentiment lexicon knowledge within the CS-knowledge graph (denoted as w/o Senticnet), and the modality interaction fusion unit (denoted as w/o FU). Specifically, for the w/o Senticnet model, the external knowledge is only obtained from the ConceptNet graph, and is combined with the text representations to perform sentiment polarity prediction,

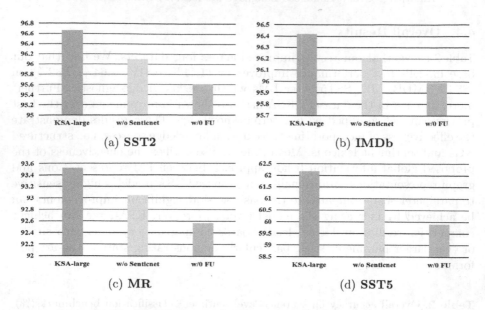

Fig. 3. Ablation study of our model components.

with a single source of knowledge. For the w/o FU model, we remove the connection of the LM to the GNN, there is not the global token h_{glo} and the global node v_{glo}, and the two modalities no longer exchange information. The external knowledge representations was encoded by GNN and combined with the LM representations for sentiment polarity analysis at the end, rather than performing multi-layers fusion. The ablation results are shown in Fig. 3. We observe that both the Senticnet and FU make great improvements to our KSA method. On the one hand, compared to simply fusing external commonsense knowledge, incorporating specific sentiment knowledge to construct heterogeneous graphs can help KSA better capture multi-hop semantic correlations between words and sentiment labels, significantly improving the model performance. On the other hand, FU helps to fully integrate external knowledge with the LM representations, promoting the learning of consistent representations between the LM and GNN, which allows the model representations to better adapt to sentiment analysis.

Based on our empirical observations, the information exchange between the LM-encoded text representations and the GNN-encoded graph representations in the fusion module is one of the most crucial parts for the overall performance of KSA. Therefore, we also studied the impact of the number of fusion module layers for this process in KSA. Specifically, we evaluated the performance of KSA by increasing the number of fusion module layers from 3 to 8 with a step size of 1. We find that the best results are achieved when N = 5 for SST2, SST5 and MR. For IMDB, the best performance was achieved when N = 7. This may be because such fusion layers strike a good balance between the complexity and efficiency of the model while achieving effective information interaction between different modalities.

4.6 Advantages and Drawbacks of Combining KGs and LMs

Combining KGs with LMs brings significant advantages, allowing for comprehensive knowledge representation. Specifically, by incorporating the structured information from KGs into LMs, we can enhance their understanding and reasoning abilities, resulting in more accurate and contextually appropriate responses. As shown in Table 2, our KSA model demonstrates significant improvement compared to LMs without integrated KGs. However, along with these benefits, it also presents challenges related to data quality and increased complexity. In terms of data quality, ensuring the accuracy and reliability of the information stored in KGs becomes paramount. Since KGs are built upon the amalgamation of data from various sources, there is a high likelihood of encountering conflicting or outdated information. This can lead to potential inaccuracies in the knowledge presented by the KG, which can then be propagated to the LMs during the fusion process. Another challenge lies in the increased complexity introduced by the integration of KGs with LMs. LMs and KGs have different ways of representing knowledge, where LMs understand natural language by learning language patterns in texts, while KGs express structured knowledge using entity-relation-entity triples. During the fusion process, it is necessary to establish an effective bridge to transform the knowledge in KGs into a format suitable for processing in LMs, or to map the language representations in LMs to entities and relations in KGs. This introduces additional complexity to the integration process. Therefore, when adopting this approach, it is essential to consider these factors. In this study, we used ConceptNet, which offers extensive and accurate knowledge, and integrated the two modalities in an appropriate manner. Although it may introduce some complexity, the overall impact is positive.

5 Conclusion

In this paper, we propose KSA, an end-to-end sentiment analysis model that leverages LMs and external knowledge. Our key innovations include (i) Constructing CS knowledge graph, which incorporates both commonsense knowledge from ConceptNet and sentiment knowledge from SenticNet, and (ii) Deep fusion of LM representations and graph representations, where we utilize fusion units to enable comprehensive interaction between the two modalities, bridging the gap between them for improving sentiment polarity prediction. Our experiments demonstrate the usefulness of both external knowledge sources in sentiment analysis task, as well as the significance of the fusion approach used in KSA.

Supplemental Material Statement: Source code and other supplemental materials for KSA are available from https://github.com/lll111000/KSA.

462   J. Li et al.

Acknowledgments. This work was supported by the National Science Foundation of China (No. U22B2019, 62276029), Beijing Academy of Artificial Intelligence (BAAI) and CCF-Zhipu.AI Large Model Fund (No. 202217).

References

1. Bing, L.: Sentiment analysis and opinion mining (synthesis lectures on human language technologies). University of Illinois, Chicago, IL, USA (2012)
2. Zhang, L., Wang, S., Liu, B.: Deep learning for sentiment analysis: a survey. Wiley Interdisc. Rev. Data Mining Knowl. Dis. **8**(4), e1253 (2018)
3. Peters, M., Neumann, M., Iyyer, M., et al.: deep contextualized word representations. In: The Conference of the North American Chapter of the Association for Computational Linguistics: Human Language Technologies, pp. 2227–2237 (2018)
4. Radford, A., Narasimhan, K., Salimans, T., et al.: Improving language understanding by generative pre-training (2018)
5. Devlin, J., Chang, M.W., Lee, K., et al.: Bert: pre-training of deep bidirectional transformers for language understanding. In: The Conference of the North American Chapter of the Association for Computational Linguistics: Human Language Technologies, pp. 4171–4186 (2019)
6. Yang, Z., Dai, Z., Yang, Y., et al.: Xlnet: generalized autoregressive pretraining for language understanding. Adv. Neural. Inf. Process. Syst. **32**, 5754–5764 (2019)
7. McCoy, R.T., Pavlick, E., Linzen, T.: Right for the wrong reasons: diagnosing syntactic heuristics in natural language inference. Annual Meeting Assoc. Comput. Ling. **57**, 3428–3448 (2019)
8. Zhou, J., Tian, J., Wang, R., et al.: Sentix: a sentiment-aware pre-trained model for cross-domain sentiment analysis. In: The 28th international conference on computational linguistics, pp. 568–579 (2020)
9. Zhang, B., Yang, M., Li, X., et al.: Enhancing cross-target stance detection with transferable semantic-emotion knowledge. In: The 58th Annual Meeting of the Association for Computational Linguistics, pp. 3188–3197 (2020)
10. Ghosal, D., Hazarika, D., Roy, A., et al.: Kingdom: knowledge-guided domain adaptation for sentiment analysis. In: The 58th Annual Meeting of the Association for Computational Linguistics, pp. 3198–3210 (2020)
11. Speer, R., Chin, J., Havasi, C.: Conceptnet 5.5: an open multilingual graph of general knowledge. In: The Association for the Advancement of Artificial Intelligence Conference on Artificial Intelligence, vol. 31(1) (2017)
12. Bollacker, K., Evans, C., Paritosh, P., et al.: Freebase: a collaboratively created graph database for structuring human knowledge. In: The Association for Computing Machinery Conference on Management of data, pp. 1247–1250 (2008)
13. Cambria, E., Poria, S., Hazarika. D, et al.: SenticNet 5: discovering conceptual primitives for sentiment analysis by means of context embeddings. In: The Association for the Advancement of Artificial Intelligence Conference on Artificial Intelligence, vol. 32(1) (2018)
14. Baccianella, S., Esuli, A., Sebastiani, F.: Sentiwordnet 3.0: an enhanced lexical resource for sentiment analysis and opinion mining. In: The 10th International Conference on Language Resources and Evaluation, pp. 2200–2204 (2010)
15. Gururangan, S., Marasovi, A., Swayamdipta, S, et al.: Don't stop pretraining: adapt language models to domains and tasks. In: The 58th Annual Meeting of the Association for Computational Linguistics, pp. 8342–8360 (2020)

16. Gu, Y., Zhang, Z., Wang, X., et al.: Train no evil: Selective masking for task-guided pre-training. In: The Conference on Empirical Methods in Natural Language Processing, pp. 6966–6974 (2020)
17. Tian, Y., Chen, G., Song, Y.: Enhancing aspect-level sentiment analysis with word dependencies. In: The 16th Conference of the European Chapter of the Association for Computational Linguistics, pp. 3726–3739 (2021)
18. Li, C., Gao, F., Bu, J., et al.: Sentiprompt: sentiment knowledge enhanced prompt-tuning for aspect-based sentiment analysis. In: Reproducibility Challenge (2022)
19. Sun, Y., Wang, S., Feng, S., et al.: Ernie 3.0: Large-scale knowledge enhanced pre-training for language understanding and generation. In: Reproducibility Challenge (2022)
20. Liu, W., Zhou, P., Zhao, Z., et al.: K-bert: enabling language representation with knowledge graph. In: The Association for the Advancement of Artificial Intelligence Conference on Artificial Intelligence, vol. 34(03), pp. 2901–2908 (2020)
21. Levine, Y., Lenz, B., Dagan, O., et al.: SenseBERT: driving some sense into BERT. In: The 58th Annual Meeting of the Association for Computational Linguistics, pp. 4656–4667 (2019)
22. Peters, M.E., Neumann, M., Logan, I.V.R. L., et al.: Knowledge enhanced contextual word representations. In: The 9th Conference on Empirical Methods in Natural Language Processing and the International Joint Conference on Natural Language Processing, pp. 43–54 (2019)
23. Wang, R., Tang, D., Duan, N., et al.: K-adapter: infusing knowledge into pre-trained models with adapters. In: The Joint Conference of the 59th Annual Meeting of the Association for Computational Linguistics and the 11th International Joint Conference on Natural Language Processing, pp. 1405–1418 (2021)
24. Zhong, Q., Ding, L., Liu, J., et al.: Knowledge graph augmented network towards multiview representation learning for aspect-based sentiment analysis. IEEE Trans. Knowl. Data Eng. (2023)
25. Yan, X., Jian, F., Sun, B.: SAKG-BERT: enabling language representation with knowledge graphs for Chinese sentiment analysis. IEEE Access 9, 101695–101701 (2021)
26. Liao, J., Wang, M., Chen, X., et al.: Dynamic commonsense knowledge fused method for Chinese implicit sentiment analysis. Inform. Process. Manag. **59**(3), 102934 (2022)
27. Tian, H., Gao, C., Xiao, X., et al.: SKEP: sentiment knowledge enhanced pre-training for sentiment analysis. In: The 58th Annual Meeting of the Association for Computational Linguistics, pp. 4067–4076 (2020)
28. Ke, P., Ji, H., Liu, S., et al.: SentiLARE: sentiment-aware language representation learning with linguistic knowledge. In: The Conference on Empirical Methods in Natural Language Processing, pp. 6975–6988 (2020)
29. Tian, Y., Chen, G., Song. Y.: Enhancing aspect-level sentiment analysis with word dependencies. In: The 16th Conference of the European Chapter of the Association for Computational Linguistics, pp. 3726–3739 (2021)
30. Li, C., Gao, F., Bu, J., et al.: Sentiprompt: sentiment knowledge enhanced prompt-tuning for aspect-based sentiment analysis. arXiv preprint arXiv:2109.08306 (2021)
31. Veličković, P., Cucurull, G., Casanova, A., et al.: Graph attention networks. In: International Conference on Learning Representations (2018)
32. Socher, R., Perelygin, A., Wu, J., et al.: Recursive deep models for semantic compositionality over a sentiment treebank. In: The Conference on Empirical Methods in Natural Language Processing, pp. 1631–1642 (2013)

33. Maas, A., Daly, R.E., Pham, P.T., et al.: Learning word vectors for sentiment analysis. In: The 49th Annual Meeting of the Association for Computational Linguistics: Human Language Technologies, pp. 142–150 (2011)
34. Pang, B., Lee, L.: Seeing stars: exploiting class relationships for sentiment categorization with respect to rating scales. In: The 43rd Annual Meeting on Association for Computational Linguistics, pp. 115–124 (2005)
35. Liu, Y., Ott, M., Goyal, N., et al.: Roberta: a robustly optimized bert pretraining approach. In: The 20th Chinese National Conference on Computational Linguistics, pp. 1218–1227 (2019)
36. Devlin, J., Chang, M.W., Lee, K., et al.: Bert: pre-training of deep bidirectional transformers for language understanding. The Conference of the North American Chapter of the Association for Computational Linguistics: Human Language Technologies, vol. 1, pp. 4171–4186 (2019)
37. Yin, D., Meng, T., Chang, K.W.: Sentibert: a transferable transformer-based architecture for compositional sentiment semantics. In: The 58th Annual Meeting of the Association for Computational Linguistics, pp. 3695–3706 (2020)
38. Zhao, Q., Ma, S., Ren, S.: KESA: a knowledge enhanced approach for sentiment analysis. In: The 2nd Conference of the Asia-Pacific Chapter of the Association for Computational Linguistics and The 12th International Joint Conference on Natural Language Processing, vol. 1, pp. 766–776 (2022)
39. Fan, S., Lin, C., Li, H., et al.: Sentiment-aware word and sentence level pre-training for sentiment analysis. In: The Conference on Empirical Methods in Natural Language Processing, pp. 4984–4994 (2022)

TEMPORALFC: A Temporal Fact Checking Approach over Knowledge Graphs

Umair Qudus[1]([✉])(iD), Michael Röder[1](iD), Sabrina Kirrane[2](iD),
and Axel-Cyrille Ngonga Ngomo[1](iD)

[1] DICE Group, Department of Computer Science, Universität Paderborn, Paderborn, Germany
{umair.qudus,michael.roeder,axel.ngonga}@uni-paderborn.de
[2] Institute for Information Systems and New Media, Vienna University of Economics and
Business, Vienna, Austria
sabrina.kirrane@wu.ac.at
https://dice-research.org

Abstract. Verifying assertions is an essential part of creating and maintaining
knowledge graphs. Most often, this task cannot be carried out manually due
to the sheer size of modern knowledge graphs. Hence, automatic fact-checking
approaches have been proposed over the last decade. These approaches aim to
compute automatically whether a given assertion is correct or incorrect. However, most fact-checking approaches are binary classifiers that fail to consider the
volatility of some assertions, i.e., the fact that such assertions are only valid at
certain times or for specific time intervals. Moreover, the few approaches able to
predict when an assertion was valid (i.e., time-point prediction approaches) rely
on manual feature engineering. This paper presents TEMPORALFC, a temporal
fact-checking approach that uses multiple sources of background knowledge to
assess the veracity and temporal validity of a given assertion. We evaluate TEM-
PORALFC on two datasets and compare it to the state of the art in fact-checking
and time-point prediction. Our results suggest that TEMPORALFC outperforms
the state of the art on the fact-checking task by 0.13 to 0.15 in terms of Area Under
the Receiver Operating Characteristic curve and on the time-point prediction task
by 0.25 to 0.27 in terms of Mean Reciprocal Rank. Our code is open-source and
can be found at https://github.com/dice-group/TemporalFC.

Keywords: temporal fact checking · ensemble learning · transfer learning ·
time-point prediction · temporal knowledge graphs

1 Introduction

The transition from an industrial civilization to an information and knowledge society during the last few decades has been fast-paced [12]. The adoption of the World
Wide Web is largely to thank for this transformation. A similar uptake of knowledge
graphs for the creation and management of knowledge has occurred in many communities around the world [19]. This uptake most certainly holds in the semantic web
community, where knowledge is commonly represented in the form of RDF knowledge graphs (KGs). The Linked Open Data Stats[1], which already holds over 9,000

---

[1] http://lodstats.aksw.org/.

© The Author(s), under exclusive license to Springer Nature Switzerland AG 2023
T. R. Payne et al. (Eds.): ISWC 2023, LNCS 14265, pp. 465–483, 2023.
https://doi.org/10.1007/978-3-031-47240-4_25

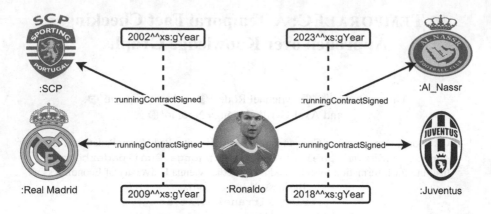

Fig. 1. A temporal knowledge graph excerpt from a large knowledge graph. The dotted line shows the time point for a given fact (in granularity of a year). Filled black lines are edges (aka predicates) with labels, and the rest are nodes of different RDF classes, which include Person, City, County, Award, and University.

KGs with more than 149 billion assertions and 3 billion entities, further supports the growing adoption of the Resource Description Framework (RDF) at Web scale [13]. WikiData [34], DBpedia [2], Knowledge Vault [11], and YAGO [48] are examples of large-scale KGs that include billions of assertions and describe millions of entities. They are used as background information in an increasing number of applications, such as in-flight entertainment [34], autonomous chatbots [1], and healthcare [27]. However, current KGs may not be fully correct. for instance, the literature assumes that roughly 20% of DBpedia's claims are erroneous [19,43]. To encourage the further adoption of KGs on a large scale on the Web, approaches that can automatically forecast the truthfulness of the assertions included in KGs must be developed. Such methods are what we refer to as fact-checking approaches.

There are several fact-checking approaches designed to verify assertions in KGs and compute their veracity scores [19,23,49–51]. However, assertions can be volatile and the majority of existing approaches do not take any temporal aspects into account. For example, Fig. 1, which we use as a running example in this paper, shows that the assertion (:Ronaldo, :runningContractSigned, :SCP) is not accurate without information about the year since :Ronaldo also signed contracts with other teams at later points in time[2]. Ergo, temporal information is critical for validating volatile assertions. However, very little attention has been given to the temporal aspect of KGs when dealing with the task at hand. Temporal-DeFacto [19] is at the time of writing the only temporal fact-checking method that looks at this aspect of KGs along with their verification. However, Temporal-DeFacto relies on tedious manual feature engineering [19,50], which has been shown to be sub-optimal w.r.t. their prediction per-

---

[2] From here on, we work with IRIs. The prefixes for these IRIs that we use are "xs" and ":". The xmlns schema is identified by the URI-Reference http://www.w3.org/2001/XMLSchema/# and is associated with the prefix 'xs'. Furthermore, we use ":" prefix for literals.

formance by representation learning approaches [4]. The approaches T-TRANSE [30], T-COMPLEX [6] and T-DYHE [35] from the knowledge base completion domain concentrate on time-point prediction as well. These approaches focus on the time prediction task and encounter limitations with respect to their Mean Reciprocal Rank (MRR) scores as well as their scalability. Furthermore, they do not consider the fact-checking aspect [35].

We alleviate the limitations of the aforementioned approaches by proposing a neural network-based approach that utilizes transfer learning (i.e., it uses pre-trained embeddings created from a Temporal Knowledge Graph TKG) for fact-checking and time-point prediction tasks. Since temporal information is also critical, our system predicts the year in which an assertion was true, along with its veracity score. For example, if an assertion (:Ronaldo, :runningContractSigned, :SCP) is given as input, our system not only validates the statement, it also predicts the year in which the assertion was true.

The main contributions of our work are as follows:

– We employ transfer learning to repurpose pre-trained TKG embeddings for the fact-checking and time-point prediction tasks.
– We present an open-source neural network-based approach for detecting the temporal scope of assertions.
– We evaluate our approach on two datasets—DBpedia124K and Yago3K—and compare it to the state of the art of time-point prediction and temporal fact-checking tasks. Our approach outperforms other approaches in the time-point prediction task by 0.25 and 0.27 MRR and temporal fact-checking task by 0.13 to 0.15 in terms of Area Under the Receiver Operating Characteristic curve (AUROC).

The rest of this paper is organized as follows. The notations necessary to comprehend the remainder of the paper are introduced in Sect. 2. In Sect. 3, we provide an overview of the related work. We present our proposed approach in Sect. 4. After that, Sect. 5 describes the experimental setup. The results are discussed in Sect. 6. In Sect. 7, we conclude and discuss potential future work.

2 Preliminaries

Fact checking and related terms have a variety of definitions that come from different fields, such as journalism [25,26,32], natural language processing [38], and KGs [29, 44,52]. We adopt the definition of fact-checking for KGs provided in [50] as follows:

Definition 1 (Fact Checking). *Fact checking implies calculating the likelihood that an assertion is true or false in the presence of a reference KG $\mathcal{G}$, and/or a reference corpus* [50].

We utilize RDF TKGs throughout the entirety of this work.

Definition 2 (Temporal Knowledge Graph (TKG)). *A TKG $\mathcal{TG}$ is a collection of RDF quadruples $\mathcal{TG} \subseteq (\mathbb{E} \cup \mathbb{B}) \times \mathbb{P} \times (\mathbb{E} \cup \mathbb{B} \cup \mathbb{L}) \times \mathbb{T}$, where each quadruple $(s, p, o, t) \in \mathcal{TG}$ consists of a subject (s), a predicate (p), an object (o), and a time*

Table 1. Scoring functions of different embedding-based approaches used in this paper. $*$ stands for the Dihedron multiplication, $\otimes$ stands for the quaternion multiplication, $\mathbb{R}$ for the space of real numbers, $\mathbb{H}$ *for the space of quaternions,* $\mathbb{D}$ *for the space of Dihedrons,* $\mathbb{C}$ for the complex numbers, Re for the real part of a complex number, $<>$ for componentwise multi-linear dot product e.g., $< a, b, c >:= \sum_k a_k b_k c_k$, conv for the convolution operator, $\overline{\varphi(\text{o})}$ for the complex conjugate of $\varphi(\text{o})$, q is the length of embedding vectors, and $\|\cdot\|_2$ for the L2 norm.

	Approach	Scoring function	Vector space
TKGE	T-TRANSE	$-\|(\varphi(s) + \varphi(p) + \varphi(t)) - \varphi(o)\|_2$	$\varphi(s), \varphi(p), \varphi(o), \varphi(t) \in \mathbb{R}^q$
	T-COMPLEX	Re $\left(< \varphi(s), \varphi(p), \varphi(t), \overline{\varphi(o)} > \right)$	$\varphi(s), \varphi(p), \varphi(t), \varphi(o) \in \mathbb{C}^q$
	T-DYHE	$-\|\varphi(s) * \varphi(p)_{1,2} + \varphi(t) - \varphi(o)\|_2$	$\varphi(s), \varphi(p)_{1,2}, \varphi(t), \varphi(o) \in \mathbb{D}^q$
KGE	TRANSE	$\|(\varphi(s) + \varphi(p)) - \varphi(o)\|_2$	$\varphi(s), \varphi(p), \varphi(o) \in \mathbb{R}^q$
	COMPLEX	Re $\left(< \varphi(s), \varphi(p), \overline{\varphi(o)} > \right)$	$\varphi(s), \varphi(p), \varphi(o) \in \mathbb{C}^q$
	QMULT	$\varphi(s) \otimes \varphi(p) \cdot \varphi(o)$	$\varphi(s), \varphi(p), \varphi(o) \in \mathbb{H}^q$
	CONEX	Re($\langle\text{conv}(\varphi(s), \varphi(p)), \varphi(s), \varphi(p), \overline{\varphi(o)}\rangle$)	$\varphi(s), \varphi(p), \varphi(o) \in \mathbb{C}^q$

point (t). $\mathbb{E}$ *is the set of all RDF resource IRIs (Internationalized Resource Identifier),* $\mathbb{P} \subseteq \mathbb{E}$ *is the set of all RDF predicates,* $\mathbb{L}$ *is the set of all literals,* $\mathbb{B}$ *is the set of all blank nodes, and* $\mathbb{T}$ *is the set of all time points* [35,51].

In this study, we treat each year as a single point in time. The time-point prediction is defined as follows:

Definition 3 (Time-point prediction). *Given an assertion (s, p, o), the task of time-point prediction is to predict the time-point t to form a correct quadruple (s, p, o, t), where t is a specific point in time that represents the occurrence of a predicate p with respect to s and o* [35].

In our running example, a time-point prediction algorithm should predict 2002 for the assertion (:Ronaldo, :runningContractSigned, :SCP).

Definition 4 (Temporal Knowledge Graph Embeddings (TKGE)). *A TKGE embedding function* φ *maps a* $\mathcal{TG}$ *to a continuous vector space. Given a quadruple (s, p, o, t),* $\varphi(s)$*,* $\varphi(p)$*,* $\varphi(o)$*, and* $\varphi(t)$ *stand for the embedding of the subject, predicate, object, and time point, respectively* [28].

Different knowledge graph embedding (KGE) and temporal knowledge graph embedding -based approaches use different scoring functions to compute embeddings [54]. The approaches considered in this paper are shown in Table 1.

3   Related Work

The research covered in this paper relates to two key areas of study: fact checking and time-point prediction of assertions in KGs. The most recent methods in each area are briefly described below, along with their limitations.

3.1 Fact Checking

The goal of fact checking is to determine which subset of a given set of assertions from a KG may be trusted [39]. Fact-checking approaches can broadly be divided into three categories: those that utilize unstructured textual sources [19,50], those that utilize structured information sources [23,49,51], and those that are hybrid and use both [41].

In the first category, approaches validate a given assertion by searching evidence in a reference text corpus. There are two examples of this category: FactCheck [50] and DeFacto [19]. Both approaches are based on RDF verbalization techniques to find textual excerpts that can be used as evidence for the stated assertion. Both approaches compute a vector representation of the texts they retrieve as evidence based on a set of manually created features.

In the second category, there are three sub-categories of approaches: 1. path-based, 2. rule-based, and 3. embedding-based. By automatically computing short paths from the subject of the assertion to its object inside the reference KG, path-based approaches seek to validate the input assertion. The input assertion is then scored using these paths. Most path-based approaches, like COPAAL [51], Knowledge stream [45], PRA [18], SFE [17], and KG-Miner [44], filter out meaningful paths using RDF semantics (e.g., class subsumption hierarchy, domain and range information). However, the T-Box of several KGs provides a limited number of RDFS statements. Furthermore, no short paths may be found within the reference KG, although the assertion is correct [51]. In these situations, path-based approaches fall short of accurately predicting whether the provided assertion is true. Rule-based approaches such as KV-Rule [23], AMIE [14, 15,29], OP [7], and RuDiK [37] extract association rules from KGs to perform the fact-checking task. These approaches are constrained by the knowledge found in the KG, and mining rules from huge KGs can be a long and tedious process (e.g., OP takes $\geq$45 h on DBpedia [29]). Embedding-based approaches express the input KG in a continuous high-dimensional vector space via a mapping function [5,10,21,31,46,53]. For example, Esther [46] computes likely paths between resources using compositional embeddings. By developing a KG embedding model and learning a scoring function, the veracity of these statements is computed. In general, the information included in the continuous representation of the KG is the fundamental constraint on embedding-based techniques. Ergo, when used with large-scale KGs, these approaches have limitations in terms of both their scalability and accuracy in fact-checking scenarios.

The third category is more pertinent to the work presented herein. To the best of our knowledge, the only state-of-the-art hybrid approach that takes full advantage of the variety of available fact-checking approach categories in an ensemble learning environment is called HybridFC [41]. By integrating the aforementioned categories of approaches, HybridFC seeks to address the issues of: 1. manual feature engineering in text-based approaches, 2. circumstances when paths between subjects and objects are not available to path-based approaches, and 3. the poor performance of pure KG-embedding-based approaches. However, HybridFC does not use time information along with the assertions in a TKG. In comparison, TEMPORALFC overcomes this limitation.

3.2 Time-Point Prediction

Knowledge Graphs (KGs) with an added temporal component are the focus of Temporal Knowledge Graph Embedding (TKGE) models. Quadruples are created from a triple-based representation. The majority of the early TKGE models were constructed on top of KGEs that already existed. One of the first TKGEs to project the subject, predicate, and object embeddings to a time space is the HyTE [8] model. HyTE uses TRANSE on the projected embeddings for the final scoring of the newly predicted facts. T-TRANSE [30] and TA-TRANSE [16] are two further TKGEs that have been proposed as expansions of TRANSE. The ConT model, which is an extension of the Tucker [3] KGE, is the other cutting-edge approach among TKGEs. For the encoding of TKGs, a number of adaptations to DistMult [57] have also been proposed, including TDist-Mult [33] and TA-DistMult [16]. Recurrent neural networks (RNNs) are the foundation of these models, and they capture the entity embeddings for the subject and object entities. Another RNN-based TKGE called RE-NET uses unique patterns from historical data between entities to capture pair-wise knowledge in the form of (subject, predicate) or (object, predicate) pairs [22]. The main difficulty with these models is that they carry over the flaws of the base models upon which they are built. For instance, the TKGEs that were constructed on top of TRANSE have problems encoding relational patterns. Recently, the TeRo model [56] was developed to address these issues with the pre-existing TKGEs regarding the inference of relational patterns. TeRo partially overcomes some of the limitations of other models; however, it does not focus on time-point prediction in TKGEs. Instead, it uses the time dimension solely for a better relation prediction. The T-COMPLEX model [6] is the temporal iteration of the COMPLEX-N3 model, which achieves better results in the relation prediction task compared with the previous approaches. For learning and predicting time-points, the DYHE embedding model uses dihedron algebra. Dihedron algebra is a rich 4D algebra of hyper-complex spaces. To the best of our knowledge, DYHE is the only approach for which the authors report the results of the time-point prediction task.

Our proposed approach performs both tasks—fact checking and time-point prediction—for a given assertion. To the best of our knowledge, Temporal-DeFacto [19] is the only state-of-the-art approach that covers both tasks as well.

4 Methodology

We propose TEMPORALFC, an approach that addresses the fact-checking and time-point prediction tasks. It takes the quadruple of a TKG as input and comprises three components as depicted in Fig. 2. First, a pre-trained `TKGE model` is used to generate TKGE vectors of the input quadruple. Second, a `fact-checking` component classifies the (s, p, o) part of the quadruple as true or false. *We designed this fact-checking component as an extension of HybridFC and,* in contrast to the related work, our component takes all 4 TKGE vectors from the first component into account. If an assertion is classified as true, the (s, p, o) TKGE vectors of the input quadruple are used as input for the third `time-point prediction` component. The `time-point prediction` component comprises a neural network, which predicts the year in which the given assertion should be true. *Our ensemble of the two latter components is in line with the task definition of Temporal-DeFacto [19], i.e., our approach checks whether the assertion is true at any point in time and then performs the time-point prediction task for the given assertion.* We describe all these components in more detail in the following.

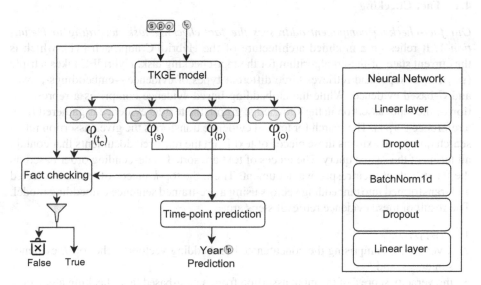

Fig. 2. Left: Overview of the architecture of TEMPORALFC. Right: A multi-layer perceptron module (ϑ_i) that is used in the fact-checking and the time-point prediction components of TEMPORALFC.

4.1 TKGE Model

We use pre-trained temporal embedding vectors, which are generated from a given TKGE model, in our approach. Given a quadruple (s, p, o, t), φ(s), φ(o), φ(p), and φ(t) stand for the embedding of the subject, predicate, object, and time point, respectively. Initially, we form an embedding vector for a given quadruple (s, p, o, t) by concatenating the embedding of its first three elements and defining the embedding mapping function φ(s,p,o) for assertions (s, p, o) as follows [41]:

$$\varphi(s,p,o) = \varphi(s) \oplus \varphi(p) \oplus \varphi(o),   \tag{1}$$

where $\oplus$ stands for the concatenation of vectors. φ(s,p,o) is used in both of the following components, while the time embedding vector φ(t) is only used in the fact-checking component.

From our running example, given (:Ronaldo, :runningContractSigned, :SCP, 2002) as input quadruple, we first gather the embedding of each component using a pre-trained TKGE model. In the next step, we transform the embeddings of φ(:Ronaldo), φ(:runningContractSigned), and φ(:SCP) into a concatenated embedding vector $\varphi($ `:Ronaldo`, `:runningContractSigned`, `:SCP`), which is the input to both the `time-point-prediction` and the `fact-checking` components. The `fact-checking` component utilizes $\varphi(2002)$ as an additional input.

4.2 Fact Checking

Our fact-checking component addresses the fact-checking task according to Definition 1. It relies on a modified architecture of the HybridFC approach [41], which is the current state-of-the-art algorithm for the fact-checking task. HybridFC takes a triple (s, p, o) as input and retrieves three different types of evidence—embeddings-, text-, and $\mathcal{G}$-based evidence. While the embedding-based evidence comprises a representation of the input assertion in the knowledge graph, the textual evidence is gathered from a reference corpus. The search for textual evidence transforms the given assertion into a search query and extracts those pieces of text from the retrieved documents that contain all terms of the search query. The pieces of text are sorted in descending order based on the PageRank of their respective document. Then, the top-k pieces of text are selected and transformed into embedding vectors using a pre-trained sentence embedding model. The result of these evidence retrieval steps are:

1. $\varphi($ s , p , o $)$,
2. a vector $\varphi_\aleph$ comprising the concatenated embedding vectors of the top-k evidence sentences, and
3. the veracity score ζ of the input assertion from a path-based fact-checking algorithm.

From our running example, $\varphi($ `:Ronaldo`, `:runningContractSigned`, `:SCP` $)$ is the embedding-based evidence retrieval output. An example for a textual evidence could be "Ronaldo began his senior career with Sporting CP (SCP)" retrieved from the reference corpus as one of the outputs for the given triple and transformed into an embedding vector. This vector is concatenated with the embedding vectors of other pieces of textual evidence to form $\varphi_\aleph$. The $\mathcal{G}$-based evidence retrieval utilizes an existing path-based approach. Such an approach searches for paths between `:Ronaldo` and `:SCP` in the reference $\mathcal{G}$ and utilizes them to calculate a single veracity score ζ. For example, COPAAL [51] returns a veracity score of 0.69 for the given triple based on DBpedia as reference graph.

Furthermore, HybridFC contains 3 multi-layer perceptron modules (ϑ_1, ϑ_2 and, ϑ_3). Each of the three multi-layer perceptron modules (ϑ_i) is defined as follows for an input vector x:

$$\vartheta_i = W_{5,i} \times D(ReLU(W_{3,i} \times (BN(W_{1,i} \times x)))), \tag{2}$$

where $W_{j,i}$ is the weight matrix of an affine transformation in the j-th layer of the multi-layer perceptron, ReLU is an activation function, D stands for a Dropout layer [55], $\times$ represents the matrix multiplication, and BN represents the Batch Normalization [20]. The Batch Normalization and Dropout layers are defined as follows.

Given $x\prime$ as input, the batch normalization is formally defined as:

$$BN(x') = \beta + \gamma \frac{x' - \mathrm{E}[x']}{\sqrt{\mathrm{Var}[x']}}, \tag{3}$$

where, $E[x']$ and $Var[x']$ are the expected value and variance of x', respectively. β and γ are weight vectors, which are learned during the training process via backpropagation to increase the accuracy [20].

Given x as input to the Dropout layer D, the elements of the layer's output vector $\bar{x}$ are computed as:

$$\bar{x}_i = \delta_i x_i, \tag{4}$$

where each δ_i is sampled from a Bernoulli distribution with parameter r, i.e., δ is 1 with probability r, and 0 otherwise.

In our approach, we add a fourth input vector that comprises the embedding vectors of a pre-trained TKGE model of the given quadruple. After adding the time embeddings $\varphi(t)$, the resultant equation of the final neural network component of HybridFC is as follows:

$$\omega = \sigma\left(w_\sigma^T \vartheta_3\left(\vartheta_1(\varphi_\aleph) \oplus \vartheta_2(\varphi(s,p,o) \oplus \zeta \oplus \varphi(t)))\right)\right), \tag{5}$$

where ω is the final veracity score of our fact-checking part, $\oplus$ stands for the concatenation of vectors, and w_σ is a weight vector that is multiplied with the output vector of the third module ϑ_3. For the given quadruple from our running example, we input $\varphi(2002)$ as the fourth input, and the fact-checking component was able to correctly classify it by producing the final veracity score of 0.95.

4.3 Time-Point Prediction

The time-point prediction component predicts the time-point in a certain range of years to form a correct quadruple (s, p, o, t) from the given assertion (s, p, o). The output concatenated vector $\varphi(s,p,o)$ of the first component is fed as input to a multi-layer perceptron. This multi-layer perceptron consists of a Linear Layer, a Dropout layer, a Batch Normalization layer, a second Dropout layer, and a final Linear layer. It can be formalized as follows:

$$\gamma(s,p,o) = W_5 \times D(BN(D(W_1 \times \varphi(s,p,o)))). \tag{6}$$

$\gamma(s,p,o)$ is a vector of size n, where n is the number of years in the targeted range of years. This vector is normalized to transform its values into probabilities and the vector into a distribution. The year with the highest predicted probability is returned as the predicted year and is the final output for the time-point prediction task. In our running example, for the given assertion (:Ronaldo, :runningContractSigned, :SCP), our time-prediction component predicts the correct year as 2002.

5 Experiments

Our evaluation has two objectives: we want to measure TEMPORALFC's abilities to a) discern between true and false assertions, and b) identify the appropriate point in time for a given, true assertion. In the following, we describe the experiment designs.

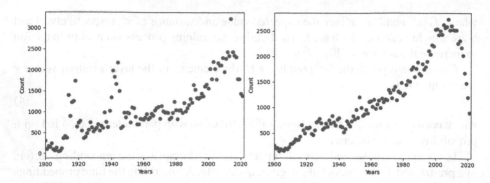

Fig. 3. The distribution of quadruples over years for the training sets of DBpedia124k (left) and Yago3k (right).

Table 2. Overview of updated DBpedia124k and Yago3k datasets used in experiments; the abbreviations are: Q/Quadruples, Ent./Entities, Rel./Relations, Tim./Time stamps, | . |/count.

Dataset	|Train-Q|	|Valid-Q|	|Test-Q|	|Ent.|	|Rel.|	|Tim.|
DBpedia124k	145k	44k	44k	124k	7	123
Yago3k	7k	2k	2k	3k	8	195

5.1 Datasets

We reuse two TKGs, DBpedia124k and Yago3k, from [35]. Due to the small size and incorrect IRIs in the original datasets, we update it by running the queries used to generate these datasets again on recent versions of the DBpedia and Yago datasets. Due to the Temporal-DeFacto requirement and, consequently, to ensure a fair comparison, we filtered all quadruples and kept those with year information between 1900 and 2022. We dubbed the resultant dataset with DBpedia124k and Yago3k due to the number of entities present in them. The statistics of the resultant datasets are shown in Table 2. Furthermore, we do not use the FactBench dataset [19] because it is based on older versions of DBpedia (i.e., 2013-10) and Freebase (i.e., 2013-08), which contain many entities (650/1813) for which $\mathcal{TG}$ model failed to produce embedding vectors.[3]

Our fact-checking component makes use of a reference corpus. We created this corpus by extracting the plain text snippets from all English Wikipedia articles and loading them into an Elasticsearch instance.[4] We use the English Wikipedia dump from March 7th, 2022. For the Elasticsearch index, we use a cluster of 3 nodes with a combined storage of 1 TB and 32 GB RAM per node. Figure 3 shows the frequency of time points for the DBpedia124k and Yago3k train sets.

The process of generating negative examples for the fact-checking task requires more effort than generating positive examples [19]. For the purpose of examining the contribution of the assertion (s, p, o) part of the quadruple and the time-point (t) part

---

[3] Fair comparison could not be possible with missing entities, which constitute many assertions.
[4] https://www.elastic.co/.

of the quadruple in the overall result, we generated two sets of negative examples: 1. The assertion-based negative example set is generated using the same strategy as defined in [28]. 2. The time-point-based negative example set is generated by randomly replacing time points as suggested in [19].

5.2 Evaluation Metrics

We use common measures to evaluate the performance of the different approaches on the two tasks. When evaluating the fact-checking task, we rely on the area under the receiver operator characteristic curve (AUROC) [23,50,51]. We use the GERBIL framework to calculate this score [36,40].

The time prediction task is based on queries of the form (s, p, o, ?), which are generated by removing the correct time point t from a set of test quadruples. The evaluated systems predict scores for all years that we have within our dataset. We rank the years according to the predicted scores and use the MRR, Hits@1, and Hits@3 to determine the ranking quality. In addition, we use the accuracy metric of multi-class classification to measure system performance in cases where only the highest-ranked year is considered.

5.3 Setup Details and Reproducibility

TEMPORALFC is designed to work with any pre-trained TKGE model to generate embedding vectors. *However, throughout our experiments, we solely use pre-trained embedding models because training large embedding models has a high footprint in terms of cost, energy, and CO_2 emissions* [47]. Within our evaluation, we use a pre-trained T-DYHE model, since this approach has been reported to outperform other approaches for the time-point prediction task [35]. The size of each embedding vector is set to $q = 100$. The range of years is between 1900 and 2022.[5] The loss functions for training our multi-layer perceptron are the *Binary Cross Entropy Loss* for the fact-checking task and the *Cross Entropy Loss* for the time-point prediction task. *We chose the Binary Cross Entropy Loss because it is widely used for binary classification and is well-suited for models with a sigmoid activation function in the output layer* [41,46,51]. *We chose the Cross Entropy Loss for analogous reasons on multi-class classification* [8,33]. With a batch size equal to one third of the training data, we set the maximum number of epochs to 1000. We calculate the validation loss after every 10th epoch and stop the training earlier if the loss is not reduced for 50 epochs to avoid overfitting.[6] Throughout our experiments, we use Adam [24] optimizer. For the fact-checking component, we use a pre-trained SBert model for sentence vector gener-

---

[5] https://doi.org/10.5281/zenodo.7913193.

[6] We report the parameters that were used to achieve the results reported in this study. Nevertheless, the user has the option to modify these parameters to suit her personal preferences. Visit the project home page to get the complete list of parameters.

Table 3. Area under the curve (AUROC) score on DBpedia124k and Yago3k train sets; the abbreviations are: Text/Text-based approaches, E./Example, Neg./negative, Path/Path-based approaches, Hybrid/Hybrid approaches, Gen./Generation, Avg./Average. Best performances are bold, second-best are underlined.

		Assertion-based Neg. E. Gen.			Time-based Neg. E. Gen.		
		DBpedia124k	Yago3k	Avg.	DBpedia124k	Yago3k	Avg.
Text	FactCheck [50]	0.69	0.66	0.67	<u>0.55</u>	<u>0.53</u>	<u>0.54</u>
	Temporal-DeFacto [19]	0.67	0.64	0.65	0.53	0.51	0.52
KG-emb	TRANSE [5]	0.71	0.78	0.75	0.50	0.50	0.50
	CONEX [10]	0.80	0.81	0.80	0.50	0.50	0.50
	COMPLEX [53]	0.72	0.70	0.71	0.50	0.50	0.50
	QMULT [9]	0.73	0.77	0.75	0.50	0.50	0.50
Hybrid	HybridFC [41]	<u>0.92</u>	<u>0.94</u>	<u>0.93</u>	0.50	0.50	0.50
	TEMPORALFC	**0.93**	**0.97**	**0.95**	**0.68**	**0.65**	**0.66**
Path	KV-Rule [23]	0.58	0.61	0.59	0.50	0.50	0.50
	COPAAL [51]	0.65	0.67	0.66	0.50	0.50	0.50

ation.[7] Furthermore, we set $k = 3$ in the sentence selection module. SBert generates sentence embedding vectors of 768, which leads to $|\varphi_{\aleph}| = (3 \times 768) + 3 = 2307$.[8]

All experiments are executed on a computer with 32 CPU cores, 128 GB of RAM, and an NVIDIA GeForce RTX 3090. For the sake of reproducibility, we uploaded scripts for hyperparameter optimization, training, and evaluation to our project home-page.

5.4 Competing Approaches

We compare our approach TEMPORALFC with HybridFC [41], FactCheck [50], Temporal-DeFacto [19], COPAAL [51], and KV-Rule [23], which are the state-of-the-art approaches in the hybrid, text-, path-, and rule-based categories of the fact-checking task. We also compare our results to the four KG embedding-based approaches TRANSE, CONEX, COMPLEX, and QMULT, which show the most effective performance for the fact-checking tasks [41].

For the time-point prediction task, we compare our approach with Temporal-DeFacto and the top-performing temporal embedding-based approaches: T-DYHE [35], T-TRANSE [30], and T-COMPLEX [28]. For the embedding-based approaches, we use the parameter configuration reported in [35].

---

[7] Among all the available pre-training models from the SBert webpage (https://www.sbert.net/docs/pretrained_models.html), we select nq-distilbert-base-v1 for our approach (as suggested in [41]).

[8] *We ran experiments with other values of k, i.e., 1, 2, 3, and 5 and found that $k = 3$ worked best for our approach. We cannot present comprehensive results in this paper due to space limitations. However, they can be found in our extended, green open-access version of the paper.*

6   Results and Discussion

In this section, we discuss the results we obtained in our evaluation. All results along with the scripts to reproduce the results are also available at the project homepage. First, we evaluate TEMPORALFC on the fact-checking task. Thereafter, we compare and evaluate the time-point prediction task with the state-of-the-art approaches.

Table 4. Area under the curve (AUROC) score on DBpedia124k and Yago3k test sets; the abbreviations are: Text/Text-based approaches, E./Example, Neg./negative, Path/Path-based approaches, Hybrid/Hybrid approaches, Gen./Generation, Avg./Average. Best performances are bold, second-best are underlined.

		Assertion-based Neg. E. Gen.			Time-based Neg. E. Gen.		
		DBpedia124k	Yago3k	Avg.	DBpedia124k	Yago3k	Avg.
Text	FactCheck [50]	0.69	0.66	0.67	<u>0.52</u>	<u>0.53</u>	<u>0.52</u>
	Temporal-DeFacto [19]	0.64	0.66	0.65	0.51	0.51	0.51
KG-emb	TRANSE [5]	0.74	<u>0.74</u>	0.74	0.50	0.50	0.50
	CONEX [10]	0.78	0.74	0.76	0.50	0.50	0.50
	COMPLEX [53]	0.74	0.70	0.72	0.50	0.50	0.50
	QMULT [9]	0.71	0.73	0.72	0.50	0.50	0.50
Hybrid	HybridFC [41]	<u>0.88</u>	**0.92**	<u>0.90</u>	0.50	0.50	0.50
	TEMPORALFC	**0.91**	**0.92**	**0.91**	**0.65**	**0.65**	**0.65**
Path	KV-Rule [23]	0.54	0.56	0.55	0.50	0.50	0.50
	COPAAL [51]	0.65	0.69	0.67	0.50	0.50	0.50

6.1   Fact Checking

Tables 3 and 4 show the results for the fact-checking task on the training and test data, respectively. In comparison to other approaches, hybrid approaches perform best.[9]

This is expected since hybrid approaches combine aspects of different categories of approaches. Among both of the hybrid approaches, TEMPORALFC performs slightly better (Avg. 0.02–0.03 on AUROC scores) than HybridFC on the DBpedia124k dataset, when using assertion-based negative examples in our dataset.[10] A potential reason for this small improvement could be that the additional temporal embeddings add more context to the data and, thus, the performance of the model increases.

When using time-based negative quadruples, TEMPORALFC outperforms other approaches by at least 0.12 AUROC on the train set and 0.13 AUROC on the test set.

---

[9] Our results are also available on the GERBIL benchmarking platform [42]: 1. Using assertion-based negative examples: http://w3id.org/gerbil/kbc/experiment?id=202301180129, http://w3id.org/gerbil/kbc/experiment?id=202301180056,   http://w3id.org/gerbil/kbc/experiment?id=202301180123, and http://w3id.org/gerbil/kbc/experiment?id=202301180125. 2. Using time-based negative examples: http://w3id.org/gerbil/kbc/experiment?id=202305020014, http://w3id.org/gerbil/kbc/experiment?id=202305020015,   http://w3id.org/gerbil/kbc/experiment?id=202305020012, and http://w3id.org/gerbil/kbc/experiment?id=202305020013.

[10] We use a Wilcoxon signed rank test with a significance threshold $\alpha = 0.05$.

Table 5. Results for the time-point prediction task on the DBpedia124k and Yago3k test datasets.

		MRR	Accuracy	Hits@1	Hits@3
DBpedia124k	Temporal-DeFacto [19]	0.16	0.10	0.17	0.19
	T-DyHE [35]	0.43	0.44	0.14	0.62
	T-TransE [30]	0.26	0.25	0.08	0.10
	T-ComplEx [28]	0.24	0.21	0.13	0.17
	TemporalFC	**0.70**	**0.66**	**0.65**	**0.71**
Yago3k	Temporal-DeFacto [19]	0.11	0.05	0.01	0.12
	T-DyHE [35]	0.58	0.56	0.24	**0.90**
	T-TransE [30]	0.24	0.25	0.02	0.13
	T-ComplEx [28]	0.21	0.20	0.17	0.19
	TemporalFC	**0.83**	**0.79**	**0.78**	0.86

This difference is also due to the fact that most other approaches do not consider the temporal aspect of quadruples. Therefore, their classifiers do not consider temporal information during the training phase. *We use these negative examples to evaluate the potential performance that the fact-checking component would have if the fact-checking task would take time into account.* We modified the behavior of FactCheck and Defacto to include the temporal aspect as well, by including time-points in their search queries to the reference corpus. However, our results in Tables 3 and 4 show that the benefit of using the temporal aspect is not pertinent for FactCheck and Defacto.

During the training phase, we observe that our approach needs more epochs (e.g., 989 for DBpedia124k) than the comparable non-temporal approach HybridFC (479 epochs for DBpedia124k). This is most probably caused by the larger input vectors of the temporal embeddings.

The text-based approaches rely on the reference corpus as background knowledge. A look into the details of their output reveals that these approaches failed to find relevant evidence for 70% of the assertions, resulting in lower performance than hybrid or KG-based approaches for assertion-based negative sampling-based datasets. KG-embedding-based approaches achieve relatively better performance than text- and path-based approaches. In fact, ConEx is the third best performing system, followed by QMult, TransE, and ComplEx. Our results also show that KV-Rule performs worse among all competing approaches. This behavior of KV-Rule could be due to the fact that the pre-generated rule set is biased towards certain properties of the DBpedia dataset. Hence, for unknown properties the performance degrades. After the KV-Rule, COPAAL has the second-worst AUROC scores. It might be because COPAAL fails to find paths for the properties of our dataset and performs better on other properties [41]. These experimental findings imply that our strategy effectively utilizes the performance variability of the approaches it comprises. It appears to rely on KG-embedding-based approach's strong performance in particular. However, it also has the ability to supplement KG-embedding-based approach's predictions with those of other categories of approaches, in cases in which KG-embedding-based approach does not perform well.

6.2 Time-Point Prediction

Table 5 shows the results of the time-point prediction experiment. The results show that TEMPORALFC significantly outperforms all competing approaches in MRR by at least 0.27 and 0.25, Accuracy by at least 0.22 and 0.23, and Hit@1 by at least 0.48 and 0.54 on the DBpedia124k and Yago3k datasets, respectively. Temporal-DeFacto, TEMPORALFC's closest competitor, performs worst in terms of MRR and Accuracy as compared to all other systems. A closer look at the results reveals two main reasons for the low performance of Temporal-DeFacto. First, it fails to extract pieces of evidence for around 30% of quadruples ($43.5k/145k$ on DBpedia124k and $2k/7k$ on Yago3k). Second, its manual feature engineering seems to be optimized for the Fact-Bench dataset [19] proposed by the authors. T-DYHE is the second best performing embedding-based approach after TEMPORALFC, scoring MRR of 0.43 and 0.58 on DBpedia124k and Yago3k datasets respectively. On the Yago3k dataset, it performs better than TEMPORALFC on Hit@3 scores.

7 Conclusion

In this study, we propose TEMPORALFC—a hybrid method for temporal fact-checking for knowledge graphs. The goal of TEMPORALFC is to address two key issues: 1. most fact checking approaches do not take the volatility of some assertions into account and 2. those that do only achieve a low performance in the time-point prediction task. In both fact-checking and time-prediction tasks, we evaluate TEMPORALFC against the current state of the art. Our findings on two datasets imply that our TEMPORALFC approach can outperform competing approaches in both fact-checking and time-point prediction tasks. In particular, on the fact-checking task TEMPORALFC achieves an Area Under the Receiver Operating Characteristic curve that is 0.13 and 0.15 higher than the best competing approaches for volatile assertions, while it achieves the same or an even slightly superior performance as the current state-of-the-art approach HybridFC for non-volatile assertions. In the time-point prediction task, TEMPORALFC outperforms all other approaches in our evaluation by at least 0.25 to 0.27 Mean Reciprocal Rank.

   In future work, we will enhance TEMPORALFC to support time-period-based assertions in $\mathcal{TG}$. In addition, we plan to extend the fact-checking component to include rule-based approaches.

Supplemental Material Statement

– The source code of TEMPORALFC, the scripts to recreate the full experimental setup, and the required libraries can be found on GitHub.[11]

• The datasets used in this paper, the pre-trained embeddings for these datasets, the prediction files, and AUROC graphs are available on our HOBBIT data server: https://files.dice-research.org/datasets/ISWC2023_TemporalFC/.

---

[11] Source code: https://github.com/dice-group/TemporalFC.

Acknowledgments. This work is part of a project that has received funding from the European Union's Horizon 2020 research and innovation programme under the Marie Skłodowska-Curie grant agreement No 860801, the German Federal Ministry of Education and Research (BMBF) within the project NEBULA under the grant no 13N16364, the Ministry of Culture and Science of North Rhine-Westphalia (MKW NRW) within the project SAIL under the grant no NW21-059D, and the European Union's Horizon Europe research and innovation programme under grant agreement No 101070305. This work is also funded by the FWF Austrian Science Fund and the Internet Foundation Austria under the FWF Elise Richter and netidee SCIENCE programmes as project number V 759-N.

References

1. Athreya, R.G., Ngonga Ngomo, A.C., Usbeck, R.: Enhancing community interactions with data-driven chatbots-the dbpedia chatbot. In: Companion Proceedings of World Wide Web, pp. 143–146. International World Wide Web Conferences Steering Committee, Republic and Canton of Geneva, CHE (2018). https://doi.org/10.1145/3184558.3186964

2. Auer, S., Bizer, C., Kobilarov, G., Lehmann, J., Cyganiak, R., Ives, Z.: DBpedia: a nucleus for a web of open data. In: Aberer, K., et al. (eds.) ASWC/ISWC -2007. LNCS, vol. 4825, pp. 722–735. Springer, Heidelberg (2007). https://doi.org/10.1007/978-3-540-76298-0_52

3. Balazevic, I., Allen, C., Hospedales, T.: TuckER: tensor factorization for knowledge graph completion. In: EMNLP-IJCNLP, pp. 5185–5194. Association for Computational Linguistics, Hong Kong (2019). https://doi.org/10.18653/v1/D19-1522. https://aclanthology.org/D19-1522

4. Bengio, Y., Courville, A., Vincent, P.: Representation learning: a review and new perspectives. IEEE Trans. Pattern Anal. Mach. Intell. **35**(8), 1798–1828 (2013)

5. Bordes, A., Usunier, N., Garcia-Durán, A., Weston, J., Yakhnenko, O.: Translating embeddings for modeling multi-relational data. In: NIPS, pp. 2787–2795. Curran Associates Inc., Red Hook (2013)

6. Chekol, M.W.: Tensor decomposition for link prediction in temporal knowledge graphs. In: Proceedings of the 11th on Knowledge Capture Conference, pp. 253–256. ACM, New York (2021). https://doi.org/10.1145/3460210.3493558

7. Chen, Y., Goldberg, S., Wang, D.Z., Johri, S.S.: Ontological pathfinding: mining first-order knowledge from large knowledge bases. In: ICMD, pp. 835–846. ACM, New York (2016). https://doi.org/10.1145/2882903.2882954

8. Dasgupta, S.S., Ray, S.N., Talukdar, P.: HyTE: hyperplane-based temporally aware knowledge graph embedding. In: EMNLP, pp. 2001–2011. Association for Computational Linguistics, Brussels (2018). https://doi.org/10.18653/v1/D18-1225. https://aclanthology.org/D18-1225

9. Demir, C., Moussallem, D., Heindorf, S., Ngomo, A.C.N.: Convolutional hypercomplex embeddings for link prediction. In: Asian Conference on Machine Learning, pp. 656–671. PMLR (2021)

10. Demir, C., Ngomo, A.-C.N.: Convolutional complex knowledge graph embeddings. In: Verborgh, R., et al. (eds.) ESWC 2021. LNCS, vol. 12731, pp. 409–424. Springer, Cham (2021). https://doi.org/10.1007/978-3-030-77385-4_24

11. Dong, X.L., et al.: Knowledge vault: a web-scale approach to probabilistic knowledge fusion. In: SIGKDD, pp. 601–610 (2014). http://www.cs.cmu.edu/nlao/publication/2014.kdd.pdf

12. Drucker, P.F.: The Age of Discontinuity: Guidelines to Our Changing Society. Transaction Publishers, Piscataway (2011)

13. Ermilov, I., Lehmann, J., Martin, M., Auer, S.: LODStats: the data web census dataset. In: Groth, P., et al. (eds.) ISWC 2016. LNCS, vol. 9982, pp. 38–46. Springer, Cham (2016). https://doi.org/10.1007/978-3-319-46547-0_5

14. Galárraga, L., Teflioudi, C., Hose, K., Suchanek, F.M.: Fast rule mining in ontological knowledge bases with amie+. VLDB J. **24**(6), 707–730 (2015). https://doi.org/10.1007/s00778-015-0394-1

15. Galárraga, L.A., Teflioudi, C., Hose, K., Suchanek, F.: Amie: association rule mining under incomplete evidence in ontological knowledge bases. In: World Wide Web, World Wide Web '13, pp. 413–422. ACM, New York (2013). https://doi.org/10.1145/2488388.2488425

16. García-Durán, A., Dumančić, S., Niepert, M.: Learning sequence encoders for temporal knowledge graph completion. In: EMNLP, pp. 4816–4821. Association for Computational Linguistics, Brussels (2018). https://doi.org/10.18653/v1/D18-1516. https://aclanthology.org/D18-1516

17. Gardner, M., Mitchell, T.: Efficient and expressive knowledge base completion using subgraph feature extraction. In: EMNLP, pp. 1488–1498 (2015)

18. Gardner, M., Talukdar, P., Krishnamurthy, J., Mitchell, T.: Incorporating vector space similarity in random walk inference over knowledge bases. In: EMNLP, pp. 397–406. Association for Computational Linguistics, Doha (2014). https://doi.org/10.3115/v1/D14-1044

19. Gerber, D., et al.: Defacto-temporal and multilingual deep fact validation. Web Semant. **35**(P2), 85–101 (2015). https://doi.org/10.1016/j.websem.2015.08.001

20. Ioffe, S., Szegedy, C.: Batch normalization: accelerating deep network training by reducing internal covariate shift. In: ICML, p. 448–456. JMLR.org (2015)

21. Ji, G., He, S., Xu, L., Liu, K., Zhao, J.: Knowledge graph embedding via dynamic mapping matrix. In: IJCNLP, pp. 687–696. Association for Computational Linguistics, Beijing (2015). https://doi.org/10.3115/v1/P15-1067. https://www.aclweb.org/anthology/P15-1067

22. Jin, W., Zhang, C., Szekely, P.A., Ren, X.: Recurrent event network for reasoning over temporal knowledge graphs. CoRR abs/1904.05530 (2019). http://arxiv.org/abs/1904.05530

23. Kim, J., Choi, K.s.: Unsupervised fact checking by counter-weighted positive and negative evidential paths in a knowledge graph. In: CICLing, pp. 1677–1686. International Committee on Computational Linguistics, Barcelona (2020). https://doi.org/10.18653/v1/2020.coling-main.147. https://www.aclweb.org/anthology/2020.coling-main.147

24. Kingma, D.P., Ba, J.: Adam: a method for stochastic optimization. CoRR arXiv:1412.6980 (2014)

25. Konstantinovskiy, L., Price, O., Babakar, M., Zubiaga, A.: Toward automated factchecking: developing an annotation schema and benchmark for consistent automated claim detection. Dig. Threats: Res. Pract. **2**(2) (2021). https://doi.org/10.1145/3412869

26. Koster, A., Bazzan, A., Souza, M.d.: Liar liar, pants on fire; or how to use subjective logic and argumentation to evaluate information from untrustworthy sources. Artif. Intell. Rev. **48** (2017). https://doi.org/10.1007/s10462-016-9499-1

27. Kotonya, N., Toni, F.: Explainable automated fact-checking for public health claims. arXiv preprint arXiv:2010.09926 (2020)

28. Lacroix, T., Obozinski, G., Usunier, N.: Tensor decompositions for temporal knowledge base completion (2020). https://doi.org/10.48550/ARXIV.2004.04926. https://arxiv.org/abs/2004.04926

29. Lajus, J., Galárraga, L., Suchanek, F.: Fast and exact rule mining with AMIE 3. In: Harth, A., Kirrane, S., Ngonga Ngomo, A.-C., Paulheim, H., Rula, A., Gentile, A.L., Haase, P., Cochez, M. (eds.) ESWC 2020. LNCS, vol. 12123, pp. 36–52. Springer, Cham (2020). https://doi.org/10.1007/978-3-030-49461-2_3

30. Leblay, J., Chekol, M.W.: Deriving validity time in knowledge graph. In: Companion Proceedings of the The Web Conference 2018, pp. 1771–1776. International World Wide Web

Conferences Steering Committee, Republic and Canton of Geneva, CHE (2018). https://doi.org/10.1145/3184558.3191639

31. Lin, Y., Liu, Z., Sun, M., Liu, Y., Zhu, X.: Learning entity and relation embeddings for knowledge graph completion. In: AAAI, vol. 29 (2015)

32. Long, Y., Lu, Q., Xiang, R., Li, M., Huang, C.R.: Fake news detection through multi-perspective speaker profiles. In: ICNLP, pp. 252–256. Asian Federation of Natural Language Processing, Taipei, Taiwan (2017). https://aclanthology.org/I17-2043

33. Ma, Y., Tresp, V., Daxberger, E.A.: Embedding models for episodic knowledge graphs. J. Web Semant. **59**, 100490 (2019). https://doi.org/10.1016/j.websem.2018.12.008. https://www.sciencedirect.com/science/article/pii/S1570826818300702

34. Malyshev, S., Krötzsch, M., González, L., Gonsior, J., Bielefeldt, A.: Getting the most out of wikidata: semantic technology usage in wikipedia's knowledge graph. In: Vrandečić, D., et al. (eds.) ISWC 2018. LNCS, vol. 11137, pp. 376–394. Springer, Cham (2018). https://doi.org/10.1007/978-3-030-00668-6_23

35. Nayyeri, M., et al.: Dihedron algebraic embeddings for spatio-temporal knowledge graph completion. In: ESWC, pp. 253–269. Springer, Cham (2022). https://doi.org/10.1007/978-3-031-06981-9_15

36. Ngonga Ngomo, A.C., Röder, M., Syed, Z.H.: Semantic web challenge 2019. Website (2019). https://github.com/dice-group/semantic-web-challenge.github.io/. Accessed 30 Mar 2022

37. Ortona, S., Meduri, V.V., Papotti, P.: Rudik: rule discovery in knowledge bases. Proc. VLDB Endow. **11**(12), 1946–1949 (2018). https://doi.org/10.14778/3229863.3236231

38. Pasternack, J., Roth, D.: Knowing what to believe (when you already know something). In: CICLing, pp. 877–885. Association for Computational Linguistics, USA (2010)

39. Pasternack, J., Roth, D.: Latent credibility analysis. In: World Wide Web, World Wide Web 2013, pp. 1009–1020. ACM, New York (2013). https://doi.org/10.1145/2488388.2488476

40. Paulheim, H., Ngonga Ngomo, A.C., Bennett, D.: Semantic web challenge 2018. Website (2018). http://iswc2018.semanticweb.org/semantic-web-challenge-2018/index.html. Accessed 30 Mar 2022

41. Qudus, U., Röder, M., Saleem, M., Ngomo, A.C.N.: Hybridfc: a hybrid fact-checking approach for knowledge graphs. In: International Semantic Web Conference, pp. 462–480. Springer International Publishing, Cham (2022). https://doi.org/10.1007/978-3-031-19433-7_27. https://papers.dice-research.org/2022/ISWC_HybridFC/public.pdf

42. Röder, M., Usbeck, R., Ngomo, A.N.: GERBIL - benchmarking named entity recognition and linking consistently. Semant. Web **9**(5), 605–625 (2018). https://doi.org/10.3233/SW-170286. http://www.semantic-web-journal.net/system/files/swj1671.pdf

43. Rula, A., et al.: Tisco: temporal scoping of facts. Web Semant. **54**(C), 72–86 (2019). https://doi.org/10.1016/j.websem.2018.09.002

44. Shi, B., Weninger, T.: Discriminative predicate path mining for fact checking in knowledge graphs. Know.-Based Syst. **104**(C), 123–133 (2016). https://doi.org/10.1016/j.knosys.2016.04.015

45. Shiralkar, P., Flammini, A., Menczer, F., Ciampaglia, G.L.: Finding streams in knowledge graphs to support fact checking. In: ICDM, pp. 859–864 (2017). https://doi.org/10.1109/ICDM.2017.105

46. da Silva, A.A.M., Röder, M., Ngomo, A.-C.N.: Using compositional embeddings for fact checking. In: Hotho, A., et al. (eds.) ISWC 2021. LNCS, vol. 12922, pp. 270–286. Springer, Cham (2021). https://doi.org/10.1007/978-3-030-88361-4_16

47. Strubell, E., Ganesh, A., McCallum, A.: Energy and policy considerations for deep learning in NLP. In: Proceedings of the 57th Annual Meeting of the Association for Computational Linguistics, pp. 3645–3650. Association for Computational Linguistics, Florence (2019). https://doi.org/10.18653/v1/P19-1355. https://aclanthology.org/P19-1355

48. Suchanek, F.M., Kasneci, G., Weikum, G.: Yago: a core of semantic knowledge. In: World Wide Web, pp. 697–706. ACM (2007)
49. Syed, Z.H., Röder, M., Ngomo, A.-C.N.: Unsupervised discovery of corroborative paths for fact validation. In: Ghidini, C., et al. (eds.) ISWC 2019. LNCS, vol. 11778, pp. 630–646. Springer, Cham (2019). https://doi.org/10.1007/978-3-030-30793-6_36
50. Syed, Z.H., Röder, M., Ngonga Ngomo, A.C.: Factcheck: Validating RDF triples using textual evidence. In: CIKM, CIKM 2018, pp. 1599–1602. ACM, New York (2018). https://doi.org/10.1145/3269206.3269308
51. Syed, Z.H., Srivastava, N., Röder, M., Ngomo, A.C.N.: Copaal - an interface for explaining facts using corroborative paths. In: International Semantic Web Conference (2019)
52. Syed, Z.H., Srivastava, N., Röder, M., Ngomo, A.N.: COPAAL - an interface for explaining facts using corroborative paths. In: International Semantic Web Conference, vol. 2456, pp. 201–204. CEUR-WS.org (2019). http://ceur-ws.org/Vol-2456/paper52.pdf
53. Trouillon, T., Welbl, J., Riedel, S., Gaussier, E., Bouchard, G.: Complex embeddings for simple link prediction. In: ICML, pp. 2071–2080 (2016)
54. Wang, Q., Mao, Z., Wang, B., Guo, L.: Knowledge graph embedding: a survey of approaches and applications. IEEE Trans. Knowl. Data Eng. 29(12), 2724–2743 (2017). https://doi.org/10.1109/TKDE.2017.2754499
55. Watt, N., du Plessis, M.C.: Dropout algorithms for recurrent neural networks. In: SAICSIT, pp. 72–78. ACM, New York (2018). https://doi.org/10.1145/3278681.3278691
56. Xu, C., Nayyeri, M., Alkhoury, F., Shariat Yazdi, H., Lehmann, J.: TeRo: a time-aware knowledge graph embedding via temporal rotation. In: CICLing, pp. 1583–1593. International Committee on Computational Linguistics, Barcelona (2020). https://doi.org/10.18653/v1/2020.coling-main.139. https://aclanthology.org/2020.coling-main.139
57. Yang, B., Yih, W., He, X., Gao, J., Deng, L.: Embedding entities and relations for learning and inference in knowledge bases. In: ICLR (2015). http://arxiv.org/abs/1412.6575

Assessing the Generalization Capabilities of Neural Machine Translation Models for SPARQL Query Generation

Samuel Reyd[✉] and Amal Zouaq

Laboratoire LAMA-WeST, Polytechnique Montréal, Montreal, Canada
{samuel.reyd,amal.zouaq}@polymtl.ca
http://www.labowest.ca/

Abstract. Recent studies in the field of Neural Machine Translation for SPARQL query generation have shown rapidly rising performance. State-of-the-art models have reached almost perfect query generation for simple datasets. However, such progress raises the question of the ability of these models to generalize and deal with unseen question-query structures and entities. In this work, we propose copy-enhanced pre-trained models with question annotation and test the ability of several models to handle unknown question-query structures and URIs. To do so, we split two popular datasets based on unknown URIs and question-query structures. Our results show that the copy mechanism effectively allows non-pre-trained models to deal with unknown URIs, and that it also improves the results of some pre-trained models. Our results also show that, when exposed to unknown question-query structures on a simple dataset, pre-trained models significantly outperform non-pre-trained models, but both non-pre-trained and pre-trained models have a considerable drop in performance on a harder dataset. However, the copy mechanism significantly boosts the results of non-pre-trained models on all settings and of the BART pre-trained model, except for the template split on LC-QuAD 2.0 dataset.

Keywords: SPARQL query generation · Generalization · Unknown templates · Unknown URIs · Out-of-vocabulary problem

1 Introduction

The Knowledge Base/Graph Question Answering (KGQA) task has seen recent progress thanks to the development of Neural Machine Translation (NMT) and encoder-decoder architectures. Instead of directly generating or extracting the answer to a question, NMT models generate a SPARQL query that is run against the Knowledge Base (KB) to retrieve the answer.

Addressing English to SPARQL translation with NMT techniques can be done by considering SPARQL as another language. However, there are specific

T. R. Payne et al. (Eds.): ISWC 2023, LNCS 14265, pp. 484–501, 2023.
https://doi.org/10.1007/978-3-031-47240-4_26

challenges that arise from the fact that SPARQL is a formal language, and substituting a word with another, even one that might appear in a similar context, might completely change the sense of the query and generate totally different answers. Notably, the most challenging issue of classic encoder-decoder models is the Out Of Vocabulary (OOV) problem. In general, for traditional NLP models, the vocabulary is fixed in advance and any word that appears in a new input or that is expected in the predicted output that has not been seen during training cannot be taken into account or be generated. This is a very real problem in SPARQL generation since most large KBs include many resources that are very rarely used and are not available to be learned by models. Recent studies address this problem by annotating the KB elements in the question and allowing models to transfer tokens or sequences of tokens from the question to the predicted query [1,10]. Even though modern technics improve the URI generation capabilities of the traditional models, this point remains one of the most challenging parts of the task, especially in the case of unseen or rare URIs. Even though some studies [10] specifically try to evaluate how their approach handles this problem, none systematically evaluate the capabilities of models to deal with unknown URIs.

Another challenge of neural SPARQL translation is the ability of state-of-the-art models to generate question-query structures unseen in training. To our knowledge, none of the previous approaches specifically evaluated this aspect. This challenge is also linked to the way most datasets are generated. Since real-world data is rarely available, most datasets feature automatically generated question-query pairs that are built by filling placeholders inside structural templates with specific KB URIs. This allows models to rely on structures that are limited. Even though some datasets feature questions that are reformulated by human experts, the training data still encourage the model to fit a finite set of question-query structures. To our knowledge, no study addresses the issue of generating queries that do not correspond to the structures seen during training.

We will therefore address the following research questions:

- How do NMT models perform with unknown URIs?
- How do NMT models perform when they face unknown question-query structures?

Our contributions are: 1) to evaluate the capabilities of modern NMT approaches (Transformers [21], ConvSeq2Seq [7], BART [15] and T5 [17]) to handle unknown URIs and question-query structures; 2) to highlight challenges in NMT-based approaches and propose an algorithm to split datasets for better generalization properties of the test set and 3) to test the ability of pretrained models enhanced with a copy mechanism to handle unknown URIs and question-query structures.

2   Related Work

KGQA with NMT Approaches. KGQA has been approached by many methods but recent studies have focused on deep learning NMT approaches. For instance,

Yin et al. [22] used encoder-decoder architectures [19] to translate English questions into SPARQL queries and outperformed traditional neural architectures using a Transformer model [21] and a ConvSeq2Seq model [7].

Hirigoyen et al. [10] proposed a copy mechanism inspired by CopyNet [8] and PGN [18] to copy URIs from questions to SPARQL queries. Their copy mechanism distinguishes itself from former copy approaches by introducing a specific knowledge base vocabulary whose tokens are hidden from the encoder-decoder block and that are the only ones that the copy mechanism can act on. By annotating the questions with the URIs found in the golden queries, this method allows improved performances by a great margin and improves OOV token handling.

The most recent approaches, such as Debayan et al. [1], used pre-trained models, namely BART [15] and T5 [17]. Debayan et al. [1] also annotate questions by placing URIs at the end of the question next to their label from the KB. They also propose a model based on an LSTM [11] encoder-decoder with BERT [5] token embeddings enhanced by a copy block as defined by PGN [18]. However, they report significantly lower results with this method than with their pre-trained models.

Generalization. Generalization in sequence-to-sequence (seq-to-seq) models has been extensively studied, and while models learn generalization as an implicit set of patterns, they may not learn explicit rules required for compositional generalization. According to Baroni [2], neural machine translation (NMT) models can adapt to unseen data, but they lack the cognitive ability to understand explicit rules. Compositional generalization refers to the ability to understand rules used for meaning construction based on how elements are composed. For instance, understanding "jump" and "jump twice" should allow generalization to "walk twice". However, NMT models struggle with explicit composition rules, as supported by experiments on the SCAN dataset [14].

In the field of SPARQL query generation from English questions, Keysers et al. [13] further specify the concept of compositional generalization by measuring the distribution of the Direct Acyclic Graphs (DAG) used for the generation of the question query pairs. They create an English-to-SPARQL dataset with appropriate compositional generalization properties and show a negative correlation between seq-to-seq models' performance and the level of compositional generalization. Gu et al. [9] defined three levels of generalization. These definitions are based on "logical forms", i.e. the underlying structures in the question-query pair. For instance, logical forms in another study [12] include the set of KB classes and properties that appear in the query, the comparison operator in the queries (e.g. $=$, $<$, etc.) and the SPARQL keyword COUNT. Based on these logical forms, each test set data d_0 can be associated to a level of generalization according to the following definitions. 1) the I.I.D. level: there is a question-query pair in the train set that has the same set logical forms as d_0. 2) the compositional level: all the logical forms in d_0 belong to the set of all logical forms in the train set, but no question-query pair of the train set had the same exact set of logical forms. 3) The zero-shot level: there is at least one logical form in d_0 that does not belong to the set of all logical forms in the train set.

Jiang et al. [12] conducted a survey of the KGQA datasets and how they comply with these levels. They also show that the models they tested (including former approaches [3,4] and BART [15]) do not generalize well on these new splits. In this work, we address specific NMT difficulties that can be interpreted as variations of these generalization levels. For instance, we aim at evaluating how models deal with unknown URIs, which is equivalent to the zero-shot level when considering that all URIs are logical forms. This is also equivalent to some definition of compositional generalization as proposed by Baroni [2] where a model must understand the meaning of new symbols as it understood how to compose with other symbols. Similarly, Hirigoyen et al. [10] attempted to evaluate how their models dealt with unknown URIs by generating test sets that do not share any URIs with the training sets. However, these test sets were very limited in size (250 entries). In this work, we test the ability of modern NMT models on popular SPARQL generation datasets and include pre-trained language models enhanced by a copy mechanism.

3 Methodology

3.1 Task and Data

The task of SPARQL query generation for KGQA uses pairs (called entries) of sequences, composed of English questions and expected SPARQL queries. For example: *Question:* "what is the office of richard coke ?" / *Query:* `select distinct ?uri where {dbr:Richard_Coke dbp:office ?uri }`.

All the datasets that we consider use automatically generated entries based on global templates. A global template is composed of a question template and a query template that have matching placeholders that are later filled with specific KB URIs. We refer distinctly to question templates, query templates, and global templates since some question templates or query templates might be shared by several global templates. The placeholder can be filled by any KB element, including URIs and literals. URIs can be resources, or refer to properties and classes. For instance, the above example was generated by the following template: *Question template:* "what is the <1> of <2> ?" / *Query template:* `select distinct ?uri where {<2> <1> ?uri}`.

We use three types of question annotation. 1) The raw questions are presented in the original datasets. 2) The tagged questions, where we use the global templates to replace the natural language mentions with their corresponding KB URIs, found in the corresponding placeholders in the SPARQL queries. This tagging methodology is inspired by [10]. The above example has the following tagged question: "what is the `dbp:office` of `dbr:Richard_Coke` ?" 3) The tag end questions, where each KB element is randomly placed next to its label at the end of the question, separated by `<sep>` tokens. This tagging methodology is inspired by [1]. The above example has the following tag-end question:

"what is the office of richard coke ? `<sep>` `dbr:Richard_Coke` richard coke `<sep>` `dbp:office` office"

3.2   NMT Models

Base Architectures. Following [22] and [10], we experimented with ConvSeq2Seq [7] and Transformer [21] models as well as a copy-enhanced architecture [10]. Similarly to [1], we also experimented with T5-small [17] and BART-base [15] as pre-trained models. Finally, we proposed and tested a copy-enhanced version of the pretrained language models.

Copy Mechanism. As explained in [10], adding a copy-mechanism on top of a non-pre-trained encoder-decoder can improve its performances by a great margin. The copy mechanism from [10] that we use is designed specifically to address the main difficulty of the task of SPARQL query generation, as it helps models to put the right URIs in the query. It is a block added on top of the raw encoder-decoder model. This copy mechanism is well-suited for the task of SPARQL query generation because it allows to not consider the KB elements in the model's vocabulary. For non-pretrained models, this means a significant reduction in the size of the vocabulary. For pre-trained models, it allows avoiding the tokenization of URIs and making "spelling" mistakes when generating the URIs.

We consider an annotated question $w_{0:m}$ with tokens from the natural language vocabulary W and the KB vocabulary K. The expected query $\hat{q}_{0:n}$ is composed of tokens from the SPARQL vocabulary S and the shared tokens from K. When producing a new token, the model will choose to generate a token from the SPARQL vocabulary or to copy a KB element (URI, literal) that belong to the KB vocabulary from the annotated question.

To perform this choice between generating and copying, we first mask the KB token from the annotated question before feeding it to the encoder-decoder. Then, the copy block will compute a copy probability by applying a linear transformation to the decoder logits. This copy probability will then be used to weight the copy distribution and the generation distribution. The generation distribution is obtained by applying a softmax on the decoder logits. This distribution therefore only covers the SPARQL vocabulary. The copy distribution is computed by applying a softmax on the cross-attention weights (from the last attention layer) between the token to be produced and the masked tokens of the question. This distribution therefore only covers the KB elements that appear in the question.

3.3   Evaluation of Generalization Capabilities

Generalization Properties of a Dataset. To evaluate the generalization capabilities of our models, we define generalization properties of our datasets and their split based on some characteristics of the question-query pairs. The characteristics of the entries are simply elements of interest, such as the global template or the URIs that the entry features. The generalization properties are assessments on the distribution of these characteristics with respect to the dataset split. More formally, let D be a dataset, let D_1 be a reference subset of this dataset (usually the test set), and $\overline{D}_1$ be the rest of the dataset (usually the train set). For all $d \in D$ let $c(d)$ be the set of characteristics of the data (in our case either the URIs or the global template of a question-query pair), we say that a generalization property gp holds if any data point d_1 of D_1 has at least one characteristic that does not appear in $\overline{D}_1$, i.e.

$$gp(D, D_1) \equiv \forall d_1 \in D_1 \; \exists c_1 \in c(d_1) : c_1 \notin \cup_{d \in \overline{D}_1}(c(d))$$

We then define two properties of our datasets that are useful for assessing the generalization capabilities of NMT models.

We first evaluate the problem of unknown URIs, since generating the right URIs is necessary to produce correct queries. This generalization capability is very important because real knowledge bases cover very large types of subjects and contain a very large number of URIs. Even though the datasets might aim at covering as many areas and concepts as possible, none may feature enough data to contain multiple examples of each possible URI. Hence, our first generalization property is: *a test set must feature only queries that have at least one URI that is unseen during training.*

We then aim to evaluate the generation of queries with structures that differ from the ones seen during training. The handling of unknown question-query structures is particularly important because it is unclear if models really generate queries based on the sentence semantics, or if they simply map them to known structures of queries. Hence, our second generalization property is: *a test set must feature only question-query pairs that were generated with different global templates than the ones used in the train set.*

Generation of Test Sets with Generalization Properties. We first partition our dataset into subsets that we call groups, such that any set of groups can constitute a reference subset of the dataset that has a generalization property. More formally, given a dataset D, a partition of this dataset into groups $\{g_1, ..., g_k\}$ and a generalization property gp, for any set of these groups $\mathcal{G} \subset \{g_1, ..., g_k\}$ we have that $gp(D, \bigcup \mathcal{G})$ holds. We then define the procedure to build these groups for each of our two generalization properties.

Groups for Unknown Templates Split. In the case of unknown question-query templates (aka unknown template split), the groups are composed of question-query pairs that share the same question-query template. These groups can then be assigned to the train set or test set. This ensures that there is no overlap.

Groups for Unknown URI Split. The URIs are exponentially distributed amongst the question-query pairs. Therefore, most pairs share common URIs and most pairs feature rare URIs that are not shared by many other pairs. The minimum frequency of a URI to be considered rare is an experimental hyperparameter of the algorithm. We explain how we choose it in Sect. 4.1. We first set aside the few question-query pairs in the dataset D that only feature common URIs, which are by default assigned to the train set. Thus our dataset $\tilde{D}$ contains only question-query pairs that feature at least one rare URI. We then define a graph where each node is a question-query pair of $\tilde{D}$, and there is an edge between two nodes if the two question-query pairs share a rare URI. We define our groups as the connected components of this graph. If we take any set of these groups, all the question-query pairs within these groups will feature at least one URI that does not appear in the rest of the groups. Indeed, if we take any rare URI in any entry of these groups, it cannot appear in other groups because if it was the case, there would have been an edge between entries from two different groups, which can't append since they are connected components of our graph.

Desired Number of Question-Query Pairs to Assign to the Train Set. For both settings, we aim at assigning 80% of the data to the train set and 20% to the test set. We define N as the desired number of question-query pairs in the groups that are assigned to the train set. In the case of the unknown template split, $N = 0.8 \times |D|$ with D being the dataset we want to split. In the case of unknown URIs, since we reserved the question-query pairs without rare URIs to the train set, we get $N = 0.8 \times |D| - (|D| - |\tilde{D}|) = |\tilde{D}| - 0.2 \times |D|$.

Split Procedure. We then execute the following procedure. We initialize the train set *train* and the test set *test* as empty sets. We then iterate over each group g. If the size of *train* is larger than N, we assign the group to *test*. Reversely, if the size of *test* is larger than $|D| - N$ we assign the group to *train*. Finally, if neither of these conditions is true, we compute a probability $p = \frac{N - |train|}{|D| - |train| - |test|}$ and assign the group to *train* with probability p or to *test* with probability $1 - p$.

By design of the groups, this ensures that the test set has the intended generalization properties. We define a metric $\delta = \frac{|N - |train||}{|D|}$ that we wish to minimize. In our procedure, once the train or test set has reached or exceeded its desired size, no more groups can be assigned to it. Thus, we obtain $\delta < |g_f|/|D|$ where g_f is the last group to be assigned. We run the procedure multiple times and keep the run with the lowest δ, i.e. the one where the last assigned group is the smallest.

4   Experiments

4.1   Data

We experimented with a simpler and a harder dataset, namely LC-QuAD 1.0 [20] and LC-QuAD 2.0 [6]. They both provide question-query pairs from English to SPARQL. We use processed versions that include the raw questions and queries, as well as two annotated versions of the questions.

Table 1 reports the number of URIs, global templates, and question query pairs of the entire dataset and each of its subsets, as well as the number of unseen elements in the test set. As can be noticed, while many URIs are unknown in LC-QuAD 2.0, global templates are all seen in training. Question-query pairs refer to specific questions and queries. Those in the test set have not, by definition, been seen in training.

Table 1. Number of URIs, global templates and question-query pairs in the datasets for the original split

	Total	Train	Validation	Test	Unseen
All URIs					
LC-QuAD 1.0	4751	4150	1068	1065	318
LC-QuAD 2.0	31018	25064	4978	9992	6724
Global templates					
LC-QuAD 1.0	35	35	32	31	0
LC-QuAD 2.0	30	30	30	30	0
Entries					
LC-QuAD 1.0	5000	4000	500	500	500
LC-QuAD 2.0	30225	21761	2418	6046	6046

We chose an 80-10-10 split proportion for the train, validation, and test sets. We used the split methodology described in Sect. 3.3 to get an 80–20 division of our datasets [6, 20] with the generalization properties introduced in the same section. We then uniformly split the 20% into 10% for the validation set and 10% for the test set.

We obtained our unknown template splits in seconds by running our split procedure around a hundred times and keeping the split with lowest δ as explained in Sect. 3.3. For the unknown URI split, we set the minimum frequency for a URI to be rare at 5. Figure 1 shows that we have the most connected component and the largest size of $\tilde{D}$ ($\tilde{D}$ being the set of entries with at least one rare URI, see Sect. 3.3) around a minimum frequency of 5.

Finding the graph's connected components took less than a second for LC-QuAD 1.0 [20] and around 1.5min for LC-QuAD 2.0 [6]. We then ran the split procedure around a hundred times, which took less than a second. We get $\delta = 6.6e^{-5}$ for the template split on LC-QuAD 2.0 [6] and $\delta = 0$ for the template split on LC-QuAD 1.0 [20] and for the URI split on both datasets [6, 20].

Table 2 reports the number of URIs, global templates, and question query pairs of the train/val/test sets obtained for the unknown URIs split and the unknown template split. We can observe that we have fewer unknown URIs in the test set of the unknown URI spit than in the test set of the original split. This is because the original split did not use an 80-10-10 split and therefore had around twice as many entries in its test set. However, our new split ensures that 100% entries of the test feature at least one unknown URI which is not the case in the original split.

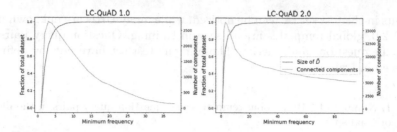

Fig. 1. Size of $\tilde{D}$ (see Sect. 3.3) and number of connected components as we raise the minimum frequency for considering a URI rare

Table 2. Number of URIs, global templates, and question-query pairs in the datasets for our splits

	Total	Train	Val	Test	Unseen	Train	Val	Test	Unseen
		Unknown template split				Unknown URIs split			
		All URIs							
LC-QuAD 1.0	4751	4183	925	912	282	3872	909	948	535
LC-QuAD 2.0	31018	27986	4403	4429	1619	25121	4738	4708	3437
		Global templates							
LC-QuAD 1.0	35	31	4	4	4	35	32	30	0
LC-QuAD 2.0	30	24	6	6	6	30	30	30	0
		Entries							
LC-QuAD 1.0	5000	4000	500	500	500	4000	500	500	500
LC-QuAD 2.0	30225	24178	3023	3024	3024	24180	3022	3023	3023

4.2   Models Training and Evaluation

Our non-pre-trained model architectures follow the ones of [22] and [10] in terms of the number of layers (6 for Transformer and 15 for ConvSe2Seq), and number of hidden units (1024 for Transformer and 512 for ConvSeq2Seq). The training methodology is also the same with similar optimizer (ADAM for Transformer and SGD for ConvSeq2Seq), learning rates (0.0005 for Transformer and 0.5 for ConvSeq2Seq) and dropout (0.3 for Transformer and 0.2 for ConvSeq2Seq). Our pre-trained models are T5-small and BART-base following [1]. We also adopt their training parameters, using the ADAM optimizer for both models with a learning rate of 0.000015 for BART and 0.0015 for T5, and a polynomial decay schedule with warmup.

We ran our models for a fixed number of epochs three times, keeping the model with the best validation loss at each run, and report the mean of the three best models. The number of epochs and the batch size are fixed based on our physical device's abilities. For non-pre-trained models, we used 500 epochs and a batch size of 32 for LC-QuAD 1.0 [20] and 150 epochs and a batch size of 16 for LC-QuAD 2.0 [6]. For pre-trained models, we used 200 epochs and a batch size of 16 for LC-QuAD 1.0 [20] and 50 epochs and a batch size of 8 for LC-QuAD 2.0 [6].

During the evaluation, we generate the outputs greedily and compute several evaluation measures, namely BLEU score [16], answer accuracy and F1 score. We first compare the predicted queries to the gold queries using the BLEU score. We also run the gold queries against a 2016 dump of DBPedia-based endpoint for LC-QuAD 1.0 [20] and on the current public endpoint for LC-QuAD 2.0 [6], and we only keep queries that return non-empty answers. We then run our predicted queries on the same endpoints and compare expected answers with predicted answers using answer accuracy, which measures if the two sets of answers are identical and using the F1-score.

5   Results

We report results rounded to integers for an easier comparison between tables.

5.1   Original Results

All results for the original split are reported in Table 3.

For non-pre-trained models, we can notice that the copy mechanism managed to bring the performance for LC-QuAD 1.0 [20] close to 100%. For LC-QuAD 2.0 [6], even with copy, the task remains really challenging. Moreover, we can see that in most settings, the Transformer architecture struggles with LC-QuAD 2.0 [6].

Contrary to non-pre-trained models, the original results of pre-trained models are quite heterogeneous. Both T5 [17] and BART [15] have low results on raw questions (even though they are better than any setting of non-pre-trained models without the copy mechanism). BART [15] without the copy mechanism is the only pre-trained architecture that has performances noticeably lower than ConSeq2Seq with the copy mechanism. In the case of LC-QuAD 1.0 [20] in its original split, both BART [15] with the copy mechanism and T5 [17] with and without the copy mechanism perform well. In the case of LC-QuAD 2.0 [6], T5 [17] performs well without the copy mechanism, whereas BART [15] performs well only with the copy mechanism.

5.2   Unknown URIs Split

All results for the unknown URIs split are reported in Table 4.

The results for non-pre-trained models show very clearly the impact of the copy mechanism on the handling of unknown URIs and also clearly highlight that our split creates a real difficulty for non-pre-trained models compared to the original dataset.

Without the copy mechanism, we can note that no non-pre-trained model reaches 10% of accuracy on LC-QuAD 1.0 [20] nor 2% on LC-QuAD 2.0 [6]. Even

Table 3. Results for the original split

		No copy			Copy			No copy			Copy		
		BLEU	Acc	F1	BLEU	Acc	F1	BLEU	Acc	F1	BLEU	Acc	F1
		Transformer						Conv					
LC-QuAD 1.0	raw	69	33	37	/	/	/	69	23	27	/	/	/
	tagged	82	41	44	98	95	95	78	28	32	98	95	95
	tag end	74	38	41	49	1.9	1.9	75	25	28	91	77	78
		BART						T5					
	raw	83	59	62	/	/	/	77	42	46	/	/	/
	tagged	96	85	85	99	97	97	98	96	96	98	96	96
	tag end	96	85	85	98	96	96	98	95	95	97	93	93
		Transformer						Conv					
LC-QuAD 2.0	raw	57	0.9	1.1	/	/	/	76	10	11	/	/	/
	tagged	59	1.5	1.6	83	69	69	76	8.8	10	88	69	70
	tag end	66	1.4	1.7	57	2.2	2.2	78	14	15	91	66	66
		BART						T5					
	raw	70	2.2	2.3	/	/	/	79	13	13	/	/	/
	tagged	88	80	80	89	72	73	92	87	87	89	72	72
	tag end	84	67	67	95	85	85	90	85	85	87	58	58

though the tagged questions lead to slightly higher performance, the annotation impact is much less noticeable than for other settings.

On the contrary, with the copy mechanism, we clearly notice that the performance of non-pre-trained models (based on all metrics) using tagged questions is much higher than without the copy mechanism. We reach and even outperform the results from the original split. This suggests that the unknown URIs are handled, particularly using tagged questions. Indeed, the introduction of unknown URIs in each test entry without any F1-score loss (as seen by comparing Table 3 and Table 4) suggests that the errors made might not be caused by unknown URIs. The tag end setting does not however help the models.

For pre-trained models, with annotated questions, the results remain similar to the original split for T5 [17]. BART [15] loses some F1 score points on LC-QuAD 2.0 [6]. However, we see a great increase in performance between raw data and annotated questions. This suggests that with question annotation, pre-trained models are able to deal with unknown URIs to a good extent. We can also see that T5 [17] with the copy mechanism slightly increases its performance on LC-QuAD 1.0 [20].

5.3 Unknown Templates Split

All results for the unknown templates split are reported in Table 5.

For non-pre-trained models, we can observe that models without the copy mechanism consistently suffer a huge drop in performance compared to the original split. For LC-QuAD 1.0 [20], we still see a consistent increase in performance with question annotation but the answer accuracy still remains below 55%. For

Table 4. Results for non-pre-trained models on the unknown URIs split

		No copy			Copy			No copy			Copy		
		Bleu	Acc	F1	Bleu	Acc	F1	Bleu	Acc	F1	Bleu	Acc	F1
		Transformer						Conv					
LC-QuAD 1.0	raw	59	7.0	10	/	/	/	64	6.9	10	/	/	/
	tagged	70	8.0	12	98	95	95	71	8.4	12	98	96	96
	tag end	67	6.1	8.6	46	0.2	0.2	70	6.9	9.6	86	60	62
		BART						T5					
	raw	77	38	41	/	/	/	72	24	26	/	/	/
	tagged	96	85	85	99	96	96	98	95	95	99	97	98
	tag end	95	83	83	96	93	94	98	94	94	98	96	96
		Transformer						Conv					
LC-QuAD 2.0	raw	61	0.3	0.5	/	/	/	75	1.8	2.7	/	/	/
	tagged	64	0.3	0.4	86	72	73	75	2.0	3.0	90	72	73
	tag end	62	0.4	0.6	55	1.8	1.8	74	1.9	3.0	88	53	53
		BART						T5					
	raw	68	0.5	0.6	/	/	/	74	0.7	0.9	/	/	/
	tagged	87	72	72	86	62	62	93	87	88	85	68	68
	tag end	86	71	71	92	78	78	91	85	86	92	77	78

LC-QuAD 2.0 [6] with Transformer, the results are even lower than in the original split and the answers are almost always wrong. For ConvSeq2Seq, the model has better performances but they remain low.

However, we can observe a noticeable impact of the copy mechanism on the non-pre-trained models' results. Even though they remain below those of the original split, they are much better than without the copy mechanism. Moreover, compared to the original split, the BLEU score is notably lower especially if we also consider the answer accuracy. This would suggest that the structure of the predicted queries does not always match the structure of the expected ones while still providing correct answers. Explanations of why this might happen are given in Sect. 6. Overall, non-pre-trained models seem to really struggle with global templates unseen during training.

Contrarily to non-pre-trained models, pre-trained models appear to handle unknown templates for simple datasets.

For LC-QuAD 1.0 [20], BART [15] and T5 [17] without the copy mechanism both remain consistent in terms of answer metrics, while they show a significant drop in BLEU score compared to the original split. However, we can observe a huge drop in performance for T5 [17] with copy on both question annotation settings (tagged, tag-end) and for BART [15] with copy on the tag-end questions. Yet, BART [15] with copy on tagged questions demonstrates impressive and almost perfect answers metrics.

In the LC-QuAD 2.0 [6] case, we can note that the results are low. No model reaches 50% accuracy. In this case, both models perform better without the copy mechanism.

Table 5. Results for the unknown template split

		No copy			Copy			No copy			Copy		
		Bleu	Acc	F1	Bleu	Acc	F1	Bleu	Acc	F1	Bleu	Acc	F1
		Transformer						Conv					
LC-QuAD 1.0	raw	37	6.9	8.0	/	/	/	43	17	19	/	/	/
	tagged	36	6.3	6.4	50	24	24	46	19	22	50	41	41
	tag end	42	11	12	37	2.8	2.8	50	18	20	60	55	55
		BART						T5					
	raw	62	41	42	/	/	/	65	52	53	/	/	/
	tagged	79	87	88	63	99	99	80	92	92	57	50	50
	tag end	80	90	90	61	42	43	75	78	79	66	51	51
		Transformer						Conv					
LC-QuAD 2.0	raw	43	0.2	0.3	/	/	/	51	4.1	4.7	/	/	/
	tagged	39	0.1	0.2	64	32	33	52	1.4	2.0	63	34	34
	tag end	41	0.2	0.2	37	0.3	0.3	55	2.7	2.9	57	13	14
		BART						T5					
	raw	50	0.4	0.4	/	/	/	59	1.1	1.2	/	/	/
	tagged	70	47	47	65	34	34	69	48	48	61	14	14
	tag end	52	21	22	62	12	12	68	47	47	62	7.9	8.2

6 Discussion

We showed that classic NMT approaches cannot handle unknown URIs or unknown question-query structures. On the contrary, adding a copy mechanism or using pre-trained models combined with question annotation allows the handling of unknown URIs since having all test instances featuring unknown URIs almost did not lower the performances. Indeed, the results of pre-trained models on the unknown URIs split remain roughly similar compared to the original split with tagged questions (-2 F1 point on average). Significant performance gains are obtained only with tagged questions on the unknown URIs split, as we observe a raise of 67.9 F1 points on average when using tagged questions instead of raw questions for pre-trained models.

We also showed that the copy mechanism or the use of pre-trained models, and sometimes specifically the combination of both, can allow models to deal with unknown question-query structures. Yet, this type of generalization remains a challenge for SPARQL query generation with NMT as our results don't show consistent handling across models, datasets, and data annotation.

Low Performances for Non-pre-trained Models on tag-End Questions in the Unknown URIs Split. We observed that the copy mechanism allowed the non-pre-trained models to reach the same performance on the unknown URIs split as on the original split for tagged questions but not on tag-end questions. This can be explained by the fact that the copy mechanism uses the label of the URI, at the end of the question to map it to its position in the question and to its position in the query. But in these settings, there are many unknown URIs, and thus a very high probability that the label reported next to the URI is also an unknown token. Even though the copy mechanism is able to overcome unknown URIs, it needs an anchor to map the position of the given URI to the position of its natural language mention in the question, which is often impossible in the tag-end questions.

Drop of BLEU Score for the Unknown Template Split. We observed that in most cases, the margin between the BLEU score and answer-based scores is lowered if not reversed on the unknown template splits. This behavior suggests that the models predict queries that do not match the expected ones but still produce the gold answers.

We found a significant example of such behavior in the case of BART with the copy mechanism on LC-QuAD 1.0 [20] with tagged questions. When we look at the generated queries, we can see that they always follow the structure of a query template in the training set. We conclude that the model has integrated the task of mapping a question template to a query template together with placeholder filling. When it is given a question from the test set, it tries to associate the unknown structure to a known one from the training set and then generates the corresponding query. An example of outputs from BART with copy and tagged questions from the most common global template in the test set of LC-QuAD 1.0 [20] can be found in Table 6. For instance, for the test question "what is the `dbp:hubs` of `dbr:Cascade_Airways`?" the model predicted `select distinct ?uri where { dbr:Cascade_Airways dbp:hubs ?uri . dbr:Cascade_Airways dbp:hubs ?uri }` instead of `select distinct ?uri where { dbr:Cascade_Airways dbp:hubs ?uri }`.

Table 6. Example of outputs generated by BART for the most common global template of the test set (376 occurrences) which is *Question:* what is the <1> of <2> ? / *Query:* `select distinct ?uri where { <2> <1> ?uri }` (one run of BART tagged copy on LC-QuAD 2.0)

Generated structure from: what is the <1> of <2> ?	Training global template it might come from
`select distinct ?uri where { <mask> <mask> ?uri . <mask> <mask> ?uri }` (298 occurrences)	- what is the <1> of the <2> and <3> ? - `select distinct ?uri where { <2> <1> ?uri. <3> <1> ?uri }`
	- who is the <1> of the <2> and <3> of the <4> ? - `select distinct ?uri where { <2> <1> ?uri. <4> <3> ?uri }`
`select distinct ?uri where { <mask> <mask> ?uri . <mask> <mask> ?uri . }` (77 occurrences)	- what is the <1> of the <2> and <3> ? - `select distinct ?uri where { <2> <1> ?uri. <3> <1> ?uri }`
	- who is the <1> of the <2> and <3> of the <4> ? - `select distinct ?uri where { <2> <1> ?uri. <4> <3> ?uri }`
`select distinct ?uri where { ?uri <mask> <mask> . }` (1 occurrence)	- what are the <0> whose <1> is <2> ? - `select distinct ?uri where {?uri <1> <2> }`

Challenging Cases. Either thanks to the copy mechanism, to pre-trained models or to the combination of both, we manage to obtain at least one model that reaches above 80% of F1 score on almost each split of each dataset. The only exception is the case of the unknown template split for LC-QuAD 2.0. In this case, no model manages to reach above 48% of F1 score. We can notably see a very strong drop of performance from the unknown template split of LC-QuAD 1.0 compared to the unknown template split of LC-QuAD 2.0. In particular, we can observe that BART's performance with the copy mechanism and tagged questions decrease from 99% of F1 score to 34% of F1 score. On both LC-QuAD 2.0 and LC-QuAD 1.0, we note that the model generates queries that match query templates from the training set that are associated to training questions close to the test questions. In the case of LC-QuAD 1.0, this allowed to generate queries that return the expected answers due to equivalent queries with different structures (see the above example) but it is not the case for LC-QuAD 2.0.

Table 7 shows an example of how BART generated incorrect queries for questions with a specific structure and used the same SPARQL templates as those in the training set.

Table 7. Example of how BART with the copy mechanism and tagged questions handles an unknown template in LC-QuAD 2.0

Question structure from the test set: How many <1> are by <2>? *Example:* how many child are by gaia ?
Expected query structures for this question structure: select (count (?sub) as ?value) { ?sub <1> <2> } *Example:* select (count (?sub) as ?value) { ?sub wdt:P40 wd:Q93172 }
Predicted query structures for this question structure: select (count (?obj) as ?value) { <2> <1> ?obj } *Example:* select (count (?obj) as ?value) { wd:Q270503 wdt:P400 ?obj }
Question template associated to this query template in the train set: how many <1> are for <2> ? *Example:* how many platform are for tomb raider ?

Standard Deviation of Performance between Runs with the Copy Mechanism. For each result that we report, we averaged the results of three different runs where the models are trained and evaluated with different random seeds. We noted that there is, in some cases, a significant standard deviation between the runs when we use models with the copy mechanism.

Complexity of Finding Unknown URIs Groups. Despite the speed of the split procedure, our methodology for unknown URI splits has a higher time complexity. Indeed, it requires finding the connected components in the graph, which is a quadratic process in the size of the dataset.

7   Conclusion and Future Work

In this study, we defined two major issues of the NMT approach of SPARQL query generation from English questions. We first show how they are related to common definitions of generalization in the context of SPARQL query generation. We then presented a split algorithm to obtain datasets that test these challenges in their train/test distribution: the unknown template split and the unknown URI split. Finally, we tested pre-trained models and copy-enhanced models with question annotation on a simple and a hard dataset. We also compared these results to non-pre-trained models.

We showed that unknown templates are very often an issue for model training and testing since most results are low and only very specific combinations of question annotation and model architecture (BART [15] with copy and tagged questions and T5 [17] without copy) allow good results on LC-QuAD 1.0 [20]. Moreover, even when models generate queries that have correct answers, they often follow structures matching those in the training set, which is an important limitation. However, we showed that even though the performance remains low, the copy mechanism allowed a significant improvement for non-pre-trained models on LC-QuAD 2.0 [6]. We also showed that pre-training and question annotation or usage of the copy mechanism allows the handling of unknown URIs contrary to non-pre-trained models (without copy).

Our future work will include other criteria to evaluate the ability of current natural language to SPARQL datasets to test generative models. For instance, LC-QuAD 1.0 [20] and LC-QuAD 2.0 [6] both include reformulated questions that are produced by humans, which can constitute a good test set for models trained on template questions. We also plan to consider other splitting criteria that would show how models generalize to harder data, based on characteristics such as the length of the query or the question, the number of placeholders, or the number of triples in the query. Finally, we plan to enhance the performance of the split algorithm for unknown URIs, by considering other graph algorithms to find groups.

Supplemental Material Statement: The code and data for this paper can be found at this link[1].

Acknowledgements. This research has been funded by the NSERC Discovery Grant Program. The authors acknowledge support from Compute Canada for providing computational resources. We would like to thank Karou Diallo for setting the DBpedia SPARQL endpoint used in this paper.

---

[1] Link to our GitHub.

References

1. Banerjee, D., Nair, P.A., Kaur, J.N., Usbeck, R., Biemann, C.: Modern baselines for SPARQL semantic parsing. In: Amigó, E., Castells, P., Gonzalo, J., Carterette, B., Shane Culpepper, J., Kazai, G. (eds.) SIGIR 2022: The 45th International ACM SIGIR Conference on Research and Development in Information Retrieval, Madrid, Spain, 11–15 July 2022, pp. 2260–2265. ACM (2022)
2. Baroni, M.: Linguistic generalization and compositionality in modern artificial neural networks. Philos. Trans. Royal Soc. B: Biol. Sci. **375**(1791), 20190307 (2019)
3. IAIS bFraunhofer. Knowledge graph question answering using graph-pattern isomorphism. In: Further with Knowledge Graphs: Proceedings of the 17th International Conference on Semantic Systems, 6–9 September 2021, Amsterdam, The Netherlands, vol. 53, p. 103. IOS Press (2021)
4. Chen, Y., Li, H., Qi, G., Wu, T., Wang, T.: Outlining and filling: hierarchical query graph generation for answering complex questions over knowledge graphs. arXiv preprint arXiv:2111.00732 (2021)
5. Devlin, J., Chang, M.-W., Lee, K., Toutanova, K.: BERT: pre-training of deep bidirectional transformers for language understanding. In: Proceedings of the 2019 Conference of the North American Chapter of the Association for Computational Linguistics: Human Language Technologies, Volume 1 (Long and Short Papers), pp. 4171–4186, Minneapolis, Minnesota. Association for Computational Linguistics (June 2019)
6. Dubey, M., Banerjee, D., Abdelkawi, A., Lehmann, J.: LC-QuAD 2.0: a large dataset for complex question answering over Wikidata and DBpedia. In: Ghidini, C., et al. (eds.) ISWC 2019. LNCS, vol. 11779, pp. 69–78. Springer, Cham (2019). https://doi.org/10.1007/978-3-030-30796-7_5
7. Gehring, J., Auli, M., Grangier, D., Yarats, D., Dauphin, Y.N.: Convolutional sequence to sequence learning. In: Precup, D., Teh, Y.W. (eds.) Proceedings of the 34th International Conference on Machine Learning, ICML 2017, Sydney, NSW, Australia, 6–11 August 2017. Proceedings of Machine Learning Research, vol. 70 , pp. 1243–1252. PMLR (2017)
8. Gu, J., Lu, Z., Li, H., Li, V.O.K.: Incorporating copying mechanism in sequence-to-sequence learning. In: Proceedings of the 54th Annual Meeting of the Association for Computational Linguistics, ACL 2016, 7–12 August 2016, Berlin, Germany, Volume 1: Long Papers, pp. 1631–1640. The Association for Computer Linguistics (2016)
9. Gu, Y., et al.: Three levels of generalization for question answering on knowledge bases. In: Proceedings of the Web Conference 2021, WWW 2021, pp. 3477–3488. Association for Computing Machinery, New York (2021)
10. Hirigoyen, R., Zouaq, A., Reyd, S.: A copy mechanism for handling knowledge base elements in SPARQL neural machine translation. In: Findings of the Association for Computational Linguistics: AACL-IJCNLP 2022, pp. 226–236, Online only. Association for Computational Linguistics (November 2022)
11. Hochreiter, S., Schmidhuber, J.: Long short-term memory. Neural Comput. **9**, 1735–1780 (1997)
12. Jiang, L., Usbeck, R.: Knowledge graph question answering datasets and their generalizability: Are they enough for future research? In: Amigó, E., Castells, P., Gonzalo, J., Carterette, B., Shane Culpepper, J., Kazai, G. (eds.) SIGIR 2022: The 45th International ACM SIGIR Conference on Research and Development in Information Retrieval, Madrid, Spain, 11–15 July 2022, pp. 3209–3218. ACM (2022)

13. Keysers, D.: Measuring Compositional Generalization: A Comprehensive Method on Realistic Data . arXiv:1912.09713 ((June 2020)
14. Lake, B., Baroni, M.: Generalization without systematicity: on the compositional skills of sequence-to-sequence recurrent networks. In: Dy, J., Krause, A. (eds.) Proceedings of the 35th International Conference on Machine Learning, 10–15 Jul. Proceedings of Machine Learning Research, vol. 80, pp. 2873–2882. PMLR (2018)
15. Lewis, M.: BART: denoising sequence-to-sequence pre-training for natural language generation, translation, and comprehension. In Jurafsky, D., Chai, J., Schluter, N., Tetreault, J.R. (eds.) Proceedings of the 58th Annual Meeting of the Association for Computational Linguistics, ACL 2020, Online, 5–10 July 2020, pp. 7871–7880. Association for Computational Linguistics (2020)
16. Papineni, K., Roukos, S., Ward, T., Zhu, W.-J.: Bleu: a method for automatic evaluation of machine translation. In: Proceedings of the 40th Annual Meeting of the Association for Computational Linguistics, 6–12 July 2002, Philadelphia, PA, USA, pp. 311–318. ACL (2002)
17. Raffel, C., et al.: Exploring the limits of transfer learning with a unified text-to-text transformer. J. Mach. Learn. Res. 21, 140:1–140:67 (2020)
18. See, A., Liu, P.J., Manning, C.D.: Get to the point: summarization with pointer-generator networks. In: Barzilay, R., Kan, M.-Y. (eds.) Proceedings of the 55th Annual Meeting of the Association for Computational Linguistics, ACL 2017, Vancouver, Canada, 30 July - 4 August, Volume 1: Long Papers, pp. 1073–1083. Association for Computational Linguistics (2017)
19. Sutskever, I., Vinyals, O., Le, Q.V.: Sequence to sequence learning with neural networks. In: Ghahramani, Z., Welling, M., Cortes, C., Lawrence, N.D., Weinberger, K.Q. (eds.) Advances in Neural Information Processing Systems 27: Annual Conference on Neural Information Processing Systems 2014, 8–13 December 2014, Montreal, Quebec, Canada, pp. 3104–3112. Curran Associates Inc (2014)
20. Trivedi, P., Maheshwari, G., Dubey, M., Lehmann, J.: LC-QuAD: a corpus for complex question answering over knowledge graphs. In: d'Amato, C., et al. (eds.) ISWC 2017. LNCS, vol. 10588, pp. 210–218. Springer, Cham (2017). https://doi.org/10.1007/978-3-319-68204-4_22
21. Vaswani, A.: Attention is all you need. In: Guyon, I., et al.: (eds.) Advances in Neural Information Processing Systems 30: Annual Conference on Neural Information Processing Systems 2017, 4–9 December 2017, Long Beach, CA, USA, pp. 5998–6008. Curran Associates Inc (2017)
22. Yin, X., Gromann, D., Rudolph, S.: Neural machine translating from natural language to SPARQL. Future Gener. Comput. Syst. 117, 510–519 (2021)

Linking Tabular Columns to Unseen Ontologies

Sarthak Dash[✉][iD], Sugato Bagchi[iD], Nandana Mihindukulasooriya[iD],
and Alfio Gliozzo[iD]

IBM Research AI, Yorktown Heights, NY, USA
{sdash,bagchi,gliozzo}@us.ibm.com, nandana@ibm.com

Abstract. We introduce a novel approach for linking table columns to types in an ontology unseen during training. As the target ontology is unknown to the model during training, this may be considered a zero-shot linking task at the ontological level. This task is often a requirement for businesses that wish to semantically enrich their tabular data with types from their custom or industry-specific ontologies without the benefit of initial supervision. In this paper, we describe specific approaches and provide datasets for this new task: training models on open domain tables using a broad source ontology and evaluating them on increasingly difficult tables with target ontologies having different levels of type granularity. We use pre-trained Transformer encoder models and a range of encoding strategies to explore methods of encoding increasing amounts of ontological knowledge, such as type glossaries and taxonomies, to obtain better zero-shot performance. We demonstrate these results empirically through extensive experiments on three new public benchmark datasets.

1 Introduction

Enterprise data assets are now increasingly stored in various types of infrastructure, ranging from in-house database management systems on owned infrastructure to rented services on cloud infrastructure. In order to manage their distributed data assets, businesses invest in "data lakes" [5] that provide a unified view of the metadata associated with the assets regardless of their location. Although this metadata may include names of databases, tables, columns, and associated database schemas, it lacks mappings to an external ontology of interest. Such mappings allow a data consumer to discover, augment, and visualize information from this data lake. In addition, given multiple data consumer roles in an enterprise, there is a need to map columns to multiple custom ontologies, taxonomies, or business term glossaries often with thousands of business terms. Current approaches on linking columns to a target ontology are either rule-based or require training on the same ontology [34]. However, building such a system for each data consumer role is not feasible because each data consumer role within an enterprise may need to link columns to a different business glossary or an ontology. In such a setting, the rule-based approaches will suffer from

© The Author(s), under exclusive license to Springer Nature Switzerland AG 2023
T. R. Payne et al. (Eds.): ISWC 2023, LNCS 14265, pp. 502–521, 2023.
https://doi.org/10.1007/978-3-031-47240-4_27

recall/accuracy issues and supervised approaches will need manual annotations with high human effort/cost. Therefore, it is essential to find strategies to link tabular columns to any given target ontology in an unsupervised manner.

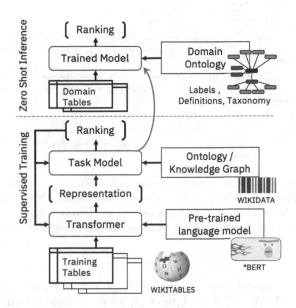

Fig. 1. System for column linking and inference. The task model is fine-tuned over pretrained transformer encoders using WikiTables with columns linked to Wikidata types. During inference, this trained model is applied as-is on tables and/or ontology from a different domain.

Existing approaches such as TABBIE [19], DODUO [31], TURL [11], SATO [33] propose table embedding models that are fine-tuned on either a subset of WebTables corpus from Viznet [16], or on the WikiTables corpus for Column Linking [11]. The ground truth in these datasets consists of only type labels, such as *Researcher*, *Institution*, etc. and does not use other associated ontological knowledge, such as glossary or taxonomy structure. Moreover, the size of the ground truth labels in these datasets is small, i.e., TABBIE and SATO are trained on 78 labels, whereas TURL is trained on 255 labels. Additionally, the ground truth labels in these datasets remain constant between the training and testing phases.

Alternatively, approaches such as [26,30] or systems participating in the SemTab challenge [22] often couple this task together with linking cell values to entities in an ontology. These approaches rely on cell-linking performance and do not generalize when the target ontology has types but no entities as commonly observed in custom enterprise ontologies.

In this paper, we train Transformer-based deep learning models on tables with known mappings to an existing ontology and assess their performance when

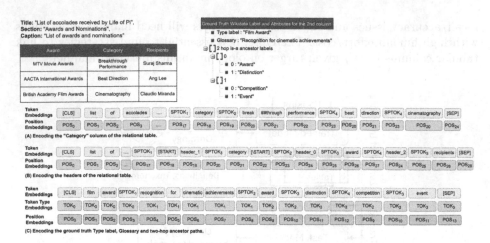

Fig. 2. Overview of encoding query columns, table headers, and the target type for the column linking task. The goal is to classify the column titled CATEGORY within the left table to the type *Film Award*. A glossary and two-hop is-a ancestor labels, i.e., additional information from the target ontology, are also available for each target type label.

those models are applied to an unseen ontology. Figure 1 illustrates an example. Here, we adapt the WikiTables dataset [4] to map table columns to Wikidata types. Moreover, we augment label of each type within our updated datasets with a glossary (using the description of the type) and verbalisation of a partial taxonomy structure (based on `rdfs:subClassOf` property) extracted from the corresponding ontology.

We introduce novel strategies to encode this ontological information and show that by doing so, we obtain models that can better link tabular columns to unseen ontologies. Here we use a Transformer's ability to encode a language model to learn the associations from columns and headers to types within an ontology.

Since most enterprise datasets and custom ontologies are highly proprietary and not openly available, in this work, we simulate a custom enterprise setting using publicly available ontologies. We use three datasets: WikiTables, BioDivTab [1], and Tough Tables [9], and three ontologies: Wikidata, DBpedia, and UMLS Semantic Network [24]. This allows for the evaluation on unseen ontologies in the same general knowledge domain (Wikidata and DBpedia) and on different domains (Wikidata and UMLS Semantic Network).

In summary, we make the following contributions,

1. We propose a new setting for the column linking task where the test ontology is unseen during the training.
2. We introduce three new datasets for the setting proposed above. These include WikiTables with columns mapped to Wikidata and DBpedia types and BioDivTab with columns mapped to UMLS Semantic Network types (Sect. 3).

These datasets and ontologies allow for evaluation within and across domains. We augment each type label in these datasets with additional glossary information and a partial taxonomy structure.

3. We propose novel strategies for encoding these semantically enriched types (Sect. 2) and empirically demonstrate their effectiveness on this task in Sect. 4.

2 Approach

In this section, we provide an overview of our proposed approach for the Column Linking task, also known as Column Type Annotation (CTA) in literature. We model this task as a *ranking* problem. Given a table containing a target column Q_c, headers H, and a list of one or more ground truth types $\mathcal{L}$, our training procedure uses Transformer encoders to learn how to associate a high similarity score between the query representation q_v and type representations from $\mathcal{L}$. The following sections describe our approach in detail.

2.1 Encoding the Query Column and the Headers

This section describes our strategies for encoding the query column Q_c and the table headers H for a given relational table. We hypothesize that the table headers provide additional context to the query column and help determine its type more accurately. Consider the relational table (on the left) in Fig. 2. Suppose that the query column Q_c is the second column with the header *Category*. The headers H consist of three entries: Award, Category, and Recipients.

We use six additional special tokens $SPTOK_1$ through $SPTOK_4$ and [START], [\START] for encoding using pre-trained Transformer encoder models and follow the strategy used by our previous work [10] to encode the query column Q_c and the headers H. For encoding Q_c, we first concatenate the title, section, and caption fields to generate the metadata text. We then append the column header, i.e., *Category*, to the metadata text using $SPTOK_1$ as the separator. Next, we concatenate the cell mentions in column Q_c using the separator $SPTOK_4$, and then append this sentence to the previous one using $SPTOK_2$. This strategy yields the overall pseudo sentence for the query column in yellow (Fig. 2(A)).

For encoding table headers, we model all those headers not belonging to the query column Q_c as a collection of texts. Yet, we also respect that these headers are present in the relational table in a specific sequence (for better understandability). Therefore, we attach additional tags of the form "header_N" where N is a natural number greater than or equal to one. The $SPTOK_3$ token separates the term "header_k" from the actual value of the header, whereas $SPTOK_2$ has the same functionality as described before. We use the $SPTOK_4$ token to concatenate with other column headers and surround Q_c's header with [START], [\START] tokens. Figure 2(B) shows the pseudo sentence for the table headers.

We use the strategy introduced by [10] for the position embeddings. The $SPTOK_2$ token acts as the pivot: Word pieces to the left of the pivot get numerically increasing position IDs, whereas, for word pieces to the right, the position

IDs are numerically increasing but are reset as soon as we hit the SPTOK$_4$ special token. The SPTOK$_4$ token always gets a position ID that is one less than the position ID of the [SEP] token. This assignment of position IDs is shown in green for Fig. 2(A), (B). Also, we use the standard strategy for encoding Token Types and attention masks. Therefore, we have omitted their illustrations for brevity.

Finally, the [CLS] vector and the [START] vector corresponding to the final Transformer layer is used as the representations for the query column Q_c and the table headers H, respectively. This encoding strategy ensures that the column representation remains unchanged even if the cell values are randomly shuffled. In other words, the column representation is invariant to the ordering of the cell values within the query column.

2.2 Encoding the Target Type

In this section, we describe our strategy for encoding the target types. The JSON structure on the right in Fig. 2 illustrates the target Wikidata type *Film Award*. Each target type also has a glossary and a list of two-hop is-a ancestor labels from the ontology. In this work, we consider the number of hops as a hyper-parameter that remains fixed throughout.

Figure 2(C) illustrates our strategy for encoding the target type. First, we *linearize* the two-hop is-a ancestor labels as follows. As observed in Fig. 2, the two-hop is-a ancestor labels can be viewed as a list of lists wherein the inner list (or a path) contains at most two type label strings. In this example, there are two inner lists (or paths) which are *Award, Distinction* and *Competition, Event*, respectively. We concatenate the type label strings for each path using the special token SPTOK$_3$ as the separator. This action results in a single list of *linearized* paths. All the paths are then concatenated together using the special token SPTOK$_4$ as the separator. This sequence of steps yields a linearized view of the two-hop is-a ancestor label attribute for a given target type.

Finally, we concatenate the type label and the glossary using the special token SPTOK$_1$ as the separator. We then concatenate the result with the linearized view of the two-hop is-a ancestor labels. For the second step, we use the special token SPTOK$_2$ as the separator. This process yields the overall pseudo sentence in yellow (Fig. 2(C)).

We use a total of *four* token type IDs TOK$_0$ through TOK$_3$ in our architecture. As shown in Fig. 2(C), we use the token ID *zero* for the type label, *one* for the glossary, *two* for the parent type labels and *three* for the grandparent type labels. We initialize TOK$_0$ and TOK$_1$ to the two pre-trained token type embeddings of a BERT-*like* model. By BERT-*like* model, we refer to a pre-trained Transformer encoder model that has two Token Type IDs. For TOK$_2$ and TOK$_3$, we discovered that initializing it with the pre-trained token type embedding for token ID *one* of a BERT-*like* model generates the best results. We also tried out other initialization strategies, whose results are shown in Table 2.

Besides, we use a similar strategy as Sect. 2.1 for assigning Position IDs. Moreover, we use the standard approach for encoding attention masks, which is why we have omitted them from Fig. 2.

2.3 Putting it All Together

Our model architecture is illustrated in Fig. 3, which puts together the contents of the previous *two* subsections. The query column Q_c and the table headers H are first encoded using the strategy described in Sect. 2.1. Once the encoding is complete, it is processed through two Transformer encoder models named Transformer$_A$ and Transformer$_B$ respectively. The [CLS] vector from Transformer$_A$ and the [START] vector from Transformer$_B$ are considered as the representations for Q_c and H respectively. Both these representations are then concatenated together, processed through a linear layer first, followed by a GELU layer [14] to yield the final query vector q_v.

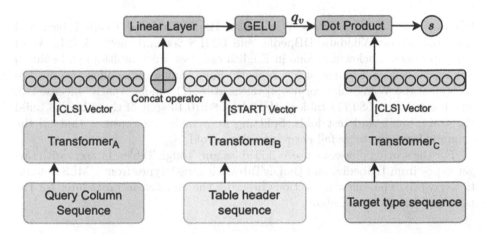

Fig. 3. Overview of our model architecture. Given a query column Q_c and table headers H, Sect. 2.1 describes how to generate the Query column and Table header sequences. Section 2.2 describes how to build the target type sequence.

On the other hand, the target type labels, together with the associated glossary and two-hop is-a ancestor labels, are first encoded using the strategy described in Sect. 2.2. It is then processed through Transformer$_C$. The overall score s is calculated as a *dot product* between the query vector q_v and the [CLS] vector from Transformer$_C$.

During the training phase, each instance, i.e., column Q_c, table headers H, and associated table metadata, may have one or more positive ground truth (GT) types. We use *random* sampling to generate *negative* types and then score both positive and negative types using the architecture described in Fig. 3. Furthermore, we use a binary cross-entropy loss for training.

During scoring, each test instance is provided a list of all possible type labels, a glossary, and information regarding two-hop is-a ancestor labels from the target ontology. This target ontology need not be the same ontology used during training; it can be a different ontology altogether bought in for scoring purposes only, which is unseen during training. As long as the target ontology has labels, a glossary, and is-a ancestor labels, we can use a Transformer model to encode this information as described above.

Since the list of all possible types from the target ontology stays fixed across all test instances, it can be processed once through Transformer$_C$, and the target type representations can be pre-computed. We can then re-use these pre-computed target type representations to generate a ranked list of types for each test instance. Alternatively, one can also use an off-the-shelf library for large-scale vector-similarity search, such as FAISS [23] for faster scoring. We use Mean Reciprocal Rank (MRR) and Hits@k metrics for evaluations.

3   Dataset Construction

We use three tabular datasets: WikiTables, BioDivTab, and Tough Tables, and three ontologies: Wikidata, DBpedia, and UMLS Semantic network [24]. All of our experiments below are done in English only; we leave multi-lingual column linking models as a source of future work. For training our models, we use the variant of the WikiTables corpus [4] released by [11] under Apache License 2.0, which consists of 580,171 tables. We did an 80:10:10 split of the tables to build the train, valid, and test folds. Splitting at a table level ensures that all the columns from one table fall entirely within a fold.

For the scoring phase, we use WikiTables and Tough Tables datasets with target types from DBpedia, and BioDivTab with target types from UMLS Semantic Network. The following sections describe the annotation procedures for the benchmarks mentioned above.

3.1   Building Datasets Using WikiTables

The WikiTables dataset contains Wikipedia page links for cell mentions, wherever available. We collect all the available Wikipedia page links for a given column and map them to Wikidata entity QIDs via a SPARQL query. Once the Wikidata QIDs are known, accumulating their corresponding types as a collection $\mathcal{T}$ is another SPARQL query. Assuming this column contains at least three Wikipedia page links, we find the *lowest common ancestor* (LCA) type of $\mathcal{T}$ within four hops. The *lowest common ancestor* (LCA) for K unique types is the closest type in the ontology graph which is a superclass to all the k types. Because the types that are too generic such as *Thing* or *Concept* are less useful for the downstream tasks, only 4 hops of super-types for each type are looked up for finding a common ancestor. If such an LCA type exists, we annotate it as the target type. Note that there can be multiple LCA types, in such cases, we consider all of them as target types.

During this annotation procedure, if the query column has less than three Wikipedia page links, or no *lowest common ancestor* exists within four hops, we assign a special NOTYPE for this column. Moreover, generic Wikidata types such as *class* or *entity* are ignored. Additionally, we under-sample columns from the NOTYPE class to reduce skewness in the training distribution. Specifically, we ensure that the size of the NoType class equals the size of the most frequent Wikidata type within the training fold.

For the validation and test folds, we use an Elastic-search-based Wikidata Lookup to generate the top twenty candidate types for each query column. If this lookup doesn't return any candidates for a query column, then that query column is removed from the fold. If this step returns less than twenty candidate types, we keep the query column and candidate types within the fold. During inference time, the model is asked to rank these candidate types for every query column. We have this lookup step because Wikidata has many types ($\geq$ 50K), and scoring all the Wikidata types for each query column is computationally expensive. In the future, we plan on investigating alternative approaches to this task that do not require a candidate generation step while working with Wikidata.

The annotation procedure, as described above, yields Wikidata types for the WikiTables dataset, whose statistics are as follows: We have 491,739 query columns for train, 61,204 for valid, and 69,135 for the test fold.

Next, we take the test fold tables of the WikiTables dataset and re-annotate the columns to types from DBpedia. We follow a similar strategy as described above. During the construction of this dataset, if we cannot find a ground truth DBpedia type for a particular column, then that column is dropped altogether.

Additionally, because DBPedia has a total of 782 types, we do not employ an Elastic-search-based candidate generation strategy; instead, we ask the model to rank all of the 782 types while scoring for a query column. This procedure yields an additional test dataset containing 47,849 columns from WikiTables test fold annotated DBpedia types.

3.2   Building Datasets Using BioDivTab

The BioDivTab dataset [2] based on biodiversity research data is a domain-specific tabular dataset consisting of 50 tables and is initially annotated with Wikidata types. Because we want to evaluate on types from an ontology different from the one used for training, we reannotated the columns within this dataset to types from UMLS Semantic Network. We had three annotators for this task; they had access to the ground truth Wikidata type and were asked to manually map the Wikidata type to the best-matching UMLS Semantic Network type. The disagreements in annotations were resolved via majority voting. Because our training dataset did not contain columns with floating point values, we removed such columns from this dataset. We leave the linking of columns containing numerical values to a type within an ontology as a future task.

This annotation procedure yielded a test set with 205 columns in total. Like DBpedia, while scoring for a query column, we ask the model to rank all 127 types belonging to the UMLS Semantic network.

3.3 Tough Tables Dataset

The Tough Tables (2T) dataset [9] is based on tables from multiple heterogeneous sources. This dataset is annotated with DBpedia type labels which are manually verified and puts particular emphasis on tables with ambiguous and misspelled mentions. This dataset has 540 query columns overall.

Table 1 below denotes the differences in the distribution of the type labels between datasets used for training and scoring. While scoring on DBpedia types, the model is given 782 types for each query instance to generate a ranking. Of the 782 type labels, only 268, i.e., 34.3%, have a non-empty description. For the others, we use an empty string.

Table 1. Statistics for WD (Wikidata) Train, DBP (DBpedia) and UMLS SN (Semantic Network). WD train represents statistics from our training dataset.

Ontology Property	WD Train	DBP	UMLS SN
Type labels	5,327	782	127
Labels with non-empty glossary	4,588	268	127
Avg 1hop ancestor *is-a* labels per type label	1.94	0.92	0.98
Avg 2hop ancestor *is-a* labels per type label	3.67	0.73	0.95
Labels with $\geq$ *five* 1hop ancestor *is-a* labels	125	0	0
Labels with $\geq$ *five* 2hop ancestor *is-a* labels	1,567	0	0

For training using Wikidata, we have non-empty descriptions for 86.1% of the Wikidata labels. Each Wikidata label, on average, has 3.67 two-hop ancestor is-a type labels. Additionally, 2.3% and 29.4% of the train Wikidata labels have at least five one-hop and two-hop ancestor is-a type labels, respectively. In contrast, DBpedia and UMLS SN have *less than one* two-hop ancestor is-a type label per target type.

4   Experiments and Analysis

We train a model once using the WikiTables training dataset annotated with Wikidata labels. We initialize using a pre-trained Transformer encoder and then fine-tune during our training procedure. Once training is complete, we evaluate independently on *three* test datasets having labels from DBpedia (same broad domain as Wikidata) and UMLS Semantic network (a more specialized biomedical domain).

4.1 Results on WikiTables and DBpedia

Table 2 shows the results on the Column Type annotation (CTA) task for the WikiTables test fold. We show results using both Wikidata (supervised task) and DBpedia, i.e., evaluating on a new ontology unseen during training.

Using Type Labels Only. We describe our results and analysis in *three* blocks depending upon the *Ontological artifacts used* (See Table 2) to build the model. In the *first* block, we use the Type labels only to encode the target type. In this baseline setting, we have *five* models depending upon the encoders used (See Fig. 3). The *first* two rows use TinyBERT [21] and BERTBase [12] to encode the query column, the table header, and the target type label.

Table 2. Results for the CTA task on the WikiTables test fold with labels from Wikidata (supervised task) and DBpedia (linking to unseen ontology). h=k indicates parent *is-a* labels upto k hops. H@k denotes Hits at k metric.

Ontological artifacts used	Encoder(s)	Wikidata		DBpedia		
		MRR	H@1	MRR	H@1	H@3
Type labels only (Baselines)	TinyBERT	0.84	0.741	0.465	0.306	0.569
	BERTBase	0.891	0.816	0.395	0.294	0.448
	BERTBase + WD-to-DBP lookup	0.891	0.816	0.192	0.154	0.210
	TAPASBase + BERTBase	0.884	0.804	0.378	0.292	0.422
	TABBIE + BERTBase	0.702	0.533	0.279	0.167	0.348
Type labels + **Glossary**	TinyBERT	0.857	0.764	0.489	0.374	0.531
	BERTBase	0.891	0.814	0.380	0.260	0.444
	TAPASBase + BERTBase	0.853	0.759	0.435	0.287	0.537
Type labels + Glossary + **is-a parent labels**	TinyBERT + GraphConv (h = 2)	0.859	0.767	0.395	0.244	0.478
	TinyBERT + GATConv (h=2)	0.857	0.766	0.445	0.313	0.497
	TinyBERT (*Baseline*1 encoding, h = 2)	0.843	0.746	0.468	0.325	0.562
	TinyBERT (*Baseline*2 encoding, h = 2)	0.859	0.770	0.424	0.267	0.520
	TinyBERT (*Our* encoding, h = 1)	0.847	0.750	0.496	0.375	0.563
	TinyBERT (*Our* encoding, h = 2)	0.854	0.762	**0.533**	**0.404**	**0.601**

The *third* row in Table 2 illustrates the CTA results for a *pipeline* approach. In this approach, we use the previous BERTBase encoder approach to generate a ranked list of Wikidata (WD) types for each query instance in the test set. For evaluating on DBpedia, we map the WD types to DBP types through a sequence of `owl:sameAs` and `rdf:type` properties using a SPARQL query to the DBpedia endpoint. We refer to this mapping as "WD-to-DBP lookup". The *fourth* row uses a pretrained TAPASBase [15] model to encode the query column and BERTBase to encode the target type label. The *fifth* row uses a pretrained TABBIE [20] model to encode the query table and separate BERTBase models to encode the table metadata and the target type label. TABBIE is the current state-of-the-art on *supervised* column linking and is table-centric, i.e., it encodes the entire table and then gets the embedding for the query column. In contrast, other models are column-centric, i.e., encode only the query column directly. TABBIE performs similarly to TaBERT on the CTA task over Viznet Web Tables [19] and outperforms SATO [33]. Thus, in our analysis, we compare against TABBIE only.

For predicting Wikidata types, we observe that BERTBase has a performance gain of roughly *five* points over TinyBERT on the MRR metric. The TAPAS-Base+BERTBase setup performs roughly similarly to BERTBase. In contrast, using a pretrained TABBIE model to encode columns, as described before, yields poorer results. Unlike [19] wherein a pretrained TABBIE is fine-tuned for CTA over a dataset containing 78 type labels only, in our experiments, we fine-tune over a training dataset containing 5,327 Wikidata Types (See Table 1). Additionally, unlike [19], our overall architecture is a Siamese network architecture designed to learn meaningful representations for the query column and the type labels to map the query column to the correct type label. The increase in the total number of target types, combined with a change in architecture, could be why fine-tuned TABBIE-based models yields poor results.

However, when evaluated on DBpedia target labels, we observe that the TinyBERT has the best performance of the lot. A plausible reason behind this could be that since BERTBase, TAPASBase, and TABBIE are bigger in size than TinyBERT, they are likely overfitting on the training distribution and are not generalizing as well as TinyBERT.

We observe that the *pipeline* approach (*third* row) performs very poorly when evaluated on DBpedia. Compared to Wikidata, this drop in performance can be attributed to errors within the "WD-to-DBP lookup". This lookup has insufficient coverage. Because it maps 50K Wikidata (WD) types to 782 DBpedia (DBP) types, many predicted WD types do not have an equivalent DBP type. Moreover, the alignments within this lookup are not consistent. For example, the WD type Q40357 (label: *prison*) does not map to the *dbo:Prison* DBP type. Due to these issues, using a human-mapped alignment can cause errors while linking to unseen ontologies. Moreover, based on the target unseen ontology, such alignments may or may not exist.

Using Type Labels and Glossary. In Rows *six* through *eight* of Table 2, we use Type labels and related glossary information to encode the target type sequence. In this setup, the type label gets the token ID zero and the glossary gets the token ID one (Sect. 2.2). Here, we use TinyBERT only, BERTBase only, and TAPASBase + BERTBase, all of which have been introduced before.

Here we are using additional glossary information compared to the *first* block in Table 2. Therefore, we believe that the models' performance *with* glossary information would be better than *without* glossary information. For TinyBERT, it is true, i.e., MRR on both Wikidata and DBpedia targets improves *with* glossary. For BERTBase, the MRR stays roughly the same *with* glossary compared to *without*. For TAPASBase + BERTBase, the MRR under DBpedia target improves *with* glossary. While comparing models in this block, we observe that TinyBERT still has the best MRR compared to others when scored against unseen DBpedia types.

Using Type Labels, Glossary, and is-a Parent Labels. In rows *nine* through *thirteen* of Table 2, we use Type labels, glossary, and is-a parent labels, i.e., a partial Taxonomy structure to encode the target type. We use TinyBERT for all experiments in this setting because of its smaller size, i.e., TinyBERT is roughly 7.5×–12× smaller than other Transformer encoders introduced in Sect. 4.1. We are interested in exploring how much we could push the envelope on the CTA task by using semantically enriched types with a smaller-sized transformer encoder.

Table 3. Results on BioDivTab and 2T datasets with types from UMLS Semantic network and DBpedia respectively.

Ontological artifacts used	Encoder(s)	BioDivTab		2T	
		MRR	Hits at 10	MRR	Hits at 1
Type labels only (Baseline)	TinyBERT	0.243	0.444	<u>0.325</u>	0.222
	BERTBase	<u>0.262</u>	<u>0.537</u>	0.296	0.219
	TAPASBase + BERTBase	0.253	0.409	0.296	0.228
	TABBIE + BERTBase	0.089	0.234	0.145	0.059
Type labels + Glossary + **2hop is-a parent labels**	TinyBERT + GATConv	**0.264**	0.444	**0.350**	<u>0.231</u>
	TinyBERT (*Our* Encoding)	0.193	**0.566**	**0.350**	**0.263**

The *ninth* and *tenth* rows of Table 2 use GraphConv [25] and GATConv [32] layers to encode the two-hop is-a partial taxonomy structure. This partial taxonomy structure can be modeled as a Graph wherein the nodes correspond to the types and edges correspond to "is-a" relation between the types. Only the target type node in this graph has a label and a glossary; all other type nodes only have a label string. We process the nodes through TinyBERT and use the [CLS] vector at the final layer as the node embedding. While building these models, we employ *two* layers of either GraphConv or GATConv, with a ReLU and a drop-out layer in between. The target type node embedding is then used to score against the query vector q_v as shown in Fig. 3.

The *eleventh* row denotes *Baseline*1 setup. Here, we use parent type labels up to two hops, and all the tokens in the target type sequence (Sect. 2.2) use a token type ID of *zero*. The *twelfth* row denotes the *Baseline*2 encoding. Compared to *Baseline*1, here we use *four* token type IDs, one each for the target type label, glossary, parent, and grand-parent types. Additionally, we initialize the two additional token type IDs (Sect. 2.2) using Xavier Initialization [13] prior to fine-tuning.

The final *two* rows denote models implementing our proposed strategy for encoding semantically enriched types. Our encoding strategy (Row *fourteen*), even when applied on TinyBERT, yields the best performance. Comparisons amongst *Baseline*1, *Baseline*2, and *Our* encodings, i.e., rows eleven, twelve, and fourteen, illustrate the ablation studies detailing the impact of different encoding and initialization strategies on this task. These results indicate that encoding richer ontological knowledge via meaningful representations results in better performance on an unseen ontology within the same general knowledge domain, i.e., from Wikidata to DBpedia in this case.

4.2   Results on BioDivTab and 2T

Table 3 illustrates the performance of our trained model when evaluated on the BioDivTab and 2T datasets with labels from UMLS Semantic Network and DBpedia respectively.

Following Sect. 4.1, we divide the results into two groups and use a total of *six* encoders for analysis. The sixth row uses TinyBERT to implement our strategy for encoding semantically enriched types. We separately analyze our results on BioDivTab and 2T datasets in the following sections.

Analysis on BioDivTab. As described before, the tables in BioDivTab belong to a biodiversity research domain and not an open domain like WikiTables. Moreover, the target UMLS Semantic network is from the biomedical domain which is more specialized than Wikidata, which was used for training. Thus, the results in Table 3 are much lower than those in Table 2.

We observe that our encoding strategy using TinyBERT yields the best Hits at 10 scores, outperforming baselines employing much larger encoders. However, in this case, TinyBERT+GATConv has the best performance overall in terms of MRR.

We manually analyzed the top-ranked predictions returned by the TinyBERT model trained using our proposed encoding strategy (Row *six* of Table 3). Unlike WikiTables, which contains English cell values, this dataset contains quite a few query columns having Latin cell values (corresponding to species names) which confuses our models trained on WikiTables. Therefore it makes errors while differentiating between organism types based on Latin cell values. Moreover, BioDivTab does not contain any metadata information to provide context. For columns containing numerical values, this absence of context promotes misclassifications, such as, our model predicts *Age Group* when the true label is *Quantitative Concept*. We show a few examples of the outputs generated by our proposed approach in Sect. A.1.

Analysis on 2T. From the results in Table 3, we observe that our proposed encoding strategy, even when applied on a smaller Transformer encoder, yields the best performance compared to baseline approaches, thereby indicating the effectiveness of our approach. Because 2T contains misspelled mentions, it likely confuses the models since they were trained on instances that did not have misspells. This could be a plausible reason why the performance on this dataset is lower than that of the WikiTables test fold with DBpedia target ontology (Table 2).

We manually analyzed the top-ranked predictions returned by the TinyBERT model trained using our proposed encoding strategy (Row *six*). We notice that, quite often, the model outputs are at a different granularity than the ground truth types. For example, there are four query columns having mentions of lakes with a ground truth type *place*; however, our above model correctly classifies it as *lake*. In another example, the model identifies *four* columns containing names of monarchs as *monarch*, with the ground truth label being *person*. Additionally, six columns contain names of cities with a ground truth type *place*. In this case, our model predicts it as *community*. We believe that the top-ranked predictions for the first two examples are better than the existing ground truth label. In contrast, it is worse for the last example.

5 Related Work

Linking tabular columns to types in an ontology is a crucial task for many business intelligence tasks such as semantic retrieval, data exploration, knowledge discovery, etc. [6,7,11] have studied this task based on cell values only, i.e., using only the available information in a table for linking columns without doing entity linking first. [11] introduce a new dataset for the supervised CTA task by annotating WikiTables columns with Freebase types.

[16] introduced Viznet, a large-scale corpus of over 31 million datasets. The dataset of particular interest here is the WebTables dataset. [33] introduce SATO, a supervised model that combines topic modeling and structured learning with single-column type prediction based on Sherlock [17]. SATO is trained on a subset of the WebTables dataset comprising relational tables with valid headers only.

The Column Type Annotation task within the SemTab challenge [22] benchmarks systems that annotate tabular data to types within a target ontology. For this task, participating systems are not given training data. They are asked to output a type for each query instance within a collection of held-out tables. Systems such as MTab [27], JenTab [1], Kepler-aSI [3], DAGOBAH [18], etc., participating in this challenge follow a pipeline architecture. The first step links cell mentions to entities within the target ontology. The second step predicts the most likely type for the query column based on the linking results. MTab and DAGOBAH also use additional information from the graph, such as entity relations, to improve cell linking accuracy. These approaches rely on the cell linking performance and suffer if the target ontology does not contain any entities to link to, which is very common in industry-specific ontologies.

Entity typing in a zero-shot fashion over textual data is a well-studied problem. FIGER [28] leverages Wikipedia descriptions of types to learn a multi-class classifier given an entity mention and its context. MZET [35] uses a memory network that models the relationship between the entity mention and the entity type and transfers the knowledge from seen entity types to the zero-shot ones. NZFET [29] uses a bi-LSTM architecture and employs entity type attention to focus on information relevant to the entity type.

MSF [8] uses additional auxiliary information such as WordNet glossaries, type hierarchy, and prototype mentions to get richer type representations. This approach independently models the interaction between the query mention and each auxiliary information. It obtains fused results in the next step. In contrast, our method jointly encodes the type label, the glossary, and the partial taxonomy structure to yield more meaningful type representations.

6   Conclusion

This paper introduces a novel approach for linking tabular columns to types in a new ontology unseen during training. We argue that this task is vital for business intelligence applications wherein data discovery needs within enterprise data lakes vary from one consumer role to another. We further argued that current academic datasets used for research in Table Understanding are unsuitable for this task and therefore introduced three new datasets. We enriched the ground truth type label within each new dataset with a glossary and a partial taxonomy structure. We show that encoding this auxiliary information for types via our proposed approach yields meaningful representations, which we can combine to build models that perform well on this task. Through extensive evaluation and analysis on these new datasets, we demonstrate the effectiveness of our proposed approach.

7   Limitations

In this work, we have used English WikiTables as the source of tabular datasets and trained a column linking model using Wikidata types. We then apply this trained model to score query columns against target ontologies having different levels of type granularities. As evidenced by results in Sect. 4.2, models trained on broad-domain WikiTables might not be reliably used to handle domain-specific jargon when working with the BioDivTab dataset, which contains cell values from the biodiversity research domain. Alternatively, if the tabular dataset contains misspells (e.g., 2T dataset), which is characteristic of many real-world datasets, hoping that a model trained on WikiTables only will generalize in such cases, might not hold.

In this work, we have shown results using Relational Tables only, i.e., tables with a well-defined 2D structure. If a user brings in, let's say, a non-relational table and queries it for Column linking against our WikiTables-only trained model, the results returned might be far from ideal. In other words, the scope of the empirical evaluations covers 2D Relational Tables only.

Summarizing the above points, we believe that, with this implementation, the Zero-shot performance on the Column linking task, when evaluated on domains far apart from the one used during training, would be less than ideal. In such cases, either building more extensive training data spanning multiple domains and using it for training or employing a human-in-the-loop approach to provide feedback to model predictions and then taking necessary corrective actions could help alleviate the limitations described above.

Supplemental Material Statement: The variant of the WikiTables corpus used in our work (and as released by [11]) are available at: https://github.com/sunlab-osu/TURL. Additionally, the original dataset files for BioDivTab annotated with Wikidata, and Tough Tables annotated with DBPedia are available at https://zenodo.org/record/6461556 and https://zenodo.org/record/6211551 respectively.

We have attached the WikiTables benchmark, annotated with Wikidata and DBPedia types, and the BioDivTab benchmark, annotated with UMLS Semantic Network types, as supplemental materials to this submission. We will provide the source code corresponding to this work, once the anonymity period ends.

The following enumerates the experimental details and the hyperparameters used in all our experiments. We performed a grid search using the validation fold of the WikiTables dataset containing Wikidata labels.

For the learning rate, we performed a grid search over {2e-5, 3e-5, 5e-5} and decided to use 2e-5. All of our experiments are run for a maximum of 40 epochs, with an early stopping criterion of 5 epochs. We had a fixed batch size of 64 in all our experiments. We used *random* negative sampling in all our experiments to generate negatives. For the transformer models in this task, we performed a grid search for the max tokenizer length parameter over {128, 256} and decided to use 128. We used a *longest first* truncation strategy, i.e., any sequence longer than 128 tokens is truncated to a maximum token length of 128.

For experiments using Graph Neural Networks (GNN), we used *two* GNN layers overall. We also used a ReLU layer and a drop-out layer between the two GNN layers. For the drop-out value, we performed a grid search over {0.1, 0.2, 0.3, 0.5} and used 0.1 for GATConv, and 0.2 for GraphConv. For experiments using TABBIE [20], we used a batch size of 2.

Furthermore, unless otherwise mentioned, we impose a max compute budget of 48 h (or 72 h if a pretrained TABBIE model is used). If a training run did not converge after 48 h (or 72 h for TABBIE), we used its last serialized checkpoint for scoring. The compute budget ensures that the carbon footprint corresponding to these training runs is bounded.

We used PyTorch v1.8.1, torch-scatter v2.0.9, torch-geometric v2.1.0.post1, and torch-sparse v0.6.12 for running our experiments on Linux RHEL v8.5 operating system using Intel x86 CPU and NVIDIA A100 GPU machines. All of our experiments use a maximum RAM of 32G and a random seed value of 73.

A   Appendix

A.1   Model Predictions

The following tables below shows examples of predictions returned by our proposed model built using a pretrained TinyBERT encoder. This model is trained using Wikidata labels and is asked to predict from the DBpedia target ontology for the top two tables. For the bottom two tables, the model predicts from the UMLS Semantic Network (UMLS SN).

The *first* row in the block titled **Top model prediction** returns model predictions using Type labels only. The *second* row returns predictions using Type labels and associated glossaries. The *final* row in this block returns predictions using our proposed encoding strategy. Note that the BioDivTab benchmark does not contain table metadata.

PageTitle SecTitle	1993-94 NBA Season Statistics leaders		PageTitle SecTitle	1970 TANFL season 1970 TANFL Ladder
Header	Player		Header	Team
Query column	David Robinson Dennis Rodman John Stockton Dikembe Mutombo Shaquille O'Neal		Query column	Sandy Bay Clarence New Norfolk North Hobart Glenorchy
Dataset Ontology	WikiTables DBpedia		Dataset Ontology	WikiTables DBpedia
Top model prediction	agent american football coach basketball player		Top model prediction	sports club sports club australian football team
True label	basketball player		True label	australian football team

Header	Species Group		Header	genus
Query column	plants bryophytes lichens moths heteroptera		Query column	ambloplites catostomus chrosomus notropis clinostomus
Dataset Ontology	BioDivTab UMLS SN		Dataset Ontology	BioDivTab UMLS SN
Top model prediction	organism attribute human organism		Top model prediction	organism attribute organism function bacterium
True label	organism		True label	fish

References

1. Abdelmageed, N., Schindler, S.: Jentab meets semtab 2021's new challenges. In: SemTab@ ISWC, pp. 42–53 (2021)
2. Abdelmageed, N., Schindler, S., König-Ries, B.: BiodivTab: a tabular benchmark based on biodiversity research data. In: SemTab@ISWC, submitted (2021)
3. Baazouzi, W., Kachroudi, M., Faiz, S.: Kepler-asi at semtab 2021. In: SemTab@ ISWC, pp. 54–67 (2021)
4. Bhagavatula, C.S., Noraset, T., Downey, D.: TabEL: entity linking in web tables. In: Arenas, M., et al. (eds.) ISWC 2015. LNCS, vol. 9366, pp. 425–441. Springer, Cham (2015). https://doi.org/10.1007/978-3-319-25007-6_25
5. Bogatu, A., Fernandes, A.A.A., Paton, N.W., Konstantinou, N.: Dataset discovery in data lakes. In: 2020 IEEE 36th International Conference on Data Engineering (ICDE), pp. 709–720 (2020)

6. Chen, J., Jiménez-Ruiz, E., Horrocks, I., Sutton, C.: Colnet: embedding the semantics of web tables for column type prediction. In: The Thirty-Third AAAI Conference on Artificial Intelligence, AAAI 2019, Honolulu, Hawaii, USA, 27 January–1 February 2019, pp. 29–36. AAAI Press (2019). https://doi.org/10.1609/aaai.v33i01.330129

7. Chen, J., Jiménez-Ruiz, E., Horrocks, I., Sutton, C.: Learning semantic annotations for tabular data. In: Kraus, S. (ed.) Proceedings of the Twenty-Eighth International Joint Conference on Artificial Intelligence, IJCAI 2019, Macao, China, 10–16 August 2019, pp. 2088–2094. ijcai.org (2019). https://doi.org/10.24963/ijcai.2019/289

8. Chen, Y., et al.: An empirical study on multiple information sources for zero-shot fine-grained entity typing. In: Moens, M., Huang, X., Specia, L., Yih, S.W. (eds.) Proceedings of the 2021 Conference on Empirical Methods in Natural Language Processing, EMNLP 2021, Virtual Event/Punta Cana, Dominican Republic, 7–11 November, 2021, pp. 2668–2678. Association for Computational Linguistics (2021). https://doi.org/10.18653/v1/2021.emnlp-main.210

9. Cutrona, V., Bianchi, F., Jiménez-Ruiz, E., Palmonari, M.: Tough tables: carefully evaluating entity linking for tabular data. In: Pan, J.Z., et al. (eds.) ISWC 2020. LNCS, vol. 12507, pp. 328–343. Springer, Cham (2020). https://doi.org/10.1007/978-3-030-62466-8_21

10. Dash, S., Bagchi, S., Mihindukulasooriya, N., Gliozzo, A.: Permutation invariant strategy using transformer encoders for table understanding. In: Findings of the Association for Computational Linguistics: NAACL 2022, pp. 788–800. Association for Computational Linguistics, Seattle (2022). https://doi.org/10.18653/v1/2022.findings-naacl.59. https://aclanthology.org/2022.findings-naacl.59

11. Deng, X., Sun, H., Lees, A., Wu, Y., Yu, C.: TURL: table understanding through representation learning. Proc. VLDB Endow. **14**(3), 307–319 (2020). https://doi.org/10.5555/3430915.3442430. http://www.vldb.org/pvldb/vol14/p307-deng.pdf

12. Devlin, J., Chang, M., Lee, K., Toutanova, K.: BERT: pre-training of deep bidirectional transformers for language understanding. In: Burstein, J., Doran, C., Solorio, T. (eds.) Proceedings of the 2019 Conference of the North American Chapter of the Association for Computational Linguistics: Human Language Technologies, NAACL-HLT 2019, Minneapolis, MN, USA, 2–7 June 2019, vol. 1 (Long and Short Papers), pp. 4171–4186. Association for Computational Linguistics (2019). https://doi.org/10.18653/v1/n19-1423

13. Glorot, X., Bengio, Y.: Understanding the difficulty of training deep feedforward neural networks. In: Teh, Y.W., Titterington, D.M. (eds.) Proceedings of the Thirteenth International Conference on Artificial Intelligence and Statistics, AISTATS 2010, Chia Laguna Resort, Sardinia, Italy, 13–15 May 2010. JMLR Proceedings, vol. 9, pp. 249–256. JMLR.org (2010). http://proceedings.mlr.press/v9/glorot10a.html

14. Hendrycks, D., Gimpel, K.: Gaussian error linear units (gelus). arXiv preprint arXiv:1606.08415 (2016)

15. Herzig, J., Nowak, P.K., Müller, T., Piccinno, F., Eisenschlos, J.: TaPas: weakly supervised table parsing via pre-training. In: Proceedings of the 58th Annual Meeting of the Association for Computational Linguistics, pp. 4320–4333. Association for Computational Linguistics, Online (2020). https://doi.org/10.18653/v1/2020.acl-main.398. https://aclanthology.org/2020.acl-main.398

16. Hu, K., et al.: Viznet: towards a large-scale visualization learning and benchmarking repository. In: Proceedings of the 2019 Conference on Human Factors in Computing Systems (CHI). ACM (2019)

17. Hulsebos, M., et al.: Sherlock: a deep learning approach to semantic data type detection. In: Teredesai, A., Kumar, V., Li, Y., Rosales, R., Terzi, E., Karypis, G. (eds.) Proceedings of the 25th ACM SIGKDD International Conference on Knowledge Discovery & Data Mining, KDD 2019, Anchorage, AK, USA, 4–8 August 2019, pp. 1500–1508. ACM (2019). https://doi.org/10.1145/3292500.3330993

18. Huynh, V.P., et al.: Dagobah: table and graph contexts for efficient semantic annotation of tabular data. In: SemTab@ISWC, pp. 19–31 (2021)

19. Iida, H., Thai, D., Manjunatha, V., Iyyer, M.: TABBIE: pretrained representations of tabular data. In: Toutanova, K., et al (eds.) Proceedings of the 2021 Conference of the North American Chapter of the Association for Computational Linguistics: Human Language Technologies, NAACL-HLT 2021, Online, 6–11 June 2021, pp. 3446–3456. Association for Computational Linguistics (2021). https://doi.org/10.18653/v1/2021.naacl-main.270

20. Iida, H., Thai, D., Manjunatha, V., Iyyer, M.: TABBIE: pretrained representations of tabular data. In: Proceedings of the 2021 Conference of the North American Chapter of the Association for Computational Linguistics: Human Language Technologies, pp. 3446–3456. Association for Computational Linguistics, Online (2021). https://doi.org/10.18653/v1/2021.naacl-main.270. https://aclanthology.org/2021.naacl-main.270

21. Jiao, X., et al.: Tinybert: distilling BERT for natural language understanding. In: Cohn, T., He, Y., Liu, Y. (eds.) Findings of the Association for Computational Linguistics: EMNLP 2020, Online Event, Findings of ACL, 16–20 November 2020, vol. EMNLP 2020, pp. 4163–4174. Association for Computational Linguistics (2020). https://doi.org/10.18653/v1/2020.findings-emnlp.372

22. Jiménez-Ruiz, E., Hassanzadeh, O., Efthymiou, V., Chen, J., Srinivas, K.: SemTab 2019: resources to benchmark tabular data to knowledge graph matching systems. In: Harth, A., et al. (eds.) ESWC 2020. LNCS, vol. 12123, pp. 514–530. Springer, Cham (2020). https://doi.org/10.1007/978-3-030-49461-2_30

23. Johnson, J., Douze, M., Jégou, H.: Billion-scale similarity search with gpus. CoRR abs/1702.08734 (2017). http://arxiv.org/abs/1702.08734

24. McCray, A.T.: An upper-level ontology for the biomedical domain. Comput. Funct. Genomics 4, 80–84 (2003)

25. Morris, C., Ritzert, M., Fey, M., Hamilton, W.L., Lenssen, J.E., Rattan, G., Grohe, M.: Weisfeiler and leman go neural: Higher-order graph neural networks. In: The Thirty-Third AAAI Conference on Artificial Intelligence, AAAI 2019, USA, 27 January–1 February 2019, pp. 4602–4609. AAAI Press (2019). https://doi.org/10.1609/aaai.v33i01.33014602

26. Mulwad, V., Finin, T., Syed, Z., Joshi, A.: Using linked data to interpret tables. In: Hartig, O., Harth, A., Sequeda, J.F. (eds.) Proceedings of the First International Workshop on Consuming Linked Data, Shanghai, China, 8 November 2010, CEUR Workshop Proceedings, vol. 665. CEUR-WS.org (2010). http://ceur-ws.org/Vol-665/MulwadEtAl_COLD2010.pdf

27. Nguyen, P., Yamada, I., Kertkeidkachorn, N., Ichise, R., Takeda, H.: Semtab 2021: Tabular data annotation with mtab tool. In: Jiménez-Ruiz, E., et al. (eds.) Proceedings of the Semantic Web Challenge on Tabular Data to Knowledge Graph Matching co-located with the 20th International Semantic Web Conference (ISWC 2021), Virtual conference, 27 October 2021, CEUR Workshop Proceedings, vol. 3103, pp. 92–101. CEUR-WS.org (2021). http://ceur-ws.org/Vol-3103/paper8.pdf

28. Obeidat, R., Fern, X., Shahbazi, H., Tadepalli, P.: Description-based zero-shot fine-grained entity typing. In: Proceedings of the 2019 Conference of the North American Chapter of the Association for Computational Linguistics: Human Language Technologies, vol. 1 (Long and Short Papers), pp. 807–814 (2019)

29. ,bibitemch27DBLP:confspswwwspsRenLZ20 Ren, Y., Lin, J., Zhou, J.: Neural zero-shot fine-grained entity typing. In: Seghrouchni, A.E.F., Sukthankar, G., Liu, T., van Steen, M. (eds.) Companion of The 2020 Web Conference 2020, Taipei, Taiwan, 20–24 April 2020. pp. 846–847. ACM/IW3C2 (2020). https://doi.org/10.1145/3366424.3382725

30. Ritze, D., Lehmberg, O., Bizer, C.: Matching HTML tables to dbpedia. In: Akerkar, R., Dikaiakos, M.D., Achilleos, A., Omitola, T. (eds.) Proceedings of the 5th International Conference on Web Intelligence, Mining and Semantics, WIMS 2015, Larnaca, Cyprus, 13–15 July 2015, pp. 10:1–10:6. ACM (2015)

31. Suhara, Y., et al.: Annotating columns with pre-trained language models. arXiv preprint arXiv:2104.01785 (2021)

32. Velickovic, P., Cucurull, G., Casanova, A., Romero, A., Liò, P., Bengio, Y.: Graph attention networks. In: 6th International Conference on Learning Representations, ICLR 2018, Vancouver, BC, Canada, 30 April–3 May 2018, Conference Track Proceedings. OpenReview.net (2018). https://openreview.net/forum?id=rJXMpikCZ

33. Zhang, D., Suhara, Y., Li, J., Hulsebos, M., Demiralp, Ç., Tan, W.: Sato: contextual semantic type detection in tables. Proc. VLDB Endow. **13**(11), 1835–1848 (2020). http://www.vldb.org/pvldb/vol13/p1835-zhang.pdf

34. Zhang, S., Balog, K.: Web table extraction, retrieval, and augmentation: a survey. ACM Trans. Intell. Syst. Technol. **11**(2), 13:1–13:35 (2020). https://doi.org/10.1145/3372117

35. Zhang, T., Xia, C., Lu, C.T., Philip, S.Y.: Mzet: memory augmented zero-shot fine-grained named entity typing. In: Proceedings of the 28th International Conference on Computational Linguistics, pp. 77–87 (2020)

Neural Multi-hop Logical Query Answering with Concept-Level Answers

Zhenwei Tang[1,3]([✉]), Shichao Pei[2], Xi Peng[3], Fuzhen Zhuang[4,5],
Xiangliang Zhang[2], and Robert Hoehndorf[3]

[1] University of Toronto, Toronto, ON, Canada
josephtang@cs.toronto.edu
[2] University of Notre Dame, Notre Dame, IN, USA
{spei2,xzhang33}@nd.com
[3] Computational Bioscience Research Center, King Abdullah University of Science
and Technology, Thuwal, Saudi Arabia
{xi.peng,robert.hoehndorf}@kaust.edu.sa
[4] Institute of Artificial Intelligence, Beihang University, Beijing, China
zhuangfuzhen@buaa.edu.cn
[5] Zhongguancun Laboratory, Beijing, China

Abstract. Neural multi-hop logical query answering (LQA) is a fundamental task to explore relational data such as knowledge graphs, which aims at answering multi-queries with logical operations based on distributed representations of queries and answers. Although previous LQA methods can give specific **instance-level** answers, they are not able to provide descriptive **concept-level** answers, where each concept is a description of a set of instances. Concept-level answers are more comprehensible to users and are of great usefulness in the field of applied ontology. In this work, we formulate the problem of LQA with concept-level answers (LQAC), solving which needs to address challenges in **incorporating, representing,** and **operating on concepts.** We propose an original solution for LQAC. Firstly, we incorporate description logic-based ontological axioms to provide the source of concepts. Then, we represent concepts and queries as fuzzy sets, i.e., sets whose elements have degrees of membership, to bridge concepts and queries with instances. Moreover, we design operators involving concepts on top of fuzzy set representation of concepts and queries for optimization and inference. Extensive experimental results on three real-world datasets demonstrate the effectiveness of our method for LQAC. In particular, we show that our method is promising in discovering complex logical biomedical facts.

Keywords: Knowledge Representation Learning · Multi-hop Logical Query Answering · Fuzzy Logic · Neuro-symbolic Reasoning

1 Introduction

Along with the rapid development of high-quality large-scale knowledge infrastructures [2,35], researchers are increasingly interested in exploiting knowledge

© The Author(s), under exclusive license to Springer Nature Switzerland AG 2023
T. R. Payne et al. (Eds.): ISWC 2023, LNCS 14265, pp. 522–540, 2023.
https://doi.org/10.1007/978-3-031-47240-4_28

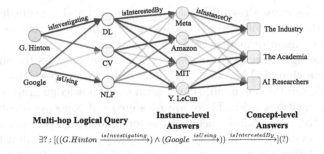

Fig. 1. An example of neural multi-hop logical query answering with concept-level answers (LQAC). The query is "Who will be interested in techniques that G. Hinton is investigating and Google is using?". The answers are not only instance-level answers as yellow circles: *Meta, Amazon, MIT*, and *Y. LeCun*, but also concept-level answers as squares: *AI Researchers, The Academia*, and *The Industry*. Such concept-level descriptive answers are more comprehensible to users.

bases for real-world applications, such as knowledge graph completion [8,34] and entity alignment [36]. Recent years have witnessed increasing interest in a fundamental yet challenging task on such relational data, i.e. neural multi-hop logical query answering (LQA), which attempts to answer complex structured queries that include logical operations and multi-hop projections given the facts in knowledge bases using learned distributed representations [15]. Efforts [15,29,30] have been made to develop LQA systems by designing strategies to learn geometric or uncertainty-aware distributed query representations, and proposing mechanisms to deal with various logical operations on these distributed representations. However, existing LQA methods are limited to providing instances of knowledge graphs as answers.

In many real-world scenarios, providing only instance-level answers is insufficient because users may also seek more descriptive concept-level answers, where each of the concepts is a description of a set of instances. For example, in online question-answering forums, as shown in Fig. 1, users may ask "Who will be interested in techniques that G. Hinton is investigating and Google is using?" and expect both instance-level answers like *Meta, Amazon, MIT*, and *Y. LeCun*, as well as concept-level answers such as *AI Researchers, The Academia*, and *The Industry*. In this example, the conceptual answer *The Academia* refers to a summary of a set of instances consisting of *Y. LeCun* and *MIT*. Such concept-level answers augment the answer set to make it more comprehensible to users and fulfill their need for both detailed and abstract answers. In biomedical applications, to find the causes of a set of symptoms, scientists expect both instance-level answers (such as *SARS-CoV-2* causing *Fever*) as well as concept-level answers (such as *Viral infections* causing *Fever*). In this case, the answer constitutes a descriptive concept-level answer (e.g., *Viral infections*) that is a summary of a set of instance-level answers. Other downstream tasks such as online chatbots [26] and conversational recommender systems [39] also need rich and comprehensive answers to provide better services. Providing both instance-level and concept-level answers can improve their capability of generating more informative responses for users and enrich the semantics in answers for downstream tasks.

Despite the significance of providing concept-level answers to multi-hop logical queries, previous LQA systems [15,29,30] do not support that for the following reasons. On the one hand, they reason over knowledge graphs where only instances and relations exist. There are no sources of concepts involved in their systems. On the other hand, mechanisms for exploiting concepts are lacking. Specifically, previous solutions only measure query–instance similarity for LQA, without considering concept representations and operators involving concepts, such as a proper measurement of query–concept similarity.

Along this line, we propose an initial solution for neural multi-hop logical queries with concept-level answers (LQAC). The key challenges for addressing LQAC are to incorporate, represent, and to operate on concepts. First, we observe that terminological axioms in ontologies include taxonomic hierarchies of concepts, concept definitions, and concept subsumption axioms [14]. To **incorporate** concepts into for LQAC, we thus introduce terminological axioms into the system to provide sources of concepts. Second, we find that fuzzy sets [21], i.e., sets whose elements have degrees of membership, can naturally bridge instances with concepts while providing a notion of vagueness for sets of instances. Therefore, we **represent** concepts as fuzzy sets for LQAC. Meanwhile, properly representing queries is the prerequisite for effectively operating on concepts. We find that fuzzy sets can also bridge instances with queries, i.e., vague sets of instance-level answers. The theoretically supported and unparameterized fuzzy set operations enable us to resolve logical operations within queries. Thus, fuzzy sets are ideal for concept and query representation for LQAC. Then, **operators** involving concepts can also be designed based on fuzzy sets, including query–concept operators for concept retrieval, concept–concept operators for concept subsumption, and instance–concept operators for concept instantiation.

The main contributions of this work are: (1) To the best of our knowledge, we are the first to focus on the LQAC problem that aims at providing not only instance-level but also concept-level answers. LQAC goes beyond LQA over knowledge graphs and better satisfies the need of users, downstream tasks, and ontological applications; (2) We propose an initial solution for LQAC that incorporates, represents, and operates on concepts. We incorporate terminological axioms to provide sources of concepts and employ fuzzy sets as the representations of concepts and queries. Logical operations are supported by the well-established fuzzy set theory and operators involving concepts are designed upon fuzzy sets.

2   Related Work

Neural Multi-hop Logical Query Answering. Great efforts have been made to develop LQA systems in recent years. GQE [15] formulated the LQA problem and proposed to use points in the embeddings space to represent logical queries. Q2B [29] use hyper-rectangles that can include multiple points in the embedding space to represent queries. HypE [11], ConE [38], and BetaE [30] extended Q2B by using more sophisticated geometric shapes or Beta distributions for query representation. More recent methods explore fuzzy logic [21] for LQA. CQD [1] used t-norm and t-conorms from the fuzzy logic theory to achieve promising performance on zero-shot settings. QTO [7] further improves CQD by introducing query tree optimization. FuzzQE [10], GNN-QE [40], and LogicE [27] directly represent entities and queries using embeddings with specially designed restrictions and interpreted them as fuzzy sets for LQA. However, these reasoners could only give instance-level answers, while we focus on the more general LQAC problem that aims at additionally providing descriptive concepts as answers. Furthermore, they either use bit-wise fuzzy logic without fuzzy **sets** or use fuzzy sets with the number of elements that coincides with the embedding dimension, while we adhere to the foundational definition of fuzzy sets [21], allowing us to fully exploit theoretically supported fuzzy set operations.

Ontology Representation Learning. Several methods have been developed to exploit ontologies using distributed representation learning [24]. ELEm [23], EmEL [28], and BoxEL [37] learn geometric embeddings for concepts in ontologies. Other approaches [9,32] rely on graph embeddings or word embeddings and apply them to ontological axioms. Another line of research [16,17] focuses on jointly embedding instances (entities) and relations in knowledge graphs together with concepts and roles (relations) in ontological axioms. Our work is related in that we incorporate description logic ontological axioms and we exploit concepts with distributed representation learning. However, previous methods are limited to link prediction tasks such as predicting protein–protein interactions or performing knowledge graph completion, which can be regarded as answering *1p* queries in Fig. 2, whereas we focus on more complex multi-hop logical queries.

3 Methodology

Incorporating, representing, and operating on concepts are key to LQAC. In this section, we first formulate the problem along with the process of incorporating concepts into the reasoning system. Then we propose an original solution for LQAC by designing concept representations and operators involving concepts.

3.1 Incorporating Concepts

Multi-hop Logical Query Answering (LQA) is defined on knowledge graphs. A knowledge graph is formulated as $\mathcal{KG} = \{\langle h, r, t \rangle\} \subseteq \mathcal{E} \times \mathcal{R} \times \mathcal{E}$, where h, r, t denote the head entity (instance), relation, and tail entity (instance) in triple $\langle h, r, t \rangle$, respectively, $\mathcal{E}$ and $\mathcal{R}$ refer to the instance set and the relation set in $\mathcal{KG}$. As shown in Fig. 2.(a), each triple $\langle h, r, t \rangle$ is regarded as a positive sample of the *1p* query $\exists ? : [h \xrightarrow{r}](?)$ with an answer t that satisfies $[h \xrightarrow{r}](t)$,

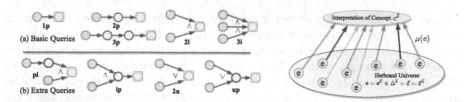

Fig. 2. Left: The considered types of queries are represented with their graphical structures. ∧ and ∨ represent the intersection and union logical operations, respectively. Squares denote concepts and circles represent instances. Right: Illustration of the interpretation of a concept $c^{\mathcal{I}}$.

where h is the anchor instance and $\xrightarrow{r}$ is the projection operation with relation r. Furthermore, LQA may also address the intersection, union, and negation operations ∧, ∨, and ¬ within queries. Thus, infinite types of queries can be found with the combinations of these logical operations. We consider the representative types of queries, which are listed and demonstrated with their graphical structures in Fig. 2. For example, queries of type pi in Fig. 2.(b) are to ask $\exists? : [(h_1 \xrightarrow{r_1} \xrightarrow{r_2}) \wedge (h_2 \xrightarrow{r_3})](?)$. LQA reasoners seek to provide a set of instances that satisfy the query as answers. We predict the possibility of each candidate instance $e \in \mathcal{E}$ satisfying a query $\exists? : [q](?)$. We then rank the $|\mathcal{E}|$ possibilities and select the top-k instances in $\mathcal{E}$ as the set of answers. Since all the candidate answers are instances, we can only retrieve instance-level answers from LQA systems.

LQA with Concept-Level Answers (LQAC) is based on a description logic-based knowledge base $\mathcal{KB}$, i.e., ontology, which is an ordered pair $(\mathcal{T}, \mathcal{A})$ for TBox $\mathcal{T}$ and ABox $\mathcal{A}$, where $\mathcal{T}$ is a finite set of terminological axioms and $\mathcal{A}$ is a finite set of assertion axioms. Specifically, terminological axioms within a TBox $\mathcal{T}$ are of the form $c_1 \sqsubseteq c_2$ where the symbol $\sqsubseteq$ denotes subsumption ($subClassOf$). In general, c_1 and c_2 can be concept descriptions that consist of concept names, quantifiers, roles (relations), and logical operators; we limit LQAC to axioms where c_1 and c_2 are concept names that will not involve roles or logical operators [3]. In the following, we do not distinguish between a concept name and a concept description unless there are special needs. In this case, a TBox is:

$$\mathcal{T} \subseteq \{c_i \sqsubseteq c_j | c_i, c_j \in \mathcal{C}\} \tag{1}$$

where $\mathcal{C}$ denotes the set of concept names in $\mathcal{KB}$. $\mathcal{T}$ accounts for the source of concepts and the pairwise concept subsumption information in the LQAC system. Assertion axioms in $\mathcal{A}$ consist of two parts, including role assertions:

$$\mathcal{A}_{ee} \subseteq \{\langle e_1, r, e_2 \rangle | e_1, e_2 \in \mathcal{E}, r \in \mathcal{R}\} \tag{2}$$

where $e_1, e_2 \in \mathcal{E}$ denote instances (entities), $\mathcal{E}$ denotes the instance set in $\mathcal{KB}$, $r \in \mathcal{R}$ denotes the role assertion between e_1 and e_2, and $\mathcal{R}$ is the role set of

$\mathcal{A}_{ee}$. $\mathcal{A}_{ee}$ accounts for the triple-wise relational information about instances and roles. $\mathcal{A}$ also include the concept instantiations between an instance $e \in \mathcal{E}$ and a concept $c \in \mathcal{C}$:

$$\mathcal{A}_{ec} = \{e \triangleleft c\} \subseteq \mathcal{E} \times \mathcal{C}, \tag{3}$$

where $e \triangleleft c$ represents e is an element in c. $\mathcal{A}_{ec}$ serves as the bridge between $\mathcal{T}$ and $\mathcal{A}_{ee}$ by providing pairwise links between instances and concepts.

Since we incorporate concepts in the LQAC systems, we are able to ask questions about concepts. In particular, for a query $\exists? : [q](?)$, we not only provide a set of instances of $\{a_e\}$ as the answers but also infer an explanation for each query result by summarizing instance-level answers with descriptive concepts, yielding another set of concept-level answers $\{a_c\}$. More specifically, as shown in Fig. 2, the answers are no longer restricted to be $e \in \mathcal{E}$ (denoted by circles), they can also be $c \in \mathcal{C}$ (denoted by squares). To achieve this, we predict the possibility of each candidate instance $e \in \mathcal{E}$ as well as the possibility of each candidate concept $c \in \mathcal{C}$ satisfying a query $\exists? : [q](?)$. We then rank $|\mathcal{E}|$ predicted scores of candidate instances and $|\mathcal{C}|$ predicted scores of candidate concepts. We select and combine the top-k results from each set of candidates as the final answers of q with instance-and-concept-level answers $\{a\} = \{a_e\} \bigcup \{a_c\}$. Note that LQA is a sub-problem of LQAC. First, an LQA reasoner can only provide a subset of the answers provided by an LQAC system, i.e., $\{a_e\} \subseteq \{a\}$. Also, the entire $\mathcal{KG}$ in the context of LQA corresponds to $\mathcal{A}_{ee}$ in LQAC, which is a subset of the ontology, i.e., $\mathcal{KG} \subseteq \mathcal{KB}$, leaving $\mathcal{T}$ and $\mathcal{A}_{ec}$ with conceptual information in the ontologies not explored. Therefore, LQAC is more general in terms of providing more answers and reasoning over more complex knowledge bases.

3.2 Representing Concepts

We are motivated to represent concepts as fuzzy sets by the relationship between concepts and instances. We gain insights into such a relationship from the definition of the semantics in description logics [6]:

Definition 1. *A terminological interpretation* $\mathcal{I} = (\Delta^{\mathcal{I}}, \cdot^{\mathcal{I}})$ *over a signature* $(\mathcal{C}, \mathcal{E}, \mathcal{R})$ *consists of:*

- *a non-empty set $\Delta^{\mathcal{I}}$ called the domain*
- *an interpretation function $\cdot^{\mathcal{I}}$ that maps:*
    - *every instance $e \in \mathcal{E}$ to an element $e^{\mathcal{I}} \in \Delta^{\mathcal{I}}$*
    - *every concept $c \in \mathcal{C}$ to a subset of $\Delta^{\mathcal{I}}$*
    - *every role (relation) $r \in \mathcal{R}$ to a subset of $\Delta^{\mathcal{I}} \times \Delta^{\mathcal{I}}$*

As we use a function-free language [3], we set $\Delta^{\mathcal{I}} = \mathcal{E}$, i.e., we focus on the Herbrand universe [25] of our knowledge base. Therefore, according to Definition 1, the interpretation of concept $c^{\mathcal{I}}$ is a subset of $\mathcal{E}$, which is finite. On the other hand, fuzzy sets [21] over the Herbrand Universe are finite sets whose elements have degrees of membership:

$$FS = \{\mu(x_1), \mu(x_2), \cdots, \mu(x_{|FS|})\}, \tag{4}$$

where $\mu(\cdot)$ is the membership function that measures the degree of membership of each element. Therefore, we further interpret all concepts as fuzzy sets over the finite domain $\Delta^{\mathcal{I}} = \mathcal{E} = \{e_1, e_2, \cdots, e_{|\mathcal{E}|}\}$ as the elements of fuzzy sets $\{x_1, x_2, \cdots, x_{|FS|}\}$. Thus, we have:

$$c^{\mathcal{I}} = \{\mu(e_1), \mu(e_2), \cdots, \mu(e_{|\mathcal{E}|})\}. \tag{5}$$

As shown in Fig. 2, since the Herbrand universe for our language is always finite, the interpretation of concept $c^{\mathcal{I}}$ is fully determined by the fuzzy membership function $\mu(\cdot)$ that assigns a degree of membership to each instance $e = e^{\mathcal{I}} \in \Delta^{\mathcal{I}} = \mathcal{E} = \mathcal{E}^{\mathcal{I}}$ for $c^{\mathcal{I}} \in \mathcal{C}^{\mathcal{I}}$, where $\mathcal{E}^{\mathcal{I}}$ and $\mathcal{C}^{\mathcal{I}}$ are the interpretation of the instance set and the concept set.

To obtain the degree of membership of instance e_i in $c^{\mathcal{I}}$, i.e., $\mu(e_i)$, we first randomly initialize the embedding matrix of concepts and instances as $\mathbf{E}_c \in \mathbb{R}^{|\mathcal{C}| \times d}$ and $\mathbf{E}_e \in \mathbb{R}^{|\mathcal{E}| \times d}$ with Xavier uniform initialization [13], where d is the embedding dimension. Then we obtain the embedding of each concept $\mathbf{c} \in \mathbb{R}^d$ by looking up the rows of $\mathbf{E}_c$. The embedding then serves as the generator of the fuzzy set representation of each concept FS_c. Thus, we compute the similarities between each concept c and every instance in our universe $e \in \mathcal{E} = \Delta^{\mathcal{I}}$ as the degrees of membership of each instance in the fuzzy set:

$$FS_c = \{\sigma(\mathbf{c} \otimes \mathbf{E}_e^T)\} = c^{\mathcal{I}}, \tag{6}$$

where symbol $\otimes$ denotes matrix multiplication and $\cdot^T$ represents the matrix transposition. The measured similarities are then normalized to $(0, 1)$ using the bit-wise sigmoid function $\sigma(\cdot)$. Here, the set-wise operation to obtain FS_c consists of $|\mathcal{E}|$ pair-wise operations on the instance–concept pairs; we use the same operator for concept instantiation, which we will explain in Sect. 3.4.

3.3   Representing Instances and Queries

Properly representing instances and queries is the prerequisite for operating on concepts. Fuzzy sets are also particularly suitable to represent instances and queries because both interpretations of instances and queries are essentially interpretations of concepts. Instances are represented as a special type of fuzzy set [31] that assigns the membership function $\mu(\cdot)$ to 1 for exactly one instance and assigns it to 0 to all other instances. Consequently, we can interpret instances as **(singleton) concepts**. Queries can be regarded as **concept (descriptions)** that are more general than concept names in $\mathcal{C}$, where concept names can be combined by logical operations and relations to form concept descriptions. Thus, we can use the same formalism designed for representing concept names to represent queries (concept descriptions). In this way, we can again use description logic semantics [5] to interpret a query: an interpretation function $\cdot^{\mathcal{I}}$ maps every query q to a subset of $\Delta^{\mathcal{I}}$. As the Herbrand universe $\Delta^{\mathcal{I}} = \mathcal{E}$ is finite, the interpretation of query $q^{\mathcal{I}}$ is fully determined by the fuzzy membership function

$$q^{\mathcal{I}} = \{\mu(e_1), \mu(e_2), \cdots, \mu(e_{|\mathcal{E}|})\}. \tag{7}$$

Note that adhering to the fuzzy logic theory [21] enables us to interpret logical operations within queries as vague and unparameterized fuzzy set operations. The preservation of vagueness is important in that LQAC requires uncertainty, rather than deductive reasoning that guarantees correctness. Unparameterized operations are desirable because they require fewer data during training and are often more interpretable. We then explain how to represent queries as fuzzy sets.

Representing Atomic Queries. Each multi-hop logical query consists of one or more Atomic Queries (AQ), where an AQ is defined as a query that only contains projection(s) $\xrightarrow{r}$ from an anchor instance without logical operations such as intersection $\land$, union $\lor$, and negation $\lnot$. Therefore, the first step is to represent AQs. We obtain the embeddings of each instance $\mathbf{e} \in \mathbb{R}^d$ and the ith relation $\mathbf{r} \in \mathbb{R}^d$ by looking up the rows of the randomly initialized instance embedding matrices $\mathbf{E}_e \in \mathbb{R}^{|\mathcal{E}| \times d}$ and $\mathbf{E}_r \in \mathbb{R}^{|\mathcal{R}| \times d}$. Then, the generator for fuzzy set representation FS_{aq} of a valid AQ $[e \xrightarrow{r_1} \cdots \xrightarrow{r_i}](?)$ is $(\mathbf{e} + \mathbf{r_1} + \cdots + \mathbf{r_i})$. Thus, we obtain the fuzzy set corresponding to the query aq as:

$$FS_{aq} = \{\sigma((\mathbf{e} + \mathbf{r_1} + \cdots + \mathbf{r_i}) \otimes \mathbf{E}_e^T)\} = aq^{\mathcal{I}}. \tag{8}$$

Similar to the process of obtaining fuzzy set representations of concepts, Eq. (8) is to acquire the degrees of membership of every candidate $e \in \mathcal{E}$ being an answer to a given AQ by computing their normalized similarities.

Fusing Atomic Queries. AQs are fused by logical operations to form multi-hop logical queries. Since AQs are already represented in fuzzy sets and we are equipped with the theoretically supported fuzzy set operations, we interpret logical operations as fuzzy set operations over concepts to fuse AQs into the final query representations. For two fuzzy sets in the domain $\Delta^{\mathcal{I}} = \mathcal{E}$: $FS_1 = \{\mu_1(e_1), \cdots, \mu_1(e_{|\mathcal{E}|})\}$ and $FS_2 = \{\mu_2(e_1), \cdots, \mu_2(e_{|\mathcal{E}|})\}$, we have the **intersection** $\land$ and the **union** $\lor$ over the two fuzzy sets as:

$$FS_\land = FS_1 \land FS_2 = \{\forall e \in \mathcal{E} : \mu_\land(e) = \top(\mu_1(e), \mu_2(e))\}, \tag{9}$$

$$FS_\lor = FS_1 \lor FS_2 = \{\forall e \in \mathcal{E} : \mu_\lor(e) = \bot(\mu_1(e), \mu_2(e))\}, \tag{10}$$

and we have the **negation** $\lnot$ over FS as:

$$FS_\lnot = \{\mu_\lnot(e_1), \cdots, \mu_\lnot(e_{|\mathcal{E}|})\} = \{\forall e \in \mathcal{E} : \mu_\lnot(e) = 1 - \mu(e)\}, \tag{11}$$

where a t-norm $\top : [0,1] \times [0,1] \mapsto [0,1]$ is a generalisation of logical conjunction [20]. Examples of t-norms include the Gödel t-norm $\top_{\min}(x,y) = \min\{x,y\}$, the product t-norm $\top_{\text{prod}}(x,y) = x \cdot y$, and the Łukasiewicz t-norm $\top_{\text{Luk}}(x,y) = \max\{0, x+y-1\}$ [22]. Analogously, a t-conorm $\bot : [0,1] \times [0,1] \mapsto [0,1]$ is complementary to t-norm and generalizes logical disjunction, which is defined by $\bot(x,y) = 1 - \top(1-x, 1-y)$ [1]. The choice of the t-norm and the corresponding t-conorm is a hyperparameter to be tuned. We found that product t-norm/t-conorm performs well for our LQAC task.

Thus, each query can be decomposed into AQs and represented as a fuzzy set with Eq. (8), and then fuzzy set representations of AQs are fused by the fuzzy set operations in Eq. (9), (10), and (11) to obtain the final representation of the query. Note that fuzzy set operations hold the property of *closure*, which means the input and output of these operations remain in fuzzy sets. Thus, the final representation of each query is also a fuzzy set FS_q.

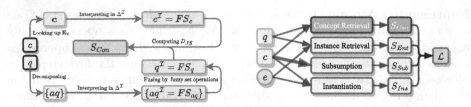

Fig. 3. Left: Representing concepts and queries to retrieve concept-level answers. Right: Illustration of obtaining $\mathcal{L}$ for optimization.

3.4   Operating on Concepts

Here we design operators involving concepts for concept retrieval, instance retrieval, concept subsumption, and concept instantiation based on the fuzzy set representations.

Concept Retrieval is to provide concept-level answers, i.e., $\{a_c\}$ as shown in Sect. 3.1. We illustrate the overall process of concept retrieval in Fig. 3. After we obtain the fuzzy set of the query FS_q and the answer FS_c, we measure the possibility of each $c \in C$ being a concept-level answer of a given query upon fuzzy set representations. More specifically, we measure how well can FS_c and FS_q align with each other based on the Jensen-Shannon divergence D_{JS} [12], which is a symmetrized and smoothed version of the Kullback-Leibler divergence D_{KL}. We choose to use D_{JS} because it is suitable for measuring the difference between probability distributions. We believe D_{JS} is better than D_{KL} because the former is symmetric while the latter is not, and the difference between two fuzzy set representations of concepts should be modeled symmetrically. The similarity function S_{Con} is defined by:

$$S_{Con} = -D_{JS}(P\|Q) = -\frac{1}{2}D_{KL}(P\|M) + \frac{1}{2}D_{KL}(Q\|M) \qquad (12)$$

where $M = \frac{1}{2}(P+Q)$, P and Q represent the normalized fuzzy set representations of the considered query and concept descriptions, which are given by:

$$P = \frac{FS_c}{\max\left(\|FS_c\|_p, \epsilon\right)}, Q = \frac{FS_q}{\max\left(\|FS_q\|_p, \epsilon\right)}, \qquad (13)$$

where ϵ is a small value to avoid division by zero and p is the exponent value in the norm formulation $\|\cdot\|_p$. S_{Con} is then used for model training and inference.

Instance Retrieval aims to provide instance-level answers; for this purpose, only query–instance similarities S_{Ent} need to be measured without the necessity of designing new mechanisms. Therefore, we follow the pioneering work [15] on LQA to represent each query as an embedding $\mathbf{q} = f(q; \Omega)$ and measure query–instance similarity S_{Ent} as:

$$S_{Ent} = \gamma - \|\mathbf{q} - \mathbf{e}\|_1 \qquad (14)$$

where γ is the margin. Here, we elaborate on the method to obtain the query embedding $\mathbf{q}$ for providing instance-level answers, i.e., $f(\cdot)$ with parameters Ω. Specifically, the **projection** operation $\mathbf{x} \xrightarrow{r}$ that projects an instance or query embedding $\mathbf{x}$ with relation r is resolved by:

$$\mathbf{q} = \mathbf{x} + \mathbf{r}, \qquad (15)$$

where $\mathbf{x} \in \mathbb{R}^d$ is another query embedding that is obtained in advance or an instance embedding obtained by looking up $\mathbf{E}_e \in \mathbb{R}^{|\mathcal{E}| \times d}$ by rows. The **intersection** of two query embeddings $\mathbf{q_1}$ and $\mathbf{q_2}$ is resolved by:

$$\mathbf{q} = a(\mathbf{q_1} \oplus \mathbf{q_2}; \Omega)_1 * \mathbf{q_1} + a(\mathbf{q_1} \oplus \mathbf{q_2}; \Omega)_2 * \mathbf{q_2}, \qquad (16)$$

where $\oplus$ denotes matrix concatenation over the last dimension, Ω denotes the parameters of $a(\cdot)$, and $a(\cdot)$ is a two-layer feed-forward network with $Relu$ activation. $a(\cdot)_1$ and $a(\cdot)_2$ represent the first and second d attention weights, respectively. The **union** of two query embeddings $\mathbf{q_1}$ and $\mathbf{q_2}$ is resolved by:

$$\mathbf{q} = \max(\mathbf{q_1}, \mathbf{q_2})_{-1}, \qquad (17)$$

where $\max(\cdot)_{-1}$ denotes the max operation over the last dimension.

Concept Subsumption. As defined by Eq. (1), $\mathcal{T}$ supplies for relational information among concepts with the form of concept subsumptions. Although concepts are represented in fuzzy sets and we already designed mechanism to measure the similarity between two fuzzy sets, we can not directly apply the method in Sect. 3.4 for concept subsumptions. It is because we need to measure the degree of inclusion of one concept to another instead of the similarities between them. The degree of inclusion is asymmetrical and more complex than the similarity measurement. Therefore, we employ a neural network $h(\cdot)$ to model the degree of inclusion:

$$S_{Sub} = h(\mathbf{c_1} \oplus \mathbf{c_2}; \theta) \qquad (18)$$

where symbol $\oplus$ denotes matrix concatenation over the last dimension, and θ denotes the parameters of $h(\cdot)$. In this work, $h(\cdot)$ is a two-layer feed-forward network with $Relu$ activation. Note that we directly use the embeddings of concepts without interpreting concept in the Herbrand universe of entities $\Delta^{\mathcal{I}} = \mathcal{E}$ because neither concept–instance relationships need to be modeled nor logical operations need to be resolved for modeling degree of subsumption.

Concept Instantiation. As defined by Eq. (3), $\mathcal{A}_{ec}$ bridges $\mathcal{T}$ and $\mathcal{A}_{cc}$ by providing links between instances and concepts. Such links instantiate concept with its describing instances and thus offer relational information with the form of concept instantiation. Recall that in Sect. 3.2, we obtain the fuzzy set representation of concepts by computing the similarities between the given c and every candidate $e \in \mathcal{E}$ with Eq. (6). In the case of concept instantiation, the set-wise computation Eq. (6) is degraded to pair-wise similarity measurement for each concept-instance pair:

$$S_{Ins} = \sigma(\mathbf{c} \otimes \mathbf{e}^T) \tag{19}$$

where $\mathbf{c} \in \mathbb{R}^d$ and $\mathbf{e} \in \mathbb{R}^d$ are concept and instance embeddings, respectively.

3.5 Optimization and Inference

The parameters in our model include the instance embedding matrix $\mathbf{E}_e$, the concept embedding matrix $\mathbf{E}_c$, the relation embedding matrix $\mathbf{E}_r$, θ in Sect. 3.4, and Ω in Sect. 3.4. In the training stage, we sample m negative samples for each positive sample of concept-level answering $[q](c^+)$ by corrupting c^+ with randomly sampled $c_i^- \in \mathcal{C}$ $(i = 1, \cdots, m)$. Similarly, negative samples for instance-level answering $[q](e_i^-)$ are obtained by corrupting e^+ in $[q](e^+)$ with randomly sampled $e_i^- \in \mathcal{E}$. For concept subsumption and concept instantiation, both sides of the concept-concept pairs and concept-instance pairs are randomly corrupted following the same procedure. We illustrate the modularized computation procedure for model training as Fig. 3. The loss is defined as

$$\mathcal{L} = -\frac{1}{4m} \sum_{n \in N} \sum_{i=1}^{m} \log \sigma(S_n^+ - S_{n_i}^-) \tag{20}$$

where $N = \{Con, Ent, Sub, Ins\}$ denotes the set of the four included tasks discussed in Sect. 3.4, S_n^+ (or $S_{n_i}^-$) denotes the predicted similarity or degree of inclusion of the positive (or negative) sample according to task n. The overall optimization process of $\mathcal{L}$ is outlined in Algorithm 1 in Supplementary Materials.

In the inference stage, we predict S_{Con} (or S_{Ent}) for every candidate concept $c \in \mathcal{C}$ (or instance $e \in \mathcal{E}$) regarding to query q and select the top-k results to be the concept-level answers $\{a_c\}$ (or instance-level answers $\{a_e\}$) for query q. Thus, we are able to achieve LQAC by providing the comprehensive answers $\{a\} = \{a_e\} \bigcup \{a_c\}$. Although concept subsumption and concept instantiation are not included in the inference stage, they empowered our LQAC system to better represent and operate concepts by providing training samples and extra supervision signals of the relational data.

4 Experiments

We conduct extensive experiments to answer the following research questions: How to properly compare our method with LQA systems (**RQ1**)? How does our method perform in concept retrieval (**RQ2**) and instance retrieval (**RQ3**)? How do concept subsumption and instantiation affect reasoning performance (**RQ4**)?

4.1 Experimental Settings

Baselines (RQ1). The considered baselines are representative methods for LQA, namely GQE [15], Q2B [29], and BetaE [30], along with a recent method FuzzQE [10] that directly represent instances and queries using embeddings with specially designed restrictions and interpreted them as fuzzy sets for LQA. Since LQA reasoners can only provide instance-level answers, we need to come up with a strategy to enforce concept retrieval, so as to compare with our method for LQAC. Therefore, we introduce the *One-more-hop* experiment. That is, we exploit all the information given by $\mathcal{KB} = (\mathcal{T}, \mathcal{A})$ and simply degrade concepts to instances in the training stage. Specifically, we first augment $\mathcal{A}_{ec}$ by the transductive links provided by $\mathcal{T}$. Then we combine the augmented $\mathcal{A}_{ec}$ and $\mathcal{A}_{ee}$ to form the new knowledge graph $\mathcal{KG}'$. Note that part of the instances in $\mathcal{KG}'$ are the degraded concepts and $\mathcal{KG}'$ contains an additional relation r_{ec} to describe the *isInstanceOf* relation between an instance and a concept. Thus, we construct training examples with various types of queries using $\mathcal{KG}'$. In the inference stage, two sets of candidate instances are prepared for each query. The first is the instance-level candidate set, which can be handled following the original papers [15,29,30]. Another set contains the degraded concepts. To predict the possibility of a concept being an answer to a query $[q](?)$, we add one more projection operation with the relation r_{ec}, i.e., $[q'](?) = [q \xrightarrow{r_{ec}}](?)$. In other words, concept-level reasoning is implicitly achieved by an additional hop asking the *isInstanceOf* upon instance retrieval queries, i.e., the *One-more-hop*.

Dataset Construction. GQE [15], Q2B [29], and BetaE [30] are a series of works that established the benchmark datasets for LQA, and they provide the integrated implementation of these methods[1]. We follow their procedure to construct instance retrieval datasets and we additionally construct concept retrieval datasets by adding one more projection from the answer instance to the answer concept. We also follow Q2B [29] to decide the query types used for training and testing our LQAC system as shown in Fig. 2. In our dataset, we make sure the query-answer pairs can't be directly found from the knowledge base by holding out part of the knowledge. This means we always evaluate query-answer pairs that were not part of the training set and the method has not seen them before. Thus, traditional graph traversal techniques would not be able to find the answers (due to missing relations) [29].

Implementation Details. We use three real-world large-scale knowledge bases: the English Wikipedia version[2] of YAGO4, 2016-10 release[3] of Dbpedia, and the same subset of Gene Ontology[4] used in well-established ontology embedding works [23,37]. We first filter out low-degree instances in $\mathcal{A}_{ee}$ and

---

[1] https://github.com/snap-stanford/KGReasoning.
[2] https://yago-knowledge.org/downloads/yago-4.
[3] http://downloads.dbpedia.org/wiki-archive/downloads-2016-10.html.
[4] https://bio2vec.cbrc.kaust.edu.sa/data/elembeddings/el-embeddings-data.zip.

Table 1. Hit@3 of concept and instance retrieval. The best results are in boldface.

		Concept-level Answers									
		1p	2p	3p	2i	3i	pi	ip	2u	up	avg
YAGO4	GQE	43.7	67.4	44.9	67.1	49.9	15.0	12.3	19.7	9.4	36.6
	Q2B	47.1	75.4	78.2	**70.0**	58.2	2.8	1.9	1.9	1.4	37.4
	BetaE	47.8	74.7	76.7	64.2	52.5	10.1	10.2	2.9	5.0	38.2
	FuzzQE	41.6	69.8	59.4	67.5	52.8	16.9	13.3	23.4	10.4	39.5
	LQAC	**60.3**	**88.8**	**88.7**	66.4	**65.5**	**60.2**	**57.1**	**59.9**	**52.5**	**66.6**
Dbpedia	GQE	28.7	42.9	40.0	32.5	36.0	13.0	14.4	7.2	10.7	25.0
	Q2B	28.2	41.4	38.0	32.7	33.5	11.7	13.0	8.4	9.3	24.0
	BetaE	34.1	45.4	50.8	37.2	41.2	14.6	10.9	4.0	8.0	27.4
	FuzzQE	29.0	39.2	38.2	30.5	29.7	15.6	15.9	11.2	12.7	24.7
	LQAC	**62.4**	**83.7**	**83.6**	**50.9**	**43.7**	**45.0**	**29.9**	**67.2**	**67.3**	**59.3**
		Instance-level Answers									
		1p	2p	3p	2i	3i	pi	ip	2u	up	avg
YAGO4	GQE	29.7	17.3	4.6	29.0	31.4	23.5	18.6	13.6	17.4	20.6
	Q2B	28.4	20.0	7.0	29.5	34.4	27.0	21.3	11.6	18.5	22.0
	BetaE	31.4	22.3	12.0	33.5	37.5	31.3	24.1	12.5	**23.8**	25.4
	FuzzQE	30.7	17.3	4.1	30.0	32.3	22.9	18.1	12.5	18.6	20.7
	LQAC	**39.6**	**27.3**	**18.4**	**56.6**	**70.2**	**34.2**	**39.1**	14.9	23.7	**36.0**
Dbpedia	GQE	25.2	18.9	19.8	26.5	43.6	17.2	33.3	12.6	21.1	24.2
	Q2B	21.3	16.5	17.7	27.5	31.9	19.7	25.7	9.1	15.4	20.7
	BetaE	20.9	23.2	21.7	27.5	32.9	27.5	28.4	13.0	25.1	24.5
	FuzzQE	18.5	16.3	18.5	26.5	33.0	32.6	25.4	8.0	16.0	21.6
	LQAC	**34.6**	**28.0**	**29.0**	**44.6**	**54.8**	21.4	**40.6**	**17.8**	23.0	**32.6**

$\mathcal{A}_{ec}$ with the threshold of 5. Then we split $\mathcal{A}_{ee}$ to leave 5% out for evaluation. We follow BetaE [30] to construct examples of logical queries from $\mathcal{A}_{ee} = \mathcal{KG}$. We summarize the statistics of datasets in Table 1 and Table 3 in the Supplementary Materials. In the training stage, the initial learning rate of the Adam [19] optimizer, the embedding dimension d, and the batch size, are tuned by grid searching within $\{1e^{-2}, 1e^{-3}, 1e^{-4}, 1e^{-5}\}$, $\{128, 256, 512\}$, and $\{256, 512, 1024\}$, respectively. We keep the number of corrupted negative samples for each positive sample m, the small value ϵ, the exponent value p, the margin γ, and the adopted type of t-norm as 4, $1e^{-12}$, 1, 12, and $\top_{\text{prod}}$, respectively. We use the filtered setting [29] for testing and report the averaged results of Mean Reciprocal Rank (MRR), Hit@3, and Hit@10 over 3 independent runs.

4.2 Experimental Results

Concept-Level Answers (RQ2). We conduct the *One-more-hop* experiment to answer RQ2. As shown in Table.1, our method consistently outperforms baselines on various evaluation metrics with large margins. For the *basic* queries in Fig. 2 that are simply projections and intersections, our method significantly improves the performance of concept-level reasoning, especially for the multi-hop queries *1p*, *2p*, and *3p*. For *extra* queries in Fig. 2 that are more complex in terms of including unions or combined logical operations, we even boosted the performance exponentially. The average performance of our method is also significantly better than the baselines.

The superior performance can be interpreted in two folds. First, due to the lack of reasoning capabilities when concepts are involved, GQE, Q2B, FuzzQE, and BetaE need to do reasoning over more complicated queries. For example, baselines need to reason over an *ipp* query $[((h_1 \xrightarrow{r_1}) \wedge (h_2 \xrightarrow{r_2})) \xrightarrow{r_{ec}}](?)$ to provide concept-level answers of an *ip* query $[(h_1 \xrightarrow{r_1}) \wedge (h_2 \xrightarrow{r_2})](?)$. Therefore, *1p* queries become *2p* queries for baseline methods, *2p* becomes *3p*, and so on. Thus, the complexity of the transformed queries limits their performance. Second, explicit supervision signals for concept-level reasoning are not provided. Since the concepts are degraded as instances, LQA methods could not explicitly feed the empirical error on concept-level answers back to update the model parameters. It is thus understandable that they cannot perform well in providing concept retrieval, especially on *extra* queries that are more complicated and require supervision signals more eagerly.

Table 2. Hit@3 of concept and instance retrieval on the biomedical GO dataset. The best results are in boldface.

		1p	2p	3p	2i	3i	pi	ip	2u	up	avg.
Concept	GQE	0.004	0.088	0.067	0.101	0.099	0.010	0.014	0.003	0.006	0.044
	Q2B	0.005	0.085	0.066	0.095	0.109	0.006	0.007	0.005	0.007	0.043
	BetaE	0.004	0.085	0.068	0.102	0.099	0.012	0.013	0.003	0.009	0.044
	FuzzQE	0.008	0.088	0.069	0.107	0.112	0.010	0.014	0.007	0.005	0.047
	LQAC	**0.031**	**0.683**	**0.860**	**0.147**	**0.149**	**0.160**	**0.165**	**0.438**	**0.805**	**0.382**
Instance	GQE	0.130	0.462	**0.641**	0.079	0.068	0.078	0.348	0.064	0.487	0.262
	Q2B	0.137	0.467	0.637	0.087	0.078	0.097	0.358	0.065	**0.508**	0.270
	BetaE	0.129	**0.463**	0.632	0.075	0.065	0.085	0.342	0.059	0.498	0.261
	FuzzQE	0.126	0.461	0.635	0.095	0.090	0.102	0.349	0.051	0.500	0.268
	LQAC	**0.236**	**0.463**	0.628	**0.200**	**0.219**	**0.237**	0.405	0.114	0.347	**0.317**

Moreover, as shown in Table 2, our method outperforms all baselines in providing concept-level answers. Note that the instances in the GO datasets are proteins, and the concepts are molecular functions, cellular components, or biological processes[5]. Therefore, such results demonstrate that the formulated LQAC

---

[5] http://geneontology.org/.

task and our solution enable effective complex logical reasoning for crucial bio-logical facts, which is promising to be applied to biomedical applications to facilitate healthcare services.

Instance-Level Answers (RQ3). Although our method is designed for LQAC, it is interesting to know its performance on instance-level reasoning only (for answering RQ3). The results in Table 1 and 2 show that our method also outperforms LQA methods on most types of queries on various metrics. The performance gain should be credited to its capability of representing and oper-ating on concepts. It thus encodes the additional information of the relationships among queries, instances, and concepts, which are helpful for instance retrieval. Additional experimental results are provided in Table 2, Table 4, and Table 5 in the Supplementary Materials.

Ablation Study (RQ4). We conduct an ablation study on the effect of incor-porating $\mathcal{T}$ and $\mathcal{A}_{ec}$ and our proposed mechanisms of exploiting them to answer RQ4. As shown in Table 3, when the *Subsumption* task is not included, i.e., ontological axioms in $\mathcal{T}$ are not used and S_{Sub} is not computed, *LQAC w/o Sub* underperforms *LQAC* on all types of queries for both tasks. Such results

Table 3. Ablation study on Concept Subsumptions and Instantiation on Dbpedia dataset. The best MRR results are in boldface.

Concept	1p	2p	3p	2i	3i	pi	ip	2u	up	avg
LQAC w/o Sub	53.3	72.4	71.5	19.0	15.8	24.1	19.3	59.9	61.7	44.1
LQAC w/o Ins	52.8	68.8	67.7	38.3	35.4	34.2	19.3	56.2	61.6	48.3
LQAC	**55.0**	**80.8**	**80.7**	**42.9**	**36.7**	**42.0**	**28.5**	**63.4**	**64.9**	**55.0**
Instance	1p	2p	3p	2i	3i	pi	ip	2u	up	avg
LQAC w/o Sub	17.7	20.1	21.0	18.0	18.8	14.9	22.7	9.1	16.0	17.6
LQAC w/o Ins	17.4	18.8	19.0	18.1	18.7	14.3	22.9	8.7	17.7	17.3
LQAC	**28.8**	**24.5**	**24.4**	**38.4**	**46.3**	**20.1**	**33.6**	**14.0**	**20.6**	**27.9**

Table 4. Case study on the Instance Realization task for complex logical query $[(\text{Manon the Moon} \xrightarrow{\text{actor}} \xrightarrow{\text{alumniOf}}) \wedge (\text{William Devane} \xrightarrow{\text{alumniOf}})](?)$, which aims to find the *most specific* concept among all true answers.

Concept	Score	Predicted	Expected
Academy	−0.310	5th	3rd
Drama_school	−0.234	3rd	1st
LocalBusiness	−0.238	4th	5th
CollegeOrUniversity	−0.159	1st	2nd
School	−0.219	2nd	4th

show the importance of incorporating the relational information between concepts, and the effectiveness of the designed operator in Sect. 3.4 for modeling such information. On the other hand, *LQAC* consistently outperforms *LQAC w/o Ins* on all types of queries. This verifies that the relational information about *isInstanceOf* in $\mathcal{A}_{ec}$ is vital, and the mechanism introduced in Sect. 3.4 is effective to tackle with *Instantiation*.

5 Discussion

Instance Realization is closely related to LQAC, which is to retrieve the **most specific** concept among all concepts that a given instance belongs to [18]. We are more interested in specific and fine-grained concepts because they are more informative. For example, from the last column of Table 4, the instance-level answer 'American Academy of Dramatic Arts' is intuitively better to be answered by concept 'Drama School' instead of 'School', where 'Drama School' is substantially more informative than 'School'. Since concept-level answers are descriptions of sets of instances, the most specific one is equivalent to the concept describing the minimal set of instances among all true concepts. However, as the predicted ranks are shown in Table 4, our method is not always able to give the most specific answer. Although our results are stable thanks to the filtered setting, the internal rank among true concepts is not tested. We recognize this as an important future research direction in neuro-symbolic reasoning. Nevertheless, instance realization takes instances instead of multi-hop logical queries as input to retrieve concepts, which fundamentally differs from LQAC.

Note that although our system supports negations, we did not report such results because several of our adopted baseline methods do not support negations. In this case, if negation is incorporated, more query types with negations are required in training. The training data would thus be different for the methods supporting and not supporting negations. Therefore, we limit our experiments to non-negation query types to ensure fair comparisons. It would be interesting to investigate the effectiveness of LQAC with negated queries by directly comparing it with negation-supported methods, we identify this as an important future work within reach.

Moreover, recall that we define TBox in our system as $\mathcal{T} \subseteq \{c_i \sqsubseteq c_j | c_i, c_j \in \mathcal{C}\}$, where $\mathcal{C}$ denotes the set of concept **names** in $\mathcal{KB}$. However, c can be concept **descriptions** in general. In one of the most widely used description logics $\mathcal{ALC}$ [4], concept descriptions are recursively defined: Every concept name is a concept description; if C and D are concept descriptions and r is a role (relation), then $C \sqcap D$, $C \sqcup D$, $\neg C$, $\forall R.C$, and $\exists r.C$ are concept descriptions. Neural reasoning over $\mathcal{ALC}$ ontologies with concept descriptions, is particularly challenging mainly because the axioms no longer form a graph structure due to their arbitrary depths and the involvement of quantifiers. However, many $\mathcal{ALC}$ ontologies have been developed to provide rich and accurate knowledge about various domains, in particular in the biomedical field where hundreds of ontologies have been created [33]. Therefore, we recognize neural logical reasoning over the full $\mathcal{ALC}$

ontologies as a highly potential future research direction that would be influential in the neuro-symbolic reasoning communities and beyond.

6 Conclusion

We formulated the LQAC problem that is of great importance for users, downstream tasks, and ontological applications. Accordingly, we propose an initial method for LQAC that properly incorporates ontological axioms, represents concepts and queries as fuzzy sets, and operates on concepts based on fuzzy sets. Experimental results and in-depth analysis demonstrate the effectiveness of our method and the significance of LQAC in biomedical knowledge discovery.

Supplemental Material Statement: Source code, statistics of datasets, data preprocessing procedures, and tuned hyperparameter settings are available from our code repository[6]. Detailed computation procedures of model training and additional experimental results are also attached to our code repository.

Acknowledgements. This work has been supported by funding from King Abdullah University of Science and Technology (KAUST) Office of Sponsored Research (OSR) under Award No. URF/1/5041-01-01, the National Key Research and Development Program of China under Grant No. 2021ZD0113602, and the National Natural Science Foundation of China under Grant Nos. 62176014, the Fundamental Research Funds for the Central Universities.

References

1. Arakelyan, E., Daza, D., Minervini, P., Cochez, M.: Complex query answering with neural link predictors. In: ICLR (2020)
2. Auer, S., Bizer, C., Kobilarov, G., Lehmann, J., Cyganiak, R., Ives, Z.: DBpedia: a nucleus for a web of open data. In: Aberer, K., et al. (eds.) ASWC/ISWC -2007. LNCS, vol. 4825, pp. 722–735. Springer, Heidelberg (2007). https://doi.org/10.1007/978-3-540-76298-0_52
3. Baader, F.: Appendix: description logic terminology. In: The Description Logic Handbook: Theory, Implementation, and Applications, pp. 485–495 (2003)
4. Baader, F., Calvanese, D., McGuinness, D., Patel-Schneider, P., Nardi, D., et al.: The Description Logic Handbook: Theory, Implementation and Applications. Cambridge University Press, Cambridge (2003)
5. Baader, F., Horrocks, I., Lutz, C., Sattler, U.: Introduction to Description Logic. Cambridge University Press, Cambridge (2017)
6. Baader, F., Horrocks, I., Sattler, U.: Description logics. Found. Artif. Intell. **3**, 135–179 (2008)
7. Bai, Y., Lv, X., Li, J., Hou, L.: Answering complex logical queries on knowledge graphs via query tree optimization. arXiv preprint arXiv:2212.09567 (2022)
8. Bordes, A., Usunier, N., Garcia-Duran, A., Weston, J., Yakhnenko, O.: Translating embeddings for modeling multi-relational data. In: NeurIPS, vol. 26 (2013)

---

[6] https://github.com/lilv98/LQAC.

9. Chen, J., Hu, P., Jimenez-Ruiz, E., Holter, O.M., Antonyrajah, D., Horrocks, I.: Owl2vec*: embedding of owl ontologies. In: Machine Learning, pp. 1–33 (2021)
10. Chen, X., Hu, Z., Sun, Y.: Fuzzy logic based logical query answering on knowledge graphs. In: Proceedings of the AAAI Conference on Artificial Intelligence, vol. 36, pp. 3939–3948 (2022)
11. Choudhary, N., Rao, N., Katariya, S., Subbian, K., Reddy, C.K.: Self-supervised hyperboloid representations from logical queries over knowledge graphs. In: WWW, pp. 1373–1384 (2021)
12. Endres, D.M., Schindelin, J.E.: A new metric for probability distributions. IEEE Trans. Inf. Theory **49**(7), 1858–1860 (2003)
13. Glorot, X., Bengio, Y.: Understanding the difficulty of training deep feedforward neural networks. In: AISTATS, pp. 249–256. JMLR Workshop and Conference Proceedings (2010)
14. Gruber, T.R.: A translation approach to portable ontology specifications. Knowl. Acquis. **5**(2), 199–220 (1993)
15. Hamilton, W.L., Bajaj, P., Zitnik, M., Jurafsky, D., Leskovec, J.: Embedding logical queries on knowledge graphs. In: NeurIPS, pp. 2030–2041 (2018)
16. Hao, J., Chen, M., Yu, W., Sun, Y., Wang, W.: Universal representation learning of knowledge bases by jointly embedding instances and ontological concepts. In: KDD, pp. 1709–1719 (2019)
17. Hao, J., Ju, C.J.T., Chen, M., Sun, Y., Zaniolo, C., Wang, W.: Bio-joie: joint representation learning of biological knowledge bases. In: Proceedings of the 11th ACM International Conference on Bioinformatics, Computational Biology and Health Informatics, pp. 1–10 (2020)
18. Huitzil, I., Bernad, J., Bobillo, F.: Algorithms for instance retrieval and realization in fuzzy ontologies. Mathematics **8**(2), 154 (2020)
19. Kingma, D.P., Ba, J.: Adam: a method for stochastic optimization. arXiv preprint arXiv:1412.6980 (2014)
20. Klement, E.P., Mesiar, R., Pap, E.: Triangular norms. position paper i: basic analytical and algebraic properties. Fuzzy Sets Syst. **143**(1), 5–26 (2004)
21. Klir, G., Yuan, B.: Fuzzy Sets and Fuzzy Logic, vol. 4. Prentice hall, Upper Saddle River (1995)
22. van Krieken, E., Acar, E., van Harmelen, F.: Analyzing differentiable fuzzy implications. In: KR, pp. 893–903. IJCAI Organization (2020)
23. Kulmanov, M., Liu-Wei, W., Yan, Y., Hoehndorf, R.: El embeddings: Geometric construction of models for the description logic el++. IJCAI (2019)
24. Kulmanov, M., Smaili, F.Z., Gao, X., Hoehndorf, R.: Semantic similarity and machine learning with ontologies. Brief. Bioinf. **22**(4), bbaa199 (2021)
25. Lee, R.C.: Fuzzy logic and the resolution principle. J. ACM (JACM) **19**(1), 109–119 (1972)
26. Liu, S., Chen, H., Ren, Z., Feng, Y., Liu, Q., Yin, D.: Knowledge diffusion for neural dialogue generation. In: ACL, pp. 1489–1498 (2018)
27. Luus, F., et al.: Logic embeddings for complex query answering. arXiv preprint arXiv:2103.00418 (2021)
28. Mondala, S., Bhatiab, S., Mutharajua, R.: Emel++: embeddings for description logic (2021)
29. Ren, H., Hu, W., Leskovec, J.: Query2box: reasoning over knowledge graphs in vector space using box embeddings. In: ICLR (2019)
30. Ren, H., Leskovec, J.: Beta embeddings for multi-hop logical reasoning in knowledge graphs. In: NeurIPS, vol. 33 (2020)

31. Rihoux, B., De Meur, G.: Crisp-set qualitative comparative analysis (csqca). In: Configurational Comparative Methods: Qualitative Comparative Analysis (QCA) and Related Techniques, vol. 51, pp. 33–68 (2009)
32. Smaili, F.Z., Gao, X., Hoehndorf, R.: Opa2vec: combining formal and informal content of biomedical ontologies to improve similarity-based prediction. Bioinformatics **35**(12), 2133–2140 (2019)
33. Smith, B., et al.: The OBO foundry: coordinated evolution of ontologies to support biomedical data integration. Nat. Biotech. **25**(11), 1251–1255 (2007)
34. Tang, Z., et al.: Positive-unlabeled learning with adversarial data augmentation for knowledge graph completion. In: IJCAI (2022)
35. Pellissier Tanon, T., Weikum, G., Suchanek, F.: YAGO 4: a reason-able knowledge base. In: Harth, A., et al. (eds.) ESWC 2020. LNCS, vol. 12123, pp. 583–596. Springer, Cham (2020). https://doi.org/10.1007/978-3-030-49461-2_34
36. Trisedya, B.D., Qi, J., Zhang, R.: Entity alignment between knowledge graphs using attribute embeddings. In: AAAI, vol. 33, pp. 297–304 (2019)
37. Xiong, B., Potyka, N., Tran, T.K., Nayyeri, M., Staab, S.: Faithful embeddings for el++ knowledge bases. In: The Semantic Web-ISWC 2022: 21st International Semantic Web Conference, Virtual Event, 23–27 October 2022, Proceedings, pp. 22–38. Springer, Heidelberg (2022). https://doi.org/10.1007/978-3-031-19433-7_2
38. Zhang, Z., Wang, J., Chen, J., Ji, S., Wu, F.: Cone: cone embeddings for multi-hop reasoning over knowledge graphs. Adv. Neural. Inf. Process. Syst. **34**, 19172–19183 (2021)
39. Zhou, K., Zhao, W.X., Bian, S., Zhou, Y., Wen, J.R., Yu, J.: Improving conversational recommender systems via knowledge graph based semantic fusion. In: KDD, pp. 1006–1014 (2020)
40. Zhu, Z., Galkin, M., Zhang, Z., Tang, J.: Neural-symbolic models for logical queries on knowledge graphs. arXiv preprint arXiv:2205.10128 (2022)

FORECASTTKGQUESTIONS: A Benchmark for Temporal Question Answering and Forecasting over Temporal Knowledge Graphs

Zifeng Ding[1,2], Zongyue Li[1,3], Ruoxia Qi[1], Jingpei Wu[1], Bailan He[1,2], Yunpu Ma[1,2], Zhao Meng[4], Shuo Chen[1,2], Ruotong Liao[1,3], Zhen Han[1(✉)], and Volker Tresp[1(✉)]

[1] LMU Munich, Geschwister-Scholl-Platz 1, 80539 Munich, Germany
{zifeng.ding,ruoxia.qi,bailan.he,shuo.chen}@campus.lmu.de,
{zongyue.li,jingpei.wu}@outlook.com, cognitive.yunpu@gmail.com,
liao@dbs.ifi.lmu.de, hanzhen02111@hotmail.com, Volker.Tresp@lmu.de
[2] Siemens AG, Otto-Hahn-Ring 6, 81739 Munich, Germany
[3] Munich Center for Machine Learning (MCML), Munich, Germany
[4] ETH Zürich, Rämistrasse 101, 8092 Zürich, Switzerland
zhmeng@ethz.ch

Abstract. Question answering over temporal knowledge graphs (TKGQA) has recently found increasing interest. Previous related works aim to develop QA systems that answer temporal questions based on the facts from a fixed time period, where a temporal knowledge graph (TKG) spanning this period can be fully used for inference. In real-world scenarios, however, it is common that given knowledge until the current instance, we wish the TKGQA systems to answer the questions asking about future. As humans constantly plan the future, building forecasting TKGQA systems is important. In this paper, we propose a novel task: forecasting TKGQA, and propose a coupled large-scale TKGQA benchmark dataset, i.e., FORECASTTKGQUESTIONS. It includes three types of forecasting questions, i.e., entity prediction, yes-unknown, and fact reasoning questions. For every question, a timestamp is annotated and QA models only have access to TKG information prior to it for answer inference. We find that previous TKGQA methods perform poorly on forecasting questions, and they are unable to answer yes-unknown and fact reasoning questions. To this end, we propose FORECASTTKGQA, a TKGQA model that employs a TKG forecasting module for future inference. Experiments show that it performs well in forecasting TKGQA.

1 Introduction

Knowledge graphs (KGs) model factual information by representing every fact with a triple, i.e., (s, r, o), where s, o, r, are the subject entity, the object entity,

---

Z. Ding, Z. Li and R. Qi— Equal contribution.

T. R. Payne et al. (Eds.): ISWC 2023, LNCS 14265, pp. 541–560, 2023.
https://doi.org/10.1007/978-3-031-47240-4_29

and the relation between s and o, respectively. To adapt to the ever-evolving knowledge, temporal knowledge graphs (TKGs) are introduced, where they additionally specify the time validity of every fact with a time constraint t (e.g., a timestamp), and represent each fact with a quadruple (s, r, o, t). Recently, TKG reasoning has drawn increasing attention. While a lot of methods focus on temporal knowledge graph completion (TKGC) where they predict missing facts at the observed timestamps, various recent methods pay more attention to forecasting the facts at unobserved future timestamps in TKGs.

Knowledge graph question answering (KGQA) is a task aiming to answer natural language questions using a KG as the knowledge base (KB). KGQA requires QA models to extract answers from KGs, rather than retrieving or summarizing answers from text contexts. [21] first introduces question answering over temporal knowledge graphs (TKGQA). It proposes a non-forecasting TKGQA dataset CRONQUESTIONS that takes a TKG as its underlying KB. Temporal reasoning techniques are required to answer these questions. Though [21] manages to combine TKG reasoning with KGQA, it has limitations. Previous KGQA datasets, including CRONQUESTIONS, do not include yes-no and multiple-choice questions, while these two question types have been extensively studied in reading comprehension QA, e.g., [13]. Besides, the questions in CRONQUESTIONS are in a non-forecasting style, where all questions are based on the TKG facts that happen in a fixed time period, and an extensive TKG that is fully observable in this period can be used to infer the answers, making the answer inference less challenging. For example, the TKG facts from *2003*, including (*Stephen Robert Jordan, member of sports team, Manchester City, 2003*), are all observable to answer the question *Which team was Stephen Robert Jordan part of in 2003?*. CRONQUESTIONS manages to bridge the gap between TKGC and KGQA, however, no previous work manages to combine TKG forecasting with KGQA, where only past TKG information can be used for answer inference.

In this work, we propose a novel task: forecasting question answering over temporal knowledge graphs (forecasting TKGQA), together with a coupled large-scale dataset, i.e., FORECASTTKGQUESTIONS. We generate forecasting questions based on the Integrated Crisis Early Warning System (ICEWS) Dataverse [2], and label every question with a timestamp. To answer a forecasting question, QA models can only access the TKG information prior to the question timestamp. The contribution of our work is three-folded: (1) We propose forecasting TKGQA, a novel task aiming to test the forecasting ability of TKGQA models. To the best of our knowledge, this is the first work binding TKG forecasting with temporal KGQA; (2) We propose a large-scale benchmark TKGQA dataset: FORECASTTKGQUESTIONS. It contains three types of questions, i.e., entity prediction questions (EPQs), yes-unknown questions (YUQs), and fact reasoning questions (FRQs), where the last two types of questions have never been considered in previous KGQA datasets[1]; (3) We propose FORECASTTKGQA, a model aiming to solve forecasting TKGQA. It employs a TKG forecasting module and a pre-trained language model (LM) for answer inference. Experimental results show that it achieves great performance on forecasting questions.

---

[1] YUQs are based on yes-no questions and FRQs are multiple-choice questions.

2 Preliminaries and Related Work

TKG Reasoning. Let $\mathcal{E}$, $\mathcal{R}$ and $\mathcal{T}$ denote a finite set of entities, relations, and timestamps, respectively. A TKG $\mathcal{G}$ is defined as a finite set of TKG facts represented by quadruples, i.e., $\mathcal{G} = \{(s, r, o, t) | s, o \in \mathcal{E}, r \in \mathcal{R}, t \in \mathcal{T}\}$. We define the TKG forecasting task (also known as TKG extrapolation) as follows. Assume we have a query $(s_q, r_q, ?, t_q)$ (or $(?, r_q, o_q, t_q)$) derived from a target quadruple (s_q, r_q, o_q, t_q), and we denote all the ground-truth quadruples as $\mathcal{F}$. TKG forecasting aims to predict the missing entity in the query, given the observed **past** TKG facts $\mathcal{O} = \{(s_i, r_i, o_i, t_i) \in \mathcal{F} | t_i < t_q\}$. Such temporal restriction is not imposed in TKG completion (TKGC, also known as TKG interpolation), where the observed TKG facts from any timestamp, including t_q and the timestamps after t_q, can be used for prediction. In recent years, there have been extensive works done for both TKGC [6,15,16] and TKG forecasting [8,9,14,18,30]. We give a more detailed discussion about the forecasting methods. RE-NET [14] employs an autoregressive architecture and models fact occurrence as a probability distribution conditioned on the temporal sequences of past related TKG information. TANGO [9] employs neural ordinary differential equations to model temporal dependencies among graph information of different timestamps. CyGNet [30] uses the copy-generation mechanism to extract hints from historical facts for forecasting. xERTE [8] constructs a historical fact-based subgraph and selects prediction answers from it. TLogic [18] is the first rule-based TKG forecasting method that learns temporal logical rules in TKGs and achieves superior results.

Question Answering over KGs. Several datasets have been proposed for QA over non-temporal KGs, such as SimpleQuestions [1], WebQuestionsSP [28], ComplexWebQuestions [24], MetaQA [29], TempQuestions [11], and Time-Questions [12]. Among these datasets, only TempQuestions and TimeQuestions involve temporal questions that require temporal reasoning for answer inference, however, their associated KGs are non-temporal. CRONQUESTIONS [21] contains questions based on a time-evolving TKG, i.e., Wikidata [27]. It is proposed for non-forecasting TKGQA. Two types of questions, i.e., entity prediction and time prediction questions, are included. To answer CRONQUESTIONS, Saxena et al. propose CRONKGQA that uses TKGC methods, along with pre-trained LMs, which shows great effectiveness. A line of methods has been proposed on top of CRONKGQA (TempoQR [19], TSQA [23], SubGTR [4]), where they better distinguish question time scopes and reason over subgraphs. CRONQUESTIONS is proposed based on the idea of TKGC, and it does not support TKG forecasting and contains no forecasting questions. One recent work, i.e., FORECASTQA [13], proposes a QA dataset fully consisting of forecasting questions. However, FORECASTQA is not related to KGQA. In FORECASTQA, answers to its questions are inferred from text contexts, while KGQA/TKGQA requires models to find the answers from the coupled KGs/TKGs without providing any additional text contexts. As a result, the methods designed for FORECASTQA have no ability to address TKGQA. To this end, we propose FORECASTTKGQUESTIONS,

Table 1. (a) KGQA dataset comparison. Statistics are taken from [12,21]. **T%** denotes the portion of temporal questions. (b) FORECASTTKGQUESTIONS statistics: number of questions of different types.

(a)

Datasets	TKG	Forecast	T%	# Questions
MetaQA	✗	✗	0%	400k
TempQuestions	✗	✗	100%	1271
TimeQuestions	✗	✗	100%	16k
CRONQUESTIONS	✓	✗	100%	410k
FORECASTTKGQUESTIONS	✓	✓	100%	727k

(b)

	Train	Valid	Test
1-Hop Entity Prediction	211,564	36,172	33,447
2-Hop Entity Prediction	85,088	12,266	10,765
Yes-Unknown	251,537	42,884	39,695
Fact Reasoning	3,164	514	517
Total	551,353	91,836	84,424

aiming to bridge the gap between TKG forecasting and KGQA. We compare FORECASTTKGQUESTIONS with recent KGQA datasets in Table 1.

Task Formulation: Forecasting TKGQA. Forecasting TKGQA aims to test the forecasting ability of TKGQA models. It requires QA models to predict future facts based on past TKG information. We formulate it as follows. Given a TKG $\mathcal{G}$ and a natural language question q generated based on a TKG fact whose valid timestamp is t_q, forecasting TKGQA aims to predict the answer to q. We label every question q with t_q, and constrain QA models to only use the TKG facts $\{(s_i, r_i, o_i, t_i)|t_i < t_q\}$ before t_q for answer inference. We propose three types of forecasting TKGQA questions, i.e., EPQs, YUQs, and FRQs. The answer to a EPQ is an entity $e \in \mathcal{E}$. The answer to a YUQ is either *yes* or *unknown*. We formulate FRQs as multiple choices and thus the answer to an FRQ corresponds to a choice c. As a novel task, forecasting TKGQA requires models to have the ability of both natural language understanding (NLU) and future forecasting. Compared with it, the traditional TKG forecasting task does not require NLU and non-forecasting TKGQA does not consider future forecasting. Thus, previous methods for TKG forecasting[2], e.g., RE-NET [14], and non-forecasting TKGQA, e.g., TempoQR [19], are not suitable for solving forecasting TKGQA.

3   FORECASTTKGQUESTIONS

3.1   Temporal Knowledge Base

A subset from ICEWS [2] is taken as the associated temporal KB for our proposed dataset. We construct a TKG ICEWS21 based on the events taken from the official website of the ICEWS weekly event data[3] [2]. ICEWS contains sociopolitical events in English. We take the events from Jan. 1, 2021, to Aug. 31,

---

[2] Relation set is provided in TKG forecasting and these methods explicitly learn relation representations. However, TKG relations are not annotated in forecasting TKGQA questions. Only question texts are provided and these methods have no way to process. Therefore, we do not consider them in experiments on our new task.

[3] https://dataverse.harvard.edu/dataverse/icews.

Table 2. ICEWS21 TKG statistics. N_{train}, N_{valid}, N_{test} denote the number of TKG facts in $\mathcal{G}_{\text{train}}$, $\mathcal{G}_{\text{valid}}$, $\mathcal{G}_{\text{test}}$, respectively. $|\mathcal{E}|$, $|\mathcal{R}|$, $|\mathcal{T}|$ denote ICEWS21's number of entities, relations, timestamps, respectively.

Dataset	N_{train}	N_{valid}	N_{test}	$|\mathcal{E}|$	$|\mathcal{R}|$	$|\mathcal{T}|$
ICEWS21	252,434	43,033	39,836	20,575	253	243

2021, and extract TKG facts in the following way. For every ICEWS event, we generate a TKG fact (s, r, o, t). We take the content of *Event Date* as the timestamp t of the TKG fact. We take the contents of *Source Name* and *Target Name* as the subject entity s and the object entity o of the TKG fact, respectively. We take the content of *Event Text* as the relation type r of the fact. We present the dataset statistics of ICEWS21 in Table 2. We split ICEWS21 into three parts $\mathcal{G}_{\text{train}} = \{(s, r, o, t) \in \mathcal{G} | t \in [t_0, t_1)\}$, $\mathcal{G}_{\text{valid}} = \{(s, r, o, t) \in \mathcal{G} | t \in [t_1, t_2)\}$, $\mathcal{G}_{\text{test}} = \{(s, r, o, t) \in \mathcal{G} | t \in [t_2, t_3]\}$, where t_0, t_1, t_2, t_3 correspond to *2021-01-01*, *2021-07-01*, *2021-08-01* and *2021-08-31*, respectively. We generate training/validation/test questions based on $\mathcal{G}_{\text{train}}/\mathcal{G}_{\text{valid}}/\mathcal{G}_{\text{test}}$. We ensure that there exists no temporal overlap between every two of them, i.e., $\mathcal{G}_{\text{train}} \cap \mathcal{G}_{\text{valid}} = \emptyset$, $\mathcal{G}_{\text{train}} \cap \mathcal{G}_{\text{test}} = \emptyset$ and $\mathcal{G}_{\text{valid}} \cap \mathcal{G}_{\text{test}} = \emptyset$. In this way, we prevent QA models from observing any information from the evaluation sets during training.

3.2 Question Categorization and Generation

We generate natural language questions based on the TKG facts in ICEWS21 and propose our QA dataset FORECASTTKGQUESTIONS. Every relation type in ICEWS21 is coupled with a CAMEO code (specified in the *CAMEO Code* column of the ICEWS weekly event data). In the official CAMEO codebook (can be found in ICEWS database), each CAMEO code is explained with examples and detailed descriptions. We use the official CAMEO codebook provided in the ICEWS dataverse for aiding the generation of natural language relation templates. We create relation templates for 250 out of 253 relation types for question generation[4]. For example, we create a relation template *engage in material cooperation with* for the relation type *engage in material cooperation, not specified below*. Questions in FORECASTTKGQUESTIONS are categorized into three categories, i.e., EPQs (including 1-hop and 2 hop EPQs), YUQs, and FRQs. We summarize the number of different types of questions in Table 1b. We use the relation templates to create natural language question templates for all types of questions (examples in Table 3) which are used for question generation. All question templates are presented in our supplementary source code and explained in Appendix C.2. Similar to previous KGQA datasets, e.g., CRONQUESTIONS, entity linking is considered as a separate problem and is not covered in our work. We assume complete entity and timestamp linking, and annotate the entities and timestamps in our questions. This applies to all three types of questions in our dataset. Distribution of question timestamps is specified in Appendix C.5.

---

[4] The rest three relation types are not ideal for question generation (Appendix C.1).

Table 3. Example question templates of all types. s_q and o_q are the annotated question entities. t_q is the annotated question timestamp. For FRQ, s_c, o_c, t_c are annotated choice entities and timestamp. We only write one choice in FRQ template for brevity. Better understand with details in Sect. 3.2.

Question Type	Example Template
1-Hop EPQ	*Who will {s_q} engage in material cooperation with on {t_q}?*
2-Hop EPQ	*Who will threaten a country, while {s_q} criticizes or denounces this country on {t_q}?*
YUQ	*Will {s_q} make a pessimistic comment about {o_q} on {t_q}?*
FRQ	*Why will {s_q} appeal to {o_q} to meet or negotiate on {t_q}?*
	A: {s_c} threatens {o_c} on {t_c}; B:...

Entity Prediction Questions. We generate two groups of EPQs, i.e., 1-hop and 2-hop EPQs. Each 1-hop EPQ is generated from a single TKG fact, e.g., the natural language question *Who will Sudan host on 2021-08-01?* is based on (*Sudan, host, Ramtane Lamamra, 2021-08-01*). Question templates are used during question generation. The underlined parts in the question denote the annotated entities and timestamps for KGQA. We consider all the facts concerning the 250 selected relations and transform them into 1-hop EPQs. Each 2-hop EPQ is generated from two associated TKG facts in ICEWS21 where they contain common entities. An example is presented in Table 4. The answer to a 2-hop EPQ (*Israel*) corresponds to a 2-hop neighbor of its annotated entity (*Iran*) at the question timestamp (*2021-08-02*). We generate 2-hop questions by utilizing AnyBURL [20], a rule-based KG reasoning model. We first split ICEWS21 into snapshots, where each snapshot $\mathcal{G}_{t_i} = \{(s, r, o, t) \in \mathcal{G} | t = t_i\}$ contains all the TKG facts happening at the same timestamp. Then we train AnyBURL on each snapshot for rule extraction. We collect the 2-hop rules with a confidence higher than 0.5 returned by AnyBURL, and manually check if two associated TKG facts in each rule potentially have a logical causation or can be used to interpret positive/negative entity relationships. After excluding the rules not meeting this requirement, we create question templates based on the remaining ones. We search for the groundings in ICEWS21 at every timestamp, where each grounding corresponds to a 2-hop EPQ. See our source code for the complete list of extracted 2-hop rules and see Appendix C.3 for more EPQ generation details.

Yes-Unknown Questions. Based on the idea of triple classification in KG reasoning[5], we introduce yes-no questions into KGQA. We then turn yes-no questions into yes-unknown questions because, according to the Open World Assumption (OWA), the facts not observed in a given TKG are not necessarily wrong [7]. We generalize triple classification to quadruple classification[6], and then translate TKG facts into natural language questions. We take answering YUQs as solving

---

[5] For a KG fact (s, r, o), triple classification aims to predict whether this fact is valid or not.

[6] Quadruple classification has never been studied in previous works. We define it as predicting whether a TKG fact (s, r, o, t) is valid or unknown, under OWA.

Table 4. 2-hop EPQ example. To avoid overlong text, we use symbols to represent relations and timestamps in TKG facts and 2-hop rules. $r_1 =accuse$; $r_2 =engage\ in\ diplomatic\ cooperation$; $t_1 =2021$-08-02. m, n are two entities that are 2-hop neighbors of each other at t_1. X is their common 1-hop neighbor at t_1. The extracted rule describes the negative relationship between *Iran* and *Israel*.

Associated TKG Facts	2-Hop Rule	Generated 2-Hop Question	Answer
(United States, r_1, Iran, t_1)	(X, r_1, m)	*Who will a country engage in diplomatic cooperation with,*	*Israel*
(United States, r_2, Israel, t_1)	$=> (X, r_2, n)$	*while this country accuses <u>Iran</u> on <u>2021-08-02</u>?*	

quadruple classification. For every TKG fact concerning the selected 250 relations, we generate either a true or an unknown question based on it. For example, for the fact *(Sudan, host, Ramtane Lamamra, 2021-08-01)*, a true question is generated as *Will <u>Sudan</u> host <u>Ramtane Lamamra</u> on <u>2021-08-01</u>?* and we label *yes* as its answer. An unknown question is generated by randomly perturbing one entity or the relation type in this fact, e.g., *Will <u>Germany</u> host <u>Ramtane Lamamra</u> on <u>2021-08-01</u>?*, and we label *unknown* as its answer. We ensure that the perturbed fact does not exist in the original TKG. We use 25% of total facts in ICEWS21 to generate true questions and the rest are used to generate unknown questions.

Fact Reasoning Questions. The motivation for proposing FRQs is to study the difference between humans and machines in finding supporting evidence for reasoning. We formulate FRQs in the form of multiple choices. Each question is coupled with four choices. Given a TKG fact from an FRQ, we ask the QA models to choose which fact in the choices is the most contributive to (the most relevant cause of) the fact mentioned in the question. We provide several examples in Fig. 1. We generate FRQs as follows. We first train a TKG forecasting model xERTE [8] on ICEWS21. Note that to predict a query $(s, r, ?, t)$, xERTE samples its related prior TKG facts and assigns contribution scores to them. It provides explainability by assigning higher scores to the more related prior facts. We perform TKG forecasting and collect the queries where the ground-truth missing entities are ranked as top 1 by xERTE. For each collected query, we find its corresponding TKG fact and pick out four related prior facts found by xERTE. We take the prior facts with the highest, the lowest, and median contribution scores as **Answer, Negative**, and **Median**, respectively. Inspired by InferWiki [3], we include a **Hard Negative** fact with the second highest contribution score, making it non-trivial for QA models to make the right decision. We generate each FRQ by turning the corresponding facts into a question and four choices (using templates), and manage to use xERTE to generate a large number of questions. However, since the answers to these questions are solely determined by xERTE, there exist numerous erroneous examples. For example, the **Hard Negative** of lots of them are more suitable than their **Answer** to be the answers. We ask five graduate students (major in computer science) to manually check all these questions and annotate them as reasonable or unreasonable according to their own knowledge or through search engines. If the majority annotate a question as unreasonable, we filter it out. See Appendix C.4 for more details of FRQ generation and annotation, including the annotation instruction and interface.

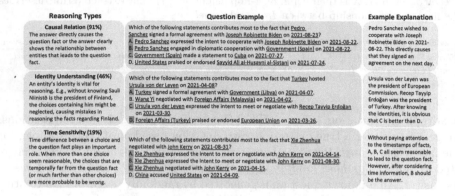

Fig. 1. Required reasoning types and proportions (%) in sampled FRQs, as well as FRQ examples. We sample 100 FRQs in each train/valid/test set. For choices, green for **Answer**, blue for **Hard Negative**, orange for **Median** and yellow for **Negative**. Multiple reasoning skills are required to answer each question, so the total proportion sum is not 100%. (Color figure online)

To better study the reasoning skills required to answer FRQs, we randomly sample 300 FRQs and manually annotate them with reasoning types. The required reasoning skills and their proportions are shown in Fig. 1.

4   FORECASTTKGQA

FORECASTTKGQA employs a TKG forecasting model TANGO [9] and a pretrained LM BERT [5] for solving forecasting questions. We illustrate its model structure in Fig. 2 with three stages. In Stage 1, a TKG forecasting model TANGO [9] is used to generate the time-aware representation for each entity at each timestamp. In Stage 2, a pre-trained LM (e.g., BERT) is used to encode questions (and choices) into question (choice) representations. Finally, in Stage 3, answers are predicted according to the scores computed using the representations from Stage 1 and 2.

4.1   TKG Forecasting Model

We train TANGO on ICEWS21 with the TKG forecasting task. We use ComplEx [26] as its scoring function. We learn the entity and relation representations in the complex space $\mathbb{C}^d$, where d is the dimension of complex vectors. The training set corresponds to all the TKG facts in $\mathcal{G}_{\text{train}}$, and we evaluate the trained model on $\mathcal{G}_{\text{valid}}$ and $\mathcal{G}_{\text{test}}$. After training, we perform a one time inference on $\mathcal{G}_{\text{valid}}$ and $\mathcal{G}_{\text{test}}$. Following the default setting of TANGO, to compute entity and

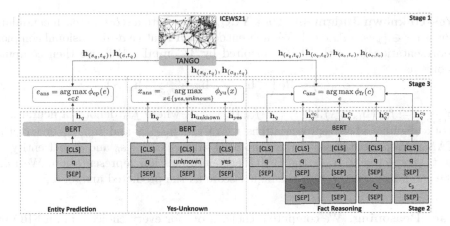

Fig. 2. Model structure of FORECASTTKGQA.

relation representations at every timestamp t, we recurrently input all the TKG facts from $t-4$ to $t-1$, i.e., snapshots from $\mathcal{G}_{t-4}$ to $\mathcal{G}_{t-1}$, into TANGO and take the output representations. Note that it infers representations based on the prior facts, thus not violating our forecasting setting. We compute the entity and relation representations at every timestamp in ICEWS21 and keep them for aiding the QA systems in Stage 1 (Fig. 2). See Appendix B.1 for more details of TANGO training and inference. To leverage the complex representations computed by TANGO with ComplEx, we map the output of BERT to $\mathbb{C}^d$. For each natural language input, we take the output representation of the [CLS] token computed by BERT and project it to a $2d$ real space to form a $2d$ real-valued vector. We take the first and second half of it as the real and imaginary part of a d-dimensional complex vector, respectively. All the representations output by BERT have already been mapped to $\mathbb{C}^d$ without further notice.

4.2   QA Model

Entity Prediction. For every EPQ q, we compute an entity score for every entity $e \in \mathcal{E}$. The entity with the highest score is predicted as the answer e_{ans}. To compute the score for e, we first input q into BERT and map its output to $\mathbb{C}^d$ to get the question representation $\mathbf{h}_q$. Inspired by ComplEx, we then define e's entity score as

$$\phi_{\text{ep}}(e) = \text{Re}\left(< \mathbf{h}'_{(s_q,t_q)}, \mathbf{h}_q, \bar{\mathbf{h}}'_{(e,t_q)} > \right). \tag{1}$$

$\mathbf{h}'_{(s_q,t_q)} = f_{\text{ep}}\left(\mathbf{h}_{(s_q,t_q)}\right)$, $\mathbf{h}'_{(e,t_q)} = f_{\text{ep}}\left(\mathbf{h}_{(e,t_q)}\right)$, where f_{ep} denotes a neural network aligning TKG representations to EPQs. $\mathbf{h}_{(s_q,t_q)}$ and $\mathbf{h}_{(e,t_q)}$ denote the TANGO representations of the annotated entity s_q and the entity e at the question timestamp t_q, respectively. Re means taking the real part of a complex vector and $\bar{\mathbf{h}}'_{(e,t_q)}$ means the complex conjugate of $\mathbf{h}'_{(e,t_q)}$.

Yes-Unknown Judgment. For a YUQ, we compute a score for each candidate answer $x \in \{yes, unknown\}$. We first encode each x into a d-dimensional complex representation $\mathbf{h}_x$ with BERT. Inspired by TComplEx [16], we then compute scores as

$$\phi_{\text{yu}}(x) = \text{Re}\left(< \mathbf{h}'_{(s_q,t_q)}, \mathbf{h}_q, \bar{\mathbf{h}}'_{(o_q,t_q)}, \mathbf{h}_x >\right). \tag{2}$$

$\mathbf{h}'_{(s_q,t_q)} = f_{\text{yu}}\left(\mathbf{h}_{(s_q,t_q)}\right), \mathbf{h}'_{(o_q,t_q)} = f_{\text{yu}}\left(\mathbf{h}_{(o_q,t_q)}\right)$, where f_{yu} denotes a neural network aligning TKG representations to YUQs. $\mathbf{h}_{(s_q,t_q)}$ and $\mathbf{h}_{(o_q,t_q)}$ denote the TANGO representations of the annotated subject entity s_q and object entity o_q at t_q, respectively. $\mathbf{h}_q$ is the BERT encoded question representation. We take the candidate answer with the higher score as the predicted answer x_{ans}.

Fact Reasoning. We compute a choice score for every choice c in an FRQ by using the following scoring function:

$$\phi_{\text{fr}}(c) = \text{Re}\left(< \mathbf{h}'_{(s_c,t_c)}, \mathbf{h}_q^c, \bar{\mathbf{h}}'_{(o_c,t_c)}, \mathbf{h}'_q >\right), \tag{3}$$

$\mathbf{h}_q^c$ is the output of BERT mapped to $\mathbb{C}^d$ given the concatenation of q and c. $\mathbf{h}'_{(s_c,t_c)} = f_{\text{fr}}\left(\mathbf{h}_{(s_c,t_c)}\right)$ and $\mathbf{h}'_{(o_c,t_c)} = f_{\text{fr}}\left(\mathbf{h}_{(o_c,t_c)}\right)$. f_{fr} is a projection network and $\mathbf{h}_{(s_c,t_c)}, \mathbf{h}_{(o_c,t_c)}$ denote the TANGO representations of the entities annotated in c. $\mathbf{h}'_q = f\left(f_{\text{fr}}\left(\mathbf{h}_{(s_q,t_q)}\right)\|\mathbf{h}_q^c\|f_{\text{fr}}\left(\mathbf{h}_{(o_q,t_q)}\right)\right)$, where f serves as a projection and $\|$ denotes concatenation. $\mathbf{h}_{(s_q,t_q)}$ and $\mathbf{h}_{(o_q,t_q)}$ denote the TANGO representations of the entities annotated in the question q. We take the choice with the highest choice score as our predicted answer c_{ans}. We give a more detailed description of Eq. 1, 2 and 3 in Appendix A.

Parameter Learning. We use cross-entropy loss to train FORECASTTKGQA on each type of questions separately. The loss functions of EPQs, FRQs and YUQs are given by $\mathcal{L}_{\text{ep}} = -\sum_{q\in\mathcal{Q}^{\text{ep}}} \log\left(\frac{\phi_{\text{ep}}(e_{\text{ans}})}{\sum_{e\in\mathcal{E}} \phi_{\text{ep}}(e)}\right)$, $\mathcal{L}_{\text{fr}} = -\sum_{q\in\mathcal{Q}^{\text{fr}}} \log\left(\frac{\phi_{\text{fr}}(c_{\text{ans}})}{\sum_c \phi_{\text{fr}}(c)}\right)$ and $\mathcal{L}_{\text{yu}} = -\sum_{q\in\mathcal{Q}^{\text{yu}}} \log\left(\frac{\phi_{\text{yu}}(x_{\text{ans}})}{\sum_{x\in\{yes,unknown\}} \phi_{\text{yu}}(x)}\right)$, respectively. $\mathcal{Q}^{\text{ep}}/\mathcal{Q}^{\text{yu}}/\mathcal{Q}^{\text{fr}}$ denotes all EPQs/YUQs/FRQs and $e_{\text{ans}}/x_{\text{ans}}/c_{\text{ans}}$ is the answer to question q.

5   Experiments

We answer several research questions (RQs) with experiments[7]. **RQ1** (Sect. 5.2, 5.4): Can a TKG forecasting model better support forecasting TKGQA than a TKGC model? **RQ2** (Sect. 5.2, 5.4): Does FORECASTTKGQA perform well in forecasting TKGQA? **RQ3** (Sect. 5.3, 5.5): Are the questions in our dataset answerable? **RQ4** (Sect. 5.7): Is the proposed dataset efficient? **RQ5** (Sect. 5.6): What are the challenges of forecasting TKGQA?

---

[7] Implementation details and further analysis of FORECASTTKGQA in Appendix B.3 and G.

5.1 Experimental Setting

Evaluation Metrics. We use mean reciprocal rank (MRR) and Hits@k as the evaluation metrics of the EPQs. For each EPQ, we compute the rank of the ground-truth answer entity among all the TKG entities. Test MRR is then computed as $\frac{1}{|\mathcal{Q}_{test}^{ep}|} \sum_{q \in \mathcal{Q}_{test}^{ep}} \frac{1}{rank_q}$, where $\mathcal{Q}_{test}^{ep}$ denotes all EPQs in the test set and $rank_q$ is the rank of the ground-truth answer entity of question q. Hits@k is the proportion of the answered questions where the ground-truth answer entity is ranked as top k. For YUQs and FRQs, we employ accuracy for evaluation. Accuracy is the proportion of the correctly answered questions out of all questions.

Baseline Methods. We consider two pre-trained LMs, BERT [5] and RoBERTa [17] as baselines. For EPQs and YUQs, we add a prediction head on top of the question representations computed by LMs, and use softmax function to compute answer probabilities. For every FRQ, we input into each LM the concatenation of the question with each choice, and follow the same prediction structure. Besides, we derive two model variants for each LM by introducing TKG representations. We train TComplEx on ICEWS21. For every EPQ and YUQ, we concatenate the question representation with the TComplEx representations of the entities and timestamps annotated in the question, and then perform prediction with a prediction head and softmax. For FRQs, we further include TComplEx representations into choices in the same way. We call this type of variant BERT_int and RoBERTa_int since TComplEx is a TKGC (TKG interpolation) method. Similarly, we also introduce TANGO representations into LMs and derive BERT_ext and RoBERTa_ext, where TANGO serves as a TKG extrapolation backend. Detailed model derivations are presented in Appendix B.2. We also consider one KGQA method EmbedKGQA [22], and two TKGQA methods, i.e., CRONKGQA [21] and TempoQR [19] as baselines. We run Embed-KGQA on top of the KG representations trained with ComplEx on ICEWS21, and run TKGQA baselines on top of the TKG representations trained with TComplEx.

5.2 Main Results

We report the experimental results in Table 5. In Table 5a, we show that our entity prediction model outperforms all baseline methods. We observe that EmbedKGQA achieves a better performance than BERT and RoBERTa, showing that employing KG representations helps TKGQA. Besides, LM variants outperform their original LMs, indicating that TKG representations help LMs perform better in TKGQA. Further, BERT_ext shows stronger performance than BERT_int (this also applies to RoBERTa_int and RoBERTa_ext), which proves that TKG forecasting models provide greater help than TKGC models in forecasting TKGQA. CRONKGQA and TempoQR employ TComplEx representations as supporting information and perform poorly, implying that employing TKG representations provided by TKGC methods may include noisy information in forecasting TKGQA. FORECASTTKGQA injects TANGO representations

Table 5. Experimental results over FORECASTTKGQUESTIONS. The best results are marked in bold.

(a) EPQs. Overall results in Appendix D.

Model	MRR 1-Hop	MRR 2-Hop	Hits@1 1-Hop	Hits@1 2-Hop	Hits@10 1-Hop	Hits@10 2-Hop
RoBERTa	0.166	0.149	0.104	0.085	0.288	0.268
BERT	0.279	0.182	0.192	0.106	0.451	0.342
EmbedKGQA	0.317	0.185	0.228	0.112	0.489	0.333
RoBERTa_int	0.283	0.157	0.190	0.094	0.467	0.290
BERT_int	0.314	0.183	0.223	0.107	0.490	0.344
CRONKGQA	0.131	0.090	0.081	0.042	0.231	0.187
TempoQR	0.145	0.107	0.094	0.061	0.243	0.199
RoBERTa_ext	0.306	0.180	0.216	0.108	0.497	0.323
BERT_ext	0.331	0.208	0.239	0.128	0.508	0.369
FORECASTTKGQA	**0.339**	**0.216**	**0.248**	**0.129**	**0.517**	**0.386**

(b) YUQs and FRQs.

Model	Accuracy YUQ	Accuracy FRQ
RoBERTa	0.721	0.645
BERT	0.813	0.634
RoBERTa_int	0.768	0.693
BERT_int	0.829	0.682
RoBERTa_ext	0.798	0.707
BERT_ext	0.837	0.746
FORECASTTKGQA	**0.870**	**0.769**
Human Performance (a)	-	0.936
Human Performance (b)	-	0.954

into a scoring module, showing its great effectiveness on EPQs. For YUQs and FRQs, FORECASTTKGQA also achieves the best performance. Table 5b shows that it is helpful to include TKG representations for answering YUQs and FRQs and our scoring functions are effective.

5.3   Human Vs. Machine on FRQs

To study the difference between humans and models in fact reasoning, we further benchmark human performance on FRQs with a survey (See Appendix E for details). We ask five graduate students to answer 100 questions randomly sampled from the test set. We consider two settings: (a) Humans answer FRQs with their own knowledge and inference ability. **Search engines are not allowed**; (b) Humans can turn to search engines and use the web information published **before the question timestamp** for aiding QA. Table 5 shows that humans achieve much stronger performance than all QA models (even in setting (a)). This calls for a great effort to build better fact reasoning TKGQA models.

5.4   Performance over FRQs with Different Reasoning Types

Considering the reasoning types listed in Fig. 1, we compare RoBERTa_int with FORECASTTKGQA on the 100 sampled test questions that are annotated with reasoning types, to justify performance gain brought by TKG forecasting model on FRQs. Experimental results in Table 6 imply that employing TKG forecasting model helps QA models better deal with any reasoning type on FRQs. We use two cases in Fig. 3 to provide insights into performance gain.

Case 1. Two reasoning skills, i.e., Causal Relation and Time Sensitivity (shown in Fig. 1), are required to correctly answer the question in Case 1. Without considering the timestamps of choices, A, B, C all seem at least somehow reasonable.

Table 6. Performance comparison across FRQs with different reasoning types.

Model	Accuracy		
	Causal Relation	Identity Understanding	Time Sensitivity
RoBERTa_int	0.670	0.529	0.444
FORECASTTKGQA	**0.787**	**0.735**	**0.611**

Which of the following statements contributes most to the fact that Xie Zhenhua negotiated with John Kerry on 2021-08-31?
A. Xie Zhenhua expressed the intent to meet or negotiate with John Kerry on 2021-04-14.
B. Xie Zhenhua expressed the intent to meet or negotiate with John Kerry on 2021-08-30.
C. Xie Zhenhua negotiated with John Kerry on 2021-04-15.
D. China accused United States on 2021-04-09.

RoBERTa_int: A   FORECASTTKGQA: **B**

(a) Case 1.

Which of the following statements contributes most to the fact that Kenya hosted Head of Government (Somalia) on 2021-08-10?
A. Kenya expressed the intent to cooperate economically with United Arab Emirates on 2021-07-28.
B. Simon Coveney appealed to European Union on 2021-06-15.
C. Kenya expressed the intent to cooperate with Somalia on 2021-08-09.
D. Kenya had a consolation or a meeting with Israel on 2021-07-30.

RoBERTa_int: D   FORECASTTKGQA: **C**

(b) Case 2.

Fig. 3. Case Studies on FRQs. We mark green for **Answer**, blue for **Hard Negative**, orange for **Median** and yellow for **Negative**. (Color figure online)

However, after considering choice timestamps, B should be the most contributive reason for the question fact. First, the timestamp of B (*2021-08-30*) is much closer to the question timestamp (*2021-08-31*). Moreover, the fact in choice B directly causes the question fact. RoBERTa_int manages to capture the causation, but fails to correctly deal with time sensitivity, while FORECASTTKGQA achieves better reasoning on both reasoning types.

Case 2. Two reasoning skills, i.e., Causal Relation and Identity Understanding (shown in Fig. 1), are required to correctly answer the question in Case 2. *Head of Government (Somalia)* and *Somalia* are two different entities in TKG, however, both entities are about Somalia. By understanding this, we are able to choose the correct answer. FORECASTTKGQA manages to understand the identity of *Head of Government (Somalia)*, match it with *Somalia* and find the cause of the question fact. RoBERTa_int makes a mistake because as a model equipped with TComplEx, it has no well-trained timestamp representations of the question and choice timestamps, which would introduce noise in decision making.

5.5 Answerability of FORECASTTKGQUESTIONS

To validate the answerability of the questions in FORECASTTKGQUESTIONS. We train TComplEx and TANGO over the whole ICEWS21, i.e., $\mathcal{G}_{train} \cup \mathcal{G}_{valid} \cup \mathcal{G}_{test}$, and use them to support QA. Note that this violates the forecasting setting of forecasting TKGQA, and thus we call the TKG models trained in this way as cheating TComplEx (CTComplEx) and cheating TANGO (CTANGO). Answering EPQs with cheating TKG models is same as non-forecasting TKGQA. We couple TempoQR with CTComplEx and see a huge performance increase

Table 7. Answerability study. Models with α means using CTComplEx and β means using CTANGO. $\uparrow$ denotes relative improvement (%) from the results in Table 5. Acc means Accuracy.

(a) EPQs.

	MRR				Hits@10			
Model	1-Hop	$\uparrow$	2-Hop	$\uparrow$	1-Hop	$\uparrow$	2-Hop	$\uparrow$
TempoQR$^\alpha$	0.713	391.7	0.233	117.8	0.883	263.4	0.419	110.6
MHS$^\alpha$	0.868	-	0.647	-	0.992	-	0.904	-
MHS$^\beta$	0.771	-	0.556	-	0.961	-	0.828	-

(b) YUQs and FRQs.

	YUQ		FRQ	
Model	Acc	$\uparrow$	Acc	$\uparrow$
BERT_int$^\alpha$	0.855	19.6	0.816	14.4
BERT_ext$^\beta$	0.873	4.3	0.836	12.1
FORECASTTKGQA$^\beta$	0.925	6.3	0.821	6.8

(Table 7a). Besides, inspired by [10], we develop a new TKGQA model Multi-Hop Scorer[8] (MHS) for EPQs. Starting from the annotated entity s_q of an EPQ, MHS updates the scores of outer entities for n-hops ($n = 2$ in our experiments) until all s_q's n-hop neighbors on the snapshot $\mathcal{G}_{t_q}$ are visited. Initially, MHS assigns a score of 1 to s_q and 0 to any other unvisited entity. For each unvisited entity e, it then computes e's score as: $\phi_{\text{ep}}(e) = \frac{1}{|\mathcal{N}_e(t_q)|} \sum_{(e',r) \in \mathcal{N}_e(t_q)} (\gamma \cdot \phi_{\text{ep}}(e') + \psi(e',r,e,t_q))$, where $\mathcal{N}_e(t_q) = \{(e',r)|(e',r,e,t_q) \in \mathcal{G}_{t_q}\}$ is e's 1-hop neighborhood on $\mathcal{G}_{t_q}$ and γ is a discount factor. We couple MHS with CTComplEx and CTANGO, and define $\psi(e',r,e,t_q)$ separately. For MHS + CTComplEx, $\psi(e',r,e,t_q) = f_2(f_1(\mathbf{h}_{e'}||\mathbf{h}_r||\mathbf{h}_e||\mathbf{h}_{t_q}||\mathbf{h}_q))$. f_1 and f_2 are two neural networks. $\mathbf{h}_e, \mathbf{h}_{e'}, \mathbf{h}_r, \mathbf{h}_{t_q}$ are the CTComplEx representations of entities e, e', relation r and timestamp t_q, respectively. For MHS + CTANGO, we take the idea of FORECASTTKGQA: $\psi(e',r,e,t_q) = \text{Re}\left(<\mathbf{h}_{(e',t_q)}, \mathbf{h}_r, \bar{\mathbf{h}}_{(e,t_q)}, \mathbf{h}_q>\right)$. $\mathbf{h}_{(e,t_q)}$, $\mathbf{h}_{(e',t_q)}$, $\mathbf{h}_r$ are the CTANGO representations of entities e, e' at t_q, and relation r, respectively. $\mathbf{h}_q$ is BERT encoded question representation. We find that MHS achieves superior performance (even on 2-hop EPQs). This is because MHS not only uses cheating TKG models, but also considers ground-truth multi-hop structural information of TKGs at t_q (which is unavailable in the forecasting setting). For YUQs and FRQs, Table 7b shows that cheating TKG models help improve performance, especially on FRQs. These results imply that given the ground-truth TKG information at question timestamps, our forecasting TKGQA questions are answerable.

5.6   Challenges of Forecasting TKGQA over FORECAST TKG QUESTIONS

From the experiments discussed in Sect. 5.3 and 5.5, we summarize the challenges of forecasting TKGQA: (1) Inferring the ground-truth TKG information $\mathcal{G}_{t_q}$ at the question timestamp t_q accurately; (2) Effectively performing multi-hop reasoning for forecasting TKGQA; (3) Developing TKGQA models for better fact reasoning. In Sect. 5.5, we have trained cheating TKG models and used them to support QA. We show in Table 7 that QA models substantially improve their performance on forecasting TKGQA with cheating TKG models. This implies

---

[8] See Appendix F for detailed model explanation and model structure illustration.

that accurately inferring the ground-truth TKG information at t_q is crucial in our task and how to optimally achieve it remains a challenge. We also observe that MHS with cheating TKG models achieves much better results on EPQs (especially on 2-hop). MHS utilizes multi-hop information of the ground-truth TKG at t_q ($\mathcal{G}_{t_q}$) for better QA. In forecasting TKGQA, by only knowing the TKG facts before t_q and not observing $\mathcal{G}_{t_q}$, it is impossible for MHS to directly utilize the ground-truth multi-hop information at t_q. This implies that how to effectively infer and exploit multi-hop information for QA in the forecasting scenario remains a challenge. Moreover, as discussed in Sect. 5.3, current TKGQA models still trail humans with great margin on FRQs. It is challenging to design novel forecasting TKGQA models for better fact reasoning.

5.7 Study of Data Efficiency

We want to know how the models will be affected with less/more training data. For each type of questions, we modify the size of its training set. We train FORECASTTKGQA on the modified training sets and evaluate our model on the original test sets. We randomly sample 10%, 25%, 50%, and 75% of the training examples to form new training sets. Figure 4 shows that for every type of question, the performance of FORECASTTKGQA steadily improves as the size of the training sets increase. This proves that our proposed dataset is efficient and useful for training forecasting TKGQA models.

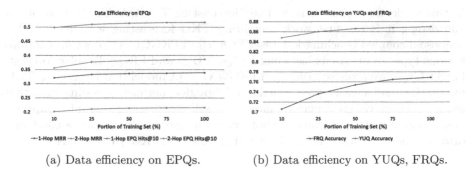

(a) Data efficiency on EPQs.   (b) Data efficiency on YUQs, FRQs.

Fig. 4. Data efficiency analysis.

6   Justification of Task Validity from Two Perspectives

(1) Perspective from Underlying TKG. We take a commonly used temporal KB, i.e., ICEWS, as the KB for constructing underlying TKG ICEWS21. ICEWS-based TKGs contain socio-political facts. It is meaningful to perform forecasting over them because this can help to improve early warning in critical socio-political situations around the globe. [25] has shown with case studies that ICEWS-based TKG datasets have underlying cause-and-effect temporal patterns and TKG forecasting models are built to capture them. This indicates that performing TKG forecasting over ICEWS-based TKGs is also valid. And therefore, developing forecasting TKGQA on top of ICEWS21 is meaningful and valid. **(2) Perspective from the Motivation of Proposing Different Types of Questions.** The motivation of proposing EPQs is to introduce TKG link forecasting (future link prediction) into KGQA, while proposing YUQs is to introduce quadruple classification (stemming from triple classification) and yes-no type questions. We view quadruple classification in the forecasting scenario as deciding if the unseen TKG facts are valid based on previously known TKG facts. To answer EPQs and YUQs, models can be considered as understanding natural language questions first and then performing TKG reasoning tasks. Since TKG reasoning tasks are considered solvable and widely studied in the TKG community, our task over EPQs and YUQs is valid. We propose FRQs aiming to study the difference between humans and machines in fact reasoning. We have summarized the reasoning skills that are required to answer every FRQ in Fig. 1, which also implies the potential direction for QA models to achieve improvement in fact reasoning in the future. We have shown in Sect. 5.3 that our proposed FRQs are answerable to humans, which directly indicates the validity of our FRQs. Thus, answering FRQs in forecasting TKGQA is also valid and meaningful.

7   Conclusion

In this work, we propose a novel task: forecasting TKGQA. To the best of our knowledge, it is the first work combining TKG forecasting with KGQA. We propose a coupled benchmark dataset FORECASTTKGQUESTIONS that contains various types of questions including EPQs, YUQs and FRQs. To solve forecasting TKGQA, we propose FORECASTTKGQA, a QA model that leverages a TKG forecasting model with a pre-trained LM. Though experimental results show that our model achieves great performance, there still exists a large room for improvement compared with humans. We hope our work can benefit future research and draw attention to studying the forecasting power of TKGQA methods.

Supplemental Material Statement: Source code and data are uploaded here[9]. Appendices are published in the arXiv version[10]. We have referred to the corresponding parts in the main body. Please check accordingly.

Acknowledgement. This work has been supported by the German Federal Ministry for Economic Affairs and Climate Action (BMWK) as part of the project CoyPu under grant number 01MK21007K.

---

[9] https://github.com/ZifengDing/ForecastTKGQA.
[10] https://arxiv.org/abs/2208.06501.

References

1. Bordes, A., Usunier, N., Chopra, S., Weston, J.: Large-scale simple question answering with memory networks (2015). arxiv.org:1506.02075
2. Boschee, E., Lautenschlager, J., O'Brien, S., Shellman, S., Starz, J., Ward, M.: ICEWS Coded Event Data (2015). https://doi.org/10.7910/DVN/28075
3. Cao, Y., Ji, X., Lv, X., Li, J., Wen, Y., Zhang, H.: Are missing links predictable? an inferential benchmark for knowledge graph completion. In: Zong, C., Xia, F., Li, W., Navigli, R. (eds.) Proceedings of the 59th Annual Meeting of the Association for Computational Linguistics and the 11th International Joint Conference on Natural Language Processing, ACL/IJCNLP 2021, (Volume 1: Long Papers), Virtual Event, August 1–6, 2021, pp. 6855–6865. Association for Computational Linguistics (2021). https://doi.org/10.18653/v1/2021.acl-long.534
4. Chen, Z., Zhao, X., Liao, J., Li, X., Kanoulas, E.: Temporal knowledge graph question answering via subgraph reasoning. Knowl. Based Syst. **251**, 109134 (2022). https://doi.org/10.1016/j.knosys.2022.109134
5. Devlin, J., Chang, M., Lee, K., Toutanova, K.: BERT: pre-training of deep bidirectional transformers for language understanding. In: Burstein, J., Doran, C., Solorio, T. (eds.) Proceedings of the 2019 Conference of the North American Chapter of the Association for Computational Linguistics: Human Language Technologies, NAACL-HLT 2019, Minneapolis, MN, USA, June 2–7, 2019, Volume 1 (Long and Short Papers), pp. 4171–4186. Association for Computational Linguistics (2019). https://doi.org/10.18653/v1/n19-1423
6. Ding, Z., Ma, Y., He, B., Han, Z., Tresp, V.: A simple but powerful graph encoder for temporal knowledge graph completion. In: NeurIPS 2022 Temporal Graph Learning Workshop (2022). https://openreview.net/forum?id=DYG8RbgAIo
7. Galárraga, L.A., Teflioudi, C., Hose, K., Suchanek, F.M.: AMIE: association rule mining under incomplete evidence in ontological knowledge bases. In: Schwabe, D., Almeida, V.A.F., Glaser, H., Baeza-Yates, R., Moon, S.B. (eds.) 22nd International World Wide Web Conference, WWW '13, Rio de Janeiro, Brazil, May 13–17, 2013, pp. 413–422. International World Wide Web Conferences Steering Committee / ACM (2013). https://doi.org/10.1145/2488388.2488425
8. Han, Z., Chen, P., Ma, Y., Tresp, V.: Explainable subgraph reasoning for forecasting on temporal knowledge graphs. In: 9th International Conference on Learning Representations, ICLR 2021, Virtual Event, Austria, May 3–7, 2021. OpenReview.net (2021). https://openreview.net/forum?id=pGIHq1m7PU
9. Han, Z., Ding, Z., Ma, Y., Gu, Y., Tresp, V.: Learning neural ordinary equations for forecasting future links on temporal knowledge graphs. In: Moens, M., Huang, X., Specia, L., Yih, S.W. (eds.) Proceedings of the 2021 Conference on Empirical Methods in Natural Language Processing, EMNLP 2021, Virtual Event / Punta Cana, Dominican Republic, 7–11 November, 2021, pp. 8352–8364. Association for Computational Linguistics (2021). https://doi.org/10.18653/v1/2021.emnlp-main.658
10. Ji, H., Ke, P., Huang, S., Wei, F., Zhu, X., Huang, M.: Language generation with multi-hop reasoning on commonsense knowledge graph. In: Webber, B., Cohn, T., He, Y., Liu, Y. (eds.) Proceedings of the 2020 Conference on Empirical Methods in Natural Language Processing, EMNLP 2020, Online, November 16–20, 2020, pp. 725–736. Association for Computational Linguistics (2020). https://doi.org/10.18653/v1/2020.emnlp-main.54

11. Jia, Z., Abujabal, A., Roy, R.S., Strötgen, J., Weikum, G.: Tempquestions: A benchmark for temporal question answering. In: Champin, P., Gandon, F., Lalmas, M., Ipeirotis, P.G. (eds.) Companion of the The Web Conference 2018 on The Web Conference 2018, WWW 2018, Lyon, France, April 23–27, 2018, pp. 1057–1062. ACM (2018). https://doi.org/10.1145/3184558.3191536

12. Jia, Z., Pramanik, S., Roy, R.S., Weikum, G.: Complex temporal question answering on knowledge graphs. In: Demartini, G., Zuccon, G., Culpepper, J.S., Huang, Z., Tong, H. (eds.) CIKM '21: The 30th ACM International Conference on Information and Knowledge Management, Virtual Event, Queensland, Australia, November 1–5, 2021, pp. 792–802. ACM (2021). https://doi.org/10.1145/3459637.3482416

13. Jin, W., et al.: Forecastqa: A question answering challenge for event forecasting with temporal text data. In: Zong, C., Xia, F., Li, W., Navigli, R. (eds.) Proceedings of the 59th Annual Meeting of the Association for Computational Linguistics and the 11th International Joint Conference on Natural Language Processing, ACL/IJCNLP 2021, (Volume 1: Long Papers), Virtual Event, August 1–6, 2021, pp. 4636–4650. Association for Computational Linguistics (2021). https://doi.org/10.18653/v1/2021.acl-long.357

14. Jin, W., Qu, M., Jin, X., Ren, X.: Recurrent event network: Autoregressive structure inferenceover temporal knowledge graphs. In: Webber, B., Cohn, T., He, Y., Liu, Y. (eds.) Proceedings of the 2020 Conference on Empirical Methods in Natural Language Processing, EMNLP 2020, Online, November 16–20, 2020, pp. 6669–6683. Association for Computational Linguistics (2020). https://doi.org/10.18653/v1/2020.emnlp-main.541

15. Jung, J., Jung, J., Kang, U.: Learning to walk across time for interpretable temporal knowledge graph completion. In: Zhu, F., Ooi, B.C., Miao, C. (eds.) KDD '21: The 27th ACM SIGKDD Conference on Knowledge Discovery and Data Mining, Virtual Event, Singapore, August 14–18, 2021, pp. 786–795. ACM (2021). https://doi.org/10.1145/3447548.3467292

16. Lacroix, T., Obozinski, G., Usunier, N.: Tensor decompositions for temporal knowledge base completion. In: 8th International Conference on Learning Representations, ICLR 2020, Addis Ababa, Ethiopia, April 26–30, 2020. OpenReview.net (2020), https://openreview.net/forum?id=rke2P1BFwS

17. Liu, Y., et al.: Roberta: A robustly optimized BERT pretraining approach (2019). https://doi.org/10.48550/ARXIV.1907.11692

18. Liu, Y., Ma, Y., Hildebrandt, M., Joblin, M., Tresp, V.: Tlogic: Temporal logical rules for explainable link forecasting on temporal knowledge graphs. In: Thirty-Sixth AAAI Conference on Artificial Intelligence, AAAI 2022, Thirty-Fourth Conference on Innovative Applications of Artificial Intelligence, IAAI 2022, The Twelveth Symposium on Educational Advances in Artificial Intelligence, EAAI 2022 Virtual Event, February 22 - March 1, 2022, pp. 4120–4127. AAAI Press (2022). https://ojs.aaai.org/index.php/AAAI/article/view/20330

19. Mavromatis, C., et al.: Tempoqr: Temporal question reasoning over knowledge graphs. In: Thirty-Sixth AAAI Conference on Artificial Intelligence, AAAI 2022, Thirty-Fourth Conference on Innovative Applications of Artificial Intelligence, IAAI 2022, The Twelveth Symposium on Educational Advances in Artificial Intelligence, EAAI 2022 Virtual Event, February 22 - March 1, 2022, pp. 5825–5833. AAAI Press (2022). https://ojs.aaai.org/index.php/AAAI/article/view/20526

20. Meilicke, C., Chekol, M.W., Fink, M., Stuckenschmidt, H.: Reinforced anytime bottom up rule learning for knowledge graph completion (2020). arxiv.org:2004.04412

21. Saxena, A., Chakrabarti, S., Talukdar, P.P.: Question answering over temporal knowledge graphs. In: Zong, C., Xia, F., Li, W., Navigli, R. (eds.) Proceedings of the 59th Annual Meeting of the Association for Computational Linguistics and the 11th International Joint Conference on Natural Language Processing, ACL/IJCNLP 2021, (Volume 1: Long Papers), Virtual Event, August 1–6, 2021, pp. 6663–6676. Association for Computational Linguistics (2021). https://doi.org/10.18653/v1/2021.acl-long.520

22. Saxena, A., Tripathi, A., Talukdar, P.: Improving multi-hop question answering over knowledge graphs using knowledge base embeddings. In: Proceedings of the 58th Annual Meeting of the Association for Computational Linguistics, pp. 4498–4507. Association for Computational Linguistics, Online (2020). https://doi.org/10.18653/v1/2020.acl-main.412, https://aclanthology.org/2020.acl-main.412

23. Shang, C., Wang, G., Qi, P., Huang, J.: Improving time sensitivity for question answering over temporal knowledge graphs. In: Muresan, S., Nakov, P., Villavicencio, A. (eds.) Proceedings of the 60th Annual Meeting of the Association for Computational Linguistics (Volume 1: Long Papers), ACL 2022, Dublin, Ireland, May 22–27, 2022, pp. 8017–8026. Association for Computational Linguistics (2022). https://aclanthology.org/2022.acl-long.552

24. Talmor, A., Berant, J.: The web as a knowledge-base for answering complex questions. In: Walker, M.A., Ji, H., Stent, A. (eds.) Proceedings of the 2018 Conference of the North American Chapter of the Association for Computational Linguistics: Human Language Technologies, NAACL-HLT 2018, New Orleans, Louisiana, USA, June 1–6, 2018, Volume 1 (Long Papers), pp. 641–651. Association for Computational Linguistics (2018). https://doi.org/10.18653/v1/n18-1059

25. Trivedi, R., Dai, H., Wang, Y., Song, L.: Know-evolve: Deep temporal reasoning for dynamic knowledge graphs. In: Precup, D., Teh, Y.W. (eds.) Proceedings of the 34th International Conference on Machine Learning, ICML 2017, Sydney, NSW, Australia, 6–11 August 2017. Proceedings of Machine Learning Research, vol. 70, pp. 3462–3471. PMLR (2017). http://proceedings.mlr.press/v70/trivedi17a.html

26. Trouillon, T., Welbl, J., Riedel, S., Gaussier, É., Bouchard, G.: Complex embeddings for simple link prediction. In: Balcan, M., Weinberger, K.Q. (eds.) Proceedings of the 33nd International Conference on Machine Learning, ICML 2016, New York City, NY, USA, June 19–24, 2016. JMLR Workshop and Conference Proceedings, vol. 48, pp. 2071–2080. JMLR.org (2016), http://proceedings.mlr.press/v48/trouillon16.html

27. Vrandecic, D., Krötzsch, M.: Wikidata: a free collaborative knowledgebase. Commun. ACM **57**(10), 78–85 (2014). https://doi.org/10.1145/2629489

28. Yih, W., Chang, M., He, X., Gao, J.: Semantic parsing via staged query graph generation: Question answering with knowledge base. In: Proceedings of the 53rd Annual Meeting of the Association for Computational Linguistics and the 7th International Joint Conference on Natural Language Processing of the Asian Federation of Natural Language Processing, ACL 2015, July 26–31, 2015, Beijing, China, Volume 1: Long Papers, pp. 1321–1331. The Association for Computer Linguistics (2015). https://doi.org/10.3115/v1/p15-1128

29. Zhang, Y., Dai, H., Kozareva, Z., Smola, A.J., Song, L.: Variational reasoning for question answering with knowledge graph. In: McIlraith, S.A., Weinberger, K.Q. (eds.) Proceedings of the Thirty-Second AAAI Conference on Artificial Intelligence, (AAAI-18), the 30th innovative Applications of Artificial Intelligence (IAAI-18), and the 8th AAAI Symposium on Educational Advances in Artificial Intelligence (EAAI-18), New Orleans, Louisiana, USA, February 2–7, 2018, pp. 6069–6076.

AAAI Press (2018). https://www.aaai.org/ocs/index.php/AAAI/AAAI18/paper/view/16983

30. Zhu, C., Chen, M., Fan, C., Cheng, G., Zhang, Y.: Learning from history: Modeling temporal knowledge graphs with sequential copy-generation networks. In: Thirty-Fifth AAAI Conference on Artificial Intelligence, AAAI 2021, Thirty-Third Conference on Innovative Applications of Artificial Intelligence, IAAI 2021, The Eleventh Symposium on Educational Advances in Artificial Intelligence, EAAI 2021, Virtual Event, February 2–9, 2021, pp. 4732–4740. AAAI Press (2021). https://ojs.aaai.org/index.php/AAAI/article/view/16604

SORBET: A Siamese Network for Ontology Embeddings Using a Distance-Based Regression Loss and BERT

Francis Gosselin[✉] and Amal Zouaq

LAMA-WeST Lab, Departement of Computer Engineering and Software Engineering,
Polytechnique Montreal, 2500 Chem. de Polytechnique, Montréal,
QC H3T 1J4, Canada
{francis.gosselin,amal.zouaq}@polymtl.ca
http://www.labowest.ca/

Abstract. Ontology embedding methods have been popular in recent years, especially when it comes to representation learning algorithms for solving ontology-related tasks. Despite the impact of large language models on knowledge graphs' related tasks, there has been less focus on adapting these models to construct ontology embeddings that are both semantically relevant and faithful to the ontological structure. In this paper, we present a novel ontology embedding method that encodes ontology classes into a pre-trained SBERT through random walks and then fine-tunes the embeddings using a distance-based regression loss. We benchmark our algorithm on four different datasets across two tasks and show the impact of transfer learning and our distance-based loss on the quality of the embeddings. Our results show that SORBET outperform state-of-the-art ontology embedding techniques for the performed tasks.

Keywords: Ontology · Ontology Embedding · Transfer Learning · Representation Learning · BERT · Sentence BERT

1 Introduction

In recent years, the field of Semantic Web has been changed by the rapidly growing techniques in representation learning [19,28]. Ontology-related tasks, such as ontology alignment or subsumption prediction, have seen an emergence of representation learning methods that have laid the foundation of future research in those fields [28]. However, there has been less focus on one of the main components of these methods: ontology embeddings. More precisely, the mapping of classes and properties of an ontology into vector representations. As representation learning gains popularity across ontology-related task, the necessity of more accurate and significant ontology embeddings is also growing. And with the rapid development of large language model that constantly outperforms state-of-the-art, such as SentenceBERT [24], there is no doubt that leveraging the

© The Author(s), under exclusive license to Springer Nature Switzerland AG 2023
T. R. Payne et al. (Eds.): ISWC 2023, LNCS 14265, pp. 561–578, 2023.
https://doi.org/10.1007/978-3-031-47240-4_30

extensive knowledge learnt by these models could be beneficial for the embedding of ontologies.

Traditional ontology embedding techniques have mainly been adapted from knowledge graph embeddings, after the known successes of the latter [12] for instance representation. TransE and TransR are good examples of well-known KG embeddings that were adapted for ontology embeddings with algorithms like DeepWalk [23] or Deep Graph Kernels [32]. However, applying the same methods and principles for ontologies and KG may not be the most adequate methodology. In comparison with KGs, ontologies contain taxonomical relations (*rdfs:subclassOf*), determining a hierarchy of parent and child concepts. KG only contains instances of those concepts, which are linked together with specific object properties. That is why rdfs:subclass relationships should be at the core of ontology embeddings methods to construct meaningful embeddings.

In this paper, we present a Siamese network for Ontology embeddings Using a Distance-based Regression Loss and BERT (SORBET), a novel ontology embedding approach. Our model is inspired by the task of ontology alignment, which learns representations of classes by bringing equivalent classes closer to each other and by pushing away the rest of the classes. We use the task of ontology alignment to obtain embeddings that are useful to represent classes and usable in other downstream tasks. More precisely, our model is inspired from the SEBMatcher system presented at OAEI 2022 [10], where BERT embeddings created from random walks based on the ontological structure was first introduced. However, SORBET changes the paradigm of the learning objective. Instead of learning to classify pairs of positive (aligned classes) and negative samples (unaligned classes), the model is asked: what should be the distance between these two classes if they were in the same ontology? This impacts the learning in a major way. First, it is flexible in that it can be used in an unsupervised or semi-supervised way. Secondly, the construction of the embeddings is driven by the structure of the ontology, leading to a major impact on their quality. Finally, as we show in the results, the training and embedding is not bound to be done on one ontology at a time, meaning SORBET can be trained on many ontologies simultaneously and transfer knowledge between them.

The contributions of this paper are summarized as follows:

- A novel ontology embedding method able to represent one or multiple ontologies in a same latent space using a pre-trained language model upon random walks. Extending our SEBMatcher model [10], SORBET is able to produce ontology embeddings in a more efficient process with a light-weight model, while yielding more accurate representations.
- A novel training objective function that injects the structure of an ontology into the latent space by reducing the distance of neighbouring classes with a regression loss.
- An improved data sampling mechanism that increases non-trivial alignment samples with an added semi-negative sampling based on graph neighbourhood.

2   Related Work

2.1   Ontology and Knowledge Graph Embeddings

In ontology embedding, the embedding of instances, known as KG embedding, has been a popular line of research in recent years [19]. KG embedding has usually been an inspiration in the development of ontology embedding later on [18, 26]. Some popular approaches in KG embedding focus on minimizing the loss in a classification task, using correct and incorrect triples as samples from the KG. This category includes the translation-based models TransR and TransE [4, 20]. Other methods use a word embedding approach, which revolves around finding some way to express KGs in natural language sentences, then uses a NLP embedding algorithm such as a Word2vec skip-gram or CBOW [22]. One of the first methods in this category was Node2vec [11], where the main idea was to create Random Walks through the KG that would be interpreted as sentences to train the word2vec model. DeepWalk [23] and Deep Graph Kernel [32] had very similar ideas but were geared towards the analysis of social network datasets like BlogCatalog, Flickr, and YouTube. Deep Graph Kernel then extended the idea of Deep Walk by modeling graph substructures instead of Random Walks. Similarly, RDF2Vec [25] was introduced as a way to embed RDF graphs into vectors, by also using random walks, and it has proved to be effective on large datasets such as DBpedia. Finally, many recent models like KEPLER [30], K-BERT [21] and CoLAKE [29] have shown how Large Language Models (LLM) can be effective for KG embedding by producing text-enhanced entity representations.

In the field of ontology embedding, many works have been done related to the word embedding approach. Onto2Vec [26] uses a reasoner combined with the axioms of ontologies to create training data for the modeling of a word2vec skip-gram. OPA2Vec [27] extends Onto2Vec by adding the meta-data information provided by an ontology such as *rdfs:comment*. El Embeddings [18], on the other hand, expands TransE for ontologies by transforming axioms into custom losses depending on the axiom type, but does not include other ontology specific information such as meta-data. OWL2Vec* [5] takes full leverage of OWL ontologies by using ontological structure and metadata as well as a reasoner to infer axioms. It blends random walks and lexical information to fine-tune a pre-trained word2vec model.

These approaches however share some limitations. Firstly, they construct embeddings that are not meant to be generalized and likewise, knowledge is not meant to be shared across embeddings of different ontologies. Secondly, they do not leverage state-of-the-art language models, which can provide significant comprehension and depth through transfer learning.

2.2   Tasks Related to Ontology Embeddings

One of the main tasks related to ontologies is ontolgy alignment (OA). The ontology alignment task can be defined mathematically as the problem of finding a mapping of semantically equivalent classes, properties or instances between two or more ontologies.

Many representation learning systems have emerged in OA in recent years. Some approaches opted for the usage of large language models as the cornerstone of their embeddings. Tom [17] and Fine-Tom [15] are both systems using the pre-trained Sentence BERT. Fine-Tom extends Tom by fine-tuning the model on the OAEI datasets. DAEOM uses BERT as part of a complex system complementing its Graph Attention Transformers (GAT). Other approaches use BERT to produce a similarity score for a pair of candidate alignment. BERTMAP [13] uses random walks to add context to the concepts and outputs a similarity score for a subset of candidate mappings. SEBMatcher [10] uses both of the methods, by leveraging Random Walks to calculate candidate alignments with BERT embeddings then doing a more accurate scoring of the pairs with a fine-tuned BERT. Other approaches using standard word embeddings have also been explored. The usage of Universal Sentence Embedding (USE) have produced good results for VeeAlign [14] and GraphMatcher [9], which are models that use path and node attention to create contextualized embeddings. LogMap-ML [6] uses OWL2Vec* embeddings fine-tuned with a supervised classification task, then use LogMap's output as anchor mappings. Finally, SCBOW+DAE [16] is a top state-of-the-art method that fine-tunes word2vec embeddings with extended knowledge coming from ConceptNet, BabelNet and WikiSynonyms. For misalignment detection, SCBOW+DAE uses a Denoising Auto Encoder (DAE) that encodes the embeddings in a smaller vector space.

Even with the success of representation learning in ontology alignment, it often face challenges when it comes to training data. Firstly, reference alignments cannot be utilized during training, or in some cases, only a small portion of such data is available. Consequently, the efficacy of systems relies heavily on the quantity of pseudo-alignments that can be generated. This challenge is amplified in cases where ontologies are small and contain minimal metadata, such as the conference track in the OAEI [2]. To overcome this hurdle, a strategy often adopted is to rely more on pre-trained word vectors, as little training can be performed. Secondly, the quality of generated training data can be poor depending of the dataset, since the high-precision positive alignments are often trivial to align. When most of the training data comprises trivial alignments, the algorithm's performance may be biased towards classifying non-trivial alignments as negative.

SORBET embeddings are partly inspired by these limitations. Indeed, it has been found that transfer learning yields state-of-the-art results [13,31], however, the quality of the embeddings can still be poor due to the mentioned problems that arise for OA. This motivates the idea of an ontology embedding technique based on transfer learning that is not bound to the training objective of traditional OA models.

3   Methodology

The foremost idea behind SORBET is to create BERT embeddings that are representative of the ontological structure. To achieve this, close pairs of classes in the ontology must be pushed together while distinct classes must be pushed apart. Hence, a siamese network architecture is employed.

3.1   Architecture

SORBET Embeddings follow a siamese architecture pattern using Sentence BERT [24], a pre-trained Siamese BERT model. Figure 1 shows the general architecture of our model. In the SentenceBERT paper, the authors fine-tuned the model on a binary classification task where pairs of sentences are either classified as synonyms or antonyms. SORBET follows the same principle, but instead of a pair of sentences, a pair of tree walks representing classes is fed to the model. The output is then filtered by the pooling layer and a regression distance-based loss is applied. The tree walks are obtained through our data sampling mechanism, which generates positive, semi-negative and negative samples in a stochastic process.

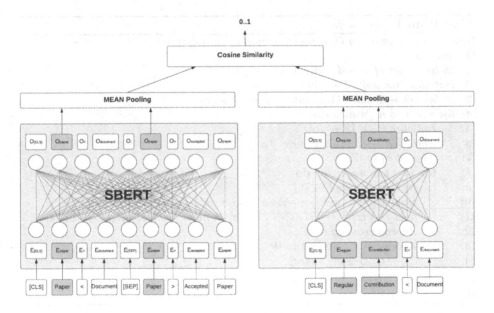

Fig. 1. General Architecture

Preprocessing. For every class and property, the associated descriptive label is tokenized and case-folded. If the tokens are not part of the pre-trained BERT vocabulary, a basic spelling corrector algorithm is applied[1] to deal with some

---

[1] https://github.com/filyp/autocorrect.

errors in input labels. For ontologies that associate more than one label or synonyms to classes, SORBET creates a list of descriptive terms for these classes and randomly chooses labels from this list during training.

Tree Walk. A tree walk is the process of finding multiple distinct random walks, where a random walk is a sequence of classes, starting from a given concept and iterating randomly through the ontological structure. Each iteration adds a subsequent class randomly chosen from the set of 1-hop neighbors of its preceding class in the random walk, by considering subclassOf and object properties relations. These random walks are used as the textual representation of the root concept and its context when they are fed into the BERT model. The algorithm of the Tree Walk, Algorithm 1, is a derivation of the original algorithm described in SEBMatcher [10]. The first change is that both the number of tree walks and the walk length are now interval hyper-parameters instead of having a fixed minimum of 0, so to increase regularization. Furthermore, the concatenation token was changed to "[SEP]" instead of ";". Experiments showed that using the pre-trained special token "[SEP]" produced slightly better results than the previous approach.

Algorithm 1. Tree walk

Input: *Source ontology O, concept c_0 from the ontology O*
Output: T
 1: *Initialize set of visited nodes: $C_v \leftarrow \{c_0\}$*
 2: *Initialize tree walk: $T \leftarrow [\,]$*
 3: *$n\_branch \leftarrow randint(1..number\ of\ neighbours)$*
 4: **for** $i := 1$ to n_branch **do**
 5:     *Initialize walk: $W \leftarrow [\,]$*
 6:     *$walk\_len \leftarrow randint(1..max\_len)$*
 7:     *Append c_0 to W*
 8:     **for** $j := 1$ to $walk\_len$ **do**
 9:         *$current\_concept \leftarrow W_j$*
10:         *$neighbours \leftarrow get\_neighbours(current\_concept)\ /C_v$*
11:         *$next\_concept,\ relation \leftarrow choose\_random\_neighbour(neighbours)$*
12:         *Append relation to W*
13:         *Append $next\_concept$ to W*
14:         *$C_v \leftarrow C_v \cup next\_concept$*
15:     *Append END_TOKEN to W*
16:     *$T \leftarrow T + W$*

Random Masks. A masking strategy is used during training with the idea of regularizing the model. In fact, an undesirable effect during training would be that the model overfits on the label of the root concepts alone without using the context provided by the Tree Walk. In order to prevent this, the root concept is entirely masked 15% of the time, while the remaining 85% of samples will have a random mask applied to 15% of the subtokens.

MEAN Pooling. The pooling layer intends to compute the final vector representation of a concept derived from the output of the BERT model. To do so, the pooling layer computes the mean vector of the BERT outputs related to the root concept (highlighted in Fig. 1). Subsequently, all other embeddings in the tree walk are discarded.

3.2 Data Sampling

Training data consists of pairs of classes that should be pushed toward or apart from each other depending on their similarity score (1 meaning they should be pushed together). It is composed of positive, semi-negative and negative samples. Positive samples are pairs of classes that have a similarity score of 1, meaning they are equivalent concepts. Semi-negative samples are pairs of distinct neighbouring classes in the ontological structure, meaning their similarity score is between 0 and 1 exclusively. Negative samples are distinct classes with disjoint neighbourhood, they have a similarity score of 0. The training data is obtained through our data sampling mechanism, which generates pairs of concepts in a stochastic process using two different sampling strategies: intra-ontology sampling and inter-ontology sampling. Intra-ontology sampling refers to pairs of concepts from the same ontology while inter-ontology sampling refers to pairs of concepts from two different ontologies. Inter-ontology sampling can only be applied if the two following conditions are met: there are 2 or more ontologies, and positive alignments can be inferred from these ontologies. The utilisation of both strategies enhances data augmentation and makes SORBET flexible for the embedding of one or several ontologies.

Positive Sampling. Firstly, we create a set of positive intra-ontology samples where each concept is paired with itself $M_{intra}^{+} : \{(c_i, c_i) : \forall c_i \in O, O'\}$. Then a set of inter-ontology samples is obtained through a String matcher, which is the simple process of matching each concept from a source and target ontology that has the exact same rdfs:label. To further augment the quality of training data, we sample a subset of positive alignments that are chosen randomly from the reference alignments of the ontology alignment task. The resulting set of alignments denoted as M_{inter}^{+} is the union of the String matched samples and the reference alignments samples.

Semi-negative Sampling. Semi-negative samples use both intra and inter-ontology sampling strategies. A semi-negative sample is obtained by choosing a random concept c_i from the ontology O and pairing it with any another concept

c_j from either the same ontology O or a different ontology O' such that $d(c_i, c_j) <$ A. The definition of the distance function d and the hyper-parameter A are described in Sect. 3.3.

Negative Sampling. Negative samples are generated much like semi-negative samples, but with the opposite condition $d(c_i, c_j) \geq A$. Additionally, cross-ontology negative pairs obtained with the inter-ontology strategy cannot have an undefined distance between them. Such case would happen if the cross-ontology distance between the pair cannot be approximated, for example if there are no positive sample $(c_i, c_j) \in M_{inter}^+$ such as $c_i \in O, c_j \in O'$.

The final training set M is built by carefully balancing the generation of samples. For every learning batch, the ratio of positive samples is set to $\lambda_{positive}$, the ratio of semi-negative to negative samples is λ_{semi} and finally the ratio of the usage of inter to intra sampling strategy is λ_{inter}. During the training, one epoch corresponds to one iteration of the model on all positive samples and for each batch, new semi-negative and negative samples are generated. It is necessary for the process to be stochastic, since there are too many possibilities of semi-negative and negative pairs to realistically iterate through them all.

3.3 Regression Distance-Based Loss

The Regression Distance-based Loss is a geometric approach that is inspired by the traditional classification losses used in ontology alignment. The objective of this function is to calculate a similarity score from a pair of classes that is proportionate to the distance between them. We compare this similarity score with the cosine similarity generated by the Siamese network using Mean Squared Error (MSE), and use this metrics for the gradient descent. The equation of the loss can be defined as the following:

$$L = \frac{1}{|M|} \sum_{(c_i, c_j) \in M} [(sim_\theta(c_i, c_j) - \frac{A - min(d(c_i, c_j), A)}{A})^2] \qquad (1)$$

where the function sim_θ is the cosine similarity of the vector representation of the concepts produced by the Siamese network. A is an upper bound on the distance between concepts, its optimal value can vary across datasets and can be tuned as a hyper-parameter. The function d is defined in the following section.

Definition 1. *Let d be a function returning the shortest distance between a source concept c_i and a target concept c_j. Where a distance can be calculated by iterating through the ontological structure only considering rdfs:subclassof relationships.*

SORBET uses a **cross-ontology distance**, which is a distance where the source c_i and target concept c_k originate from different ontologies. Since there are no direct connections between 2 different ontologies, a distance cannot be

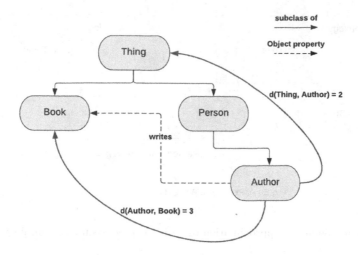

Fig. 2. Example in which the distance between Author and Person in the source Ontology is 1, while the distance between Author and Book is 3.

fetched directly. However we can utilize a positive mapping $(c_i, c_j) \in M^+_{inter}$ to approximate the distance $d(c_i, c_j)$ to $d(c_j, c_k)$ instead.

$$d(c_i, c_k) \approx d(c_j, c_k | (c_i, c_j) \in M^+_{inter}) \tag{2}$$

where $c_i \in O$ and $c_j, c_k \in O'$

The distance function can be visualized in both Fig. 2 and Fig. 3. In Fig. 2, the path between Author and Thing is obtained with two iterations through the hierarchical structure, it can also be observed that the distance between Author and Book is three even if they are linked by an object property. In Fig. 3, the knowledge of the alignment of Person and Human allows the model to approximate the distance between Book and Human.

4 Experiments

We experiment with SORBET embeddings on two downstream tasks: ontology alignment and ontology subsumption.

Formally, given two ontologies O and O', the ontology alignment task can be defined as finding a mapping M between the set of concepts C in O and the concepts C' in O', such that M is a subset of CxC', and each pair of concepts in M is a pair of equivalent concepts.

The subsumption prediction task is a task that involves predicting whether one concept in an ontology O is a subclass of another concept in the same or another ontology. It is a classification problem, where the input is a pair of concepts (A, B), and the output is a binary label indicating whether A is subsumed by B or not.

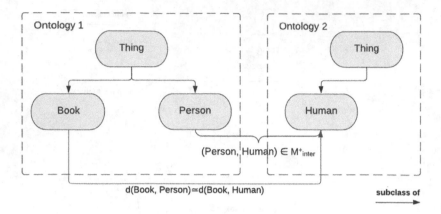

Fig. 3. Example of the approximation of a distance between cross-ontology concepts

4.1 Datasets

Table 1 shows some descriptive statistics on our datasets.

For the evaluation on the ontology alignment task, the OAEI 2022[2] tracks Anatomy and Conference were used as the evaluation datasets. The Conference track is a combination of 16 small ontologies totaling 867 classes describing the conference organization domain. The evaluation is performed with the reference alignments of a subset of 7 of those ontologies, using the *ra1-m1* subset. The Anatomy track is the alignment of the mouse anatomy (MA) and the human anatomy (NCI), with respectively 2744 and 3304 classes. These tracks were trained and evaluated simultaneously with the same SORBET model.

For the subsumption task, our model is benchmarked on two different datasets: FoodOn [8] and Gene Ontology (GO) [3,7] . FoodOn[3] is an ontology capturing a vast amount of information about food, it has 28,182 classes and 29,778 subsumption relations. GO[4] is a well-known bioinformatic ontology, that captures information about the functions of genes, with 44,244 classes and 72,601 subsumption relations.

4.2 Model

The SORBET model used in the experiments is fine-tuned from the pre-trained Sentence BERT weights trained on the natural language inference (NLI) dataset, it is available in Huggingface using *sentence-transformers/bert-base-nli-mean-tokens*. This version of SentenceBERT was used since it has the advantage of being already pre-trained on the similar task of scoring similar inputs.

---

[2] https://oaei.ontologymatching.org/2022/.
[3] https://foodon.org/.
[4] http://geneontology.org/ontology/ accessed on the 2020-09-08.

Table 1. Statistics of the benchmarked datasets and their ontologies

Datasets	Number of ontologies	Avg. number of classes	Avg. number of subsumptions
Conference	16	54	78
Anatomy	2	3,024	4,958
FoodOn	1	28,182	29,778
GO	1	44,244	72, 601

Hyperparameters. For the loss function, we set the upper maximum bound $A = 4$. In the alignment sampling, we set $\lambda_{positive} = 0.5$, $\lambda_{semi} = 0.6$, $\lambda_{inter} = 0.8$, and 20% of the available reference alignments in the tracks are used in training. Moreover, the set of considered neighbours in the construction of the Random Walks for contextual data is composed of parents, children and object properties. The impacts of those hyper-parameter are kept for future works. Each epoch iterates over all positive alignments and the batch size is set to 32. The training lasts for 3 epochs. During both training and prediction, the number of paths in the tree walk is randomly chosen in the interval $[0, 5]$, and the length of each path in the interval $[2, 6]$.

4.3 Experiments on the Ontology Alignment Task

In this section, SORBET embeddings, as well as other baseline embeddings, are evaluated on the ontology alignment task. To achieve this, we use the embeddings obtained through various methods to compute the similarity of pairs of concepts, and sort them in decreasing order. Then for each reference alignment, we evaluate how far off the pair was in the ordered list of predicted pairs. Since our model is trained on part of the reference alignments, the testing dataset excludes all of the training alignments. Our evaluation metric is Hits@K:

$$Hits@K = \frac{|\{m \in M_{ref}/M_{ref}^+ | Rank(m) \leq K\}|}{|M_{ref}/M_{ref}^+|} \quad (3)$$

where M_{ref} is the set of reference alignments, M_{ref}^+ is the subset (20%) of the reference alignments used in training. The function $Rank()$ is a function that determines how far off the algorithm was to giving the right alignment. To achieve this, it outputs the rank of the reference alignment (c_i, c_j) the list of predicted pairs of alignments $[(c_i, c_0), (c_i, c_1), ...(c_i, c_j)...(c_i, c_n)]$ where pairs are listed in descending order according to the cosine similarity between the two embeddings produced by the model in Table 2.

Table 2 presents the performance of SORBET embeddings for the ontology alignment tasks on the anatomy and conference tracks of the OAEI 2022. For this task, we compare our model with the baseline OWL2Vec*, a state-of-the-art model in ontology embeddings. We also compare our model with SentenceBERT, a state-of-the-art sentence embedding model, for which the embeddings of classes are fetched by passing their preprocessed label in the model. OWL2Vec* embeddings were obtained using the code provided by its authors[5], while the SentenceBERT model can be obtained through its main version on *huggingface*.[6]. Another aspect of this study is the comparison of regression distance-based loss (SORBET) to the traditional classification loss used in OA models. Therefore, we ran another version of SORBET for which the regression distanced-based loss is replaced with a classification loss (SORBET(Classification)). This is done by omitting the creation of semi-negative samples ($\lambda_{semi} = 0.0$).

Table 2. Comparison of different embeddings for the ontology alignment task

Models	Conference			Anatomy		
	Hits@1	Hits@5	Hits@10	Hits@1	Hits@5	Hits@10
SORBET(Classification)	0.8108	0.9034	0.9305	0.8502	0.9307	0.9426
SentenceBert	0.7568	0.8687	0.8996	0.7784	0.8740	0.8984
Owl2Vec*	0.7876	0.9073	0.9343	0.7427	0.8232	0.8470
SORBET Embeddings	**0.9095**	**0.9809**	**0.9904**	**0.9024**	**0.9636**	**0.9760**

As the result shows, SORBET outperforms the baselines for all metrics. It can also be noticed that the performance is not affected by the training of SORBET on different domains and ontology sizes simultaneously.

4.4   Experiments on the Subsumption Task

Table 3 shows the performance of SORBET embeddings on the subsumption task using the FoodOn and GO case studies. For this task, the employed baselines are: RDF2Vec [25], a well-known KG embedding algorithm, Onto2Vec [26], which is a more traditional ontology embeddings model, OWL2Vec*, SentenceBert and SORBET(classification). The performance of baselines models are taken from the benchmark of the Owl2Vec* paper [5]. The following Hits@K is computed, where M_{sub} is a test set of subclass axioms that were removed from the ontology used in training.

$$Hits@K = \frac{|\{m \in M_{sub} | Rank(m) \leq K\}|}{|M_{sub}|} \qquad (4)$$

The $Rank()$ function is similar to the one in the OA task, however, the similarity score is changed to follow the same methodology of the OWL2Vec* paper [5]. In this evaluation framework, the embeddings of every concept is obtained using one of the models in Table 3. Then, using those embeddings, a Random Forest classifier is trained to classify a dataset of true and false subclass relationship pairs. Finally, for every pair of concepts, instead of the cosine similarity,

---

[5] https://github.com/KRR-Oxford/OWL2Vec-Star.
[6] https://huggingface.co/sentence-transformers/bert-base-nli-mean-tokens.

their embeddings are fed to the Random Forest classifier and the output is used as the similarity score.

Table 3. Comparison of different embeddings for the subsumption prediction task

Models	FoodOn			GO		
	Hits@1	Hits@5	Hits@10	Hits@1	Hits@5	Hits@10
RDF2Vec	0.053	0.097	0.119	0.017	0.057	0.087
Onto2Vec	0.014	0.047	0.064	0.008	0.031	0.053
OWL2Vec*	0.143	0.287	0.357	0.076	0.258	0.376
SentenceBERT	0.074	0.186	0.256	0.059	0.171	0.225
SORBET (classification)	0.040	0.060	0.080	0.039	0.120	0.158
SORBET embeddings	**0.169**	**0.417**	**0.521**	**0.090**	**0.310**	**0.423**

Overall, SORBET embeddings outperform the state-of-the-art for both the ontology alignment and subsumption tasks. Without surprise, the task of OA has the most noticeable difference. Not only because the training objective is partly a OA task objective, but also because the conference dataset does not gather much training data, meaning transfer learning has the uttermost importance. It is also noticeable that while the results are high, no hyper-parameter tuning is done for the different datasets and tasks, therefore showing the regularization of the model. Finally, as the same embeddings were all learnt and utilized simultaneously for the benchmark of the datasets, the model is able to generalize while preventing overfitting on a single ontology.

4.5 Ablation Study

In this ablation study, we measure how specific components of the model have an impact on the final result.

The pre-training p of the BERT refers to the usage of the pre-trained Sentence BERT. w indicates whether the model used Tree Walks in training, if not, only the label of concepts are used as input. Finally, r indicates if a portion (20%) of the reference alignments were used as positive alignments.

The results of the ablation study, Table 4, demonstrate the importance of the different aspects of SORBET embeddings. First of all, the regression loss makes most of the boost in performance in both tested datasets compared to the traditional classification loss. The augmented input with context had a large impact for the conference dataset, however the same cannot be said for the anatomy track. This could be because of the difference in the nature of both datasets. In fact, the labels of concepts in the conference dataset tend to be less detailed, which may be why the use of the context makes such difference. Finally, as expected, the use of reference alignments in training increases the performance by a significant margin. Even though the Hits@5 and Hits@10 do not seem impacted by this change, the small performance gap could be due to the already very high scores.

Table 4. Results of the ablation study

Models	Conference			Anatomy		
	Hits@1	Hits@5	Hits@10	Hits@1	Hits@5	Hits@10
SORBET	0.7374	0.8996	0.9112	0.7790	0.8760	0.9010
SORBET$_p$	0.8069	0.9537	0.9730	0.8845	0.9512	0.9611
SORBET$_{p+w}$	0.8764	0.9652	0.9846	0.8812	0.9538	0.9690
SORBET$_{p+w+r}$ (Classification)	0.8108	0.9034	0.9305	0.8502	0.9307	0.9426
SORBET$_{p+w+r}$	**0.9095**	**0.9809**	**0.9904**	**0.9024**	**0.9636**	**0.9760**

5   Discussion

5.1   Ontological Representation

The main goal of SORBET embeddings is to obtain a more accurate representation of the ontological structure in the latent space. This goal is achieved by tweaking a OA classification loss so that every neighbour concepts have a gradually higher loss the further they are apart from each other. This constraint inherently builds the latent space in the desired way because the embeddings that would produce the minimum possible loss are the ones where the ontological structure could be perfectly deduced from the latent space. One could view this as a web of concepts being held together by subclassOf relationships. Conversely, with a classification loss, a model does not have any way of keeping neighbouring concepts together in a structured way. Equivalent concepts are indeed pushed together, however, negative samples push every other pair of concepts away from each other. This results into a very chaotic latent space.

The experiment in Fig. 4 demonstrates this phenomenon. We initially plot the latent space of the embeddings created by SORBET into a 2D space using PCA for a single ontology. Secondly, we plot the same ontology but with embeddings resulting from SORBET trained with a classification loss. We then plot every rdfs:subclass relationship in order to visualise the structure of the ontology in the latent space. The results show undoubtedly that the regression loss creates a more organised space. The tree-like structure depicted in the projection imitates the hierarchical structure of the ontology: the leaf nodes aggregate into a larger group of nodes which then aggregate to the root (top-level class). Furthermore, the model creates separate clusters for different aspects of the ontology. The cluster on the left represent every element that is a derivative of "Event", while the ontology on the right regroups all derivatives of "Person". Isolated concepts are separated from any of these clusters.

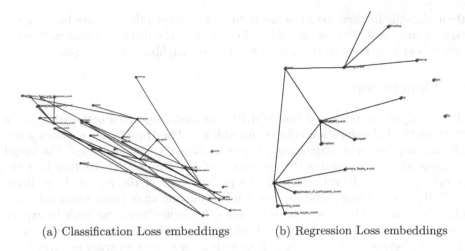

(a) Classification Loss embeddings   (b) Regression Loss embeddings

Fig. 4. Comparison of embeddings obtained with different loss functions, using the ontology "confof" in the Conference track

5.2   Superposed Ontologies

An important feature of SORBET embeddings is that the concepts of any ontologies can be trained and superposed in the same latent space. As the previous analysis showed, the nature of the training objective leads to clusters of tree-like structures for each distinct ontologies to be distributed across the vector space. But the training objective of the regression loss is also directed at making overlaps of similar clusters. For example, a cluster of the ontology O associated with the concept "Person", and another cluster from the ontology O' associated with concept "User" should have an overlap. This can be achieved in our loss function with inter-ontology positive and negative sampling if there is at least one mapping that anchors the clusters. In this example, if "User" and "Person" both have the child concept "Member", the two clusters will be pushed towards each other, resulting in an overlap. Consequently, the embeddings are much more coherent, and this enables the possibility of training on multiple domains simultaneously.

5.3   Limitations of Our Approach

While SORBET has many perks, there are still drawbacks to our approach. The most evident one is that, in order to construct training data, there must be a high amount of *rdfs:subclassOf* relationships. In fact, the more an ontology has an average depth closer to 0, the more the learning objective becomes a classification task. Consequently, the usage of the regression loss become much more advantageous when trained on deep and complex ontologies. Another flaw of the approach is the immutable value of a distance between 2 concepts related by a single $rdfs : subclassOf$ relationship. The underlying fact for this hypothesis is that concepts closer to the root of an ontology have different taxonomic relations than concepts further down the hierarchy. For example, the distance between the pair "Thing" and "Person" should be higher than the distance between "Paper" and "Short Paper", even though both pairs are neighbouring concepts.

6   Conclusion

In this paper, we presented how SORBET embeddings are a better alternative to traditional classification-refined embeddings. The Hits@K have shown a significant improvement, indicating a higher quality of the embeddings. The visual analysis also demonstrates the continuity of the ontology's structure into the latent space, and how this affects the performance of the model. In addition SORBET embeddings tend to be much less chaotic than those obtained using classification, yielding more robust results. In future work, we plan to experiment with different combinations of rules that could improve the estimation of distances between concepts, as well as finding new ways to train our model on shallow ontologies.

Supplemental Material Statement. Source code and datasets can be found on its Github repository.[7]

Acknowledgment. This research has been funded by the NSERC Discovery Grant Program. The authors acknowledge support from Compute Canada for providing computational resources.

References

1. Ontology Matching 2021. Proceedings of the 16th International Workshop on Ontology Matching Co-located with the 20th International Semantic Web Conference (ISWC 2021), CEUR Workshop Proceedings, vol. 3063. CEUR-WS.org (2021)
2. Ontology Matching 2022. Proceedings of the 17th International Workshop on Ontology Matching (OM 2022) Co-located with the 21th International Semantic Web Conference (ISWC 2022), Hangzhou, Virtual Conference, 23 October 2022, CEUR Workshops Proceedings, vol. 3324. CEUR-WS.org (2022)
3. Ashburner, M., et al.: Gene ontology: tool for the unification of biology. Nat. Genet. **25**(1), 25–29 (2000). https://doi.org/10.1038/75556
4. Bordes, A., Usunier, N., Garcia-Duran, A., Weston, J., Yakhnenko, O.: Translating embeddings for modeling multi-relational data. Adv. Neural Inf. Process. Syst. **26** (2013)
5. Chen, J., Hu, P., Jimenez-Ruiz, E., Holter, O.M., Antonyrajah, D., Horrocks, I.: OWL2Vec*: embedding of OWL ontologies. Mach. Learn. **110**(7), 1813–1845 (2021). https://doi.org/10.1007/s10994-021-05997-6
6. Chen, J., Jiménez-Ruiz, E., Horrocks, I., Antonyrajah, D., Hadian, A., Lee, J.: Augmenting ontology alignment by semantic embedding and distant supervision. In: Verborgh, R., et al. (eds.) ESWC 2021. LNCS, vol. 12731, pp. 392–408. Springer, Cham (2021). https://doi.org/10.1007/978-3-030-77385-4_23

---

[7] https://github.com/Lama-West/SORBET_ISWC23.

7. Consortium, T.G.O.: The gene ontology resource: enriching a gold mine. Nucl. Acids Res. **49**(D1), D325–D334 (12 2020). https://doi.org/10.1093/nar/gkaa1113

8. Dooley, D.M., et al.: Foodon: a harmonized food ontology to increase global food traceability, quality control and data integration. NPJ Sci. Food **2**(1), 23 (2018). https://doi.org/10.1038/s41538-018-0032-6

9. Efeoglu, S.: Graphmatcher: A graph representation learning approach for ontology matching. In: Ontology Matching 2022 : Proceedings of the 17th International Workshop on Ontology Matching (OM 2022) Co-located with the 21th International Semantic Web Conference (ISWC 2022), Hangzhou, Virtual Conference, 23 October 2022 [2], pp. 174–180 (2022)

10. Gosselin, F., Zouaq, A.: Sebmatcher results for OAEI 2022. In: Ontology Matching 2022: Proceedings of the 17th International Workshop on Ontology Matching (OM 2022) Co-located with the 21th International Semantic Web Conference (ISWC 2022), Hangzhou, Virtual Conference, 23 October 2022 [2], pp. 202–209 (2022)

11. Grover, A., Leskovec, J.: node2vec: scalable feature learning for networks. In: Proceedings of the 22nd ACM SIGKDD International Conference on Knowledge Discovery and Data Mining, pp. 855–864 (2016)

12. Gutiérrez-Basulto, V., Schockaert, S.: From knowledge graph embedding to ontology embedding? an analysis of the compatibility between vector space representations and rules. In: International Conference on Principles of Knowledge Representation and Reasoning (2018)

13. He, Y., Chen, J., Antonyrajah, D., Horrocks, I.: Bertmap: a bert-based ontology alignment system. In: Proceedings of the AAAI Conference on Artificial Intelligence, vol. 36, pp. 5684–5691 (2022)

14. Iyer, V., Agarwal, A., Kumar, H.: VeeAlign: multifaceted context representation using dual attention for ontology alignment. In: Proceedings of the 2021 Conference on Empirical Methods in Natural Language Processing. pp. 10780–10792. Association for Computational Linguistics, Punta Cana (2021). https://doi.org/10.18653/v1/2021.emnlp-main.842

15. Knorr, L., Portisch, J.: Fine-tom matcher results for OAEI 2021. In: Ontology Matching 2021: Proceedings of the 16th International Workshop on Ontology Matching Co-located with the 20th International Semantic Web Conference (ISWC 2021) [1], pp. 144–151 (2021)

16. Kolyvakis, P., Kalousis, A., Smith, B., Kiritsis, D.: Biomedical ontology alignment: an approach based on representation learning. J. Biomed. Semant. **9**(1), 1–20 (2018)

17. Kossack, D., Borg, N., Knorr, L., Portisch, J.: Tom matcher results for OAEI 2021. In: Ontology Matching 2021: Proceedings of the 16th International Workshop on Ontology Matching co-located with the 20th International Semantic Web Conference (ISWC 2021) [1], pp. 193–198 (2021)

18. Kulmanov, M., Liu-Wei, W., Yan, Y., Hoehndorf, R.: El embeddings: geometric construction of models for the description logic el ++. Int. Joint Conf. Artif. Intell. (2019)

19. Li, C., Li, A., Wang, Y., Tu, H., Song, Y.: A survey on approaches and applications of knowledge representation learning. In: 2020 IEEE Fifth International Conference on Data Science in Cyberspace (DSC), pp. 312–319. IEEE (2020)

20. Lin, Y., Liu, Z., Sun, M., Liu, Y., Zhu, X.: Learning entity and relation embeddings for knowledge graph completion. In: Proceedings of the AAAI Conference on Artificial Intelligence, vol. 29 (2015)

21. Liu, W., et al.: K-bert: enabling language representation with knowledge graph. In: AAAI Conference on Artificial Intelligence (2019). https://api.semanticscholar.org/CorpusID:202583325
22. Mikolov, T., Chen, K., Corrado, G., Dean, J.: Efficient estimation of word representations in vector space. In: 1st International Conference on Learning Representations, ICLR 2013, Scottsdale, 2–4 May 2013, Workshop Track Proceedings (2013)
23. Perozzi, B., Al-Rfou, R., Skiena, S.: Deepwalk: online learning of social representations. In: Proceedings of the 20th ACM SIGKDD International Conference on Knowledge Discovery and Data Mining, pp. 701–710 (2014)
24. Reimers, N., Gurevych, I.: Sentence-bert: sentence embeddings using siamese bert-networks. In: Conference on Empirical Methods in Natural Language Processing (2019)
25. Ristoski, P., Rosati, J., Di Noia, T., De Leone, R., Paulheim, H.: Rdf2vec: Rdf graph embeddings and their applications. Semant. Web 10(4), 721–752 (2019)
26. Smaili, F.Z., Gao, X., Hoehndorf, R.: Onto2vec: joint vector-based representation of biological entities and their ontology-based annotations. Bioinformatics 34(13), i52–i60 (2018)
27. Smaili, F.Z., Gao, X., Hoehndorf, R.: Opa2vec: combining formal and informal content of biomedical ontologies to improve similarity-based prediction. Bioinformatics 35(12), 2133–2140 (2019)
28. Sousa, G., Lima, R., Trojahn, C.: An eye on representation learning in ontology matching. In: Ontology Matching 2022: Proceedings of the 17th International Workshop on Ontology Matching (OM 2022) Co-located with the 21th International Semantic Web Conference (ISWC 2022), Hangzhou, Virtual Conference, October 23, 2022 [2], pp. 49–60 (2022)
29. Sun, T., et al.: Colake: contextualized language and knowledge embedding. arXiv preprint arXiv:2010.00309 (2020)
30. Wang, X., Gao, T., Zhu, Z., Liu, Z., Li, J.Z., Tang, J.: Kepler: a unified model for knowledge embedding and pre-trained language representation. Trans. Assoc. Comput. Linguist. 9, 176–194 (2019)
31. Wu, J., Lv, J., Guo, H., Ma, S.: Daeom: a deep attentional embedding approach for biomedical ontology matching. Appl. Sci. 10, 7909 (2020)
32. Yanardag, P., Vishwanathan, S.: Deep graph kernels. In: Proceedings of the 21th ACM SIGKDD International Conference on Knowledge Discovery and Data Mining, pp. 1365–1374 (2015)

Visualizing Mappings Between Pairwise Ontologies - An Empirical Study of Matrix and Linked Indented List in Their User Support During Class Mapping Creation and Evaluation

Bo Fu(✉) [ORCID], Allison Austin, and Max Garcia

California State University Long Beach, Long Beach, CA 90840, USA
Bo.Fu@csulb.edu, {Allison.Austin,Max.Garcia}@student.csulb.edu

Abstract. Visual support designed to facilitate human interaction with semantic data has largely focused on visualizing entities such as classes and relationships within an ontology. Comparatively speaking, less attention has focused on visualizing mappings established between independent ontologies and determining the effectiveness of mapping visualizations. This paper presents a user study of the matrix and the linked indented list visualization in their visual support for users during creation and evaluation of class mappings between pairwise ontologies. A total of 81 participants took part in a task-based controlled experiment, with the aim of assessing the extent to which a given visualization supports recognition of visual cues, validation of existing mappings, and creation of new results. Based on empirical evidence collected from the participants in their speed to complete the tasks, their success in answering various questions, as well as their physiological sensory data such as eye gaze, we aim to quantify user performance and visual attention demanded in the use of the two aforementioned mapping visualizations. The experimental results indicate that the linked indented lists and the matrix visualization are comparable in terms of effectiveness and efficiency when assisting users in the given task scenarios with marginal differences. However, linked indented lists are likely to demand less effort from the users' visual perceptual systems with statistically significant differences found in several gaze measures, including the physical distances needed to locate relevant visual information, number of fixations and time required to process visual cues, and the overall efforts in scanning the visual scene.

Keywords: Ontology Mapping Visualization · Matrix · Linked Indented List · Eye Tracking

1 Introduction

A growing body of research aimed to overcome challenges in providing user-centered tools and systems to support and enhance human interaction with semantic data and semantically empowered systems has pushed advances in the Semantic Web to beyond simply improving the efficiencies and accuracies of various algorithms. While leveraging

T. R. Payne et al. (Eds.): ISWC 2023, LNCS 14265, pp. 579–598, 2023.
https://doi.org/10.1007/978-3-031-47240-4_31

semantic technologies and computational intelligence in problem-solving remains a critical component in the Semantic Web, cohorts of research in interfaces for the Semantic Web as well as semantically empowered systems have contributed to recent innovations in interactive Semantic Web. Within this context, the *Interactive Semantic Web* (ISW) refers to the design, development, and refinement in all aspects of human interaction with the Semantic Web, whereby the integration of interfaces and interactions bridged between human users and semantic content and technologies contribute to enhanced and improved use of the Semantic Web and all its constituents.

Well-known Semantic Web tools and systems designed to support humans (experts and non-experts alike) in the loop often incorporate interactive visualizations and visual analytics in order to best assist users, such as Protégé[1]/WebProtégé[2] for ontology editing, the Wikidata Query Service[3] for querying semantic content, and Punya[4] for building semantically enriched mobile applications, to name just a few. Other efforts to assist novice users in the navigation and querying of knowledge graphs is also demonstrated in [1], where traditional SPARQL queries are simplified by means of visual queries. A more recent example of a knowledge graph empowered search and visualization system is presented in [2], which aims to facilitate researchers in their explorations of relevant scientific publications by leveraging thematic rule-based associations, networks of co-publications, and co-occurring topics. To accelerate biomedical research and discovery in the fight against COVID-19, a tool to automatically extract and visualize argumentative graphs of clinical articles is demonstrated in [3], whereby information extraction is enhanced by a continuously enriched knowledge graph to assist with human decision-making in healthcare.

Evidentially, appropriate integrations of interaction and visualization techniques lie at the center of ISW systems, where visual cues have continued to provide the necessary means for users to better understand, explore, correct, and modify semantic data and semantically empowered systems. As such, assessing the effectiveness of interactive visual support in their capacity to support users in the ISW has been investigated in prior work such as [4–6], where commonly used tools and techniques to visualize ontologies have been evaluated extensively. In comparison, less research focus has been placed on relationships established between independent ontologies, such as ontology mapping visualization. To this end, this paper focuses on a relatively unexplored area in mapping visualizations between pairwise ontologies. Through an empirical user study involving 81 participants in the context of creating and evaluating class mappings between pairwise ontologies, we report on the effectiveness and efficiency of two popular techniques in mapping visualization, namely the linked indented list and matrix visualization. In addition, we analyzed user gaze to investigate how users divided their visual attention when interacting with the aforementioned mapping visualizations, and report on a number of observations in gaze tendencies in each visualization technique through eye tracking. A main contribution of this paper lies in the generation of new knowledge on the user experience with two interactive mapping visualization techniques frequently found in

---

[1] protege.stanford.edu, last accessed 07/31/2023.

[2] webprotege.stanford.edu, last accessed 07/31/2023.

[3] query.wikidata.org, last accessed 07/31/2023.

[4] punya.mit.edu, last accessed 07/31/2023.

current tools and systems. With knowledge graph and ontology development environments amongst some of the most impactful and widely adopted technologies derived from the Semantic Web community, the empirical findings collected from a reasonably large user group shown in this paper will likely inform future design and development of these environments to be more user-centered with viable visual and interactive support for the average user.

2 Related Work

User involvement and how best to support human users remain a critical research area in ontology mapping given that automatically generated mappings typically require further refinement and user intervention. An example system aimed to support users in ontology and entity matching is presented in [7], which provides an environment for users to generate mappings based on element descriptions and system-generated matching suggestions. Visual assistance is provided in the form of interactive indented lists of the source and target ontologies, while visualizations of the mappings themselves are not supported. A review of mapping systems[5] designed to support various stages of ontology mapping is presented in [8]. Amongst the eight systems surveyed, five [9–18] use connecting links to visualize mappings between ontological nodes belonging to different ontologies, whereby the ontologies themselves are often arranged as indented lists in the visualization. Such techniques to visualize mappings (as links) between ontologies (as indented lists) are referred to as *linked indented lists* (LIL) in this paper. LIL remains a popular technique to visualize relationships between structured datasets as also seen in the RBA tool [23], which is designed to facilitate mappings between relational databases and ontologies. Subsequent research has also focused on reducing visual clutter in LIL when a large number of mappings is present, through layout techniques such as edge bundling [24].

Later systems have utilized matrices or grids when visualizing pairwise mappings, whereby mappings are illustrated as occurrences of vectors in a 2D plane, and the associated ontological entities are displayed along horizontal and vertical axes. In this paper, such visualization techniques are referred to as *matrix* visualization. An example of a matrix visualization is shown in [25] with mappings visualized at the ontology level as well as at the node level. To facilitate visual search, a user can sort the source and target ontologies/nodes displayed along the axes in alphabetical order. Another example can be found in ProvenanceMatrix [16], where the user can sort the matrix axes in breadth-first, depth-first, and similarity orderings. In addition to 2D matrices, later research has investigated adding a third dimension to utilize 3D cubes when visualizing mappings such as [27] with the goal of providing various levels of granularity when exploring and evaluating ontology mappings. Other visualization systems have utilized multiple views when presenting mappings to the user, in an effort to better support various viewpoints during visual search such as VOAR 3.0 [28] that visualizes mappings in both LIL and node-link diagrams, AlignmentVis [29] that uses LIL, matrices, scatterplots, and parallel

---

[5] The review includes the following systems: AgreementMaker [9–11, VOILA 2015], AlViz [12], AML [13, 14], CogZ/Prompt [15–17], COMA [18], LogMap [19], SAMBO [20, 21], and RepOSE [22].

coordinates to visualize mappings and related statistics in a mapping scenario, as well as BioMixer [30] that visualizes mappings as timelines and node-link diagrams with multiple coordinated layouts.

Recent research has also investigated the application of block metaphors that are frequently used in visual programming languages in the context of semantic mapping such as [31] and the use of pie charts in large scale ontology mappings [32]. Moreover, efforts to broaden ontology visualization to beyond visualizing hierarchies but to also include non-hierarchical relationships in large ontologies is proposed in [33], where icicle plots coupled with visual compression have been shown to improve space-efficiency and reduce visual structural complexity. Given that node-link diagrams are often used to visualize ontological entities as nodes in a network with connecting edges illustrating ontological relationships such as *is-a* relations, a natural expansion is to also include mappings amongst ontological entities, by inserting visual associations (i.e., more edges that can be visually distinguished, often by line color or style, from those of *is-a* relations) into the visualization to illustrate additional relationships such as mappings among otherwise isolated nodes. This node-link technique can be observed in a number of systems such as [33–37] and studied extensively in [4–6, 39–44]. Recent efforts to advance node-link diagrams in the Information Visualization (InfoVis) community include determining the effects of progressively increasing encoded information in node/node-link/node-link-group diagrams [39], comparing different methods to visualize long, dense, complex, and piecewise linear spatial trajectories [40], displaying clusters overlaid using node coloring, GMap, BubbleSets, and LineSets [41], encoding multivariate and continuous data on edges in 3D node-link diagrams [42], developing novel exemplar-based layout to adjust substructures [43], and improving readability via layered layout that considers crossing reduction, edge bendiness, nested and multi-layer groups simultaneously [44]. Other efforts to improve matrix visualization in the InfoVis community have investigated ways to enhance visual analysis with hierarchy matrix [45] and ordering effects within matrices [46]. A recent evaluation study [47] from the Info-Vis community compares bipartite, node-link, and matrix-based network presentation in a range of tasks such as network class identification, cluster detection, network density estimation, to demonstrate overall network structures are best illustrated with bipartite layouts.

There is however limited research focusing on the evaluation of interactive visualizations designed for ISW. In the context of ontological data modelling, prior evaluations have largely focused on assessing user experience with visualizations of class hierarchies. For instance, the usability of indented lists and node-link diagrams when visualizing class relationships are assessed in [4] with eye tracking results [5] providing further insights on the strengths and weaknesses of each visualization technique. In the context of supporting users in large-scale ontology alignment, a study [48] using heuristic evaluations and feedback from 8 participants across three mapping systems (that all utilize LIL including CogZ [15], COMA [18], and SAMBO [20, 21]) aims to elicit system design requirements. Given the frequent use of LIL and matrices across a number of existing tools and systems as outlined above, and with a lack of evaluations of the two, there is a pressing need to assess these visualizations designed specifically for mappings. To this end, this paper presents a controlled, between-subject user study utilizing eye tracking in the assessment of the LIL and matrix visualizations in the context of human mapping creation and evaluation.

3 Experimental Setup

3.1 Tasks and Visualizations

The goal of the experiment is to compare if one visualization technique may be better suited for a particular type of mapping creation and/or evaluation tasks than the other. To simulate an environment where the user tasks would require human interaction and comprehension of the given visual cues, we asked participants to answer a series of 15 questions while supported by mapping visualizations between an ontology pair. Table 1 presents an overview of the questions in two domains. These questions can be categorized as i) *identification* tasks (Q.1–6), where successful completion requires a participant to recognize what is and is not already visually displayed in the mapping visualization; ii) *validation* tasks (Q.7–12), where successful completion requires participants to verify the accuracy of a mapping displayed or the lack thereof; and iii) *creation* tasks (Q.13–15), where successful completion requires a participant to generate new knowledge (i.e., new mappings) that is not already displayed in the visualization. These questions are not intended to be exhaustive, but as examples of typical scenarios during mapping creation and evaluation where a human user needs to comprehend visual cues in the process of establishing correct and complete mappings between pairwise ontologies. The goal of these questions is to simulate a necessary environment for the purpose of enabling comparative studies between the matrix and LIL visualization in the context of class mappings with a range of example conditions where different visual needs may be demanded during human decision-making.

Where appropriate, some questions are presented as multiple-choice questions with a dropdown menu containing 2 or 4 options with one correct answer (e.g., in Q.1, 4 numbers are shown in a dropdown menu where one of them is the correct answer; in Q.4, yes or no options are given in a dropdown menu), and others are presented as open-ended questions with textboxes to fill in (e.g., Q.15). Identification tasks direct users to decode a given visual cue (e.g., Q.3 requires a user to describe what a link or solid/dotted cell between two entities entails, and Q.4 requires a user to interpret what a non-existent link or empty cell entails), validation tasks require a user to assess existing mapping quality (is a link/solid cell correct or wrong), and creation tasks ask a user to generate new knowledge by creating additional mappings not already shown in the visualization (e.g., in Q.15, users can create new mappings if they believe there are absent mappings such as those prompted in Q.4 and Q.6). The same set of mappings (containing the same correct, incorrect, and incomplete results) were visualized in each domain, so that the only difference between user groups remain as the mapping visualization themselves as opposed to differing mapping results shown to the user, to ensure the comparison between LIL and matrix visualization is made fair.

Table 1. Mapping Creation and Evaluation Questions Used in the Study.

	Conference Domain	Anatomy Domain
Identification	1. How many mappings are shown in the visualization in total? 2. How many classes is *Author* (in the source ontology) mapped to? 3. What is *SlideSet* (in the source ontology) mapped to? 4. Can *Person* (in the source ontology) be mapped to another class (in the target ontology)? 5. What is *ConferenceDinner* (in the source ontology) mapped to (in the target ontology)? 6. Can *Workshop* (in the source ontology) be mapped to another class (in the target ontology)?	1. How many mappings are shown in the visualization in total? 2. How many classes is *Skin* (in the source ontology) mapped to? 3. What is *Viscera* (in the source ontology) mapped to? 4. Can *Joint* (in the source ontology) be mapped to another class (in the target ontology)? 5. What is *Skull* (in the source ontology) mapped to (in the target ontology)? 6. Can *Arm* (in the source ontology) be mapped to another class (in the target ontology)?
Validation	7. Is there a mapping between *AcademicEvent* (in the source ontology) and *Scientific_Event* (in the target ontology)? 8. Is *AcademiaOrganization* (in the source ontology) correctly mapped? 9. *SecurityTopic* (in the source ontology) is mapped to *Research_Topic* (in the target ontology). Is this correct? 10. *Place* (in the source ontology) is mapped to *Location* (in the target ontology). Is this correct? 11. *RejectedPaper* (in the source ontology) is mapped to *Assigned_Paper* (in the target ontology). Is this correct? 12. *IndustryOrganization* (in the source ontology) is mapped to *Organisation* (in the right ontology). Is this correct?	7. Is there a mapping between *Blood* (in the source ontology) and *blood* (in the target ontology)? 8. Is *Cartilage* (in the source ontology) correctly mapped? 9. *Urinary_System_Part* (in the source ontology) is mapped to *muscle* (in the target ontology). Is this correct? 10. *Cheek* (in the source ontology) is mapped to *cuticle* (in the target ontology). Is this correct? 11. *Skin* (in the source ontology) is mapped to *skin* (in the target ontology). Is this correct? 12. *Mucus* (in the source ontology) is mapped to *nasal mucus* (in the target ontology). Is this correct?
Creation	13. Which class could *Attendee* (in the source ontology) be mapped to (in the target ontology)? 14. Which class could *ConferenceDinner* (in the left ontology) mapped to (in the right ontology)? 15. Is there any other mapping(s) that should be created between the ontologies but is currently absent from the visualization?	13. Which class could *Heart* (in the source ontology) be mapped to (in the target ontology)? 14. Which class could *Lip* (in the source ontology) be mapped to (in the target ontology)? 15. Is there any other mapping(s) that should be created between the ontologies but is currently absent from the visualization?

Two pairs of ontologies are used in this study. These ontologies and their respective mappings are based on the conference and biomedical tracks at the Ontology Alignment Evaluation Initiative (OAEI)[6]. Mappings in the OAEI gold standards have been modified

---

[6] oaei.ontologymatching.org, last accessed 07/31/2023.

in the study for the purpose of presenting a mixture of correct, incorrect, and incomplete mappings in the visualization, so that participants can complete a range of creation and evaluation scenarios as discussed above. An overview of the characteristics of the ontologies used in the study is presented in Table 2. The conference ontologies, taken as is from the OAEI, have 97 and 73 classes in the source and target ontology respectively. In order to ensure comparable sizes, for the biomedical ontologies, we used the portions that focus on the human anatomy, whereby there are 115 and 97 classes in the source and target ontology respectively. For each domain, the accompanying mapping visualizations show a total of 10 mappings between the ontology pair, amongst which, 5 are correct and 5 are incorrect. There are also 5 additional mappings that are missing from the visualization. The experiment variables such as the ontology size, task scenario, and the number of mappings were controlled in the study to ensure their potential impact on user performance is minimized so that a given mapping visualization (i.e., either the LIL or matrix visualization) can be assessed as the independent variable in the experiment. In other words, if a difference were to be found in user success or completion time, the underlying cause is likely attributed to the visualization used as opposed to a simple result of a smaller ontology pair or fewer mappings to inspect. The domains, ontologies, and mappings used in our study are not intended to be exhaustive, but as example scenarios aimed to provide the necessary experimental conditions to compare the LIL and matrix visualization. For those interested in specific domains or ontologies with certain characteristics, it would be necessary to target other mapping scenarios/domains not presented in this paper.

Table 2. Ontologies and Mappings Used in the Study. The longest path to root defines the depth of a class hierarchy, the largest sibling pool refers to the most number of subclasses for a given class, multiple inheritances refer to instances of classes with more than one superclass.

	Conference Ontologies		Anatomy Ontologies	
	Source	Target	Source	Target
Number of Classes	97	93	115	97
Longest path to root	4	6	6	5
Largest sibling pool	21	9	12	26
Multiple inheritance	–	1	2	–
Correct mappings	5		5	
Incorrect mappings	5		5	
Incomplete mappings	5		5	

The matrix and LIL visualization used in this study are implemented using the D3 JavaScript Library[7]. Figure 1 presents a screenshot of the study interface showing how questions and mapping visualizations are presented to a participant in a Web browser. In the matrix visualization (Fig. 1a), the source and target ontologies are visualized as

---

[7] d3js.org, last accessed 07/31/2023.

indented lists along the axes. Toggling a node on the axis will expand or collapse child nodes (if any), where solid blue triangles indicate subclasses that can be further revealed, hollow blue triangles indicate fully expanded child nodes, and blue dots indicate childless nodes. Mappings are illustrated as cells associating pairwise entities shown along the vertical and horizontal axes. Solid blue cells indicate mappings of entities that are already fully visible in the visualization, e.g., *ConferenceEvent* is mapped to *Event*. Dotted blue cells indicate mappings exist amongst child nodes of the corresponding entities and are yet to be revealed in the visualization, e.g., there is at least one mapping amongst the child nodes of *ConferenceEvent* and *Scientific_Event*, and a user will need to toggle these entities to further reveal the exact mapping(s) at the child level. As nodes are expanded, the matrix grows in both length and width and a user can scroll vertically and horizontally during interaction, while the entity labels along the axes remain fixed in position to facilitate readability.

In the LIL visualization (Fig. 1b), the source and target ontologies are visualized as two separate indented lists, and mappings are visualized as links connecting pairwise entities belonging to different ontologies. Users can toggle nodes to expand or collapse an entity, with solid triangles indicating expandable nodes, hollow triangles indicating nonexpendable nodes, and dotted nodes indicating childless entities. Solid blue links denote mappings of two entities that are already fully visible in the visualization, e.g., *Mucus* is mapped to *nasal mucus*. Dotted links denote at least one mapping exists amongst the children of the associated entities and the user must toggle the associated entities to reveal the mappings beneath, e.g., *Lower_Extermity_Part* in the source ontology should be toggled to reveal the child node that is mapped to *leg* in the target ontology. Finally, users can scroll vertically and horizontally during the interaction as nodes are expanded and the indented lists grow in the visualization.

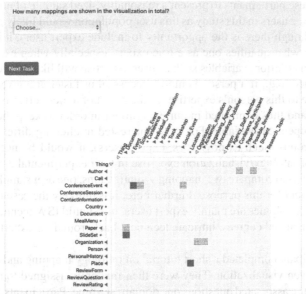

(a) Mapping Visualized in A Matrix in the Conference Domain

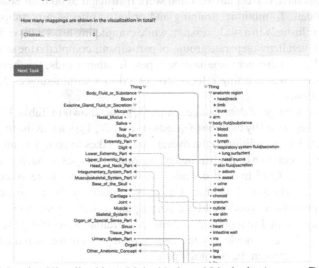

(b) Mapping Visualized in A Linked Indented List in the Anatomy Domain

Fig. 1. Study Interface Displaying Questions and Visualizations.

3.2 Participants, Protocol, and Data Collection

A total of 81 participants (with approximately 20% of them having taken a semester long graduate level introductory course on the Semantic Web) took part in this study, including a mixture of undergraduate and graduate students majoring in Computer Science, Computer Engineering, Mechanical Engineering, Applied Math, and Political Science.

We recruited these participants to present a reasonably sized sample of novice users. We focused on novice users in this study as this user population would likely need most help and support. Though there is the opportunity to include expert users, it is a frequently debatable topic what qualifies one as a true expert, especially when expertise is often self-reported. In addition, variables such as user expertise will likely have an impact on user performance (e.g., if a person is more successful or faster at a given task, is such an outcome due to this person's expertise, or the result of a more effective and efficient visualization), and thus controlled in our experiment in order to keep the visualization type as the independent variable. For those interested in eliciting differences between distinct user groups (such as novice vs. expert users), it would be necessary to also include domain/ontology/visualization expertise in their experimental design. Since the goal of our study is to compare two mapping visualizations, one user sample with novices would be sufficient for this purpose. Furthermore, it is unlikely the case that real-world users of ISW technologies are mainly expert users, nor should ISW technologies require users to hold advanced degrees, intricate technical background, or expert knowledge in order to use.

Each participant completed a short tutorial on ontology mapping and the interactive features in a given visualization. They were then randomly assigned to a visualization and completed the associated questions one domain at a time. Participants were informed that all questions have correct answers and were instructed to do their best while being as fast as they can. To minimize training and ordering effects, a participant used one visualization exclusively in a study session, while completing tasks with varied orderings of the domain. Overall, two separate groups of participants completed the same questions, but supported by two distinct visualization types. In other words, this between-subject design ensures minimal learning effects (compared to a within-subject design) on the given visualization.

We collected a range of data from each participant, shown in Table 3. Time on task can be further categorized by the type of questions (T_i, T_v, T_c) such as the three categories outlined in Sect. 3.1, in addition to the overall time it takes to complete all 15 questions (T_o). Likewise, success can be determined by the question type (S_i, S_v, S_c). For the open-ended question (i.e., Q.15 in each domain) where participants were asked to generate new mappings, we computed additional metrics to quantify the precision, recall, and f-measure of the answers produced by a participant in that question (S_p, S_r, $S_{f\text{-}m}$), in the same way automated mapping algorithms are evaluated, whereby the correctness, completeness, and overall quality of the new mappings were measured against known missing mappings between the ontology pair.

To quantify how participants divided their visual attention during their interaction with a given mapping visualization, we used physiological sensors to collect eye gaze from each participant. More specifically, we used a Gazepoint GP3 HD eye tracker[8] with a 150 Hz sample rate and a 24" Full HD Dell monitor[9] with 1920 × 1080p at 165 Hz and 1ms response time to collect gaze data. Each participant completed a 9-point calibration before each eye tracking session to ensure maximized gaze data accuracy. Participants

---

[8] gazept.com/product/gp3hd, last accessed 07/31/2023.

[9] www.dell.com/en-us/shop/dell-24-gaming-monitor-g2422hs/apd/210-bdpw/monitors-mon itor-accessories, last accessed 07/31/2023.

Table 3. Data Collected from Each Participant.

Data Type		Description
Time on Task (min)	T_i:	Time it takes a participant to complete all *identification* tasks
	T_v:	Time it takes a participant to complete all *validation* tasks
	T_c:	Time it takes a participant to complete all *creation* tasks
	T_o:	Overall time it takes a participant to complete all questions
Task Success (0,1)	S_i:	Correct answers contained in all *identification* tasks as a ratio
	S_v:	Correct answers contained in all *validation* tasks as a ratio
	S_c:	Correct answers contained in all *creation* tasks as a ratio
	C_p:	The precision of the new mappings generated in Q.15
	C_r:	The recall of the new mappings generated in Q.15
	$C_{f\text{-}m}$:	The f-measure of the new mappings generated in Q.15
	S_o:	Overall success in all 15 questions

were seated on non-wheeled and non-swiveled office chairs and maintained relatively unchanged distances to the eye tracker, which tolerates a range of 35 cm (horizontal) × 22cm (vertical) × ± 15 cm (depth) movement. Based on the raw gaze data generated from the eye tracker, a set of descriptive gaze measures (DGM) are computed for each participant after the person has completed all 15 questions using a given visualization. The goal of the DGM is to capture one's ability in selecting and maintaining awareness of specific locations and attributes of a visual scene presented. To compute the DGM, the raw gaze data produced from the eye tracker underwent a cleaning process, whereby invalid (per validity codes reported by the eye tracker, negative numbers, and when entries are off-screen), incomplete (e.g., when only one eye was captured, missing x and y coordinates), and corrupted entries (e.g., pupil dilation exceeding possible ranges, whereby anisocoria or asymmetric pupils is rarely greater than 1mm [49], and normal pupil size in adults typically varies from 2–4 mm in diameter in bright light and 4–8 mm in the dark [50]) were discarded.

In this paper, we report on the most notable DGM that reflect distinct behaviors for participants using one visualization versus the other such as those related to fixations and scanpaths. Fixations refer to those moments where the eyes are relatively stationary and holding a vision of focus in place, which are typically understood as information processing behaviors as a person stops scanning the visual scene at large but concentrating on extracting information from the targeted visual cues. Descriptive statistics of fixations are typically measured as sums and durations, which are indicative of the number of fixations required and the time needed to process information [51]. As a person scans for various fixations to focus on in a visual scene, the rapid eye movements between fixations are captured as saccades, which are typically understood as information searching behaviors. Saccades are typically quantified through counts and durations. In addition, a useful measure to capture the distances between successive fixations is saccadic length (in pixel). As a person searches and processes visual information, a sequence of fixations and saccades can be captured, whereby the sum of all saccadic lengths (known as scanpath length) is typically used to reflect the complete visual journey commenced [51]. In this paper, average saccadic lengths and their standard deviations (StDev) are used to describe gaze behaviors sampled from the participants. Furthermore, fixation count, scanpath length, and the StDev of fixation durations are correlated to participant success.

4   Results

To prevent data distortion, out of all data collected from 81 participants, we discarded those from 8 participants who experienced various issues during the experiment, such as reflective wear (e.g., earrings) being sampled in gaze, leaning too close (e.g., placing elbows on desk) or too far (e.g., beyond the tolerated range as discussed in Sect. 3.2) from the eye tracker. The findings shown in this paper are aggregated results of the remaining 73 individuals, whereby 35 participants completed the given tasks using LIL and 38 participants completed the same tasks using the matrix visualization.

Figure 2 presents the findings of participant success by task type. Across domains and irrespective of the type of task, participants were marginally more successful using the LIL (Fig. 2a-d). When creating new mappings, as shown in Fig. 3, those who used LIL produced higher quality mappings, which is evident in the higher precision (Fig. 3a), recall (Fig. 3b), and f-measure (Fig. 3c) compared to the group of participants who used the matrix visualization. Figure 4 presents the time it takes a participant to complete the series of given tasks. Those who used LIL were found to be marginally faster compared to the others who used the matrix visualization in the identification and validation task scenarios (Fig. 4a and Fig. 4b). Notably, when creating new mappings, those who used the matrix visualization were found to be faster at task completion (Fig. 4c). Overall, time on task is comparable irrespective of the visualization used, though a greater difference is evident in the Conference domain, whereby those who used the matrix visualization were faster at task completion (Fig. 4d). In the identification tasks, participants who used LIL were faster at completing the given tasks and yielded higher success in the Conference domain. This is also echoed in the validation tasks across both domains, whereby the participants supported by LIL achieved higher success while needing less time. In the creation tasks however, participants who used the matrix visualization were faster at completing the given questions while being more successful in the Conference domain. When evaluating the quality of the new mappings participants generated in the open-ended question Q.15, those who were supported by LIL had generally produced more correct and complete results, yielding to better overall f-measure scores consequently. The difference found across all aspects of success, time, and the quality of new mappings produced are marginal and relatively comparable. This result suggest that the LIL and the matrix visualization are relatively comparable to one another, since irrespective of the visualization used, the participants performed almost equally well in all questions across both domains. All differences shown in Fig. 2–4 reported greater than 0.05 p-value, suggesting the differences found are not statistically significant. One notable finding is that in the Anatomy domain, participants were equally successful in the identification tasks irrespective of the visualization used (shown in Fig. 2a, where p > 0.05), though those who used the LIL were faster (shown in Fig. 4a, where p > 0.05).

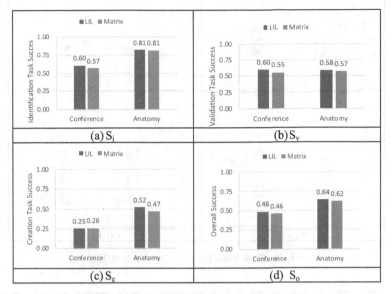

Fig. 2. Task Success by Task Type (p > 0.05).

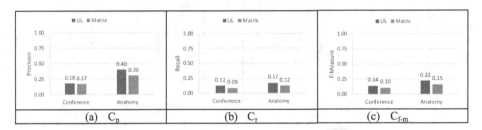

Fig. 3. Precision, Recall, and F-Measure of the New Mappings Created (p > 0.05).

When comparing how participants divided their visual attention while interacting with the two visualizations, one notable observation is the statistically significant differences found in the participants' saccadic lengths and their StDev, as shown in Fig. 5. Across both domains, the participants exhibited consistently smaller saccadic lengths (Fig. 5a) as well as smaller StDev in the dispersion of these saccadic lengths (Fig. 5b) when using the LIL. This result indicates that when using the LIL, participants generally fixated on visual cues that are closer by and that the disparity of various points of interest was smaller. In other words, this finding suggests that the matrix visualization in comparison requires visual searches of fixations that are located further apart and that there is a greater dispersion among various visual cues relevant to the participants. As such, the matrix visualization likely demands greater efforts from one's visual perceptual system in completing the given tasks shown in this paper.

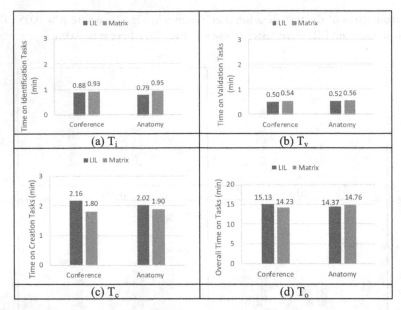

Fig. 4. Task Time by Task Type (p > 0.05).

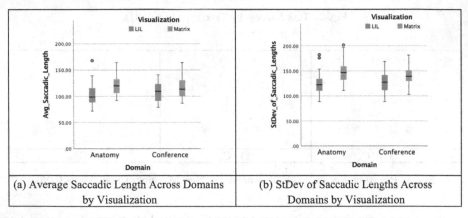

(a) Average Saccadic Length Across Domains by Visualization

(b) StDev of Saccadic Lengths Across Domains by Visualization

Fig. 5. Saccadic Length Mean and Dispersion (p < 0.01).

In order to examine relationships between one's performance and this person's visual attention spent during the interaction, we performed correlation coefficient tests as shown in Fig. 6 and Fig. 7. In the Anatomy domain, a participant's creation success is found to be correlated with this person's total fixation count (Fig. 6a), scanpath length (Fig. 6b), and the StDev of fixation durations (Fig. 6c). The r values indicate weak but statistically significant positive relationships between a person's success in creation tasks (Q.13–15) and the number of fixations this person sampled during the interaction, coupled with how extensive the entire scanpath was and how dispersed the person divided their attention processing information at various fixations. Notably, to achieve the same level of success,

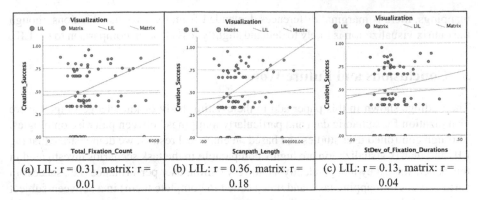

(a) LIL: r = 0.31, matrix: r = 0.01	(b) LIL: r = 0.36, matrix: r = 0.18	(c) LIL: r = 0.13, matrix: r = 0.04

Fig. 6. Correlations in the Anatomy Domain (p < 0.05).

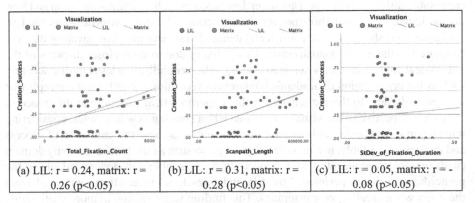

(a) LIL: r = 0.24, matrix: r = 0.26 (p<0.05)	(b) LIL: r = 0.31, matrix: r = 0.28 (p<0.05)	(c) LIL: r = 0.05, matrix: r = - 0.08 (p>0.05)

Fig. 7. Correlations in the Conference Domain.

a participant using the LIL typically generated fewer fixations, shorter scanpath, and more variation in the time spent on processing information. This finding suggests that in the context of mapping creation, the LIL may require less effort from the user while assisting them in accomplishing the same level of success compared to the matrix visualization, which likely demands greater numbers of fixations to be sampled and longer scanpaths from the user.

In the Conference domain, similar weak correlations are found though with reduced differences between the two visualizations as well as the correlative relationships themselves. Creation success and scanpath length continue to demonstrate a positive relationship (Fig. 7b), although the two visualization techniques exhibit almost exactly the same degree of correlations with a negligible difference. In contrast to the findings shown in Fig. 6a, participants with the same level of success in the creation tasks sampled fewer fixations (Fig. 7a) when using the matrix visualization. In addition, participants who achieved higher success in the creation tasks exhibited greater consistency in the time spent on processing visual information at various fixations (Fig. 7c) when using the matrix visualization, though this result is not statically significant and the relationship is almost linear. This finding suggests that in the Conference domain when creating new mappings, there is marginal differences demanded from the two visualizations, though the matrix visualization is likely to demand slightly less effort in comparison to the LIL.

5   Conclusions and Future Work

The findings shown in this paper add to the existing body of knowledge in interactive visualization for semantic data and particularly mappings between pairwise ontologies. Through controlled user studies and based on empirical results, we demonstrate that the LIL and matrix visualization are highly comparable in the task scenarios investigated in this paper, since they independently led to very similar user performance (i.e., success in various types of mapping task, and time needed to complete them) in a between-subject experimental setting across domains. In other words, the participants were as successful and efficient as one another irrespective of which visualization was used. However, there are notable differences in visual attention demanded in each visualization group and how the participants arrived at those performance outcomes. Firstly, across domains, the LIL visualization is shown to have consistently demanded shorter physical travels of the eyes compared to the matrix visualization. This is likely due to their closer displays of the ontological entities that are visualized side-by-side. Secondly, in a less familiar scenario such as the organization of academic conferences (containing ontological concepts that are generally new to the participants in this experiment), it makes little difference to the user irrespective of the visualization used when creating new mappings, considering that all participants exhibited similar gaze behaviors to achieve the same level of success and task speed. Notably, in a more familiar scenario such as the human anatomy domain (with ontological concepts that are generally recognizable and understandable to the participants in this experiment), the LIL indicates less visual effort demanded from the users when creating new mappings. This finding suggests that in more challenging scenarios (be it domain related or otherwise), it is likely that the LIL may be more appropriate to support novice users than the matrix visualization.

While this study focuses on the mapping visualizations of ontology classes, future research may broaden the scope to include visualizations of instance and property associations made between two or more ontologies, as well as investigating effective visualizations for other types of mapping relationships beyond equivalences (e.g., part-of, disjoints, etc.) and one-to-one mappings (e.g., one-to-many). In addition, while there are infinite numbers of scenarios and domains that can also be investigated, further efforts focusing on specific types of mapping scenarios such as mismatches at the language level (e.g., due to syntax, expressiveness, etc.) vs. structure level (e.g., due to differing ontology modeling convention, paradigms, granularity, coverage, etc.) may be useful in identifying effective visual primitives that are helpful in overcoming targeted issues for the average user.

The ontologies and mapping sets used in this study are relatively small in size, as such, we have not investigated how the LIL and matrix visualization would perform in large-scale ontology mappings. There is an opportunity to measure user experience in the context of creating and evaluating large sets of ontology mappings in future studies. Furthermore, though we did not find any statistically significant differences in Computer Science vs. non-Computer Science participants or results across the two domains in this particular study, it may be speculated that distinct user backgrounds, domain knowledge, and personal preferences are potential attributing factors dictating various visual needs, future research focusing on eliciting gaze trends in novice vs. expert user groups in experiments designed specifically to extract differing behaviors from various user groups are needed in the refinement of mapping visualizations.

Finally, empowered with the knowledge of user gaze during an interaction such as how one is searching and processing visual cues in real time, intelligent visualizations with adaptative features can be developed in the advancement of visualizations for the ISW, whereby we can envision adaptive ISW visualization systems (such as predicting user success and failure in real time based on gaze data during user interaction with ontology visualizations to recognize those potential moments to provide visual intervention [52, 53]) suggesting differing visualization techniques and modifying visual primitives in an existing visualization in order to tailor to users' changing needs in a visual scene with the overall goal of improving user success and reducing cognitive efforts.

Supplemental Material Statement: Source code of the ontology pairs, their mapping visualizations, and the user tasks are available at https://github.com/ TheD2Lab/OntoMapVis. `Source code used to analyze the partici-pants' eye gaze data is available at` https://github.com/TheD2Lab/Eye. Tracking.Data.Analysis.For.Tobii.2150. *The raw user data generated from the study is available upon request.*

References

1. Vargas, H., Buil-Aranda, C., Hogan, A., López, C.: RDF explorer: a visual SPARQL query builder. In: Ghidini, C., et al. The Semantic Web – ISWC 2019. ISWC 2019. LNCS, vol. 11778, pp. 647–663. Springer, Cham (2019). https://doi.org/10.1007/978-3-030-30793-6_37
2. Toulet, A., et al.: ISSA: generic pipeline, knowledge model and visualization tools to help scientists search and make sense of a scientific archive. In: Sattler, U., et al. The Semantic Web – ISWC 2022. ISWC 2022. LNCS, vol. 13489, pp. 660–677. Springer, Cham (2022). https://doi.org/10.1007/978-3-031-19433-7_38
3. Michel, F., et al.: Covid-on-the-web: knowledge graph and services to advance COVID-19 research. In: Pan, J.Z., et al. The Semantic Web – ISWC 2020. ISWC 2020. LNCS, vol. 12507, pp 294–310. Springer, Cham (2020). https://doi.org/10.1007/978-3-030-62466-8_19
4. Fu, B., Noy, N.F., Storey, M.-A.: Eye tracking the user experience - an evaluation of ontology visualization techniques. Semantic Web J. Interoperability Usability Applicability 8(1), 23–41 (2017)
5. Fu, B., Noy, N.F., Storey, M.A.: Indented tree or graph? A usability study of ontology visualization techniques in the context of class mapping evaluation. In: Alani, H., et al. The Semantic Web – ISWC 2013. ISWC 2013. LNCS, vol. 8218, pp. 117–134. Springer, Berlin (2013). https://doi.org/10.1007/978-3-642-41335-3_8
6. Asmat, M.R.A., Wiens, V., Lohmann, S.: A comparative user evaluation on visual ontology modeling using node-link diagrams. VOILA@ISWC 2018, CERU-WS **2187**, 25–36 (2018)
7. Karampatakis, S., Bratsas, C., Sváb-Zamazal, O., Filippidis, P., Antoniou, I.: Alignment: a hybrid, interactive and collaborative ontology and entity matching service. Information **9**, 281 (2018)
8. Dragisic, Z., Ivanova, V., Lambrix, P., Faria, D., Jiménez-Ruiz, E., Pesquita, C.: User validation in ontology alignment. In: Groth, P., et al. The Semantic Web – ISWC 2016. ISWC

2016. LNCS, vol. 9981, pp. 200–217. Springer, Cham (2016). https://doi.org/10.1007/978-3-319-46523-4_13

9. Cruz, I., Stroe, C., Palmonari, M.: Interactive user feedback in ontology matching using signature vectors. In: IEE 28th International Conference on Data Engineering, pp. 1321–1324 (2012)

10. Cruz, I., Antonelli, F., Stroe, C.: Agreementmaker: efficient matching for large real-world schemas and ontologies. Proc. VLDB Endowment **2**(2) 1586–1589 (2009)

11. Cruz, I., Sunna, W., Makar, N., Bathala, S.: A visual tool for ontology alignment to enable geospatial interoperability. Vis. Lang. Comput. **18**(3), 230–254 (2007)

12. Lanzenberger, M., Sampson, J., Rester, M., Naudet, Y., Latour, T.: Visual ontology alignment for knowledge sharing and reuse. Knowl. Manag. **12**(6), 102–120 (2008)

13. Faria, D., et al.: AML results for OAEI 2015. In: OM@ISWC 2015 (2015)

14. Pesquita, C., Faria, D., Santos, E., Neefs, J.M., Couto, F.M.: Towards visualizing the alignment of large biomedical ontologies. In: Galhardas, H., Rahm, E. (eds.) Data Integration in the Life Sciences. DILS 2014. LNCS, vol. 8574. Springer, Cham (2014). https://doi.org/10.1007/978-3-319-08590-6_10

15. Falconer, S., Bull, R., Grammel, L., Storey, M.-A. Creating visualizations through ontology mapping. In: Proceedings of the International Conference on Complex, Intelligent and Software Intensive Systems, pp. 688–693 (2009)

16. Falconer, S.M., Storey, M.A.: A cognitive support framework for ontology mapping. In: Aberer, K., et al. The Semantic Web. ISWC ASWC 2007 2007. LNCS, vol. 4825, pp. 114–127. Springer, Berlin (2007). https://doi.org/10.1007/978-3-540-76298-0_9

17. Noy, N., Musen, M.: Algorithm and tool for automated ontology merging and alignment. In AAAI **2000**, 450–455 (2000)

18. Aumueller, D., Do, H., Massmann, S., Rahm, E.: Schema and ontology matching with COMA++. In: Proceedings of the ACM SIGMOD International Conference on Management of Data, pp. 906–908 (2005)

19. Jiménez-Ruiz, E., Grau, B.C., Zhou, Y., Horrocks, I.: Large-scale interactive ontology matching: algorithms and implementation. Front. Artif. Intell. Appl. **242**, 444–449 (2012)

20. Lambrix, P., Kaliyaperumal, R.: A session-based approach for aligning large ontologies. In: Cimiano, P., Corcho, O., Presutti, V., Hollink, L., Rudolph, S. (eds.) The Semantic Web: Semantics and Big Data. ESWC 2013. LNCS, vol. 7882. Springer, Berlin (2013). https://doi.org/10.1007/978-3-642-38288-8_4

21. Lambrix, P., Tan. H., SAMBO - a system for aligning and merging biomedical ontologies. J. Web Semantics **4**(3), 196–206 (2006)

22. Ivanova, V., Lambrix, P.: A unified approach for aligning taxonomies and debugging taxonomies and their alignments. In: Cimiano, P., Corcho, O., Presutti, V., Hollink, L., Rudolph, S. (eds.) The Semantic Web: Semantics and Big Data. ESWC 2013. LNCS, vol 7882, pp. 1–15. Springer, Berlin (2013). https://doi.org/10.1007/978-3-642-38288-8_1

23. Neto, L.E.T., Vidal, V.M.P., Casanova, M.A., Monteiro, J.M.: R2RML by assertion: a semi-automatic tool for generating customised R2RML mappings. In: Cimiano, P., Fernández, M., Lopez, V., Schlobach, S., Völker, J. (eds.) The Semantic Web: ESWC 2013 Satellite Events. ESWC 2013. LNCS, vol. 7955, pp. 248–252. Springer, Berlin (2013). https://doi.org/10.1007/978-3-642-41242-4_33

24. Nasir, M., Hoeber, O., Evermann, J.: Supporting ontology alignment tasks with edge bundling. In Proceedings of the 13th International Conference on Knowledge Management and Knowledge Technologies, Article 11, pp. 1–8, ACM (2013)

25. Voyloshnikova, E., Fu, B., Grammel, L., Storey, M.-A.: BioMixer: visualizing mappings of biomedical ontologies. In: The 3rd International Conference on Biomedical Ontology, CEUR-WS, vol. 897 (2012)

26. Dang, T., Franz, N., Ludäscher, B., Forbes, A.G.: ProvenanceMatrix: a visualization tool for multi-taxonomy alignments. In: Proceedings of the International Workshop on Visualizations and User Interfaces for Ontologies and Linked Data, co-located with ISWC 2015, CEUR-WS, vol. 1456, pp. 13–24 (2015)

27. Ivanova, V., Bach, B., Pietriga, E., Lambrix, P.: Alignment cubes: towards interactive visual exploration and evaluation of multiple ontology alignments. In: d'Amato, C., et al. The Semantic Web – ISWC 2017. ISWC 2017. LNCS, vol. 10587, pp. 400–417. Springer, Cham (2017). https://doi.org/10.1007/978-3-319-68288-4_24

28. Severo, B., Trojahn, C., Vieira, R.: VOAR 3.0: a configurable environment for manipulating multiple ontology alignments. In: Proceedings of the ISWC 2017 Posters & Demonstrations and Industry Tracks, CEUR-WS, vol. 1963 (2017)

29. Aurisano, J., Nanavaty, A., Cruz, I.: Visual analytics for ontology matching using multi-linked views. In: Proceedings of the International Workshop on Visualizations and User Interfaces for Ontologies and Linked Data, co-located with ISWC 2015, CEUR-WS, vol. 1456, pp. 25–36 (2015)

30. Fu, B., Grammel, L., Storey, M.-A.: BioMixer: a web-based collaborative ontology visualization tool. In: Proceedings of the 3rd International Conference on Biomedical Ontology, CEUR-WS, vol. 897, ISSN 1613–0073 (2012)

31. Junior, A.C., Debruyne, C., O'Sullivan, D.: An editor that uses a block metaphor for representing semantic mappings in linked data. In: Gangemi, A., et al. The Semantic Web: ESWC 2018 Satellite Events. ESWC 2018. LNCS, vol. 11155, pp. 28–33. Springer, Cham (2018). https://doi.org/10.1007/978-3-319-98192-5_6

32. Li, Y., Stroe, C., Cruz, I.: Interactive visualization of large ontology matching results. In: VOILA@ISWC 2015, CEUR-WS, vol. 1456, pp. 37–48 (2015)

33. Heyvaert, P., et al.: Specification and implementation of mapping rule visualization and editing: MapVOWL and the RMLEditor. J. Web Semantics 49, 31–50 (2018)

34. Sicilia, A., Nemirovski, G., Nolle, A.: Map-on: a web-based editor for visual ontology mapping. Semantic Web – Interoperability Usability Applicability. 8, 969–980 (2017)

35. Heyvaert, P., et al.: RMLEditor: a graph-based mapping editor for linked data mappings. In: Sack, H., Blomqvist, E., d'Aquin, M., Ghidini, C., Ponzetto, S., Lange, C. (eds.) The Semantic Web. Latest Advances and New Domains. ESWC 2016. LNCS, vol. 9678, pp 709–723. Springer, Cham (2016). https://doi.org/10.1007/978-3-319-34129-3_43

36. Lembo, D., Rosati, R., Ruzzi, M., Savo, D.F., Tocci, E.: Visualization and management of mappings in ontology-based data access. In: Informal Proceedings of the 27th International Workshop on Description Logics, CERU, vol. 1193, pp. 595–607 (2014)

37. Falconer, S.M., Callendar, C., Storey, M.A.: A visualization service for the semantic web. In: Cimiano, P., Pinto, H.S. (eds.) Knowledge Engineering and Management by the Masses. EKAW 2010. LNCS, vol. 6317, pp. 554–564. Springer, Berlin (2010). https://doi.org/10.1007/978-3-642-16438-5_45

38. Liu, G.T., Volpe, N.J., Galetta, S.: Neuro-ophthalmology diagnosis and management, 3rd edition, Chapter 13, ISBN: 9780323340441, Elsevier (2018)

39. Spector R.H.: The Pupils. Clinical Methods: The History, Physical, and Laboratory Examinations, 3rd edition, Chapter 58, Butterworths, Boston (1990)

40. Goldberg, J.H., Kotval, X.P.: Computer interface evaluation using eye movements: methods and constructs. Int. J. Ind. Ergon. 24(6), 631–645 (1999)

41. Ivanova, V., Lambrix, P., Åberg, J.: Requirements for and evaluation of user support for large-scale ontology alignment. In: Gandon, F., Sabou, M., Sack, H., d'Amato, C., Cudré-Mauroux, P., Zimmermann, A. (eds.) The Semantic Web. Latest Advances and New Domains. ESWC 2015. LNCS, vol. 9088, pp. 3–20. Springer, Cham (2015). https://doi.org/10.1007/978-3-319-18818-8_1

42. Fu, B., Steichen, B., McBride, A.: Tumbling to succeed: a predictive analysis of user success in interactive ontology visualization. In: Proceedings of the 10th International Conference on Web Intelligence, Mining and Semantics (WIMS 2020), pp. 78–87. ACM (2020)

43. Fu, B., Steichen, B.: Impending success or failure? An investigation of gaze-based user predictions during interaction with ontology visualizations. In: Proceedings of the International Conference on Advanced Visual Interfaces (AVI 2022), Article No. 7, pp. 1–9. ACM (2022)

44. Yang, Y., Wybrow, M., Li, Y.-F., Czauderna, T., He, Y.: OntoPlot: a novel visualisation for non-hierarchical associations in large ontologies. IEEE Trans. Visual Comput. Graphics 26(1), 1140–1150 (2020)

45. Saket, B., Simonetto, P., Kobourov, S., Borner, K.: Node, node-link, and node-link-group diagrams: an evaluation. IEEE Trans. Vis. Comput. Graph. 20(12), 2231–2240 (2014)

46. Netzel, R., Burch, M., Weiskopf, D.: Comparative eye tracking study on node-link visualizations of trajectories. IEEE Trans. Visual Comput. Graphics 20(12), 2221–2230 (2014)

47. Jianu, R., Rusu, A., Hu, Y., Taggart, D.: How to display group information on node-link diagrams: an evaluation. IEEE Trans. Visual Comput. Graphics 20(11), 1530–1541 (2014)

48. Büschel, W., Vogt, S., Dachselt, R.: Augmented reality graph visualizations: investigation of visual styles in 3d node-link diagrams. IEEE Comput. Graphics Appl. 39(3), 29–40 (2019)

49. Pan, J., et al.: Exemplar-based layout fine-tuning for node-link diagrams. IEEE Trans. Vis. Comput. Graph. 27(2), 1655–1665 (2021)

50. di Bartolomeo, S., Riedewald, M., Gatterbauer, W., Dunne, C.: STRATISFIMAL LAYOUT: a modular optimization model for laying out layered node-link network visualizations. IEEE Trans. Visual Comput. Graphics 28(1), 324–334 (2022)

51. Shimabukuro, M., Zipf, J., El-Assady M., Collins, C., H-Matrix: hierarchical matrix for visual analysis of cross-linguistic features in large learner corpora. In: 2019 IEEE Visualization Conference, pp. 61–65 (2019)

52. van Beusekom, N., Meulemans, W., Speckmann, B.: Simultaneous matrix orderings for graph collections. IEEE Trans. Visual Comput. Graphics 28(1), 1–10 (2022)

53. Abdelaal, M., Schiele, N.D., Angerbauer, K., Kurzhals, K., Sedlmair, M., Weiskopf, D.: Comparative evaluation of bipartite, node-link, and matrix-based network representations. IEEE Trans. Visual Comput. GraphicsComput. Graphics 29(1), 896–906 (2023)

FeaBI: A Feature Selection-Based Framework for Interpreting KG Embeddings

Youmna Ismaeil[1,2]($\boxtimes$), Daria Stepanova[1], Trung-Kien Tran[1], and Hendrik Blockeel[2]

[1] Bosch Center for Artificial Intelligence, Renningen, Germany
{youmna.ismaeil,daria.stepanova,trung-kien.tran}@de.bosch.com
[2] KU Leuven, Leuven, Belgium
{youmna.ismaeil,hendrik.blockeel}@kuleuven.be

Abstract. Knowledge Graph (KG) embedding methods represent KG entities as vectors in an embedding space, and they have been successfully used for a variety of tasks, including link prediction and entity classification. While some of the recent embedding methods outperform traditional approaches on these tasks, their main drawback is the lack of interpretability. Several methods for explaining predictions made by KG embeddings have been proposed in the literature. However, none of them targeted the problem of constructing model explanations for embeddings, i.e., interpretable KG representations that behave similarly to embeddings on certain tasks. We address this problem and propose a novel method for generating interpretable vectors for entity embeddings. To achieve this, we employ embedded feature selection techniques to extract from the KG, on which the embedding model was trained, propositional features that are important for a given KG embedding model. Our approach sheds light on the information in the KG captured by embeddings and provides valuable insights that can be used to further enhance the embedding models. Additionally, we demonstrate the usefulness of our method for explaining embedding-based entity similarity.

1 Introduction

Motivation. Knowledge Graphs (KG) describe facts about a certain domain of interest by representing them using entities interconnected via relations. Existing KGs such as YAGO [36], Freebase [5], and DBpedia [1] contain millions of facts about people, places, organizations, etc. over hundreds of relations. For instance, an example of a KG presenting information about companies, people, products, and relations among them is presented on the left side of Fig. 1.

Deep learning techniques, such as Knowledge Graph embeddings (see [41] for an overview) are increasingly being applied to solve various machine learning tasks (e.g., link prediction [6,39,43] or entity classification [18,31]) that use KGs as input data. However, these techniques typically learn a latent representation for the entities of interest, which is often not comprehensible to humans. Thus, deep learning techniques are usually considered to be black boxes.

© The Author(s), under exclusive license to Springer Nature Switzerland AG 2023
T. R. Payne et al. (Eds.): ISWC 2023, LNCS 14265, pp. 599–617, 2023.
https://doi.org/10.1007/978-3-031-47240-4_32

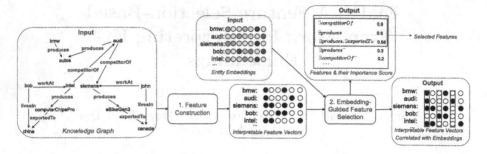

Fig. 1. Embedding-guided feature vector generation for KG entities

State-of-the-Art and Its Limitations. There has been a surge of interest in understanding how deep learning models work. Two distinct types of explanations have emerged: prediction explanations and model explanations [9]. While prediction explanations justify a particular prediction generated by a given black-box model, different definitions for model explanations exist in the literature (see, e.g., [22] for an extensive discussion). In this work, with model explanations we refer to the identification of parts of the input data that contributed most to the construction of the model, also known as feature importance-based model explanations [4]. Several works have focused on constructing prediction explanations for embeddings [3,7,14,32]. E.g., [32] generates explanations for the link prediction task by perturbing the training data, while [7] constructs prediction explanations for link prediction and triple classification using entity co-occurrence statistics. However, none of the above methods target the problem of computing model explanations, which are complementary to prediction explanations and can be exploited for model analysis. Some methods [35] construct interpretable embeddings, but these are not designed to explain or analyze other deep learning-based models. In this paper, we address the respective issue.

Our Approach and Contributions. We present a novel method (see Fig. 1 for overview), which computes explainable vectors for entity embeddings and generates KG embedding model explanations in the form of KG features important for the given embedding model.

Our method proceeds as follows. First, we extract propositional features from the KG and express them in Description Logic [2]. Then, we use these features to construct Boolean vectors (a.k.a. feature vectors) for each entity relying on its neighborhood. For example, in the KG from Fig. 1, the Boolean feature vector representation of the entity *siemens* contains the information that *siemens* produces some products that are exported to *canada* and *audi* is among its competitors. Next, given a pre-computed embedding model that we want to explain (i.e., a function mapping entities to vectors in some d-dimensional space), we train a regression random forest on the task of reconstructing embedding-based entity representations using features defined in the first step of our method. The regression random forest model ranks features based on their importance for the reconstruction task. We consider the highest-scoring features as the KG embedding model explanations.

Intuitively, the obtained feature vector and embedding entity representations are two ways of representing entities in the KG. Thus, if there is a regression model that can accurately reconstruct KG embeddings from feature vector-based representations, then the feature vectors and the embeddings contain comparable information. We use the list of the computed most important features as an explanation for the KG embedding model. Finally, we reduce the Boolean feature vector of each entity such that it contains only the features that exist in the list of most important features obtained in the previous step. For instance, in the KG from Fig. 1, the resulting Boolean feature vector representation for *siemens* will contain only selected features.

Our main contributions are summarized as follows:

- We present an automated method for generating model explanations for KG embeddings in the form of KG features most relevant for the given embedding. These identified important KG features are used to construct interpretable feature vector representations (entity-level explanations) for each KG entity, approximating their respective embedding vectors.
- We empirically demonstrate that the generated interpretable feature vectors behave similarly to the respective entity embeddings on the entity and relation classification tasks.
- We show how the interpretable entity representations generated by our method can facilitate the analysis of the behavior of embedding models.
- We provide evidence that our interpretable entity representations can be leveraged to explain similarities between entity embeddings.

2   Preliminaries

Knowledge Graphs. Knowledge Graphs (KGs) represent interlinked collections of factual information, encoded as a set of ⟨*subject predicate object*⟩ triples, *e.g.*, ⟨*bmw produces autos*⟩ which can also be represented as ground binary predicates in predicate logic format, e.g., *produces*(*bmw, autos*). A signature of a KG $\mathcal{G}$ is $\Sigma_{\mathcal{G}} = \langle \mathbf{R}, \mathbf{E} \rangle$, where $\mathbf{R}$ is a set of binary predicates, *i.e.*, relations and $\mathbf{E}$ is a set of constants, *i.e.*, entities, in the knowledge graph $\mathcal{G}$. Concepts can be built over KGs following the Description Logic (DL) [2] syntax. In this work we mainly rely on concepts described in Table 1.

KG Embeddings. Deep learning methods (in particular, KG embeddings) have been proposed to perform different machine learning tasks on top of KGs, such as link prediction or entity classification. KG embeddings aim at representing all entities and relations in a continuous vector space, usually as vectors or matrices called *embeddings*. Embeddings can be used to estimate the likelihood of a triple being true via a scoring function: $f : \mathbf{E} \times \mathbf{R} \times \mathbf{E} \to \mathbb{R}$, or to classify entities [18,31,44,46]. In this work, we only make use of entity-based embedding representations leaving the exploitation of relation embeddings for future work.

Table 1. Description Logic concepts where r is an (atomic) relation or its inverse, R is any relation or its inverse, e is an entity, $\top$ is the universal (top) concept.

DL concept	Informal description
$\exists r.\top$	Existence of some relation r
$\exists r.\{e\}$	Existence of some relation r to the entity e
$\exists R.\{e\}$	Existence of any relation to the entity e
$\exists r_1.\exists r_2...\exists r_k.\top$	Existence of a chain of relations $r_1, r_2, \ldots, r_k$
$\leq kR.\top,\ \geq kR.\top$	Less (greater) than or equal to k overall number of relations

Thus, without loss of generality, we assume that an embedding model is given a function: $\mathcal{E} : \mathbf{E} \mapsto \mathbb{R}^d$, which maps entities from $\mathbf{E}$ to d-dimensional real vectors.

One of the earliest and most popular embeddings is *e.g.*, TransE [6], which embeds entities and relations as vectors and assumes $\mathbf{v_s} + \mathbf{v_r} \approx \mathbf{v_o}$ for true triples, where $\mathbf{v_s}, \mathbf{v_r}, \mathbf{v_o}$ are vector embeddings for subject s, relation r and object o, resp. The likelihood that the above assumption holds should be higher for triples in the KG than for those outside. The learning process is done by minimizing the error induced by the respective assumption given the considered loss function.

Several KG embeddings that are based on graph neural networks have also been proposed in the literature (e.g., [40]) and, to the best of our knowledge, currently, they demonstrate the state-of-the-art performance on link prediction and entity classification tasks [12,47]. One of the prominent representatives of this group of embeddings is CompGCN [40], which leverages a variety of entity-relation composition operations from KG embedding techniques as well as several existing multi-relational graph convolutional neural network methods.

3　Embedding-Guided Feature Construction

KG embedding models achieve promising results on different popular tasks; however, they are not interpretable. To address this issue, our work aims at providing insights into the effectiveness of pre-computed KG embedding models in capturing information in the KG by identifying the most important features in the training data for the embedding models and generating interpretable feature vector representations for KG entities. This can help in improving KG embedding models traditionally considered as black boxes.

More formally, given a KG $\mathcal{G}$ and an embedding model $\mathcal{E} : \mathbf{E} \mapsto \mathbb{R}^d$, which maps KG entities to numerical vectors, we aim at investigating the following questions: (a) Can we find a set of features F and an encoding $\mathcal{F}$ of entities using these features such that a function $\mathcal{W}$ exists that maps feature-based encoding $\mathcal{F}(e)$ of any entity $e \in \mathbf{E}$ to $\mathcal{E}(e)$? (b) If we use $\mathcal{F}(\mathbf{E})$ instead of $\mathcal{E}(\mathbf{E})$ as the input for downstream tasks, do we get similar results for these tasks?

In this section, we propose a method for constructing $\mathcal{F}$ according to criterion (a). Then in Sect. 4, we evaluate its practical usefulness according to (b) using entity and relation classification as downstream tasks.

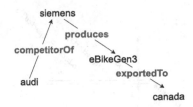

Fig. 2. Fragment of a KG from Fig. 1

Fig. 3. Feature vector for the entity *siemens* for KG from Fig. 2

The overview of our method for constructing an interpretable model based on a given KG embedding is presented in Fig. 1. We take as input a knowledge graph and a pre-computed embedding model (e.g., TransE [6], CompGCN [40], or any other model). We then construct interpretable feature vectors for entities as described in Sect. 3.1. The obtained features are used for the embedding-guided feature selection to identify only those features that are important for approximating the given embedding model (see Sect. 3.2). The resulting features are then used to encode each KG entity and serve as embedding explanations, which are further evaluated in Sect. 4.

3.1 Feature Construction

In the first step of our method, we construct interpretable feature vector representations for KG entities relevant to a given embedding model. To achieve this, several proposionalization techniques [8,19,21,30,35] can be invoked, including methods that rely on rule learning [20,23]. In this work, we incorporate four types of features. In addition to relations and relations with entities features proposed in INK [35], we introduce two new features: graph structural statistics (capturing patterns important for graph-based embedding models) and surrounding entities (necessary for embedding models lacking relations and paths with labeled edges, such as Snore [24]). To ensure that the features used in our analysis originated from the triples, on which the embedding models were initially trained, we focus on the above simple feature types. While more complex features extracted from rules or ontologies could be utilized, we choose features (represented in DL) that are more likely to be learned by the embedding models, as they are used explicitly as part of the input during training.

Relations. The first feature type indicates whether an entity takes part in a given relation or not. For each relation r, there are features $\exists r.\top$ and $\exists r^-.\top$ that

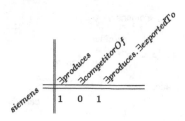

Fig. 4. Feature vector for the entity *siemens* from Fig. 3 after feature selection based on the important features in Fig. 1.

describe for each entity whether it has an outgoing or incoming relation with the respective label r. For example, for the entity *siemens* in Fig. 2 we have the following set of *relation* features: $\exists produces.\top$, $\exists competitorOf^-.\top$.

Entities. The second group of features is formed by collecting for each entity e, the entities e' to which e is connected via relations with some label. In the Description Logic syntax, this amounts to $\exists R.\{e'\}$ and $\exists R^-.\{e'\}$. E.g., *siemens* in Fig. 2 has $\exists R.\{eBikeGen3\}$ and $\exists R^-.\{audi\}$ among its *entity* features.

Relations with Entities. The third type of features indicates whether a given entity is connected to another entity via a certain relation. For each entity e we consider its outgoing or incoming relations along with the entities to which the given entity is connected. In the Description Logic syntax, this results in the features of the following form: $\exists r.\{e'\}$ and $\exists r^-.\{e'\}$. E.g., for *siemens* in Fig. 2 we have the following features $\exists produces.\{eBikeGen3\}$, $\exists competitorOf^-.\{audi\}$.

Paths. Another type of features corresponds to paths with a predefined length k $\exists r_1.\exists r_2. \ldots .\exists r_k$. E.g., when considering the entity *siemens* and $k = 2$, a single path feature is generated: $\exists produces.\exists exportedTo$.

Statistics. Finally, we consider the number of outgoing and incoming relations r and r^- for each entity e. In the DL syntax, this amounts to the following constructors $\geq k.R \sqcap \leq k.R$ and $\geq k.R^- \sqcap \leq k.R^-$ respectively, for which (with some abuse of notation) we use the shortcuts $= k.R$ and $= k.R^-$ to save space. For instance, for *siemens* in Fig. 2 we have $= 1.R$, and $= 1.R^-$, as there is 1 outgoing and 1 incoming relation for this entity. Similar to Statistics, additional information about the entities (e.g., textual or numerical attributes) can be considered as an extra entry in the feature vector.

Building on the work in [35], we compute all features including paths for a predefined depth k. We then collect all features of the described types into the set $F = \{f_1, \ldots, f_p\}$, where p is the total number of features extracted from the KG $\mathcal{G}$. Based on the knowledge graph and the respective set of features F, we form an interpretable Boolean vector $\mathbf{fv}_e = [f_0^e, f_1^e, \ldots, f_p^e]$ for each entity e, such that $|\mathbf{fv}_e| = |F| = p$ and $f_i^e = 1$ iff the feature f_i holds for the entity e in the KG $\mathcal{G}$, and $f_i^e = 0$ otherwise. E.g., the resulting representation for the entity *siemens* for a small KG fragment from Fig. 2 is presented in Fig. 3.

3.2 Feature Selection

The pre-constructed set of features generated as described in Sect. 3.1 encodes information about the entities based on their neighborhood. However, it is unclear which of these features are relevant to the embedding model. To identify the most relevant features in the KG for embedding reconstruction, we adopt an embedded feature selection technique inspired by [37]. This approach allows us to use the embeddings to guide us in identifying and scoring the crucial features in the KG needed to reconstruct the embeddings. For the step of embedded feature selection, various models (e.g., decision trees, MLP) providing feature scores can be in principle utilized. In our case, we use random regression forest due to its simplicity, interpretability and resistance to overfitting [33]. The model, denoted as M, is trained to reconstruct the corresponding embeddings from their feature-based entity representations.

The random regression forest constructs a separate regression tree for predicting each embedding dimension using a subset of the features in the input. The respective trees are then combined to make predictions for all the embedding dimensions at once by averaging the predictions made by each regression tree for each dimension. During training, the random forest regression model scores the input features based on their importance (a.k.a. feature importance score) for the reconstruction task. The features with the highest importance score are used to explain the info captured by the KG embedding.

Formally, let $F = \{f_1, \ldots, f_p\}$ be a set of features computed in the previous step, e.g., $\exists competitorOf, \exists produces$, etc. As mentioned in Sect. 3.1, each entity $e \in \mathbf{E}$ is represented as a Boolean vector of the form $\mathbf{fv}_e = [f_0^e, \ldots, f_p^e]$, where f_i^e reflects the presence or absence of the respective feature f_i for the entity e. For the training input to the random forest regression model for each entity $e \in \mathbf{E}$, we have its Boolean feature vector $\mathbf{fv}_e = [f_0^e, f_1^e, \ldots, f_p^e]$ with the label being the embedding of e, i.e., $\mathbf{v}_e \in \mathbb{R}^d$ computed by the target embedding model $\mathcal{E}$ which we aim at explaining. The random forest regression model [33] is used to find the mapping between the feature vectors and embeddings. Additionally, the model outputs the importance score for each feature, which is computed relying on the mean squared error on the respective predictive task of reconstructing entity embeddings from feature vector-based entity representations. Once the model M is trained, the scores assigned to the features are extracted, and only the features with scores that are greater than a certain threshold θ are deemed essential. In our experiments, we set the threshold for the feature selection parameter to be the mean of the feature importance scores, as commonly done in practice.

The features selected by our feature selection algorithm reflect the parts of the KG that the embedding model focuses on most. Therefore, we refer to them as model explanations. Next, we utilize the selected features to obtain instance-level explanations for each entity embedding. This is achieved by keeping only the selected features within each entity representation. For example, if we have a set of selected features for a KG embedding model (Fig. 1), we obtain the corresponding feature vector-based representation for entity *siemens* (Fig. 4).

Table 2. Knowledge graph data statistics. The train and test splits are used for training the respective embedding models

KG elements	FB15K-237	DBpedia50K
Entities	14,541	49,900
Relations	237	654
Train triples	272,115	32,388
Validation triples	17,535	399
Test triples	20,466	10,969

4   Experiments

We evaluate the quality and usefulness of the interpretable feature-based entity representations computed by our method. To evaluate the quality, we compare the behavior of the original embedding-based entity representations and our interpretable entity representations on the two tasks: 1) the entity classification following [17], and 2) the relation classification, i.e., given a pair of entities, predict a relation that holds between the entities. Additionally, to demonstrate the usefulness of our method, we consider the entity similarity task and show how our feature-based entity representations can be exploited to compute explanations for entities being close to each other in the embedding space.

4.1   Experimental Setup

Datasets. We experiment with two widely used knowledge graphs namely, Freebase15k-237 (a.k.a. FB15k-237) [38] and DBpedia50K [34] (see Table 2).

Embedding Models. For embeddings, we consider (1) TransE [6] as one of the first and most popular models; (2) CompGCN [40] as one of the latest GNN-based models which achieves state-of-the-art results on the entity classification tasks; (3) NodePiece [12] as a shallow path-based embedding model; and (4) Snore [24] and INK [35] as embeddings that are interpretable by construction.

Evaluation Tasks. We consider entity classification and relation classification as the tasks on which we evaluate whether our feature vectors encompass the same information as the corresponding embedding-based entity representations.
• **Feature Selection Evaluation.** To evaluate our feature selection module, we apply the proposed framework to approximate Boolean INK [35] embeddings, for which interpretable features are known. More specifically, we compute the F1 score reflecting the similarity between the most important features generated by our method and the features used for constructing INK embeddings.

- **Entity Classification.** Entity classification is concerned with the prediction of a label from a given set of labels for KG entities. The goal of this evaluation is to verify whether different classifiers when trained on feature vector-based entity representations and embedding-based entity representations, align with each other by making the same correct and incorrect predictions for the entity classification task. For the FB15K-237 KG, we consider the labels for entities from [17], and for the DBPedia50K KG, we extract the entity types as labels. Similar to [28], we have selected the following classifiers: (1) Random forest [33]; (2) K-nearest neighbor classifier [10]; (3) Multi-layer perceptron (MLP) [15]. For all the models used in this work, we used the default parameter setup defined by the scikit-learn library [27] for the respective model.

We train the respective classifiers on the train set of labeled KG entity embeddings and the train set of our feature vector representations approximating the target embedding. We then use the respective classifiers to predict the labels for entities in the test set, pick the classifier that shows the best performance for the embedding-based entity classification, and use its predictions to compute the alignment score (weighted average F1 score) between the predictions made by the embedding-based and feature-vector based classifiers. The alignment score evaluates the consistency between predictions using embeddings and those using feature-vectors. Accounting for false positives and negatives, the F1 score quantifies the overall agreement. A perfect alignment score is 1, reflecting that the behavior of both embeddings and feature vectors is identical on a specific task.

Since, to the best of our knowledge, no previous works have targeted the problem of computing model explanations for KG embedding models, as a baseline, we use the feature vectors constructed by our method but without the feature selection step. If the feature selection step removes a large percentage of features, but this does not impact the weighted average F1 score, one can conclude that the removed features are indeed not important for the embedding model on the respective task.

- **Relation Classification.** In the relation classification task, we randomly select a set $\mathbf{R}'$ of 50 relations from the KG, resulting in 39,273 (resp. 24,832) entity pairs $E = \{(e_1, e_2) \mid \langle e_1, r, e_2 \rangle, r \in R\}$ for FB15k-237 (resp. for DBpedia50k). We split the set E into the train (70 % of entity pairs) and the test (30 %) sets.

We proceed with evaluating the alignment between the embedding-based entity representations and the feature-vector-based entity representations in the same way as for the entity classification task. The only difference is that the task considered in this experiment is rather concerned with classifying pairs of entities from the test set into a class r from the set of 50 classes in $\mathbf{R}'$. Intuitively, the meaning of a pair being classified to a specific class r is that the relation r holds between the respective entities.

Applications. Our feature vector-based entity representations can be exploited for analyzing and comparing different embedding models. To this end, we report and examine the types of features in the model explanations computed by our method for different embeddings and datasets as well as present examples of

Table 3. Mean squared error of the random forest regression model used to learn important features for the regeneration of the embeddings.

	Mean squared error (MSE)	
Embedding model	DBPedia50K	FB15K-237
Random	55.70	54.76
INK	0.0001	0.0003
TransE	0.026	0.0257
CompGCN	0.007	0.005
NodePiece	0.016	0.035
Snore	0.138	0.076

selected features along with computed entity representations. Another application of our method is explainable entity similarity. Given the embeddings learned by an embedding model and their corresponding interpretable feature vectors **fv** computed by our method, one can generate explanations for the similarity between any pair of entities e_i and its neighbor e_j in the embedding space as the intersection between their respective feature vectors, i.e., $\mathbf{fv}_{e_i} \cap \mathbf{fv}_{e_j}$.

4.2   Experimental Results

Evaluation of Feature Selection. We report the mean squared error (MSE) of the random forest regression model, trained to regenerate the embeddings from feature vectors in Table 3. As a baseline, we consider a simple model that outputs a vector of random numbers of size 50 (average size of the embeddings used) when given a feature vector as input. The respective baseline is referred to as Random in Table 3. The low MSE values for all models apart from the baseline witness that the random forest regression model is capable of identifying a meaningful relationship between the input feature vectors and the corresponding KG embeddings. For the random embeddings, the model failed to find a connection between the input feature vectors and the randomly generated embeddings, leading to high MSE.

Additionally, we also computed the alignment F1 score between the features selected by our feature selection algorithm and the original features present in the INK embeddings. For FB15k-237, the F1 score is 0.77 and for DBpedia50K it is 0.82, indicating that the majority of the selected features were indeed in the input embeddings. These results further confirm the effectiveness of the feature selection method in accurately retrieving the content of embeddings. More results on custom embeddings are in Table 16 in Sec. 7.3 in the Appendix.

Entity and Relation Classification. In Table 4, we report the weighted average F1 score for the alignment between the classification results computed by the respective embedding models and the feature vector-based entity representations before (columns 4 and 6) and after (columns 5 and 7) the feature selection step.

Table 4. The alignment F1 score between embedding-based classifiers and our feature-vector-based classifiers (before and after the feature selection step) on the entity and relation classification tasks. The third column represents the percentage of the selected features out of the total number of features.

Interpreted model	Dataset	Selected feature %	Entity-classification (F1)		Relation classification (F1)	
			Before selection	After selection	Before selection	After selection
INK [35]	FB15K-237	75.5	0.93	0.80	0.90	0.90
	DBpedia50k	50.5	0.73	0.78	0.97	0.96
TransE [6]	FB15k-237	19.7	0.84	0.84	0.73	0.78
	DBpedia50k	13.9	0.61	0.64	0.53	0.54
CompGCN [40]	FB15k-237	24.4	0.64	0.64	0.57	0.61
	DBpedia50k	31.8	0.52	0.69	0.63	0.65
NodePiece [12]	FB15k-237	20.0	0.68	0.68	0.47	0.51
	DBpedia50k	22.7	0.73	0.73	0.75	0.75
Snore [24]	FB15k-237	11.9	0.66	0.69	0.23	0.23
	DBpedia50k	2.5	0.59	0.59	0.50	0.51

We also report the percentage of all features left after the feature selection step (column 3). One can observe that the alignment scores reach 0.84 for entity classification and 0.78 for relation classification tasks, respectively. The alignment score for Snore on the relation classification task was low, which is attributed to the fact that its embeddings do not consider relations as mentioned in [24]. As a consequence, the performance of Snore on the relation classification task is rather poor, with the F1 score of 0.16. Our feature selection-based method also manages to reproduce this, which is witnessed by the results in Fig. 6, where the top 10 features selected as the most important ones for Snore on DBPedia50K correspond to entities. Moreover, we found that this result is invariant to the value of θ, as the performance was poor even before feature selection. Furthermore, we observed that the alignment with INK is the highest, which can be attributed to the interpretable nature of the INK embeddings and the intersection of features used in our method with those used in INK. Based on the percentage of selected features, the results show that NodePiece uses less features than CompGCN but more than TransE. This is due to the facts that NodePiece retains small amount of information about explicit nodes without sacrificing its performance on down stream tasks.

Table 4 shows that the feature selection discards up to 97.5% of the features without negative impact on the alignment F1 score. This indicates that the embeddings do not utilize all of the information in the neighborhood of entities.

KG Embedding Analysis. In Fig. 5, we present detailed information regarding the contribution of each feature type to the total number of features before and after the feature selection step for the models TransE, CompGCN, NodePiece, and Snore on FB15k-237 and DBpedia50k. Figure 5 shows that even though inward relations with entities constitute more than 50% of all features, they are mostly ignored by our selection mechanism (at most 16% were selected for TransE and 17% for CompGCN across all considered datasets). This might indicate that the embedding models learn to represent each entity in terms of

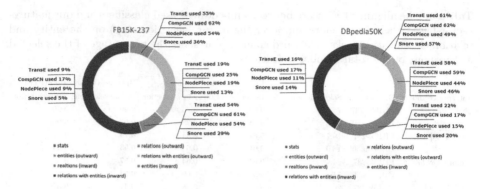

Fig. 5. The percentage of each feature type out of the total number of features for FB15k-237 (left) and DBPedia50k (right). Labels reflect the percentage of features per feature type selected by our method for the considered models.

FB15K-237		**DBpedia50K**	
TransE	**CompGCN**	**Snore**	**NodePiece**
$\exists profession$	$= 0.R^-$	$\exists genre$	$= 1.R$
$\exists film^-$	$= 1.R^-$	$\exists R.\{germany\}$	$\exists team$
$\exists award^-$	$= 2.R^-$	$\exists R.\{london\}$	$\exists musical Artist^-$
$\exists genre$	$= 3.R^-$	$= 0.R$	$\exists birthplace$
$\exists artists^-$	$= 2.R$	$\exists R.\{drumKit\}$	$= 1.R^-$
$\exists institution^-$	$= 1.R$	$\exists recordLabel$	$\exists staring$
$\exists role^-$	$= 4.R$	$\exists R.\{iran\}$	$\exists genre$
$= 0.R^-$	$= 0.R$	$\exists R.\{insect\}$	$\exists team^-$
$\exists team^-$	$\exists placeOfBirth$	$\exists R.\{southKorea\}$	$\exists producer$
$= 1.R^-$	$= 3.R$	$\exists kingdom.\{plant\}$	$\exists writer$

Fig. 6. The top 10 most important features identified by our method for FB15K-237 and DBpedia50k, sorted in descending order of their importance scores.

outward (paths of) relations and entities rather than inward ones. This behavior was consistent over all four knowledge graph embedding models used.

We can observe that the portion of features filtered out by our selection method within each feature type is significant, reaching more than 60% for some feature types. Our feature selection technique filtered out more features for Snore and NodePiece models than for other models. The selected feature types are consistent with the methods for constructing the respective embeddings [12,24]. For the CompGCN model the majority of the features were retained. In Fig. 6, we also present the top 10 features selected by our framework for FB15k-237 on TransE and CompGCN. One can notice that CompGCN focuses more on the information about the number of inward and outward relations and entities with large numbers of incoming and outgoing relations which aligns with the limitations of GNNs in [42]. A similar behavior has been observed for DBpedia50k.

The model explanations can also be used to analyze the behavior of the embedding models throughout training phases (see Sec. 7.4 in the Appendix).

Table 5. Feature vector of entity *"América de Cali Club"* from DBpedia50k KG computed by our method for different models.

Model	Feature vector representation
Original (no feature selection)	$\exists team^-, \exists team^-.\{AndrsAndrade\}, \exists team^-.\{ChristianMontao\},$ $\exists team^-.\{DanielTlger\}, \exists team^-.\{DavidFerreira\}, \exists team^-.\{DiegoGmez\},$ $\exists team^-.\{EduardoFerreira\}, \exists team^-.\{ErnestoFaras\}, \exists team^-.\{GiovanniHernndez\},$ $\exists team^-.\{HugoSosa\}, \exists team^-.\{JairReinoso\}, \exists team^-.\{JavierArizala\},$ $\exists team^-.\{JohnCrdoba\}, \exists team^-.\{JohnHaroldLozano\}, \exists team^-.\{JuanCamiloAngulo\},$ $\exists team^-.\{LeandroCastellanos\}, \exists team^-.\{LuisBarbat\}, \exists team^-.\{LuisEduardoZapata\},$ $\exists team^-.\{LuisMarcoleta\}, \exists team^-.\{RobertoCabaas\}, \exists team^-.\{WilsonMorelo\},$ $= 20.R^-, = 0.R, \exists R^-.\{AndrsAndrade\}, \exists R^-.\{ChristianMontao\},$ $\exists R^-.\{DanielTlger\}, \exists R^-.\{DavidFerreira\}, \exists R^-.\{DiegoGmez\},$ $\exists R^-.\{EduardoFerreira\}, \exists R^-.\{ErnestoFaras\}, \exists R^-.\{GiovanniHernndez\},$ $\exists R^-.\{HugoSosa\}, \exists R^-.\{JairReinoso\}, \exists R^-.\{JavierArizala\},$ $\exists R^-.\{JohnCrdoba\}, \exists R^-.\{JohnHaroldLozano\}, \exists R^-.\{JuanCamiloAngulo\},$ $\exists R^-.\{LeandroCastellanos\}, \exists R^-.\{LuisBarbat\}, \exists R^-.\{LuisEduardoZapata\},$ $\exists R^-.\{LuisMarcoleta\}, \exists R^-.\{RobertoCabaas\}, \exists R^-.\{WilsonMorelo\}$
TransE	$\exists team^-, = 0.R, \exists team^-.\{DanielTlger\}, \exists R.\{JohnCrdoba\}$
CompGCN	$\exists team^-.\{JavierArizala\}, \exists team^-.\{LuisEduardoZapata\}, = 20.R, = 0.R^-,$ $\exists R^-.\{JavierArizala\}, \exists R^-.\{LuisEduardoZapata\}, \exists R^-.\{LuisMarcoleta\}$
NodePiece	$\exists team^-.\{EduardoFerreira\}, \exists team^-, = 20.R^-, = 0.R, \exists R^-.\{EduardoFerreira\},$
Snore	$\exists team^-, = 20.R^-, = 0.R$

Example Feature Vectors. In Table 5 and 6, we present example feature-based representations computed by our method for entities *"América de Cali Club"* and *"Fox Channel (Asia)"* from DBPedia50K KG. For these entities the CompGCN embedding model tends to capture more inward relations with entities than other models. For TransE the majority of the selected features are relations with entities with different relations, which aligns well with its limitation to capture one-to-many relations [41].

Although CompGCN better grasps inward relations with entities compared to other models, it fails to capture all the entities with dense neighborhood, i.e., entities having numerous inward relations with the same label. We observed this behavior for the entity *"América de Cali Club"*, which has 20 inward relations with entities labeled with the same relation type (see Table 5). The same holds for the outward relations with entities for *"Fox Channel (Asia)"* in Table 6. More examples are in the appendix. After conducting the feature selection process, we observed an average of around 29K-19K selected features for FB15K-236 and DBPedia50k, respectively. Despite the high average, individual entities typically possess a limited number of features in their representations, 6-54 features per entity on average for FB15K-236 and DBPedia50k, respectively. Hence, feature representations are easily comprehensible by humans, making them suitable for manual examination (see Table 9 and 10 in the appendix).

Explainable Entity Similarity. Our explanations for embedding models can be utilized to explain similarity between entities. To exemplify this application, in Table 7 we report the closest and the 100th closest entity to *"Christina*

Table 6. Feature vector of the entity *"Fox Channel (Asia)"* from DBpedia50k KG computed by our method.

Model	Feature vector representation
Original (no feature selection)	$\exists broadcastArea, \exists broadcastArea.\{SouthKorea\}), \exists language,$ $\exists language.\{EnglishLanguage\}, \exists sisterStation, \exists sisterStation.\{FoxFilipino\},$ $\exists sisterStation.\{NatGeoPeople\}, \exists sisterStation.\{NatGeoWild\},$ $\exists sisterStation.\{StarSports\}, \exists sisterStation.\{StarWorld\}, = 7.R, = 0.R^-,$ $\exists R.\{SouthKorea\}), \exists R.\{EnglishLanguage\}, \exists R.\{FoxFilipino\},$ $\exists R.\{NatGeoPeople\}, \exists R.\{NatGeoWild\}, \exists R.\{StarSports\}, \exists R.\{StarWorld\}$
TransE	$\exists broadcastArea, \exists broadcastArea.\{SouthKorea\}), \exists language,$ $\exists language.\{EnglishLanguage\}, \exists sisterStation, = 0.R^-, \exists R.\{SouthKorea\}),$ $\exists R.\{EnglishLanguage\}, \exists R.\{NatGeoPeople\}$
CompGCN	$\exists broadcastArea, \exists language, \exists language.\{EnglishLanguage\},$ $\exists sisterStation, \exists sisterStation.\{FoxFilipino\}, \exists sisterStation.\{NatGeoPeople\},$ $\exists sisterStation.\{NatGeoWild\}, = 7.R, = 0.R^-, \exists R.\{SouthKorea\}),$ $\exists R.\{EnglishLanguage\}, \exists R.\{FoxFilipino\}, \exists R.\{NatGeoPeople\}, \exists R.\{NatGeoWild\}$

Aguilera" based on the cosine similarity of the respective vectors for TransE model on the FB15K-237 dataset along with the features computed by our method that the respective entities share. The results reveal that *"Christina Aguilera"* shares more features with its closest neighbor *"Katy Perry"* than with *"Ice Cube"*, which explains why the respective entities are closer in the embedding space. We provide further results for the entity similarity application in appendix. These results show insights into the embedding space learned by the embedding models, allowing for a better understanding of possible reasons for the respective positions of entities in the embedding space.

5 Related Work

Explanations of KG Embedding Models. In recent years, a variety of KG embeddings have been proposed, e.g., [6,12,26,31,40] (see [41] for an overview). While some of the methods achieve state-of-the-art performance on certain tasks [12,40,47], the models often remain to be black boxes. This has raised interest in explaining KG embeddings and led to works targeting outcome explanations for embeddings on the link prediction task [3,7,11,13,25,32]. In [32] a Kelpie framework has been introduced, which explains predictions made by a given embedding by identifying the combinations of training facts that have enabled the respective predictions. The works [3,13] exploit rule learning techniques for identifying triples which are logical explanations for a particular prediction. Generation of post-hoc explanation for triples inferred by a (factorization-based) embedding model has been considered in [25]. This method first augments the underlying KG by introducing weighted edges between entities relying on their embedding-based similarity and then computes human-understandable explanations in the form of paths. All of the above methods

Table 7. The list of explanations for the similarity of "*Christina Aguilera*" to its nearest neighbours. The entity is from FB15K-237 and its 1st and 100th nearest neighbors are based on TransE embeddings.

n^{th} Neighbor	Neighbor	Similarity Explanation
1st	Katy Perry	$\exists artists^{-}.\{dancepop\}, \exists artists^{-}.\{popmusic\},$ $\exists award.\{GrammyAwardforBestFemalePopVocalPerformance\},$ $\exists award.\{MTVVideoMusicAwardoftheYear\}$ $\exists award.\{MTVVideoMusicAwardforBestNewArtist\},$ $\exists award.\{(MTVVideoMusicAwardForBestFemaleVideo\},$ $\exists netWorthCurrency.\{USdollar\}, \exists gender.\{femaleorganism\},$ $\exists profession.\{actor\}, \exists vacationer^{-}, \exists participant^{-},$ $\exists awardWinner^{-}, \exists person^{-}, \exists artist^{-}, \exists award,$ $\exists specialPerformanceType, \exists awardNominee, \exists profession,$ $\exists origin, \exists film, \exists participant, \exists netWorthCurrency,$ $\exists religion, \exists nationality, \exists R^{-}.\{poprock\},$ $\exists R^{-}.\{popmusic\}, \exists R^{-}.\{dancepop\}, = 43.R^{-},$ $\exists R.\{MTVVideoMusicAwardforVideooftheYear\},$ $\exists R.\{MTVVideoMusicAwardforBestFemaleVideo\},$ $\exists R.\{MTVVideoMusicAwardforBestNewArtist\},$ $\exists R.\{MTVVideoMusicAwardforBestPopVideo\},$ $\exists R.\{MTVVideoMusicAwardforBestArtDirection\},$ $\exists R.\{GrammyAwardforBestFemalePopVocalPerformance\},$ $\exists R.\{femaleorganism\}, \exists R.\{actor\}, \exists R.\{USdollar\}, \exists R.\{friend\},$
100th	Ice Cube	$\exists profession.\{recordproducer\}, \exists languages.\{English\},$ $\exists netWorthCurrency.\{USdollar\}, \exists artists^{-},$ $\exists awardNominee^{-}, \exists awardWinner^{-}, \exists profession,$ $\exists film, \exists gender, \exists languages, \exists award, \exists netWorthCurrency,$ $\exists nationality, \exists religion, \exists location, \exists awardNominee,$ $\exists awardWinner, \exists R.\{USdollar\}, \exists R.\{recordproducer\}, \exists R.\{English\}$

focus on explaining the *outcome* of an embedding model rather than generating interpretable feature-based representations of entities that would mimic the behavior of embeddings on downstream tasks as we do. The recent work [12] is aligned with our idea of representing entities using a fixed-size entity vocabulary, but the respective model targets a different task of making embedding models space efficient, and in contrast to our entity representations, the representations generated by NodePiece are not interpretable.

In contrast, the works [24, 35] generate KG embeddings that are interpretable by construction. Their feature-driven entity encodings are similar to ours, but these methods do not approximate existing black box models as we do.

Interpretable Propositionalization-Based Embeddings. Propositionalization, the task of constructing table-based representations, has been proposed for relational data [19]. It has also been studied in the context of knowledge graphs [21, 29–31, 35]. While these existing propositionalization methods are interpretable by nature, they were developed and used as an alternative to black box KG embedding models, rather than for explaining existing KGE embedding models. Thus, these methods complement our work, and any interpretable propositionalization method can be incorporated during the feature construction step of our approach. To the best of our knowledge, none of the existing propositionalization methods targeted the problem of approximating the behavior of a given embedding model, which is our main focus.

6   Conclusion

Knowledge Graph embedding models are widely used for various tasks, but their numeric vector representations are not interpretable. Even with KG embedding models that create embeddings from interpretable features like NodePiece [12] and Snore [24], an extra embedding layer that is not reversible is used to turn the feature vectors into numerical vectors that are not interpretable. To address this issue, we have presented a feature selection-based approach to explain the behavior of knowledge graph embedding models. The results demonstrate that the proposed approach is effective in identifying the most important features for a given embedding model by finding the alignment between feature-based entity representations and the embedding-based entity representations. The findings reveal that KG embeddings do not capture all the information in the neighborhood of entities and that the feature selection process can discard up to 86% of the features without sacrificing the F1 alignment score. Furthermore, our method can be used to explain similarities of entities in the embedding space. We believe that our work offers interesting perspectives for debugging embedding models and makes a further step towards revealing relations between embeddings and propositionalization methods following [21].

While the presented framework provides insights into the behavior of embeddings, it still could be further extended by accounting for embeddings of relations along with entity embeddings, more complex features like longer paths or trees as well as textual and numerical attributes. Despite the advantages of propositionalization for interpretable feature vector construction, it also has limitations. The size of the feature vector naturally scales with the knowledge graph size. Additionally, for larger KGs, the search space for the feature selection algorithm increases, which may lead to scalability issues. Thus, for ongoing and future work, we plan to integrate embeddings of relations into our method and exploit the information coming from the embeddings already at the feature generation stage. This can be achieved by relying on frequent pattern mining methods or rule learning approaches [20, 23], especially those that already account for embeddings during rule construction [16, 45]. We also plan to identify ways for concise representation of feature vectors to adapt for large KGs.

Last but not least, as another ongoing and future work direction we are analyzing the performance of our method on other interpretable embeddings.

Supplemental Material Statement: Source code, datasets and a version of the paper with appendix are available for reproducing the results.[1]

Acknowledgements. We thank anonymous reviews for their useful feedback, and Dr. Blaž Škrlj for helpful comments on the initial version of this work.

References

1. Auer, S., Bizer, C., Kobilarov, G., Lehmann, J., Cyganiak, R., Ives, Z.: DBpedia: a nucleus for a web of open data. In: ISWC/ASWC, pp. 722–735 (2007)
2. Baader, F., Calvanese, D., McGuinness, D., Patel-Schneider, P., Nardi, D., et al.: The Description Logic Handbook: Theory, Implementation and Applications. Cambridge University Press (2003)
3. Betz, P., Meilicke, C., Stuckenschmidt, H.: Adversarial explanations for knowledge graph embeddings. In: Raedt, L.D. (ed.) IJCAI 2022, pp. 2820–2826 (2022)
4. Bhatt, U., Xiang, A., Shubham Sharma, t.: Explainable machine learning in deployment. In: FAT* 2020, pp. 648–657 (2020)
5. Bollacker, K., Evans, C., Paritosh, P., Sturge, T., Taylor, J.: Freebase: a collaboratively created graph database for structuring human knowledge. In: SIGMOD 2008, pp. 1247–1250 (2008)
6. Bordes, A., Usunier, N., García-Durán, A., Weston, J., Yakhnenko, O.: Translating embeddings for modeling multi-relational data. In: NeurIPs, pp. 2787–2795 (2013)
7. Chandrahas, Sengupta, T., Pragadeesh, C., Talukdar, P.P.: Inducing interpretability in knowledge graph embeddings. In: Bhattacharyya, P., Sharma, D.M., Sangal, R. (eds.) ICON 2020, pp. 70–75 (2020)
8. Cheng, W., Kasneci, G., Graepel, T., Stern, D.H., Herbrich, R.: Automated feature generation from structured knowledge. In: CIKM, 2011, pp. 1395–1404 (2011)
9. Costabello, L., et al.: On explainable AI: from theory to motivation, applications and limitations. In: A Tutorial at AAAI 2019 (2019)
10. Cover, T.M., Hart, P.E.: Nearest neighbor pattern classification. IEEE Trans. Inf. Theory **13**(1), 21–27 (1967)
11. Galárraga, L.: Effects of locality and rule language on explanations for knowledge graph embeddings. CoRR abs/2302.06967 (2023)
12. Galkin, M., Denis, E.G., Wu, J., Hamilton, W.L.: NodePiece: compositional and parameter-efficient representations of large knowledge graphs. In: ICLR 2022 (2022)
13. Gusmão, A.C., Correia, A.H.C., Bona, G.D., Cozman, F.G.: Interpreting embedding models of knowledge bases: a pedagogical approach. CoRR abs/1806.09504 (2018)
14. Halliwell, N., Gandon, F., Lécué, F.: User scored evaluation of non-unique explanations for relational graph convolutional network link prediction on knowledge graphs. In: K-CAP, pp. 57–64 (2021)
15. Haykin, S.: Neural Networks: A Comprehensive Foundation (1994)
16. Ho, V.T., Stepanova, D., Gad-Elrab, M.H., Kharlamov, E., Weikum, G.: Rule Learning from Knowledge Graphs Guided by Embedding Models. In: Vrandečić, D., Bontcheva, K., Suárez-Figueroa, M.C., Presutti, V., Celino, I., Sabou, M., Kaffee, L.-A., Simperl, E. (eds.) ISWC 2018. LNCS, vol. 11136, pp. 72–90. Springer, Cham (2018). https://doi.org/10.1007/978-3-030-00671-6_5

---

[1] https://shorturl.at/lGV49.

17. Jain, N., Kalo, J.C., Balke, W.T., Krestel, R.: Do embeddings actually capture knowledge graph semantics? In: ESWC (2021)
18. Kipf, T.N., Welling, M.: Semi-supervised classification with graph convolutional networks. In: ICLR 2017 (2017)
19. Krogel, M., Rawles, S.A., Zelezný, F., Flach, P.A., Lavrac, N., Wrobel, S.: In: ILP 2003, vol. 2835, pp. 197–214 (2003)
20. Lajus, J., Galárraga, L., Suchanek, F.: Fast and exact rule mining with AMIE 3. In: Harth, A., et al. (eds.) ESWC 2020. LNCS, vol. 12123, pp. 36–52. Springer, Cham (2020). https://doi.org/10.1007/978-3-030-49461-2_3
21. Lavrač, N., Škrlj, B., Robnik-Šikonja, M.: Propositionalization and embeddings: two sides of the same coin. Mach. Learn. **109**(7), 1465–1507 (2020)
22. Lawler, I., Sullivan, E.: Model explanation versus model-induced explanation. Found. Sci. **26**, 1049–1074 (2021)
23. Meilicke, C., Chekol, M.W., Ruffinelli, D., Stuckenschmidt, H.: Anytime bottom-up rule learning for knowledge graph completion. In: IJCAI 2019, pp. 3137–3143 (2019)
24. Mežnar, S., Lavrač, N., Škrlj, B.: Snore: scalable unsupervised learning of symbolic node representations. IEEE Access **8**, 212568–212588 (2020)
25. Nandwani, Y., Gupta, A., Agrawal, A., Chauhan, M.S., Singla, P., Mausam: OXKBC: outcome explanation for factorization based knowledge base completion. In: AKBC 2020 (2020)
26. Nguyen, D.Q., Nguyen, T.D., Nguyen, D.Q., Phung, D.Q.: A novel embedding model for knowledge base completion based on convolutional neural network. In: NAACL (2018)
27. Pedregosa, F., et al.: Scikit-learn: machine learning in Python. J. Mach. Learn. Res. **12**, 2825–2830 (2011)
28. Pellegrino, M.A., Altabba, A., Garofalo, M., Ristoski, P., Cochez, M.: GEval: a modular and extensible evaluation framework for graph embedding techniques. In: Harth, A., et al. (eds.) ESWC 2020. LNCS, vol. 12123, pp. 565–582. Springer, Cham (2020). https://doi.org/10.1007/978-3-030-49461-2_33
29. Portisch, J., Heist, N., Paulheim, H.: Knowledge graph embedding for data mining vs. knowledge graph embedding for link prediction - two sides of the same coin? Semant. Web **13**(3), 399–422 (2022)
30. Ristoski, P., Paulheim, H.: A comparison of propositionalization strategies for creating features from linked open data. In: Tiddi, I., d'Aquin, M., Jay, N. (eds.) LOD Workshop at ECML PKDD 2014 (2014)
31. Ristoski, P., Rosati, J., Noia, T.D., Leone, R.D., Paulheim, H.: RDF2Vec: RDF graph embeddings and their applications. Semant. Web **10**(4), 721–752 (2019)
32. Rossi, A., Firmani, D., Merialdo, P., Teofili, T.: Explaining link prediction systems based on knowledge graph embeddings. In: SIGMOD 2022, pp. 2062–2075 (2022)
33. Segal, M., Xiao, Y.: Multivariate random forests. WIREs Data Min. Knowl. Disc. **1**, 80–87 (2011)
34. Shi, B., Weninger, T.: Open-world knowledge graph completion. ArXiv abs/1711.03438 (2018)
35. Steenwinckel, B., Vandewiele, G., Weyns, M., Agozzino, T., Turck, F.D., Ongenae, F.: INK: knowledge graph embeddings for node classification. Data Min. Knowl. Discov. **36**(2), 620–667 (2022)
36. Suchanek, F.M., Kasneci, G., Weikum, G.: Yago: A core of semantic knowledge. In: WWW 2007 (2007)

37. Tang, J., et al.: Computational advances of tumor marker selection and sample classification in cancer proteomics. Comput. Struct. Biotechnol. J. **18**, 2012–2025 (2020)
38. Toutanova, K., Chen, D.: Observed versus latent features for knowledge base and text inference. In: Proceedings of the 3rd Workshop on Continuous Vector Space Models and their Compositionality (2015)
39. Trouillon, T., Welbl, J., Riedel, S., Gaussier, É., Bouchard, G.: Complex embeddings for simple link prediction. In: ICML, pp. 2071–2080 (2016)
40. Vashishth, S., Sanyal, S., Nitin, V., Talukdar, P.P.: Composition-based multi-relational graph convolutional networks. In: ICLR 2020 (2020)
41. Wang, Q., Mao, Z., Wang, B., Guo, L.: Knowledge graph embedding: a survey of approaches and applications. IEEE Trans. Knowl. Data Eng. **29**(12), 2724–2743 (2017)
42. Xu, K., Hu, W., Leskovec, J., Jegelka, S.: How powerful are graph neural networks? CoRR abs/1810.00826 (2018)
43. Yang, B., Yih, W., He, X., Gao, J., Deng, L.: Embedding entities and relations for learning and inference in knowledge bases. In: ICLR (2015)
44. Yogatama, D., Gillick, D., Lazic, N.: Embedding methods for fine grained entity type classification. In: ACL 2015, pp. 291–296 (2015)
45. Zhang, W., et al.: Iteratively learning embeddings and rules for knowledge graph reasoning. In: WWW 2019, pp. 2366–2377 (2019)
46. Zhao, Y., Zhang, A., Xie, R., Liu, K., Wang, X.: Connecting embeddings for knowledge graph entity typing. In: Jurafsky, D., Chai, J., Schluter, N., Tetreault, J.R. (eds.) ACL 2020, pp. 6419–6428 (2020)
47. Zhu, Z., Zhang, Z., Xhonneux, L.A.C., Tang, J.: Neural bellman-ford networks: a general graph neural network framework for link prediction. In: NeurIPS 2021, pp. 29476–29490 (2021)

CapsKG: Enabling Continual Knowledge Integration in Language Models for Automatic Knowledge Graph Completion

Janna Omeliyanenko[(✉)], Albin Zehe, Andreas Hotho, and Daniel Schlör

Julius-Maximilians-University Würzburg, Am Hubland, 97074 Würzburg, Germany
{omeliyanenko,zehe,hotho,daniel.schloer}@informatik.uni-wuerzburg.de

Abstract. Automated completion of knowledge graphs is a popular topic in the Semantic Web community that aims to automatically and continuously integrate new appearing knowledge into knowledge graphs using artificial intelligence. Recently, approaches that leverage implicit knowledge from language models for this task have shown promising results. However, by fine-tuning language models directly to the domain of knowledge graphs, models forget their original language representation and associated knowledge. An existing solution to address this issue is a trainable adapter, which is integrated into a frozen language model to extract the relevant knowledge without altering the model itself. However, this constrains the generalizability to the specific extraction task and by design requires new and independent adapters to be trained for new knowledge extraction tasks. This effectively prevents the model from benefiting from existing knowledge incorporated in previously trained adapters.

In this paper, we propose to combine the benefits of adapters for knowledge graph completion with the idea of integrating capsules, introduced in the field of continual learning. This allows the continuous integration of knowledge into a joint model by sharing and reusing previously trained capsules. We find that our approach outperforms solutions using traditional adapters, while requiring notably fewer parameters for continuous knowledge integration. Moreover, we show that this architecture benefits significantly from knowledge sharing in low-resource situations, outperforming adapter-based models on the task of link prediction.

Keywords: knowledge graph completion · language model · link prediction · continual learning

1 Introduction

Our work is at the intersection of two research areas that have received significant attention in recent years: Knowledge Graphs (KGs) and Language Models (LMs). KGs have gained increasing attention over the past decade and have improved the state of the art in natural language approaches through their integration into

T. R. Payne et al. (Eds.): ISWC 2023, LNCS 14265, pp. 618–636, 2023.
https://doi.org/10.1007/978-3-031-47240-4_33

many downstream tasks such as question answering [31] and sentiment analysis [40]. However, KGs are incomplete and in continuous development. Much work has been done on the prediction of relations missing between two entities, the so-called link prediction. Moreover, over time, new concepts and relation types emerge that need to be captured in KGs, or even give rise to new KGs. On the other hand, powerful pre-trained LMs such as GPT-2 [24] and BERT [9] have been shown to incorporate a certain amount of factual and common sense knowledge that has been automatically extracted from their unstructured training data, without explicit common sense training. Since this knowledge is extracted from unstructured texts and may not be available in structured form, leveraging these models for KG completion by prompting facts with MASK tokens has emerged in recent research. In the past, pre-trained LMs have been successfully used to improve KGs in two directions: (A) to rate the quality of information contained in KGs [20] and (B) to complete given KGs through fine-tuning these models and conducting link prediction [3,11].

Previous approaches to this have usually fine-tuned the entire language model to all relation types in a KGs at once, which has two main drawbacks: First, fine-tuning the entire LM is very resource intensive, due to the large number of parameters contained in the model. Secondly, if a knowledge graph is updated to include new relation types, or if a new knowledge graph is supposed to be included into the model, the fine-tuning process needs to be redone on the full dataset, rather than only updating it with the new information. For the second case, simply performing fine-tuning on the new relations frequently leads to a problem commonly called *catastrophic forgetting* [17], where the model learns about the new relations, but forgets the ones it had previously learned.

In order to solve these problems, we propose to transfer ideas from the areas of *multi-task learning* and *continual learning*, specifically the use of Adapters and Capsules. Both of these approaches aim to make fine-tuning a model to different sub-tasks (in our case, link prediction for different relation types) as efficient as possible. Adapters (cf. Sect. 4.2) keep large parts of the model fixed during fine-tuning, allowing to retain the originally learned information within the LM. However, they do not allow for continuously fine-tuning the knowledge contained in a previously trained adapter when new knowledge becomes available or new aspects and sub-tasks become relevant for which information from the LM shall be extracted. The knowledge contained within the adapter to be retrained or fine-tuned to the new dataset would still be subject to catastrophic forgetting. Since KGs are continuously evolving and new facts emerge or new relations become important that can be queried from the LM, new adapters can be trained on these new facts. However, multiple adapters do not communicate with each other even if their purpose is to extract similar information and they could therefore potentially benefit from each other's training progress. Capsules additionally add the capability of sharing knowledge between different sub-tasks, enabling the model to make use of previously learned information (cf. Sect. 4.2).

We transfer and combine these ideas to the task of link prediction by modelling each relation type in a KG as one sub-task and fine-tuning on them iteratively. This enables both of the desiderata described above: We avoid the high

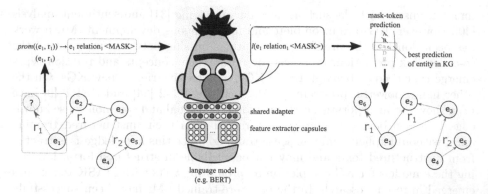

Fig. 1. Overview of our continual relation learning approach within CapsKG. To predict links within a given KG, a query containing a known entity and relation from the KG is obtained and converted to natural language prompt with a <MASK> token. This prompt is forwarded to a relation adapted LM to obtain likely candidate entities. Finally, a filter ensures that predicted candidates correspond to entities contained in the KG. For a detailed view of the relation adapted LM architecture, see Fig. 2.

cost of updating the entire language model and we can update a trained Capsule-based model with new relation types by simply fine-tuning the trained model with the new relations. An overview of the task and our proposed model is depicted in Fig. 1.

Our resulting model CapsKG demonstrates the benefit of applying continual learning to the task of KG link prediction on three common KG datasets, WN18, YAGO3-10, and FB15k. Results show consistent improvement across all datasets, comparable to existing related work [36], while requiring significantly fewer trainable parameters. CapsKG also shows superior results in a low resource setting, when only small amounts of data are available for training, especially when relation types are similar in the sense of sharing similar entities or relations are semantically similar.[1]

The remainder of this work is structured as follows: Section 2 introduces the scientific context of link prediction through LMs, while Sect. 4 describes the chosen adapter-based capsule network in detail. Experiments on multiple datasets are conducted and discussed in Sect. 5. Section 6 concludes the paper.

2   Related Work

The task of completing KGs via link prediction is a well-established field of research within the semantic web community that aims to explore new knowledge by extrapolating from observed existing facts [7]. This task is commonly approached through learning KG representations, e.g. through classical translation-based or tensor factorization-based graph embedding techniques,

---

[1] Our code is available at https://professor-x.de/code-capskg.

such as TransE [33] or RotatE [39], as well as complex neural network architectures [7]. In this context, capsule networks have been used as a specialized architecture that extracts low level features to improve graph embeddings [19,32]. However, their usage in previous work is so far limited to capsules as simple feature extractors. Additionally, within traditional KG representation learning, several works have identified the use of so called continual learning schemes, where architectures are designed to be continuously trained on newly incoming training data without forgetting previously learned information [8,26].

Beyond the use of traditional KG embedding techniques, a recent trend of works has identified the potential of large LMs for link prediction in KGs. In the past, LMs have been effectively utilized for two purposes: testing the quality of existing information contained in KGs [20], and extracting additional facts to complete KGs [11]. Successful applications of LMs for KG link prediction convert factual triples from a KG to natural language either through relation-specific sentence templates or through leveraging available textual descriptions of entities [3,5,11,12,22,27,30,35,37,38]. The resulting textual inputs are then used to fine-tune pre-trained LMs to extract predictions of likely entities.

Wang et al. [31] have further improved this procedure by incorporating adapters, which is an architecture designed to prevent catastrophic forgetting in LMs. In this architecture, additional neuron layers are inserted between the layers of a pre-trained LM for fine-tuning, while all weights belonging to the original LM are frozen to prevent overwriting learned information. This approach allows the LM to retain its learned high quality language representations, but does not allow for the training of multiple adapters that can exchange information and thus support each other.

Pfeiffer et al. [23] address this issue by proposing AdapterFusion, a two stage training process that first trains multiple adapters and afterwards learns a knowledge composition through training data. While this approach is capable of aggregating the knowledge of multiple adapters, it does not allow individual adapters to support each other during training. Moreover, it is not suitable for continual learning, as the entire composition training process has to be repeated when new training data is available.

In contrast to these existing works, our work jointly leverages continual learning strategies, large LMs, and adapters for KG link prediction. This allows for the use of powerful LMs for KG link prediction, while continuously integrating new information into the learned model and facilitating communication of individual adapters during the training process.

3   Task Definition: Link Prediction

KGs are structural representations of real-world factual knowledge in the form of triples (e_1, r, e_2) where e_1 and e_2 represent the head and tail entities describing world objects and r represents a specific relation connecting these two entities, for example (Berlin, CapitalOf, Germany). Although existing KGs such as YAGO and WikiData cover a large portion of factual knowledge, they often suffer from

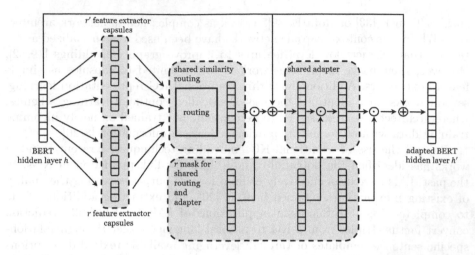

Fig. 2. Continual relation learning adapter showcasing two exemplary relations. The adapter is attached to LM hidden layer h, where relation-specific features are extracted. Feature extractors of a previously trained relation r' (green) may influence the currently trained relation r (orange) through similarity routing. Results are passed through a shared adapter (grey) that is biased through relation-specific masks. Note that most weights in the architecture are contained within the shared layers, leading it to share most trainable weights. (Color figure online)

incompleteness [10,34]. To address this problem, link prediction was introduced that aims to learn a function f that predicts missing relations between entities in a given graph. Given a head entity e_1 and a relation r, the function f predicts the tail entity e_2 that is most likely to be connected via this relation:

$$f_{KG}(e_1, r) \rightarrow e_2 \tag{1}$$

4   Methodology

In this chapter, we describe in detail the architecture we have chosen to solve the link prediction task by continuously adapting an LM to the different knowledge sub-tasks. The architecture is also illustrated in Fig. 2.

4.1   Base Model: LM for Link Prediction

For our base model, we follow the idea of prompting a pre-trained LM for the task of link prediction [3,22]. To access the model's knowledge, facts are converted into a natural language representation in the form of a sequence of tokens, where the desired unit of information is omitted or masked and the model is prompted to complete the given text sequence. For example, given a tuple (Berlin, CapitalOf), we transform the tuple into the following (masked) sentence: "Berlin is a capital of <MASK>." This sentence is then input to the LM, which predicts the most likely token for <MASK> – in this case Germany. Note that the quality of the extracted information strongly depends on the prompt sentence, and therefore the generation of well-performing prompts has been focus of several scientific works [4,13,25]. More formally, given a function *prom* that maps tuples (e_1, r) to a natural language representation prompt p, and a pre-trained LM l, prompting for link prediction is defined as follows:

$$prom((e_1, r)) \rightarrow p, \qquad l(p) \rightarrow e_2 \qquad (2)$$

In the example above, this becomes $prom((\texttt{Berlin}, \texttt{CapitalOf})) \rightarrow$ "Berlin is a capital of <MASK>." $=: p$, and $l(p) \rightarrow$ Germany.

We fine-tune this model to the task of link prediction by converting all tuples in the train set of a dataset (cf. Sect. 5.1) to natural language sentences and performing regular masked LM training. However, this approach comes with the disadvantage that the model is prone to catastrophic forgetting, thereby potentially losing its generalizability and language modeling performance, as well as missing the possibility of extending the trained model with additional relation types.

4.2   Continual Learning for Link Prediction

Continual learning [21] studies this problem of avoiding catastrophic forgetting, i.e., the general ability of the system to maintain its performance in a previously learned task or domain without access to the previous training data while learning a new task. This becomes relevant to incorporating LMs for KG completion from two perspectives. First, the knowledge that the LM has learned during its pre-training and training to perform natural language modeling should be retained and not forgotten, although the specific domain of the KG including the different relations, relevant entities and grammar cover only a very small subset of the previously acquired knowledge. Second, the KGs themselves continuously expand. This means that by the integration of new entities or relations, the previously learned KG knowledge might also become subject to catastrophic forgetting.

One solution to address both issues following the idea of continual learning is the adapter architecture [31]. This architecture has been proven useful as it allows to freeze the underlying LM while training new knowledge into specific adapter layers, added to the original architecture. Furthermore, new adapters can be added for new relations and facts to be learned without altering the weights of other adapters.

Basic Adapter. To be precise, the adapter [31] is a small set of additional trainable neural layers that are inserted between the layers of a pre-trained base LM l to learn new features relevant for a new task, for example, link prediction for a new relation type r. During training, the base model is frozen and only the parameters of the adapter are trainable. In our work, following [15], the adapter consists of two fully connected layers, which are inserted into each transformer layer in our LM. The input to the adapter is the output of the intermediate layer $h^{(r)} \in \mathbb{R}^{d_s \times d_e}$ of the base model, with the sequence length d_s and the dimension of the base model's hidden state output d_e. Adapter layers map the input to an intermediate adapter dimensionality free of choice and back to the hidden state space of the model. Finally, the intermediate output of the original base model is added via skip connections, where f_c and f_d are fully connected layers by

$$h'^{(r)} = f_c(f_d(h^{(r)}))) + h^{(r)}. \tag{3}$$

Shared Adapter. In a basic adapter architecture, a new adapter is added for each type of relation. With a growing number of relations, this highly increases the number of trainable parameters, as for each relation a separate adapter with independent weights is provided. Inspired by [15], we propose to share the adapter layers for all relation types making the model more parameter efficient with increasing number of relations. To prevent catastrophic forgetting that may occur when continuously training adapter layers with new data, a masking procedure is introduced into the adapter. For each relation r, a mask $m^{(r)}$ with same dimensionality as each adapter layer is calculated from relation embeddings $e^{(r)}$ based on the task's id. These relation embeddings are then converted to a pseudo-gating function through a Sigmoid activation and a scale hyper-parameter s as follows:

$$m^{(r)} = \sigma(se^{(r)}) \tag{4}$$

The hyper-parameter s is chosen as positive scalar that gradually increases in value to $\gg 1$ during training, forcing the learned mask $m^{(r)}$ to contain values closer to 0 or 1. The resulting pseudo-binary masks $m_d^{(r)}$ and $m_c^{(r)}$ for the adapter layers f_c and f_d are multiplied element-wise with the respective shared adapter layer, giving:

$$h'^{(r)} = f_c(f_d(h^{(r)}) \otimes m_d^{(r)}) \otimes m_c^{(r)} + h^{(r)} \tag{5}$$

As we observe that the pseudo-gate function commonly produces non binary masks that still lead to catastrophic forgetting, we additionally follow [14] and binarize all masks for a sub-task once this sub-task has been fully trained.

$$m_{eval}^{(r)} = \begin{cases} 1 & \text{if } \sigma(se^{(r)}) > 0.5 \\ 0 & \text{otherwise.} \end{cases} \tag{6}$$

To prevent the gradient flow through neurons that were already used by previously learned tasks, or in this case relation types, the overall use of neurons by previous task masks is calculated by

$$m^{(prev)} = \text{MaxPool}(\{m_{eval}^{(r')}, r' \in \{\text{previously trained } r\}\}) \tag{7}$$

and applied to the gradients $g^{(r)}$ to limit the updates on these neurons during backpropagation through

$$g'^{(r)} = g^{(r)} \otimes (1 - m^{(prev)}). \tag{8}$$

As we calculate previous masks $m^{(prev)}$ for gradient gating from these binarized masks, this allows trained relations to truly reserve neurons within the adapter preventing any gradient updates that could cause forgetting. Conversely, other relations may still utilize reserved neurons during the forward pass, allowing them to use shared information of previously learned relations while preventing problematic updates.

As trained relations are capable of reserving neurons through the masks which prevents them from being trained by new relations, sparse masks are required to prevent a single relation from occupying the entire architecture. To achieve sparse masks, a regularization term is added to the loss function $\mathcal{L}$, which regularizes the values of $m^{(r)}$ during training depending on the number of neurons that are not already occupied by previously trained relations:

$$\mathcal{L}' = \mathcal{L} + \lambda \cdot \frac{\|m^{(r)}\|_1}{d_m - \|m^{(r)}_{eval}\|_1}, \tag{9}$$

where d_m denotes the dimensionality of $m^{(r)}$ and λ is a weighting hyperparameter.

To summarize, this shared adapter architecture allows parameter efficient continual learning and the utilization of weights from previously learned relations if they are helpful without risking catastrophic forgetting as these weights are not changed during back-propagation. This idea is further extended by capsules as low-level feature extractors, which instead of masking rely on a routing mechanism. This approach brings the flexibility to incorporate additional capsules in a trained model when required for continual learning.

Relation Specific Capsules with Knowledge Transfer. To enable further information transfer and reuse of previously learned knowledge between relation types, we apply a capsule architecture to train low-level feature extractors with a similarity based routing to share extractors between relation types [15]. Relation specific capsules consist of three components: relation capsule layer, transfer capsule layer and a transfer routing mechanism. Relation-specific extractor capsules f_i in the relation capsule layer are used as low-level feature extractors that learn relation-relevant information from intermediate layers of a given base model through

$$p_i^{(r)} = f_i(h^{(r)}), \tag{10}$$

parameterized as small fully connected layers. Capsules in the transfer capsule layer are used to represent transferable features extracted by relation specific capsules. A special routing mechanism consisting of several steps is used to transfer features between lower layer relation capsules and higher layer transfer capsules. To share the extracted features between relation capsule $p_i^{(r)}$ and a transfer capsule $t_j^{(r)}$, a pre-routing vector is generated that extracts relevant features from relation capsule i for transfer capsule j as

$$u_{j|i}^{(r)} = W_{ij}p_i^{(r)}, \tag{11}$$

where $W_{ij} \in \mathbb{R}^{d_c \times d_k}$ is a transformation matrix learned during training, with d_c denoting the dimension of relation capsule $p_i^{(r)}$ and d_k denoting the dimension of transfer capsule $t_j^{(r)}$.

In order to transfer useful knowledge between relation types, the similarity between relation types i and the relation type r is estimated using multiple convolution layers that form a learned similarity estimator comparing the relation capsules of i and r:

$$q_{j|r}^{(r)} = \mathrm{MaxPool}(\mathrm{ReLU}(u_{j|r}^{(r)} * W_q + b_q)) \tag{12}$$

$$a_{j|i}^{(r)} = \mathrm{MaxPool}(\mathrm{ReLU}(u_{j|i}^{(r)} * W_a + f_a(q_{j|r}^{(r)}) + b_a)) \tag{13}$$

Convolutions over $u_{j|r}$ and $u_{j|i}$ extract the relevant features of the relation type r and i respectively. The similarity score $a_{j|i}^{(r)}$ is calculated in Eq. (13), where f_a is a linear layer for matching the dimensions of $q_{j|r}^{(r)}$ and $u_{j|i}^{(r)}$, $b_a, b_q \in \mathbb{R}$ are biases, $W_a, W_q \in \mathbb{R}^{d_e \times d_\omega}$ convolution filters and d_ω denotes the window size.

To keep knowledge exchange constrained to only similar relation types, a binary differentiable gating function is calculated using convolution with Gumbel Softmax

$$\delta_{j|r}^{(r)} = \mathrm{Gumbel\_softmax}(a_{j|i}^{(r)} * W_\delta + b_\delta), \tag{14}$$

resulting in a gating function for similar tasks. The overall output is obtained by aggregating over the element-wise product of all similar extractor capsules with their corresponding learned similarities to the relation that is currently trained by

$$v_j^{(r)} = \sum_{i=1|\delta_{i|j}^{(r)}=1}^{n+1} v_{j|i}^{\mathrm{tran}(r)}, \qquad v_{j|i}^{\mathrm{tran}(r)} = a_{j|i}^{(r)} \otimes u_{j|i}^{(r)} \tag{15}$$

with $\delta_{j|r}^{(r)} \in \{0: \text{disconnected}, 1: \text{connected}\}$. Note that this gating allows for gradient updates to apply to the extractor capsules of previously learned relation types if similarity to the current relation type is found by the Gumbel Softmax, thus facilitating a backward knowledge transfer to previously trained relation types. We additionally investigate model performance when preventing these updates even on similar relations following [15], allowing only forward knowledge transfer from previously learned relations to the new relations.

The generated output $v^{(r)}$ is forwarded through a fully connected layer f_b to match the base model's hidden dimension. The base model's intermediate output $h^{(r)}$ is added again through a skip connection, giving

$$v'^{(r)} = f_b(v^{(r)}) + h^{(r)}. \tag{16}$$

Finally, $v'^{(r)}$ contains the aggregated relation-specific information of all extractor capsules and is given as input to the shared adapter.

Table 1. Dataset characteristics of the used link prediction datasets after filtering according to Sect. 5.1.

dataset	relation types	entities	train triples	dev triples	test triples	total
WN18	5	23324	27045	9017	9018	45080
YAGO	8	92991	75774	25260	25262	126296
FB15k	18	10754	38178	12734	12736	63648

5   Experiments

In the following, we showcase the introduced architecture on three KG link prediction datasets.

5.1   Datasets

For our experiments, we use three established KG datasets commonly used in link prediction settings, namely (1) the WN18 dataset [2] with triples from the WordNet KG, (2) the YAGO3-10 dataset [18, 29] (called YAGO from hereon) with triples from the YAGO KG, and (3) the FB15k dataset [28] that contains data from the FreeBase KG. WN18 has a strict hierarchical structure, with most triples representing the hyponym and hypernym relation. YAGO is a subset of YAGO3, with most triples covering descriptive factual information about people, including birthplace, nationality, and more. FB15k is a subset of FreeBase that contain a rich collection of factual information about a diverse range of subjects including movies, actors, people, places and more.

Following previous work that prompts LMs through the use of entity masking, we remove all triples from the datasets where the target entity is (1) larger than one token or (2) not known within the LM's vocabulary [6,11,22]. As we evaluate the distinct relations within the dataset separately, which results in very small and unbalanced splits for some relations after filtering, we join the original train, development, and test splits to one dataset, remove all relations that contain less than 1200 triples, and split the remaining relations back into train, development, and test sets of 60%, 20%, and 20% respectively. The statistics of the resulting datasets can be found in Table 1.

5.2   Experimental Setup

In this section, we describe our evaluation setup, including the sentence generation, evaluation metrics, methods that we evaluated, as well as hyperparameters used.

Sentence Generation. To convert the KG triples into natural language (*prom* in Eq. (2)), we use the sentence templates of [22] where applicable and design sentence templates in the same style for relations not covered by their work. The full list of used templates is listed in the repository.

Evaluation Metric. To evaluate link prediction performance of the investigated models, we use the established hits at one accuracy (Hits@1), which corresponds to the ratio of exact matches between prediction and correct KG entity. Since there may be multiple correct completions e_2 for a given tuple (e_1, r), we follow [11] and filter out all correct alternative entities from the model prediction to avoid penalizing the models for the correct answers that differ from the current label entity. More formally, let $P = l(prom(e_1, r))$ be the probability distribution over tokens returned by the LM l. We count the prediction as correct if

$$e_2 = argmax_e \{P(e) \mid (e_1, r, e) \notin (\text{train} \cup \text{test}) \backslash \{(e_1, r, e_2)\} \}. \quad (17)$$

Scores are always reported as averages over all sub-tasks. To prevent results being skewed by statistical fluctuation, we repeat all experiments with 5 random seeds and report means and standard deviations of all metrics.

Models. While the general adapter framework is LM agnostic, we use a pre-trained BERT model in this experimental setup due to its public availability, computational efficiency, and established use within the domain of KG completion [5,11]. We compare the following models in our experiments:

BERT$_{\text{frozen}}$. A BERT base model that is prompted without any fine tuning.

BERT. An independent BERT base model is trained and evaluated for each relation type [11].

BERT-CL. A BERT base model is iteratively trained for all relation types and evaluated once at the end.

Adapter. An independent BERT base model with frozen parameters and one trainable Adapter is trained and evaluated for each relation type [9,31].

Adapter-CL. A frozen BERT base model with one trainable Adapter is iteratively trained for all relation types and evaluated once at the end.

Table 2. Number of trainable model parameters for the YAGO, WN18, and FB15k data. The number of parameters depends on the number of relation types in the dataset, since in the non-CL settings, a separate model is trained for each relation type, while in the CL settings, additional Capsules are added to the model for each relation type.

Dataset	Model	specific per r (M)	shared across r (M)	total (M)
WN18	BERT	301.99	0.00	1,509.95
	Adapter	73.83	0.00	369.16
	CapsKG	0.16	75.53	76.33
YAGO	BERT	301.99	0.00	2,415.92
	Adapter	73.83	0.00	590.65
	CapsKG	0.16	75.53	76.81
FB15k	BERT	301.99	0.00	5,435.83
	Adapter	73.83	0.00	1,328.96
	CapsKG	0.16	75.53	78.41

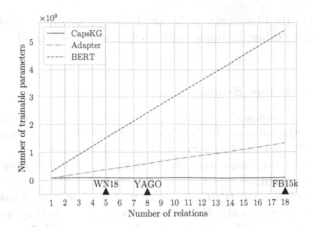

Fig. 3. Visualization showing trainable parameters in billions for BERT, Adapter and CapsKG on an increasing numbers of relations, marking the datasets used in this study. CapsKG scales very conservatively due to the large numbers of shared parameters.

CapsKG$_{forward}$. The full CapsKG model (Sect. 4.2) is iteratively trained for all relation types and evaluated once at the end, *not* allowing the capsules for previous relation types to be updated even if similarity to the current relation type is given by the Gumbel Softmax.

CapsKG$_{backward}$. The full CapsKG model (Sect. 4.2) is iteratively trained for all relation types and evaluated once at the end, allowing the capsules for previous similar relation types to be updated.

In BERT and BERT-CL, the entire model is updated during fine-tuning, leading to a very expensive training process and very high capacity of the model. In Adapter and Adapter-CL, the number of trained parameters is greatly reduced, leading to a more efficient training process. The resulting number of trainable parameters of used models on all datasets is reported in Table 2. We additionally visualize the increase in trainable parameters for each model with increasing numbers of relations in Fig. 3. The CapsKG-variations use Capsules to enable the model to share knowledge between the different relation types and simultaneously avoid catastrophic forgetting. Note that CapsKG still requires increasing numbers of trainable parameters when adding new relations, which is required to prevent catastrophic forgetting [31]. Nevertheless, the increase in trainable parameters per relation is vastly reduced in CapsKG in comparison to other models, due to the efficient parameter sharing.

Model Hyperparameters. For the adapter and capsule models, we follow the setup of [15]. We use an adapter size of 2000, adding adapter modules before each layer normalization within the 12 BERT transformer layers. Knowledge extractor capsules are set to 3 extractor capsules of hidden size 3 per relation. Training was carried out on a single A100 GPU for 30 epochs using a regularization parameter

λ (cf. Eq. (9)) of 10, a batch size of 64, and learning rate of 5e−5 using the Adam optimizer [16], choosing the model with lowest validation loss after training each relation.

5.3 Link Prediction Evaluation

We evaluate our proposed CapsKG architecture on a link prediction task for three different KG datasets, WN18, YAGO, and FB15k to systematically investigate its benefit compared to previous architectures.

The results of this comparison on all three datasets are shown in Table 3, measured through Hits@1 accuracy on the test set.

The first section with BERT$_{frozen}$ shows that prompting a pre-trained LM without any training on the KG data results in poor performance across all datasets. Due to the significantly lower performance of BERT$_{frozen}$ compared to all other approaches, we omit this baseline in the following experiments.

The second section comprises BERT and Adapter and represents the resource intensive training of one individual model per relation. As these models are trained independently by design, they denote the performance achievable without leveraging inter-relation dependencies and are evaluated without the threat of catastrophic forgetting. In comparison to BERT, the Adapter-based model performs slightly better on all datasets, despite its significantly lower number of trainable parameters (cf. Table 2). This highlights the potential of the general model decision to freeze the underlying LM and incorporate additional trainable layers, even if no continual learning setting with the danger of catastrophic forgetting is given.

The third block of our results contains all models trained in a continual learning setting, including both variants of our CapsKG. By iteratively incorporating new relations and presenting the respective training data to the model, this setting is prone to catastrophic forgetting. For both of the architectures not specifically optimized for continual learning, training in the continual learning setting as BERT-CL and Adapter-CL shows the severe impact of catastrophic

Table 3. Results for link prediction on WN18, YAGO, and FB15k with 5 random seeds, reporting mean and standard deviation of Hits@1 performance.

Model/Dataset	WN18	YAGO	FB15k
BERT$_{frozen}$	10.7 ± 0.0	27.0 ± 0.0	5.5 ± 0.0
BERT	25.8 ± 0.5	48.0 ± 0.1	34.7 ± 0.7
Adapter	26.4 ± 0.5	48.7 ± 0.4	35.6 ± 0.2
BERT-CL	20.2 ± 1.2	40.4 ± 4.0	11.4 ± 3.2
Adapter-CL	18.4 ± 1.2	41.5 ± 0.7	16.3 ± 1.4
CapsKG$_{forward}$	$\mathbf{27.4 \pm 0.4}$	49.4 ± 0.3	$\mathbf{36.1 \pm 0.3}$
CapsKG$_{backward}$	27.2 ± 0.4	$\mathbf{49.5 \pm 0.3}$	34.9 ± 0.3

forgetting as their performance is impaired significantly for all datasets, occasionally losing more than half of their prediction power. An in-depth analysis of the training course shows that they do indeed suffer from catastrophic forgetting, as the relation most recently learned shows good performance, while the performance of previously learned relations deteriorates over time. The FB15k dataset especially suffers from this forgetting effect, which may be attributed to its large number of different relation types that all have the potential to disrupt trained knowledge of previous relation types. BERT-CL achieves a very low performance on this dataset due to only retaining good prediction accuracy on the relation type trained last, entirely failing to predict previous relation types. Adapter-CL manages to retain more information compared to the BERT-CL model on the FB15k dataset, but still performs significantly worse in this continual learning scenario.

Our CapsKG model, however, performs considerably better in the continual learning setting, strongly outperforming the other approaches throughout all datasets. Additionally, our CapsKG model even consistently outperforms the non-continual models that train on individual relations. This can be attributed to the internal structures that route and reuse previously learned low-level feature extractors. The performance gain, even in comparison to the much more parameter-intensive BERT and Adapter models (cf. Table 2), suggests that iterative training emphasizes the sharing of knowledge from different but related relations reminiscent of the concept of curriculum learning [1].

Finally, we compare both variants of CapsKG, $CapsKG_{forward}$ that allows only to use parameters of previously learned relation types and $CapsKG_{backward}$ that allows to update the model parameters of knowledge capsules from previously trained relation types. One can observe that both models perform comparably with $CapsKG_{forward}$ slightly outperforming $CapsKG_{backward}$ which might be a consequence of the significantly larger number of relation types in FB15k accumulating disturbance on early learned relations over the course of the training.

Overall our results highlight the superior performance of the CapsKG architecture on all link prediction datasets.

5.4   Low Resource Evaluation

Since [15] found the capsule architecture to be more efficient in low-resource scenarios where shared knowledge may be used to overcome the limited training data, we further evaluate the model's performance with only a limited number of training instances for each relation. This is particularly relevant for the task of KG-completion, as some of the knowledge graph (KG) relations are very sparse.

To evaluate the performance of our model in a low-resource setting, we build low-resource subsets of the datasets used in the previous experiment by reducing the number of training samples to only 200 triples per relation. We follow the architectural parameters and experimental setup of our previous experiments, other than that we set the regularization parameter λ to a large number of 2000, as we observe that the limited number of training samples severely impedes the

Table 4. Link prediction on WN18, YAGO, and FB15k using only 200 triples for training each relation, repeated with 5 seeds and reporting mean and standard deviation of Hits@1 performance.

Model/Dataset	$WN18_{200}$	$YAGO_{200}$	$FB15k_{200}$
BERT	19.1 ± 0.5	45.8 ± 0.6	30.7 ± 0.5
Adapter	18.8 ± 0.2	44.9 ± 0.7	32.2 ± 0.6
BERT-CL	13.1 ± 0.5	29.5 ± 6.5	5.5 ± 0.0
Adapter-CL	13.6 ± 0.4	26.1 ± 1.1	6.7 ± 1.1
$CapsKG_{forward}$	$\mathbf{19.7 \pm 0.4}$	$\mathbf{46.4 \pm 0.2}$	$\mathbf{33.7 \pm 0.1}$
$CapsKG_{backward}$	19.1 ± 0.4	46.3 ± 0.2	32.2 ± 0.2

regularization of weight sharing (cf. Eq. (9)) within CapsKG. We train the model on a single RTX 2080 ti using a batch size of 16.

The results of this low resource evaluation are summarized in Table 4. CapsKG outperforms BERT and Adapter on all datasets, while requiring fewer parameters. Note that both architectures have been explicitly fine-tuned for each relation individually. This suggests that the parameter sharing and routing between similar feature extractor capsules allows the model to access knowledge extracted by previously trained relations that a model trained individually per relation cannot leverage.

The remarkably lower performances for BERT-CL and Adapter-CL suggest, that even though the number of training samples has been reduced by magnitudes, the effect of catastrophic forgetting is not mitigated in this setting, such that this effect outweighs the lower number of training samples overall.

5.5   Topic Evaluation

To verify our hypothesis that relation types learned with CapsKG iteratively profit from previously learned similar relations, we conduct a topic evaluation experiment in the low-resource setting from Sect. 5.4. We therefore sample four topic groups from the FreeBase hierarchy, *people*, *music*, *sport*, and *film*, each consisting of more than one relation type, topically related. The goal is to examine to what extent CapsKG based models benefit from topically similar relations while *similar* can be understood in terms of overlap of similar entity pairs and semantics from the LM. The results of the experiments are shown in Table 5 and support our hypothesis, as CapsKG outperforms all other models. The largest improvement is observed in the smallest topic group consisting of only two relation types which are the direct inverse relations and thus highly relevant for each other: location/contains and location/containedby. Our experiment shows that, when considering topic-specific similar relations, our model can leverage knowledge from prior relations for all topic groups, showing its potential in the low-resource continual learning setting.

Table 5. Link prediction on FB15k relations grouped by topic according to the KG relation types, each with 5 random seeds.

Model/Topic	people	music	location	film
BERT	41.1 ± 1.6	20.7 ± 1.3	48.0 ± 1.2	36.4 ± 1.6
Adapter	42.4 ± 0.7	23.4 ± 0.7	47.4 ± 0.4	37.9 ± 0.6
CapsKG-Forward	43.8 ± 0.4	$\mathbf{24.2 \pm 0.3}$	50.8 ± 0.4	$\mathbf{38.8 \pm 0.5}$
CapsKG-Backward	$\mathbf{44.0 \pm 0.3}$	22.9 ± 0.8	$\mathbf{50.9 \pm 0.4}$	38.7 ± 0.2

6 Conclusion

In this work, we have proposed to transfer architectures from continual learning to KG completion using LMs, and demonstrated the performance of an Adapter- and Capsule-based architecture on the task of link prediction in KGs in CapsKG. CapsKG combines the benefits of adapters for the extraction of knowledge from LMs with capsules as feature extractors to perform link prediction in KGs in a continual learning scenario. Our experiments on three common KG datasets, WN18, YAGO, and FB15k demonstrate the benefit of the proposed architecture, outperforming even fine-tuned BERT that has 20 to 70 times more trainable parameters and Adapters that have 5 to 17 times more trainable parameters. We have also shown that our CapsKG model maintains and partially even improves in performance when trained in a continual learning scenario, while other models show the devastating behavior of catastrophic forgetting. Our low-resource experiment demonstrates the benefit of knowledge sharing across different sub-tasks, especially when only few training instances per sub-task are available.

Our findings suggest that our proposed model-agnostic architecture allows continual learning for KG completion using LMs even in low resource scenarios, making it a promising foundation for future research in the Semantic Web community. In our consecutive research, we plan to systematically evaluate a variety of base-LMs with CapsKG on top, to examine their potential for generic KG completion as well as link prediction with specific domain adapted LMs in their particular domain, for example for medical KGs. Moreover, different approaches to precisely model similarity for the low-level feature extraction capsules and their routing mechanism is an interesting field for future work as well.

Supplemental Material Statement: Source code for CapsKG and used baselines is available at https://professor-x.de/code-capskg. The used datasets are publicly available at https://everest.hds.utc.fr/doku.php?id=en:transe for both WN18 and FB15k, and at https://pykeen.readthedocs.io/ for YAGO3-10.

References

1. Bengio, Y., Louradour, J., Collobert, R., Weston, J.: Curriculum learning. In: Proceedings of the 26th Annual International Conference on Machine Learning, pp. 41–48 (2009)
2. Bordes, A., Usunier, N., Garcia-Duran, A., Weston, J., Yakhnenko, O.: Translating embeddings for modeling multi-relational data. In: Advances in Neural Information Processing Systems, vol. 26. Curran Associates, Inc. (2013)
3. Bosselut, A., Rashkin, H., Sap, M., Malaviya, C., Celikyilmaz, A., Choi, Y.: COMET: commonsense transformers for automatic knowledge graph construction. In: Proceedings of the 57th Annual Meeting of the Association for Computational Linguistics, pp. 4762–4779. Association for Computational Linguistics, Florence, Italy, July 2019
4. Bouraoui, Z., Camacho-Collados, J., Schockaert, S.: Inducing relational knowledge from BERT. In: Proceedings of the AAAI Conference on Artificial Intelligence, vol. 34, pp. 7456–7463 (2020)
5. Brayne, A., Wiatrak, M., Corneil, D.: On masked language models for contextual link prediction. In: Proceedings of Deep Learning Inside Out (DeeLIO 2022): The 3rd Workshop on Knowledge Extraction and Integration for Deep Learning Architectures, pp. 87–99. Association for Computational Linguistics, Dublin, Ireland and Online, May 2022
6. Cao, B., et al.: Knowledgeable or educated guess? Revisiting language models as knowledge bases, June 2021
7. Dai, Y., Wang, S., Xiong, N.N., Guo, W.: A survey on knowledge graph embedding: approaches, applications and benchmarks. Electronics $9(5)$, 750 (2020)
8. Daruna, A., Gupta, M., Sridharan, M., Chernova, S.: Continual learning of knowledge graph embeddings. IEEE Rob. Autom. Lett. $6(2)$, 1128–1135 (2021)
9. Devlin, J., Chang, M.W., Lee, K., Toutanova, K.: BERT: pre-training of deep bidirectional transformers for language understanding, May 2019
10. Ebisu, T., Ichise, R.: TorusE: knowledge graph embedding on a lie group. In: Proceedings of the AAAI Conference on Artificial Intelligence, vol. 32 (2018)
11. Fichtel, L., Kalo, J.C., Balke, W.T.: Prompt tuning or fine-tuning - investigating relational knowledge in pre-trained language models. In: 3rd Conference on Automated Knowledge Base Construction, September 2021
12. Hao, S., et al.: BertNet: harvesting knowledge graphs from pretrained language models, December 2022
13. Haviv, A., Berant, J., Globerson, A.: BERTese: learning to speak to BERT. arXiv preprint arXiv:2103.05327 (2021)
14. Ke, Z., Lin, H., Shao, Y., Xu, H., Shu, L., Liu, B.: Continual training of language models for few-shot learning. arXiv preprint arXiv:2210.05549 (2022)
15. Ke, Z., Liu, B., Ma, N., Xu, H., Shu, L.: Achieving forgetting prevention and knowledge transfer in continual learning. In: Advances in Neural Information Processing Systems, vol. 34, pp. 22443–22456. Curran Associates, Inc. (2021)
16. Kingma, D.P., Ba, J.: Adam: a method for stochastic optimization, December 2014
17. Kirkpatrick, J., et al.: Overcoming catastrophic forgetting in neural networks. Proc. Natl. Acad. Sci. $114(13)$, 3521–3526 (2017)
18. Mahdisoltani, F., Biega, J., Suchanek, F.M.: YAGO3: a knowledge base from multilingual Wikipedias (2016)

19. Nguyen, D.Q., Vu, T., Nguyen, T.D., Nguyen, D.Q., Phung, D.: A capsule network-based embedding model for knowledge graph completion and search personalization. In: Proceedings of the 2019 Conference of the North American Chapter of the Association for Computational Linguistics: Human Language Technologies, Volume 1 (Long and Short Papers), pp. 2180–2189. Association for Computational Linguistics, Minneapolis, Minnesota, June 2019

20. Omeliyanenko, J., Zehe, A., Hettinger, L., Hotho, A.: LM4KG: improving common sense knowledge graphs with language models. In: Pan, J.Z., et al. (eds.) ISWC 2020. LNCS, vol. 12506, pp. 456–473. Springer, Cham (2020). https://doi.org/10.1007/978-3-030-62419-4_26

21. Parisi, G.I., Kemker, R., Part, J.L., Kanan, C., Wermter, S.: Continual lifelong learning with neural networks: a review. Neural Netw. **113**, 54–71 (2019)

22. Petroni, F., et al.: Language models as knowledge bases? September 2019

23. Pfeiffer, J., Kamath, A., Rücklé, A., Cho, K., Gurevych, I.: AdapterFusion: non-destructive task composition for transfer learning, January 2021

24. Radford, A., Wu, J., Child, R., Luan, D., Amodei, D., Sutskever, I.: Language models are unsupervised multitask learners (2019)

25. Shin, T., Razeghi, Y., Logan IV, R.L., Wallace, E., Singh, S.: AutoPrompt: eliciting knowledge from language models with automatically generated prompts. arXiv preprint arXiv:2010.15980 (2020)

26. Song, H.J., Park, S.B.: Enriching translation-based knowledge graph embeddings through continual learning. IEEE Access **6**, 60489–60497 (2018)

27. Teru, K.K., Denis, E., Hamilton, W.L.: Inductive relation prediction by subgraph reasoning, February 2020

28. Toutanova, K., Chen, D.: Observed versus latent features for knowledge base and text inference. In: Proceedings of the 3rd Workshop on Continuous Vector Space Models and Their Compositionality, pp. 57–66. Association for Computational Linguistics, Beijing, China, July 2015

29. Tran, H.N., Takasu, A.: MEIM: multi-partition embedding interaction beyond block term format for efficient and expressive link prediction, October 2022

30. Wang, B., Shen, T., Long, G., Zhou, T., Wang, Y., Chang, Y.: Structure-augmented text representation learning for efficient knowledge graph completion. In: Proceedings of the Web Conference 2021, pp. 1737–1748. ACM, Ljubljana Slovenia, April 2021

31. Wang, R., et al.: K-adapter: infusing knowledge into pre-trained models with adapters, December 2020

32. Wang, Y., Xiao, W., Tan, Z., Zhao, X.: Caps-OWKG: a capsule network model for open-world knowledge graph. Int. J. Mach. Learn. Cybern. **12**(6), 1627–1637 (2021)

33. Wang, Z., Zhang, J., Feng, J., Chen, Z.: Knowledge graph embedding by translating on hyperplanes. In: Proceedings of the AAAI Conference on Artificial Intelligence, vol. 28, no. 1, June 2014

34. West, R., Gabrilovich, E., Murphy, K., Sun, S., Gupta, R., Lin, D.: Knowledge base completion via search-based question answering. In: Proceedings of the 23rd International Conference on World Wide Web, pp. 515–526 (2014)

35. Yao, L., Mao, C., Luo, Y.: KG-BERT: BERT for knowledge graph completion, September 2019

36. Youn, J., Tagkopoulos, I.: KGLM: integrating knowledge graph structure in language models for link prediction. arXiv preprint arXiv:2211.02744 (2022)

37. Youn, J., Tagkopoulos, I.: KGLM: integrating knowledge graph structure in language models for link prediction, November 2022

38. Zha, H., Chen, Z., Yan, X.: Inductive relation prediction by BERT. In: Proceedings of the AAAI Conference on Artificial Intelligence, vol. 36, no. 5, pp. 5923–5931 (2022)
39. Zhang, S., Tay, Y., Yao, L., Liu, Q.: Quaternion knowledge graph embeddings. In: Advances in Neural Information Processing Systems, vol. 32. Curran Associates, Inc. (2019)
40. Zhao, A., Yu, Y.: Knowledge-enabled BERT for aspect-based sentiment analysis. Knowl.-Based Syst. **227**, 107220 (2021)

Author Index

A

Ahrabian, Kian I-271
Aimonier-Davat, Julien II-285
Aïssaoui, François II-325
Akrami, Farahnaz II-113
Akter, Mst. Mahfuja I-388
Alam, Mirza Mohtashim I-388
Angioni, Simone II-400
Archer, Dave II-345
Arenas-Guerrero, Julián II-152
Ascencion Arevalo, Kiara M. II-3
Asprino, Luigi I-197
Auer, Sören I-408
Aung, Linn II-94
Austin, Allison I-579

B

Babaei Giglou, Hamed I-408
Bagchi, Sugato I-502
Bai, Quan I-234
Bernasconi, Eleonora II-435
Berrío, Cristian I-80
Birukou, Aliaksandr II-400
Blockeel, Hendrik I-599
Blum, Ralph II-3
Bolle, Sébastien II-325
Bouazzouni, Syphax II-38
Boyer, Fabienne II-325
Bryant, Mike II-362

C

Cao, Xudong II-59
Carriero, Valentina Anita II-302
Ceriani, Miguel I-197, II-435
Chaves-Fraga, David II-152
Chen, Gaode I-61
Chen, Huajun I-121, I-290
Chen, Jiaoyan I-121
Chen, Mingyang I-253, I-290

Chen, Qiaosheng I-23
Chen, Shuo I-541
Chen, Xiangnan I-253
Chen, Yongrui I-348
Chen, Zhuo I-121
Cheng, Gong I-23, II-211
Corcho, Oscar I-271
Cuddihy, Paul II-345

D

D'Souza, Jennifer I-408
Damiano, Rossana II-435
Dang, Minh-Hoang II-285
Dash, Sarthak I-502
de Berardinis, Jacopo II-302
De Meester, Ben II-152
De Palma, Noel II-325
Debruyne, Christophe II-152
Demidova, Elena I-179, I-216
Dimou, Anastasia II-152
Ding, Guoxuan I-61
Ding, Jingyi I-159
Ding, Zifeng I-541
Dorf, Michael II-38
Dsouza, Alishiba I-179, I-216
Du, Wen II-18

E

Enguix, Carlos F. II-247

F

Fang, Xiaolin I-159
Fang, Yin I-121
Färber, Michael II-94
Ferilli, Stefano II-435
Fernández, Javier D. I-309
Fiore, Nicola II-38
Foley, Catherine II-419
Fu, Bo I-579

T. R. Payne et al. (Eds.): ISWC 2023, LNCS 14265, pp. 637–640, 2023.
https://doi.org/10.1007/978-3-031-47240-4

G
Garcia, Max   I-579
García-González, Herminio   II-362
García-Silva, Andrés   I-80
Garijo, Daniel   II-76
Gautrais, Thomas   I-309
Germano, Stefano   II-76
Giese, Martin   I-41
Gimenez-Garcia, Jose M.   I-309
Gliozzo, Alfio   I-502
Gnabasik, David   II-134
Goeke-Smith, Jeff   II-419
Gómez-Pérez, Jose Manuel   I-80
Gong, Tianling   II-59
Gonzalez, Irlan-Grangel   II-453
Gonzalez-Estrecha, Seila   II-419
Gosselin, Francis   I-561
Graybeal, John   II-38
Guittoum, Amal   II-325
Guo, Lingbing   I-121
Guo, Xiaobo   I-61

H
Haase, Peter   II-94
Han, Zhen   I-541
Harth, Andreas   II-176
Hartig, Olaf   II-285
He, Bailan   I-541
He, Zhidong   II-18
Hitzler, Pascal   II-419
Hoehndorf, Robert   I-522
Hotho, Andreas   I-618
Hu, Chenhao   I-140
Hu, Linmei   I-447
Hu, Nan   I-348
Huang, Shuhua   I-140
Huang, Ziqi   II-453
Huang, Zixian   I-23

I
Iglesias-Molina, Ana   I-271, II-152
Ilievski, Filip   I-271
Ismaeil, Youmna   I-599

J
Jain, Nitisha   II-302
Jin, Jiahui   I-159
Jin, Long   I-290

Jing, Shenqi   II-59
Jonquet, Clement   II-38
Jozashoori, Samaneh   II-152

K
Ke, Wenjun   I-101
Kechagioglou, Xeni   II-38
Kefalidis, Sergios-Anestis   II-266
Kharlamov, Evgeny   II-380, II-453
Kirrane, Sabrina   I-465
Klíma, Karel   II-194
Kong, Weiyang   I-140
Koubarakis, Manolis   II-266
Krause, Johan   II-94

L
Lamprecht, David   II-94
Lata, Kusum   II-247
Lazzari, Nicolas   II-302
Le Crom, Yotlan   II-285
Lefrançois, Maxime   II-134
Lehmann, Jens   I-388
Li, Chengkai   II-113
Li, Jie   I-447
Li, Junwen   II-18
Li, Weihua   I-234
Li, Wenbo   I-348
Li, Xuan   I-447
Li, Yangning   I-121
Li, Yu   I-348
Li, Zongyue   I-541
Liao, Ruotong   I-541
Lin, Tengteng   I-23
Liu, Jiajun   I-101
Liu, Jingping   II-18
Liu, Qing   I-234
Liu, Yongbin   I-328
Liu, Yubao   I-140
Liu, Yuzhang   I-101
Luo, Weiqing   I-23
Luo, Xianghui   II-380

M
Ma, Yunpu   I-541
Mann, Genivika   I-179
Maret, Pierre   II-266
Maria, Pano   II-152
Markovic, Milan   II-76

Martínez-Prieto, Miguel A. I-309
Meckler, Sascha II-176
Meloni, Antonello II-400
Meng, Zhao I-541
Meroño-Peñuela, Albert II-302
Mertens, Eric II-345
Michel, Franck II-152
Mihindukulasooriya, Nandana I-502, II-247
Min, Dehai I-348
Mitsios, Michail II-266
Molli, Pascal II-285
Morgan, Jackson II-230
Motta, Enrico II-400
Musen, Mark II-38

N
Naja, Iman II-76
Nayyeri, Mojtaba I-388
Nečaský, Martin II-194
Neunsinger, Christoph II-3
Ngomo, Axel-Cyrille Ngonga I-465
Nikolov, Nikolay II-380

O
Omeliyanenko, Janna I-618
Osborne, Francesco II-400
Ouyang, Chunping I-328

P
Pan, Jeff Z. I-121, II-211
Patti, Viviana II-435
Paulheim, Heiko I-428
Pei, Shichao I-522
Peng, Xi I-522
Pesquita, Catia I-428
Plas, Konstantinos II-266
Pollali, Mariangela II-266
Poltronieri, Andrea II-302
Presutti, Valentina II-302
Pujara, Jay I-271
Punjani, Dharmen II-266

Q
Qi, Guilin I-348
Qi, Ruoxia I-541
Qian, Jianguo I-159
Qiu, Jingyi I-159
Qudus, Umair I-465

R
Razniewski, Simon I-368
Redmond, Timothy II-38
Reforgiato Recupero, Diego II-400
Rehberger, Dean II-419
Ren, Lin I-328
Reyd, Samuel I-484
Röder, Michael I-465
Roman, Dumitru II-380
Romero, Julien I-368
Rony, Md Rashad Al Hasan I-388
Rosati, Ilaria II-38
Ruan, Tong II-18
Russell, Daniel II-345

S
Saeef, Mohammed Samiul II-113
Salatino, Angelo II-400
Savkovic, Ognjen II-380, II-453
Schlör, Daniel I-618
Shang, Ziyu I-101
Sheill, Alicia II-419
Shi, Qing I-23, II-211
Shi, Xiao II-113
Shimizu, Cogan II-419
Shirvani-Mahdavi, Nasim II-113
Silva, Sara I-428
Siu, Kit II-345
Skaf-Molli, Hala II-285
Skrenchuk, Alex II-38
Song, Aibo I-159
Sousa, Rita T. I-428
Soylu, Ahmet II-380, II-453
Staab, Steffen I-388
Stepanova, Daria I-599
Stranisci, Marco Antonio II-435

T
Taelman, Ruben I-3, II-194
Tan, Yiming I-348
Tan, Zhipeng II-453
Tang, Siliang I-253
Tang, Zhenwei I-522
Thapa, Ratan Bahadur I-41
Tiwari, Sanju II-247
Tran, Trung-Kien I-599
Tresp, Volker I-541
Tsalapati, Eleni II-266
Tsokanaridou, Myrto II-266

V

Van Assche, Dylan   II-152
Vendetti, Jennifer L.   II-38
Verborgh, Ruben   I-3

W

Wang, Haofen   II-18
Wang, Jinrui   I-447
Wang, Junrui   II-211
Wang, Lei   I-61
Wang, Peng   I-101
Wang, Yuxiang   II-59
Wang, Zihao   I-388
Weakly, Kendra   II-3
Williams, Jenny   II-345
Windoffer, Moritz   I-216
Wu, Feiyue   II-59
Wu, Jingpei   I-541
Wu, Tianxing   II-59
Wu, Xiaowei   II-18
Wu, Yinan   II-18

Y

Yang, Yi   I-234
Yao, Naimeng   I-234
Yao, Zhen   I-253, I-290
Yu, Ran   I-179, I-216

Z

Zehe, Albin   I-618
Zha, Daren   I-61
Zhang, Tianbo   I-159
Zhang, Wen   I-121, I-253, I-290
Zhang, Xiangliang   I-522
Zhang, Yichi   I-121
Zhang, Yirui   I-447
Zhang, Yue   II-18
Zhang, Zhiyang   I-23
Zheng, Zhuoxun   II-380, II-453
Zhou, Baifan   II-380, II-453
Zhu, Yipeng   II-59
Zhuang, Fuzhen   I-522
Zimmermann, Roland   II-3
Zouaq, Amal   I-484, I-561